The State of the Union
Messages of the Presidents of
the United States

Volume II

The State of the Union Messages of the Presidents

1790-1966

★ ★ ★

with an introduction by

ARTHUR M. SCHLESINGER JR.

Editor: Fred L. Israel

VOLUME

II

1861–1904

NEW YORK
CHELSEA HOUSE PUBLISHERS
in association with the
R. R. BOWKER COMPANY
1967

Preface

Volume II begins with Lincoln's eloquent defense of the Union and concludes with Theodore Roosevelt's justification of his expansionist philosophy. Lincoln's compact essays contain an average of 8,000 words while Roosevelt's discourses approximate 22,000 words. Both Lincoln and Roosevelt spoke about a positive presidency. "I suppose I have a right to take *any* measure which may best subdue the enemy," Lincoln told Chicago friends. And his annual messages to Congress adequately illustrate his concept of strong executive authority. Theodore Roosevelt recorded how he considered himself "a steward of the people bound actively and affirmatively to do all he could for the people, and not to content himself with the negative merit of keeping his talents undamaged in a napkin." Roosevelt used his messages to assert and defend his Presidential leadership in foreign and domestic affairs. In the generation which separates these two men, the United States passed through the trying Reconstruction period and forged ahead to the front rank of the manufacturing nations. The new age brought with it all the hazards posed by a mechanized society and raised fundamental questions for a democracy. In foreign affairs, the United States, by the turn of the century, had taken its place as a world power.

It is generally assumed that the men who occupied the White House from the end of Reconstruction to the twentieth century appeared to ignore the major problems inherent in an industrial society that had subjugated a vast continent. To the contrary, the texts of the messages clearly illustrate that the Presidents made specific recommendations to Congress on a multitude of issues. The Index at the end of Volume III underscores the range of Presidential concern: civil service, internal improvements, tariff reform, agriculture, land sales, conservation, Indian relations, banking and currency reforms, education, immigration, plus scores of other detailed domestic issues. In foreign affairs, a grandiose Pacific policy emerges—a two ocean navy, the purchase of Alaska, coaling stations in Hawaii, trade with the Far East, and an Isthmian canal. In the Caribbean the United States continued to uphold the Monroe Doctrine, adding to it the spirit of "manifest destiny." For all practical purposes American isolationism ended as trade now extended to all parts of the world.

The years 1861 to 1904 are marked by a new American consciousness—the consciousness of national pride and strength. At the turn of the century Americans could look back to a generation of progress unparalleled in history.

Fred L. Israel

Contents

The State of the Union Messages of the Presidents of the United States

Volume II

Abraham Lincoln

March 4, 1861 to April 15, 1865

FIRST ANNUAL MESSAGE.

WASHINGTON, *December 3, 1861.*

Fellow-Citizens of the Senate and House of Representatives:

In the midst of unprecedented political troubles we have cause of great gratitude to God for unusual good health and most abundant harvests.

You will not be surprised to learn that in the peculiar exigencies of the times our intercourse with foreign nations has been attended with profound solicitude, chiefly turning upon our own domestic affairs.

A disloyal portion of the American people have during the whole year been engaged in an attempt to divide and destroy the Union. A nation which endures factious domestic division is exposed to disrespect abroad, and one party, if not both, is sure sooner or later to invoke foreign intervention.

Nations thus tempted to interfere are not always able to resist the counsels of seeming expediency and ungenerous ambition, although measures adopted under such influences seldom fail to be unfortunate and injurious to those adopting them.

The disloyal citizens of the United States who have offered the ruin of our country in return for the aid and comfort which they have invoked abroad have received less patronage and encouragement than they probably expected. If it were just to suppose, as the insurgents have seemed to assume, that foreign nations in this case, discarding all moral, social, and treaty obligations, would act solely and selfishly for the most speedy restoration of commerce, including especially the acquisition of cotton, those nations appear as yet not to have seen their way to their object more directly or clearly through the destruction than through the preservation of the Union. If we could dare to believe that foreign nations are actuated by no higher principle than this, I am quite sure a sound argument could be made to show them that they can reach their aim more readily and easily by aiding to crush this rebellion than by giving encouragement to it.

The principal lever relied on by the insurgents for exciting foreign nations to hostility against us, as already intimated, is the embarrassment of commerce. Those nations, however, not improbably saw from the first that it was the Union which made as well our foreign as our domestic commerce. They can scarcely have failed to perceive that the effort for disunion produces the existing difficulty, and that one strong nation promises more durable peace and a more extensive, valuable, and reliable commerce than can the same nation broken into hostile fragments.

It is not my purpose to review our discussions with foreign states, because, whatever might be their wishes or dispositions, the integrity of our country and the stability of our Government mainly depend not upon them, but on the loyalty, virtue, patriotism, and intelligence of the American people. The correspondence itself, with the usual reservations, is herewith submitted.

I venture to hope it will appear that we have practiced prudence and liberality toward foreign powers, averting causes of irritation and with firmness maintaining our own rights and honor.

Since, however, it is apparent that here, as in every other state, foreign dangers necessarily attend domestic difficulties, I recommend that adequate and ample measures be adopted for maintaining the public defenses on every side. While under this general recommendation provision for defending our seacoast line readily occurs to the mind, I also in the same connection ask the attention of Congress to our great lakes and rivers. It is believed that some fortifications and depots of arms and munitions, with harbor and navigation improvements, all at well-selected points upon these, would be of great importance to the national defense and preservation. I ask attention to the views of the Secretary of War, expressed in his report, upon the same general subject.

I deem it of importance that the loyal regions of east Tennessee and western North Carolina should be connected with Kentucky and other faithful parts of the Union by railroad. I therefore recommend, as a military measure, that Congress provide for the construction of such road as speedily as possible. Kentucky no doubt will cooperate, and through her legislature make the most judicious selection of a line. The northern terminus must connect with some existing railroad, and whether the route shall be from Lexington or Nicholasville to the Cumberland Gap, or from Lebanon to the Tennessee line, in the direction of Knoxville, or on some still different line, can easily be determined. Kentucky and the General Government cooperating, the work can be completed in a very short time, and when done it will be not only of vast present usefulness, but also a valuable permanent improvement, worth its cost in all the future.

Some treaties, designed chiefly for the interests of commerce, and having no grave political importance, have been negotiated, and will be submitted to the Senate for their consideration.

Although we have failed to induce some of the commercial powers to adopt a desirable melioration of the rigor of maritime war, we have removed all obstructions from the way of this humane reform except such as are merely of temporary and accidental occurrence.

I invite your attention to the correspondence between Her Britannic Majesty's minister accredited to this Government and the Secretary of State relative to the detention of the British ship *Perthshire* in June last by the United States steamer *Massachusetts* for a supposed breach of the blockade. As this detention was occasioned by an obvious misapprehension of the facts, and as justice requires that we should commit no belligerent act not founded in strict right as sanctioned by public law, I recommend that an appropriation be made to satisfy the reasonable demand of the owners of the vessel for her detention.

I repeat the recommendation of my predecessor in his annual message to Congress in December last in regard to the disposition of the surplus which will probably remain after satisfying the claims of American citizens against China, pursuant to the awards of the commissioners under the act of the 3d of March, 1859. If, however, it should not be deemed advisable to carry that recommendation into effect, I would suggest that authority be given for investing the principal, over the proceeds of the surplus referred to, in good securities, with a view to the satisfaction of such other just claims of our citizens against China as are not unlikely to arise hereafter in the course of our extensive trade with that Empire.

By the act of the 5th of August last Congress authorized the President to instruct the commanders of suitable vessels to defend themselves against and to capture pirates. This authority has been exercised in a single instance only. For the more effectual protection of our extensive and valuable commerce in the Eastern seas especially, it seems to me that it would also be advisable to authorize the commanders of sailing vessels to recapture any prizes which pirates may make of United States vessels and their cargoes, and the consular courts now established by law in Eastern countries to adjudicate the cases in the event that this should not be objected to by the local authorities.

If any good reason exists why we should persevere longer in withholding our recognition of the independence and sovereignty of Hayti and Liberia, I am unable to discern it. Unwilling, however, to inaugurate a novel policy in regard to them without the approbation of Congress, I submit for your consideration the expediency of an appropriation for maintaining a chargé d'affaires near each of those new States. It does not admit of doubt that important commercial advantages might be secured by favorable treaties with them.

The operations of the Treasury during the period which has elapsed since your adjournment have been conducted with signal success. The patriotism of the people has placed at the disposal of the Government the large means demanded by the public exigencies. Much of the national loan has been taken by citizens of the industrial classes, whose confidence in their country's faith and zeal for their country's deliverance from present peril have induced them to contribute to the support of the Government the whole of their limited acquisitions. This fact imposes peculiar obligations to economy in disbursement and energy in action.

The revenue from all sources, including loans, for the financial year ending on the 30th of June, 1861, was $86,835,900.27, and the expenditures for the same period, including payments on account of the public debt, were $84,578,834.47, leaving a balance in the Treasury on the 1st of July of $2,257,065.80. For the first quarter of the financial year ending on the 30th of September, 1861, the receipts from all sources, including the balance of the 1st of July, were $102,532,509.27, and the expenses $98,239,733.09, leaving a balance on the 1st of October, 1861, of $4,292,776.18.

Estimates for the remaining three quarters of the year and for the financial year 1863, together with his views of ways and means for meeting the demands contemplated by them, will be submitted to Congress by the Secretary of the Treasury. It is gratifying to know that the expenditures made necessary by the rebellion are not beyond the resources of the loyal people, and to believe that the same patriotism which has thus far sustained the Government will continue to sustain it till peace and union shall again bless the land.

I respectfully refer to the report of the Secretary of War for information respecting the numerical strength of the Army and for recommendations having in view an increase of its efficiency and the well-being of the various branches of the service intrusted to his care. It is gratifying to know that the patriotism of the people has proved equal to the occasion, and that the number of troops tendered greatly exceeds the force which Congress authorized me to call into the field.

I refer with pleasure to those portions of his report which make allusion to the creditable degree of discipline already attained by our troops and to the excellent sanitary condition of the entire Army.

The recommendation of the Secretary for an organization of the militia upon a uniform basis is a subject of vital importance to the future safety of the country, and is commended to the serious attention of Congress.

The large addition to the Regular Army, in connection with the defection that has so considerably diminished the number of its officers, gives peculiar importance to his recommendation for increasing the corps of cadets to the greatest capacity of the Military Academy.

By mere omission, I presume, Congress has failed to provide chaplains for hospitals occupied by volunteers. This subject was brought to my notice, and I was induced to draw up the form of a letter, one copy of which, properly addressed, has been delivered to each of the persons, and at the dates respectively named and stated in a schedule, containing also the form of the letter marked A, and herewith transmitted.

These gentlemen, I understand, entered upon the duties designated at the times respectively stated in the schedule, and have labored faithfully therein ever since. I therefore recommend that they be compensated at the same rate as chaplains in the Army. I further suggest that general provision be made for chaplains to serve at hospitals, as well as with regiments.

The report of the Secretary of the Navy presents in detail the operations of that branch of the service, the activity and energy which have characterized its administration, and the results of measures to increase its efficiency and power. Such have been the additions, by construction and purchase, that it may almost be said a navy has been created and brought into service since our difficulties commenced.

Besides blockading our extensive coast, squadrons larger than ever before assembled under our flag have been put afloat and performed deeds which have increased our naval renown.

I would invite special attention to the recommendation of the Secretary for a more perfect organization of the Navy by introducing additional grades in the service.

The present organization is defective and unsatisfactory, and the suggestions submitted by the Department will, it is believed, if adopted, obviate the difficulties alluded to, promote harmony, and increase the efficiency of the Navy.

There are three vacancies on the bench of the Supreme Court—two by the decease of Justices Daniel and McLean and one by the resignation of Justice Campbell. I have so far forborne making nominations to fill these vacancies for reasons which I will now state. Two of the outgoing judges resided within the States now overrun by revolt, so that if successors were appointed in the same localities they could not now serve upon their circuits; and many of the most competent men there probably would not take the personal hazard of accepting to serve, even here, upon the Supreme bench. I have been unwilling to throw all the appointments northward, thus disabling myself from doing justice to the South on the return of peace; although I may remark that to transfer to the North one which has heretofore been in the South would not, with reference to territory and population, be unjust.

During the long and brilliant judicial career of Judge McLean his circuit grew into an empire—altogether too large for any one judge to give the courts therein more than a nominal attendance—rising in population from 1,470,018 in 1830 to 6,151,405 in 1860.

Besides this, the country generally has outgrown our present judicial system. If uniformity was at all intended, the system requires that all the States shall be accommodated with circuit courts, attended by Supreme judges, while, in fact, Wisconsin, Minnesota, Iowa, Kansas, Florida, Texas, California, and Oregon have never had any such courts. Nor can this well be remedied without a change in the system, because the adding of judges to the Supreme Court, enough for the accommodation of all parts of the country with circuit courts, would create a court altogether too numerous for a judicial body of any sort. And the evil, if it be one, will increase as new States come into the Union. Circuit courts are useful or they are not useful. If useful, no State should be denied them; if not useful, no State should have them. Let them be provided for all or abolished as to all.

Three modifications occur to me, either of which, I think, would be an improvement upon our present system. Let the Supreme Court be of convenient number in every event; then, first, let the whole country be divided into circuits of convenient size, the Supreme judges to serve in a number of them corresponding to their own number, and independent circuit judges be provided for all the rest; or, secondly, let the Supreme judges be relieved from circuit duties and circuit judges provided for all the circuits; or, thirdly, dispense with circuit courts altogether, leaving the judicial functions wholly to the district courts and an independent Supreme Court.

I respectfully recommend to the consideration of Congress the present condition of the statute laws, with the hope that Congress will be able to find an easy remedy for many of the inconveniences and evils which constantly embarrass those engaged in the practical administration of them. Since the organization of the Government Congress has enacted some 5,000 acts and joint resolutions, which fill more than 6,000 closely printed pages and are scattered through many volumes. Many of these acts have been drawn in haste and without sufficient caution, so that their provisions are often obscure in themselves or in conflict with each other, or at least so doubtful as to render it very difficult for even the best-informed persons to ascertain precisely what the statute law really is.

It seems to me very important that the statute laws should be made as plain and intelligible as possible, and be reduced to as small a compass as may consist with the fullness and precision of the will of the Legislature and the perspicuity of its language. This well done would, I think, greatly facilitate the labors of those whose duty it is to assist in the administration of the laws, and would be a lasting benefit to the people, by placing before them in a more accessible and intelligible form the laws which so deeply concern their interests and their duties.

I am informed by some whose opinions I respect that all the acts of Congress now in force and of a permanent and general nature might be revised and rewritten so as to be embraced in one volume (or at most two volumes) of ordinary and convenient size; and I respectfully recommend to Congress to consider of the subject, and if my suggestion be approved to devise such plan as to their wisdom shall seem most proper for the attainment of the end proposed.

One of the unavoidable consequences of the present insurrection is the entire suppression in many places of all the ordinary means of administering civil justice by the officers and in the forms of existing law. This is the case, in whole or in part, in all the insurgent States; and as our armies advance upon and take possession of parts of those States the practical evil becomes more apparent. There are no courts nor officers to whom the citizens of other States may apply for the enforcement of their lawful claims against citizens of the insurgent States, and there is a vast amount of debt constituting such claims. Some have estimated it as high as $200,000,000, due in large part from insurgents in open rebellion to loyal citizens who are even now making great sacrifices in the discharge of their patriotic duty to support the Government.

Under these circumstances I have been urgently solicited to establish by military power courts to administer summary justice in such cases. I have thus far declined to do it, not because I had any doubt that the end proposed—the collection of the debts—was just and right in itself, but because I have been unwilling to go beyond the pressure of necessity in the unusual exercise of power. But the powers of Congress, I suppose, are equal to the anomalous occasion, and therefore I refer the whole matter to Congress, with the hope that a plan may be devised for the administration of justice in all such parts of the insurgent States and Territories as may be under the control of this Government, whether by a voluntary return to allegiance and order or by the power of our arms; this, however, not to be a permanent institution, but a temporary substitute, and to cease as soon as the ordinary courts can be reestablished in peace.

It is important that some more convenient means should be provided, if possible, for the adjustment of claims against the Government, especially in view of their increased number by reason of the war. It is as much the duty of Government to render prompt justice against itself in favor of citizens as it is to administer the same between private individuals. The investigation and adjudication of claims in their nature belong to the judicial department. Besides, it is apparent that the attention of Congress will be more than usually engaged for some time to come with great national questions. It was intended by the organization of the Court of Claims mainly to remove this branch of business from the halls of Congress; but while the court has proved to be an effective and valuable means of investigation, it in great degree fails to effect the object of its creation for want of power to make its judgments final.

Fully aware of the delicacy, not to say the danger, of the subject, I commend to your careful consideration whether this power of making judgments final may not properly be given to the court, reserving the right of appeal on questions of law to the Supreme Court, with such other provisions as experience may have shown to be necessary.

I ask attention to the report of the Postmaster-General, the following being a summary statement of the condition of the Department:

The revenue from all sources during the fiscal year ending June 30, 1861, including the annual permanent appropriation of $700,000 for the transportation of "free mail matter," was $9,049,296.40, being about 2 per cent less than the revenue for 1860.

The expenditures were $13,606,759.11, showing a decrease of more than 8 per cent as compared with those of the previous year and leaving an excess of expenditure over the revenue for the last fiscal year of $4,557,462.71.

The gross revenue for the year ending June 30, 1863, is estimated at an increase of 4 per cent on that of 1861, making $8,683,000, to which should be added the earnings of the Department in carrying free matter, viz, $700,000, making $9,383,000.

The total expenditures for 1863 are estimated at $12,528,000, leaving an estimated deficiency of $3,145,000 to be supplied from the Treasury in addition to the permanent appropriation.

The present insurrection shows, I think, that the extension of this District across the Potomac River at the time of establishing the capital here was eminently wise, and consequently that the relinquishment of that portion of it which lies within the State of Virginia was unwise and dangerous. I submit for your consideration the expediency of regaining that part of the District and the restoration of the original boundaries thereof through negotiations with the State of Virginia.

The report of the Secretary of the Interior, with the accompanying documents, exhibits the condition of the several branches of the public business pertaining to that Department. The depressing influences of the insurrection have been specially felt in the operations of the Patent and General Land Offices. The cash receipts from the sales of public lands during the past year have exceeded the expenses of our land system only about $200,000. The sales have been entirely suspended in the Southern States, while the interruptions to the business of the country and the diversion of large numbers of men from labor to military service have obstructed settlements in the new States and Territories of the Northwest.

The receipts of the Patent Office have declined in nine months about $100,000, rendering a large reduction of the force employed necessary to make it self-sustaining.

The demands upon the Pension Office will be largely increased by the insurrection. Numerous applications for pensions, based upon the casualties of the existing war, have already been made. There is reason to believe that many who are now upon the pension rolls and in receipt of the bounty of the Government are in the ranks of the insurgent army or giving them aid and comfort. The Secretary of the Interior has directed a suspension of the payment of the pensions of such persons upon proof of their disloyalty. I recommend that Congress authorize that officer to cause the names of such persons to be stricken from the pension rolls.

The relations of the Government with the Indian tribes have been greatly disturbed by the insurrection, especially in the southern superintendency and in that of New Mexico. The Indian country south of Kansas is in the possession of insurgents from Texas and Arkansas. The agents of the United States appointed since the 4th of March for this superintendency have been unable to reach their posts, while the most of those who were in office before that time have espoused the insurrectionary cause, and assume to exercise the powers of agents by virtue of commissions from the insurrectionists. It has been stated in the public press that a portion of those Indians have been organized as a military force and are attached to the army of the insurgents. Although the Government has no official information upon this subject, letters have been written to the Commissioner of Indian Affairs by several prominent chiefs giving assurance of their loyalty to the United States and expressing a wish for the presence of Federal troops to protect them. It is believed that upon the repossession of the country by the Federal forces the Indians will readily cease all hostile demonstrations and resume their former relations to the Government.

Agriculture, confessedly the largest interest of the nation, has not a department nor a bureau, but a clerkship only, assigned to it in the Government. While it is fortunate that this great interest is so independent in its nature as to not have demanded and extorted more from the Government, I respectfully ask Congress to consider whether something more can not be given voluntarily with general advantage.

Annual reports exhibiting the condition of our agriculture, commerce, and manufactures would present a fund of information of great practical value to the country. While I make no suggestion as to details, I venture the opinion that an agricultural and statistical bureau might profitably be organized.

The execution of the laws for the suppression of the African slave trade has been confided to the Department of the Interior. It is a subject of gratulation that the efforts which have been made for the suppression of this inhuman traffic have been recently attended with unusual success. Five vessels being fitted out for the slave trade have been seized and condemned. Two mates of vessels engaged in the trade and one person in equipping a vessel as a slaver have been convicted and subjected to the penalty of fine and imprisonment, and one captain, taken with a cargo of Africans on board his vessel, has been convicted of the highest grade of offense under our laws, the punishment of which is death.

The Territories of Colorado, Dakota, and Nevada, created by the last Congress, have been organized, and civil administration has been inaugurated therein under auspices especially gratifying when it is considered that the leaven of treason was found existing in some of these new countries when the Federal officers arrived there.

The abundant natural resources of these Territories, with the security and protection afforded by organized government, will doubtless invite to them a large immigration when peace shall restore the business of the country to its accustomed channels. I submit the resolutions of the legislature of Colorado, which evidence the patriotic spirit of the people of the Territory. So far the authority of the United States has been upheld in all the Territories, as it is hoped it will be in the future. I commend their interests and defense to the enlightened and generous care of Congress.

I recommend to the favorable consideration of Congress the interests of the District of Columbia. The insurrection has been the cause of much suffering and sacrifice to its inhabitants, and as they have no representative in Congress that body should not overlook their just claims upon the Government.

At your late session a joint resolution was adopted authorizing the President to take measures for facilitating a proper representation of the industrial interests of the United States at the exhibition of the industry of all nations to be holden at London in the year 1862. I regret to say I have been unable to give personal attention to this subject—a subject at once so interesting in itself and so extensively and intimately connected with the material prosperity of the world. Through the Secretaries of State and of the Interior a plan or system has been devised and partly matured, and which will be laid before you.

Under and by virtue of the act of Congress entitled "An act to confiscate property used for insurrectionary purposes," approved August 6, 1861, the legal claims of certain persons to the labor and service of certain other persons have become forfeited, and numbers of the latter thus liberated are already dependent on the United States and must be provided for in some way. Besides this, it is not impossible that some of the States will pass similar enactments for their own benefit respectively, and by operation of which persons of the same class will be thrown upon them for disposal. In such case I recommend that Congress provide for accepting such persons from such States, according to some mode of valuation, in lieu, *pro tanto*, of direct taxes, or upon some other plan to be agreed on with such States respectively; that such persons, on such acceptance by the General Government, be at once deemed free, and that in any event steps be taken for colonizing both classes (or the one first mentioned if the other shall not be brought into existence) at some place or places in a climate congenial to them. It might be well to consider, too, whether the free colored people already in the United States could not, so far as individuals may desire, be included in such colonization.

To carry out the plan of colonization may involve the acquiring of territory, and also the appropriation of money beyond that to be expended in the territorial acquisition. Having practiced the acquisition of territory for nearly sixty years, the question of constitutional power to do so is no longer an open one with us. The power was questioned at first by Mr. Jefferson, who, however, in the purchase of Louisiana, yielded his scruples on the plea of great expediency. If it be said that the only legitimate object of acquiring territory is to furnish homes for white men, this measure effects that object, for the emigration of colored men leaves additional room for white men remaining or coming here. Mr. Jefferson, however, placed the importance of procuring Louisiana more on political and commercial grounds than on providing room for population.

On this whole proposition, including the appropriation of money with the acquisition of territory, does not the expediency amount to absolute necessity—that without which the Government itself can not be perpetuated?

The war continues. In considering the policy to be adopted for suppressing the insurrection I have been anxious and careful that the inevitable conflict for this purpose shall not degenerate into a violent and remorseless revolutionary struggle. I have therefore in every case thought it proper to keep the integrity of the Union prominent as the primary object of the contest on our part, leaving all questions which are not of vital military importance to the more deliberate action of the Legislature.

In the exercise of my best discretion I have adhered to the blockade of the ports held by the insurgents, instead of putting in force by proclamation the law of Congress enacted at the late session for closing those ports.

So also, obeying the dictates of prudence, as well as the obligations of law, instead of transcending I have adhered to the act of Congress to confiscate property used for insurrectionary purposes. If a new law upon the same subject shall be proposed, its propriety will be duly considered. The Union must be preserved, and hence all indispensable means must be employed. We should not be in haste to determine that radical and extreme measures, which may reach the loyal as well as the disloyal, are indispensable.

The inaugural address at the beginning of the Administration and the message to Congress at the late special session were both mainly devoted to the domestic controversy out of which the insurrection and consequent war have sprung. Nothing now occurs to add or subtract to or from the principles or general purposes stated and expressed in those documents.

The last ray of hope for preserving the Union peaceably expired at the assault upon Fort Sumter, and a general review of what has occurred since may not be unprofitable. What was painfully uncertain then is much better defined and more distinct now, and the progress of events is plainly in the right direction. The insurgents confidently claimed a strong support from north of Mason and Dixon's line, and the friends of the Union were not free from apprehension on the point. This, however, was soon settled definitely, and on the right side. South of the line noble little Delaware led off right from the first. Maryland was made to *seem* against the Union. Our soldiers were assaulted, bridges were burned, and railroads torn up within her limits, and we were many days at one time without the ability to bring a single regiment over her soil to the capital. Now her bridges and railroads are repaired and open to the Government; she already gives seven regiments to the cause of the Union, and none to the enemy; and her people, at a regular election, have sustained the Union by a larger majority and a larger aggregate vote than they ever before gave to any candidate or any question. Kentucky, too, for some time in doubt, is now decidedly and, I think, unchangeably ranged on the side of the Union. Missouri is comparatively quiet, and, I believe, can not again be overrun by the insurrectionists. These three States of Maryland, Kentucky, and Missouri, neither of which would promise a single soldier at first, have now an aggregate of not less than 40,000 in the field for the Union, while of their citizens certainly not more than a third of that number, and they of doubtful whereabouts and doubtful existence, are in arms against us. After a somewhat bloody struggle of months, winter closes on the Union people of western Virginia, leaving them masters of their own country.

An insurgent force of about 1,500, for months dominating the narrow peninsular region constituting the counties of Accomac and Northampton, and known as Eastern Shore of Virginia, together with some contiguous parts of Maryland, have laid down their arms, and the people there have renewed their allegiance to and accepted the protection of the old flag. This leaves no armed insurrectionist north of the Potomac or east of the Chesapeake.

Also we have obtained a footing at each of the isolated points on the southern coast of Hatteras, Port Royal, Tybee Island (near Savannah), and Ship Island; and we likewise have some general accounts of popular movements in behalf of the Union in North Carolina and Tennessee.

These things demonstrate that the cause of the Union is advancing steadily and certainly southward.

Since your last adjournment Lieutenant-General Scott has retired from the head of the Army. During his long life the nation has not been unmindful of his merit; yet on calling to mind how faithfully, ably, and brilliantly he has served the country, from a time far back in our history, when few of the now living had been born, and thenceforward continually, I can not but think we are still his debtors. I submit, therefore, for your consideration what further mark of recognition is due to him, and to ourselves as a grateful people.

With the retirement of General Scott came the Executive duty of appointing in his stead a General in Chief of the Army. It is a fortunate circumstance that neither in council nor country was there, so far as I know, any difference of opinion as to the proper person to be selected. The retiring chief repeatedly expressed his judgment in favor of General McClellan for the position, and in this the nation seemed to give a unanimous concurrence. The designation of General McClellan is therefore in considerable degree the selection of the country as well as of the Executive, and hence there is better reason to hope there will be given him the confidence and cordial support thus by fair implication promised, and without which he can not with so full efficiency serve the country.

It has been said that one bad general is better than two good ones, and the saying is true if taken to mean no more than that an army is better directed by a single mind, though inferior, than by two superior ones at variance and cross-purposes with each other.

And the same is true in all joint operations wherein those engaged *can* have none but a common end in view and *can* differ only as to the choice of means. In a storm at sea no one on board *can* wish the ship to sink, and yet not unfrequently all go down together because too many will direct and no single mind can be allowed to control.

It continues to develop that the insurrection is largely, if not exclusively, a war upon the first principle of popular government—the rights of the people. Conclusive evidence of this is found in the most grave and maturely considered public documents, as well as in the general tone of the insurgents. In those documents we find the abridgment of the existing right of suffrage and the denial to the people of all right to participate in the selection of public officers except the legislative boldly advocated, with labored arguments to prove that large control of the people in government is the source of all political evil. Monarchy itself is sometimes hinted at as a possible refuge from the power of the people.

In my present position I could scarcely be justified were I to omit raising a warning voice against this approach of returning despotism.

It is not needed nor fitting here that a general argument should be made in favor of popular institutions, but there is one point, with its connections, not so hackneyed as most others, to which I ask a brief attention. It is the effort to place *capital* on an equal footing with, if not above, *labor* in the structure of government. It is assumed that labor is available only in connection with capital; that nobody labors unless somebody else, owning capital, somehow by the use of it induces him to labor. This assumed, it is next considered whether it is best that capital shall *hire* laborers, and thus induce them to work by their own consent, or *buy* them and drive them to it without their consent. Having proceeded so far, it is naturally concluded that all laborers are either *hired* laborers or what we call slaves. And further, it is assumed that whoever is once a hired laborer is fixed in that condition for life.

Now there is no such relation between capital and labor as assumed, nor is there any such thing as a free man being fixed for life in the condition of a hired laborer. Both these assumptions are false, and all inferences from them are groundless.

Labor is prior to and independent of capital. Capital is only the fruit of labor, and could never have existed if labor had not first existed. Labor is the superior of capital, and deserves much the higher consideration. Capital has its rights, which are as worthy of protection as any other rights. Nor is it denied that there is, and probably always will be, a relation between labor and capital producing mutual benefits. The error is in assuming that the whole labor of community exists within that relation. A few men own capital, and that few avoid labor themselves, and with their capital hire or buy another few to labor for them. A large majority belong to neither class—neither work for others nor have others working for them. In most of the Southern States a majority of the whole people of all colors are neither slaves nor masters, while in the Northern a large majority are neither hirers nor hired. Men, with their families—wives, sons, and daughters—work for themselves on their farms, in their houses, and in their shops, taking the whole product to themselves, and asking no favors of capital on the one hand nor of hired laborers or slaves on the other. It is not forgotten that a considerable number of persons mingle their own labor with capital; that is, they labor with their own hands and also buy or hire others to labor for them; but this is only a mixed and not a distinct class. No principle stated is disturbed by the existence of this mixed class.

Again, as has already been said, there is not of necessity any such thing as the free hired laborer being fixed to that condition for life. Many independent men everywhere in these States a few years back in their lives were hired laborers. The prudent, penniless beginner in the world labors for wages awhile, saves a surplus with which to buy tools or land for himself, then labors on his own account another while, and at length hires another new beginner to help him. This is the just and generous and prosperous system which opens the way to all, gives hope to all, and consequent energy and progress and improvement of condition to all. No men living are more worthy to be trusted than those who toil up from poverty; none less inclined to take or touch aught which they have not honestly earned. Let them beware of surrendering a political power which they already possess, and which if surrendered will surely be used to close the door of advancement against such as they and to fix new disabilities and burdens upon them till all of liberty shall be lost.

From the first taking of our national census to the last are seventy years and we find our population at the end of the period eight times as great as it was at the beginning. The increase of those other things which men deem desirable has been even greater. We thus have at one view what the popular principle, applied to Government through the machinery of the States and the Union, has produced in a given time, and also what if firmly maintained it promises for the future. There are already among us those who if the Union be preserved will live to see it contain 250,000,000. The struggle *of* to-day is not altogether *for* to-day; it is for a vast future also. With a reliance on Providence all the more firm and earnest, let us proceed in the great task which events have devolved upon us.

SECOND ANNUAL MESSAGE.

DECEMBER 1, 1862.

Fellow-Citizens of the Senate and House of Representatives:

Since your last annual assembling another year of health and bountiful harvests has passed, and while it has not pleased the Almighty to bless us with a return of peace, we can but press on, guided by the best light He gives us, trusting that in His own good time and wise way all will yet be well.

The correspondence touching foreign affairs which has taken place during the last year is herewith submitted, in virtual compliance with a request to that effect made by the House of Representatives near the close of the last session of Congress.

If the condition of our relations with other nations is less gratifying than it has usually been at former periods, it is certainly more satisfactory than a nation so unhappily distracted as we are might reasonably have apprehended. In the month of June last there were some grounds to expect that the maritime powers which at the beginning of our domestic difficulties so unwisely and unnecessarily, as we think, recognized the insurgents as a belligerent would soon recede from that position, which has proved only less injurious to themselves than to our own country. But the temporary reverses which afterwards befell the national arms, and which were exaggerated by our own disloyal citizens abroad, have hitherto delayed that act of simple justice.

The civil war, which has so radically changed for the moment the occupations and habits of the American people, has necessarily disturbed the social condition and affected very deeply the prosperity of the nations with which we have carried on a commerce that has been steadily increasing throughout a period of half a century. It has at the same time excited political ambitions and apprehensions which have produced a profound agitation throughout the civilized world. In this unusual agitation we have forborne from taking part in any controversy between foreign states and between parties or factions in such states. We have attempted no propagandism and acknowledged no revolution. But we have left to every nation the exclusive conduct and management of its own affairs. Our struggle has been, of course, contemplated by foreign nations with reference less to its own merits than to its supposed and often exaggerated effects and consequences resulting to those nations themselves. Nevertheless, complaint on the part of this Government, even if it were just, would certainly be unwise.

The treaty with Great Britain for the suppression of the slave trade has been put into operation with a good prospect of complete success. It is an occasion of special pleasure to acknowledge that the execution of it on the part of Her Majesty's Government has been marked with a jealous respect for the authority of the United States and the rights of their moral and loyal citizens.

The convention with Hanover for the abolition of the Stade dues has been carried into full effect under the act of Congress for that purpose.

. A blockade of 3,000 miles of seacoast could not be established and vigorously enforced in a season of great commercial activity like the present without committing occasional mistakes and inflicting unintentional injuries upon foreign nations and their subjects.

A civil war occurring in a country where foreigners reside and carry on trade under treaty stipulations is necessarily fruitful of complaints of the violation of neutral rights. All such collisions tend to excite misapprehensions, and possibly to produce mutual reclamations between nations which have a common interest in preserving peace and friendship. In clear cases of these kinds I have so far as possible heard and redressed complaints which have been presented by friendly powers. There is still, however, a large and an augmenting number of doubtful cases upon which the Government is unable to agree with the governments whose protection is demanded by the claimants. There are, moreover, many cases in which the United States or their citizens suffer wrongs from the naval or military authorities of foreign nations which the governments of those states are not at once prepared to redress. I have proposed to some of the foreign states thus interested mutual conventions to examine and adjust such complaints. This proposition has been made especially to Great Britain, to France, to Spain, and to Prussia. In each case it has been kindly received, but has not yet been formally adopted.

I deem it my duty to recommend an appropriation in behalf of the owners of the Norwegian bark *Admiral P. Tordenskiold*, which vessel was in May, 1861, prevented by the commander of the blockading force off Charleston from leaving that port with cargo, notwithstanding a similar privilege had shortly before been granted to an English vessel. I have directed the Secretary of State to cause the papers in the case to be communicated to the proper committees.

Applications have been made to me by many free Americans of African descent to favor their emigration, with a view to such colonization as was contemplated in recent acts of Congress. Other parties, at home and abroad—some from interested motives, others upon patriotic considerations, and still others influenced by philanthropic sentiments—have suggested similar measures, while, on the other hand, several of the Spanish American Republics have protested against the sending of such colonies to their respective territories. Under these circumstances I have declined to move any such colony to any state without first obtaining the consent of its government, with an agreement on its part to receive and protect such emigrants in all the rights of freemen; and I have at the same time offered to the several States situated within the Tropics, or having colonies there, to negotiate with them, subject to the advice and consent of the Senate, to favor the voluntary emigration of persons of that class to their respective territories, upon conditions which shall be equal, just, and humane.   Liberia and Hayti are as yet the only countries to which colonists of African descent from here could go with certainty of being received and adopted as citizens; and I regret to say such persons contemplating colonization do not seem so willing to migrate to those countries as to some others, nor so willing as I think their interest demands.   I believe, however, opinion among them in this respect is improving, and that ere long there will be an augmented and considerable migration to both these countries from the United States.

The new commercial treaty between the United States and the Sultan of Turkey has been carried into execution.

A commercial and consular treaty has been negotiated, subject to the Senate's consent, with Liberia, and a similar negotiation is now pending with the Republic of Hayti.   A considerable improvement of the national commerce is expected to result from these measures.

Our relations with Great Britain, France, Spain, Portugal, Russia, Prussia, Denmark, Sweden, Austria, the Netherlands, Italy, Rome, and the other European States remain undisturbed.   Very favorable relations also continue to be maintained with Turkey, Morocco, China, and Japan.

During the last year there has not only been no change of our previous relations with the independent States of our own continent, but more friendly sentiments than have heretofore existed are believed to be entertained by these neighbors, whose safety and progress are so intimately connected with our own.   This statement especially applies to Mexico, Nicaragua, Costa Rica, Honduras, Peru, and Chile.

The commission under the convention with the Republic of New Granada closed its session without having audited and passed upon all the claims which were submitted to it.   A proposition is pending to revive the convention, that it may be able to do more complete justice.   The joint commission between the United States and the Republic of Costa Rica has completed its labors and submitted its report.

I have favored the project for connecting the United States with Europe by an Atlantic telegraph, and a similar project to extend the telegraph from San Francisco to connect by a Pacific telegraph with the line which is being extended across the Russian Empire.

The Territories of the United States, with unimportant exceptions, have remained undisturbed by the civil war; and they are exhibiting such evidence of prosperity as justifies an expectation that some of them will soon be in a condition to be organized as States and be constitutionally admitted into the Federal Union.

The immense mineral resources of some of those Territories ought to be developed as rapidly as possible.   Every step in that direction would have a tendency to improve the revenues of the Government and diminish the burdens of the people. It is worthy of your serious consideration whether some extraordinary measures to promote that end can not be adopted. The means which suggests itself as most likely to be effective is a scientific exploration of the mineral regions in those Territories with a view to the publication of its results at home and in foreign countries—results which can not fail to be auspicious.

The condition of the finances will claim your most diligent consideration. The vast expenditures incident to the military and naval operations required for the suppression of the rebellion have hitherto been met with a promptitude and certainty unusual in similar circumstances, and the public credit has been fully maintained. The continuance of the war, however, and the increased disbursements made necessary by the augmented forces now in the field demand your best reflections as to the best modes of providing the necessary revenue without injury to business and with the least possible burdens upon labor.

The suspension of specie payments by the banks soon after the commencement of your last session made large issues of United States notes unavoidable. In no other way could the payment of the troops and the satisfaction of other just demands be so economically or so well provided for. The judicious legislation of Congress, securing the receivability of these notes for loans and internal duties and making them a legal tender for other debts, has made them an universal currency, and has satisfied, partially at least, and for the time, the long-felt want of an uniform circulating medium, saving thereby to the people immense sums in discounts and exchanges.

A return to specie payments, however, at the earliest period compatible with due regard to all interests concerned should ever be kept in view. Fluctuations in the value of currency are always injurious, and to reduce these fluctuations to the lowest possible point will always be a leading purpose in wise legislation. Convertibility, prompt and certain convertibility, into coin is generally acknowledged to be the best and surest safeguard against them; and it is extremely doubtful whether a circulation of United States notes payable in coin and sufficiently large for the wants of the people can be permanently, usefully, and safely maintained.

Is there, then, any other mode in which the necessary provision for the public wants can be made and the great advantages of a safe and uniform currency secured?

I know of none which promises so certain results and is at the same time so unobjectionable as the organization of banking associations, under a general act of Congress, well guarded in its provisions. To such associations the Government might furnish circulating notes on the security of United States bonds deposited in the Treasury. These notes, prepared under the supervision of proper officers, being uniform in appearance and security and convertible always into coin, would at once protect labor against the evils of a vicious currency and facilitate commerce by cheap and safe exchanges.

A moderate reservation from the interest on the bonds would compensate the United States for the preparation and distribution of the notes and a general supervision of the system, and would lighten the burden of that part of the public debt employed as securities. The public credit, moreover, would be greatly improved and the negotiation of new loans greatly facilitated by the steady market demand for Government bonds which the adoption of the proposed system would create.

It is an additional recommendation of the measure, of considerable weight, in my judgment, that it would reconcile as far as possible all existing interests by the opportunity offered to existing institutions to reorganize under the act, substituting only the secured uniform national circulation for the local and various circulation, secured and unsecured, now issued by them.

The receipts into the Treasury from all sources, including loans and balance from the preceding year, for the fiscal year ending on the 30th June, 1862, were $583,885,247.06, of which sum $49,056,397.62 were derived from customs; $1,795,331.73 from the direct tax; from public lands, $152,203.77; from miscellaneous sources, $931,787.64; from loans in all forms, $529,692,460.50. The remainder, $2,257,065.80, was the balance from last year.

The disbursements during the same period were: For Congressional, executive, and judicial purposes, $5,939,009.29; for foreign intercourse, $1,339,710.35; for miscellaneous expenses, including the mints, loans, Post-Office deficiencies, collection of revenue, and other like charges, $14,129,771.50; for expenses under the Interior Department, $3,102,-985.52; under the War Department, $394,368,407.36; under the Navy Department, $42,674,569.69; for interest on public debt, $13,190,324.45; and for payment of public debt, including reimbursement of temporary loan and redemptions, $96,096,922.09; making an aggregate of $570,-841,700.25, and leaving a balance in the Treasury on the 1st day of July, 1862, of $13,043,546.81.

It should be observed that the sum of $96,096,922.09, expended for reimbursements and redemption of public debt, being included also in the loans made, may be properly deducted both from receipts and expenditures, leaving the actual receipts for the year $487,788,324.97, and the expenditures $474,744,778.16.

Other information on the subject of the finances will be found in the report of the Secretary of the Treasury, to whose statements and views I invite your most candid and considerate attention.

The reports of the Secretaries of War and of the Navy are herewith transmitted. These reports, though lengthy, are scarcely more than brief abstracts of the very numerous and extensive transactions and operations conducted through those Departments. Nor could I give a summary of them here upon any principle which would admit of its being much shorter than the reports themselves. I therefore content myself with laying the reports before you and asking your attention to them.

It gives me pleasure to report a decided improvement in the financial condition of the Post-Office Department as compared with several preceding years. The receipts for the fiscal year 1861 amounted to $8,349,296.40, which embraced the revenue from all the States of the Union for three quarters of that year. Notwithstanding the cessation of revenue from the so-called seceded States during the last fiscal year, the increase of the correspondence of the loyal States has been sufficient to produce a revenue during the same year of $8,299,820.90, being only $50,000 less than was derived from all the States of the Union during the previous year. The expenditures show a still more favorable result. The amount expended in 1861 was $13,606,759.11. For the last year the amount has been reduced to $11,125,364.13, showing a decrease of about $2,481,000 in the expenditures as compared with the preceding year, and about $3,750,000 as compared with the fiscal year 1860. The deficiency in the Department for the previous year was $4,551,966.98. For the last fiscal year it was reduced to $2,112,814.57. These favorable results are in part owing to the cessation of mail service in the insurrectionary States and in part to a careful review of all expenditures in that Department in the interest of economy. The efficiency of the postal service, it is believed, has also been much improved. The Postmaster-General has also opened a correspondence through the Department of State with foreign governments proposing a convention of postal representatives for the purpose of simplifying the rates of foreign postage and to expedite the foreign mails. This proposition, equally important to our adopted citizens and to the commercial interests of this country, has been favorably entertained and agreed to by all the governments from whom replies have been received.

I ask the attention of Congress to the suggestions of the Postmaster-General in his report respecting the further legislation required, in his opinion, for the benefit of the postal service.

The Secretary of the Interior reports as follows in regard to the public lands:

The public lands have ceased to be a source of revenue. From the 1st July, 1861, to the 30th September, 1862, the entire cash receipts from the sale of lands were $137,476.26—a sum much less than the expenses of our land system during the same period. The homestead law, which will take effect on the 1st of January next, offers such inducements to settlers that sales for cash can not be expected to an extent sufficient to meet the expenses of the General Land Office and the cost of surveying and bringing the land into market.

The discrepancy between the sum here stated as arising from the sales of the public lands and the sum derived from the same source as reported from the Treasury Department arises, as I understand, from the fact that the periods of time, though apparently, were not really coincident at the beginning point, the Treasury report including a considerable sum now which had previously been reported from the Interior, sufficiently large to greatly overreach the sum derived from the three months now reported upon by the Interior and not by the Treasury.

The Indian tribes upon our frontiers have during the past year manifested a spirit of insubordination, and at several points have engaged in open hostilities against the white settlements in their vicinity. The tribes occupying the Indian country south of Kansas renounced their allegiance to the United States and entered into treaties with the insurgents. Those who remained loyal to the United States were driven from the country. The chief of the Cherokees has visited this city for the purpose of restoring the former relations of the tribe with the United States. He alleges that they were constrained by superior force to enter into treaties with the insurgents, and that the United States neglected to furnish the protection which their treaty stipulations required.

In the month of August last the Sioux Indians in Minnesota attacked the settlements in their vicinity with extreme ferocity, killing indiscriminately men, women, and children. This attack was wholly unexpected, and therefore no means of defense had been provided. It is estimated that not less than 800 persons were killed by the Indians, and a large amount of property was destroyed. How this outbreak was induced is not definitely known, and suspicions, which may be unjust, need not to be stated. Information was received by the Indian Bureau from different sources about the time hostilities were commenced that a simultaneous attack was to be made upon the white settlements by all the tribes between the Mississippi River and the Rocky Mountains. The State of Minnesota has suffered great injury from this Indian war. A large portion of her territory has been depopulated, and a severe loss has been sustained by the destruction of property. The people of that State manifest much anxiety for the removal of the tribes beyond the limits of the State as a guaranty against future hostilities. The Commissioner of Indian Affairs will furnish full details. I submit for your especial consideration whether our Indian system shall not be remodeled. Many wise and good men have impressed me with the belief that this can be profitably done.

I submit a statement of the proceedings of commissioners, which shows the progress that has been made in the enterprise of constructing the Pacific Railroad. And this suggests the earliest completion of this road, and also the favorable action of Congress upon the projects now pending before them for enlarging the capacities of the great canals in New York and Illinois, as being of vital and rapidly increasing importance to the whole nation, and especially to the vast interior region hereinafter to be noticed at some greater length. I purpose having prepared and laid before you at an early day some interesting and valuable statistical information upon this subject. The military and commercial importance of enlarging the Illinois and Michigan Canal and improving the Illinois River is presented in the report of Colonel Webster to the Secretary of War, and now transmitted to Congress. I respectfully ask attention to it.

To carry out the provisions of the act of Congress of the 15th of May last, I have caused the Department of Agriculture of the United States to be organized.

The Commissioner informs me that within the period of a few months this Department has established an extensive system of correspondence and exchanges, both at home and abroad, which promises to effect highly beneficial results in the development of a correct knowledge of recent improvements in agriculture, in the introduction of new products, and in the collection of the agricultural statistics of the different States.

Also, that it will soon be prepared to distribute largely seeds, cereals, plants, and cuttings, and has already published and liberally diffused much valuable information in anticipation of a more elaborate report, which will in due time be furnished, embracing some valuable tests in chemical science now in progress in the laboratory.

The creation of this Department was for the more immediate benefit of a large class of our most valuable citizens, and I trust that the liberal basis upon which it has been organized will not only meet your approbation, but that it will realize at no distant day all the fondest anticipations of its most sanguine friends and become the fruitful source of advantage to all our people.

On the 22d day of September last a proclamation was issued by the Executive, a copy of which is herewith submitted.

In accordance with the purpose expressed in the second paragraph of that paper, I now respectfully recall your attention to what may be called "compensated emancipation."

A nation may be said to consist of its territory, its people, and its laws. The territory is the only part which is of certain durability. "One generation passeth away and another generation cometh, but the earth abideth forever." It is of the first importance to duly consider and estimate this ever-enduring part. That portion of the earth's surface which is owned and inhabited by the people of the United States is well adapted to be the home of one national family, and it is not well adapted for two or more. Its vast extent and its variety of climate and productions are of advantage in this age for one people, whatever they might have been in former ages. Steam, telegraphs, and intelligence have brought these to be an advantageous combination for one united people.

In the inaugural address I briefly pointed out the total inadequacy of disunion as a remedy for the differences between the people of the two sections. I did so in language which I can not improve, and which, therefore, I beg to repeat:

One section of our country believes slavery is *right* and ought to be extended, while the other believes it is *wrong* and ought not to be extended. This is the only substantial dispute. The fugitive-slave clause of the Constitution and the law for the suppression of the foreign slave trade are each as well enforced, perhaps, as any law can ever be in a community where the moral sense of the people imperfectly supports the law itself. The great body of the people abide by the dry legal obligation in both cases, and a few break over in each. This, I think, can not be perfectly cured, and it would be worse in both cases *after* the separation of the sections than before. The foreign slave trade, now imperfectly suppressed, would be ultimately revived without restriction in one section, while fugitive slaves, now only partially surrendered, would not be surrendered at all by the other.

Physically speaking, we can not separate. We can not remove our respective sections from each other nor build an impassable wall between them. A husband and wife may be divorced and go out of the presence and beyond the reach of each other, but the different parts of our country can not do this. They can not but remain face to face, and intercourse, either amicable or hostile, must continue between them. Is it possible, then, to make that intercourse more advantageous or more satisfactory *after* separation than *before*? Can aliens make treaties easier than friends can make laws? Can treaties be more faithfully enforced between aliens than laws can among friends? Suppose you go to war, you can not fight always; and when, after much loss on both sides and no gain on either, you cease fighting, the identical old questions, as to terms of intercourse, are again upon you.

There is no line, straight or crooked, suitable for a national boundary upon which to divide. Trace through, from east to west, upon the line between the free and slave country, and we shall find a little more than one-third of its length are rivers, easy to be crossed, and populated, or soon to be populated, thickly upon both sides; while nearly all its remaining length are merely surveyors' lines, over which people may walk back and forth without any consciousness of their presence. No part of this line can be made any more difficult to pass by writing it down on paper or parchment as a national boundary. The fact of separation, if it comes, gives up on the part of the seceding section the fugitive-slave clause, along with all other constitutional obligations upon the section seceded from, while I should expect no treaty stipulation would ever be made to take its place.

But there is another difficulty. The great interior region bounded east by the Alleghanies, north by the British dominions, west by the Rocky Mountains, and south by the line along which the culture of corn and cotton meets, and which includes part of Virginia, part of Tennessee, all of Kentucky, Ohio, Indiana, Michigan, Wisconsin, Illinois, Missouri, Kansas, Iowa, Minnesota, and the Territories of Dakota, Nebraska, and part of Colorado, already has above 10,000,000 people, and will have 50,000,000 within fifty years if not prevented by any political folly or mistake. It contains more than one-third of the country owned by the United States—certainly more than 1,000,000 square miles. Once half as populous as Massachusetts already is, it would have more than 75,000,000 people. A glance at the map shows that, territorially speaking, it is the great body of the Republic. The other parts are but marginal borders to it, the magnificent region sloping west from the Rocky Mountains to the Pacific being the deepest and also the richest in undeveloped resources. In the production of provisions, grains, grasses, and all which proceed from them this great interior region is naturally one of the most important in the world. Ascertain from the statistics the small proportion of the region which has as yet been brought into cultivation, and also the large and rapidly increasing amount of its products, and we shall be overwhelmed with the magnitude of the prospect presented. And yet this region has no seacoast—touches no ocean anywhere. As part of one nation, its people now find, and may forever find, their way to Europe by New York, to South America and Africa by New Orleans, and to Asia by San Francisco; but separate our common country into two nations, as designed by the present rebellion, and every man of this great interior region is thereby cut off from some one or more of these outlets, not perhaps by a physical barrier, but by embarrassing and onerous trade regulations.

And this is true, *wherever* a dividing or boundary line may be fixed. Place it between the now free and slave country, or place it south of Kentucky or north of Ohio, and still the truth remains that none south of it can trade to any port or place north of it, and none north of it can trade to any port or place south of it, except upon terms dictated by a government foreign to them. These outlets, east, west, and south, are indispensable to the well-being of the people inhabiting and to inhabit this vast interior region. *Which* of the three may be the best is no proper question. All are better than either, and all of right belong to that people and to their successors forever. True to themselves, they will not ask *where* a line of separation shall be, but will vow rather that there shall be no such line. Nor are the marginal regions less interested in these communications to and through them to the great outside world. They, too, and each of them, must have access to this Egypt of the West without paying toll at the crossing of any national boundary.

Our national strife springs not from our permanent part; not from the land we inhabit; not from our national homestead. There is no possible severing of this but would multiply and not mitigate evils among us. In all its adaptations and aptitudes it demands union and abhors separation. In fact, it would ere long force reunion, however much of blood and treasure the separation might have cost.

Our strife pertains to ourselves—to the passing generations of men—and it can without convulsion be hushed forever with the passing of one generation.

In this view I recommend the adoption of the following resolution and articles amendatory to the Constitution of the United States:

Resolved by the Senate and House of Representatives of the United States of America in Congress assembled (two-thirds of both Houses concurring), That the following articles be proposed to the legislatures (or conventions) of the several States as amendments to the Constitution of the United States, all or any of which articles, when ratified by three-fourths of the said legislatures (or conventions), to be valid as part or parts of the said Constitution, viz:

ART. —. Every State wherein slavery now exists which shall abolish the same therein at any time or times before the 1st day of January, A. D. 1900, shall receive compensation from the United States as follows, to wit:

The President of the United States shall deliver to every such State bonds of the United States bearing interest at the rate of —— per cent per annum to an amount equal to the aggregate sum of —————— for each slave shown to have been therein by the Eighth Census of the United States, said bonds to be delivered to such State by installments or in one parcel at the completion of the abolishment, accordingly as the same shall have been gradual or at one time within such State; and interest shall begin to run upon any such bond only from the proper time of its delivery as aforesaid. Any State having received bonds as aforesaid and afterwards reintroducing or tolerating slavery therein shall refund to the United States the bonds so received, or the value thereof, and all interest paid thereon.

ART. —. All slaves who shall have enjoyed actual freedom by the chances of the war at any time before the end of the rebellion shall be forever free; but all owners of such who shall not have been disloyal shall be compensated for them at the same rates as is provided for States adopting abolishment of slavery, but in such way that no slave shall be twice accounted for.

ART. —. Congress may appropriate money and otherwise provide for colonizing free colored persons with their own consent at any place or places without the United States.

I beg indulgence to discuss these proposed articles at some length. Without slavery the rebellion could never have existed; without slavery it could not continue.

Among the friends of the Union there is great diversity of sentiment and of policy in regard to slavery and the African race amongst us. Some would perpetuate slavery; some would abolish it suddenly and without compensation; some would abolish it gradually and with compensation; some would remove the freed people from us, and some would retain them with us; and there are yet other minor diversities. Because of these diversities we waste much strength in struggles among ourselves. By mutual concession we should harmonize and act together. This would be compromise, but it would be compromise among the friends and not with the enemies of the Union. These articles are intended to embody a plan of such mutual concessions. If the plan shall be adopted, it is assumed that emancipation will follow, at least in several of the States.

As to the first article, the main points are, first, the emancipation; secondly, the length of time for consummating it (thirty-seven years); and, thirdly, the compensation.

The emancipation will be unsatisfactory to the advocates of perpetual slavery, but the length of time should greatly mitigate their dissatisfaction. The time spares both races from the evils of sudden derangement—in fact, from the necessity of any derangement—while most of those whose habitual course of thought will be disturbed by the measure will have passed away before its consummation. They will never see it. Another class will hail the prospect of emancipation, but will deprecate the length of time. They will feel that it gives too little to the now living slaves. But it really gives them much. It saves them from the vagrant destitution which must largely attend immediate emancipation in localities where their numbers are very great, and it gives the inspiring assurance that their posterity shall be free forever. The plan leaves to each State choosing to act under it to abolish slavery now or at the end of the century, or at any intermediate time, or by degrees extending over the whole or any part of the period, and it obliges no two States to proceed alike. It also provides for compensation, and generally the mode of making it. This, it would seem, must further mitigate the dissatisfaction of those who favor perpetual slavery, and especially of those who are to receive the compensation. Doubtless some of those who are to pay and not to receive will object. Yet the measure is both just and economical. In a certain sense the liberation of slaves is the destruction of property—property acquired by descent or by purchase, the same as any other property. It is no less true for having been often said that the people of the South are not more responsible for the original introduction of this property than are the people of the North; and when it is remembered how unhesitatingly we all use cotton and sugar and share the profits of dealing in them, it may not be quite safe to say that the South has been more responsible than the North for its continuance. If, then, for a common object this property is to be sacrificed, is it not just that it be done at a common charge?

And if with less money, or money more easily paid, we can preserve the benefits of the Union by this means than we can by the war alone, is it not also economical to do it? Let us consider it, then. Let us ascertain the sum we have expended in the war since compensated emancipation was proposed last March, and consider whether if that measure had been promptly accepted by even some of the slave States the same sum would not have done more to close the war than has been otherwise done. If so, the measure would save money, and in that view would be a prudent and economical measure. Certainly it is not so easy to pay *something* as it is to pay *nothing*, but it is easier to pay a *large* sum than it is to pay a *larger* one. And it is easier to pay any sum *when* we are able than it is to pay it *before* we are able. The war requires large sums, and requires them at once. The aggregate sum necessary for compensated emancipation of course would be large. But it would require no ready cash, nor the bonds even any faster than the emancipation progresses. This might not, and probably would not, close before the end of the thirty-seven years. At that time we shall probably have a hundred millions of people to share the burden, instead of thirty-one millions as now. And not only so, but the increase of our population may be expected to continue for a long time after that period as rapidly as before, because our territory will not have become full. I do not state this inconsiderately. At the same ratio of increase which we have maintained, on an average, from our first national census, in 1790, until that of 1860, we should in 1900 have a population of 103,208,415. And why may we not continue that ratio far beyond that period? Our abundant room, our

broad national homestead, is our ample resource.   Were our territory as
limited as are the British Isles, very certainly our population could not
expand as stated.   Instead of receiving the foreign born as now, we
should be compelled to send part of the native born away.   But such
is not our condition.   We have 2,963,000 square miles.   Europe has
3,800,000, with a population averaging 73⅓ persons to the square mile.
Why may not our country at some time average as many?   Is it less
fertile?   Has it more waste surface by mountains, rivers, lakes, deserts,
or other causes?   Is it inferior to Europe in any natural advantage?   If,
then, we are at some time to be as populous as Europe, how soon?   As
to when this *may* be, we can judge by the past and the present; as to
when it *will* be, if ever, depends much on whether we maintain the Union.
Several of our States are already above the average of Europe—73⅓ to
the square mile.   Massachusetts has 157; Rhode Island, 133; Connecticut, 99; New York and New Jersey, each 80.   Also two other great States,
Pennsylvania and Ohio, are not far below, the former having 63 and the
latter 59.   The States already above the European average, except New
York, have increased in as rapid a ratio since passing that point as ever
before, while no one of them is equal to some other parts of our country
in natural capacity for sustaining a dense population.

Taking the nation in the aggregate, and we find its population and ratio
of increase for the several decennial periods to be as follows:

Year.	Population.	Ratio of increase.
		Per cent.
1790..	3,929,827	....
1800..	5,305,937	35.02
1810..	7,239,814	36.45
1820..	9,638,131	33.13
1830..	12,866,020	33.49
1840..	17,069,453	32.67
1850..	23,191,876	35.87
1860..	31,443,790	35.58

This shows an average decennial increase of 34.60 per cent in population through the seventy years from our first to our last census yet taken.
It is seen that the ratio of increase at no one of these seven periods is
either 2 per cent below or 2 per cent above the average, thus showing
how inflexible, and consequently how reliable, the law of increase in our
case is.   Assuming that it will continue, it gives the following results:

Year.	Population.
1870	42,323,341
1880	56,967,216
1890	76,677,872
1900	103,208,415
1910	138,918,526
1920	186,984,335
1930	251,680,914

These figures show that our country *may* be as populous as Europe now is at some point between 1920 and 1930—say about 1925—our territory, at 73⅓ persons to the square mile, being of capacity to contain 217,186,000.

And we *will* reach this, too, if we do not ourselves relinquish the chance by the folly and evils of disunion or by long and exhausting war springing from the only great element of national discord among us. While it can not be foreseen exactly how much one huge example of secession, breeding lesser ones indefinitely, would retard population, civilization, and prosperity, no one can doubt that the extent of it would be very great and injurious.

The proposed emancipation would shorten the war, perpetuate peace, insure this increase of population, and proportionately the wealth of the country. With these we should pay all the emancipation would cost, together with our other debt, easier than we should pay our other debt without it. If we had allowed our old national debt to run at 6 per cent per annum, simple interest, from the end of our revolutionary struggle until to-day, without paying anything on either principal or interest, each man of us would owe less upon that debt now than each man owed upon it then; and this because our increase of men through the whole period has been greater than 6 per cent—has run faster than the interest upon the debt. Thus time alone relieves a debtor nation, so long as its population increases faster than unpaid interest accumulates on its debt.

This fact would be no excuse for delaying payment of what is justly due, but it shows the great importance of time in this connection—the great advantage of a policy by which we shall not have to pay until we number 100,000,000 what by a different policy we would have to pay now, when we number but 31,000,000. In a word, it shows that a dollar will be much harder to pay for the war than will be a dollar for emancipation on the proposed plan. And then the latter will cost no blood, no precious life. It will be a saving of both.

As to the second article, I think it would be impracticable to return to bondage the class of persons therein contemplated. Some of them, doubtless, in the property sense belong to loyal owners, and hence provision is made in this article for compensating such.

The third article relates to the future of the freed people. It does not oblige, but merely authorizes Congress to aid in colonizing such as may consent. This ought not to be regarded as objectionable on the one hand or on the other, insomuch as it comes to nothing unless by the mutual consent of the people to be deported and the American voters, through their representatives in Congress.

I can not make it better known than it already is that I strongly favor colonization; and yet I wish to say there is an objection urged against free colored persons remaining in the country which is largely imaginary, if not sometimes malicious.

It is insisted that their presence would injure and displace white labor and white laborers. If there ever could be a proper time for mere catch arguments, that time surely is not now. In times like the present men should utter nothing for which they would not willingly be responsible through time and in eternity. Is it true, then, that colored people can displace any more white labor by being free than by remaining slaves? If they stay in their old places, they jostle no white laborers; if they leave their old places, they leave them open to white laborers. Logically, there is neither more nor less of it. Emancipation, even without deportation, would probably enhance the wages of white labor, and very surely would not reduce them. Thus the customary amount of labor would still have to be performed—the freed people would surely not do more than their old proportion of it, and very probably for a time would do less, leaving an increased part to white laborers, bringing their labor into greater demand, and consequently enhancing the wages of it. With deportation, even to a limited extent, enhanced wages to white labor is mathematically certain. Labor is like any other commodity in the market—increase the demand for it and you increase the price of it. Reduce the supply of black labor by colonizing the black laborer out of the country, and by precisely so much you increase the demand for and wages of white labor.

But it is dreaded that the freed people will swarm forth and cover the whole land. Are they not already in the land? Will liberation make them any more numerous? Equally distributed among the whites of the whole country, and there would be but one colored to seven whites. Could the one in any way greatly disturb the seven? There are many communities now having more than one free colored person to seven whites and this without any apparent consciousness of evil from it. The District of Columbia and the States of Maryland and Delaware are all in this condition. The District has more than one free colored to six whites, and yet in its frequent petitions to Congress I believe it has never presented the presence of free colored persons as one of its grievances. But why should emancipation South send the free people North? People of any color seldom run unless there be something to run from. *Heretofore* colored people to some extent have fled North from bondage, and *now*, perhaps, from both bondage and destitution. But if gradual emancipation and deportation be adopted, they will have neither to flee from. Their old masters will give them wages at least until new laborers can be procured, and the freedmen in turn will gladly give their labor for the wages till new homes can be found for them in congenial climes and with people of their own blood and race. This proposition can be trusted on the mutual interests involved. And in any event, can not the North decide for itself whether to receive them?

Again, as practice proves more than theory in any case, has there been any irruption of colored people northward because of the abolishment of slavery in this District last spring?

What I have said of the proportion of free colored persons to the whites in the District is from the census of 1860, having no reference to persons called contrabands nor to those made free by the act of Congress abolishing slavery here.

The plan consisting of these articles is recommended, not but that a restoration of the national authority would be accepted without its adoption.

Nor will the war nor proceedings under the proclamation of September 22, 1862, be stayed because of the *recommendation* of this plan. Its timely *adoption*, I doubt not, would bring restoration, and thereby stay both.

And notwithstanding this plan, the recommendation that Congress provide by law for compensating any State which may adopt emancipation before this plan shall have been acted upon is hereby earnestly renewed. Such would be only an advance part of the plan, and the same arguments apply to both.

This plan is recommended as a means, not in exclusion of, but additional to, all others for restoring and preserving the national authority throughout the Union. The subject is presented exclusively in its economical aspect. The plan would, I am confident, secure peace more speedily and maintain it more permanently than can be done by force alone, while all it would cost, considering amounts and manner of payment and times of payment, would be easier paid than will be the additional cost of the war if we rely solely upon force. It is much, very much, that it would cost no blood at all.

The plan is proposed as permanent constitutional law. It can not become such without the concurrence of, first, two-thirds of Congress, and afterwards three-fourths of the States. The requisite three-fourths of the States will necessarily include seven of the slave States. Their concurrence, if obtained, will give assurance of their severally adopting emancipation at no very distant day upon the new constitutional terms. This assurance would end the struggle now and save the Union forever.

I do not forget the gravity which should characterize a paper addressed to the Congress of the nation by the Chief Magistrate of the nation, nor do I forget that some of you are my seniors, nor that many of you have more experience than I in the conduct of public affairs. Yet I trust that in view of the great responsibility resting upon me you will perceive no want of respect to yourselves in any undue earnestness I may seem to display.

Is it doubted, then, that the plan I propose, if adopted, would shorten the war, and thus lessen its expenditure of money and of blood? Is it doubted that it would restore the national authority and national prosperity and perpetuate both indefinitely? Is it doubted that we here—Congress and Executive—can secure its adoption? Will not the good people respond to a united and earnest appeal from us? Can we, can they, by any other means so certainly or so speedily assure these vital objects? We can succeed only by concert. It is not "Can *any* of us *imagine* better?" but "Can we *all* do better?" Object whatsoever is possible, still the question recurs, "Can we do better?" The dogmas of the quiet past are inadequate to the stormy present. The occasion is piled high with difficulty, and we must rise with the occasion. As our case is new, so we must think anew and act anew. We must disenthrall ourselves, and then we shall save our country.

Fellow-citizens, *we* can not escape history. We of this Congress and this Administration will be remembered in spite of ourselves. No personal significance or insignificance can spare one or another of us. The fiery trial through which we pass will light us down in honor or dishonor to the latest generation. We *say* we are for the Union. The world will not forget that we say this. We know how to save the Union. The world knows we do know how to save it. We, even *we here*, hold the power and bear the responsibility. In *giving* freedom to the *slave* we *assure* freedom to the *free*—honorable alike in what we give and what we preserve. We shall nobly save or meanly lose the last best hope of earth. Other means may succeed; this could not fail. The way is plain, peaceful, generous, just—a way which if followed the world will forever applaud and God must forever bless.

THIRD ANNUAL MESSAGE.

DECEMBER 8, 1863.

Fellow-Citizens of the Senate and House of Representatives:

Another year of health and of sufficiently abundant harvests has passed. For these, and especially for the improved condition of our national affairs, our renewed and profoundest gratitude to God is due.

We remain in peace and friendship with foreign powers.

The efforts of disloyal citizens of the United States to involve us in foreign wars to aid an inexcusable insurrection have been unavailing. Her Britannic Majesty's Government, as was justly expected, have exercised their authority to prevent the departure of new hostile expeditions from British ports. The Emperor of France has by a like proceeding promptly vindicated the neutrality which he proclaimed at the beginning of the contest. Questions of great intricacy and importance have arisen out of the blockade and other belligerent operations between the Government and several of the maritime powers, but they have been discussed and, as far as was possible, accommodated in a spirit of frankness, justice, and mutual good will. It is especially gratifying that our prize courts, by the impartiality of their adjudications, have commanded the respect and confidence of maritime powers.

The supplemental treaty between the United States and Great Britain for the suppression of the African slave trade, made on the 17th day of February last, has been duly ratified and carried into execution. It is believed that so far as American ports and American citizens are concerned that inhuman and odious traffic has been brought to an end.

I shall submit for the consideration of the Senate a convention for the adjustment of possessory claims in Washington Territory arising out of the treaty of the 15th June, 1846, between the United States and Great Britain, and which have been the source of some disquiet among the citizens of that now rapidly improving part of the country.

A novel and important question, involving the extent of the maritime jurisdiction of Spain in the waters which surround the island of Cuba, has been debated without reaching an agreement, and it is proposed in an amicable spirit to refer it to the arbitrament of a friendly power. A convention for that purpose will be submitted to the Senate.

I have thought it proper, subject to the approval of the Senate, to concur with the interested commercial powers in an arrangement for the liquidation of the Scheldt dues, upon the principles which have been heretofore adopted in regard to the imposts upon navigation in the waters of Denmark.

The long-pending controversy between this Government and that of Chile touching the seizure at Sitana, in Peru, by Chilean officers, of a large amount in treasure belonging to citizens of the United States has been brought to a close by the award of His Majesty the King of the Belgians, to whose arbitration the question was referred by the parties. The subject was thoroughly and patiently examined by that justly respected magistrate, and although the sum awarded to the claimants may not have been as large as they expected there is no reason to distrust the wisdom of His Majesty's decision. That decision was promptly complied with by Chile when intelligence in regard to it reached that country.

The joint commission under the act of the last session for carrying into effect the convention with Peru on the subject of claims has been organized at Lima, and is engaged in the business intrusted to it.

Difficulties concerning interoceanic transit through Nicaragua are in course of amicable adjustment.

In conformity with principles set forth in my last annual message, I have received a representative from the United States of Colombia, and have accredited a minister to that Republic.

Incidents occurring in the progress of our civil war have forced upon my attention the uncertain state of international questions touching the rights of foreigners in this country and of United States citizens abroad. In regard to some governments these rights are at least partially defined by treaties.   In no instance, however, is it expressly stipulated that in the event of civil war a foreigner residing in this country within the lines of the insurgents is to be exempted from the rule which classes him as a belligerent, in whose behalf the Government of his country can not expect any privileges or immunities distinct from that character.   I regret to say, however, that such claims have been put forward, and in some instances in behalf of foreigners who have lived in the United States the greater part of their lives.

There is reason to believe that many persons born in foreign countries who have declared their intention to become citizens, or who have been fully naturalized, have evaded the military duty required of them by denying the fact and thereby throwing upon the Government the burden of proof.   It has been found difficult or impracticable to obtain this proof, from the want of guides to the proper sources of information.   These might be supplied by requiring clerks of courts where declarations of intention may be made or naturalizations effected to send periodically lists of the names of the persons naturalized or declaring their intention to become citizens to the Secretary of the Interior, in whose Department those names might be arranged and printed for general information.

There is also reason to believe that foreigners frequently become citizens of the United States for the sole purpose of evading duties imposed by the laws of their native countries, to which on becoming naturalized here they at once repair, and though never returning to the United States they still claim the interposition of this Government as citizens.   Many altercations and great prejudices have heretofore arisen out of this abuse. It is therefore submitted to your serious consideration.   It might be advisable to fix a limit beyond which no citizen of the United States residing abroad may claim the interposition of his Government.

The right of suffrage has often been assumed and exercised by aliens under pretenses of naturalization, which they have disavowed when drafted into the military service.   I submit the expediency of such an amendment of the law as will make the fact of voting an estoppel against any plea of exemption from military service or other civil obligation on the ground of alienage.

In common with other Western powers, our relations with Japan have been brought into serious jeopardy through the perverse opposition of the hereditary aristocracy of the Empire to the enlightened and liberal policy of the Tycoon, designed to bring the country into the society of nations. It is hoped, although not with entire confidence, that these difficulties may be peacefully overcome. I ask your attention to the claim of the minister residing there for the damages he sustained in the destruction by fire of the residence of the legation at Yedo.

Satisfactory arrangements have been made with the Emperor of Russia, which, it is believed, will result in effecting a continuous line of telegraph through that Empire from our Pacific coast.

I recommend to your favorable consideration the subject of an international telegraph across the Atlantic Ocean, and also of a telegraph between this capital and the national forts along the Atlantic seaboard and the Gulf of Mexico. Such communications, established with any reasonable outlay, would be economical as well as effective aids to the diplomatic, military, and naval service.

The consular system of the United States, under the enactments of the last Congress, begins to be self-sustaining, and there is reason to hope that it may become entirely so with the increase of trade which will ensue whenever peace is restored. Our ministers abroad have been faithful in defending American rights. In protecting commercial interests our consuls have necessarily had to encounter increased labors and responsibilities growing out of the war. These they have for the most part met and discharged with zeal and efficiency. This acknowledgment justly includes those consuls who, residing in Morocco, Egypt, Turkey, Japan, China, and other Oriental countries, are charged with complex functions and extraordinary powers.

The condition of the several organized Territories is generally satisfactory, although Indian disturbances in New Mexico have not been entirely suppressed. The mineral resources of Colorado, Nevada, Idaho, New Mexico, and Arizona are proving far richer than has been heretofore understood. I lay before you a communication on this subject from the governor of New Mexico. I again submit to your consideration the expediency of establishing a system for the encouragement of immigration. Although this source of national wealth and strength is again flowing with greater freedom than for several years before the insurrection occurred, there is still a great deficiency of laborers in every field of industry, especially in agriculture and in our mines, as well of iron and coal as of the precious metals. While the demand for labor is much increased here, tens of thousands of persons, destitute of remunerative occupation, are thronging our foreign consulates and offering to emigrate to the United States if essential, but very cheap, assistance can be afforded them. It is easy to see that under the sharp discipline of civil war the nation is beginning a new life. This noble effort demands the aid and ought to receive the attention and support of the Government.

Injuries unforeseen by the Government and unintended may in some cases have been inflicted on the subjects or citizens of foreign countries, both at sea and on land, by persons in the service of the United States. As this Government expects redress from other powers when similar injuries are inflicted by persons in their service upon citizens of the United States, we must be prepared to do justice to foreigners. If the existing judicial tribunals are inadequate to this purpose, a special court may be authorized, with power to hear and decide such claims of the character referred to as may have arisen under treaties and the public law. Conventions for adjusting the claims by joint commission have been proposed to some governments, but no definitive answer to the proposition has yet been received from any.

In the course of the session I shall probably have occasion to request you to provide indemnification to claimants where decrees of restitution have been rendered and damages awarded by admiralty courts, and in other cases where this Government may be acknowledged to be liable in principle and where the amount of that liability has been ascertained by an informal arbitration.

The proper officers of the Treasury have deemed themselves required by the law of the United States upon the subject to demand a tax upon the incomes of foreign consuls in this country. While such a demand may not in strictness be in derogation of public law, or perhaps of any existing treaty between the United States and a foreign country, the expediency of so far modifying the act as to exempt from tax the income of such consuls as are not citizens of the United States, derived from the emoluments of their office or from property not situated in the United States, is submitted to your serious consideration. I make this suggestion upon the ground that a comity which ought to be reciprocated exempts our consuls in all other countries from taxation to the extent thus indicated. The United States, I think, ought not to be exceptionally illiberal to international trade and commerce.

The operations of the Treasury during the last year have been successfully conducted. The enactment by Congress of a national banking law has proved a valuable support of the public credit, and the general legislation in relation to loans has fully answered the expectations of its favorers. Some amendments may be required to perfect existing laws, but no change in their principles or general scope is believed to be needed.

Since these measures have been in operation all demands on the Treasury, including the pay of the Army and Navy, have been promptly met and fully satisfied. No considerable body of troops, it is believed, were ever more amply provided and more liberally and punctually paid, and it may be added that by no people were the burdens incident to a great war ever more cheerfully borne.

The receipts during the year from all sources, including loans and balance in the Treasury at its commencement, were $901,125,674.86, and the aggregate disbursements $895,796,630.65, leaving a balance on the 1st of

July, 1863, of $5,329,044.21. Of the receipts there were derived from customs $69,059,642.40, from internal revenue $37,640,787.95, from direct tax $1,485,103.61, from lands $167,617.17, from miscellaneous sources $3,046,615.35, and from loans $776,682,361.57, making the aggregate $901,125,674.86. Of the disbursements there were for the civil service $23,253,922.08, for pensions and Indians $4,216,520.79, for interest on public debt $24,729,846.51, for the War Department $599,298,600.83, for the Navy Department $63,211,105.27, for payment of funded and temporary debt $181,086,635.07, making the aggregate $895,796,630.65 and leaving the balance of $5,329,044.21. But the payment of funded and temporary debt, having been made from moneys borrowed during the year, must be regarded as merely nominal payments and the moneys borrowed to make them as merely nominal receipts, and their amount, $181,086,635.07, should therefore be deducted both from receipts and disbursements. This being done there remains as actual receipts $720,039,039.79 and the actual disbursements $714,709,995.58, leaving the balance as already stated.

The actual receipts and disbursements for the first quarter and the estimated receipts and disbursements for the remaining three quarters of the current fiscal year (1864) will be shown in detail by the report of the Secretary of the Treasury, to which I invite your attention. It is sufficient to say here that it is not believed that actual results will exhibit a state of the finances less favorable to the country than the estimates of that officer heretofore submitted, while it is confidently expected that at the close of the year both disbursements and debt will be found very considerably less than has been anticipated.

The report of the Secretary of War is a document of great interest. It consists of—

1. The military operations of the year, detailed in the report of the General in Chief.

2. The organization of colored persons into the war service.

3. The exchange of prisoners, fully set forth in the letter of General Hitchcock.

4. The operations under the act for enrolling and calling out the national forces, detailed in the report of the Provost-Marshal-General.

5. The organization of the invalid corps, and

6. The operation of the several departments of the Quartermaster-General, Commissary-General, Paymaster-General, Chief of Engineers, Chief of Ordnance, and Surgeon-General.

It has appeared impossible to make a valuable summary of this report, except such as would be too extended for this place, and hence I content myself by asking your careful attention to the report itself.

The duties devolving on the naval branch of the service during the year and throughout the whole of this unhappy contest have been discharged with fidelity and eminent success. The extensive blockade has been constantly increasing in efficiency as the Navy has expanded, yet on so long a line it has so far been impossible to entirely suppress illicit trade. From returns received at the Navy Department it appears that more than 1,000 vessels have been captured since the blockade was instituted, and that the value of prizes already sent in for adjudication amounts to over $13,000,000.

The naval force of the United States consists at this time of 588 vessels completed and in the course of completion, and of these 75 are ironclad or armored steamers. The events of the war give an increased interest and importance to the Navy which will probably extend beyond the war itself.

The armored vessels in our Navy completed and in service, or which are under contract and approaching completion, are believed to exceed in number those of any other power; but while these may be relied upon for harbor defense and coast service, others of greater strength and capacity will be necessary for cruising purposes and to maintain our rightful position on the ocean.

The change that has taken place in naval vessels and naval warfare since the introduction of steam as a motive power for ships of war demands either a corresponding change in some of our existing navy-yards or the establishment of new ones for the construction and necessary repair of modern naval vessels. No inconsiderable embarrassment, delay, and public injury have been experienced from the want of such governmental establishments. The necessity of such a navy-yard, so furnished, at some suitable place upon the Atlantic seaboard has on repeated occasions been brought to the attention of Congress by the Navy Department, and is again presented in the report of the Secretary which accompanies this communication. I think it my duty to invite your special attention to this subject, and also to that of establishing a yard and depot for naval purposes upon one of the Western rivers. A naval force has been created on those interior waters, and under many disadvantages, within little more than two years, exceeding in numbers the whole naval force of the country at the commencement of the present Administration. Satisfactory and important as have been the performances of the heroic men of the Navy at this interesting period, they are scarcely more wonderful than the success of our mechanics and artisans in the production of war vessels, which has created a new form of naval power.

Our country has advantages superior to any other nation in our resources of iron and timber, with inexhaustible quantities of fuel in the immediate vicinity of both, and all available and in close proximity to navigable waters. Without the advantage of public works, the resources of the nation have been developed and its power displayed in the construction of a Navy of such magnitude, which has at the very period of its creation rendered signal service to the Union.

The increase of the number of seamen in the public service from 7,500 men in the spring of 1861 to about 34,000 at the present time has been accomplished without special legislation or extraordinary bounties to promote that increase. It has been found, however, that the operation of the draft, with the high bounties paid for army recruits, is beginning to affect injuriously the naval service, and will, if not corrected, be likely to impair its efficiency by detaching seamen from their proper vocation and inducing them to enter the Army. I therefore respectfully suggest that Congress might aid both the army and naval services by a definite provision on this subject which would at the same time be equitable to the communities more especially interested.

I commend to your consideration the suggestions of the Secretary of the Navy in regard to the policy of fostering and training seamen and also the education of officers and engineers for the naval service. The Naval Academy is rendering signal service in preparing midshipmen for the highly responsible duties which in after life they will be required to perform. In order that the country should not be deprived of the proper quota of educated officers, for which legal provision has been made at the naval school, the vacancies caused by the neglect or omission to make nominations from the States in insurrection have been filled by the Secretary of the Navy. The school is now more full and complete than at any former period, and in every respect entitled to the favorable consideration of Congress.

During the past fiscal year the financial condition of the Post-Office Department has been one of increasing prosperity, and I am gratified in being able to state that the actual postal revenue has nearly equaled the entire expenditures, the latter amounting to $11,314,206.84 and the former to $11,163,789.59, leaving a deficiency of but $150,417.25. In 1860, the year immediately preceding the rebellion, the deficiency amounted to $5,656,705.49, the postal receipts of that year being $2,645,722.19 less than those of 1863. The decrease since 1860 in the annual amount of transportation has been only about 25 per cent, but the annual expenditure on account of the same has been reduced 35 per cent. It is manifest, therefore, that the Post-Office Department may become self-sustaining in a few years, even with the restoration of the whole service.

The international conference of postal delegates from the principal countries of Europe and America, which was called at the suggestion of the Postmaster-General, met at Paris on the 11th of May last and concluded its deliberations on the 8th of June. The principles established by the conference as best adapted to facilitate postal intercourse between nations and as the basis of future postal conventions inaugurate a general system of uniform international charges at reduced rates of postage, and can not fail to produce beneficial results.

I refer you to the report of the Secretary of the Interior, which is herewith laid before you, for useful and varied information in relation to the public lands, Indian affairs, patents, pensions, and other matters of public concern pertaining to his Department.

The quantity of land disposed of during the last and the first quarter of the present fiscal years was 3,841,549 acres, of which 161,911 acres were sold for cash, 1,456,514 acres were taken up under the homestead law, and the residue disposed of under laws granting lands for military bounties, for railroad and other purposes.   It also appears that the sale of the public lands is largely on the increase.

It has long been a cherished opinion of some of our wisest statesmen that the people of the United States had a higher and more enduring interest in the early settlement and substantial cultivation of the public lands than in the amount of direct revenue to be derived from the sale of them. This opinion has had a controlling influence in shaping legislation upon the subject of our national domain.   I may cite as evidence of this the liberal measures adopted in reference to actual settlers; the grant to the States of the overflowed lands within their limits, in order to their being reclaimed and rendered fit for cultivation; the grants to railway companies of alternate sections of land upon the contemplated lines of their roads, which when completed will so largely multiply the facilities for reaching our distant possessions.   This policy has received its most signal and beneficent illustration in the recent enactment granting homesteads to actual settlers.   Since the 1st day of January last the before-mentioned quantity of 1,456,514 acres of land have been taken up under its provisions.   This fact and the amount of sales furnish gratifying evidence of increasing settlement upon the public lands, notwithstanding the great struggle in which the energies of the nation have been engaged, and which has required so large a withdrawal of our citizens from their accustomed pursuits.   I cordially concur in the recommendation of the Secretary of the Interior suggesting a modification of the act in favor of those engaged in the military and naval service of the United States.   I doubt not that Congress will cheerfully adopt such measures as will, without essentially changing the general features of the system, secure to the greatest practicable extent its benefits to those who have left their homes in the defense of the country in this arduous crisis.

I invite your attention to the views of the Secretary as to the propriety of raising by appropriate legislation a revenue from the mineral lands of the United States.

The measures provided at your last session for the removal of certain Indian tribes have been carried into effect.   Sundry treaties have been negotiated, which will in due time be submitted for the constitutional action of the Senate.   They contain stipulations for extinguishing the possessory rights of the Indians to large and valuable tracts of lands.   It is hoped that the effect of these treaties will result in the establishment of permanent friendly relations with such of these tribes as have been brought into frequent and bloody collision with our outlying settlements and emigrants.   Sound policy and our imperative duty to these wards of the Government demand our anxious and constant attention to their material well-being, to their progress in the arts of civilization, and, above all, to that moral training which under the blessing of Divine Providence will confer upon them the elevated and sanctifying influences, the hopes and consolations, of the Christian faith.

I suggested in my last annual message the propriety of remodeling our Indian system. Subsequent events have satisfied me of its necessity. The details set forth in the report of the Secretary evince the urgent need for immediate legislative action.

I commend the benevolent institutions established or patronized by the Government in this District to your generous and fostering care.

The attention of Congress during the last session was engaged to some extent with a proposition for enlarging the water communication between the Mississippi River and the northeastern seaboard, which proposition, however, failed for the time. Since then, upon a call of the greatest respectability, a convention has been held at Chicago upon the same subject, a summary of whose views is contained in a memorial addressed to the President and Congress, and which I now have the honor to lay before you. That this interest is one which ere long will force its own way I do not entertain a doubt, while it is submitted entirely to your wisdom as to what can be done now. Augmented interest is given to this subject by the actual commencement of work upon the Pacific Railroad, under auspices so favorable to rapid progress and completion. The enlarged navigation becomes a palpable need to the great road.

I transmit the second annual report of the Commissioner of the Department of Agriculture, asking your attention to the developments in that vital interest of the nation.

When Congress assembled a year ago, the war had already lasted nearly twenty months, and there had been many conflicts on both land and sea, with varying results; the rebellion had been pressed back into reduced limits; yet the tone of public feeling and opinion, at home and abroad, was not satisfactory. With other signs, the popular elections then just past indicated uneasiness among ourselves, while, amid much that was cold and menacing, the kindest words coming from Europe were uttered in accents of pity that we were too blind to surrender a hopeless cause. Our commerce was suffering greatly by a few armed vessels built upon and furnished from foreign shores, and we were threatened with such additions from the same quarter as would sweep our trade from the sea and raise our blockade. We had failed to elicit from European Governments anything hopeful upon this subject. The preliminary emancipation proclamation, issued in September, was running its assigned period to the beginning of the new year. A month later the final proclamation came, including the announcement that colored men of suitable condition would be received into the war service. The policy of emancipation and of employing black soldiers gave to the future a new aspect, about which hope and fear and doubt contended in uncertain conflict. According to our political system, as a matter of civil administration, the General Government had no lawful power to effect emancipation in any State, and for a long time it had been hoped that the rebellion could be suppressed without resorting to it as a military measure. It was all the while deemed possible that the necessity for it might come, and that if it should the crisis of the contest would then be presented. It came, and, as was anticipated, it was followed by dark and doubtful days. Eleven months having now passed, we are permitted to take another review. The rebel borders are pressed still farther back, and by the complete opening of the Mississippi the country dominated by the rebellion is divided into distinct parts, with no practical communication between them. Tennessee and Arkansas have been substantially cleared of insurgent control, and influential citizens in each, owners of slaves and advocates of slavery at the beginning of the rebellion, now declare openly for emancipation in their respective States. Of those States not included in the emancipation proclamation, Maryland and Missouri, neither of which three years ago would tolerate any restraint upon the extension of slavery into new Territories, only dispute now as to the best mode of removing it within their own limits.

Of those who were slaves at the beginning of the rebellion full 100,000 are now in the United States military service, about one-half of which number actually bear arms in the ranks, thus giving the double advantage of taking so much labor from the insurgent cause and supplying the places which otherwise must be filled with so many white men. So far as tested, it is difficult to say they are not as good soldiers as any. No servile insurrection or tendency to violence or cruelty has marked the measures of emancipation and arming the blacks. These measures have been much discussed in foreign countries, and, contemporary with such discussion, the tone of public sentiment there is much improved. At home the same measures have been fully discussed, supported, criticised, and denounced, and the annual elections following are highly encouraging to those whose official duty it is to bear the country through this great trial. Thus we have the new reckoning. The crisis which threatened to divide the friends of the Union is past.

Looking now to the present and future, and with reference to a resumption of the national authority within the States wherein that authority has been suspended, I have thought fit to issue a proclamation, a copy of which is herewith transmitted. On examination of this proclamation it will appear, as is believed, that nothing will be attempted beyond what is amply justified by the Constitution. True, the form of an oath is given, but no man is coerced to take it. The man is only promised a pardon in case he voluntarily takes the oath. The Constitution authorizes the Executive to grant or withhold the pardon at his own absolute discretion, and this includes the power to grant on terms, as is fully established by judicial and other authorities.

It is also proffered that if in any of the States named a State government shall be in the mode prescribed set up, such government shall be recognized and guaranteed by the United States, and that under it the State shall, on the constitutional conditions, be protected against invasion and domestic violence. The constitutional obligation of the United States to guarantee to every State in the Union a republican form of government and to protect the State in the cases stated is explicit and full. But why tender the benefits of this provision only to a State government set up in this particular way? This section of the Constitution contemplates a case wherein the element within a State favorable to republican government in the Union may be too feeble for an opposite and hostile element external to or even within the State, and such are precisely the cases with which we are now dealing.

An attempt to guarantee and protect a revived State government, constructed in whole or in preponderating part from the very element against whose hostility and violence it is to be protected, is simply absurd. There must be a test by which to separate the opposing elements, so as to build only from the sound; and that test is a sufficiently liberal one which accepts as sound whoever will make a sworn recantation of his former unsoundness.

But if it be proper to require as a test of admission to the political body an oath of allegiance to the Constitution of the United States and to the Union under it, why also to the laws and proclamations in regard to slavery? Those laws and proclamations were enacted and put forth for the purpose of aiding in the suppression of the rebellion. To give them their fullest effect there had to be a pledge for their maintenance. In my judgment, they have aided and will further aid the cause for which they were intended. To now abandon them would be not only to relinquish a lever of power, but would also be a cruel and an astounding breach of faith. I may add at this point that while I remain in my present position I shall not attempt to retract or modify the emancipation proclamation, nor shall I return to slavery any person who is free by the terms of that proclamation or by any of the acts of Congress. For these and other reasons it is thought best that support of these measures shall be included in the oath, and it is believed the Executive may lawfully claim it in return for pardon and restoration of forfeited rights, which he has clear constitutional power to withhold altogether or grant upon the terms which he shall deem wisest for the public interest. It should be observed also that this part of the oath is subject to the modifying and abrogating power of legislation and supreme judicial decision.

The proposed acquiescence of the National Executive in any reasonable temporary State arrangement for the freed people is made with the view of possibly modifying the confusion and destitution which must at best attend all classes by a total revolution of labor throughout whole States.

It is hoped that the already deeply afflicted people in those States may be somewhat more ready to give up the cause of their affliction if to this extent this vital matter be left to themselves, while no power of the National Executive to prevent an abuse is abridged by the proposition.

The suggestion in the proclamation as to maintaining the political framework of the States on what is called reconstruction is made in the hope that it may do good without danger of harm. It will save labor and avoid great confusion.

But why any proclamation now upon this subject? This question is beset with the conflicting views that the step might be delayed too long or be taken too soon. In some States the elements for resumption seem ready for action, but remain inactive apparently for want of a rallying point—a plan of action. Why shall A adopt the plan of B rather than B that of A? And if A and B should agree, how can they know but that the General Government here will reject their plan? By the proclamation a plan is presented which may be accepted by them as a rallying point, and which they are assured in advance will not be rejected here. This may bring them to act sooner than they otherwise would.

The objections to a premature presentation of a plan by the National Executive consist in the danger of committals on points which could be more safely left to further developments. Care has been taken to so shape the document as to avoid embarrassments from this source. Saying that on certain terms certain classes will be pardoned with rights restored, it is not said that other classes or other terms will never be included. Saying that reconstruction will be accepted if presented in a specified way, it is not said it will never be accepted in any other way.

The movements by State action for emancipation in several of the States not included in the emancipation proclamation are matters of profound gratulation. And while I do not repeat in detail what I have heretofore so earnestly urged upon this subject, my general views and feelings remain unchanged; and I trust that Congress will omit no fair opportunity of aiding these important steps to a great consummation.

In the midst of other cares, however important, we must not lose sight of the fact that the war power is still our main reliance. To that power alone can we look yet for a time to give confidence to the people in the contested regions that the insurgent power will not again overrun them. Until that confidence shall be established little can be done anywhere for what is called reconstruction. Hence our chiefest care must still be directed to the Army and Navy, who have thus far borne their harder part so nobly and well; and it may be esteemed fortunate that in giving the greatest efficiency to these indispensable arms we do also honorably recognize the gallant men, from commander to sentinel, who compose them, and to whom more than to others the world must stand indebted for the home of freedom disenthralled, regenerated, enlarged, and perpetuated.

FOURTH ANNUAL MESSAGE.

DECEMBER 6, 1864.

Fellow-Citizens of the Senate and House of Representatives:

Again the blessings of health and abundant harvests claim our profoundest gratitude to Almighty God.

The condition of our foreign affairs is reasonably satisfactory.

Mexico continues to be a theater of civil war. While our political relations with that country have undergone no change, we have at the same time strictly maintained neutrality between the belligerents.

At the request of the States of Costa Rica and Nicaragua, a competent engineer has been authorized to make a survey of the river San Juan and the port of San Juan. It is a source of much satisfaction that the difficulties which for a moment excited some political apprehensions and caused a closing of the interoceanic transit route have been amicably adjusted, and that there is a good prospect that the route will soon be reopened with an increase of capacity and adaptation. We could not exaggerate either the commercial or the political importance of that great improvement.

It would be doing injustice to an important South American State not to acknowledge the directness, frankness, and cordiality with which the United States of Colombia have entered into intimate relations with this Government. A claims convention has been constituted to complete the unfinished work of the one which closed its session in 1861.

The new liberal constitution of Venezuela having gone into effect with the universal acquiescence of the people, the Government under it has been recognized and diplomatic intercourse with it has opened in a cordial and friendly spirit. The long-deferred Aves Island claim has been satis‧factorily paid and discharged.

Mutual payments have been made of the claims awarded by the late joint commission for the settlement of claims between the United States and Peru. An earnest and cordial friendship continues to exist between the two countries, and such efforts as were in my power have been used to remove misunderstanding and avert a threatened war between Peru and Spain.

Our relations are of the most friendly nature with Chile, the Argentine Republic, Bolivia, Costa Rica, Paraguay, San Salvador, and Hayti.

During the past year no differences of any kind have arisen with any of those Republics, and, on the other hand, their sympathies with the United States are constantly expressed with cordiality and earnestness.

The claim arising from the seizure of the cargo of the brig *Macedonian* in 1821 has been paid in full by the Government of Chile.

Civil war continues in the Spanish part of San Domingo, apparently without prospect of an early close.

Official correspondence has been freely opened with Liberia, and it gives us a pleasing view of social and political progress in that Republic. It may be expected to derive new vigor from American influence, improved by the rapid disappearance of slavery in the United States.

I solicit your authority to furnish to the Republic a gunboat at moderate cost, to be reimbursed to the United States by installments. Such a vessel is needed for the safety of that State against the native African races, and in Liberian hands it would be more effective in arresting the African slave trade than a squadron in our own hands. The possession of the least organized naval force would stimulate a generous ambition in the Republic, and the confidence which we should manifest by furnishing it would win forbearance and favor toward the colony from all civilized nations.

The proposed overland telegraph between America and Europe, by the way of Behrings Straits and Asiatic Russia, which was sanctioned by Congress at the last session, has been undertaken, under very favorable circumstances, by an association of American citizens, with the cordial good will and support as well of this Government as of those of Great Britain and Russia. Assurances have been received from most of the South American States of their high appreciation of the enterprise and their readiness to cooperate in constructing lines tributary to that world-encircling communication. I learn with much satisfaction that the noble design of a telegraphic communication between the eastern coast of America and Great Britain has been renewed, with full expectation of its early accomplishment.

Thus it is hoped that with the return of domestic peace the country will be able to resume with energy and advantage its former high career of commerce and civilization.

Our very popular and estimable representative in Egypt died in April last. An unpleasant altercation which arose between the temporary incumbent of the office and the Government of the Pasha resulted in a suspension of intercourse. The evil was promptly corrected on the arrival of the successor in the consulate, and our relations with Egypt, as well as our relations with the Barbary Powers, are entirely satisfactory.

The rebellion which has so long been flagrant in China has at last been suppressed, with the cooperating good offices of this Government and of the other Western commercial States. The judicial consular establishment there has become very difficult and onerous, and it will need legislative revision to adapt it to the extension of our commerce and to the more intimate intercourse which has been instituted with the Government and people of that vast Empire. China seems to be accepting with hearty good will the conventional laws which regulate commercial and social intercourse among the Western nations.

Owing to the peculiar situation of Japan and the anomalous form of its Government, the action of that Empire in performing treaty stipula-tions is inconstant and capricious. Nevertheless, good progress has been effected by the Western powers, moving with enlightened concert. Our own pecuniary claims have been allowed or put in course of settlement, and the inland sea has been reopened to commerce. There is reason also to believe that these proceedings have increased rather than diminished the friendship of Japan toward the United States.

The ports of Norfolk, Fernandina, and Pensacola have been opened by proclamation. It is hoped that foreign merchants will now consider whether it is not safer and more profitable to themselves, as well as just to the United States, to resort to these and other open ports than it is to pursue, through many hazards and at vast cost, a contraband trade with other ports which are closed, if not by actual military occupation, at least by a lawful and effective blockade.

For myself, I have no doubt of the power and duty of the Executive, under the law of nations, to exclude enemies of the human race from an asylum in the United States. If Congress should think that proceedings in such cases lack the authority of law, or ought to be further regulated by it, I recommend that provision be made for effectually preventing for-eign slave traders from acquiring domicile and facilities for their criminal occupation in our country.

It is possible that if it were a new and open question the maritime pow-ers, with the lights they now enjoy, would not concede the privileges of a naval belligerent to the insurgents of the United States, destitute, as they are, and always have been, equally of ships of war and of ports and har-bors. Disloyal emissaries have been neither less assiduous nor more successful during the last year than they were before that time in their efforts, under favor of that privilege, to embroil our country in foreign wars. The desire and determination of the governments of the maritime states to defeat that design are believed to be as sincere as and can not be more earnest than our own. Nevertheless, unforeseen political difficul-ties have arisen, especially in Brazilian and British ports and on the north-ern boundary of the United States, which have required, and are likely to continue to require, the practice of constant vigilance and a just and con-ciliatory spirit on the part of the United States, as well as of the nations concerned and their governments.

Commissioners have been appointed under the treaty with Great Brit-ain on the adjustment of the claims of the Hudsons Bay and Pugets Sound Agricultural Companies, in Oregon, and are now proceeding to the exe-cution of the trust assigned to them.

In view of the insecurity of life and property in the region adjacent to the Canadian border, by reason of recent assaults and depredations com-mitted by inimical and desperate persons who are harbored there, it has been thought proper to give notice that after the expiration of six months, the period conditionally stipulated in the existing arrangement with Great Britain, the United States must hold themselves at liberty to increase their naval armament upon the Lakes if they shall find that proceeding necessary. The condition of the border will necessarily come into consideration in connection with the question of continuing or modifying the rights of transit from Canada through the United States, as well as the regulation of imposts, which were temporarily established by the reciprocity treaty of the 5th June, 1854.

I desire, however, to be understood while making this statement that the colonial authorities of Canada are not deemed to be intentionally unjust or unfriendly toward the United States, but, on the contrary, there is every reason to expect that, with the approval of the Imperial Government, they will take the necessary measures to prevent new incursions across the border.

The act passed at the last session for the encouragement of immigration has so far as was possible been put into operation. It seems to need amendment which will enable the officers of the Government to prevent the practice of frauds against the immigrants while on their way and on their arrival in the ports, so as to secure them here a free choice of avocations and places of settlement. A liberal disposition toward this great national policy is manifested by most of the European States, and ought to be reciprocated on our part by giving the immigrants effective national protection. I regard our immigrants as one of the principal replenishing streams which are appointed by Providence to repair the ravages of internal war and its wastes of national strength and health. All that is necessary is to secure the flow of that stream in its present fullness, and to that end the Government must in every way make it manifest that it neither needs nor designs to impose involuntary military service upon those who come from other lands to cast their lot in our country.

The financial affairs of the Government have been successfully administered during the last year. The legislation of the last session of Congress has beneficially affected the revenues, although sufficient time has not yet elapsed to experience the full effect of several of the provisions of the acts of Congress imposing increased taxation.

The receipts during the year from all sources, upon the basis of warrants signed by the Secretary of the Treasury, including loans and the balance in the Treasury on the 1st day of July, 1863, were $1,394,796,007.62, and the aggregate disbursements, upon the same basis, were $1,298,056,-101.89, leaving a balance in the Treasury, as shown by warrants, of $96,739,905.73.

Deduct from these amounts the amount of the principal of the public debt redeemed and the amount of issues in substitution therefor, and the actual cash operations of the Treasury were: Receipts, $884,076,646.57; disbursements, $865,234,087.86; which leaves a cash balance in the Treasury of $18,842,558.71.

Of the receipts there were derived from customs $102,316,152.99, from lands $588,333.29, from direct taxes $475,648.96, from internal revenue $109,741,134.10, from miscellaneous sources $47,511,448.10, and from loans applied to actual expenditures, including former balance, $623,-443,929.13.

There were disbursed for the civil service $27,505,599.46, for pensions and Indians $7,517,930.97, for the War Department $690,791,842.97, for the Navy Department $85,733,292.77, for interest on the public debt $53,685,421.69, making an aggregate of $865,234,087.86 and leaving a balance in the Treasury of $18,842,558.71, as before stated.

For the actual receipts and disbursements for the first quarter and the estimated receipts and disbursements for the three remaining quarters of the current fiscal year, and the general operations of the Treasury in detail, I refer you to the report of the Secretary of the Treasury. I concur with him in the opinion that the proportion of moneys required to meet the expenses consequent upon the war derived from taxation should be still further increased; and I earnestly invite your attention to this subject, to the end that there may be such additional legislation as shall be required to meet the just expectations of the Secretary.

The public debt on the 1st day of July last, as appears by the books of the Treasury, amounted to $1,740,690,489.49.   Probably, should the war continue for another year, that amount may be increased by not far from five hundred millions.   Held, as it is, for the most part by our own people, it has become a substantial branch of national, though private, property.   For obvious reasons the more nearly this property can be distributed among all the people the better.   To favor such general distribution, greater inducements to become owners might, perhaps, with good effect and without injury be presented to persons of limited means. With this view I suggest whether it might not be both competent and expedient for Congress to provide that a limited amount of some future issue of public securities might be held by any *bona fide* purchaser exempt from taxation and from seizure for debt, under such restrictions and limitations as might be necessary to guard against abuse of so important a privilege.   This would enable every prudent person to set aside a small annuity against a possible day of want.

Privileges like these would render the possession of such securities to the amount limited most desirable to every person of small means who might be able to save enough for the purpose.   The great advantage of citizens being creditors as well as debtors with relation to the public debt is obvious.   Men readily perceive that they can not be much oppressed by a debt which they owe to themselves.

The public debt on the 1st day of July last, although somewhat exceeding the estimate of the Secretary of the Treasury made to Congress at the commencement of the last session, falls short of the estimate of that officer made in the preceding December as to its probable amount at the beginning of this year by the sum of $3,995,097.31.   This fact exhibits a satisfactory condition and conduct of the operations of the Treasury.

The national banking system is proving to be acceptable to capitalists and to the people. On the 25th day of November 584 national banks had been organized, a considerable number of which were conversions from State banks. Changes from State systems to the national system are rapidly taking place, and it is hoped that very soon there will be in the United States no banks of issue not authorized by Congress and no bank-note circulation not secured by the Government. That the Government and the people will derive great benefit from this change in the banking systems of the country can hardly be questioned. The national system will create a reliable and permanent influence in support of the national credit and protect the people against losses in the use of paper money. Whether or not any further legislation is advisable for the suppression of State-bank issues it will be for Congress to determine. It seems quite clear that the Treasury can not be satisfactorily conducted unless the Government can exercise a restraining power over the bank-note circulation of the country.

The report of the Secretary of War and the accompanying documents will detail the campaigns of the armies in the field since the date of the last annual message, and also the operations of the several administrative bureaus of the War Department during the last year. It will also specify the measures deemed essential for the national defense and to keep up and supply the requisite military force.

The report of the Secretary of the Navy presents a comprehensive and satisfactory exhibit of the affairs of that Department and of the naval service. It is a subject of congratulation and laudable pride to our countrymen that a Navy of such vast proportions has been organized in so brief a period and conducted with so much efficiency and success.

The general exhibit of the Navy, including vessels under construction on the 1st of December, 1864, shows a total of 671 vessels, carrying 4,610 guns, and of 510,396 tons, being an actual increase during the year, over and above all losses by shipwreck or in battle, of 83 vessels, 167 guns, and 42,427 tons.

The total number of men at this time in the naval service, including officers, is about 51,000.

There have been captured by the Navy during the year 324 vessels, and the whole number of naval captures since hostilities commenced is 1,379, of which 267 are steamers.

The gross proceeds arising from the sale of condemned prize property thus far reported amount to $14,396,250.51. A large amount of such proceeds is still under adjudication and yet to be reported.

The total expenditure of the Navy Department of every description, including the cost of the immense squadrons that have been called into existence from the 4th of March, 1861, to the 1st of November, 1864, is $238,647,262.35.

Your favorable consideration is invited to the various recommendations of the Secretary of the Navy, especially in regard to a navy-yard and suitable establishment for the construction and repair of iron vessels and the machinery and armature for our ships, to which reference was made in my last annual message.

Your attention is also invited to the views expressed in the report in relation to the legislation of Congress at its last session in respect to prize on our inland waters.

I cordially concur in the recommendation of the Secretary as to the propriety of creating the new rank of vice-admiral in our naval service.

Your attention is invited to the report of the Postmaster-General for a detailed account of the operations and financial condition of the Post-Office Department.

The postal revenues for the year ending June 30, 1864, amounted to $12,438,253.78 and the expenditures to $12,644,786.20, the excess of expenditures over receipts being $206,652.42.

The views presented by the Postmaster-General on the subject of special grants by the Government in aid of the establishment of new lines of ocean mail steamships and the policy he recommends for the development of increased commercial intercourse with adjacent and neighboring countries should receive the careful consideration of Congress.

It is of noteworthy interest that the steady expansion of population, improvement, and governmental institutions over the new and unoccupied portions of our country have scarcely been checked, much less impeded or destroyed, by our great civil war, which at first glance would seem to have absorbed almost the entire energies of the nation.

The organization and admission of the State of Nevada has been completed in conformity with law, and thus our excellent system is firmly established in the mountains, which once seemed a barren and uninhabitable waste between the Atlantic States and those which have grown up on the coast of the Pacific Ocean.

The Territories of the Union are generally in a condition of prosperity and rapid growth. Idaho and Montana, by reason of their great distance and the interruption of communication with them by Indian hostilities, have been only partially organized; but it is understood that these difficulties are about to disappear, which will permit their governments, like those of the others, to go into speedy and full operation.

As intimately connected with and promotive of this material growth of the nation, I ask the attention of Congress to the valuable information and important recommendations relating to the public lands, Indian affairs, the Pacific Railroad, and mineral discoveries contained in the report of the Secretary of the Interior which is herewith transmitted, and which report also embraces the subjects of patents, pensions, and other topics of public interest pertaining to his Department.

The quantity of public land disposed of during the five quarters ending on the 30th of September last was 4,221,342 acres, of which 1,538,614 acres were entered under the homestead law. The remainder was located with military land warrants, agricultural scrip certified to States for railroads, and sold for cash. The cash received from sales and location fees was $1,019,446.

The income from sales during the fiscal year ending June 30, 1864, was $678,007.21, against $136,077.95 received during the preceding year. The aggregate number of acres surveyed during the year has been equal to the quantity disposed of, and there is open to settlement about 133,000,000 acres of surveyed land.

The great enterprise of connecting the Atlantic with the Pacific States by railways and telegraph lines has been entered upon with a vigor that gives assurance of success, notwithstanding the embarrassments arising from the prevailing high prices of materials and labor. The route of the main line of the road has been definitely located for 100 miles westward from the initial point at Omaha City, Nebr., and a preliminary location of the Pacific Railroad of California has been made from Sacramento eastward to the great bend of the Truckee River in Nevada.

Numerous discoveries of gold, silver, and cinnabar mines have been added to the many heretofore known, and the country occupied by the Sierra Nevada and Rocky mountains and the subordinate ranges now teems with enterprising labor, which is richly remunerative. It is believed that the product of the mines of precious metals in that region has during the year reached, if not exceeded, one hundred millions in value.

It was recommended in my last annual message that our Indian system be remodeled. Congress at its last session, acting upon the recommendation, did provide for reorganizing the system in California, and it is believed that under the present organization the management of the Indians there will be attended with reasonable success. Much yet remains to be done to provide for the proper government of the Indians in other parts of the country, to render it secure for the advancing settler, and to provide for the welfare of the Indian. The Secretary reiterates his recommendations, and to them the attention of Congress is invited.

The liberal provisions made by Congress for paying pensions to invalid soldiers and sailors of the Republic and to the widows, orphans, and dependent mothers of those who have fallen in battle or died of disease contracted or of wounds received in the service of their country have been diligently administered. There have been added to the pension rolls during the year ending the 30th day of June last the names of 16,770 invalid soldiers and of 271 disabled seamen, making the present number of army invalid pensioners 22,767 and of navy invalid pensioners 712.

Of widows, orphans, and mothers 22,198 have been placed on the army pension rolls and 248 on the navy rolls. The present number of army pensioners of this class is 25,433 and of navy pensioners 793. At the beginning of the year the number of Revolutionary pensioners was 1,430. Only 12 of them were soldiers, of whom 7 have since died. The remainder are those who under the law receive pensions because of relationship to Revolutionary soldiers. During the year ending the 30th of June, 1864, $4,504,616.92 have been paid to pensioners of all classes.

I cheerfully commend to your continued patronage the benevolent institutions of the District of Columbia which have hitherto been established or fostered by Congress, and respectfully refer for information concerning them and in relation to the Washington Aqueduct, the Capitol, and other matters of local interest to the report of the Secretary.

The Agricultural Department, under the supervision of its present energetic and faithful head, is rapidly commending itself to the great and vital interest it was created to advance It is peculiarly the people's Department, in which they feel more directly concerned than in any other. I commend it to the continued attention and fostering care of Congress.

The war continues. Since the last annual message all the important lines and positions then occupied by our forces have been maintained and our arms have steadily advanced, thus liberating the regions left in rear, so that Missouri, Kentucky, Tennessee, and parts of other States have again produced reasonably fair crops.

The most remarkable feature in the military operations of the year is General Sherman's attempted march of 300 miles directly through the insurgent region. It tends to show a great increase of our relative strength that our General in Chief should feel able to confront and hold in check every active force of the enemy, and yet to detach a well-appointed large army to move on such an expedition. The result not yet being known, conjecture in regard to it is not here indulged.

Important movements have also occurred during the year to the effect of molding society for durability in the Union. Although short of complete success, it is much in the right direction that 12,000 citizens in each of the States of Arkansas and Louisiana have organized loyal State governments, with free constitutions, and are earnestly struggling to maintain and administer them. The movements in the same direction, more extensive though less definite, in Missouri, Kentucky, and Tennessee should not be overlooked. But Maryland presents the example of complete success. Maryland is secure to liberty and union for all the future. The genius of rebellion will no more claim Maryland. Like another foul spirit being driven out, it may seek to tear her, but it will woo her no more.

At the last session of Congress a proposed amendment of the Constitution abolishing slavery throughout the United States passed the Senate, but failed for lack of the requisite two-thirds vote in the House of Representatives. Although the present is the same Congress and nearly the same members, and without questioning the wisdom or patriotism of those who stood in opposition, I venture to recommend the reconsideration and passage of the measure at the present session. Of course the abstract question is not changed; but an intervening election shows almost certainly that the next Congress will pass the measure if this does not. Hence there is only a question of *time* as to when the proposed amendment will go to the States for their action. And as it is to so go at all events, may we not agree that the sooner the better? It is not claimed that the election has imposed a duty on members to change their views or their votes any further than, as an additional element to be considered, their judgment may be affected by it. It is the voice of the people now for the first time heard upon the question. In a great national crisis like ours unanimity of action among those seeking a common end is very desirable— almost indispensable. And yet no approach to such unanimity is attainable unless some deference shall be paid to the will of the majority simply because it is the will of the majority. In this case the common end is the maintenance of the Union, and among the means to secure that end such will, through the election, is most clearly declared in favor of such constitutional amendment.

The most reliable indication of public purpose in this country is derived through our popular elections. Judging by the recent canvass and its result, the purpose of the people within the loyal States to maintain the integrity of the Union was never more firm nor more nearly unanimous than now. The extraordinary calmness and good order with which the millions of voters met and mingled at the polls give strong assurance of this. Not only all those who supported the Union ticket, so called, but a great majority of the opposing party also may be fairly claimed to entertain and to be actuated by the same purpose. It is an unanswerable argument to this effect that no candidate for any office whatever, high or low, has ventured to seek votes on the avowal that he was for giving up the Union. There have been much impugning of motives and much heated controversy as to the proper means and best mode of advancing the Union cause, but on the distinct issue of Union or no Union the politicians have shown their instinctive knowledge that there is no diversity among the people. In affording the people the fair opportunity of showing one to another and to the world this firmness and unanimity of purpose, the election has been of vast value to the national cause.

The election has exhibited another fact not less valuable to be known— the fact that we do not approach exhaustion in the most important branch of national resources, that of living men. While it is melancholy to reflect that the war has filled so many graves and carried mourning to so many hearts, it is some relief to know that, compared with the surviving, the fallen have been so few. While corps and divisions and brigades and regiments have formed and fought and dwindled and gone out of existence, a great majority of the men who composed them are still living. The same is true of the naval service. The election returns prove this. So many voters could not else be found. The States regularly holding elections, both now and four years ago, to wit, California, Connecticut, Delaware, Illinois, Indiana, Iowa, Kentucky, Maine, Maryland, Massachusetts, Michigan, Minnesota, Missouri, New Hampshire, New Jersey, New York, Ohio, Oregon, Pennsylvania, Rhode Island, Vermont, West Virginia, and Wisconsin, cast 3,982,011 votes now, against 3,870,222 cast then, showing an aggregate now of 3,982,011. To this is to be added 33,762 cast now in the new States of Kansas and Nevada, which States did not vote in 1860, thus swelling the aggregate to 4,015,773 and the net increase during the three years and a half of war to 145,551. A table is appended showing particulars. To this again should be added the number of all soldiers in the field from Massachusetts, Rhode Island, New Jersey, Delaware, Indiana, Illinois, and California, who by the laws of those States could not vote away from their homes, and which number can not be less than 90,000. Nor yet is this all. The number in organized Territories is triple now what it was four years ago, while thousands, white and black, join us as the national arms press back the insurgent lines. So much is shown, affirmatively and negatively, by the election. It is not material to inquire *how* the increase has been produced or to show that it would have been *greater* but for the war, which is probably true. The important fact remains demonstrated that we have *more* men *now* than we had when the war *began;* that we are not exhausted nor in process of exhaustion; that we are *gaining* strength and may if need be maintain the contest indefinitely. This as to men. Material resources are now more complete and abundant than ever.

The national resources, then, are unexhausted, and, as we believe, inexhaustible. The public purpose to reestablish and maintain the national authority is unchanged, and, as we believe, unchangeable. The manner of continuing the effort remains to choose. On careful consideration of all the evidence accessible it seems to me that no attempt at negotiation with the insurgent leader could result in any good. He would accept nothing short of severance of the Union, precisely what we will not and can not give. His declarations to this effect are explicit and oft repeated. He does not attempt to deceive us. He affords us no excuse to deceive ourselves. He can not voluntarily reaccept the Union; we can not voluntarily yield it. Between him and us the issue is distinct, simple, and inflexible. It is an issue which can only be tried by war and decided by victory. If we yield, we are beaten; if the Southern people fail him, he is beaten. Either way it would be the victory and defeat following war. What is true, however, of him who heads the insurgent cause is not necessarily true of those who follow. Although he can not reaccept the Union, they can. Some of them, we know, already desire peace and reunion. The number of such may increase. They can at any moment have peace simply by laying down their arms and submitting to the national authority under the Constitution. After so much the Government could not, if it would, maintain war against them. The loyal people would not sustain or allow it. If questions should remain, we would adjust them by the peaceful means of legislation, conference, courts, and votes, operating only in constitutional and lawful channels. Some certain, and other possible, questions are and would be beyond the Executive power to adjust; as, for instance, the admission of members into Congress and whatever might require the appropriation of money. The Executive power itself would be greatly diminished by the cessation of actual war. Pardons and remissions of forfeitures, however, would still be within Executive control. In what spirit and temper this control would be exercised can be fairly judged of by the past.

A year ago general pardon and amnesty, upon specified terms, were offered to all except certain designated classes, and it was at the same time made known that the excepted classes were still within contemplation of special clemency. During the year many availed themselves of the general provision, and many more would, only that the signs of bad faith in some led to such precautionary measures as rendered the practical process less easy and certain. During the same time also special pardons have been granted to individuals of the excepted classes, and no voluntary application has been denied. Thus practically the door has been for a full year open to all except such as were not in condition to make free choice; that is, such as were in custody or under constraint. It is still so open to all. But the time may come, probably will come, when public duty shall demand that it be closed and that in lieu more rigorous measures than heretofore shall be adopted.

In presenting the abandonment of armed resistance to the national authority on the part of the insurgents as the only indispensable condition to ending the war on the part of the Government, I retract nothing heretofore said as to slavery. I repeat the declaration made a year ago, that "while I remain in my present position I shall not attempt to retract or modify the emancipation proclamation, nor shall I return to slavery any person who is free by the terms of that proclamation or by any of the acts of Congress." If the people should, by whatever mode or means, make it an Executive duty to reenslave such persons, another, and not I, must be their instrument to perform it.

In stating a single condition of peace I mean simply to say that the war will cease on the part of the Government whenever it shall have ceased on the part of those who began it.

Table showing the aggregate votes in the States named at the Presidential elections respectively, in 1860 and 1864.

State.	1860.	1864.
California	118,840	*110,000
Connecticut	77,246	86,616
Delaware	16,039	16,924
Illinois	339,693	348,235
Indiana	272,143	280,645
Iowa	128,331	143,331
Kentucky	146,216	*91,300
Maine	97,918	115,141
Maryland	92,502	72,703
Massachusetts	169,533	175,487
Michigan	154,747	162,413
Minnesota	34,799	42,534
Missouri	165,538	*90,000
New Hampshire	65,953	69,111
New Jersey	121,125	128,680
New York	675,156	730,664
Ohio	442,441	470,745
Oregon	14,410	†14,410
Pennsylvania	476,442	572,697
Rhode Island	19,931	22,187
Vermont	42,844	55,811
West Virginia	46,195	33,874
Wisconsin	152,180	148,513
	3,870,222	3,982,011
Kansas		17,234
Nevada		16,528
		33,762
		3,982,011
Total		4,015,773
		3,870,222
Net increase		145,551

* Nearly.   † Estimated.

Andrew Johnson

April 15, 1865 to March 4, 1869

FIRST ANNUAL MESSAGE.

WASHINGTON, *December 4, 1865.*

Fellow-Citizens of the Senate and House of Representatives:

To express gratitude to God in the name of the people for the preservation of the United States is my first duty in addressing you. Our thoughts next revert to the death of the late President by an act of parricidal treason. The grief of the nation is still fresh. It finds some solace in the consideration that he lived to enjoy the highest proof of its confidence by entering on the renewed term of the Chief Magistracy to which he had been elected; that he brought the civil war substantially to a close; that his loss was deplored in all parts of the Union, and that foreign nations have rendered justice to his memory. His removal cast upon me a heavier weight of cares than ever devolved upon any one of his predecessors. To fulfill my trust I need the support and confidence of all who are associated with me in the various departments of Government and the support and confidence of the people. There is but one way in which I can hope to gain their necessary aid. It is to state with frankness the principles which guide my conduct, and their application to the present state of affairs, well aware that the efficiency of my labors will in a great measure depend on your and their undivided approbation.

The Union of the United States of America was intended by its authors to last as long as the States themselves shall last. "The Union shall be perpetual" are the words of the Confederation. "To form a more perfect Union," by an ordinance of the people of the United States, is the declared purpose of the Constitution. The hand of Divine Providence was never more plainly visible in the affairs of men than in the framing and the adopting of that instrument. It is beyond comparison the greatest event in American history, and, indeed, is it not of all events in modern times the most pregnant with consequences for every people of the earth? The members of the Convention which prepared it brought to their work the experience of the Confederation, of their several States, and of other republican governments, old and new; but they needed and they obtained a wisdom superior to experience. And when for its validity it required the approval of a people that occupied a large part of a continent and acted separately in many distinct conventions, what is more wonderful than that, after earnest contention and long discussion, all feelings and all opinions were ultimately drawn in one way to its support? The Constitution to which life was thus imparted contains within itself ample resources for its own preservation. It has power to enforce the laws, punish treason, and insure domestic tranquillity. In case of the usurpation of the government of a State by one man or an oligarchy, it becomes a duty of the United States to make good the guaranty to that State of a republican form of government, and so to maintain the homogeneousness of all. Does the lapse of time reveal defects? A simple mode of amendment is provided in the Constitution itself, so that its conditions can always be made to conform to the requirements of advancing civilization. No room is allowed even for the thought of a possibility of its coming to an end. And these powers of self-preservation have always been asserted in their complete integrity by every patriotic Chief Magistrate—by Jefferson and Jackson not less than by Washington and Madison. The parting advice of the Father of his Country, while yet President, to the people of the United States was that the free Constitution, which was the work of their hands, might be sacredly maintained; and the inaugural words of President Jefferson held up "the preservation of the General Government in its whole constitutional vigor as the sheet anchor of our peace at home and safety abroad." The Constitution is the work of "the people of the United States," and it should be as indestructible as the people.

It is not strange that the framers of the Constitution, which had no model in the past, should not have fully comprehended the excellence of their own work. Fresh from a struggle against arbitrary power, many patriots suffered from harassing fears of an absorption of the State governments by the General Government, and many from a dread that the States would break away from their orbits. But the very greatness of our country should allay the apprehension of encroachments by the General Government. The subjects that come unquestionably within its jurisdiction are so numerous that it must ever naturally refuse to be embarrassed by questions that lie beyond it. Were it otherwise the Executive would sink beneath the burden, the channels of justice would be choked, legislation would be obstructed by excess, so that there is a greater temptation to exercise some of the functions of the General Government through the States than to trespass on their rightful sphere. The "absolute acquiescence in the decisions of the majority" was at the beginning of the century enforced by Jefferson as "the vital principle of republics;" and the events of the last four years have established, we will hope forever, that there lies no appeal to force.

The maintenance of the Union brings with it "the support of the State governments in all their rights," but it is not one of the rights of any State government to renounce its own place in the Union or to nullify the laws of the Union. The largest liberty is to be maintained in the discussion of the acts of the Federal Government, but there is no appeal from its laws except to the various branches of that Government itself, or to the people, who grant to the members of the legislative and of the executive departments no tenure but a limited one, and in that manner always retain the powers of redress.

"The sovereignty of the States" is the language of the Confederacy, and not the language of the Constitution. The latter contains the emphatic words—

> This Constitution and the laws of the United States which shall be made in pursuance thereof, and all treaties made or which shall be made under the authority of the United States, shall be the supreme law of the land, and the judges in every State shall be bound thereby, anything in the constitution or laws of any State to the contrary notwithstanding.

Certainly the Government of the United States is a limited government, and so is every State government a limited government. With us this idea of limitation spreads through every form of administration—general, State, and municipal—and rests on the great distinguishing principle of the recognition of the rights of man. The ancient republics absorbed the individual in the state—prescribed his religion and controlled his activity. The American system rests on the assertion of the equal right of every man to life, liberty, and the pursuit of happiness, to freedom of conscience, to the culture and exercise of all his faculties. As a consequence the State government is limited—as to the General Government in the interest of union, as to the individual citizen in the interest of freedom.

States, with proper limitations of power, are essential to the existence of the Constitution of the United States. At the very commencement, when we assumed a place among the powers of the earth, the Declaration of Independence was adopted by States; so also were the Articles of Confederation; and when "the people of the United States" ordained and established the Constitution it was the assent of the States, one by one, which gave it vitality. In the event, too, of any amendment to the Constitution, the proposition of Congress needs the confirmation of States. Without States one great branch of the legislative government would be wanting. And if we look beyond the letter of the Constitution to the character of our country, its capacity for comprehending within its jurisdiction a vast continental empire is due to the system of States. The best security for the perpetual existence of the States is the "supreme authority" of the Constitution of the United States. The perpetuity of the Constitution brings with it the perpetuity of the States; their mutual relation makes us what we are, and in our political system their connection is indissoluble. The whole can not exist without the parts, nor the parts without the whole. So long as the Constitution of the United States endures, the States will endure. The destruction of the one is the destruction of the other; the preservation of the one is the preservation of the other.

I have thus explained my views of the mutual relations of the Constitution and the States, because they unfold the principles on which I have sought to solve the momentous questions and overcome the appalling difficulties that met me at the very commencement of my Administration. It has been my steadfast object to escape from the sway of momentary passions and to derive a healing policy from the fundamental and unchanging principles of the Constitution.

I found the States suffering from the effects of a civil war. Resistance to the General Government appeared to have exhausted itself. The United States had recovered possession of their forts and arsenals, and their armies were in the occupation of every State which had attempted to secede. Whether the territory within the limits of those States should be held as conquered territory, under military authority emanating from the President as the head of the Army, was the first question that presented itself for decision.

Now military governments, established for an indefinite period, would have offered no security for the early suppression of discontent, would have divided the people into the vanquishers and the vanquished, and would have envenomed hatred rather than have restored affection. Once established, no precise limit to their continuance was conceivable. They would have occasioned an incalculable and exhausting expense. Peaceful emigration to and from that portion of the country is one of the best means that can be thought of for the restoration of harmony, and that emigration would have been prevented; for what emigrant from abroad, what industrious citizen at home, would place himself willingly undei military rule? The chief persons who would have followed in the train of the Army would have been dependents on the General Government or men who expected profit from the miseries of their erring fellow-citizens. The powers of patronage and rule which would have been exercised, under the President, over a vast and populous and naturally wealthy region are greater than, unless under extreme necessity, I shculd be will ing to intrust to any one man. They are such as, for myself, I could never, unless on occasions of great emergency, consent to exercise. The willful use of such powers, if continued through a period of years, would have endangered the purity of the general administration and the liberties of the States which remained loyal.

Besides, the policy of military rule over a conquered territory would have implied that the States whose inhabitants may have taken part in the rebellion had by the act of those inhabitants ceased to exist. But the true theory is that all pretended acts of secession were from the beginning null and void. The States can not commit treason nor screen the individual citizens who may have committed treason any more than they can make valid treaties or engage in lawful commerce with any foreign power. The States attempting to secede placed themselves in a condition where their vitality was impaired, but not extinguished; their functions suspended, but not destroyed.

But if any State neglects or refuses to perform its offices there is the more need that the General Government should maintain all its authority and as soon as practicable resume the exercise of all its functions. On this principle I have acted, and have gradually and quietly, and by almost imperceptible steps, sought to restore the rightful energy of the

General Government and of the States.   To that end provisional governors have been appointed for the States, conventions called, governors elected, legislatures assembled, and Senators and Representatives chosen to the Congress of the United States.   At the same time the courts of the United States, as far as could be done, have been reopened, so that the laws of the United States may be enforced through their agency. The blockade has been removed and the custom-houses reestablished in ports of entry, so that the revenue of the United States may be collected. The Post-Office Department renews its ceaseless activity, and the General Government is thereby enabled to communicate promptly with its officers and agents.   The courts bring security to persons and property; the opening of the ports invites the restoration of industry and commerce; the post-office renews the facilities of social intercourse and of business.   And is it not happy for us all that the restoration of each one of these functions of the General Government brings with it a blessing to the States over which they are extended?   Is it not a sure promise of harmony and renewed attachment to the Union that after all that has happened the return of the General Government is known only as a beneficence?

I know very well that this policy is attended with some risk; that for its success it requires at least the acquiescence of the States which it concerns; that it implies an invitation to those States, by renewing their allegiance to the United States, to resume their functions as States of the Union.   But it is a risk that must be taken.   In the choice of difficulties it is the smallest risk; and to diminish and if possible to remove all danger, I have felt it incumbent on me to assert one other power of the General Government—the power of pardon.   As no State can throw a defense over the crime of treason, the power of pardon is exclusively vested in the executive government of the United States.   In exercising that power I have taken every precaution to connect it with the clearest recognition of the binding force of the laws of the United States and an unqualified acknowledgment of the great social change of condition in regard to slavery which has grown out of the war.

The next step which I have taken to restore the constitutional relations of the States has been an invitation to them to participate in the high office of amending the Constitution.   Every patriot must wish for a general amnesty at the earliest epoch consistent with public safety. For this great end there is need of a concurrence of all opinions and the spirit of mutual conciliation.   All parties in the late terrible conflict must work together in harmony.   It is not too much to ask, in the name of the whole people, that on the one side the plan of restoration shall proceed in conformity with a willingness to cast the disorders of the past into oblivion, and that on the other the evidence of sincerity in the future maintenance of the Union shall be put beyond any doubt by the ratification of the proposed amendment to the Constitution, which provides for the abolition of slavery forever within the limits of our country. So long as the adoption of this amendment is delayed, so long will doubt and jealousy and uncertainty prevail. This is the measure which will efface the sad memory of the past: this is the measure which will most certainly call population and capital and security to those parts of the Union that need them most. Indeed, it is not too much to ask of the States which are now resuming their places in the family of the Union to give this pledge of perpetual loyalty and peace. Until it is done the past, however much we may desire it, will not be forgotten. The adoption of the amendment reunites us beyond all power of disruption; it heals the wound that is still imperfectly closed; it removes slavery, the element which has so long perplexed and divided the country; it makes of·us once more a united people, renewed and strengthened, bound more than ever to mutual affection and support.

The amendment to the Constitution being adopted, it would remain for the States whose powers have been so long in abeyance to resume their places in the two branches of the National Legislature, and thereby complete the work of restoration. Here it is for you, fellow-citizens of the Senate, and for you, fellow-citizens of the House of Representatives, to judge, each of you for yourselves, of the elections, returns, and qualifications of your own members.

The full assertion of the powers of the General Government requires the holding of circuit courts of the United States within the districts where their authority has been interrupted. In the present posture of our public affairs strong objections have been urged to holding those courts in any of the States where the rebellion has existed; and it was ascertained by inquiry that the circuit court of the United States would not be held within the district of Virginia during the autumn or early winter, nor until Congress should have "an opportunity to consider and act on the whole subject." To your deliberations the restoration of this branch of the civil authority of the United States is therefore necessarily referred, with the hope that early provision will be made for the resumption of all its functions. It is manifest that treason, most flagrant in character, has been committed. Persons who are charged with its commission should have fair and impartial trials in the highest civil tribunals of the country, in order that the Constitution and the laws may be fully vindicated, the truth clearly established and affirmed that treason is a crime, that traitors should be punished and the offense made infamous, and, at the same time, that the question may be judicially settled, finally and forever, that no State of its own will has the right to renounce its place in the Union.

The relations of the General Government toward the 4,000,000 inhabitants whom the war has called into freedom have engaged my most serious consideration. On the propriety of attempting to make the freedmen electors by the proclamation of the Executive I took for my counsel the Constitution itself, the interpretations of that instrument by its authors and their contemporaries, and recent legislation by Congress. When, at the first movement toward independence, the Congress of the United States instructed the several States to institute governments of their own, they left each State to decide for itself the conditions for the enjoyment of the elective franchise. During the period of the Confederacy there continued to exist a very great diversity in the qualifications of electors in the several States, and even within a State a distinction of qualifications prevailed with regard to the officers who were to be chosen. The Constitution of the United States recognizes these diversities when it enjoins that in the choice of members of the House of Representatives of the United States "the electors in each State shall have the qualifications requisite for electors of the most numerous branch of the State legislature." After the formation of the Constitution it remained, as before, the uniform usage for each State to enlarge the body of its electors according to its own judgment, and under this system one State after another has proceeded to increase the number of its electors, until now universal suffrage, or something very near it, is the general rule. So fixed was this reservation of power in the habits of the people and so unquestioned has been the interpretation of the Constitution that during the civil war the late President never harbored the purpose—certainly never avowed the purpose—of disregarding it; and in the acts of Congress during that period nothing can be found which, during the continuance of hostilities, much less after their close, would have sanctioned any departure by the Executive from a policy which has so uniformly obtained. Moreover, a concession of the elective franchise to the freedmen by act of the President of the United States must have been extended to all colored men, wherever found, and so must have established a change of suffrage in the Northern, Middle, and Western States, not less than in the Southern and Southwestern. Such an act would have created a new class of voters, and would have been an assumption of power by the President which nothing in the Constitution or laws of the United States would have warranted.

On the other hand, every danger of conflict is avoided when the settlement of the question is referred to the several States. They can, each for itself, decide on the measure, and whether it is to be adopted at once and absolutely or introduced gradually and with conditions. In my judgment the freedmen, if they show patience and manly virtues, will sooner obtain a participation in the elective franchise through the States than through the General Government, even if it had power to intervene. When the tumult of emotions that have been raised by the suddenness of the social change shall have subsided, it may prove that they will receive the kindest usage from some of those on whom they have heretofore most closely depended.

But while I have no doubt that now, after the close of the war, it is not competent for the General Government to extend the elective franchise in the several States, it is equally clear that good faith requires the security of the freedmen in their liberty and their property, their right to labor, and their right to claim the just return of their labor. I can not too strongly urge a dispassionate treatment of this subject, which should be carefully kept aloof from all party strife. We must equally avoid hasty assumptions of any natural impossibility for the two races to live side by side in a state of mutual benefit and good will. The experiment involves us in no inconsistency; let us, then, go on and make that experiment in good faith, and not be too easily disheartened. The country is in need of labor, and the freedmen are in need of employment, culture, and protection. While their right of voluntary migration and expatriation is not to be questioned, I would not advise their forced removal and colonization. Let us rather encourage them to honorable and useful industry, where it may be beneficial to themselves and to the country; and, instead of hasty anticipations of the certainty of failure, let there be nothing wanting to the fair trial of the experiment. The change in their condition is the substitution of labor by contract for the status of slavery. The freedman can not fairly be accused of unwillingness to work so long as a doubt remains about his freedom of choice in his pursuits and the certainty of his recovering his stipulated wages. In this the interests of the employer and the employed coincide. The employer desires in his workmen spirit and alacrity, and these can be permanently secured in no other way. And if the one ought to be able to enforce the contract. so ought the other. The public interest will be best promoted if the several States will provide adequate protection and remedies for the freedmen. Until this is in some way accomplished there is no chance for the advantageous use of their labor, and the blame of ill success will not rest on them.

I know that sincere philanthropy is earnest for the immediate realization of its remotest aims; but time is always an element in reform. It is one of the greatest acts on record to have brought 4,000,000 people into freedom. The career of free industry must be fairly opened to them, and then their future prosperity and condition must, after all, rest mainly on themselves. If they fail, and so perish away, let us be careful that the failure shall not be attributable to any denial of justice. In all that relates to the destiny of the freedmen we need not be too anxious to read the future; many incidents which, from a speculative point of view, might raise alarm will quietly settle themselves. Now that slavery is at an end, or near its end, the greatness of its evil in the point of view of public economy becomes more and more apparent. Slavery was essentially a monopoly of labor, and as such locked the States where it prevailed against the incoming of free industry. Where labor was the property of the capitalist, the white man was excluded from employment, or had but the second best chance of finding it; and the foreign emigrant turned away from the region where his condition would be so precarious. With the destruction of the monopoly free labor will hasten from all parts of the civilized world to assist in developing various and immeasurable resources which have hitherto lain dormant. The eight or nine States nearest the Gulf of Mexico have a soil of exuberant fertility, a climate friendly to long life, and can sustain a denser population than is found as yet in any part of our country. And the future influx of population to them will be mainly from the North or from the most cultivated nations in Europe. From the sufferings that have attended them during our late struggle let us look away to the future, which is sure to be laden for them with greater prosperity than has ever before been known. The removal of the monopoly of slave labor is a pledge that those regions will be peopled by a numerous and enterprising population, which will vie with any in the Union in compactness, inventive genius, wealth, and industry.

Our Government springs from and was made for the people—not the people for the Government. To them it owes allegiance; from them it must derive its courage, strength, and wisdom. But while the Government is thus bound to defer to the people, from whom it derives its existence, it should, from the very consideration of its origin, be strong in its power of resistance to the establishment of inequalities. Monopolies, perpetuities, and class legislation are contrary to the genius of free government, and ought not to be allowed. Here there is no room for favored classes or monopolies; the principle of our Government is that of equal laws and freedom of industry. Wherever monopoly attains a foothold, it is sure to be a source of danger, discord, and trouble. We shall but fulfill our duties as legislators by according "equal and exact justice to all men," special privileges to none. The Government is subordinate to the people; but, as the agent and representative of the people, it must be held superior to monopolies, which in themselves ought never to be granted, and which, where they exist, must be subordinate and yield to the Government.

The Constitution confers on Congress the right to regulate commerce among the several States. It is of the first necessity, for the maintenance of the Union, that that commerce should be free and unobstructed. No State can be justified in any device to tax the transit of travel and commerce between States. The position of many States is such that if they were allowed to take advantage of it for purposes of local revenue the commerce between States might be injuriously burdened, or even virtually prohibited. It is best, while the country is still young and while the tendency to dangerous monopolies of this kind is still feeble, to use the power of Congress so as to prevent any selfish impediment to the free circulation of men and merchandise. A tax on travel and merchandise in their transit constitutes one of the worst forms of monopoly, and the evil is increased if coupled with a denial of the choice of route. When the vast extent of our country is considered, it is plain that every obstacle to the free circulation of commerce between the States ought to be sternly guarded against by appropriate legislation within the limits of the Constitution.

The report of the Secretary of the Interior explains the condition of the public lands, the transactions of the Patent Office and the Pension Bureau, the management of our Indian affairs, the progress made in the construction of the Pacific Railroad, and furnishes information in reference to matters of local interest in the District of Columbia. It also presents evidence of the successful operation of the homestead act, under the provisions of which 1,160,533 acres of the public lands were entered during the last fiscal year—more than one-fourth of the whole number of acres sold or otherwise disposed of during that period. It is estimated that the receipts derived from this source are sufficient to cover the expenses incident to the survey and disposal of the lands entered under this act, and that payments in cash to the extent of from 40 to 50 per cent will be made by settlers who may thus at any time acquire title before the expiration of the period at which it would otherwise vest. The homestead policy was established only after long and earnest resistance; experience proves its wisdom. The lands in the hands of industrious settlers, whose labor creates wealth and contributes to the public resources, are worth more to the United States than if they had been reserved as a solitude for future purchasers.

The lamentable events of the last four years and the sacrifices made by the gallant men of our Army and Navy have swelled the records of the Pension Bureau to an unprecedented extent. On the 30th day of June last the total number of pensioners was 85,986, requiring for their annual pay, exclusive of expenses, the sum of $8,023,445. The number of applications that have been allowed since that date will require a large increase of this amount for the next fiscal year. The means for the payment of the stipends due under existing laws to our disabled soldiers and sailors and to the families of such as have perished in the service of the country will no doubt be cheerfully and promptly granted. A grateful people will not hesitate to sanction any measures having for their object the relief of soldiers mutilated and families made fatherless in the efforts to preserve our national existence.

The report of the Postmaster-General presents an encouraging exhibit of the operations of the Post-Office Department during the year. The revenues of the past year, from the loyal States alone, exceeded the maximum annual receipts from all the States previous to the rebellion in the sum of $6,038,091; and the annual average increase of revenue during the last four years, compared with the revenues of the four years immediately preceding the rebellion, was $3,533,845. The revenues of the last fiscal year amounted to $14,556,158 and the expenditures to $13,694,728, leaving a surplus of receipts over expenditures of $861,430. Progress has been made in restoring the postal service in the Southern States. The views presented by the Postmaster-General against the policy of granting subsidies to the ocean mail steamship lines upon established routes and in favor of continuing the present system, which limits the compensation for ocean service to the postage earnings, are recommended to the careful consideration of Congress.

It appears from the report of the Secretary of the Navy that while at the commencement of the present year there were in commission 530 vessels of all classes and descriptions, armed with 3,000 guns and manned by 51,000 men, the number of vessels at present in commission is 117, with 830 guns and 12,128 men. By this prompt reduction of the naval forces the expenses of the Government have been largely diminished, and a number of vessels purchased for naval purposes from the merchant marine have been returned to the peaceful pursuits of commerce. Since the suppression of active hostilities our foreign squadrons have been reestablished, and consist of vessels much more efficient than those employed on similar service previous to the rebellion. The suggestion for the enlargement of the navy-yards, and especially for the establishment of one in fresh water for ironclad vessels, is deserving of consideration, as is also the recommendation for a different location and more ample grounds for the Naval Academy.

In the report of the Secretary of War a general summary is given of the military campaigns of 1864 and 1865, ending in the suppression of armed resistance to the national authority in the insurgent States. The operations of the general administrative bureaus of the War Department during the past year are detailed and an estimate made of the appropriations that will be required for military purposes in the fiscal year commencing the 1st day of July, 1866. The national military force on the 1st of May, 1865, numbered 1,000,516 men. It is proposed to reduce the military establishment to a peace footing, comprehending 50,000 troops of all arms, organized so as to admit of an enlargement by filling up the ranks to 82,600 if the circumstances of the country should require an augmentation of the Army. The volunteer force has already been reduced by the discharge from service of over 800,000 troops, and the Department is proceeding rapidly in the work of further reduction. The war estimates are reduced from $516,240,131 to $33,814,461, which amount, in the opinion of the Department, is adequate for a peace establishment. The measures of retrenchment in each bureau and branch of the service exhibit a diligent economy worthy of commendation. Reference is also made in the report to the necessity of providing for a uniform militia system and to the propriety of making suitable provision for wounded and disabled officers and soldiers.

The revenue system of the country is a subject of vital interest to its honor and prosperity, and should command the earnest consideration of Congress. The Secretary of the Treasury will lay before you a full and detailed report of the receipts and disbursements of the last fiscal year, of the first quarter of the present fiscal year, of the probable receipts and expenditures for the other three quarters, and the estimates for the year following the 30th of June, 1866. I might content myself with a reference to that report, in which you will find all the information required for your deliberations and decision, but the paramount importance of the subject so presses itself on my own mind that I can not but lay before you my views of the measures which are required for the good character, and I might almost say for the existence, of this people. The life of a republic lies certainly in the energy, virtue, and intelligence of its citizens; but it is equally true that a good revenue system is the life of an organized government. I meet you at a time when the nation has voluntarily burdened itself with a debt unprecedented in our annals. Vast as is its amount, it fades away into nothing when compared with the countless blessings that will be conferred upon our country and upon man by the preservation of the nation's life. Now, on the first occasion of the meeting of Congress since the return of peace, it is of the utmost importance to inaugurate a just policy, which shall at once be put in motion, and which shall commend itself to those who come after us for its continuance. We must aim at nothing less than the complete effacement of the financial evils that necessarily followed a state of civil war. We must endeavor to apply the earliest remedy to the deranged state of the currency, and not shrink from devising a policy which, without being oppressive to the people, shall immediately begin to effect a reduction of the debt, and, if persisted in, discharge it fully within a definitely fixed number of years.

It is our first duty to prepare in earnest for our recovery from the ever-increasing evils of an irredeemable currency without a sudden revulsion, and yet without untimely procrastination. For that end we must each, in our respective positions, prepare the way. I hold it the duty of the Executive to insist upon frugality in the expenditures, and a sparing economy is itself a great national resource. Of the banks to which authority has been given to issue notes secured by bonds of the United States we may require the greatest moderation and prudence, and the law must be rigidly enforced when its limits are exceeded. We may each one of us counsel our active and enterprising countrymen to be constantly on their guard, to liquidate debts contracted in a paper currency, and by conducting business as nearly as possible on a system of cash payments or short credits to hold themselves prepared to return to the standard of gold and silver. To aid our fellow-citizens in the prudent management of their monetary affairs, the duty devolves on us to diminish by law the amount of paper money now in circulation. Five years ago the bank-note circulation of the country amounted to not much more than two hundred millions; now the circulation, bank and national, exceeds seven hundred millions. The simple statement of the fact recommends more strongly than any words of mine could do the necessity of our restraining this expansion. The gradual reduction of the currency is the only measure that can save the business of the country from disastrous calamities, and this can be almost imperceptibly accomplished by gradually funding the national circulation in securities that may be made redeemable at the pleasure of the Government.

Our debt is doubly secure—first in the actual wealth and still greater undeveloped resources of the country, and next in the character of our institutions. The most intelligent observers among political economists have not failed to remark that the public debt of a country is safe in proportion as its people are free; that the debt of a republic is the safest of all. Our history confirms and establishes the theory, and is, I firmly believe, destined to give it a still more signal illustration. The secret of this superiority springs not merely from the fact that in a republic the national obligations are distributed more widely through countless numbers in all classes of society; it has its root in the character of our laws. Here all men contribute to the public welfare and bear their fair share of the public burdens. During the war, under the impulses of patriotism, the men of the great body of the people, without regard to their own comparative want of wealth, thronged to our armies and filled our fleets of war, and held themselves ready to offer their lives for the public good. Now, in their turn, the property and income of the country should bear their just proportion of the burden of taxation, while in our impost system, through means of which increased vitality is incidentally imparted to all the industrial interests of the nation, the duties should be so adjusted as to fall most heavily on articles of luxury, leaving the necessaries of life as free from taxation as the absolute wants of the Government economically administered will justify. No favored class should demand freedom from assessment, and the taxes should be so distributed as not to fall unduly on the poor, but rather on the accumulated wealth of the country. We should look at the national debt just as it is—not as a national blessing, but as a heavy burden on the industry of the country, to be discharged without unnecessary delay.

It is estimated by the Secretary of the Treasury that the expenditures for the fiscal year ending the 30th of June, 1866, will exceed the receipts $112,194,947. It is gratifying, however, to state that it is also estimated that the revenue for the year ending the 30th of June, 1867, will exceed the expenditures in the sum of $111,682,818. This amount, or so much as may be deemed sufficient for the purpose, may be applied to the reduction of the public debt, which on the 31st day of October, 1865, was $2,740,854,750. Every reduction will diminish the total amount of interest to be paid, and so enlarge the means of still further reductions, until the whole shall be liquidated; and this, as will be seen from the estimates of the Secretary of the Treasury, may be accomplished by annual payments even within a period not exceeding thirty years. I have faith that we shall do all this within a reasonable time; that as we have amazed the world by the suppression of a civil war which was thought to be beyond the control of any government, so we shall equally show the superiority of our institutions by the prompt and faithful discharge of our national obligations.

The Department of Agriculture under its present direction is accomplishing much in developing and utilizing the vast agricultural capabilities of the country, and for information respecting the details of its management reference is made to the annual report of the Commissioner.

I have dwelt thus fully on our domestic affairs because of their transcendent importance. Under any circumstances our great extent of territory and variety of climate, producing almost everything that is necessary for the wants and even the comforts of man, make us singularly independent of the varying policy of foreign powers and protect us against every temptation to "entangling alliances," while at the present moment the reestablishment of harmony and the strength that comes from harmony will be our best security against "nations who feel power and forget right." For myself, it has been and it will be my constant aim to promote peace and amity with all foreign nations and powers, and I have every reason to believe that they all, without exception, are animated by the same disposition. Our relations with the Emperor of China, so recent in their origin, are most friendly. Our commerce with his dominions is receiving new developments, and it is very pleasing to find that the Government of that great Empire manifests satisfaction with our policy and reposes just confidence in the fairness which marks our intercourse. The unbroken harmony between the United States and the Emperor of Russia is receiving a new support from an enterprise designed to carry telegraphic lines across the continent of Asia, through his dominions, and so to connect us with all Europe by a new channel of intercourse. Our commerce with South America is about to receive encouragement by a direct line of mail steamships to the rising Empire of Brazil. The distinguished party of men of science who have recently left our country to make a scientific exploration of the natural history and rivers and mountain ranges of that region have received from the Emperor that generous welcome which was to have been expected from his constant friendship for the United States and his well-known zeal in promoting the advancement of knowledge. A hope is entertained that our commerce with the rich and populous countries that border the Mediterranean Sea may be largely increased. Nothing will be wanting on the part of this Government to extend the protection of our flag over the enterprise of our fellow-citizens. We receive from the powers in that region assurances of good will ; and it is worthy of note that a special envoy has brought us messages of condolence on the death of our late Chief Magistrate from the Bey of Tunis, whose rule includes the old dominions of Carthage, on the African coast.

Our domestic contest, now happily ended, has left some traces in our relations with one at least of the great maritime powers. The formal accordance of belligerent rights to the insurgent States was unprecedented, and has not been justified by the issue. But in the systems of neutrality pursued by the powers which made that concession there was a marked difference. The materials of war for the insurgent States were furnished, in a great measure, from the workshops of Great Britain, and British ships, manned by British subjects and prepared for receiving British armaments, sallied from the ports of Great Britain to make war on American commerce under the shelter of a commission from the insurgent States. These ships, having once escaped from British ports, ever afterwards entered them in every part of the world to refit, and so to renew their depredations. The consequences of this conduct were most disastrous to the States then in rebellion, increasing their desolation and misery by the prolongation of our civil contest. It had, moreover, the effect, to a great extent, to drive the American flag from the sea, and to transfer much of our shipping and our commerce to the very power whose subjects had created the necessity for such a change. These events took place before I was called to the administration of the Government. The sincere desire for peace by which I am animated led me to approve the proposal, already made, to submit the question which had thus arisen between the countries to arbitration. These questions are of such moment that they must have commanded the attention of the great powers, and are so interwoven with the peace and interests of every one of them as to have insured an impartial decision. I regret to inform you that Great Britain declined the arbitrament, but, on the other hand, invited us to the formation of a joint commission to settle mutual claims between the two countries, from which those for the depredations before mentioned should be excluded. The proposition, in that very unsatisfactory form, has been declined.

The United States did not present the subject as an impeachment of the good faith of a power which was professing the most friendly dispositions, but as involving questions of public law of which the settlement is essential to the peace of nations; and though pecuniary reparation to their injured citizens would have followed incidentally on a decision against Great Britain, such compensation was not their primary object. They had a higher motive, and it was in the interests of peace and justice to establish important principles of international law. The correspondence will be placed before you. The ground on which the British minister rests his justification is, substantially, that the municipal law of a nation and the domestic interpretations of that law are the measure of its duty as a neutral, and I feel bound to declare my opinion before you and before the world that that justification can not be sustained before the tribunal of nations. At the same time, I do not advise to any present attempt at redress by acts of legislation. For the future, friendship between the two countries must rest on the basis of mutual justice.

From the moment of the establishment of our free Constitution the civilized world has been convulsed by revolutions in the interests of democracy or of monarchy, but through all those revolutions the United States have wisely and firmly refused to become propagandists of republicanism. It is the only government suited to our condition; but we have never sought to impose it on others, and we have consistently followed the advice of Washington to recommend it only by the careful preservation and prudent use of the blessing. During all the intervening period the policy of European powers and of the United States has, on the whole, been harmonious. Twice, indeed, rumors of the invasion of some parts of America in the interest of monarchy have prevailed; twice my predecessors have had occasion to announce the views of this nation in respect to such interference. On both occasions the remonstrance of the United States was respected from a deep conviction on the part of European Governments that the system of noninterference and mutual abstinence from propagandism was the true rule for the two hemispheres. Since those times we have advanced in wealth and power, but we retain the same purpose to leave the nations of Europe to choose their own dynasties and form their own systems of government. This consistent moderation may justly demand a corresponding moderation. We should regard it as a great calamity to ourselves, to the cause of good government, and to the peace of the world should any European power challenge the American people, as it were, to the defense of republicanism against foreign interference. We can not foresee and are unwilling to consider what opportunities might present themselves, what combinations might offer to protect ourselves against designs inimical to our form of government. The United States desire to act in the future as they have ever acted heretofore; they never will be driven from that course but by the aggression of European powers, and we rely on the wisdom and justice of those powers to respect the system of noninterference which has so long been sanctioned by time, and which by its good results has approved itself to both continents.

The correspondence between the United States and France in reference to questions which have become subjects of discussion between the two Governments will at a proper time be laid before Congress.

When, on the organization of our Government under the Constitution, the President of the United States delivered his inaugural address to the two Houses of Congress, he said to them, and through them to the country and to mankind, that—

The preservation of the sacred fire of liberty and the destiny of the republican model of government are justly considered, perhaps, as *deeply*, as *finally*, staked on the experiment intrusted to the hands of the American people.

And the House of Representatives answered Washington by the voice of Madison:

We adore the Invisible Hand which has led the American people, through so many difficulties, to cherish a conscious responsibility for the destiny of republican liberty.

More than seventy-six years have glided away since these words were spoken; the United States have passed through severer trials than were foreseen; and now, at this new epoch in our existence as one nation, with our Union purified by sorrows and strengthened by conflict and established by the virtue of the people, the greatness of the occasion invites us once more to repeat with solemnity the pledges of our fathers to hold ourselves answerable before our fellow-men for the success of the republican form of government. Experience has proved its sufficiency in peace and in war; it has vindicated its authority through dangers and afflictions, and sudden and terrible emergencies, which would have crushed any system that had been less firmly fixed in the hearts of the people. At the inauguration of Washington the foreign relations of the country were few and its trade was repressed by hostile regulations; now all the civilized nations of the globe welcome our commerce, and their governments profess toward us amity. Then our country felt its way hesitatingly along an untried path, with States so little bound together by rapid means of communication as to be hardly known to one another, and with historic traditions extending over very few years; now intercourse between the States is swift and intimate; the experience of centuries has been crowded into a few generations, and has created an intense, indestructible nationality. Then our jurisdiction did not reach beyond the inconvenient boundaries of the territory which had achieved independence; now, through cessions of lands, first colonized by Spain and France, the country has acquired a more complex character, and has for its natural limits the chain of lakes, the Gulf of Mexico, and on the east and the west the two great oceans. Other nations were wasted by civil wars for ages before they could establish for themselves the necessary degree of unity; the latent conviction that our form of government is the best ever known to the world has enabled us to emerge from civil war within four years with a complete vindication of the constitutional authority of the General Government and with our local liberties and State institutions unimpaired.

The throngs of emigrants that crowd to our shores are witnesses of the confidence of all peoples in our permanence. Here is the great land of free labor, where industry is blessed with unexampled rewards and the bread of the workingman is sweetened by the consciousness that the cause of the country "is his own cause, his own safety, his own dignity." Here everyone enjoys the free use of his faculties and the choice of activity as a natural right. Here, under the combined influence of a fruitful soil, genial climes, and happy institutions, population has increased fifteenfold within a century. Here, through the easy development of boundless resources, wealth has increased with twofold greater rapidity than numbers, so that we have become secure against the financial vicissitudes of other countries and, alike in business and in opinion, are self-centered and truly independent. Here more and more care is given to provide education for everyone born on our soil.   Here religion, released from political connection with the civil government, refuses to subserve the craft of statesmen, and becomes in its independence the spiritual life of the people.   Here toleration is extended to every opinion, in the quiet certainty that truth needs only a fair field to secure the victory.   Here the human mind goes forth unshackled in the pursuit of science, to collect stores of knowledge and acquire an ever-increasing mastery over the forces of nature.   Here the national domain is offered and held in millions of separate freeholds, so that our fellow-citizens, beyond the occupants of any other part of the earth, constitute in reality a people.   Here exists the democratic form of government; and that form of government, by the confession of European statesmen, "gives a power of which no other form is capable, because it incorporates every man with the state and arouses everything that belongs to the soul."

Where in past history does a parallel exist to the public happiness which is within the reach of the people of the United States?   Where in any part of the globe can institutions be found so suited to their habits or so entitled to their love as their own free Constitution?   Every one of them, then, in whatever part of the land he has his home, must wish its perpetuity.   Who of them will not now acknowledge, in the words of Washington, that "every step by which the people of the United States have advanced to the character of an independent nation seems to have been distinguished by some token of providential agency"?   Who will not join with me in the prayer that the Invisible Hand which has led us through the clouds that gloomed around our path will so guide us onward to a perfect restoration of fraternal affection that we of this day may be able to transmit our great inheritance of State governments in all their rights, of the General Government in its whole constitutional vigor, to our posterity, and they to theirs through countless generations?

SECOND ANNUAL MESSAGE.

WASHINGTON, *December 3, 1866.*

Fellow-Citizens of the Senate and House of Representatives:

After a brief interval the Congress of the United States resumes its annual legislative labors.   An all-wise and merciful Providence has abated the pestilence which visited our shores, leaving its calamitous traces upon some portions of our country.   Peace, order, tranquillity, and civil authority have been formally declared to exist throughout the whole of the

United States.   In all of the States civil authority has superseded the
coercion of arms, and the people, by their voluntary action, are maintaining their governments in full activity and complete operation.   The
enforcement of the laws is no longer "obstructed in any State by combinations too powerful to be suppressed by the ordinary course of judicial
proceedings," and the animosities engendered by the war are rapidly
yielding to the beneficent influences of our free institutions and to the
kindly effects of unrestricted social and commercial intercourse.   An
entire restoration of fraternal feeling must be the earnest wish of every
patriotic heart; and we will have accomplished our grandest national
achievement when, forgetting the sad events of the past and remembering only their instructive lessons, we resume our onward career as a free,
prosperous, and united people.

In my message of the 4th of December, 1865, Congress was informed of
the measures which had been instituted by the Executive with a view
to the gradual restoration of the States in which the insurrection occurred
to their relations with the General Government.   Provisional governors
had been appointed, conventions called, governors elected, legislatures
assembled, and Senators and Representatives chosen to the Congress of
the United States.   Courts had been opened for the enforcement of laws
long in abeyance.   The blockade had been removed, custom-houses reestablished, and the internal-revenue laws put in force, in order that the
people might contribute to the national income.   Postal operations had
been renewed, and efforts were being made to restore them to their former
condition of efficiency.   The States themselves had been asked to take
part in the high function of amending the Constitution, and of thus sanc-
tioning the extinction of African slavery as one of the legitimate results
of our internecine struggle.

Having progressed thus far, the executive department found that it had
accomplished nearly all that was within the scope of its constitutional
authority.   One thing, however, yet remained to be done before the work
of restoration could be completed, and that was the admission to Congress
of loyal Senators and Representatives from the States whose people had
rebelled against the lawful authority of the General Government.   This
question devolved upon the respective Houses, which by the Constitution
are made the judges of the elections, returns, and qualifications of their
own members, and its consideration at once engaged the attention of
Congress.

In the meantime the executive department—no other plan having been
proposed by Congress—continued its efforts to perfect, as far as was practicable, the restoration of the proper relations between the citizens of the
respective States, the States, and the Federal Government, extending
from time to time, as the public interests seemed to require, the judicial,
revenue, and postal systems of the country.   With the advice and consent of the Senate, the necessary officers were appointed and appropria-

tions made by Congress for the payment of their salaries. The proposition to amend the Federal Constitution, so as to prevent the existence of slavery within the United States or any place subject to their jurisdiction, was ratified by the requisite number of States, and on the 18th day of December, 1865, it was officially declared to have become valid as a part of the Constitution of the United States. All of the States in which the insurrection had existed promptly amended their constitutions so as to make them conform to the great change thus effected in the organic law of the land; declared null and void all ordinances and laws of secession; repudiated all pretended debts and obligations created for the revolutionary purposes of the insurrection, and proceeded in good faith to the enactment of measures for the protection and amelioration of the condition of the colored race. Congress, however, yet hesitated to admit any of these States to representation, and it was not until toward the close of the eighth month of the session that an exception was made in favor of Tennessee by the admission of her Senators and Representatives.

I deem it a subject of profound regret that Congress has thus far failed to admit to seats loyal Senators and Representatives from the other States whose inhabitants, with those of Tennessee, had engaged in the rebellion. Ten States—more than one-fourth of the whole number—remain without representation; the seats of fifty members in the House of Representatives and of twenty members in the Senate are yet vacant, not by their own consent, not by a failure of election, but by the refusal of Congress to accept their credentials. Their admission, it is believed, would have accomplished much toward the renewal and strengthening of our relations as one people and removed serious cause for discontent on the part of the inhabitants of those States. It would have accorded with the great principle enunciated in the Declaration of American Independence that no people ought to bear the burden of taxation and yet be denied the right of representation. It would have been in consonance with the express provisions of the Constitution that "each State shall have at least one Representative" and "that no State, without its consent, shall be deprived of its equal suffrage in the Senate." These provisions were intended to secure to every State and to the people of every State the right of representation in each House of Congress; and so important was it deemed by the framers of the Constitution that the equality of the States in the Senate should be preserved that not even by an amendment of the Constitution can any State, without its consent, be denied a voice in that branch of the National Legislature.

It is true it has been assumed that the existence of the States was terminated by the rebellious acts of their inhabitants, and that, the insurrection having been suppressed, they were thenceforward to be considered merely as conquered territories. The legislative, executive, and judicial departments of the Government have, however, with great distinctness and uniform consistency, refused to sanction an assumption so incompatible with the nature of our republican system and with the professed objects of the war. Throughout the recent legislation of Congress the undeniable fact makes itself apparent that these ten political communities are nothing less than States of this Union. At the very commencement of the rebellion each House declared, with a unanimity as remarkable as it was significant, that the war was not "waged upon our part in any spirit of oppression, nor for any purpose of conquest or subjugation, nor purpose of overthrowing or interfering with the rights or established institutions of those States, but to defend and maintain the supremacy of the Constitution and all laws made in pursuance thereof, and to preserve the Union, with all the dignity, equality, and rights of the several States unimpaired; and that as soon as these objects" were "accomplished the war ought to cease." In some instances Senators were permitted to continue their legislative functions, while in other instances Representatives were elected and admitted to seats after their States had formally declared their right to withdraw from the Union and were endeavoring to maintain that right by force of arms. All of the States whose people were in insurrection, as States, were included in the apportionment of the direct tax of $20,000,000 annually laid upon the United States by the act approved 5th August, 1861. Congress, by the act of March 4, 1862, and by the apportionment of representation thereunder also recognized their presence as States in the Union; and they have, for judicial purposes, been divided into districts, as States alone can be divided. The same recognition appears in the recent legislation in reference to Tennessee, which evidently rests upon the fact that the functions of the State were not destroyed by the rebellion, but merely suspended; and that principle is of course applicable to those States which, like Tennessee, attempted to renounce their places in the Union.

The action of the executive department of the Government upon this subject has been equally definite and uniform, and the purpose of the war was specifically stated in the proclamation issued by my predecessor on the 22d day of September, 1862. It was then solemnly proclaimed and declared "that hereafter, as heretofore, the war will be prosecuted for the object of practically restoring the constitutional relation between the United States and each of the States and the people thereof in which States that relation is or may be suspended or disturbed."

The recognition of the States by the judicial department of the Government has also been clear and conclusive in all proceedings affecting them as States had in the Supreme, circuit, and district courts.

In the admission of Senators and Representatives from any and all of the States there can be no just ground of apprehension that persons who are disloyal will be clothed with the powers of legislation, for this could not happen when the Constitution and the laws are enforced by a vigilant and faithful Congress. Each House is made the "judge of the elections, returns, and qualifications of its own members," and may, "with the concurrence of two-thirds, expel a member." When a Senator or Representative presents his certificate of election, he may at once be admitted or rejected; or, should there be any question as to his eligibility, his credentials may be referred for investigation to the appropriate committee. If admitted to a seat, it must be upon evidence satisfactory to the House of which he thus becomes a member that he possesses the requisite constitutional and legal qualifications. If refused admission as a member for want of due allegiance to the Government and returned to his constituents, they are admonished that none but persons loyal to the United States will be allowed a voice in the legislative councils of the nation, and the political power and moral influence of Congress are thus effectively exerted in the interests of loyalty to the Government and fidelity to the Union. Upon this question, so vitally affecting the restoration of the Union and the permanency of our present form of government, my convictions, heretofore expressed, have undergone no change, but, on the contrary, their correctness has been confirmed by reflection and time. If the admission of loyal members to seats in the respective Houses of Congress was wise and expedient a year ago, it is no less wise and expedient now. If this anomalous condition is right now—if in the exact condition of these States at the present time it is lawful to exclude them from representation—I do not see that the question will be changed by the efflux of time. Ten years hence, if these States remain as they are, the right of representation will be no stronger, the right of exclusion will be no weaker.

The Constitution of the United States makes it the duty of the President to recommend to the consideration of Congress "such measures as he shall judge necessary and expedient." I know of no measure more imperatively demanded by every consideration of national interest, sound policy, and equal justice than the admission of loyal members from the now unrepresented States. This would consummate the work of restoration and exert a most salutary influence in the reestablishment of peace, harmony, and fraternal feeling. It would tend greatly to renew the confidence of the American people in the vigor and stability of their institutions. It would bind us more closely together as a nation and enable us to show to the world the inherent and recuperative power of a government founded upon the will of the people and established upon the principles of liberty, justice, and intelligence. Our increased strength and enhanced prosperity would irrefragably demonstrate the fallacy of the arguments against free institutions drawn from our recent national disorders by the enemies of republican government. The admission of loyal members from the States now excluded from Congress, by allaying doubt and apprehension, would turn capital now awaiting an opportunity for investment into the channels of trade and industry. It would alleviate the present troubled condition of those States, and by inducing emigration aid in the settlement of fertile regions now uncultivated and lead to an increased production of those staples which have added so greatly to the wealth of the nation and commerce of the world.   New fields of enterprise would be opened to our progressive people, and soon the devastations of war would be repaired and all traces of our domestic differences effaced from the minds of our countrymen.

In our efforts to preserve "the unity of government which constitutes as one people" by restoring the States to the condition which they held prior to the rebellion, we should be cautious, lest, having rescued our nation from perils of threatened disintegration, we resort to consolidation, and in the end absolute despotism, as a remedy for the recurrence of simi lar troubles.   The war having terminated, and with it all occasion for the exercise of powers of doubtful constitutionality, we should hasten to bring legislation within the boundaries prescribed by the Constitution and to return to the ancient landmarks established by our fathers for the guidance of succeeding generations.

> The constitution which at any time exists till changed by an explicit and authentic act of the whole people is sacredly obligatory upon all. * * * If in the opinion of the people the distribution or modification of the constitutional powers be in any particular wrong, let it be corrected by an amendment in the way which the Constitution designates; but let there be no change by usurpation, for * * * it is the customary weapon by which free governments are destroyed.

Washington spoke these words to his countrymen when, followed by their love and gratitude, he voluntarily retired from the cares of public life.   "To keep in all things within the pale of our constitutional powers and cherish the Federal Union as the only rock of safety" were prescribed by Jefferson as rules of action to endear to his "countrymen the true principles of their Constitution and promote a union of sentiment and action, equally auspicious to their happiness and safety."   Jackson held that the action of the General Government should always be strictly confined to the sphere of its appropriate duties, and justly and forcibly urged that our Government is not to be maintained nor our Union preserved "by invasions of the rights and powers of the several States.   In thus attempting to make our General Government strong we make it weak. Its true strength consists in leaving individuals and States as much as possible to themselves; in making itself felt, not in its power, but in its beneficence; not in its control, but in its protection; not in binding the States more closely to the center, but leaving each to move unobstructed in its proper constitutional orbit."   These are the teachings of men whose deeds and services have made them illustrious, and who, long since withdrawn from the scenes of life, have left to their country the rich legacy of their example, their wisdom, and their patriotism.   Drawing fresh inspiration from their lessons, let us emulate them in love of country and respect for the Constitution and the laws.

The report of the Secretary of the Treasury affords much information respecting the revenue and commerce of the country.   His views upon the currency and with reference to a proper adjustment of our revenue system, internal as well as impost, are commended to the careful consideration of Congress. In·my last annual message I expressed my general views upon these subjects. I need now only call attention to the necessity of carrying into every department of the Government a system of rigid accountability, thorough retrenchment, and wise economy. With no exceptional nor unusual expenditures, the oppressive burdens of taxation can be lessened by such a modification of our revenue laws as will be consistent with the public faith and the legitimate and necessary wants of the Government.

The report presents a much more satisfactory condition of our finances than one year ago the most sanguine could have anticipated. During the fiscal year ending the 30th June, 1865 (the last year of the war), the public debt was increased $941,902,537, and on the 31st of October, 1865, it amounted to $2,740,854,750. On the 31st day of October, 1866, it had been reduced to $2,551,310,006, the diminution during a period of fourteen months, commencing September 1, 1865, and ending October 31, 1866, having been $206,379,565. In the last annual report on the state of the finances it was estimated that during the three quarters of the fiscal year ending the 30th of June last the debt would be increased $112,194,947. During that period, however, it was reduced $31,196,387, the receipts of the year having been $89,905,905 more and the expenditures $200,529,235 less than the estimates. Nothing could more clearly indicate than these statements the extent and availability of the national resources and the rapidity and safety with which, under our form of government, great military and naval establishments can be disbanded and expenses reduced from a war to a peace footing.

During the fiscal year ending June 30, 1866, the receipts were $558,-032,620 and the expenditures $520,750,940, leaving an available surplus of $37,281,680. It is estimated that the receipts for the fiscal year ending the 30th June, 1867, will be $475,061,386, and that the expenditures will reach the sum of $316,428,078, leaving in the Treasury a surplus of $158,633,308. For the fiscal year ending June 30, 1886, it is estimated that the receipts will amount to $436,000,000 and that the expenditures will be $350,247,641, showing an excess of $85,752,359 in favor of the Government. These estimated receipts may be diminished by a reduction of excise and import duties, but after all necessary reductions shall have been made the revenue of the present and of following years will doubtless be sufficient to cover all legitimate charges upon the Treasury and leave a large annual surplus to be applied to the payment of the principal of the debt. There seems now to be no good reason why taxes may not be reduced as the country advances in population and wealth, and yet the debt be extinguished within the next quarter of a century.

The report of the Secretary of War furnishes valuable and important information in reference to the operations of his Department during the past year.   Few volunteers now remain in the service, and they are being discharged as rapidly as they can be replaced by regular troops.   The Army has been promptly paid, carefully provided with medical treatment, well sheltered and subsisted, and is to be furnished with breech-loading small arms.   The military strength of the nation has been unimpaired by the discharge of volunteers, the disposition of unserviceable or perishable stores, and the retrenchment of expenditure.   Sufficient war material to meet any emergency has been retained, and from the disbanded volunteers standing ready to respond to the national call large armies can be rapidly organized, equipped, and concentrated.   Fortifications on the coast and frontier have received or are being prepared for more powerful armaments; lake surveys and harbor and river improvements are in course of energetic prosecution.   Preparations have been made for the payment of the additional bounties authorized during the recent session of Congress, under such regulations as will protect the Government from fraud and secure to the honorably discharged soldier the well-earned reward of his faithfulness and gallantry.   More than 6,000 maimed soldiers have received artificial limbs or other surgical apparatus, and 41 national cemeteries, containing the remains of 104,526 Union soldiers, have already been established.   The total estimate of military appropriations is $25,205,669.

It is stated in the report of the Secretary of the Navy that the naval force at this time consists of 278 vessels, armed with 2,351 guns.   Of these, 115 vessels, carrying 1,029 guns, are in commission, distributed chiefly among seven squadrons.   The number of men in the service is 13,600.   Great activity and vigilance have been displayed by all the squadrons, and their movements have been judiciously and efficiently arranged in such manner as would best promote American commerce and protect the rights and interests of our countrymen abroad.   The vessels unemployed are undergoing repairs or are laid up until their services may be required.   Most of the ironclad fleet is at League Island, in the vicinity of Philadelphia, a place which, until decisive action should be taken by Congress, was selected by the Secretary of the Navy as the most eligible location for that class of vessels.   It is important that a suitable public station should be provided for the ironclad fleet. It is intended that these vessels shall be in proper condition for any emergency, and it is desirable that the bill accepting League Island for naval purposes, which passed the House of Representatives at its last session, should receive final action at an early period, in order that there may be a suitable public station for this class of vessels, as well as a navy-yard of area sufficient for the wants of the service on the Delaware River. The naval pension fund amounts to $11,750,000, having been increased $2,750,000 during the year.   The expenditures of the Department for the fiscal year ending 30th June last were $43,324,526, and the estimates for the coming year amount to $23,568,436.   Attention is invited to the condition of our seamen and the importance of legislative measures for their relief and improvement. The suggestions in behalf of this deserving class of our fellow-citizens are earnestly recommended to the favorable attention of Congress.

The report of the Postmaster-General presents a most satisfactory condition of the postal service and submits recommendations which deserve the consideration of Congress. The revenues of the Department for the year ending June 30, 1866, were $14,386,986 and the expenditures $15,352,079, showing an excess of the latter of $965,093. In anticipation of this deficiency, however, a special appropriation was made by Congress in the act approved July 28, 1866. Including the standing appropriation of $700,000 for free mail matter as a legitimate portion of the revenues, yet remaining unexpended, the actual deficiency for the past year is only $265,093—a sum within $51,141 of the amount estimated in the annual report of 1864. The decrease of revenue compared with the previous year was 1⅕ per cent, and the increase of expenditures, owing principally to the enlargement of the mail service in the South, was 12 per cent. On the 30th of June last there were in operation 6,930 mail routes, with an aggregate length of 180,921 miles, an aggregate annual transportation of 71,837,914 miles, and an aggregate annual cost, including all expenditures, of $8,410,184. The length of railroad routes is 32,092 miles and the annual transportation 30,609,467 miles. The length of steamboat routes is 14,346 miles and the annual transportation 3,411,962 miles. The mail service is rapidly increasing throughout the whole country, and its steady extension in the Southern States indicates their constantly improving condition. The growing importance of the foreign service also merits attention. The post-office department of Great Britain and our own have agreed upon a preliminary basis for a new postal convention, which it is believed will prove eminently beneficial to the commercial interests of the United States, inasmuch as it contemplates a reduction of the international letter postage to one-half the existing rates; a reduction of postage with all other countries to and from which correspondence is transmitted in the British mail, or in closed mails through the United Kingdom; the establishment of uniform and reasonable charges for the sea and territorial transit of correspondence in closed mails; and an allowance to each post-office department of the right to use all mail communications established under the authority of the other for the dispatch of correspondence, either in open or closed mails, on the same terms as those applicable to the inhabitants of the country providing the means of transmission.

The report of the Secretary of the Interior exhibits the condition of those branches of the public service which are committed to his supervision. During the last fiscal year 4,629,312 acres of public land were disposed of, 1,892,516 acres of which were entered under the homestead act. The policy originally adopted relative to the public lands has undergone essential modifications.   Immediate revenue, and not their rapid settlement, was the cardinal feature of our land system.   Long experience and earnest discussion have resulted in the conviction that the early development of our agricultural resources and the diffusion of an energetic population over our vast territory are objects of far greater importance to the national growth and prosperity than the proceeds of the sale of the land to the highest bidder in open market.   The preemption laws confer upon the pioneer who complies with the terms they impose the privilege of purchasing a limited portion of "unoffered lands" at the minimum price.   The homestead enactments relieve the settler from the payment of purchase money, and secure him a permanent home upon the condition of residence for a term of years.   This liberal policy invites emigration from the Old and from the more crowded portions of the New World.   Its propitious results are undoubted, and will be more signally manifested when time shall have given to it a wider development.

Congress has made liberal grants of public land to corporations in aid of the construction of railroads and other internal improvements.   Should this policy hereafter prevail, more stringent provisions will be required to secure a faithful application of the fund.   The title to the lands should not pass, by patent or otherwise, but remain in the Government and subject to its control until some portion of the road has been actually built. Portions of them might then from time to time be conveyed to the corporation, but never in a greater ratio to the whole quantity embraced by the grant than the completed parts bear to the entire length of the projected improvement.   This restriction would not operate to the prejudice of any undertaking conceived in good faith and executed with reasonable energy, as it is the settled practice to withdraw from market the lands falling within the operation of such grants, and thus to exclude the inception of a subsequent adverse right.   A breach of the conditions which Congress may deem proper to impose should work a forfeiture of claim to the lands so withdrawn but unconveyed, and of title to the lands conveyed which remain unsold.

Operations on the several lines of the Pacific Railroad have been prosecuted with unexampled vigor and success.   Should no unforeseen causes of delay occur, it is confidently anticipated that this great thoroughfare will be completed before the expiration of the period designated by Congress.

During the last fiscal year the amount paid to pensioners, including the expenses of disbursement, was $13,459,996, and 50,177 names were added to the pension rolls.   The entire number of pensioners June 30, 1866, was 126,722.   This fact furnishes melancholy and striking proof of the sacrifices made to vindicate the constitutional authority of the Federal Government and to maintain inviolate the integrity of the Union They impose upon us corresponding obligations.   It is estimated that $33,000,000 will be required to meet the exigencies of this branch of the service during the next fiscal year.

Treaties have been concluded with the Indians, who, enticed into armed opposition to our Government at the outbreak of the rebellion, have unconditionally submitted to our authority and manifested an earnest desire for a renewal of friendly relations.

During the year ending September 30, 1866, 8,716 patents for useful inventions and designs were issued, and at that date the balance in the Treasury to the credit of the patent fund was $228,297.

As a subject upon which depends an immense amount of the production and commerce of the country, I recommend to Congress such legislation as may be necessary for the preservation of the levees of the Mississippi River. It is a matter of national importance that early steps should be taken, not only to add to the efficiency of these barriers against destructive inundations, but for the removal of all obstructions to the free and safe navigation of that great channel of trade and commerce.

The District of Columbia under existing laws is not entitled to that representation in the national councils which from our earliest history has been uniformly accorded to each Territory established from time to time within our limits. It maintains peculiar relations to Congress, to whom the Constitution has granted the power of exercising exclusive legislation over the seat of Government. Our fellow-citizens residing in the District, whose interests are thus confided to the special guardianship of Congress, exceed in number the population of several of our Territories, and no just reason is perceived why a Delegate of their choice should not be admitted to a seat in the House of Representatives. No mode seems so appropriate and effectual of enabling them to make known their peculiar condition and wants and of securing the local legislation adapted to them. I therefore recommend the passage of a law authorizing the electors of the District of Columbia to choose a Delegate, to be allowed the same rights and privileges as a Delegate representing a Territory. The increasing enterprise and rapid progress of improvement in the District are highly gratifying, and I trust that the efforts of the municipal authorities to promote the prosperity of the national metropolis will receive the efficient and generous cooperation of Congress.

The report of the Commissioner of Agriculture reviews the operations of his Department during the past year, and asks the aid of Congress in its efforts to encourage those States which, scourged by war, are now earnestly engaged in the reorganization of domestic industry.

It is a subject of congratulation that no foreign combinations against our domestic peace and safety or our legitimate influence among the nations have been formed or attempted. While sentiments of reconciliation, loyalty, and patriotism have increased at home, a more just consideration of our national character and rights has been manifested by foreign nations.

The entire success of the Atlantic telegraph between the coast of Ireland and the Province of Newfoundland is an achievement which has been justly celebrated in both hemispheres as the opening of an era in the progress of civilization. There is reason to expect that equal success will attend and even greater results follow the enterprise for connecting the two continents through the Pacific Ocean by the projected line of telegraph between Kamchatka and the Russian possessions in America.

The resolution of Congress protesting against pardons by foreign governments of persons convicted of infamous offenses on condition of emigration to our country has been communicated to the states with which we maintain intercourse, and the practice, so justly the subject of complaint on our part, has not been renewed.

The congratulations of Congress to the Emperor of Russia upon his escape from attempted assassination have been presented to that humane and enlightened ruler and received by him with expressions of grateful appreciation.

The Executive, warned of an attempt by Spanish American adventurers to induce the emigration of freedmen of the United States to a foreign country, protested against the project as one which, if consummated, would reduce them to a bondage even more oppressive than that from which they have just been relieved. Assurance has been received from the Government of the State in which the plan was matured that the proceeding will meet neither its encouragement nor approval. It is a question worthy of your consideration whether our laws upon this subject are adequate to the prevention or punishment of the crime thus meditated.

In the month of April last, as Congress is aware, a friendly arrangement was made between the Emperor of France and the President of the United States for the withdrawal from Mexico of the French expeditionary military forces. This withdrawal was to be effected in three detachments, the first of which, it was understood, would leave Mexico in November, now past, the second in March next, and the third and last in November, 1867. Immediately upon the completion of the evacuation the French Government was to assume the same attitude of nonintervention in regard to Mexico as is held by the Government of the United States. Repeated assurances have been given by the Emperor since that agreement that he would complete the promised evacuation within the period mentioned, or sooner.

It was reasonably expected that the proceedings thus contemplated would produce a crisis of great political interest in the Republic of Mexico. The newly appointed minister of the United States, Mr. Campbell, was therefore sent forward on the 9th day of November last to assume his proper functions as minister plenipotentiary of the United States to that Republic. It was also thought expedient that he should be attended in the vicinity of Mexico by the Lieutenant-General of the Army of the United States, with the view of obtaining such information as might be important to determine the course to be pursued by the United States in reestablishing and maintaining necessary and proper intercourse with the Republic of Mexico. Deeply interested in the cause of liberty and humanity, it seemed an obvious duty on our part to exercise whatever influence we possessed for the restoration and permanent establishment in that country of a domestic and republican form of government.

Such was the condition of our affairs in regard to Mexico when, on the 22d of November last, official information was received from Paris that the Emperor of France had some time before decided not to withdraw a detachment of his forces in the month of November past, according to engagement, but that this decision was made with the purpose of withdrawing the whole of those forces in the ensuing spring. Of this determination, however, the United States had not received any notice or intimation, and so soon as the information was received by the Government care was taken to make known its dissent to the Emperor of France.

I can not forego the hope that France will reconsider the subject and adopt some resolution in regard to the evacuation of Mexico which will conform as nearly as practicable with the existing engagement, and thus meet the just expectations of the United States. The papers relating to the subject will be laid before you. It is believed that with the evacuation of Mexico by the expeditionary forces no subject for serious differences between France and the United States would remain. The expressions of the Emperor and people of France warrant a hope that the traditionary friendship between the two countries might in that case be renewed and permanently restored.

A claim of a citizen of the United States for indemnity for spoliations committed on the high seas by the French authorities in the exercise of a belligerent power against Mexico has been met by the Government of France with a proposition to defer settlement until a mutual convention for the adjustment of all claims of citizens and subjects of both countries arising out of the recent wars on this continent shall be agreed upon by the two countries. The suggestion is not deemed unreasonable, but it belongs to Congress to direct the manner in which claims for indemnity by foreigners as well as by citizens of the United States arising out of the late civil war shall be adjudicated and determined. I have no doubt that the subject of all such claims will engage your attention at a convenient and proper time.

It is a matter of regret that no considerable advance has been made toward an adjustment of the differences between the United States and Great Britain arising out of the depredations upon our national commerce and other trespasses committed during our civil war by British subjects, in violation of international law and treaty obligations. The delay, however, may be believed to have resulted in no small degree from the domestic situation of Great Britain. An entire change of ministry occurred in that country during the last session of Parliament. The attention of the new ministry was called to the subject at an early day, and there is some reason to expect that it will now be considered in a becoming and friendly spirit. The importance of an early disposition of the question can not be exaggerated. Whatever might be the wishes of the two Governments, it is manifest that good will and friendship between the two countries can not be established until a reciprocity in the practice of good faith and neutrality shall be restored between the respective nations.

On the 6th of June last, in violation of our neutrality laws, a military expedition and enterprise against the British North American colonies was projected and attempted to be carried on within the territory and jurisdiction of the United States. In obedience to the obligation imposed upon the Executive by the Constitution to see that the laws are faithfully executed, all citizens were warned by proclamation against taking part in or aiding such unlawful proceedings, and the proper civil, military, and naval officers were directed to take all necessary measures for the enforcement of the laws. The expedition failed, but it has not been without its painful consequences. Some of our citizens who, it was alleged, were engaged in the expedition were captured, and have been brought to trial as for a capital offense in the Province of Canada. Judgment and sentence of death have been pronounced against some, while others have been acquitted. Fully believing in the maxim of government that severity of civil punishment for misguided persons who have engaged in revolutionary attempts which have disastrously failed is unsound and unwise, such representations have been made to the British Government in behalf of the convicted persons as, being sustained by an enlightened and humane judgment, will, it is hoped, induce in their cases an exercise of clemency and a judicious amnesty to all who were engaged in the movement. Counsel has been employed by the Government to defend citizens of the United States on trial for capital offenses in Canada, and a discontinuance of the prosecutions which were instituted in the courts of the United States against those who took part in the expedition has been directed.

I have regarded the expedition as not only political in its nature, but as also in a great measure foreign from the United States in its causes, character, and objects. The attempt was understood to be made in sympathy with an insurgent party in Ireland, and by striking at a British Province on this continent was designed to aid in obtaining redress for political grievances which, it was assumed, the people of Ireland had suffered at the hands of the British Government during a period of several centuries. The persons engaged in it were chiefly natives of that country, some of whom had, while others had not, become citizens of the United States under our general laws of naturalization. Complaints of misgovernment in Ireland continually engage the attention of the British nation, and so great an agitation is now prevailing in Ireland that the British Government have deemed it necessary to suspend the writ of *habeas corpus* in that country. These circumstances must necessarily modify the opinion which we might otherwise have entertained in regard to an expedition expressly prohibited by our neutrality laws. So long as those laws remain upon our statute books they should be faithfully executed, and if they operate harshly, unjustly, or oppressively Congress alone can apply the remedy by their modification or repeal.

Political and commercial interests of the United States are not unlikely to be affected in some degree by events which are transpiring in the eastern regions of Europe, and the time seems to have come when our Government ought to have a proper diplomatic representation in Greece.

This Government has claimed for all persons not convicted or accused or suspected of crime an absolute political right of self-expatriation and a choice of new national allegiance. Most of the European States have dissented from this principle, and have claimed a right to hold such of their subjects as have emigrated to and been naturalized in the United States and afterwards returned on transient visits to their native countries to the performance of military service in like manner as resident subjects. Complaints arising from the claim in this respect made by foreign states have heretofore been matters of controversy between the United States and some of the European powers, and the irritation consequent upon the failure to settle this question increased during the war in which Prussia, Italy, and Austria were recently engaged. While Great Britain has never acknowledged the right of expatriation, she has not for some years past practically insisted upon the opposite doctrine. France has been equally forbearing, and Prussia has proposed a compromise, which, although evincing increased liberality, has not been accepted by the United States. Peace is now prevailing everywhere in Europe, and the present seems to be a favorable time for an assertion by Congress of the principle so long maintained by the executive department that naturalization by one state fully exempts the native-born subject of any other state from the performance of military service under any foreign government, so long as he does not voluntarily renounce its rights and benefits.

In the performance of a duty imposed upon me by the Constitution I have thus submitted to the representatives of the States and of the people such information of our domestic and foreign affairs as the public interests seem to require. Our Government is now undergoing its most trying ordeal, and my earnest prayer is that the peril may be successfully and finally passed without impairing its original strength and symmetry. The interests of the nation are best to be promoted by the revival of fraternal relations, the complete obliteration of our past differences, and the reinauguration of all the pursuits of peace. Directing our efforts to the early accomplishment of these great ends, let us endeavor to preserve harmony between the coordinate departments of the Government, that each in its proper sphere may cordially cooperate with the other in securing the maintenance of the Constitution, the preservation of the Union, and the perpetuity of our free institutions.

THIRD ANNUAL MESSAGE.

WASHINGTON, *December 3, 1867.*

Fellow-Citizens of the Senate and House of Representatives:

The continued disorganization of the Union, to which the President has so often called the attention of Congress, is yet a subject of profound and patriotic concern. We may, however, find some relief from that anxiety in the reflection that the painful political situation, although before untried by ourselves, is not new in the experience of nations. Political science, perhaps as highly perfected in our own time and country as in any other, has not yet disclosed any means by which civil wars can be absolutely prevented. An enlightened nation, however, with a wise and beneficent constitution of free government, may diminish their frequency and mitigate their severity by directing all its proceedings in accordance with its fundamental law.

When a civil war has been brought to a close, it is manifestly the first interest and duty of the state to repair the injuries which the war has inflicted, and to secure the benefit of the lessons it teaches as fully and as speedily as possible. This duty was, upon the termination of the rebellion, promptly accepted, not only by the executive department, but by the insurrectionary States themselves, and restoration in the first moment of peace was believed to be as easy and certain as it was indispensable. The expectations, however, then so reasonably and confidently entertained were disappointed by legislation from which I felt constrained by my obligations to the Constitution to withhold my assent.

It is therefore a source of profound regret that in complying with the obligation imposed upon the President by the Constitution to give to Congress from time to time information of the state of the Union I am unable to communicate any definitive adjustment, satisfactory to the American people, of the questions which since the close of the rebellion have agitated the public mind. On the contrary, candor compels me to declare that at this time there is no Union as our fathers understood the term, and as they meant it to be understood by us. The Union which they established can exist only where all the States are represented in both Houses of Congress; where one State is as free as another to regulate its internal concerns according to its own will, and where the laws of the central Government, strictly confined to matters of national jurisdiction, apply with equal force to all the people of every section. That such is not the present "state of the Union" is a melancholy fact, and we must all acknowledge that the restoration of the States to their proper legal relations with the Federal Government and with one another, according to the terms of the original compact, would be the greatest temporal blessing which God, in His kindest providence, could bestow upon this nation. It becomes our imperative duty to consider whether or not it is impossible to effect this most desirable consummation.

The Union and the Constitution are inseparable. As long as one is obeyed by all parties, the other will be preserved; and if one is destroyed, both must perish together. The destruction of the Constitution will be followed by other and still greater calamities. It was ordained not only to form a more perfect union between the States, but to "establish justice, insure domestic tranquillity, provide for the common defense, promote the general welfare, and secure the blessings of liberty to ourselves and our posterity." Nothing but implicit obedience to its requirements in all parts of the country will accomplish these great ends. Without that obedience we can look forward only to continual outrages upon individual rights, incessant breaches of the public peace, national weakness, financial dishonor, the total loss of our prosperity, the general corruption of morals, and the final extinction of popular freedom. To save our country from evils so appalling as these, we should renew our efforts again and again.

To me the process of restoration seems perfectly plain and simple. It consists merely in a faithful application of the Constitution and laws. The execution of the laws is not now obstructed or opposed by physical force. There is no military or other necessity, real or pretended, which can prevent obedience to the Constitution, either North or South. All the rights and all the obligations of States and individuals can be protected and enforced by means perfectly consistent with the fundamental law. The courts may be everywhere open, and if open their process would be unimpeded. Crimes against the United States can be prevented or punished by the proper judicial authorities in a manner entirely practicable and legal. There is therefore no reason why the Constitution should not be obeyed, unless those who exercise its powers have determined that it shall be disregarded and violated. The mere naked will of this Government, or of some one or more of its branches, is the only obstacle that can exist to a perfect union of all the States.

On this momentous question and some of the measures growing out of it I have had the misfortune to differ from Congress, and have expressed my convictions without reserve, though with becoming deference to the opinion of the legislative department.   Those convictions are not only unchanged, but strengthened by subsequent events and further reflection The transcendent importance of the subject will be a sufficient excuse for calling your attention to some of the reasons which have so strongly influenced my own judgment.   The hope that we may all finally concur in a mode of settlement consistent at once with our true interests and with our sworn duties to the Constitution is too natural and too just to be easily relinquished.

It is clear to my apprehension that the States lately in rebellion are still members of the National Union.   When did they cease to be so?   The "ordinances of secession" adopted by a portion (in most of them a very small portion) of their citizens were mere nullities.   If we admit now that they were valid and effectual for the purpose intended by their authors, we sweep from under our feet the whole ground upon which we justified the war.   Were those States afterwards expelled from the Union by the war?   The direct contrary was averred by this Government to be its purpose, and was so understood by all those who gave their blood and treasure to aid in its prosecution.   It can not be that a successful war, waged for the preservation of the Union, had the legal effect of dissolving it.   The victory of the nation's arms was not the disgrace of her policy; the defeat of secession on the battlefield was not the triumph of its lawless principle. Nor could Congress, with or without the consent of the Executive, do anything which would have the effect, directly or indirectly, of separating the States from each other.   To dissolve the Union is to repeal the Constitution which holds it together, and that is a power which does not belong to any department of this Government, or to all of them united.

This is so plain that it has been acknowledged by all branches of the Federal Government.   The Executive (my predecessor as well as myself) and the heads of all the Departments have uniformly acted upon the principle that the Union is not only undissolved, but indissoluble.   Congress submitted an amendment of the Constitution to be ratified by the Southern States, and accepted their acts of ratification as a necessary and lawful exercise of their highest function.   If they were not States, or were States out of the Union, their consent to a change in the fundamental law of the Union would have been nugatory, and Congress in asking it committed a political absurdity.   The judiciary has also given the solemn sanction of its authority to the same view of the case.   The judges of the Supreme Court have included the Southern States in their circuits, and they are constantly, *in banc* and elsewhere, exercising jurisdiction which does not belong to them unless those States are States of the Union.

If the Southern States are component parts of the Union, the Constitution is the supreme law for them, as it is for all the other States. They are bound to obey it, and so are we.   The right of the Federal Government, which is clear and unquestionable, to enforce the Constitution upon them implies the correlative obligation on our part to observe its limitations and execute its guaranties. Without the Constitution we are nothing; by, through, and under the Constitution we are what it makes us. We may doubt the wisdom of the law, we may not approve of its provisions, but we can not violate it merely because it seems to confine our powers within limits narrower than we could wish. It is not a question of individual or class or sectional interest, much less of party predominance, but of duty—of high and sacred duty—which we are all sworn to perform. If we can not support the Constitution with the cheerful alacrity of those who love and believe in it, we must give to it at least the fidelity of public servants who act under solemn obligations and commands which they dare not disregard.

The constitutional duty is not the only one which requires the States to be restored. There is another consideration which, though of minor importance, is yet of great weight. On the 22d day of July, 1861, Congress declared by an almost unanimous vote of both Houses that the war should be conducted solely for the purpose of preserving the Union and maintaining the supremacy of the Federal Constitution and laws, without impairing the dignity, equality, and rights of the States or of individuals, and that when this was done the war should cease. I do not say that this declaration is personally binding on those who joined in making it, any more than individual members of Congress are personally bound to pay a public debt created under a law for which they voted. But it was a solemn, public, official pledge of the national honor, and I can not imagine upon what grounds the repudiation of it is to be justified. If it be said that we are not bound to keep faith with rebels, let it be remembered that this promise was not made to rebels only. Thousands of true men in the South were drawn to our standard by it, and hundreds of thousands in the North gave their lives in the belief that it would be carried out. It was made on the day after the first great battle of the war had been fought and lost. All patriotic and intelligent men then saw the necessity of giving such an assurance, and believed that without it the war would end in disaster to our cause. Having given that assurance in the extremity of our peril, the violation of it now, in the day of our power, would be a rude rending of that good faith which holds the moral world together; our country would cease to have any claim upon the confidence of men; it would make the war not only a failure, but a fraud.

Being sincerely convinced that these views are correct, I would be unfaithful to my duty if I did not recommend the repeal of the acts of Congress which place ten of the Southern States under the domination of military masters. If calm reflection shall satisfy a majority of your honorable bodies that the acts referred to are not only a violation of the national faith, but in direct conflict with the Constitution, I dare not permit myself to doubt that you will immediately strike them from the statute book.

To demonstrate the unconstitutional character of those acts I need do no more than refer to their general provisions. It must be seen at once that they are not authorized. To dictate what alterations shall be made in the constitutions of the several States; to control the elections of State legislators and State officers, members of Congress and electors of President and Vice-President, by arbitrarily declaring who shall vote and who shall be excluded from that privilege; to dissolve State legislatures or prevent them from assembling; to dismiss judges and other civil functionaries of the State and appoint others without regard to State law; to organize and operate all the political machinery of the States; to regulate the whole administration of their domestic and local affairs according to the mere will of strange and irresponsible agents, sent among them for that purpose—these are powers not granted to the Federal Government or to any one of its branches. Not being granted, we violate our trust by assuming them as palpably as we would by acting in the face of a positive interdict; for the Constitution forbids us to do whatever it does not affirmatively authorize, either by express words or by clear implication. If the authority we desire to use does not come to us through the Constitution, we can exercise it only by usurpation, and usurpation is the most dangerous of political crimes. By that crime the enemies of free government in all ages have worked out their designs against public liberty and private right. It leads directly and immediately to the establishment of absolute rule, for undelegated power is always unlimited and unrestrained.

The acts of Congress in question are not only objectionable for their assumption of ungranted power, but many of their provisions are in conflict with the direct prohibitions of the Constitution. The Constitution commands that a republican form of government shall be guaranteed to all the States; that no person shall be deprived of life, liberty, or property without due process of law, arrested without a judicial warrant, or punished without a fair trial before an impartial jury; that the privilege of *habeas corpus* shall not be denied in time of peace, and that no bill of attainder shall be passed even against a single individual. Yet the system of measures established by these acts of Congress does totally subvert and destroy the form as well as the substance of republican government in the ten States to which they apply. It binds them hand and foot in absolute slavery, and subjects them to a strange and hostile power, more unlimited and more likely to be abused than any other now known among civilized men. It tramples down all those rights in which the essence of liberty consists, and which a free government is always most careful to protect. It denies the *habeas corpus* and the trial by jury. Personal freedom, property, and life, if assailed by the passion, the prejudice, or the rapacity of the ruler, have no security whatever. It has the effect of a bill of attainder or bill of pains and penalties, not upon a few individuals, but upon whole masses, including the millions who inhabit the subject States, and even their unborn children. These wrongs, being expressly forbidden, can not be constitutionally inflicted upon any portion of our people, no matter how they may have come within our jurisdiction, and no matter whether they live in States, Territories, or districts.

I have no desire to save from the proper and just consequences of their great crime those who engaged in rebellion against the Government, but as a mode of punishment the measures under consideration are the most unreasonable that could be invented. Many of those people are perfectly innocent; many kept their fidelity to the Union untainted to the last; many were incapable of any legal offense; a large proportion even of the persons able to bear arms were forced into rebellion against their will, and of those who are guilty with their own consent the degrees of guilt are as various as the shades of their character and temper. But these acts of Congress confound them all together in one common doom. Indiscriminate vengeance upon classes, sects, and parties, or upon whole communities, for offenses committed by a portion of them against the governments to which they owed obedience was common in the barbarous ages of the world; but Christianity and civilization have made such progress that recourse to a punishment so cruel and unjust would meet with the condemnation of all unprejudiced and right-minded men. The punitive justice of this age, and especially of this country, does not consist in stripping whole States of their liberties and reducing all their people, without distinction, to the condition of slavery. It deals separately with each individual, confines itself to the forms of law, and vindicates its own purity by an impartial examination of every case before a competent judicial tribunal. If this does not satisfy all our desires with regard to Southern rebels, let us console ourselves by reflecting that a free Constitution, triumphant in war and unbroken in peace, is worth far more to us and our children than the gratification of any present feeling.

I am aware it is assumed that this system of government for the Southern States is not to be perpetual. It is true this military government is to be only provisional, but it is through this temporary evil that a greater evil is to be made perpetual. If the guaranties of the Constitution can be broken provisionally to serve a temporary purpose, and in a part only of the country, we can destroy them everywhere and for all time. Arbitrary measures often change, but they generally change for the worse. It is the curse of despotism that it has no halting place. The intermitted exercise of its power brings no sense of security to its subjects, for they can never know what more they will be called to endure when its red right hand is armed to plague them again. Nor is it possible to conjecture how or where power, unrestrained by law, may seek its next victims. The States that are still free may be enslaved at any moment; for if the Constitution does not protect all, it protects none.

It is manifestly and avowedly the object of these laws to confer upon negroes the privilege of voting and to disfranchise such a number of white citizens as will give the former a clear majority at all elections in the

Southern States. This, to the minds of some persons, is so important that a violation of the Constitution is justified as a means of bringing it about. The morality is always false which excuses a wrong because it proposes to accomplish a desirable end. We are not permitted to do evil that good may come. But in this case the end itself is evil, as well as the means. The subjugation of the States to negro domination would be worse than the military despotism under which they are now suffering. It was believed beforehand that the people would endure any amount of military oppression for any length of time rather than degrade themselves by subjection to the negro race. Therefore they have been left without a choice. Negro suffrage was established by act of Congress, and the military officers were commanded to superintend the process of clothing the negro race with the political privileges torn from white men.

The blacks in the South are entitled to be well and humanely governed, and to have the protection of just laws for all their rights of person and property. If it were practicable at this time to give them a Government exclusively their own, under which they might manage their own affairs in their own way, it would become a grave question whether we ought to do so, or whether common humanity would not require us to save them from themselves. But under the circumstances this is only a speculative point. It is not proposed merely that they shall govern themselves, but that they shall rule the white race, make and administer State laws, elect Presidents and members of Congress, and shape to a greater or less extent the future destiny of the whole country. Would such a trust and power be safe in such hands?

The peculiar qualities which should characterize any people who are fit to decide upon the management of public affairs for a great state have seldom been combined. It is the glory of white men to know that they have had these qualities in sufficient measure to build upon this continent a great political fabric and to preserve its stability for more than ninety years, while in every other part of the world all similar experiments have failed. But if anything can be proved by known facts, if all reasoning upon evidence is not abandoned, it must be acknowledged that in the progress of nations negroes have shown less capacity for government than any other race of people. No independent government of any form has ever been successful in their hands. On the contrary, wherever they have been left to their own devices they have shown a constant tendency to relapse into barbarism. In the Southern States, however, Congress has undertaken to confer upon them the privilege of the ballot. Just released from slavery, it may be doubted whether as a class they know more than their ancestors how to organize and regulate civil society. Indeed, it is admitted that the blacks of the South are not only regardless of the rights of property, but so utterly ignorant of public affairs that their voting can consist in nothing more than carrying a ballot to the place where they are directed to deposit it. I need not remind you that the exercise of the elective franchise is the highest attribute of an American citizen, and that when guided by virtue, intelligence, patriotism, and a proper appreciation of our free institutions it constitutes the true basis of a democratic form of government, in which the sovereign power is lodged in the body of the people. A trust artificially created, not for its own sake, but solely as a means of promoting the general welfare, its influence for good must necessarily depend upon the elevated character and true allegiance of the elector. It ought, therefore, to be reposed in none except those who are fitted morally and mentally to administer it well; for if conferred upon persons who do not justly estimate its value and who are indifferent as to its results, it will only serve as a means of placing power in the hands of the unprincipled and ambitious, and must eventuate in the complete destruction of that liberty of which it should be the most powerful conservator. I have therefore heretofore urged upon your attention the great danger—

to be apprehended from an untimely extension of the elective franchise to any new class in our country, especially when the large majority of that class, in wielding the power thus placed in their hands, can not be expected correctly to comprehend the duties and responsibilities which pertain to suffrage. Yesterday, as it were, 4,000,000 persons were held in a condition of slavery that had existed for generations; to-day they are freemen and are assumed by law to be citizens. It can not be presumed, from their previous condition of servitude, that as a class they are as well informed as to the nature of our Government as the intelligent foreigner who makes our land the home of his choice. In the case of the latter neither a residence of five years and the knowledge of our institutions which it gives nor attachment to the principles of the Constitution are the only conditions upon which he can be admitted to citizenship; he must prove in addition a good moral character, and thus give reasonable ground for the belief that he will be faithful to the obligations which he assumes as a citizen of the Republic. Where a people—the source of all political power—speak by their suffrages through the instrumentality of the ballot box, it must be carefully guarded against the control of those who are corrupt in principle and enemies of free institutions, for it can only become to our political and social system a safe conductor of healthy popular sentiment when kept free from demoralizing influences. Controlled through fraud and usurpation by the designing, anarchy and despotism must inevitably follow. In the hands of the patriotic and worthy our Government will be preserved upon the principles of the Constitution inherited from our fathers. It follows, therefore, that in admitting to the ballot box a new class of voters not qualified for the exercise of the elective franchise we weaken our system of government instead of adding to its strength and durability.

* * * * * * *

I yield to no one in attachment to that rule of general suffrage which distinguishes our policy as a nation. But there is a limit, wisely observed hitherto, which makes the ballot a privilege and a trust, and which requires of some classes a time suitable for probation and preparation. To give it indiscriminately to a new class, wholly unprepared by previous habits and opportunities to perform the trust which it demands, is to degrade it, and finally to destroy its power, for it may be safely assumed that no political truth is better established than that such indiscriminate and all-embracing extension of popular suffrage must end at last in its destruction.

I repeat the expression of my willingness to join in any plan within the scope of our constitutional authority which promises to better the condition of the negroes in the South, by encouraging them in industry, enlightening their minds, improving their morals, and giving protection to all their just rights as freedmen. But the transfer of our political inheritance to them would, in my opinion, be an abandonment of a duty which we owe alike to the memory of our fathers and the rights of our children.

The plan of putting the Southern States wholly and the General Government partially into the hands of negroes is proposed at a time peculiarly unpropitious. The foundations of society have been broken up by civil war. Industry must be reorganized, justice reestablished, public credit maintained, and order brought out of confusion. To accomplish these ends would require all the wisdom and virtue of the great men who formed our institutions originally. I confidently believe that their descendants will be equal to the arduous task before them, but it is worse than madness to expect that negroes will perform it for us. Certainly we ought not to ask their assistance till we despair of our own competency.

The great difference between the two races in physical, mental, and moral characteristics will prevent an amalgamation or fusion of them together in one homogeneous mass. If the inferior obtains the ascendency over the other, it will govern with reference only to its own interests—for it will recognize no common interest—and create such a tyranny as this continent has never yet witnessed. Already the negroes are influenced by promises of confiscation and plunder. They are taught to regard as an enemy every white man who has any respect for the rights of his own race. If this continues it must become worse and worse, until all order will be subverted, all industry cease, and the fertile fields of the South grow up into a wilderness. Of all the dangers which our nation has yet encountered, none are equal to those which must result from the success of the effort now making to Africanize the half of our country.

I would not put considerations of money in competition with justice and right; but the expenses incident to "reconstruction" under the system adopted by Congress aggravate what I regard as the intrinsic wrong of the measure itself. It has cost uncounted millions already, and if persisted in will add largely to the weight of taxation, already too oppressive to be borne without just complaint, and may finally reduce the Treasury of the nation to a condition of bankruptcy. We must not delude ourselves. It will require a strong standing army and probably more than $200,000,000 per annum to maintain the supremacy of negro governments after they are established. The sum thus thrown away would, if properly used, form a sinking fund large enough to pay the whole national debt in less than fifteen years. It is vain to hope that negroes will maintain their ascendency themselves. Without military power they are wholly incapable of holding in subjection the white people of the South.

I submit to the judgment of Congress whether the public credit may not be injuriously affected by a system of measures like this. With our debt and the vast private interests which are complicated with it, we can not be too cautious of a policy which might by possibility impair the confidence of the world in our Government. That confidence can only be retained by carefully inculcating the principles of justice and honor on the popular mind and by the most scrupulous fidelity to all our engagements of every sort. Any serious breach of the organic law, persisted in for a considerable time, can not but create fears for the stability of our institutions. Habitual violation of prescribed rules, which we bind ourselves to observe, must demoralize the people. Our only standard of civil duty being set at naught, the sheet anchor of our political morality is lost, the public conscience swings from its moorings and yields to every impulse of passion and interest. If we repudiate the Constitution, we will not be expected to care much for mere pecuniary obligations. The violation of such a pledge as we made on the 22d day of July, 1861, will assuredly diminish the market value of our other promises. Besides, if we acknowledge that the national debt was created, not to hold the States in the Union, as the taxpayers were led to suppose, but to expel them from it and hand them over to be governed by negroes, the moral duty to pay it may seem much less clear. I say it may *seem* so, for I do not admit that this or any other argument in favor of repudiation can be entertained as sound; but its influence on some classes of minds may well be apprehended. The financial honor of a great commercial nation, largely indebted and with a republican form of government administered by agents of the popular choice, is a thing of such delicate texture and the destruction of it would be followed by such unspeakable calamity that every true patriot must desire to avoid whatever might expose it to the slightest danger.

The great interests of the country require immediate relief from these enactments. Business in the South is paralyzed by a sense of general insecurity, by the terror of confiscation, and the dread of negro supremacy. The Southern trade, from which the North would have derived so great a profit under a government of law, still languishes, and can never be revived until it ceases to be fettered by the arbitrary power which makes all its operations unsafe. That rich country—the richest in natural resources the world ever saw—is worse than lost if it be not soon placed under the protection of a free constitution. Instead of being, as it ought to be, a source of wealth and power, it will become an intolerable burden upon the rest of the nation.

Another reason for retracing our steps will doubtless be seen by Congress in the late manifestations of public opinion upon this subject. We live in a country where the popular will always enforces obedience to itself, sooner or later. It is vain to think of opposing it with anything short of legal authority backed by overwhelming force. It can not have escaped your attention that from the day on which Congress fairly and formally presented the proposition to govern the Southern States by military force, with a view to the ultimate establishment of negro supremacy, every expression of the general sentiment has been more or less adverse to it. The affections of this generation can not be detached from the institutions of their ancestors. Their determination to preserve the inheritance of free government in their own hands and transmit it undivided and unimpaired to their own posterity is too strong to be successfully opposed. Every weaker passion will disappear before that love of liberty and law for which the American people are distinguished above all others in the world.

How far the duty of the President "to preserve, protect, and defend the Constitution" requires him to go in opposing an unconstitutional act of Congress is a very serious and important question, on which I have deliberated much and felt extremely anxious to reach a proper conclusion. Where an act has been passed according to the forms of the Constitution by the supreme legislative authority, and is regularly enrolled among the public statutes of the country, Executive resistance to it, especially in times of high party excitement, would be likely to produce violent collision between the respective adherents of the two branches of the Government. This would be simply civil war, and civil war must be resorted to only as the last remedy for the worst of evils. Whatever might tend to provoke it should be most carefully avoided. A faithful and conscientious magistrate will concede very much to honest error, and something even to perverse malice, before he will endanger the public peace; and he will not adopt forcible measures, or such as might lead to force, as long as those which are peaceable remain open to him or to his constituents. It is true that cases may occur in which the Executive would be compelled to stand on its rights, and maintain them regardless of all consequences. If Congress should pass an act which is not only in palpable conflict with the Constitution, but will certainly, if carried out, produce immediate and irreparable injury to the organic structure of the Government, and if there be neither judicial remedy for the wrongs it inflicts nor power in the people to protect themselves without the official aid of their elected defender—if, for instance, the legislative department should pass an act even through all the forms of law to abolish a coordinate department of the Government—in such a case the President must take the high responsibilities of his office and save the life of the nation at all hazards. The so-called reconstruction acts, though as plainly unconstitutional as any that can be imagined, were not believed to be within the class last mentioned. The people were not wholly disarmed of the power of self-defense. In all the Northern States they still held in their hands the sacred right of the ballot, and it was safe to believe that in due time they would come to the rescue of their own institutions. It gives me pleasure to add that the appeal to our common constituents was not taken in vain, and that my confidence in their wisdom and virtue seems not to have been misplaced.

It is well and publicly known that enormous frauds have been perpetrated on the Treasury and that colossal fortunes have been made at the public expense. This species of corruption has increased, is increasing, and if not diminished will soon bring us into total ruin and disgrace. The public creditors and the taxpayers are alike interested in an honest administration of the finances, and neither class will long endure the large-handed robberies of the recent past. For this discreditable state of things there are several causes. Some of the taxes are so laid as to present an irresistible temptation to evade payment. The great sums which officers may win by connivance at fraud create a pressure which is more than the virtue of many can withstand, and there can be no doubt that the open disregard of constitutional obligations avowed by some of the highest and most influential men in the country has greatly weakened the moral sense of those who serve in subordinate places. The expenses of the United States, including interest on the public debt, are more than six times as much as they were seven years ago. To collect and disburse this vast amount requires careful supervision as well as systematic vigilance. The system, never perfected, was much disorganized by the "tenure-of-office bill," which has almost destroyed official accountability. The President may be thoroughly convinced that an officer is incapable, dishonest, or unfaithful to the Constitution, but under the law which I have named the utmost he can do is to complain to the Senate and ask the privilege of supplying his place with a better man. If the Senate be regarded as personally or politically hostile to the President, it is natural, and not altogether unreasonable, for the officer to expect that it will take his part as far as possible, restore him to his place, and give him a triumph over his Executive superior. The officer has other chances of impunity arising from accidental defects of evidence, the mode of investigating it, and the secrecy of the hearing. It is not wonderful that official malfeasance should become bold in proportion as the delinquents learn to think themselves safe. I am entirely persuaded that under such a rule the President can not perform the great duty assigned to him of seeing the laws faithfully executed, and that it disables him most especially from enforcing that rigid accountability which is necessary to the due execution of the revenue laws.

The Constitution invests the President with authority to *decide* whether a removal should be made in any given case; the act of Congress declares in substance that he shall only *accuse* such as he supposes to be unworthy of their trust. The Constitution makes him sole *judge* in the premises, but the statute takes away his jurisdiction, transfers it to the Senate, and leaves him nothing but the odious and sometimes impracticable duty of becoming a *prosecutor*. The prosecution is to be conducted before a tribunal whose members are not, like him, responsible to the whole people, but to separate constituent bodies, and who may hear his accusation with great disfavor. The Senate is absolutely without any known standard of decision applicable to such a case. Its judgment can not be anticipated, for it is not governed by any rule. The law does not define what shall be deemed good cause for removal. It is impossible even to conjecture what may or may not be so considered by the Senate. The nature of the subject forbids clear proof. If the charge be incapacity, what evidence will support it? Fidelity to the Constitution may be understood or misunderstood in a thousand different ways, and by violent party men, in violent party times, unfaithfulness to the Constitution may even come to be considered meritorious. If the officer be accused of dishonesty, 'how shall it be made out? Will it be inferred from acts unconnected with public duty, from private history, or from general reputation, or must the President await the commission of an actual misdemeanor in office? Shall he in the meantime risk the character and interest of the nation in the hands of men to whom he can not give his confidence? Must he forbear his complaint until the mischief is done and can not be prevented? If his zeal in the public service should impel him to anticipate the overt act, must he move at the peril of being tried himself for the offense of slandering his subordinate? In the present circumstances of the country someone must be held responsible for official delinquency of every kind. It is extremely difficult to say where that responsibility should be thrown if it be not left where it has been placed by the Constitution. But all just men will admit that the President ought to be entirely relieved from such responsibility if he can not meet it by reason of restrictions placed by law upon his action.

The unrestricted power of removal from office is a very great one to be trusted even to a magistrate chosen by the general suffrage of the whole people and accountable directly to them for his acts. It is undoubtedly liable to abuse, and at some periods of our history perhaps has been abused. If it be thought desirable and constitutional that it should be so limited as to make the President merely a common informer against other public agents, he should at least be permitted to act in that capacity before some open tribunal, independent of party politics, ready to investigate the merits of every case, furnished with the means of taking evidence, and bound to decide according to established rules. This would guarantee the safety of the accuser when he acts in good faith, and at the same time secure the rights of the other party. I speak, of course, with all proper respect for the present Senate, but it does not seem to me that any legislative body can be so constituted as to insure its fitness for these functions.

It is not the theory of this Government that public offices are the property of those who hold them. They are given merely as a trust for the public benefit, sometimes for a fixed period, sometimes during good behavior, but generally they are liable to be terminated at the pleasure of the appointing power, which represents the collective majesty and speaks the will of the people. The forced retention in office of a single dishonest person may work great injury to the public interests. The danger to the public service comes not from the power to remove, but from the power to appoint. Therefore it was that the framers of the Constitution left the power of removal unrestricted, while they gave the Senate a right to reject all appointments which in its opinion were not fit to be made. A little reflection on this subject will probably satisfy all who have the good of the country at heart that our best course is to take the Constitution for our guide, walk in the path marked out by the founders of the Republic, and obey the rules made sacred by the observance of our great predecessors.

The present condition of our finances and circulating medium is one to which your early consideration is invited.

The proportion which the currency of any country should bear to the whole value of the annual produce circulated by its means is a question upon which political economists have not agreed. Nor can it be controlled by legislation, but must be left to the irrevocable laws which everywhere regulate commerce and trade. The circulating medium will ever irresistibly flow to those points where it is in greatest demand. The law of demand and supply is as unerring as that which regulates the tides of the ocean; and, indeed, currency, like the tides, has its ebbs and flows throughout the commercial world.

At the beginning of the rebellion the bank-note circulation of the country amounted to not much more than $200,000,000; now the circulation of national-bank notes and those known as "legal-tenders" is nearly seven hundred millions. While it is urged by some that this amount should be increased, others contend that a decided reduction is absolutely essential to the best interests of the country. In view of these diverse opinions, it may be well to ascertain the real value of our paper issues when compared with a metallic or convertible currency. For this purpose let us inquire how much gold and silver could be purchased by the seven hundred millions of paper money now in circulation. Probably not more than half the amount of the latter, showing that when our paper currency is compared with gold and silver its commercial value is compressed into three hundred and fifty millions. This striking fact makes it the obvious duty of the Government, as early as may be consistent with the principles of sound political economy, to take such measures as will enable the holder of its notes and those of the national banks to convert them without loss into specie or its equivalent. A reduction of our paper circulating medium need not necessarily follow. This, however, would depend upon the law of demand and supply, though it should be borne in mind that by making legal-tender and bank notes convertible into coin or its equivalent their present specie value in the hands of their holders would be enhanced 100 per cent.

Legislation for the accomplishment of a result so desirable is demanded by the highest public considerations. The Constitution contemplates that the circulating medium of the country shall be uniform in quality and value. At the time of the formation of that instrument the country had just emerged from the War of the Revolution, and was suffering from the effects of a redundant and worthless paper currency. The sages of that period were anxious to protect their posterity from the evils that they themselves had experienced. Hence in providing a circulating medium they conferred upon Congress the power to coin money and regulate the value thereof, at the same time prohibiting the States from making anything but gold and silver a tender in payment of debts.

The anomalous condition of our currency is in striking contrast with that which was originally designed. Our circulation now embraces, first, notes of the national banks, which are made receivable for all dues to the Government, excluding imposts, and by all its creditors, excepting in payment of interest upon its bonds and the securities themselves; second, legal-tender notes, issued by the United States, and which the law requires shall be received as well in payment of all debts between citizens as of all Government dues, excepting imposts; and, third, gold and silver coin. By the operation of our present system of finance, however, the metallic currency, when collected, is reserved only for one class of Government creditors, who, holding its bonds, semiannually receive their interest in coin from the National Treasury. They are thus made to occupy an invidious position, which may be used to strengthen the arguments of those who would bring into disrepute the obligations of the nation. In the payment of all its debts the plighted faith of the Government should be inviolably maintained. But while it acts with fidelity toward the bondholder who loaned his money that the integrity of the Union might be preserved, it should at the same time observe good faith with the great masses of the people, who, having rescued the Union from the perils of rebellion, now bear the burdens of taxation, that the Government may be able to fulfill its engagements. There is no reason which will be accepted as satisfactory by the people why those who defend us on the land and protect us on the sea; the pensioner upon the gratitude of the nation, bearing the scars and wounds received while in its service; the public servants in the various Departments of the Government; the farmer who supplies the soldiers of the Army and the sailors of the Navy; the artisan who toils in the nation's workshops, or the mechanics and laborers who build its edifices and construct its forts and vessels of war, should, in payment of their just and hard-earned dues, receive depreciated paper, while another class of their countrymen, no more deserving, are paid in coin of gold and silver. Equal and exact justice requires that all the creditors of the Government should be paid in a currency possessing a uniform value. This can only be accomplished by the restoration of the currency to the standard established by the Constitution; and by this means we would remove a discrimination which may, if it has not already done so, create a prejudice that may become deep rooted and widespread and imperil the national credit.

The feasibility of making our currency correspond with the constitutional standard may be seen by reference to a few facts derived from our commercial statistics.

The production of precious metals in the United States from 1849 to 1857, inclusive, amounted to $579,000,000; from 1858 to 1860, inclusive, to $137,500,000, and from 1861 to 1867, inclusive, to $457,500,000—making the grand aggregate of products since 1849 $1,174,000,000. The amount of specie coined from 1849 to 1857 inclusive, was $439,000,000; from 1858 to 1860, inclusive, $125,000,000, and from 1861 to 1867, inclusive, $310,000,000—making the total coinage since 1849 $874,000,000. From 1849 to 1857, inclusive, the net exports of specie amounted to $271,000,000; from 1858 to 1860, inclusive, to $148,000,000, and from 1861 to 1867, inclusive, $322,000,000—making the aggregate of net exports since 1849 $741,000,000. These figures show an excess of product over net exports of $433,000,000. There are in the Treasury $111,000,000 in coin, something more than $40,000,000 in circulation on the Pacific Coast, and a few millions in the national and other banks—in all about $160,000,000. This, however, taking into account the specie in the country prior to 1849, leaves more than $300,000,000 which have not been accounted for by exportation, and therefore may yet remain in the country.

These are important facts and show how completely the inferior currency will supersede the better, forcing it from circulation among the masses and causing it to be exported as a mere article of trade, to add to the money capital of foreign lands. They show the necessity of retiring our paper money, that the return of gold and silver to the avenues of trade may be invited and a demand created which will cause the retention at home of at least so much of the productions of our rich and inexhaustible gold-bearing fields as may be sufficient for purposes of circulation. It is unreasonable to expect a return to a sound currency so long as the Government by continuing to issue irredeemable notes fills the channels of circulation with depreciated paper. Notwithstanding a coinage by our mints, since 1849, of $874,000,000, the people are now strangers to the currency which was designed for their use and benefit, and specimens of the precious metals bearing the national device are seldom seen, except when produced to gratify the interest excited by their novelty. If depreciated paper is to be continued as the permanent currency of the country, and all our coin is to become a mere article of traffic and speculation, to the enhancement in price of all that is indispensable to the comfort of the people, it would be wise economy to abolish our mints, thus saving the nation the care and expense incident to such establishments, and let all our precious metals be exported in bullion. The time has come, however, when the Government and national banks should be required to take the most efficient steps and make all necessary arrangements for a resumption of specie payments at the earliest practicable period. Specie payments having been once resumed by the Government and banks, all notes or bills of paper issued by either of a less denomination than $20 should by law be excluded from circulation, so that the people may have the benefit and convenience of a gold and silver currency which in all their business transactions will be uniform in value at home and abroad.

Every man of property or industry, every man who desires to preserve what he honestly possesses or to obtain what he can honestly earn, has a direct interest in maintaining a safe circulating medium—such a medium as shall be real and substantial, not liable to vibrate with opinions, not subject to be blown up or blown down by the breath of speculation, but to be made stable and secure. A disordered currency is one of the greatest political evils. It undermines the virtues necessary for the support of the social system and encourages propensities destructive of its happiness; it wars against industry, frugality, and economy, and it fosters the evil spirits of extravagance and speculation.

It has been asserted by one of our profound and most gifted statesmen that—

Of all the contrivances for cheating the laboring classes of mankind, none has been more effectual than that which deludes them with paper money. This is the most effectual of inventions to fertilize the rich man's fields by the sweat of the poor man's brow. Ordinary tyranny, oppression, excessive taxation—these bear lightly on the happiness of the mass of the community compared with a fraudulent currency and the robberies committed by depreciated paper. Our own history has recorded for our instruction enough, and more than enough, of the demoralizing tendency, the injustice, and the intolerable oppression on the virtuous and well disposed of a degraded paper currency authorized by law or in any way countenanced by government.

It is one of the most successful devices, in times of peace or war, expansions or revulsions, to accomplish the transfer of all the precious metals from the great mass of the people into the hands of the few, where they are hoarded in secret places or deposited in strong boxes under bolts and bars, while the people are left to endure all the inconvenience, sacrifice, and demoralization resulting from the use of a depreciated and worthless paper money.

The condition of our finances and the operations of our revenue system are set forth and fully explained in the able and instructive report of the Secretary of the Treasury. On the 30th of June, 1866, the public debt amounted to $2,783,425,879; on the 30th of June last it was $2,692,199,215, showing a reduction during the fiscal year of $91,226,664. During the fiscal year ending June 30, 1867, the receipts were $490,634,010 and the expenditures $346,729,129, leaving an available surplus of $143,904,880. It is estimated that the receipts for the fiscal year ending June 30, 1868, will be $417,161,928 and that the expenditures will reach the sum of $393,269,226, leaving in the Treasury a surplus of $23,892,702. For the fiscal year ending June 30, 1869, it is estimated that the receipts will amount to $381,000,000 and that the expenditures will be $372,000,000, showing an excess of $9,000,000 in favor of the Government.

The attention of Congress is earnestly invited to the necessity of a thorough revision of our revenue system. Our internal-revenue laws and impost system should be so adjusted as to bear most heavily on articles of luxury, leaving the necessaries of life as free from taxation as may be consistent with the real wants of the Government, economically administered. Taxation would not then fall unduly on the man of moderate means; and while none would be entirely exempt from assessment, all, in proportion to their pecuniary abilities, would contribute toward the support of the State. A modification of the internal-revenue system, by a large reduction in the number of articles now subject to tax, would be followed by results equally advantageous to the citizen and the Government. It would render the execution of the law less expensive and more certain, remove obstructions to industry, lessen the temptations to evade the law, diminish the violations and frauds perpetrated upon its provisions, make its operations less inquisitorial, and greatly reduce in numbers the army of taxgatherers created by the system, who "take from the mouth of honest labor the bread it has earned." Retrenchment, reform, and economy should be carried into every branch of the public service, that the expenditures of the Government may be reduced and the people relieved from oppressive taxation; a sound currency should be restored, and the public faith in regard to the national debt sacredly observed. The accomplishment of these important results, together with the restoration of the Union of the States upon the principles of the Constitution, would inspire confidence at home and abroad in the stability of our institutions and bring to the nation prosperity, peace, and good will.

The report of the Secretary of War *ad interim* exhibits the operations of the Army and of the several bureaus of the War Department. The aggregate strength of our military force on the 30th of September last was 56,315. The total estimate for military appropriations is $77,124,707, including a deficiency in last year's appropriation of $13,600,000. The payments at the Treasury on account of the service of the War Department from January 1 to October 29, 1867—a period of ten months— amounted to $109,807,000. The expenses of the military establishment, as well as the numbers of the Army, are now three times as great as they have ever been in time of peace, while the discretionary power is vested in the Executive to add millions to this expenditure by an increase of the Army to the maximum strength allowed by the law.

The comprehensive report of the Secretary of the Interior furnishes interesting information in reference to the important branches of the public service connected with his Department. The menacing attitude of some of the warlike bands of Indians inhabiting the district of country between the Arkansas and Platte rivers and portions of Dakota Territory required the presence of a large military force in that region. Instigated by real or imaginary grievances, the Indians occasionally committed acts of barbarous violence upon emigrants and our frontier settlements;

but a general Indian war has been providentially averted. The commissioners under the act of 20th July, 1867, were invested with full power to adjust existing difficulties, negotiate treaties with the disaffected bands, and select for them reservations remote from the traveled routes between the Mississippi and the Pacific. They entered without delay upon the execution of their trust, but have not yet made any official report of their proceedings. It is of vital importance that our distant Territories should be exempt from Indian outbreaks, and that the construction of the Pacific Railroad, an object of national importance, should not be interrupted by hostile tribes. These objects, as well as the material interests and the moral and intellectual improvement of the Indians, can be most effectually secured by concentrating them upon portions of country set apart for their exclusive use and located at points remote from our highways and encroaching white settlements.

Since the commencement of the second session of the Thirty-ninth Congress 510 miles of road have been constructed on the main line and branches of the Pacific Railway. The line from Omaha is rapidly approaching the eastern base of the Rocky Mountains, while the terminus of the last section of constructed road in California, accepted by the Government on the 24th day of October last, was but 11 miles distant from the summit of the Sierra Nevada. The remarkable energy evinced by the companies offers the strongest assurance that the completion of the road from Sacramento to Omaha will not be long deferred.

During the last fiscal year 7,041,114 acres of public land were disposed of, and the cash receipts from sales and fees exceeded by one-half million dollars the sum realized from those sources during the preceding year. The amount paid to pensioners, including expenses of disbursements, was $18,619,956, and 36,482 names were added to the rolls. The entire number of pensioners on the 30th of June last was 155,474. Eleven thousand six hundred and fifty-five patents and designs were issued during the year ending September 30, 1867, and at that date the balance in the Treasury to the credit of the patent fund was $286,607.

The report of the Secretary of the Navy states that we have seven squadrons actively and judiciously employed, under efficient and able commanders, in protecting the persons and property of American citizens, maintaining the dignity and power of the Government, and promoting the commerce and business interests of our countrymen in every part of the world. Of the 238 vessels composing the present Navy of the United States, 56, carrying 507 guns, are in squadron service. During the year the number of vessels in commission has been reduced 12, and there are 13 less on squadron duty than there were at the date of the last report. A large number of vessels were commenced and in the course of construction when the war terminated, and although Congress had made the necessary appropriations for their completion, the Department has either suspended work upon them or limited the slow completion of the steam vessels, so as to meet the contracts for machinery made with private establishments. The total expenditures of the Navy Department for the fiscal year ending June 30, 1867, were $31,034,011. No appropriations have been made or required since the close of the war for the construction and repair of vessels, for steam machinery, ordnance, provisions and clothing, fuel, hemp, etc., the balances under these several heads having been more than sufficient for current expenditures. It should also be stated to the credit of the Department that, besides asking no appropriations for the above objects for the last two years, the Secretary of the Navy, on the 30th of September last, in accordance with the act of May 1, 1820, requested the Secretary of the Treasury to carry to the surplus fund the sum of $65,000,000, being the amount received from the sales of vessels and other war property and the remnants of former appropriations.

The report of the Postmaster-General shows the business of the Post-Office Department and the condition of the postal service in a very favorable light, and the attention of Congress is called to its practical recommendations. The receipts of the Department for the year ending June 30, 1867, including all special appropriations for sea and land service and for free mail matter, were $19,978,693. The expenditures for all purposes were $19,235,483, leaving an unexpended balance in favor of the Department of $743,210, which can be applied toward the expenses of the Department for the current year. The increase of postal revenue, independent of specific appropriations, for the year 1867 over that of 1866 was $850,040. The increase of revenue from the sale of stamps and stamped envelopes was $783,404. The increase of expenditures for 1867 over those of the previous year was owing chiefly to the extension of the land and ocean mail service. During the past year new postal conventions have been ratified and exchanged with the United Kingdom of Great Britain and Ireland, Belgium, the Netherlands, Switzerland, the North German Union, Italy, and the colonial government at Hong Kong, reducing very largely the rates of ocean and land postages to and from and within those countries.

The report of the Acting Commissioner of Agriculture concisely presents the condition, wants, and progress of an interest eminently worthy the fostering care of Congress, and exhibits a large measure of useful results achieved during the year to which it refers.

The reestablishment of peace at home and the resumption of extended trade, travel, and commerce abroad have served to increase the number and variety of questions in the Department for Foreign Affairs. None of these questions, however, have seriously disturbed our relations with other states.

The Republic of Mexico, having been relieved from foreign intervention, is earnestly engaged in efforts to reestablish her constitutional system of government. A good understanding continues to exist between our Government and the Republics of Hayti and San Domingo, and our cordial relations with the Central and South American States remain unchanged. The tender, made in conformity with a resolution of Congress, of the good offices of the Government with a view to an amicable adjustment of peace between Brazil and her allies on one side and Paraguay on the other, and between Chile and her allies on the one side and Spain on the other, though kindly received, has in neither case been fully accepted by the belligerents. The war in the valley of the Parana is still vigorously maintained. On the other hand, actual hostilities between the Pacific States and Spain have been more than a year suspended. I shall, on any proper occasion that may occur, renew the conciliatory recommendations which have been already made. Brazil, with enlightened sagacity and comprehensive statesmanship, has opened the great channels of the Amazon and its tributaries to universal commerce. One thing more seems needful to assure a rapid and cheering progress in South America. I refer to those peaceful habits without which states and nations can not in this age well expect material prosperity or social advancement.

The Exposition of Universal Industry at Paris has passed, and seems to have fully realized the high expectations of the French Government. If due allowance be made for the recent political derangement of industry here, the part which the United States has borne in this exhibition of invention and art may be regarded with very high satisfaction. During the exposition a conference was held of delegates from several nations, the United States being one, in which the inconveniences of commerce and social intercourse resulting from the diverse standards of money value were very fully discussed, and plans were developed for establishing by universal consent a common principle for the coinage of gold. These conferences are expected to be renewed, with the attendance of many foreign states not hitherto represented. A report of these interesting proceedings will be submitted to Congress, which will, no doubt, justly appreciate the great object and be ready to adopt any measure which may tend to facilitate its ultimate accomplishment.

On the 25th of February, 1862, Congress declared by law that Treasury notes, without interest, authorized by that act should be legal tender in payment of all debts, public and private, within the United States. An annual remittance of $30,000, less stipulated expenses, accrues to claimants under the convention made with Spain in 1834. These remittances, since the passage of that act, have been paid in such notes. The claimants insist that the Government ought to require payment in coin. The subject may be deemed worthy of your attention.

No arrangement has yet been reached for the settlement of our claims for British depredations upon the commerce of the United States. I have felt it my duty to decline the proposition of arbitration made by Her Majesty's Government, because it has hitherto been accompanied by reservations and limitations incompatible with the rights, interest, and honor of our country. It is not to be apprehended that Great Britain will persist in her refusal to satisfy these just and reasonable claims, which involve the sacred principle of nonintervention—a principle henceforth not more important to the United States than to all other commercial nations.

The West India islands were settled and colonized by European States simultaneously with the settlement and colonization of the American continent. Most of the colonies planted here became independent nations in the close of the last and the beginning of the present century. Our own country embraces communities which at one period were colonies of Great Britain, France, Spain, Holland, Sweden, and Russia. The people in the West Indies, with the exception of those of the island of Hayti, have neither attained nor aspired to independence, nor have they become prepared for self-defense. Although possessing considerable commercial value, they have been held by the several European States which colonized or at some time conquered them, chiefly for purposes of military and naval strategy in carrying out European policy and designs in regard to this continent. In our Revolutionary War ports and harbors in the West India islands were used by our enemy, to the great injury and embarrassment of the United States. We had the same experience in our second war with Great Britain. The same European policy for a long time excluded us even from trade with the West Indies, while we were at peace with all nations. In our recent civil war the rebels and their piratical and blockade-breaking allies found facilities in the same ports for the work, which they too successfully accomplished, of injuring and devastating the commerce which we are now engaged in rebuilding. We labored especially under this disadvantage, that European steam vessels employed by our enemies found friendly shelter, protection, and supplies in West Indian ports, while our naval operations were necessarily carried on from our own distant shores. There was then a universal feeling of the want of an advanced naval outpost between the Atlantic coast and Europe. The duty of obtaining such an outpost peacefully and lawfully, while neither doing nor menacing injury to other states, earnestly engaged the attention of the executive department before the close of the war, and it has not been lost sight of since that time. A not entirely dissimilar naval want revealed itself during the same period on the Pacific coast. The required foothold there was fortunately secured by our late treaty with the Emperor of Russia, and it now seems imperative that the more obvious necessities of the Atlantic coast should not be less carefully provided for. A good and convenient port and harbor, capable of easy defense, will supply that want. With the possession of such a station by the United States, neither we nor any other American nation need longer apprehend injury or offense from any transatlantic enemy. I agree with our early statesmen that the West Indies naturally gravitate to, and may be expected ultimately to be absorbed by, the continental States, including our own. I agree with them also that it is wise to leave the question of such absorption to this process of natural political gravitation. The islands of St. Thomas and St. John, which constitute a part of the group called the Virgin Islands, seemed to offer us advantages immediately desirable, while their acquisition could be secured in harmony with the principles to which I have alluded. A treaty has therefore been concluded with the King of Denmark for the cession of those islands, and will be submitted to the Senate for consideration.

It will hardly be necessary to call the attention of Congress to the subject of providing for the payment to Russia of the sum stipulated in the treaty for the cession of Alaska. Possession having been formally delivered to our commissioner, the territory remains for the present in care of a military force, awaiting such civil organization as shall be directed by Congress.

The annexation of many small German States to Prussia and the reorganization of that country under a new and liberal constitution have induced me to renew the effort to obtain a just and prompt settlement of the long-vexed question concerning the claims of foreign states for military service from their subjects naturalized in the United States.

In connection with this subject the attention of Congress is respectfully called to a singular and embarrassing conflict of laws. The executive department of this Government has hitherto uniformly held, as it now holds, that naturalization in conformity with the Constitution and laws of the United States absolves the recipient from his native allegiance. The courts of Great Britain hold that allegiance to the British Crown is indefeasible, and is not absolved by our laws of naturalization. British judges cite courts and law authorities of the United States in support of that theory against the position held by the executive authority of the United States. This conflict perplexes the public mind concerning the rights of naturalized citizens and impairs the national authority abroad. I called attention to this subject in my last annual message, and now again respectfully appeal to Congress to declare the national will unmistakably upon this important question.

The abuse of our laws by the clandestine prosecution of the African slave trade from American ports or by American citizens has altogether ceased, and under existing circumstances no apprehensions of its renewal in this part of the world are entertained. Under these circumstances it becomes a question whether we shall not propose to Her Majesty's Government a suspension or discontinuance of the stipulations for maintaining a naval force for the suppression of that trade.

FOURTH ANNUAL MESSAGE.

WASHINGTON, *December 9, 1868.*

Fellow-Citizens of the Senate and House of Representatives:

Upon the reassembling of Congress it again becomes my duty to call your attention to the state of the Union and to its continued disorganized condition under the various laws which have been passed upon the subject of reconstruction.

It may be safely assumed as an axiom in the government of states that the greatest wrongs inflicted upon a people are caused by unjust and arbitrary legislation, or by the unrelenting decrees of despotic rulers, and that the timely revocation of injurious and oppressive measures is the greatest good that can be conferred upon a nation. The legislator or ruler who has the wisdom and magnanimity to retrace his steps when convinced of error will sooner or later be rewarded with the respect and gratitude of an intelligent and patriotic people.

Our own history, although embracing a period less than a century, affords abundant proof that most, if not all, of our domestic troubles are directly traceable to violations of the organic law and excessive legislation. The most striking illustrations of this fact are furnished by the enactments of the past three years upon the question of reconstruction. After a fair trial they have substantially failed and proved pernicious in their results, and there seems to be no good reason why they should longer remain upon the statute book. States to which the Constitution guarantees a republican form of government have been reduced to military dependencies, in each of which the people have been made subject to the arbitrary will of the commanding general. Although the Constitution requires that each State shall be represented in Congress, Virginia, Mississippi, and Texas are yet excluded from the two Houses, and, contrary to the express provisions of that instrument, were denied participation in the recent election for a President and Vice-President of the United States. The attempt to place the white population under the domination of persons of color in the South has impaired, if not destroyed, the kindly relations that had previously existed between them; and mutual distrust has engendered a feeling of animosity which, leading in some instances to collision and bloodshed, has prevented that cooperation between the two races so essential to the success of industrial enterprise in the Southern States. Nor have the inhabitants of those States alone suffered from the disturbed condition of affairs growing out of these Congressional enactments. The entire Union has been agitated by grave apprehensions of troubles which might again involve the peace of the nation; its interests have been injuriously affected by the derangement of business and labor, and the consequent want of prosperity throughout that portion of the country.

The Federal Constitution—the *magna charta* of American rights, under whose wise and salutary provisions we have successfully conducted all our domestic and foreign affairs, sustained ourselves in peace and in war, and become a great nation among the powers of the earth—must assuredly be now adequate to the settlement of questions growing out of the civil war, waged alone for its vindication.   This great fact is made most manifest by the condition of the country when Congress assembled in the month of December, 1865.   Civil strife had ceased, the spirit of rebellion had spent its entire force, in the Southern States the people had warmed into national life, and throughout the whole country a healthy reaction in public sentiment had taken place.   By the application of the simple yet effective provisions of the Constitution the executive department, with the voluntary aid of the States, had brought the work of restoration as near completion as was within the scope of its authority, and the nation was encouraged by the prospect of an early and satisfactory adjustment of all its difficulties.   Congress, however, intervened, and, refusing to perfect the work so nearly consummated, declined to admit members from the unrepresented States, adopted a series of measures which arrested the progress of restoration, frustrated all that had been so successfully accomplished, and, after three years of agitation and strife, has left the country further from the attainment of union and fraternal feeling than at the inception of the Congressional plan of reconstruction.   It needs no argument to show that legislation which has produced such baneful consequences should be abrogated, or else made to conform to the genuine principles of republican government.

Under the influence of party passion and sectional prejudice, other acts have been passed not warranted by the Constitution.   Congress has already been made familiar with my views respecting the "tenure-of-office bill."   Experience has proved that its repeal is demanded by the best interests of the country, and that while it remains in force the President can not enjoin that rigid accountability of public officers so essential to an honest and efficient execution of the laws.   Its revocation would enable the executive department to exercise the power of appointment and removal in accordance with the original design of the Federal Constitution.

The act of March 2, 1867, making appropriations for the support of the Army for the year ending June 30, 1868, and for other purposes, contains provisions which interfere with the President's constitutional functions as Commander in Chief of the Army and deny to States of the Union the right to protect themselves by means of their own militia.   These provisions should be at once annulled; for while the first might, in times of great emergency, seriously embarrass the Executive in efforts to employ and direct the common strength of the nation for its protection and preservation, the other is contrary to the express declaration of the Constitution that "a well-regulated militia being necessary to the security of a free state, the right of the people to keep and bear arms shall not be infringed."

It is believed that the repeal of all such laws would be accepted by the American people as at least a partial return to the fundamental principles of the Government, and an indication that hereafter the Constitution is to be made the nation's safe and unerring guide. They can be productive of no permanent benefit to the country, and should not be permitted to stand as so many monuments of the deficient wisdom which has characterized our recent legislation.

The condition of our finances demands the early and earnest consideration of Congress. Compared with the growth of our population, the public expenditures have reached an amount unprecedented in our history.

The population of the United States in 1790 was nearly 4,000,000 people. Increasing each decade about 33 per cent, it reached in 1860 31,000,000, an increase of 700 per cent on the population in 1790. In 1869 it is estimated that it will reach 38,000,000, or an increase of 868 per cent in seventy-nine years.

The annual expenditures of the Federal Government in 1791 were $4,200,000; in 1820, $18,200,000; in 1850, forty-one millions; in 1860, sixty-three millions; in 1865, nearly thirteen hundred millions; and in 1869 it is estimated by the Secretary of the Treasury, in his last annual report, that they will be three hundred and seventy-two millions.

By comparing the public disbursements of 1869, as estimated, with those of 1791, it will be seen that the increase of expenditure since the beginning of the Government has been 8,618 per cent, while the increase of the population for the same period was only 868 per cent. Again, the expenses of the Government in 1860, the year of peace immediately preceding the war, were only sixty-three millions, while in 1869, the year of peace three years after the war, it is estimated they will be three hundred and seventy-two millions, an increase of 489 per cent, while the increase of population was only 21 per cent for the same period.

These statistics further show that in 1791 the annual national expenses, compared with the population, were little more than $1 per capita, and in 1860 but $2 per capita; while in 1869 they will reach the extravagant sum of $9.78 per capita.

It will be observed that all these statements refer to and exhibit the disbursements of peace periods. It may, therefore, be of interest to compare the expenditures of the three war periods—the war with Great Britain, the Mexican War, and the War of the Rebellion.

In 1814 the annual expenses incident to the War of 1812 reached their highest amount—about thirty-one millions—while our population slightly exceeded 8,000,000, showing an expenditure of only $3.80 per capita. In 1847 the expenditures growing out of the war with Mexico reached fifty-five millions, and the population about 21,000,000, giving only $2.60

per capita for the war expenses of that year. In 1865 the expenditures called for by the rebellion reached the vast amount of twelve hundred and ninety millions, which, compared with a population of 34,000,000, gives $38.20 per capita.

From the 4th day of March, 1789, to the 30th of June, 1861, the entire expenditures of the Government were $1,700,000,000. During that period we were engaged in wars with Great Britain and Mexico, and were involved in hostilities with powerful Indian tribes; Louisiana was purchased from France at a cost of $15,000,000; Florida was ceded to us by Spain for five millions; California was acquired from Mexico for fifteen millions, and the territory of New Mexico was obtained from Texas for the sum of ten millions. Early in 1861 the War of the Rebellion commenced; and from the 1st of July of that year to the 30th of June, 1865, the public expenditures reached the enormous aggregate of thirty-three hundred millions. Three years of peace have intervened, and during that time the disbursements of the Government have successively been five hundred and twenty millions, three hundred and forty-six millions, and three hundred and ninety-three millions. Adding to these amounts three hundred and seventy-two millions, estimated as necessary for the fiscal year ending the 30th of June, 1869, we obtain a total expenditure of $1,600,000,000 during the four years immediately succeeding the war, or nearly as much as was expended during the seventy-two years that preceded the rebellion and embraced the extraordinary expenditures already named.

These startling facts clearly illustrate the necessity of retrenchment in all branches of the public service. Abuses which were tolerated during the war for the preservation of the nation will not be endured by the people, now that profound peace prevails. The receipts from internal revenues and customs have during the past three years gradually diminished, and the continuance of useless and extravagant expenditures will involve us in national bankruptcy, or else make inevitable an increase of taxes, already too onerous and in many respects obnoxious on account of their inquisitorial character. One hundred millions annually are expended for the military force, a large portion of which is employed in the execution of laws both unnecessary and unconstitutional; one hundred and fifty millions are required each year to pay the interest on the public debt; an army of taxgatherers impoverishes the nation, and public agents, placed by Congress beyond the control of the Executive, divert from their legitimate purposes large sums of money which they collect from the people in the name of the Government. Judicious legislation and prudent economy can alone remedy defects and avert evils which, if suffered to exist, can not fail to diminish confidence in the public councils and weaken the attachment and respect of the people toward their political institutions. Without proper care the small balance which it is estimated will remain in the Treasury at the close of the present fiscal year will not be realized, and additional millions be added to a debt which is now enumerated by billions.

It is shown by the able and comprehensive report of the Secretary of the Treasury that the receipts for the fiscal year ending June 30, 1868, were $405,638,083, and that the expenditures for the same period were $377,340,284, leaving in the Treasury a surplus of $28,297,798. It is estimated that the receipts during the present fiscal year, ending June 30, 1869, will be $341,392,868 and the expenditures $336,152,470, showing a small balance of $5,240,398 in favor of the Government. For the fiscal year ending June 30, 1870, it is estimated that the receipts will amount to $327,000,000 and the expenditures to $303,000,000, leaving an estimated surplus of $24,000,000.

It becomes proper in this connection to make a brief reference to our public indebtedness, which has accumulated with such alarming rapidity and assumed such colossal proportions.

In 1789, when the Government commenced operations under the Federal Constitution, it was burdened with an indebtedness of $75,000,000, created during the War of the Revolution. This amount had been reduced to $45,000,000 when, in 1812, war was declared against Great Britain. The three years' struggle that followed largely increased the national obligations, and in 1816 they had attained the sum of $127,000,000. Wise and economical legislation, however, enabled the Government to pay the entire amount within a period of twenty years, and the extinguishment of the national debt filled the land with rejoicing and was one of the great events of President Jackson's Administration. After its redemption a large fund remained in the Treasury, which was deposited for safe-keeping with the several States, on condition that it should be returned when required by the public wants. In 1849—the year after the termination of an expensive war with Mexico—we found ourselves involved in a debt of $64,000,000; and this was the amount owed by the Government in 1860, just prior to the outbreak of the rebellion. In the spring of 1861 our civil war commenced. Each year of its continuance made an enormous addition to the debt; and when, in the spring of 1865, the nation successfully emerged from the conflict, the obligations of the Government had reached the immense sum of $2,873,992,909. The Secretary of the Treasury shows that on the 1st day of November, 1867, this amount had been reduced to $2,491,504,450; but at the same time his report exhibits an increase during the past year of $35,625,102, for the debt on the 1st day of November last is stated to have been $2,527,129,552. It is estimated by the Secretary that the returns for the past month will add to our liabilities the further sum of $11,000,000, making a total increase during thirteen months of $46,500,000.

In my message to Congress December 4, 1865, it was suggested that a policy should be devised which, without being oppressive to the people, would at once begin to effect a reduction of the debt, and, if persisted in,

discharge it fully within a definite number of years. The Secretary of
the Treasury forcibly recommends legislation of this character, and justly
urges that the longer it is deferred the more difficult must become its
accomplishment. We should follow the wise precedents established in
1789 and 1816, and without further delay make provision for the payment of our obligations at as early a period as may be practicable. The
fruits of their labors should be enjoyed by our citizens rather than used
to build up and sustain moneyed monopolies in our own and other lands.
Our foreign debt is already computed by the Secretary of the Treasury
at $850,000,000; citizens of foreign countries receive interest upon a
large portion of our securities, and American taxpayers are made to contribute large sums for their support. The idea that such a debt is to
become permanent should be at all times discarded as involving taxation
too heavy to be borne, and payment once in every sixteen years, at the
present rate of interest, of an amount equal to the original sum. This
vast debt, if permitted to become permanent and increasing, must eventually be gathered into the hands of a few, and enable them to exert a
dangerous and controlling power in the affairs of the Government. The
borrowers would become servants to the lenders, the lenders the masters
of the people. We now pride ourselves upon having given freedom to
4,000,000 of the colored race; it will then be our shame that 40,000,000
of people, by their own toleration of usurpation and profligacy, have
suffered themselves to become enslaved, and merely exchanged slave
owners for new taskmasters in the shape of bondholders and taxgatherers. Besides, permanent debts pertain to monarchical governments,
and, tending to monopolies, perpetuities, and class legislation, are totally
irreconcilable with free institutions. Introduced into our republican
system, they would gradually but surely sap its foundations, eventually
subvert our governmental fabric, and erect upon its ruins a moneyed aristocracy. It is our sacred duty to transmit unimpaired to our posterity
the blessings of liberty which were bequeathed to us by the founders
of the Republic, and by our example teach those who are to follow us
carefully to avoid the dangers which threaten a free and independent
people.

Various plans have been proposed for the payment of the public debt.
However they may have varied as to the time and mode in which it
should be redeemed, there seems to be a general concurrence as to the
propriety and justness of a reduction in the present rate of interest. The
Secretary of the Treasury in his report recommends 5 per cent; Congress, in a bill passed prior to adjournment on the 27th of July last,
agreed upon 4 and 4½ per cent; while by many 3 per cent has been held
to be an amply sufficient return for the investment. The general impression as to the exorbitancy of the existing rate of interest has led to
an inquiry in the public mind respecting the consideration which the
Government has actually received for its bonds, and the conclusion is

becoming prevalent that the amount which it obtained was in real money three or four hundred per cent less than the obligations which it issued in return. It can not be denied that we are paying an extravagant percentage for the use of the money borrowed, which was paper currency, greatly depreciated below the value of coin. This fact is made apparent when we consider that bondholders receive from the Treasury upon each dollar they own in Government securities 6 per cent in gold, which is nearly or quite equal to 9 per cent in currency; that the bonds are then converted into capital for the national banks, upon which those institutions issue their circulation, bearing 6 per cent interest; and that they are exempt from taxation by the Government and the States, and thereby enhanced 2 per cent in the hands of the holders. We thus have an aggregate of 17 per cent which may be received upon each dollar by the owners of Government securities. A system that produces such results is justly regarded as favoring a few at the expense of the many, and has led to the further inquiry whether our bondholders, in view of the large profits which they have enjoyed, would themselves be averse to a settlement of our indebtedness upon a plan which would yield them a fair remuneration and at the same time be just to the taxpayers of the nation. Our national credit should be sacredly observed, but in making provision for our creditors we should not forget what is due to the masses of the people. It may be assumed that the holders of our securities have already received upon their bonds a larger amount than their original investment, measured by a gold standard. Upon this statement of facts it would seem but just and equitable that the 6 per cent interest now paid by the Government should be applied to the reduction of the principal in semi-annual installments, which in sixteen years and eight months would liquidate the entire national debt. Six per cent in gold would at present rates be equal to 9 per cent in currency, and equivalent to the payment of the debt one and a half times in a fraction less than seventeen years. This, in connection with all the other advantages derived from their investment, would afford to the public creditors a fair and liberal compensation for the use of their capital, and with this they should be satisfied. The lessons of the past admonish the lender that it is not well to be over-anxious in exacting from the borrower rigid compliance with the letter of the bond.

If provision be made for the payment of the indebtedness of the Government in the manner suggested, our nation will rapidly recover its wonted prosperity. Its interests require that some measure should be taken to release the large amount of capital invested in the securities of the Government. It is not now merely unproductive, but in taxation annually consumes $150,000,000, which would otherwise be used by our enterprising people in adding to the wealth of the nation. Our commerce, which at one time successfully rivaled that of the great maritime powers, has rapidly diminished, and our industrial interests are in a depressed and languishing condition. The development of our inexhaustible resources is checked, and the fertile fields of the South are becoming waste for want of means to till them. With the release of capital, new life would be infused into the paralyzed energies of our people and activity and vigor imparted to every branch of industry. Our people need encouragement in their efforts to recover from the effects of the rebellion and of injudicious legislation, and it should be the aim of the Government to stimulate them by the prospect of an early release from the burdens which impede their prosperity. If we can not take the burdens from their shoulders, we should at least manifest a willingness to help to bear them.

In referring to the condition of the circulating medium, I shall merely reiterate substantially that portion of my last annual message which relates to that subject.

The proportion which the currency of any country should bear to the whole value of the annual produce circulated by its means is a question upon which political economists have not agreed. Nor can it be controlled by legislation, but must be left to the irrevocable laws which everywhere regulate commerce and trade. The circulating medium will ever irresistibly flow to those points where it is in greatest demand. The law of demand and supply is as unerring as that which regulates the tides of the ocean; and, indeed, currency, like the tides, has its ebbs and flows throughout the commercial world.

At the beginning of the rebellion the bank-note circulation of the country amounted to not much more than $200,000,000; now the circulation of national-bank notes and those known as "legal-tenders" is nearly seven hundred millions. While it is urged by some that this amount should be increased, others contend that a decided reduction is absolutely essential to the best interests of the country. In view of these diverse opinions, it may be well to ascertain the real value of our paper issues when compared with a metallic or convertible currency. For this purpose let us inquire how much gold and silver could be purchased by the seven hundred millions of paper money now in circulation. Probably not more than half the amount of the latter; showing that when our paper currency is compared with gold and silver its commercial value is compressed into three hundred and fifty millions. This striking fact makes it the obvious duty of the Government, as early as may be consistent with the principles of sound political economy, to take such measures as will enable the holders of its notes and those of the national banks to convert them, without loss, into specie or its equivalent. A reduction of our paper circulating medium need not necessarily follow. This, however, would depend upon the law of demand and supply, though it should be borne in mind that by making legal-tender and bank notes convertible into coin or its equivalent their present specie value in the hands of their holders would be enhanced 100 per cent.

Legislation for the accomplishment of a result so desirable is demanded by the highest public considerations. The Constitution contemplates that the circulating medium of the country shall be uniform in quality and value. At the time of the formation of that instrument the country had just emerged from the War of the Revolution, and was suffering from the effects of a redundant and worthless paper currency. The sages of that period were anxious to protect their posterity from the evils which they themselves had experienced. Hence in providing a circulating medium they conferred upon Congress the power to coin money and regulate the value thereof, at the same time prohibiting the States from making anything but gold and silver a tender in payment of debts.

The anomalous condition of our currency is in striking contrast with that which was originally designed. Our circulation now embraces, first, notes of the national banks, which are made receivable for all dues to the Government, excluding imposts, and by all its creditors, excepting in payment of interest upon its bonds and the securities themselves; second, legal tender, issued by the United States, and which the law requires shall be received as well in payment of all debts between citizens as of all Government dues, excepting imposts; and, third, gold and silver coin. By the operation of our present system of finance, however, the metallic currency, when collected, is reserved only for one class of Government creditors, who, holding its bonds, semiannually receive their interest in coin from the National Treasury. There is no reason which will be accepted as satisfactory by the people why those who defend us on the land and protect us on the sea; the pensioner upon the gratitude of the nation, bearing the scars and wounds received while in its service; the public servants in the various departments of the Government; the farmer who supplies the soldiers of the Army and the sailors of the Navy; the artisan who toils in the nation's workshops, or the mechanics and laborers who build its edifices and construct its forts and vessels of war, should, in payment of their just and hard-earned dues, receive depreciated paper, while another class of their countrymen, no more deserving, are paid in coin of gold and silver. Equal and exact justice requires that all the creditors of the Government should be paid in a currency possessing a uniform value. This can only be accomplished by the restoration of the currency to the standard established by the Constitution, and by this means we would remove a discrimination which may, if it has not already done so, create a prejudice that may become deep-rooted and widespread and imperil the national credit.

The feasibility of making our currency correspond with the constitutional standard may be seen by reference to a few facts derived from our commercial statistics.

The aggregate product of precious metals in the United States from 1849 to 1867 amounted to $1,174,000,000, while for the same period the net exports of specie were $741,000,000. This shows an excess of product over net exports of $433,000,000. There are in the Treasury

$103,407,985 in coin; in circulation in the States on the Pacific Coast about $40,000,000, and a few millions in the national and other banks— in all less than $160,000,000. Taking into consideration the specie in the country prior to 1849 and that produced since 1867, and we have more than $300,000,000 not accounted for by exportation or by returns of the Treasury, and therefore most probably remaining in the country.

These are important facts, and show how completely the inferior currency will supersede the better, forcing it from circulation among the masses and causing it to be exported as a mere article of trade, to add to the money capital of foreign lands. They show the necessity of retiring our paper money, that the return of gold and silver to the avenues of trade may be invited and a demand created which will cause the retention at home of at least so much of the productions of our rich and inexhaustible gold-bearing fields as may be sufficient for purposes of circulation. It is unreasonable to expect a return to a sound currency so long as the Government and banks, by continuing to issue irredeemable notes, fill the channels of circulation with depreciated paper. Notwithstanding a coinage by our mints since 1849 of $874,000,000, the people are now strangers to the currency which was designed for their use and benefit, and specimens of the precious metals bearing the national device are seldom seen, except when produced to gratify the interest excited by their novelty. If depreciated paper is to be continued as the permanent currency of the country, and all our coin is to become a mere article of traffic and speculation, to the enhancement in price of all that is indispensable to the comfort of the people, it would be wise economy to abolish our mints, thus saving the nation the care and expense incident to such establishments, and let our precious metals be exported in bullion. The time has come, however, when the Government and national banks should be required to take the most efficient steps and make all necessary arrangements for a resumption of specie payments. Let specie payments once be earnestly inaugurated by the Government and banks, and the value of the paper circulation would directly approximate a specie standard.

Specie payments having been resumed by the Government and banks, all notes or bills of paper issued by either of a less denomination than $20 should by law be excluded from circulation, so that the people may have the benefit and convenience of a gold and silver currency which in all their business transactions will be uniform in value at home and abroad.

Every man of property or industry, every man who desires to preserve what he honestly possesses or to obtain what he can honestly earn, has a direct interest in maintaining a safe circulating medium—such a medium as shall be real and substantial, not liable to vibrate with opinions, not subject to be blown up or blown down by the breath of speculation, but to be made stable and secure. A disordered currency is one of the greatest political evils. It undermines the virtues necessary for the support of the social system and encourages propensities destructive of its happiness; it wars against industry, frugality, and economy, and it fosters the evil spirits of extravagance and speculation.

It has been asserted by one of our profound and most gifted statesmen that—

Of all the contrivances for cheating the laboring classes of mankind, none has been more effectual than that which deludes them with paper money. This is the most effectual of inventions to fertilize the rich man's fields by the sweat of the poor man's brow. Ordinary tyranny, oppression, excessive taxation—these bear lightly on the happiness of the mass of the community compared with a fraudulent currency and the robberies committed by depreciated paper. Our own history has recorded for our instruction enough, and more than enough, of the demoralizing tendency, the injustice, and the intolerable oppression on the virtuous and well-disposed of a degraded paper currency authorized by law or in any way countenanced by government.

It is one of the most successful devices, in times of peace or war, of expansions or revulsions, to accomplish the transfer of all the precious metals from the great mass of the people into the hands of the few, where they are hoarded in secret places or deposited under bolts and bars, while the people are left to endure all the inconvenience, sacrifice, and demoralization resulting from the use of depreciated and worthless paper.

The Secretary of the Interior in his report gives valuable information in reference to the interests confided to the supervision of his Department, and reviews the operations of the Land Office, Pension Office, Patent Office, and Indian Bureau.

During the fiscal year ending June 30, 1868, 6,655,700 acres of public land were disposed of. The entire cash receipts of the General Land Office for the same period were $1,632,745, being greater by $284,883 than the amount realized from the same sources during the previous year. The entries under the homestead law cover 2,328,923 acres, nearly one-fourth of which was taken under the act of June 21, 1866, which applies only to the States of Alabama, Mississippi, Louisiana, Arkansas, and Florida.

On the 30th of June, 1868, 169,643 names were borne on the pension rolls, and during the year ending on that day the total amount paid for pensions, including the expenses of disbursement, was $24,010,982, being $5,391,025 greater than that expended for like purposes during the preceding year.

During the year ending the 30th of September last the expenses of the Patent Office exceeded the receipts by $171, and, including reissues and designs, 14,153 patents were issued.

Treaties with various Indian tribes have been concluded, and will be submitted to the Senate for its constitutional action. I cordially sanction the stipulations which provide for reserving lands for the various tribes, where they may be encouraged to abandon their nomadic habits and engage in agricultural and industrial pursuits. This policy, inaugurated many years since, has met with signal success whenever it has

been pursued in good faith and with becoming liberality by the United
States.   The necessity for extending it as far as practicable in our relations with the aboriginal population is greater now than at any preceding
period.   Whilst we furnish subsistence and instruction to the Indians
and guarantee the undisturbed enjoyment of their treaty rights, we
should habitually insist upon the faithful observance of their agreement
to remain within their respective reservations.   This is the only mode
by which collisions with other tribes and with the whites can be avoided
and the safety of our frontier settlements secured.

The companies constructing the railway from Omaha to Sacramento
have been most energetically engaged in prosecuting the work, and it is
believed that the line will be completed before the expiration of the next
fiscal year.   The 6 per cent bonds issued to these companies amounted
on the 5th instant to $44,337,000, and additional work had been per-
formed to the extent of $3,200,000.

The Secretary of the Interior in August last invited my attention to
the report of a Government director of the Union Pacific Railroad Company who had been specially instructed to examine the location, construction, and equipment of their road.   I submitted for the opinion of
the Attorney-General certain questions in regard to the authority of the
Executive which arose upon this report and those which had from time
to time been presented by the commissioners appointed to inspect each
successive section of the work.   After carefully considering the law of
the case, he affirmed the right of the Executive to order, if necessary, a
thorough revision of the entire road.   Commissioners were thereupon
appointed to examine this and other lines, and have recently submitted a
statement of their investigations, of which the report of the Secretary of
the Interior furnishes specific information.

The report of the Secretary of War contains information of interest and
importance respecting the several bureaus of the War Department and the
operations of the Army.   The strength of our military force on the 30th
of September last was 48,000 men, and it is computed that by the 1st of
January next this number will be decreased to 43,000.   It is the opinion
of the Secretary of War that within the next year a considerable diminution of the infantry force may be made without detriment to the interests
of the country; and in view of the great expense attending the military
peace establishment and the absolute necessity of retrenchment wherever
it can be applied, it is hoped that Congress will sanction the reduction
which his report recommends.   While in 1860 sixteen thousand three
hundred men cost the nation $16,472,000, the sum of $65,682,000 is estimated as necessary for the support of the Army during the fiscal year
ending June 30, 1870.   The estimates of the War Department for the last
two fiscal years were, for 1867, $33,814,461, and for 1868 $25,205,669.
The actual expenditures during the same periods were, respectively,
$95,224,415 and $123,246,648.   The estimate submitted in December last

for the fiscal year ending June 30, 1869, was $77,124,707; the expenditures for the first quarter, ending the 30th of September last, were $27,219,117, and the Secretary of the Treasury gives $66,000,000 as the amount which will probably be required during the remaining three quarters, if there should be no reduction of the Army—making its aggregate cost for the year considerably in excess of ninety-three millions. The difference between the estimates and expenditures for the three fiscal years which have been named is thus shown to be $175,545,343 for this single branch of the public service.

The report of the Secretary of the Navy exhibits the operations of that Department and of the Navy during the year. A considerable reduction of the force has been effected. There are 42 vessels, carrying 411 guns, in the six squadrons which are established in different parts of the world. Three of these vessels are returning to the United States and 4 are used as storeships, leaving the actual cruising force 35 vessels, carrying 356 guns. The total number of vessels in the Navy is 206, mounting 1,743 guns. Eighty-one vessels of every description are in use, armed with 696 guns. The number of enlisted men in the service, including apprentices, has been reduced to 8,500. An increase of navy-yard facilities is recommended as a measure which will in the event of war be promotive of economy and security. A more thorough and systematic survey of the North Pacific Ocean is advised in view of our recent acquisitions, our expanding commerce, and the increasing intercourse between the Pacific States and Asia. The naval pension fund, which consists of a moiety of the avails of prizes captured during the war, amounts to $14,000,000. Exception is taken to the act of 23d July last, which reduces the interest on the fund loaned to the Government by the Secretary, as trustee, to 3 per cent instead of 6 per cent, which was originally stipulated when the investment was made. An amendment of the pension laws is suggested to remedy omissions and defects in existing enactments. The expenditures of the Department during the last fiscal year were $20,120,394, and the estimates for the coming year amount to $20,993,414.

The Postmaster-General's report furnishes a full and clear exhibit of the operations and condition of the postal service. The ordinary postal revenue for the fiscal year ending June 30, 1868, was $16,292,600, and the total expenditures, embracing all the service for which special appropriations have been made by Congress, amounted to $22,730,592, showing an excess of expenditures of $6,437,991. Deducting from the expenditures the sum of $1,896,525, the amount of appropriations for ocean-steamship and other special service, the excess of expenditures was $4,541,466. By using an unexpended balance in the Treasury of $3,800,000 the actual sum for which a special appropriation is required to meet the deficiency is $741,466. The causes which produced this large excess of expenditure over revenue were the restoration of service in the late insurgent States and the putting into operation of new service established by acts of Congress, which amounted within the last two years and a half to about 48,700 miles—equal to more than one-third of the whole amount of the service at the close of the war. New postal conventions with Great Britain, North Germany, Belgium, the Netherlands, Switzerland, and Italy, respectively, have been carried into effect. Under their provisions important improvements have resulted in reduced rates of international postage and enlarged mail facilities with European countries. The cost of the United States transatlantic ocean mail service since January 1, 1868, has been largely lessened under the operation of these new conventions, a reduction of over one-half having been effected under the new arrangements for ocean mail steamship service which went into effect on that date. The attention of Congress is invited to the practical suggestions and recommendations made in his report by the Postmaster-General.

No important question has occurred during the last year in our accustomed cordial and friendly intercourse with Costa Rica, Guatemala, Honduras, San Salvador, France, Austria, Belgium, Switzerland, Portugal, the Netherlands, Denmark, Sweden and Norway, Rome, Greece, Turkey, Persia, Egypt, Liberia, Morocco, Tripoli, Tunis, Muscat, Siam, Borneo, and Madagascar.

Cordial relations have also been maintained with the Argentine and the Oriental Republics. The expressed wish of Congress that our national good offices might be tendered to those Republics, and also to Brazil and Paraguay, for bringing to an end the calamitous war which has so long been raging in the valley of the La Plata, has been assiduously complied with and kindly acknowledged by all the belligerents. That important negotiation, however, has thus far been without result.

Charles A. Washburn, late United States minister to Paraguay, having resigned, and being desirous to return to the United States, the rear-admiral commanding the South Atlantic Squadron was early directed to send a ship of war to Asuncion, the capital of Paraguay, to receive Mr. Washburn and his family and remove them from a situation which was represented to be endangered by faction and foreign war. The Brazilian commander of the allied invading forces refused permission to the *Wasp* to pass through the blockading forces, and that vessel returned to its accustomed anchorage. Remonstrance having been made against this refusal, it was promptly overruled, and the *Wasp* therefore resumed her errand, received Mr. Washburn and his family, and conveyed them to a safe and convenient seaport. In the meantime an excited controversy had arisen between the President of Paraguay and the late United States minister, which, it is understood, grew out of his proceedings in giving asylum in the United States legation to alleged enemies of that Republic. The question of the right to give asylum is one always difficult and often productive of great embarrassment. In states well organized and established, foreign powers refuse either to concede or exercise that right, except as to persons actually belonging to the diplomatic service.   On the other hand, all such powers insist upon exercising the right of asylum in states where the law of nations is not fully acknowledged, respected, and obeyed.

The President of Paraguay is understood to have opposed to Mr. Washburn's proceedings the injurious and very improbable charge of personal complicity in insurrection and treason.   The correspondence, however, has not yet reached the United States.

Mr. Washburn, in connection with this controversy, represents that two United States citizens attached to the legation were arbitrarily seized at his side, when leaving the capital of Paraguay, committed to prison, and there subjected to torture for the purpose of procuring confessions of their own criminality and testimony to support the President's allegations against the United States minister.   Mr. McMahon, the newly appointed minister to Paraguay, having reached the La Plata, has been instructed to proceed without delay to Asuncion, there to investigate the whole subject.   The rear-admiral commanding the United States South Atlantic Squadron has been directed to attend the new minister with a proper naval force to sustain such just demands as the occasion may require, and to vindicate the rights of the United States citizens referred to and of any others who may be exposed to danger in the theater of war.   With these exceptions, friendly relations have been maintained between the United States and Brazil and Paraguay.

Our relations during the past year with Bolivia, Ecuador, Peru, and Chile have become especially friendly and cordial.   Spain and the Republics of Peru, Bolivia, and Ecuador have expressed their willingness to accept the mediation of the United States for terminating the war upon the South Pacific coast.   Chile has not finally declared upon the question.   In the meantime the conflict has practically exhausted itself, since no belligerent or hostile movement has been made by either party during the last two years, and there are no indications of a present purpose to resume hostilities on either side.   Great Britain and France have cordially seconded our proposition of mediation, and I do not forego the hope that it may soon be accepted by all the belligerents and lead to a secure establishment of peace and friendly relations between the Spanish American Republics of the Pacific and Spain—a result which would be attended with common benefits to the belligerents and much advantage to all commercial nations.   I communicate, for the consideration of Congress, a correspondence which shows that the Bolivian Republic has established the extremely liberal principle of receiving into its citizenship any citizen of the United States, or of any other of the American Republics, upon the simple condition of voluntary registry.

The correspondence herewith submitted will be found painfully replete with accounts of the ruin and wretchedness produced by recent earthquakes, of unparalleled severity, in the Republics of Peru, Ecuador, and

Bolivia.   The diplomatic agents and naval officers of the United States who were present in those countries at the time of those disasters furnished all the relief in their power to the sufferers, and were promptly rewarded with grateful and touching acknowledgments by the Congress of Peru.   An appeal to the charity of our fellow-citizens has been answered by much liberality.   In this connection I submit an appeal which has been made by the Swiss Republic, whose Government and institutions are kindred to our own, in behalf of its inhabitants, who are suffering extreme destitution, produced by recent devastating inundations.

Our relations with Mexico during the year have been marked by an increasing growth of mutual confidence.   The Mexican Government has not yet acted upon the three treaties celebrated here last summer for establishing the rights of naturalized citizens upon a liberal and just basis, for regulating consular powers, and for the adjustment of mutual claims.

All commercial nations, as well as all friends of republican institutions, have occasion to regret the frequent local disturbances which occur in some of the constituent States of Colombia.   Nothing has occurred, however, to affect the harmony and cordial friendship which have for several years existed between that youthful and vigorous Republic and our own.

Negotiations are pending with a view to the survey and construction of a ship canal across the Isthmus of Darien, under the auspices of the United States.   I hope to be able to submit the results of that negotiation to the Senate during its present session.

The very liberal treaty which was entered into last year by the United States and Nicaragua has been ratified by the latter Republic.

Costa Rica, with the earnestness of a sincerely friendly neighbor, solicits a reciprocity of trade, which I commend to the consideration of Congress.

The convention created by treaty between the United States and Venezuela in July, 1865, for the mutual adjustment of claims, has been held, and its decisions have been received at the Department of State.   The heretofore-recognized Government of the United States of Venezuela has been subverted.   A provisional government having been instituted under circumstances which promise durability, it has been formally recognized.

I have been reluctantly obliged to ask explanation and satisfaction for national injuries committed by the President of Hayti.   The political and social condition of the Republics of Hayti and St. Domingo is very unsatisfactory and painful.   The abolition of slavery, which has been carried into effect throughout the island of St. Domingo and the entire West Indies, except the Spanish islands of Cuba and Porto Rico, has been followed by a profound popular conviction of the rightfulness of republican institutions and an intense desire to secure them.   The attempt, however, to establish republics there encounters many obstacles, most of which may be supposed to result from long-indulged habits of colonial supineness and dependence upon European monarchical powers.   While the United States have on all occasions professed a decided unwillingness that any part of this continent or of its adjacent islands shall be made a theater for a new establishment of monarchical power, too little has been done by us, on the other hand, to attach the communities by which we are surrounded to our own country, or to lend even a moral support to the efforts they are so resolutely and so constantly making to secure republican institutions for themselves. It is indeed a question of grave consideration whether our recent and present example is not calculated to check the growth and expansion of free principles, and make those communities distrust, if not dread, a government which at will consigns to military domination States that are integral parts of our Federal Union, and, while ready to resist any attempts by other nations to extend to this hemisphere the monarchical institutions of Europe, assumes to establish over a large portion of its people a rule more absolute, harsh, and tyrannical than any known to civilized powers.

The acquisition of Alaska was made with the view of extending national jurisdiction and republican principles in the American hemisphere. Believing that a further step could be taken in the same direction, I last year entered into a treaty with the King of Denmark for the purchase of the islands of St. Thomas and St. John, on the best terms then attainable, and with the express consent of the people of those islands. This treaty still remains under consideration in the Senate. A new convention has been entered into with Denmark, enlarging the time fixed for final ratification of the original treaty.

Comprehensive national policy would seem to sanction the acquisition and incorporation into our Federal Union of the several adjacent continental and insular communities as speedily as it can be done peacefully, lawfully, and without any violation of national justice, faith, or honor. Foreign possession or control of those communities has hitherto hindered the growth and impaired the influence of the United States. Chronic revolution and anarchy there would be equally injurious. Each one of them, when firmly established as an independent republic, or when incorporated into the United States, would be a new source of strength and power. Conforming my Administration to these principles, I have on no occasion lent support or toleration to unlawful expeditions set on foot upon the plea of republican propagandism or of national extension or aggrandizement. The necessity, however, of repressing such unlawful movements clearly indicates the duty which rests upon us of adapting our legislative action to the new circumstances of a decline of European monarchical power and influence and the increase of American republican ideas, interests, and sympathies.

It can not be long before it will become necessary for this Government to lend some effective aid to the solution of the political and social problems which are continually kept before the world by the two Republics of the island of St. Domingo, and which are now disclosing themselves more distinctly than heretofore in the island of Cuba. The subject is commended to your consideration with all the more earnestness because I am satisfied that the time has arrived when even so direct a proceeding as a proposition for an annexation of the two Republics of the island of St. Domingo would not only receive the consent of the people interested, but would also give satisfaction to all other foreign nations.

I am aware that upon the question of further extending our possessions it is apprehended by some that our political system can not successfully be applied to an area more extended than our continent; but the conviction is rapidly gaining ground in the American mind that with the increased facilities for intercommunication between all portions of the earth the principles of free government, as embraced in our Constitution, if faithfully maintained and carried out, would prove of sufficient strength and breadth to comprehend within their sphere and influence the civilized nations of the world.

The attention of the Senate and of Congress is again respectfully invited to the treaty for the establishment of commercial reciprocity with the Hawaiian Kingdom entered into last year, and already ratified by that Government. The attitude of the United States toward these islands is not very different from that in which they stand toward the West Indies. It is known and felt by the Hawaiian Government and people that their Government and institutions are feeble and precarious; that the United States, being so near a neighbor, would be unwilling to see the islands pass under foreign control. Their prosperity is continually disturbed by expectations and alarms of unfriendly political proceedings, as well from the United States as from other foreign powers. A reciprocity treaty, while it could not materially diminish the revenues of the United States, would be a guaranty of the good will and forbearance of all nations until the people of the islands shall of themselves, at no distant day, voluntarily apply for admission into the Union.

The Emperor of Russia has acceded to the treaty negotiated here in January last for the security of trade-marks in the interest of manufacturers and commerce. I have invited his attention to the importance of establishing, now while it seems easy and practicable, a fair and equal regulation of the vast fisheries belonging to the two nations in the waters of the North Pacific Ocean.

The two treaties between the United States and Italy for the regulation of consular powers and the extradition of criminals, negotiated and ratified here during the last session of Congress, have been accepted and confirmed by the Italian Government. A liberal consular convention which has been negotiated with Belgium will be submitted to the Senate. The very important treaties which were negotiated between the United States and North Germany and Bavaria for the regulation of the rights of naturalized citizens have been duly ratified and exchanged, and similar treaties have been entered into with the Kingdoms of Belgium and Wurtemberg and with the Grand Duchies of Baden and Hesse-Darmstadt. I hope soon to be able to submit equally satisfactory conventions of the same character now in the course of negotiation with the respective Governments of Spain, Italy, and the Ottoman Empire.

Examination of claims against the United States by the Hudsons Bay Company and the Puget Sound Agricultural Company, on account of certain possessory rights in the State of Oregon and Territory of Washington, alleged by those companies in virtue of provisions of the treaty between the United States and Great Britain of June 15, 1846, has been diligently prosecuted, under the direction of the joint international commission to which they were submitted for adjudication by treaty between the two Governments of July 1, 1863, and will, it is expected, be concluded at an early day.

No practical regulation concerning colonial trade and the fisheries can be accomplished by treaty between the United States and Great Britain until Congress shall have expressed their judgment concerning the principles involved. Three other questions, however, between the United States and Great Britain remain open for adjustment. These are the mutual rights of naturalized citizens, the boundary question involving the title to the island of San Juan, on the Pacific coast, and mutual claims arising since the year 1853 of the citizens and subjects of the two countries for injuries and depredations committed under the authority of their respective Governments. Negotiations upon these subjects are pending, and I am not without hope of being able to lay before the Senate, for its consideration during the present session, protocols calculated to bring to an end these justly exciting and long-existing controversies.

We are not advised of the action of the Chinese Government upon the liberal and auspicious treaty which was recently celebrated with its plenipotentiaries at this capital.

Japan remains a theater of civil war, marked by religious incidents and political severities peculiar to that long-isolated Empire. The Executive has hitherto maintained strict neutrality among the belligerents, and acknowledges with pleasure that it has been frankly and fully sustained in that course by the enlightened concurrence and cooperation of the other treaty powers, namely, Great Britain, France, the Netherlands, North Germany, and Italy.

Spain having recently undergone a revolution marked by extraordinary unanimity and preservation of order, the provisional government established at Madrid has been recognized, and the friendly intercourse which has so long happily existed between the two countries remains unchanged.

I renew the recommendation contained in my communication to Congress dated the 18th July last—a copy of which accompanies this message—that the judgment of the people should be taken on the propriety of so amending the Federal Constitution that it shall provide—

First. For an election of President and Vice-President by a direct vote of the people, instead of through the agency of electors, and making them ineligible for reelection to a second term.

Second. For a distinct designation of the person who shall discharge the duties of President in the event of a vacancy in that office by the death, resignation, or removal of both the President and Vice-President.

Third. For the election of Senators of the United States directly by the people of the several States, instead of by the legislatures; and

Fourth. For the limitation to a period of years of the terms of Federal judges.

Profoundly impressed with the propriety of making these important modifications in the Constitution, I respectfully submit them for the early and mature consideration of Congress. We should, as far as possible, remove all pretext for violations of the organic law, by remedying such imperfections as time and experience may develop, ever remembering that "the constitution which at any time exists until changed by an explicit and authentic act of the whole people is sacredly obligatory upon all."

In the performance of a duty imposed upon me by the Constitution, I have thus communicated to Congress information of the state of the Union and recommended for their consideration such measures as have seemed to me necessary and expedient. If carried into effect, they will hasten the accomplishment of the great and beneficent purposes for which the Constitution was ordained, and which it comprehensively states were "to form a more perfect Union, establish justice, insure domestic tranquillity, provide for the common defense, promote the general welfare, and secure the blessings of liberty to ourselves and our posterity." In Congress are vested all legislative powers, and upon them devolves the responsibility as well for framing unwise and excessive laws as for neglecting to devise and adopt measures absolutely demanded by the wants of the country. Let us earnestly hope that before the expiration of our respective terms of service, now rapidly drawing to a close, an all-wise Providence will so guide our counsels as to strengthen and preserve the Federal Union, inspire reverence for the Constitution, restore prosperity and happiness to our whole people, and promote "on earth peace, good will toward men."

Ulysses S. Grant

March 4, 1869 to March 4, 1877

FIRST ANNUAL MESSAGE.

EXECUTIVE MANSION,
Washington, D. C., December 6, 1869.

To the Senate and House of Representatives:

In coming before you for the first time as Chief Magistrate of this great nation, it is with gratitude to the Giver of All Good for the many benefits we enjoy. We are blessed with peace at home, and are without entangling alliances abroad to forebode trouble; with a territory unsurpassed in fertility, of an area equal to the abundant support of 500,000,000 people, and abounding in every variety of useful mineral in quantity sufficient to supply the world for generations; with exuberant crops; with a variety of climate adapted to the production of every species of earth's riches and suited to the habits, tastes, and requirements of every living thing; with a population of 40,000,000 free people, all speaking one language; with facilities for every mortal to acquire an education; with institutions closing to none the avenues to fame or any blessing of fortune that may be coveted; with freedom of the pulpit, the press, and the school; with a revenue flowing into the National Treasury beyond the requirements of the Government. Happily, harmony is being rapidly restored within our own borders. Manufactures hitherto unknown in our country are springing up in all sections, producing a degree of national independence unequaled by that of any other power.

These blessings and countless others are intrusted to your care and mine for safe-keeping for the brief period of our tenure of office. In a short time we must, each of us, return to the ranks of the people, who have conferred upon us our honors, and account to them for our stewardship. I earnestly desire that neither you nor I may be condemned by a free and enlightened constituency nor by our own consciences.

Emerging from a rebellion of gigantic magnitude, aided, as it was, by the sympathies and assistance of nations with which we were at peace, eleven States of the Union were, four years ago, left without legal State governments. A national debt had been contracted; American commerce was almost driven from the seas; the industry of one-half of the country had been taken from the control of the capitalist and placed where all labor rightfully belongs—in the keeping of the laborer. The work of restoring State governments loyal to the Union, of protecting and fostering free labor, and providing means for paying the interest on the public debt has received ample attention from Congress. Although your efforts have not met with the success in all particulars that might have been desired, yet on the whole they have been more successful than could have been reasonably anticipated.

Seven States which passed ordinances of secession have been fully restored to their places in the Union. The eighth (Georgia) held an election at which she ratified her constitution, republican in form, elected a governor, Members of Congress, a State legislature, and all other officers required. The governor was duly installed, and the legislature met and performed all the acts then required of them by the reconstruction acts of Congress. Subsequently, however, in violation of the constitution which they had just ratified (as since decided by the supreme court of the State), they unseated the colored members of the legislature and admitted to seats some members who are disqualified by the third clause of the fourteenth amendment to the Constitution—an article which they themselves had contributed to ratify. Under these circumstances I would submit to you whether it would not be wise, without delay, to enact a law authorizing the governor of Georgia to convene the members originally elected to the legislature, requiring each member to take the oath prescribed by the reconstruction acts, and none to be admitted who are ineligible under the third clause of the fourteenth amendment.

The freedmen, under the protection which they have received, are making rapid progress in learning, and no complaints are heard of lack of industry on their part where they receive fair remuneration for their labor. The means provided for paying the interest on the public debt, with all other expenses of Government, are more than ample. The loss of our commerce is the only result of the late rebellion which has not received sufficient attention from you. To this subject I call your earnest attention. I will not now suggest plans by which this object may be effected, but will, if necessary, make it the subject of a special message during the session of Congress.

At the March term Congress by joint resolution authorized the Executive to order elections in the States of Virginia, Mississippi, and Texas, to submit to them the constitutions which each had previously, in convention, framed, and submit the constitutions, either entire or in separate parts, to be voted upon, at the discretion of the Executive. Under this authority elections were called. In Virginia the election took place on the 6th of July, 1869. The governor and lieutenant-governor elected have been installed. The legislature met and did all required by this resolution and by all the reconstruction acts of Congress, and abstained from all doubtful authority. I recommend that her Senators and Representatives be promptly admitted to their seats, and that the State be fully restored to its place in the family of States. Elections were called in Mississippi and Texas, to commence on the 30th of November, 1869, and to last two days in Mississippi and four days in Texas. The elections have taken place, but the result is not known. It is to be hoped that the acts of the legislatures of these States, when they meet, will be such as to receive your approval, and thus close the work of reconstruction.

Among the evils growing out of the rebellion, and not yet referred to, is that of an irredeemable currency. It is an evil which I hope will receive your most earnest attention. It is a duty, and one of the highest duties, of Government to secure to the citizen a medium of exchange of fixed, unvarying value. This implies a return to a specie basis, and no substitute for it can be devised. It should be commenced now and reached at the earliest practicable moment consistent with a fair regard to the interests of the debtor class. Immediate resumption, if practicable, would not be desirable. It would compel the debtor class to pay, beyond their contracts, the premium on gold at the date of their purchase, and would bring bankruptcy and ruin to thousands. Fluctuation, however, in the paper value of the measure of all values (gold) is detrimental to the interests of trade. It makes the man of business an involuntary gambler, for in all sales where future payment is to be made both parties speculate as to what will be the value of the currency to be paid and received. I earnestly recommend to you, then, such legislation as will insure a gradual return to specie payments and put an immediate stop to fluctuations in the value of currency.

The methods to secure the former of these results are as numerous as are the speculators on political economy. To secure the latter I see but one way, and that is to authorize the Treasury to redeem its own paper, at a fixed price, whenever presented, and to withhold from circulation all currency so redeemed until sold again for gold.

The vast resources of the nation, both developed and undeveloped, ought to make our credit the best on earth. With a less burden of taxation than the citizen has endured for six years past, the entire public debt could be paid in ten years. But it is not desirable that the people should be taxed to pay it in that time. Year by year the ability to pay increases in a rapid ratio. But the burden of interest ought to be reduced as rapidly as can be done without the violation of contract. The public debt is represented in great part by bonds having from five to twenty and from ten to forty years to run, bearing interest at the rate of 6 per cent and 5 per cent, respectively. It is optional with the Government to pay these bonds at any period after the expiration of the least time mentioned upon their face. The time has already expired when a great part of them may be taken up, and is rapidly approaching when all may be. It is believed that all which are now due may be replaced by bonds bearing a rate of interest not exceeding 4½ per cent, and as rapidly as the remainder become due that they may be replaced in the same way. To accomplish this it may be necessary to authorize the interest to be paid at either of three or four of the money centers of Europe, or by any assistant treasurer of the United States, at the option of the holder of the bond. I suggest this subject for the consideration of Congress, and also, simultaneously with this, the propriety of redeeming our currency, as before suggested, at its market value at the time the law goes into effect, increasing the rate at which currency shall be bought and sold from day to day or week to week, at the same rate of interest as Government pays upon its bonds.

The subjects of tariff and internal taxation will necessarily receive your attention. The revenues of the country are greater than the requirements, and may with safety be reduced. But as the funding of the debt in a 4 or a 4½ per cent loan would reduce annual current expenses largely, thus, after funding, justifying a greater reduction of taxation than would be now expedient, I suggest postponement of this question until the next meeting of Congress.

It may be advisable to modify taxation and tariff in instances where unjust or burdensome discriminations are made by the present laws, but a general revision of the laws regulating this subject I recommend the postponement of for the present. I also suggest the renewal of the tax on incomes, but at a reduced rate, say of 3 per cent, and this tax to expire in three years.

With the funding of the national debt, as here suggested, I feel safe in saying that taxes and the revenue from imports may be reduced safely from sixty to eighty millions per annum at once, and may be still further reduced from year to year, as the resources of the country are developed.

The report of the Secretary of the Treasury shows the receipts of the Government for the fiscal year ending June 30, 1869, to be $370,943,747, and the expenditures, including interest, bounties, etc., to be $321,490,597. The estimates for the ensuing year are more favorable to the Government, and will no doubt show a much larger decrease of the public debt.

The receipts in the Treasury beyond expenditures have exceeded the amount necessary to place to the credit of the sinking fund, as provided by law. To lock up the surplus in the Treasury and withhold it from circulation would lead to such a contraction of the currency as to cripple trade and seriously affect the prosperity of the country. Under these circumstances the Secretary of the Treasury and myself heartily concurred in the propriety of using all the surplus currency in the Treasury in the purchase of Government bonds, thus reducing the interest-bearing indebtedness of the country, and of submitting to Congress the question of the disposition to be made of the bonds so purchased. The bonds now held by the Treasury amount to about seventy-five millions, including those belonging to the sinking fund. I recommend that the whole be placed to the credit of the sinking fund.

Your attention is respectfully invited to the recommendations of the Secretary of the Treasury for the creation of the office of commissioner of customs revenue; for the increase of salaries to certain classes of officials; the substitution of increased national-bank circulation to replace the outstanding 3 per cent certificates; and most especially to his recommendation for the repeal of laws allowing shares of fines, penalties, forfeitures, etc., to officers of the Government or to informers.

The office of Commissioner of Internal Revenue is one of the most arduous and responsible under the Government. It falls but little, if any, short of a Cabinet position in its importance and responsibilities. I would ask for it, therefore, such legislation as in your judgment will place the office upon a footing of dignity commensurate with its importance and with the character and qualifications of the class of men required to fill it properly.

As the United States is the freest of all nations, so, too, its people sympathize with all people struggling for liberty and self-government; but while so sympathizing it is due to our honor that we should abstain from enforcing our views upon unwilling nations and from taking an interested part, *without invitation*, in the quarrels between different nations or between governments and their subjects. Our course should always be in conformity with strict justice and law, international and local. Such has been the policy of the Administration in dealing with these questions. For more than a year a valuable province of Spain, and a near neighbor of ours, in whom all our people can not but feel a deep interest, has been struggling for independence and freedom. The people and Government of the United States entertain the same warm feelings and sympathies for the people of Cuba in their pending struggle that they manifested throughout the previous struggles between Spain and her former colonies in behalf of the latter. But the contest has at no time assumed the conditions which amount to a war in the sense of international law, or which would show the existence of a *de facto* political organization of the insurgents sufficient to justify a recognition of belligerency.

The principle is maintained, however, that this nation is its own judge when to accord the rights of belligerency, either to a people struggling to free themselves from a government they believe to be oppressive or to independent nations at war with each other.

The United States have no disposition to interfere with the existing relations of Spain to her colonial possessions on this continent. They believe that in due time Spain and other European powers will find their interest in terminating those relations and establishing their present dependencies as independent powers—members of the family of nations. These dependencies are no longer regarded as subject to transfer from one European power to another. When the present relation of colonies ceases, they are to become independent powers, exercising the right of choice and of self-control in the determination of their future condition and relations with other powers.

The United States, in order to put a stop to bloodshed in Cuba, and in the interest of a neighboring people, proposed their good offices to bring the existing contest to a termination. The offer, not being accepted by Spain on a basis which we believed could be received by Cuba, was withdrawn. It is hoped that the good offices of the United States may yet prove advantageous for the settlement of this unhappy strife. Meanwhile a number of illegal expeditions against Cuba have been broken up. It has been the endeavor of the Administration to execute the neutrality laws in good faith, no matter how unpleasant the task, made so by the sufferings we have endured from lack of like good faith toward us by other nations.

On the 26th of March last the United States schooner *Lizzie Major* was arrested on the high seas by a Spanish frigate, and two passengers taken from it and carried as prisoners to Cuba. Representations of these facts were made to the Spanish Government as soon as official information of them reached Washington. The two passengers were set at liberty, and the Spanish Government assured the United States that the captain of the frigate in making the capture had acted without law, that he had been reprimanded for the irregularity of his conduct, and that the Spanish authorities in Cuba would not sanction any act that could violate the rights or treat with disrespect the sovereignty of this nation.

The question of the seizure of the brig *Mary Lowell* at one of the Bahama Islands by Spanish authorities is now the subject of correspondence between this Government and those of Spain and Great Britain.

The Captain-General of Cuba about May last issued a proclamation authorizing search to be made of vessels on the high seas. Immediate remonstrance was made against this, whereupon the Captain-General issued a new proclamation limiting the right of search to vessels of the United States so far as authorized under the treaty of 1795. This proclamation, however, was immediately withdrawn.

I have always felt that the most intimate relations should be cultivated between the Republic of the United States and all independent nations on this continent. It may be well worth considering whether new treaties between us and them may not be profitably entered into, to secure more intimate relations—friendly, commercial, and otherwise.

The subject of an interoceanic canal to connect the Atlantic and Pacific oceans through the Isthmus of Darien is one in which commerce is greatly interested. Instructions have been given to our minister to the Republic of the United States of Colombia to endeavor to obtain authority for a survey by this Government, in order to determine the practicability of such an undertaking, and a charter for the right of way to build, by private enterprise, such a work, if the survey proves it to be practicable.

In order to comply with the agreement of the United States as to a mixed commission at Lima for the adjustment of claims, it became necessary to send a commissioner and secretary to Lima in August last. No appropriation having been made by Congress for this purpose, it is now asked that one be made covering the past and future expenses of the commission.

The good offices of the United States to bring about a peace between Spain and the South American Republics with which she is at war having been accepted by Spain, Peru, and Chile, a congress has been invited to be held in Washington during the present winter.

A grant has been given to Europeans of an exclusive right of transit over the territory of Nicaragua, to which Costa Rica has given its assent, which, it is alleged, conflicts with vested rights of citizens of the United States. The Department of State has now this subject under consideration.

The minister of Peru having made representations that there was a state of war between Peru and Spain, and that Spain was constructing, in and near New York, thirty gunboats, which might be used by Spain in such a way as to relieve the naval force at Cuba, so as to operate against Peru, orders were given to prevent their departure. No further steps having been taken by the representative of the Peruvian Government to prevent the departure of these vessels, and I not feeling authorized to detain the property of a nation with which we are at peace on a mere Executive order, the matter has been referred to the courts to decide.

The conduct of the war between the allies and the Republic of Paraguay has made the intercourse with that country so difficult that it has been deemed advisable to withdraw our representative from there.

Toward the close of the last Administration a convention was signed at London for the settlement of all outstanding claims between Great Britain and the United States, which failed to receive the advice and consent of the Senate to its ratification. The time and the circumstances attending the negotiation of that treaty were unfavorable to its acceptance by the people of the United States, and its provisions were wholly inadequate for the settlement of the grave wrongs that had been sustained by this Government, as well as by its citizens. The injuries resulting to the United States by reason of the course adopted by Great Britain during our late civil war—in the increased rates of insurance; in the diminution of exports and imports, and other obstructions to domestic industry and production; in its effect upon the foreign commerce of the country; in the decrease and transfer to Great Britain of our commercial marine; in the prolongation of the war and the increased cost (both in treasure and in lives) of its suppression—could not be adjusted and satisfied as ordinary commercial claims, which continually arise between commercial nations; and yet the convention treated them simply as such ordinary claims, from which they differ more widely in the gravity of their character than in the magnitude of their amount, great even as is that difference. Not a word was found in the treaty, and not an inference could be drawn from it, to remove the sense of the unfriendliness of the course of Great Britain in our struggle for existence, which had so deeply and universally impressed itself upon the people of this country.

Believing that a convention thus misconceived in its scope and inadequate in its provisions would not have produced the hearty, cordial settlement of pending questions, which alone is consistent with the relations which I desire to have firmly established between the United States and Great Britain, I regarded the action of the Senate in rejecting the treaty to have been wisely taken in the interest of peace and as a necessary step in the direction of a perfect and cordial friendship between the two countries. A sensitive people, conscious of their power, are more at ease under a great wrong wholly unatoned than under the restraint of a settlement which satisfies neither their ideas of justice nor their grave sense of the grievance they have sustained. The rejection of the treaty was followed by a state of public feeling on both sides which I thought not favorable to an immediate attempt at renewed negotiations. I accordingly so instructed the minister of the United States to Great Britain, and found that my views in this regard were shared by Her Majesty's ministers. I hope that the time may soon arrive when the two Governments can approach the solution of this momentous question with an appreciation of what is due to the rights, dignity, and honor of each, and with the determination not only to remove the causes of complaint in the past, but to lay the foundation of a broad principle of public law which will prevent future differences and tend to firm and continued peace and friendship.

This is now the only grave question which the United States has with any foreign nation.

The question of renewing a treaty for reciprocal trade between the United States and the British Provinces on this continent has not been favorably considered by the Administration. The advantages of such a treaty would be wholly in favor of the British producer. Except, possibly, a few engaged in the trade between the two sections, no citizen of the United States would be benefited by reciprocity. Our internal taxation would prove a protection to the British producer almost equal to the protection which our manufacturers now receive from the tariff. Some arrangement, however, for the regulation of commercial intercourse between the United States and the Dominion of Canada may be desirable.

The commission for adjusting the claims of the "Hudsons Bay and Puget Sound Agricultural Company" upon the United States has terminated its labors. The award of $650,000 has been made and all rights and titles of the company on the territory of the United States have been extinguished. Deeds for the property of the company have been delivered. An appropriation by Congress to meet this sum is asked.

The commissioners for determining the northwestern land boundary between the United States and the British possessions under the treaty of 1856 have completed their labors, and the commission has been dissolved.

In conformity with the recommendation of Congress, a proposition was early made to the British Government to abolish the mixed courts created under the treaty of April 7, 1862, for the suppression of the slave trade. The subject is still under negotiation.

It having come to my knowledge that a corporate company, organized under British laws, proposed to land upon the shores of the United States and to operate there a submarine cable, under a concession from His Majesty the Emperor of the French of an exclusive right for twenty years of telegraphic communication between the shores of France and the United States, with the very objectionable feature of subjecting all messages conveyed thereby to the scrutiny and control of the French Government, I caused the French and British legations at Washington to be made acquainted with the probable policy of Congress on this subject, as foreshadowed by the bill which passed the Senate in March last. This drew from the representatives of the company an agreement to accept as the basis of their operations the provisions of that bill, or of such other enactment on the subject as might be passed during the approaching session of Congress; also, to use their influence to secure from the French Government a modification of their concession, so as to permit the landing upon French soil of any cable belonging to any company incorporated by the authority of the United States or of any State in the Union, and, on their part, not to oppose the establishment of any such cable. In consideration of this agreement I directed the withdrawal of all opposition by the United States authorities to the landing of the cable and to the working of it until the meeting of Congress. I regret to say that there has been no modification made in the company's concession, nor, so far as I can learn, have they attempted to secure one. Their concession excludes the capital and the citizens of the United States from competition upon the shores of France. I recommend legislation to protect the rights of citizens of the United States, as well as the dignity and sovereignty of the nation, against such an assumption. I shall also endeavor to secure, by negotiation, an abandonment of the principle of monopolies in ocean telegraphic cables. Copies of this correspondence are herewith furnished.

The unsettled political condition of other countries, less fortunate than our own, sometimes induces their citizens to come to the United States for the sole purpose of becoming naturalized. Having secured this, they return to their native country and reside there, without disclosing their change of allegiance. They accept official positions of trust or honor, which can only be held by citizens of their native land; they journey under passports describing them as such citizens; and it is only when civil discord, after perhaps years of quiet, threatens their persons or their property, or when their native state drafts them into its military service, that the fact of their change of allegiance is made known. They reside permanently away from the United States, they contribute nothing to its revenues, they avoid the duties of its citizenship, and they only make themselves known by a claim of protection. I have directed the diplomatic and consular officers of the United States to scrutinize carefully all such claims for protection. The citizen of the United States, whether native or adopted, who discharges his duty to his country, is entitled to its complete protection. While I have a voice in the direction of affairs

I shall not consent to imperil this sacred right by conferring it upon fictitious or fraudulent claimants.

On the accession of the present Administration it was found that the minister for North Germany had made propositions for the negotiation of a convention for the protection of emigrant passengers, to which no response had been given. It was concluded that to be effectual all the maritime powers engaged in the trade should join in such a measure. Invitations have been extended to the cabinets of London, Paris, Florence, Berlin, Brussels, The Hague, Copenhagen, and Stockholm to empower their representatives at Washington to simultaneously enter into negotiations and to conclude with the United States conventions identical in form, making uniform regulations as to the construction of the parts of vessels to be devoted to the use of emigrant passengers, as to the quality and quantity of food, as to the medical treatment of the sick, and as to the rules to be observed during the voyage, in order to secure ventilation, to promote health, to prevent intrusion, and to protect the females; and providing for the establishment of tribunals in the several countries for enforcing such regulations by summary process.

Your attention is respectfully called to the law regulating the tariff on Russian hemp, and to the question whether to fix the charges on Russian hemp higher than they are fixed upon manila is not a violation of our treaty with Russia placing her products upon the same footing with those of the most favored nations.

Our manufactures are increasing with wonderful rapidity under the encouragement which they now receive. With the improvements in machinery already effected, and still increasing, causing machinery to take the place of skilled labor to a large extent, our imports of many articles must fall off largely within a very few years. Fortunately, too, manufactures are not confined to a few localities, as formerly, and it is to be hoped will become more and more diffused, making the interest in them equal in all sections. They give employment and support to hundreds of thousands of people at home, and retain with us the means which otherwise would be shipped abroad. The extension of railroads in Europe and the East is bringing into competition with our agricultural products like products of other countries. Self-interest, if not self-preservation, therefore dictates caution against disturbing any industrial interest of the country. It teaches us also the necessity of looking to other markets for the sale of our surplus. Our neighbors south of us, and China and Japan, should receive our special attention. It will be the endeavor of the Administration to cultivate such relations with all these nations as to entitle us to their confidence and make it their interest, as well as ours, to establish better commercial relations.

Through the agency of a more enlightened policy than that heretofore pursued toward China, largely due to the sagacity and efforts of one of our own distinguished citizens, the world is about to commence largely increased relations with that populous and hitherto exclusive nation. As the United States have been the initiators in this new policy, so they should be the most earnest in showing their good faith in making it a success.   In this connection I advise such legislation as will forever preclude the enslavement of the Chinese upon our soil under the name of coolies, and also prevent American vessels from engaging in the transportation of coolies to any country tolerating the system.   I also recommend that the mission to China be raised to one of the first class.

On my assuming the responsible duties of Chief Magistrate of the United States it was with the conviction that three things were essential to its peace, prosperity, and fullest development.   First among these is strict integrity in fulfilling all our obligations; second, to secure protection to the person and property of the citizen of the United States in each and every portion of our common country, wherever he may choose to move, without reference to original nationality, religion, color, or politics, demanding of him only obedience to the laws and proper respect for the rights of others; third, union of all the States, with equal rights, indestructible by any constitutional means.

To secure the first of these, Congress has taken two essential steps: First, in declaring by joint resolution that the public debt shall be paid, principal and interest, in coin; and, second, by providing the means for paying.   Providing the means, however, could not secure the object desired without a proper administration of the laws for the collection of the revenues and an economical disbursement of them.   To this subject the Administration has most earnestly addressed itself, with results, I hope, satisfactory to the country.   There has been no hesitation in changing officials in order to secure an efficient execution of the laws, sometimes, too, when, in a mere party view, undesirable political results were likely to follow; nor any hesitation in sustaining efficient officials against remonstrances wholly political.

It may be well to mention here the embarrassment possible to arise from leaving on the statute books the so-called "tenure-of-office acts," and to earnestly recommend their total repeal.   It could not have been the intention of the framers of the Constitution, when providing that appointments made by the President should receive the consent of the Senate, that the latter should have the power to retain in office persons placed there by Federal appointment against the will of the President. The law is inconsistent with a faithful and efficient administration of the Government.   What faith can an Executive put in officials forced upon him, and those, too, whom he has suspended for reason?   How will such officials be likely to serve an Administration which they know does not trust them?

For the second requisite to our growth and prosperity time and a firm but humane administration of existing laws (amended from time to time as they may prove ineffective or prove harsh and unnecessary) are probably all that are required.

The third can not be attained by special legislation, but must be regarded as fixed by the Constitution itself and gradually acquiesced in by force of public opinion.

From the foundation of the Government to the present the manage-ment of the original inhabitants of this continent—the Indians—has been a subject of embarrassment and expense, and has been attended with continuous robberies, murders, and wars. From my own experience upon the frontiers and in Indian countries, I do not hold either legisla-tion or the conduct of the whites who come most in contact with the Indian blameless for these hostilities. The past, however, can not be undone, and the question must be met as we now find it. I have attempted a new policy toward these wards of the nation (they can not be regarded in any other light than as wards), with fair results so far as tried, and which I hope will be attended ultimately with great success. The Society of Friends is well known as having succeeded in living in peace with the Indians in the early settlement of Pennsylvania, while their white neighbors of other sects in other sections were con-stantly embroiled. They are also known for their opposition to all strife, violence, and war, and are generally noted for their strict integrity and fair dealings. These considerations induced me to give the management of a few reservations of Indians to them and to throw the burden of the selection of agents upon the society itself. The result has proven most satisfactory. It will be found more fully set forth in the report of the Commissioner of Indian Affairs. For superintendents and Indian agents not on the reservations, officers of the Army were selected. The rea-sons for this are numerous. Where Indian agents are sent, there, or near there, troops must be sent also. The agent and the commander of troops are independent of each other, and are subject to orders from different Departments of the Government. The army officer holds a position for life; the agent, one at the will of the President. The former is person-ally interested in living in harmony with the Indian and in establishing a permanent peace, to the end that some portion of his life may be spent within the limits of civilized society; the latter has no such personal interest. Another reason is an economic one; and still another, the hold which the Government has upon a life officer to secure a faithful discharge of duties in carrying out a given policy.

The building of railroads, and the access thereby given to all the agri-cultural and mineral regions of the country, is rapidly bringing civilized settlements into contact with all the tribes of Indians. No matter what ought to be the relations between such settlements and the aborigines, the fact is they do not harmonize well, and one or the other has to give way in the end. A system which looks to the extinction of a race is too horrible for a nation to adopt without entailing upon itself the wrath of all Christendom and engendering in the citizen a disregard for human life and the rights of others, dangerous to society.   I see no substitute for such a system, except in placing all the Indians on large reservations, as rapidly as it can be done, and giving them absolute protection there. As soon as they are fitted for it they should be induced to take their lands in severalty and to set up Territorial governments for their own protection.   For full details on this subject I call your special attention to the reports of the Secretary of the Interior and the Commissioner of Indian Affairs.

The report of the Secretary of War shows the expenditures of the War Department for the year ending June 30, 1869, to be $80,644,042, of which $23,882,310 was disbursed in the payment of debts contracted during the war, and is not chargeable to current army expenses.   His estimate of $34,531,031 for the expenses of the Army for the next fiscal year is as low as it is believed can be relied on.   The estimates of bureau officers have been carefully scrutinized, and reduced wherever it has been deemed practicable.   If, however, the condition of the country should be such by the beginning of the next fiscal year as to admit of a greater concentration of troops, the appropriation asked for will not be expended.

The appropriations estimated for river and harbor improvements and for fortifications are submitted separately.   Whatever amount Congress may deem proper to appropriate for these purposes will be expended.

The recommendation of the General of the Army that appropriations be made for the forts at Boston, Portland, New York, Philadelphia, New Orleans, and San Francisco, if for no other, is concurred in.   I also ask your special attention to the recommendation of the general commanding the Military Division of the Pacific for the sale of the seal islands of St. Paul and St. George, Alaska Territory, and suggest that it either be complied with or that legislation be had for the protection of the seal fisheries from which a revenue should be derived.

The report of the Secretary of War contains a synopsis of the reports of the heads of bureaus, of the commanders of military divisions, and of the districts of Virginia, Mississippi, and Texas, and the report of the General of the Army in full.   The recommendations therein contained have been well considered, and are submitted for your action.   I, however, call special attention to the recommendation of the Chief of Ordnance for the sale of arsenals and lands no longer of use to the Government; also, to the recommendation of the Secretary of War that the act of 3d March, 1869, prohibiting promotions and appointments in the staff corps of the Army, be repealed.   The extent of country to be garrisoned and the number of military posts to be occupied is the same with a reduced Army as with a large one.   The number of staff officers required is more dependent upon the latter than the former condition.

The report of the Secretary of the Navy accompanying this shows the condition of the Navy when this Administration came into office and the changes made since.   Strenuous efforts have been made to place as many vessels "in commission," or render them fit for service if required, as possible, and to substitute the sail for steam while cruising, thus materially reducing the expenses of the Navy and adding greatly to its efficiency. Looking to our future, I recommend a liberal, though not extravagant, policy toward this branch of the public service.

The report of the Postmaster-General furnishes a clear and comprehensive exhibit of the operations of the postal service and of the financial condition of the Post-Office Department. The ordinary postal revenues for the year ending the 30th of June, 1869, amounted to $18,344,510, and the expenditures to $23,698,131, showing an excess of expenditures over receipts of $5,353,620. The excess of expenditures over receipts for the previous year amounted to $6,437,992. The increase of revenues for 1869 over those of 1868 was $2,051,909, and the increase of expenditures was $967,538. The increased revenue in 1869 exceeded the increased revenue in 1868 by $996,336, and the increased expenditure in 1869 was $2,527,570 less than the increased expenditure in 1868, showing by comparison this gratifying feature of improvement, that while the increase of expenditures over the increase of receipts in 1868 was $2,439,535, the increase of receipts over the increase of expenditures in 1869 was $1,084,371.

Your attention is respectfully called to the recommendations made by the Postmaster-General for authority to change the rate of compensation to the main trunk railroad lines for their services in carrying the mails; for having post-route maps executed; for reorganizing and increasing the efficiency of the special-agency service; for increase of the mail service on the Pacific, and for establishing mail service, under the flag of the Union, on the Atlantic; and most especially do I call your attention to his recommendation for the total abolition of the franking privilege. This is an abuse from which no one receives a commensurate advantage; it reduces the receipts for postal service from 25 to 30 per cent and largely increases the service to be performed. The method by which postage should be paid upon public matter is set forth fully in the report of the Postmaster-General.

The report of the Secretary of the Interior shows that the quantity of public lands disposed of during the year ending the 30th of June, 1869, was 7,666,152 acres, exceeding that of the preceding year by 1,010,409 acres. Of this amount 2,899,544 acres were sold for cash and 2,737,365 acres entered under the homestead laws. The remainder was granted to aid in the construction of works of internal improvement, approved to the States as swamp land, and located with warrants and scrip. The cash receipts from all sources were $4,472,886, exceeding those of the preceding year $2,840,140.

During the last fiscal year 23,196 names were added to the pension rolls and 4,876 dropped therefrom, leaving at its close 187,963. The amount paid to pensioners, including the compensation of disbursing agents, was $28,422,884, an increase of $4,411,902 on that of the previous year. The munificence of Congress has been conspicuously manifested in its legislation for the soldiers and sailors who suffered in the recent struggle to maintain "that unity of government which makes us one people." The additions to the pension rolls of each successive year since the conclusion of hostilities result in a great degree from the repeated amendments of the act of the 14th of July, 1862, which extended its provisions to cases not falling within its original scope. The large outlay which is thus occasioned is further increased by the more liberal allowance bestowed since that date upon those who in the line of duty were wholly or permanently disabled. Public opinion has given an emphatic sanction to these measures of Congress, and it will be conceded that no part of our public burden is more cheerfully borne than that which is imposed by this branch of the service. It necessitates for the next fiscal year, in addition to the amount justly chargeable to the naval pension fund, an appropriation of $30,000,000.

During the year ending the 30th of September, 1869, the Patent Office issued 13,762 patents, and its receipts were $686,389, being $213,926 more than the expenditures.

I would respectfully call your attention to the recommendation of the Secretary of the Interior for uniting the duties of supervising the education of freedmen with the other duties devolving upon the Commissioner of Education.

If it is the desire of Congress to make the census which must be taken during the year 1870 more complete and perfect than heretofore, I would suggest early action upon any plan that may be agreed upon. As Congress at the last session appointed a committee to take into consideration such measures as might be deemed proper in reference to the census and report a plan, I desist from saying more.

I recommend to your favorable consideration the claims of the Agricultural Bureau for liberal apppropriations. In a country so diversified in climate and soil as ours, and with a population so largely dependent upon agriculture, the benefits that can be conferred by properly fostering this Bureau are incalculable.

I desire respectfully to call the attention of Congress to the inadequate salaries of a number of the most important offices of the Government. In this message I will not enumerate them, but will specify only the justices of the Supreme Court. No change has been made in their salaries for fifteen years. Within that time the labors of the court have largely increased and the expenses of living have at least doubled. During the same time Congress has twice found it necessary to increase largely the compensation of its own members, and the duty which it owes to another department of the Government deserves, and will undoubtedly receive, its due consideration.

There are many subjects not alluded to in this message which might with propriety be introduced, but I abstain, believing that your patriotism and statesmanship will suggest the topics and the legislation most conducive to the interests of the whole people. On my part I promise a rigid adherence to the laws and their strict enforcement.

SECOND ANNUAL MESSAGE.

EXECUTIVE MANSION, *December 5, 1870.*

To the Senate and House of Representatives:

A year of peace and general prosperity to this nation has passed since the last assembling of Congress. We have, through a kind Providence, been blessed with abundant crops, and have been spared from complications and war with foreign nations. In our midst comparative harmony has been restored. It is to be regretted, however, that a free exercise of the elective franchise has by violence and intimidation been denied to citizens in exceptional cases in several of the States lately in rebellion, and the verdict of the people has thereby been reversed. The States of Virginia, Mississippi, and Texas have been restored to representation in our national councils. Georgia, the only State now without representation, may confidently be expected to take her place there also at the beginning of the new year, and then, let us hope, will be completed the work of reconstruction. With an acquiescence on the part of the whole people in the national obligation to pay the public debt created as the price of our Union, the pensions to our disabled soldiers and sailors and their widows and orphans, and in the changes to the Constitution which have been made necessary by a great rebellion, there is no reason why we should not advance in material prosperity and happiness as no other nation ever did after so protracted and devastating a war.

Soon after the existing war broke out in Europe the protection of the United States minister in Paris was invoked in favor of North Germans domiciled in French territory. Instructions were issued to grant the protection. This has been followed by an extension of American protection to citizens of Saxony, Hesse and Saxe-Coburg, Gotha, Colombia, Portugal, Uruguay, the Dominican Republic, Ecuador, Chile, Paraguay, and Venezuela in Paris. The charge was an onerous one, requiring constant and severe labor, as well as the exercise of patience, prudence, and good judgment. It has been performed to the entire satisfaction of this Government, and, as I am officially informed, equally so to the satisfaction of the Government of North Germany.

As soon as I learned that a republic had been proclaimed at Paris and that the people of France had acquiesced in the change, the minister of the United States was directed by telegraph to recognize it and to tender my congratulations and those of the people of the United States. The reestablishment in France of a system of government disconnected with the dynastic traditions of Europe appeared to be a proper subject for the felicitations of Americans. Should the present struggle result in attaching the hearts of the French to our simpler forms of representative government, it will be a subject of still further satisfaction to our people. While we make no effort to impose our institutions upon the inhabitants of other countries, and while we adhere to our traditional neutrality in civil contests elsewhere, we can not be indifferent to the spread of American political ideas in a great and highly civilized country like France.

We were asked by the new Government to use our good offices, jointly with those of European powers, in the interests of peace. Answer was made that the established policy and the true interests of the United States forbade them to interfere in European questions jointly with European powers. I ascertained, informally and unofficially, that the Government of North Germany was not then disposed to listen to such representations from any power, and though earnestly wishing to see the blessings of peace restored to the belligerents, with all of whom the United States are on terms of friendship, I declined on the part of this Government to take a step which could only result in injury to our true interests without advancing the object for which our intervention was invoked. Should the time come when the action of the United States can hasten the return of peace by a single hour, that action will be heartily taken. I deemed it prudent, in view of the number of persons of German and French birth living in the United States, to issue, soon after official notice of a state of war had been received from both belligerents, a proclamation defining the duties of the United States as a neutral and the obligations of persons residing within their territory to observe their laws and the laws of nations. This proclamation was followed by others, as circumstances seemed to call for them. The people, thus acquainted in advance of their duties and obligations, have assisted in preventing violations of the neutrality of the United States.

It is not understood that the condition of the insurrection in Cuba has materially changed since the close of the last session of Congress. In an early stage of the contest the authorities of Spain inaugurated a system of arbitrary arrests, of close confinement, and of military trial and execution of persons suspected of complicity with the insurgents, and of summary embargo of their properties, and sequestration of their revenues by executive warrant. Such proceedings, so far as they affected the persons or property of citizens of the United States, were in violation of the provisions of the treaty of 1795 between the United States and Spain.

Representations of injuries resulting to several persons claiming to be citizens of the United States by reason of such violations were made to the Spanish Government. From April, 1869, to June last the Spanish minister at Washington had been clothed with a limited power to aid in redressing such wrongs. That power was found to be withdrawn, "in view," as it was said, "of the favorable situation in which the island of Cuba" then "was," which, however, did not lead to a revocation or suspension of the extraordinary and arbitrary functions exercised by the executive power in Cuba, and we were obliged to make our complaints at Madrid. In the negotiations thus opened, and still pending there, the United States only claimed that for the future the rights secured to their citizens by treaty should be respected in Cuba, and that as to the past a joint tribunal should be established in the United States with full jurisdiction over all such claims. Before such an impartial tribunal each claimant would be required to prove his case. On the other hand, Spain would be at liberty to traverse every material fact, and thus complete equity would be done. A case which at one time threatened seriously to affect the relations between the United States and Spain has already been disposed of in this way. The claim of the owners of the *Colonel Lloyd Aspinwall* for the illegal seizure and detention of that vessel was referred to arbitration by mutual consent, and has resulted in an award to the United States, for the owners, of the sum of $19,702.50 in gold. Another and long-pending claim of like nature, that of the whaleship *Canada*, has been disposed of by friendly arbitrament during the present year. It was referred, by the joint consent of Brazil and the United States, to the decision of Sir Edward Thornton, Her Britannic Majesty's minister at Washington, who kindly undertook the laborious task of examining the voluminous mass of correspondence and testimony submitted by the two Governments, and awarded to the United States the sum of $100,740.09 in gold, which has since been paid by the Imperial Government. These recent examples show that the mode which the United States have proposed to Spain for adjusting the pending claims is just and feasible, and that it may be agreed to by either nation without dishonor. It is to be hoped that this moderate demand may be acceded to by Spain without further delay. Should the pending negotiations, unfortunately and unexpectedly, be without result, it will then become my duty to communicate that fact to Congress and invite its action on the subject.

The long-deferred peace conference between Spain and the allied South American Republics has been inaugurated in Washington under the auspices of the United States. Pursuant to the recommendation contained in the resolution of the House of Representatives of the 17th of December, 1866, the executive department of the Government offered its friendly offices for the promotion of peace and harmony between Spain and the allied Republics. Hesitations and obstacles occurred to the acceptance of the offer. Ultimately, however, a conference was arranged, and was opened in this city on the 29th of October last, at which I authorized the Secretary of State to preside. It was attended by the ministers of Spain, Peru, Chile, and Ecuador.   In consequence of the absence of a representative from Bolivia, the conference was adjourned until the attendance of a plenipotentiary from that Republic could be secured or other measures could be adopted toward compassing its objects.

The allied and other Republics of Spanish origin on this continent may see in this fact a new proof of our sincere interest in their welfare, of our desire to see them blessed with good governments, capable of maintaining order and of preserving their respective territorial integrity, and of our sincere wish to extend our own commercial and social relations with them.   The time is not probably far distant when, in the natural course of events, the European political connection with this continent will cease.   Our policy should be shaped, in view of this probability, so as to ally the commercial interests of the Spanish American States more closely to our own, and thus give the United States all the preeminence and all the advantage which Mr. Monroe, Mr. Adams, and Mr. Clay contemplated when they proposed to join in the congress of Panama.

During the last session of Congress a treaty for the annexation of the Republic of San Domingo to the United States failed to receive the requisite two-thirds vote of the Senate.   I was thoroughly convinced then that the best interests of this country, commercially and materially, demanded its ratification.   Time has only confirmed me in this view.   I now firmly believe that the moment it is known that the United States have entirely abandoned the project of accepting as a part of its territory the island of San Domingo a free port will be negotiated for by European nations in the Bay of Samana.   A large commercial city will spring up, to which we will be tributary without receiving corresponding benefits, and then will be seen the folly of our rejecting so great a prize.   The Government of San Domingo has voluntarily sought this annexation.   It is a weak power, numbering probably less than 120,000 souls, and yet possessing one of the richest territories under the sun, capable of supporting a population of 10,000,000 people in luxury.   The people of San Domingo are not capable of maintaining themselves in their present condition, and must look for outside support.   They yearn for the protection of our free institutions and laws, our progress and civilization.   Shall we refuse them?

The acquisition of San Domingo is desirable because of its geographical position.   It commands the entrance to the Caribbean Sea and the Isthmus transit of commerce.   It possesses the richest soil, best and most capacious harbors, most salubrious climate, and the most valuable products of the forests, mine, and soil of any of the West India Islands.   Its possession by us will in a few years build up a coastwise commerce of immense magnitude, which will go far toward restoring to us our lost merchant marine.   It will give to us those articles which we consume so largely and do not produce, thus equalizing our exports and imports. In case of foreign war it will give us command of all the islands referred to, and thus prevent an enemy from ever again possessing himself of rendezvous upon our very coast. At present our coast trade between the States bordering on the Atlantic and those bordering on the Gulf of Mexico is cut into by the Bahamas and the Antilles. Twice we must, as it were, pass through foreign countries to get by sea from Georgia to the west coast of Florida.

San Domingo, with a stable government, under which her immense resources can be developed, will give remunerative wages to tens of thousands of laborers not now upon the island. This labor will take advantage of every available means of transportation to abandon the adjacent islands and seek the blessings of freedom and its sequence—each inhabitant receiving the reward of his own labor. Porto Rico and Cuba will have to abolish slavery, as a measure of self-preservation, to retain their laborers.

San Domingo will become a large consumer of the products of Northern farms and manufactories. The cheap rate at which her citizens can be furnished with food, tools, and machinery will make it necessary that contiguous islands should have the same advantages in order to compete in the production of sugar, coffee, tobacco, tropical fruits, etc. This will open to us a still wider market for our products. The production of our own supply of these articles will cut off more than one hundred millions of our annual imports, besides largely increasing our exports. With such a picture it is easy to see how our large debt abroad is ultimately to be extinguished. With a balance of trade against us (including interest on bonds held by foreigners and money spent by our citizens traveling in foreign lands) equal to the entire yield of the precious metals in this country, it is not so easy to see how this result is to be otherwise accomplished.

The acquisition of San Domingo is an adherence to the " Monroe doctrine;" it is a measure of national protection; it is asserting our just claim to a controlling influence over the great commercial traffic soon to flow from west to east by way of the Isthmus of Darien; it is to build up our merchant marine; it is to furnish new markets for the products of our farms, shops, and manufactories; it is to make slavery insupportable in Cuba and Porto Rico at once, and ultimately so in Brazil; it is to settle the unhappy condition of Cuba and end an exterminating conflict; it is to provide honest means of paying our honest debts without overtaxing the people; it is to furnish our citizens with the necessaries of everyday life at cheaper rates than ever before; and it is, in fine, a rapid stride toward that greatness which the intelligence, industry, and enterprise of the citizens of the United States entitle this country to assume among nations.

In view of the importance of this question, I earnestly urge upon Congress early action expressive of its views as to the best means of acquiring San Domingo. My suggestion is that by joint resolution of the two Houses of Congress the Executive be authorized to appoint a commission to negotiate a treaty with the authorities of San Domingo for the acquisition of that island, and that an appropriation be made to defray the expenses of such a commission. The question may then be determined, either by the action of the Senate upon the treaty or the joint action of the two Houses of Congress upon a resolution of annexation, as in the case of the acquisition of Texas. So convinced am I of the advantages to flow from the acquisition of San Domingo, and of the great disadvantages—I might almost say calamities—to flow from nonacquisition, that I believe the subject has only to be investigated to be approved.

It is to be regretted that our representations in regard to the injurious effects, especially upon the revenue of the United States, of the policy of the Mexican Government in exempting from impost duties a large tract of its territory on our borders have not only been fruitless, but that it is even proposed in that country to extend the limits within which the privilege adverted to has hitherto been enjoyed. The expediency of taking into your serious consideration proper measures for countervailing the policy referred to will, it is presumed, engage your earnest attention.

It is the obvious interest, especially of neighboring nations, to provide against impunity to those who may have committed high crimes within their borders and who may have sought refuge abroad. For this purpose extradition treaties have been concluded with several of the Central American Republics, and others are in progress.

The sense of Congress is desired, as early as may be convenient, upon the proceedings of the commission on claims against Venezuela, as communicated in my messages of March 16, 1869, March 1, 1870, and March 31, 1870. It has not been deemed advisable to distribute any of the money which has been received from that Government until Congress shall have acted on the subject.

The massacres of French and Russian residents at Tien-Tsin, under circumstances of great barbarity, was supposed by some to have been premeditated, and to indicate a purpose among the populace to exterminate foreigners in the Chinese Empire. The evidence fails to establish such a supposition, but shows a complicity between the local authorities and the mob. The Government at Peking, however, seems to have been disposed to fulfill its treaty obligations so far as it was able to do so. Unfortunately, the news of the war between the German States and France reached China soon after the massacre. It would appear that the popular mind became possessed with the idea that this contest, extending to Chinese waters, would neutralize the Christian influence and power, and that the time was coming when the superstitious masses might expel all foreigners and restore mandarin influence. Anticipating trouble from this cause, I invited France and North Germany to make an authorized suspension of hostilities in the East (where they were temporarily suspended by act of the commanders), and to act together for the future protection in China of the lives and properties of Americans and Europeans.

Since the adjournment of Congress the ratifications of the treaty with Great Britain for abolishing the mixed courts for the suppression of the slave trade have been exchanged. It is believed that the slave trade is now confined to the eastern coast of Africa, whence the slaves are taken to Arabian markets.

The ratifications of the naturalization convention between Great Britain and the United States have also been exchanged during the recess, and thus a long-standing dispute between the two Governments has been settled in accordance with the principles always contended for by the United States.

In April last, while engaged in locating a military reservation near Pembina, a corps of engineers discovered that the commonly received boundary line between the United States and the British possessions at that place is about 4,700 feet south of the true position of the forty-ninth parallel, and that the line, when run on what is now supposed to be the true position of that parallel, would leave the fort of the Hudsons Bay Company at Pembina within the territory of the United States. This information being communicated to the British Government, I was requested to consent, and did consent, that the British occupation of the fort of the Hudsons Bay Company should continue for the present. I deem it important, however, that this part of the boundary line should be definitely fixed by a joint commission of the two Governments, and I submit herewith estimates of the expense of such a commission on the part of the United States and recommend that an appropriation be made for that purpose. The land boundary has already been fixed and marked from the summit of the Rocky Mountains to the Georgian Bay. It should now be in like manner marked from the Lake of the Woods to the summit of the Rocky Mountains.

I regret to say that no conclusion has been reached for the adjustment of the claims against Great Britain growing out of the course adopted by that Government during the rebellion. The cabinet of London, so far as its views have been expressed, does not appear to be willing to concede that Her Majesty's Government was guilty of any negligence, or did or permitted any act during the war by which the United States has just cause of complaint. Our firm and unalterable convictions are directly the reverse. I therefore recommend to Congress to authorize the appointment of a commission to take proof of the amount and the ownership of these several claims, on notice to the representative of Her Majesty at Washington, and that authority be given for the settlement of these claims by the United States, so that the Government shall have the ownership of the private claims, as well as the responsible control of all the demands against Great Britain. It can not be necessary to add that whenever Her Majesty's Government shall entertain a desire for a full and friendly adjustment of these claims the United States will enter upon their consideration with an earnest desire for a conclusion consistent with the honor and dignity of both nations.

The course pursued by the Canadian authorities toward the fishermen of the United States during the past season has not been marked by a friendly feeling. By the first article of the convention of 1818 between Great Britain and the United States it was agreed that the inhabitants of the United States should have forever, in common with British subjects, the right of taking fish in certain waters therein defined. In the waters not included in the limits named in the convention (within 3 miles of parts of the British coast) it has been the custom for many years to give to intruding fishermen of the United States a reasonable warning of their violation of the technical rights of Great Britain. The Imperial Government is understood to have delegated the whole or a share of its jurisdiction or control of these inshore fishing grounds to the colonial authority known as the Dominion of Canada, and this semi-independent but irresponsible agent has exercised its delegated powers in an unfriendly way. Vessels have been seized without notice or warning, in violation of the custom previously prevailing, and have been taken into the colonial ports, their voyages broken up, and the vessels condemned. There is reason to believe that this unfriendly and vexatious treatment was designed to bear harshly upon the hardy fishermen of the United States, with a view to political effect upon this Government. The statutes of the Dominion of Canada assume a still broader and more untenable jurisdiction over the vessels of the United States. They authorize officers or persons to bring vessels hovering within 3 marine miles of any of the coasts, bays, creeks, or harbors of Canada into port, to search the cargo, to examine the master on oath touching the cargo and voyage, and to inflict upon him a heavy pecuniary penalty if true answers are not given; and if such a vessel is found "preparing to fish" within 3 marine miles of any of such coasts, bays, creeks, or harbors without a license, or after the expiration of the period named in the last license granted to it, they provide that the vessel, with her tackle, etc., shall be forfeited. It is not known that any condemnations have been made under this statute. Should the authorities of Canada attempt to enforce it, it will become my duty to take such steps as may be necessary to protect the rights of the citizens of the United States.

It has been claimed by Her Majesty's officers that the fishing vessels of the United States have no right to enter the open ports of the British possessions in North America, except for the purposes of shelter and repairing damages, of purchasing wood and obtaining water; that they have no right to enter at the British custom-houses or to trade there except in the purchase of wood and water, and that they must depart within twenty-four hours after notice to leave. It is not known that any seizure of a fishing vessel carrying the flag of the United States has been made under this claim. So far as the claim is founded on an alleged construction of the convention of 1818, it can not be acquiesced in by the United States. It is hoped that it will not be insisted on by Her Majesty's Government.

During the conferences which preceded the negotiation of the convention of 1818 the British commissioners proposed to expressly exclude the fishermen of the United States from "the privilege of carrying on trade with any of His Britannic Majesty's subjects residing within the limits assigned for their use;" and also that it should not be "lawful for the vessels of the United States engaged in said fishery to have on board any goods, wares, or merchandise whatever, except such as may be necessary for the prosecution of their voyages to and from the said fishing grounds: and any vessel of the United States which shall contravene this regulation may be seized, condemned, and confiscated, with her cargo."

This proposition, which is identical with the construction now put upon the language of the convention, was emphatically rejected by the American commissioners, and thereupon was abandoned by the British plenipotentiaries, and Article I, as it stands in the convention, was substituted.

If, however, it be said that this claim is founded on provincial or colonial statutes, and not upon the convention, this Government can not but regard them as unfriendly, and in contravention of the spirit, if not of the letter, of the treaty, for the faithful execution of which the Imperial Government is alone responsible.

Anticipating that an attempt may possibly be made by the Canadian authorities in the coming season to repeat their unneighborly acts toward our fishermen, I recommend you to confer upon the Executive the power to suspend by proclamation the operation of the laws authorizing the transit of goods, wares, and merchandise in bond across the territory of the United States to Canada, and, further, should such an extreme measure become necessary, to suspend the operation of any laws whereby the vessels of the Dominion of Canada are permitted to enter the waters of the United States.

A like unfriendly disposition has been manifested on the part of Canada in the maintenance of a claim of right to exclude the citizens of the United States from the navigation of the St. Lawrence. This river constitutes a natural outlet to the ocean for eight States, with an aggregate population of about 17,600,000 inhabitants, and with an aggregate tonnage of 651,367 tons upon the waters which discharge into it. The foreign commerce of our ports on these waters is open to British competition, and the major part of it is done in British bottoms.

If the American seamen be excluded from this natural avenue to the ocean, the monopoly of the direct commerce of the lake ports with the Atlantic would be in foreign hands, their vessels on transatlantic voyages having an access to our lake ports which would be denied to American vessels on similar voyages. To state such a proposition is to refute its justice.

During the Administration of Mr. John Quincy Adams Mr. Clay unanswerably demonstrated the natural right of the citizens of the United States to the navigation of this river, claiming that the act of the congress of Vienna in opening the Rhine and other rivers to all nations showed the judgment of European jurists and statesmen that the inhabitants of a country through which a navigable river passes have a natural right to enjoy the navigation of that river to and into the sea, even though passing through the territories of another power. This right does not exclude the coequal right of the sovereign possessing the territory through which the river debouches into the sea to make such regulations relative to the police of the navigation as may be reasonably necessary; but those regulations should be framed in a liberal spirit of comity, and should not impose needless burdens upon the commerce which has the right of transit. It has been found in practice more advantageous to arrange these regulations by mutual agreement. The United States are ready to make any reasonable arrangement as to the police of the St. Lawrence which may be suggested by Great Britain.

If the claim made by Mr. Clay was just when the population of States bordering on the shores of the Lakes was only 3,400,000, it now derives greater force and equity from the increased population, wealth, production, and tonnage of the States on the Canadian frontier. Since Mr. Clay advanced his argument in behalf of our right the principle for which he contended has been frequently, and by various nations, recognized by law or by treaty, and has been extended to several other great rivers. By the treaty concluded at Mayence in 1831 the Rhine was declared free from the point where it is first navigable into the sea. By the convention between Spain and Portugal concluded in 1835 the navigation of the Douro throughout its whole extent was made free for the subjects of both Crowns. In 1853 the Argentine Confederation by treaty threw open the free navigation of the Parana and the Uruguay to the merchant vessels of all nations. In 1856 the Crimean War was closed by a treaty which provided for the free navigation of the Danube. In 1858 Bolivia by treaty declared that it regarded the rivers Amazon and La Plata, in accordance with fixed principles of national law, as highways or channels opened by nature for the commerce of all nations. In 1859 the Paraguay was made free by treaty, and in December, 1866, the Emperor of Brazil by imperial decree declared the Amazon to be open to the frontier of Brazil to the merchant ships of all nations. The greatest living British authority on this subject, while asserting the abstract right of the British claim, says:

It seems difficult to deny that Great Britain may ground her refusal upon strict *law*, but it is equally difficult to deny, first, that in so doing she exercises harshly an extreme and hard law; secondly, that her conduct with respect to the navigation of the St. Lawrence is in glaring and discreditable inconsistency with her conduct with respect to the navigation of the Mississippi. On the ground that she possessed a small domain in which the Mississippi took its rise, she insisted on the right to navigate the entire volume of its waters. On the ground that she possesses both banks of the St. Lawrence, where it disembogues itself into the sea, she denies to the United States the right of navigation, though about one-half of the waters of Lakes Ontario, Erie, Huron, and Superior, and the whole of Lake Michigan, through which the river flows, are the property of the United States.

The whole nation is interested in securing cheap transportation from the agricultural States of the West to the Atlantic Seaboard. To the citizens of those States it secures a greater return for their labor; to the inhabitants of the seaboard it affords cheaper food; to the nation, an increase in the annual surplus of wealth. It is hoped that the Government of Great Britain will see the justice of abandoning the narrow and inconsistent claim to which her Canadian Provinces have urged her adherence.

Our depressed commerce is a subject to which I called your special attention at the last session, and suggested that we will in the future have to look more to the countries south of us, and to China and Japan, for its revival. Our representatives to all these Governments have exerted their influence to encourage trade between the United States and the countries to which they are accredited. But the fact exists that the carrying is done almost entirely in foreign bottoms, and while this state of affairs exists we can not control our due share of the commerce of the world; that between the Pacific States and China and Japan is about all the carrying trade now conducted in American vessels. I would recommend a liberal policy toward that line of American steamers—one that will insure its success, and even increased usefulness.

The cost of building iron vessels, the only ones that can compete with foreign ships in the carrying trade, is so much greater in the United States than in foreign countries that without some assistance from the Government they can not be successfully built here. There will be several propositions laid before Congress in the course of the present session looking to a remedy for this evil. Even if it should be at some cost to the National Treasury, I hope such encouragement will be given as will secure American shipping on the high seas and American shipbuilding at home.

The condition of the archives at the Department of State calls for the early action of Congress. The building now rented by that Department is a frail structure, at an inconvenient distance from the Executive Mansion and from the other Departments, is ill adapted to the purpose for which it is used, has not capacity to accommodate the archives, and is not fireproof. Its remote situation, its slender construction, and the absence of a supply of water in the neighborhood leave but little hope of safety for either the building or its contents in case of the accident of a fire. Its destruction would involve the loss of the rolls containing the original acts and resolutions of Congress, of the historic records of the Revolution and of the Confederation, of the whole series of diplomatic and consular archives since the adoption of the Constitution, and of the many other valuable records and papers left with that Department when it was the principal depository of the governmental archives.   I recommend an appropriation for the construction of a building for the Department of State.

I recommend to your consideration the propriety of transferring to the Department of the Interior, to which they seem more appropriately to belong, all powers and duties in relation to the Territories with which the Department of State is now charged by law or usage; and from the Interior Department to the War Department the Pension Bureau, so far as it regulates the payment of soldiers' pensions.   I would further recommend that the payment of naval pensions be transferred to one of the bureaus of the Navy Department.

The estimates for the expenses of the Government for the next fiscal year are $18,244,346.01 less than for the current one, but exceed the appropriations for the present year for the same items $8,972,127.56. In this estimate, however, is included $22,338,278.37 for public works heretofore begun under Congressional provision, and of which only so much is asked as Congress may choose to give.   The appropriation for the same works for the present fiscal year was $11,984,518.08.

The average value of gold, as compared with national currency, for the whole of the year 1869 was about 134, and for eleven months of 1870 the same relative value has been about 115.   The approach to a specie basis is very gratifying, but the fact can not be denied that the instability of the value of our currency is prejudicial to our prosperity, and tends to keep up prices, to the detriment of trade.   The evils of a depreciated and fluctuating currency are so great that now, when the premium on gold has fallen so much, it would seem that the time has arrived when by wise and prudent legislation Congress should look to a policy which would place our currency at par with gold at no distant day.

The tax collected from the people has been reduced more than $80,-000,000 per annum.   By steadiness in our present course there is no reason why in a few short years the national taxgatherer may not disappear from the door of the citizen almost entirely.   With the revenue stamp dispensed by postmasters in every community, a tax upon liquors of all sorts and tobacco in all its forms, and by a wise adjustment of the tariff, which will put a duty only upon those articles which we could dispense with, known as luxuries, and on those which we use more of than we produce, revenue enough may be raised after a few years of peace and consequent reduction of indebtedness to fulfill all our obligations.   A further reduction of expenses, in addition to a reduction of interest account, may be relied on to make this practicable.   Revenue reform, if it means this, has my hearty support.   If it implies a collection of all the revenue for the support of the Government, for the payment of principal and interest of the public debt, pensions, etc., by directly taxing the people, then I am against revenue reform, and confidently believe the people are with me.

If it means failure to provide the necessary means to defray all the expenses of Government, and thereby repudiation of the public debt and pensions, then I am still more opposed to such kind of revenue reform. Revenue reform has not been defined by any of its advocates to my knowledge, but seems to be accepted as something which is to supply every man's wants without any cost or effort on his part.

A true revenue reform can not be made in a day, but must be the work of national legislation and of time. As soon as the revenue can be dispensed with, all duty should be removed from coffee, tea and other articles of universal use not produced by ourselves. The necessities of the country compel us to collect revenue from our imports. An army of assessors and collectors is not a pleasant sight to the citizen, but that of a tariff for revenue is necessary. Such a tariff, so far as it acts as an encouragement to home production, affords employment to labor at living wages, in contrast to the pauper labor of the Old World, and also in the development of home resources.

Under the act of Congress of the 15th day of July, 1870, the Army has gradually been reduced, so that on the 1st day of January, 1871, the number of commissioned officers and men will not exceed the number contemplated by that law.

The War Department building is an old structure, not fireproof, and entirely inadequate in dimensions to our present wants. Many thousands of dollars are now paid annually for rent of private buildings to accommodate the várious bureaus of the Department. I recommend an appropriation for a new War Department building, suited to the present and growing wants of the nation.

The report of the Secretary of War shows a very satisfactory reduction in the expenses of the Army for the last fiscal year. For details you are referred to his accompanying report.

The expenses of the Navy for the whole of the last year—*i. e.*, from December 1, 1869, the date of the last report—are less than $19,000,000, or about $1,000,000 less than they were the previous year. The expenses since the commencement of this fiscal year— *i. e.*, since July 1—show for the five months a decrease of over $2,400,000 from those of the corresponding months last year. The estimates for the current year were $28,205,671.37. Those for next year are $20,683,317, with $955,100 additional for necessary permanent improvements. These estimates are made closely for the mere maintenance of the naval establishment as it now is, without much in the nature of permanent improvement. The appropriations made for the last and current years were evidently intended by Congress, and are sufficient only, to keep the Navy on its present footing by the repairing and refitting of our old ships.

This policy must, of course, gradually but surely destroy the Navy, and it is in itself far from economical, as each year that it is pursued the necessity for mere repairs in ships and navy-yards becomes more imperative and more costly, and our current expenses are annually increased for the mere repair of ships, many of which must soon become unsafe and useless. I hope during the present session of Congress to be able to submit to it a plan by which naval vessels can be built and repairs made with great saving upon the present cost.

It can hardly be wise statesmanship in a Government which represents a country with over 5,000 miles of coast line on both oceans, exclusive of Alaska, and containing 40,000,000 progressive people, with relations of every nature with almost every foreign country, to rest with such inadequate means of enforcing any foreign policy, either of protection or redress. Separated by the ocean from the nations of the Eastern Continent, our Navy is our only means of direct protection to our citizens abroad or for the enforcement of any foreign policy.

The accompanying report of the Postmaster-General shows a most satisfactory working of that Department. With the adoption of the recommendations contained therein, particularly those relating to a reform in the franking privilege and the adoption of the "correspondence cards," a self-sustaining postal system may speedily be looked for, and at no distant day a further reduction of the rate of postage be attained.

I recommend authorization by Congress to the Postmaster-General and Attorney-General to issue all commissions to officials appointed through their respective Departments. At present these commissions, where appointments are Presidential, are issued by the State Department. The law in all the Departments of Government, except those of the Post-Office and of Justice, authorizes each to issue its own commissions.

Always favoring practical reforms, I respectfully call your attention to one abuse of long standing which I would like to see remedied by this Congress. It is a reform in the civil service of the country. I would have it go beyond the mere fixing of the tenure of office of clerks and employees who do not require "the advice and consent of the Senate" to make their appointments complete. I would have it govern, not the tenure, but the manner of making all appointments. There is no duty which so much embarrasses the Executive and heads of Departments as that of appointments, nor is there any such arduous and thankless labor imposed on Senators and Representatives as that of finding places for constituents. The present system does not secure the best men, and often not even fit men, for public place. The elevation and purification of the civil service of the Government will be hailed with approval by the whole people of the United States.

Reform in the management of Indian affairs has received the special attention of the Administration from its inauguration to the present day. The experiment of making it a missionary work was tried with a few agencies given to the denomination of Friends, and has been found to work most advantageously. All agencies and superintendencies not so disposed of were given to officers of the Army. The act of Congress reducing the Army renders army officers ineligible for civil positions. Indian agencies being civil offices, I determined to give all the agencies to such religious denominations as had heretofore established missionaries among the Indians, and perhaps to some other denominations who would undertake the work on the same terms — *i. e.*, as a missionary work. The societies selected are allowed to name their own agents, subject to the approval of the Executive, and are expected to watch over them and aid them as missionaries, to Christianize and civilize the Indian, and to train him in the arts of peace. The Government watches over the official acts of these agents, and requires of them as strict an accountability as if they were appointed in any other manner. I entertain the confident hope that the policy now pursued will in a few years bring all the Indians upon reservations, where they will live in houses, and have schoolhouses and churches, and will be pursuing peaceful and self-sustaining avocations, and where they may be visited by the law-abiding white man with the same impunity that he now visits the civilized white settlements. I call your special attention to the report of the Commissioner of Indian Affairs for full information on this subject.

During the last fiscal year 8,095,413 acres of public land were disposed of. Of this quantity 3,698,910.05 acres were taken under the homestead law and 2,159,515.81 acres sold for cash. The remainder was located with military warrants, college or Indian scrip, or applied in satisfaction of grants to railroads or for other public uses. The entries under the homestead law during the last year covered 961,545 acres more than those during the preceding year. Surveys have been vigorously prosecuted to the full extent of the means applicable to the purpose. The quantity of land in market will amply supply the present demand. The claim of the settler under the homestead or the preemption laws is not, however, limited to lands subject to sale at private entry. Any unappropriated surveyed public land may, to a limited amount, be acquired under the former laws if the party entitled to enter under them will comply with the requirements they prescribe in regard to the residence and cultivation. The actual settler's preference right of purchase is even broader, and extends to lands which were unsurveyed at the time of his settlement. His right was formerly confined within much narrower limits, and at one period of our history was conferred only by special statutes. They were enacted from time to time to legalize what was then regarded as an unauthorized intrusion upon the national domain. The opinion that the public lands should be regarded chiefly as a source of revenue is no longer maintained. The rapid settlement and successful cultivation of them are now justly considered of more importance to our well-being than is the fund which the sale of them would produce. The remarkable growth and prosperity of our new States and Territories attest the wisdom of the legislation which invites the tiller of the soil to secure a permanent home on terms within the reach of all. The pioneer who incurs the dangers and privations of a frontier life, and thus aids in laying the foundation of new commonwealths, renders a signal service to his country, and is entitled to its special favor and protection. These laws secure that object and largely promote the general welfare. They should **therefore be cherished as** a permanent feature of our land system.

Good faith requires us to give full effect to existing grants. The time-honored and beneficent policy of setting apart certain sections of public land for educational purposes in the new States should be continued. When ample provision shall have been made for these objects, I submit as a question worthy of serious consideration whether the residue of our national domain should not be wholly disposed of under the provisions of the homestead and preemption laws.

In addition to the swamp and overflowed lands granted to the States in which they are situated, the lands taken under the agricultural-college acts and for internal-improvement purposes under the act of September, 1841, and the acts supplemental thereto, there had been conveyed up to the close of the last fiscal year, by patent or other equivalent title, to States and corporations 27,836,257.63 acres for railways, canals, and wagon roads. It is estimated that an additional quantity of 174,735,523 acres is still due under grants for like uses. The policy of thus aiding the States in building works of internal improvement was inaugurated more than forty years since in the grants to Indiana and Illinois, to aid those States in opening canals to connect the waters of the Wabash with those of Lake Erie and the waters of the Illinois with those of Lake Michigan. It was followed, with some modifications, in the grant to Illinois of alternate sections of public land within certain limits of the Illinois Central Railway. Fourteen States and sundry corporations have received similar subsidies in connection with railways completed or in process of construction. As the reserved sections are rated at the double minimum, the sale of them at the enhanced price has thus in many instances indemnified the Treasury for the granted lands. The construction of some of these thoroughfares has undoubtedly given a vigorous impulse to the development of our resources and the settlement of the more distant portions of the country. It may, however, be well insisted that much of our legislation in this regard has been characterized by indiscriminate and profuse liberality. The United States should not loan their credit in aid of any enterprise undertaken by States or corporations, nor grant lands in any instance, unless the projected work is of acknowledged national importance. I am strongly inclined to the opinion that it is inexpedient and unnecessary to bestow subsidies of either description; but should Congress determine otherwise I earnestly recommend that the right of settlers and of the public be more effectually secured and protected by appropriate legislation.

During the year ending September 30, 1870, there were filed in the

Patent Office 19,411 applications for patents, 3,374 caveats, and 160 applications for the extension of patents.   Thirteen thousand six hundred and twenty-two patents, including reissues and designs, were issued, 1,010 extended, and 1,089 allowed, but not issued by reason of the non-payment of the final fees.   The receipts of the office during the fiscal year were $136,304.29 in excess of its expenditures.

The work of the Census Bureau has been energetically prosecuted. The preliminary report, containing much information of special value and interest, will be ready for delivery during the present session.   The remaining volumes will be completed with all the dispatch consistent with perfect accuracy in arranging and classifying the returns.   We shall thus at no distant day be furnished with an authentic record of our condition and resources.   It will, I doubt not, attest the growing prosperity of the country, although during the decade which has just closed it was so severely tried by the great war waged to maintain its integrity and to secure and perpetuate our free institutions.

During the last fiscal year the sum paid to pensioners, including the cost of disbursement, was $27,780,811.11, and 1,758 bounty-land warrants were issued.   At its close 198,686 names were on the pension rolls.

The labors of the Pension Office have been directed to the severe scrutiny of the evidence submitted in favor of new claims and to the discovery of fictitious claims which have been heretofore allowed.   The appropriation for the employment of special agents for the investigation of frauds has been judiciously used, and the results obtained have been of unquestionable benefit to the service.

The subjects of education and agriculture are of great interest to the success of our republican institutions, happiness, and grandeur as a nation.   In the interest of one a bureau has been established in the Interior Department—the Bureau of Education; and in the interest of the other, a separate Department, that of Agriculture.   I believe great general good is to flow from the operations of both these Bureaus if properly fostered. I can not commend to your careful consideration too highly the reports of the Commissioners of Education and of Agriculture, nor urge too strongly such liberal legislation as to secure their efficiency.

In conclusion I would sum up the policy of the Administration to be a thorough enforcement of every law; a faithful collection of every tax provided for; economy in the disbursement of the same; a prompt payment of every debt of the nation; a reduction of taxes as rapidly as the requirements of the country will admit; reductions of taxation and tariff, to be so arranged as to afford the greatest relief to the greatest number; honest and fair dealings with all other peoples, to the end that war, with all its blighting consequences, may be avoided, but without surrendering any right or obligation due to us; a reform in the treatment of Indians and in the whole civil service of the country; and, finally, in securing a pure, untrammeled ballot, where every man entitled to cast a vote may do so, just once at each election, without fear of molestation or proscription on account of his political faith, nativity, or color.

THIRD ANNUAL MESSAGE.

EXECUTIVE MANSION, *December 4, 1871.*

To the Senate and House of Representatives:

In addressing my third annual message to the law-making branch of the Government it is gratifying to be able to state that during the past year success has generally attended the effort to execute all laws found upon the statute books. The policy has been not to inquire into the wisdom of laws already enacted, but to learn their spirit and intent and to enforce them accordingly.

The past year has, under a wise Providence, been one of general prosperity to the nation. It has, however, been attended with more than usual chastisements in the loss of life and property by storm and fire. These disasters have served to call forth the best elements of human nature in our country and to develop a friendship for us on the part of foreign nations which goes far toward alleviating the distresses occasioned by these calamities. The benevolent, who have so generously shared their means with the victims of these misfortunes, will reap their reward in the consciousness of having performed a noble act and in receiving the grateful thanks of men, women, and children whose sufferings they have relieved.

The relations of the United States with foreign powers continue to be friendly. The year has been an eventful one in witnessing two great nations, speaking one language and having one lineage, settling by peaceful arbitration disputes of long standing and liable at any time to bring those nations into bloody and costly conflict. An example has thus been set which, if successful in its final issue, may be followed by other civilized nations, and finally be the means of returning to productive industry millions of men now maintained to settle the disputes of nations by the bayonet and the broadside.

I transmit herewith a copy of the treaty alluded to, which has been concluded since the adjournment of Congress with Her Britannic Majesty, and a copy of the protocols of the conferences of the commissioners by whom it was negotiated. This treaty provides methods for adjusting the questions pending between the two nations.

Various questions are to be adjusted by arbitration. I recommend Congress at an early day to make the necessary provision for the tribunal at Geneva and for the several commissioners on the part of the United States called for by the treaty.

His Majesty the King of Italy, the President of the Swiss Confederation, and His Majesty the Emperor of Brazil have each consented, on the joint request of the two powers, to name an arbiter for the tribunal at Geneva. I have caused my thanks to be suitably expressed for the readiness with which the joint request has been complied with, by the appointment of gentlemen of eminence and learning to these important positions.

His Majesty the Emperor of Germany has been pleased to comply with the joint request of the two Governments, and has consented to act as the arbitrator of the disputed water boundary between the United States and Great Britain.

The contracting parties in the treaty have undertaken to regard as between themselves certain principles of public law, for which the United States have contended from the commencement of their history. They have also agreed to bring those principles to the knowledge of the other maritime powers and to invite them to accede to them. Negotiations are going on as to the form of the note by which the invitation is to be extended to the other powers.

I recommend the legislation necessary on the part of the United States to bring into operation the articles of the treaty relating to the fisheries and to the other matters touching the relations of the United States toward the British North American possessions, to become operative so soon as the proper legislation shall be had on the part of Great Britain and its possessions. It is much to be desired that this legislation may become operative before the fishermen of the United States begin to make their arrangements for the coming season.

I have addressed a communication, of which a copy is transmitted herewith, to the governors of New York, Pennsylvania, Ohio, Indiana, Michigan, Illinois, and Wisconsin, urging upon the governments of those States, respectively, the necessary action on their part to carry into effect the object of the article of the treaty which contemplates the use of the canals, on either side, connected with the navigation of the lakes and rivers forming the boundary, on terms of equality, by the inhabitants of both countries. It is hoped that the importance of the object and the benefits to flow therefrom will secure the speedy approval and legislative sanction of the States concerned.

I renew the recommendation for an appropriation for determining the true position of the forty-ninth parallel of latitude where it forms the boundary between the United States and the British North American possessions, between the Lake of the Woods and the summit of the Rocky Mountains. The early action of Congress on this recommendation would put it in the power of the War Department to place a force in the field during the next summer.

The resumption of diplomatic relations between France and Germany has enabled me to give directions for the withdrawal of the protection extended to Germans in France by the diplomatic and consular representatives of the United States in that country. It is just to add that the delicate duty of this protection has been performed by the minister and the consul-general at Paris, and the various consuls in France under the supervision of the latter, with great kindness as well as with prudence and tact. Their course has received the commendation of the German Government, and has wounded no susceptibility of the French.

The Government of the Emperor of Germany continues to manifest a friendly feeling toward the United States, and a desire to harmonize with the moderate and just policy which this Government maintains in its relations with Asiatic powers, as well as with the South American Republics. I have given assurances that the friendly feelings of that Government are fully shared by the United States.

The ratifications of the consular and naturalization conventions with the Austro-Hungarian Empire have been exchanged.

I have been officially informed of the annexation of the States of the Church to the Kingdom of Italy, and the removal of the capital of that Kingdom to Rome. In conformity with the established policy of the United States, I have recognized this change. The ratifications of the new treaty of commerce between the United States and Italy have been exchanged. The two powers have agreed in this treaty that private property at sea shall be exempt from capture in case of war between the two powers. The United States have spared no opportunity of incorporating this rule into the obligation of nations.

The Forty-first Congress, at its third session, made an appropriation for the organization of a mixed commission for adjudicating upon the claims of citizens of the United States against Spain growing out of the insurrection in Cuba. That commission has since been organized. I transmit herewith the correspondence relating to its formation and its jurisdiction. It is to be hoped that this commission will afford the claimants a complete remedy for their injuries.

It has been made the agreeable duty of the United States to preside over a conference at Washington between the plenipotentiaries of Spain and the allied South American Republics, which has resulted in an armistice, with the reasonable assurance of a permanent peace.

The intimate friendly relations which have so long existed between the United States and Russia continue undisturbed. The visit of the third son of the Emperor is a proof that there is no desire on the part of his Government to diminish the cordiality of those relations. The hospitable reception which has been given to the Grand Duke is a proof that on our side we share the wishes of that Government. The inexcusable course of the Russian minister at Washington rendered it necessary to ask his recall and to decline to longer receive that functionary as a diplomatic representative. It was impossible, with self-respect or with a just regard to the dignity of the country, to permit Mr. Catacazy to continue to hold intercourse with this Government after his personal abuse of Government officials, and during his persistent interferences, through various means, with the relations between the United States and other powers. In accordance with my wishes, this Government has been relieved of further intercourse with Mr. Catacazy, and the management of the affairs of the imperial legation has passed into the hands of a gentleman entirely unobjectionable.

With Japan we continue to maintain intimate relations. The cabinet of the Mikado has since the close of the last session of Congress selected citizens of the United States to serve in offices of importance in several departments of Government. I have reason to think that this selection is due to an appreciation of the disinterestedness of the policy which the United States have pursued toward Japan. It is our desire to continue to maintain this disinterested and just policy with China as well as Japan. The correspondence transmitted herewith shows that there is no disposition on the part of this Government to swerve from its established course

Prompted by a desire to put an end to the barbarous treatment of our shipwrecked sailors on the Korean coast, I instructed our minister at Peking to endeavor to conclude a convention with Korea for securing the safety and humane treatment of such mariners.

Admiral Rodgers was instructed to accompany him with a sufficient force to protect him in case of need.

A small surveying party sent out, on reaching the coast was treacherously attacked at a disadvantage. Ample opportunity was given for explanation and apology for the insult. Neither came. A force was then landed. After an arduous march over a rugged and difficult country, the forts from which the outrages had been committed were reduced by a gallant assault and were destroyed. Having thus punished the criminals, and having vindicated the honor of the flag, the expedition returned, finding it impracticable under the circumstances to conclude the desired convention. I respectfully refer to the correspondence relating thereto, herewith submitted, and leave the subject for such action as Congress may see fit to take.

The Republic of Mexico has not yet repealed the very objectionable laws establishing what is known as the "free zone" on the frontier of the United States. It is hoped that this may yet be done, and also that more stringent measures may be taken by that Republic for restraining lawless persons on its frontiers. I hope that Mexico by its own action will soon relieve this Government of the difficulties experienced from these causes.

Our relations with the various Republics of Central and South America continue, with one exception, to be cordial and friendly.

I recommend some action by Congress regarding the overdue installments under the award of the Venezuelan Claims Commission of 1866.
The internal dissensions of this Government present no justification for
the absence of effort to meet their solemn treaty obligations.

The ratification of an extradition treaty with Nicaragua has been
exchanged.

It is a subject for congratulation that the great Empire of Brazil has
taken the initiatory step toward the abolition of slavery. Our relations
with that Empire, always cordial, will naturally be made more so by
this act. It is not too much to hope that the Government of Brazil may
hereafter find it for its interest, as well as intrinsically right, to advance
toward entire emancipation more rapidly than the present act contemplates.

The true prosperity and greatness of a nation is to be found in the
elevation and education of its laborers.

It is a subject for regret that the reforms in this direction which were
voluntarily promised by the statesmen of Spain have not been carried out
in its West India colonies. The laws and regulations for the apparent
abolition of slavery in Cuba and Porto Rico leave most of the laborers
in bondage, with no hope of release until their lives become a burden to
their employers.

I desire to direct your attention to the fact that citizens of the United
States, or persons claiming to be citizens of the United States, are large
holders in foreign lands of this species of property, forbidden by the
fundamental law of their alleged country. I recommend to Congress to
provide by stringent legislation a suitable remedy against the holding,
owning, or dealing in slaves, or being interested in slave property, in
foreign lands, either as owners, hirers, or mortgagors, by citizens of the
United States.

It is to be regretted that the disturbed condition of the island of Cuba
continues to be a source of annoyance and of anxiety. The existence of
a protracted struggle in such close proximity to our own territory, without apparent prospect of an early termination, can not be other than an
object of concern to a people who, while abstaining from interference
in the affairs of other powers, naturally desire to see every country in
the undisturbed enjoyment of peace, liberty, and the blessings of free
institutions.

Our naval commanders in Cuban waters have been instructed, in case
it should become necessary, to spare no effort to protect the lives and
property of *bona fide* American citizens and to maintain the dignity of
the flag.

It is hoped that all pending questions with Spain growing out of the
affairs in Cuba may be adjusted in the spirit of peace and conciliation
which has hitherto guided the two powers in their treatment of such

questions.

To give importance to and to add to the efficiency of our diplomatic relations with Japan and China, and to further aid in retaining the good opinion of those peoples, and to secure to the United States its share of the commerce destined to flow between those nations and the balance of the commercial world, I earnestly recommend that an appropriation be made to support at least four American youths in each of those countries, to serve as a part of the official family of our ministers there. Our representatives would not even then be placed upon an equality with the representatives of Great Britain and of some other powers. As now situated, our representatives in Japan and China have to depend for interpreters and translators upon natives of those countries who know our language imperfectly, or procure for the occasion the services of employees in foreign business houses or the interpreters to other foreign ministers.

I would also recommend liberal measures for the purpose of supporting the American lines of steamers now plying between San Francisco and Japan and China, and the Australian line—almost our only remaining lines of ocean steamers—and of increasing their services.

The national debt has been reduced to the extent of $86,057,126.80 during the year, and by the negotiation of national bonds at a lower rate of interest the interest on the public debt has been so far diminished that now the sum to be raised for the interest account is nearly $17,000,000 less than on the 1st of March, 1869. It was highly desirable that this rapid diminution should take place, both to strengthen the credit of the country and to convince its citizens of their entire ability to meet every dollar of liability without bankrupting them. But in view of the accomplishment of these desirable ends: of the rapid development of the resources of the country; its increasing ability to meet large demands, and the amount already paid, it is not desirable that the present resources of the country should continue to be taxed in order to continue this rapid payment. I therefore recommend a modification of both the tariff and internal-tax law. I recommend that all taxes from internal sources be abolished, except those collected from spirituous, vinous, and malt liquors, tobacco in its various forms, and from stamps.

In readjusting the tariff I suggest that a careful estimate be made of the amount of surplus revenue collected under the present laws, after providing for the current expenses of the Government, the interest account, and a sinking fund, and that this surplus be reduced in such a manner as to afford the greatest relief to the greatest number. There are many articles not produced at home, but which enter largely into general consumption through articles which are manufactured at home, such as medicines compounded, etc., etc., from which very little revenue is derived, but which enter into general use. All such articles I recommend to be placed on the "free list." Should a further reduction prove advisable, I would then recommend that it be made upon those articles which can best bear it without disturbing home production or reducing the wages of American labor.

I have not entered into figures, because to do so would be to repeat what will be laid before you in the report of the Secretary of the Treasury The present laws for collecting revenue pay collectors of customs small salaries, but provide for moieties (shares in all seizures), which, at principal ports of entry particularly, raise the compensation of those officials to a large sum.   It has always seemed to me as if this system must at times work perniciously.   It holds out an inducement to dishonest men, should such get possession of those offices, to be lax in their scrutiny of goods entered, to enable them finally to make large seizures. Your attention is respectfully invited to this subject.

Continued fluctuations in the value of gold, as compared with the national currency, has a most damaging effect upon the increase and development of the country, in keeping up prices of all articles necessary in everyday life.   It fosters a spirit of gambling, prejudicial alike to national morals and the national finances.   If the question can be met as to how to get a fixed value to our currency, that value constantly and uniformly approaching par with specie, a very desirable object will be gained.

For the operations of the Army in the past year, the expense of maintaining it, the estimate for the ensuing year, and for continuing seacoast and other improvements conducted under the supervision of the War Department, I refer you to the accompanying report of the Secretary of War.

I call your attention to the provisions of the act of Congress approved March 3, 1869, which discontinues promotions in the staff corps of the Army until provided for by law.   I recommend that the number of officers in each grade in the staff corps be fixed, and that whenever the number in any one grade falls below the number so fixed, that the vacancy may be filled by promotion from the grade below.   I also recommend that when the office of chief of a corps becomes vacant the place may be filled by selection from the corps in which the vacancy exists.

The report of the Secretary of the Navy shows an improvement in the number and efficiency of the naval force, without material increase in the expense of supporting it.   This is due to the policy which has been adopted, and is being extended as fast as our material will admit, of using smaller vessels as cruisers on the several stations.   By this means we have been enabled to occupy at once a larger extent of cruising grounds, to visit more frequently the ports where the presence of our flag is desirable, and generally to discharge more efficiently the appropriate duties of the Navy in time of peace, without exceeding the number of men or the expenditure authorized by law.

During the past year the Navy has, in addition to its regular service, supplied the men and officers for the vessels of the Coast Survey, and has completed the surveys authorized by Congress of the isthmuses of Darien and Tehuantepec, and, under like authority, has sent out an expedition, completely furnished and equipped, to explore the unknown ocean of the north.

The suggestions of the report as to the necessity for increasing and improving the *matériel* of the Navy, and the plan recommended for reducing the *personnel* of the service to a peace standard, by the gradual abolition of certain grades of officers, the reduction of others, and the employment of some in the service of the commercial marine, are well considered and deserve the thoughtful attention of Congress.

I also recommend that all promotions in the Navy above the rank of captain be by selection instead of by seniority. This course will secure in the higher grades greater efficiency and hold out an incentive to young officers to improve themselves in the knowledge of their profession.

The present cost of maintaining the Navy, its cost compared with that of the preceding year, and the estimates for the ensuing year are contained in the accompanying report of the Secretary of the Navy.

The enlarged receipts of the Post-Office Department, as shown by the accompanying report of the Postmaster-General, exhibit a gratifying increase in that branch of the public service. It is the index of the growth of education and of the prosperity of the people, two elements highly conducive to the vigor and stability of republics. With a vast territory like ours, much of it sparsely populated, but all requiring the services of the mail, it is not at present to be expected that this Department can be made self-sustaining. But a gradual approach to this end from year to year is confidently relied on, and the day is not far distant when the Post-Office Department of the Government will prove a much greater blessing to the whole people than it is now.

The suggestions of the Postmaster-General for improvements in the Department presided over by him are earnestly recommended to you special attention. Especially do I recommend favorable consideration of the plan for uniting the telegraphic system of the United States with the postal system. It is believed that by such a course the cost of telegraphing could be much reduced, and the service as well, if not better, rendered. It would secure the further advantage of extending the telegraph through portions of the country where private enterprise will not construct it. Commerce, trade, and, above all, the efforts to bring a people widely separated into a community of interest are always benefited by a rapid intercommunication. Education, the groundwork of republican institutions, is encouraged by increasing the facilities to gather speedy news from all parts of the country. The desire to reap the benefit of such improvements will stimulate education. I refer you to the report of the Postmaster-General for full details of the operations of last year and for comparative statements of results with former years.

There has been imposed upon the executive branch of the Government the execution of the act of Congress approved April 20, 1871, and commonly known as the Kuklux law, in a portion of the State of South Carolina. The necessity of the course pursued will be demonstrated by the report of the Committee to Investigate Southern Outrages. Under the provisions of the above act I issued a proclamation calling the attention of the people of the United States to the same, and declaring my reluctance to exercise any of the extraordinary powers thereby conferred upon me, except in case of imperative necessity, but making known my purpose to exercise such powers whenever it should become necessary to do so for the purpose of securing to all citizens of the United States the peaceful enjoyment of the rights guaranteed to them by the Constitution and the laws.

After the passage of this law information was received from time to time that combinations of the character referred to in this law existed and were powerful in many parts of the Southern States, particularly in certain counties in the State of South Carolina.

Careful investigation was made, and it was ascertained that in nine counties of that State such combinations were active and powerful, embracing a sufficient portion of the citizens to control the local authority, and having, among other things, the object of depriving the emancipated class of the substantial benefits of freedom and of preventing the free political action of those citizens who did not sympathize with their own views. Among their operations were frequent scourgings and occasional assassinations, generally perpetrated at night by disguised persons, the victims in almost all cases being citizens of different political sentiments from their own or freed persons who had shown a disposition to claim equal rights with other citizens. Thousands of inoffensive and well-disposed citizens were the sufferers by this lawless violence.

Thereupon, on the 12th of October, 1871, a proclamation was issued, in terms of the law, calling upon the members of those combinations to disperse within five days and to deliver to the marshal or military officers of the United States all arms, ammunition, uniforms, disguises, and other means and implements used by them for carrying out their unlawful purposes.

This warning not having been heeded, on the 17th of October another proclamation was issued, suspending the privileges of the writ of *habeas corpus* in nine counties in that State.

Direction was given that within the counties so designated persons supposed, upon creditable information, to be members of such unlawful combinations should be arrested by the military forces of the United States and delivered to the marshal, to be dealt with according to law. In two of said counties, York and Spartanburg, many arrests have been made. At the last account the number of persons thus arrested was 168. Several hundred, whose criminality was ascertained to be of an inferior degree, were released for the present. These have generally made confessions of their guilt.

Great caution has been exercised in making these arrests, and, notwithstanding the large number, it is believed that no innocent person is now in custody. The prisoners will be held for regular trial in the judicial tribunals of the United States.

As soon as it appeared that the authorities of the United States were about to take vigorous measures to enforce the law, many persons absconded, and there is good ground for supposing that all of such persons have violated the law. A full report of what has been done under this law will be submitted to Congress by the Attorney-General.

In Utah there still remains a remnant of barbarism, repugnant to civilization, to decency, and to the laws of the United States. Territorial officers, however, have been found who are willing to perform their duty in a spirit of equity and with a due sense of the necessity of sustaining the majesty of the law. Neither polygamy nor any other violation of existing statutes will be permitted within the territory of the United States. It is not with the religion of the self-styled Saints that we are now dealing, but with their practices. They will be protected in the worship of God according to the dictates of their consciences, but they will not be permitted to violate the laws under the cloak of religion.

It may be advisable for Congress to consider what, in the execution of the laws against polygamy, is to be the status of plural wives and their offspring. The propriety of Congress passing an enabling act authorizing the Territorial legislature of Utah to legitimize all children born prior to a time fixed in the act might be justified by its humanity to these innocent children. This is a suggestion only, and not a recommendation.

The policy pursued toward the Indians has resulted favorably, so far as can be judged from the limited time during which it has been in operation. Through the exertions of the various societies of Christians to whom has been intrusted the execution of the policy, and the board of commissioners authorized by the law of April 10, 1869, many tribes of Indians have been induced to settle upon reservations, to cultivate the soil, to perform productive labor of various kinds, and to partially accept civilization. They are being cared for in such a way, it is hoped, as to induce those still pursuing their old habits of life to embrace the only opportunity which is left them to avoid extermination.

I recommend liberal appropriations to carry out the Indian peace policy, not only because it is humane, Christianlike, and economical, but because it is right.

I recommend to your favorable consideration also the policy of granting a Territorial government to the Indians in the Indian Territory west of Arkansas and Missouri and south of Kansas. In doing so every right guaranteed to the Indian by treaty should be secured. Such a course might in time be the means of collecting most of the Indians now between the Missouri and the Pacific and south of the British possessions into

one Territory or one State.   The Secretary of the Interior has treated
upon this subject at length, and I commend to you his suggestions.

I renew my recommendation that the public lands be regarded as a
heritage to our children, to be disposed of only as required for occupation and to actual settlers.   Those already granted have been in great
part disposed of in such a way as to secure access to the balance by the
hardy settler who may wish to avail himself of them, but caution should
be exercised even in attaining so desirable an object.

Educational interest may well be served by the grant of the proceeds
of the sale of public lands to settlers.   I do not wish to be understood as
recommending in the least degree a curtailment of what is being done by
the General Government for the encouragement of education.

The report of the Secretary of the Interior submitted with this will
give you all the information collected and prepared for publication in
regard to the census taken during the year 1870; the operations of the
Bureau of Education for the year; the Patent Office; the Pension Office;
the Land Office, and the Indian Bureau.

The report of the Commissioner of Agriculture gives the operations of
his Department for the year.   As agriculture is the groundwork of our
prosperity, too much importance can not be attached to the labors of this
Department.   It is in the hands of an able head, with able assistants, all
zealously devoted to introducing into the agricultural productions of the
nation all useful products adapted to any of the various climates and
soils of our vast territory, and to giving all useful information as to the
method of cultivation, the plants, cereals, and other products adapted
to particular localities.   Quietly but surely the Agricultural Bureau is
working a great national good, and if liberally supported the more widely
its influence will be extended and the less dependent we shall be upon
the products of foreign countries.

The subject of compensation to the heads of bureaus and officials holding positions of responsibility, and requiring ability and character to fill
properly, is one to which your attention is invited.   But few of the officials receive a compensation equal to the respectable support of a family,
while their duties are such as to involve millions of interest.   In private
life services demand compensation equal to the services rendered; a wise
economy would dictate the same rule in the Government service.

I have not given the estimates for the support of Government for the
ensuing year, nor the comparative statement between the expenditures
for the year just passed and the one just preceding, because all these
figures are contained in the accompanying reports or in those presented
directly to Congress.   These estimates have my approval.

More than six years having elapsed since the last hostile gun was fired
between the armies then arrayed against each other—one for the perpetuation, the other for the destruction, of the Union—it may well be
considered whether it is not now time that the disabilities imposed by the

fourteenth amendment should be removed. That amendment does not exclude the ballot, but only imposes the disability to hold offices upon certain classes. When the purity of the ballot is secure, majorities are sure to elect officers reflecting the views of the majority. I do not see the advantage or propriety of excluding men from office merely because they were before the rebellion of standing and character sufficient to be elected to positions requiring them to take oaths to support the Constitution, and admitting to eligibility those entertaining precisely the same views, but of less standing in their communities. It may be said that the former violated an oath, while the latter did not; the latter did not have it in their power to do so. If they had taken this oath, it can not be doubted they would have broken it as did the former class. If there are any great criminals, distinguished above all others for the part they took in opposition to the Government, they might, in the judgment of Congress, be excluded from such an amnesty.

This subject is submitted for your careful consideration.

The condition of the Southern States is, unhappily, not such as all true patriotic citizens would like to see. Social ostracism for opinion's sake, personal violence or threats toward persons entertaining political views opposed to those entertained by the majority of the old citizens, prevents immigration and the flow of much-needed capital into the States lately in rebellion. It will be a happy condition of the country when the old citizens of these States will take an interest in public affairs, promulgate ideas honestly entertain d, vote for men representing their views, and tolerate the same freedom of expression and ballot in those entertaining different political convictions.

Under the provisions of the act of Congress approved February 21, 1871, a Territorial government was organized in the District of Columbia. Its results have thus far fully realized the expectations of its advocates. Under the direction of the Territorial officers, a system of improvements has been inaugurated by means of which Washington is rapidly becoming a city worthy of the nation's capital. The citizens of the District having voluntarily taxed themselves to a large amount for the purpose of contributing to the adornment of the seat of Government, I recommend liberal appropriations on the part of Congress, in order that the Government may bear its just share of the expense of carrying out a judicious system of improvements.

By the great fire in Chicago the most important of the Government buildings in that city were consumed. Those burned had already become inadequate to the wants of the Government in that growing city, and, looking to the near future, were totally inadequate. I recommend, therefore, that an appropriation be made immediately to purchase the remainder of the square on which the burned buildings stood, provided it can be purchased at a fair valuation, or provided that the legislature of Illinois will pass a law authorizing its condemnation for Government purposes; and also an appropriation of as much money as can properly be expended toward the erection of new buildings during this fiscal year.

The number of immigrants ignorant of our laws, habits, etc., coming into our country annually has become so great and the impositions practiced upon them so numerous and flagrant that I suggest Congressional action for their protection. It seems to me a fair subject of legislation by Congress. I can not now state as fully as I desire the nature of the complaints made by immigrants of the treatment they receive, but will endeavor to do so during the session of Congress, particularly if the subject should receive your attention.

It has been the aim of the Administration to enforce honesty and efficiency in all public offices. Every public servant who has violated the trust placed in him has been proceeded against with all the rigor of the law. If bad men have secured places, it has been the fault of the system established by law and custom for making appointments, or the fault of those who recommend for Government positions persons not sufficiently well known to them personally, or who give letters indorsing the characters of office seekers without a proper sense of the grave responsibility which such a course devolves upon them. A civil-service reform which can correct this abuse is much desired. In mercantile pursuits the business man who gives a letter of recommendation to a friend to enable him to obtain credit from a stranger is regarded as morally responsible for the integrity of his friend and his ability to meet his obligations. A reformatory law which would enforce this principle against all indorsers of persons for public place would insure great caution in making recommendations. A salutary lesson has been taught the careless and the dishonest public servant in the great number of prosecutions and convictions of the last two years.

It is gratifying to notice the favorable change which is taking place throughout the country in bringing to punishment those who have proven recreant to the trusts confided to them and in elevating to public office none but those who possess the confidence of the honest and the virtuous, who, it will always be found, comprise the majority of the community in which they live.

In my message to Congress one year ago I urgently recommended a reform in the civil service of the country. In conformity with that recommendation Congress, in the ninth section of "An act making appropriations for sundry civil expenses of the Government, and for other purposes," approved March 3, 1871, gave the necessary authority to the Executive to inaugurate a civil-service reform, and placed upon him the responsibility of doing so. Under the authority of said act I convened a board of gentlemen eminently qualified for the work to devise rules and regulations to effect the needed reform. Their labors are not yet complete, but it is believed that they will succeed in devising a plan that can be adopted to the great relief of the Executive, the heads of Departments, and members of Congress, and which will redound to the true interest of the public service. At all events, the experiment shall have a fair trial.

I have thus hastily summed up the operations of the Government during the last year, and made such suggestions as occur to me to be proper for your consideration. I submit them with a confidence that your combined action will be wise, statesmanlike, and in the best interests of the whole country.

FOURTH ANNUAL MESSAGE.

EXECUTIVE MANSION, *December 2, 1872.*

To the Senate and House of Representatives:

In transmitting to you this my fourth annual message it is with thankfulness to the Giver of All Good that as a nation we have been blessed for the past year with peace at home, peace abroad, and a general prosperity vouchsafed to but few peoples.

With the exception of the recent devastating fire which swept from the earth with a breath, as it were, millions of accumulated wealth in the city of Boston, there has been no overshadowing calamity within the year to record. It is gratifying to note how, like their fellow-citizens of the city of Chicago under similar circumstances a year earlier, the citizens of Boston are rallying under their misfortunes, and the prospect that their energy and perseverance will overcome all obstacles and show the same prosperity soon that they would had no disaster befallen them. Otherwise we have been free from pestilence, war, and calamities, which often overtake nations; and, as far as human judgment can penetrate the future, no cause seems to exist to threaten our present peace.

When Congress adjourned in June last, a question had been raised by Great Britain, and was then pending, which for a time seriously imperiled the settlement by friendly arbitration of the grave differences between this Government and that of Her Britannic Majesty, which by the treaty of Washington had been referred to the tribunal of arbitration which had met at Geneva, in Switzerland.

The arbitrators, however, disposed of the question which had jeoparded the whole of the treaty and threatened to involve the two nations in most unhappy relations toward each other in a manner entirely satisfactory to this Government and in accordance with the views and the policy which it had maintained.

The tribunal, which had convened at Geneva in December, concluded its laborious session on the 14th day of September last, on which day.

having availed itself of the discretionary power given to it by the treaty to award a sum in gross, it made its decision, whereby it awarded the sum of $15,500,000 in gold as the indemnity to be paid by Great Britain to the United States for the satisfaction of all the claims referred to its consideration.

This decision happily disposes of a long-standing difference between the two Governments, and, in connection with another award, made by the German Emperor under a reference to him by the same treaty, leaves these two Governments without a shadow upon the friendly relations which it is my sincere hope may forever remain equally unclouded.

The report of the agent of the United States appointed to attend the Geneva tribunal, accompanied by the protocols of the proceedings of the arbitrators, the arguments of the counsel of both Governments, the award of the tribunal, and the opinions given by the several arbitrators, is transmitted herewith.

I have caused to be communicated to the heads of the three friendly powers who complied with the joint request made to them under the treaty the thanks of this Government for the appointment of arbitrators made by them respectively, and also my thanks to the eminent personages named by them, and my appreciation of the dignity, patience, impartiality, and great ability with which they discharged their arduous and high functions.

Her Majesty's Government has communicated to me the appreciation by Her Majesty of the ability and indefatigable industry displayed by Mr. Adams, the arbitrator named on the part of this Government during the protracted inquiries and discussions of the tribunal. I cordially unite with Her Majesty in this appreciation.

It is due to the agent of the United States before the tribunal to record my high appreciation of the marked ability, unwearied patience, and the prudence and discretion with which he has conducted the very responsible and delicate duties committed to him, as it is also due to the learned and eminent counsel who attended the tribunal on the part of this Government to express my sense of the talents and wisdom which they brought to bear in the attainment of the result so happily reached.

It will be the province of Congress to provide for the distribution among those who may be entitled to it of their respective shares of the money to be paid. Although the sum awarded is not payable until a year from the date of the award, it is deemed advisable that no time be lost in making a proper examination of the several cases in which indemnification may be due. I consequently recommend the creation of a board of commissioners for the purpose.

By the thirty-fourth article of the treaty of Washington the respective claims of the United States and of Great Britain in their construction of the treaty of the 15th of June, 1846, defining the boundary line between their respective territories, were submitted to the arbitration and award of His Majesty the Emperor of Germany, to decide which of those claims is most in accordance with the true interpretation of the treaty of 1846.

His Majesty the Emperor of Germany, having been pleased to undertake the arbitration, has the earnest thanks of this Government and of the people of the United States for the labor, pains, and care which he has devoted to the consideration of this long-pending difference. I have caused an expression of my thanks to be communicated to His Majesty. Mr. Bancroft, the representative of this Government at Berlin, conducted the case and prepared the statement on the part of the United States with the ability that his past services justified the public in expecting at his hands. As a member of the Cabinet at the date of the treaty which has given rise to the discussion between the two Governments, as the minister to Great Britain when the construction now pronounced unfounded was first advanced, and as the agent and representative of the Government to present the case and to receive the award, he has been associated with the question in all of its phases, and in every stage has manifested a patriotic zeal and earnestness in maintenance of the claim of the United States. He is entitled to much credit for the success which has attended the submission.

After a patient investigation of the case and of the statements of each party, His Majesty the Emperor, on the 21st day of October last, signed his award in writing, decreeing that the claim of the Government of the United States, that the boundary line between the territories of Her Britannic Majesty and the United States should be drawn through the Haro Channel, is most in accordance with the true interpretation of the treaty concluded on the 15th of June, 1846, between the Governments of Her Britannic Majesty and of the United States.

Copies of the "case" presented on behalf of each Government, and of the "statement in reply" of each, and a translation of the award, are transmitted herewith.

This award confirms the United States in their claim to the important archipelago of islands lying between the continent and Vancouvers Island, which for more than twenty-six years (ever since the ratification of the treaty) Great Britain has contested, and leaves us, for the first time in the history of the United States as a nation, without a question of disputed boundary between our territory and the possessions of Great Britain on this continent.

It is my grateful duty to acknowledge the prompt, spontaneous action of Her Majesty's Government in giving effect to the award. In anticipation of any request from this Government, and before the reception in the United States of the award signed by the Emperor, Her Majesty had given instructions for the removal of her troops which had been stationed there and for the cessation of all exercise or claim of jurisdiction, so as to leave the United States in the exclusive possession of the lately disputed territory. I am gratified to be able to announce that the orders for the removal of the troops have been executed, and that the military joint occupation of San Juan has ceased. The islands are now in the exclusive possession of the United States.

It now becomes necessary to complete the survey and determination of that portion of the boundary line (through the Haro Channel) upon which the commission which determined the remaining part of the line were unable to agree. I recommend the appointment of a commission to act jointly with one which may be named by Her Majesty for that purpose.

Experience of the difficulties attending the determination of our admitted line of boundary, after the occupation of the territory and its settlement by those owing allegiance to the respective Governments, points to the importance of establishing, by natural objects or other monuments, the actual line between the territory acquired by purchase from Russia and the adjoining possessions of Her Britannic Majesty. The region is now so sparsely occupied that no conflicting interests of individuals or of jurisdiction are likely to interfere to the delay or embarrassment of the actual location of the line. If deferred until population shall enter and occupy the territory, some trivial contest of neighbors may again array the two Governments in antagonism. I therefore recommend the appointment of a commission, to act jointly with one that may be appointed on the part of Great Britain, to determine the line between our Territory of Alaska and the conterminous possessions of Great Britain.

In my last annual message I recommended the legislation necessary on the part of the United States to bring into operation the articles of the treaty of Washington of May 8, 1871, relating to the fisheries and to other matters touching the relations of the United States toward the British North American possessions, to become operative so soon as the proper legislation should be had on the part of Great Britain and its possessions.

That legislation on the part of Great Britain and its possessions had not then been had, and during the session of Congress a question was raised which for the time raised a doubt whether any action by Congress in the direction indicated would become important. This question has since been disposed of, and I have received notice that the Imperial Parliament and the legislatures of the provincial governments have passed laws to carry the provisions of the treaty on the matters referred to into operation. I therefore recommend your early adoption of the egislation in the same direction necessary on the part of this Government.

The joint commission for determining the boundary line between the United States and the British possessions between the Lake of the Woods and the Rocky Mountains has organized and entered upon its work. It is desirable that the force be increased, in order that the completion of the survey and determination of the line may be the sooner attained. To this end I recommend that a sufficient appropriation be made.

With France, our earliest ally; Russia, the constant and steady friend of the United States; Germany, with whose Government and people we have so many causes of friendship and so many common sympathies, and the other powers of Europe, our relations are maintained on the most friendly terms.

Since my last annual message the exchange has been made of the ratifications of a treaty with the Austro-Hungarian Empire relating to naturalization; also of a treaty with the German Empire respecting consuls and trade-marks; also of a treaty with Sweden and Norway relating to naturalization; all of which treaties have been duly proclaimed.

Congress at its last session having made an appropriation to defray the expense of commissioners on the part of the United States to the International Statistical Congress at St. Petersburg, the persons appointed in that character proceeded to their destination and attended the sessions of the congress. Their report shall in due season be laid before you. This congress meets at intervals of about three years, and has held its sessions in several of the countries of Europe. I submit to your consideration the propriety of extending an invitation to the congress to hold its next meeting in the United States. The Centennial Celebration to be held in 1876 would afford an appropriate occasion for such meeting.

Preparations are making for the international exposition to be held during the next year in Vienna, on a scale of very great magnitude. The tendency of these expositions is in the direction of advanced civilization, and of the elevation of industry and of labor, and of the increase of human happiness, as well as of greater intercourse and good will between nations. As this exposition is to be the first which will have been held in eastern Europe, it is believed that American inventors and manufacturers will be ready to avail themselves of the opportunity for the presentation of their productions if encouraged by proper aid and protection.

At the last session of Congress authority was given for the appointment of one or more agents to represent this Government at the exposition. The authority thus given has been exercised, but, in the absence of any appropriation, there is danger that the important benefits which the occasion offers will in a large degree be lost to citizens of the United States. I commend the subject strongly to your consideration, and recommend that an adequate appropriation be made for the purpose.

To further aid American exhibitors at the Vienna Exposition, I would recommend, in addition to an appropriation of money, that the Secretary of the Navy be authorized to fit up two naval vessels to transport between our Atlantic cities and Trieste, or the most convenient port to Vienna, and back, their articles for exhibition.

Since your last session the President of the Mexican Republic, distinguished by his high character and by his services to his country, has died. His temporary successor has now been elected with great unanimity by the people—a proof of confidence on their part in his patriotism and wisdom which it is believed will be confirmed by the results of his administration.   It is particularly desirable that nothing should be left undone by the Government of either Republic to strengthen their relations as neighbors and friends.

It is much to be regretted that many lawless acts continue to disturb the quiet of the settlements on the border between our territory and that of Mexico, and that complaints of wrongs to American citizens in various parts of the country are made.   The revolutionary condition in which the neighboring Republic has so long been involved has in some degree contributed to this disturbance.   It is to be hoped that with a more settled rule of order through the Republic, which may be expected from the present Government, the acts of which just complaint is made will cease.

The proceedings of the commission under the convention with Mexico of the 4th of July, 1868, on the subject of claims, have, unfortunately, been checked by an obstacle, for the removal of which measures have been taken by the two Governments which it is believed will prove successful.

The commissioners appointed, pursuant to the joint resolution of Congress of the 7th of May last, to inquire into depredations on the Texan frontier have diligently made investigations in that quarter.   Their report upon the subject will be communicated to you.   Their researches were necessarily incomplete, partly on account of the limited appropriation made by Congress.   Mexico, on the part of that Government, has appointed a similar commission to investigate these outrages.   It is not announced officially, but the press of that country states that the fullest investigation is desired, and that the cooperation of all parties concerned is invited to secure that end.   I therefore recommend that a special appropriation be made at the earliest day practicable, to enable the commissioners on the part of the United States to return to their labors without delay.

It is with regret that I have again to announce a continuance of the disturbed condition of the island of Cuba.   No advance toward the pacification of the discontented part of the population has been made. While the insurrection has gained no advantages and exhibits no more of the elements of power or of the prospects of ultimate success than were exhibited a year ago, Spain, on the other hand, has not succeeded in its repression, and the parties stand apparently in the same relative attitude which they have occupied for a long time past.

This contest has lasted now for more than four years.   Were its scene at a distance from our neighborhood, we might be indifferent to its result, although humanity could not be unmoved by many of its incidents wherever they might occur.   It is, however, at our door.

I can not doubt that the continued maintenance of slavery in Cuba is among the strongest inducements to the continuance of this strife.   A terrible wrong is the natural cause of a terrible evil.   The abolition of slavery and the introduction of other reforms in the administration of government in Cuba could not fail to advance the restoration of peace and order. It is greatly to be hoped that the present liberal Government of Spain will voluntarily adopt this view.

The law of emancipation, which was passed more than two years since, has remained unexecuted in the absence of regulations for its enforcement. It was but a feeble step toward emancipation, but it was the recognition of right, and was hailed as such, and exhibited Spain in harmony with sentiments of humanity and of justice and in sympathy with the other powers of the Christian and civilized world.

Within the past few weeks the regulations for carrying out the law of emancipation have been announced, giving evidence of the sincerity of intention of the present Government to carry into effect the law of 1870. I have not failed to urge the consideration of the wisdom, the policy, and the justice of a more effective system for the abolition of the great evil which oppresses a race and continues a bloody and destructive contest close to our border, as well as the expediency and the justice of conceding reforms of which the propriety is not questioned.

Deeply impressed with the conviction that the continuance of slavery is one of the most active causes of the continuance of the unhappy condition in Cuba, I regret to believe that citizens of the United States, or those claiming to be such, are large holders in Cuba of what is there claimed as property, but which is forbidden and denounced by the laws of the United States. They are thus, in defiance of the spirit of our own laws, contributing to the continuance of this distressing and sickening contest. In my last annual message I referred to this subject, and I again recommend such legislation as may be proper to denounce, and, if not prevent, at least to discourage American citizens from holding or dealing in slaves.

It is gratifying to announce that the ratifications of the convention concluded under the auspices of this Government between Spain on the one part and the allied Republics of the Pacific on the other, providing for an armistice, have been exchanged. A copy of the instrument is herewith submitted. It is hoped that this may be followed by a permanent peace between the same parties.

The differences which at one time threatened the maintenance of peace between Brazil and the Argentine Republic it is hoped are in the way of satisfactory adjustment.

With these States, as with the Republics of Central and of South America, we continue to maintain the most friendly relations.

It is with regret, however, I announce that the Government of Venezuela has made no further payments on account of the awards under the convention of the 25th of April, 1866. That Republic is understood to be now almost, if not quite, tranquilized. It is hoped, therefore, that it will lose no time in providing for the unpaid balance of its debt to the

United States, which, having originated in injuries to our citizens by Venezuelan authorities, and having been acknowledged, pursuant to a treaty, in the most solemn form known among nations, would seem to deserve a preference over debts of a different origin and contracted in a different manner. This subject is again recommended to the attention of Congress for such action as may be deemed proper.

Our treaty relations with Japan remain unchanged. An imposing embassy from that interesting and progressive nation visited this country during the year that is passing, but, being unprovided with powers for the signing of a convention in this country, no conclusion in that direction was reached. It is hoped, however, that the interchange of opinions which took place during their stay in this country has led to a mutual appreciation of the interests which may be promoted when the revision of the existing treaty shall be undertaken.

In this connection I renew my recommendation of one year ago, that—

To give importance to and to add to the efficiency of our diplomatic relations with Japan and China, and to further aid in retaining the good opinion of those peoples, and to secure to the United States its share of the commerce destined to flow between those nations and the balance of the commercial world, an appropriation be made to support at least four American youths in each of those countries, to serve as a part of the official family of our ministers there. Our representatives would not even then be placed upon an equality with the representatives of Great Britain and of some other powers. As now situated, our representatives in Japan and China have to depend for interpreters and translators upon natives of those countries, who know our language imperfectly, or procure for the occasion the services of employees in foreign business houses or the interpreters to other foreign ministers.

I renew the recommendation made on a previous occasion, of the transfer to the Department of the Interior, to which they seem more appropriately to belong, of all the powers and duties in relation to the Territories with which the Department of State is now charged by law or by custom.

Congress from the beginning of the Government has wisely made provision for the relief of distressed seamen in foreign countries. No similar provision, however, has hitherto been made for the relief of citizens in distress abroad other than seamen. It is understood to be customary with other governments to authorize consuls to extend such relief to their citizens or subjects in certain cases. A similar authority and an appropriation to carry it into effect are recommended in the case of citizens of the United States destitute or sick under such circumstances. It is well known that such citizens resort to foreign countries in great numbers. Though most of them are able to bear the expenses incident to locomotion, there are some who, through accident or otherwise, become penniless, and have no friends at home able to succor them. Persons in this situation must either perish, cast themselves upon the charity of foreigners, or be relieved at the private charge of our own officers, who usually, even with the most benevolent dispositions, have nothing to spare for such purposes.

Should the authority and appropriation asked for be granted, care will be taken so to carry the beneficence of Congress into effect that it shall not be unnecessarily or unworthily bestowed.

TREASURY.

The moneys received and covered into the Treasury during the fiscal year ended June 30, 1872, were:

From customs	$216,370,286.77
From sales of public lands	2,575,714.19
From internal revenue	130,642,177.72
From tax on national-bank circulation, etc.	6,523,396.39
From Pacific railway companies	749,861.87
From customs fines, etc.	1,136,442.34
From fees—consular, patent, land, etc.	2,284,095.92
From miscellaneous sources	4,412,254.71
Total ordinary receipts	364,694,229.91
From premium on sales of coin	9,412,637.65
Total net receipts	374,106,867.56
Balance in Treasury June 30, 1871 (including $18,228.35 received from "unavailable")	109,935,705.59
Total available cash	484,042,573.15

The net expenditures by warrants during the same period were:

For civil expenses		$16,187,059.20
For foreign intercourse		1,839,369.14
For Indians		7,061,728.82
For pensions		28,533,402.76
For military establishment, including fortifications, river and harbor improvements, and arsenals		35,372,157.20
For naval establishment, including vessels and machinery and improvements at navy-yards		21,249,809.99
For miscellaneous civil, including public buildings, light-houses, and collecting the revenue		42,958,329.08
For interest on the public debt		117,357,839.72
Total, exclusive of principal and premium on the public debt		270,559,695.91
For premium on bonds purchased	$6,958,266.76	
For redemption of the public debt	99,960,253.54	
		106,918,520.30
Total net disbursements		377,478,216.21
Balance in Treasury June 30, 1872		106,564,356.94
Total		484,042,573.15

From the foregoing statement it appears that the net reduction of the principal of the debt during the fiscal year ending June 30, 1872, was $99,960,253.54.

The source of this reduction is as follows:

Net ordinary receipts during the year	$364,694,229.91
Net ordinary expenditures, including interest on the public debt	270,559,695.91
Leaving surplus revenue	94,134,534.00
Add amount received from premium on sales of gold, in excess of the premium paid on bonds purchased	2,454,370.89
Add the amount of the reduction of the cash balance at the close of the year, accompanied with same at commencement of the year	3,371,348.65
Total	99,960,253.54

This statement treats solely of the principal of the public debt.

By the monthly statement of the public debt, which adds together the principal, interest due and unpaid, and interest accrued to date, not due, and deducts the cash in the Treasury as ascertained on the day of publication, the reduction was $100,544,491.28.

The source of this reduction is as follows:

Reduction in principal account	$99,960,003.54
Reduction in unpaid-interest account	3,330,952.96
	103,290,956.50
Reduction in cash on hand	2,746,465.22
	100,544,491.28

On the basis of the last table the statements show a reduction of the public debt from the 1st of March, 1869, to the present time as follows:

From March 1, 1869, to March 1, 1870	$87,134,782.84
From March 1, 1870, to March 1, 1871	117,619,630.25
From March 1, 1871, to March 1, 1872	94,895,348.94
From March 1, 1872, to November 1, 1872 (eight months)	64,047,237.84
Total	363,696,999.87

With the great reduction of taxation by the acts of Congress at its last session, the expenditure of the Government in collecting the revenue will be much reduced for the next fiscal year. It is very doubtful, however, whether any further reduction of so vexatious a burden upon any people will be practicable for the present. At all events, as a measure of justice to the holders of the nation's certificates of indebtedness, I would recommend that no more legislation be had on this subject, unless it be to correct errors of omission or commission in the present laws, until sufficient time has elapsed to prove that it can be done and still leave sufficient revenue to meet current expenses of Government, pay interest on the public debt, and provide for the sinking fund established by law. The preservation of our national credit is of the highest importance; next in importance to this comes a solemn duty to provide a national currency of fixed, unvarying value as compared with gold, and as soon as practicable, having due regard for the interests of the debtor class and the vicissitudes of trade and commerce, convertible into gold at par.

WAR DEPARTMENT.

The report of the Secretary of War shows the expenditures of the War Department for the fiscal year ending June 30, 1871, to be $35,799,991.82, and for the fiscal year ending June 30, 1872, to be $35,372,157.20, showing a reduction in favor of the last fiscal year of $427,834.62.

The estimates for military appropriations for the next fiscal year, ending June 30, 1874, are $33,801,378.78.

The estimates of the Chief of Engineers are submitted separately for fortifications, river and harbor improvements, and for public buildings and grounds and the Washington Aqueduct.

The affairs of the Freedmen's Bureau have all been transferred to the War Department, and regulations have been put into execution for the speedy payment of bounty, pay, etc., due colored soldiers, properly coming under that Bureau. All war accounts, for money and property, prior to 1871 have been examined and transmitted to the Treasury for final settlement.

During the fiscal year there has been paid for transportation on railroads $1,300,000, of which $800,857 was over the Pacific railroads; for transportation by water $626,373.52, and by stage $48,975.84; for the purchase of transportation animals, wagons, hire of teamsters, etc., $924,650.64.

About $370,000 have been collected from Southern railroads during the year, leaving about $4,000,000 still due.

The Quartermaster has examined and transmitted to the accounting officers for settlement $367,172.72 of claims by loyal citizens for quartermaster stores taken during the war.

Subsistence supplies to the amount of $89,048.12 have been issued to Indians.

The annual average mean strength of the Army was 24,101 white and 2,494 colored soldiers. The total deaths for the year reported were 367 white and 54 colored.

The distribution of the Medical and Surgical History of the War is yet to be ordered by Congress.

There exists an absolute necessity for a medical corps of the full number established by act of Congress of July 28, 1866, there being now fifty-nine vacancies, and the number of successful candidates rarely exceeds eight or ten in any one year.

The river and harbor improvements have been carried on with energy and economy. Though many are only partially completed, the results have saved to commerce many times the amount expended. The increase of commerce, with greater depths of channels, greater security in navigation, and the saving of time, adds millions to the wealth of the country and increases the resources of the Government.

The bridge across the Mississippi River at Rock Island has been completed, and the proper site has been determined upon for the bridge at La Crosse.

The able and exhaustive report made by the commission appointed to investigate the Sutro Tunnel has been transmitted to Congress.

The observations and reports of the Signal Office have been continued. Stations have been maintained at each of the principal lake, seaport, and river cities. Ten additional stations have been established in the United States, and arrangements have been made for an exchange of reports with Canada, and a similar exchange of observations is contemplated with the West India Islands.

The favorable attention of Congress is invited to the following recommendations of the Secretary of War:

A discontinuance of the appointment of extra lieutenants to serve as

adjutants and quartermasters; the adoption of a code providing specific penalties for well-defined offenses, so that the inequality of sentences adjudged by courts-martial may be adjusted; the consolidation of accounts under which expenditures are made, as a measure of economy; a reappropriation of the money for the construction of a depot at San Antonio, the title to the site being now perfected; a special act placing the cemetery at the City of Mexico on the same basis as other national cemeteries; authority to purchase sites for military posts in Texas; the appointment of commissary sergeants from noncommissioned officers, as a measure for securing the better care and protection of supplies; an appropriation for the publication of the catalogue and tables of the anatomical section of the Army Medical Museum; a reappropriation of the amount for the manufacture of breech-loading arms, should the selection be so delayed by the board of officers as to leave the former appropriation unexpended at the close of the fiscal year; the sale of such arsenals east of the Mississippi as can be spared, and the proceeds applied to the establishment of one large arsenal of construction and repair upon the Atlantic Coast and the purchase of a suitable site for a proving and experimental ground for heavy ordnance; the abrogation of laws which deprive inventors in the United States service from deriving any benefit from their inventions; the repeal of the law prohibiting promotions in the staff corps; a continuance of the work upon coast defenses; the repeal of the seventh section of the act of July 13, 1866, taking from engineer soldiers the per diem granted to other troops; a limitation of time for presentation of old war claims for subsistence supplies under act of July 4, 1864; and a modification in the mode of the selection of cadets for the Military Academy, in order to enhance the usefulness of the Academy, which is impaired by reason of the large amount of time necessarily expended in giving new cadets a thorough knowledge of the more elementary branches of learning, which they should acquire before entering the Academy. Also an appropriation for philosophical apparatus and an increase in the numbers and pay of the Military Academy band.

The attention of Congress will be called during its present session to various enterprises for the more certain and cheaper transportation of the constantly increasing surplus of Western and Southern products to the Atlantic Seaboard. The subject is one that will force itself upon the legislative branch of the Government sooner or later, and I suggest, therefore, that immediate steps be taken to gain all available information to insure equable and just legislation.

One route to connect the Mississippi Valley with the Atlantic, at Charleston, S. C., and Savannah, Ga., by water, by the way of the Ohio and Tennessee rivers, and canals and slack-water navigation to the Savannah and Ocmulgee rivers, has been surveyed, and report made by an accomplished engineer officer of the Army. Second and third new routes will be proposed for the consideration of Congress, namely, by an extension of the Kanawha and James River Canal to the Ohio, and by extension of the Chesapeake and Ohio Canal.

I am not prepared to recommend Government aid to these or other enterprises until it is clearly shown that they are not only of national interest, but that when completed they will be of a value commensurate with their cost.

That production increases more rapidly than the means of transportation in our country has been demonstrated by past experience. That the unprecedented growth in population and products of the whole country will require additional facilities—and cheaper ones for the more bulky articles of commerce to reach tide water and a market will be demanded in the near future—is equally demonstrable. I would therefore suggest either a committee or a commission to be authorized to consider this whole question, and to report to Congress at some future day for its better guidance in legislating on this important subject.

The railroads of the country have been rapidly extended during the last few years to meet the growing demands of producers, and reflect much credit upon the capitalists and managers engaged in their construction.

In addition to these, a project to facilitate commerce by the building of a ship canal around Niagara Falls, on the United States side, which has been agitated for many years, will no doubt be called to your attention at this session.

Looking to the great future growth of the country and the increasing demands of commerce, it might be well while on this subject not only to have examined and reported upon the various practicable routes for connecting the Mississippi with tide water on the Atlantic, but the feasibility of an almost continuous landlocked navigation from Maine to the Gulf of Mexico. Such a route along our coast would be of great value at all times, and of inestimable value in case of a foreign war. Nature has provided the greater part of this route, and the obstacles to overcome are easily within the skill of the engineer.

I have not alluded to this subject with the view of having any further expenditure of public money at this time than may be necessary to procure and place all the necessary information before Congress in an authentic form, to enable it hereafter, if deemed practicable and worthy, to legislate on the subject without delay.

NAVY DEPARTMENT.

The report of the Secretary of the Navy herewith accompanying explains fully the condition of that branch of the public service, its wants and deficiencies, expenses incurred during the past year, and appropriations for the same. It also gives a complete history of the services of the Navy for the past year in addition to its regular service.

It is evident that unless early steps are taken to preserve our Navy in a very few years the United States will be the weakest nation upon the ocean, of all great powers. With an energetic, progressive, business people like ours, penetrating and forming business relations with every part of the known world, a navy strong enough to command the respect of our flag abroad is necessary for the full protection of their rights.

I recommend careful consideration by Congress of the recommendations made by the Secretary of the Navy.

POST-OFFICE DEPARTMENT.

The accompanying report of the Postmaster-General furnishes a full and satisfactory exhibit of the operations of the Post-Office Department during the year. The ordinary revenues of the Department for the fiscal year ending June 30, 1872, amounted to $21,915,426.37, and the expenditures to $26,658,192.31. Compared with the previous fiscal year the increase of revenue was $1,878,330.95, or 9.37 per cent, and the increase of expenditures $2,268,088.23, or 9.29 per cent. Adding to the ordinary revenues the annual appropriation of $700,000 for free matter and the amounts paid to the subsidized mail steamship lines from special appropriations, the deficiency paid out of the General Treasury was $3,317,-765.94, an excess of $389,707.28 over the deficiency for the year 1871.

Other interesting statistical information relating to our rapidly extending postal service is furnished in this report. The total length of railroad mail routes on the 30th of June, 1872, was 57,911 miles, 8,077 additional miles of such service having been put into operation during the year. Eight new lines of railway post-offices have been established, with an aggregate length of 2,909 miles. The number of letters exchanged in the mails with foreign countries was 24,362,500, an increase of 4,066,502, or 20 per cent, over the number in 1871; and the postage thereon amounted to $1,871,257.25. The total weight of the mails exchanged with European countries exceeded 820 tons. The cost of the United States transatlantic mail steamship service was $220,301.70. The total cost of the United States ocean steamship service, including the amounts paid to the subsidized lines of mail steamers, was $1,027,020.97.

The following are the only steamship lines now receiving subsidies for mail service under special acts of Congress: The Pacific Mail Steamship Company receive $500,000 per annum for conveying a monthly mail between San Francisco, Japan, and China, which will be increased to $1,000,000 per annum for a semimonthly mail on and after October 1, 1873; the United States and Brazil Mail Steamship Company receive $150,000 per annum for conveying a monthly mail between New York and Rio de Janeiro, Brazil; and the California, Oregon and Mexican Steamship Company receive $75,000 per annum for conveying a monthly mail between San Francisco and Honolulu (Hawaiian Islands), making the total amount of mail steamship subsidies at present $725,000 per annum.

Our postal communications with all parts of the civilized world have been placed upon a most advantageous footing by the improved postal conventions and arrangements recently concluded with the leading commercial countries of Europe and America, and the gratifying statement is made that with the conclusion of a satisfactory convention with France, the details of which have been definitely agreed to by the head of the French postal department, subject to the approval of the minister of finance, little remains to be accomplished by treaty for some time to come with respect either to reduction of rates or improved facilities of postal intercourse.

Your favorable consideration is respectfully invited to the recommendations made by the Postmaster-General for an increase of service from monthly to semimonthly trips on the mail steamship route to Brazil; for a subsidy in aid of the establishment of an American line of mail steamers between San Francisco, New Zealand, and Australia; for the establishment of post-office savings banks, and for the increase of the salaries of the heads of bureaus. I have heretofore recommended the abolition of the franking privilege, and see no reason now for changing my views on that subject. It not having been favorably regarded by Congress, however, I now suggest a modification of that privilege to correct its glaring and costly abuses. I would recommend also the appointment of a committee or commission to take into consideration the best method (equitable to private corporations who have invested their time and capital in the establishment of telegraph lines) of acquiring the title to all telegraph lines now in operation, and of connecting this service with the postal service of the nation. It is not probable that this subject could receive the proper consideration during the limits of a short session of Congress, but it may be initiated, so that future action may be fair to the Government and to private parties concerned.

There are but three lines of ocean steamers—namely, the Pacific Mail Steamship Company, between San Francisco, China, and Japan, with provision made for semimonthly service after October 1, 1873; the United States and Brazil line, monthly; and the California, New Zealand, and Australian line, monthly—plying between the United States and foreign ports, and owned and operated under our flag. I earnestly recommend that such liberal contracts for carrying the mails be authorized with these lines as will insure their continuance.

If the expediency of extending the aid of Government to lines of steamers which hitherto have not received it should be deemed worthy of the consideration of Congress, political and commercial objects make it advisable to bestow such aid on a line under our flag between Panama and the western South American ports. By this means much trade now diverted to other countries might be brought to us, to the mutual advantage of this country and those lying in that quarter of the continent of America.

The report of the Secretary of the Treasury will show an alarming falling off in our carrying trade for the last ten or twelve years, and even for the past year.   I do not believe that public treasure can be better expended in the interest of the whole people than in trying to recover this trade.   An expenditure of $5,000,000 per annum for the next five years, if it would restore to us our proportion of the carrying trade of the world, would be profitably expended.

The price of labor in Europe has so much enhanced within the last few years that the cost of building and operating ocean steamers in the United States is not so much greater than in Europe; and I believe the time has arrived for Congress to take this subject into serious consideration.

DEPARTMENT OF JUSTICE.

Detailed statements of the disbursements through the Department of Justice will be furnished by the report of the Attorney-General, and though these have been somewhat increased by the recent acts of Congress "to enforce the rights of citizens of the United States to vote in the several States of the Union," and "to enforce the provisions of the fourteenth amendment to the Constitution of the United States," and the amendments thereto, I can not question the necessity and salutary effect of those enactments.   Reckless and lawless men, I regret to say, have associated themselves together in some localities to deprive other citizens of those rights guaranteed to them by the Constitution of the United States, and to that end have committed deeds of blood and violence; but the prosecution and punishment of many of these persons have tended greatly to the repression of such disorders.   I do not doubt that a great majority of the people in all parts of the country favor the full enjoyment by all classes of persons of those rights to which they are entitled under the Constitution and laws, and I invoke the aid and influence of all good citizens to prevent organizations whose objects are by unlawful means to interfere with those rights.   I look with confidence to the time, not far distant, when the obvious advantages of good order and peace will induce an abandonment of all combinations prohibited by the acts referred to, and when it will be unnecessary to carry on prosecutions or inflict punishment to protect citizens from the lawless doings of such combinations.

Applications have been made to me to pardon persons convicted of a violation of said acts, upon the ground that clemency in such cases would tend to tranquilize the public mind, and to test the virtue of that policy I am disposed, as far as my sense of justice will permit, to give to these applications a favorable consideration; but any action thereon is not to be construed as indicating any change in my determination to enforce with vigor such acts so long as the conspiracies and combinations therein named disturb the peace of the country.

It is much to be regretted, and is regretted by no one more than myself, that a necessity has ever existed to execute the "enforcement act." No one can desire more than I that the necessity of applying it may never again be demanded.

INTERIOR DEPARTMENT.

The Secretary of the Interior reports satisfactory improvement and progress in each of the several bureaus under the control of the Interior Department. They are all in excellent condition. The work which in some of them for some years has been in arrears has been brought down to a recent date, and in all the current business is being promptly dispatched.

INDIANS.

The policy which was adopted at the beginning of this Administration with regard to the management of the Indians has been as successful as its most ardent friends anticipated within so short a time. It has reduced the expense of their management; decreased their forays upon the white settlements; tended to give the largest opportunity for the extension of the great railways through the public domain and the pushing of settlements into more remote districts of the country, and at the same time improved the condition of the Indians. The policy will be maintained without any change excepting such as further experience may show to be necessary to render it more efficient.

The subject of converting the so-called Indian Territory south of Kansas into a home for the Indian, and erecting therein a Territorial form of government, is one of great importance as a complement of the existing Indian policy. The question of removal to that Territory has within the past year been presented to many of the tribes resident upon other and less desirable portions of the public domain, and has generally been received by them with favor. As a preliminary step to the organization of such a Territory, it will be necessary to confine the Indians now resident therein to farms of proper size, which should be secured to them in fee; the residue to be used for the settlement of other friendly Indians. Efforts will be made in the immediate future to induce the removal of as many peaceably disposed Indians to the Indian Territory as can be settled properly without disturbing the harmony of those already there. There is no other location now available where a people who are endeavoring to acquire a knowledge of pastoral and agricultural pursuits can be as well accommodated as upon the unoccupied lands in the Indian Territory. A Territorial government should, however, protect the Indians from the inroads of whites for a term of years, until they become sufficiently advanced in the arts and civilization to guard their own rights, and from the disposal of the lands held by them for the same period.

LANDS.

During the last fiscal year there were disposed of out of the public lands 11,864,975 acres, a quantity greater by 1,099,270 acres than was disposed of the previous year. Of this amount 1,370,320 acres were sold for cash, 389,460 acres located with military warrants, 4,671,332 acres taken for homesteads, 693,613 acres located with college scrip, 3,554,887 acres granted to railroads, 465,347 acres granted to wagon roads, 714,255 acres given to States as swamp land, 5,760 acres located by Indian scrip. The cash receipts from all sources in the Land Office amounted to $3,218,100. During the same period 22,016,608 acres of the public lands were surveyed, which, added to the quantity before surveyed, amounts to 583,364,780 acres, leaving 1,257,633,628 acres of the public lands still unsurveyed.

The reports from the subordinates of the Land Office contain interesting information in regard to their respective districts. They uniformly mention the fruitfulness of the soil during the past season and the increased yields of all kinds of produce. Even in those States and Territories where mining is the principal business agricultural products have exceeded the local demand, and liberal shipments have been made to distant points.

PATENTS.

During the year ending September 30, 1872, there were issued from the Patent Office 13,626 patents, 233 extensions, and 556 certificates and registries of trade-marks. During the same time 19,587 applications for patents, including reissues and designs, have been received and 3,100 caveats filed. The fees received during the same period amounted to $700,954.86, and the total expenditures to $623,553.90, making the net receipts over the expenditures $77,400.96.

Since 1836 200,000 applications for patents have been filed and about 133,000 patents issued. The office is being conducted under the same laws and general organization as were adopted at its original inauguration, when only from 100 to 500 applications were made per annum. The Commissioner shows that the office has outgrown the original plan, and that a new organization has become necessary. This subject was presented to Congress in a special communication in February last, with my approval and the approval of the Secretary of the Interior, and the suggestions contained in said communication were embraced in the bill that was reported to the House by the Committee on Patents at the last session. The subject of the reorganization of the Patent Office, as contemplated by the bill referred to, is one of such importance to the industrial interests of the country that I commend it to the attention of Congress.

The Commissioner also treats the subject of the separation of the Patent Office from the Department of the Interior. This subject is also embraced in the bill heretofore referred to. The Commissioner complains of the want of room for the model gallery and for the working force and necessary files of the office. It is impossible to transact the business of the office properly without more room in which to arrange files and drawings, that must be consulted hourly in the transaction of business. The whole of the Patent Office building will soon be needed, if it is not already, for the accommodation of the business of the Patent Office.

PENSIONS.

The amount paid for pensions in the last fiscal year was $30,169,340, an amount larger by $3,708,434 than was paid during the preceding year. Of this amount $2,313,409 were paid under the act of Congress of February 17, 1871, to survivors of the War of 1812. The annual increase of pensions by the legislation of Congress has more than kept pace with the natural yearly losses from the rolls. The act of Congress of June 8, 1872, has added an estimated amount of $750,000 per annum to the rolls, without increasing the number of pensioners. We can not, therefore, look for any substantial decrease in the expenditures of this Department for some time to come, or so long as Congress continues to so change the rates of pension.

The whole number of soldiers enlisted in the War of the Rebellion was 2,688,523. The total number of claims for invalid pensions is 176,000, being but 6 per cent of the whole number of enlisted men. The total number of claims on hand at the beginning of the year was 91,689; the number received during the year was 26,574; the number disposed of was 39,178, making a net gain of 12,604. The number of claims now on file is 79,085.

On the 30th of June, 1872, there were on the rolls the names of 95,405 invalid military pensioners, 113,518 widows, orphans, and dependent relatives, making an aggregate of 208,923 army pensioners. At the same time there were on the rolls the names of 1,449 navy pensioners and 1,730 widows, orphans, and dependent relatives, making the whole number of naval pensioners 3,179. There have been received since the passage of the act to provide pensions for the survivors of the War of 1812 36,551 applications, prior to June 30, 1872. Of these there were allowed during the last fiscal year 20,126 claims; 4,845 were rejected during the year, leaving 11,580 claims pending at that date. The number of pensions of all classes granted during the last fiscal year was 33,838. During that period there were dropped from the rolls, for various causes, 9,104 names, leaving a grand total of 232,229 pensioners on the rolls on the 30th of June, 1872.

It is thought that the claims for pensions on account of the War of 1812 will all be disposed of by the 1st of May, 1873. It is estimated that $30,480,000 will be required for the pension service during the next fiscal year.

THE CENSUS.

The Ninth Census is about completed. Its early completion is a subject of congratulation, inasmuch as the use to be made of the statistics therein contained depends very greatly on the promptitude of publication.

The Secretary of the Interior recommends that a census be taken in 1875, which recommendation should receive the early attention of Congress. The interval at present established between the Federal census is so long that the information obtained at the decennial period as to the material condition, wants, and resources of the nation is of little practical value after the expiration of the first half of that period. It would probably obviate the constitutional provision regarding the decennial census if a census taken in 1875 should be divested of all political character and no reapportionment of Congressional representation be made under it. Such a census, coming, as it would, in the last year of the first century of our national existence, would furnish a noble monument of the progress of the United States during that century.

EDUCATION.

The rapidly increasing interest in education is a most encouraging feature in the current history of the country, and it is no doubt true that this is due in a great measure to the efforts of the Bureau of Education. That office is continually receiving evidences, which abundantly prove its efficiency, from the various institutions of learning and educators of all kinds throughout the country.

The report of the Commissioner contains a vast amount of educational details of great interest. The bill now pending before Congress, providing for the appropriation of the net proceeds of the sales of public lands for educational purposes, to aid the States in the general education of their rising generation, is a measure of such great importance to our real progress and is so unanimously approved by the leading friends of education that I commend it to the favorable attention of Congress.

TERRITORIES.

Affairs in the Territories are generally satisfactory. The energy and business capacity of the pioneers who are settling up the vast domains not yet incorporated into States are keeping pace in internal improvements and civil government with the older communities. In but one of them (Utah) is the condition of affairs unsatisfactory, except so far as the quiet of the citizen may be disturbed by real or imaginary danger of Indian hostilities. It has seemed to be the policy of the legislature of Utah to evade all responsibility to the Government of the United States, and even to hold a position in hostility to it.

I recommend a careful revision of the present laws of the Territory by Congress, and the enactment of such a law (the one proposed in Congress at its last session, for instance, or something similar to it) as will secure peace, the equality of all citizens before the law, and the ultimate extinguishment of polygamy.

Since the establishment of a Territorial government for the District of Columbia the improvement of the condition of the city of Washington and surroundings and the increased prosperity of the citizens are observable to the most casual visitor. The nation, being a large owner of property in the city, should bear, with the citizens of the District, its just share of the expense of these improvements.

I recommend, therefore, an appropriation to reimburse the citizens for the work done by them along and in front of public grounds during the past year, and liberal appropriations in order that the improvements and embellishments of the public buildings and grounds may keep pace with the improvements made by the Territorial authorities.

AGRICULTURE.

The report of the Commissioner of Agriculture gives a very full and interesting account of the several divisions of that Department—the horticultural, agricultural, statistical, entomological, and chemical—and the benefits conferred by each upon the agricultural interests of the country. The whole report is a complete history, in detail, of the workings of that Department in all its branches, showing the manner in which the farmer, merchant, and miner is informed, and the extent to which he is aided in his pursuits.

The Commissioner makes one recommendation—that measures be taken by Congress to protect and induce the planting of forests—and suggests that no part of the public lands should be disposed of without the condition that one-tenth of it should be reserved in timber where it exists, and where it does not exist inducements should be offered for planting it.

CENTENNIAL CELEBRATION.

In accordance with the terms of the act of Congress approved March 3, 1871, providing for the celebration of the one hundredth anniversary of American independence, a commission has been organized, consisting of two members from each of the States and Territories. This commission has held two sessions, and has made satisfactory progress in the organization and in the initiatory steps necessary for carrying out the provisions of the act, and for executing also the provisions of the act of June 1, 1872, creating a centennial board of finance. A preliminary report of progress has been received from the president of the commission, and is herewith transmitted. It will be the duty of the commission at your coming session to transmit a full report of the progress made, and to lay before you the details relating to the exhibition of American and foreign arts, products, and manufactures, which by the terms of the act is to be held under the auspices of the Government of the United States in the city of Philadelphia in the year 1876.

This celebration will be looked forward to by American citizens with great interest, as marking a century of greater progress and prosperity than is recorded in the history of any other nation, and as serving a further good purpose in bringing together on our soil peoples of all the commercial nations of the earth in a manner calculated to insure international good feeling.

CIVIL SERVICE.

An earnest desire has been felt to correct abuses which have grown up in the civil service of the country through the defective method of making appointments to office. Heretofore Federal offices have been regarded too much as the reward of political services. Under authority of Congress rules have been established to regulate the tenure of office and the mode of appointments. It can not be expected that any system of rules can be entirely effective and prove a perfect remedy for the existing evils until they have been thoroughly tested by actual practice and amended according to the requirements of the service. During my term of office it shall be my earnest endeavor to so apply the rules as to secure the greatest possible reform in the civil service of the Government, but it will require the direct action of Congress to render the enforcement of the system binding upon my successors; and I hope that the experience of the past year, together with appropriate legislation by Congress, may reach a satisfactory solution of this question and secure to the public service for all time a practical method of obtaining faithful and efficient officers and employees.

FIFTH ANNUAL MESSAGE.

EXECUTIVE MANSION, *December 1, 1873.*

To the Senate and House of Representatives:

The year that has passed since the submission of my last message to Congress has, especially during the latter part of it, been an eventful one to the country. In the midst of great national prosperity a financial crisis has occurred that has brought low fortunes of gigantic proportions; political partisanship has almost ceased to exist, especially in the agricultural regions; and, finally, the capture upon the high seas of a vessel bearing our flag has for a time threatened the most serious consequences, and has agitated the public mind from one end of the country to the other. But this, happily, now is in the course of satisfactory adjustment, honorable to both nations concerned.

The relations of the United States, however, with most of the other powers continue to be friendly and cordial. With France, Germany, Russia, Italy, and the minor European powers; with Brazil and most of the South American Republics, and with Japan, nothing has occurred during the year to demand special notice. The correspondence between the Department of State and various diplomatic representatives in or from those countries is transmitted herewith.

In executing the will of Congress, as expressed in its joint resolution of the 14th of February last, and in accordance with the provisions of the resolution, a number of "practical artisans," of "scientific men," and of "honorary commissioners" were authorized to attend the exposition at Vienna as commissioners on the part of the United States. It is believed that we have obtained the object which Congress had in view when it passed the joint resolution—"in order to enable the people of the United States to participate in the advantages of the International Exhibition of the Products of Agriculture, Manufactures, and the Fine Arts to be held at Vienna." I take pleasure in adding that the American exhibitors have received a gratifying number of diplomas and of medals.

During the exposition a conference was held at Vienna for the purpose of consultation on the systems prevailing in different countries for the protection of inventions. I authorized a representative from the Patent Office to be present at Vienna at the time when this conference was to take place, in order to aid as far as he might in securing any possible additional protection to American inventors in Europe. The report of this agent will be laid before Congress.

It is my pleasant duty to announce to Congress that the Emperor of China, on attaining his majority, received the diplomatic representatives of the Western powers in person. An account of these ceremonies and of the interesting discussions which preceded them will be found in the documents transmitted herewith. The accompanying papers show that some advance, although slight, has been made during the past year toward the suppression of the infamous Chinese cooly trade. I recommend Congress to inquire whether additional legislation be not needed on this subject.

The money awarded to the United States by the tribunal of arbitration at Geneva was paid by Her Majesty's Government a few days in advance of the time when it would have become payable according to the terms of the treaty. In compliance with the provisions of the act of March 3, 1873, it was at once paid into the Treasury, and used to redeem, so far as it might, the public debt of the United States; and the amount so redeemed was invested in a 5 per cent registered bond of the United States for $15,500,000, which is now held by the Secretary of State, subject to the future disposition of Congress.

I renew my recommendation, made at the opening of the last session of Congress, that a commission be created for the purpose of auditing and determining the amounts of the several "direct losses growing out of the destruction of vessels and their cargoes" by the *Alabama*, the *Florida*, or the *Shenandoah* after leaving Melbourne, for which the sufferers have received no equivalent or compensation, and of ascertaining the names of the persons entitled to receive compensation for the same, making the computations upon the basis indicated by the tribunal of arbitration at Geneva; and that payment of such losses be authorized to an extent not to exceed the awards of the tribunal at Geneva.

By an act approved on the 14th day of February last Congress made provision for completing, jointly with an officer or commissioner to be named by Her Britannic Majesty, the determination of so much of the boundary line between the territory of the United States and the possessions of Great Britain as was left uncompleted by the commissioners appointed under the act of Congress of August 11, 1856. Under the provisions of this act the northwest water boundary of the United States has been determined and marked in accordance with the award of the Emperor of Germany. A protocol and a copy of the map upon which the line was thus marked are contained in the papers submitted herewith.

I also transmit a copy of the report of the commissioner for marking the northern boundary between the United States and the British possessions west of the Lake of the Woods, of the operations of the commission during the past season. Surveys have been made to a point 497 miles west of the Lake of the Woods, leaving about 350 miles to be surveyed, the field work of which can be completed during the next season.

The mixed commission organized under the provisions of the treaty of Washington for settling and determining the claims of citizens of either power against the other arising out of acts committed against their persons or property during the period between April 13, 1861, and April 9, 1865, made its final award on the 25th day of September last. It was awarded that the Government of the United States should pay to the Government of Her Britannic Majesty, within twelve months from the date of the award, the sum of $1,929,819 in gold. The commission disallowed or dismissed all other claims of British subjects against the United States. The amount of the claims presented by the British Government, but disallowed or dismissed, is understood to be about $93,000,000. It also disallowed all the claims of citizens of the United States against Great Britain which were referred to it.

I recommend the early passage of an act appropriating the amount necessary to pay this award against the United States.

I have caused to be communicated to the Government of the King of Italy the thanks of this Government for the eminent services rendered by Count Corti as the third commissioner on this commission. With dignity, learning, and impartiality he discharged duties requiring great labor and constant patience, to the satisfaction, I believe, of both Governments. I recommend legislation to create a special court, to consist of three judges, who shall be empowered to hear and determine all claims of aliens upon the United States arising out of acts committed against their persons or property during the insurrection. The recent reference under the treaty of Washington was confined to claims of British subjects arising during the period named in the treaty; but it is understood that there are other British claims of a similar nature, arising after the 9th of April, 1865, and it is known that other claims of a like nature are advanced by citizens or subjects of other powers. It is desirable to have these claims also examined and disposed of.

Official information being received from the Dutch Government of a state of war between the King of the Netherlands and the Sultan of Acheen, the officers of the United States who were near the seat of the war were instructed to observe an impartial neutrality. It is believed that they have done so.

The joint commission under the convention with Mexico of 1868, having again been legally prolonged, has resumed its business, which, it is hoped, may be brought to an early conclusion. The distinguished representative of Her Britannic Majesty at Washington has kindly consented, with the approval of his Government, to assume the arduous and responsible duties of umpire in this commission, and to lend the weight of his character and name to such decisions as may not receive the acquiescence of both the arbitrators appointed by the respective Governments.

The commissioners appointed pursuant to the authority of Congress to examine into the nature and extent of the forays by trespassers from that country upon the herds of Texas have made a report, which will be submitted for your consideration.

The Venezuelan Government has been apprised of the sense of Congress in regard to the awards of the joint commission under the convention of 25th April, 1866, as expressed in the act of the 25th of February last.

It is apprehended that that Government does not realize the character of its obligations under that convention. As there is reason to believe, however, that its hesitancy in recognizing them springs, in part at least, from real difficulty in discharging them in connection with its obligations to other governments, the expediency of further forbearance on our part is believed to be worthy of your consideration.

The Ottoman Government and that of Egypt have latterly shown a disposition to relieve foreign consuls of the judicial powers which heretofore they have exercised in the Turkish dominions, by organizing other tribunals. As Congress, however, has by law provided for the discharge of judicial functions by consuls of the United States in that quarter under the treaty of 1830, I have not felt at liberty formally to accept the proposed change without the assent of Congress, whose decision upon the subject at as early a period as may be convenient is earnestly requested.

I transmit herewith, for the consideration and determination of Congress, an application of the Republic of Santo Domingo to this Government to exercise a protectorate over that Republic.

Since the adjournment of Congress the following treaties with foreign powers have been proclaimed: A naturalization convention with Denmark; a convention with Mexico for renewing the Claims Commission; a convention of friendship, commerce, and extradition with the Orange Free State, and a naturalization convention with Ecuador.

I renew the recommendation made in my message of December, 1870, that Congress authorize the Postmaster-General to issue all commissions to officials appointed through his Department.

I invite the earnest attention of Congress to the existing laws of the United States respecting expatriation and the election of nationality by individuals. Many citizens of the United States reside permanently abroad with their families. Under the provisions of the act approved February 10, 1855, the children of such persons are to be deemed and taken to be citizens of the United States, but the rights of citizenship are not to descend to persons whose fathers never resided in the United States.

It thus happens that persons who have never resided within the United States have been enabled to put forward a pretension to the protection of the United States against the claim to military service of the government under whose protection they were born and have been reared. In some cases even naturalized citizens of the United States have returned to the land of their birth, with intent to remain there, and their children, the issue of a marriage contracted there after their return, and who have never been in the United States, have laid claim to our protection when the lapse of many years had imposed upon them the duty of military service to the only government which had ever known them personally.

Until the year 1868 it was left, embarrassed by conflicting opinions of courts and of jurists, to determine how far the doctrine of perpetual allegiance derived from our former colonial relations with Great Britain was applicable to American citizens. Congress then wisely swept these doubts away by enacting that—

Any declaration, instruction, opinion, order, or decision of any officer of this Government which denies, restricts, impairs, or questions the right of expatriation is inconsistent with the fundamental principles of this Government.

But Congress did not indicate in that statute, nor has it since done so, what acts are to be deemed to work expatriation. For my own guidance in determining such questions I required (under the provisions of the Constitution) the opinion in writing of the principal officer in each of the Executive Departments upon certain questions relating to this subject. The result satisfies me that further legislation has become necessary. I therefore commend the subject to the careful consideration of

Congress, and I transmit herewith copies of the several opinions of the principal officers of the Executive Departments, together with other correspondence and pertinent information on the same subject.

The United States, who led the way in the overthrow of the feudal doctrine of perpetual allegiance, are among the last to indicate how their own citizens may elect another nationality. The papers submitted herewith indicate what is necessary to place us on a par with other leading nations in liberality of legislation on this international question. We have already in our treaties assented to the principles which would need to be embodied in laws intended to accomplish such results. We have agreed that citizens of the United States may cease to be citizens and may voluntarily render allegiance to other powers. We have agreed that residence in a foreign land without intent to return, shall of itself work expatriation. We have agreed in some instances upon the length of time necessary for such continued residence to work a presumption of such intent. I invite Congress now to mark out and define when and how expatriation can be accomplished; to regulate by law the condition of American women marrying foreigners; to fix the status of children born in a foreign country of American parents residing more or less permanently abroad, and to make rules for determining such other kindred points as may seem best to Congress.

In compliance with the request of Congress, I transmitted to the American minister at Madrid, with instructions to present it to the Spanish Government, the joint resolution approved on the 3d of March last, tendering to the people of Spain, in the name and on the behalf of the American people, the congratulations of Congress upon the efforts to consolidate in Spain the principles of universal liberty in a republican form of government.

The existence of this new Republic was inaugurated by striking the fetters from the slaves in Porto Rico. This beneficent measure was followed by the release of several thousand persons illegally held as slaves in Cuba. Next, the Captain-General of that colony was deprived of the power to set aside the orders of his superiors at Madrid, which had pertained to the office since 1825. The sequestered estates of American citizens, which had been the cause of long and fruitless correspondence, were ordered to be restored to their owners. All these liberal steps were taken in the face of a violent opposition directed by the reactionary slaveholders of Havana, who are vainly striving to stay the march of ideas which has terminated slavery in Christendom, Cuba only excepted. Unhappily, however, this baneful influence has thus far succeeded in defeating the efforts of all liberal-minded men in Spain to abolish slavery in Cuba, and in preventing the promised reform in that island. The struggle for political supremacy continues there.

The proslavery and aristocratic party in Cuba is gradually arraigning itself in more and more open hostility and defiance of the home govern-

ment, while it still maintains a political connection with the Republic
in the peninsula; and although usurping and defying the authority of
the home government whenever such usurpation or defiance tends in the
direction of oppression or of the maintenance of abuses, it is still a power
in Madrid, and is recognized by the Government.   Thus an element more
dangerous to continued colonial relations between Cuba and Spain than
that which inspired the insurrection at Yara—an element opposed to
granting any relief from misrule and abuse, with no aspirations after
freedom, commanding no sympathies in generous breasts, aiming to rivet
still stronger the shackles of slavery and oppression—has seized many
of the emblems of power in Cuba, and, under professions of loyalty to the
mother country, is exhausting the resources of the island, and is doing
acts which are at variance with those principles of justice, of liberality,
and of right which give nobility of character to a republic.   In the
interests of humanity, of civilization, and of progress, it is to be hoped
that this evil influence may be soon averted.

The steamer *Virginius* was on the 26th day of September, 1870, duly
registered at the port of New York as a part of the commercial marine
of the United States.   On the 4th of October, 1870, having received the
certificate of her register in the usual legal form, she sailed from the port
of New York and has not since been within the territorial jurisdiction of
the United States.   On the 31st day of October last, while sailing under
the flag of the United States on the high seas, she was forcibly seized
by the Spanish gunboat *Tornado*, and was carried into the port of Santiago de Cuba, where fifty-three of her passengers and crew were inhu-
manly, and, so far at least as relates to those who were citizens of the
United States, without due process of law, put to death.

It is a well-established principle, asserted by the United States from the
beginning of their national independence, recognized by Great Britain and
other maritime powers, and stated by the Senate in a resolution passed
unanimously on the 16th of June, 1858, that—

American vessels on the high seas in time of peace, bearing the American flag,
remain under the jurisdiction of the country to which they belong, and therefore any
visitation, molestation, or detention of such vessel by force, or by the exhibition of
force, on the part of a foreign power is in derogation of the sovereignty of the United
States.

In accordance with this principle, the restoration of the *Virginius* and
the surrender of the survivors of her passengers and crew, and a due reparation to the flag, and the punishment of the authorities who had been
guilty of the illegal acts of violence, were demanded.   The Spanish Government has recognized the justice of the demand, and has arranged for
the immediate delivery of the vessel, and for the surrender of the survivors of the passengers and crew, and for a salute to the flag, and for proceedings looking to the punishment of those who may be proved to have
been guilty of illegal acts of violence toward citizens of the United States,

and also toward indemnifying those who may be shown to be entitled to indemnity. A copy of a protocol of a conference between the Secretary of State and the Spanish minister, in which the terms of this arrangement were agreed to, is transmitted herewith.

The correspondence on this subject with the legation of the United States in Madrid was conducted in cipher and by cable, and needs the verification of the actual text of the correspondence. It has seemed to me to be due to the importance of the case not to submit this correspondence until the accurate text can be received by mail. It is expected shortly, and will be submitted when received.

In taking leave of this subject for the present I wish to renew the expression of my conviction that the existence of African slavery in Cuba is a principal cause of the lamentable condition of the island. I do not doubt that Congress shares with me the hope that it will soon be made to disappear, and that peace and prosperity may follow its abolition.

The embargoing of American estates in Cuba, cruelty to American citizens detected in no act of hostility to the Spanish Government, the murdering of prisoners taken with arms in their hands, and, finally, the capture upon the high seas of a vessel sailing under the United States flag and bearing a United States registry have culminated in an outburst of indignation that has seemed for a time to threaten war. Pending negotiations between the United States and the Government of Spain on the subject of this capture, I have authorized the Secretary of the Navy to put our Navy on a war footing, to the extent, at least, of the entire annual appropriation for that branch of the service, trusting to Congress and the public opinion of the American people to justify my action.

Assuming from the action of the last Congress in appointing a Committee on Privileges and Elections to prepare and report to this Congress a constitutional amendment to provide a better method of electing the President and Vice-President of the United States, and also from the necessity of such an amendment, that there will be submitted to the State legislatures for ratification such an improvement in our Constitution, I suggest two others for your consideration:

First. To authorize the Executive to approve of so much of any measure passing the two Houses of Congress as his judgment may dictate, without approving the whole, the disapproved portion or portions to be subjected to the same rules as now, to wit, to be referred back to the House in which the measure or measures originated, and, if passed by a two-thirds vote of the two Houses, then to become a law without the approval of the President. I would add to this a provision that there should be no legislation by Congress during the last twenty-four hours of its sitting, except upon vetoes, in order to give the Executive an opportunity to examine and approve or disapprove bills understandingly.

Second. To provide by amendment that when an extra session of

Congress is convened by Executive proclamation legislation during the continuance of such extra session shall be confined to such subjects as the Executive may bring before it from time to time in writing.

The advantages to be gained by these two amendments are too obvious for me to comment upon them.   One session in each year is provided for by the Constitution, in which there are no restrictions as to the subjects of legislation by Congress.   If more are required, it is always in the power of Congress, during their term of office, to provide for sessions at any time.   The first of these amendments would protect the public against the many abuses and waste of public moneys which creep into appropriation bills and other important measures passing during the expiring hours of Congress, to which otherwise due consideration can not be given.

TREASURY DEPARTMENT.

The receipts of the Government from all sources for the last fiscal year were $333,738,204, and expenditures on all accounts $290,345,245, thus showing an excess of receipts over expenditures of $43,392,959. But it is not probable that this favorable exhibit will be shown for the present fiscal year.   Indeed, it is very doubtful whether, except with great economy on the part of Congress in making appropriations and the same economy in administering the various Departments of Government, the revenues will not fall short of meeting actual expenses, including interest on the public debt.

I commend to Congress such economy, and point out two sources where it seems to me it might commence, to wit, in the appropriations for public buildings in the many cities where work has not yet been commenced; in the appropriations for river and harbor improvement in those localities where the improvements are of but little benefit to general commerce, and for fortifications.

There is a still more fruitful source of expenditure, which I will point out later in this message.   I refer to the easy method of manufacturing claims for losses incurred in suppressing the late rebellion.

I would not be understood here as opposing the erection of good, substantial, and even ornamental buildings by the Government wherever such buildings are needed.   In fact, I approve of the Government owning its own buildings in all sections of the country, and hope the day is not far distant when it will not only possess them, but will erect in the capital suitable residences for all persons who now receive commutation for quarters or rent at Government expense, and for the Cabinet, thus setting an example to the States which may induce them to erect buildings for their Senators.   But I would have this work conducted at a time when the revenues of the country would abundantly justify it.

The revenues have materially fallen off for the first five months of the present fiscal year from what they were expected to produce, owing to the general panic now prevailing, which commenced about the middle of September last. The full effect of this disaster, if it should not prove a "blessing in disguise," is yet to be demonstrated. In either event it is your duty to heed the lesson and to provide by wise and well-considered legislation, as far as it lies in your power, against its recurrence, and to take advantage of all benefits that may have accrued.

My own judgment is that, however much individuals may have suffered, one long step has been taken toward specie payments; that we can never have permanent prosperity until a specie basis is reached; and that a specie basis can not be reached and maintained until our exports, exclusive of gold, pay for our imports, interest due abroad, and other specie obligations, or so nearly so as to leave an appreciable accumulation of the precious metals in the country from the products of our mines.

The development of the mines of precious metals during the past year and the prospective development of them for years to come are gratifying in their results. Could but one-half of the gold extracted from the mines be retained at home, our advance toward specie payments would be rapid.

To increase our exports sufficient currency is required to keep all the industries of the country employed. Without this national as well as individual bankruptcy must ensue. Undue inflation, on the other hand, while it might give temporary relief, would only lead to inflation of prices, the impossibility of competing in our own markets for the products of home skill and labor, and repeated renewals of present experiences. Elasticity to our circulating medium, therefore, and just enough of it to transact the legitimate business of the country and to keep all industries employed, is what is most to be desired. The exact medium is specie, the recognized medium of exchange the world over. That obtained, we shall have a currency of an exact degree of elasticity. If there be too much of it for the legitimate purposes of trade and commerce, it will flow out of the country. If too little, the reverse will result. To hold what we have and to appreciate our currency to that standard is the problem deserving of the most serious consideration of Congress.

The experience of the present panic has proven that the currency of the country, based, as it is, upon the credit of the country, is the best that has ever been devised. Usually in times of such trials currency has become worthless, or so much depreciated in value as to inflate the values of all the necessaries of life as compared with the currency. Everyone holding it has been anxious to dispose of it on any terms. Now we witness the reverse. Holders of currency hoard it as they did gold in former experiences of a like nature.

It is patent to the most casual observer that much more currency, or money, is required to transact the legitimate trade of the country during the fall and winter months, when the vast crops are being removed, than

during the balance of the year. With our present system the amount
in the country remains the same throughout the entire year, resulting in
an accumulation of all the surplus capital of the country in a few centers
when not employed in the moving of crops, tempted there by the offer of
interest on call loans.   Interest being paid, this surplus capital must
earn this interest paid with a profit. Being subject to "call," it can not
be loaned, only in part at best, to the merchant or manufacturer for a
fixed term.   Hence, no matter how much currency there might be in
the country, it would be absorbed, prices keeping pace with the volume,
and panics, stringency, and disasters would ever be recurring with the
autumn.   Elasticity in our monetary system, therefore, is the object to
be attained first, and next to that, as far as possible, a prevention of the
use of other people's money in stock and other species of speculation.
To prevent the latter it seems to me that one great step would be taken
by prohibiting the national banks from paying interest on deposits, by
requiring them to hold their reserves in their own vaults, and by forcing
them into resumption, though it would only be in legal-tender notes.
For this purpose I would suggest the establishment of clearing houses
for your consideration.

To secure the former many plans have been suggested, most, if not all,
of which look to me more like inflation on the one hand, or compelling
the Government, on the other, to pay interest, without corresponding
benefits, upon the surplus funds of the country during the seasons when
otherwise unemployed.

I submit for your consideration whether this difficulty might not be
overcome by authorizing the Secretary of the Treasury to issue at any
time to national banks of issue any amount of their own notes below a
fixed percentage of their issue (say 40 per cent), upon the banks' depositing with the Treasurer of the United States an amount of Government
bonds equal to the amount of notes demanded, the banks to forfeit to the
Government, say, 4 per cent of the interest accruing on the bonds so
pledged during the time they remain with the Treasurer as security for
the increased circulation, the bonds so pledged to be redeemable by the
banks at their pleasure, either in whole or in part, by returning their
own bills for cancellation to an amount equal to the face of the bonds
withdrawn.   I would further suggest for your consideration the propriety of authorizing national banks to diminish their standing issue at
pleasure, by returning for cancellation their own bills and withdrawing so many United States bonds as are pledged for the bills returned.

In view of the great actual contraction that has taken place in the
currency and the comparative contraction continuously going on, due to
the increase of population, increase of manufactories and all the industries, I do not believe there is too much of it now for the dullest period
of the year.   Indeed, if clearing houses should be established, thus forcing redemption, it is a question for your consideration whether banking

should not be made free, retaining all the safeguards now required to secure bill holders. In any modification of the present laws regulating national banks, as a further step toward preparing for resumption of specie payments, I invite your attention to a consideration of the propriety of exacting from them the retention as a part of their reserve either the whole or a part of the gold interest accruing upon the bonds pledged as security for their issue. I have not reflected enough on the bearing this might have in producing a scarcity of coin with which to pay duties on imports to give it my positive recommendation. But your attention is invited to the subject.

During the last four years the currency has been contracted, directly, by the withdrawal of 3 per cent certificates, compound-interest notes, and "seven-thirty" bonds outstanding on the 4th of March, 1869, all of which took the place of legal-tenders in the bank reserves to the extent of $63,000,000.

During the same period there has been a much larger comparative contraction of the currency. The population of the country has largely increased. More than 25,000 miles of railroad have been built, requiring the active use of capital to operate them. Millions of acres of land have been opened to cultivation, requiring capital to move the products. Manufactories have multiplied beyond all precedent in the same period of time, requiring capital weekly for the payment of wages and for the purchase of material; and probably the largest of all comparative contraction arises from the organizing of free labor in the South. Now every laborer there receives his wages, and, for want of savings banks, the greater part of such wages is carried in the pocket or hoarded until required for use.

These suggestions are thrown out for your consideration, without any recommendation that they shall be adopted literally, but hoping that the best method may be arrived at to secure such an elasticity of the currency as will keep employed all the industries of the country and prevent such an inflation as will put off indefinitely the resumption of specie payments, an object so devoutly to be wished for by all, and by none more earnestly than the class of people most directly interested—those who "earn their bread by the sweat of their brow." The decisions of Congress on this subject will have the hearty support of the Executive.

In previous messages I have called attention to the decline in American shipbuilding and recommended such legislation as would secure to us our proportion of the carrying trade. Stimulated by high rates and abundance of freight, the progress for the last year in shipbuilding has been very satisfactory. There has been an increase of about 3 per cent in the amount transported in American vessels over the amount of last year. With the reduced cost of material which has taken place, it may reasonably be hoped that this progress will be maintained, and even increased. However, as we pay about $80,000,000 per annum to foreign vessels for the transportation to a market of our surplus products, thus increasing the balance of trade against us to this amount, the subject is one worthy of your serious consideration.

"Cheap transportation" is a subject that has attracted the attention of both producers and consumers for the past few years, and has contributed to, if it has not been the direct cause of, the recent panic and stringency.

As Congress, at its last session, appointed a special committee to investigate this whole subject during the vacation and report at this session, I have nothing to recommend until their report is read.

There is one work, however, of a national character, in which the greater portion of the East and the West, the North and the South, are equally interested, to which I will invite your attention.

The State of New York has a canal connecting Lake Erie with tide water on the Hudson River. The State of Illinois has a similar work connecting Lake Michigan with navigable water on the Illinois River, thus making water communication inland between the East and the West and South. These great artificial water courses are the property of the States through which they pass, and pay toll to those States. Would it not be wise statesmanship to pledge these States that if they will open these canals for the passage of large vessels the General Government will look after and keep in navigable condition the great public highways with which they connect, to wit, the Overslaugh on the Hudson, the St. Clair Flats, and the Illinois and Mississippi rivers? This would be a national work; one of great value to the producers of the West and South in giving them cheap transportation for their produce to the seaboard and a market, and to the consumers in the East in giving them cheaper food, particularly of those articles of food which do not find a foreign market, and the prices of which, therefore, are not regulated by foreign demands. The advantages of such a work are too obvious for argument. I submit the subject to you, therefore, without further comment.

In attempting to regain our lost commerce and carrying trade I have heretofore called attention to the States south of us offering a field where much might be accomplished. To further this object I suggest that a small appropriation be made, accompanied with authority for the Secretary of the Navy to fit out a naval vessel to ascend the Amazon River to the mouth of the Madeira; thence to explore that river and its tributaries into Bolivia, and to report to Congress at its next session, or as soon as practicable, the accessibility of the country by water, its resources, and the population so reached. Such an exploration would cost but little; it can do no harm, and may result in establishing a trade of value to both nations.

In further connection with the Treasury Department I would recommend a revision and codification of the tariff laws and the opening of more mints for coining money, with authority to coin for such nations as may apply.

WAR DEPARTMENT.

The attention of Congress is invited to the recommendations contained in the report of the Secretary of War herewith accompanying.

The apparent great cost of supporting the Army is fully explained by this report, and I hope will receive your attention.

While inviting your general attention to all the recommendations made by the Secretary of War, there are two which I would especially invite you to consider: First, the importance of preparing for war in time of peace by providing proper armament for our seacoast defenses. Proper armament is of vastly more importance than fortifications. The latter can be supplied very speedily for temporary purposes when needed; the former can not. The second is the necessity of reopening promotion in the staff corps of the Army. Particularly is this necessity felt in the Medical, Pay, and Ordnance departments.

At this time it is necessary to employ "contract surgeons" to supply the necessary medical attendance required by the Army.

With the present force of the Pay Department it is now difficult to make the payments to troops provided for by law. Long delays in payments are productive of desertions and other demoralization, and the law prohibits the payment of troops by other than regular army paymasters.

There are now sixteen vacancies in the Ordnance Department, thus leaving that branch of the service without sufficient officers to conduct the business of the different arsenals on a large scale if ever required.

NAVY DEPARTMENT.

During the past year our Navy has been depleted by the sale of some vessels no longer fit for naval service and by the condemnation of others not yet disposed of. This, however, has been more than compensated for by the repair of six of the old wooden ships and by the building of eight new sloops of war, authorized by the last Congress. The building of these latter has occurred at a doubly fortunate time. They are about being completed at a time when they may possibly be much needed, and the work upon them has not only given direct employment to thousands of men, but has no doubt been the means of keeping open establishments for other work at a time of great financial distress.

Since the commencement of the last month, however, the distressing occurrences which have taken place in the waters of the Caribbean Sea, almost on our very seaboard, while they illustrate most forcibly the necessity always existing that a nation situated like ours should maintain in a state of possible efficiency a navy adequate to its responsibilities, has at the same time demanded that all the effective force we really have shall be put in immediate readiness for warlike service. This has been and is being done promptly and effectively, and I am assured that all the available ships and every authorized man of the American Navy will be ready for whatever action is required for the safety of our citizens or the maintenance of our honor. This, of course, will require the expenditure in a short time of some of the appropriations which were calculated to extend through the fiscal year, but Congress will, I doubt not, understand and appreciate the emergency, and will provide adequately not only for the present preparation, but for the future maintenance of our naval force. The Secretary of the Navy has during the past year been quietly putting some of our most effective monitors in condition for service, and thus the exigency finds us in a much better condition for work than we could possibly have been without his action.

POST-OFFICE DEPARTMENT.

A complete exhibit is presented in the accompanying report of the Postmaster-General of the operations of the Post-Office Department during the year. The ordinary postal revenues for the fiscal year ended June 30, 1873, amounted to $22,996,741.57, and the expenditures of all kinds to $29,084.945.67. The increase of revenues over 1872 was $1,081,315.20, and the increase of expenditures $2,426,753.36.

Independent of the payments made from special appropriations for mail steamship lines, the amount drawn from the General Treasury to meet deficiencies was $5,265,475. The constant and rapid extension of our postal service, particularly upon railways, and the improved facilities for the collection, transmission, distribution, and delivery of the mails which are constantly being provided account for the increased expenditures of this popular branch of the public service.

The total number of post-offices in operation on June 30, 1873, was 33,244, a net increase of 1,381 over the number reported the preceding year. The number of Presidential offices was 1,363, an increase of 163 during the year. The total length of railroad mail routes at the close of the year was 63,457 miles, an increase of 5,546 miles over the year 1872. Fifty-nine railway post-office lines were in operation June 30, 1873, extending over 14,866 miles of railroad routes and performing an aggregate service of 34,925 miles daily.

The number of letters exchanged with foreign countries was 27,459,- 185, an increase of 3,096,685 over the previous year, and the postage thereon amounted to $2,021,310.86. The total weight of correspondence exchanged in the mails with European countries exceeded 912 tons, an increase of 92 tons over the previous year. The total cost of the United States ocean steamship service, including $725,000 paid from special appropriations to subsidized lines of mail steamers, was $1,047,271.35.

New or additional postal conventions have been concluded with Sweden, Norway, Belgium, Germany, Canada, Newfoundland, and Japan, reducing postage rates on correspondence exchanged with those countries; and further efforts have been made to conclude a satisfactory postal convention with France, but without success.

I invite the favorable consideration of Congress to the suggestions and recommendations of the Postmaster-General for an extension of the free-delivery system in all cities having a population of not less than 10,000; for the prepayment of postage on newspapers and other printed matter of the second class; for a uniform postage and limit of weight on miscellaneous matter; for adjusting the compensation of all postmasters not appointed by the President, by the old method of commissions on the actual receipts of the office, instead of the present mode of fixing the salary in advance upon special returns; and especially do I urge favorable action by Congress on the important recommendations of the Postmaster-General for the establishment of United States postal savings depositories.

Your attention is also again called to a consideration of the question of postal telegraphs and the arguments adduced in support thereof, in the hope that you may take such action in connection therewith as in your judgment will most contribute to the best interests of the country.

DEPARTMENT OF JUSTICE.

Affairs in Utah require your early and special attention. The Supreme Court of the United States, in the case of Clinton *vs.* Englebrecht, decided that the United States marshal of that Territory could not lawfully summon jurors for the district courts; and those courts hold that the Territorial marshal can not lawfully perform that duty, because he is elected by the legislative assembly, and not appointed as provided for in the act organizing the Territory. All proceedings at law are practically abolished by these decisions, and there have been but few or no jury trials in the district courts of that Territory since the last session of Congress. Property is left without protection by the courts, and crimes go unpunished. To prevent anarchy there it is absolutely necessary that Congress provide the courts with some mode of obtaining jurors, and I recommend legislation to that end, and also that the probate courts of the Territory, now assuming to issue writs of injunction and *habeas corpus* and to try criminal cases and questions as to land titles, be denied all jurisdiction not possessed ordinarily by courts of that description.

I have become impressed with the belief that the act approved March 2, 1867, entitled "An act to establish a uniform system of bankruptcy throughout the United States," is productive of more evil than good at this time. Many considerations might be urged for its total repeal, but, if this is not considered advisable, I think it will not be seriously questioned that those portions of said act providing for what is called involuntary bankruptcy operate to increase the financial embarrassments of the country. Careful and prudent men very often become involved in debt in the transaction of their business, and though they may possess ample property, if it could be made available for that purpose, to meet all their liabilities, yet, on account of the extraordinary scarcity of money, they may be unable to meet all their pecuniary obligations as they become due, in consequence of which they are liable to be prostrated in their business by proceedings in bankruptcy at the instance of unrelenting creditors. People are now so easily alarmed as to monetary matters that the mere filing of a petition in bankruptcy by an unfriendly creditor will necessarily embarrass, and oftentimes accomplish the financial ruin, of a responsible business man. Those who otherwise might make lawful and just arrangements to relieve themselves from difficulties produced by the present stringency in money are prevented by their constant exposure to attack and disappointment by proceedings against them in bankruptcy, and, besides, the law is made use of in many cases by obdurate creditors to frighten or force debtors into a compliance with their wishes and into acts of injustice to other creditors and to themselves. I recommend that so much of said act as provides for involuntary bankruptcy on account of the suspension of payment be repealed.

Your careful attention is invited to the subject of claims against the Government and to the facilities afforded by existing laws for their prosecution. Each of the Departments of State, Treasury, and War has demands for many millions of dollars upon its files, and they are rapidly accumulating. To these may be added those now pending before Congress, the Court of Claims, and the Southern Claims Commission, making in the aggregate an immense sum. Most of these grow out of the rebellion, and are intended to indemnify persons on both sides for their losses during the war; and not a few of them are fabricated and supported by false testimony. Projects are on foot, it is believed, to induce Congress to provide for new classes of claims, and to revive old ones through the repeal or modification of the statute of limitations, by which they are now barred. I presume these schemes, if proposed, will be received with little favor by Congress, and I recommend that persons having claims against the United States cognizable by any tribunal or Department thereof be required to present them at an early day, and that legislation be directed as far as practicable to the defeat of unfounded and unjust demands upon the Government; and I would suggest, as a means of preventing fraud, that witnesses be called upon to appear in person to testify before those tribunals having said claims before them for adjudication. Probably the largest saving to the National Treasury can be secured by timely legislation on these subjects of any of the economic measures that will be proposed.

You will be advised of the operations of the Department of Justice by the report of the Attorney-General, and I invite your attention to the amendments of existing laws suggested by him, with the view of reducing the expenses of that Department.

DEPARTMENT OF THE INTERIOR.

The policy inaugurated toward the Indians at the beginning of the last Administration has been steadily pursued, and, I believe, with beneficial results. It will be continued with only such modifications as time and experience may demonstrate as necessary.

With the encroachment of civilization upon the Indian reservations and hunting grounds, disturbances have taken place between the Indians and whites during the past year, and probably will continue to do so until each race appreciates that the other has rights which must be respected.

The policy has been to collect the Indians as rapidly as possible on reservations, and as far as practicable within what is known as the Indian Territory, and to teach them the arts of civilization and self-support. Where found off their reservations, and endangering the peace and safety of the whites, they have been punished, and will continue to be for like offenses.

The Indian Territory south of Kansas and west of Arkansas is sufficient in area and agricultural resources to support all the Indians east of the Rocky Mountains. In time, no doubt, all of them, except a few who may elect to make their homes among white people, will be collected there. As a preparatory step for this consummation, I am now satisfied that a Territorial form of government should be given them, which will secure the treaty rights of the original settlers and protect their homesteads from alienation for a period of twenty years.

The operations of the Patent Office are growing to such a magnitude and the accumulation of material is becoming so great that the necessity of more room is becoming more obvious day by day. I respectfully invite your attention to the reports of the Secretary of the Interior and Commissioner of Patents on this subject.

The business of the General Land Office exhibits a material increase in all its branches during the last fiscal year. During that time there were disposed of out of the public lands 13,030,606 acres, being an amount greater by 1,165,631 acres than was disposed of during the preceding year. Of the amount disposed of, 1,626,266 acres were sold for cash, 214,940 acres were located with military land warrants, 3,793,612 acres were taken for homesteads, 653,446 acres were located with agricultural-college scrip, 6,083,536 acres were certified by railroads, 76,576 acres were granted to wagon roads, 238,548 acres were approved to States as swamp lands, 138,681 acres were certified for agricultural colleges, common schools, universities, and seminaries, 190,775 acres were approved to States for internal improvements, and 14,222 acres were located with Indian scrip. The cash receipts during the same time were $3,408,-515.50, being $190,415.50 in excess of the receipts of the previous year. During the year 30,488,132 acres of public land were surveyed, an increase over the amount surveyed the previous year of 1,037,193 acres, and, added to the area previously surveyed, aggregates 616,554,895 acres which have been surveyed, leaving 1,218,443,505 acres of the public land still unsurveyed.

The increased and steadily increasing facilities for reaching our unoccupied public domain and for the transportation of surplus products enlarge the available field for desirable homestead locations, thus stimulating settlement and extending year by year in a gradually increasing ratio the area of occupation and cultivation.

The expressed desire of the representatives of a large colony of citizens of Russia to emigrate to this country, as is understood, with the consent of their Government, if certain concessions can be made to enable them to settle in a compact colony, is of great interest, as going to show the light in which our institutions are regarded by an industrious, intelligent, and wealthy people, desirous of enjoying civil and religious liberty; and the acquisition of so large an immigration of citizens of a superior class would without doubt be of substantial benefit to the country. I invite attention to the suggestion of the Secretary of the Interior in this behalf.

There was paid during the last fiscal year for pensions, including the expense of disbursement, $29,185,289.62, being an amount less by $984,050.98 than was expended for the same purpose the preceding year. Although this statement of expenditures would indicate a material reduction in amount compared with the preceding year, it is believed that the changes in the pension laws at the last session of Congress will absorb that amount the curren. year. At the close of the last fiscal year there were on the pension rolls 99,804 invalid military pensioners and 112,088 widows, orphans, and dependent relatives of deceased soldiers, making a total of that class of 211,892; 18,266 survivors of the War of 1812 and 5,053 widows of soldiers of that war pensioned under the act of Congress of February 14, 1871, making a total of that class of 23,319; 1,430 invalid navy pensioners and 1,770 widows, orphans, and dependent relatives of deceased officers, sailors, and marines of the Navy, making a total of navy pensioners of 3,200, and a grand total of pensioners of all classes of 238,411, showing a net increase during the last fiscal year of 6,182. During the last year the names of 16,405 pensioners were added to the rolls, and 10,223 names were dropped therefrom for various causes.

The system adopted for the detection of frauds against the Government in the matter of pensions has been productive of satisfactory results, but legislation is needed to provide, if possible, against the perpetration of such frauds in future.

The evidently increasing interest in the cause of education is a most encouraging feature in the general progress and prosperity of the country, and the Bureau of Education is earnest in its efforts to give proper direction to the new appliances and increased facilities which are being offered to aid the educators of the country in their great work.

The Ninth Census has been completed, the report thereof published and distributed, and the working force of the Bureau disbanded. The Secretary of the Interior renews his recommendation for a census to be taken in 1875, to which subject the attention of Congress is invited. The original suggestion in that behalf has met with the general approval of the country; and even if it be not deemed advisable at present to provide for a regular quinquennial census, a census taken in 1875, the report of which could be completed and published before the one hundredth anniversary of our national independence, would be especially interesting and valuable, as showing the progress of the country during the first century of our national existence. It is believed, however, that a regular census every five years would be of substantial benefit to the country, inasmuch as our growth hitherto has been so rapid that the results of the decennial census are necessarily unreliable as a basis of estimates for the latter years of a decennial period.

DISTRICT OF COLUMBIA.

Under the very efficient management of the governor and the board of public works of this District the city of Washington is rapidly assuming the appearance of a capital of which the nation may well be proud. From being a most unsightly place three years ago, disagreeable to pass through in summer in consequence of the dust arising from unpaved streets, and almost impassable in the winter from the mud, it is now one of the most sightly cities in the country, and can boast of being the best paved.

The work has been done systematically, the plans, grades, location of sewers, water and gas mains being determined upon before the work was commenced, thus securing permanency when completed. I question whether so much has ever been accomplished before in any American city for the same expenditures. The Government having large reservations in the city, and the nation at large having an interest in their capital, I recommend a liberal policy toward the District of Columbia, and that the Government should bear its just share of the expense of these improvements. Every citizen visiting the capital feels a pride in its growing beauty, and that he too is part owner in the investments made here.

I would suggest to Congress the propriety of promoting the establishment in this District of an institution of learning, or university of the highest class, by the donation of lands. There is no place better suited for such an institution than the national capital. There is no other place in which every citizen is so directly interested.

CIVIL-SERVICE REFORM.

In three successive messages to Congress I have called attention to the subject of "civil-service reform."

Action has been taken so far as to authorize the appointment of a board to devise rules governing methods of making appointments and promotions, but there never has been any action making these rules, or any rules, binding, or even entitled to observance, where persons desire the appointment of a friend or the removal of an official who may be disagreeable to them.

To have any rules effective they must have the acquiescence of Congress as well as of the Executive.   I commend, therefore, the subject to your attention, and suggest that a special committee of Congress might confer with the Civil-Service Board during the present session for the purpose of devising such rules as can be maintained, and which will secure the services of honest and capable officials, and which will also protect them in a degree of independence while in office.

Proper rules will protect Congress, as well as the Executive, from much needless persecution, and will prove of great value to the public at large.

I would recommend for your favorable consideration the passage of an enabling act for the admission of Colorado as a State in the Union.   It possesses all the elements of a prosperous State, agricultural and mineral, and, I believe, has a population now to justify such admission.   In connection with this I would also recommend the encouragement of a canal for purposes of irrigation from the eastern slope of the Rocky Mountains to the Missouri River.   As a rule I am opposed to further donations of public lands for internal improvements owned and controlled by private corporations, but in this instance I would make an exception.   Between the Missouri River and the Rocky Mountains there is an arid belt of public land from 300 to 500 miles in width, perfectly valueless for the occupation of man, for the want of sufficient rain to secure the growth of any product.   An irrigating canal would make productive a belt as wide as the supply of water could be made to spread over across this entire country, and would secure a cordon of settlements connecting the present population of the mountain and mining regions with that of the older States.   All the land reclaimed would be clear gain.   If alternate sections are retained by the Government, I would suggest that the retained sections be thrown open to entry under the homestead laws, or sold to actual settlers for a very low price.

I renew my previous recommendation to Congress for general amnesty. The number engaged in the late rebellion yet laboring under disabilities is very small, but enough to keep up a constant irritation.   No possible danger can accrue to the Government by restoring them to eligibility to hold office.

I suggest for your consideration the enactment of a law to better secure the civil rights which freedom should secure, but has not effectually secured, to the enfranchised slave.

SIXTH ANNUAL MESSAGE.

EXECUTIVE MANSION, *December 7, 1874.*

To the Senate and House of Representatives:

Since the convening of Congress one year ago the nation has undergone a prostration in business and industries such as has not been witnessed with us for many years. Speculation as to the causes for this prostration might be indulged in without profit, because as many theories would be advanced as there would be independent writers—those who expressed their own views without borrowing—upon the subject. Without indulging in theories as to the cause of this prostration, therefore, I will call your attention only to the fact, and to some plain questions as to which it would seem there should be no disagreement.

During this prostration two essential elements of prosperity have been most abundant—labor and capital. Both have been largely unemployed. Where security has been undoubted, capital has been attainable at very moderate rates. Where labor has been wanted, it has been found in abundance, at cheap rates compared with what—of necessaries and comforts of life—could be purchased with the wages demanded. Two great elements of prosperity, therefore, have not been denied us. A third might be added: Our soil and climate are unequaled, within the limits of any contiguous territory under one nationality, for its variety of products to feed and clothe a people and in the amount of surplus to spare to feed less favored peoples. Therefore, with these facts in view, it seems to me that wise statesmanship, at this session of Congress, would dictate legislation ignoring the past; directing in proper channels these great elements of prosperity to any people. Debt, debt abroad, is the only element that can, with always a sound currency, enter into our affairs to cause any continued depression in the industries and prosperity of our people.

A great conflict for national existence made necessary, for temporary purposes, the raising of large sums of money from whatever source attainable. It made it necessary, in the wisdom of Congress—and I do not doubt their wisdom in the premises, regarding the necessity of the times—to devise a system of national currency which it proved to be impossible to keep on a par with the recognized currency of the civilized world. This begot a spirit of speculation involving an extravagance and luxury not required for the happiness or prosperity of a people, and involving, both directly and indirectly, foreign indebtedness. The currency, being of fluctuating value, and therefore unsafe to hold for legitimate transactions requiring money, became a subject of speculation within itself. These two causes, however, have involved us in a foreign indebtedness, contracted in good faith by borrower and lender, which should be paid in coin, and according to the bond agreed upon when the debt was contracted—gold or its equivalent. The good faith of the Government can not be violated toward creditors without national disgrace. But our commerce should be encouraged; American shipbuilding and carrying capacity increased; foreign markets sought for products of the soil and manufactories, to the end that we may be able to pay these debts. Where a new market can be created for the sale of our products, either of the soil, the mine, or the manufactory, a new means is discovered of utilizing our idle capital and labor to the advantage of the whole people. But, in my judgment, the first step toward accomplishing this object is to secure a currency of fixed, stable value; a currency good wherever civilization reigns; one which, if it becomes superabundant with one people, will find a market with some other; a currency which has as its basis the labor necessary to produce it, which will give to it its value. Gold and silver are now the recognized medium of exchange the civilized world over, and to this we should return with the least practicable delay. In view of the pledges of the American Congress when our present legal-tender system was adopted, and debt contracted, there should be no delay—certainly no unnecessary delay—in fixing by legislation a method by which we will return to specie. To the accomplishment of this end I invite your special attention. I believe firmly that there can be no prosperous and permanent revival of business and industries until a policy is adopted—with legislation to carry it out—looking to a return to a specie basis. It is easy to conceive that the debtor and speculative classes may think it of value to them to make so-called money abundant until they can throw a portion of their burdens upon others. But even these, I believe, would be disappointed in the result if a course should be pursued which will keep in doubt the value of the legal-tender medium of exchange. A revival of productive industry is needed by all classes; by none more than the holders of property, of whatever sort, with debts to liquidate from realization upon its sale. But admitting that these two classes of citizens are to be benefited by expansion, would it be honest to give it? Would not the general loss be too great to justify such relief? Would it not be just as honest and prudent to authorize each debtor to issue his own legal-tenders to the extent of his liabilities? Than to do this, would it not be safer, for fear of overissues by unscrupulous creditors, to say that all debt obligations are obliterated in the United States, and now we commence anew, each possessing all he has at the time free from incumbrance? These propositions are too absurd to be entertained for a moment by thinking or honest people. Yet every delay in preparation for final resumption partakes of this dishonesty, and is only less in degree as the hope is held out that a convenient season will at last arrive for the good work of redeeming our pledges to commence. It will never come, in my opinion, except by positive action by Congress, or by national disasters which will destroy, for a time at least, the credit of the individual and the State at large. A sound currency might be reached by total bankruptcy and discredit of the integrity of the nation and of individuals. I believe it is in the power of Congress at this session to devise such legislation as will renew confidence, revive all the industries, start us on a career of prosperity to last for many years and to save the credit of the nation and of the people. Steps toward the return to a specie basis are the great requisites to this devoutly to be sought for end. There are others which I may touch upon hereafter.

A nation dealing in a currency below that of specie in value labors under two great disadvantages: First, having no use for the world's acknowledged medium of exchange, gold and silver, these are driven out of the country because there is no need for their use; second, the medium of exchange in use being of a fluctuating value—for, after all, it is only worth just what it will purchase of gold and silver, metals having an intrinsic value just in proportion to the honest labor it takes to produce them—a larger margin must be allowed for profit by the manufacturer and producer. It is months from the date of production to the date of realization. Interest upon capital must be charged, and risk of fluctuation in the value of that which is to be received in payment added. Hence high prices, acting as a protection to the foreign producer, who receives nothing in exchange for the products of his skill and labor except a currency good, at a stable value, the world over. It seems to me that nothing is clearer than that the greater part of the burden of existing prostration, for the want of a sound financial system, falls upon the working man, who must after all produce the wealth, and the salaried man, who superintends and conducts business. The burden falls upon them in two ways—by the deprivation of employment and by the decreased purchasing power of their salaries. It is the duty of Congress to devise the method of correcting the evils which are acknowledged to exist, and not mine. But I will venture to suggest two or three things which seem to me as absolutely necessary to a return to specie payments, the first great requisite in a return to prosperity. The legal-tender clause to the law authorizing the issue of currency by the National Government should be repealed, to take effect as to all contracts entered into after a day fixed in the repealing act—not to apply, however, to payments of salaries by Government, or for other expenditures now provided by law to be paid in currency, in the interval pending between repeal and final resumption. Provision should be made by which the Secretary of the Treasury can obtain gold as it may become necessary from time to time from the date when specie redemption commences. To this might and should be added a revenue sufficiently in excess of expenses to insure an accumulation of gold in the Treasury to sustain permanent redemption.

I commend this subject to your careful consideration, believing that a favorable solution is attainable, and if reached by this Congress that the present and future generations will ever gratefully remember it as their deliverer from a thraldom of evil and disgrace.

With resumption, free banking may be authorized with safety, giving the same full protection to bill holders which they have under existing laws. Indeed, I would regard free banking as essential. It would give proper elasticity to the currency. As more currency should be required for the transaction of legitimate business, new banks would be started, and in turn banks would wind up their business when it was found that there was a superabundance of currency. The experience and judgment of the people can best decide just how much currency is required for the transaction of the business of the country. It is unsafe to leave the settlement of this question to Congress, the Secretary of the Treasury, or the Executive. Congress should make the regulation under which banks may exist, but should not make banking a monopoly by limiting the amount of redeemable paper currency that shall be authorized. Such importance do I attach to this subject, and so earnestly do I commend it to your attention, that I give it prominence by introducing it at the beginning of this message.

During the past year nothing has occurred to disturb the general friendly and cordial relations of the United States with other powers.

The correspondence submitted herewith between this Government and its diplomatic representatives, as also with the representatives of other countries, shows a satisfactory condition of all questions between the United States and the most of those countries, and with few exceptions, to which reference is hereafter made, the absence of any points of difference to be adjusted.

The notice directed by the resolution of Congress of June 17, 1874, to be given to terminate the convention of July 17, 1858, between the United States and Belgium has been given, and the treaty will accordingly terminate on the 1st day of July, 1875. This convention secured to certain Belgian vessels entering the ports of the United States exceptional privileges which are not accorded to our own vessels. Other features of the convention have proved satisfactory, and have tended to the cultivation of mutually beneficial commercial intercourse and friendly relations between the two countries. I hope that negotiations which have been invited will result in the celebration of another treaty which may tend to the interests of both countries.

Our relations with China continue to be friendly. During the past year the fear of hostilities between China and Japan, growing out of the landing of an armed force upon the island of Formosa by the latter, has occasioned uneasiness. It is earnestly hoped, however, that the difficulties arising from this cause will be adjusted, and that the advance of civilization in these Empires may not be retarded by a state of war. In consequence of the part taken by certain citizens of the United States in this expedition, our representatives in those countries have been instructed to impress upon the Governments of China and Japan the firm intention of this country to maintain strict neutrality in the event of hostilities, and to carefully prevent any infraction of law on the part of our citizens.

In connection with this subject I call the attention of Congress to a generally conceded fact—that the great proportion of the Chinese immigrants who come to our shores do not come voluntarily, to make their homes with us and their labor productive of general prosperity, but come under contracts with headmen, who own them almost absolutely. In a worse form does this apply to Chinese women. Hardly a perceptible percentage of them perform any honorable labor, but they are brought for shameful purposes, to the disgrace of the communities where settled and to the great demoralization of the youth of those localities. If this evil practice can be legislated against, it will be my pleasure as well as duty to enforce any regulation to secure so desirable an end.

It is hoped that negotiations between the Government of Japan and the treaty powers, looking to the further opening of the Empire and to the removal of various restrictions upon trade and travel, may soon produce the results desired, which can not fail to inure to the benefit of all the parties. Having on previous occasions submitted to the consideration of Congress the propriety of the release of the Japanese Government from the further payment of the indemnity under the convention of October 22, 1864, and as no action had been taken thereon, it became my duty to regard the obligations of the convention as in force; and as the other powers interested had received their portion of the indemnity in full, the minister of the United States in Japan has, in behalf of this Government, received the remainder of the amount due to the United States under the convention of Simonosaki. I submit the propriety of applying the income of a part, if not of the whole, of this fund to the education in the Japanese language of a number of young men to be under obligations to serve the Government for a specified time as interpreters at the legation and the consulates in Japan. A limited number of Japanese youths might at the same time be educated in our own vernacular, and mutual benefits would result to both Governments. The importance of having our own citizens, competent and familiar with the language of Japan, to act as interpreters and in other capacities connected with the legation and the consulates in that country can not readily be overestimated.

The amount awarded to the Government of Great Britain by the mixed commission organized under the provisions of the treaty of Washington in settlement of the claims of British subjects arising from acts committed between April 13, 1861, and April 9, 1865, became payable, under the terms of the treaty, within the past year, and was paid upon the 21st day of September, 1874. In this connection I renew my recommendation, made at the opening of the last session of Congress, that a special court be created to hear and determine all claims of aliens against the United States arising from acts committed against their persons or property during the insurrection. It appears equitable that opportunity should be offered to citizens of other states to present their claims, as well as to those British subjects whose claims were not admissible under the late commission, to the early decision of some competent tribunal. To this end I recommend the necessary legislation to organize a court to dispose of all claims of aliens of the nature referred to in an equitable and satisfactory manner, and to relieve Congress and the Departments from the consideration of these questions.

The legislation necessary to extend to the colony of Newfoundland certain articles of the treaty of Washington of the 8th day of May, 1871, having been had, a protocol to that effect was signed in behalf of the United States and of Great Britain on the 28th day of May last, and was duly proclaimed on the following day. A copy of the proclamation* is submitted herewith.

A copy of the report of the commissioner appointed under the act of March 19, 1872, for surveying and marking the boundary between the United States and the British possessions from the Lake of the Woods to the summit of the Rocky Mountains is herewith transmitted. I am happy to announce that the field work of the commission has been completed, and the entire line from the northwest corner of the Lake of the Woods to the summit of the Rocky Mountains has been run and marked upon the surface of the earth. It is believed that the amount remaining unexpended of the appropriation made at the last session of Congress will be sufficient to complete the office work. I recommend that the authority of Congress be given to the use of the unexpended balance of the appropriation in the completion of the work of the commission in making its report and preparing the necessary maps.

The court known as the Court of Commissioners of Alabama Claims, created by an act of Congress of the last session, has organized and commenced its work, and it is to be hoped that the claims admissible under the provisions of the act may be speedily ascertained and paid.

It has been deemed advisable to exercise the discretion conferred upon the Executive at the last session by accepting the conditions required by the Government of Turkey for the privilege of allowing citizens of the United States to hold real estate in the former country, and by assenting to a certain change in the jurisdiction of courts in the latter. A copy of the proclamation* upon these subjects is herewith communicated.

There has been no material change in our relations with the independent States of this hemisphere which were formerly under the dominion of Spain. Marauding on the frontiers between Mexico and Texas still frequently takes place, despite the vigilance of the civil and military authorities in that quarter. The difficulty of checking such trespasses along the course of a river of such length as the Rio Grande, and so often fordable, is obvious. It is hoped that the efforts of this Government will be seconded by those of Mexico to the effectual suppression of these acts of wrong.

From a report upon the condition of the business before the American and Mexican Joint Claims Commission, made by the agent on the part of the United States, and dated October 28, 1874, it appears that of the 1,017 claims filed on the part of citizens of the United States, 483 had been finally decided and 75 were in the hands of the umpire, leaving 462 to be disposed of; and of the 998 claims filed against the United States, 726 had been finally decided, 1 was before the umpire, and 271 remained to be disposed of. Since the date of such report other claims have been disposed of, reducing somewhat the number still pending; and others have been passed upon by the arbitrators. It has become apparent, in view of these figures and of the fact that the work devolving on the umpire is particularly laborious, that the commission will be unable to dispose of the entire number of claims pending prior to the 1st day of February, 1875—the date fixed for its expiration. Negotiations are pending looking to the securing of the results of the decisions which have been reached and to a further extension of the commission for a limited time, which it is confidently hoped will suffice to bring all the business now before it to a final close.

The strife in the Argentine Republic is to be deplored, both on account of the parties thereto and from the probable effects on the interests of those engaged in the trade to that quarter, of whom the United States are among the principal. As yet, so far as I am aware, there has been no violation of our neutrality rights, which, as well as our duties in that respect, it shall be my endeavor to maintain and observe.

It is with regret I announce that no further payment has been received from the Government of Venezuela on account of awards in favor of citizens of the United States. Hopes have been entertained that if that Republic could escape both foreign and civil war for a few years its great natural resources would enable it to honor its obligations. Though it is now understood to be at peace with other countries, a serious insurrection is reported to be in progress in an important region of that Republic. This may be taken advantage of as another reason to delay the payment of the dues of our citizens.

The deplorable strife in Cuba continues without any marked change in the relative advantages of the contending forces. The insurrection continues, but Spain has gained no superiority. Six years of strife give to the insurrection a significance which can not be denied. Its duration and the tenacity of its adherence, together with the absence of manifested power of suppression on the part of Spain, can not be controverted, and may make some positive steps on the part of other powers a matter of self-necessity. I had confidently hoped at this time to be able to announce the arrangement of some of the important questions between this Government and that of Spain, but the negotiations have been protracted. The unhappy intestine dissensions of Spain command our profound sympathy, and must be accepted as perhaps a cause of some delay. An early settlement, in part at least, of the questions between the Governments is hoped.   In the meantime, awaiting the results of immediately pending negotiations, I defer a further and fuller communication on the subject of the relations of this country and Spain.

I have again to call the attention of Congress to the unsatisfactory condition of the existing laws with reference to expatriation and the election of nationality.   Formerly, amid conflicting opinions and decisions, it was difficult to exactly determine how far the doctrine of perpetual allegiance was applicable to citizens of the United States.   Congress by the act of the 27th of July, 1868, asserted the abstract right of expatriation as a fundamental principle of this Government.   Notwithstanding such assertion and the necessity of frequent application of the principle, no legislation has been had defining what acts or formalities shall work expatriation or when a citizen shall be deemed to have renounced or to have lost his citizenship.   The importance of such definition is obvious. The representatives of the United States in foreign countries are continually called upon to lend their aid and the protection of the United States to persons concerning the good faith or the reality of whose citizenship there is at least great question.   In some cases the provisions of the treaties furnish some guide; in others it seems left to the person claiming the benefits of citizenship, while living in a foreign country, contributing in no manner to the performance of the duties of a citizen of the United States, and without intention at any time to return and undertake those duties, to use the claims to citizenship of the United States simply as a shield from the performance of the obligations of a citizen elsewhere.

The status of children born of American parents residing in a foreign country, of American women who have married aliens, of American citizens residing abroad where such question is not regulated by treaty, are all sources of frequent difficulty and discussion.   Legislation on these and similar questions, and particularly defining when and under what circumstances expatriation can be accomplished or is to be presumed, is especially needed.   In this connection I earnestly call the attention of Congress to the difficulties arising from fraudulent naturalization.   The United States wisely, freely, and liberally offers its citizenship to all who may come in good faith to reside within its limits on their complying with certain prescribed reasonable and simple formalities and conditions. Among the highest duties of the Government is that to afford firm, sufficient, and equal protection to all its citizens, whether native born or naturalized.   Care should be taken that a right carrying with it such support from the Government should not be fraudulently obtained, and should be bestowed only upon full proof of a compliance with the law; and yet frequent instances are brought to the attention of the Government of illegal and fraudulent naturalization and of the unauthorized use of certificates thus improperly obtained.   In some cases the fraudulent character of the naturalization has appeared upon the face of the certificate itself; in others examination discloses that the holder had not complied with the law, and in others certificates have been obtained where the persons holding them not only were not entitled to be naturalized, but had not even been within the United States at the time of the pretended naturalization. Instances of each of these classes of fraud are discovered at our legations, where the certificates of naturalization are presented either for the purpose of obtaining passports or in demanding the protection of the legation. When the fraud is apparent on the face of such certificates, they are taken up by the representatives of the Government and forwarded to the Department of State. But even then the record of the court in which the fraudulent naturalization occurred remains, and duplicate certificates are readily obtainable. Upon the presentation of these for the issue of passports or in demanding protection of the Government, the fraud sometimes escapes notice, and such certificates are not infrequently used in transactions of business to the deception and injury of innocent parties. Without placing any additional obstacles in the way of the obtainment of citizenship by the worthy and well-intentioned foreigner who comes in good faith to cast his lot with ours, I earnestly recommend further legislation to punish fraudulent naturalization and to secure the ready cancellation of the record of every naturalization made in fraud.

Since my last annual message the exchange has been made of the ratification of treaties of extradition with Belgium, Ecuador, Peru, and Salvador; also of a treaty of commerce and navigation with Peru, and one of commerce and consular privileges with Salvador; all of which have been duly proclaimed, as has also a declaration with Russia with reference to trade-marks.

The report of the Secretary of the Treasury, which by law is made directly to Congress, and forms no part of this message, will show the receipts and expenditures of the Government for the last fiscal year, the amount received from each source of revenue, and the amount paid out for each of the Departments of Government. It will be observed from this report that the amount of receipts over expenditures has been but $2,344,882.30 for the fiscal year ending June 30, 1874, and that for the current fiscal year the estimated receipts over expenditures will not much exceed $9,000,000. In view of the large national debt existing and the obligation to add 1 per cent per annum to the sinking fund, a sum amounting now to over $34,000,000 per annum, I submit whether revenues should not be increased or expenditures diminished to reach this amount of surplus. Not to provide for the sinking fund is a partial failure to comply with the contracts and obligations of the Government. At the last session of Congress a very considerable reduction was made in rates of taxation and in the number of articles submitted to taxation; the question may well be asked, whether or not, in some instances, un-

wisely.   In connection with this subject, too, I venture the opinion that
the means of collecting the revenue, especially from imports, have been
so embarrassed by legislation as to make it questionable whether or not
large amounts are not lost by failure to collect, to the direct loss of the
Treasury and to the prejudice of the interests of honest importers and
taxpayers.

The Secretary of the Treasury in his report favors legislation looking
to an early return to specie payments, thus supporting views previously
expressed in this message.   He also recommends economy in appropriations; calls attention to the loss of revenue from repealing the tax on tea
and coffee, without benefit to the consumer; recommends an increase of
10 cents a gallon on whisky, and, further, that no modification be made
in the banking and currency bill passed at the last session of Congress,
unless modification should become necessary by reason of the adoption of
measures for returning to specie payments.   In these recommendations I
cordially join.

I would suggest to Congress the propriety of readjusting the tariff so
as to increase the revenue, and at the same time decrease the number of
articles upon which duties are levied.   Those articles which enter into
our manufactures and are not produced at home, it seems to me, should
be entered free.   Those articles of manufacture which we produce a constituent part of, but do not produce the whole, that part which we do not
produce should enter free also.   I will instance fine wool, dyes, etc.   These
articles must be imported to form a part of the manufacture of the higher
grades of woolen goods.   Chemicals used as dyes, compounded in medicines, and used in various ways in manufactures come under this class.
The introduction free of duty of such wools as we do not produce would
stimulate the manufacture of goods requiring the use of those we do produce, and therefore would be a benefit to home production.   There are
many articles entering into "home manufactures" which we do not produce ourselves the tariff upon which increases the cost of producing the
manufactured article.   All corrections in this regard are in the direction
of bringing labor and capital in harmony with each other and of supplying
one of the elements of prosperity so much needed.

The report of the Secretary of War herewith attached, and forming a
part of this message, gives all the information concerning the operations,
wants, and necessities of the Army, and contains many suggestions and
recommendations which I commend to your special attention.

There is no class of Government employees who are harder worked
than the Army—officers and men; none who perform their tasks more
cheerfully and efficiently and under circumstances of greater privations
and hardships.

Legislation is desirable to render more efficient this branch of the public service.   All the recommendations of the Secretary of War I regard as
judicious, and I especially commend to your attention the following: The

consolidation of Government arsenals; the restoration of mileage to officers traveling under orders; the exemption of money received from the sale of subsistence stores from being covered into the Treasury; the use of appropriations for the purchase of subsistence stores without waiting for the beginning of the fiscal year for which the appropriation is made; for additional appropriations for the collection of torpedo material; for increased appropriations for the manufacture of arms; for relieving the various States from indebtedness for arms charged to them during the rebellion; for dropping officers from the rolls of the Army without trial for the offense of drawing pay more than once for the same period; for the discouragement of the plan to pay soldiers by check, and for the establishment of a professorship of rhetoric and English literature at West Point. The reasons for these recommendations are obvious, and are set forth sufficiently in the reports attached. I also recommend that the status of the staff corps of the Army be fixed, where this has not already been done, so that promotions may be made and vacancies filled as they occur in each grade when reduced below the number to be fixed by law. The necessity for such legislation is specially felt now in the Pay Department. The number of officers in that department is below the number adequate to the performance of the duties required of them by law.

The efficiency of the Navy has been largely increased during the last year. Under the impulse of the foreign complications which threatened us at the commencement of the last session of Congress, most of our efficient wooden ships were put in condition for immediate service, and the repairs of our ironclad fleet were pushed with the utmost vigor. The result is that most of these are now in an effective state and need only to be manned and put in commission to go at once into service.

Some of the new sloops authorized by Congress are already in commission, and most of the remainder are launched and wait only the completion of their machinery to enable them to take their places as part of our effective force.

Two iron torpedo ships have been completed during the last year, and four of our large double-turreted ironclads are now undergoing repairs. When these are finished, everything that is useful of our Navy, as now authorized, will be in condition for service, and with the advance in the science of torpedo warfare the American Navy, comparatively small as it is, will be found at any time powerful for the purposes of a peaceful nation.

Much has been accomplished during the year in aid of science and to increase the sum of general knowledge and further the interests of commerce and civilization. Extensive and much-needed soundings have been made for hydrographic purposes and to fix the proper routes of ocean telegraphs. Further surveys of the great Isthmus have been undertaken and completed, and two vessels of the Navy are now employed, in conjunction with those of England, France, Germany, and Russia, in observations connected with the transit of Venus, so useful and interesting to the scientific world.

The estimates for this branch of the public service do not differ materially from those of last year, those for the general support of the service being somewhat less and those for permanent improvements at the various stations rather larger than the corresponding estimate made a year ago. The regular maintenance and a steady increase in the efficiency of this most important arm in proportion to the growth of our maritime intercourse and interests is recommended to the attention of Congress.

The use of the Navy in time of peace might be further utilized by a direct authorization of the employment of naval vessels in explorations and surveys of the supposed navigable waters of other nationalities on this continent, especially the tributaries of the two great rivers of South America, the Orinoco and the Amazon. Nothing prevents, under existing laws, such exploration, except that expenditures must be made in such expeditions beyond those usually provided for in the appropriations. The field designated is unquestionably one of interest and one capable of large development of commercial interests—advantageous to the peoples reached and to those who may establish relations with them.

Education of the people entitled to exercise the right of franchise I regard essential to general prosperity everywhere, and especially so in republics, where birth, education, or previous condition does not enter into account in giving suffrage. Next to the public school, the post-office is the great agent of education over our vast territory. The rapidity with which new sections are being settled, thus increasing the carrying of mails in a more rapid ratio than the increase of receipts, is not alarming. The report of the Postmaster-General herewith attached shows that there was an increase of revenue in his Department in 1873 over the previous year of $1,674,411, and an increase of cost of carrying the mails and paying employees of $3,041,468.91. The report of the Postmaster-General gives interesting statistics of his Department, and compares them with the corresponding statistics of a year ago, showing a growth in every branch of the Department.

A postal convention has been concluded with New South Wales, an exchange of postal cards established with Switzerland, and the negotiations pending for several years past with France have been terminated in a convention with that country, which went into effect last August.

An international postal congress was convened in Berne, Switzerland, in September last, at which the United States was represented by an officer of the Post-Office Department of much experience and of qualification for the position. A convention for the establishment of an international postal union was agreed upon and signed by the delegates of the countries represented, subject to the approval of the proper authorities of those countries.

I respectfully direct your attention to the report of the Postmaster-

General and to his suggestions in regard to an equitable adjustment of the question of compensation to railroads for carrying the mails.

Your attention will be drawn to the unsettled condition of affairs in some of the Southern States.

On the 14th of September last the governor of Louisiana called upon me, as provided by the Constitution and laws of the United States, to aid in suppressing domestic violence in that State. This call was made in view of a proclamation issued on that day by D. B. Penn, claiming that he was elected lieutenant-governor in 1872, and calling upon the militia of the State to arm, assemble, and drive from power the usurpers, as he designated the officers of the State government. On the next day I issued my proclamation commanding the insurgents to disperse within five days from the date thereof, and subsequently learned that on that day they had taken forcible possession of the statehouse. Steps were taken by me to support the existing and recognized State government, but before the expiration of the five days the insurrectionary movement was practically abandoned, and the officers of the State government, with some minor exceptions, resumed their powers and duties. Considering that the present State administration of Louisiana has been the only government in that State for nearly two years; that it has been tacitly acknowledged and acquiesced in as such by Congress, and more than once expressly recognized by me, I regarded it as my clear duty, when legally called upon for that purpose, to prevent its overthrow by an armed mob under pretense of fraud and irregularity in the election of 1872. I have heretofore called the attention of Congress to this subject, stating that on account of the frauds and forgeries committed at said election, and because it appears that the returns thereof were never legally canvassed, it was impossible to tell thereby who were chosen; but from the best sources of information at my command I have always believed that the present State officers received a majority of the legal votes actually cast at that election. I repeat what I said in my special message of February 23, 1873, that in the event of no action by Congress I must continue to recognize the government heretofore recognized by me.

I regret to say that with preparations for the late election decided indications appeared in some localities in the Southern States of a determination, by acts of violence and intimidation, to deprive citizens of the freedom of the ballot because of their political opinions. Bands of men, masked and armed, made their appearance; White Leagues and other societies were formed; large quantities of arms and ammunition were imported and distributed to these organizations; military drills, with menacing demonstrations, were held, and with all these murders enough were committed to spread terror among those whose political action was to be suppressed, if possible, by these intolerant and criminal proceedings. In some places colored laborers were compelled to vote according to the wishes of their employers, under threats of discharge if they acted otherwise; and there are too many instances in which, when these threats were disregarded, they were remorselessly executed by those who made them. I understand that the fifteenth amendment to the Constitution was made to prevent this and a like state of things, and the act of May 31, 1870, with amendments, was passed to enforce its provisions, the object of both being to guarantee to all citizens the right to vote and to protect them in the free enjoyment of that right.   Enjoined by the Constitution "to take care that the laws be faithfully executed," and convinced by undoubted evidence that violations of said act had been committed and that a widespread and flagrant disregard of it was contemplated, the proper officers were instructed to prosecute the offenders, and troops were stationed at convenient points to aid these officers, if necessary, in the performance of their official duties.   Complaints are made of this interference by Federal authority; but if said amendment and act do not provide for such interference under the circumstances as above stated, then they are without meaning, force, or effect, and the whole scheme of colored enfranchisement is worse than mockery and little better than a crime.   Possibly Congress may find it due to truth and justice to ascertain, by means of a committee, whether the alleged wrongs to colored citizens for political purposes are real or the reports thereof were manufactured for the occasion.

The whole number of troops in the States of Louisiana, Alabama, Georgia, Florida, South Carolina, North Carolina, Kentucky, Tennessee, Arkansas, Mississippi, Maryland, and Virginia at the time of the election was 4,082.   This embraces the garrisons of all the forts from the Delaware to the Gulf of Mexico.

Another trouble has arisen in Arkansas.   Article 13 of the constitution of that State (which was adopted in 1868, and upon the approval of which by Congress the State was restored to representation as one of the States of the Union) provides in effect that before any amendments proposed to this constitution shall become a part thereof they shall be passed by two successive assemblies and then submitted to and ratified by a majority of the electors of the State voting thereon.   On the 11th of May, 1874, the governor convened an extra session of the general assembly of the State, which on the 18th of the same month passed an act providing for a convention to frame a new constitution.   Pursuant to this act, and at an election held on the 30th of June, 1874, the convention was approved, and delegates were chosen thereto, who assembled on the 14th of last July and framed a new constitution, the schedule of which provided for the election of an entire new set of State officers in a manner contrary to the then existing election laws of the State.   On the 13th of October, 1874, this constitution, as therein provided, was submitted to the people for their approval or rejection, and according to the election returns was approved by a large majority of those qualified to vote thereon; and at the same election persons were chosen to fill all the State, county, and township offices. The governor elected in 1872 for the term of four years turned over his office to the governor chosen under the new constitution, whereupon the lieutenant-governor, also elected in 1872 for a term of four years, claiming to act as governor, and alleging that said proceedings by which the new constitution was made and a new set of officers elected were unconstitutional, illegal, and void, called upon me, as provided in section 4, Article IV, of the Constitution, to protect the State against domestic violence. As Congress is now investigating the political affairs of Arkansas, I have declined to interfere.

The whole subject of Executive interference with the affairs of a State is repugnant to public opinion, to the feelings of those who, from their official capacity, must be used in such interposition, and to him or those who must direct. Unless most clearly on the side of law, such interference becomes a crime; with the law to support it, it is condemned without a hearing. I desire, therefore, that all necessity for Executive direction in local affairs may become unnecessary and obsolete. I invite the attention, not of Congress, but of the people of the United States, to the causes and effects of these unhappy questions. Is there not a disposition on one side to magnify wrongs and outrages, and on the other side to belittle them or justify them? If public opinion could be directed to a correct survey of what is and to rebuking wrong and aiding the proper authorities in punishing it, a better state of feeling would be inculcated, and the sooner we would have that peace which would leave the States free indeed to regulate their own domestic affairs. I believe on the part of our citizens of the Southern States—the better .part of them—there is a disposition to be law abiding, and to do no violence either to individuals or to the laws existing. But do they do right in ignoring the existence of violence and bloodshed in resistance to constituted authority? I sympathize with their prostrate condition, and would do all in my power to relieve them, acknowledging that in some instances they have had most trying governments to live under, and very oppressive ones in the way of taxation for nominal improvements, not giving benefits equal to the hardships imposed. But can they proclaim themselves entirely irresponsible for this condition? They can not. Violence has been rampant in some localities, and has either been justified or denied by those who could have prevented it. The theory is even raised that there is to be no further interference on the part of the General Government to protect citizens within a State where the State authorities fail to give protection. This is a great mistake. While I remain Executive all the laws of Congress and the provisions of the Constitution, including the recent amendments added thereto, will be enforced with rigor, but with regret that they should have added one jot or tittle to Executive duties or powers. Let there be fairness in the discussion of Southern questions, the advocates of both or all political parties giving honest, truthful reports of occurrences, condemning the wrong and upholding the right, and soon all will be well.

Under existing conditions the negro votes the Republican ticket because he knows his friends are of that party.   Many a good citizen votes the opposite, not because he agrees with the great principles of state which separate parties, but because, generally, he is opposed to negro rule.   This is a most delusive cry.   Treat the negro as a citizen and a voter, as he is and must remain, and soon parties will be divided, not on the color line, but on principle.   Then we shall have no complaint of sectional interference.

The report of the Attorney-General contains valuable recommendations relating to the administration of justice in the courts of the United States, to which I invite your attention.

I respectfully suggest to Congress the propriety of increasing the number of judicial districts in the United States to eleven (the present number being nine) and the creation of two additional judgeships.   The territory to be traversed by the circuit judges is so great and the business of the courts so steadily increasing that it is growing more and more impossible for them to keep up with the business requiring their attention.   Whether this would involve the necessity of adding two more justices of the Supreme Court to the present number I submit to the judgment of Congress.

The attention of Congress is invited to the report of the Secretary of the Interior and to the legislation asked for by him.   The domestic interests of the people are more intimately connected with this Department than with either of the other Departments of Government.   Its duties have been added to from time to time until they have become so onerous that without the most perfect system and order it will be impossible for any Secretary of the Interior to keep trace of all official transactions having his sanction and done in his name, and for which he is held personally responsible.

The policy adopted for the management of Indian affairs, known as the peace policy, has been adhered to with most beneficial results.   It is confidently hoped that a few years more will relieve our frontiers from danger of Indian depredations.

I commend the recommendation of the Secretary for the extension of the homestead laws to the Indians and for some sort of Territorial government for the Indian Territory.   A great majority of the Indians occupying this Territory are believed yet to be incapable of maintaining their rights against the more civilized and enlightened white man. Any Territorial form of government given them, therefore, should protect them in their homes and property for a period of at least twenty years, and before its final adoption should be ratified by a majority of those affected.

The report of the Secretary of the Interior herewith attached gives much interesting statistical information, which I abstain from giving an abstract of, but refer you to the report itself.

The act of Congress providing the oath which pensioners must sub-scribe to before drawing their pensions cuts off from this bounty a few survivors of the War of 1812 residing in the Southern States. I recom-mend the restoration of this bounty to all such. The number of persons whose names would thus be restored to the list of pensioners is not large. They are all old persons, who could have taken no part in the rebellion, and the services for which they were awarded pensions were in defense of the whole country.

The report of the Commissioner of Agriculture herewith contains sug-gestions of much interest to the general public, and refers to the ap-proaching Centennial and the part his Department is ready to take in it. I feel that the nation at large is interested in having this exposition a success, and commend to Congress such action as will secure a greater general interest in it. Already many foreign nations have signified their intention to be represented at it, and it may be expected that every civi-lized nation will be represented.

The rules adopted to improve the civil service of the Government have been adhered to as closely as has been practicable with the opposition with which they meet. The effect, I believe, has been beneficial on the whole, and has tended to the elevation of the service. But it is impracticable to maintain them without direct and positive support of Congress. Gen-erally the support which this reform receives is from those who give it their support only to find fault when the rules are apparently departed from. Removals from office without preferring charges against parties removed are frequently cited as departures from the rules adopted, and the retention of those against whom charges are made by irresponsible persons and without good grounds is also often condemned as a viola-tion of them. Under these circumstances, therefore, I announce that if Congress adjourns without positive legislation on the subject of "civil-service reform" I will regard such action as a disapproval of the system, and will abandon it, except so far as to require examinations for certain appointees, to determine their fitness. Competitive examinations will be abandoned.

The gentlemen who have given their services, without compensation, as members of the board to devise rules and regulations for the govern-ment of the civil service of the country have shown much zeal and ear-nestness in their work, and to them, as well as to myself, it will be a source of mortification if it is to be thrown away. But I repeat that it is impossible to carry this system to a successful issue without general approval and assistance and positive law to support it.

I have stated that three elements of prosperity to the nation—capital, labor, skilled and unskilled, and products of the soil—still remain with us. To direct the employment of these is a problem deserving the most serious attention of Congress. If employment can be given to all the labor offering itself, prosperity necessarily follows. I have expressed the opinion, and repeat it, that the first requisite to the accomplishment of this end is the substitution of a sound currency in place of one of a fluctuating value. This secured, there are many interests that might be fostered to the great profit of both labor and capital. How to induce capital to employ labor is the question. The subject of cheap transportation has occupied the attention of Congress. Much new light on this question will without doubt be given by the committee appointed by the last Congress to investigate and report upon this subject.

A revival of shipbuilding, and particularly of iron steamship building, is of vast importance to our national prosperity. The United States is now paying over $100,000,000 per annum for freights and passage on foreign ships—to be carried abroad and expended in the employment and support of other peoples—beyond a fair percentage of what should go to foreign vessels, estimating on the tonnage and travel of each respectively. It is to be regretted that this disparity in the carrying trade exists, and to correct it I would be willing to see a great departure from the usual course of Government in supporting what might usually be termed private enterprise. I would not suggest as a remedy direct subsidy to American steamship lines, but I would suggest the direct offer of ample compensation for carrying the mails between Atlantic Seaboard cities and the Continent on American-owned and American-built steamers, and would extend this liberality to vessels carrying the mails to South American States and to Central America and Mexico, and would pursue the same policy from our Pacific seaports to foreign seaports on the Pacific. It might be demanded that vessels built for this service should come up to a standard fixed by legislation in tonnage, speed, and all other qualities, looking to the possibility of Government requiring them at some time for war purposes. The right also of taking possession of them in such emergency should be guarded.

I offer these suggestions, believing them worthy of consideration, in all seriousness, affecting all sections and all interests alike. If anything better can be done to direct the country into a course of general prosperity, no one will be more ready than I to second the plan.

Forwarded herewith will be found the report of the commissioners appointed under an act of Congress approved June 20, 1874, to wind up the affairs of the District government. It will be seen from the report that the net debt of the District of Columbia, less securities on hand and available, is:

Bonded debt issued prior to July 1, 1874		$8,883,940.43
3.65 bonds, act of Congress June 20, 1874		2,088,168.73
Certificates of the board of audit		4,770,558.45
		15,742,667.61
Less special-improvement assessments (chargeable to private property) in excess of any demand against such assessments	$1,614,054.37	
Less Chesapeake and Ohio Canal bonds	75,000.00	
And Washington and Alexandria Railroad bonds	59,000.00	
In the hands of the commissioners of the sinking fund		1,748,054.37
Leaving actual debt, less said assets		13,994,613.24

In addition to this there are claims preferred against the government of the District amounting, in the estimated aggregate reported by the board of audit, to $3,147,787.48, of which the greater part will probably be rejected. This sum can with no more propriety be included in the debt account of the District government than can the thousands of claims against the General Government be included as a portion of the national debt. But the aggregate sum thus stated includes something more than the funded debt chargeable exclusively to the District of Columbia. The act of Congress of June 20, 1874, contemplates an apportionment between the United States Government and the District of Columbia in respect of the payment of the principal and interest of the 3.65 bonds. Therefore in computing with precision the bonded debt of the District the aggregate sums above stated as respects 3.65 bonds now issued, the outstanding certificates of the board of audit, and the unadjusted claims pending before that board should be reduced to the extent of the amount to be apportioned to the United States Government in the manner indicated in the act of Congress of June 20, 1874.

I especially invite your attention to the recommendations of the commissioners of the sinking fund relative to the ambiguity of the act of June 20, 1874, the interest on the District bonds, and the consolidation of the indebtedness of the District.

I feel much indebted to the gentlemen who consented to leave their private affairs and come from a distance to attend to the business of this District, and for the able and satisfactory manner in which it has been conducted. I am sure their services will be equally appreciated by the entire country.

It will be seen from the accompanying full report of the board of health that the sanitary condition of the District is very satisfactory.

In my opinion the District of Columbia should be regarded as the grounds of the national capital, in which the entire people are interested. I do not allude to this to urge generous appropriations to the District, but to draw the attention of Congress, in framing a law for the government of the District, to the magnificent scale on which the city was planned by the founders of the Government; the manner in which, for ornamental purposes, the reservations, streets, and avenues were laid out, and the proportion of the property actually possessed by the General Government. I think the proportion of the expenses of the government and improvements to be borne by the General Government, the cities of Washington and Georgetown, and the county should be carefully and equitably defined.

In accordance with section 3, act approved June 23, 1874, I appointed a board to make a survey of the mouth of the Mississippi River with a view to determine the best method of obtaining and maintaining a depth of water sufficient for the purposes of commerce, etc.; and in accordance with an act entitled "An act to provide for the appointment of a commission of engineers to investigate and report a permanent plan for the reclamation of the alluvial basin of the Mississippi River subject to inundation," I appointed a commission of engineers. Neither board has yet completed its labors. When their reports are received, they will be forwarded to Congress without delay.

SEVENTH ANNUAL MESSAGE.

EXECUTIVE MANSION, *December 7, 1875.*

To the Senate and House of Representatives:

In submitting my seventh annual message to Congress, in this centennial year of our national existence as a free and independent people, it affords me great pleasure to recur to the advancement that has been made from the time of the colonies, one hundred years ago. We were then a people numbering only 3,000,000. Now we number more than 40,000,000. Then industries were confined almost exclusively to the tillage of the soil. Now manufactories absorb much of the labor of the country.

Our liberties remain unimpaired; the bondmen have been freed from slavery; we have become possessed of the respect, if not the friendship, of all civilized nations. Our progress has been great in all the arts—in science, agriculture, commerce, navigation, mining, mechanics, law, medicine, etc.; and in general education the progress is likewise encouraging. Our thirteen States have become thirty-eight, including Colorado (which has taken the initiatory steps to become a State), and eight Territories, including the Indian Territory and Alaska, and excluding Colorado, making a territory extending from the Atlantic to the Pacific. On the south we have extended to the Gulf of Mexico, and in the west from the Mississippi to the Pacific.

One hundred years ago the cotton gin, the steamship, the railroad, the telegraph, the reaping, sewing, and modern printing machines, and numerous other inventions of scarcely less value to our business and happiness were entirely unknown.

In 1776 manufactories scarcely existed even in name in all this vast erritory. In 1870 more than 2,000,000 persons were employed in manıfactories, producing more than $2,100,000,000 of products in amount annually, nearly equal to our national debt. From nearly the whole of the population of 1776 being engaged in the one occupation of agriculture, in 1870 so numerous and diversified had become the occupation of our people that less than 6,000,000 out of more than 40,000,000 were so engaged. The extraordinary effect produced in our country by a resort to diversified occupations has built a market for the products of fertile lands distant from the seaboard and the markets of the world.

The American system of locating various and extensive manufactories next to the plow and the pasture, and adding connecting railroads and steamboats, has produced in our distant interior country a result noticeable by the intelligent portions of all commercial nations. The ingenuity and skill of American mechanics have been demonstrated at home and abroad in a manner most flattering to their pride. But for the extraordinary genius and ability of our mechanics, the achievements of our agriculturists, manufacturers, and transporters throughout the country would have been impossible of attainment.

The progress of the miner has also been great. Of coal our production was small; now many millions of tons are mined annually. So with iron, which formed scarcely an appreciable part of our products half a century ago, we now produce more than the world consumed at the beginning of our national existence. Lead, zinc, and copper, from being articles of import, we may expect to be large exporters of in the near future. The development of gold and silver mines in the United States and Territories has not only been remarkable, but has had a large influence upon the business of all commercial nations. Our merchants in the last hundred years have had a success and have established a reputation for enterprise, sagacity, progress, and integrity unsurpassed by peoples of older nationalities. This "good name" is not confined to their homes, but goes out upon every sea and into every port where commerce enters. With equal pride we can point to our progress in all of the learned professions.

As we are now about to enter upon our second centennial—commencing our manhood as a nation—it is well to look back upon the past and study what will be best to preserve and advance our future greatness From the fall of Adam for his transgression to the present day no nation has ever been free from threatened danger to its prosperity and happiness. We should look to the dangers threatening us, and remedy them so far as lies in our power. We are a republic whereof one man is as good as another before the law. Under such a form of government it is of the greatest importance that all should be possessed of education and intelligence enough to cast a vote with a right understanding of its meaning. A large association of ignorant men can not for any considerable period oppose a successful resistance to tyranny and oppression from the educated few, but will inevitably sink into acquiescence to the will of intelligence, whether directed by the demagogue or by priestcraft. Hence the education of the masses becomes of the first necessity for the preservation of our institutions. They are worth preserving, because they have secured the greatest good to the greatest proportion of the population of any form of government yet devised. All other forms of government approach it just in proportion to the general diffusion of education and independence of thought and action. As the primary step, therefore, to our advancement in all that has marked our progress in the past century, I suggest for your earnest consideration, and most earnestly recommend it, that a constitutional amendment be submitted to the legislatures of the several States for ratification, making it the duty of each of the several States to establish and forever maintain free public schools adequate to the education of all the children in the rudimentary branches within their respective limits, irrespective of sex, color, birthplace, or religions; forbidding the teaching in said schools of religious, atheistic, or pagan tenets; and prohibiting the granting of any school funds or school taxes, or any part thereof, either by legislative, municipal, or other authority, for the benefit or in aid, directly or indirectly, of any religious sect or denomination, or in aid or for the benefit of any other object of any nature or kind whatever.

In connection with this important question I would also call your attention to the importance of correcting an evil that, if permitted to continue, will probably lead to great trouble in our land before the close of the nineteenth century. It is the accumulation of vast amounts of untaxed church property.

In 1850, I believe, the church property of the United States which paid no tax, municipal or State, amounted to about $83,000,000. In 1860 the amount had doubled; in 1875 it is about $1,000,000,000. By 1900, without check, it is safe to say this property will reach a sum exceeding $3,000,000,000. So vast a sum, receiving all the protection and benefits of Government without bearing its proportion of the burdens and expenses of the same, will not be looked upon acquiescently by those who have to pay the taxes. In a growing country, where real estate enhances so rapidly with time, as in the United States, there is scarcely a limit to the wealth that may be acquired by corporations, religious or otherwise, if allowed to retain real estate without taxation. The contemplation of so vast a property as here alluded to, without taxation, may lead to sequestration without constitutional authority and through blood.

I would suggest the taxation of all property equally, whether church or corporation, exempting only the last resting place of the dead and possibly, with proper restrictions, church edifices.

Our relations with most of the foreign powers continue on a satisfactory and friendly footing.

Increased intercourse, the extension of commerce, and the cultivation of mutual interests have steadily improved our relations with the large majority of the powers of the world, rendering practicable the peaceful solution of questions which from time to time necessarily arise, leaving few which demand extended or particular notice.

The correspondence of the Department of State with our diplomatic representatives abroad is transmitted herewith.

I am happy to announce the passage of an act by the General Cortes of Portugal, proclaimed since the adjournment of Congress, for the abolition of servitude in the Portuguese colonies. It is to be hoped that such legislation may be another step toward the great consummation to be reached, when no man shall be permitted, directly or indirectly, under any guise, excuse, or form of law, to hold his fellow-man in bondage. I am of opinion also that it is the duty of the United States, as contributing toward that end, and required by the spirit of the age in which we live, to provide by suitable legislation that no citizen of the United States shall hold slaves as property in any other country or be interested therein.

Chile has made reparation in the case of the whale ship *Good Return*, seized without sufficient cause upward of forty years ago. Though she had hitherto denied her accountability, the denial was never acquiesced in by this Government, and the justice of the claim has been so earnestly contended for that it has been gratifying that she should have at last acknowledged it.

The arbitrator in the case of the United States steamer *Montijo*, for the seizure and detention of which the Government of the United States of Colombia was held accountable, has decided in favor of the claim. This decision has settled a question which had been pending for several years, and which, while it continued open, might more or less disturb the good understanding which it is desirable should be maintained between the two Republics.

A reciprocity treaty with the King of the Hawaiian Islands was concluded some months since. As it contains a stipulation that it shall not take effect until Congress shall enact the proper legislation for that purpose, copies of the instrument are herewith submitted, in order that, if such should be the pleasure of Congress, the necessary legislation upon the subject may be adopted.

In March last an arrangement was made, through Mr. Cushing, our minister in Madrid, with the Spanish Government for the payment by the latter to the United States of the sum of $80,000 in coin, for the purpose of the relief of the families or persons of the ship's company and certain passengers of the *Virginius*. This sum was to have been paid in three installments at two months each. It is due to the Spanish Government that I should state that the payments were fully and spontaneously anticipated by that Government, and that the whole amount was paid within but a few days more than two months from the date of the agreement, a copy of which is herewith transmitted. In pursuance of the terms of the adjustment, I have directed the distribution of the amount among the parties entitled thereto, including the ship's company and such of the passengers as were American citizens. Payments are made accordingly, on the application by the parties entitled thereto.

The past year has furnished no evidence of an approaching termination of the ruinous conflict which has been raging for seven years in the neighboring island of Cuba.   The same disregard of the laws of civilized warfare and of the just demands of humanity which has heretofore called forth expressions of condemnation from the nations of Christendom has continued to blacken the sad scene.   Desolation, ruin, and pillage are pervading the rich fields of one of the most fertile and productive regions of the earth, and the incendiary's torch, firing plantations and valuable factories and buildings, is the agent marking the alternate advance or retreat of contending parties.

The protracted continuance of this strife seriously affects the interests of all commercial nations, but those of the United States more than others, by reason of close proximity, its larger trade and intercourse with Cuba, and the frequent and intimate personal and social relations which have grown up between its citizens and those of the island.   Moreover, the property of our citizens in Cuba is large, and is rendered insecure and depreciated in value and in capacity of production by the continuance of the strife and the unnatural mode of its conduct.   The same is true, differing only in degree, with respect to the interests and people of other nations; and the absence of any reasonable assurance of a near termination of the conflict must of necessity soon compel the States thus suffering to consider what the interests of their own people and their duty toward themselves may demand.

I have hoped that Spain would be enabled to establish peace in her colony, to afford security to the property and the interests of our citizens, and allow legitimate scope to trade and commerce and the natural productions of the island.   Because of this hope, and from an extreme reluctance to interfere in the most remote manner in the affairs of another and a friendly nation, especially of one whose sympathy and friendship in the struggling infancy of our own existence must ever be remembered with gratitude, I have patiently and anxiously waited the progress of events.   Our own civil conflict is too recent for us not to consider the difficulties which surround a government distracted by a dynastic rebellion at home at the same time that it has to cope with a separate insurrection in a distant colony.   But whatever causes may have produced the situation which so grievously affects our interests, it exists, with all its attendant evils operating directly upon this country and its people.   Thus far all the efforts of Spain have proved abortive, and time has marked no improvement in the situation.   The armed bands of either side now occupy nearly the same ground as in the past, with the difference, from time to time, of more lives sacrificed, more property destroyed, and wider extents of fertile and productive fields and more and more of valuable property constantly wantonly sacrificed to the incendiary's torch.

In contests of this nature, where a considerable body of people who have attempted to free themselves of the control of the superior government have reached such point in occupation of territory, in power, and in general organization as to constitute in fact a body politic; having a government in substance as well as in name; possessed of the elements of stability and equipped with the machinery for the administration of internal policy and the execution of its laws; prepared and able to administer justice at home, as well as in its dealings with other powers, it is within the province of those other powers to recognize its existence as a new and independent nation. In such cases other nations simply deal with an actually existing condition of things, and recognize as one of the powers of the earth that body politic which, possessing the necessary elements, has in fact become a new power. In a word, the creation of a new state is a fact.

To establish the condition of things essential to the recognition of this fact there must be a people occupying a known territory, united under some known and defined form of government, acknowledged by those subject thereto, in which the functions of government are administered by usual methods, competent to mete out justice to citizens and strangers, to afford remedies for public and for private wrongs, and able to assume the correlative international obligations and capable of performing the corresponding international duties resulting from its acquisition of the rights of sovereignty. A power should exist complete in its organization, ready to take and able to maintain its place among the nations of the earth.

While conscious that the insurrection in Cuba has shown a strength and endurance which make it at least doubtful whether it be in the power of Spain to subdue it, it seems unquestionable that no such civil organization exists which may be recognized as an independent government capable of performing its international obligations and entitled to be treated as one of the powers of the earth. A recognition under such circumstances would be inconsistent with the facts, and would compel the power granting it soon to support by force the government to which it had really given its only claim of existence. In my judgment the United States should adhere to the policy and the principles which have heretofore been its sure and safe guides in like contests between revolted colonies and their mother country, and, acting only upon the clearest evidence, should avoid any possibility of suspicion or of imputation.

A recognition of the independence of Cuba being, in my opinion, impracticable and indefensible, the question which next presents itself is that of the recognition of belligerent rights in the parties to the contest.

In a former message to Congress I had occasion to consider this question, and reached the conclusion that the conflict in Cuba, dreadful and devastating as were its incidents, did not rise to the fearful dignity of war. Regarding it now, after this lapse of time, I am unable to see that any notable success or any marked or real advance on the part of the insurgents has essentially changed the character of the contest. It has acquired greater age, but not greater or more formidable proportions.   It is possible that the acts of foreign powers, and even acts of Spain herself, of this very nature, might be pointed to in defense of such recognition.   But now, as in its past history, the United States should carefully avoid the false lights which might lead it into the mazes of doubtful law and of questionable propriety, and adhere rigidly and sternly to the rule, which has been its guide, of doing only that which is right and honest and of good report.   The question of according or of withholding rights of belligerency must be judged in every case in view of the particular attending facts.   Unless justified by necessity, it is always, and justly, regarded as an unfriendly act and a gratuitous demonstration of moral support to the rebellion.   It is necessary, and it is required, when the interests and rights of another government or of its people are so far affected by a pending civil conflict as to require a definition of its relations to the parties thereto.   But this conflict must be one which will be recognized in the sense of international law as war.   Belligerence, too, is a fact.   The mere existence of contending armed bodies and their occasional conflicts do not constitute war in the sense referred to.   Applying to the existing condition of affairs in Cuba the tests recognized by publicists and writers on international law, and which have been observed by nations of dignity, honesty, and power when free from sensitive or selfish and unworthy motives, I fail to find in the insurrection the existence of such a substantial political organization, real, palpable, and manifest to the world, having the forms and capable of the ordinary functions of government toward its own people and to other states, with courts for the administration of justice, with a local habitation, possessing such organization of force, such material, such occupation of territory, as to take the contest out of the category of a mere rebellious insurrection or occasional skirmishes and place it on the terrible footing of war, to which a recognition of belligerency would aim to elevate it.   The contest, moreover, is solely on land; the insurrection has not possessed itself of a single seaport whence it may send forth its flag, nor has it any means of communication with foreign powers except through the military lines of its adversaries.   No apprehension of any of those sudden and difficult complications which a war upon the ocean is apt to precipitate upon the vessels, both commercial and national, and upon the consular officers of other powers calls for the definition of their relations to the parties to the contest.   Considered as a question of expediency, I regard the accordance of belligerent rights still to be as unwise and premature as I regard it to be, at present, indefensible as a measure of right.   Such recognition entails upon the country according the rights which flow from it difficult and complicated duties, and requires the exaction from the contending parties of the strict observance of their rights and obligations; it confers the right of search upon the high seas by vessels of both parties; it would subject the carrying of arms and munitions of war, which now may be transported freely and without interruption in the vessels of the United States, to detention and to possible seizure; it would give rise to countless vexatious questions, would release the parent Government from responsibility for acts done by the insurgents, and would invest Spain with the right to exercise the supervision recognized by our treaty of 1795 over our commerce on the high seas, a very large part of which, in its traffic between the Atlantic and the Gulf States and between all of them and the States on the Pacific, passes through the waters which wash the shores of Cuba. The exercise of this supervision could scarce fail to lead, if not to abuses, certainly to collisions perilous to the peaceful relations of the two States. There can be little doubt to what result such supervision would before long draw this nation. It would be unworthy of the United States to inaugurate the possibilities of such result by measures of questionable right or expediency or by any indirection. Apart from any question of theoretical right, I am satisfied that while the accordance of belligerent rights to the insurgents in Cuba might give them a hope and an inducement to protract the struggle, it would be but a delusive hope, and would not remove the evils which this Government and its people are experiencing, but would draw the United States into complications which it has waited long and already suffered much to avoid. The recognition of independence or of belligerency being thus, in my judgment, equally inadmissible, it remains to consider what course shall be adopted should the conflict not soon be brought to an end by acts of the parties themselves, and should the evils which result therefrom, affecting all nations, and particularly the United States, continue. In such event I am of opinion that other nations will be compelled to assume the responsibility which devolves upon them, and to seriously consider the only remaining measures possible—mediation and intervention. Owing, perhaps, to the large expanse of water separating the island from the peninsula, the want of harmony and of personal sympathy between the inhabitants of the colony and those sent thither to rule them, and want of adaptation of the ancient colonial system of Europe to the present times and to the ideas which the events of the past century have developed, the contending parties appear to have within themselves no depository of common confidence to suggest wisdom when passion and excitement have their sway and to assume the part of peacemaker. In this view in the earlier days of the contest the good offices of the United States as a mediator were tendered in good faith, without any selfish purpose, in the interest of humanity and in sincere friendship for both parties, but were at the time declined by Spain, with the declaration, nevertheless, that at a future time they would be indispensable. No intimation has been received that in the opinion of Spain that time has been reached. And yet the strife continues, with all its dread horrors and all its injuries to the interests of the United States, and of other nations. Each party seems quite capable of working great injury and damage to the other, as well as to all the relations and interests dependent on the existence of peace in the island; but they seem incapable of reaching any adjustment, and both have thus far failed of achieving any success whereby one party shall possess and control the island to the exclusion of the other. Under these circumstances the agency of others, either by mediation or by intervention, seems to be the only alternative which must, sooner or later, be invoked for the termination of the strife. At the same time, while thus impressed I do not at this time recommend the adoption of any measure of intervention. I shall be ready at all times, and as the equal friend of both parties, to respond to a suggestion that the good offices of the United States will be acceptable to aid in bringing about a peace honorable to both. It is due to Spain, so far as this Government is concerned, that the agency of a third power, to which I have adverted, shall be adopted only as a last expedient. Had it been the desire of the United States to interfere in the affairs of Cuba, repeated opportunities for so doing have been presented within the last few years; but we have remained passive, and have performed our whole duty and all international obligations to Spain with friendship, fairness, and fidelity, and with a spirit of patience and forbearance which negatives every possible suggestion of desire to interfere or to add to the difficulties with which she has been surrounded.

The Government of Spain has recently submitted to our minister at Madrid certain proposals which it is hoped may be found to be the basis, if not the actual submission, of terms to meet the requirements of the particular griefs of which this Government has felt itself entitled to complain. These proposals have not yet reached me in their full text. On their arrival they will be taken into careful examination, and may, I hope, lead to a satisfactory adjustment of the questions to which they refer and remove the possibility of future occurrences such as have given rise to our just complaints.

It is understood also that renewed efforts are being made to introduce reforms in the internal administration of the island. Persuaded, however, that a proper regard for the interests of the United States and of its citizens entitles it to relief from the strain to which it has been subjected by the difficulties of the questions and the wrongs and losses which arise from the contest in Cuba, and that the interests of humanity itself demand the cessation of the strife before the whole island shall be laid waste and larger sacrifices of life be made, I shall feel it my duty, should my hopes of a satisfactory adjustment and of the early restoration of peace and the removal of future causes of complaint be, unhappily, disappointed, to make a further communication to Congress at some period not far remote, and during the present session, recommending what may then seem to me to be necessary.

The free zone, so called, several years since established by the Mexican Government in certain of the States of that Republic adjacent to our frontier, remains in full operation. It has always been materially injurious to honest traffic, for it operates as an incentive to traders in Mexico to supply without customs charges the wants of inhabitants on this side of the line, and prevents the same wants from being supplied by merchants of the United States, thereby to a considerable extent defrauding our revenue and checking honest commercial enterprise.

Depredations by armed bands from Mexico on the people of Texas near the frontier continue. Though the main object of these incursions is robbery, they frequently result in the murder of unarmed and peaceably disposed persons, and in some instances even the United States post-offices and mail communications have been attacked. Renewed remonstrances upon this subject have been addressed to the Mexican Government, but without much apparent effect. The military force of this Government disposable for service in that quarter is quite inadequate to effectually guard the line, even at those points where the incursions are usually made. An experiment of an armed vessel on the Rio Grande for that purpose is on trial, and it is hoped that, if not thwarted by the shallowness of the river and other natural obstacles, it may materially contribute to the protection of the herdsmen of Texas.

The proceedings of the joint commission under the convention between the United States and Mexico of the 4th of July, 1868, on the subject of claims, will soon be brought to a close. The result of those proceedings will then be communicated to Congress.

I am happy to announce that the Government of Venezuela has, upon further consideration, practically abandoned its objection to pay to the United States that share of its revenue which some years since it allotted toward the extinguishment of the claims of foreigners generally. In thus reconsidering its determination that Government has shown a just sense of self-respect which can not fail to reflect credit upon it in the eyes of all disinterested persons elsewhere. It is to be regretted, however, that its payments on account of claims of citizens of the United States are still so meager in amount, and that the stipulations of the treaty in regard to the sums to be paid and the periods when those payments were to take place should have been so signally disregarded.

Since my last annual message the exchange has been made of the ratification of a treaty of commerce and navigation with Belgium, and of conventions with the Mexican Republic for the further extension of the joint commission respecting claims; with the Hawaiian Islands for commercial reciprocity, and with the Ottoman Empire for extradition; all of which have been duly proclaimed.

The Court of Commissioners of Alabama Claims has prosecuted its important duties very assiduously and very satisfactorily. It convened and was organized on the 22d day of July, 1874, and by the terms of the act under which it was created was to exist for one year from that date. The act provided, however, that should it be found impracticable to complete the work of the court before the expiration of the year the President might by proclamation extend the time of its duration to a period not more than six months beyond the expiration of the one year.

Having received satisfactory evidence that it would be impracticable to complete the work within the time originally fixed, I issued a proclamation (a copy of which is presented herewith) extending the time of duration of the court for a period of six months from and after the 22d day of July last.

A report made through the clerk of the court (communicated herewith) shows the condition of the calendar on the 1st of November last and the large amount of work which has been accomplished. One thousand three hundred and eighty-two claims have been presented, of which 682 had been disposed of at the date of the report. I am informed that 170 cases were decided during the month of November. Arguments are being made and decisions given in the remaining cases with all the dispatch consistent with the proper consideration of the questions submitted. Many of these claims are in behalf of mariners, or depend on the evidence of mariners, whose absence has delayed the taking or the return of the necessary evidence.

It is represented to me that it will be impracticable for the court to finally dispose of all the cases before it within the present limit of its duration. Justice to the parties claimant, who have been at large expense in preparing their claims and obtaining the evidence in their support, suggests a short extension, to enable the court to dispose of all of the claims which have been presented.

I recommend the legislation which may be deemed proper to enable the court to complete the work before it.

I recommend that some suitable provision be made, by the creation of a special court or by conferring the necessary jurisdiction upon some appropriate tribunal, for the consideration and determination of the claims of aliens against the Government of the United States which have arisen within some reasonable limitation of time, or which may hereafter arise, excluding all claims barred by treaty provisions or otherwise. It has been found impossible to give proper consideration to these claims by the Executive Departments of the Government. Such a tribunal would afford an opportunity to aliens other than British subjects to present their claims on account of acts committed against their persons or property during the rebellion, as also to those subjects of Great Britain whose claims, having arisen subsequent to the 9th day of April, 1865, could not be presented to the late commission organized pursuant to the provisions of the treaty of Washington.

The electric telegraph has become an essential and indispensable agent in the transmission of business and social messages. Its operation on land, and within the limit of particular states, is necessarily under the control of the jurisdiction within which it operates. The lines on the high seas, however, are not subject to the particular control of any one government.

In 1869 a concession was granted by the French Government to a company which proposed to lay a cable from the shores of France to the United States. At that time there was a telegraphic connection between the United States and the continent of Europe (through the possessions of Great Britain at either end of the line), under the control of an association which had, at large outlay of capital and at great risk, demonstrated the practicability of maintaining such means of communication. The cost of correspondence by this agency was great, possibly not too large at the time for a proper remuneration for so hazardous and so costly an enterprise. It was, however, a heavy charge upon a means of communication which the progress in the social and commercial intercourse of the world found to be a necessity, and the obtaining of this French concession showed that other capital than that already invested was ready to enter into competition, with assurance of adequate return for their outlay. Impressed with the conviction that the interests, not only of the people of the United States, but of the world at large, demanded, or would demand, the multiplication of such means of communication between separated continents, I was desirous that the proposed connection should be made; but certain provisions of this concession were deemed by me to be objectionable, particularly one which gave for a long term of years the exclusive right of telegraphic communication by submarine cable between the shores of France and the United States. I could not concede that any power should claim the right to land a cable on the shores of the United States and at the same time deny to the United States, or to its citizens or grantees, an equal right to land a cable on its shores. The right to control the conditions for the laying of a cable within the jurisdictional waters of the United States, to connect our shores with those of any foreign state, pertains exclusively to the Government of the United States, under such limitations and conditions as Congress may impose. In the absence of legislation by Congress I was unwilling, on the one hand, to yield to a foreign state the right to say that its grantees might land on our shores while it denied a similar right to our people to land on its shores, and, on the other hand, I was reluctant to deny to the great interests of the world and of civilization the facilities of such communication as were proposed. I therefore withheld any resistance to the landing of the cable on condition that the offensive monopoly feature of the concession be abandoned, and that the right of any cable which may be established by authority of this Government to land upon French territory and to connect with French land lines and enjoy all the necessary facilities or privileges incident to the use thereof upon as favorable terms as any other company be conceded. As the result thereof the company in question renounced the exclusive privilege, and the representative of France was informed that, understanding this relinquishment to be construed as granting the

entire reciprocity and equal facilities which had been demanded, the opposition to the landing of the cable was withdrawn.   The cable, under
this French concession, was landed in the month of July, 1869, and has
been an efficient and valuable agent of communication between this
country and the other continent.   It soon passed under the control,
however, of those who had the management of the cable connecting
Great Britain with this continent, and thus whatever benefit to the public might have ensued from competition between the two lines was lost,
leaving only the greater facilities of an additional line and the additional security in case of accident to one of them.   But these increased
facilities and this additional security, together with the control of the
combined capital of the two companies, gave also greater power to prevent the future construction of other lines and to limit the control of
telegraphic communication between the two continents to those possessing the lines already laid.   Within a few months past a cable has
been laid, known as the United States Direct Cable Company, connecting
the United States directly with Great Britain.   As soon as this cable was
reported to be laid and in working order the rates of the then existing
consolidated companies were greatly reduced.   Soon, however, a break
was announced in this new cable, and immediately the rates of the other
line, which had been reduced, were again raised.   This cable being now
repaired, the rates appear not to be reduced by either line from thos?
formerly charged by the consolidated companies.

There is reason to believe that large amounts of capital, both at home
and abroad, are ready to seek profitable investment in the advancement of
this useful and most civilizing means of intercourse and correspondence.
They await, however, the assurance of the means and conditions on which
they may safely be made tributary to the general good.

As these cable telegraph lines connect separate states, there are questions as to their organization and control which probably can be best,
if not solely, settled by conventions between the respective states.   In
the absence, however, of international conventions on the subject, municipal legislation may secure many points which appear to me important,
if not indispensable for the protection of the public against the extortions which may result from a monopoly of the right of operating cable
telegrams or from a combination between several lines:

I. No line should be allowed to land on the shores of the United States
under the concession from another power which does not admit the right
of any other line or lines, formed in the United States, to land and freely
connect with and operate through its land lines.

II. No line should be allowed to land on the shores of the United States
which is not, by treaty stipulation with the government from whose shores
it proceeds, or by prohibition in its charter, or otherwise to the satisfaction of this Government, prohibited from consolidating or amalgamating
with any other cable telegraph line, or combining therewith for the pur-

pose of regulating and maintaining the cost of telegraphing.

III. All lines should be bound to give precedence in the transmission of the official messages of the governments of the two countries between which it may be laid.

IV. A power should be reserved to the two governments, either conjointly or to each, as regards the messages dispatched from its shores, to fix a limit to the charges to be demanded for the transmission of messages.

I present this subject to the earnest consideration of Congress.

In the meantime, and unless Congress otherwise direct, I shall not oppose the landing of any telegraphic cable which complies with and assents to the points above enumerated, but will feel it my duty to prevent the landing of any which does not conform to the first and second points as stated, and which will not stipulate to concede to this Government the precedence in the transmission of its official messages and will not enter into a satisfactory arrangement with regard to its charges.

Among the pressing and important subjects to which, in my opinion, the attention of Congress should be directed are those relating to fraudulent naturalization and expatriation.

The United States, with great liberality, offers its citizenship to all who in good faith comply with the requirements of law. These requirements are as simple and upon as favorable terms to the emigrant as the high privilege to which he is admitted can or should permit. I do not propose any additional requirements to those which the law now demands; but the very simplicity and the want of unnecessary formality in our law have made fraudulent naturalization not infrequent, to the discredit and injury of all honest citizens, whether native or naturalized. Cases of this character are continually being brought to the notice of the Government by our representatives abroad, and also those of persons resident in other countries, most frequently those who, if they have remained in this country long enough to entitle them to become naturalized, have generally not much overpassed that period, and have returned to the country of their origin, where they reside, avoiding all duties to the United States by their absence, and claiming to be exempt from all duties to the country of their nativity and of their residence by reason of their alleged naturalization. It is due to this Government itself and to the great mass of the naturalized citizens who entirely, both in name and in fact, become citizens of the United States that the high privilege of citizenship of the United States should not be held by fraud or in derogation of the laws and of the good name of every honest citizen. On many occasions it has been brought to the knowledge of the Government that certificates of naturalization are held and protection or interference claimed by parties who admit that not only they were not within the United States at the time of the pretended naturalization, but that they have never resided in the United States; in others the certificate and record of the court show on their face that the person claiming to be naturalized had not resided the required time in the United States; in others it is admitted upon examination that the requirements of law have not been complied with; in some cases, even, such certificates have been matter of purchase.   These are not isolated cases, arising at rare intervals, but of common occurrence, and which are reported from all quarters of the globe.   Such occurrences can not, and do not, fail to reflect upon the Government and injure all honest citizens.   Such a fraud being discovered, however, there is no practicable means within the control of the Government by which the record of naturalization can be vacated; and should the certificate be taken up, as it usually is, by the diplomatic and consular representatives of the Government to whom it may have been presented, there is nothing to prevent the person claiming to have been naturalized from obtaining a new certificate from the court in place of that which has been taken from him.

The evil has become so great and of such frequent occurrence that I can not too earnestly recommend that some effective measures be adopted to provide a proper remedy and means for the vacating of any record thus fraudulently made, and of punishing the guilty parties to the transaction.

In this connection I refer also to the question of expatriation and the election of nationality.

The United States was foremost in upholding the right of expatriation and was principally instrumental in overthrowing the doctrine of perpetual allegiance.   Congress has declared the right of expatriation to be a natural and inherent right of all people ; but while many other nations have enacted laws providing what formalities shall be necessary to work a change of allegiance, the United States has enacted no provisions of law and has in no respect marked out how and when expatriation may be accomplished by its citizens.   Instances are brought to the attention of the Government where citizens of the United States, either naturalized or native born, have formally become citizens or subjects of foreign powers, but who, nevertheless, in the absence of any provisions of legislation on this question, when involved in difficulties or when it seems to be their interest, claim to be citizens of the United States and demand the intervention of a Government which they have long since abandoned and to which for years they have rendered no service nor held themselves in any way amenable.

In other cases naturalized citizens, immediately after naturalization, have returned to their native country; have become engaged in business; have accepted offices or pursuits inconsistent with American citizenship, and evidence no intent to return to the United States until called upon to discharge some duty to the country where they are residing, when at once they assert their citizenship and call upon the representatives of the Government to aid them in their unjust pretensions.   It is but justice to all *bona fide* citizens that no doubt should exist on such questions, and that Congress should determine by enactment of law how expatriation may be accomplished and change of citizenship be established.

I also invite your attention to the necessity of regulating by law the status of American women who may marry foreigners, and of defining more fully that of children born in a foreign country of American parents who may reside abroad; and also of some further provision regulating or giving legal effect to marriages of American citizens contracted in foreign countries. The correspondence submitted herewith shows a few of the constantly occurring questions on these points presented to the consideration of the Government. There are few subjects to engage the attention of Congress on which more delicate relations or more important interests are dependent.

In the month of July last the building erected for the Department of State was taken possession of and occupied by that Department. I am happy to announce that the archives and valuable papers of the Government in the custody of that Department are now safely deposited and properly cared for.

The report of the Secretary of the Treasury shows the receipts from customs for the fiscal year ending June 30, 1874, to have been $163,-103,833.69, and for the fiscal year ending June 30, 1875, to have been $157,167,722.35, a decrease for the last fiscal year of $5,936,111.34. Receipts from internal revenue for the year ending the 30th of June, 1874, were $102,409,784.90, and for the year ending June 30, 1875, $110,007,493.58; increase, $7,597,708.68.

The report also shows a complete history of the workings of the Department for the last year, and contains recommendations for reforms and for legislation which I concur in, but can not comment on so fully as I should like to do if space would permit, but will confine myself to a few suggestions which I look upon as vital to the best interests of the whole people—coming within the purview of "Treasury;" I mean specie resumption. Too much stress can not be laid upon this question, and I hope Congress may be induced, at the earliest day practicable, to insure the consummation of the act of the last Congress, at its last session, to bring about specie resumption "on and after the 1st of January, 1879," at furthest. It would be a great blessing if this could be consummated even at an earlier day.

Nothing seems to me more certain than that a full, healthy, and permanent reaction can not take place in favor of the industries and financial welfare of the country until we return to a measure of values recognized throughout the civilized world. While we use a currency not equivalent to this standard the world's recognized standard, specie, becomes a commodity like the products of the soil, the surplus seeking a market wherever there is a demand for it.

Under our present system we should want none, nor would we have any, were it not that customs dues must be paid in coin and because of the pledge to pay interest on the public debt in coin. The yield of precious metals would flow out for the purchase of foreign productions and leave the United States "hewers of wood and drawers of water," because of wiser legislation on the subject of finance by the nations with whom we have dealings. I am not prepared to say that I can suggest the best legislation to secure the end most heartily recommended. It will be a source of great gratification to me to be able to approve any measure of Congress looking effectively toward securing "resumption."

Unlimited inflation would probably bring about specie payments more speedily than any legislation looking to redemption of the legal-tenders in coin; but it would be at the expense of honor. The legal-tenders would have no value beyond settling present liabilities, or, properly speaking, re-pudiating them. They would buy nothing after debts were all settled.

There are a few measures which seem to me important in this connec-tion and which I commend to your earnest consideration:

A repeal of so much of the legal-tender act as makes these notes receiv-able for debts contracted after a date to be fixed in the act itself, say not later than the 1st of January, 1877. We should then have quotations at real values, not fictitious ones. Gold would no longer be at a premium, but currency at a discount. A healthy reaction would set in at once, and with it a desire to make the currency equal to what it purports to be. The merchants, manufacturers, and tradesmen of every calling could do business on a fair margin of profit, the money to be received having an unvarying value. Laborers and all classes who work for stipulated pay or salary would receive more for their income, because extra profits would no longer be charged by the capitalists to compensate for the risk of a downward fluctuation in the value of the currency.

Second. That the Secretary of the Treasury be authorized to redeem, say, not to exceed $2,000,000 monthly of legal-tender notes, by issuing in their stead a long bond, bearing interest at the rate of 3.65 per cent per annum, of denominations ranging from $50 up to $1,000 each. This would in time reduce the legal-tender notes to a volume that could be kept afloat without demanding redemption in large sums suddenly.

Third. That additional power be given to the Secretary of the Treasury to accumulate gold for final redemption, either by increasing revenue, curtailing expenses, or both (it is preferable to do both); and I recom-mend that reduction of expenditures be made wherever it can be done without impairing Government obligations or crippling the due execu-tion thereof. One measure for increasing the revenue—and the only one I think of—is the restoration of the duty on tea and coffee. These duties would add probably $18,000,000 to the present amount received from imports, and would in no way increase the prices paid for those articles by the consumers.

These articles are the products of countries collecting revenue from exports, and as we, the largest consumers, reduce the duties they propor-tionately increase them. With this addition to the revenue, many duties now collected, and which give but an insignificant return for the cost of collection, might be remitted, and to the direct advantage of consumers at home.

I would mention those articles which enter into manufactures of all sorts. All duty paid upon such articles goes directly to the cost of the article when manufactured here, and must be paid for by the consumers. These duties not only come from the consumers at home, but act as a protection to foreign manufacturers of the same completed articles in our own and distant markets.

I will suggest or mention another subject bearing upon the problem of ''how to enable the Secretary of the Treasury to accumulate balances.'' It is to devise some better method of verifying claims against the Government than at present exists through the Court of Claims, especially those claims growing out of the late war. Nothing is more certain than that a very large percentage of the amounts passed and paid are either wholly fraudulent or are far in excess of the real losses sustained. The large amount of losses proven—on good testimony according to existing laws, by affidavits of fictitious or unscrupulous persons—to have been sustained on small farms and plantations are not only far beyond the possible yield of those places for any one year, but, as everyone knows who has had experience in tilling the soil and who has visited the scenes of these spoliations, are in many instances more than the individual claimants were ever worth, including their personal and real estate.

The report of the Attorney-General, which will be submitted to Congress at an early day, will contain a detailed history of awards made and of claims pending of the class here referred to.

The report of the Secretary of War, accompanying this message, gives a detailed account of Army operations for the year just passed, expenses for maintenance, etc., with recommendations for legislation to which I respectfully invite your attention. To some of these I invite special attention:

First. The necessity of making $300,000 of the appropriation for the Subsistence Department available before the beginning of the next fiscal year. Without this provision troops at points distant from supply production must either go without food or existing laws must be violated. It is not attended with cost to the Treasury.

Second. His recommendation for the enactment of a system of annuities for the families of deceased officers by voluntary deductions from the monthly pay of officers. This again is not attended with burden upon the Treasury, and would for the future relieve much distress which every old army officer has witnessed in the past—of officers dying suddenly or being killed, leaving families without even the means of reaching their friends, if fortunate enough to have friends to aid them.

Third. The repeal of the law abolishing mileage, and a return to the old system.

Fourth. The trial with torpedoes under the Corps of Engineers, and appropriation for the same. Should war ever occur between the United States and any maritime power, torpedoes will be among if not the most effective and cheapest auxiliary for the defense of harbors, and also in aggressive operations, that we can have. Hence it is advisable to learn by experiment their best construction and application, as well as effect.

Fifth. A permanent organization for the Signal-Service Corps. This service has now become a necessity of peace as well as war, under the advancement made by the present able management.

Sixth. A renewal of the appropriation for compiling the official records of the war, etc.

The condition of our Navy at this time is a subject of satisfaction. It does not contain, it is true, any of the powerful cruising ironclads which make so much of the maritime strength of some other nations, but neither our continental situation nor our foreign policy requires that we should have a large number of ships of this character, while this situation and the nature of our ports combine to make those of other nations little dangerous to us under any circumstances.

Our Navy does contain, however, a considerable number of ironclads of the monitor class, which, though not properly cruisers, are powerful and effective for harbor defense and for operations near our own shores. Of these all the single-turreted ones, fifteen in number, have been substantially rebuilt, their rotten wooden beams replaced with iron, their hulls strengthened, and their engines and machinery thoroughly repaired, so that they are now in the most efficient condition and ready for sea as soon as they can be manned and put in commission.

The five double-turreted ironclads belonging to our Navy, by far the most powerful of our ships for fighting purposes, are also in hand undergoing complete repairs, and could be ready for sea in periods varying from four to six months. With these completed according to the present design and our two iron torpedo boats now ready, our ironclad fleet will be, for the purposes of defense at home, equal to any force that can readily be brought against it.

Of our wooden navy also cruisers of various sizes, to the number of about forty, including those now in commission, are in the Atlantic, and could be ready for duty as fast as men could be enlisted for those not already in commission. Of these, one-third are in effect new ships, and though some of the remainder need considerable repairs to their boilers and machinery, they all are, or can readily be made, effective.

This constitutes a fleet of more than fifty war ships, of which fifteen are ironclad, now in hand on the Atlantic coast. The Navy has been brought to this condition by a judicious and practical application of what could be spared from the current appropriations of the last few years and from that made to meet the possible emergency of two years ago. It has been done quietly, without proclamation or display, and though it has necessarily straitened the Department in its ordinary expenditure, and, as far as the ironclads are concerned, has added nothing to the cruising force of the Navy, yet the result is not the less satisfactory because it is to be found in a great increase of real rather than apparent force. The expenses incurred in the maintenance of an effective naval force in all its branches are necessarily large, but such force is essential to our position, relations, and character, and affects seriously the weight of our principles and policy throughout the whole sphere of national responsibilities.

The estimates for the regular support of this branch of the service for the next year amount to a little less in the aggregate than those made for the current year; but some additional appropriations are asked for objects not included in the ordinary maintenance of the Navy, but believed to be of pressing importance at this time. It would, in my opinion, be wise at once to afford sufficient means for the immediate completion of the five double-turreted monitors now undergoing repairs, which must otherwise advance slowly, and only as money can be spared from current expenses. Supplemented by these, our Navy, armed with the destructive weapons of modern warfare, manned by our seamen, and in charge of our instructed officers, will present a force powerful for the home purposes of a responsible though peaceful nation.

The report of the Postmaster-General herewith transmitted gives a full history of the workings of the Department for the year just past. It will be observed that the deficiency to be supplied from the General Treasury is increased over the amount required for the preceding year. In a country so vast in area as the United States, with large portions sparsely settled, it must be expected that this important service will be more or less a burden upon the Treasury for many years to come. But there is no branch of the public service which interests the whole people more than that of cheap and rapid transmission of the mails to every inhabited part of our territory. Next to the free school, the post-office is the great educator of the people, and it may well receive the support of the General Government.

The subsidy of $150,000 per annum given to vessels of the United States for carrying the mails between New York and Rio de Janeiro having ceased on the 30th day of September last, we are without direct mail facilities with the South American States. This is greatly to be regretted, and I do not hesitate to recommend the authorization of a renewal of that contract, and also that the service may be increased from monthly to semi-monthly trips. The commercial advantages to be gained by a direct line of American steamers to the South American States will far outweigh the expense of the service.

By act of Congress approved March 3, 1875, almost all matter, whether properly mail matter or not, may be sent any distance through the mails, in packages not exceeding 4 pounds in weight, for the sum of 16 cents per pound. So far as the transmission of real mail matter goes, this would seem entirely proper; but I suggest that the law be so amended as to exclude from the mails merchandise of all descriptions, and limit this transportation to articles enumerated, and which may be classed as mail matter proper.

The discovery of gold in the Black Hills, a portion of the Sioux Reservation, has had the effect to induce a large emigration of miners to that point. Thus far the effort to protect the treaty rights of the Indians to that section has been successful, but the next year will certainly witness a large increase of such emigration. The negotiations for the relinquishment of the gold fields having failed, it will be necessary for Congress to adopt some measures to relieve the embarrassment growing out of the causes named. The Secretary of the Interior suggests that the supplies now appropriated for the sustenance of that people, being no longer obligatory under the treaty of 1868, but simply a gratuity, may be issued or withheld at his discretion.

The condition of the Indian Territory, to which I have referred in several of my former annual messages, remains practically unchanged. The Secretary of the Interior has taken measures to obtain a full report of the condition of that Territory, and will make it the subject of a special report at an early day. It may then be necessary to make some further recommendation in regard to legislation for the government of that Territory.

The steady growth and increase of the business of the Patent Office indicates in some measure the progress of the industrial activity of the country. The receipts of the office are in excess of its expenditures, and the office generally is in a prosperous and satisfactory condition.

The report of the General Land Office shows that there were 2,459,601 acres less disposed of during this than during the last year. More than one-half of this decrease was in lands disposed of under the homestead and timber-culture laws. The cause of this decrease is supposed to be found in the grasshopper scourge and the droughts which prevailed so extensively in some of the frontier States and Territories during that time as to discourage and deter entries by actual settlers. The cash receipts were less by $690,322.23 than during the preceding year.

The entire surveyed area of the public domain is 680,253,094 acres, of which 26,077,531 acres were surveyed during the past year, leaving 1,154,471,762 acres still unsurveyed.

The report of the Commissioner presents many interesting suggestions in regard to the management and disposition of the public domain and the modification of existing laws, the apparent importance of which should insure for them the careful consideration of Congress.

The number of pensioners still continues to decrease, the highest number having been reached during the year ending June 30, 1873. During the last year 11,557 names were added to the rolls, and 12,977 were dropped therefrom, showing a net decrease of 1,420. But while the number of pensioners has decreased, the annual amount due on the pension rolls has increased $44,733.13. This is caused by the greatly increased average rate of pensions, which, by the liberal legislation of Congress, has increased from $90.26 in 1872 to $103.91 in 1875 to each invalid pensioner, an increase in the average rate of 15 per cent in the three years. During the year ending June 30, 1875, there was paid on account of pensions, including the expenses of disbursement, $29,683,116, being $910,632 less than was paid the preceding year. This reduction in amount of expenditures was produced by the decrease in the amount of arrearages due on allowed claims and on pensions the rate of which was increased by the legislation of the preceding session of Congress. At the close of the last fiscal year there were on the pension rolls 234,821 persons, of whom 210,363 were army pensioners, 105,478 being invalids and 104,885 widows and dependent relatives; 3,420 were navy pensioners, of whom 1,636 were invalids and 1,784 widows and dependent relatives; 21,038 were pensioners of the War of 1812, 15,875 of whom were survivors and 5,163 were widows.

It is estimated that $29,535,000 will be required for the payment of pensions for the next fiscal year, an amount $965,000 less than the estimate for the present year.

The geological explorations have been prosecuted with energy during the year, covering an area of about 40,000 square miles in the Territories of Colorado, Utah, and New Mexico, developing the agricultural and mineral resources and furnishing interesting scientific and topographical details of that region.

The method for the treatment of the Indians adopted at the beginning of my first term has been steadily pursued, and with satisfactory and encouraging results. It has been productive of evident improvement in the condition of that race, and will be continued, with only such modifications as further experience may indicate to be necessary.

The board heretofore appointed to take charge of the articles and materials pertaining to the War, the Navy, the Treasury, the Interior. and the Post-Office Departments, and the Department of Agriculture, the Smithsonian Institution, and the Commission of Food Fishes, to be contributed, under the legislation of last session, to the international exhibition to be held at Philadelphia during the centennial year 1876, has been diligent in the discharge of the duties which have devolved upon it; and the preparations so far made with the means at command give assurance that the governmental contribution will be made one of the marked characteristics of the exhibition. The board has observed commendable economy in the matter of the erection of a building for the governmental exhibit, the expense of which it is estimated will not exceed, say, $80,000. This amount has been withdrawn, under the law, from the appropriations of five of the principal Departments, which leaves some of those Departments without sufficient means to render their respective practical exhibits complete and satisfactory.   The exhibition being an international one, and the Government being a voluntary contributor, it is my opinion that its contribution should be of a character, in quality and extent, to sustain the dignity and credit of so distinguished a contributor.   The advantages to the country of a creditable display are, in an international point of view, of the first importance, while an indifferent or uncreditable participation by the Government would be humiliating to the patriotic feelings of our people themselves.   I commend the estimates of the board for the necessary additional appropriations to the favorable consideration of Congress.

The powers of Europe almost without exception, many of the South American States, and even the more distant Eastern powers have manifested their friendly sentiments toward the United States and the interest of the world in our progress by taking steps to join with us in celebrating the centennial of the nation, and I strongly recommend that a more national importance be given to this exhibition by such legislation and by such appropriation as will insure its success.   Its value in bringing to our shores innumerable useful works of art and skill, the commingling of the citizens of foreign countries and our own, and the interchange of ideas and manufactures will far exceed any pecuniary outlay we may make.

I transmit herewith the report of the Commissioner of Agriculture, together with the reports of the Commissioners, the board of audit, and the board of health of the District of Columbia, to all of which I invite your attention.

The Bureau of Agriculture has accomplished much in disseminating useful knowledge to the agriculturist, and also in introducing new and useful productions adapted to our soil and climate, and is worthy of the continued encouragement of the Government.

The report of the Commissioner of Education, which accompanies the report of the Secretary of the Interior, shows a gratifying progress in educational matters.

In nearly every annual message that I have had the honor of transmitting to Congress I have called attention to the anomalous, not to say scandalous, condition of affairs existing in the Territory of Utah, and have asked for definite legislation to correct it.   That polygamy should exist in a free, enlightened, and Christian country, without the power to punish so flagrant a crime against decency and morality, seems preposterous. True, there is no law to sustain this unnatural vice; but what is needed is a law to punish it as a crime, and at the same time to fix the status of the innocent children, the offspring of this system, and of the possibly innocent plural wives.   But as an institution polygamy should be banished from the land.

While this is being done I invite the attention of Congress to another, though perhaps no less an evil—the importation of Chinese women, but few of whom are brought to our shores to pursue honorable or useful occupations.

Observations while visiting the Territories of Wyoming, Utah, and Colorado during the past autumn convinced me that existing laws regulating the disposition of public lands, timber, etc., and probably the mining laws themselves, are very defective and should be carefully amended, and at an early day. Territory where cultivation of the soil can only be followed by irrigation, and where irrigation is not practicable the lands can only be used as pasturage, and this only where stock can reach water (to quench its thirst), can not be governed by the same laws as to entries as lands every acre of which is an independent estate by itself.

Land must be held in larger quantities to justify the expense of conducting water upon it to make it fruitful, or to justify utilizing it as pasturage. The timber in most of the Territories is principally confined to the mountain regions, which are held for entry in small quantities only, and as mineral lands. The timber is the property of the United States, for the disposal of which there is now no adequate law. The settler must become a consumer of this timber, whether he lives upon the plain or engages in working the mines. Hence every man becomes either a tres-passer himself or knowingly a patron of trespassers.

My opportunities for observation were not sufficient to justify me in recommending specific legislation on these subjects, but I do recommend that a joint committee of the two Houses of Congress, sufficiently large to be divided into subcommittees, be organized to visit all the mining States and Territories during the coming summer, and that the committee shall report to Congress at the next session such laws or amendments to laws as it may deem necessary to secure the best interests of the Government and the people of these Territories, who are doing so much for their development.

I am sure the citizens occupying the territory described do not wish to be trespassers, nor will they be if legal ways are provided for them to become owners of these actual necessities of their position.

As this will be the last annual message which I shall have the honor of transmitting to Congress before my successor is chosen, I will repeat or recapitulate the questions which I deem of vital importance which may be legislated upon and settled at this session:

First. That the States shall be required to afford the opportunity of a good common-school education to every child within their limits.

Second. No sectarian tenets shall ever be taught in any school supported in whole or in part by the State, nation, or by the proceeds of any tax levied upon any community. Make education compulsory so far as to deprive all persons who can not read and write from becoming voters after the year 1890, disfranchising none, however, on grounds of illiteracy who may be voters at the time this amendment takes effect.

Third. Declare church and state forever separate and distinct, but each free within their proper spheres; and that all church property shall bear its own proportion of taxation.

Fourth. Drive out licensed immorality, such as polygamy and the importation of women for illegitimate purposes. To recur again to the centennial year, it would seem as though now, as we are about to begin the second century of our national existence, would be a most fitting time for these reforms.

Fifth. Enact such laws as will insure a speedy return to a sound currency, such as will command the respect of the world.

Believing that these views will commend themselves to the great majority of the right-thinking and patriotic citizens of the United States, I submit the rest to Congress.

EIGHTH ANNUAL MESSAGE.

EXECUTIVE MANSION, *December 5, 1876.*

To the Senate and House of Representatives:

In submitting my eighth and last annual message to Congress it seems proper that I should refer to and in some degree recapitulate the events and official acts of the past eight years.

It was my fortune, or misfortune, to be called to the office of Chief Executive without any previous political training. From the age of 17 I had never even witnessed the excitement attending a Presidential campaign but twice antecedent to my own candidacy, and at but one of them was I eligible as a voter.

Under such circumstances it is but reasonable to suppose that errors of judgment must have occurred. Even had they not, differences of opinion between the Executive, bound by an oath to the strict performance of his duties, and writers and debaters must have arisen. It is not necessarily evidence of blunder on the part of the Executive because there are these differences of views. Mistakes have been made, as all can see and I admit, but it seems to me oftener in the selections made of the assistants appointed to aid in carrying out the various duties of administering the Government—in nearly every case selected without a personal acquaintance with the appointee, but upon recommendations of the representatives chosen directly by the people. It is impossible, where so many trusts are to be allotted, that the right parties should be chosen in every instance. History shows that no Administration from the time of Washington to the present has been free from these mistakes. But I leave comparisons to history, claiming only that I have acted in every instance from a conscientious desire to do what was right, constitutional, within the law, and for the very best interests of the whole people. Failures have been errors of judgment, not of intent.

My civil career commenced, too, at a most critical and difficult time. Less than four years before, the country had emerged from a conflict such as no other nation had ever survived. Nearly one-half of the States had revolted against the Government, and of those remaining faithful to the Union a large percentage of the population sympathized with the rebellion and made an "enemy in the rear" almost as dangerous as the more honorable enemy in the front. The latter committed errors of judgment, but they maintained them openly and courageously; the former received the protection of the Government they would see destroyed, and reaped all the pecuniary advantage to be gained out of the then existing state of affairs, many of them by obtaining contracts and by swindling the Government in the delivery of their goods.

Immediately on the cessation of hostilities the then noble President, who had carried the country so far through its perils, fell a martyr to his patriotism at the hands of an assassin.

The intervening time to my first inauguration was filled up with wranglings between Congress and the new Executive as to the best mode of "reconstruction," or, to speak plainly, as to whether the control of the Government should be thrown immediately into the hands of those who had so recently and persistently tried to destroy it, or whether the victors should continue to have an equal voice with them in this control. Reconstruction, as finally agreed upon, means this and only this, except that the late slave was enfranchised, giving an increase, as was supposed, to the Union-loving and Union-supporting votes. If *free* in the full sense of the word, they would not disappoint this expectation. Hence at the beginning of my first Administration the work of reconstruction, much embarrassed by the long delay, virtually commenced. It was the work of the legislative branch of the Government. My province was wholly in approving their acts, which I did most heartily, urging the legislatures of States that had not yet done so to ratify the fifteenth amendment to the Constitution. The country was laboring under an enormous debt, contracted in the suppression of rebellion, and taxation was so oppressive as to discourage production. Another danger also threatened us—a foreign war. The last difficulty had to be adjusted and was adjusted without a war and in a manner highly honorable to all parties concerned. Taxes have been reduced within the last seven years nearly $300,000,000, and the national debt has been reduced in the same time over $435,000,000. By refunding the 6 per cent bonded debt for bonds bearing 5 and 4½ per cent interest, respectively, the annual interest has been reduced from over $130,000,000 in 1869 to but little over $100,000,000 in 1876. The balance of trade has been changed from over $130,000,000 against the United States in 1869 to more than $120,000,000 in our favor in 1876.

It is confidently believed that the balance of trade in favor of the United States will increase, not diminish, and that the pledge of Congress to resume specie payments in 1879 will be easily accomplished, even in the absence of much-desired further legislation on the subject.

A policy has been adopted toward the Indian tribes inhabiting a large portion of the territory of the United States which has been humane and has substantially ended Indian hostilities in the whole land except in a portion of Nebraska, and Dakota, Wyoming, and Montana Territories— the Black Hills region and approaches thereto. Hostilities there have grown out of the avarice of the white man, who has violated our treaty stipulations in his search for gold. The question might be asked why the Government has not enforced obedience to the terms of the treaty prohibiting the occupation of the Black Hills region by whites. The answer is simple: The first immigrants to the Black Hills were removed by troops, but rumors of rich discoveries of gold took into that region increased numbers. Gold has actually been found in paying quantity, and an effort to remove the miners would only result in the desertion of the bulk of the troops that might be sent there to remove them. All difficulty in this matter has, however, been removed—subject to the approval of Congress—by a treaty ceding the Black Hills and approaches to settlement by citizens.

The subject of Indian policy and treatment is so fully set forth by the Secretary of the Interior and the Commissioner of Indian Affairs, and my views so fully expressed therein, that I refer to their reports and recommendations as my own.

The relations of the United States with foreign powers continue on a friendly footing.

Questions have arisen from time to time in the foreign relations of the Government, but the United States have been happily free during the past year from the complications and embarrassments which have surrounded some of the foreign powers.

The diplomatic correspondence submitted herewith contains information as to certain of the matters which have occupied the Government.

The cordiality which attends our relations with the powers of the earth has been plainly shown by the general participation of foreign nations in the exhibition which has just closed and by the exertions made by distant powers to show their interest in and friendly feelings toward the United States in the commemoration of the centennial of the nation. The Government and people of the United States have not only fully appreciated this exhibition of kindly feeling, but it may be justly and fairly expected that no small benefits will result both to ourselves and other nations from a better acquaintance, and a better appreciation of our mutual advantages and mutual wants.

Congress at its last session saw fit to reduce the amount usually appropriated for foreign intercourse by withholding appropriations for representatives of the United States in certain foreign countries and for certain consular officers, and by reducing the amounts usually appropriated for certain other diplomatic posts, and thus necessitating a change in the grade of the representatives. For these reasons, immediately upon the passage of the bill making appropriations for the diplomatic and consular service for the present fiscal year, instructions were issued to the representatives of the United States at Bolivia, Ecuador, and Colombia, and to the consular officers for whom no appropriation had been made, to close their respective legations and consulates and cease from the performance of their duties; and in like manner steps were immediately taken to substitute chargés d'affaires for ministers resident in Portugal, Denmark, Greece, Switzerland, and Paraguay.

While thoroughly impressed with the wisdom of sound economy in the foreign service, as in other branches of the Government, I can not escape the conclusion that in some instances the withholding of appropriations will prove an expensive economy, and that the small retrenchment secured by a change of grade in certain diplomatic posts is not an adequate consideration for the loss of influence and importance which will attend our foreign representatives under this reduction. I am of the opinion that a reexamination of the subject will cause a change in some instances in the conclusions reached on these subjects at the last session of Congress.

The Court of Commissioners of Alabama Claims, whose functions were continued by an act of the last session of Congress until the 1st day of January, 1877, has carried on its labors with diligence and general satisfaction. By a report from the clerk of the court, transmitted herewith, bearing date November 14, 1876, it appears that within the time now allowed by law the court will have disposed of all the claims presented for adjudication. This report also contains a statement of the general results of the labors of the court to the date thereof. It is a cause of satisfaction that the method adopted for the satisfaction of the classes of claims submitted to the court, which are of long standing and justly entitled to early consideration, should have proved successful and acceptable.

It is with satisfaction that I am enabled to state that the work of the joint commission for determining the boundary line between the United States and British possessions from the northwest angle of the Lake of the Woods to the Rocky Mountains, commenced in 1872, has been completed. The final agreements of the commissioners, with the maps, have been duly signed, and the work of the commission is complete.

The fixing of the boundary upon the Pacific coast by the protocol of March 10, 1873, pursuant to the award of the Emperor of Germany by Article XXXIV of the treaty of Washington, with the termination of the work of this commission, adjusts and fixes the entire boundary between the United States and the British possessions, except as to the portion of territory ceded by Russia to the United States under the treaty of 1867. The work intrusted to the commissioner and the officers of the Army attached to the commission has been well and satisfactorily performed. The original of the final agreement of the commissioners, signed upon the 29th of May, 1876, with the original official "lists of astronomical stations observed," the original official "list of monuments marking the international boundary line," and the maps, records, and general reports relating to the commission, have been deposited in the Department of State. The official report of the commissioner on the part of the United States, with the report of the chief astronomer of the United States, will be submitted to Congress within a short time.

I reserve for a separate communication to Congress a statement of the condition of the questions which lately arose with Great Britain respecting the surrender of fugitive criminals under the treaty of 1842.

The Ottoman Government gave notice, under date of January 15, 1874, of its desire to terminate the treaty of 1862, concerning commerce and navigation, pursuant to the provisions of the twenty-second article thereof. Under this notice the treaty terminated upon the 5th day of June, 1876. That Government has invited negotiations toward the conclusion of a new treaty.

By the act of Congress of March 23, 1874, the President was authorized, when he should receive satisfactory information that the Ottoman Government or that of Egypt had organized new tribunals likely to secure to citizens of the United States the same impartial justice enjoyed under the exercise of judicial functions by diplomatic and consular officers of the United States, to suspend the operation of the act of June 22, 1860, and to accept for citizens of the United States the jurisdiction of the new tribunals. Satisfactory information having been received of the organization of such new tribunals in Egypt, I caused a proclamation* to be issued upon the 27th of March last, suspending the operation of the act of June 22, 1860, in Egypt, according to the provisions of the act. A copy of the proclamation accompanies this message. The United States has united with the other powers in the organization of these courts. It is hoped that the jurisdictional questions which have arisen may be readily adjusted, and that this advance in judicial reform may be hindered by no obstacles.

The necessary legislation to carry into effect the convention respecting commercial reciprocity concluded with the Hawaiian Islands in 1875 having been had, the proclamation to carry into effect the convention, as provided by the act approved August 15, 1876, was duly issued upon the 9th day of September last. A copy thereof accompanies this message.

The commotions which have been prevalent in Mexico for some time past, and which, unhappily, seem to be not yet wholly quieted, have led to complaints of citizens of the United States of injuries by persons in authority. It is hoped, however, that these will ultimately be adjusted to the satisfaction of both Governments. The frontier of the United States in that quarter has not been exempt from acts of violence by citizens of one Republic on those of the other. The frequency of these is supposed to be increased and their adjustment made more difficult by the considerable changes in the course of the lower part of the Rio Grande River, which river is a part of the boundary between the two countries. These changes have placed on either side of that river portions of land which by existing conventions belong to the jurisdiction of the Government on the opposite side of the river. The subject of adjustment of this cause of difficulty is under consideration between the two Republics.

The Government of the United States of Colombia has paid the award in the case of the steamer *Montijo*, seized by authorities of that Government some years since, and the amount has been transferred to the claimants.

It is with satisfaction that I am able to announce that the joint commission for the adjustment of claims between the United States and Mexico under the convention of 1868, the duration of which has been several times extended, has brought its labors to a close. From the report of the agent of the United States, which accompanies the papers transmitted herewith, it will be seen that within the time limited by the commission 1,017 claims on the part of citizens of the United States against Mexico were referred to the commission. Of these claims 831 were dismissed or disallowed, and in 186 cases awards were made in favor of the claimants against the Mexican Republic, amounting in the aggregate to $4,125,622.20. Within the same period 998 claims on the part of citizens of the Mexican Republic against the United States were referred to the commission. Of these claims 831 were dismissed or disallowed, and in 167 cases awards were made in favor of the claimants against the United States, amounting in the aggregate to $150,498.41.

By the terms of the convention the amount of these awards is to be deducted from the amount awarded in favor of our citizens against Mexico, and the balance only to be paid by Mexico to the United States, leaving the United States to make provision for this proportion of the awards in favor of its own citizens.

I invite your attention to the legislation which will be necessary to provide for the payment.

In this connection I am pleased to be able to express the acknowledgments due to Sir Edward Thornton, the umpire of the commission, who has given to the consideration of the large number of claims submitted to him much time, unwearied patience, and that firmness and intelligence which are well known to belong to the accomplished representative of Great Britain, and which are likewise recognized by the representative in this country of the Republic of Mexico.

Monthly payments of a very small part of the amount due by the Government of Venezuela to citizens of the United States on account of claims of the latter against that Government continue to be made with reasonable punctuality. That Government has proposed to change the system which it has hitherto pursued in this respect by issuing bonds for part of the amount of the several claims. The proposition, however, could not, it is supposed, properly be accepted, at least without the consent of the holders of certificates of the indebtedness of Venezuela. These are so much dispersed that it would be difficult, if not impossible, to ascertain their disposition on the subject.

In former messages I have called the attention of Congress to the necessity of legislation with regard to fraudulent naturalization and to the subject of expatriation and the election of nationality.

The numbers of persons of foreign birth seeking a home in the United States, the ease and facility with which the honest emigrant may, after the lapse of a reasonable time, become possessed of all the privileges of citizenship of the United States, and the frequent occasions which induce such adopted citizens to return to the country of their birth render the subject of naturalization and the safeguards which experience has proved necessary for the protection of the honest naturalized citizen of paramount importance. The very simplicity in the requirements of law on this question affords opportunity for fraud, and the want of uniformity in the proceedings and records of the various courts and in the forms of the certificates of naturalization issued affords a constant source of difficulty.

I suggest no additional requirements to the acquisition of citizenship beyond those now existing, but I invite the earnest attention of Congress to the necessity and wisdom of some provisions regarding uniformity in the records and certificates, and providing against the frauds which frequently take place and for the vacating of a record of naturalization obtained in fraud.

These provisions are needed in aid and for the protection of the honest citizen of foreign birth, and for the want of which he is made to suffer not infrequently. The United States has insisted upon the right of expatriation, and has obtained, after a long struggle, an admission of the principle contended for by acquiescence therein on the part of many foreign powers and by the conclusion of treaties on that subject. It is, however, but justice to the government to which such naturalized citizens have formerly owed allegiance, as well as to the United States, that certain fixed and definite rules should be adopted governing such cases and providing how expatriation may be accomplished.

While emigrants in large numbers become citizens of the United States, it is also true that persons, both native born and naturalized, once citizens of the United States, either by formal acts or as the effect of a series of facts and circumstances, abandon their citizenship and cease to be entitled to the protection of the United States, but continue on conven-

rent occasions to assert a claim to protection in the absence of provisions on these questions.

And in this connection I again invite your attention to the necessity of legislation concerning the marriages of American citizens contracted abroad, and concerning the status of American women who may marry foreigners and of children born of American parents in a foreign country.

The delicate and complicated questions continually occurring with reference to naturalization, expatriation, and the status of such persons as I have above referred to induce me to earnestly direct your attention again to these subjects.

In like manner I repeat my recommendation that some means be provided for the hearing and determination of the just and subsisting claims of aliens upon the Government of the United States within a reasonable limitation, and of such as may hereafter arise. While by existing provisions of law the Court of Claims may in certain cases be resorted to by an alien claimant, the absence of any general provisions governing all such cases and the want of a tribunal skilled in the disposition of such cases upon recognized fixed and settled principles, either provides no remedy in many deserving cases or compels a consideration of such claims by Congress or the executive department of the Government.

It is believed that other governments are in advance of the United States upon this question, and that the practice now adopted is entirely unsatisfactory.

Congress, by an act approved the 3d day of March, 1875, authorized the inhabitants of the Territory of Colorado to form a State government, with the name of the State of Colorado, and therein provided for the admission of said State, when formed, into the Union upon an equal footing with the original States.

A constitution having been adopted and ratified by the people of that State, and the acting governor having certified to me the facts as provided by said act, together with a copy of such constitution and ordinances as provided for in the said act, and the provisions of the said act of Congress having been duly complied with, I issued a proclamation upon the 1st of August, 1876, a copy of which is hereto annexed.

The report of the Secretary of War shows that the Army has been actively employed during the year in subduing, at the request of the Indian Bureau, certain wild bands of the Sioux Indian Nation and in preserving the peace at the South during the election. The commission constituted under the act of July 24, 1876, to consider and report on the "whole subject of the reform and reorganization of the Army" met in August last, and has collected a large mass of statistics and opinions bearing on the subject before it. These are now under consideration, and their report is progressing. I am advised, though, by the president of the commission that it will be impracticable to comply with the clause of the act requiring the report to be presented, through

me, to Congress on the first day of this session, as there has not yet
been time for that mature deliberation which the importance of the
subject demands.   Therefore I ask that the time of making the report
be extended to the 29th day of January, 1877.

In accordance with the resolution of August 15, 1876, the Army regulations prepared under the act of March 1, 1875, have not been promulgated,
but are held until after the report of the above-mentioned commission
shall have been received and acted on.

By the act of August 15, 1876, the cavalry force of the Army was
increased by 2,500 men, with the proviso that they should be discharged
on the expiration of hostilities.   Under this authority the cavalry regiments have been strengthened, and a portion of them are now in the field
pursuing the remnants of the Indians with whom they have been engaged
during the summer.

The estimates of the War Department are made up on the basis of the
number of men authorized by law, and their requirements as shown by
years of experience, and also with the purpose on the part of the bureau
officers to provide for all contingencies that may arise during the time
for which the estimates are made.   Exclusive of engineer estimates (presented in accordance with acts of Congress calling for surveys and estimates for improvements at various localities), the estimates now presented
are about six millions in excess of the appropriations for the years 1874–75
and 1875–76.   This increase is asked in order to provide for the increased
cavalry force (should their services be necessary), to prosecute economically work upon important public buildings, to provide for armament of
fortifications and manufacture of small arms, and to replenish the working stock in the supply departments.   The appropriations for these last
named have for the past few years been so limited that the accumulations
in store will be entirely exhausted during the present year, and it will be
necessary to at once begin to replenish them.

I invite your special attention to the following recommendations of
the Secretary of War:

First. That the claims under the act of July 4. 1864, for supplies taken
by the Army during the war be removed from the offices of the Quartermaster and Commissary Generals and transferred to the Southern
Claims Commission.   These claims are of precisely similar nature to those
now before the Southern Claims Commission, and the War Department
bureaus have not the clerical force for their examination nor proper
machinery for investigating the loyalty of the claimants.

Second. That Congress sanction the scheme of an annuity fund for
the benefit of the families of deceased officers, and that it also provide
for the permanent organization of the Signal Service, both of which were
recommended in my last annual message.

Third. That the manufacturing operations of the Ordnance Department be concentrated at three arsenals and an armory, and that the

remaining arsenals be sold and the proceeds applied to this object by the Ordnance Department.

The appropriations for river and harbor improvements for the current year were $5,015,000. With my approval, the Secretary of War directed that of this amount $2,000,000 should be expended, and no new works should be begun and none prosecuted which were not of national importance. Subsequently this amount was increased to $2,237,600, and the works are now progressing on this basis.

The improvement of the South Pass of the Mississippi River, under James B. Eads and his associates, is progressing favorably. At the present time there is a channel of 20.3 feet in depth between the jetties at the mouth of the pass and 18.5 feet at the head of the pass. Neither channel, however, has the width required before payments can be made by the United States. A commission of engineer officers is now examining these works, and their reports will be presented as soon as received.

The report of the Secretary of the Navy shows that branch of the service to be in condition as effective as it is possible to keep it with the means and authority given the Department. It is, of course, not possible to rival the costly and progressive establishments of great European powers with the old material of our Navy, to which no increase has been authorized since the war, except the eight small cruisers built to supply the place of others which had gone to decay. Yet the most has been done that was possible with the means at command; and by substantially rebuilding some of our old ships with durable material and completely repairing and refitting our monitor fleet the Navy has been gradually so brought up that, though it does not maintain its relative position among the progressive navies of the world, it is now in a condition more powerful and effective than it ever has been in time of peace.

The complete repairs of our five heavy ironclads are only delayed on account of the inadequacy of the appropriations made last year for the working bureaus of the Department, which were actually less in amount than those made before the war, notwithstanding the greatly enhanced price of labor and materials and the increase in the cost of the naval service growing out of the universal use and great expense of steam machinery. The money necessary for these repairs should be provided at once, that they may be completed without further unnecessary delay and expense.

When this is done, all the strength that there is in our Navy will be developed and useful to its full capacity, and it will be powerful for purposes of defense, and also for offensive action, should the necessity for that arise within a reasonable distance from our shores.

The fact that our Navy is not more modern and powerful than it is has been made a cause of complaint against the Secretary of the Navy by persons who at the same time criticise and complain of his endeavors to bring the Navy that we have to its best and most efficient condition; but the good sense of the country will understand that it is really due to his practical action that we have at this time any effective naval force at command.

The report of the Postmaster-General shows the excess of expenditures (excluding expenditures on account of previous years) over receipts for the fiscal year ended June 30, 1876, to be $4,151,988.66.

Estimated expenditures for the fiscal year ending June 30, 1878, are $36,723,432.43.

Estimated revenue for same period is $30,645,165, leaving estimated excess of expenditure, to be appropriated as a deficiency, of $6,078,267.43.

The Postmaster-General, like his predecessor, is convinced that a change in the basis of adjusting the salaries of postmasters of the fourth class is necessary for the good of the service as well as for the interests of the Government, and urgently recommends that the compensation of the class of postmasters above mentioned be based upon the business of their respective offices, as ascertained from the sworn returns to the Auditor of stamps canceled.

A few postmasters in the Southern States have expressed great apprehension of their personal safety on account of their connection with the postal service, and have specially requested that their reports of apprehended danger should not be made public lest it should result in the loss of their lives.   But no positive testimony of interference has been submitted, except in the case of a mail messenger at Spartanburg, in South Carolina, who reported that he had been violently driven away while in charge of the mails on account of his political affiliations.   An assistant superintendent of the Railway Mail Service investigated this case and reported that the messenger had disappeared from his post, leaving his work to be performed by a substitute.   The Postmaster-General thinks this case is sufficiently suggestive to justify him in recommending that a more severe punishment should be provided for the offense of assaulting any person in charge of the mails or of retarding or otherwise obstructing them by threats of personal injury.

"A very gratifying result is presented in the fact that the deficiency of this Department during the last fiscal year was reduced to $4,081,790.18, as against $6,169,938.88 of the preceding year.   The difference can be traced to the large increase in its ordinary receipts (which greatly exceed the estimates therefor) and a slight decrease in its expenditures."

The ordinary *receipts* of the Post-Office Department for the past seven fiscal years have increased at an average of over 8 per cent per annum, while the increase of *expenditures* for the same period has been but about 5.50 per cent per annum, and the *decrease* of *deficiency* in the revenues has been at the rate of nearly 2 per cent per annum.

The report of the Commissioner of Agriculture accompanying this message will be found one of great interest, marking, as it does, the great progress of the last century in the variety of products of the soil; increased knowledge and skill in the labor of producing, saving, and manipulating the same to prepare them for the use of man; in the improvements in machinery to aid the agriculturist in his labors, and in a knowledge of those scientific subjects necessary to a thorough system of economy in agricultural production, namely, chemistry, botany, entomology, etc. A study of this report by those interested in agriculture and deriving their support from it will find it of value in pointing out those articles which are raised in greater quantity than the needs of the world require, and must sell, therefore, for less than the cost of production, and those which command a profit over cost of production because there is not an over-production.

I call special attention to the need of the Department for a new gallery for the reception of the exhibits returned from the Centennial Exhibition, including the exhibits donated by very many foreign nations, and to the recommendations of the Commissioner of Agriculture generally.

The reports of the District Commissioners and the board of health are just received—too late to read them and to make recommendations thereon—and are herewith submitted.

The international exhibition held in Philadelphia this year, in commemoration of the one hundredth anniversary of American independence, has proven a great success, and will, no doubt, be of enduring advantage to the country. It has shown the great progress in the arts, sciences, and mechanical skill made in a single century, and demonstrated that we are but little behind older nations in any one branch, while in some we scarcely have a rival. It has served, too, not only to bring peoples and products of skill and labor from all parts of the world together, but in bringing together people from all sections of our own country, which must prove a great benefit in the information imparted and pride of country engendered.

It has been suggested by scientists interested in and connected with the Smithsonian Institution, in a communication herewith, that the Government exhibit be removed to the capital and a suitable building be erected or purchased for its accommodation as a permanent exhibit. I earnestly recommend this; and believing that Congress would second this view, I directed that all Government exhibits at the Centennial Exhibition should remain where they are, except such as might be injured by remaining in a building not intended as a protection in inclement weather, or such as may be wanted by the Department furnishing them, until the question of permanent exhibition is acted on.

Although the moneys appropriated by Congress to enable the participation of the several Executive Departments in the International Exhibition of 1876 were not sufficient to carry out the undertaking to the full extent at first contemplated, it gives me pleasure to refer to the very efficient and creditable manner in which the board appointed from these several Departments to provide an exhibition on the part of the Government have discharged their duties with the funds placed at their command. Without a precedent to guide them in the preparation of such a display, the success of their labors was amply attested by the sustained attention which the contents of the Government building attracted during the period of the exhibition from both foreign and native visitors.

I am strongly impressed with the value of the collection made by the Government for the purposes of the exhibition, illustrating, as it does, the mineral resources of the country, the statistical and practical evidences of our growth as a nation, and the uses of the mechanical arts and the applications of applied science in the administration of the affairs of Government.

Many nations have voluntarily contributed their exhibits to the United States to increase the interest in any permanent exhibition Congress may provide for. For this act of generosity they should receive the thanks of the people, and I respectfully suggest that a resolution of Congress to that effect be adopted.

The attention of Congress can not be too earnestly called to the necessity of throwing some greater safeguard over the method of choosing and declaring the election of a President. Under the present system there seems to be no provided remedy for contesting the election in any one State. The remedy is partially, no doubt, in the enlightenment of electors. The compulsory support of the free school and the disfranchisement of all who can not read and write the English language, after a fixed probation, would meet my hearty approval. I would not make this apply, however, to those already voters, but I would to all becoming so after the expiration of the probation fixed upon. Foreigners coming to this country to become citizens, who are educated in their own language, should acquire the requisite knowledge of ours during the necessary residence to obtain naturalization. If they did not take interest enough in our language to acquire sufficient knowledge of it to enable them to study the institutions and laws of the country intelligently, I would not confer upon them the right to make such laws nor to select those who do.

I append to this message, for convenient reference, a synopsis of administrative events and of all recommendations to Congress made by me during the last seven years. Time may show some of these recommendations not to have been wisely conceived, but I believe the larger part will do no discredit to the Administration. One of these recommendations met with the united opposition of one political party in the Senate and with a strong opposition from the other, namely, the treaty for the annexation of Santo Domingo to the United States, to which I will specially refer, maintaining, as I do, that if my views had been concurred in the country would be in a more prosperous condition to-day, both politically and financially.

Santo Domingo is fertile, and upon its soil may be grown just those tropical products of which the United States use so much, and which are produced or prepared for market now by slave labor almost exclusively, namely, sugar, coffee, dyewoods, mahogany, tropical fruits, tobacco, etc. About 75 per cent of the exports of Cuba are consumed in the United States. A large percentage of the exports of Brazil also find the same market. These are paid for almost exclusively in coin, legislation, particularly in Cuba, being unfavorable to a mutual exchange of the products of each country. Flour shipped from the Mississippi River to Havana can pass by the very entrance to the city on its way to a port in Spain. there pay a duty fixed upon articles to be reexported, transferred to a Spanish vessel and brought back almost to the point of starting, paying a second duty, and still leave a profit over what would be received by direct shipment. All that is produced in Cuba could be produced in Santo Domingo. Being a part of the United States, commerce between the island and mainland would be free. There would be no export duties on her shipments nor import duties on those coming here. There would be no import duties upon the supplies, machinery, etc., going from the States. The effect that would have been produced upon Cuban commerce, with these advantages to a rival, is observable at a glance. The Cuban question would have been settled long ago in favor of "free Cuba." Hundreds of American vessels would now be advantageously used in transporting the valuable woods and other products of the soil of the island to a market and in carrying supplies and emigrants to it. The island is but sparsely settled, while it has an area sufficient for the profitable employment of several millions of people. The soil would have soon fallen into the hands of United States capitalists. The products are so valuable in commerce that emigration there would have been encouraged; the emancipated race of the South would have found there a congenial home, where their civil rights would not be disputed and where their labor would be so much sought after that the poorest among them could have found the means to go. Thus in cases of great oppression and cruelty, such as has been practiced upon them in many places within the last eleven years, whole communities would have sought refuge in Santo Domingo. I do not suppose the whole race would have gone, nor is it desirable that they should go. Their labor is desirable—indispensable almost—where they now are. But the possession of this territory would have left the negro "master of the situation," by enabling him to demand his rights at home on pain of finding them elsewhere.

I do not present these views now as a recommendation for a renewal of the subject of annexation, but I do refer to it to vindicate my previous action in regard to it.

With the present term of Congress my official life terminates. It is not probable that public affairs will ever again receive attention from me further than as a citizen of the Republic, always taking a deep interest in the honor, integrity, and prosperity of the whole land.

Rutherford B. Hayes

March 4, 1877 to March 4, 1881

FIRST ANNUAL MESSAGE.

DECEMBER 3, 1877.

Fellow-Citizens of the Senate and House of Representatives:

With devout gratitude to the bountiful Giver of All Good, I congratulate you that at the beginning of your first regular session you find our country blessed with health and peace and abundant harvests, and with encouraging prospects of an early return of general prosperity.

To complete and make permanent the pacification of the country continues to be, and until it is fully accomplished must remain, the most important of all our national interests. The earnest purpose of good citizens generally to unite their efforts in this endeavor is evident. It found decided expression in the resolutions announced in 1876 by the national conventions of the leading political parties of the country. There was a widespread apprehension that the momentous results in our progress as a nation marked by the recent amendments to the Constitution were in imminent jeopardy; that the good understanding which prompted their adoption, in the interest of a loyal devotion to the general welfare, might prove a barren truce, and that the two sections of the country, once engaged in civil strife, might be again almost as widely severed and disunited as they were when arrayed in arms against each other.

The course to be pursued, which, in my judgment, seemed wisest in the presence of this emergency, was plainly indicated in my inaugural address. It pointed to the time, which all our people desire to see, when a genuine love of our whole country and of all that concerns its true welfare shall supplant the destructive forces of the mutual animosity of races and of sectional hostility. Opinions have differed widely as to the measures best calculated to secure this great end. This was to be expected. The measures adopted by the Administration have been subjected to severe and varied criticism. Any course whatever which might have been entered upon would certainly have encountered distrust and opposition. These measures were, in my judgment, such as were most in harmony with the Constitution and with the genius of our people, and best adapted, under all the circumstances, to attain the end in view. Beneficent results, already apparent, prove that these endeavors are not to be regarded as a mere experiment, and should sustain and encourage us in our efforts. Already, in the brief period which has elapsed, the immediate effectiveness, no less than the justice, of the course pursued is demonstrated, and I have an abiding faith that time will furnish its ample vindication in the minds of the great majority of my fellow-citizens. The discontinuance of the use of the Army for the purpose of upholding local governments in two States of the Union was no less a constitutional duty and requirement, under the circumstances existing at the time, than it was a much-needed measure for the restoration of local self-government and the promotion of national harmony. The withdrawal of the troops from such employment was effected deliberately, and with solicitous care for the peace and good order of society and the protection of the property and persons and every right of all classes of citizens.

The results that have followed are indeed significant and encouraging. All apprehension of danger from remitting those States to local self-government is dispelled, and a most salutary change in the minds of the people has begun and is in progress in every part of that section of the country once the theater of unhappy civil strife, substituting for suspicion, distrust, and aversion, concord, friendship, and patriotic attachment to the Union. No unprejudiced mind will deny that the terrible and often fatal collisions which for several years have been of frequent occurrence and have agitated and alarmed the public mind have almost entirely ceased, and that a spirit of mutual forbearance and hearty national interest has succeeded. There has been a general reestablishment of order and of the orderly administration of justice. Instances of remaining lawlessness have become of rare occurrence; political turmoil and turbulence have disappeared; useful industries have been resumed; public credit in the Southern States has been greatly strengthened, and the encouraging benefits of a revival of commerce between the sections of the country lately embroiled in civil war are fully enjoyed. Such are some of the results already attained, upon which the country is to be congratulated. They are of such importance that we may with confidence patiently await the desired consummation that will surely come with the natural progress of events.

It may not be improper here to say that it should be our fixed and unalterable determination to protect by all available and proper means under the Constitution and the laws the lately emancipated race in the enjoyment of their rights and privileges; and I urge upon those to whom heretofore the colored people have sustained the relation of bondmen the wisdom and justice of humane and liberal local legislation with respect to their education and general welfare. A firm adherence to the laws, both national and State, as to the civil and political rights of the colored people, now advanced to full and equal citizenship; the immediate repression and sure punishment by the national and local authorities, within their respective jurisdictions, of every instance of lawlessness and violence toward them, is required for the security alike of both races, and is justly demanded by the public opinion of the country and the age. In this way the restoration of harmony and good will and the complete protection of every citizen in the full enjoyment of every constitutional right will surely be attained. Whatever authority rests with me to this end I shall not hesitate to put forth.

Whatever belongs to the power of Congress and the jurisdiction of the courts of the Union, they may confidently be relied upon to provide and perform; and to the legislatures, the courts, and the executive authorities of the several States I earnestly appeal to secure, by adequate, appropriate, and seasonable means, within their borders, these common and uniform rights of a united people which loves liberty, abhors oppression, and reveres justice. These objects are very dear to my heart. I shall continue most earnestly to strive for their attainment. The cordial cooperation of all classes, of all sections of the country and of both races, is required for this purpose; and with these blessings assured, and not otherwise, we may safely hope to hand down our free institutions of government unimpaired to the generations that will succeed us.

Among the other subjects of great and general importance to the people of this country, I can not be mistaken, I think, in regarding as preeminent the policy and measures which are designed to secure the restoration of the currency to that normal and healthful condition in which, by the resumption of specie payments, our internal trade and foreign commerce may be brought into harmony with the system of exchanges which is based upon the precious metals as the intrinsic money of the world. In the public judgment that this end should be sought and compassed as speedily and securely as the resources of the people and the wisdom of their Government can accomplish, there is a much greater degree of unanimity than is found to concur in the specific measures which will bring the country to this desired end or the rapidity of the steps by which it can be safely reached.

Upon a most anxious and deliberate examination, which I have felt it my duty to give to the subject, I am but the more confirmed in the opinion which I expressed in accepting the nomination for the Presidency, and again upon my inauguration, that the policy of resumption should be pursued by every suitable means, and that no legislation would be wise that should disparage the importance or retard the attainment of that result. I have no disposition, and certainly no right, to question the sincerity or the intelligence of opposing opinions, and would neither conceal nor undervalue the considerable difficulties, and even occasional distresses, which may attend the progress of the nation toward this primary condition to its general and permanent prosperity. I must, however, adhere to my most earnest conviction that any wavering in purpose or unsteadiness in methods, so far from avoiding or reducing the inconvenience inseparable from the transition from an irredeemable to a redeemable paper currency, would only tend to increased and prolonged disturbance in values, and unless retrieved must end in serious disorder, dishonor, and disaster in the financial affairs of the Government and of the people.

The mischiefs which I apprehend and urgently deprecate are confined to no class of the people, indeed, but seem to me most certainly to threaten the industrious masses, whether their occupations are of skilled or common labor. To them, it seems to me, it is of prime importance that their labor should be compensated in money which is itself fixed in exchangeable value by being irrevocably measured by the labor necessary to its production. This permanent quality of the money of the people is sought for, and can only be gained by the resumption of specie payments. The rich, the speculative, the operating, the money-dealing classes may not always feel the mischiefs of, or may find casual profits in, a variable currency, but the misfortunes of such a currency to those who are paid salaries or wages are inevitable and remediless.

Closely connected with this general subject of the resumption of specie payments is one of subordinate, but still of grave, importance; I mean the readjustment of our coinage system by the renewal of the silver dollar as an element in our specie currency, endowed by legislation with the quality of legal tender to a greater or less extent.

As there is no doubt of the power of Congress under the Constitution "to coin money and regulate the value thereof," and as this power covers the whole range of authority applicable to the metal, the rated value and the legal-tender quality which shall be adopted for the coinage, the considerations which should induce or discourage a particular measure connected with the coinage, belong clearly to the province of legislative discretion and of public expediency. Without intruding upon this province of legislation in the least, I have yet thought the subject of such critical importance, in the actual condition of our affairs, as to present an occasion for the exercise of the duty imposed by the Constitution on the President of recommending to the consideration of Congress "such measures as he shall judge necessary and expedient."

Holding the opinion, as I do, that neither the interests of the Government nor of the people of the United States would be promoted by disparaging silver as one of the two precious metals which furnish the coinage of the world, and that legislation which looks to maintaining the volume of intrinsic money to as full a measure of both metals as their relative commercial values will permit would be neither unjust nor inexpedient, I must ask your indulgence to a brief and definite statement of certain essential features in any such legislative measure which I feel it my duty to recommend.

I do not propose to enter the debate, represented on both sides by such able disputants in Congress and before the people and in the press, as to the extent to which the legislation of any one nation can control this question, even within its own borders, against the unwritten laws of trade or the positive laws of other governments. The wisdom of Congress in shaping any particular law that may be presented for my approval may wholly supersede the necessity of my entering into these considerations, and I willingly avoid either vague or intricate inquiries. It is only certain plain and practical traits of such legislation that I desire to recommend to your attention.

In any legislation providing for a silver coinage, regulating its value, and imparting to it the quality of legal tender, it seems to me of great importance that Congress should not lose sight of its action as operating in a twofold capacity and in two distinct directions. If the United States Government were free from a public debt, its legislative dealing with the question of silver coinage would be purely sovereign and governmental, under no restraints but those of constitutional power and the public good as affected by the proposed legislation. But in the actual circumstances of the nation, with a vast public debt distributed very widely among our own citizens and held in great amounts also abroad, the nature of the silver-coinage measure, as affecting this relation of the Government to the holders of the public debt, becomes an element, in any proposed legislation, of the highest concern. The obligation of the public faith transcends all questions of profit or public advantage otherwise. Its unquestionable maintenance is the dictate as well of the highest expediency as of the most necessary duty, and will ever be carefully guarded by Congress and people alike.

The public debt of the United States to the amount of $729,000,000 bears interest at the rate of 6 per cent, and $708,000,000 at the rate of 5 per cent, and the only way in which the country can be relieved from the payment of these high rates of interest is by advantageously refunding the indebtedness. Whether the debt is ultimately paid in gold or in silver coin is of but little moment compared with the possible reduction of interest one-third by refunding it at such reduced rate. If the United States had the unquestioned right to pay its bonds in silver coin, the little benefit from that process would be greatly overbalanced by the injurious effect of such payment if made or proposed against the honest convictions of the public creditors.

All the bonds that have been issued since February 12, 1873, when gold became the only unlimited legal-tender metallic currency of the country, are justly payable in gold coin or in coin of equal value. During the time of these issues the only dollar that could be or was received by the Government in exchange for bonds was the gold dollar. To require the public creditors to take in repayment any dollar of less commercial value would be regarded by them as a repudiation of the full obligation assumed. The bonds issued prior to 1873 were issued at a time when the gold dollar was the only coin in circulation or contemplated by either the Government or the holders of the bonds as the coin in which they were to be paid. It is far better to pay these bonds in that coin than to seem to take advantage of the unforeseen fall in silver bullion to pay in a new issue of silver coin thus made so much less valuable. The power of the United States to coin money and to regulate the value thereof ought never to be exercised for the purpose of enabling the Government to pay its obligations in a coin of less value than that contemplated by the parties when the bonds were issued. Any attempt to pay the national indebtedness in a coinage of less commercial value than the money of the world would involve a violation of the public faith and work irreparable injury to the public credit.

It was the great merit of the act of March, 1869, in strengthening the public credit, that it removed all doubt as to the purpose of the United States to pay their bonded debt in coin. That act was accepted as a pledge of public faith. The Government has derived great benefit from it in the progress thus far made in refunding the public debt at low rates of interest. An adherence to the wise and just policy of an exact observance of the public faith will enable the Government rapidly to reduce the burden of interest on the national debt to an amount exceeding $20,000,000 per annum, and effect an aggregate saving to the United States of more than $300,000,000 before the bonds can be fully paid.

In adapting the new silver coinage to the ordinary uses of currency in the everyday transactions of life and prescribing the quality of legal tender to be assigned to it, a consideration of the first importance should be so to adjust the ratio between the silver and the gold coinage, which now constitutes our specie currency, as to accomplish the desired end of maintaining the circulation of the two metallic currencies and keeping up the volume of the two precious metals as our intrinsic money. It is a mixed question, for scientific reasoning and historical experience to determine, how far and by what methods a practical equilibrium can be maintained which will keep both metals in circulation in their appropriate spheres of common use.

An absolute equality of commercial value, free from disturbing fluctuations, is hardly attainable, and without it an unlimited legal tender for private transactions assigned to both metals would irresistibly tend to drive out of circulation the dearer coinage and disappoint the principal object proposed by the legislation in view. I apprehend, therefore, that the two conditions of a near approach to equality of commercial value between the gold and silver coinage of the same denomination and of a limitation of the amounts for which the silver coinage is to be a legal tender are essential to maintaining both in circulation. If these conditions can be successfully observed, the issue from the mint of silver dollars would afford material assistance to the community in the transition to redeemable paper money, and would facilitate the resumption of specie payment and its permanent establishment. Without these conditions I fear that only mischief and misfortune would flow from a coinage of silver dollars with the quality of unlimited legal tender, even in private transactions.

Any expectation of temporary ease from an issue of silver coinage to pass as a legal tender at a rate materially above its commercial value is, I am persuaded, a delusion. Nor can I think that there is any substantial distinction between an original issue of silver dollars at a nominal value materially above their commercial value and the restoration of the silver dollar at a rate which once was, but has ceased to be, its commercial value. Certainly the issue of our gold coinage, reduced in weight materially below its legal-tender value, would not be any the less a present debasement of the coinage by reason of its equaling, or even exceeding, in weight a gold coinage which at some past time had been commercially equal to the legal-tender value assigned to the new issue.

In recommending that the regulation of any silver coinage which may be authorized by Congress should observe these conditions of commercial value and limited legal tender, I am governed by the feeling that every possible increase should be given to the volume of metallic money which can be kept in circulation, and thereby every possible aid afforded to the people in the process of resuming specie payments. It is because of my firm conviction that a disregard of these conditions would frustrate the good results which are desired from the proposed coinage, and embarrass with new elements of confusion and uncertainty the business of the country, that I urge upon your attention these considerations.

I respectfully recommend to Congress that in any legislation providing for a silver coinage and imparting to it the quality of legal tender there be impressed upon the measure a firm provision exempting the public debt heretofore issued and now outstanding from payment, either of principal or interest, in any coinage of less commercial value than the present gold coinage of the country.

The organization of the civil service of the country has for a number of years attracted more and more of the public attention. So general has become the opinion that the methods of admission to it and the conditions of remaining in it are unsound that both the great political parties have agreed in the most explicit declarations of the necessity of reform and in the most emphatic demands for it. I have fully believed these declarations and demands to be the expression of a sincere conviction of the intelligent masses of the people upon the subject, and that they should be recognized and followed by earnest and prompt action on the part of the legislative and executive departments of the Government, in pursuance of the purpose indicated.

Before my accession to office I endeavored to have my own views distinctly understood, and upon my inauguration my accord with the public opinion was stated in terms believed to be plain and unambiguous. My experience in the executive duties has strongly confirmed the belief in the great advantage the country would find in observing strictly the plan of the Constitution, which imposes upon the Executive the sole duty and responsibility of the selection of those Federal officers who by law are appointed, not elected, and which in like manner assigns to the Senate the complete right to advise and consent to or to reject the nominations so made, whilst the House of Representatives stands as the public censor of the performance of official duties, with the prerogative of investigation and prosecution in all cases of dereliction. The blemishes and imperfections in the civil service may, as I think, be traced in most cases to a practical confusion of the duties assigned to the several Departments of the Government. My purpose in this respect has been to return to the system established by the fundamental law, and to do this with the heartiest cooperation and most cordial understanding with the Senate and House of Representatives.

The practical difficulties in the selection of numerous officers for posts of widely varying responsibilities and duties are acknowledged to be very great. No system can be expected to secure absolute freedom from mistakes, and the beginning of any attempted change of custom is quite likely to be more embarrassed in this respect than any subsequent period. It is here that the Constitution seems to me to prove its claim to the great wisdom accorded to it. It gives to the Executive the assistance of the knowledge and experience of the Senate, which, when acting upon nominations as to which they may be disinterested and impartial judges, secures as strong a guaranty of freedom from errors of importance as is perhaps possible in human affairs.

In addition to this, I recognize the public advantage of making all nominations, as nearly as possible, impersonal, in the sense of being free from mere caprice or favor in the selection; and in those offices in which special training is of greatly increased value I believe such a rule as to the tenure of office should obtain as may induce men of proper qualifications to apply themselves industriously to the task of becoming proficients. Bearing these things in mind, I have endeavored to reduce the number of changes in subordinate places usually made upon the change of the general administration, and shall most heartily cooperate with Congress in the better systematizing of such methods and rules of admission to the public service and of promotion within it as may promise to be most successful in making thorough competency, efficiency, and character the decisive tests in these matters.

I ask the renewed attention of Congress to what has already been done by the Civil Service Commission, appointed, in pursuance of an act of Congress, by my predecessor, to prepare and revise civil-service rules. In regard to much of the departmental service, especially at Washington, it may be difficult to organize a better system than that which has thus been provided, and it is now being used to a considerable extent under my direction. The Commission has still a legal existence, although for several years no appropriation has been made for defraying its expenses. Believing that this Commission has rendered valuable service and will be a most useful agency in improving the administration of the civil service, I respectfully recommend that a suitable appropriation, to be immediately available, be made to enable it to continue its labors.

It is my purpose to transmit to Congress as early as practicable a report by the chairman of the Commission, and to ask your attention to such measures on this subject as in my opinion will further promote the improvement of the civil service.

During the past year the United States have continued to maintain peaceful relations with foreign powers.

The outbreak of war between Russia and Turkey, though at one time attended by grave apprehension as to its effect upon other European nations, has had no tendency to disturb the amicable relations existing between the United States and each of the two contending powers. An attitude of just and impartial neutrality has been preserved, and I am gratified to state that in the midst of their hostilities both the Russian and the Turkish Governments have shown an earnest disposition to adhere to the obligations of all treaties with the United States and to give due regard to the rights of American citizens.

By the terms of the treaty defining the rights, immunities, and privileges of consuls, between Italy and the United States, ratified in 1868, either Government may, after the lapse of ten years, terminate the existence of the treaty by giving twelve months' notice of its intention. The Government of Italy, availing itself of this faculty, has now given the required notice, and the treaty will accordingly end on the 17th of September, 1878. It is understood, however, that the Italian Government wishes to renew it in its general scope, desiring only certain modifications in some of its articles. In this disposition I concur, and shall hope that no serious obstacles may intervene to prevent or delay the negotiation of a satisfactory treaty.

Numerous questions in regard to passports, naturalization, and exemption from military service have continued to arise in cases of emigrants from Germany who have returned to their native country. The provisions of the treaty of February 22, 1868, however, have proved to be so ample and so judicious that the legation of the United States at Berlin has been able to adjust all claims arising under it, not only without detriment to the amicable relations existing between the two Governments, but, it is believed, without injury or injustice to any duly naturalized American citizen. It is desirable that the treaty originally made with the North German Union in 1868 should now be extended so as to apply equally to all the States of the Empire of Germany.

The invitation of the Government of France to participate in the Exposition of the Products of Agriculture, Industry, and the Fine Arts to be held at Paris during the coming year was submitted for your consideration at the extra session. It is not doubted that its acceptance by the United States, and a well-selected exhibition of the products of American industry on that occasion, will tend to stimulate international commerce and emigration, as well as to promote the traditional friendship between the two countries.

A question arose some time since as to the proper meaning of the extradition articles of the treaty of 1842 between the United States and Great Britain. Both Governments, however, are now in accord in the belief that the question is not one that should be allowed to frustrate the ends of justice or to disturb the friendship between the two nations. No serious difficulty has arisen in accomplishing the extradition of criminals when necessary. It is probable that all points of disagreement will in due time be settled, and, if need be, more explicit declarations be made in a new treaty.

The Fishery Commission under Articles XVIII to XXV of the treaty of Washington has concluded its session at Halifax. The result of the deliberations of the commission, as made public by the commissioners, will be communicated to Congress.

A treaty for the protection of trade-marks has been negotiated with Great Britain, which has been submitted to the Senate for its consideration.

The revolution which recently occurred in Mexico was followed by the accession of the successful party to power and the installation of its chief, General Porfirio Diaz, in the Presidential office. It has been the custom of the United States, when such changes of government have heretofore occurred in Mexico, to recognize and enter into official relations with the *de facto* government as soon as it should appear to have the approval of the Mexican people and should manifest a disposition to adhere to the obligations of treaties and international friendship. In the present case such official recognition has been deferred by the occurrences on the Rio Grande border, the records of which have been already communicated to each House of Congress in answer to their respective resolutions of inquiry. Assurances have been received that the authorities at the seat of the Mexican Government have both the disposition and the power to prevent and punish such unlawful invasions and depredations. It is earnestly to be hoped that events may prove these assurances to be well founded. The best interests of both countries require the maintenance of peace upon the border and the development of commerce between the two Republics.

It is gratifying to add that this temporary interruption of official relations has not prevented due attention by the representatives of the United States in Mexico to the protection of American citizens, so far as practicable; nor has it interfered with the prompt payment of the amounts due from Mexico to the United States under the treaty of July 4, 1868, and the awards of the joint commission. While I do not anticipate an interruption of friendly relations with Mexico, yet I can not but look with some solicitude upon a continuance of border disorders as exposing the two countries to initiations of popular feeling and mischances of action which are naturally unfavorable to complete amity. Firmly determined that nothing shall be wanting on my part to promote a good understanding between the two nations, I yet must ask the attention of Congress to the actual occurrences on the border, that the lives and property of our citizens may be adequately protected and peace preserved.

Another year has passed without bringing to a close the protracted contest between the Spanish Government and the insurrection in the island of Cuba. While the United States have sedulously abstained from any intervention in this contest, it is impossible not to feel that it is attended with incidents affecting the rights and interests of American citizens. Apart from the effect of the hostilities upon trade between the United States and Cuba, their progress is inevitably accompanied by complaints, having more or less foundation, of searches, arrests, embargoes, and oppressive taxes upon the property of American residents, and of unprovoked interference with American vessels and commerce. It is due to the Government of Spain to say that during the past year it has promptly disavowed and offered reparation for any unauthorized acts of unduly zealous subordinates whenever such acts have been brought to its attention. Nevertheless, such occurrences can not but tend to excite feelings of annoyance, suspicion, and resentment, which are greatly to be deprecated, between the respective subjects and citizens of two friendly powers.

Much delay (consequent upon accusations of fraud in some of the awards) has occurred in respect to the distribution of the limited amounts received from Venezuela under the treaty of April 25, 1866, applicable to the awards of the joint commission created by that treaty. So long as these matters are pending in Congress the Executive can not assume either to pass upon the questions presented or to distribute the fund received. It is eminently desirable that definite legislative action should be taken, either affirming the awards to be final or providing some method for reexamination of the claims. Our relations with the Republics of Central and South America and with the Empire of Brazil have continued without serious change, further than the temporary interruption of diplomatic intercourse with Venezuela and with Guatemala. Amicable relations have already been fully restored with Venezuela, and it is not doubted that all grounds of misunderstanding with Guatemala will speedily be removed. From all these countries there are favorable indications of a disposition on the part of their Governments and people to reciprocate our efforts in the direction of increased commercial intercourse.

The Government of the Samoan Islands has sent an envoy, in the person of its secretary of state, to invite the Government of the United States to recognize and protect their independence, to establish commercial relations with their people, and to assist them in their steps toward regulated and responsible government. The inhabitants of these islands, having made considerable progress in Christian civilization and the development of trade, are doubtful of their ability to maintain peace and independence without the aid of some stronger power. The subject is deemed worthy of respectful attention, and the claims upon our assistance by this distant community will be carefully considered.

The long commercial depression in the United States has directed attention to the subject of the possible increase of our foreign trade and the methods for its development, not only with Europe, but with other countries, and especially with the States and sovereignties of the Western Hemisphere. Instructions from the Department of State were issued to the various diplomatic and consular officers of the Government, asking them to devote attention to the question of methods by which trade between the respective countries of their official residence and the United States could be most judiciously fostered. In obedience to these instructions, examinations and reports upon this subject have been made by many of these officers and transmitted to the Department, and the same are submitted to the consideration of Congress.

The annual report of the Secretary of the Treasury on the state of the finances presents important questions for the action of Congress, upon some of which I have already remarked.

The revenues of the Government during the fiscal year ending June 30, 1877, were $269,000,586.62; the total expenditures for the same period were $238,660,008.93, leaving a surplus revenue of $30,340,-577.69. This has substantially supplied the requirements of the sinking fund for that year. The estimated revenues of the current fiscal year are $265,500,000, and the estimated expenditures for the same period are $232,430,643.72. If these estimates prove to be correct, there will be a surplus revenue of $33,069,356.28—an amount nearly sufficient for the sinking fund for that year. The estimated revenues for the next fiscal year are $269,250,000. It appears from the report that during the last fiscal year the revenues of the Government, compared with the previous year, have largely decreased. This decrease, amounting to the sum of $18,481,452.54, was mainly in customs duties, caused partly by a large falling off of the amount of imported dutiable goods and partly by the general fall of prices in the markets of production of such articles as pay *ad valorem* taxes.

While this is felt injuriously in the diminution of the revenue, it has been accompanied with a very large increase of exportations. The total exports during the last fiscal year, including coin, have been $658,637,457, and the imports have been $492,097,540, leaving a balance of trade in favor of the United States amounting to the sum of $166,539,917, the beneficial effects of which extend to all branches of business.

The estimated revenue for the next fiscal year will impose upon Congress the duty of strictly limiting appropriations, including the requisite sum for the maintenance of the sinking fund, within the aggregate estimated receipts.

While the aggregate of taxes should not be increased, amendments might be made to the revenue laws that would, without diminishing the revenue, relieve the people from unnecessary burdens. A tax on tea and coffee is shown by the experience not only of our own country, but of other countries, to be easily collected, without loss by undervaluation or fraud, and largely borne in the country of production. A tax of 10 cents a pound on tea and 2 cents a pound on coffee would produce a revenue exceeding $12,000,000, and thus enable Congress to repeal a multitude of annoying taxes yielding a revenue not exceeding that sum. The internal-revenue system grew out of the necessities of the war, and most of the legislation imposing taxes upon domestic products under this system has been repealed. By the substitution of a tax on tea and coffee all forms of internal taxation may be repealed, except that on whisky, spirits, tobacco, and beer. Attention is also called to the necessity of enacting more vigorous laws for the protection of the revenue and for the punishment of frauds and smuggling. This can best be done by judicious provisions that will induce the disclosure of attempted fraud by undervaluation and smuggling. All revenue laws should be simple in their provisions and easily understood. So far as practicable, the rates of taxation should be in the form of specific duties, and not *ad valorem*, requiring the judgment of experienced men to ascertain values and exposing the revenue to the temptation of fraud.

My attention has been called during the recess of Congress to abuses existing in the collection of the customs, and strenuous efforts have been made for their correction by Executive orders. The recommendations submitted to the Secretary of the Treasury by a commission appointed to examine into the collection of customs duties at the port of New York contain many suggestions for the modification of the customs laws, to which the attention of Congress is invited.

It is matter of congratulation that notwithstanding the severe burdens caused by the war the public faith with all creditors has been preserved, and that as the result of this policy the public credit has continuously advanced and our public securities are regarded with the highest favor in the markets of the world. I trust that no act of the Government will cast a shadow upon its credit.

The progress of refunding the public debt has been rapid and satisfactory. Under the contract existing when I entered upon the discharge of the duties of my office, bonds bearing interest at the rate of 4½ per cent were being rapidly sold, and within three months the aggregate sales of these bonds had reached the sum of $200,000,000. With my sanction the Secretary of the Treasury entered into a new contract for the sale of 4 per cent bonds, and within thirty days after the popular subscription for such bonds was opened subscriptions were had amounting to $75,496,550, which were paid for within ninety days after the date of subscription. By this process, within but little more than one year, the annual interest on the public debt was reduced in the sum of $3,775,000.

I recommended that suitable provision be made to enable the people to easily convert their savings into Government securities, as the best mode in which small savings may be well secured and yield a moderate interest. It is an object of public policy to retain among our own people the securities of the United States. In this way our country is guarded against their sudden return from foreign countries, caused by war or other disturbances beyond our limits.

The commerce of the United States with foreign nations, and especially the export of domestic productions, has of late years largely increased; but the greater portion of this trade is conducted in foreign vessels. The importance of enlarging our foreign trade, and especially by direct and speedy interchange with countries on this continent, can not be overestimated; and it is a matter of great moment that our own shipping interest should receive, to the utmost practical extent, the benefit of our commerce with other lands. These considerations are forcibly urged by all the large commercial cities of the country, and public attention is generally and wisely attracted to the solution of the problems they present. It is not doubted that Congress will take them up in the broadest spirit of liberality and respond to the public demand by practical legislation upon this important subject.

The report of the Secretary of War shows that the Army has been actively employed during the year, and has rendered very important service in suppressing hostilities in the Indian country and in preserving peace and protecting life and property in the interior as well as along the Mexican border. A long and arduous campaign has been prosecuted, with final complete success, against a portion of the Nez Percé tribe of Indians. A full account of this campaign will be found in the report of the General of the Army. It will be seen that in its course several severe battles were fought, in which a number of gallant officers and men lost their lives. I join with the Secretary of War and the General of the Army in awarding to the officers and men employed in the long and toilsome pursuit and in the final capture of these Indians the honor and praise which are so justly their due.

The very serious riots which occurred in several of the States in July last rendered necessary the employment of a considerable portion of the Army to preserve the peace and maintain order. In the States of West Virginia, Maryland, Pennsylvania, and Illinois these disturbances were so formidable as to defy the local and State authorities, and the National Executive was called upon, in the mode provided by the Constitution and laws, to furnish military aid. I am gratified to be able to state that the troops sent in response to these calls for aid in the suppression of domestic violence were able, by the influence of their presence in the disturbed regions, to preserve the peace and restore order without the use of force. In the discharge of this delicate and important duty both officers and men acted with great prudence and courage, and for their services deserve the thanks of the country.

Disturbances along the Rio Grande in Texas, to which I have already referred, have rendered necessary the constant employment of a military force in that vicinity. A full report of all recent military operations in that quarter has been transmitted to the House of Representatives in answer to a resolution of that body, and it will therefore not be necessary to enter into details. I regret to say that these lawless incursions into our territory by armed bands from the Mexican side of the line, for the purpose of robbery, have been of frequent occurrence, and in spite of the most vigilant efforts of the commander of our forces the marauders have generally succeeded in escaping into Mexico with their plunder. In May last I gave orders for the exercise of the utmost vigilance on the part of our troops for the suppression of these raids and the punishment of the guilty parties, as well as the recapture of property stolen by them. General Ord, commanding in Texas, was directed to invite the coopera-tion of the Mexican authorities in efforts to this end, and to assure them that I was anxious to avoid giving the least offense to Mexico. At the same time, he was directed to give notice of my determination to put an end to the invasion of our territory by lawless bands intent upon the plunder of our peaceful citizens, even if the effectual punishment of the outlaws should make the crossing of the border by our troops in their pursuit necessary. It is believed that this policy has had the effect to check somewhat these depredations, and that with a considerable increase of our force upon that frontier and the establishment of several additional military posts along the Rio Grande, so as more effectually to guard that extensive border, peace may be preserved and the lives and property of our citizens in Texas fully protected.

Prior to the 1st day of July last the Army was, in accordance with law, reduced to the maximum of 25,000 enlisted men, being a reduction of 2,500 below the force previously authorized. This reduction was made, as required by law, entirely from the infantry and artillery branches of the service, without any reduction of the cavalry. Under the law as it now stands it is necessary that the cavalry regiments be recruited to 100 men in each company for service on the Mexican and Indian frontiers. The necessary effect of this legislation is to reduce the infantry and artillery arms of the service below the number required for efficiency, and I concur with the Secretary of War in recommending that authority be given to recruit all companies of infantry to at least 50 men and all batteries of artillery to at least 75 men, with the power, in case of emer-gency, to increase the former to 100 and the latter to 122 men each.

I invite your special attention to the following recommendations of the Secretary of War:

First. That provision be made for supplying to the Army a more abun-dant and better supply of reading matter.

Second. That early action be taken by Congress looking to a complete revision and republication of the Army Regulations.

Third. That section 1258 of the Revised Statutes, limiting the number of officers on the retired list, be repealed.

Fourth. That the claims arising under the act of July 4, 1864, for sup-plies taken by the Army during the war, be taken from the offices of the

Quartermaster and Commissary Generals and transferred to the Southern Claims Commission, or some other tribunal having more time and better facilities for their prompt investigation and decision than are possessed by these officers.

Fifth. That Congress provide for an annuity fund for the families of deceased soldiers, as recommended by the Paymaster-General of the Army.

The report of the Secretary of the Navy shows that we have six squadrons now engaged in the protection of our foreign commerce and other duties pertaining to the naval service. The condition and operations of the Department are also shown. The total expenditures for the fiscal year ending June 30, 1877, were $16,077,974.54. There are unpaid claims against the Department chargeable to the last year, which are presented to the consideration of Congress by the report of the Secretary. The estimates for the fiscal year commencing July 1, 1878, are $16,233,234.40, exclusive of the sum of $2,314,231 submitted for new buildings, repairs, and improvements at the several navy-yards. The appropriations for the present fiscal year, commencing July 1, 1877, are $13,592,932.90. The amount drawn from the Treasury from July 1 to November 1, 1877, is $5,343,037.40, of which there is estimated to be yet available $1,029,528.30, showing the amount of actual expenditure during the first four months of the present fiscal year to have been $4,313,509.10.

The report of the Postmaster-General contains a full and clear statement of the operations and condition of the Post-Office Department. The ordinary revenues of the Department for the fiscal year ending June 30, 1877, including receipts from the money-order business and from official stamps and stamped envelopes, amounted to the sum of $27,531,-585.26. The additional sum of $7,013,000 was realized from appropriations from the general Treasury for various purposes, making the receipts from all sources $34,544,885.26. The total expenditures during the fiscal year amounted to $33,486,322.44, leaving an excess of total receipts over total expenditures of $1,058,562.82, and an excess of total expenditures over ordinary receipts of $5,954,737.18. Deducting from the total receipts the sum of $63,261.84, received from international money orders of the preceding fiscal year, and deducting from the total expenditures the sum of $1,163,818.20, paid on liabilities incurred in previous fiscal years, the expenditures and receipts appertaining to the business of the last fiscal year were as follows:

Expenditures...	$32,322,504.24
Receipts (ordinary, from money-order business and from official postage stamps)...	27,468,323.42
Excess of expenditures	4,854,180.82

The ordinary revenues of the Post-Office Department for the year ending June 30, 1879, are estimated at an increase of 3 per cent over those of 1877, making $29,034,098.28, and the expenditures for the same year are estimated at $36,427,771, leaving an estimated deficiency for the year 1879 of $7,393,672.72. The additional legislation recommended by the Postmaster-General for improvements of the mail service and to protect the postal revenues from the abuses practiced under existing laws is respectfully commended to the careful consideration of Congress.

The report of the Attorney-General contains several suggestions as to the administration of justice, to which I invite your attention. The pressure of business in the Supreme Court and in certain circuit courts of the United States is now such that serious delays, to the great injury, and even oppression, of suitors, occur, and a remedy should be sought for this condition of affairs. Whether it will be found in the plan briefly sketched in the report, of increasing the number of judges of the circuit courts, and, by means of this addition to the judicial force, of creating an intermediate court of errors and appeals, or whether some other mode can be devised for obviating the difficulties which now exist, I leave to your mature consideration.

The present condition of the Indian tribes in the territory of the United States and our relations with them are fully set forth in the reports of the Secretary of the Interior and the Commissioner of Indian Affairs. After a series of most deplorable conflicts—the successful termination of which, while reflecting honor upon the brave soldiers who accomplished it, can not lessen our regret at their occurrence—we are now at peace with all the Indian tribes within our borders. To preserve that peace by a just and humane policy will be the object of my earnest endeavors. Whatever may be said of their character and savage propensities, of the difficulties of introducing among them the habits of civilized life, and of the obstacles they have offered to the progress of settlement and enter-prise in certain parts of the country, the Indians are certainly entitled to our sympathy and to a conscientious respect on our part for their claims upon our sense of justice. They were the aboriginal occupants of the land we now possess. They have been driven from place to place. The purchase money paid to them in some cases for what they called their own has still left them poor. In many instances, when they had settled down upon land assigned to them by compact and begun to support them-selves by their own labor, they were rudely jostled off and thrust into the wilderness again. Many, if not most, of our Indian wars have had their origin in broken promises and acts of injustice upon our part, and the advance of the Indians in civilization has been slow because the treatment they received did not permit it to be faster and more general. We can not expect them to improve and to follow our guidance unless we keep faith with them in respecting the rights they possess, and un-less, instead of depriving them of their opportunities, we lend them a helping hand.

I cordially approve the policy regarding the management of Indian affairs outlined in the reports of the Secretary of the Interior and of the Commissioner of Indian Affairs. The faithful performance of our promises is the first condition of a good understanding with the Indians. I can not too urgently recommend to Congress that prompt and liberal provision be made for the conscientious fulfillment of all engagements entered into by the Government with the Indian tribes. To withhold the means necessary for the performance of a promise is always false economy, and is apt to prove disastrous in its consequences. Especial care is recommended to provide for Indians settled on their reservations cattle and agricultural implements, to aid them in whatever efforts they may make to support themselves, and by the establishment and maintenance of schools to bring them under the control of civilized influences. I see no reason why Indians who can give satisfactory proof of having by their own labor supported their families for a number of years, and who are willing to detach themselves from their tribal relations, should not be admitted to the benefit of the homestead act and the privileges of citizenship, and I recommend the passage of a law to that effect. It will be an act of justice as well as a measure of encouragement. Earnest efforts are being made to purify the Indian service, so that every dollar appropriated by Congress shall redound to the benefit of the Indians, as intended. Those efforts will have my firm support. With an improved service and every possible encouragement held out to the Indians to better their condition and to elevate themselves in the scale of civilization, we may hope to accomplish at the same time a good work for them and for ourselves.

I invite the attention of Congress to the importance of the statements and suggestions made by the Secretary of the Interior concerning the depredations committed on the timber lands of the United States and the necessity for the preservation of forests. It is believed that the measures taken in pursuance of existing laws to arrest those depredations will be entirely successful if Congress, by an appropriation for that purpose, renders their continued enforcement possible. The experience of other nations teaches us that a country can not be stripped of its forests with impunity, and we shall expose ourselves to the gravest consequences unless the wasteful and improvident manner in which the forests in the United States are destroyed be effectually checked. I earnestly recommend that the measures suggested by the Secretary of the Interior for the suppression of depredations on the public timber lands of the United States, for the selling of timber from the public lands, and for the preservation of forests be embodied in a law, and that, considering the urgent necessity of enabling the people of certain States and Territories to purchase timber from the public lands in a legal manner, which at present they can not do, such a law be passed without unavoidable delay. I would also call the attention of Congress to the statements made by the Secretary of the Interior concerning the disposition that might be made of the desert lands, not irrigable, west of the one hundredth meridian. These lands are practically unsalable under existing laws, and the suggestion is worthy of consideration that a system of leasehold tenure would make them a source of profit to the United States, while at the same time legalizing the business of cattle raising which is at present carried on upon them.

The report of the Commissioner of Agriculture contains the gratifying announcement of the extraordinary success which has rewarded the agricultural industry of the country for the past year. With the fair prices which obtain for the products of the soil, especially for the surplus which our people have to export, we may confidently turn to this as the most important of all our resources for the revival of the depressed industries of the country. The report shows our agricultural progress during the year, and contains a statement of the work done by this Department for the advancement of agricultural industry, upon which the prosperity of our people so largely depends. Matters of information are included of great interest to all who seek, by the experience of others, to improve their own methods of cultivation. The efforts of the Department to increase the production of important articles of consumption will, it is hoped, improve the demand for labor and advance the business of the country, and eventually result in saving some of the many millions that are now annually paid to foreign nations for sugar and other staple products which habitual use has made necessary in our domestic everyday life.

The board on behalf of the United States Executive Departments at the International Exhibition of 1876 has concluded its labors. The final report of the board was transmitted to Congress by the President near the close of the last session. As these papers are understood to contain interesting and valuable information, and will constitute the only report emanating from the Government on the subject of the exhibition, I invite attention to the matter and recommend that the report be published for general information.

Congress is empowered by the Constitution with the authority of exclusive legislation over the District of Columbia, in which the seat of Government of the nation is located. The interests of the District, having no direct representation in Congress, are entitled to especial consideration and care at the hands of the General Government. The capital of the United States belongs to the nation, and it is natural that the American people should take pride in the seat of their National Government and desire it to be an ornament to the country. Much has been done to render it healthful, convenient, and attractive, but much remains to be done, which its permanent inhabitants are not able and ought not to be expected to do. To impose upon them a large proportion of the cost required for public improvements, which are in a great measure planned and executed for the convenience of the Government and of the many thousands of visitors from all parts of the country who temporarily reside at the capital of the nation, is an evident injustice. Special attention is asked by the Commissioners of the District in their report, which is herewith transmitted, to the importance of a permanent adjustment by Congress of the financial relations between the United States and the District, involving the regular annual contribution by the United States of its just proportion of the expenses of the District government and of the outlay for all needed public improvements, and such measure of relief from the burden of taxation now resting upon the people of the District as in the wisdom of Congress may be deemed just.

The report of the Commissioners shows that the affairs of the District are in a condition as satisfactory as could be expected in view of the heavy burden of debt resting upon it and its very limited means for necessary expenses.

The debt of the District is as follows:

Old funded debt	$8,379,691.96
3.65 bonds, guaranteed by the United States	13,743,250.00
Total bonded debt	22,122,941.96
To which should be added certain outstanding claims, as explained in the report of the Commissioners	1,187,204.52
Making the total debt of the District	23,310,146.48

The Commissioners also ask attention to the importance of the improvement of the Potomac River and the reclamation of the marshes bordering the city of Washington, and their views upon this subject are concurred in by the members of the board of health, whose report is also herewith transmitted. Both the commercial and sanitary interests of the District will be greatly promoted, I doubt not, by this improvement.

Your attention is invited to the suggestion of the Commissioners and of the board of health for the organization of a board of charities, to have supervision and control of the disbursement of all moneys for charitable purposes from the District treasury. I desire also to ask your especial attention to the need of adding to the efficiency of the public schools of the District by supplemental aid from the National Treasury. This is especially just, since so large a number of those attending these schools are children of employees of the Government. I earnestly commend to your care the interests of the people of the District, who are so intimately associated with the Government establishments, and to whose enterprise the good order and attractiveness of the capital are largely due; and I ask your attention to the request of the Commissioners for legislation in behalf of the interests intrusted to their care. The appropriations asked for the care of the reservations belonging to the Government within the city, by the Commissioner of Public Buildings and Grounds, are also commended to your favorable consideration.

The report of the joint commission created by the act approved 2d of August, 1876, entitled "An act providing for the completion of the Washington Monument," is also herewith transmitted, with accompanying documents. The board of engineer officers detailed to examine the monument, in compliance with the second section of the act, have reported that the foundation is insufficient. No authority exists for making the expenditure necessary to secure its stability. I therefore recommend that the commission be authorized to expend such portion of the sum appropriated by the act as may be necessary for the purpose. The present unfinished condition of the monument, begun so long ago, is a reproach to the nation. It can not be doubted that the patriotic sense of the country will warmly respond to such prompt provision as may be made for its completion at an early day, and I urge upon Congress the propriety and necessity of immediate legislation for this purpose.

The wisdom of legislation upon the part of Congress, in aid of the States, for the education of the whole people in those branches of study which are taught in the common schools of the country is no longer a question. The intelligent judgment of the country goes still further, regarding it as also both constitutional and expedient for the General Government to extend to technical and higher education such aid as is deemed essential to the general welfare and to our due prominence among the enlightened and cultured nations of the world. The ultimate settlement of all questions of the future, whether of administration or finance or of true nationality of sentiment, depends upon the virtue and intelligence of the people. It is vain to hope for the success of a free government without the means of insuring the intelligence of those who are the source of power. No less than one-seventh of the entire voting population of our country are yet unable to read and write.

It is encouraging to observe, in connection with the growth of fraternal feeling in those States in which slavery formerly existed, evidences of increasing interest in universal education, and I shall be glad to give my approval to any appropriate measures which may be enacted by Congress for the purpose of supplementing with national aid the local systems of education in those States and in all the States; and, having already invited your attention to the needs of the District of Columbia with respect to its public-school system, I here add that I believe it desirable, not so much with reference to the local wants of the District, but to the great and lasting benefit of the entire country, that this system should be crowned with a university in all respects in keeping with the national capital, and thereby realize the cherished hopes of Washington on this subject.

I also earnestly commend the request of the Regents of the Smithsonian Institution that an adequate appropriation be made for the establishment and conduct of a national museum under their supervision.

The question of providing for the preservation and growth of the

Library of Congress is also one of national importance. As the depository of all copyright publications and records, this library has outgrown the provisions for its accommodation; and the erection, on such site as the judgment of Congress may approve, of a fireproof library building, to preserve the treasures and enlarge the usefulness of this valuable collection, is recommended. I recommend also such legislation as will render available and efficient for the purposes of instruction, so far as is consistent with the public service, the cabinets or museums of invention, of surgery, of education, and of agriculture, and other collections the property of the National Government.

The capital of the nation should be something more than a mere political center. We should avail ourselves of all the opportunities which Providence has here placed at our command to promote the general intelligence of the people and increase the conditions most favorable to the success and perpetuity of our institutions.

SECOND ANNUAL MESSAGE.

EXECUTIVE MANSION, *December 2, 1878.*

Fellow-Citizens of the Senate and House of Representatives:

Our heartfelt gratitude is due to the Divine Being who holds in His hands the destinies of nations for the continued bestowal during the last year of countless blessings upon our country.

We are at peace with all other nations. Our public credit has greatly improved, and is perhaps now stronger than ever before. Abundant harvests have rewarded the labors of those who till the soil, our manufacturing industries are reviving, and it is believed that general prosperity, which has been so long anxiously looked for, is at last within our reach.

The enjoyment of health by our people generally has, however, been interrupted during the past season by the prevalence of a fatal pestilence (the yellow fever) in some portions of the Southern States, creating an emergency which called for prompt and extraordinary measures of relief. The disease appeared as an epidemic at New Orleans and at other places on the Lower Mississippi soon after midsummer. It was rapidly spread by fugitives from the infected cities and towns, and did not disappear until early in November. The States of Louisiana, Mississippi, and Tennessee have suffered severely. About 100,000 cases are believed to have occurred, of which about 20,000, according to intel-

ligent estimates, proved fatal.   It is impossible to estimate with any
approach to accuracy the loss to the country occasioned by this epidemic
It is to be reckoned by the hundred millions of dollars.   The suffering
and destitution that resulted excited the deepest sympathy in all parts of
the Union.   Physicians and nurses hastened from every quarter to the
assistance of the afflicted communities.   Voluntary contributions of money
and supplies, in every needed form, were speedily and generously furnished.   The Government was able to respond in some measure to the
call for help, by providing tents, medicines, and food for the sick and destitute, the requisite directions for the purpose being given in the confident expectation that this action of the Executive would receive the
sanction of Congress.   About 1,800 tents, and rations of the value of
about $25,000, were sent to cities and towns which applied for them, full
details of which will be furnished to Congress by the proper Department.

The fearful spread of this pestilence has awakened a very general
public sentiment in favor of national sanitary administration, which shall
not only control quarantine, but have the sanitary supervision of internal commerce in times of epidemics, and hold an advisory relation to
the State and municipal health authorities, with power to deal with
whatever endangers the public health, and which the municipal and
State authorities are unable to regulate.   The national quarantine act
approved April 29, 1878, which was passed too late in the last session of
Congress to provide the means for carrying it into practical operation
during the past season, is a step in the direction here indicated.   In
view of the necessity for the most effective measures, by quarantine and
otherwise, for the protection of our seaports and the country generally
from this and other epidemics, it is recommended that Congress give to
the whole subject early and careful consideration.

The permanent pacification of the country by the complete protection
of all citizens in every civil and political right continues to be of paramount interest with the great body of our people.   Every step in this
direction is welcomed with public approval, and every interruption of
steady and uniform progress to the desired consummation awakens general uneasiness and widespread condemnation.   The recent Congressional
elections have furnished a direct and trustworthy test of the advance
thus far made in the practical establishment of the right of suffrage secured by the Constitution to the liberated race in the Southern States.
All disturbing influences, real or imaginary, had been removed from all
of these States.

The three constitutional amendments which conferred freedom and
equality of civil and political rights upon the colored people of the South
were adopted by the concurrent action of the great body of good citizens
who maintained the authority of the National Government and the integrity and perpetuity of the Union at such a cost of treasure and life,
as a wise and necessary embodiment in the organic law of the just results

of the war. The people of the former slaveholding States accepted these results, and gave in every practicable form assurances that the thirteenth, fourteenth, and fifteenth amendments, and laws passed in pursuance thereof, should in good faith be enforced, rigidly and impartially, in letter and spirit, to the end that the humblest citizen, without distinction of race or color, should under them receive full and equal protection in person and property and in political rights and privileges. By these constitutional amendments the southern section of the Union obtained a large increase of political power in Congress and in the electoral college, and the country justly expected that elections would proceed, as to the enfranchised race, upon the same circumstances of legal and constitutional freedom and protection which obtained in all the other States of the Union. The friends of law and order looked forward to the conduct of these elections as offering to the general judgment of the country an important opportunity to measure the degree in which the right of suffrage could be exercised by the colored people and would be respected by their fellow-citizens; but a more general enjoyment of freedom of suffrage by the colored people and a more just and generous protection of that freedom by the communities of which they form a part were generally anticipated than the record of the elections discloses. In some of those States in which the colored people have been unable to make their opinions felt in the elections the result is mainly due to influences not easily measured or remedied by legal protection; but in the States of Louisiana and South Carolina at large, and in some particular Congressional districts outside of those States, the records of the elections seem to compel the conclusion that the rights of the colored voters have been overridden and their participation in the elections not permitted to be either general or free.

It will be for the Congress for which these elections were held to make such examinations into their conduct as may be appropriate to determine the validity of the claims of members to their seats. In the meanwhile it becomes the duty of the executive and judicial departments of the Government, each in its province, to inquire into and punish violations of the laws of the United States which have occurred. I can but repeat what I said in this connection in my last message, that whatever authority rests with me to this end I shall not hesitate to put forth; and I am unwilling to forego a renewed appeal to the legislatures, the courts, the executive authorities, and the people of the States where these wrongs have been perpetrated to give their assistance toward bringing to justice the offenders and preventing a repetition of the crimes. No means within my power will be spared to obtain a full and fair investigation of the alleged crimes and to secure the conviction and just punishment of the guilty.

It is to be observed that the principal appropriation made for the Department of Justice at the last session contained the following clause:

And for defraying the expenses which may be incurred in the enforcement of the act approved February 28, 1871, entitled "An act to amend an act approved May 31, 1870, entitled 'An act to enforce the rights of citizens of the United States to vote in the several States of this Union, and for other purposes,'" or any acts amendatory thereof or supplementary thereto.

It is the opinion of the Attorney-General that the expenses of these proceedings will largely exceed the amount which was thus provided, and I rely confidently upon Congress to make adequate appropriations to enable the executive department to enforce the laws.

I respectfully urge upon your attention that the Congressional elections, in every district, in a very important sense, are justly a matter of political interest and concern throughout the whole country. Each State, every political party, is entitled to the share of power which is conferred by the legal and constitutional suffrage. It is the right of every citizen possessing the qualifications prescribed by law to cast one unintimidated ballot and to have his ballot honestly counted. So long as the exercise of this power and the enjoyment of this right are common and equal, practically as well as formally, submission to the results of the suffrage will be accorded loyally and cheerfully, and all the departments of Government will feel the true vigor of the popular will thus expressed. No temporary or administrative interests of Government, however urgent or weighty, will ever displace the zeal of our people in defense of the primary rights of citizenship. They understand that the protection of liberty requires the maintenance in full vigor of the manly methods of free speech, free press, and free suffrage, and will sustain the full authority of Government to enforce the laws which are framed to preserve these inestimable rights. The material progress and welfare of the States depend on the protection afforded to their citizens. There can be no peace without such protection, no prosperity without peace, and the whole country is deeply interested in the growth and prosperity of all its parts.

While the country has not yet reached complete unity of feeling and reciprocal confidence between the communities so lately and so seriously estranged, I feel an absolute assurance that the tendencies are in that direction, and with increasing force. The power of public opinion will override all political prejudices and all sectional or State attachments in demanding that all over our wide territory the name and character of citizen of the United States shall mean one and the same thing and carry with them unchallenged security and respect.

Our relations with other countries continue peaceful. Our neutrality in contests between foreign powers has been maintained and respected.

The Universal Exposition held at Paris during the past summer has been attended by large numbers of our citizens. The brief period allowed for the preparation and arrangement of the contributions of our citizens to this great exposition was well employed in energetic and judicious efforts to overcome this disadvantage. These efforts, led and directed by the commissioner-general, were remarkably successful, and the exhibition of the products of American industry was creditable and gratifying in scope and character. The reports of the United States commissioners, giving its results in detail, will be duly laid before you. Our participation in this international competition for the favor and the trade of the world may be expected to produce useful and important results—in promoting intercourse, friendship, and commerce with other nations.

In accordance with the provisions of the act of February 28, 1878, three commissioners were appointed to an international conference on the subject of adopting a common ratio between gold and silver, for the purpose of establishing internationally the use of bimetallic money and securing fixity of relative value between those metals.

Invitations were addressed to the various governments which had expressed a willingness to participate in its deliberations. The conference held its meetings in Paris in August last. The report of the commissioners, herewith submitted, will show its results. No common ratio between gold and silver could be agreed upon by the conference. The general conclusion was reached that it is necessary to maintain in the world the monetary functions of silver as well as of gold, leaving the selection of the use of one or the other of these two metals, or of both, to be made by each state.

Congress having appropriated at its last session the sum of $5,500,000 to pay the award of the joint commission at Halifax, if, after correspondence with the British Government on the subject of the conformity of the award to the requirements of the treaty and to the terms of the question thereby submitted to the commission, the President shall deem it his duty to make the payment, communications upon these points were addressed to the British Government through the legation of the United States at London. Failing to obtain the concurrence of the British Government in the views of this Government respecting the award, I have deemed it my duty to tender the sum named within the year fixed by the treaty, accompanied by a notice of the grounds of the payment and a protest against any other construction of the same. The correspondence upon this subject will be laid before you.

The Spanish Government has officially announced the termination of the insurrection in Cuba and the restoration of peace throughout that island. Confident expectations are expressed of a revival of trade and prosperity, which it is earnestly hoped may prove well founded. Numerous claims of American citizens for relief for injuries or restoration of property have been among the incidents of the long-continued hostilities. Some of these claims are in process of adjustment by Spain, and the others are promised early and careful consideration.

The treaty made with Italy in regard to reciprocal consular privileges has been duly ratified and proclaimed.

No questions of grave importance have arisen with any other of the European powers.

The Japanese Government has been desirous of a revision of such parts of its treaties with foreign powers as relate to commerce, and it is understood has addressed to each of the treaty powers a request to open negotiations with that view. The United States Government has been inclined to regard the matter favorably. Whatever restrictions upon trade with Japan are found injurious to that people can not but affect injuriously nations holding commercial intercourse with them. Japan, after a long period of seclusion, has within the past few years made rapid strides in the path of enlightenment and progress, and, not unreasonably, is looking forward to the time when her relations with the nations of Europe and America shall be assimilated to those which they hold with each other. A treaty looking to this end has been made, which will be submitted for the consideration of the Senate.

After an interval of several years the Chinese Government has again sent envoys to the United States. They have been received, and a permanent legation is now established here by that Government. It is not doubted that this step will be of advantage to both nations in promoting friendly relations and removing causes of difference.

The treaty with the Samoan Islands, having been duly ratified and accepted on the part of both Governments, is now in operation, and a survey and soundings of the harbor of Pago-Pago have been made by a naval vessel of the United States, with a view of its occupation as a naval station if found desirable to the service.

Since the resumption of diplomatic relations with Mexico correspondence has been opened and still continues between the two Governments upon the various questions which at one time seemed to endanger their relations. While no formal agreement has been reached as to the troubles on the border, much has been done to repress and diminish them. The effective force of United States troops on the Rio Grande, by a strict and faithful compliance with instructions, has done much to remove the sources of dispute, and it is now understood that a like force of Mexican troops on the other side of the river is also making an energetic movement against the marauding Indian tribes. This Government looks with the greatest satisfaction upon every evidence of strength in the national authority of Mexico, and upon every effort put forth to prevent or to punish incursions upon our territory. Reluctant to assume any action or attitude in the control of these incursions by military movements across the border not imperatively demanded for the protection of the lives and property of our own citizens, I shall take the earliest opportunity consistent with the proper discharge of this plain duty to recognize the ability of the Mexican Government to restrain effectively violations of our territory. It is proposed to hold next year an international exhibition in Mexico, and it is believed that the display of the agricultural and manufacturing products of the two nations will tend to better understanding and increased commercial intercourse between their people.

With Brazil and the Republics of Central and South America some steps have been taken toward the development of closer commercial intercourse. Diplomatic relations have been resumed with Colombia and with Bolivia. A boundary question between the Argentine Republic and Paraguay has been submitted by those Governments for arbitration to the President of the United States, and I have, after careful examination, given a decision upon it.

A naval expedition up the Amazon and Madeira rivers has brought back information valuable both for scientific and commercial purposes. A like expedition is about visiting the coast of Africa and the Indian Ocean. The reports of diplomatic and consular officers in relation to the development of our foreign commerce have furnished many facts that have proved of public interest and have stimulated to practical exertion the enterprise of our people.

The report of the Secretary of the Treasury furnishes a detailed statement of the operations of that Department of the Government and of the condition of the public finances.

The ordinary revenues from all sources for the fiscal year ended June 30, 1878, were $257,763,878.70; the ordinary expenditures for the same period were $236,964,326.80, leaving a surplus revenue for the year of $20,799,551.90. The receipts for the present fiscal year, ending June 30, 1879, actual and estimated, are as follows: Actual receipts for the first quarter, commencing July 1, 1878, $73,389,743.43; estimated receipts for the remaining three quarters of the year, $191,110,256.57; total receipts for the current fiscal year, actual and estimated, $264,500,000. The expenditures for the same period will be, actual and estimated, as follows: For the quarter commencing July 1, 1878, actual expenditures, $73,344,573.27; and for the remaining three quarters of the year the expenditures are estimated at $166,755,426.73, making the total expenditures $240,100,000, and leaving an estimated surplus revenue for the year ending June 30, 1879, of $24,400,000. The total receipts during the next fiscal year, ending June 30, 1880, estimated according to existing laws, will be $264,500,000, and the estimated ordinary expenditures for the same period will be $236,320,412.68, leaving a surplus of $28,179,587.32 for that year.

In the foregoing statements of expenditures, actual and estimated, no amount is allowed for the sinking fund provided for by the act approved February 25, 1862, which requires that 1 per cent of the entire debt of the United States shall be purchased or paid within each fiscal year, to be set apart as a sinking fund. There has been, however, a substantial compliance with the conditions of the law. By its terms the public debt should have been reduced between 1862 and the close of the last fiscal year $518,361,806.28; the actual reduction of the ascertained debt in that period has been $720,644,739.61, being in excess of the reduction required by the sinking fund act $202,282,933.33.

The amount of the public debt, less cash in the Treasury, November 1, 1878, was $2,024,200,083.18, a reduction since the same date last year of $23,150,617.39.

The progress made during the last year in refunding the public debt at lower rates of interest is very gratifying. The amount of 4 per cent bonds sold during the present year prior to November 23, 1878, is $100,270,900, and 6 per cent bonds, commonly known as five-twenties, to an equal amount, have been or will be redeemed as calls mature.

It has been the policy of the Department to place the 4 per cent bonds within easy reach of every citizen who desires to invest his savings, whether small or great, in these securities. The Secretary of the Treasury recommends that the law be so modified that small sums may be invested, and that through the post-offices or other agents of the Government the freest opportunity may be given in all parts of the country for such investments.

The best mode suggested is that the Department be authorized to issue certificates of deposit, of the denomination of $10, bearing interest at the rate of 3.65 per cent per annum and convertible at any time within one year after their issue into the 4 per cent bonds authorized by the refunding act, and to be issued only in exchange for United States notes sent to the Treasury by mail or otherwise. Such a provision of law, supported by suitable regulations, would enable any person readily, without cost or risk, to convert his money into an interest-bearing security of the United States, and the money so received could be applied to the redemption of 6 per cent bonds.

The coinage of gold during the last fiscal year was $52,798,980. The coinage of silver dollars under the act passed February 28, 1878, amounted on the 23d of November, 1878, to $19,814,550, of which amount $4,984,947 are in circulation, and the balance, $14,829,603, is still in the possession of the Government.

With views unchanged with regard to the act under which the coinage of silver proceeds, it has been the purpose of the Secretary faithfully to execute the law and to afford a fair trial to the measure.

In the present financial condition of the country I am persuaded that the welfare of legitimate business and industry of every description will be best promoted by abstaining from all attempts to make radical changes in the existing financial legislation. Let it be understood that during the coming year the business of the country will be undisturbed by governmental interference with the laws affecting it, and we may confidently expect that the resumption of specie payments, which will take place at the appointed time, will be successfully and easily maintained, and that it will be followed by a healthful and enduring revival of business prosperity.

Let the healing influence of time, the inherent energies of our people, and the boundless resources of our country have a fair opportunity, and relief from present difficulties will surely follow.

The report of the Secretary of War shows that the Army has been well and economically supplied; that our small force has been actively employed and has faithfully performed all the service required of it. The morale of the Army has improved and the number of desertions has materially decreased during the year.

The Secretary recommends—

1. That a pension be granted to the widow of the late Lieutenant Henry H. Benner, Eighteenth Infantry, who lost his life by yellow fever while in command of the steamer *J. M. Chambers*, sent with supplies for the relief of sufferers in the South from that disease.

2. The establishment of the annuity scheme for the benefit of the heirs of deceased officers, as suggested by the Paymaster-General.

3. The adoption by Congress of a plan for the publication of the records of the War of the Rebellion, now being prepared for that purpose.

4. The increase of the extra per diem of soldier teachers employed in post schools, and liberal appropriations for the erection of buildings for schools and libraries at the different posts.

5. The repeal or amendment of the act of June 18, 1878, forbidding the use of the Army "as a *posse comitatus,* or otherwise, for the purpose of executing the laws, except in such cases and under such circumstances as such employment of said force may be expressly authorized by the Constitution or by act of Congress."

6. The passage of a joint resolution of Congress legalizing the issues of rations, tents, and medicines which were made for the relief of sufferers from yellow fever.

7. That provision be made for the erection of a fireproof building for the preservation of certain valuable records, now constantly exposed to destruction by fire.

These recommendations are all commended to your favorable consideration.

The report of the Secretary of the Navy shows that the Navy has improved during the last fiscal year. Work has been done on seventy-five vessels, ten of which have been thoroughly repaired and made ready for sea. Two others are in rapid progress toward completion. The total expenditures of the year, including the amount appropriated for the deficiencies of the previous year, were $17,468,392.65. The actual expenses chargeable to the year, exclusive of these deficiencies, were $13,306,914.09, or $767,199.18 less than those of the previous year, and $4,928,677.74 less than the expenses including the deficiencies. The estimates for the fiscal year ending June 30, 1880, are $14,562,381.45, exceeding the appropriations of the present year only $33,949.75, which excess is occasioned by the demands of the Naval Academy and the

Marine Corps, as explained in the Secretary's report. The appropriations for the present fiscal year are $14,528,431.70, which, in the opinion of the Secretary, will be ample for all the current expenses of the Department during the year. The amount drawn from the Treasury from July 1 to November 1, 1878, is $4,740,544.14, of which $70,980.75 has been refunded, leaving as the expenditure for that period $4,669,563.39, or $520,899.24 less than the corresponding period of the last fiscal year.

The report of the Postmaster-General embraces a detailed statement of the operations of the Post-Office Department. The expenditures of that Department for the fiscal year ended June 30, 1878, were $34,165,084.49. The receipts, including sales of stamps, money-order business, and official stamps, were $29,277,516.95. The sum of $290,436.90, included in the foregoing statement of expenditures, is chargeable to preceding years, so that the actual expenditures for the fiscal year ended June 30, 1878, are $33,874,647.59. The amount drawn from the Treasury on appropriations, in addition to the revenues of the Department, was $5,307,652.82. The expenditures for the fiscal year ending June 30, 1880, are estimated at $36,571,900 and the receipts from all sources at $30,664,023.90, leaving a deficiency to be appropriated out of the Treasury of $5,907,876.10. The report calls attention to the fact that the compensation of postmasters and of railroads for carrying the mail is regulated by law, and that the failure of Congress to appropriate the amounts required for these purposes does not relieve the Government of responsibility, but necessarily increases the deficiency bills which Congress will be called upon to pass.

In providing for the postal service the following questions are presented: Should Congress annually appropriate a sum for its expenses largely in excess of its revenues or should such rates of postage be established as will make the Department self-sustaining? Should the postal service be reduced by excluding from the mails matter which does not pay its way? Should the number of post routes be diminished? Should other methods be adopted which will increase the revenues or diminish the expenses of the postal service?

The International Postal Congress which met at Paris May 1, 1878, and continued in session until June 4 of the same year, was composed of delegates from nearly all the civilized countries of the world. It adopted a new convention (to take the place of the treaty concluded at Berne October 9, 1874), which goes into effect on the 1st of April, 1879, between the countries whose delegates have signed it. It was ratified and approved, by and with the consent of the President, August 13, 1878. A synopsis of this Universal Postal Convention will be found in the report of the Postmaster-General, and the full text in the appendix thereto. In its origin the Postal Union comprised twenty-three countries, having a population of 350,000,000 people. On the 1st of April next it will comprise forty-three countries and colonies, with a population of more than 650,000,000 people, and will soon, by the accession of the few remaining countries and colonies which maintain organized postal services, constitute in fact as well as in name, as its new title indicates, a universal union, regulating, upon a uniform basis of cheap postage rates, the postal intercourse between all civilized nations.

Some embarrassment has arisen out of the conflict between the customs laws of this country and the provisions of the Postal Convention in regard to the transmission of foreign books and newspapers to this country by mail. It is hoped that Congress will be able to devise some means of reconciling the difficulties which have thus been created, so as to do justice to all parties involved.

The business of the Supreme Court and of the courts in many of the circuits has increased to such an extent during the past year that additional legislation is imperative to relieve and prevent the delay of justice and possible oppression to suitors which is thus occasioned. The encumbered condition of these dockets is presented anew in the report of the Attorney-General, and the remedy suggested is earnestly urged for Congressional action. The creation of additional circuit judges, as proposed, would afford a complete remedy, and would involve an expense, at the present rate of salaries, of not more than $60,000 a year.

The annual reports of the Secretary of the Interior and of the Commissioner of Indian Affairs present an elaborate account of the present condition of the Indian tribes and of that branch of the public service which ministers to their interests. While the conduct of the Indians generally has been orderly and their relations with their neighbors friendly and peaceable, two local disturbances have occurred, which were deplorable in their character, but remained, happily, confined to a comparatively small number of Indians. The discontent among the Bannocks, which led first to some acts of violence on the part of some members of the tribe and finally to the outbreak, appears to have been caused by an insufficiency of food on the reservation, and this insufficiency to have been owing to the inadequacy of the appropriations made by Congress to the wants of the Indians at a time when the Indians were prevented from supplying the deficiency by hunting. After an arduous pursuit by the troops of the United States, and several engagements, the hostile Indians were reduced to subjection, and the larger part of them surrendered themselves as prisoners. In this connection I desire to call attention to the recommendation made by the Secretary of the Interior, that a sufficient fund be placed at the disposal of the Executive, to be used, with proper accountability, at discretion, in sudden emergencies of the Indian service.

The other case of disturbance was that of a band of Northern Cheyennes, who suddenly left their reservation in the Indian Territory and marched rapidly through the States of Kansas and Nebraska in the direction of their old hunting grounds, committing murders and other crimes on their way. From documents accompanying the report of the Secretary of the Interior it appears that this disorderly band was as fully supplied with the necessaries of life as the 4,700 other Indians who remained quietly on the reservation, and that the disturbance was caused by men of a restless and mischievous disposition among the Indians themselves. Almost the whole of this band have surrendered to the military authorities; and it is a gratifying fact that when some of them had taken refuge in the camp of the Red Cloud Sioux, with whom they had been in friendly relations, the Sioux held them as prisoners and readily gave them up to the officers of the United States, thus giving new proof of the loyal spirit which, alarming rumors to the contrary notwithstanding, they have uniformly shown ever since the wishes they expressed at the council of September, 1877, had been complied with.

Both the Secretary of the Interior and the Secretary of War unite in the recommendation that provision be made by Congress for the organization of a corps of mounted "Indian auxiliaries," to be under the control of the Army and to be used for the purpose of keeping the Indians on their reservations and preventing or repressing disturbance on their part. I earnestly concur in this recommendation. It is believed that the organization of such a body of Indian cavalry, receiving a moderate pay from the Government, would considerably weaken the restless element among the Indians by withdrawing from it a number of young men and giving them congenial employment under the Government, it being a matter of experience that Indians in our service almost without exception are faithful in the performance of the duties assigned to them. Such an organization would materially aid the Army in the accomplishment of a task for which its numerical strength is sometimes found insufficient.

But while the employment of force for the prevention or repression of Indian troubles is of occasional necessity, and wise preparation should be made to that end, greater reliance must be placed on humane and civilizing agencies for the ultimate solution of what is called the Indian problem. It may be very difficult and require much patient effort to curb the unruly spirit of the savage Indian to the restraints of civilized life, but experience shows that it is not impossible. Many of the tribes which are now quiet and orderly and self-supporting were once as savage as any that at present roam over the plains or in the mountains of the far West, and were then considered inaccessible to civilizing influences. It may be impossible to raise them fully up to the level of the white population of the United States; but we should not forget that they are the aborigines of the country, and called the soil their own on which our people have grown rich, powerful, and happy. We owe it to them as a moral duty to help them in attaining at least that degree of civilization which they may be able to reach. It is not only our duty, it is also our interest to do so. Indians who have become agriculturists or herdsmen, and feel an interest in property, will thenceforth cease to be a warlike and disturbing element. It is also a well-authenticated fact that Indians are apt to be peaceable and quiet when their children are at school, and I am gratified to know, from the expressions of Indians themselves and from many concurring reports, that there is a steadily increasing desire, even among Indians belonging to comparatively wild tribes, to have their children educated. I invite attention to the reports of the Secretary of the Interior and the Commissioner of Indian Affairs touching the experiment recently inaugurated, in taking fifty Indian children, boys and girls, from different tribes, to the Hampton Normal Agricultural Institute in Virginia, where they are to receive an elementary English education and training in agriculture and other useful works, to be returned to their tribes, after the completed course, as interpreters, instructors, and examples. It is reported that the officer charged with the selection of those children might have had thousands of young Indians sent with him had it been possible to make provision for them. I agree with the Secretary of the Interior in saying that "the result of this interesting experiment, if favorable, may be destined to become an important factor in the advancement of civilization among the Indians."

The question whether a change in the control of the Indian service should be made was at the last session of Congress referred to a committee for inquiry and report. Without desiring to anticipate that report, I venture to express the hope that in the decision of so important a question the views expressed above may not be lost sight of, and that the decision, whatever it may be, will arrest further agitation of this subject, such agitation being apt to produce a disturbing effect upon the service, as well as on the Indians themselves.

In the enrollment of the bill making appropriations for sundry civil expenses, at the last session of Congress, that portion which provided for the continuation of the Hot Springs Commission was omitted. As the commission had completed the work of taking testimony on the many conflicting claims, the suspension of their labors, before determining the rights of claimants, threatened for a time to embarrass the interests, not only of the Government, but also of a large number of the citizens of Hot Springs, who were waiting for final action on their claims before beginning contemplated improvements. In order to prevent serious difficulties, which were apprehended, and at the solicitation of many leading citizens of Hot Springs and others interested in the welfare of the town, the Secretary of the Interior was authorized to request the late commissioners to take charge of the records of their proceedings and to perform such work as could properly be done by them under such circumstances to facilitate the future adjudication of the claims at an early day and to preserve the status of the claimants until their rights should be finally determined. The late commissioners complied with that request, and report that the testimony in all the cases has been written out, examined, briefed, and so arranged as to facilitate an early settlement when authorized by law. It is recommended that the requisite authority be given at as early a day in the session as possible, and that a fair compensation be allowed the late commissioners for the expense incurred and the labor performed by them since the 25th of June last.

I invite the attention of Congress to the recommendations made by the Secretary of the Interior with regard to the preservation of the timber on the public lands of the United States. The protection of the public property is one of the first duties of the Government. The Department of the Interior should therefore be enabled by sufficient appropriations to enforce the laws in that respect. But this matter appears still more important as a question of public economy. The rapid destruction of our forests is an evil fraught with the gravest consequences, especially in the mountainous districts, where the rocky slopes, once denuded of their trees, will remain so forever. There the injury, once done, can not be repaired. I fully concur with the Secretary of the Interior in the opinion that for this reason legislation touching the public timber in the mountainous States and Territories of the West should be especially well considered, and that existing laws in which the destruction of the forests is not sufficiently guarded against should be speedily modified. A general law concerning this important subject appears to me to be a matter of urgent public necessity.

From the organization of the Government the importance of encouraging by all possible means the increase of our agricultural productions has been acknowledged and urged upon the attention of Congress and the people as the surest and readiest means of increasing our substantial and enduring prosperity.

The words of Washington are as applicable to-day as when, in his eighth annual message, he said:

It will not be doubted that, with reference either to individual or national welfare, agriculture is of primary importance. In proportion as nations advance in population and other circumstances of maturity this truth becomes more apparent, and renders the cultivation of the soil more and more an object of public patronage. Institutions for promoting it grow up, supported by the public purse; and to what object can it be dedicated with greater propriety? Among the means which have been employed to this end none have been attended with greater success than the establishment of boards (composed of proper characters) charged with collecting and diffusing information, and enabled by premiums and small pecuniary aids to encourage and assist a spirit of discovery and improvement. This species of establishment contributes doubly to the increase of improvement, by stimulating to enterprise and experiment, and by drawing to a common center the results everywhere of individual skill and observation and spreading them thence over the whole nation. Experience accordingly hath shewn that they are very cheap instruments of immense national benefits.

The preponderance of the agricultural over any other interest in the United States entitles it to all the consideration claimed for it by Washington. About one-half of the population of the United States is engaged in agriculture. The value of the agricultural products of the United States for the year 1878 is estimated at $3,000,000,000. The exports of agricultural products for the year 1877, as appears from the report of the Bureau of Statistics, were $524,000,000. The great extent of our country, with its diversity of soil and climate, enables us to produce within our own borders and by our own labor not only the necessaries, but most of the luxuries, that are consumed in civilized countries. Yet, notwithstanding our advantages of soil, climate, and intercommunication, it appears from the statistical statements in the report of the Commissioner of Agriculture that we import annually from foreign lands many millions of dollars worth of agricultural products which could be raised in our own country.

Numerous questions arise in the practice of advanced agriculture which can only be answered by experiments, often costly and sometimes fruitless, which are beyond the means of private individuals and are a just and proper charge on the whole nation for the benefit of the nation. It is good policy, especially in times of depression and uncertainty in other business pursuits, with a vast area of uncultivated, and hence unproductive, territory, wisely opened to homestead settlement, to encourage by every proper and legitimate means the occupation and tillage of the soil. The efforts of the Department of Agriculture to stimulate old and introduce new agricultural industries, to improve the quality and increase the quantity of our products, to determine the value of old or establish the importance of new methods of culture, are worthy of your careful and favorable consideration, and assistance by such appropriations of money and enlargement of facilities as may seem to be demanded by the present favorable conditions for the growth and rapid development of this important interest.

The abuse of animals in transit is widely attracting public attention. A national convention of societies specially interested in the subject has recently met at Baltimore, and the facts developed, both in regard to cruelties to animals and the effect of such cruelties upon the public health, would seem to demand the careful consideration of Congress and the enactment of more efficient laws for the prevention of these abuses.

The report of the Commissioner of the Bureau of Education shows very gratifying progress throughout the country in all the interests committed to the care of this important office. The report is especially encouraging with respect to the extension of the advantages of the common-school system in sections of the country where the general enjoyment of the privilege of free schools is not yet attained.

To education more than to any other agency we are to look as the resource for the advancement of the people in the requisite knowledge and appreciation of their rights and responsibilities as citizens, and I desire to repeat the suggestion contained in my former message in behalf of the enactment of appropriate measures by Congress for the purpose of supplementing with national aid the local systems of education in the several States.

Adequate accommodations for the great library, which is overgrowing the capacity of the rooms now occupied at the Capitol, should be provided without further delay. This invaluable collection of books, manuscripts, and illustrative art has grown to such proportions, in connection with the copyright system of the country, as to demand the prompt and careful attention of Congress to save it from injury in its present crowded and insufficient quarters. As this library is national in its character, and must from the nature of the case increase even more rapidly in the future than in the past, it can not be doubted that the people will sanction any wise expenditure to preserve it and to enlarge its usefulness.

The appeal of the Regents of the Smithsonian Institution for the means to organize, exhibit, and make available for the public benefit the articles now stored away belonging to the National Museum I heartily recommend to your favorable consideration.

The attention of Congress is again invited to the condition of the river front of the city of Washington. It is a matter of vital importance to the health of the residents of the national capital, both temporary and permanent, that the lowlands in front of the city, now subject to tidal overflow, should be reclaimed. In their present condition these flats obstruct the drainage of the city and are a dangerous source of malarial poison. The reclamation will improve the navigation of the river by restricting, and consequently deepening, its channel, and is also of importance when considered in connection with the extension of the public ground and the enlargement of the park west and south of the Washington Monument. The report of the board of survey, heretofore ordered by act of Congress, on the improvement of the harbor of Washington and Georgetown, is respectfully commended to consideration.

The report of the Commissioners of the District of Columbia presents a detailed statement of the affairs of the District.

The relative expenditures by the United States and the District for local purposes is contrasted, showing that the expenditures by the people of the District greatly exceed those of the General Government. The exhibit is made in connection with estimates for the requisite repair of the defective pavements and sewers of the city, which is a work of immediate necessity; and in the same connection a plan is presented for the permanent funding of the outstanding securities of the District.

The benevolent, reformatory, and penal institutions of the District are all entitled to the favorable attention of Congress. The Reform School needs additional buildings and teachers. Appropriations which will place all of these institutions in a condition to become models of usefulness and beneficence will be regarded by the country as liberality wisely bestowed.

The Commissioners, with evident justice, request attention to the discrimination made by Congress against the District in the donation of land for the support of the public schools, and ask that the same liberality that has been shown to the inhabitants of the various States and Territories of the United States may be extended to the District of Columbia.

The Commissioners also invite attention to the damage inflicted upon public and private interests by the present location of the depots and switching tracks of the several railroads entering the city, and ask for legislation looking to their removal. The recommendations and suggestions contained in the report will, I trust, receive the careful consideration of Congress.

Sufficient time has, perhaps, not elapsed since the reorganization of the government of the District under the recent legislation of Congress for the expression of a confident opinion as to its successful operation, but the practical results already attained are so satisfactory that the friends of the new government may well urge upon Congress the wisdom of its continuance, without essential modification, until by actual experience its advantages and defects may be more fully ascertained.

THIRD ANNUAL MESSAGE.

EXECUTIVE MANSION, *December 1, 1879.*

Fellow-Citizens of the Senate and House of Representatives:

The members of the Forty-sixth Congress have assembled in their first regular session under circumstances calling for mutual congratulation and grateful acknowledgment to the Giver of All Good for the large and unusual measure of national prosperity which we now enjoy.

The most interesting events which have occurred in our public affairs since my last annual message to Congress are connected with the financial operations of the Government, directly affecting the business interests of the country. I congratulate Congress on the successful execution of the resumption act. At the time fixed, and in the manner contemplated by law, United States notes began to be redeemed in coin. Since the 1st of January last they have been promptly redeemed on presentation, and in all business transactions, public and private, in all parts of the country, they are received and paid out as the equivalent of coin. The demand upon the Treasury for gold and silver in exchange for United States notes has been comparatively small, and the voluntary deposit of coin and bullion in exchange for notes has been very large. The excess of the precious metals deposited or exchanged for United States notes over the amount of United States notes redeemed is about $40,000,000.

The resumption of specie payments has been followed by a very great revival of business. With a currency equivalent in value to the money of the commercial world, we are enabled to enter upon an equal competition with other nations in trade and production. The increasing foreign demand for our manufactures and agricultural products has caused a large balance of trade in our favor, which has been paid in gold, from the 1st of July last to November 15, to the amount of about $59,000,000. Since the resumption of specie payments there has also been a marked and gratifying improvement of the public credit. The bonds of the Government bearing only 4 per cent interest have been sold at or above par, sufficient in amount to pay off all of the national debt which was redeemable under present laws. The amount of interest saved annually by the process of refunding the debt since March 1, 1877, is $14,297,177. The bonds sold were largely in small sums, and the number of our citizens now holding the public securities is much greater than ever before. The amount of the national debt which matures within less than two years is $792,121,700, of which $500,000,000 bear interest at the rate of 5 per cent, and the balance is in bonds bearing 6 per cent interest. It is believed that this part of the public debt can be refunded by the issue of 4 per cent bonds, and, by the reduction of interest which will thus be effected, about $11,000,000 can be annually saved to the Treasury. To secure this important reduction of interest to be paid by the United States further legislation is required, which it is hoped will be provided by Congress during its present session.

The coinage of gold by the mints of the United States during the last fiscal year was $40,986,912. The coinage of silver dollars since the passage of the act for that purpose up to November 1, 1879, was $45,000,850, of which $12,700,344 have been issued from the Treasury and are now in circulation, and $32,300,506 are still in the possession of the Government.

The pendency of the proposition for unity of action between the United States and the principal commercial nations of Europe to effect a permanent system for the equality of gold and silver in the recognized money of the world leads me to recommend that Congress refrain from new legislation on the general subject. The great revival of trade, internal and foreign, will supply during the coming year its own instructions, which may well be awaited before attempting further experimental measures with the coinage. I would, however, strongly urge upon Congress the importance of authorizing the Secretary of the Treasury to suspend the coinage of silver dollars upon the present legal ratio. The market value of the silver dollar being uniformly and largely less than the market value of the gold dollar, it is obviously impracticable to maintain them at par with each other if both are coined without limit. If the cheaper coin is forced into circulation, it will, if coined without limit, soon become the sole standard of value, and thus defeat the desired object, which is a currency of both gold and silver which shall be of equivalent value, dollar for dollar, with the universally recognized money of the world.

The retirement from circulation of United States notes with the capacity of legal tender in private contracts is a step to be taken in our progress toward a safe and stable currency which should be accepted as the policy and duty of the Government and the interest and security of the people. It is my firm conviction that the issue of legal-tender paper money based wholly upon the authority and credit of the Government, except in extreme emergency, is without warrant in the Constitution and a violation of sound financial principles. The issue of United States notes during the late civil war with the capacity of legal tender between private individuals was not authorized except as a means of rescuing the country from imminent peril. The circulation of these notes as paper money for any protracted period of time after the accomplishment of this purpose was not contemplated by the framers of the law under which they were issued. They anticipated the redemption and withdrawal of these notes at the earliest practicable period consistent with the attainment of the object for which they were provided.

The policy of the United States, steadily adhered to from the adoption of the Constitution, has been to avoid the creation of a national debt; and when, from necessity in time of war, debts have been created, they have been paid off, on the return of peace, as rapidly as possible. With this view, and for this purpose, it is recommended that the existing laws for the accumulation of a sinking fund sufficient to extinguish the public debt within a limited period be maintained. If any change of the objects or rates of taxation is deemed necessary by Congress, it is suggested that experience has shown that a duty can be placed on tea and coffee which will not enhance the price of those articles to the consumer, and which will add several millions of dollars annually to the Treasury.

The continued deliberate violation by a large number of the prominent and influential citizens of the Territory of Utah of the laws of the United States for the prosecution and punishment of polygamy demands the attention of every department of the Government. This Territory has a population sufficient to entitle it to admission as a State, and the general interests of the nation, as well as the welfare of the citizens of the Territory, require its advance from the Territorial form of government to the responsibilities and privileges of a State. This important change will not, however, be approved by the country while the citizens of Utah in very considerable number uphold a practice which is condemned as a crime by the laws of all civilized communities throughout the world.

The law for the suppression of this offense was enacted with great unanimity by Congress more than seventeen years ago, but has remained until recently a dead letter in the Territory of Utah, because of the peculiar difficulties attending its enforcement. The opinion widely prevailed among the citizens of Utah that the law was in contravention of the constitutional guaranty of religious freedom. This objection is now removed. The Supreme Court of the United States has decided the law to be within the legislative power of Congress and binding as a rule of action for all who reside within the Territories. There is no longer any reason for delay or hesitation in its enforcement. It should be firmly and effectively executed. If not sufficiently stringent in its provisions, it should be amended; and in aid of the purpose in view I recommend that more comprehensive and more searching methods for preventing as well as punishing this crime be provided. If necessary to secure obedience to the law, the enjoyment and exercise of the rights and privileges of citizenship in the Territories of the United States may be withheld or withdrawn from those who violate or oppose the enforcement of the law on this subject.

The elections of the past year, though occupied only with State officers, have not failed to elicit in the political discussions which attended them all over the country new and decisive evidence of the deep interest which the great body of citizens take in the progress of the country toward a more general and complete establishment, at whatever cost, of universal security and freedom in the exercise of the elective franchise. While many topics of political concern demand great attention from our people, both in the sphere of national and State authority, I find no reason to qualify the opinion I expressed in my last annual message, that no temporary or administrative interests of government, however urgent or weighty, will ever displace the zeal of our people in defense of the primary rights of citizenship, and that the power of public opinion will override all political prejudices, and all sectional and State attachments in demanding that all over our wide territory the name and character of citizen of the United States shall mean one and the same thing and carry with them unchallenged security and respect. I earnestly appeal to the intelligence and patriotism of all good citizens of every part of the country, however much they may be divided in opinions on other political subjects, to unite in compelling obedience to existing laws aimed at the protection of the right of suffrage. I respectfully urge upon Congress to supply any defects in these laws which experience has shown and which it is within its power to remedy. I again invoke the cooperation of the executive and legislative authorities of the States in this great purpose. I am fully convinced that if the public mind can be set at rest on this paramount question of popular rights no serious obstacle will thwart or delay the complete pacification of the country or retard the general diffusion of prosperity.

In a former message I invited the attention of Congress to the subject of the reformation of the civil service of the Government, and expressed the intention of transmitting to Congress as early as practicable a report upon this subject by the chairman of the Civil Service Commission.

In view of the facts that during a considerable period the Government of Great Britain has been dealing with administrative problems and abuses in various particulars analogous to those presented in this country, and that in recent years the measures adopted were understood to have been effective and in every respect highly satisfactory, I thought it desirable to have fuller information upon the subject, and accordingly requested the chairman of the Civil Service Commission to make a thorough investigation for this purpose. The result has been an elaborate and comprehensive report.

The report sets forth the history of the partisan spoils system in Great Britain, and of the rise and fall of the parliamentary patronage, and of official interference with the freedom of elections. It shows that after long trials of various kinds of examinations those which are competitive and open on equal terms to all, and which are carried on under the superintendence of a single commission, have, with great advantage, been established as conditions of admission to almost every official place in the subordinate administration of that country and of British India. The completion of the report, owing to the extent of the labor involved in its preparation and the omission of Congress to make any provision either for the compensation or the expenses of the Commission, has been postponed until the present time. It is herewith transmitted to Congress.

While the reform measures of another government are of no authority for us, they are entitled to influence to the extent to which their intrinsic wisdom and their adaptation to our institutions and social life may commend them to our consideration. The views I have heretofore expressed concerning the defects and abuses in our civil administration remain unchanged, except in so far as an enlarged experience has deepened my sense of the duty both of officers and of the people themselves to cooperate for their removal. The grave evils and perils of a partisan spoils system of appointment to office and of office tenure are now generally recognized. In the resolutions of the great parties, in the reports of Departments, in the debates and proceedings of Congress, in the messages of Executives, the gravity of these evils has been pointed out and the need of their reform has been admitted.

To command the necessary support, every measure of reform must be based on common right and justice, and must be compatible with the healthy existence of great parties, which are inevitable and essential in a free state.

When the people have approved a policy at a national election, confidence on the part of the officers they have selected and of the advisers who, in accordance with our political institutions, should be consulted in the policy which it is their duty to carry into effect is indispensable. It is eminently proper that they should explain it before the people, as well as illustrate its spirit in the performance of their official duties.

Very different considerations apply to the greater number of those who fill the subordinate places in the civil service. Their responsibility is to their superiors in official position. It is their duty to obey the legal instructions of those upon whom that authority is devolved, and their best public service consists in the discharge of their functions irrespective of partisan politics. Their duties are the same whatever party is in power and whatever policy prevails. As a consequence it follows that their tenure of office should not depend on the prevalence of any policy or the supremacy of any party, but should be determined by their capacity to serve the people most usefully quite irrespective of partisan interests. The same considerations that should govern the tenure should also prevail in the appointment, discipline, and removal of these subordinates. The authority of appointment and removal is not a perquisite, which may be used to aid a friend or reward a partisan, but is a trust, to be exercised in the public interest under all the sanctions which attend the obligation to apply the public funds only for public purposes.

Every citizen has an equal right to the honor and profit of entering the public service of his country. The only just ground of discrimination is the measure of character and capacity he has to make that service most useful to the people. Except in cases where, upon just and recognized principles—as upon the theory of pensions—offices and promotions are bestowed as rewards for past services, their bestowal upon any theory which disregards personal merit is an act of injustice to the citizen, as well as a breach of that trust subject to which the appointing power is held.

In the light of these principles it becomes of great importance to provide just and adequate means, especially for every Department and large administrative office, where personal discrimination on the part of its head is not practicable, for ascertaining those qualifications to which appointments and removals should have reference. To fail to provide such means is not only to deny the opportunity of ascertaining the facts upon which the most righteous claim to office depends, but of necessity to discourage all worthy aspirants by handing over appointments and removals to mere influence and favoritism. If it is the right of the worthiest claimant to gain the appointment and the interest of the people to bestow it upon him, it would seem clear that a wise and just method of ascertaining personal fitness for office must be an important and permanent function of every just and wise government. It has long since become impossible in the great offices for those having the duty of nomination and appointment to personally examine into the individual qualifications of more than a small proportion of those seeking office, and with the enlargement of the civil service that proportion must continue to become less.

In the earlier years of the Government the subordinate offices were so few in number that it was quite easy for those making appointments and promotions to personally ascertain the merits of candidates. Party managers and methods had not then become powerful agencies of coercion, hostile to the free and just exercise of the appointing power.

A large and responsible part of the duty of restoring the civil service to the desired purity and efficiency rests upon the President, and it is my purpose to do what is within my power to advance such prudent and gradual measures of reform as will most surely and rapidly bring about that radical change of system essential to make our administrative methods satisfactory to a free and intelligent people. By a proper exercise of authority it is in the power of the Executive to do much to promote such a reform. But it can not be too clearly understood that nothing adequate can be accomplished without cooperation on the part of Congress and considerate and intelligent support among the people. Reforms which challenge the generally accepted theories of parties and demand changes in the methods of Departments are not the work of a day. Their permanent foundations must be laid in sound principles and in an experience which demonstrates their wisdom and exposes the errors of their adversaries. Every worthy officer desires to make his official action a gain and an honor to his country; but the people themselves, far more than their officers in public station, are interested in a pure, economical, and vigorous administration.

By laws enacted in 1853 and 1855, and now in substance incorporated in the Revised Statutes, the practice of arbitrary appointments to the several subordinate grades in the great Departments was condemned, and examinations as to capacity, to be conducted by departmental boards of examiners, were provided for and made conditions of admission to the public service. These statutes are a decision by Congress that examinations of some sort as to attainments and capacity are essential to the well-being of the public service. The important questions since the enactment of these laws have been as to the character of these examinations, and whether official favor and partisan influence or common right and merit were to control the access to the examinations. In practice these examinations have not always been open to worthy persons generally who might wish to be examined. Official favoritism and partisan influence, as a rule, appear to have designated those who alone were permitted to go before the examining boards, subjecting even the examiners to a pressure from the friends of the candidates very difficult to resist. As a consequence the standard of admission fell below that which the public interest demanded. It was also almost inevitable that a system which provided for various separate boards of examiners, with no common supervision or uniform method of procedure, should result in confusion, inconsistency, and inadequate tests of capacity, highly detrimental to the public interest. A further and more radical change was obviously required.

In the annual message of December, 1870, my predecessor declared that—

There is no duty which so much embarrasses the Executive and heads of Departments as that of appointments, nor is there any such arduous and thankless labor imposed on Senators and Representatives as that of finding places for constituents. The present system does not secure the best men, and often not even fit men, for public place. The elevation and purification of the civil service of the Government will be hailed with approval by the whole people of the United States.

Congress accordingly passed the act approved March 3, 1871, "to regulate the civil service of the United States and promote the efficiency thereof," giving the necessary authority to the Executive to inaugurate a civil-service reform.

Acting under this statute, which was interpreted as intended to secure a system of just and effectual examinations under uniform supervision, a number of eminently competent persons were selected for the purpose, who entered with zeal upon the discharge of their duties, prepared with an intelligent appreciation of the requirements of the service the regulations contemplated, and took charge of the examinations, and who in their capacity as a board have been known as the "Civil Service Commission." Congress for two years appropriated the money needed for the compensation and for the expense of carrying on the work of the Commission.

It appears from the report of the Commission submitted to the President in April, 1874, that examinations had been held in various sections of the country, and that an appropriation of about $25,000 would be required to meet the annual expenses, including salaries, involved in discharging the duties of the Commission. The report was transmitted to Congress by special message of April 18, 1874, with the following favorable comment upon the labors of the Commission:

If sustained by Congress, I have no doubt the rules can, after the experience gained, be so improved and enforced as to still more materially benefit the public service and relieve the Executive, members of Congress, and the heads of Departments from influences prejudicial to good administration. The rules, as they have hitherto been enforced, have resulted beneficially, as is shown by the opinions of the members of the Cabinet and their subordinates in the Departments, and in that opinion I concur.

And in the annual message of December of the same year similar views are expressed and an appropriation for continuing the work of the Commission again advised.

The appropriation was not made, and as a consequence the active work of the Commission was suspended, leaving the Commission itself still in existence. Without the means, therefore, of causing qualifications to be tested in any systematic manner or of securing for the public service the advantages of competition upon any extensive plan, I recommended in my annual message of December, 1877, the making of an appropriation for the resumption of the work of the Commission.

In the meantime, however, competitive examinations, under many embarrassments, have been conducted within limited spheres in the Executive Departments in Washington and in a number of the custom-houses and post-offices of the principal cities of the country, with a view to further test their effects, and in every instance they have been found to be as salutary as they are stated to have been under the Administration of my predecessor. I think the economy, purity, and efficiency of the public service would be greatly promoted by their systematic introduction, wherever practicable, throughout the entire civil service of the Government, together with ample provision for their general supervision in order to secure consistency and uniform justice.

Reports from the Secretary of the Interior, from the Postmaster-General, from the postmaster in the city of New York, where such examinations have been some time on trial, and also from the collector of the port, the naval officer, and the surveyor in that city, and from the postmasters and collectors in several of the other large cities, show that the competitive system, where applied, has in various ways contributed to improve the public service.

The reports show that the results have been salutary in a marked degree, and that the general application of similar rules can not fail to be of decided benefit to the service.

The reports of the Government officers, in the city of New York especially, bear decided testimony to the utility of open competitive examinations in their respective offices, showing that—

These examinations and the excellent qualifications of those admitted to the service through them have had a marked incidental effect upon the persons previously in the service, and particularly upon those aspiring to promotion. There has been on the part of these latter an increased interest in the work and a desire to extend acquaintance with it beyond the particular desk occupied, and thus the morale of the entire force has been raised. * * * The examinations have been attended by many citizens, who have had an opportunity to thoroughly investigate the scope and character of the tests and the method of determining the results, and those visitors have without exception approved the methods employed, and several of them have publicly attested their favorable opinion.

Upon such considerations I deem it my duty to renew the recommendation contained in my annual message of December, 1877, requesting Congress to make the necessary appropriation for the resumption of the work of the Civil Service Commission. Economy will be promoted by authorizing a moderate compensation to persons in the public service who may perform extra labor upon or under the Commission, as the Executive may direct.

I am convinced that if a just and adequate test of merit is enforced for admission to the public service and in making promotions such abuses as removals without good cause and partisan and official interference with the proper exercise of the appointing power will in large measure disappear.

There are other administrative abuses to which the attention of Congress should be asked in this connection. Mere partisan appointments and the constant peril of removal without cause very naturally lead to an absorbing and mischievous political activity on the part of those thus appointed, which not only interferes with the due discharge of official duty, but is incompatible with the freedom of elections. Not without warrant in the views of several of my predecessors in the Presidential office, and directly within the law of 1871, already cited, I endeavored, by regulation made on the 22d day of June, 1877, to put some reasonable limits to such abuses. It may not be easy, and it may never perhaps be necessary, to define with precision the proper limit of political action on the part of Federal officers. But while their right to hold and freely express their opinions can not be questioned, it is very plain that they should neither be allowed to devote to other subjects the time needed for the proper discharge of their official duties nor to use the authority of their office to enforce their own opinions or to coerce the political action of those who hold different opinions.

Reasons of justice and public policy quite analogous to those which forbid the use of official power for the oppression of the private citizen impose upon the Government the duty of protecting its officers and agents from arbitrary exactions. In whatever aspect considered, the practice of making levies for party purposes upon the salaries of officers is highly demoralizing to the public service and discreditable to the country. Though an officer should be as free as any other citizen to give his own money in aid of his opinions or his party, he should also be as free as any other citizen to refuse to make such gifts. If salaries are but a fair compensation for the time and labor of the officer, it is gross injustice to levy a tax upon them. If they are made excessive in order that they may bear the tax, the excess is an indirect robbery of the public funds.

I recommend, therefore, such a revision and extension of present statutes as shall secure to those in every grade of official life or public employment the protection with which a great and enlightened nation should guard those who are faithful in its service.

Our relations with foreign countries have continued peaceful.

With Great Britain there are still unsettled questions, growing out of the local laws of the maritime provinces and the action of provincial authorities deemed to be in derogation of rights secured by treaty to American fishermen. The United States minister in London has been instructed to present a demand for $105,305.02 in view of the damages received by American citizens at Fortune Bay on the 6th day of January, 1878. The subject has been taken into consideration by the British Government, and an early reply is anticipated.

Upon the completion of the necessary preliminary examinations the subject of our participation in the provincial fisheries, as regulated by treaty, will at once be brought to the attention of the British Government, with a view to an early and permanent settlement of the whole question, which was only temporarily adjusted by the treaty of Washington.

Efforts have been made to obtain the removal of restrictions found injurious to the exportation of cattle to the United Kingdom.

Some correspondence has also occurred with regard to the rescue and saving of life and property upon the Lakes, which has resulted in important modifications of the previous regulations of the Dominion government on the subject in the interest of humanity and commerce.

In accordance with the joint resolution of the last session of Congress, commissioners were appointed to represent the United States at the two international exhibitions in Australia, one of which is now in progress at Sydney, and the other to be held next year at Melbourne. A desire has been expressed by our merchants and manufacturers interested in the important and growing trade with Australia that an increased provision should be made by Congress for the representation of our industries at the Melbourne exhibition of next year, and the subject is respectfully submitted to your favorable consideration.

The assent of the Government has been given to the landing on the coast of Massachusetts of a new and independent transatlantic cable between France, by way of the French island of St. Pierre, and this country, subject to any future legislation of Congress on the subject. The conditions imposed before allowing this connection with our shores to be established are such as to secure its competition with any existing or future lines of marine cable and preclude amalgamation therewith, to provide for entire equality of rights to our Government and people with those of France in the use of the cable, and prevent any exclusive possession of the privilege as accorded by France to the disadvantage of any future cable communication between France and the United States which may be projected and accomplished by our citizens. An important reduction of the present rates of cable communication with Europe, felt to be too burdensome to the interests of our commerce, must necessarily flow from the establishment of this competing line.

The attention of Congress was drawn to the propriety of some general regulation by Congress of the whole subject of transmarine cables by my predecessor in his message of December 7, 1875, and I respectfully submit to your consideration the importance of Congressional action in the matter.

The questions of grave importance with Spain growing out of the incidents of the Cuban insurrection have been for the most part happily and honorably settled. It may reasonably be anticipated that the commission now sitting in Washington for the decision of private cases in this connection will soon be able to bring its labors to a conclusion.

The long-standing question of East Florida claims has lately been renewed as a subject of correspondence, and may possibly require Congressional action for its final disposition.

A treaty with the Netherlands with respect to consular rights and privileges similar to those with other powers has been signed and ratified, and the ratifications were exchanged on the 31st of July last. Negotiations for extradition treaties with the Netherlands and with Denmark are now in progress.

Some questions with Switzerland in regard to pauper and convict emigrants have arisen, but it is not doubted that they will be arranged upon a just and satisfactory basis. A question has also occurred with respect to an asserted claim by Swiss municipal authorities to exercise tutelage over persons and property of Swiss citizens naturalized in this country. It is possible this may require adjustment by treaty.

With the German Empire frequent questions arise in connection with the subjects of naturalization and expatriation, but the Imperial Government has constantly manifested a desire to strictly maintain and comply with all treaty stipulations in regard to them.

In consequence of the omission of Congress to provide for a diplomatic representative at Athens, the legation to Greece has been withdrawn. There is now no channel of diplomatic communication between the two countries, and the expediency of providing for one in some form is submitted to Congress.

Relations with Austria, Russia, Italy, Portugal, Turkey, and Belgium continue amicable, and marked by no incident of especial importance.

A change of the personal head of the Government of Egypt has taken place. No change, however, has occurred in the relations between Egypt and the United States. The action of the Egyptian Government in presenting to the city of New York one of the ancient obelisks, which possess such historic interest, is highly appreciated as a generous mark of international regard. If prosperity should attend the enterprise of its transportation across the Atlantic, its erection in a conspicuous position in the chief commercial city of the nation will soon be accomplished.

The treaty recently made between Japan and the United States in regard to the revision of former commercial treaties it is now believed will be followed by similar action on the part of other treaty powers. The attention of Congress is again invited to the subject of the indemnity funds received some years since from Japan and China, which, with their accumulated interest, now amount to considerable sums. If any part of these funds is justly due to American citizens, they should receive it promptly; and whatever may have been received by this Government in excess of strictly just demands should in some form be returned to the nations to whom it equitably belongs.

The Government of China has signified its willingness to consider the question of the emigration of its subjects to the United States with a dispassionate fairness and to cooperate in such measures as may tend to prevent injurious consequences to the United States. The negotiations are still proceeding, and will be pressed with diligence.

A question having arisen between China and Japan about the Lew

Chew Islands, the United States Government has taken measures to inform those powers of its readiness to extend its good offices for the maintenance of peace if they shall mutually deem it desirable and find it practicable to avail themselves of the proffer.

It is a gratification to be able to announce that, through the judicious and energetic action of the military commanders of the two nations on each side of the Rio Grande, under the instructions of their respective Governments, raids and depredations have greatly decreased, and in the localities where formerly most destructive have now almost wholly ceased. In view of this result, I entertain a confident expectation that the prevalence of quiet on the border will soon become so assured as to justify a modification of the present orders to our military commanders as to crossing the border, without encouraging such disturbances as would endanger the peace of the two countries.

The third installment of the award against Mexico under the claims commission of July 4, 1868, was duly paid, and has been put in course of distribution in pursuance of the act of Congress providing for the same. This satisfactory situation between the two countries leads me to anticipate an expansion of our trade with Mexico and an increased contribution of capital and industry by our people to the development of the great resources of that country. I earnestly commend to the wisdom of Congress the provision of suitable legislation looking to this result.

Diplomatic intercourse with Colombia is again fully restored by the arrival of a minister from that country to the United States. This is especially fortunate in view of the fact that the question of an interoceanic canal has recently assumed a new and important aspect and is now under discussion with the Central American countries through whose territory the canal, by the Nicaragua route, would have to pass. It is trusted that enlightened statesmanship on their part will see that the early prosecution of such a work will largely inure to the benefit, not only of their own citizens and those of the United States, but of the commerce of the civilized world. It is not doubted that should the work be undertaken under the protective auspices of the United States, and upon satisfactory concessions for the right of way and its security by the Central American Governments, the capital for its completion would be readily furnished from this country and Europe, which might, failing such guaranties, prove inaccessible.

Diplomatic relations with Chile have also been strengthened by the reception of a minister from that country.

The war between Peru, Bolivia, and Chile still continues. The United States have not deemed it proper to interpose in the matter further than to convey to all the Governments concerned the assurance that the friendly offices of the Government of the United States for the restoration of peace upon an honorable basis will be extended in case the belligerents shall exhibit a readiness to accept them.

Cordial relations continue with Brazil and the Argentine Republic, and trade with those countries is improving. A provision for regular and more frequent mail communication, in our own ships, between the ports of this country and the nations of South America seems to me to deserve the attention of Congress as an essential precursor of an enlargement of our commerce with them and an extension of our carrying trade.

A recent revolution in Venezuela has been followed by the establishment of a provisional government. This government has not yet been formally recognized, and it is deemed desirable to await the proposed action of the people which is expected to give it the sanction of constitutional forms.

A naval vessel has been sent to the Samoan Islands to make surveys and take possession of the privileges ceded to the United States by Samoa in the harbor of Pago-Pago. A coaling station is to be established there, which will be convenient and useful to United States vessels.

The subject of opening diplomatic relations with Roumania and Servia, now become independent sovereignties, is at present under consideration, and is the subject of diplomatic correspondence.

There is a gratifying increase of trade with nearly all European and American countries, and it is believed that with judicious action in regard to its development it can and will be still more enhanced and that American products and manufactures will find new and expanding markets. The reports of diplomatic and consular officers upon this subject, under the system now adopted, have resulted in obtaining much valuable information, which has been and will continue to be laid before Congress and the public from time to time.

The third article of the treaty with Russia of March 30, 1867, by which Alaska was ceded to the United States, provides that the inhabitants of the ceded territory, with the exception of the uncivilized native tribes, shall be admitted to the enjoyment of all the rights of citizens of the United States and shall be maintained and protected in the free enjoyment of their liberty, property, and religion. The uncivilized tribes are subject to such laws and regulations as the United States may from time to time adopt in regard to the aboriginal tribes of that country.

Both the obligations of this treaty and the necessities of the people require that some organized form of government over the Territory of Alaska be adopted.

There appears to be no law for the arrest of persons charged with common-law offenses, such as assault, robbery, and murder, and no magistrate authorized to issue or execute process in such cases. Serious difficulties have already arisen from offenses of this character, not only among the original inhabitants, but among citizens of the United States and other countries who have engaged in mining, fishing, and other business operations within the territory. A bill authorizing the appointment of justices of the peace and constables and the arrest and detention of persons charged with criminal offenses, and providing for an appeal to United States courts for the district of Oregon in suitable cases, will at a proper time be submitted to Congress.

The attention of Congress is called to the annual report of the Secretary of the Treasury on the condition of the public finances.

The ordinary revenues from all sources for the fiscal year ended June 30, 1879, were $273,827,184.46; the ordinary expenditures for the same period were $266,947,883.53, leaving a surplus revenue for the year of $6,879,300.93.

The receipts for the present fiscal year, ending June 30, 1880, actual and estimated, are as follows: Actual receipts for the first quarter, commencing July 1, 1879, $79,843,663.61; estimated receipts for the remaining three quarters of the year, $208,156,336.39; total receipts for the current fiscal year, actual and estimated, $288,000,000.

The expenditures for the same period will be, actual and estimated, as follows: For the quarter commencing July 1, 1879, actual expenditures, $91,683,385.10; and for the remaining three quarters of the year the expenditures are estimated at $172,316,614.90, making the total expenditures $264,000,000, and leaving an estimated surplus revenue for the year ending June 30, 1880, of $24,000,000. The total receipts during the next fiscal year, ending June 30, 1881, estimated according to existing laws, will be $288,000,000, and the estimated ordinary expenditures for the same period will be $278,097,364.39, leaving a surplus of $9,902,-635.61 for that year.

The large amount expended for arrears of pensions during the last and the present fiscal year, amounting to $21,747,249.60, has prevented the application of the full amount required by law to the sinking fund for the current year; but these arrears having been substantially paid, it is believed that the sinking fund can hereafter be maintained without any change of existing law.

The Secretary of War reports that the War Department estimates for the fiscal year ending June 30, 1881, are $40,380,428.93, the same being for a less sum of money than any annual estimate rendered to Congress from that Department during a period of at least twelve years.

He concurs with the General of the Army in recommending such legislation as will authorize the enlistment of the full number of 25,000 men for the line of the Army, exclusive of the 3,463 men required for detached duty, and therefore not available for service in the field.

He also recommends that Congress be asked to provide by law for the disposition of a large number of abandoned military posts and reservations, which, though very valuable in themselves, have been rendered useless for military purposes by the advance of civilization and settlement.

He unites with the Quartermaster-General in recommending that an appropriation be made for the construction of a cheap and perfectly fireproof building for the safe storage of a vast amount of money accounts, vouchers, claims, and other valuable records now in the Quartermaster-General's Office, and exposed to great risk of total destruction by fire.

He also recommends, in conformity with the views of the Judge-Advocate-General, some declaratory legislation in reference to the military statute of limitations as applied to the crime of desertion.

In these several recommendations I concur.

The Secretary of War further reports that the work for the improvement of the South Pass of the Mississippi River, under contract with Mr. James B. Eads, made in pursuance of an act of Congress, has been prosecuted during the past year with a greater measure of success in the attainment of results than during any previous year. The channel through the South Pass, which at the beginning of operations in June, 1875, had a depth of only 7½ feet of water, had on the 8th of July, 1879, a minimum depth of 26 feet, having a width of not less than 200 feet and a central depth of 30 feet. Payments have been made in accordance with the statute, as the work progressed, amounting in the aggregate to $4,250,000; and further payments will become due, as provided by the statute, in the event of success in maintaining the channel now secured.

The reports of the General of the Army and of his subordinates present a full and detailed account of the military operations for the suppression of hostilities among the Indians of the Ute and Apache tribes, and praise is justly awarded to the officers and troops engaged for promptness, skill, and courage displayed.

The past year has been one of almost unbroken peace and quiet on the Mexican frontier, and there is reason to believe that the efforts of this Government and of Mexico to maintain order in that region will prove permanently successful.

This Department was enabled during the past year to find temporary, though crowded, accommodations and a safe depository for a portion of its records in the completed east wing of the building designed for the State, War, and Navy Departments. The construction of the north wing of the building, a part of the structure intended for the use of the War Department, is being carried forward with all possible dispatch, and the work should receive from Congress such liberal appropriations as will secure its speedy completion.

The report of the Secretary of the Navy shows continued improvement in that branch of the service during the last fiscal year. Extensive repairs have been made upon vessels, and two new ships have been completed and made ready for sea.

The total expenditures of the year ended June 30, 1879, including specific appropriations not estimated for by the Department, were $13,555,710.09. The expenses chargeable to the year, after deducting the amount of these specific appropriations, were $13,343,317.79; but this is subject to a reduction of $283,725.99, that amount having been drawn upon warrants, but not paid out during the year. The amount of appropriations applicable to the last fiscal year was $14,538,646.17. There was, therefore, a balance of $1,479,054.37 remaining unexpended and to the credit of the Department on June 30, 1879. The estimates for the fiscal year ending June 30, 1881, are $14,864,147.95, which exceeds the appropriations for the present fiscal year $361,897.28. The reason for this increase is explained in the Secretary's report. The appropriations available for the present fiscal year are $14,502,250.67, which will, in the opinion of the Secretary, answer all the ordinary demands of the service. The amount drawn from the Treasury from July 1 to November 1, 1879 was $5,770,404.12, of which $1,095,440.33 has been refunded, leaving as the expenditure for that period $4,674,963.79. If the expenditures of the remaining two-thirds of the year do not exceed the proportion for these four months, there will remain unexpended at the end of the year $477,359.30 of the current appropriations. The report of the Secretary shows the gratifying fact that among all the disbursing officers of the Pay Corps of the Navy there is not one who is a defaulter to the extent of a single dollar. I unite with him in recommending the removal of the observatory to a more healthful location. That institution reflects credit upon the nation, and has obtained the approbation of scientific men in all parts of the world. Its removal from its present location would not only be conducive to the health of its officers and professors, but would greatly increase its usefulness.

The appropriation for judicial expenses, which has heretofore been made for the Department of Justice in gross, was subdivided at the last session of Congress, and no appropriation whatever was made for the payment of the fees of marshals and their deputies, either in the service of process or for the discharge of other duties; and since June 30 these officers have continued the performance of their duties without compensation from the Government, taking upon themselves the necessary incidental outlays, as well as rendering their own services. In only a few unavoidable instances has the proper execution of the process of the United States failed by reason of the absence of the requisite appropriation. This course of official conduct on the part of these officers, highly creditable to their fidelity, was advised by the Attorney-General, who informed them, however, that they would necessarily have to rely for their compensation upon the prospect of future legislation by Congress. I therefore especially recommend that immediate appropriation be made by Congress for this purpose.

The act making the principal appropriation for the Department of Justice at previous sessions has uniformly contained the following clause:

And for defraying the expenses which may be incurred in the enforcement of the act approved February 28, 1871, entitled "An act to amend an act approved May 31, 1870, entitled 'An act to enforce the rights of citizens of the United States to vote in the several States of this Union, and for other purposes,'" or any acts amendatory thereof or supplementary thereto.

No appropriation was made for this purpose for the current year. As no general election for Members of Congress occurred, the omission was a matter of little practical importance. Such election will, however, take place during the ensuing year, and the appropriation made for the pay of marshals and deputies should be sufficient to embrace compensation for the services they may be required to perform at such elections.

The business of the Supreme Court is at present largely in arrears. It can not be expected that more causes can be decided than are now disposed of in its annual session, or that by any assiduity the distinguished magistrates who compose the court can accomplish more than is now done. In the courts of many of the circuits also the business has increased to such an extent that the delay of justice will call the attention of Congress to an appropriate remedy. It is believed that all is done in each circuit which can fairly be expected from its judicial force. The evils arising from delay are less heavily felt by the United States than by private suitors, as its causes are advanced by the courts when it is seen that they involve the discussion of questions of a public character.

The remedy suggested by the Attorney-General is the appointment of additional circuit judges and the creation of an intermediate court of errors and appeals, which shall relieve the Supreme Court of a part of its jurisdiction, while a larger force is also obtained for the performance of circuit duties.

I commend this suggestion to the consideration of Congress. It would seem to afford a complete remedy, and would involve, if ten additional circuit judges are appointed, an expenditure, at the present rate of salaries, of not more than $60,000 a year, which would certainly be small in comparison with the objects to be attained.

The report of the Postmaster-General bears testimony to the general revival of business throughout the country. The receipts of the Post-Office Department for the fiscal year ended June 30, 1879, were $30,041,-982.86, being $764,465.91 more than the revenues of the preceding year. The amount realized from the sale of postage stamps, stamped envelopes, and postal cards was $764,465.91 **more than** in the preceding year, and $2,387,559.23 more than in 1877. The expenditures of the Department were $33,449,899.45, of which the sum of $376,461.63 was paid on liabilities incurred in preceding years.

The expenditures during the year were $801,209.77 less than in the preceding year. This reduction is to be attributed mainly to the operation of the law passed June 17, 1878, changing the compensation of postmasters from a commission on the value of stamps sold to a commission on stamps canceled.

The amount drawn from the Treasury on appropriations, in addition to the revenues of the Department, was $3,031,454.96, being $2,276,197.86 less than in the preceding year.

The expenditures for the fiscal year ending June 30, 1881, are estimated at $39,920,900 and the receipts from all sources at $32,210,000, leaving a deficiency to be appropriated for out of the Treasury of $7,710,900.

The relations of the Department with railroad companies have been harmonized, notwithstanding the general reduction by Congress of their compensation by the appropriation for special facilities, and the railway post-office lines have been greatly extended, especially in the Southern States. The interests of the Railway Mail Service and of the public would be greatly promoted and the expenditures could be more readily controlled by the classification of the employees of the Railway Mail Service as recommended by the Postmaster-General, the appropriation for salaries, with respect to which the maximum limit is already fixed by law, to be made in gross.

The Postmaster-General recommends an amendment of the law regulating the increase of compensation for increased service and increased speed on star routes, so as to enable him to advertise for proposals for such increased service and speed. He also suggests the advantages to accrue to the commerce of the country from the enactment of a general law authorizing contracts with American-built steamers, carrying the American flag, for transporting the mail between ports of the United States and ports of the West Indies and South America, at a fixed maximum price per mile, the amount to be expended being regulated by annual appropriations, in like manner with the amount paid for the domestic star service.

The arrangement made by the Postmaster-General and the Secretary of the Treasury for the collection of duty upon books received in the mail from foreign countries has proved so satisfactory in its practical operation that the recommendation is now made that Congress shall extend the provisions of the act of March 3, 1879, under which this arrangement was made, so as to apply to all other dutiable articles received in the mails from foreign countries.

The reports of the Secretary of the Interior and of the Commissioner of Indian Affairs, setting forth the present state of our relations with the Indian tribes on our territory, the measures taken to advance their civilization and prosperity, and the progress already achieved by them, will be found of more than ordinary interest. The general conduct of our Indian population has been so satisfactory that the occurrence of two disturbances, which resulted in bloodshed and destruction of property, is all the more to be lamented.

The history of the outbreak on the White River Ute Reservation, in western Colorado, has become so familiar by elaborate reports in the public press that its remarkable incidents need not be stated here in detail. It is expected that the settlement of this difficulty will lead to such arrangements as will prevent further hostile contact between the Indians and the border settlements in western Colorado.

The other disturbance occurred at the Mescalero Agency, in New

Mexico, where Victoria, at the head of a small band of marauders, after committing many atrocities, being vigorously chased by a military force, made his way across the Mexican border and is now on foreign soil.

While these occurrences, in which a conparatively small number of Indians were engaged, are most deplorable, a vast majority of our Indian population have fully justified the expectations of those who believe that by humane and peaceful influences the Indian can be led to abandon the habits of savage life and to develop a capacity for useful and civilized occupations. What they have already accomplished in the pursuit of agricultural and mechanical work, the remarkable success which has attended the experiment of employing as freighters a class of Indians hitherto counted among the wildest and most intractable, and the general and urgent desire expressed by them for the education of their children may be taken as sufficient proof that they will be found capable of accomplishing much more if they continue to be wisely and fairly guided. The "Indian policy" sketched in the report of the Secretary of the Interior, the object of which is to make liberal provision for the education of Indian youth, to settle the Indians upon farm lots in severalty, to give them title in fee to their farms, inalienable for a certain number of years, and when their wants are thus provided for to dispose by sale of the lands on their reservations not occupied and used by them, a fund to be formed out of the proceeds for the benefit of the Indians which will gradually relieve the Government of the expenses now provided for by annual appropriations, must commend itself as just and beneficial to the Indians, and as also calculated to remove those obstructions which the existence of large reservations presents to the settlement and development of the country. I therefore earnestly recommend the enactment of a law enabling the Government to give Indians a title in fee, inalienable for twenty-five years, to the farm lands assigned to them by allotment. I also repeat the recommendation made in my first annual message, that a law be passed admitting Indians who can give satisfactory proof of having by their own labor supported their families for a number of years, and who are willing to detach themselves from their tribal relations, to the benefit of the homestead act, and to grant them patents containing the same provision of inalienability for a certain period.

The experiment of sending a number of Indian children of both sexes to the Hampton Normal and Agricultural Institute, in Virginia, to receive an elementary English education and practical instruction in farming and other useful industries, has led to results so promising that it was thought expedient to turn over the cavalry barracks at Carlisle, in Pennsylvania, to the Interior Department for the establishment of an Indian school on a larger scale. This school has now 158 pupils, selected from various tribes, and is in full operation. Arrangements are also made for the education of a number of Indian boys and girls belonging to tribes on the Pacific Slope in a similar manner, at Forest Grove, in Oregon.

These institutions will commend themselves to the liberality of Congress and to the philanthropic munificence of the American people.

Last spring information was received of the organization of an extensive movement in the Western States, the object of which was the occupation by unauthorized persons of certain lands in the Indian Territory ceded by the Cherokees to the Government for the purpose of settlement by other Indian tribes.

On the 26th of April I issued a proclamation warning all persons against participation in such an attempt, and by the cooperation of a military force the invasion was promptly checked. It is my purpose to protect the rights of the Indian inhabitants of that Territory to the full extent of the executive power; but it would be unwise to ignore the fact that a territory so large and so fertile, with a population so sparse and with so great a wealth of unused resources, will be found more exposed to the repetition of such attempts as happened this year when the surrounding States are more densely settled and the westward movement of our population looks still more eagerly for fresh lands to occupy. Under such circumstances the difficulty of maintaining the Indian Territory in its present state will greatly increase, and the Indian tribes inhabiting it would do well to prepare for such a contingency. I therefore fully approve of the advice given to them by the Secretary of the Interior on a recent occasion, to divide among themselves in severalty as large a quantity of their lands as they can cultivate; to acquire individual title in fee instead of their present tribal ownership in common, and to consider in what manner the balance of their lands may be disposed of by the Government for their benefit. By adopting such a policy they would more certainly secure for themselves the value of their possessions, and at the same time promote their progress in civilization and prosperity, than by endeavoring to perpetuate the present state of things in the Territory.

The question whether a change in the control of the Indian service should be made was in the Forty-fifth Congress referred to a joint committee of both Houses for inquiry and report. In my last annual message I expressed the hope that the decision of that question, then in prospect, would "arrest further agitation of this subject, such agitation being apt to produce a disturbing effect upon the service as well as on the Indians themselves." Since then, the committee having reported, the question has been decided in the negative by a vote in the House of Representatives.

For the reasons here stated, and in view of the fact that further uncertainty on this point will be calculated to obstruct other much-needed legislation, to weaken the discipline of the service, and to unsettle salutary measures now in progress for the government and improvement of the Indians, I respectfully recommend that the decision arrived at by Congress at its last session be permitted to stand.

The efforts made by the Department of the Interior to arrest the depredations on the timber lands of the United States have been continued, and have met with considerable success. A large number of cases of trespass have been prosecuted in the courts of the United States; others have been settled, the trespassers offering to make payment to the Government for the value of the timber taken by them. The proceeds of these prosecutions and settlements turned into the Treasury far exceed in amount the sums appropriated by Congress for this purpose. A more important result, however, consists in the fact that the destruction of our public forests by depredation, although such cases still occur, has been greatly reduced in extent, and it is probable that if the present policy is vigorously pursued and sufficient provision to that end is made by Congress such trespasses, at least those on a large scale, can be entirely suppressed, except in the Territories, where timber for the daily requirements of the population can not, under the present state of the law, be otherwise obtained. I therefore earnestly invite the attention of Congress to the recommendation made by the Secretary of the Interior, that a law be enacted enabling the Government to sell timber from the public lands without conveying the fee, where such lands are principally valuable for the timber thereon, such sales to be so regulated as to conform to domestic wants and business requirements, while at the same time guarding against a sweeping destruction of the forests. The enactment of such a law appears to become a more pressing necessity every day.

My recommendations in former messages are renewed in favor of enlarging the facilities of the Department of Agriculture. Agriculture is the leading interest and the permanent industry of our people. It is to the abundance of agricultural production, as compared with our home consumption, and the largely increased and highly profitable market abroad which we have enjoyed in recent years, that we are mainly indebted for our present prosperity as a people. We must look for its continued maintenance to the same substantial resource. There is no branch of industry in which labor, directed by scientific knowledge, yields such increased production in comparison with unskilled labor, and no branch of the public service to which the encouragement of liberal appropriations can be more appropriately extended. The omission to render such aid is not a wise economy, but, on the contrary, undoubtedly results in losses of immense sums annually that might be saved through well-directed efforts by the Government to promote this vital interest.

The results already accomplished with the very limited means heretofore placed at the command of the Department of Agriculture is an earnest of what may be expected with increased appropriations for the several purposes indicated in the report of the Commissioner, with a view to placing the Department upon a footing which will enable it to prosecute more effectively the objects for which it is established.

Appropriations are needed for a more complete laboratory, for the establishment of a veterinary division and a division of forestry, and for an increase of force.

The requirements for these and other purposes, indicated in the report of the Commissioner under the head of the immediate necessities of the Department, will not involve any expenditure of money that the country can not with propriety now undertake in the interests of agriculture.

It is gratifying to learn from the Bureau of Education the extent to which educational privileges throughout the United States have been advanced during the year. No more fundamental responsibility rests upon Congress than that of devising appropriate measures of financial aid to education, supplemental to local action in the States and Territories and in the District of Columbia. The wise forethought of the founders of our Government has not only furnished the basis for the support of the common-school systems of the newer States, but laid the foundations for the maintenance of their universities and colleges of agriculture and the mechanic arts. Measures in accordance with this traditional policy, for the further benefit of all these interests and the extension of the same advantages to every portion of the country, it is hoped will receive your favorable consideration.

To preserve and perpetuate the national literature should be among the foremost cares of the National Legislature. The library gathered at the Capitol still remains unprovided with any suitable accommodations for its rapidly increasing stores. The magnitude and importance of the collection, increased as it is by the deposits made under the law of copyright, by domestic and foreign exchanges, and by the scientific library of the Smithsonian Institution, call for building accommodations which shall be at once adequate and fireproof. The location of such a public building, which should provide for the pressing necessities of the present and for the vast increase of the nation's books in the future, is a matter which addresses itself to the discretion of Congress. It is earnestly recommended as a measure which should unite all suffrages and which should no longer be delayed.

The joint commission created by the act of Congress of August 2, 1876, for the purpose of supervising and directing the completion of the Washington National Monument, of which commission the President is a member, has given careful attention to this subject, and already the strengthening of the foundation has so far progressed as to insure the entire success of this part of the work. A massive layer of masonry has been introduced below the original foundation, widening the base, increasing the stability of the structure, and rendering it possible to carry the shaft to completion. It is earnestly recommended that such further appropriations be made for the continued prosecution of the work as may be necessary for the completion of this national monument at an early day.

In former messages, impressed with the importance of the subject, I have taken occasion to commend to Congress the adoption of a generous policy toward the District of Columbia. The report of the Commissioners of the District, herewith transmitted, contains suggestions and recommendations, to all of which I earnestly invite your careful attention. I ask your early and favorable consideration of the views which they express as to the urgent need of legislation for the reclamation of the marshes of the Potomac and its Eastern Branch within the limits of the city, and for the repair of the streets of the capital, heretofore laid with wooden blocks and now by decay rendered almost impassable and a source of imminent danger to the health of its citizens. The means at the disposal of the Commissioners are wholly inadequate for the accomplishment of these important works, and should be supplemented by timely appropriations from the Federal Treasury.

The filling of the flats in front of the city will add to the adjacent lands and parks now owned by the United States a large and valuable domain, sufficient, it is thought, to reimburse its entire cost, and will also, as an incidental result, secure the permanent improvement of the river for the purposes of navigation.

The Constitution having invested Congress with supreme and exclusive jurisdiction over the District of Columbia, its citizens must of necessity look to Congress alone for all needful legislation affecting their interests; and as the territory of this District is the common property of the people of the United States, who equally with its resident citizens are interested in the prosperity of their capital, I can not doubt that you will be amply sustained by the general voice of the country in any measures you may adopt for this purpose.

I also invite the favorable consideration of Congress to the wants of the public schools of this District, as exhibited in the report of the Commissioners. While the number of pupils is rapidly increasing, no adequate provision exists for a corresponding increase of school accommodation, and the Commissioners are without the means to meet this urgent need. A number of the buildings now used for school purposes are rented, and are in important particulars unsuited for the purpose. The cause of popular education in the District of Columbia is surely entitled to the same consideration at the hands of the National Government as in the several States and Territories, to which munificent grants of the public lands have been made for the endowment of schools and universities.

FOURTH ANNUAL MESSAGE.

EXECUTIVE MANSION, *December 6, 1880.*

Fellow-Citizens of the Senate and House of Representatives:

I congratulate you on the continued and increasing prosperity of our country. By the favor of Divine Providence we have been blessed during the past year with health, with abundant harvests, with profitable employment for all our people, and with contentment at home, and with peace and friendship with other nations. The occurrence of the twenty-fourth election of Chief Magistrate has afforded another opportunity to the people of the United States to exhibit to the world a significant example of the peaceful and safe transmission of the power and authority of government from the public servants whose terms of office are about to expire to their newly chosen successors. This example can not fail to impress profoundly thoughtful people of other countries with the advantages which republican institutions afford. The immediate, general, and cheerful acquiescence of all good citizens in the result of the election gives gratifying assurance to our country and to its friends throughout the world that a government based on the free consent of an intelligent and patriotic people possesses elements of strength, stability, and permanency not found in any other form of government.

Continued opposition to the full and free enjoyment of the rights of citizenship conferred upon the colored people by the recent amendments to the Constitution still prevails in several of the late slaveholding States. It has, perhaps, not been manifested in the recent election to any large extent in acts of violence or intimidation. It has, however, by fraudulent practices in connection with the ballots, with the regulations as to the places and manner of voting, and with counting, returning, and canvassing the votes cast, been successful in defeating the exercise of the right preservative of all rights—the right of suffrage—which the Constitution expressly confers upon our enfranchised citizens.

It is the desire of the good people of the whole country that sectionalism as a factor in our politics should disappear. They prefer that no section of the country should be united in solid opposition to any other section. The disposition to refuse a prompt and hearty obedience to the equal-rights amendments to the Constitution is all that now stands in the way of a complete obliteration of sectional lines in our political contests. As long as either of these amendments is flagrantly violated or disregarded, it is safe to assume that the people who placed them in the Constitution, as embodying the legitimate results of the war for the Union, and who believe them to be wise and necessary, will continue to act together and to insist that they shall be obeyed. The paramount question still is as to the enjoyment of the right by every American citizen who has the requisite qualifications to freely cast his vote and to have it honestly counted. With this question rightly settled, the country will be relieved of the contentions of the past; bygones will indeed be bygones, and political and party issues, with respect to economy and efficiency of administration, internal improvements, the tariff, domestic taxation, education, finance, and other important subjects, will then receive their full share of attention; but resistance to and nullification of the results of the war will unite together in resolute purpose for their support all who maintain the authority of the Government and the perpetuity of the Union, and who adequately appreciate the value of the victory achieved. This determination proceeds from no hostile sentiment or feeling to any part of the people of our country or to any of their interests. The inviolability of the amendments rests upon the fundamental principle of our Government. They are the solemn expression of the will of the people of the United States.

The sentiment that the constitutional rights of all our citizens must be maintained does not grow weaker. It will continue to control the Government of the country. Happily, the history of the late election shows that in many parts of the country where opposition to the fifteenth amendment has heretofore prevailed it is diminishing, and is likely to cease altogether if firm and well-considered action is taken by Congress. I trust the House of Representatives and the Senate, which have the right to judge of the elections, returns, and qualifications of their own members, will see to it that every case of violation of the letter or spirit of the fifteenth amendment is thoroughly investigated, and that no benefit from such violation shall accrue to any person or party. It will be the duty of the Executive, with sufficient appropriations for the purpose, to prosecute unsparingly all who have been engaged in depriving citizens of the rights guaranteed to them by the Constitution.

It is not, however, to be forgotten that the best and surest guaranty of the primary rights of citizenship is to be found in that capacity for self-protection which can belong only to a people whose right to universal suffrage is supported by universal education. The means at the command of the local and State authorities are in many cases wholly inadequate to furnish free instruction to all who need it. This is especially true where before emancipation the education of the people was neglected or prevented, in the interest of slavery. Firmly convinced that the subject of popular education deserves the earnest attention of the people of the whole country, with a view to wise and comprehensive action by the Government of the United States, I respectfully recommend that Congress, by suitable legislation and with proper safeguards, supplement the local educational funds in the several States where the grave duties and responsibilities of citizenship have been devolved on uneducated people by devoting to the purpose grants of the public lands and, if necessary, by appropriations from the Treasury of the United States. Whatever

Government can fairly do to promote free popular education ought to be done. Wherever general education is found, peace, virtue, and social order prevail and civil and religious liberty are secure.

In my former annual messages I have asked the attention of Congress to the urgent necessity of a reformation of the civil-service system of the Government. My views concerning the dangers of patronage, or appointments for personal or partisan considerations, have been strengthened by my observation and experience in the Executive office, and I believe these dangers threaten the stability of the Government. Abuses so serious in their nature can not be permanently tolerated. They tend to become more alarming with the enlargement of administrative service, as the growth of the country in population increases the number of officers and placemen employed.

The reasons are imperative for the adoption of fixed rules for the regulation of appointments, promotions, and removals, establishing a uniform method having exclusively in view in every instance the attainment of the best qualifications for the position in question. Such a method alone is consistent with the equal rights of all citizens and the most economical and efficient administration of the public business.

Competitive examinations in aid of impartial appointments and promotions have been conducted for some years past in several of the Executive Departments, and by my direction this system has been adopted in the custom-houses and post-offices of the larger cities of the country. In the city of New York over 2,000 positions in the civil service have been subject in their appointments and tenure of place to the operation of published rules for this purpose during the past two years. The results of these practical trials have been very satisfactory, and have confirmed my opinion in favor of this system of selection. All are subjected to the same tests, and the result is free from prejudice by personal favor or partisan influence. It secures for the position applied for the best qualifications attainable among the competing applicants. It is an effectual protection from the pressure of importunity, which under any other course pursued largely exacts the time and attention of appointing officers, to their great detriment in the discharge of other official duties preventing the abuse of the service for the mere furtherance of private or party purposes, and leaving the employee of the Government, freed from the obligations imposed by patronage, to depend solely upon merit for retention and advancement, and with this constant incentive to exertion and improvement.

These invaluable results have been attained in a high degree in the offices where the rules for appointment by competitive examination have been applied.

A method which has so approved itself by experimental tests at points where such tests may be fairly considered conclusive should be extended to all subordinate positions under the Government. I believe that a strong and growing public sentiment demands immediate measures for securing and enforcing the highest possible efficiency in the civil service and its protection from recognized abuses, and that the experience referred to has demonstrated the feasibility of such measures.

The examinations in the custom-houses and post-offices have been held under many embarrassments and without provision for compensation for the extra labor performed by the officers who have conducted them, and whose commendable interest in the improvement of the public service has induced this devotion of time and labor without pecuniary reward. A continuance of these labors gratuitously ought not to be expected, and without an appropriation by Congress for compensation it is not practicable to extend the system of examinations generally throughout the civil service. It is also highly important that all such examinations should be conducted upon a uniform system and under general supervision. Section 1753 of the Revised Statutes authorizes the President to prescribe the regulations for admission to the civil service of the United States, and for this purpose to employ suitable persons to conduct the requisite inquiries with reference to "the fitness of each candidate, in respect to age, health, character, knowledge, and ability for the branch of service into which he seeks to enter;" but the law is practically inoperative for want of the requisite appropriation.

I therefore recommend an appropriation of $25,000 per annum to meet the expenses of a commission, to be appointed by the President in accordance with the terms of this section, whose duty it shall be to devise a just, uniform, and efficient system of competitive examinations and to supervise the application of the same throughout the entire civil service of the Government. I am persuaded that the facilities which such a commission will afford for testing the fitness of those who apply for office will not only be as welcome a relief to members of Congress as it will be to the President and heads of Departments, but that it will also greatly tend to remove the causes of embarrassment which now inevitably and constantly attend the conflicting claims of patronage between the legislative and executive departments. The most effectual check upon the pernicious competition of influence and official favoritism in the bestowal of office will be the substitution of an open competition of merit between the applicants, in which everyone can make his own record with the assurance that his success will depend upon this alone.

I also recommend such legislation as, while leaving every officer as free as any other citizen to express his political opinions and to use his means for their advancement, shall also enable him to feel as safe as any private citizen in refusing all demands upon his salary for political purposes. A law which should thus guarantee true liberty and justice to all who are engaged in the public service, and likewise contain stringent provisions against the use of official authority to coerce the political action of private citizens or of official subordinates, is greatly to be desired.

The most serious obstacle, however, to an improvement of the civil service, and especially to a reform in the method of appointment and removal, has been found to be the practice, under what is known as the spoils system, by which the appointing power has been so largely encroached upon by members of Congress. The first step in the reform of the civil service must be a complete divorce between Congress and the Executive in the matter of appointments. The corrupting doctrine that "to the victors belong the spoils" is inseparable from Congressional patronage as the established rule and practice of parties in power. It comes to be understood by applicants for office and by the people generally that Representatives and Senators are entitled to disburse the patronage of their respective districts and States. It is not necessary to recite at length the evils resulting from this invasion of the Executive functions. The true principles of Government on the subject of appointments to office, as stated in the national conventions of the leading parties of the country, have again and again been approved by the American people, and have not been called in question in any quarter. These authentic expressions of public opinion upon this all-important subject are the statement of principles that belong to the constitutional structure of the Government.

Under the Constitution the President and heads of Departments are to make nominations for office. The Senate is to advise and consent to appointments, and the House of Representatives is to accuse and prosecute faithless officers. The best interest of the public service demands that these distinctions be respected; that Senators and Representatives, who may be judges and accusers, should not dictate appointments to office.

To this end the cooperation of the legislative department of the Government is required alike by the necessities of the case and by public opinion. Members of Congress will not be relieved from the demands made upon them with reference to appointments to office until by legislative enactment the pernicious practice is condemned and forbidden.

It is therefore recommended that an act be passed defining the relations of members of Congress with respect to appointment to office by the President; and I also recommend that the provisions of section 1767 and of the sections following of the Revised Statutes, comprising the tenure-of-office act of March 2, 1867, be repealed.

Believing that to reform the system and methods of the civil service in our country is one of the highest and most imperative duties of statesmanship, and that it can be permanently done only by the cooperation of the legislative and executive departments of the Government, I again commend the whole subject to your considerate attention.

It is the recognized duty and purpose of the people of the United States to suppress polygamy where it now exists in our Territories and to prevent its extension.   Faithful and zealous efforts have been made by the United States authorities in Utah to enforce the laws against it. Experience has shown that the legislation upon this subject, to be effective, requires extensive modification and amendment.   The longer action is delayed the more difficult it will be to accomplish what is desired. Prompt and decided measures are necessary.   The Mormon sectarian organization which upholds polygamy has the whole power of making and executing the local legislation of the Territory.   By its control of the grand and petit juries it possesses large influence over the administration of justice.   Exercising, as the heads of this sect do, the local political power of the Territory, they are able to make effective their hostility to the law of Congress on the subject of polygamy, and, in fact, do prevent its enforcement.   Polygamy will not be abolished if the enforcement of the law depends on those who practice and uphold the crime.   It can only be suppressed by taking away the political power of the sect which encourages and sustains it.

The power of Congress to enact suitable laws to protect the Territories is ample.   It is not a case for halfway measures.   The political power of the Mormon sect is increasing.   It controls now one of our wealthiest and most populous Territories.   It is extending steadily into other Territories.   Wherever it goes it establishes polygamy and sectarian political power.   The sanctity of marriage and the family relation are the corner stone of our American society and civilization.   Religious liberty and the separation of church and state are among the elementary ideas of free institutions.   To reestablish the interests and principles which polygamy and Mormonism have imperiled, and to fully reopen to intelligent and virtuous immigrants of all creeds that part of our domain which has been in a great degree closed to general immigration by intolerant and immoral institutions, it is recommended that the government of the Territory of Utah be reorganized.

I recommend that Congress provide for the government of Utah by a governor and judges, or commissioners, appointed by the President and confirmed by the Senate—a government analogous to the provisional government established for the territory northwest of the Ohio by the ordinance of 1787.   If, however, it is deemed best to continue the existing form of local government, I recommend that the right to vote, hold office, and sit on juries in the Territory of Utah be confined to those who neither practice nor uphold polygamy.   If thorough measures are adopted, it is believed that within a few years the evils which now afflict Utah will be eradicated, and that this Territory will in good time become one of the most prosperous and attractive of the new States of the Union.

Our relations with all foreign countries have been those of undisturbed peace, and have presented no occasion for concern as to their continued maintenance.

My anticipation of an early reply from the British Government to the demand of indemnity to our fishermen for the injuries suffered by that industry at Fortune Bay in January, 1878, which I expressed in my last annual message, was disappointed. This answer was received only in the latter part of April in the present year, and when received exhibited a failure of accord between the two Governments as to the measure of the inshore fishing privilege secured to our fishermen by the treaty of Washington of so serious a character that I made it the subject of a communication to Congress, in which I recommended the adoption of the measures which seemed to me proper to be taken by this Government in maintenance of the rights accorded to our fishermen under the treaty and toward securing an indemnity for the injury these interests had suffered. A bill to carry out these recommendations was under consideration by the House of Representatives at the time of the adjournment of Congress in June last.

Within a few weeks I have received a communication from Her Majesty's Government renewing the consideration of the subject, both of the indemnity for the injuries at Fortune Bay and of the interpretation of the treaty in which the previous correspondence had shown the two Governments to be at variance. Upon both these topics the disposition toward a friendly agreement is manifested by a recognition of our right to an indemnity for the transaction at Fortune Bay, leaving the measure of such indemnity to further conference, and by an assent to the view of this Government, presented in the previous correspondence, that the regulation of conflicting interests of the shore fishery of the provincial sea-coasts and the vessel fishery of our fishermen should be made the subject of conference and concurrent arrangement between the two Governments.

I sincerely hope that the basis may be found for a speedy adjustment of the very serious divergence of views in the interpretation of the fishery clauses of the treaty of Washington, which, as the correspondence between the two Governments stood at the close of the last session of Congress, seemed to be irreconcilable.

In the important exhibition of arts and industries which was held last year at Sydney, New South Wales, as well as in that now in progress at Melbourne, the United States have been efficiently and honorably represented. The exhibitors from this country at the former place received a large number of awards in some of the most considerable departments, and the participation of the United States was recognized by a special mark of distinction. In the exhibition at Melbourne the share taken by our country is no less notable, and an equal degree of success is confidently expected.

The state of peace and tranquillity now enjoyed by all the nations of the continent of Europe has its favorable influence upon our diplomatic and commercial relations with them. We have concluded and ratified a convention with the French Republic for the settlement of claims of the citizens of either country against the other. Under this convention a

commission, presided over by a distinguished publicist, appointed in pur·
suance of the request of both nations by His Majesty the Emperor of
Brazil, has been organized and has begun its sessions in this city.   A
congress to consider means for the protection of industrial property has
recently been in session in Paris, to which I have appointed the ministers
of the United States in France and in Belgium as delegates.   The International Commission upon Weights and Measures also continues its work
in Paris.   I invite your attention to the necessity of an appropriation to
be made in time to enable this Government to comply with its obligations under the metrical convention.

Our friendly relations with the German Empire continue without interruption.   At the recent International Exhibition of Fish and Fisheries at Berlin the participation of the United States, notwithstanding the
haste with which the commission was forced to make its preparations,
was extremely successful and meritorious, winning for private exhibitors
numerous awards of a high class and for the country at large the principal prize of honor offered by His Majesty the Emperor.   The results of
this great success can not but be advantageous to this important and
growing industry.   There have been some questions raised between the
two Governments as to the proper effect and interpretation of our treaties of naturalization, but recent dispatches from our minister at Berlin
show that favorable progress is making toward an understanding in
accordance with the views of this Government, which makes and admits
no distinction whatever between the rights of a native and a naturalized
citizen of the United States.   In practice the complaints of molestation
suffered by naturalized citizens abroad have never been fewer than at
present.

There is nothing of importance to note in our unbroken friendly relations with the Governments of Austria-Hungary, Russia, Portugal,
Sweden and Norway, Switzerland, Turkey, and Greece.

During the last summer several vessels belonging to the merchant
marine of this country, sailing in neutral waters of the West Indies, were
fired at, boarded, and searched by an armed cruiser of the Spanish Government.   The circumstances as reported involve not only a private
injury to the persons concerned, but also seemed too little observant of
the friendly relations existing for a century between this country and
Spain.   The wrong was brought to the attention of the Spanish Government in a serious protest and remonstrance, and the matter is undergoing investigation by the royal authorities with a view to such explanation
or reparation as may be called for by the facts.

The commission sitting in this city for the adjudication of claims of
our citizens against the Government of Spain is, I hope, approaching
the termination of its labors.

The claims against the United States under the Florida treaty with
Spain were submitted to Congress for its action at the late session, and

I again invite your attention to this long-standing question, with a view to a final disposition of the matter.

At the invitation of the Spanish Government, a conference has recently been held at the city of Madrid to consider the subject of protection by foreign powers of native Moors in the Empire of Morocco. The minister of the United States in Spain was directed to take part in the deliberations of this conference, the result of which is a convention signed on behalf of all the powers represented. The instrument will be laid before the Senate for its consideration. The Government of the United States has also lost no opportunity to urge upon that of the Emperor of Morocco the necessity, in accordance with the humane and enlightened spirit of the age, of putting an end to the persecutions, which have been so prevalent in that country, of persons of a faith other than the Moslem, and especially of the Hebrew residents of Morocco.

The consular treaty concluded with Belgium has not yet been officially promulgated, owing to the alteration of a word in the text by the Senate of the United States, which occasioned a delay, during which the time allowed for ratification expired. The Senate will be asked to extend the period for ratification.

The attempt to negotiate a treaty of extradition with Denmark failed on account of the objection of the Danish Government to the usual clause providing that each nation should pay the expense of the arrest of the persons whose extradition it asks.

The provision made by Congress at its last session for the expense of the commission which had been appointed to enter upon negotiations with the Imperial Government of China on subjects of great interest to the relations of the two countries enabled the commissioners to proceed at once upon their mission. The Imperial Government was prepared to give prompt and respectful attention to the matters brought under negotiation, and the conferences proceeded with such rapidity and success that on the 17th of November last two treaties were signed at Peking, one relating to the introduction of Chinese into this country and one relating to commerce. Mr. Trescot, one of the commissioners, is now on his way home bringing the treaties, and it is expected that they will be received in season to be laid before the Senate early in January.

Our minister in Japan has negotiated a convention for the reciprocal relief of shipwrecked seamen. I take occasion to urge once more upon Congress the propriety of making provision for the erection of suitable fireproof buildings at the Japanese capital for the use of the American legation and the court-house and jail connected with it. The Japanese Government, with great generosity and courtesy, has offered for this purpose an eligible piece of land.

In my last annual message I invited the attention of Congress to the subject of the indemnity funds received some years ago from China and Japan. I renew the recommendation then made that whatever portions of these runas are due to American citizens should be promptly paid and the residue returned to the nations, respectively, to which they justly and equitably belong.

The extradition treaty with the Kingdom of the Netherlands, which has been for some time in course of negotiation, has during the past year been concluded and duly ratified.

Relations of friendship and amity have been established between the Government of the United States and that of Roumania. We have sent a diplomatic representative to Bucharest, and have received at this capital the special envoy who has been charged by His Royal Highness Prince Charles to announce the independent sovereignty of Roumania. We hope for a speedy development of commercial relations between the two countries.

In my last annual message I expressed the hope that the prevalence of quiet on the border between this country and Mexico would soon become so assured as to justify the modification of the orders then in force to our military commanders in regard to crossing the frontier, without encouraging such disturbances as would endanger the peace of the two countries. Events moved in accordance with these expectations, and the orders were accordingly withdrawn, to the entire satisfaction of our own citizens and the Mexican Government. Subsequently the peace of the border was again disturbed by a savage foray under the command of the Chief Victoria, but by the combined and harmonious action of the military forces of both countries his band has been broken up and substantially destroyed.

There is reason to believe that the obstacles which have so long prevented rapid and convenient communication between the United States and Mexico by railways are on the point of disappearing, and that several important enterprises of this character will soon be set on foot, which can not fail to contribute largely to the prosperity of both countries.

New envoys from Guatemala, Colombia, Bolivia, Venezuela, and Nicaragua have recently arrived at this capital, whose distinction and enlightenment afford the best guaranty of the continuance of friendly relations between ourselves and these sister Republics.

The relations between this Government and that of the United States of Colombia have engaged public attention during the past year, mainly by reason of the project of an interoceanic canal across the Isthmus of Panama, to be built by private capital under a concession from the Colombian Government for that purpose. The treaty obligations subsisting between the United States and Colombia, by which we guarantee the neutrality of the transit and the sovereignty and property of Colombia in the Isthmus, make it necessary that the conditions under which so stupendous a change in the region embraced in this guaranty should be effected— transforming, as it would, this Isthmus from a barrier between the Atlantic and Pacific oceans into a gateway and thoroughfare between them for the navies and the merchant ships of the world—should receive the approval of this Government, as being compatible with the discharge of these obligations on our part and consistent with our interests as the principal commercial power of the Western Hemisphere. The views which I expressed in a special message to Congress in March last in relation to this project I deem it my duty again to press upon your attention. Subsequent consideration has but confirmed the opinion "that it is the right and duty of the United States to assert and maintain such supervision and authority over any interoceanic canal across the isthmus that connects North and South America as will protect our national interest."

The war between the Republic of Chile on the one hand and the allied Republics of Peru and Bolivia on the other still continues. This Government has not felt called upon to interfere in a contest that is within the belligerent rights of the parties as independent states. We have, however, always held ourselves in readiness to aid in accommodating their difference, and have at different times reminded both belligerents of our willingness to render such service.

Our good offices in this direction were recently accepted by all the belligerents, and it was hoped they would prove efficacious; but I regret to announce that the measures which the ministers of the United States at Santiago and Lima were authorized to take with the view to bring about a peace were not successful. In the course of the war some questions have arisen affecting neutral rights. In all of these the ministers of the United States have, under their instructions, acted with promptness and energy in protection of American interests.

The relations of the United States with the Empire of Brazil continue to be most cordial, and their commercial intercourse steadily increases, to their mutual advantage.

The internal disorders with which the Argentine Republic has for some time past been afflicted, and which have more or less influenced its external trade, are understood to have been brought to a close. This happy result may be expected to redound to the benefit of the foreign commerce of that Republic, as well as to the development of its vast interior resources.

In Samoa the Government of King Malietoa, under the support and recognition of the consular representatives of the United States, Great Britain, and Germany, seems to have given peace and tranquillity to the islands. While it does not appear desirable to adopt as a whole the scheme of tripartite local government which has been proposed, the common interests of the three great treaty powers require harmony in their relations to the native frame of government, and this may be best secured by a simple diplomatic agreement between them. It would be well if the consular jurisdiction of our representative at Apia were increased in extent and importance so as to guard American interests in the surrounding and outlying islands of Oceanica.

The obelisk generously presented by the Khedive of Egypt to the city of New York has safely arrived in this country, and will soon be erected in that metropolis. A commission for the liquidation of the Egyptian debt has lately concluded its work, and this Government, at the earnest solicitation of the Khedive, has acceded to the provisions adopted by it, which will be laid before Congress for its information. A commission for the revision of the judicial code of the reform tribunal of Egypt is now in session in Cairo. Mr. Farman, consul-general, and J. M. Batchelder, esq., have been appointed as commissioners to participate in this work. The organization of the reform tribunals will probably be continued for another period of five years.

In pursuance of the act passed at the last session of Congress, invitations have been extended to foreign maritime states to join in a sanitary conference in Washington, beginning the 1st of January. The acceptance of this invitation by many prominent powers gives promise of success in this important measure, designed to establish a system of international notification by which the spread of infectious or epidemic diseases may be more effectively checked or prevented. The attention of Congress is invited to the necessary appropriations for carrying into effect the provisions of the act referred to.

The efforts of the Department of State to enlarge the trade and commerce of the United States, through the active agency of consular officers and through the dissemination of information obtained from them, have been unrelaxed. The interest in these efforts, as developed in our commercial communities, and the value of the information secured by this means to the trade and manufactures of the country were recognized by Congress at its last session, and provision was made for the more frequent publication of consular and other reports by the Department of State. The first issue of this publication has now been prepared, and subsequent issues may regularly be expected. The importance and interest attached to the reports of consular officers are witnessed by the general demand for them by all classes of merchants and manufacturers engaged in our foreign trade. It is believed that the system of such publications is deserving of the approval of Congress, and that the necessary appropriations for its continuance and enlargement will commend itself to your consideration.

The prosperous energies of our domestic industries and their immense production of the subjects of foreign commerce invite, and even require, an active development of the wishes and interests of our people in that direction. Especially important is it that our commercial relations with the Atlantic and Pacific coasts of South America, with the West Indies and the Gulf of Mexico, should be direct, and not through the circuit of European systems, and should be carried on in our own bottoms. The full appreciation of the opportunities which our front on the Pacific Ocean gives to commerce with Japan, China, and the East Indies, with Australia and the island groups which lie along these routes of navigation, should inspire equal efforts to appropriate to our own shipping and to administer by our own capital a due proportion of this trade. Whatever modifications of our regulations of trade and navigation may be necessary or useful to meet and direct these impulses to the enlargement of our exchanges and of our carrying trade I am sure the wisdom of Congress will be ready to supply. One initial measure, however, seems to me so clearly useful and efficient that I venture to press it upon your earnest attention. It seems to be very evident that the provision of regular steam postal communication by aid from government has been the forerunner of the commercial predominance of Great Britain on all these coasts and seas, a greater share in whose trade is now the desire and the intent of our people. It is also manifest that the efforts of other European nations to contend with Great Britain for a share of this commerce have been successful in proportion with their adoption of regular steam postal communication with the markets whose trade they sought. Mexico and the States of South America are anxious to receive such postal communication with this country and to aid in their development. Similar cooperation may be looked for in due time from the Eastern nations and from Australia. It is difficult to see how the lead in this movement can be expected from private interests. In respect of foreign commerce quite as much as in internal trade postal communication seems necessarily a matter of common and public administration, and thus pertaining to Government. I respectfully recommend to your prompt attention such just and efficient measures as may conduce to the development of our foreign commercial exchanges and the building up of our carrying trade.

In this connection I desire also to suggest the very great service which might be expected in enlarging and facilitating our commerce on the Pacific Ocean were a transmarine cable laid from San Francisco to the Sandwich Islands, and thence to Japan at the north and Australia at the south. The great influence of such means of communication on these routes of navigation in developing and securing the due share of our Pacific Coast in the commerce of the world needs no illustration or enforcement. It may be that such an enterprise, useful, and in the end profitable, as it would prove to private investment, may need to be accelerated by prudent legislation by Congress in its aid, and I submit the matter to your careful consideration.

An additional and not unimportant, although secondary, reason for fostering and enlarging the Navy may be found in the unquestionable service to the expansion of our commerce which would be rendered by the frequent circulation of naval ships in the seas and ports of all quarters of the globe. Ships of the proper construction and equipment to be of the greatest efficiency in case of maritime war might be made constant and active agents in time of peace in the advancement and protection of our foreign trade and in the nurture and discipline of young seamen, who would naturally in some numbers mix with and improve the crews of our merchant ships. Our merchants at home and abroad recognize the value to foreign commerce of an active movement of our naval vessels, and the intelligence and patriotic zeal of our naval officers in promoting every interest of their countrymen is a just subject of national pride.

The condition of the financial affairs of the Government, as shown by the report of the Secretary of the Treasury, is very satisfactory. It is believed that the present financial situation of the United States, whether considered with respect to trade, currency, credit, growing wealth, or the extent and variety of our resources, is more favorable than that of any other country of our time, and has never been surpassed by that of any country at any period of its history. All our industries are thriving; the rate of interest is low; new railroads are being constructed; a vast immigration is increasing our population, capital, and labor; new enterprises in great number are in progress, and our commercial relations with other countries are improving.

The ordinary revenues from all sources for the fiscal year ended June 30, 1880, were—

From customs`...	$186, 522, 064.60
From internal revenue..	124, 009, 373.92
From sales of public lands	1, 016, 506.60
From tax on circulation and deposits of national banks..................	7, 014, 971.44
From repayment of interest by Pacific Railway companies...............	1, 707, 367.18
From sinking fund for Pacific Railway companies.......................	786, 621.22
From customs fees, fines, penalties, etc	1, 148, 800.16
From fees—consular, letters patent, and lands...........................	2, 337, 029.00
From proceeds of sales of Government property.........................	282, 616.50
From profits on coinage, etc...	2, 792, 186.78
From revenues of the District of Columbia	1, 809, 469.70
From miscellaneous sources...	4, 099, 603.88
Total ordinary receipts...	333, 526, 610.98

The ordinary expenditures for the same period were—

For civil expenses..	$15, 693, 963.55
For foreign intercourse...	1, 211, 490.58
For Indians ....:................................	5, 945, 457.09
For pensions (including $19,341,025.20 arrears of pensions)...............	56, 777, 174.44
For the military establishment, including river and harbor improvements and arsenals..	38, 116, 916.22
For the naval establishment, including vessels, machinery, and improvements at navy-yards..	13, 536, 984.74
For miscellaneous expenditures, including public buildings, light-houses, and collecting the revenue..	34, 535, 691.00
For expenditures on account of the District of Columbia.................	3, 272, 384.63
For interest on the public debt...	95, 757, 575.11
For premium on bonds purchased.......................................	2, 795, 320.42

leaving a surplus revenue of $65,883,653.20, which, with an amount drawn from the cash balance in Treasury of $8,084,434.21, making $73,968,087.41, was applied to the redemption—

Of bonds for the sinking fund...	$73, 652, 900.00
Of fractional currency	251, 717.41
Of the loan of 1858...	40, 000.00
Of temporary loan	100.00
Of bounty-land scrip..	25.00
Of compound-interest notes	16, 500.00
Of 7.30 notes of 1864–65	2, 650.00
Of one and two year notes..	3, 700.00
Of old demand notes..	495.00
Total..	73, 968, 087.41

The amount due the sinking fund for this year was $37,931,643.55. There was applied thereto the sum of $73,904,617.41, being $35,972,-973.86 in excess of the actual requirements for the year.

The aggregate of the revenues from all sources during the fiscal year ended June 30, 1880, was $333,526,610.98, an increase over the preceding year of $59,699,426.52. The receipts thus far of the current year, together with the estimated receipts for the remainder of the year, amount to $350,000,000, which will be sufficient to meet the estimated expenditures of the year and leave a surplus of $90,000,000.

It is fortunate that this large surplus revenue occurs at a period when it may be directly applied to the payment of the public debt soon to be redeemable. No public duty has been more constantly cherished in the United States than the policy of paying the nation's debt as rapidly as possible.

The debt of the United States, less cash in the Treasury and exclusive of accruing interest, attained its maximum of $2,756,431,571.43 in August, 1865, and has since that time been reduced to $1,886,019,504.65. Of the principal of the debt, $108,758,100 has been paid since March 1, 1877, effecting an annual saving of interest of $6,107,593. The burden of interest has also been diminished by the sale of bonds bearing a low rate of interest and the application of the proceeds to the redemption of bonds bearing a higher rate. The annual saving thus secured since March 1, 1877, is $14,290,453.50. Within a short period over six hundred millions of 5 and 6 per cent bonds will become redeemable. This presents a very favorable opportunity not only to further reduce the principal of the debt, but also to reduce the rate of interest on that which will remain unpaid. I call the attention of Congress to the views expressed on this subject by the Secretary of the Treasury in his annual report, and recommend prompt legislation to enable the Treasury Department to complete the refunding of the debt which is about to mature.

The continuance of specie payments has not been interrupted or endangered since the date of resumption. It has contributed greatly to the revival of business and to our remarkable prosperity. The fears that preceded and accompanied resumption have proved groundless. No considerable amount of United States notes have been presented for redemption, while very large sums of gold bullion, both domestic and imported, are taken to the mints and exchanged for coin or notes. The increase of coin and bullion in the United States since January 1, 1879, is estimated at $227,399,428.

There are still in existence, uncanceled, $346,681,016 of United States legal-tender notes. These notes were authorized as a war measure, made necessary by the exigencies of the conflict in which the United States was then engaged. The preservation of the nation's existence required, in the judgment of Congress, an issue of legal-tender paper money. That it served well the purpose for which it was created is not questioned, but the employment of the notes as paper money indefinitely, after the accomplishment of the object for which they were provided, was not contemplated by the framers of the law under which they were issued. These notes long since became, like any other pecuniary obligation of the Government, a debt to be paid, and when paid to be canceled as mere evidence of an indebtedness no longer existing.   I therefore repeat what was said in the annual message of last year, that the retirement from circulation of United States notes with the capacity of legal tender in private contracts is a step to be taken in our progress toward a safe and stable currency which should be accepted as the policy and duty of the Government and the interest and security of the people.

At the time of the passage of the act now in force requiring the coinage of silver dollars, fixing their value, and giving them legal-tender character it was believed by many of the supporters of the measure that the silver dollar which it authorized would speedily become, under the operations of the law, of equivalent value to the gold dollar.   There were other supporters of the bill, who, while they doubted as to the probability of this result, nevertheless were willing to give the proposed experiment a fair trial, with a view to stop the coinage if experience should prove that the silver dollar authorized by the bill continued to be of less commercial value than the standard gold dollar.

The coinage of silver dollars under the act referred to began in March, 1878, and has been continued as required by the act.   The average rate per month to the present time has been $2,276,492.   The total amount coined prior to the 1st of November last was $72,847,750.   Of this amount $47,084,450 remain in the Treasury, and only $25,763,291 are in the hands of the people.   A constant effort has been made to keep this currency in circulation, and considerable expense has been necessarily incurred for this purpose; but its return to the Treasury is prompt and sure.   Contrary to the confident anticipation of the friends of the measure at the time of its adoption, the value of the silver dollar containing 412½ grains of silver has not increased.   During the year prior to the passage of the bill authorizing its coinage the market value of the silver which it contained was from 90 to 92 cents as compared with the standard gold dollar.   During the last year the average market value of the silver dollar has been 88½ cents.

It is obvious that the legislation of the last Congress in regard to silver, so far as it was based on an anticipated rise in the value of silver as a result of that legislation, has failed to produce the effect then predicted. The longer the law remains in force, requiring, as it does, the coinage of a nominal dollar which in reality is not a dollar, the greater becomes the danger that this country will be forced to accept a single metal as the sole legal standard of value in circulation, and this a standard of less value than it purports to be worth in the recognized money of the world.

The Constitution of the United States, sound financial principles, and our best interests all require that the country should have as its legal-tender money both gold and silver coin of an intrinsic value, as bullion, equivalent to that which upon its face it purports to possess. The Constitution in express terms recognizes both gold and silver as the only true legal-tender money. To banish either of these metals from our currency is to narrow and limit the circulating medium of exchange to the disparagement of important interests. The United States produces more silver than any other country, and is directly interested in maintaining it as one of the two precious metals which furnish the coinage of the world. It will, in my judgment, contribute to this result if Congress will repeal so much of existing legislation as requires the coinage of silver dollars containing only 412½ grains of silver, and in its stead will authorize the Secretary of the Treasury to coin silver dollars of equivalent value, as bullion, with gold dollars. This will defraud no man, and will be in accordance with familiar precedents. Congress on several occasions has altered the ratio of value between gold and silver, in order to establish it more nearly in accordance with the actual ratio of value between the two metals.

In financial legislation every measure in the direction of greater fidelity in the discharge of pecuniary obligations has been found by experience to diminish the rates of interest which debtors are required to pay and to increase the facility with which money can be obtained for every legitimate purpose. Our own recent financial history shows how surely money becomes abundant whenever confidence in the exact performance of moneyed obligations is established.

The Secretary of War reports that the expenditures of the War Department for the fiscal year ended June 30, 1880, were $39,924,773.03. The appropriations for this Department for the current fiscal year amount to $41,993,630.40.

With respect to the Army, the Secretary invites attention to the fact that its strength is limited by statute (U. S. Revised Statutes, sec. 1115) to not more than 30,000 enlisted men, but that provisos contained in appropriation bills have limited expenditures to the enlistment of but 25,000. It is believed the full legal strength is the least possible force at which the present organization can be maintained, having in view efficiency, discipline, and economy. While the enlistment of this force would add somewhat to the appropriation for pay of the Army, the saving made in other respects would be more than an equivalent for this additional outlay, and the efficiency of the Army would be largely increased.

The rapid extension of the railroad system west of the Mississippi River and the great tide of settlers which has flowed in upon new territory impose on the military an entire change of policy. The maintenance of small posts along wagon and stage routes of travel is no longer necessary. Permanent quarters at points selected, of a more substantial character than those heretofore constructed, will be required. Under existing laws permanent buildings can not be erected without the sanction of Congress, and when sales of military sites and buildings have been authorized the moneys received have reverted to the Treasury and could only become available through a new appropriation. It is recommended that provision be made by a general statute for the sale of such abandoned military posts and buildings as are found to be unnecessary and for the application of the proceeds to the construction of other posts. While many of the present posts are of but slight value for military purposes, owing to the changed condition of the country, their occupation is continued at great expense and inconvenience, because they afford the only available shelter for troops.

The absence of a large number of officers of the line, in active duty, from their regiments is a serious detriment to the maintenance of the service. The constant demand for small detachments, each of which should be commanded by a commissioned officer, and the various details of officers for necessary service away from their commands occasion a scarcity in the number required for company duties. With a view to lessening this drain to some extent, it is recommended that the law authorizing the detail of officers from the active list as professors of tactics and military science at certain colleges and universities be so amended as to provide that all such details be made from the retired list of the Army.

Attention is asked to the necessity of providing by legislation for organizing, arming, and disciplining the *active* militia of the country, and liberal appropriations are recommended in this behalf. The reports of the Adjutant-General of the Army and the Chief of Ordnance touching this subject fully set forth its importance.

The report of the officer in charge of education in the Army shows that there are 78 schools now in operation in the Army, with an aggregate attendance of 2,305 enlisted men and children. The Secretary recommends the enlistment of 150 schoolmasters, with the rank and pay of commissary-sergeants. An appropriation is needed to supply the judge-advocates of the Army with suitable libraries, and the Secretary recommends that the Corps of Judge-Advocates be placed upon the same footing as to promotion with the other staff corps of the Army. Under existing laws the Bureau of Military Justice consists of one officer (the Judge-Advocate-General), and the Corps of Judge-Advocates of eight officers of equal rank (majors), with a provision that the limit of the corps shall remain at four when reduced by casualty or resignation to that number. The consolidation of the Bureau of Military Justice and the Corps of Judge-Advocates upon the same basis with the other staff corps of the Army would remove an unjust discrimination against deserving officers and subserve the best interests of the service.

Especial attention is asked to the report of the Chief of Engineers upon the condition of our national defenses. From a personal inspection of many of the fortifications referred to, the Secretary is able to emphasize the recommendations made and to state that their incomplete and defenseless condition is discreditable to the country. While other nations have been increasing their means for carrying on offensive warfare and attacking maritime cities, we have been dormant in preparation for defense. Nothing of importance has been done toward strengthening and finishing our casemated works since our late civil war, during which the great guns of modern warfare and the heavy armor of modern fortifications and ships came into use among the nations; and our earthworks, left by a sudden failure of appropriations some years since in all stages of incompletion, are now being rapidly destroyed by the elements.

The two great rivers of the North American continent, the Mississippi and the Columbia, have their navigable waters wholly within the limits of the United States, and are of vast importance to our internal and foreign commerce. The permanency of the important work on the South Pass of the Mississippi River seems now to be assured. There has been no failure whatever in the maintenance of the maximum channel during the six months ended August 9 last. This experiment has opened a broad, deep highway to the ocean, and is an improvement upon the permanent success of which congratulations may be exchanged among people abroad and at home, and especially among the communities of the Mississippi Valley, whose commercial exchanges float in an unobstructed channel safely to and from the sea.

A comprehensive improvement of the Mississippi and its tributaries is a matter of transcendent importance. These great waterways comprise a system of inland transportation spread like network over a large portion of the United States, and navigable to the extent of many thousands of miles. Producers and consumers alike have a common interest in such unequaled facilities for cheap transportation. Geographically, commercially, and politically, they are the strongest tie between the various sections of the country. These channels of communication and interchange are the property of the nation. Its jurisdiction is paramount over their waters, and the plainest principles of public interest require their intelligent and careful supervision, with a view to their protection, improvement, and the enhancement of their usefulness.

The channel of the Columbia River for a distance of about 100 miles from its mouth is obstructed by a succession of bars, which occasion serious delays in navigation and heavy expense for lighterage and towage. A depth of at least 20 feet at low tide should be secured and maintained to meet the requirements of the extensive and growing inland and ocean commerce it subserves. The most urgent need, however, for this great waterway is a permanent improvement of the channel at the mouth of the river.

From Columbia River to San Francisco, a distance of over 600 miles, there is no harbor on our Pacific coast which can be approached during stormy weather.   An appropriation of $150,000 was made by the Forty-fifth Congress for the commencement of a breakwater and harbor of refuge, to be located at some point between the Straits of Fuca and San Francisco at which the necessities of commerce, local and general, will be best accommodated.   The amount appropriated is thought to be quite inadequate for the purpose intended.   The cost of the work, when finished, will be very great, owing to the want of natural advantages for a site at any point on the coast between the designated limits, and it has not been thought to be advisable to undertake the work without a larger appropriation.   I commend the matter to the attention of Congress.

The completion of the new building for the War Department is urgently needed, and the estimates for continuing its construction are especially recommended.

The collections of books, specimens, and records constituting the Army Medical Museum and Library are of national importance.   The library now contains about 51,500 volumes and 57,000 pamphlets relating to medicine, surgery, and allied topics.   The contents of the Army Medical Museum consist of 22,000 specimens, and are unique in the completeness with which both military surgery and the diseases of armies are illustrated.   Their destruction would be an irreparable loss, not only to the United States, but to the world.   There are filed in the Record and Pension Division over 16,000 bound volumes of hospital records, together with a great quantity of papers, embracing the original records of the hospitals of our armies during the civil war.   Aside from their historical value, these records are daily searched for evidence needed in the settlement of large numbers of pension and other claims, for the protection of the Government against attempted frauds, as well as for the benefit of honest claimants.   These valuable collections are now in a building which is peculiarly exposed to the danger of destruction by fire.   It is therefore earnestly recommended that an appropriation be made for a new fireproof building, adequate for the present needs and reasonable future expansion of these valuable collections.   Such a building should be absolutely fireproof; no expenditure for mere architectural display is required.   It is believed that a suitable structure can be erected at a cost not to exceed $250,000.

I commend to the attention of Congress the great services of the Commander in Chief of our armies during the war for the Union, whose wise, firm, and patriotic conduct did so much to bring that momentous conflict to a close.   The legislation of the United States contains many precedents for the recognition of distinguished military merit, authorizing rank and emoluments to be conferred for eminent services to the country.   An act of Congress authorizing the appointment of a Captain-General of the Army, with suitable provisions relating to compensation, retirement, and other details, would, in my judgment, be altogether fitting and proper, and would be warmly approved by the country.

The report of the Secretary of the Navy exhibits the successful and satisfactory management of that Department during the last fiscal year. The total expenditures for the year were $12,916,639.45, leaving unexpended at the close of the year $2,141,682.23 of the amount of available appropriations. The appropriations for the present fiscal year, ending June 30, 1881, are $15,095,061.45, and the total estimates for the next fiscal year, ending June 30, 1882, are $15,953,751.61. The amount drawn by warrant from July 1, 1880, to November 1, 1880, is $5,041,570.45.

The recommendation of the Secretary of the Navy that provision be made for the establishment of some form of civil government for the people of Alaska is approved. At present there is no protection of persons or property in that Territory except such as is afforded by the officers of the United States ship *Jamestown*. This vessel was dispatched to Sitka because of the fear that without the immediate presence of the national authority there was impending danger of anarchy. The steps taken to restore order have been accepted in good faith by both white and Indian inhabitants, and the necessity for this method of restraint does not, in my opinion, now exist. If, however, the *Jamestown* should be withdrawn, leaving the people, as at present, without the ordinary judicial and administrative authority of organized local government, serious consequences might ensue.

The laws provide only for the collection of revenue, the protection of public property, and the transmission of the mails. The problem is to supply a local rule for a population so scattered and so peculiar in its origin and condition. The natives are reported to be teachable and self-supporting, and if properly instructed doubtless would advance rapidly in civilization, and a new factor of prosperity would be added to the national life. I therefore recommend the requisite legislation upon this subject.

The Secretary of the Navy has taken steps toward the establishment of naval coaling stations at the Isthmus of Panama, to meet the requirements of our commercial relations with Central and South America, which are rapidly growing in importance. Locations eminently suitable, both as regards our naval purposes and the uses of commerce, have been selected, one on the east side of the Isthmus, at Chiriqui Lagoon, in the Caribbean Sea, and the other on the Pacific coast, at the Bay of Golfito. The only safe harbors, sufficiently commodious, on the Isthmus are at these points, and the distance between them is less than 100 miles. The report of the Secretary of the Navy concludes with valuable suggestions with respect to the building up of our merchant marine service, which deserve the favorable consideration of Congress.

The report of the Postmaster-General exhibits the continual growth and the high state of efficiency of the postal service. The operations of no Department of the Government, perhaps, represent with greater exactness the increase in the population and the business of the country. In 1860 the postal receipts were $8,518,067.40; in 1880 the receipts were $33,315,479.34. All the inhabitants of the country are directly and personally interested in having proper mail facilities, and naturally watch the Post-Office very closely. This careful oversight on the part of the people has proved a constant stimulus to improvement. During the past year there was an increase of 2,134 post-offices, and the mail routes were extended 27,177 miles, making an additional annual transportation of 10,804,191 miles. The revenues of the postal service for the ensuing year are estimated at $38,845,174.10, and the expenditures at $42,475,932, leaving a deficiency to be appropriated out of the Treasury of $3,630,757.90.

The Universal Postal Union has received the accession of almost all the countries and colonies of the world maintaining organized postal services, and it is confidently expected that all the other countries and colonies now outside the union will soon unite therewith, thus realizing the grand idea and aim of the founders of the union of forming, for purposes of international mail communication, a single postal territory, embracing the world, with complete uniformity of postal charges and conditions of international exchange for all descriptions of correspondence. To enable the United States to do its full share of this great work, additional legislation is asked by the Postmaster-General, to whose recommendations especial attention is called.

The suggestion of the Postmaster-General that it would be wise to encourage, by appropriate legislation, the establishment of American lines of steamers by our own citizens to carry the mails between our own ports and those of Mexico, Central America, South America, and of transpacific countries is commended to the serious consideration of Congress.

The attention of Congress is also invited to the suggestions of the Postmaster-General in regard to postal savings.

The necessity for additional provision to aid in the transaction of the business of the Federal courts becomes each year more apparent. The dockets of the Supreme Court and of the circuit courts in the greater number of the circuits are encumbered with the constant accession of cases. In the former court, and in many instances in the circuit courts, years intervene before it is practicable to bring cases to hearing.

The Attorney-General recommends the establishment of an intermediate court of errors and appeals. It is recommended that the number of judges of the circuit court in each circuit, with the exception of the second circuit, should be increased by the addition of another judge; in the second circuit, that two should be added; and that an intermediate appellate court should be formed in each circuit, to consist of the circuit judges and the circuit justice, and that in the event of the absence of either of these judges the place of the absent judge should be supplied by the judge of one of the district courts in the circuit. Such an appellate court could be safely invested with large jurisdiction, and its decisions would satisfy suitors in many cases where appeals would still be allowed to the Supreme Court. The expense incurred for this intermediate court will require a very moderate increase of the appropriations for the expenses of the Department of Justice. This recommendation is commended to the careful consideration of Congress.

It is evident that a delay of justice, in many instances oppressive and disastrous to suitors, now necessarily occurs in the Federal courts, which will in this way be remedied.

The report of the Secretary of the Interior presents an elaborate account of the operations of that Department during the past year. It gives me great pleasure to say that our Indian affairs appear to be in a more hopeful condition now than ever before. The Indians have made gratifying progress in agriculture, herding, and mechanical pursuits. Many who were a few years ago in hostile conflict with the Government are quietly settling down on farms where they hope to make their permanent homes, building houses and engaging in the occupations of civilized life. The introduction of the freighting business among them has been remarkably fruitful of good results, in giving many of them congenial and remunerative employment and in stimulating their ambition to earn their own support. Their honesty, fidelity, and efficiency as carriers are highly praised. The organization of a police force of Indians has been equally successful in maintaining law and order upon the reservations and in exercising a wholesome moral influence among the Indians themselves. I concur with the Secretary of the Interior in the recommendation that the pay of this force be increased, as an inducement to the best class of young men to enter it.

Much care and attention has been devoted to the enlargement of educational facilities for the Indians. The means available for this important object have been very inadequate. A few additional boarding schools at Indian agencies have been established and the erection of buildings has been begun for several more; but an increase of the appropriations for this interesting undertaking is greatly needed to accommodate the large number of Indian children of school age. The number offered by their parents from all parts of the country for education in the Government schools is much larger than can be accommodated with the means at present available for that purpose. The number of Indian pupils at the normal school at Hampton, Va., under the direction of General Armstrong, has been considerably increased, and their progress is highly encouraging. The Indian school established by the Interior Department in 1879 at Carlisle, Pa., under the direction of Captain Pratt, has been equally successful. It has now nearly 200 pupils of both sexes, representing a great variety of the tribes east of the Rocky Mountains. The pupils in both these institutions receive not only an elementary English education, but are also instructed in housework, agriculture, and useful mechanical pursuits. A similar school was established this year at For-est Grove, Oreg., for the education of Indian youth on the Pacific Coast. In addition to this, thirty-six Indian boys and girls were selected from the Eastern Cherokees and placed in boarding schools in North Carolina, where they are to receive an elementary English education and training in industrial pursuits. The interest shown by Indian parents, even among the so-called wild tribes, in the education of their children is very gratifying, and gives promise that the results accomplished by the efforts now making will be of lasting benefit.

The expenses of Indian education have so far been drawn from the per-manent civilization fund at the disposal of the Department of the Interior, but the fund is now so much reduced that the continuance of this bene-ficial work will in the future depend on specific appropriations by Con-gress for the purpose; and I venture to express the hope that Congress will not permit institutions so fruitful of good results to perish for want of means for their support. On the contrary, an increase of the num-ber of such schools appears to me highly advisable.

The past year has been unusually free from disturbances among the Indian tribes. An agreement has been made with the Utes by which they surrender their large reservation in Colorado in consideration of an annuity to be paid to them, and agree to settle in severalty on certain lands designated for that purpose, as farmers, holding individual title to their land in fee simple, inalienable for a certain period. In this way a costly Indian war has been avoided, which at one time seemed imminent, and for the first time in the history of the country an Indian nation has given up its tribal existence to be settled in severalty and to live as indi-viduals under the common protection of the laws of the country.

The conduct of the Indians throughout the country during the past year, with but few noteworthy exceptions, has been orderly and peaceful. The guerrilla warfare carried on for two years by Victoria and his band of Southern Apaches has virtually come to an end by the death of that chief and most of his followers on Mexican soil. The disturbances caused on our northern frontier by Sitting Bull and his men, who had taken refuge in the British dominions, are also likely to cease. A large majority of his followers have surrendered to our military forces, and the remainder are apparently in progress of disintegration.

I concur with the Secretary of the Interior in expressing the earnest hope that Congress will at this session take favorable action on the bill providing for the allotment of lands on the different reservations in sev-eralty to the Indians, with patents conferring fee-simple title inalienable for a certain period, and the eventual disposition of the residue of the reservations for general settlement, with the consent and for the benefit of the Indians, placing the latter under the equal protection of the laws of the country. This measure, together with a vigorous prosecution of our educational efforts, will work the most important and effective advance toward the solution of the Indian problem, in preparing for the gradual merging of our Indian population in the great body of American citizenship.

A large increase is reported in the disposal of public lands for settlement during the past year, which marks the prosperous growth of our agricultural industry and a vigorous movement of population toward our unoccupied lands. As this movement proceeds, the codification of our land laws, as well as proper legislation to regulate the disposition of public lands, become of more pressing necessity, and I therefore invite the consideration of Congress to the report and the accompanying draft of a bill made by the Public Lands Commission, which were communicated by me to Congress at the last session. Early action upon this important subject is highly desirable.

The attention of Congress is again asked to the wasteful depredations committed on our public timber lands and the rapid and indiscriminate destruction of our forests. The urgent necessity for legislation to this end is now generally recognized. In view of the lawless character of the depredations committed and the disastrous consequences which will inevitably follow their continuance, legislation has again and again been recommended to arrest the evil and to preserve for the people of our Western States and Territories the timber needed for domestic and other essential uses.

The report of the Director of the Geological Survey is a document of unusual interest. The consolidation of the various geological and geographical surveys and exploring enterprises, each of which has heretofore operated upon an independent plan, without concert, can not fail to be of great benefit to all those industries of the country which depend upon the development of our mineral resources. The labors of the scientific men, of recognized merit, who compose the corps of the Geological Survey, during the first season of their field operations and inquiries, appear to have been very comprehensive, and will soon be communicated to Congress in a number of volumes. The Director of the Survey recommends that the investigations carried on by his bureau, which so far have been confined to the so-called public-land States and Territories, be extended over the entire country, and that the necessary appropriation be made for this purpose. This would be particularly beneficial to the iron, coal, and other mining interests of the Mississippi Valley and of the Eastern and Southern States. The subject is commended to the careful consideration of Congress.

The Secretary of the Interior asks attention to the want of room in the public buildings of the capital, now existing and in progress of construction, for the accommodation of the clerical force employed and of the public records. Necessity has compelled the renting of private buildings in different parts of the city for the location of public offices, for which a large amount of rent is annually paid, while the separation of offices belonging to the same Department impedes the transaction of current business. The Secretary suggests that the blocks surrounding Lafayette Square on the east, north, and west be purchased as the sites for new edifices for the accommodation of the Government offices, leaving the square itself intact, and that if such buildings were constructed upon a harmonious plan of architecture they would add much to the beauty of the national capital, and would, together with the Treasury and the new State, Navy, and War Department building, form one of the most imposing groups of public edifices in the world.

The Commissioner of Agriculture expresses the confident belief that his efforts in behalf of the production of our own sugar and tea have been encouragingly rewarded. The importance of the results attained have attracted marked attention at home and have received the special consideration of foreign nations. The successful cultivation of our own tea and the manufacture of our own sugar would make a difference of many millions of dollars annually in the wealth of the nation.

The report of the Commissioner asks attention particularly to the continued prevalence of an infectious and contagious cattle disease known and dreaded in Europe and Asia as cattle plague, or pleuro-pneumonia. A mild type of this disease in certain sections of our country is the occasion of great loss to our farmers and of serious disturbance to our trade with Great Britain, which furnishes a market for most of our live stock and dressed meats. The value of neat cattle exported from the United States for the eight months ended August 31, 1880, was more than $12,000,000, and nearly double the value for the same period in 1879— an unexampled increase of export trade. Your early attention is solicited to this important matter.

The Commissioner of Education reports a continued increase of public interest in educational affairs, and that the public schools generally throughout the country are well sustained. Industrial training is attracting deserved attention, and colleges for instruction, theoretical and practical, in agriculture and mechanic arts, including the Government schools recently established for the instruction of Indian youth, are gaining steadily in public estimation. The Commissioner asks special attention to the depredations committed on the lands reserved for the future support of public instruction, and to the very great need of help from the nation for schools in the Territories and in the Southern States. The recommendation heretofore made is repeated and urged, that an educational fund be set apart from the net proceeds of the sales of the public lands annually, the income of which and the remainder of the net annual proceeds to be distributed on some satisfactory plan to the States and the Territories and the District of Columbia.

The success of the public schools of the District of Columbia, and the progress made, under the intelligent direction of the board of education and the superintendent, in supplying the educational requirements of the

District with thoroughly trained and efficient teachers, is very gratifying. The acts of Congress, from time to time, donating public lands to the several States and Territories in aid of educational interests have proved to be wise measures of public policy, resulting in great and lasting benefit. It would seem to be a matter of simple justice to extend the benefits of this legislation, the wisdom of which has been so fully vindicated by experience, to the District of Columbia.

I again commend the general interests of the District of Columbia to the favorable consideration of Congress. The affairs of the District, as shown by the report of the Commissioners, are in a very satisfactory condition.

In my annual messages heretofore and in my special message of December 19, 1879, I have urged upon the attention of Congress the necessity of reclaiming the marshes of the Potomac adjacent to the capital, and I am constrained by its importance to advert again to the subject. These flats embrace an area of several hundred acres. They are an impediment to the drainage of the city and seriously impair its health. It is believed that with this substantial improvement of its river front the capital would be in all respects one of the most attractive cities in the world. Aside from its permanent population, this city is necessarily the place of residence of persons from every section of the country engaged in the public service. Many others reside here temporarily for the transaction of business with the Government.

It should not be forgotten that the land acquired will probably be worth the cost of reclaiming it and that the navigation of the river will be greatly improved. I therefore again invite the attention of Congress to the importance of prompt provision for this much needed and too long delayed improvement.

The water supply of the city is inadequate. In addition to the ordinary use throughout the city, the consumption by Government is necessarily very great in the navy-yard, arsenal, and the various Departments, and a large quantity is required for the proper preservation of the numerous parks and the cleansing of sewers. I recommend that this subject receive the early attention of Congress, and that in making provision for an increased supply such means be adopted as will have in view the future growth of the city. Temporary expedients for such a purpose can not but be wasteful of money, and therefore unwise. A more ample reservoir, with corresponding facilities for keeping it filled, should, in my judgment, be constructed. I commend again to the attention of Congress the subject of the removal from their present location of the depots of the several railroads entering the city; and I renew the recommendations of my former messages in behalf of the erection of a building for the Congressional Library, the completion of the Washington Monument, and of liberal appropriations in support of the benevolent, reformatory, and penal institutions of the District.

James A. Garfield

March 4, 1881 to September 19, 1881

(Assassinated prior to delivering

any Annual Messages)

Chester A. Arthur

September 19, 1881 to March 4, 1885

FIRST ANNUAL MESSAGE.

WASHINGTON, *December 6, 1881.*

To the Senate and House of Representatives of the United States:

An appalling calamity has befallen the American people since their chosen representatives last met in the halls where you are now assembled. We might else recall with unalloyed content the rare prosperity with which throughout the year the nation has been blessed. Its harvests have been plenteous; its varied industries have thriven; the health of its people has been preserved; it has maintained with foreign governments the undisturbed relations of amity and peace. For these manifestations of His favor we owe to Him who holds our destiny in His hands the tribute of our grateful devotion.

To that mysterious exercise of His will which has taken from us the loved and illustrious citizen who was but lately the head of the nation we bow in sorrow and submission.

The memory of his exalted character, of his noble achievements, and of his patriotic life will be treasured forever as a sacred possession of the whole people.

The announcement of his death drew from foreign governments and peoples tributes of sympathy and sorrow which history will record as signal tokens of the kinship of nations and the federation of mankind.

The feeling of good will between our own Government and that of Great Britain was never more marked than at present. In recognition of this pleasing fact I directed, on the occasion of the late centennial celebration at Yorktown, that a salute be given to the British flag.

Save for the correspondence to which I shall refer hereafter in relation to the proposed canal across the Isthmus of Panama, little has occurred worthy of mention in the diplomatic relations of the two countries.

Early in the year the Fortune Bay claims were satisfactorily settled by the British Government paying in full the sum of £15,000, most of which has been already distributed. As the terms of the settlement included compensation for injuries suffered by our fishermen at Aspee Bay, there has been retained from the gross award a sum which is deemed adequate for those claims.

The participation of Americans in the exhibitions at Melbourne and Sydney will be approvingly mentioned in the reports of the two exhibitions, soon to be presented to Congress. They will disclose the readiness of our countrymen to make successful competition in distant fields of enterprise.

Negotiations for an international copyright convention are in hopeful progress.

The surrender of Sitting Bull and his forces upon the Canadian frontier has allayed apprehension, although bodies of British Indians still cross the border in quest of sustenance. Upon this subject a correspondence has been opened which promises an adequate understanding. Our troops have orders to avoid meanwhile all collisions with alien Indians.

The presence at the Yorktown celebration of representatives of the French Republic and descendants of Lafayette and of his gallant compatriots who were our allies in the Revolution has served to strengthen the spirit of good will which has always existed between the two nations.

You will be furnished with the proceedings of the Bimetallic Conference held during the summer at the city of Paris. No accord was reached, but a valuable interchange of views was had, and the conference will next year be renewed.

At the Electrical Exhibition and Congress, also held at Paris, this country was creditably represented by eminent specialists, who, in the absence of an appropriation, generously lent their efficient aid at the instance of the State Department. While our exhibitors in this almost distinctively American field of achievement have won several valuable awards, I recommend that Congress provide for the repayment of the personal expenses incurred in the public interest by the honorary commissioners and delegates.

No new questions respecting the status of our naturalized citizens in Germany have arisen during the year, and the causes of complaint, especially in Alsace and Lorraine, have practically ceased through the liberal action of the Imperial Government in accepting our often-expressed views on the subject. The application of the treaty of 1868 to the lately acquired Rhenish provinces has received very earnest attention, and a definite and lasting agreement on this point is confidently expected. The participation of the descendants of Baron von Steuben in the Yorktown festivities, and their subsequent reception by their American kinsmen, strikingly evinced the ties of good will which unite the German people and our own.

Our intercourse with Spain has been friendly. An agreement concluded in February last fixes a term for the labors of the Spanish and American Claims Commission. The Spanish Government has been requested to pay the late awards of that Commission, and will, it is believed, accede to the request as promptly and courteously as on former occasions.

By recent legislation onerous fines have been imposed upon American shipping in Spanish and colonial ports for slight irregularities in manifests. One case of hardship is specially worthy of attention. The bark *Masonic*, bound for Japan, entered Manila in distress, and is there sought to be confiscated under Spanish revenue laws for an alleged shortage in her transshipped cargo. Though efforts for her relief have thus far proved unavailing, it is expected that the whole matter will be adjusted in a friendly spirit.

The Senate resolutions of condolence on the assassination of the Czar Alexander II were appropriately communicated to the Russian Government, which in turn has expressed its sympathy in our late national bereavement. It is desirable that our cordial relations with Russia should be strengthened by proper engagements assuring to peaceable Americans who visit the Empire the consideration which is due to them as citizens of a friendly state. This is especially needful with respect to American Israelites, whose classification with the native Hebrews has evoked energetic remonstrances from this Government.

A supplementary consular agreement with Italy has been sanctioned and proclaimed, which puts at rest conflicts of jurisdiction in the case of crimes on shipboard.

Several important international conferences have been held in Italy during the year. At the Geographical Congress of Venice, the Beneficence Congress of Milan, and the Hygienic Congress of Turin this country was represented by delegates from branches of the public service or by private citizens duly accredited in an honorary capacity. It is hoped that Congress will give such prominence to the results of their participation as they may seem to deserve.

The abolition of all discriminating duties against such colonial productions of the Dutch East Indies as are imported hither from Holland has been already considered by Congress. I trust that at the present session the matter may be favorably concluded.

The insecurity of life and property in many parts of Turkey has given rise to correspondence with the Porte looking particularly to the better protection of American missionaries in the Empire. The condemned murderer of the eminent missionary Dr. Justin W. Parsons has not yet been executed, although this Government has repeatedly demanded that exemplary justice be done.

The Swiss Government has again solicited the good offices of our diplomatic and consular agents for the protection of its citizens in countries where it is not itself represented. This request has, within proper limits, been granted.

Our agents in Switzerland have been instructed to protest against the conduct of the authorities of certain communes in permitting the emigration to this country of criminals and other objectionable persons. Several such persons, through the cooperation of the commissioners of emigration at New York, have been sent back by the steamers which brought them. A continuance of this course may prove a more effectual remedy than diplomatic remonstrance.

Treaties of commerce and navigation and for the regulation of consular privileges have been concluded with Roumania and Servia since their admission into the family of European States.

As is natural with contiguous states having like institutions and like aims of advancement and development, the friendship of the United States and Mexico has been constantly maintained. This Government has lost no occasion of encouraging the Mexican Government to a beneficial realization of the mutual advantages which will result from more intimate commercial intercourse and from the opening of the rich interior of Mexico to railway enterprise. I deem it important that means be provided to restrain the lawlessness unfortunately so common on the frontier and to suppress the forays of the reservation Indians on either side of the Rio Grande.

The neighboring States of Central America have preserved internal peace, and their outward relations toward us have been those of intimate friendship. There are encouraging signs of their growing disposition to subordinate their local interests to those which are common to them by reason of their geographical relations.

The boundary dispute between Guatemala and Mexico has afforded this Government an opportunity to exercise its good offices for preventing a rupture between those States and for procuring a peaceable solution of the question. I cherish strong hope that in view of our relations of amity with both countries our friendly counsels may prevail.

A special envoy of Guatemala has brought to me the condolences of his Government and people on the death of President Garfield.

The Costa Rican Government lately framed an engagement with Colombia for settling by arbitration the boundary question between those countries, providing that the post of arbitrator should be offered successively to the King of the Belgians, the King of Spain, and the President of the Argentine Confederation. The King of the Belgians has declined to act, but I am not as yet advised of the action of the King of Spain. As we have certain interests in the disputed territory which are protected by our treaty engagements with one of the parties, it is important that the arbitration should not without our consent affect our rights, and this Government has accordingly thought proper to make its views known to the parties to the agreement, as well as to intimate them to the Belgian and Spanish Governments.

The questions growing out of the proposed interoceanic waterway across the Isthmus of Panama are of grave national importance. This Government has not been unmindful of the solemn obligations imposed upon it by its compact of 1846 with Colombia, as the independent and sovereign mistress of the territory crossed by the canal, and has sought to render them effective by fresh engagements with the Colombian Republic looking to their practical execution. The negotiations to this end, after they had reached what appeared to be a mutually satisfactory solution here, were met in Colombia by a disavowal of the powers which its envoy had assumed and by a proposal for renewed negotiation on a modified basis.

Meanwhile this Government learned that Colombia had proposed to the European powers to join in a guaranty of the neutrality of the proposed Panama canal—a guaranty which would be in direct contravention of our obligation as the sole guarantor of the integrity of Colombian territory and of the neutrality of the canal itself. My lamented predecessor felt it his duty to place before the European powers the reasons which make the prior guaranty of the United States indispensable, and for which the interjection of any foreign guaranty might be regarded as a superfluous and unfriendly act.

Foreseeing the probable reliance of the British Government on the provisions of the Clayton-Bulwer treaty of 1850 as affording room for a share in the guaranties which the United States covenanted with Colombia four years before, I have not hesitated to supplement the action of my predecessor by proposing to Her Majesty's Government the modification of that instrument and the abrogation of such clauses thereof as do not comport with the obligations of the United States toward Colombia or with the vital needs of the two friendly parties to the compact.

This Government sees with great concern the continuance of the hostile relations between Chile, Bolivia, and Peru. An early peace between these Republics is much to be desired, not only that they may themselves be spared further misery and bloodshed, but because their continued antagonism threatens consequences which are, in my judgment, dangerous to the interests of republican government on this continent and calculated to destroy the best elements of our free and peaceful civilization.

As in the present excited condition of popular feeling in these countries there has been serious misapprehension of the position of the United States, and as separate diplomatic intercourse with each through independent ministers is sometimes subject, owing to the want of prompt reciprocal communication, to temporary misunderstanding, I have deemed it judicious at the present time to send a special envoy accredited to all and each of them, and furnished with general instructions which will, I trust, enable him to bring these powers into friendly relations.

The Government of Venezuela maintains its attitude of warm friendship and continues with great regularity its payment of the monthly quota of the diplomatic debt. Without suggesting the direction in which Congress should act, I ask its attention to the pending questions affecting the distribution of the sums thus far received.

The relations between Venezuela and France growing out of the same debt have been for some time past in an unsatisfactory state, and this Government, as the neighbor and one of the largest creditors of Venezuela, has interposed its influence with the French Government with the view of producing a friendly and honorable adjustment.

I regret that the commercial interests between the United States and Brazil, from which great advantages were hoped a year ago, have suffered from the withdrawal of the American lines of communication between the Brazilian ports and our own.

Through the efforts of our minister resident at Buenos Ayres and the United States minister at Santiago, a treaty has been concluded between the Argentine Republic and Chile, disposing of the long-pending Patagonian boundary question. It is a matter of congratulation that our Government has been afforded the opportunity of successfully exerting its good influence for the prevention of disagreements between these Republics of the American continent.

I am glad to inform you that the treaties lately negotiated with China have been duly ratified on both sides and the exchange made at Peking. Legislation is necessary to carry their provisions into effect. The prompt and friendly spirit with which the Chinese Government, at the request of the United States, conceded the modification of existing treaties should secure careful regard for the interests and susceptibilities of that Government in the enactment of any laws relating to Chinese immigration.

Those clauses of the treaties which forbid the participation of citizens or vessels of the United States in the opium trade will doubtless receive your approval. They will attest the sincere interest which our people and Government feel in the commendable efforts of the Chinese Government to put a stop to this demoralizing and destructive traffic.

In relation both to China and Japan some changes are desirable in our present system of consular jurisdiction. I hope at some future time to lay before you a scheme for its improvement in the entire East.

The intimacy between our own country and Japan, the most advanced of the Eastern nations, continues to be cordial. I am advised that the Emperor contemplates the establishment of full constitutional government, and that he has already summoned a parliamentary congress for the purpose of effecting the change. Such a remarkable step toward complete assimilation with the Western system can not fail to bring Japan into closer and more beneficial relationship with ourselves as the chief Pacific power.

A question has arisen in relation to the exercise in that country of the judicial functions conferred upon our ministers and consuls. The indictment, trial, and conviction in the consular court at Yokohama of John Ross, a merchant seaman on board an American vessel, have made it necessary for the Government to institute a careful examination into the nature and methods of this jurisdiction.

It appeared that Ross was regularly shipped under the flag of the United States, but was by birth a British subject. My predecessor felt it his duty to maintain the position that during his service as a regularly shipped seaman on board an American merchant vessel Ross was subject to the laws of that service and to the jurisdiction of the United States consular authorities.

I renew the recommendation which has been heretofore urged by the Executive upon the attention of Congress, that after the deduction of such amount as may be found due to American citizens the balance of the indemnity funds heretofore obtained from China and Japan, and which are now in the hands of the State Department, be returned to the

Governments of those countries.

The King of Hawaii, in the course of his homeward return after a journey around the world, has lately visited this country. While our relations with that Kingdom are friendly, this Government has viewed with concern the efforts to seek replenishment of the diminishing population of the islands from outward sources, to a degree which may impair the native sovereignty and independence, in which the United States was among the first to testify a lively interest.

Relations of unimpaired amity have been maintained throughout the year with the respective Governments of Austria-Hungary, Belgium, Denmark, Hayti, Paraguay and Uruguay, Portugal, and Sweden and Norway. This may also be said of Greece and Ecuador, although our relations with those States have for some years been severed by the withdrawal of appropriations for diplomatic representatives at Athens and Quito. It seems expedient to restore those missions, even on a reduced scale, and I decidedly recommend such a course with respect to Ecuador, which is likely within the near future to play an important part among the nations of the Southern Pacific.

At its last extra session the Senate called for the text of the Geneva convention for the relief of the wounded in war. I trust that this action foreshadows such interest in the subject as will result in the adhesion of the United States to that humane and commendable engagement.

I invite your attention to the propriety of adopting the new code of international rules for the prevention of collisions on the high seas and of conforming the domestic legislation of the United States thereto, so that no confusion may arise from the application of conflicting rules in the case of vessels of different nationalities meeting in tidal waters. These international rules differ but slightly from our own. They have been adopted by the Navy Department for the governance of the war ships of the United States on the high seas and in foreign waters, and, through the action of the State Department in disseminating the rules and in acquainting shipmasters with the option of conforming to them without the jurisdictional waters of the United States, they are now very generally known and obeyed.

The State Department still continues to publish to the country the trade and manufacturing reports received from its officers abroad. The success of this course warrants its continuance and such appropriation as may be required to meet the rapidly increasing demand for these publications. With special reference to the Atlanta Cotton Exposition, the October number of the reports was devoted to a valuable collection of papers on the cotton-goods trade of the world.

The International Sanitary Conference for which, in 1879, Congress made provision assembled in this city early in January last, and its sessions were prolonged until March. Although it reached no specific conclusions affecting the future action of the participant powers, the interchange of views proved to be most valuable. The full protocols of the sessions have been already presented to the Senate.

As pertinent to this general subject, I call your attention to the operations of the National Board of Health. Established by act of Congress approved March 3, 1879, its sphere of duty was enlarged by the act of June 2 in the same year. By the last-named act the board was required to institute such measures as might be deemed necessary for preventing the introduction of contagious or infectious diseases from foreign countries into the United States or from one State into another.

The execution of the rules and regulations prepared by the board and approved by my predecessor has done much to arrest the progress of epidemic disease, and has thus rendered substantial service to the nation.

The International Sanitary Conference, to which I have referred, adopted a form of a bill of health to be used by all vessels seeking to enter the ports of the countries whose representatives participated in its deliberations. This form has since been prescribed by the National Board of Health and incorporated with its rules and regulations, which have been approved by me in pursuance of law.

The health of the people is of supreme importance. All measures looking to their protection against the spread of contagious diseases and to the increase of our sanitary knowledge for such purposes deserve attention of Congress.

The report of the Secretary of the Treasury presents in detail a highly satisfactory exhibit of the state of the finances and the condition of the various branches of the public service administered by that Department.

The ordinary revenues from all sources for the fiscal year ending June 30, 1881, were:

From customs	$198,159,676.02
From internal revenue	135,264,385.51
From sales of public lands	2,201,863.17
From tax on circulation and deposits of national banks	8,116,115.72
From repayment of interest by Pacific Railway companies	810,833.80
From sinking fund for Pacific Railway companies	805,180.54
From customs fees, fines, penalties, etc.	1,225,514.86
From fees—consular, letters patent, and lands	2,244,983.98
From proceeds of sales of Government property	262,174.00
From profits on coinage	3,468,485.61
From revenues of the District of Columbia	2,016,199.23
From miscellaneous sources	6,206,880.13
Total ordinary receipts	360,782,292.57

The ordinary expenditures for the same period were:

For civil expenses	$17,941,177.19
For foreign intercourse	1,093,954.92
For Indians	6,514,161.09
For pensions	50,059,279.62
For the military establishment, including river and harbor improvements and arsenals	40,466,460.55
For the naval establishment, including vessels, machinery, and improvements at navy-yards	15,686,671.66
For miscellaneous expenditures, including public buildings, light-houses, and collecting the revenue	41,837,280.57
For expenditures on account of the District of Columbia	3,543,912.03

For interest on the public debt.. 82, 508, 741. 18
For premium on bonds purchased................................. .... 1, 061, 248. 78

    Total ordinary expenditures..................................... 260, 712, 887. 59

Leaving a surplus revenue of $100,069,404.98, which was applied as follows:

To the redemption of—
Bonds for the sinking fund $74, 371, 200. 00
Fractional currency for the sinking fund 109, 001. 05
Loan of February, 1861.. 7, 418, 000. 00
Ten-forties of 1864.. 2, 016, 150. 00
Five-twenties of 1862 .... 18, 300. 00
Five-twenties of 1864 .... 3, 400. 00
Five-twenties of 1865 .... 37, 300. 00
Consols of 1865 .... 143, 150. 00
Consols of 1867.. 959, 150. 00
Consols of 1868.. 337, 400 .00
Texan indemnity stock 1, 000. 00
Old demand, compound-interest, and other notes 18, 330. 00
And to the increase of cash in the Treasury........................ 14, 637, 023. 93

                    100, 069, 404. 98

The requirements of the sinking fund for the year amounted to $90,786,064.02, which sum included a balance of $49,817,128.78, not provided for during the previous fiscal year. The sum of $74,480,201.05 was applied to this fund, which left a deficit of $16,305,873.47. The increase of the revenues for 1881 over those of the previous year was $29,352,901.10. It is estimated that the receipts during the present fiscal year will reach $400,000,000 and the expenditures $270,000,000, leaving a surplus of $130,000,000 applicable to the sinking fund and the redemption of the public debt.

I approve the recommendation of the Secretary of the Treasury that provision be made for the early retirement of silver certificates and that the act requiring their issue be repealed. They were issued in pursuance of the policy of the Government to maintain silver at or near the gold standard, and were accordingly made receivable for all customs, taxes, and public dues. About sixty-six millions of them are now outstanding. They form an unnecessary addition to the paper currency, a sufficient amount of which may be readily supplied by the national banks.

In accordance with the act of February 28, 1878, the Treasury Department has monthly caused at least two millions in value of silver bullion to be coined into standard silver dollars. One hundred and two millions of these dollars have been already coined, while only about thirty-four millions are in circulation.

For the reasons which he specifies, I concur in the Secretary's recommendation that the provision for coinage of a fixed amount each month be repealed, and that hereafter only so much be coined as shall be necessary to supply the demand.

The Secretary advises that the issue of gold certificates should not for the present be resumed, and suggests that the national banks may properly be forbidden by law to retire their currency except upon reasonable notice of their intention so to do. Such legislation would seem to be justified by the recent action of certain banks on the occasion referred to in the Secretary's report.

Of the fifteen millions of fractional currency still outstanding, only about eighty thousand has been redeemed the past year. The suggestion that this amount may properly be dropped from future statements of the public debt seems worthy of approval.

So also does the suggestion of the Secretary as to the advisability of relieving the calendar of the United States courts in the southern district of New York by the transfer to another tribunal of the numerous suits there pending against collectors.

The revenue from customs for the past fiscal year was $198,159,676.02, an increase of $11,637,611.42 over that of the year preceding. One hundred and thirty-eight million ninety-eight thousand five hundred and sixty-two dollars and thirty-nine cents of this amount was collected at the port of New York, leaving $50,251,113.63 as the amount collected at all the other ports of the country. Of this sum $47,977,137.63 was collected on sugar, melado, and molasses; $27,285,624.78 on wool and its manufactures; $21,462,534.34 on iron and steel and manufactures thereof; $19,038,665.81 on manufactures of silk; $10,825,115.21 on manufactures of cotton, and $6,469,643.04 on wines and spirits, making a total revenue from these sources of $133,058,720.81.

The expenses of collection for the past year were $6,419,345.20, an increase over the preceding year of $387,410.04. Notwithstanding the increase in the revenue from customs over the preceding year, the gross value of the imports, including free goods, decreased over $25,000,000. The most marked decrease was in the value of unmanufactured wool, $14,023,682, and in that of scrap and pig iron, $12,810,671. The value of imported sugar, on the other hand, showed an increase of $7,457,474; of steel rails, $4,345,521; of barley, $2,154,204, and of steel in bars, ingots, etc., $1,620,046.

Contrasted with the imports during the last fiscal year, the exports were as follows:

Domestic merchandise	$883,925,947
Foreign merchandise	18,451,399
Total	902,377,346
Imports of merchandise	642,664,628
Excess of exports over imports of merchandise	259,712,718
Aggregate of exports and imports	1,545,041,974

Compared with the previous year, there was an increase of $66,738,688 in the value of exports of merchandise and a decrease of $25,290,118 in the value of imports. The annual average of the excess of imports of merchandise over exports thereof for ten years previous to June 30, 1873, was $104,706,922, but for the last six years there has been an excess of exports over imports of merchandise amounting to $1,180,668,105, an annual average of $196,778,017. The specie value of the exports of domestic merchandise was $376,616,473 in 1870 and $883,925,947 in 1881, an increase of $507,309,474, or 135 per cent. The value of imports was $435,958,408 in 1870 and $642,664,628 in 1881, an increase of $206,706,220, or 47 per cent.

During each year from 1862 to 1879, inclusive, the exports of specie exceeded the imports. The largest excess of such exports over imports was reached during the year 1864, when it amounted to $92,280,929. But during the year ended June 30, 1880, the imports of coin and bullion exceeded the exports by $75,891,391, and during the last fiscal year the excess of imports over exports was $91,168,650.

In the last annual report of the Secretary of the Treasury the attention of Congress was called to the fact that $469,651,050 in 5 per cent bonds and $203,573,750 in 6 per cent bonds would become redeemable during the year, and Congress was asked to authorize the refunding of these bonds at a lower rate of interest. The bill for such refunding having failed to become a law, the Secretary of the Treasury in April last notified the holders of the $195,690,400 6 per cent bonds then outstanding that the bonds would be paid at par on the 1st day of July following, or that they might be "continued" at the pleasure of the Government, to bear interest at the rate of 3½ per cent per annum.

Under this notice $178,055,150 of the 6 per cent bonds were continued at the lower rate and $17,635,250 were redeemed.

In the month of May a like notice was given respecting the redemption or continuance of the $439,841,350 of 5 per cent bonds then outstanding, and of these $401,504,900 were continued at 3½ per cent per annum and $38,336,450 redeemed.

The 6 per cent bonds of the loan of February 8, 1861, and of the Oregon war debt, amounting together to $14,125,800, having matured during the year, the Secretary of the Treasury gave notice of his intention to redeem the same, and such as have been presented have been paid from the surplus revenues. There have also been redeemed at par $16,179,100 of the 3½ per cent "continued" bonds, making a total of bonds redeemed or which have ceased to bear interest during the year of $123,969,650.

The reduction of the annual interest on the public debt through these transactions is as follows:

By reduction of interest to 3½ per cent... $10,473,952.25
By redemption of bonds.. 6,352,340.00
                                                                                                                        _____
    Total.............. .... 16,826,292.25

The 3½ per cent bonds, being payable at the pleasure of the Government, are available for the investment of surplus revenues without the payment of premiums.

Unless these bonds can be funded at a much lower rate of interest than they now bear, I agree with the Secretary of the Treasury that no legislation respecting them is desirable.

It is a matter for congratulation that the business of the country has been so prosperous during the past year as to yield by taxation a large surplus of income to the Government. If the revenue laws remain unchanged, this surplus must year by year increase, on account of the reduction of the public debt and its burden of interest and because of the rapid increase of our population. In 1860, just prior to the institution of our internal-revenue system, our population but slightly exceeded 30,000,000; by the census of 1880 it is now found to exceed 50,000,000. It is estimated that even if the annual receipts and expenditures should continue as at present the entire debt could be paid in ten years.

In view, however, of the heavy load of taxation which our people have already borne, we may well consider whether it is not the part of wisdom to reduce the revenues, even if we delay a little the payment of the debt.

It seems to me that the time has arrived when the people may justly demand some relief from their present onerous burden, and that by due economy in the various branches of the public service this may readily be afforded.

I therefore concur with the Secretary in recommending the abolition of all internal-revenue taxes except those upon tobacco in its various forms and upon distilled spirits and fermented liquors, and except also the special tax upon the manufacturers of and dealers in such articles. The retention of the latter tax is desirable as affording the officers of the Government a proper supervision of these articles for the prevention of fraud. I agree with the Secretary of the Treasury that the law imposing a stamp tax upon matches, proprietary articles, playing cards, checks, and drafts may with propriety be repealed, and the law also by which banks and bankers are assessed upon their capital and deposits. There seems to be a general sentiment in favor of this course.

In the present condition of our revenues the tax upon deposits is especially unjust. It was never imposed in this country until it was demanded by the necessities of war, and was never exacted, I believe, in any other country even in its greatest exigencies. Banks are required to secure their circulation by pledging with the Treasurer of the United States bonds of the General Government. The interest upon these bonds, which at the time when the tax was imposed was 6 per cent, is now in most instances 3½ per cent. Besides, the entire circulation was originally limited by law and no increase was allowable. When the existing banks had practically a monopoly of the business, there was force in the suggestion that for the franchise to the favored grantees the Government might very properly exact a tax on circulation; but for years the system has been free and the amount of circulation regulated by the public demand.

The retention of this tax has been suggested as a means of reimbursing the Government for the expense of printing and furnishing the circulating notes. If the tax should be repealed, it would certainly seem proper to require the national banks to pay the amount of such expense to the Comptroller of the Currency.

It is perhaps doubtful whether the immediate reduction of the rate of taxation upon liquors and tobacco is advisable, especially in view of the drain upon the Treasury which must attend the payment of arrears of pensions. A comparison, however, of the amount of taxes collected under the varying rates of taxation which have at different times prevailed suggests the intimation that some reduction may soon be made without material diminution of the revenue.

The tariff laws also need revision; but, that a due regard may be paid to the conflicting interests of our citizens, important changes should be made with caution. If a careful revision can not be made at this session, a commission such as was lately approved by the Senate and is now recommended by the Secretary of the Treasury would doubtless lighten the labors of Congress whenever this subject shall be brought to its consideration.

The accompanying report of the Secretary of War will make known to you the operations of that Department for the past year.

He suggests measures for promoting the efficiency of the Army without adding to the number of its officers, and recommends the legislation necessary to increase the number of enlisted men to 30,000, the maximum allowed by law.

This he deems necessary to maintain quietude on our ever-shifting frontier; to preserve peace and suppress disorder and marauding in new settlements; to protect settlers and their property against Indians, and Indians against the encroachments of intruders; and to enable peaceable immigrants to establish homes in the most remote parts of our country.

The Army is now necessarily scattered over such a vast extent of territory that whenever an outbreak occurs reenforcements must be hurried from many quarters, over great distances, and always at heavy cost for transportation of men, horses, wagons, and supplies.

I concur in the recommendations of the Secretary for increasing the Army to the strength of 30,000 enlisted men.

It appears by the Secretary's report that in the absence of disturbances on the frontier the troops have been actively employed in collecting the Indians hitherto hostile and locating them on their proper reservations; that Sitting Bull and his adherents are now prisoners at Fort Randall; that the Utes have been moved to their new reservation in Utah; that during the recent outbreak of the Apaches it was necessary to reenforce the garrisons in Arizona by troops withdrawn from New Mexico; and that some of the Apaches are now held prisoners for trial, while some have escaped, and the majority of the tribe are now on their reservation.

There is need of legislation to prevent intrusion upon the lands set apart for the Indians. A large military force, at great expense, is now required to patrol the boundary line between Kansas and the Indian Territory. The only punishment that can at present be inflicted is the forcible removal of the intruder and the imposition of a pecuniary fine, which in most cases it is impossible to collect. There should be a penalty by imprisonment in such cases.

The separate organization of the Signal Service is urged by the Secretary of War, and a full statement of the advantages of such permanent organization is presented in the report of the Chief Signal Officer. A detailed account of the useful work performed by the Signal Corps and the Weather Bureau is also given in that report.

I ask attention to the statements of the Secretary of War regarding the requisitions frequently made by the Indian Bureau upon the Subsistence Department of the Army for the casual support of bands and tribes of Indians whose appropriations are exhausted. The War Department should not be left, by reason of inadequate provision for the Indian Bureau, to contribute for the maintenance of Indians.

The report of the Chief of Engineers furnishes a detailed account of the operations for the improvement of rivers and harbors.

I commend to your attention the suggestions contained in this report in regard to the condition of our fortifications, especially our coast defenses, and recommend an increase of the strength of the Engineer Battalion, by which the efficiency of our torpedo system would be improved.

I also call your attention to the remarks upon the improvement of the South Pass of the Mississippi River, the proposed free bridge over the Potomac River at Georgetown, the importance of completing at an early day the north wing of the War Department building, and other recommendations of the Secretary of War which appear in his report.

The actual expenditures of that Department for the fiscal year ending June 30, 1881, were $42,122,201.39. The appropriations for the year 1882 were $44,889,725.42. The estimates for 1883 are $44,541,276.91.

The report of the Secretary of the Navy exhibits the condition of that branch of the service and presents valuable suggestions for its improvement. I call your especial attention also to the appended report of the Advisory Board which he convened to devise suitable measures for increasing the efficiency of the Navy, and particularly to report as to the character and number of vessels necessary to place it upon a footing commensurate with the necessities of the Government.

I can not too strongly urge upon you my conviction that every consideration of national safety, economy, and honor imperatively demands a thorough rehabilitation of our Navy.

With a full appreciation of the fact that compliance with the suggestions of the head of that Department and of the Advisory Board must involve a large expenditure of the public moneys, I earnestly recommend such appropriations as will accomplish an end which seems to me so desirable.

Nothing can be more inconsistent with true public economy than withholding the means necessary to accomplish the objects intrusted by the Constitution to the National Legislature. One of those objects, and one which is of paramount importance, is declared by our fundamental law to be the provision for the "common defense." Surely nothing is more essential to the defense of the United States and of all our people than the efficiency of our Navy.

We have for many years maintained with foreign governments the relations of honorable peace, and that such relations may be permanent is desired by every patriotic citizen of the Republic. But if we heed the teachings of history we shall not forget that in the life of every nation emergencies may arise when a resort to arms can alone save it from dishonor.

No danger from abroad now threatens this people, nor have we any cause to distrust the friendly professions of other governments. But for avoiding as well as for repelling dangers that may threaten us in the future we must be prepared to enforce any policy which we think wise to adopt.

We must be ready to defend our harbors against aggression; to protect, by the distribution of our ships of war over the highways of commerce, the varied interests of our foreign trade and the persons and property of our citizens abroad; to maintain everywhere the honor of our flag and the distinguished position which we may rightfully claim among the nations of the world.

The report of the Postmaster-General is a gratifying exhibit of the growth and efficiency of the postal service.

The receipts from postage and other ordinary sources during the past fiscal year were $36,489,816.58. The receipts from the money-order business were $295,581.39, making a total of $36,785,397.97. The expenditure for the fiscal year was $39,251,736.46. The deficit supplied out of the general Treasury was $2,481,129.35, or 6.3 per cent of the amount expended. The receipts were $3,469,918.63 in excess of those of the previous year, and $4,575,397.97 in excess of the estimate made two years ago, before the present period of business prosperity had fairly begun.

The whole number of letters mailed in this country in the last fiscal year exceeded 1,000,000,000.

The registry system is reported to be in excellent condition, having been remodeled during the past four years with good results. The amount of registration fees collected during the last fiscal year was $712,882.20, an increase over the fiscal year ending June 30, 1877, of $345,443.40.

The entire number of letters and packages registered during the year was 8,338,919, of which only 2,061 were lost or destroyed in transit.

The operations of the money-order system are multiplying yearly under the impulse of immigration, of the rapid development of the newer States and Territories, and the consequent demand for additional means of intercommunication and exchange.

During the past year 338 additional money-order offices have been established, making a total of 5,499 in operation at the date of this report.

During the year the domestic money orders aggregated in value $105,-075,769.35.

A modification of the system is suggested, reducing the fees for money orders not exceeding $5 from 10 cents to 5 cents and making the maximum limit $100 in place of $50.

Legislation for the disposition of unclaimed money orders in the possession of the Post-Office Department is recommended, in view of the fact that their total value now exceeds $1,000,000.

The attention of Congress is again invited to the subject of establishing a system of savings depositories in connection with the Post-Office Department.

The statistics of mail transportation show that during the past year railroad routes have been increased in length 6,249 miles and in cost $1,114,382, while steamboat routes have been decreased in length 2,182 miles and in cost $134,054. The so-called star routes have been decreased in length 3,949 miles and in cost $364,144.

Nearly all of the more expensive routes have been superseded by railroad service. The cost of the star service must therefore rapidly decrease in the Western States and Territories.

The Postmaster-General, however, calls attention to the constantly increasing cost of the railway mail service as a serious difficulty in the way of making the Department self-sustaining.

Our postal intercourse with foreign countries has kept pace with the growth of the domestic service. Within the past year several countries and colonies have declared their adhesion to the Postal Union. It now includes all those which have an organized postal service except Bolivia, Costa Rica, New Zealand, and the British colonies in Australia.

As has been already stated, great reductions have recently been made in the expense of the star-route service. The investigations of the Department of Justice and the Post-Office Department have resulted in the presentation of indictments against persons formerly connected with that service, accusing them of offenses against the United States. I have enjoined upon the officials who are charged with the conduct of the cases on the part of the Government, and upon the eminent counsel who before my accession to the Presidency were called to their assistance, the duty of prosecuting with the utmost vigor of the law all persons who may be found chargeable with frauds upon the postal service.

The Acting Attorney-General calls attention to the necessity of modifying the present system of the courts of the United States—a necessity due to the large increase of business, especially in the Supreme Court.

Litigation in our Federal tribunals became greatly expanded after the close of the late war. So long as that expansion might be attributable to the abnormal condition in which the community found itself immediately after the return of peace, prudence required that no change be made in the constitution of our judicial tribunals. But it has now become apparent that an immense increase of litigation has directly resulted from the wonderful growth and development of the country. There is no ground for belief that the business of the United States courts will ever be less in volume than at present. Indeed, that it is likely to be much greater is generally recognized by the bench and bar.

In view of the fact that Congress has already given much consideration to this subject, I make no suggestion as to detail, but express the hope that your deliberations may result in such legislation as will give early relief to our overburdened courts.

The Acting Attorney-General also calls attention to the disturbance of the public tranquillity during the past year in the Territory of Arizona. A band of armed desperadoes known as "Cowboys," probably numbering from fifty to one hundred men, have been engaged for months in committing acts of lawlessness and brutality which the local authorities have been unable to repress. The depredations of these "Cowboys" have also extended into Mexico, which the marauders reach from the Arizona frontier. With every disposition to meet the exigencies of the case, I am embarrassed by lack of authority to deal with them effectually. The punishment of crimes committed within Arizona should ordinarily, of course, be left to the Territorial authorities; but it is worthy consideration whether acts which necessarily tend to embroil the United States with neighboring governments should not be declared crimes against the United States. Some of the incursions alluded to may perhaps be within the scope of the law (U. S. Revised Statutes, sec. 5286) forbidding "military expeditions or enterprises" against friendly states; but in view of the speedy assembling of your body I have preferred to await such legislation as in your wisdom the occasion may seem to demand.

It may perhaps be thought proper to provide that the setting on foot within our own territory of brigandage and armed marauding expeditions against friendly nations and their citizens shall be punishable as an offense against the United States.

I will add that in the event of a request from the Territorial government for protection by the United States against "domestic violence" this Government would be powerless to render assistance.

The act of 1795, chapter 36, passed at a time when Territorial governments received little attention from Congress, enforced this duty of the United States only as to the State governments. But the act of 1807, chapter 39, applied also to Territories. This law seems to have remained in force until the revision of the statutes, when the provision for the Territories was dropped. I am not advised whether this alteration was intentional or accidental; but as it seems to me that the Territories should be offered the protection which is accorded to the States by the Constitution, I suggest legislation to that end.

It seems to me, too, that whatever views may prevail as to the policy of recent legislation by which the Army has ceased to be a part of the *posse comitatus*, an exception might well be made for permitting the military to assist the civil Territorial authorities in enforcing the laws of the United States. This use of the Army would not seem to be within the alleged evil against which that legislation was aimed. From sparseness of population and other circumstances it is often quite impracticable to summon a civil posse in places where officers of justice require assistance and where a military force is within easy reach.

The report of the Secretary of the Interior, with accompanying documents, presents an elaborate account of the business of that Department. A summary of it would be too extended for this place. I ask your careful attention to the report itself.

Prominent among the matters which challenge the attention of Congress at its present session is the management of our Indian affairs. While this question has been a cause of trouble and embarrassment from the infancy of the Government, it is but recently that any effort has been made for its solution at once serious, determined, consistent, and promising success.

It has been easier to resort to convenient makeshifts for tiding over temporary difficulties than to grapple with the great permanent problem, and accordingly the easier course has almost invariably been pursued.

It was natural, at a time when the national territory seemed almost illimitable and contained many millions of acres far outside the bounds of civilized settlements, that a policy should have been initiated which more than aught else has been the fruitful source of our Indian complications.

I refer, of course, to the policy of dealing with the various Indian tribes as separate nationalities, of relegating them by treaty stipulations to the occupancy of immense reservations in the West, and of encouraging them to live a savage life, undisturbed by any earnest and well-directed efforts to bring them under the influences of civilization.

The unsatisfactory results which have sprung from this policy are becoming apparent to all.

As the white settlements have crowded the borders of the reservations, the Indians, sometimes contentedly and sometimes against their will, have been transferred to other hunting grounds, from which they have again been dislodged whenever their new-found homes have been desired by the adventurous settlers.

These removals and the frontier collisions by which they have often been preceded have led to frequent and disastrous conflicts between the races.

It is profitless to discuss here which of them has been chiefly responsible for the disturbances whose recital occupies so large a space upon the pages of our history.

We have to deal with the appalling fact that though thousands of lives have been sacrificed and hundreds of millions of dollars expended in the attempt to solve the Indian problem, it has until within the past few years seemed scarcely nearer a solution than it was half a century ago. But the Government has of late been cautiously but steadily feeling its way to the adoption of a policy which has already produced gratifying results, and which, in my judgment, is likely, if Congress and the Executive accord in its support, to relieve us ere long from the difficulties which have hitherto beset us.

For the success of the efforts now making to introduce among the Indians the customs and pursuits of civilized life and gradually to absorb them into the mass of our citizens, sharing their rights and holden to their responsibilities, there is imperative need for legislative action.

My suggestions in that regard will be chiefly such as have been already called to the attention of Congress and have received to some extent its consideration.

First. I recommend the passage of an act making the laws of the various States and Territories applicable to the Indian reservations within their borders and extending the laws of the State of Arkansas to the portion of the Indian Territory not occupied by the Five Civilized Tribes.

The Indian should receive the protection of the law. He should be allowed to maintain in court his rights of person and property. He has repeatedly begged for this privilege. Its exercise would be very valuable to him in his progress toward civilization.

Second. Of even greater importance is a measure which has been frequently recommended by my predecessors in office, and in furtherance of which several bills have been from time to time introduced in both Houses of Congress. The enactment of a general law permitting the allotment in severalty, to such Indians, at least, as desire it, of a reasonable quantity of land secured to them by patent, and for their own protection made inalienable for twenty or twenty-five years, is demanded for their present welfare and their permanent advancement.

In return for such considerate action on the part of the Government, there is reason to believe that the Indians in large numbers would be persuaded to sever their tribal relations and to engage at once in agricultural pursuits. Many of them realize the fact that their hunting days are over and that it is now for their best interests to conform their manner of life to the new order of things. By no greater inducement than the assurance of permanent title to the soil can they be led to engage in the occupation of tilling it.

The well-attested reports of their increasing interest in husbandry justify the hope and belief that the enactment of such a statute as I recommend would be at once attended with gratifying results. A resort to the allotment system would have a direct and powerful influence in dissolving the tribal bond, which is so prominent a feature of savage life, and which tends so strongly to perpetuate it.

Third. I advise a liberal appropriation for the support of Indian schools, because of my confident belief that such a course is consistent with the wisest economy.

Even among the most uncultivated Indian tribes there is reported to be a general and urgent desire on the part of the chiefs and older members for the education of their children. It is unfortunate, in view of this fact, that during the past year the means which have been at the command of the Interior Department for the purpose of Indian instruction have proved to be utterly inadequate.

The success of the schools which are in operation at Hampton, Carlisle, and Forest Grove should not only encourage a more generous provision for the support of those institutions, but should prompt the establishment of others of a similar character.

They are doubtless much more potent for good than the day schools upon the reservation, as the pupils are altogether separated from the surroundings of savage life and brought into constant contact with civilization.

There are many other phases of this subject which are of great interest, but which can not be included within the becoming limits of this communication. They are discussed ably in the reports of the Secretary of the Interior and the Commissioner of Indian Affairs.

For many years the Executive, in his annual message to Congress, has urged the necessity of stringent legislation for the suppression of polygamy in the Territories, and especially in the Territory of Utah. The existing statute for the punishment of this odious crime, so revolting to the moral and religious sense of Christendom, has been persistently and contemptuously violated ever since its enactment. Indeed, in spite of commendable efforts on the part of the authorities who represent the United States in that Territory, the law has in very rare instances been enforced, and, for a cause to which reference will presently be made, is practically a dead letter.

The fact that adherents of the Mormon Church, which rests upon polygamy as its corner stone, have recently been peopling in large numbers Idaho, Arizona, and other of our Western Territories is well calculated to excite the liveliest interest and apprehension. It imposes upon Congress and the Executive the duty of arraying against this barbarous system all the power which under the Constitution and the law they can wield for its destruction.

Reference has been already made to the obstacles which the United States officers have encountered in their efforts to punish violations of law. Prominent among these obstacles is the difficulty of procuring legal evidence sufficient to warrant a conviction even in the case of the most notorious offenders.

Your attention is called to a recent opinion of the Supreme Court of the United States, explaining its judgment of reversal in the case of Miles, who had been convicted of bigamy in Utah. The court refers to the fact that the secrecy attending the celebration of marriages in that Territory makes the proof of polygamy very difficult, and the propriety is suggested of modifying the law of evidence which now makes a wife incompetent to testify against her husband.

This suggestion is approved. I recommend also the passage of an act providing that in the Territories of the United States the fact that a woman has been married to a person charged with bigamy shall not disqualify her as a witness upon his trial for that offense. I further recommend legislation by which any person solemnizing a marriage in any of the Territories shall be required, under stringent penalties for neglect or refusal, to file a certificate of such marriage in the supreme court of the Territory.

Doubtless Congress may devise other practicable measures for obviating the difficulties which have hitherto attended the efforts to suppress this iniquity. I assure you of my determined purpose to cooperate with you in any lawful and discreet measures which may be proposed to that end.

Although our system of government does not contemplate that the nation should provide or support a system for the education of our people, no measures calculated to promote that general intelligence and virtue upon which the perpetuity of our institutions so greatly depends have ever been regarded with indifference by Congress or the Executive.

A large portion of the public domain has been from time to time devoted to the promotion of education.

There is now a special reason why, by setting apart the proceeds of its sales of public lands or by some other course, the Government should aid the work of education. Many who now exercise the right of suffrage are unable to read the ballot which they cast. Upon many who had just emerged from a condition of slavery were suddenly devolved the responsibilities of citizenship in that portion of the country most impoverished by war. I have been pleased to learn from the report of the Commissioner of Education that there has lately been a commendable increase of interest and effort for their instruction; but all that can be done by local legislation and private generosity should be supplemented by such aid as can be constitutionally afforded by the National Government.

I would suggest that if any fund be dedicated to this purpose it may be wisely distributed in the different States according to the ratio of illiteracy, as by this means those localities which are most in need of such assistance will reap its special benefits.

The report of the Commissioner of Agriculture exhibits the results of the experiments in which that Department has been engaged during the past year and makes important suggestions in reference to the agricultural development of the country.

The steady increase of our population and the consequent addition to the number of those engaging in the pursuit of husbandry are giving to this Department a growing dignity and importance. The Commissioner's suggestions touching its capacity for greater usefulness deserve attention, as it more and more commends itself to the interests which it was created to promote.

It appears from the report of the Commissioner of Pensions that since 1860 789,063 original pension claims have been filed; 450,949 of these have been allowed and inscribed on the pension roll; 72,539 have been rejected and abandoned, being 13+ per cent of the whole number of claims settled.

There are now pending for settlement 265,575 original pension claims, 227,040 of which were filed prior to July 1, 1880. These, when allowed, will involve the payment of arrears from the date of discharge in case of an invalid and from date of death or termination of a prior right in all other cases.

From all the data obtainable it is estimated that 15 per cent of the number of claims now pending will be rejected or abandoned. This would show the probable rejection of 34,040 cases and the probable admission of about 193,000 claims, all of which involve the payment of arrears of pension.

With the present force employed, the number of adjudications remaining the same and no new business intervening, this number of claims (193,000) could be acted upon in a period of six years; and taking January 1, 1884, as a near period from which to estimate in each case an average amount of arrears, it is found that every case allowed would require for the first payment upon it the sum of $1,350. Multiplying this amount by the whole number of probable admissions gives $250,-000,000 as the sum required for first payment. This represents the sum which must be paid upon claims which were filed before July 1, 1880, and are now pending and entitled to the benefits of the arrears act. From this amount ($250,000,000) may be deducted from ten to fifteen millions for cases where, the claimant dying, there is no person who under the law would be entitled to succeed to the pension, leaving $235,000,000 as the probable amount to be paid.

In these estimates no account has been taken of the 38,500 cases filed since June 30, 1880, and now pending, which must receive attention as current business, but which do not involve the payment of any arrears beyond the date of filing the claim. Of this number it is estimated that 86 per cent will be allowed.

As has been stated, with the present force of the Pension Bureau (675 clerks) it is estimated that it will take six years to dispose of the claims now pending.

It is stated by the Commissioner of Pensions that by an addition of 250 clerks (increasing the adjudicating force rather than the mechanical) double the amount of work could be accomplished, so that these cases could be acted upon within three years.

Aside from the considerations of justice which may be urged for a speedy settlement of the claims now on the files of the Pension Office, it is no less important on the score of economy, inasmuch as fully one-third of the clerical force of the office is now wholly occupied in giving attention to correspondence with the thousands of claimants whose cases have been on the files for the past eighteen years. The fact that a sum so enormous must be expended by the Government to meet demands for arrears of pensions is an admonition to Congress and the Executive to give cautious consideration to any similar project in the future. The great temptation to the presentation of fictitious claims afforded by the fact that the average sum obtained upon each application is $1,300 leads me to suggest the propriety of making some special appropriation for the prevention of fraud.

I advise appropriations for such internal improvements as the wisdom of Congress may deem to be of public importance. The necessity of improving the navigation of the Mississippi River justifies a special allusion to that subject. I suggest the adoption of some measure for the removal of obstructions which now impede the navigation of that great channel of commerce.

In my letter accepting the nomination for the Vice-Presidency I stated that in my judgment—

No man should be the incumbent of an office the duties of which he is for any cause unfit to perform; who is lacking in the ability, fidelity, or integrity which a proper administration of such office demands. This sentiment would doubtless meet with general acquiescence, but opinion has been widely divided upon the wisdom and practicability of the various reformatory schemes which have been suggested and of certain proposed regulations governing appointments to public office.

The efficiency of such regulations has been distrusted mainly because they have seemed to exalt mere educational and abstract tests above general business capacity and even special fitness for the particular work in hand. It seems to me that the rules which should be applied to the management of the public service may properly conform in the main to such as regulate the conduct of successful private business:

Original appointments should be based upon ascertained fitness.

The tenure of office should be stable.

Positions of responsibility should, so far as practicable, be filled by the promotion of worthy and efficient officers.

The investigation of all complaints and the punishment of all official misconduct should be prompt and thorough.

The views expressed in the foregoing letter are those which will govern my administration of the executive office. They are doubtless shared by all intelligent and patriotic citizens, however divergent in their opinions as to the best methods of putting them into practical operation.

For example, the assertion that "original appointments should be based upon ascertained fitness" is not open to dispute.

But the question how in practice such fitness can be most effectually ascertained is one which has for years excited interest and discussion. The measure which, with slight variations in its details, has lately been urged upon the attention of Congress and the Executive has as its principal feature the scheme of competitive examination. Save for certain exceptions, which need not here be specified, this plan would allow admission to the service only in its lowest grade, and would accordingly demand that all vacancies in higher positions should be filled by promotion alone. In these particulars it is in conformity with the existing civil-service system of Great Britain; and indeed the success which has attended that system in the country of its birth is the strongest argument which has been urged for its adoption here.

The fact should not, however, be overlooked that there are certain features of the English system which have not generally been received with favor in this country, even among the foremost advocates of civil-service reform. Among them are:

1. A tenure of office which is substantially a life tenure.

2. A limitation of the maximum age at which an applicant can enter the service, whereby all men in middle life or older are, with some exceptions, rigidly excluded.

3. A retiring allowance upon going out of office.

These three elements are as important factors of the problem as any of the others. To eliminate them from the English system would effect a most radical change in its theory and practice.

The avowed purpose of that system is to induce the educated young men of the country to devote their lives to public employment by an assurance that having once entered upon it they need never leave it, and that after voluntary retirement they shall be the recipients of an annual pension. That this system as an entirety has proved very successful in Great Britain seems to be generally conceded even by those who once opposed its adoption.

To a statute which should incorporate all its essential features I should feel bound to give my approval; but whether it would be for the best interests of the public to fix upon an expedient for immediate and extensive application which embraces certain features of the English system, but excludes or ignores others of equal importance, may be seriously doubted, even by those who are impressed, as I am myself, with the grave importance of correcting the evils which inhere in the present methods of appointment.

If, for example, the English rule which shuts out persons above the age of 25 years from a large number of public employments is not to be made an essential part of our own system, it is questionable whether the attainment of the highest number of marks at a competitive examination should be the criterion by which all applications for appointment should be put to test. And under similar conditions it may also be questioned whether admission to the service should be strictly limited to its lowest ranks.

There are very many characteristics which go to make a model civil servant. Prominent among them are probity, industry, good sense, good habits, good temper, patience, order, courtesy, tact, self-reliance, manly deference to superior officers, and manly consideration for inferiors. The absence of these traits is not supplied by wide knowledge of books, or by promptitude in answering questions, or by any other quality likely to be brought to light by competitive examination.

To make success in such a contest, therefore, an indispensable condition of public employment would very likely result in the practical exclusion of the older applicants, even though they might possess qualifications far superior to their younger and more brilliant competitors.

These suggestions must not be regarded as evincing any spirit of opposition to the competitive plan, which has been to some extent successfully employed already, and which may hereafter vindicate the claim of its most earnest supporters; but it ought to be seriously considered whether the application of the same educational standard to persons of mature years and to young men fresh from school and college would not be likely to exalt mere intellectual proficiency above other qualities of equal or greater importance.

Another feature of the proposed system is the selection by promotion of all officers of the Government above the lowest grade, except such as would fairly be regarded as exponents of the policy of the Executive and the principles of the dominant party.

To afford encouragement to faithful public servants by exciting in their minds the hope of promotion if they are found to merit it is much to be desired.

But would it be wise to adopt a rule so rigid as to permit no other mode of supplying the intermediate walks of the service?

There are many persons who fill subordinate positions with great credit, but lack those qualities which are requisite for higher posts of duty; and, besides, the modes of thought and action of one whose service in a governmental bureau has been long continued are often so cramped by routine procedure as almost to disqualify him from instituting changes required by the public interests. An infusion of new blood from time to time into the middle ranks of the service might be very beneficial in its results.

The subject under discussion is one of grave importance. The evils which are complained of can not be eradicated at once; the work must be gradual.

The present English system is a growth of years, and was not created by a single stroke of executive or legislative action.

Its beginnings are found in an order in council promulgated in 1855, and it was after patient and cautious scrutiny of its workings that fifteen years later it took its present shape.

Five years after the issuance of the order in council, and at a time when resort had been had to competitive examinations as an experiment much more extensively than has yet been the case in this country, a select committee of the House of Commons made a report to that House which, declaring its approval of the competitive plan, deprecated, nevertheless, any precipitancy in its general adoption as likely to endanger its ultimate success.

During this tentative period the results of the two methods of pass examination and competitive examination were closely watched and compared. It may be that before we confine ourselves upon this important question within the stringent bounds of statutory enactment we may profitably await the result of further inquiry and experiment.

The submission of a portion of the nominations to a central board of examiners selected solely for testing the qualifications of applicants may perhaps, without resort to the competitive test, put an end to the mischiefs which attend the present system of appointment, and it may be feasible to vest in such a board a wide discretion to ascertain the characteristics and attainments of candidates in those particulars which I have already referred to as being no less important than mere intellectual attainment.

If Congress should deem it advisable at the present session to establish competitive tests for admission to the service, no doubts such as have been suggested shall deter me from giving the measure my earnest support.

And I urgently recommend, should there be a failure to pass any other act upon this subject, that an appropriation of $25,000 per year may be made for the enforcement of section 1753 of the Revised Statutes.

With the aid thus afforded me I shall strive to execute the provisions of that law according to its letter and spirit.

I am unwilling, in justice to the present civil servants of the Government, to dismiss this subject without declaring my dissent from the severe and almost indiscriminate censure with which they have been recently assailed. That they are as a class indolent, inefficient, and corrupt is a statement which has been often made and widely credited; but when the extent, variety, delicacy, and importance of their duties are considered the great majority of the employees of the Government are, in my judgment, deserving of high commendation.

The continuing decline of the merchant marine of the United States is greatly to be deplored. In view of the fact that we furnish so large a proportion of the freights of the commercial world and that our shipments are steadily and rapidly increasing, it is cause of surprise that not only is our navigation interest diminishing, but it is less than when our exports and imports were not half so large as now, either in bulk or value.

There must be some peculiar hindrance to the development of this interest, or the enterprise and energy of American mechanics and capitalists would have kept this country at least abreast of our rivals in the friendly contest for ocean supremacy.

The substitution of iron for wood and of steam for sail have wrought great revolutions in the carrying trade of the world; but these changes could not have been adverse to America if we had given to our navigation interests a portion of the aid and protection which have been so wisely bestowed upon our manufactures. I commend the whole subject to the wisdom of Congress, with the suggestion that no question of greater magnitude or farther reaching importance can engage their attention.

In 1875 the Supreme Court of the United States declared unconstitutional the statutes of certain States which imposed upon shipowners or consignees a tax of $1.50 for each passenger arriving from a foreign country, or in lieu thereof required a bond to indemnify the State and local authorities against expense for the future relief or support of such passenger. Since this decision the expense attending the care and supervision of immigrants has fallen on the States at whose ports they have landed. As a large majority of such immigrants, immediately upon their arrival, proceed to the inland States and the Territories to seek permanent homes, it is manifestly unjust to impose upon the State whose shores they first reach the burden which it now bears. For this reason, and because of the national importance of the subject, I recommend legislation regarding the supervision and transitory care of immigrants at the ports of debarkation.

I regret to state that the people of Alaska have reason to complain that they are as yet unprovided with any form of government by which life or property can be protected. While the extent of its population does not justify the application of the costly machinery of Territorial administration, there is immediate necessity for constituting such a form of government as will promote the education of the people and secure the administration of justice.

The Senate at its last session passed a bill providing for the construction of a building for the Library of Congress, but it failed to become a law. The provision of suitable protection for this great collection of books and for the copyright department connected with it has become a subject of national importance and should receive prompt attention.

The report of the Commissioners of the District of Columbia herewith transmitted will inform you fully of the condition of the affairs of the District.

They urge the vital importance of legislation for the reclamation and improvement of the marshes and for the establishment of the harbor lines along the Potomac River front.

It is represented that in their present condition these marshes seriously affect the health of the residents of the adjacent parts of the city, and that they greatly mar the general aspect of the park in which stands the Washington Monument. This improvement would add to that park and to the park south of the Executive Mansion a large area of valuable land, and would transform what is now believed to be a dangerous nuisance into an attractive landscape extending to the river front.

They recommend the removal of the steam railway lines from the surface of the streets of the city and the location of the necessary depots in such places as may be convenient for the public accommodation, and they call attention to the deficiency of the water supply, which seriously affects the material prosperity of the city and the health and comfort of its inhabitants.

I commend these subjects to your favorable consideration.

The importance of timely legislation with respect to the ascertainment and declaration of the vote for Presidential electors was sharply called to the attention of the people more than four years ago.

It is to be hoped that some well-defined measure may be devised before another national election which will render unnecessary a resort to any expedient of a temporary character for the determination of questions upon contested returns.

Questions which concern the very existence of the Government and the liberties of the people were suggested by the prolonged illness of the late President and his consequent incapacity to perform the functions of his office.

It is provided by the second article of the Constitution, in the fifth clause of its first section, that "in case of the removal of the President from office, or of his death, resignation, or inability to discharge the powers and duties of the said office, the same shall devolve on the Vice-President."

What is the intendment of the Constitution in its specification of "inability to discharge the powers and duties of the said office" as one of the contingencies which calls the Vice-President to the exercise of Presidential functions?

Is the inability limited in its nature to long-continued intellectual incapacity, or has it a broader import?

What must be its extent and duration?

How must its existence be established?

Has the President whose inability is the subject of inquiry any voice in determining whether or not it exists, or is the decision of that momentous and delicate question confided to the Vice-President, or is it contemplated by the Constitution that Congress should provide by law precisely what should constitute inability and how and by what tribunal or authority it should be ascertained?

If the inability proves to be temporary in its nature, and during its continuance the Vice-President lawfully exercises the functions of the

Executive, by what tenure does he hold his office?

Does he continue as President for the remainder of the four years' term?

Or would the elected President, if his inability should cease in the interval, be empowered to resume his office?

And if, having such lawful authority, he should exercise it, would the Vice-President be thereupon empowered to resume his powers and duties as such?

I can not doubt that these important questions will receive your early and thoughtful consideration.

Deeply impressed with the gravity of the responsibilities which have so unexpectedly devolved upon me, it will be my constant purpose to cooperate with you in such measures as will promote the glory of the country and the prosperity of its people.

SECOND ANNUAL MESSAGE.

WASHINGTON, *December 4, 1882.*

To the Senate and House of Representatives of the United States:

It is provided by the Constitution that the President shall from time to time give to the Congress information of the state of the Union and recommend to their consideration such measures as he shall judge necessary and expedient.

In reviewing the events of the year which has elapsed since the commencement of your sessions, I first call your attention to the gratifying condition of our foreign affairs. Our intercourse with other powers has continued to be of the most friendly character.

Such slight differences as have arisen during the year have been already settled or are likely to reach an early adjustment. The arrest of citizens of the United States in Ireland under recent laws which owe their origin to the disturbed condition of that country has led to a somewhat extended correspondence with the Government of Great Britain. A disposition to respect our rights has been practically manifested by the release of the arrested parties.

The claim of this nation in regard to the supervision and control of any interoceanic canal across the American Isthmus has continued to be the subject of conference.

It is likely that time will be more powerful than discussion in removing the divergence between the two nations whose friendship is so closely cemented by the intimacy of their relations and the community of their interests.

Our long-established friendliness with Russia has remained unshaken. It has prompted me to proffer the earnest counsels of this Government that measures be adopted for suppressing the proscription which the Hebrew race in that country has lately suffered. It has not transpired that any American citizen has been subjected to arrest or injury, but our courteous remonstrance has nevertheless been courteously received. There is reason to believe that the time is not far distant when Russia will be able to secure toleration to all faiths within her borders.

At an international convention held at Paris in 1880, and attended by representatives of the United States, an agreement was reached in respect to the protection of trade-marks, patented articles, and the rights of manufacturing firms and corporations. The formulating into treaties of the recommendations thus adopted is receiving the attention which it merits.

The protection of submarine cables is a subject now under consideration by an international conference at Paris. Believing that it is clearly the true policy of this Government to favor the neutralization of this means of intercourse, I requested our minister to France to attend the convention as a delegate. I also designated two of our eminent scientists to attend as our representatives at the meeting of an international committee at Paris for considering the adoption of a common unit to measure electric force.

In view of the frequent occurrence of conferences for the consideration of important matters of common interest to civilized nations, I respectfully suggest that the Executive be invested by Congress with discretionary powers to send delegates to such conventions, and that provision be made to defray the expenses incident thereto.

The difference between the United States and Spain as to the effect of a judgment and certificate of naturalization has not yet been adjusted, but it is hoped and believed that negotiations now in progress will result in the establishment of the position which seems to this Government so reasonable and just.

I have already called the attention of Congress to the fact that in the ports of Spain and its colonies onerous fines have lately been imposed upon vessels of the United States for trivial technical offenses against local regulations. Efforts for the abatement of these exactions have thus far proved unsuccessful.

I regret to inform you also that the fees demanded by Spanish consuls in American ports are in some cases so large, when compared with the value of the cargo, as to amount in effect to a considerable export duty, and that our remonstrances in this regard have not as yet received the attention which they seem to deserve.

The German Government has invited the United States to participate in an international exhibition of domestic cattle to be held at Hamburg in July, 1883.   If this country is to be represented, it is important that in the early days of this session Congress should make a suitable appropriation for that purpose.

The death of Mr. Marsh, our late minister to Italy, has evoked from that Government expressions of profound respect for his exalted character and for his honorable career in the diplomatic service of his country.   The Italian Government has raised a question as to the propriety of recognizing in his dual capacity the representative of this country recently accredited both as secretary of legation and as consul-general at Rome.   He has been received as secretary, but his exequatur as consul-general has thus far been withheld.

The extradition convention with Belgium, which has been in operation since 1874, has been lately supplanted by another.   The Senate has signified its approval, and ratifications have been duly exchanged between the contracting countries.   To the list of extraditable crimes has been added that of the assassination or attempted assassination of the chief of the State.

Negotiations have been opened with Switzerland looking to a settlement by treaty of the question whether its citizens can renounce their allegiance and become citizens of the United States without obtaining the consent of the Swiss Government.

I am glad to inform you that the immigration of paupers and criminals from certain of the Cantons of Switzerland has substantially ceased and is no longer sanctioned by the authorities.

The consideration of this subject prompts the suggestion that the act of August 3, 1882, which has for its object the return of foreign convicts to their own country, should be so modified as not to be open to the interpretation that it affects the extradition of criminals on preferred charges of crime.

The Ottoman Porte has not yet assented to the interpretation which this Government has put upon the treaty of 1830 relative to its jurisdictional rights in Turkey.   It may well be, however, that this difference will be adjusted by a general revision of the system of jurisdiction of the United States in the countries of the East, a subject to which your attention has been already called by the Secretary of State.

In the interest of justice toward China and Japan, I trust that the question of the return of the indemnity fund to the Governments of those countries will reach at the present session the satisfactory solution which I have already recommended, and which has recently been foreshadowed by Congressional discussion.

The treaty lately concluded with Korea awaits the action of the Senate.

During the late disturbance in Egypt the timely presence of American vessels served as a protection to the persons and property of many of our own citizens and of citizens of other countries, whose governments have expressed their thanks for this assistance.

The recent legislation restricting immigration of laborers from China has given rise to the question whether Chinese proceeding to or from another country may lawfully pass through our own.

Construing the act of May 6, 1882, in connection with the treaty of November 7, 1880, the restriction would seem to be limited to Chinese immigrants coming to the United States as laborers, and would not forbid a mere transit across our territory. I ask the attention of Congress to the subject, for such action, if any, as may be deemed advisable.

This Government has recently had occasion to manifest its interest in the Republic of Liberia by seeking to aid the amicable settlement of the boundary dispute now pending between that Republic and the British possession of Sierra Leone.

The reciprocity treaty with Hawaii will become terminable after September 9, 1883, on twelve months' notice by either party. While certain provisions of that compact may have proved onerous, its existence has fostered commercial relations which it is important to preserve. I suggest, therefore, that early consideration be given to such modifications of the treaty as seem to be demanded by the interests of our people.

In view of our increasing trade with both Hayti and Santo Domingo, I advise that provision be made for diplomatic intercourse with the latter by enlarging the scope of the mission at Port au Prince.

I regret that certain claims of American citizens against the Government of Hayti have thus far been urged unavailingly.

A recent agreement with Mexico provides for the crossing of the frontier by the armed forces of either country in pursuit of hostile Indians. In my message of last year I called attention to the prevalent lawlessness upon the borders and to the necessity of legislation for its suppression. I again invite the attention of Congress to the subject.

A partial relief from these mischiefs has been sought in a convention, which now awaits the approval of the Senate, as does also another touching the establishment of the international boundary between the United States and Mexico. If the latter is ratified, the action of Congress will be required for establishing suitable commissions of survey. The boundary dispute between Mexico and Guatemala, which led this Government to proffer its friendly counsels to both parties, has been amicably settled.

No change has occurred in our relations with Venezuela. I again invoke your action in the matter of the pending awards against that Republic, to which reference was made by a special message from the Executive at your last session.

An invitation has been received from the Government of Venezuela to send representatives in July, 1883, to Caracas for participating in the centennial celebration of the birth of Bolivar, the founder of South American independence. In connection with this event it is designed to commence the erection at Caracas of a statue of Washington and to conduct an industrial exhibition which will be open to American products. I recommend that the United States be represented and that suitable provision be made therefor.

The elevation of the grade of our mission in Central America to the plenipotentiary rank, which was authorized by Congress at its late session, has been since effected.

The war between Peru and Bolivia on the one side and Chile on the other began more than three years ago. On the occupation by Chile in 1880 of all the littoral territory of Bolivia, negotiations for peace were conducted under the direction of the United States. The allies refused to concede any territory, but Chile has since become master of the whole coast of both countries and of the capital of Peru. A year since, as you have already been advised by correspondence transmitted to you in January last, this Government sent a special mission to the belligerent powers to express the hope that Chile would be disposed to accept a money indemnity for the expenses of the war and to relinquish her demand for a portion of the territory of her antagonist.

This recommendation, which Chile declined to follow, this Government did not assume to enforce; nor can it be enforced without resort to measures which would be in keeping neither with the temper of our people nor with the spirit of our institutions.

The power of Peru no longer extends over its whole territory, and in the event of our interference to dictate peace would need to be supplemented by the armies and navies of the United States. Such interference would almost inevitably lead to the establishment of a protectorate— a result utterly at odds with our past policy, injurious to our present interests, and full of embarrassments for the future.

For effecting the termination of hostilities upon terms at once just to the victorious nation and generous to its adversaries, this Government has spared no efforts save such as might involve the complications which I have indicated.

It is greatly to be deplored that Chile seems resolved to exact such rigorous conditions of peace and indisposed to submit to arbitration the terms of an amicable settlement. No peace is likely to be lasting that is not sufficiently equitable and just to command the approval of other nations.

About a year since invitations were extended to the nations of this continent to send representatives to a peace congress to assemble at Washington in November, 1882. The time of meeting was fixed at a period then remote, in the hope, as the invitation itself declared, that in the meantime the disturbances between the South American Republics would be adjusted. As that expectation seemed unlikely to be realized, I asked in April last for an expression of opinion from the two Houses of Congress as to the advisability of holding the proposed convention at the time appointed. This action was prompted in part by doubts which mature reflection had suggested whether the diplomatic usage and traditions of the Government did not make it fitting that the Executive should consult the representatives of the people before pursuing a line of policy somewhat novel in its character and far reaching in its possible consequences. In view of the fact that no action was taken by Congress in the premises and that no provision had been made for necessary expenses, I subsequently decided to postpone the convocation, and so notified the several Governments which had been invited to attend.

I am unwilling to dismiss this subject without assuring you of my support of any measures the wisdom of Congress may devise for the promotion of peace on this continent and throughout the world, and I trust that the time is nigh when, with the universal assent of civilized peoples, all international differences shall be determined without resort to arms by the benignant processes of arbitration.

Changes have occurred in the diplomatic representation of several foreign powers during the past year. New ministers from the Argentine Republic, Austria-Hungary, Brazil, Chile, China, France, Japan, Mexico, the Netherlands, and Russia have presented their credentials. The missions of Denmark and Venezuela at this capital have been raised in grade. Switzerland has created a plenipotentiary mission to this Government, and an embassy from Madagascar and a minister from Siam will shortly arrive.

Our diplomatic intercourse has been enlarged by the establishment of relations with the new Kingdom of Servia, by the creation of a mission to Siam, and by the restoration of the mission to Greece. The Shah of Persia has expressed his gratification that a chargé d'affaires will shortly be sent to that country, where the rights of our citizens have been hitherto courteously guarded by the representatives of Great Britain.

I renew my recommendation of such legislation as will place the United States in harmony with other maritime powers with respect to the international rules for the prevention of collisions at sea.

In conformity with your joint resolution of the 3d of August last, I have directed the Secretary of State to address foreign governments in respect to a proposed conference for considering the subject of the universal adoption of a common prime meridian to be used in the reckoning of longitude and in the regulation of time throughout the civilized world. Their replies will in due time be laid before you.

An agreement was reached at Paris in 1875 between the principal powers for the interchange of official publications through the medium of their respective foreign departments.

The admirable system which has been built up by the enterprise of the Smithsonian Institution affords a practical basis for our cooperation in this scheme, and an arrangement has been effected by which that institution will perform the necessary labor, under the direction of the Department of State. A reasonable compensation therefor should be provided by law.

A clause in the act making appropriations for the diplomatic and consular service contemplates the reorganization of both branches of such service on a salaried basis, leaving fees to inure to the benefit of the Treasury. I cordially favor such a project, as likely to correct abuses in the present system. The Secretary of State will present to you at an early day a plan for such reorganization.

A full and interesting exhibit of the operations of the Treasury Department is afforded by the report of the Secretary.

It appears that the ordinary revenues from all sources for the fiscal year ended June 30, 1882, were as follows:

From customs	$220,410,730.25
From internal revenue	146,497,595.45
From sales of public lands	4,753,140.37
From tax on circulation and deposits of national banks	8,956,794.45
From repayment of interest by Pacific Railway companies	840,554.37
From sinking fund for Pacific Railway companies	796,271.42
From customs fees, fines, penalties, etc	1,343,348.00
From fees—consular, letters patent, and lands	2,638,990.97
From proceeds of sales of Government property	314,959.85
From profits on coinage, bullion deposits, and assays	4,116,693.73
From Indian trust funds	5,705,243.22
From deposits by individuals for surveying public lands	2,052,306.36
From revenues of the District of Columbia	1,715,176.41
From miscellaneous sources	3,383,445.43
Total ordinary receipts	403,525,250.28

The ordinary expenditures for the same period were—

For civil expenses	$18,042,386.42
For foreign intercourse	1,307,583.19
For Indians	9,736,747.40
For pensions	61,345,193.95
For the military establishment, including river and harbor improvements, and arsenals	43,570,494.19
For the naval establishment, including vessels, machinery, and improvements at navy-yards	15,032,046.26
For miscellaneous expenditures, including public buildings, light-houses, and collecting the revenue	34,539,237.50
For expenditures on account of the District of Columbia	3,330,543.87
For interest on the public debt	71,077,206.79
Total ordinary expenditures	257,981,439.57

Leaving a surplus revenue of $145,543,810.71, which, with an amount drawn from the cash balance in the Treasury of $20,737,694.84, making $166,281,505.55, was applied to the redemption—

Of bonds for the sinking fund	$60,079,150.00
Of fractional currency for the sinking fund	58,705.55
Of loan of July and August, 1861	62,572,050.00
Of loan of March, 1863	4,472,900.00
Of funded loan of 1881	37,194,450.00
Of loan of 1858	1,000.00
Of loan of February, 1861	303,000.00
Of five-twenties of 1862	2,100.00
Of five-twenties of 1864	7,400.00
Of five-twenties of 1865	6,500.00
Of ten-forties of 1864	254,550.00
Of consols of 1865	86,450.00
Of consols of 1867	408,250.00
Of consols of 1868	141,400.00
Of Oregon War debt	675,250.00
Of old demand, compound-interest, and other notes	18,350.00
	166,281,505.55

The foreign commerce of the United States during the last fiscal year, including imports and exports of merchandise and specie, was as follows:

```
Exports:
    Merchandise..................................................... $750,542,257
    Specie .........................................................   49,417,479
                                                                      ------------
        Total......................................................   799,959,736
                                                                      ============
Imports:
    Merchandise ...................................................  724,639,574
    Specie ........................................................   42,472,390
                                                                      ------------
        Total .....................................................  767,111,964
                                                                      ============
Excess of exports over imports of merchandise.....................   25,902,683
```

This excess is less than it has been before for any of the previous six years, as appears by the following table:

Year ended June 30—	Excess of exports over imports of merchandise.
1876...	$79,643,481
1877...	151,152,094
1878...	257,814,234
1879...	264,661,666
1880...	167,683,912
1881...	259,712,718
1882...	25,902,683

During the year there have been organized 171 national banks, and of those institutions there are now in operation 2,269, a larger number than ever before. The value of their notes in active circulation on July 1, 1882, was $324,656,458.

I commend to your attention the Secretary's views in respect to the likelihood of a serious contraction of this circulation, and to the modes by which that result may, in his judgment, be averted.

In respect to the coinage of silver dollars and the retirement of silver certificates, I have seen nothing to alter but much to confirm the sentiments to which I gave expression last year.

A comparison between the respective amounts of silver-dollar circulation on November 1, 1881, and on November 1, 1882, shows a slight increase of a million and a half of dollars; but during the interval there had been in the whole number coined an increase of twenty-six millions. Of the one hundred and twenty-eight millions thus far minted, little more than thirty-five millions are in circulation. The mass of accumulated coin has grown so great that the vault room at present available for storage is scarcely sufficient to contain it. It is not apparent why it is desirable to continue this coinage, now so enormously in excess of the public demand.

As to the silver certificates, in addition to the grounds which seemed last year to justify their retirement may be mentioned the effect which is likely to ensue from the supply of gold certificates for whose issuance Congress recently made provision, and which are now in active circulation.

You can not fail to note with interest the discussion by the Secretary as to the necessity of providing by legislation some mode of freeing the Treasury of an excess of assets in the event that Congress fails to reach an early agreement for the reduction of taxation.

I heartily approve the Secretary's recommendation of immediate and extensive reductions in the annual revenues of the Government.

It will be remembered that I urged upon the attention of Congress at its last session the importance of relieving the industry and enterprise of the country from the pressure of unnecessary taxation. It is one of the tritest maxims of political economy that all taxes are burdensome, however wisely and prudently imposed; and though there have always been among our people wide differences of sentiment as to the best methods of raising the national revenues, and, indeed, as to the principles upon which taxation should be based, there has been substantial accord in the doctrine that only such taxes ought to be levied as are necessary for a wise and economical administration of the Government. Of late the public revenues have far exceeded that limit, and unless checked by appropriate legislation such excess will continue to increase from year to year. For the fiscal year ended June 30, 1881, the surplus revenue amounted to $100,000,000; for the fiscal year ended on the 30th of June last the surplus was more than one hundred and forty-five millions.

The report of the Secretary shows what disposition has been made of these moneys. They have not only answered the requirements of the sinking fund, but have afforded a large balance applicable to other reductions of the public debt.

But I renew the expression of my conviction that such rapid extinguishment of the national indebtedness as is now taking place is by no means a cause for congratulation; it is a cause rather for serious apprehension.

If it continues, it must speedily be followed by one of the evil results so clearly set forth in the report of the Secretary.

Either the surplus must lie idle in the Treasury or the Government will be forced to buy at market rates its bonds not then redeemable, and which under such circumstances can not fail to command an enormous premium, or the swollen revenues will be devoted to extravagant expenditure, which, as experience has taught, is ever the bane of an overflowing treasury.

It was made apparent in the course of the animated discussions which this question aroused at the last session of Congress that the policy of diminishing the revenue by reducing taxation commanded the general approval of the members of both Houses.

I regret that because of conflicting views as to the best methods by which that policy should be made operative none of its benefits have as yet been reaped.

In fulfillment of what I deem my constitutional duty, but with little hope that I can make valuable contribution to this vexed question, I shall proceed to intimate briefly my own views in relation to it.

Upon the showing of our financial condition at the close of the last fiscal year, I felt justified in recommending to Congress the abolition of all internal revenue taxes except those upon tobacco in its various forms and upon distilled spirits and fermented liquors, and except also the special tax upon the manufacturers of and dealers in such articles.

I venture now to suggest that unless it shall be ascertained that the probable expenditures of the Government for the coming year have been underestimated all internal taxes save those which relate to distilled spirits can be prudently abrogated.

Such a course, if accompanied by a simplification of the machinery of collection, which would then be easy of accomplishment, might reasonably be expected to result in diminishing the cost of such collection by at least $2,500,000 and in the retirement from office of from 1,500 to 2,000 persons.

The system of excise duties has never commended itself to the favor of the American people, and has never been resorted to except for supplying deficiencies in the Treasury when, by reason of special exigencies, the duties on imports have proved inadequate for the needs of the Government. The sentiment of the country doubtless demands that the present excise tax shall be abolished as soon as such a course can be safely pursued.

It seems to me, however, that, for various reasons, so sweeping a measure as the total abolition of internal taxes would for the present be an unwise step.

Two of these reasons are deserving of special mention:

First. It is by no means clear that even if the existing system of duties on imports is continued without modification those duties alone will yield sufficient revenue for all the needs of the Government. It is estimated that $100,000,000 will be required for pensions during the coming year, and it may well be doubted whether the maximum annual demand for that object has yet been reached. Uncertainty upon this question would alone justify, in my judgment, the retention for the present of that portion of the system of internal revenue which is least objectionable to the people.

Second. A total abolition of excise taxes would almost inevitably prove a serious if not an insurmountable obstacle to a thorough revision of the tariff and to any considerable reduction in import duties.

The present tariff system is in many respects unjust. It makes unequal distributions both of its burdens and its benefits. This fact was practically recognized by a majority of each House of Congress in the passage of the act creating the Tariff Commission. The report of that commission will be placed before you at the beginning of this session, and will, I trust, afford you such information as to the condition and prospects of the various commercial, agricultural, manufacturing, mining, and other interests of the country and contain such suggestions for statutory revision as will practically aid your action upon this important subject.

The revenue from customs for the fiscal year ended June 30, 1879, amounted to $137,000,000.

It has in the three succeeding years reached, first, $186,000,000, then $198,000,000, and finally, as has been already stated, $220,000,000.

The income from this source for the fiscal year which will end on June 30, 1883, will doubtless be considerably in excess of the sum last mentioned.

If the tax on domestic spirits is to be retained, it is plain, therefore, that large reductions from the customs revenue are entirely feasible. While recommending this reduction, I am far from advising the abandonment of the policy of so discriminating in the adjustment of details as to afford aid and protection to domestic labor. But the present system should be so revised as to equalize the public burden among all classes and occupations and bring it into closer harmony with the present needs of industry.

Without entering into minute detail, which under present circumstances is quite unnecessary, I recommend an enlargement of the free list so as to include within it the numerous articles which yield inconsiderable revenue, a simplification of the complex and inconsistent schedule of duties upon certain manufactures, particularly those of cotton, iron, and steel, and a substantial reduction of the duties upon those articles and upon sugar, molasses, silk, wool, and woolen goods.

If a general revision of the tariff shall be found to be impracticable at this session, I express the hope that at least some of the more conspicuous inequalities of the present law may be corrected before your final adjournment. One of them is specially referred to by the Secretary. In view of a recent decision of the Supreme Court, the necessity of amending the law by which the Dutch standard of color is adopted as the test of the saccharine strength of sugars is too obvious to require comment.

From the report of the Secretary of War it appears that the only outbreaks of Indians during the past year occurred in Arizona and in the southwestern part of New Mexico. They were promptly quelled, and the quiet which has prevailed in all other parts of the country has permitted such an addition to be made to the military force in the region endangered by the Apaches that there is little reason to apprehend trouble in the future.

Those parts of the Secretary's report which relate to our seacoast defenses and their armament suggest the gravest reflections. Our existing fortifications are notoriously inadequate to the defense of the great harbors and cities for whose protection they were built.

The question of providing an armament suited to our present necessities has been the subject of consideration by a board, whose report was transmitted to Congress at the last session. Pending the consideration of that report, the War Department has taken no steps for the manufacture or conversion of any heavy cannon, but the Secretary expresses the hope that authority and means to begin that important work will be soon provided. I invite the attention of Congress to the propriety of making more adequate provision for arming and equipping the militia than is afforded by the act of 1808, which is still upon the statute book. The matter has already been the subject of discussion in the Senate, and a bill which seeks to supply the deficiencies of existing laws is now upon its calendar.

The Secretary of War calls attention to an embarrassment growing out of the recent act of Congress making the retirement of officers of the Army compulsory at the age of 64. The act of 1878 is still in force, which limits to 400 the number of those who can be retired for disability or upon their own application. The two acts, when construed together, seem to forbid the relieving, even for absolute incapacity, of officers who do not fall within the purview of the later statute, save at such times as there chance to be less than 400 names on the retired list. There are now 420. It is not likely that Congress intended this result, and I concur with the Secretary that the law ought to be amended.

The grounds that impelled me to withhold my signature from the bill entitled "An act making appropriations for the construction, repair, and preservation of certain works on rivers and harbors," which became a law near the close of your last session, prompt me to express the hope that no similar measure will be deemed necessary during the present session of Congress. Indeed, such a measure would now be open to a serious objection in addition to that which was lately urged upon your attention. I am informed by the Secretary of War that the greater portion of the sum appropriated for the various items specified in that act remains unexpended.

Of the new works which it authorized, expenses have been incurred upon two only, for which the total appropriation was $210,000. The present available balance is disclosed by the following table:

Amount of appropriation by act of August 2, 1882	$18,738,875
Amount of appropriation by act of June 19, 1882	10,000
Amount of appropriation for payments to J. B. Eads	304,000
Unexpended balance of former appropriations	4,738,263
	23,791,138
Less amount drawn from Treasury between July 1, 1882, and November 30, 1882	6,056,194
	17,734,944

It is apparent by this exhibit that so far as concerns most of the items to which the act of August 2, 1882, relates there can be no need of further appropriations until after the close of the present session.   If, however, any action should seem to be necessary in respect to particular objects, it will be entirely feasible to provide for those objects by appropriate legislation.   It is possible, for example, that a delay until the assembling of the next Congress to make additional provision for the Mississippi River improvements might be attended with serious consequences.   If such should appear to be the case, a just bill relating to that subject would command my approval.

This leads me to offer a suggestion which I trust will commend itself to the wisdom of Congress.   Is it not advisable that grants of considerable sums of money for diverse and independent schemes of internal improvement should be made the subjects of separate and distinct legislative enactments?   It will scarcely be gainsaid, even by those who favor the most liberal expenditures for such purposes as are sought to be accomplished by what is commonly called the river and harbor bill, that the practice of grouping in such a bill appropriations for a great diversity of objects, widely separated either in their nature or in the locality with which they are concerned, or in both, is one which is much to be deprecated unless it is irremediable.   It inevitably tends to secure the success of the bill as a whole, though many of the items, if separately considered, could scarcely fail of rejection.   By the adoption of the course I have recommended every member of Congress, whenever opportunity should arise for giving his influence and vote for meritorious appropriations, would be enabled so to do without being called upon to sanction others undeserving his approval.   So also would the Executive be afforded thereby full opportunity to exercise his constitutional prerogative of opposing whatever appropriations seemed to him objectionable without imperiling the success of others which commended themselves to his judgment.

It may be urged in opposition to these suggestions that the number of works of internal improvement which are justly entitled to governmental aid is so great as to render impracticable separate appropriation bills therefor, or even for such comparatively limited number as make disposition of large sums of money.   This objection may be well founded, and, whether it be or not, the advantages which would be likely to ensue from the adoption of the course I have recommended may perhaps be more effectually attained by another, which I respectfully submit to Congress as an alternative proposition.

It is provided by the constitutions of fourteen of our States that the executive may disapprove any item or items of a bill appropriating money, whereupon the part of the bill approved shall be law and the part disapproved shall fail to become law unless repassed according to the provisions prescribed for the passage of bills over the veto of the executive.   The States wherein some such provision as the foregoing is a part of the fundamental law are Alabama, California, Colorado, Florida, Georgia, Louisiana, Minnesota, Missouri, Nebraska, New Jersey, New York, Pennsylvania, Texas, and West Virginia. I commend to your careful consideration the question whether an amendment of the Federal Constitution in the particular indicated would not afford the best remedy for what is often a grave embarrassment both to members of Congress and to the Executive, and is sometimes a serious public mischief.

The report of the Secretary of the Navy states the movements of the various squadrons during the year, in home and foreign waters, where our officers and seamen, with such ships as we possess, have continued to illustrate the high character and excellent discipline of the naval organization.

On the 21st of December, 1881, information was received that the exploring steamer *Jeannette* had been crushed and abandoned in the Arctic Ocean. The officers and crew, after a journey over the ice, embarked in three boats for the coast of Siberia. One of the parties, under the command of Chief Engineer George W. Melville, reached the land, and, falling in with the natives, was saved. Another, under Lieutenant-Commander De Long, landed in a barren region near the mouth of the Lena River. After six weeks had elapsed all but two of the number had died from fatigue and starvation. No tidings have been received from the party in the third boat, under the command of Lieutenant Chipp, but a long and fruitless investigation leaves little doubt that all its members perished at sea. As a slight tribute to their heroism I give in this communication the names of the gallant men who sacrificed their lives on this expedition: Lieutenant-Commander George W. De Long, Surgeon James M. Ambler, Jerome J. Collins, Hans Halmer Erichsen, Heinrich H. Kaacke, George W. Boyd, Walter Lee, Adolph Dressler, Carl A. Görtz, Nelse Iverson, the cook Ah Sam, and the Indian Alexy. The officers and men in the missing boat were Lieutenant Charles W. Chipp, commanding; William Dunbar, Alfred Sweetman, Walter Sharvell, Albert C. Kuehne, Edward Star, Henry D. Warren, and Peter E. Johnson.

Lieutenant Giles B. Harber and Master William H. Scheutze are now bringing home the remains of Lieutenant De Long and his comrades, in pursuance of the directions of Congress.

The *Rodgers*, fitted out for the relief of the *Jeannette* in accordance with the act of Congress of March 3, 1881, sailed from San Francisco June 16 under the command of Lieutenant Robert M. Berry. On November 30 she was accidentally destroyed by fire while in winter quarters in St. Lawrence Bay, but the officers and crew succeeded in escaping to the shore. Lieutenant Berry and one of his officers, after making a search for the *Jeannette* along the coast of Siberia, fell in with Chief Engineer Melville's party and returned home by way of Europe. The other officers and the crew of the *Rodgers* were brought from St. Lawrence Bay by the whaling steamer *North Star*. Master Charles F. Putnam, who had been placed in charge of a depot of supplies at Cape Serdze, returning to his post from St. Lawrence Bay across the ice in a blinding snow-storm, was carried out to sea and lost, notwithstanding all efforts to rescue him.

It appears by the Secretary's report that the available naval force of the United States consists of 37 cruisers, 14 single-turreted monitors, built during the rebellion, a large number of smoothbore guns and Parrott rifles, and 87 rifled cannon.

The cruising vessels should be gradually replaced by iron or steel ships, the monitors by modern armored vessels, and the armament by high-power rifled guns.

The reconstruction of our Navy, which was recommended in my last message, was begun by Congress authorizing, in its recent act, the construction of two large unarmored steel vessels of the character recommended by the late Naval Advisory Board, and subject to the final approval of a new advisory board to be organized as provided by that act. I call your attention to the recommendation of the Secretary and the board that authority be given to construct two more cruisers of smaller dimensions and one fleet dispatch vessel, and that appropriations be made for high-power rifled cannon for the torpedo service and for other harbor defenses.

Pending the consideration by Congress of the policy to be hereafter adopted in conducting the eight large navy-yards and their expensive establishments, the Secretary advocates the reduction of expenditures therefor to the lowest possible amounts.

For the purpose of affording the officers and seamen of the Navy opportunities for exercise and discipline in their profession, under appropriate control and direction, the Secretary advises that the Light-House Service and Coast Survey be transferred, as now organized, from the Treasury to the Navy Department; and he also suggests, for the reasons which he assigns, that a similar transfer may wisely be made of the cruising revenue vessels.

The Secretary forcibly depicts the intimate connection and interdependence of the Navy and the commercial marine, and invites attention to the continued decadence of the latter and the corresponding transfer of our growing commerce to foreign bottoms.

This subject is one of the utmost importance to the national welfare. Methods of reviving American shipbuilding and of restoring the United States flag in the ocean carrying trade should receive the immediate attention of Congress. We have mechanical skill and abundant material for the manufacture of modern iron steamships in fair competition with our commercial rivals. Our disadvantage in building ships is the greater cost of labor, and in sailing them, higher taxes, and greater interest on capital, while the ocean highways are already monopolized by our formidable competitors. These obstacles should in some way be overcome, and for our rapid communication with foreign lands we should not continue to depend wholly upon vessels built in the yards of other countries and sailing under foreign flags. With no United States steamers on the principal ocean lines or in any foreign ports, our facilities for extending our commerce are greatly restricted, while the nations which build and sail the ships and carry the mails and passengers obtain thereby conspicuous advantages in increasing their trade.

The report of the Postmaster-General gives evidence of the satisfactory condition of that Department and contains many valuable data and accompanying suggestions which can not fail to be of interest.

The information which it affords that the receipts for the fiscal year have exceeded the expenditures must be very gratifying to Congress and to the people of the country.

As matters which may fairly claim particular attention, I refer you to his observations in reference to the advisability of changing the present basis for fixing salaries and allowances, of extending the money-order system, and of enlarging the functions of the postal establishment so as to put under its control the telegraph system of the country, though from this last and most important recommendation I must withhold my concurrence.

At the last session of Congress several bills were introduced into the House of Representatives for the reduction of letter postage to the rate of 2 cents per half ounce.

I have given much study and reflection to this subject, and am thoroughly persuaded that such a reduction would be for the best interests of the public.

It has been the policy of the Government from its foundation to defray as far as possible the expenses of carrying the mails by a direct tax in the form of postage. It has never been claimed, however, that this service ought to be productive of a net revenue.

As has been stated already, the report of the Postmaster-General shows that there is now a very considerable surplus in his Department and that henceforth the receipts are likely to increase at a much greater ratio than the necessary expenditures. Unless some change is made in the existing laws, the profits of the postal service will in a very few years swell the revenues of the Government many millions of dollars. The time seems auspicious, therefore, for some reduction in the rates of postage. In what shall that reduction consist?

A review of the legislation which has been had upon this subject during the last thirty years discloses that domestic letters constitute the only class of mail matter which has never been favored by a substantial reduction of rates. I am convinced that the burden of maintaining the service falls most unequally upon that class, and that more than any other it is entitled to present relief.

That such relief may be extended without detriment to other public interests will be discovered upon reviewing the results of former reductions.

Immediately prior to the act of 1845 the postage upon a letter composed of a single sheet was as follows:

If conveyed—	Cents.
30 miles or less	6
Between 30 and 80 miles	10
Between 80 and 150 miles	12½
Between 150 and 400 miles	18¾
Over 400 miles	25

By the act of 1845 the postage upon a single letter conveyed for any distance under 300 miles was fixed at 5 cents and for any greater distance at 10 cents.

By the act of 1851 it was provided that a single letter, if prepaid, should be carried any distance not exceeding 3,000 miles for 3 cents and any greater distance for 6 cents.

It will be noticed that both of these reductions were of a radical character and relatively quite as important as that which is now proposed.

In each case there ensued a temporary loss of revenue, but a sudden and large influx of business, which substantially repaired that loss within three years.

Unless the experience of past legislation in this country and elsewhere goes for naught, it may be safely predicted that the stimulus of 33⅓ per cent reduction in the tax for carriage would at once increase the number of letters consigned to the mails.

The advantages of secrecy would lead to a very general substitution of sealed packets for postal cards and open circulars, and in divers other ways the volume of first-class matter would be enormously augmented. Such increase amounted in England, in the first year after the adoption of penny postage, to more than 125 per cent.

As a result of careful estimates, the details of which can not be here set out, I have become convinced that the deficiency for the first year after the proposed reduction would not exceed 7 per cent of the expenditures, or $3,000,000, while the deficiency after the reduction of 1845 was more than 14 per cent, and after that of 1851 was 27 per cent.

Another interesting comparison is afforded by statistics furnished me by the Post-Office Department.

The act of 1845 was passed in face of the fact that there existed a deficiency of more than $30,000. That of 1851 was encouraged by the slight surplus of $132,000. The excess of revenue in the next fiscal year is likely to be $3,500,000.

If Congress should approve these suggestions, it may be deemed desirable to supply to some extent the deficiency which must for a time result by increasing the charge for carrying merchandise, which is now only 16 cents per pound; but even without such an increase I am confident that the receipts under the diminished rates would equal the expenditures after the lapse of three or four years.

The report of the Department of Justice brings anew to your notice the necessity of enlarging the present system of Federal jurisprudence so as effectually to answer the requirements of the ever-increasing litigation with which it is called upon to deal.

The Attorney-General renews the suggestions of his predecessor that in the interests of justice better provision than the existing laws afford should be made in certain judicial districts for fixing the fees of witnesses and jurors.

In my message of December last I referred to pending criminal proceedings growing out of alleged frauds in what is known as the star-route service of the Post-Office Department, and advised you that I had enjoined upon the Attorney-General and associate counsel, to whom the interests of the Government were intrusted, the duty of prosecuting with the utmost vigor of the law all persons who might be found chargeable with those offenses. A trial of one of these cases has since occurred. It occupied for many weeks the attention of the supreme court of this District and was conducted with great zeal and ability. It resulted in a disagreement of the jury, but the cause has been again placed upon the calendar and will shortly be retried. If any guilty persons shall finally escape punishment for their offenses, it will not be for lack of diligent and earnest efforts on the part of the prosecution.

I trust that some agreement may be reached which will speedily enable Congress, with the concurrence of the Executive, to afford the commercial community the benefits of a national bankrupt law.

The report of the Secretary of the Interior, with its accompanying documents, presents a full statement of the varied operations of that Department. In respect to Indian affairs nothing has occurred which has changed or seriously modified the views to which I devoted much space in a former communication to Congress. I renew the recommendations therein contained as to extending to the Indian the protection of the law, allotting land in severalty to such as desire it, and making suitable provision for the education of youth. Such provision, as the Secretary forcibly maintains, will prove unavailing unless it is broad enough to include all those who are able and willing to make use of it, and should not solely relate to intellectual training, but also to instruction in such manual labor and simple industrial arts as can be made practically available.

Among other important subjects which are included within the Secretary's report, and which will doubtless furnish occasion for Congressional action, may be mentioned the neglect of the railroad companies to which large grants of land were made by the acts of 1862 and 1864 to take title thereto, and their consequent inequitable exemption from local taxation.

No survey of our material condition can fail to suggest inquiries as to the moral and intellectual progress of the people.

The census returns disclose an alarming state of illiteracy in certain portions of the country, where the provision for schools is grossly inadequate.

It is a momentous question for the decision of Congress whether immediate and substantial aid should not be extended by the General Government for supplementing the efforts of private beneficence and of State and Territorial legislation in behalf of education.

The regulation of interstate commerce has already been the subject of your deliberations. One of the incidents of the marvelous extension of the railway system of the country has been the adoption of such measures by the corporations which own or control the roads as have tended to impair the advantages of healthful competition and to make hurtful discriminations in the adjustment of freightage.

These inequalities have been corrected in several of the States by appropriate legislation, the effect of which is necessarily restricted to the limits of their own territory.

So far as such mischiefs affect commerce between the States or between any one of the States and a foreign country, they are subjects of national concern, and Congress alone can afford relief.

The results which have thus far attended the enforcement of the recent statute for the suppression of polygamy in the Territories are reported by the Secretary of the Interior. It is not probable that any additional legislation in this regard will be deemed desirable until the effect of existing laws shall be more closely observed and studied.

I congratulate you that the commissioners under whose supervision those laws have been put in operation are encouraged to believe that the evil at which they are aimed may be suppressed without resort to such radical measures as in some quarters have been thought indispensable for success.

The close relation of the General Government to the Territories preparing to be great States may well engage your special attention. It is there that the Indian disturbances mainly occur and that polygamy has found room for its growth. I can not doubt that a careful survey of Territorial legislation would be of the highest utility. Life and property would become more secure. The liability of outbreaks between Indians and whites would be lessened. The public domain would be more securely guarded and better progress be made in the instruction of the young.

Alaska is still without any form of civil government. If means were provided for the education of its people and for the protection of their lives and property, the immense resources of the region would invite permanent settlements and open new fields for industry and enterprise.

The report of the Commissioner of Agriculture presents an account of the labors of that Department during the past year and includes information of much interest to the general public.

The condition of the forests of the country and the wasteful manner in which their destruction is taking place give cause for serious apprehension. Their action in protecting the earth's surface, in modifying the extremes of climate, and in regulating and sustaining the flow of springs and streams is now well understood, and their importance in relation to the growth and prosperity of the country can not be safely disregarded. They are fast disappearing before destructive fires and the legitimate requirements of our increasing population, and their total extinction can not be long delayed unless better methods than now prevail shall be adopted for their protection and cultivation. The attention of Congress is invited to the necessity of additional legislation to secure the preservation of the valuable forests still remaining on the public domain, especially in the extreme Western States and Territories, where the necessity for their preservation is greater than in less mountainous regions, and where the prevailing dryness of the climate renders their restoration, if they are once destroyed, well-nigh impossible.

The communication which I made to Congress at its first session, in December last, contained a somewhat full statement of my sentiments in relation to the principles and rules which ought to govern appointments to public service.

Referring to the various plans which had theretofore been the subject of discussion in the National Legislature (plans which in the main were modeled upon the system which obtains in Great Britain, but which lacked certain of the prominent features whereby that system is distinguished), I felt bound to intimate my doubts whether they, or any of them, would afford adequate remedy for the evils which they aimed to correct.

I declared, nevertheless, that if the proposed measures should prove acceptable to Congress they would receive the unhesitating support of the Executive.

Since these suggestions were submitted for your consideration there has been no legislation upon the subject to which they relate, but there has meanwhile been an increase in the public interest in that subject, and the people of the country, apparently without distinction of party, have in various ways and upon frequent occasions given expression to their earnest wish for prompt and definite action. In my judgment such action should no longer be postponed.

I may add that my own sense of its pressing importance has been quickened by observation of a practical phase of the matter, to which attention has more than once been called by my predecessors.

The civil list now comprises about 100,000 persons, far the larger part of whom must, under the terms of the Constitution, be selected by the President either directly or through his own appointees.

In the early years of the administration of the Government the personal direction of appointments to the civil service may not have been an irksome task for the Executive, but now that the burden has increased fully a hundredfold it has become greater than he ought to bear, and it necessarily diverts his time and attention from the proper discharge of other duties no less delicate and responsible, and which in the very nature of things can not be delegated to other hands.

In the judgment of not a few who have given study and reflection to this matter, the nation has outgrown the provisions which the Constitution has established for filling the minor offices in the public service.

But whatever may be thought of the wisdom or expediency of changing the fundamental law in this regard, it is certain that much relief may be afforded, not only to the President and to the heads of the Departments, but to Senators and Representatives in Congress, by discreet legislation. They would be protected in a great measure by the bill now pending before the Senate, or by any other which should embody its important features, from the pressure of personal importunity and from the labor of examining conflicting claims and pretensions of candidates.

I trust that before the close of the present session some decisive action may be taken for the correction of the evils which inhere in the present methods of appointment, and I assure you of my hearty cooperation in any measures which are likely to conduce to that end.

As to the most appropriate term and tenure of the official life of the subordinate employees of the Government, it seems to be generally agreed that, whatever their extent or character, the one should be definite and the other stable, and that neither should be regulated by zeal in the service of party or fidelity to the fortunes of an individual.

It matters little to the people at large what competent person is at the head of this department or of that bureau if they feel assured that the removal of one and the accession of another will not involve the retirement of honest and faithful subordinates whose duties are purely administrative and have no legitimate connection with the triumph of any political principles or the success of any political party or faction. It is to this latter class of officers that the Senate bill, to which I have already referred, exclusively applies.

While neither that bill nor any other prominent scheme for improving the civil service concerns the higher grade of officials, who are appointed by the President and confirmed by the Senate, I feel bound to correct a prevalent misapprehension as to the frequency with which the present Executive has displaced the incumbent of an office and appointed another in his stead.

It has been repeatedly alleged that he has in this particular signally departed from the course which has been pursued under recent Administrations of the Government. The facts are as follows:

The whole number of Executive appointments during the four years immediately preceding Mr. Garfield's accession to the Presidency was 2,696. Of this number 244, or 9 per cent, involved the removal of previous incumbents.

The ratio of removals to the whole number of appointments was much the same during each of those four years.

In the first year, with 790 appointments, there were 74 removals, or 9.3 per cent; in the second, with 917 appointments, there were 85 removals, or 8.5 per cent; in the third, with 480 appointments, there were 48 removals, or 10 per cent; in the fourth, with 429 appointments, there were 37 removals, or 8.6 per cent. In the four months of President Garfield's Administration there were 390 appointments and 89 removals, or 22.7 per cent. Precisely the same number of removals (89) has taken place in the fourteen months which have since elapsed, but they constitute only 7.8 per cent of the whole number of appointments (1,118) within that period and less than 2.6 of the entire list of officials (3,459), exclusive of the Army and Navy, which is filled by Presidential appointment.

I declare my approval of such legislation as may be found necessary for supplementing the existing provisions of law in relation to political assessments.

In July last I authorized a public announcement that employees of the Government should regard themselves as at liberty to exercise their pleasure in making or refusing to make political contributions, and that their action in that regard would in no manner affect their official status.

In this announcement I acted upon the view, which I had always maintained and still maintain, that a public officer should be as absolutely free as any other citizen to give or to withhold a contribution for the aid of the political party of his choice. It has, however, been urged, and doubtless not without foundation in fact, that by solicitation of official superiors and by other modes such contributions have at times been obtained from persons whose only motive for giving has been the fear of what might befall them if they refused. It goes without saying that such contributions are not voluntary, and in my judgment their collection should be prohibited by law. A bill which will effectually suppress them will receive my cordial approval.

I hope that, however numerous and urgent may be the demands upon your attention, the interests of this District will not be forgotten.

The denial to its residents of the great right of suffrage in all its relations to national, State, and municipal action imposes upon Congress the duty of affording them the best administration which its wisdom can devise.

The report of the District Commissioners indicates certain measures whose adoption would seem to be very desirable. I instance in particular those which relate to arrears of taxes, to steam railroads, and to assessments of real property.

Among the questions which have been the topic of recent debate in the halls of Congress none are of greater gravity than those relating to the ascertainment of the vote for Presidential electors and the intendment of the Constitution in its provisions for devolving Executive functions upon the Vice-President when the President suffers from inability to discharge the powers and duties of his office.

I trust that no embarrassments may result from a failure to determine these questions before another national election.

The closing year has been replete with blessings, for which we owe to the Giver of All Good our reverent acknowledgment. For the uninterrupted harmony of our foreign relations, for the decay of sectional animosities, for the exuberance of our harvests and the triumphs of our mining and manufacturing industries, for the prevalence of health, the spread of intelligence, and the conservation of the public credit, for the growth of the country in all the elements of national greatness—for these and countless other blessings we should rejoice and be glad. I trust that under the inspiration of this great prosperity our counsels may be harmonious, and that the dictates of prudence, patriotism, justice, and economy may lead to the adoption of measures in which the Congress and the Executive may heartily unite.

THIRD ANNUAL MESSAGE.

WASHINGTON, *December 4, 1883.*

To the Congress of the United States:

At the threshold of your deliberations I congratulate you upon the favorable aspect of the domestic and foreign affairs of this Government.

Our relations with other countries continue to be upon a friendly footing. With the Argentine Republic, Austria, Belgium, Brazil, Denmark, Hayti, Italy, Santo Domingo, and Sweden and Norway no incident has occurred which calls for special comment. The recent opening of new lines of telegraphic communication with Central America and Brazil permitted the interchange of messages of friendship with the Governments of those countries.

During the year there have been perfected and proclaimed consular and commercial treaties with Servia and a consular treaty with Roumania, thus extending our intercourse with the Danubian countries, while our Eastern relations have been put upon a wider basis by treaties with Korea and Madagascar. The new boundary-survey treaty with Mexico, a trade-marks convention and a supplementary treaty of extradition with Spain, and conventions extending the duration of the Franco-American Claims Commission have also been proclaimed.

Notice of the termination of the fisheries articles of the treaty of Washington was duly given to the British Government, and the reciprocal privileges and exemptions of the treaty will accordingly cease on July 1, 1885. The fisheries industries, pursued by a numerous class of our citizens on the northern coasts, both of the Atlantic and Pacific oceans, are worthy of the fostering care of Congress. Whenever brought into competition with the like industries of other countries, our fishermen, as well as our manufacturers of fishing appliances and preparers of fish products, have maintained a foremost place. I suggest that Congress create a commission to consider the general question of our rights in the fisheries and the means of opening to our citizens, under just and enduring conditions, the richly stocked fishing waters and sealing grounds of British North America.

Question has arisen touching the deportation to the United States from the British Islands, by governmental or municipal aid, of persons unable there to gain a living and equally a burden on the community here. Such of these persons as fall under the pauper class as defined by law have been sent back in accordance with the provisions of our statutes. Her Majesty's Government has insisted that precautions have been taken before shipment to prevent these objectionable visitors from coming hither without guaranty of support by their relatives in this country. The action of the British authorities in applying measures for relief has, however, in so many cases proved ineffectual, and especially so in certain recent instances of needy emigrants reaching our territory through Canada, that a revision of our legislation upon this subject may be deemed advisable.

Correspondence relative to the Clayton-Bulwer treaty has been continued and will be laid before Congress.

The legislation of France against the importation of prepared swine products from the United States has been repealed. That result is due no less to the friendly representations of this Government than to a growing conviction in France that the restriction was not demanded by any real danger to health.

Germany still prohibits the introduction of all swine products from America. I extended to the Imperial Government a friendly invitation to send experts to the United States to inquire whether the use of those products was dangerous to health. This invitation was declined. I have believed it of such importance, however, that the exact facts should be ascertained and promulgated that I have appointed a competent commission to make a thorough investigation of the subject. Its members have shown their public spirit by accepting their trust without pledge of compensation, but I trust that Congress will see in the national and international bearings of the matter a sufficient motive for providing at least for reimbursement of such expenses as they may necessarily incur.

The coronation of the Czar at Moscow afforded to this Government an occasion for testifying its continued friendship by sending a special envoy and a representative of the Navy to attend the ceremony.

While there have arisen during the year no grave questions affecting the status in the Russian Empire of American citizens of other faith than that held by the national church, this Government remains firm in its conviction that the rights of its citizens abroad should be in no wise affected by their religious belief.

It is understood that measures for the removal of the restrictions which now burden our trade with Cuba and Puerto Rico are under consideration by the Spanish Government.

The proximity of Cuba to the United States and the peculiar methods of administration which there prevail necessitate constant discussion and appeal on our part from the proceedings of the insular authorities. I regret to say that the just protests of this Government have not as yet produced satisfactory results.

The commission appointed to decide certain claims of our citizens against the Spanish Government, after the recognition of a satisfactory rule as to the validity and force of naturalization in the United States, has finally adjourned. Some of its awards, though made more than two years ago, have not yet been paid. Their speedy payment is expected.

Claims to a large amount which were held by the late commission to be without its jurisdiction have been diplomatically presented to the Spanish Government. As the action of the colonial authorities which has given rise to these claims was admittedly illegal, full reparation for the injury sustained by our citizens should be no longer delayed.

The case of the *Masonic* has not yet reached a settlement. The Manila court has found that the proceedings of which this Government has complained were unauthorized, and it is hoped that the Government of Spain will not withhold the speedy reparation which its sense of justice should impel it to offer for the unusual severity and unjust action of its subordinate colonial officers in the case of this vessel.

The Helvetian Confederation has proposed the inauguration of a class of international treaties for the referment to arbitration of grave questions between nations. This Government has assented to the proposed negotiation of such a treaty with Switzerland.

Under the treaty of Berlin liberty of conscience and civil rights are assured to all strangers in Bulgaria. As the United States have no distinct conventional relations with that country and are not a party to the treaty, they should, in my opinion, maintain diplomatic representation at Sofia for the improvement of intercourse and the proper protection of the many American citizens who resort to that country as missionaries and teachers. I suggest that I be given authority to establish an agency and consulate-general at the Bulgarian capital.

The United States are now participating in a revision of the tariffs of the Ottoman Empire. They have assented to the application of a license tax to foreigners doing business in Turkey, but have opposed the oppressive storage tax upon petroleum entering the ports of that country.

The Government of the Khedive has proposed that the authority of the mixed judicial tribunals in Egypt be extended so as to cover citizens of the United States accused of crime, who are now triable before consular courts. This Government is not indisposed to accept the change, but believes that its terms should be submitted for criticism to the commission appointed to revise the whole subject.

At no time in our national history has there been more manifest need of close and lasting relations with a neighboring state than now exists with respect to Mexico. The rapid influx of our capital and enterprise into that country shows, by what has already been accomplished, the vast reciprocal advantages which must attend the progress of its internal development. The treaty of commerce and navigation of 1848 has been terminated by the Mexican Government, and in the absence of conventional engagements the rights of our citizens in Mexico now depend upon the domestic statutes of that Republic. There have been instances of harsh enforcement of the laws against our vessels and citizens in Mexico and of denial of the diplomatic resort for their protection. The initial step toward a better understanding has been taken in the negotiation by the commission authorized by Congress of a treaty which is still before the Senate awaiting its approval.

The provisions for the reciprocal crossing of the frontier by the troops in pursuit of hostile Indians have been prolonged for another year. The operations of the forces of both Governments against these savages have been successful, and several of their most dangerous bands have been captured or dispersed by the skill and valor of United States and Mexican soldiers fighting in a common cause.

The convention for the resurvey of the boundary from the Rio Grande to the Pacific having been ratified and exchanged, the preliminary reconnoissance therein stipulated has been effected. It now rests with Congress to make provision for completing the survey and relocating the boundary monuments.

A convention was signed with Mexico on July 13, 1882, providing for the rehearing of the cases of Benjamin Weil and the Abra Silver Mining Company, in whose favor awards were made by the late American and Mexican Claims Commission. That convention still awaits the consent of the Senate. Meanwhile, because of those charges of fraudulent awards which have made a new commission necessary, the Executive has directed the suspension of payments of the distributive quota received from Mexico.

Our geographical proximity to Central America and our political and commercial relations with the States of that country justify, in my judgment, such a material increase of our consular corps as will place at each capital a consul-general.

The contest between Bolivia, Chile, and Peru has passed from the stage of strategic hostilities to that of negotiation, in which the counsels of this Government have been exercised. The demands of Chile for absolute cession of territory have been maintained and accepted by the party of General Iglesias to the extent of concluding a treaty of peace with the Government of Chile in general conformity with the terms of the protocol signed in May last between the Chilean commander and General Iglesias. As a result of the conclusion of this treaty General Iglesias has been formally recognized by Chile as President of Peru and his government installed at Lima, which has been evacuated by the Chileans. A call has been issued by General Iglesias for a representative assembly, to be elected on the 13th of January, and to meet at Lima on the 1st of March next. Meanwhile the provisional government of General Iglesias has applied for recognition to the principal powers of America and Europe. When the will of the Peruvian people shall be manifested, I shall not hesitate to recognize the government approved by them.

Diplomatic and naval representatives of this Government attended at Caracas the centennial celebration of the birth of the illustrious Bolivar. At the same time the inauguration of the statue of Washington in the Venezuelan capital testified to the veneration in which his memory is there held.

Congress at its last session authorized the Executive to propose to Venezuela a reopening of the awards of the mixed commission of Caracas. The departure from this country of the Venezuelan minister has delayed the opening of negotiations for reviving the commission. This Government holds that until the establishment of a treaty upon this subject the Venezuelan Government must continue to make the payments provided for in the convention of 1866.

There is ground for believing that the dispute growing out of the unpaid obligations due from Venezuela to France will be satisfactorily adjusted. The French cabinet has proposed a basis of settlement which meets my approval, but as it involves a recasting of the annual quotas of the foreign debt it has been deemed advisable to submit the proposal to the judgment of the cabinets of Berlin, Copenhagen, The Hague, London, and Madrid.

At the recent coronation of His Majesty King Kalakaua this Government was represented both diplomatically and by the formal visit of a vessel of war.

The question of terminating or modifying the existing reciprocity treaty with Hawaii is now before Congress. I am convinced that the charges of abuses and frauds under that treaty have been exaggerated, and I renew the suggestion of last year's message that the treaty be modified wherever its provisions have proved onerous to legitimate trade between the two countries. I am not disposed to favor the entire cessation of the treaty relations which have fostered good will between the countries and contributed toward the equality of Hawaii in the family of nations.

In pursuance of the policy declared by this Government of extending our intercourse with the Eastern nations, legations have during the past year been established in Persia, Siam, and Korea. It is probable that permanent missions of those countries will ere long be maintained in the United States. A special embassy from Siam is now on its way hither.

Treaty relations with Korea were perfected by the exchange at Seoul, on the 19th of May last, of the ratifications of the lately concluded convention, and envoys from the King of Tah Chosen have visited this country and received a cordial welcome. Korea, as yet unacquainted with the methods of Western civilization, now invites the attention of those interested in the advancement of our foreign trade, as it needs the implements and products which the United States are ready to supply. We seek no monopoly of its commerce and no advantages over other nations, but as the Chosenese, in reaching for a higher civilization, have confided in this Republic, we can not regard with indifference any encroachment on their rights.

China, by the payment of a money indemnity, has settled certain of the long-pending claims of our citizens, and I have strong hopes that the remainder will soon be adjusted.

Questions have arisen touching the rights of American and other foreign manufacturers in China under the provisions of treaties which permit aliens to exercise their industries in that country. On this specific point our own treaty is silent, but under the operation of the most-favored-nation clause we have like privileges with those of other powers. While it is the duty of the Government to see that our citizens have the full enjoyment of every benefit secured by treaty, I doubt the expediency of leading in a movement to constrain China to admit an interpretation which we have only an indirect treaty right to exact. The transference to China of American capital for the employment there of Chinese labor would in effect inaugurate a competition for the control of markets now supplied by our home industries.

There is good reason to believe that the law restricting the immigration of Chinese has been violated, intentionally or otherwise, by the officials of China upon whom is devolved the duty of certifying that the immigrants belong to the excepted classes.

Measures have been taken to ascertain the facts incident to this supposed infraction, and it is believed that the Government of China will cooperate with the United States in securing the faithful observance of the law.

The same considerations which prompted Congress at its last session to return to Japan the Simonoseki indemnity seem to me to require at its hands like action in respect to the Canton indemnity fund, now amounting to $300,000.

The question of the general revision of the foreign treaties of Japan has been considered in an international conference held at Tokyo, but without definite result as yet. This Government is disposed to concede the requests of Japan to determine its own tariff duties, to provide such proper judicial tribunals as may commend themselves to the Western powers for the trial of causes to which foreigners are parties, and to assimilate the terms and duration of its treaties to those of other civilized states.

Through our ministers at London and at Monrovia this Government has endeavored to aid Liberia in its differences with Great Britain touching the northwestern boundary of that Republic.   There is a prospect of adjustment of the dispute by the adoption of the Mannah River as the line.   This arrangement is a compromise of the conflicting territorial claims and takes from Liberia no country over which it has maintained effective jurisdiction.

The rich and populous valley of the Kongo is being opened to commerce by a society called the International African Association, of which the King of the Belgians is the president and a citizen of the United States the chief executive officer.   Large tracts of territory have been ceded to the association by native chiefs, roads have been opened, steamboats placed on the river, and the nuclei of states established at twenty-two stations under one flag which offers freedom to commerce and prohibits the slave trade.   The objects of the society are philanthropic.   It does not aim at permanent political control, but seeks the neutrality of the valley.   The United States can not be indifferent to this work nor to the interests of their citizens involved in it.   It may become advisable for us to cooperate with other commercial powers in promoting the rights of trade and residence in the Kongo Valley free from the interference or political control of any one nation.

In view of the frequency of invitations from foreign governments to participate in social and scientific congresses for the discussion of important matters of general concern, I repeat the suggestion of my last message that provision be made for the exercise of discretionary power by the Executive in appointing delegates to such convocations.   Able specialists are ready to serve the national interests in such capacity without personal profit or other compensation than the defrayment of expenses actually incurred, and this a comparatively small annual appropriation would suffice to meet.

I have alluded in my previous messages to the injurious and vexatious restrictions suffered by our trade in the Spanish West Indies. Brazil, whose natural outlet for its great national staple, coffee, is in and through the United States, imposes a heavy export duty upon that product.   Our petroleum exports are hampered in Turkey and in other Eastern ports by restrictions as to storage and by onerous taxation. For these mischiefs adequate relief is not always afforded by reciprocity treaties like that with Hawaii or that lately negotiated with Mexico and now awaiting the action of the Senate.   Is it not advisable to provide some measure of equitable retaliation in our relations with governments which discriminate against our own?   If, for example, the Executive were empowered to apply to Spanish vessels and cargoes from Cuba and Puerto Rico the same rules of treatment and scale of penalties for technical faults which are applied to our vessels and cargoes in the Antilles, a resort to that course might not be barren of good results.

The report of the Secretary of the Treasury gives a full and interesting exhibit of the financial condition of the country.

It shows that the ordinary revenues from all sources for the fiscal year ended June 30, 1883, amounted to $398,287,581.95, whereof there was received—

From customs	$214,706,496.93
From internal revenue	144,720,368.98
From sales of public lands	7,955,864.42
From tax on circulation and deposits of national banks	9,111,008.85
From profits on coinage, bullion deposits, and assays	4,460,205.17
From other sources	17,333,637.60
Total	398,287,581.95

For the same period the ordinary expenditures were:

For civil expenses	$22,343,285.76
For foreign intercourse	2,419,275.24
For Indians	7,362,590.34
For pensions	$66,012,573.64
For the military establishment, including river and harbor improvements and arsenals	48,911,382.93
For the naval establishment, including vessels, machinery, and improvements at navy-yards	15,283,437.17
For miscellaneous expenditures, including public buildings, light-houses, and collecting the revenue	40,098,432.73
For expenditures on account of the District of Columbia	3,817,028.48
For interest on the public debt	59,160,131.25
Total	265,408,137.54

Leaving a surplus revenue of $132,879,444.41, which, with an amount drawn from the cash balance in the Treasury of $1,299,312.55, making $134,178,756.96, was applied to the redemption—

Of bonds for the sinking fund	$44,850,700.00
Of fractional currency for the sinking fund	46,556.96
Of funded loan of 1881, continued at 3½ per cent	65,380,250.00
Of loan of July and August, 1861, continued at 3½ per cent	20,594,600.00
Of funded loan of 1907	1,418,850.00
Of funded loan of 1881	719,150.00
Of loan of February, 1861	18,000.00
Of loan of July and August, 1861	266,600.00
Of loan of March, 1863	116,650.00
Of loan of July, 1882	47,650.00
Of five-twenties of 1862	10,300.00
Of five-twenties of 1864	7,050.00
Of five-twenties of 1865	9,600.00
Of ten-forties of 1864	133,550.00
Of consols of 1865	40,800.00
Of consols of 1867	235,700.00
Of consols of 1868	154,650.00
Of Oregon War debt	5,450.00
Of refunding certificates	109,150.00
Of old demand, compound-interest, and other notes	13,300.00
Total	134,178,756.96

The revenue for the present fiscal year, actual and estimated, is as follows:

Source.	For the quarter ended September 30, 1883 (actual).	For the remaining three quarters of the year (estimated).
From customs...................................	$57,402,975.67	$137,597,024.33
From internal revenue.........................	29,662,078.60	90,337,921.40
From sales of public lands	2,932,635.17	5,067,364.83
From tax on circulation and deposits of national banks	1,557,800.88	1,542,199.12
From repayment of interest and sinking fund, Pacific Railway companies.....................	521,059.51	1,478,940.49
From customs fees, fines, penalties, etc...........	298,696.78	901,303.22
From fees—consular, letters patent, and lands...	863,209.80	2,436,790.20
From proceeds of sales of Government property.	112,562.23	167,437.77
From profits on coinage, etc.....................	950,229.46	3,149,770.54
From deposits for surveying public lands.......	172,461.31	327,538.69
From revenues of the District of Columbia	256,017.99	1,643,982.01
From miscellaneous sources.....................	1,237,189.63	2,382,810.37
Total receipts...............................	95,966,917.03	247,033,082.97

The actual and estimated expenses for the same period are:

Object.	For the quarter ended September 30, 1883 (actual).	For the remaining three quarters of the year (estimated).
For civil and miscellaneous expenses, including public buildings, light-houses, and collecting the revenue....................................	$15,385,799.42	$51,114,200.58
For Indians..............................	2,623,390.54	4,126,609.46
For pensions...................................	16,285,261.98	53,714,738.02
For military establishment, including fortifications, river and harbor improvements, and arsenals......................................	13,512,204.33	26,487,795.67
For naval establishment, including vessels and machinery, and improvements at navy-yards..	4,199,299.69	12,300,700.31
For expenditures on account of the District of Columbia...........	1,138,836.41	2,611,163.59
For interest on the public debt..................	14,797,297.96	39,702,702.04
Total ordinary expenditures..............	67,942,090.33	190,057,909.67

Total receipts, actual and estimated... $343,000,000.00
Total expenditures, actual and estimated............................. .... 258,000,000.00

                   85,000,000.00
Estimated amount due the sinking fund................................... 45,816,741.07

Leaving a balance of... 39,183,258.93

  If the revenue for the fiscal year which will end on June 30, 1885, be estimated upon the basis of existing laws, the Secretary is of the opinion that for that year the receipts will exceed by $60,000,000 the ordinary expenditures including the amount devoted to the sinking fund.

  Hitherto the surplus, as rapidly as it has accumulated, has been devoted to the reduction of the national debt.

  As a result the only bonds now outstanding which are redeemable at the pleasure of the Government are the 3 percents, amounting to about $305,000,000.

The 4½ percents, amounting to $250,000,000, and the $737,000,000 4 percents are not payable until 1891 and 1907, respectively.

If the surplus shall hereafter be as large as the Treasury estimates now indicate, the 3 per cent bonds may all be redeemed at least four years before any of the 4½ percents can be called in. The latter at the same rate of accumulation of surplus can be paid at maturity, and the moneys requisite for the redemption of the 4 percents will be in the Treasury many years before those obligations become payable.

There are cogent reasons, however, why the national indebtedness should not be thus rapidly extinguished. Chief among them is the fact that only by excessive taxation is such rapidity attainable.

In a communication to the Congress at its last session I recommended that all excise taxes be abolished except those relating to distilled spirits and that substantial reductions be also made in the revenues from customs. A statute has since been enacted by which the annual tax and tariff receipts of the Government have been cut down to the extent of at least fifty or sixty millions of dollars.

While I have no doubt that still further reductions may be wisely made, I do not advise the adoption at this session of any measures for large diminution of the national revenues. The results of the legislation of the last session of the Congress have not as yet become sufficiently apparent to justify any radical revision or sweeping modifications of existing law.

In the interval which must elapse before the effects of the act of March 3, 1883, can be definitely ascertained a portion at least of the surplus revenues may be wisely applied to the long-neglected duty of rehabilitating our Navy and providing coast defenses for the protection of our harbors. This is a matter to which I shall again advert.

Immediately associated with the financial subject just discussed is the important question what legislation is needed regarding the national currency.

The aggregate amount of bonds now on deposit in the Treasury to support the national-bank circulation is about $350,000,000. Nearly $200,000,000 of this amount consists of 3 percents, which, as already stated, are payable at the pleasure of the Government and are likely to be called in within less than four years unless meantime the surplus revenues shall be diminished.

The probable effect of such an extensive retirement of the securities which are the basis of the national-bank circulation would be such a contraction of the volume of the currency as to produce grave commercial embarrassments.

How can this danger be obviated? The most effectual plan, and one whose adoption at the earliest practicable opportunity I shall heartily approve, has already been indicated.

If the revenues of the next four years shall be kept substantially commensurate with the expenses, the volume of circulation will not be likely to suffer any material disturbance; but if, on the other hand, there shall be great delay in reducing taxation, it will become necessary either to substitute some other form of currency in place of the national-bank notes or to make important changes in the laws by which their circulation is now controlled.

In my judgment the latter course is far preferable. I commend to your attention the very interesting and thoughtful suggestions upon this subject which appear in the Secretary's report.

The objections which he urges against the acceptance of any other securities than the obligations of the Government itself as a foundation for national-bank circulation seem to me insuperable.

For averting the threatened contraction two courses have been suggested, either of which is probably feasible. One is the issuance of new bonds, having many years to run, bearing a low rate of interest, and exchangeable upon specified terms for those now outstanding. The other course, which commends itself to my own judgment as the better, is the enactment of a law repealing the tax on circulation and permitting the banks to issue notes for an amount equal to 90 per cent of the market value instead of, as now, the face value of their deposited bonds. I agree with the Secretary in the belief that the adoption of this plan would afford the necessary relief.

The trade dollar was coined for the purpose of traffic in countries where silver passed at its value as ascertained by its weight and fineness. It never had a legal-tender quality. Large numbers of these coins entered, however, into the volume of our currency. By common consent their circulation in domestic trade has now ceased, and they have thus become a disturbing element. They should not be longer permitted to embarrass our currency system. I recommend that provision be made for their reception by the Treasury and the mints, as bullion, at a small percentage above the current market price of silver of like fineness.

The Secretary of the Treasury advises a consolidation of certain of the customs districts of the country, and suggests that the President be vested with such power in relation thereto as is now given him in respect to collectors of internal revenue by section 3141 of the Revised Statutes. The statistics upon this subject which are contained in his report furnish of themselves a strong argument in defense of his views.

At the adjournment of Congress the number of internal-revenue collection districts was 126. By Executive order dated June 25, 1883, I directed that certain of these districts be consolidated. The result has been a reduction of one-third their number, which at present is but 83.

From the report of the Secretary of War it will be seen that in only a single instance has there been any disturbance of the quiet condition of our Indian tribes. A raid from Mexico into Arizona was made in March last by a small party of Indians, which was pursued by General Crook into the mountain regions from which it had come. It is confidently hoped that serious outbreaks will not again occur and that the Indian tribes which have for so many years disturbed the West will hereafter remain in peaceable submission.

I again call your attention to the present condition of our extended seacoast, upon which are so many large cities whose wealth and importance to the country would in time of war invite attack from modern armored ships, against which our existing defensive works could give no adequate protection. Those works were built before the introduction of modern heavy rifled guns into maritime warfare, and if they are not put in an efficient condition we may easily be subjected to humiliation by a hostile power greatly inferior to ourselves. As germane to this subject, I call your attention to the importance of perfecting our submarine-torpedo defenses. The board authorized by the last Congress to report upon the method which should be adopted for the manufacture of heavy ordnance adapted to modern warfare has visited the principal iron and steel works in this country and in Europe. It is hoped that its report will soon be made, and that Congress will thereupon be disposed to provide suitable facilities and plant for the manufacture of such guns as are now imperatively needed.

On several occasions during the past year officers of the Army have at the request of the State authorities visited their militia encampments for inspection of the troops. From the reports of these officers I am induced to believe that the encouragement of the State militia organizations by the National Government would be followed by very gratifying results, and would afford it in sudden emergencies the aid of a large body of volunteers educated in the performance of military duties.

The Secretary of the Navy reports that under the authority of the acts of August 5, 1882, and March 3, 1883, the work of strengthening our Navy by the construction of modern vessels has been auspiciously begun. Three cruisers are in process of construction—the *Chicago*, of 4,500 tons displacement, and the *Boston* and *Atlanta*, each of 2,500 tons. They are to be built of steel, with the tensile strength and ductility prescribed by law, and in the combination of speed, endurance, and armament are expected to compare favorably with the best unarmored war vessels of other nations. A fourth vessel, the *Dolphin*, is to be constructed of similar material, and is intended to serve as a fleet dispatch boat.

The double-turreted monitors *Puritan, Amphitrite,* and *Terror* have been launched on the Delaware River and a contract has been made for the supply of their machinery. A similar monitor, the *Monadnock*, has been launched in California.

The Naval Advisory Board and the Secretary recommend the completion of the monitors, the construction of four gunboats, and also of three additional steel vessels like the *Chicago, Boston*, and *Dolphin*.

As an important measure of national defense, the Secretary urges also the immediate creation of an interior coast line of waterways across the peninsula of Florida, along the coast from Florida to Hampton Roads, between the Chesapeake Bay and the Delaware River, and through Cape Cod.

I feel bound to impress upon the attention of Congress the necessity of continued progress in the reconstruction of the Navy. The condition of the public Treasury, as I have already intimated, makes the present an auspicious time for putting this branch of the service in a state of efficiency.

It is no part of our policy to create and maintain a Navy able to cope with that of the other great powers of the world.

We have no wish for foreign conquest, and the peace which we have long enjoyed is in no seeming danger of interruption.

But that our naval strength should be made adequate for the defense of our harbors, the protection of our commercial interests, and the maintenance of our national honor is a proposition from which no patriotic citizen can withhold his assent.

The report of the Postmaster-General contains a gratifying exhibit of the condition and prospects of the interesting branch of the public service committed to his care.

It appears that on June 30, 1883, the whole number of post-offices was 47,863, of which 1,632 were established during the previous fiscal year. The number of offices operating under the system of free delivery was 154.

At these latter offices the postage on local matter amounted to $4,195,230.52, a sum exceeding by $1,021,894.01 the entire cost of the carrier service of the country.

The rate of postage on drop letters passing through these offices is now fixed by law at 2 cents per half ounce or fraction thereof. In offices where the carrier system has not been established the rate is only half as large.

It will be remembered that in 1863, when free delivery was first established by law, the uniform single-rate postage upon local letters was 1 cent, and so it remained until 1872, when in those cities where carrier service was established it was increased in order to defray the expense of such service.

It seems to me that the old rate may now with propriety be restored, and that, too, even at the risk of diminishing, for a time at least, the receipts from postage upon local letters.

I can see no reason why that particular class of mail matter should be held accountable for the entire cost of not only its own collection and delivery, but the collection and delivery of all other classes; and I am confident, after full consideration of the subject, that the reduction of rate would be followed by such a growing accession of business as to occasion but slight and temporary loss to the revenues of the Post-Office. The Postmaster-General devotes much of his report to the consideration in its various aspects of the relations of the Government to the telegraph. Such reflection as I have been able to give to this subject since my last annual message has not led me to change the views which I there expressed in dissenting from the recommendation of the then Postmaster-General that the Government assume the same control over the telegraph which it has always exercised over the mail.

Admitting that its authority in the premises is as ample as has ever been claimed for it, it would not, in my judgment, be a wise use of that authority to purchase or assume the control of existing telegraph lines, or to construct others with a view of entering into general competition with private enterprise.

The objections which may be justly urged against either of those projects, and indeed against any system which would require an enormous increase in the civil-service list, do not, however, apply to some of the plans which have lately provoked public comment and discussion. It has been claimed, for example, that Congress might wisely authorize the Postmaster-General to contract with some private persons or corporation for the transmission of messages, or of a certain class of messages, at specified rates and under Government supervision. Various such schemes, of the same general nature, but widely differing in their special characteristics, have been suggested in the public prints, and the arguments by which they have been supported and opposed have doubtless attracted your attention.

It is likely that the whole subject will be considered by you at the present session.

In the nature of things it involves so many questions of detail that your deliberations would probably be aided slightly, if at all, by any particular suggestions which I might now submit.

I avow my belief, however, that the Government should be authorized by law to exercise some sort of supervision over interstate telegraphic communication, and I express the hope that for attaining that end some measure may be devised which will receive your approbation.

The Attorney-General criticises in his report the provisions of existing law fixing the fees of jurors and witnesses in the Federal courts. These provisions are chiefly contained in the act of February 26, 1853, though some of them were introduced into that act from statutes which had been passed many years previous. It is manifest that such compensation as might when these laws were enacted have been just and reasonable would in many instances be justly regarded at the present day as inadequate. I concur with the Attorney-General in the belief that the statutes should be revised by which these fees are regulated.

So, too, should the laws which regulate the compensation of district attorneys and marshals. They should be paid wholly by salaries instead of in part by fees, as is now the case.

The change would prove to be a measure of economy and would discourage the institution of needless and oppressive legal proceedings, which it is to be feared have in some instances been conducted for the mere sake of personal gain.

Much interesting and varied information is contained in the report of the Secretary of the Interior.

I particularly call your attention to his presentation of certain phases of the Indian question, to his recommendations for the repeal of the preemption and timber-culture acts, and for more stringent legislation to prevent frauds under the pension laws. The statutes which prescribe the definitions and punishments of crimes relating to pensions could doubtless be made more effective by certain amendments and additions which are pointed out in the Secretary's report.

I have previously referred to the alarming state of illiteracy in certain portions of the country, and again submit for the consideration of Congress whether some Federal aid should not be extended to public primary education wherever adequate provision therefor has not already been made.

The Utah Commission has submitted to the Secretary of the Interior its second annual report. As a result of its labors in supervising the recent election in that Territory, pursuant to the act of March 22, 1882, it appears that persons by that act disqualified to the number of about 12,000, were excluded from the polls. This fact, however, affords little cause for congratulation, and I fear that it is far from indicating any real and substantial progress toward the extirpation of polygamy. All the members elect of the legislature are Mormons. There is grave reason to believe that they are in sympathy with the practices that this Government is seeking to suppress, and that its efforts in that regard will be more likely to encounter their opposition than to receive their encouragement and support. Even if this view should happily be erroneous, the law under which the commissioners have been acting should be made more effective by the incorporation of some such stringent amendments as they recommend, and as were included in bill No. 2238 on the Calendar of the Senate at its last session.

I am convinced, however, that polygamy has become so strongly intrenched in the Territory of Utah that it is profitless to attack it with any but the stoutest weapons which constitutional legislation can fashion. I favor, therefore, the repeal of the act upon which the existing government depends, the assumption by the National Legislature of the entire political control of the Territory, and the establishment of a commission with such powers and duties as shall be delegated to it by law.

The Department of Agriculture is accomplishing much in the direction of the agricultural development of the country, and the report of the Commissioner giving the results of his investigations and experiments will be found interesting and valuable.

At his instance a convention of those interested in the cattle industry of the country was lately held at Chicago. The prevalence of pleuropneumonia and other contagious diseases of animals was one of the chief topics of discussion. A committee of the convention will invite your cooperation in investigating the causes of these diseases and providing methods for their prevention and cure.

I trust that Congress will not fail at its present session to put Alaska under the protection of law. Its people have repeatedly remonstrated against our neglect to afford them the maintenance and protection expressly guaranteed by the terms of the treaty whereby that Territory was ceded to the United States. For sixteen years they have pleaded in vain for that which they should have received without the asking.

They have no law for the collection of debts, the support of education, the conveyance of property, the administration of estates, or the **enforce**-ment of contracts; none, indeed, for the punishment of criminals, except such as offend against certain customs, commerce, and navigation acts.

The resources of Alaska especially in fur, mines, and lumber, are considerable in extent and capable of large development, while its geographical situation is one of political and commercial importance.

The promptings of interest, therefore, as well as considerations of honor and good faith, demand the immediate establishment of civil government in that Territory.

Complaints have lately been numerous and urgent that certain corporations, controlling in whole or in part the facilities for the interstate carriage of persons and merchandise over the great railroads of the country, have resorted in their dealings with the public to divers measures unjust and oppressive in their character.

In some instances the State governments have attacked and suppressed these evils, but in others they have been unable to afford adequate relief because of the jurisdictional limitations which are imposed upon them by the Federal Constitution.

The question how far the National Government may lawfully interfere in the premises, and what, if any, supervision or control it ought to exercise, is one which merits your careful consideration.

While we can not fail to recognize the importance of the vast railway systems of the country and their great and beneficent influences upon the development of our material wealth, we should, on the other hand, remember that no individual and no corporation ought to be invested with absolute power over the interest of any other citizen or class of citizens. The right of these railway corporations to a fair and profitable return upon their investments and to reasonable freedom in their regulations must be recognized; but it seems only just that, so far as its constitutional authority will permit, Congress should protect the people at large in their interstate traffic against acts of injustice which the State governments are powerless to prevent.

In my last annual message I called attention to the necessity of protecting by suitable legislation the forests situated upon the public domain. In many portions of the West the pursuit of general agriculture is only made practicable by resort to irrigation, while successful irrigation would itself be impossible without the aid afforded by forests in contributing to the regularity and constancy of the supply of water.

During the past year severe suffering and great loss of property have been occasioned by profuse floods followed by periods of unusually low water in many of the great rivers of the country.

These irregularities were in great measure caused by the removal from about the sources of the streams in question of the timber by which the water supply had been nourished and protected.

The preservation of such portions of the forests on the national domain as essentially contribute to the equable flow of important water courses is of the highest consequence.

Important tributaries of the Missouri, the Columbia, and the Saskatchewan rise in the mountain region of Montana, near the northern boundary of the United States, between the Blackfeet and Flathead Indian reservations. This region is unsuitable for settlement, but upon the rivers which flow from it depends the future agricultural development of a vast tract of country. The attention of Congress is called to the necessity of withdrawing from public sale this part of the public domain and establishing there a forest preserve.

The industrial exhibitions which have been held in the United States during the present year attracted attention in many foreign countries, where the announcement of those enterprises had been made public through the foreign agencies of this Government. The Industrial Exhibition at Boston and the Southern Exposition at Louisville were largely attended by the exhibitors of foreign countries, notwithstanding the absence of any professed national character in those undertakings.

The Centennial Exposition to be held next year at New Orleans in commemoration of the centenary of the first shipment of cotton from a port of the United States bids fair to meet with like gratifying success. Under the act of Congress of the 10th of February, 1883, declaring that exposition to be national and international in its character, all foreign governments with which the United States maintain relations have been invited to participate.

The promoters of this important undertaking have already received assurances of the lively interest which it has excited abroad.

The report of the Commissioners of the District of Columbia is herewith transmitted. I ask for it your careful attention, especially for those portions which relate to assessments, arrears of taxes, and increase of water supply.

The commissioners who were appointed under the act of January 16, 1883, entitled "An act to regulate and improve the civil service of the United States," entered promptly upon the discharge of their duties.

A series of rules, framed in accordance with the spirit of the statute, was approved and promulgated by the President.

In some particulars wherein they seemed defective those rules were subsequently amended. It will be perceived that they discountenance any political or religious tests for admission to those offices of the public service to which the statute relates.

The act is limited in its original application to the classified clerkships in the several Executive Departments at Washington (numbering about 5,600) and to similar positions in customs districts and post-offices where as many as fifty persons are employed. A classification of these positions analogous to that existing in the Washington offices was duly made before the law went into effect. Eleven customs districts and twenty-three post-offices were thus brought under the immediate operation of the statute.

The annual report of the Civil Service Commission which will soon be submitted to Congress will doubtless afford the means of a more definite judgment than I am now prepared to express as to the merits of the new system. I am persuaded that its effects have thus far proved beneficial. Its practical methods appear to be adequate for the ends proposed, and there has been no serious difficulty in carrying them into effect. Since the 16th of July last no person, so far as I am aware, has been appointed to the public service in the classified portions thereof at any of the Departments, or at any of the post-offices and customs districts above named, except those certified by the Commission to be the most competent on the basis of the examinations held in conformity to the rules.

At the time when the present Executive entered upon his office his death, removal, resignation, or inability to discharge his duties would have left the Government without a constitutional head.

It is possible, of course, that a similar contingency may again arise unless the wisdom of Congress shall provide against its recurrence.

The Senate at its last session, after full consideration, passed an act relating to this subject, which will now, I trust, commend itself to the approval of both Houses of Congress.

The clause of the Constitution upon which must depend any law regulating the Presidential succession presents also for solution other questions of paramount importance.

These questions relate to the proper interpretation of the phrase "inability to discharge the powers and duties of said office," our organic law providing that when the President shall suffer from such inability the Presidential office shall devolve upon the Vice-President, who must himself under like circumstances give place to such officer as Congress may by law appoint to act as President.

I need not here set forth the numerous and interesting inquiries which are suggested by these words of the Constitution. They were fully stated in my first communication to Congress and have since been the subject of frequent deliberations in that body.

It is greatly to be hoped that these momentous questions will find speedy solution, lest emergencies may arise when longer delay will be impossible and any determination, albeit the wisest, may furnish cause for anxiety and alarm.

For the reasons fully stated in my last annual message I repeat my recommendation that Congress propose an amendment to that provision of the Constitution which prescribes the formalities for the enactment of laws, whereby, in respect to bills for the appropriation of public moneys, the Executive may be enabled, while giving his approval to particular items, to interpose his veto as to such others as do not commend themselves to his judgment.

The fourteenth amendment of the Constitution confers the rights of citizenship upon all persons born or naturalized in the United States and subject to the jurisdiction thereof. It was the special purpose of this amendment to insure to members of the colored race the full enjoyment of civil and political rights. Certain statutory provisions intended to secure the enforcement of those rights have been recently declared unconstitutional by the Supreme Court.

Any legislation whereby Congress may lawfully supplement the guaranties which the Constitution affords for the equal enjoyment by all the citizens of the United States of every right, privilege, and immunity of citizenship will receive my unhesitating approval.

FOURTH ANNUAL MESSAGE.

WASHINGTON, *December 1, 1884.*

To the Congress of the United States:

Since the close of your last session the American people, in the exercise of their highest right of suffrage, have chosen their Chief Magistrate for the four years ensuing.

When it is remembered that at no period in the country's history has the long political contest which customarily precedes the day of the national election been waged with greater fervor and intensity, it is a subject of general congratulation that after the controversy at the polls was over, and while the slight preponderance by which the issue had been determined was as yet unascertained, the public peace suffered no disturbance, but the people everywhere patiently and quietly awaited the result.

Nothing could more strikingly illustrate the temper of the American citizen, his love of order, and his loyalty to law. Nothing could more signally demonstrate the strength and wisdom of our political institutions.

Eight years have passed since a controversy concerning the result of a national election sharply called the attention of the Congress to the necessity of providing more precise and definite regulations for counting the electoral vote.

It is of the gravest importance that this question be solved before conflicting claims to the Presidency shall again distract the country, and I am persuaded that by the people at large any of the measures of relief thus far proposed would be preferred to continued inaction.

Our relations with all foreign powers continue to be amicable.

With Belgium a convention has been signed whereby the scope of present treaties has been so enlarged as to secure to citizens of either country within the jurisdiction of the other equal rights and privileges in the acquisition and alienation of property. A trade-marks treaty has also been concluded.

The war between Chile and Peru is at an end. For the arbitration of the claims of American citizens who during its continuance suffered through the acts of the Chilean authorities a convention will soon be negotiated.

The state of hostilities between France and China continues to be an embarrassing feature of our Eastern relations. The Chinese Government has promptly adjusted and paid the claims of American citizens whose property was destroyed in the recent riots at Canton. I renew the recommendation of my last annual message, that the Canton indemnity fund be returned to China.

The true interpretation of the recent treaty with that country permitting the restriction of Chinese immigration is likely to be again the subject of your deliberations. It may be seriously questioned whether the statute passed at the last session does not violate the treaty rights of certain Chinese who left this country with return certificates valid under the old law, and who now seem to be debarred from relanding for lack of the certificates required by the new.

The recent purchase by citizens of the United States of a large trading fleet heretofore under the Chinese flag has considerably enhanced our commercial importance in the East. In view of the large number of vessels built or purchased by American citizens in other countries and exclusively employed in legitimate traffic between foreign ports under the recognized protection of our flag, it might be well to provide a uniform rule for their registration and documentation, so that the *bona fide* property rights of our citizens therein shall be duly evidenced and properly guarded.

Pursuant to the advice of the Senate at the last session, I recognized the flag of the International Association of the Kongo as that of a friendly government, avoiding in so doing any prejudgment of conflicting territorial claims in that region. Subsequently, in execution of the expressed wish of the Congress, I appointed a commercial agent for the Kongo basin.

The importance of the rich prospective trade of the Kongo Valley has led to the general conviction that it should be open to all nations upon equal terms. At an international conference for the consideration of this subject called by the Emperor of Germany, and now in session at Berlin, delegates are in attendance on behalf of the United States. Of the results of the conference you will be duly advised.

The Government of Korea has generously aided the efforts of the United States minister to secure suitable premises for the use of the legation. As the conditions of diplomatic intercourse with Eastern nations demand that the legation premises be owned by the represented power, I advise that an appropriation be made for the acquisition of this property by the Government. The United States already possess valuable premises at Tangier as a gift from the Sultan of Morocco. As is stated hereafter, they have lately received a similar gift from the Siamese Government. The Government of Japan stands ready to present to us extensive grounds at Tokyo whereon to erect a suitable building for the legation, court-house, and jail, and similar privileges can probably be secured in China and Persia. The owning of such premises would not only effect a large saving of the present rentals, but would permit of the due assertion of extraterritorial rights in those countries, and would the better serve to maintain the dignity of the United States.

The failure of Congress to make appropriation for our representation at the autonomous court of the Khedive has proved a serious embarrassment in our intercourse with Egypt; and in view of the necessary intimacy of diplomatic relationship due to the participation of this Government as one of the treaty powers in all matters of administration there affecting the rights of foreigners, I advise the restoration of the agency and consulate-general at Cairo on its former basis. I do not conceive it to be the wish of Congress that the United States should withdraw altogether from the honorable position they have hitherto held with respect to the Khedive, or that citizens of this Republic residing or sojourning in Egypt should hereafter be without the aid and protection of a competent representative.

With France the traditional cordial relationship continues. The colossal statue of Liberty Enlightening the World, the generous gift of the people of France, is expected to reach New York in May next. I suggest that Congressional action be taken in recognition of the spirit which has prompted this gift and in aid of the timely completion of the pedestal upon which it is to be placed.

Our relations with Germany, a country which contributes to our own some of the best elements of citizenship, continue to be cordial. The United States have extradition treaties with several of the German

States, but by reason of the confederation of those States under the imperial rule the application of such treaties is not as uniform and comprehensive as the interests of the two countries require. I propose, therefore, to open negotiations for a single convention of extradition to embrace all the territory of the Empire.

It affords me pleasure to say that our intercourse with Great Britain continues to be of a most friendly character.

The Government of Hawaii has indicated its willingness to continue for seven years the provisions of the existing reciprocity treaty. Such continuance, in view of the relations of that country to the American system of States, should, in my judgment, be favored.

The revolution in Hayti against the established Government has terminated. While it was in progress it became necessary to enforce our neutrality laws by instituting proceedings against individuals and vessels charged with their infringement. These prosecutions were in all cases successful.

Much anxiety has lately been displayed by various European Governments, and especially by the Government of Italy, for the abolition of our import duties upon works of art. It is well to consider whether the present discrimination in favor of the productions of American artists abroad is not likely to result, as they themselves seem very generally to believe it may, in the practical exclusion of our painters and sculptors from the rich fields for observation, study, and labor which they have hitherto enjoyed.

There is prospect that the long-pending revision of the foreign treaties of Japan may be concluded at a new conference to be held at Tokyo. While this Government fully recognizes the equal and independent station of Japan in the community of nations, it would not oppose the general adoption of such terms of compromise as Japan may be disposed to offer in furtherance of a uniform policy of intercourse with Western nations.

During the past year the increasing good will between our own Government and that of Mexico has been variously manifested. The treaty of commercial reciprocity concluded January 20, 1883, has been ratified and awaits the necessary tariff legislation of Congress to become effective. This legislation will, I doubt not, be among the first measures to claim your attention.

A full treaty of commerce, navigation, and consular rights is much to be desired, and such a treaty I have reason to believe that the Mexican Government stands ready to conclude.

Some embarrassment has been occasioned by the failure of Congress at its last session to provide means for the due execution of the treaty of July 29, 1882, for the resurvey of the Mexican boundary and the relocation of boundary monuments.

With the Republic of Nicaragua a treaty has been concluded which authorizes the construction by the United States of a canal, railway, and telegraph line across the Nicaraguan territory.

By the terms of this treaty 60 miles of the river San Juan, as well as Lake Nicaragua, an inland sea 40 miles in width, are to constitute a part of the projected enterprise.

This leaves for actual canal construction 17 miles on the Pacific side and 36 miles on the Atlantic. To the United States, whose rich territory on the Pacific is for the ordinary purposes of commerce practically cut off from communication by water with the Atlantic ports, the political and commercial advantages of such a project can scarcely be overestimated.

It is believed that when the treaty is laid before you the justice and liberality of its provisions will command universal approval at home and abroad.

The death of our representative at Russia while at his post at St. Petersburg afforded to the Imperial Government a renewed opportunity to testify its sympathy in a manner befitting the intimate friendliness which has ever marked the intercourse of the two countries.

The course of this Government in raising its representation at Bangkok to the diplomatic rank has evoked from Siam evidences of warm friendship and augurs well for our enlarged intercourse. The Siamese Government has presented to the United States a commodious mansion and grounds for the occupancy of the legation, and I suggest that by joint resolution Congress attest its appreciation of this generous gift.

This government has more than once been called upon of late to take action in fulfillment of its international obligations toward Spain. Agitation in the island of Cuba hostile to the Spanish Crown having been fomented by persons abusing the sacred rights of hospitality which our territory affords, the officers of this Government have been instructed to exercise vigilance to prevent infractions of our neutrality laws at Key West and at other points near the Cuban coast. I am happy to say that in the only instance where these precautionary measures were successfully eluded the offenders, when found in our territory, were subsequently tried and convicted.

The growing need of close relationship of intercourse and traffic between the Spanish Antilles and their natural market in the United States led to the adoption in January last of a commercial agreement looking to that end. This agreement has since been superseded by a more carefully framed and comprehensive convention, which I shall submit to the Senate for approval. It has been the aim of this negotiation to open such a favored reciprocal exchange of productions carried under the flag of either country as to make the intercourse between Cuba and Puerto Rico and ourselves scarcely less intimate than the commercial movement between our domestic ports, and to insure a removal of the burdens on shipping in the Spanish Indies, of which in the past our shipowners and shipmasters have so often had cause to complain.

The negotiation of this convention has for a time postponed the prosecution of certain claims of our citizens which were declared to be without the jurisdiction of the late Spanish-American Claims Commission, and which are therefore remitted to diplomatic channels for adjustment. The speedy settlement of these claims will now be urged by this Government.

Negotiations for a treaty of commercial reciprocity with the Dominican Republic have been successfully concluded, and the result will shortly be laid before the Senate.

Certain questions between the United States and the Ottoman Empire still remain unsolved. Complaints on behalf of our citizens are not satisfactorily adjusted. The Porte has sought to withhold from our commerce the right of favored treatment to which we are entitled by existing conventional stipulations, and the revision of the tariffs is unaccomplished.

The final disposition of pending questions with Venezuela has not as yet been reached, but I have good reason to expect an early settlement which will provide the means of reexamining the Caracas awards in conformity with the expressed desire of Congress, and which will recognize the justice of certain claims preferred against Venezuela.

The Central and South American Commission appointed by authority of the act of July 7, 1884, will soon proceed to Mexico. It has been furnished with instructions which will be laid before you. They contain a statement of the general policy of the Government for enlarging its commercial intercourse with American States. The commissioners have been actively preparing for their responsible task by holding conferences in the principal cities with merchants and others interested in Central and South American trade.

The International Meridian Conference lately convened in Washington upon the invitation of the Government of the United States was composed of representatives from twenty-five nations. The conference concluded its labors on the 1st of November, having with substantial unanimity agreed upon the meridian of Greenwich as the starting point whence longitude is to be computed through 180 degrees eastward and westward, and upon the adoption, for all purposes for which it may be found convenient, of a universal day which shall begin at midnight on the initial meridian and whose hours shall be counted from zero up to twenty-four.

The formal report of the transactions of this conference will be hereafter transmitted to the Congress.

This Government is in frequent receipt of invitations from foreign states to participate in international exhibitions, often of great interest and importance. Occupying, as we do, an advanced position in the world's production, and aiming to secure a profitable share for our industries in the general competitive markets, it is a matter of serious concern that the want of means for participation in these exhibitions should so often exclude our producers from advantages enjoyed by those of other countries. During the past year the attention of Congress was drawn to the formal invitations in this regard tendered by the Governments of England, Holland, Belgium, Germany, and Austria. The Executive has in some instances appointed honorary commissioners. This is, however, a most unsatisfactory expedient, for without some provision to meet the necessary working expenses of a commission it can effect little or nothing in behalf of exhibitors. An International Inventions Exhibition is to be held in London next May. This will cover a field of special importance, in which our country holds a foremost rank; but the Executive is at present powerless to organize a proper representation of our vast national interests in this direction.

I have in several previous messages referred to this subject. It seems to me that a statute giving to the Executive general discretionary authority to accept such invitations and to appoint honorary commissioners, without salary, and placing at the disposal of the Secretary of State a small fund for defraying their reasonable expenses, would be of great public utility.

This Government has received official notice that the revised international regulations for preventing collisions at sea have been adopted by all the leading maritime powers except the United States, and came into force on the 1st of September last. For the due protection of our shipping interests the provisions of our statutes should at once be brought into conformity with these regulations.

The question of securing to authors, composers, and artists copyright privileges in this country in return for reciprocal rights abroad is one that may justly challenge your attention. It is true that conventions will be necessary for fully accomplishing this result; but until Congress shall by statute fix the extent to which foreign holders of copyright shall be here privileged it has been deemed inadvisable to negotiate such conventions. For this reason the United States were not represented at the recent conference at Berne.

I recommend that the scope of the neutrality laws of the United States be so enlarged as to cover all patent acts of hostility committed in our territory and aimed against the peace of a friendly nation. Existing statutes prohibit the fitting out of armed expeditions and restrict the shipment of explosives, though the enactments in the latter respect were not framed with regard to international obligations, but simply for the protection of passenger travel. All these statutes were intended to meet special emergencies that had already arisen. Other emergencies have arisen since, and modern ingenuity supplies means for the organization of hostilities without open resort to armed vessels or to filibustering parties.

I see no reason why overt preparations in this country for the commission of criminal acts such as are here under consideration should not be alike punishable whether such acts are intended to be committed in our own country or in a foreign country with which we are at peace.

The prompt and thorough treatment of this question is one which intimately concerns the national honor.

Our existing naturalization laws also need revision. Those sections relating to persons residing within the limits of the United States in 1795 and 1798 have now only a historical interest. Section 2172, recognizing the citizenship of the children of naturalized parents, is ambiguous in its terms and partly obsolete. There are special provisions of law favoring the naturalization of those who serve in the Army or in merchant vessels, while no similar privileges are granted those who serve in the Navy or the Marine Corps.

"An uniform rule of naturalization" such as the Constitution contemplates should, among other things, clearly define the status of persons born within the United States subject to a foreign power (section 1992) and of minor children of fathers who have declared their intention to become citizens but have failed to perfect their naturalization. It might be wise to provide for a central bureau of registry, wherein should be filed authenticated transcripts of every record of naturalization in the several Federal and State courts, and to make provision also for the vacation or cancellation of such record in cases where fraud had been practiced upon the court by the applicant himself or where he had renounced or forfeited his acquired citizenship. A just and uniform law in this respect would strengthen the hands of the Government in protecting its citizens abroad and would pave the way for the conclusion of treaties of naturalization with foreign countries.

The legislation of the last session effected in the diplomatic and consular service certain changes and reductions which have been productive of embarrassment. The population and commercial activity of our country are steadily on the increase, and are giving rise to new, varying, and often delicate relationships with other countries. Our foreign establishment now embraces nearly double the area of operations that it occupied twenty years ago. The confinement of such a service within the limits of expenditure then established is not, it seems to me, in accordance with true economy. A community of 60,000,000 people should be adequately represented in its intercourse with foreign nations.

A project for the reorganization of the consular service and for recasting the scheme of extraterritorial jurisdiction is now before you. If the limits of a short session will not allow of its full consideration, I trust that you will not fail to make suitable provision for the present needs of the service.

It has been customary to define in the appropriation acts the rank of each diplomatic office to which a salary is attached. I suggest that this course be abandoned and that it be left to the President, with the advice and consent of the Senate, to fix from time to time the diplomatic grade of the representatives of this Government abroad as may seem advisable, provision being definitely made, however, as now, for the amount of salary attached to the respective stations.

The condition of our finances and the operations of the various branches of the public service which are connected with the Treasury Department are very fully discussed in the report of the Secretary.

It appears that the ordinary revenues for the fiscal year ended June 30, 1884, were:

From customs	$195,067,489.76
From internal revenue	121,586,072.51
From all other sources	31,866,307.65
Total ordinary revenues	348,519,869.92

The public expenditures during the same period were:

For civil expenses	$22,312,907.71
For foreign intercourse	1,260,766.37
For Indians	6,475,999.29
For pensions	55,429,228.06
For the military establishment, including river and harbor improvements and arsenals	39,429,603.36
For the naval establishment, including vessels, machinery, and improvements at navy-yards	17,292,601.44
For miscellaneous expenditures, including public buildings, light-houses, and collecting the revenue	43,939,710.00
For expenditures on account of the District of Columbia	3,407,049.62
For interest on the public debt	54,578,378.48
For the sinking fund	46,790,229.50
Total ordinary expenditures	290,916,473.83
Leaving a surplus of	57,603,396.09

As compared with the preceding fiscal year, there was a net decrease of over $21,000,000 in the amount of expenditures. The aggregate receipts were less than those of the year previous by about $54,000,000. The falling off in revenue from customs made up nearly $20,000,000 of this deficiency, and about $23,000,000 of the remainder was due to the diminished receipts from internal taxation.

The Secretary estimates the total receipts for the fiscal year which will end June 30, 1885, at $330,000,000 and the total expenditures at $290,620,201.16, in which sum are included the interest on the debt and the amount payable to the sinking fund. This would leave a surplus for the entire year of about $39,000,000.

The value of exports from the United States to foreign countries during the year ending June 30, 1884, was as follows:

Domestic merchandise	$724,964,852
Foreign merchandise	15,548,757
Total merchandise	740,513,609
Specie	67,133,383
Total exports of merchandise and specie	807,646,992

The cotton and cotton manufactures included in this statement were valued at $208,900,415; the breadstuffs at $162,544,715; the provisions at $114,416,547, and the mineral oils at $47,103,248.

During the same period the imports were as follows:

Merchandise $667,697,693
Gold and silver.. 37,426,262

Total 705,123,955

More than 63 per cent of the entire value of imported merchandise consisted of the following articles:

Sugar and molasses $103,884,274
Wool and woolen manufactures 53,542,292
Silk and its manufactures.. 49,949,128
Coffee... 49,686,705
Iron and steel and manufactures thereof.. 41,464,599
Chemicals 38,464,965
Flax, hemp, jute, and like substances, and manufactures thereof 33,463,398
Cotton and manufactures of cotton 30,454,476
Hides and skins other than fur skins 22,350,906

I concur with the Secretary of the Treasury in recommending the immediate suspension of the coinage of silver dollars and of the issuance of silver certificates. This is a matter to which in former communications I have more than once invoked the attention of the National Legislature.

It appears that annually for the past six years there have been coined, in compliance with the requirements of the act of February 28, 1878, more than 27,000,000 silver dollars.

The number now outstanding is reported by the Secretary to be nearly 185,000,000, whereof but little more than 40,000,000, or less than 22 per cent, are in actual circulation. The mere existence of this fact seems to me to furnish of itself a cogent argument for the repeal of the statute which has made such fact possible.

But there are other and graver considerations that tend in the same direction.

The Secretary avows his conviction that unless this coinage and the issuance of silver certificates be suspended silver is likely at no distant day to become our sole metallic standard. The commercial disturbance and the impairment of national credit that would be thus occasioned can scarcely be overestimated.

I hope that the Secretary's suggestions respecting the withdrawal from circulation of the $1 and $2 notes will receive your approval. It is likely that a considerable portion of the silver now encumbering the vaults of the Treasury might thus find its way into the currency.

While trade dollars have ceased, for the present at least, to be an element of active disturbance in our currency system, some provision should be made for their surrender to the Government. In view of the circumstances under which they were coined and of the fact that they have never had a legal-tender quality, there should be offered for them only a slight advance over their bullion value.

The Secretary in the course of his report considers the propriety of beautifying the designs of our subsidiary silver coins and of so increasing their weight that they may bear their due ratio of value to the standard dollar. His conclusions in this regard are cordially approved.

In my annual message of 1882 I recommended the abolition of all excise taxes except those relating to distilled spirits. This recommendation is now renewed. In case these taxes shall be abolished the revenues that will still remain to the Government will, in my opinion, not only suffice to meet its reasonable expenditures, but will afford a surplus large enough to permit such tariff reduction as may seem to be advisable when the results of recent revenue laws and commercial treaties shall have shown in what quarters those reductions can be most judiciously effected.

One of the gravest of the problems which appeal to the wisdom of Congress for solution is the ascertainment of the most effective means for increasing our foreign trade and thus relieving the depression under which our industries are now languishing. The Secretary of the Treasury advises that the duty of investigating this subject be intrusted in the first instance to a competent commission. While fully recognizing the considerations that may be urged against this course, I am nevertheless of the opinion that upon the whole no other would be likely to effect speedier or better results.

That portion of the Secretary's report which concerns the condition of our shipping interests can not fail to command your attention. He emphatically recommends that as an incentive to the investment of American capital in American steamships the Government shall, by liberal payments for mail transportation or otherwise, lend its active assistance to individual enterprise, and declares his belief that unless that course be pursued our foreign carrying trade must remain, as it is to-day, almost exclusively in the hands of foreigners.

One phase of this subject is now especially prominent in view of the repeal by the act of June 26, 1884, of all statutory provisions arbitrarily compelling American vessels to carry the mails to and from the United States. As it is necessary to make provision to compensate the owners of such vessels for performing that service after April, 1885, it is hoped that the whole subject will receive early consideration that will lead to the enactment of such measures for the revival of our merchant marine as the wisdom of Congress may devise.

The 3 per cent bonds of the Government to the amount of more than $100,000,000 have since my last annual message been redeemed by the Treasury. The bonds of that issue still outstanding amount to little over $200,000,000, about one-fourth of which will be retired through the operations of the sinking fund during the coming year. As these bonds still constitute the chief basis for the circulation of the national banks, the question how to avert the contraction of the currency caused by their retirement is one of constantly increasing importance.

It seems to be generally conceded that the law governing this matter exacts from the banks excessive security, and that upon their present bond deposits a larger circulation than is now allowed may be granted with safety. I hope that the bill which passed the Senate at the last session, permitting the issue of notes equal to the face value of the deposited bonds, will commend itself to the approval of the House of Representatives.

In the expenses of the War Department the Secretary reports a decrease of more than $9,000,000. Of this reduction $5,600,000 was effected in the expenditures for rivers and harbors and $2,700,000 in expenditures for the Quartermaster's Department.

Outside of that Department the annual expenses of all the Army bureaus proper (except possibly the Ordnance Bureau) are substantially fixed charges, which can not be materially diminished without a change in the numerical strength of the Army. The expenditures in the Quartermaster's Department can readily be subjected to administrative discretion, and it is reported by the Secretary of War that as a result of exercising such discretion in reducing the number of draft and pack animals in the Army the annual cost of supplying and caring for such animals is now $1,108,085.90 less than it was in 1881.

The reports of military commanders show that the last year has been notable for its entire freedom from Indian outbreaks.

In defiance of the President's proclamation of July 1, 1884, certain intruders sought to make settlements in the Indian Territory. They were promptly removed by a detachment of troops.

During the past session of Congress a bill to provide a suitable fire-proof building for the Army Medical Museum and the library of the Surgeon-General's Office received the approval of the Senate. A similar bill, reported favorably to the House of Representatives by one of its committees, is still pending before that body. It is hoped that during the coming session the measure may become a law, and that thereafter immediate steps may be taken to secure a place of safe deposit for these valuable collections, now in a state of insecurity.

The funds with which the works for the improvement of rivers and harbors were prosecuted during the past year were derived from the appropriations of the act of August 2, 1882, together with such few balances as were on hand from previous appropriations. The balance in the Treasury subject to requisition July 1, 1883, was $10,021,649.55. The amount appropriated during the fiscal year 1884 was $1,319,634.62, and the amount drawn from the Treasury during the fiscal year was $8,228,703.54, leaving a balance of $3,112,580.63 in the Treasury subject to requisition July 1, 1884.

The Secretary of War submits the report of the Chief of Engineers as to the practicability of protecting our important cities on the seaboard by fortifications and other defenses able to repel modern methods of attack. The time has now come when such defenses can be prepared with confidence that they will not prove abortive, and when the possible result of delay in making such preparation is seriously considered delay seems inexcusable. For the most important cities—those whose destruction or capture would be a national humiliation—adequate defenses, inclusive of guns, may be made by the gradual expenditure of $60,000,000—a sum much less than a victorious enemy could levy as a contribution. An appropriation of about one-tenth of that amount is asked to begin the work, and I concur with the Secretary of War in urging that it be granted.

The War Department is proceeding with the conversion of 10-inch smoothbore guns into 8-inch rifles by lining the former with tubes of forged steel or of coil wrought iron. Fifty guns will be thus converted within the year. This, however, does not obviate the necessity of providing means for the construction of guns of the highest power both for the purposes of coast defense and for the armament of war vessels.

The report of the Gun Foundry Board, appointed April 2, 1883, in pursuance of the act of March 3, 1883, was transmitted to Congress in a special message of February 18, 1884. In my message of March 26, 1884, I called attention to the recommendation of the board that the Government should encourage the production at private steel works of the required material for heavy cannon, and that two Government factories, one for the Army and one for the Navy, should be established for the fabrication of guns from such material. No action having been taken, the board was subsequently reconvened to determine more fully the plans and estimates necessary for carrying out its recommendation. It has received information which indicates that there are responsible steel manufacturers in this country who, although not provided at present with the necessary plant, are willing to construct the same and to make bids for contracts with the Government for the supply of the requisite material for the heaviest guns adapted to modern warfare if a guaranteed order of sufficient magnitude, accompanied by a positive appropriation extending over a series of years, shall be made by Congress. All doubts as to the feasibility of the plan being thus removed, I renew my recommendation that such action be taken by Congress as will enable the Government to construct its own ordnance upon its own territory, and so to provide the armaments demanded by considerations of national safety and honor.

The report of the Secretary of the Navy exhibits the progress which has been made on the new steel cruisers authorized by the acts of August 5, 1882, and March 3, 1883. Of the four vessels under contract, one, the *Chicago*, of 4,500 tons, is more than half finished; the *Atlanta*, of 3,000 tons, has been successfully launched, and her machinery is now fitting; the *Boston*, also of 3,000 tons, is ready for launching, and the *Dolphin*, a dispatch steamer of 1,500 tons, is ready for delivery.

Certain adverse criticisms upon the designs of these cruisers are discussed by the Secretary, who insists that the correctness of the conclusions reached by the Advisory Board and by the Department has been demonstrated by recent developments in shipbuilding abroad.

The machinery of the double-turreted monitors *Puritan*, *Terror*, and *Amphitrite*, contracted for under the act of March 3, 1883, is in process of construction. No work has been done during the past year on their armor for lack of the necessary appropriations. A fourth monitor, the *Monadnock*, still remains unfinished at the navy-yard in California. It is recommended that early steps be taken to complete these vessels and to provide also an armament for the monitor *Miantonomoh*.

The recommendations of the Naval Advisory Board, approved by the Department, comprise the construction of one steel cruiser of 4,500 tons, one cruiser of 3,000 tons, two heavily armed gunboats, one light cruising gunboat, one dispatch vessel armed with Hotchkiss cannon, one armored ram, and three torpedo boats. The general designs, all of which are calculated to meet the existing wants of the service, are now well advanced, and the construction of the vessels can be undertaken as soon as you shall grant the necessary authority.

The act of Congress approved August 7, 1882, authorized the removal to the United States of the bodies of Lieutenant-Commander George W. De Long and his companions of the *Jeannette* expedition. This removal has been successfully accomplished by Lieutenants Harber and Schuetze. The remains were taken from their grave in the Lena Delta in March, 1883, and were retained at Yakutsk until the following winter, the season being too far advanced to admit of their immediate transportation. They arrived at New York February 20, 1884, where they were received with suitable honors.

In pursuance of the joint resolution of Congress approved February 13, 1884, a naval expedition was fitted out for the relief of Lieutenant A. W. Greely, United States Army, and of the party who had been engaged under his command in scientific observations at Lady Franklin Bay. The fleet consisted of the steam sealer *Thetis*, purchased in England; the *Bear*, purchased at St. Johns, Newfoundland, and the *Alert*, which was generously provided by the British Government. Preparations for the expedition were promptly made by the Secretary of the Navy, with the active cooperation of the Secretary of War. Commander George W. Coffin was placed in command of the *Alert* and Lieutenant William H. Emory in command of the *Bear*. The *Thetis* was intrusted to Commander Winfield S. Schley, to whom also was assigned the superintendence of the entire expedition.

Immediately upon its arrival at Upernavik the fleet began the dangerous navigation of Melville Bay, and in spite of every obstacle reached Littleton Island on June 22, a fortnight earlier than any vessel had before attained that point. On the same day it crossed over to Cape Sabine, where Lieutenant Greely and the other survivors of his party were discovered. After taking on board the living and the bodies of the dead, the relief ships sailed for St. Johns, where they arrived on July 17. They were appropriately received at Portsmouth, N. H., on August 1 and at New York on August 8.   One of the bodies was landed at the former place.   The others were put on shore at Governors Island, and, with the exception of one, which was interred in the national cemetery, were forwarded thence to the destinations indicated by friends.   The organization and conduct of this relief expedition reflects great credit upon all who contributed to its success.

In this the last of the stated messages that I shall have the honor to transmit to the Congress of the United States I can not too strongly urge upon its attention the duty of restoring our Navy as rapidly as possible to the high state of efficiency which formerly characterized it. As the long peace that has lulled us into a sense of fancied security may at any time be disturbed, it is plain that the policy of strengthening this arm of the service is dictated by considerations of wise economy, of just regard for our future tranquillity, and of true appreciation of the dignity and honor of the Republic.

The report of the Postmaster-General acquaints you with the present condition and needs of the postal service.

It discloses the gratifying fact that the loss of revenue from the reduction in the rate of letter postage recommended in my message of December 4, 1882, and effected by the act of March 3, 1883, has been much less than was generally anticipated.   My recommendation of this reduction was based upon the belief that the actual falling off in receipts from letter postages for the year immediately succeeding the change of rate would be $3,000,000.   It has proved to be only $2,275,000.

This is a trustworthy indication that the revenue will soon be restored to its former volume by the natural increase of sealed correspondence.

I confidently repeat, therefore, the recommendation of my last annual message that the single-rate postage upon drop letters be reduced to 1 cent wherever the payment of 2 cents is now required by law.   The double rate is only exacted at offices where the carrier system is in operation, and it appears that at those offices the increase in the tax upon local letters defrays the cost not only of its own collection and delivery, but of the collection and delivery of all other mail matter.   This is an inequality that ought no longer to exist.

I approve the recommendation of the Postmaster-General that the unit of weight in the rating of first-class matter should be 1 ounce instead of one-half ounce, as it now is.   In view of the statistics furnished by the Department, it may well be doubted whether the change would result in any loss of revenue.   That it would greatly promote the convenience of the public is beyond dispute.

The free-delivery system has been lately applied to five cities, and the total number of offices in which it is now in operation is 159.   Experience shows that its adoption, under proper conditions, is equally an accommodation to the public and an advantage to the postal service.   It is more than self-sustaining, and for the reasons urged by the Postmaster-

General may properly be extended.

In the opinion of that officer it is important to provide means whereby exceptional dispatch in dealing with letters in free-delivery offices may be secured by payment of extraordinary postage. This scheme might be made effective by employment of a special stamp whose cost should be commensurate with the expense of the extra service.

In some of the large cities private express companies have undertaken to outstrip the Government mail carriers by affording for the prompt transmission of letters better facilities than have hitherto been at the command of the Post-Office.

It has always been the policy of the Government to discourage such enterprises, and in no better mode can that policy be maintained than in supplying the public with the most efficient mail service that, with due regard to its own best interests, can be furnished for its accommodation.

The Attorney-General renews the recommendation contained in his report of last year touching the fees of witnesses and jurors.

He favors radical changes in the fee bill, the adoption of a system by which attorneys and marshals of the United States shall be compensated solely by salaries, and the erection by the Government of a penitentiary for the confinement of offenders against its laws.

Of the varied governmental concerns in charge of the Interior Department the report of its Secretary presents an interesting summary. Among the topics deserving particular attention I refer you to his observations respecting our Indian affairs, the preemption and timber-culture acts, the failure of railroad companies to take title to lands granted by the Government, and the operations of the Pension Office, the Patent Office, the Census Bureau, and the Bureau of Education.

Allusion has been made already to the circumstance that, both as between the different Indian tribes and as between the Indians and the whites, the past year has been one of unbroken peace.

In this circumstance the President is glad to find justification for the policy of the Government in its dealing with the Indian question and confirmation of the views which were fully expressed in his first communication to the Forty-seventh Congress.

The Secretary urges anew the enactment of a statute for the punishment of crimes committed on the Indian reservations, and recommends the passage of the bill now pending in the House of Representatives for the purchase of a tract of 18,000 square miles from the Sioux Reservation. Both these measures are worthy of approval.

I concur with him also in advising the repeal of the preemption law, the enactment of statutes resolving the present legal complications touching lapsed grants to railroad companies, and the funding of the debt of the several Pacific railroads under such guaranty as shall effectually secure its ultimate payment.

The report of the Utah Commission will be read with interest.

It discloses the results of recent legislation looking to the prevention and punishment of polygamy in that Territory. I still believe that if that abominable practice can be suppressed by law it can only be by the most radical legislation consistent with the restraints of the Constitution.

I again recommend, therefore, that Congress assume absolute political control of the Territory of Utah and provide for the appointment of commissioners with such governmental powers as in its judgment may justly and wisely be put into their hands.

In the course of this communication reference has more than once been made to the policy of this Government as regards the extension of our foreign trade. It seems proper to declare the general principles that should, in my opinion, underlie our national efforts in this direction.

The main conditions of the problem may be thus stated:

We are a people apt in mechanical pursuits and fertile in invention. We cover a vast extent of territory rich in agricultural products and in nearly all the raw materials necessary for successful manufacture. We have a system of productive establishments more than sufficient to supply our own demands. The wages of labor are nowhere else so great. The scale of living of our artisan classes is such as tends to secure their personal comfort and the development of those higher moral and intellectual qualities that go to the making of good citizens. Our system of tax and tariff legislation is yielding a revenue which is in excess of the present needs of the Government.

These are the elements from which it is sought to devise a scheme by which, without unfavorably changing the condition of the workingman, our merchant marine shall be raised from its enfeebled condition and new markets provided for the sale beyond our borders of the manifold fruits of our industrial enterprises.

The problem is complex and can be solved by no single measure of innovation or reform.

The countries of the American continent and the adjacent islands are for the United States the natural marts of supply and demand. It is from them that we should obtain what we do not produce or do not produce in sufficiency, and it is to them that the surplus productions of our fields, our mills, and our workshops should flow, under conditions that will equalize or favor them in comparison with foreign competition.

Four paths of policy seem to point to this end:

First. A series of reciprocal commercial treaties with the countries of America which shall foster between us and them an unhampered movement of trade. The conditions of these treaties should be the free admission of such merchandise as this country does not produce, in return for the admission free or under a favored scheme of duties of our own products, the benefits of such exchange to apply only to goods carried under the flag of the parties to the contract; the removal on both sides from the vessels so privileged of all tonnage dues and national imposts, so that those vessels may ply unhindered between our ports and those of the other contracting parties, though without infringing on the reserved home coasting trade; the removal or reduction of burdens on the exported products of those countries coming within the benefits of the treaties, and the avoidance of the technical restrictions and penalties by which our intercourse with those countries is at present hampered.

Secondly. The establishment of the consular service of the United States on a salaried footing, thus permitting the relinquishment of consular fees not only as respects vessels under the national flag, but also as respects vessels of the treaty nations carrying goods entitled to the benefits of the treaties.

Thirdly. The enactment of measures to favor the construction and maintenance of a steam carrying marine under the flag of the United States.

Fourthly. The establishment of an uniform currency basis for the countries of America, so that the coined products of our mines may circulate on equal terms throughout the whole system of commonwealths. This would require a monetary union of America, whereby the output of the bullion-producing countries and the circulation of those which yield neither gold nor silver could be adjusted in conformity with the population, wealth, and commercial needs of each. As many of the countries furnish no bullion to the common stock, the surplus production of our mines and mints might thus be utilized and a step taken toward the general remonetization of silver.

To the accomplishment of these ends, so far as they can be attained by separate treaties, the negotiations already concluded and now in progress have been directed; and the favor which this enlarged policy has thus far received warrants the belief that its operations will ere long embrace all, or nearly all, the countries of this hemisphere.

It is by no means desirable, however, that the policy under consideration should be applied to these countries alone. The healthful enlargement of our trade with Europe, Asia, and Africa should be sought by reducing tariff burdens on such of their wares as neither we nor the other American States are fitted to produce, and thus enabling ourselves to obtain in return a better market for our supplies of food, of raw materials, and of the manufactures in which we excel.

It seems to me that many of the embarrassing elements in the great national conflict between protection and free trade may thus be turned to good account; that the revenue may be reduced so as no longer to overtax the people; that protective duties may be retained without becoming burdensome; that our shipping interests may be judiciously encouraged, the currency fixed on firm bases, and, above all, such an unity of interests established among the States of the American system as will be of great and ever-increasing advantage to them all.

All treaties in the line of this policy which have been negotiated or are in process of negotiation contain a provision deemed to be requisite under the clause of the Constitution limiting to the House of Representatives the authority to originate bills for raising revenue.

On the 29th of February last I transmitted to the Congress the first annual report of the Civil Service Commission, together with communications from the heads of the several Executive Departments of the Government respecting the practical workings of the law under which the Commission had been acting. The good results therein foreshadowed have been more than realized.

The system has fully answered the expectations of its friends in securing competent and faithful public servants and in protecting the appointing officers of the Government from the pressure of personal importunity and from the labor of examining the claims and pretensions of rival candidates for public employment.

The law has had the unqualified support of the President and of the heads of the several Departments, and the members of the Commission have performed their duties with zeal and fidelity. Their report will shortly be submitted, and will be accompanied by such recommendations for enlarging the scope of the existing statute as shall commend themselves to the Executive and the Commissioners charged with its administration.

In view of the general and persistent demand throughout the commercial community for a national bankrupt law, I hope that the differences of sentiment which have hitherto prevented its enactment may not outlast the present session.

The pestilence which for the past two years has been raging in the countries of the East recently made its appearance in European ports with which we are in constant communication.

The then Secretary of the Treasury, in pursuance of a proclamation of the President, issued certain regulations restricting and for a time prohibiting the importation of rags and the admission of baggage of immigrants and of travelers arriving from infected quarters. Lest this course may have been without strict warrant of law, I approve the recommendation of the present Secretary that the Congress take action in the premises, and I also recommend the immediate adoption of such measures as will be likely to ward off the dreaded epidemic and to mitigate its severity in case it shall unhappily extend to our shores.

The annual report of the Commissioners of the District of Columbia reviews the operations of the several departments of its municipal government. I ask your careful consideration of its suggestions in respect to legislation, especially commending such as relate to a revision of the civil and criminal code, the performance of labor by persons sentenced to imprisonment in the jail, the construction and occupation of wharves along the river front, and the erection of a suitable building for District offices.

I recommend that in recognition of the eminent services of Ulysses S.

Grant, late General of the armies of the United States and twice President of this nation, the Congress confer upon him a suitable pension.

Certain of the measures that seem to me necessary and expedient I have now, in obedience to the Constitution, recommended for your adoption.

As respects others of no less importance I shall content myself with renewing the recommendations already made to the Congress, without restating the grounds upon which such recommendations were based.

The preservation of forests on the public domain, the granting of Government aid for popular education, the amendment of the Federal Constitution so as to make effective the disapproval by the President of particular items in appropriation bills, the enactment of statutes in regard to the filling of vacancies in the Presidential office, and the determining of vexed questions respecting Presidential inability are measures which may justly receive your serious consideration.

As the time draws nigh when I am to retire from the public service, I can not refrain from expressing to the members of the National Legislature with whom I have been brought into personal and official intercourse my sincere appreciation of their unfailing courtesy and of their harmonious cooperation with the Executive in so many measures calculated to promote the best interests of the nation.

And to my fellow-citizens generally I acknowledge a deep sense of obligation for the support which they have accorded me in my administration of the executive department of this Government.

Grover Cleveland

March 4, 1885 to March 4, 1889

FIRST ANNUAL MESSAGE.

WASHINGTON, *December 8, 1885.*

To the Congress of the United States:

Your assembling is clouded by a sense of public bereavement, caused by the recent and sudden death of Thomas A. Hendricks, Vice-President of the United States. His distinguished public services, his complete integrity and devotion to every duty, and his personal virtues will find honorable record in his country's history.

Ample and repeated proofs of the esteem and confidence in which he was held by his fellow-countrymen were manifested by his election to offices of the most important trust and highest dignity ; and at length, full of years and honors, he has been laid at rest amid universal sorrow and benediction.

The Constitution, which requires those chosen to legislate for the people to annually meet in the discharge of their solemn trust, also requires the President to give to Congress information of the state of the Union and recommend to their consideration such measures as he shall deem necessary and expedient. At the threshold of a compliance with these constitutional directions it is well for us to bear in mind that our usefulness to the people's interests will be promoted by a constant appreciation of the scope and character of our respective duties as they relate to Federal legislation. While the Executive may recommend such measures as he shall deem expedient, the responsibility for legislative action must and should rest upon those selected by the people to make their laws.

Contemplation of the grave and responsible functions assigned to the respective branches of the Government under the Constitution will disclose the partitions of power between our respective departments and their necessary independence, and also the need for the exercise of all the power intrusted to each in that spirit of comity and cooperation which is essential to the proper fulfillment of the patriotic obligations which rest upon us as faithful servants of the people.

The jealous watchfulness of our constituencies, great and small, supplements their suffrages, and before the tribunal they establish every public servant should be judged.

It is gratifying to announce that the relations of the United States with all foreign powers continue to be friendly. Our position after nearly a century of successful constitutional government, maintenance of good faith in all our engagements, the avoidance of complications with other nations, and our consistent and amicable attitude toward the strong and weak alike furnish proof of a political disposition which renders professions of good will unnecessary. There are no questions of difficulty pending with any foreign government.

The Argentine Government has revived the long dormant question of the Falkland Islands by claiming from the United States indemnity for their loss, attributed to the action of the commander of the sloop of war *Lexington* in breaking up a piratical colony on those islands in 1831, and their subsequent occupation by Great Britain. In view of the ample justification for the act of the *Lexington* and the derelict condition of the islands before and after their alleged occupation by Argentine colonists, this Government considers the claim as wholly groundless.

Question has arisen with the Government of Austria-Hungary touching the representation of the United States at Vienna. Having under my constitutional prerogative appointed an estimable citizen of unimpeached probity and competence as minister at that court, the Government of Austria-Hungary invited this Government to take cognizance of certain exceptions, based upon allegations against the personal acceptability of Mr. Keiley, the appointed envoy, asking that in view thereof the appointment should be withdrawn. The reasons advanced were such as could not be acquiesced in without violation of my oath of office and the precepts of the Constitution, since they necessarily involved a limitation in favor of a foreign government upon the right of selection by the Executive and required such an application of a religious test as a qualification for office under the United States as would have resulted in the practical disfranchisement of a large class of our citizens and the abandonment of a vital principle in our Government. The Austro-Hungarian Government finally decided not to receive Mr. Keiley as the envoy of the United States, and that gentleman has since resigned his commission, leaving the post vacant. I have made no new nomination, and the interests of this Government at Vienna are now in the care of the secretary of legation, acting as chargé d'affaires *ad interim*.

Early in March last war broke out in Central America, caused by the attempt of Guatemala to consolidate the several States into a single government. In these contests between our neighboring States the United States forebore to interfere actively, but lent the aid of their friendly offices in deprecation of war and to promote peace and concord among the belligerents, and by such counsel contributed importantly to the restoration of tranquillity in that locality.

Emergencies growing out of civil war in the United States of Colombia demanded of the Government at the beginning of this Administration the employment of armed forces to fulfill its guaranties under the thirty-fifth article of the treaty of 1846, in order to keep the transit open across the Isthmus of Panama. Desirous of exercising only the powers expressly reserved to us by the treaty, and mindful of the rights of Colombia, the forces sent to the Isthmus were instructed to confine their action to "positively and efficaciously" preventing the transit and its accessories from being "interrupted or embarrassed."

The execution of this delicate and responsible task necessarily involved police control where the local authority was temporarily powerless, but always in aid of the sovereignty of Colombia.

The prompt and successful fulfillment of its duty by this Government was highly appreciated by the Government of Colombia. and has been followed by expressions of its satisfaction.

High praise is due to the officers and men engaged in this service.

The restoration of peace on the Isthmus by the reestablishment of the constituted Government there being thus accomplished, the forces of the United States were withdrawn.

Pending these occurrences a question of much importance was presented by decrees of the Colombian Government proclaiming the closure of certain ports then in the hands of insurgents and declaring vessels held by the revolutionists to be piratical and liable to capture by any power. To neither of these propositions could the United States assent. An effective closure of ports not in the possession of the Government, but held by hostile partisans, could not be recognized; neither could the vessels of insurgents against the legitimate sovereignty be deemed *hostes humani generis* within the precepts of international law, whatever might be the definition and penalty of their acts under the municipal law of the State against whose authority they were in revolt. The denial by this Government of the Colombian propositions did not, however, imply the admission of a belligerent status on the part of the insurgents.

The Colombian Government has expressed its willingness to negotiate conventions for the adjustment by arbitration of claims by foreign citizens arising out of the destruction of the city of Aspinwall by the insurrectionary forces.

The interest of the United States in a practicable transit for ships across the strip of land separating the Atlantic from the Pacific has been repeatedly manifested during the last half century.

My immediate predecessor caused to be negotiated with Nicaragua a treaty for the construction, by and at the sole cost of the United States, of a canal through Nicaraguan territory, and laid it before the Senate. Pending the action of that body thereon, I withdrew the treaty for reexamination. Attentive consideration of its provisions leads me to withhold it from resubmission to the Senate.

Maintaining, as I do, the tenets of a line of precedents from Washington's day, which proscribe entangling alliances with foreign states, I do not favor a policy of acquisition of new and distant territory or the incorporation of remote interests with our own.

The laws of progress are vital and organic, and we must be conscious of that irresistible tide of commercial expansion which, as the concomitant of our active civilization, day by day is being urged onward by those increasing facilities of production, transportation, and communication to which steam and electricity have given birth; but our duty in the present instructs us to address ourselves mainly to the development of the vast resources of the great area committed to our charge and to the cultivation of the arts of peace within our own borders, though jealously alert in preventing the American hemisphere from being involved in the political problems and complications of distant governments. Therefore I am unable to recommend propositions involving paramount privileges of ownership or right outside of our own territory, when coupled with absolute and unlimited engagements to defend the territorial integrity of the state where such interests lie. While the general project of connecting the two oceans by means of a canal is to be encouraged, I am of opinion that any scheme to that end to be considered with favor should be free from the features alluded to.

The Tehuantepec route is declared by engineers of the highest repute and by competent scientists to afford an entirely practicable transit for vessels and cargoes, by means of a ship railway, from the Atlantic to the Pacific. The obvious advantages of such a route, if feasible, over others more remote from the axial lines of traffic between Europe and the Pacific, and particularly between the Valley of the Mississippi and the western coast of North and South America, are deserving of consideration.

Whatever highway may be constructed across the barrier dividing the two greatest maritime areas of the world must be for the world's benefit—a trust for mankind, to be removed from the chance of domination by any single power, nor become a point of invitation for hostilities or a prize for warlike ambition. An engagement combining the construction, ownership, and operation of such a work by this Government, with an offensive and defensive alliance for its protection, with the foreign state whose responsibilities and rights we would share is, in my judgment, inconsistent with such dedication to universal and neutral use, and would, moreover, entail measures for its realization beyond the scope of our national polity or present means.

The lapse of years has abundantly confirmed the wisdom and foresight of those earlier Administrations which, long before the conditions of maritime intercourse were changed and enlarged by the progress of the age, proclaimed the vital need of interoceanic transit across the American Isthmus and consecrated it in advance to the common use of mankind by their positive declarations and through the formal obligation of treaties. Toward such realization the efforts of my Administration will be applied, ever bearing in mind the principles on which it must rest, and which were declared in no uncertain tones by Mr. Cass, who, while Secretary of State, in 1858, announced that "what the United States want in Central America, next to the happiness of its people, is the security and neutrality of the interoceanic routes which lead through it."

The construction of three transcontinental lines of railway, all in successful operation, wholly within our territory, and uniting the Atlantic and the Pacific oceans, has been accompanied by results of a most interesting and impressive nature, and has created new conditions, not in the routes of commerce only, but in political geography, which powerfully affect our relations toward and necessarily increase our interests in any transisthmian route which may be opened and employed for the ends of peace and traffic, or, in other contingencies, for uses inimical to both.

Transportation is a factor in the cost of commodities scarcely second to that of their production, and weighs as heavily upon the consumer.

Our experience already has proven the great importance of having the competition between land carriage and water carriage fully developed, each acting as a protection to the public against the tendencies to monopoly which are inherent in the consolidation of wealth and power in the hands of vast corporations.

These suggestions may serve to emphasize what I have already said on the score of the necessity of a neutralization of any interoceanic transit; and this can only be accomplished by making the uses of the route open to all nations and subject to the ambitions and warlike necessities of none.

The drawings and report of a recent survey of the Nicaragua Canal route, made by Chief Engineer Menocal, will be communicated for your information.

The claims of citizens of the United States for losses by reason of the late military operations of Chile in Peru and Bolivia are the subject of negotiation for a claims convention with Chile, providing for their submission to arbitration.

The harmony of our relations with China is fully sustained.

In the application of the acts lately passed to execute the treaty of 1880, restrictive of the immigration of Chinese laborers into the United States, individual cases of hardship have occurred beyond the power of the Executive to remedy, and calling for judicial determination.

The condition of the Chinese question in the Western States and Territories is, despite this restrictive legislation, far from being satisfactory. The recent outbreak in Wyoming Territory, where numbers of unoffending Chinamen, indisputably within the protection of the treaties and the law, were murdered by a mob, and the still more recent threatened outbreak of the same character in Washington Territory, are fresh in the minds of all, and there is apprehension lest the bitterness of feeling against the Mongolian race on the Pacific Slope may find vent in similar lawless demonstrations. All the power of this Government should be exerted to maintain the amplest good faith toward China in the treatment of these men, and the inflexible sternness of the law in bringing the wrongdoers to justice should be insisted upon.

Every effort has been made by this Government to prevent these violent outbreaks and to aid the representatives of China in their investigation of these outrages; and it is but just to say that they are traceable to the lawlessness of men not citizens of the United States engaged in competition with Chinese laborers.

Race prejudice is the chief factor in originating these disturbances, and it exists in a large part of our domain, jeopardizing our domestic peace and the good relationship we strive to maintain with China.

The admitted right of a government to prevent the influx of elements hostile to its internal peace and security may not be questioned, even where there is no treaty stipulation on the subject. That the exclusion of Chinese labor is demanded in other countries where like conditions prevail is strongly evidenced in the Dominion of Canada, where Chinese immigration is now regulated by laws more exclusive than our own. If existing laws are inadequate to compass the end in view, I shall be prepared to give earnest consideration to any further remedial measures, within the treaty limits, which the wisdom of Congress may devise.

The independent State of the Kongo has been organized as a government under the sovereignty of His Majesty the King of the Belgians, who assumes its chief magistracy in his personal character only, without making the new State a dependency of Belgium. It is fortunate that a benighted region, owing all it has of quickening civilization to the beneficence and philanthropic spirit of this monarch, should have the advantage and security of his benevolent supervision.

The action taken by this Government last year in being the first to recognize the flag of the International Association of the Kongo has been followed by formal recognition of the new nationality which succeeds to its sovereign powers.

A conference of delegates of the principal commercial nations was held at Berlin last winter to discuss methods whereby the Kongo basin might be kept open to the world's trade. Delegates attended on behalf of the United States on the understanding that their part should be merely deliberative, without imparting to the results any binding character so far as the United States were concerned. This reserve was due to the indisposition of this Government to share in any disposal by an international congress of jurisdictional questions in remote foreign territories. The results of the conference were embodied in a formal act of the nature of an international convention, which laid down certain obligations purporting to be binding on the signatories, subject to ratification within one year. Notwithstanding the reservation under which the delegates of the United States attended, their signatures were attached to the general act in the same manner as those of the plenipotentiaries of other governments, thus making the United States appear, without reserve or qualification, as signatories to a joint international engagement imposing on the signers the conservation of the territorial integrity of distant regions where we have no established interests or control.

This Government does not, however, regard its reservation of liberty of action in the premises as at all impaired; and holding that an engagement to share in the obligation of enforcing neutrality in the remote valley of the Kongo would be an alliance whose responsibilities we are not in a position to assume, I abstain from asking the sanction of the Senate to that general act.

The correspondence will be laid before you, and the instructive and interesting report of the agent sent by this Government to the Kongo country and his recommendations for the establishment of commercial agencies on the African coast are also submitted for your consideration.

The commission appointed by my predecessor last winter to visit the Central and South American countries and report on the methods of enlarging the commercial relations of the United States therewith has submitted reports, which will be laid before you.

No opportunity has been omitted to testify the friendliness of this Government toward Korea, whose entrance into the family of treaty powers the United States were the first to recognize. I regard with favor the application made by the Korean Government to be allowed to employ American officers as military instructors, to which the assent of Congress becomes necessary, and I am happy to say this request has the concurrent sanction of China and Japan.

The arrest and imprisonment of Julio R. Santos, a citizen of the United States, by the authorities of Ecuador gave rise to a contention with that Government, in which his right to be released or to have a speedy and impartial trial on announced charges and with all guaranties of defense stipulated by treaty was insisted upon by us. After an elaborate correspondence and repeated and earnest representations on our part Mr. Santos was, after an alleged trial and conviction, eventually included in a general decree of amnesty and pardoned by the Ecuadorian Executive and released, leaving the question of his American citizenship denied by the Ecuadorian Government, but insisted upon by our own.

The amount adjudged by the late French and American Claims Commission to be due from the United States to French claimants on account of injuries suffered by them during the War of Secession, having been appropriated by the last Congress, has been duly paid to the French Government.

The act of February 25, 1885, provided for a preliminary search of the records of French prize courts for evidence bearing on the claims of American citizens against France for spoliations committed prior to 1801. The duty has been performed, and the report of the agent will be laid before you.

I regret to say that the restrictions upon the importation of our pork into France continue, notwithstanding the abundant demonstration of the absence of sanitary danger in its use; but I entertain strong hopes that with a better understanding of the matter this vexatious prohibition will be removed. It would be pleasing to be able to say as much with respect to Germany, Austria, and other countries, where such food products are absolutely excluded, without present prospect of reasonable change.

The interpretation of our existing treaties of naturalization by Germany during the past year has attracted attention by reason of an apparent tendency on the part of the Imperial Government to extend the scope of the residential restrictions to which returning naturalized citizens of German origin are asserted to be liable under the laws of the Empire. The temperate and just attitude taken by this Government with regard to this class of questions will doubtless lead to a satisfactory understanding.

The dispute of Germany and Spain relative to the domination of the Caroline Islands has attracted the attention of this Government by reason of extensive interests of American citizens having grown up in those parts during the past thirty years, and because the question of ownership involves jurisdiction of matters affecting the status of our citizens under civil and criminal law. While standing wholly aloof from the proprietary issues raised between powers to both of which the United States are friendly, this Government expects that nothing in the present contention shall unfavorably affect our citizens carrying on a peaceful commerce or there domiciled, and has so informed the Governments of Spain and Germany.

The marked good will between the United States and Great Britain has been maintained during the past year.

The termination of the fishing clauses of the treaty of Washington, in pursuance of the joint resolution of March 3, 1883, must have resulted in the abrupt cessation on the 1st of July of this year, in the midst of their ventures, of the operations of citizens of the United States engaged in fishing in British American waters but for a diplomatic understanding reached with Her Majesty's Government in June last, whereby assurance was obtained that no interruption of those operations should take place during the current fishing season.

In the interest of good neighborhood and of the commercial intercourse of adjacent communities, the question of the North American fisheries is one of much importance. Following out the intimation given by me when the extensory arrangement above described was negotiated, I recommend that the Congress provide for the appointment of a commission in which the Governments of the United States and Great Britain shall be respectively represented, charged with the consideration and settlement, upon a just, equitable, and honorable basis, of the entire question of the fishing rights of the two Governments and their respective citizens on the coasts of the United States and British North America. The fishing interests being intimately related to other general questions dependent upon contiguity and intercourse, consideration thereof in all their equities might also properly come within the purview of such a commission, and the fullest latitude of expression on both sides should be permitted.

The correspondence in relation to the fishing rights will be submitted.

The arctic exploring steamer *Alert*, which was generously given by Her Majesty's Government to aid in the relief of the Greely expedition, was, after the successful attainment of that humane purpose, returned to Great Britain, in pursuance of the authority conferred by the act of March 3, 1885.

The inadequacy of the existing engagements for extradition between the United States and Great Britain has been long apparent. The tenth article of the treaty of 1842, one of the earliest compacts in this regard entered into by us, stipulated for surrender in respect of a limited number of offenses. Other crimes no less inimical to the social welfare should be embraced and the procedure of extradition brought in harmony with present international practice. Negotiations with Her Majesty's Government for an enlarged treaty of extradition have been pending since 1870, and I entertain strong hopes that a satisfactory result may be soon attained.

The frontier line between Alaska and British Columbia, as defined by the treaty of cession with Russia, follows the demarcation assigned in a prior treaty between Great Britain and Russia. Modern exploration discloses that this ancient boundary is impracticable as a geographical fact. In the unsettled condition of that region the question has lacked importance, but the discovery of mineral wealth in the territory the line is supposed to traverse admonishes that the time has come when an accurate knowledge of the boundary is needful to avert jurisdictional complications. I recommend, therefore, that provision be made for a preliminary reconnoissance by officers of the United States, to the end of acquiring more precise information on the subject. I have invited Her Majesty's Government to consider with us the adoption of a more convenient line, to be established by meridian observations or by known geographical features without the necessity of an expensive survey of the whole.

The late insurrectionary movements in Hayti having been quelled, the Government of that Republic has made prompt provision for adjudicating the losses suffered by foreigners because of hostilities there, and the claims of certain citizens of the United States will be in this manner determined.

The long-pending claims of two citizens of the United States, Pelletier and Lazare, have been disposed of by arbitration, and an award in favor of each claimant has been made, which by the terms of the engagement is final. It remains for Congress to provide for the payment of the stipulated moiety of the expenses.

A question arose with Hayti during the past year by reason of the exceptional treatment of an American citizen, Mr. Van Bokkelen, a resident of Port-au-Prince, who, on suit by creditors residing in the United States, was sentenced to imprisonment, and, under the operation of a Haytian statute, was denied relief secured to a native Haytian. This Government asserted his treaty right to equal treatment with natives of Hayti in all suits at law. Our contention was denied by the Haytian Government, which, however, while still professing to maintain the ground taken against Mr. Van Bokkelen's right, terminated the controversy by setting him at liberty without explanation.

An international conference to consider the means of arresting the spread of cholera and other epidemic diseases was held at Rome in May last, and adjourned to meet again on further notice. An expert delegate on behalf of the United States has attended its sessions and will submit a report.

Our relations with Mexico continue to be most cordial, as befits those of neighbors between whom the strongest ties of friendship and commercial intimacy exist, as the natural and growing consequence of our similarity of institutions and geographical propinquity.

The relocation of the boundary line between the United States and Mexico westward of the Rio Grande, under the convention of July 29, 1882, has been unavoidably delayed, but I apprehend no difficulty in securing a prolongation of the period for its accomplishment.

The lately concluded commercial treaty with Mexico still awaits the stipulated legislation to carry its provisions into effect, for which one year's additional time has been secured by a supplementary article signed in February last and since ratified on both sides.

As this convention, so important to the commercial welfare of the two adjoining countries, has been constitutionally confirmed by the treaty-making branch, I express the hope that legislation needed to make it effective may not be long delayed.

The large influx of capital and enterprise to Mexico from the United States continues to aid in the development of the resources and in augmenting the material well-being of our sister Republic. Lines of railway, penetrating to the heart and capital of the country, bring the two peoples into mutually beneficial intercourse, and enlarged facilities of transit add to profitable commerce, create new markets, and furnish avenues to otherwise isolated communities.

I have already adverted to the suggested construction of a ship railway across the narrow formation of the territory of Mexico at Tehuantepec.

With the gradual recovery of Peru from the effects of her late disastrous conflict with Chile, and with the restoration of civil authority in that distracted country, it is hoped that pending war claims of our citizens will be adjusted.

In conformity with notification given by the Government of Peru, the existing treaties of commerce and extradition between the United States and that country will terminate March 31; 1886.

Our good relationship with Russia continues.

An officer of the Navy, detailed for the purpose, is now on his way to Siberia bearing the testimonials voted by Congress to those who generously succored the survivors of the unfortunate *Jeannette* expedition.

It is gratifying to advert to the cordiality of our intercourse with Spain.

The long-pending claim of the owners of the ship *Masonic* for loss suffered through the admitted dereliction of the Spanish authorities in the Philippine Islands has been adjusted by arbitration and an indemnity awarded. The principle of arbitration in such cases, to which the United States have long and consistently adhered, thus receives a fresh and gratifying confirmation.

Other questions with Spain have been disposed of or are under diplomatic consideration with a view to just and honorable settlement.

The operation of the commercial agreement with Spain of January 2–February 13, 1884, has been found inadequate to the commercial needs of the United States and the Spanish Antilles, and the terms of the agreement are subjected to conflicting interpretations in those islands.

Negotiations have been instituted at Madrid for a full treaty not open to these objections and in the line of the general policy touching the neighborly intercourse of proximate communities, to which I elsewhere advert, and aiming, moreover, at the removal of existing burdens and annoying restrictions; and although a satisfactory termination is promised, I am compelled to delay its announcement.

An international copyright conference was held at Berne in September, on the invitation of the Swiss Government. The envoy of the United States attended as a delegate, but refrained from committing this Government to the results, even by signing the recommendatory protocol adopted. The interesting and important subject of international copyright has been before you for several years. Action is certainly desirable to effect the object in view; and while there may be question as to the relative advantage of treating it by legislation or by specific treaty, the matured views of the Berne conference can not fail to aid your consideration of the subject.

The termination of the commercial treaty of 1862 between the United States and Turkey has been sought by that Government. While there is question as to the sufficiency of the notice of termination given, yet as the commercial rights of our citizens in Turkey come under the favored-nation guaranties of the prior treaty of 1830, and as equal treatment is admitted by the Porte, no inconvenience can result from the assent of this Government to the revision of the Ottoman tariffs, in which the treaty powers have been invited to join.

Questions concerning our citizens in Turkey may be affected by the Porte's nonacquiescence in the right of expatriation and by the imposition of religious tests as a condition of residence, in which this Government can not concur. The United States must hold in their intercourse with every power that the status of their citizens is to be respected and equal civil privileges accorded to them without regard to creed, and affected by no considerations save those growing out of domiciliary return to the land of original allegiance or of unfulfilled personal obligations which may survive, under municipal laws, after such voluntary return.

The negotiation with Venezuela relative to the rehearing of the awards of the mixed commission constituted under the treaty of 1866 was resumed in view of the recent acquiescence of the Venezuelan envoy in the principal point advanced by this Government, that the effects of the old treaty could only be set aside by the operation of a new convention. A result in substantial accord with the advisory suggestions contained in the joint resolution of March 3, 1883, has been agreed upon and will shortly be submitted to the Senate for ratification.

Under section 3659 of the Revised Statutes all funds held in trust by the United States and the annual interest accruing thereon, when not otherwise required by treaty, are to be invested in stocks of the United States bearing a rate of interest not less than 5 per cent per annum. There being now no procurable stocks paying so high a rate of interest, the letter of the statute is at present inapplicable, but its spirit is subserved by continuing to make investments of this nature in current stocks bearing the highest interest now paid. The statute, however, makes no provision for the disposal of such accretions. It being contrary to the general rule of this Government to allow interest on claims, I recommend the repeal of the provision in question and the disposition, under a uniform rule, of the present accumulations from investment of trust funds.

The inadequacy of existing legislation touching citizenship and naturalization demands your consideration.

While recognizing the right of expatriation, no statutory provision exists providing means for renouncing citizenship by an American citizen, native born or naturalized, nor for terminating and vacating an improper acquisition of citizenship. Even a fraudulent decree of naturalization can not now be canceled. The privilege and franchise of American citizenship should be granted with care, and extended to those only who intend in good faith to assume its duties and responsibilities when attaining its privileges and benefits. It should be withheld from those who merely go through the forms of naturalization with the intent of escaping the duties of their original allegiance without taking upon themselves those of their new status, or who may acquire the rights of American citizenship for no other than a hostile purpose toward their original governments. These evils have had many flagrant illustrations.

I regard with favor the suggestion put forth by one of my predecessors that provision be made for a central bureau of record of the decrees of naturalization granted by the various courts throughout the United States now invested with that power.

The rights which spring from domicile in the United States, especially when coupled with a declaration of intention to become a citizen, are worthy of definition by statute. The stranger coming hither with intent to remain, establishing his residence in our midst, contributing to the general welfare, and by his voluntary act declaring his purpose to assume the responsibilities of citizenship, thereby gains an inchoate status which

legislation may properly define.   The laws of certain States and Territories admit a domiciled alien to the local franchise, conferring on him
the rights of citizenship to a degree which places him in the anomalous
position of being a citizen of a State and yet not of the United States
within the purview of Federal and international law.

It is important within the scope of national legislation to define this
right of alien domicile as distinguished from Federal naturalization.

The commercial relations of the United States with their immediate
neighbors and with important areas of traffic near our shores suggest
especially liberal intercourse between them and us.

Following the treaty of 1883 with Mexico, which rested on the basis
of a reciprocal exemption from customs duties, other similar treaties were
initiated by my predecessor.

Recognizing the need of less obstructed traffic with Cuba and Puerto
Rico, and met by the desire of Spain to succor languishing interests in the
Antilles, steps were taken to attain those ends by a treaty of commerce.
A similar treaty was afterwards signed by the Dominican Republic.   Sub-
sequently overtures were made by Her Britannic Majesty's Government
for a like mutual extension of commercial intercourse with the British
West Indian and South American dependencies, but without result.

On taking office I withdrew for reexamination the treaties signed with
Spain and Santo Domingo, then pending before the Senate.   The result
has been to satisfy me of the inexpediency of entering into engagements
of this character not covering the entire traffic.

These treaties contemplated the surrender by the United States of
large revenues for inadequate considerations.   Upon sugar alone duties
were surrendered to an amount far exceeding all the advantages offered
in exchange.   Even were it intended to relieve our consumers, it was
evident that so long as the exemption but partially covered our importation such relief would be illusory.   To relinquish a revenue so essential
seemed highly improvident at a time when new and large drains upon
the Treasury were contemplated.   Moreover, embarrassing questions
would have arisen under the favored-nation clauses of treaties with other
nations.

As a further objection, it is evident that tariff regulation by treaty
diminishes that independent control over its own revenues which is essential for the safety and welfare of any government.   Emergency calling
for an increase of taxation may at any time arise, and no engagement with
a foreign power should exist to hamper the action of the Government.

By the fourteenth section of the shipping act approved June 26, 1884,
certain reductions and contingent exemptions from tonnage dues were
made as to vessels entering ports of the United States from any foreign
port in North and Central America, the West India Islands, the Bahamas
and Bermudas, Mexico, and the Isthmus as far as Aspinwall and Panama.
The Governments of Belgium, Denmark, Germany, Portugal, and Sweden

and Norway have asserted, under the favored-nation clause in their treaties with the United States, a claim to like treatment in respect of vessels coming to the United States from their home ports. This Government, however, holds that the privileges granted by the act are purely geographical, inuring to any vessel of any foreign power that may choose to engage in traffic between this country and any port within the defined zone, and no warrant exists under the most-favored-nation clause for the extension of the privileges in question to vessels sailing to this country from ports outside the limitation of the act.

Undoubtedly the relations of commerce with our near neighbors, whose territories form so long a frontier line difficult to be guarded, and who find in our country, and equally offer to us, natural markets, demand special and considerate treatment. It rests with Congress to consider what legislative action may increase facilities of intercourse which contiguity makes natural and desirable.

I earnestly urge that Congress recast the appropriations for the maintenance of the diplomatic and consular service on a footing commensurate with the importance of our national interests. At every post where a representative is necessary the salary should be so graded as to permit him to live with comfort. With the assignment of adequate salaries the so-called notarial extraofficial fees, which our officers abroad are now permitted to treat as personal perquisites, should be done away with. Every act requiring the certification and seal of the officer should be taxable at schedule rates and the fee therefor returned to the Treasury. By restoring these revenues to the public use the consular service would be self-supporting, even with a liberal increase of the present low salaries.

In further prevention of abuses a system of consular inspection should be instituted.

The appointment of a limited number of secretaries of legation at large, to be assigned to duty wherever necessary, and in particular for temporary service at missions which for any cause may be without a head, should also be authorized.

I favor also authorization for the detail of officers of the regular service as military or naval attachés at legations.

Some foreign governments do not recognize the union of consular with diplomatic functions. Italy and Venezuela will only receive the appointee in one of his two capacities, but this does not prevent the requirement of a bond and submission to the responsibilities of an office whose duties he can not discharge. The superadded title of consul-general should be abandoned at all missions.

I deem it expedient that a well-devised measure for the reorganization of the extraterritorial courts in Oriental countries should replace the present system, which labors under the disadvantage of combining judicial and executive functions in the same office.

In several Oriental countries generous offers have been made of prem-

ises for housing the legations of the United States.   A grant of land for
that purpose was made some years since by Japan, and has been referred
to in the annual messages of my predecessor.   The Siamese Government
has made a gift to the United States of commodious quarters in Bangkok.   In Korea the late minister was permitted to purchase a building
from the Government for legation use.   In China the premises rented
for the legation are favored as to local charges.   At Tangier the house
occupied by our representative has been for many years the property of
this Government, having been given for that purpose in 1822 by the
Sultan of Morocco.   I approve the suggestion heretofore made, that, in
view of the conditions of life and administration in the Eastern countries, the legation buildings in China, Japan, Korea, Siam, and perhaps
Persia, should be owned and furnished by the Government with a view
to permanency and security.   To this end I recommend that authority
be given to accept the gifts adverted to in Japan and Siam, and to purchase in the other countries named, with provision for furniture and
repairs.   A considerable saving in rentals would result.

The World's Industrial Exposition, held at New Orleans last winter,
with the assistance of the Federal Government, attracted a large number of foreign exhibits, and proved of great value in spreading among
the concourse of visitors from Mexico and Central and South America
a wider knowledge of the varied manufactures and productions of this
country and their availability in exchange for the productions of those
regions.

Past Congresses have had under consideration the advisability of abolishing the discrimination made by the tariff laws in favor of the works
of American artists.   The odium of the policy which subjects to a high
rate of duty the paintings of foreign artists and exempts the productions
of American artists residing abroad, and who receive gratuitously advantages and instruction, is visited upon our citizens engaged in art culture
in Europe, and has caused them with practical unanimity to favor the
abolition of such an ungracious distinction; and in their interest, and for
other obvious reasons, I strongly recommend it.

The report of the Secretary of the Treasury fully exhibits the condition of the public finances and of the several branches of the Government connected with his Department.   The suggestions of the Secretary
relating to the practical operations of this important Department, and
his recommendations in the direction of simplification and economy, particularly in the work of collecting customs duties, are especially urged
upon the attention of Congress.

The ordinary receipts from all sources for the fiscal year ended June
30, 1885, were $322,690,706.38.   Of this sum $181,471,939.34 was received from customs and $112,498,725.54 from internal revenue.   The
total receipts, as given above, were $24,829,163.54 less than those for
the year ended June 30, 1884.   This diminution embraces a falling off of

$13,595,550.42 in the receipts from customs and $9,687,346.97 in the receipts from internal revenue.

The total ordinary expenditures of the Government for the fiscal year were $260,226,935.50, leaving a surplus in the Treasury at the close of the year of $63,463,771.27. This is $40,929,854.32 less than the surplus reported at the close of the previous year.

The expenditures are classified as follows:

For civil expenses	$23,826,942.11
For foreign intercourse	5,439,609.11
For Indians	6,552,494.63
For pensions	56,102,267.49
For the military, including river and harbor improvements and arsenals	42,670,578.47
For the Navy, including vessels, machinery, and improvements of navy-yards	16,021,079.69
For interest on the public debt	51,386,256.47
For the District of Columbia	3,499,650.95
For miscellaneous expenditures, including public buildings, light-houses, and collecting the revenue	54,728,056.21

The amount paid on the public debt during the fiscal year ended June 30, 1885, was $45,993,235.43, and there has been paid since that date and up to November 1, 1885, the sum of $369,828, leaving the amount of the debt at the last-named date $1,514,475,860.47. There was, however, at that time in the Treasury, applicable to the general purposes of the Government, the sum of $66,818,292.38.

The total receipts for the current fiscal year ending June 30, 1886, ascertained to October 1, 1885, and estimated for the remainder of the year, are $315,000,000. The expenditures ascertained and estimated for the same time are $245,000,000, leaving a surplus at the close of the year estimated at $70,000,000.

The value of the exports from the United States to foreign countries during the last fiscal year was as follows:

Domestic merchandise	$726,682,946.00
Foreign merchandise	15,506,809.00
	742,189,755.00
Gold	8,477,892.00
Silver	33,753,633.00
	784,421,280.00

Some of the principal exports, with their values and the percentage they respectively bear to the total exportation, are given as follows:

Articles.	Value.	Percentage.
Cotton and cotton manufactures	$213,799,049	29.42
Breadstuffs	160,370,821	22.07
Provisions	107,332,456	14.77
Oils—mineral, vegetable, and animal	54,326,202	7.48
Tobacco and its manufactures	24,767,305	3.41
Wood and its manufactures	21,464,322	2.95

Our imports during the year were as follows:

Merchandise	$579,580,053.80
Gold	26,691,696.00
Silver	16,550,627.00
	622,822,376.80

The following are given as prominent articles of import during the year, with their values and the percentage they bear to the total importation:

Articles.	Value.	Percent-age.
Sugar and molasses	$76,738,713	13.29
Coffee	46,723,318	8.09
Wool and its manufactures	44,656,482	7.73
Silk and its manufactures	40,393,002	6.99
Chemicals, dyes, drugs, and medicines	35,070,816	6.07
Iron and steel and their manufactures	34,563,689	5.98
Flax, hemp, jute, and their manufactures	32,854,874	5.69
Cotton and its manufactures	28,152,001	4.88
Hides and skins other than fur skins	20,586,443	3.56

Of the entire amount of duties collected 70 per cent was collected from the following articles of import:

	Percentage.
Sugar and molasses	29
Wool and its manufactures	15
Silk and its manufactures	8
Iron and steel and their manufactures	7
Cotton manufactures	6
Flax, hemp, and jute, and their manufactures	5

The fact that our revenues are in excess of the actual needs of an economical administration of the Government justifies a reduction in the amount exacted from the people for its support. Our Government is but the means established by the will of a free people by which certain principles are applied which they have adopted for their benefit and protection; and it is never better administered and its true spirit is never better observed than when the people's taxation for its support is scrupulously limited to the actual necessity of expenditure and distributed according to a just and equitable plan.

The proposition with which we have to deal is the reduction of the revenue received by the Government, and indirectly paid by the people, from customs duties. The question of free trade is not involved, nor is there now any occasion for the general discussion of the wisdom or expediency of a protective system.

Justice and fairness dictate that in any modification of our present laws relating to revenue the industries and interests which have been encouraged by such laws, and in which our citizens have large investments, should not be ruthlessly injured or destroyed. We should also deal with the subject in such manner as to protect the interests of

American labor, which is the capital of our workingmen. Its stability and proper remuneration furnish the most justifiable pretext for a protective policy.

Within these limitations a certain reduction should be made in our customs revenue. The amount of such reduction having been determined, the inquiry follows, Where can it best be remitted and what articles can best be released from duty in the interest of our citizens?

I think the reduction should be made in the revenue derived from a tax upon the imported necessaries of life. We thus directly lessen the cost of living in every family of the land and release to the people in every humble home a larger measure of the rewards of frugal industry.

During the year ended November 1, 1885, 145 national banks were organized, with an aggregate capital of $16,938,000, and circulating notes have been issued to them amounting to $4,274,910. The whole number of these banks in existence on the day above mentioned was 2,727.

The very limited amount of circulating notes issued by our national banks, compared with the amount the law permits them to issue upon a deposit of bonds for their redemption, indicates that the volume of our circulating medium may be largely increased through this instrumentality.

Nothing more important than the present condition of our currency and coinage can claim your attention.

Since February, 1878, the Government has, under the compulsory provisions of law, purchased silver bullion and coined the same at the rate of more than $2,000,000 every month. By this process up to the present date 215,759,431 silver dollars have been coined.

A reasonable appreciation of a delegation of power to the General Government would limit its exercise, without express restrictive words, to the people's needs and the requirements of the public welfare.

Upon this theory the authority to "coin money" given to Congress by the Constitution, if it permits the purchase by the Government of bullion for coinage in any event, does not justify such purchase and coinage to an extent beyond the amount needed for a sufficient circulating medium.

The desire to utilize the silver product of the country should not lead to a misuse or the perversion of this power.

The necessity for such an addition to the silver currency of the nation as is compelled by the silver-coinage act is negatived by the fact that up to the present time only about 50,000,000 of the silver dollars so coined have actually found their way into circulation, leaving more than 165,000,000 in the possession of the Government, the custody of which has entailed a considerable expense for the construction of vaults for its deposit. Against this latter amount there are outstanding silver certificates amounting to about $93,000,000.

Every month two millions of gold in the public Treasury are paid out for two millions or more of silver dollars, to be added to the idle mass already accumulated.

If continued long enough, this operation will result in the substitution of silver for all the gold the Government owns applicable to its general purposes. It will not do to rely upon the customs receipts of the Government to make good this drain of gold, because the silver thus coined having been made legal tender for all debts and dues, public and private, at times during the last six months 58 per cent of the receipts for duties has been in silver or silver certificates, while the average within that period has been 20 per cent. The proportion of silver and its certificates received by the Government will probably increase as time goes on, for the reason that the nearer the period approaches when it will be obliged to offer silver in payment of its obligations the greater inducement there will be to hoard gold against depreciation in the value of silver or for the purpose of speculating.

This hoarding of gold has already begun.

When the time comes that gold has been withdrawn from circulation, then will be apparent the difference between the real value of the silver dollar and a dollar in gold, and the two coins will part company. Gold, still the standard of value and necessary in our dealings with other countries, will be at a premium over silver; banks which have substituted gold for the deposits of their customers may pay them with silver bought with such gold, thus making a handsome profit; rich speculators will sell their hoarded gold to their neighbors who need it to liquidate their foreign debts, at a ruinous premium over silver, and the laboring men and women of the land, most defenseless of all, will find that the dollar received for the wage of their toil has sadly shrunk in its purchasing power. It may be said that the latter result will be but temporary, and that ultimately the price of labor will be adjusted to the change; but even if this takes place the wage-worker can not possibly gain, but must inevitably lose, since the price he is compelled to pay for his living will not only be measured in a coin heavily depreciated and fluctuating and uncertain in its value, but this uncertainty in the value of the purchasing medium will be made the pretext for an advance in prices beyond that justified by actual depreciation.

The words uttered in 1834 by Daniel Webster in the Senate of the United States are true to-day:

The very man of all others who has the deepest interest in a sound currency, and who suffers most by mischievous legislation in money matters, is the man who earns his daily bread by his daily toil.

The most distinguished advocate of bimetallism, discussing our silver coinage, has lately written:

No American citizen's hand has yet felt the sensation of cheapness, either in receiving or expending the silver-act dollars.

And those who live by labor or legitimate trade never will feel that sensation of cheapness. However plenty silver dollars may become, they will not be distributed as gifts among the people; and if the laboring man should receive four depreciated dollars where he now receives but two, he will pay in the depreciated coin more than double the price he now pays for all the necessaries and comforts of life.

Those who do not fear any disastrous consequences arising from the continued compulsory coinage of silver as now directed by law, and who suppose that the addition to the currency of the country intended as its result will be a public benefit, are reminded that history demonstrates that the point is easily reached in the attempt to float at the same time two sorts of money of different excellence when the better will cease to be in general circulation. The hoarding of gold which has already taken place indicates that we shall not escape the usual experience in such cases. So if this silver coinage be continued we may reasonably expect that gold and its equivalent will abandon the field of circulation to silver alone. This of course must produce a severe contraction of our circulating medium, instead of adding to it.

It will not be disputed that any attempt on the part of the Government to cause the circulation of silver dollars worth 80 cents side by side with gold dollars worth 100 cents, even within the limit that legislation does not run counter to the laws of trade, to be successful must be seconded by the confidence of the people that both coins will retain the same purchasing power and be interchangeable at will. A special effort has been made by the Secretary of the Treasury to increase the amount of our silver coin in circulation; but the fact that a large share of the limited amount thus put out has soon returned to the public Treasury in payment of duties leads to the belief that the people do not now desire to keep it in hand, and this, with the evident disposition to hoard gold, gives rise to the suspicion that there already exists a lack of confidence among the people touching our financial processes. There is certainly not enough silver now in circulation to cause uneasiness, and the whole amount coined and now on hand might after a time be absorbed by the people without apprehension; but it is the ceaseless stream that threatens to overflow the land which causes fear and uncertainty.

What has been thus far submitted upon this subject relates almost entirely to considerations of a home nature, unconnected with the bearing which the policies of other nations have upon the question. But it is perfectly apparent that a line of action in regard to our currency can not wisely be settled upon or persisted in without considering the attitude on the subject of other countries with whom we maintain intercourse through commerce, trade, and travel. An acknowledgment of this fact is found in the act by virtue of which our silver is compulsorily coined. It provides that—

The President shall invite the governments of the countries composing the Latin Union, so called, and of such other European nations as he may deem advisable, to join the United States in a conference to adopt a common ratio between gold and silver for the purpose of establishing internationally the use of bimetallic money and securing fixity of relative value between those metals.

This conference absolutely failed, and a similar fate has awaited all subsequent efforts in the same direction. And still we continue our coinage of silver at a ratio different from that of any other nation. The most vital part of the silver-coinage act remains inoperative and unexecuted, and without an ally or friend we battle upon the silver field in an illogical and losing contest.

To give full effect to the design of Congress on this subject I have made careful and earnest endeavor since the adjournment of the last Congress.

To this end I delegated a gentleman well instructed in fiscal science to proceed to the financial centers of Europe and, in conjunction with our ministers to England, France, and Germany, to obtain a full knowledge of the attitude and intent of those governments in respect of the establishment of such an international ratio as would procure free coinage of both metals at the mints of those countries and our own. By my direction our consul-general at Paris has given close attention to the proceedings of the congress of the Latin Union, in order to indicate our interest in its objects and report its action.

It may be said in brief, as the result of these efforts, that the attitude of the leading powers remains substantially unchanged since the monetary conference of 1881, nor is it to be questioned that the views of these governments are in each instance supported by the weight of public opinion.

The steps thus taken have therefore only more fully demonstrated the uselessness of further attempts at present to arrive at any agreement on the subject with other nations.

In the meantime we are accumulating silver coin, based upon our own peculiar ratio, to such an extent, and assuming so heavy a burden to be provided for in any international negotiations, as will render us an undesirable party to any future monetary conference of nations.

It is a significant fact that four of the five countries composing the Latin Union mentioned in our coinage act, embarrassed with their silver currency, have just completed an agreement among themselves that no more silver shall be coined by their respective Governments and that such as has been already coined and in circulation shall be redeemed in gold by the country of its coinage. The resort to this expedient by these countries may well arrest the attention of those who suppose that we can succeed without shock or injury in the attempt to circulate upon its merits all the silver we may coin under the provisions of our silver-coinage act.

The condition in which our Treasury may be placed by a persistence in our present course is a matter of concern to every patriotic citizen who does not desire his Government to pay in silver such of its obligations as should be paid in gold. Nor should our condition be such as to oblige us, in a prudent management of our affairs, to discontinue the calling in and payment of interest-bearing obligations which we have the right now to discharge, and thus avoid the payment of further interest thereon.

The so-called debtor class, for whose benefit the continued compulsory coinage of silver is insisted upon, are not dishonest because they are in debt, and they should not be suspected of a desire to jeopardize the financial safety of the country in order that they may cancel their present debts by paying the same in depreciated dollars. Nor should it be forgotten that it is not the rich nor the money lender alone that must submit to such a readjustment, enforced by the Government and their debtors. The pittance of the widow and the orphan and the incomes of helpless beneficiaries of all kinds would be disastrously reduced. The depositors in savings banks and in other institutions which hold in trust the savings of the poor, when their little accumulations are scaled down to meet the new order of things, would in their distress painfully realize the delusion of the promise made to them that plentiful money would improve their condition.

We have now on hand all the silver dollars necessary to supply the present needs of the people and to satisfy those who from sentiment wish to see them in circulation, and if their coinage is suspended they can be readily obtained by all who desire them. If the need of more is at any time apparent, their coinage may be renewed.

That disaster has not already overtaken us furnishes no proof that danger does not wait upon a continuation of the present silver coinage. We have been saved by the most careful management and unusual expedients, by a combination of fortunate conditions, and by a confident expectation that the course of the Government in regard to silver coinage would be speedily changed by the action of Congress.

Prosperity hesitates upon our threshold because of the dangers and uncertainties surrounding this question. Capital timidly shrinks from trade, and investors are unwilling to take the chance of the questionable shape in which their money will be returned to them, while enterprise halts at a risk against which care and sagacious management do not protect.

As a necessary consequence, labor lacks employment and suffering and distress are visited upon a portion of our fellow-citizens especially entitled to the careful consideration of those charged with the duties of legislation. No interest appeals to us so strongly for a safe and stable currency as the vast army of the unemployed.

I recommend the suspension of the compulsory coinage of silver dollars, directed by the law passed in February, 1878.

The Steamboat-Inspection Service on the 30th day of June, 1885, was composed of 140 persons, including officers, clerks, and messengers. The expenses of the service over the receipts were $138,822.22 during the fiscal year. The special inspection of foreign steam vessels, organized under a law passed in 1882, was maintained during the year at an expense of $36,641.63. Since the close of the fiscal year reductions have been made in the force employed which will result in a saving during the current year of $17,000 without affecting the efficiency of the service.

The Supervising Surgeon-General reports that during the fiscal year 41,714 patients have received relief through the Marine-Hospital Service, of whom 12,803 were treated in hospitals and 28,911 at the dispensaries.

Active and effective efforts have been made through the medium of this service to protect the country against an invasion of cholera, which has prevailed in Spain and France, and the smallpox, which recently broke out in Canada.

The most gratifying results have attended the operations of the Life-Saving Service during the last fiscal year. The observance of the provision of law requiring the appointment of the force employed in this service to be made "solely with reference to their fitness, and without reference to their political or party affiliation," has secured the result which may confidently be expected in any branch of public employment where such a rule is applied. As a consequence, this service is composed of men well qualified for the performance of their dangerous and exceptionally important duties.

The number of stations in commission at the close of the year was 203. The number of disasters to vessels and craft of all kinds within their field of action was 371. The number of persons endangered in such disasters was 2,439, of whom 2,428 were saved and only 11 lost. Other lives which were imperiled, though not by disasters to shipping, were also rescued, and a large amount of property was saved through the aid of this service. The cost of its maintenance during the year was $828,474.43.

The work of the Coast and Geodetic Survey was during the last fiscal year carried on within the boundaries and off the coasts of thirty-two States, two Territories, and the District of Columbia. In July last certain irregularities were found to exist in the management of this Bureau, which led to a prompt investigation of its methods. The abuses which were brought to light by this examination and the reckless disregard of duty and the interests of the Government developed on the part of some of those connected with the service made a change of superintendency and a few of its other officers necessary. Since the Bureau has been in new hands an introduction of economies and the application of business methods have produced an important saving to the Government and a promise of more useful results.

This service has never been regulated by anything but the most indefinite legal enactments and the most unsatisfactory rules. It was many years ago sanctioned apparently for a purpose regarded as temporary and related to a survey of our coast. Having gained a place in the appropriations made by Congress, it has gradually taken to itself powers and objects not contemplated in its creation and extended its operations until it sadly needs legislative attention.

So far as a further survey of our coast is concerned, there seems to be a propriety in transferring that work to the Navy Department. The other duties now in charge of this establishment, if they can not be profitably attached to some existing Department or other bureau, should be prosecuted under a law exactly defining their scope and purpose, and with a careful discrimination between the scientific inquiries which may properly be assumed by the Government and those which should be undertaken by State authority or by individual enterprise.

It is hoped that the report of the Congressional committee heretofore appointed to investigate this and other like matters will aid in the accomplishment of proper legislation on this subject.

The report of the Secretary of War is herewith submitted. The attention of Congress is invited to the detailed account which it contains of the administration of his Department, and his recommendations and suggestions for the improvement of the service.

The Army consisted, at the date of the last consolidated returns, of 2,154 officers and 24,705 enlisted men.

The expenses of the Departments for the fiscal year ended June 30, 1885, including $13,164,394.60 for public works and river and harbor improvements, were $45,850,999.54.

Besides the troops which were dispatched in pursuit of the small band of Indians who left their reservation in Arizona and committed murders and outrages, two regiments of cavalry and one of infantry were sent last July to the Indian Territory to prevent an outbreak which seemed imminent. They remained to aid, if necessary, in the expulsion of intruders upon the reservation, who seemed to have caused the discontent among the Indians, but the Executive proclamation* warning them to remove was complied with without their interference.

Troops were also sent to Rock Springs, in Wyoming Territory, after the massacre of Chinese there, to prevent further disturbance, and afterwards to Seattle, in Washington Territory, to avert a threatened attack upon Chinese laborers and domestic violence there. In both cases the mere presence of the troops had the desired effect.

It appears that the number of desertions has diminished, but that during the last fiscal year they numbered 2,927; and one instance is given by the Lieutenant-General of six desertions by the same recruit. I am convinced that this number of desertions can be much diminished by better discipline and treatment; but the punishment should be increased for repeated offenses.

These desertions might also be reduced by lessening the term of first enlistments, thus allowing a discontented recruit to contemplate a nearer discharge and the Army a profitable riddance. After one term of service a reenlistment would be quite apt to secure a contented recruit.

The Acting Judge-Advocate-General reports that the number of trials by general courts-martial during the year was 2,328, and that 11,851 trials took place before garrison and regimental courts-martial. The suggestion that probably more than half the Army have been tried for offenses, great and small, in one year may well arrest attention. Of course many of these trials before garrison and regimental courts-martial were for offenses almost frivolous, and there should, I think, be a way devised to dispose of these in a more summary and less inconvenient manner than by court-martial.

If some of the proceedings of courts-martial which I have had occasion to examine present the ideas of justice which generally prevail in these tribunals, I am satisfied that they should be much reformed if the honor and the honesty of the Army and Navy are by their instrumentality to be vindicated and protected.

The Board on Fortifications or other defenses, appointed in pursuance of the provisions of the act of Congress approved March 3, 1885, will in a short time present their report, and it is hoped that this may greatly aid the legislation so necessary to remedy the present defenseless condition of our seacoasts.

The work of the Signal Service has been prosecuted during the last year with results of increasing benefit to the country. The field of instruction has been enlarged with a view of adding to its usefulness. The number of stations in operation June 30, 1885, was 489. Telegraphic reports are received daily from 160 stations. Reports are also received from 25 Canadian stations, 375 volunteer observers, 52 army surgeons at military posts, and 333 foreign stations. The expense of the service during the fiscal year, after deducting receipts from military telegraph lines, was $792,592.97. In view of the fact referred to by the Secretary of War, that the work of this service ordinarily is of a scientific nature, and the further fact that it is assuming larger proportions constantly and becoming more and more unsuited to the fixed rules which must govern the Army, I am inclined to agree with him in the opinion that it should be separately established. If this is done, the scope and extent of its operations should, as nearly as possible, be definitely prescribed by law and always capable of exact ascertainment.

The Military Academy at West Point is reported as being in a high state of efficiency and well equipped for the satisfactory accomplishment of the purposes of its maintenance.

The fact that the class which graduates next year is an unusually large one has constrained me to decline to make appointments to second lieutenancies in the Army from civil life, so that such vacancies as exist in these places may be reserved for such graduates; and yet it is not probable that there will be enough vacancies to provide positions for them all when they leave the military school. Under the prevailing law and usage those not thus assigned to duty never actively enter the military service.

It is suggested that the law on this subject be changed so that such of these young men as are not at once assigned to duty after graduation may be retained as second lieutenants in the Army if they desire it, subject to assignment when opportunity occurs, and under proper rules as to priority of selection.

The expenditures on account of the Military Academy for the last fiscal year, exclusive of the sum taken for its purposes from appropriations for the support of the Army, were $290,712.07.

The act approved March 3, 1885, designed to compensate officers and enlisted men for loss of private property while in the service of the United States, is so indefinite in its terms and apparently admits so many claims the adjustment of which could not have been contemplated that if it is to remain upon the statute book it needs amendment.

There should be a general law of Congress prohibiting the construction of bridges over navigable waters in such manner as to obstruct navigation, with provisions for preventing the same. It seems that under existing statutes the Government can not intervene to prevent such a construction when entered upon without its consent, though when such consent is asked and granted upon condition the authority to insist upon such condition is clear. Thus it is represented that while the officers of the Government are with great care guarding against the obstruction of navigation by a bridge across the Mississippi River at St. Paul a large pier for a bridge has been built just below this place directly in the navigable channel of the river. If such things are to be permitted, a strong argument is presented against the appropriation of large sums of money to improve the navigation of this and other important highways of commerce.

The report of the Secretary of the Navy gives a history of the operations of his Department and the present condition of the work committed to his charge.

He details in full the course pursued by him to protect the rights of the Government in respect of certain vessels unfinished at the time of his accession to office, and also concerning the dispatch boat *Dolphin*, claimed to be completed and awaiting the acceptance of the Department. No one can fail to see from recitals contained in this report that only the application of business principles has been insisted upon in the treatment of these subjects, and that whatever controversy has arisen was caused by the exaction on the part of the Department of contract obligations as they were legally construed. In the case of the *Dolphin*, with entire justice to the contractor, an agreement has been entered into providing for the ascertainment by a judicial inquiry of the complete or partial compliance with the contract in her construction, and further providing for the assessment of any damages to which the Government may be entitled on account of a partial failure to perform such contract, or the payment of the sum still remaining unpaid upon her price in case a full performance is adjudged.

The contractor, by reason of his failure in business, being unable to complete the other three vessels, they were taken possession of by the Government in their unfinished state under a clause in the contract permitting such a course, and are now in process of completion in the yard of the contractor, but under the supervision of the Navy Department.

Congress at its last session authorized the construction of two additional new cruisers and two gunboats, at a cost not exceeding in the aggregate $2,995,000. The appropriation for this purpose having become available on the 1st day of July last, steps were at once taken for the procurement of such plans for the construction of these vessels as would be likely to insure their usefulness when completed. These are of the utmost importance, considering the constant advance in the art of building vessels of this character, and the time is not lost which is spent in their careful consideration and selection.

All must admit the importance of an effective navy to a nation like ours, having such an extended seacoast to protect; and yet we have not a single vessel of war that could keep the seas against a first-class vessel of any important power. Such a condition ought not longer to continue. The nation that can not resist aggression is constantly exposed to it. Its foreign policy is of necessity weak and its negotiations are conducted with disadvantage because it is not in condition to enforce the terms dictated by its sense of right and justice.

Inspired, as I am, by the hope, shared by all patriotic citizens, that the day is not very far distant when our Navy will be such as befits our standing among the nations of the earth, and rejoiced at every step that leads in the direction of such a consummation, I deem it my duty to especially direct the attention of Congress to the close of the report of the Secretary of the Navy, in which the humiliating weakness of the present organization of his Department is exhibited and the startling abuses and waste of its present methods are exposed. The conviction is forced upon us with the certainty of mathematical demonstration that before we proceed further in the restoration of a Navy we need a thoroughly reorganized Navy Department. The fact that within seventeen years more than $75,000,000 have been spent in the construction, repair, equipment, and armament of vessels, and the further fact that instead of an effective and creditable fleet we have only the discontent and apprehension of a nation undefended by war vessels, added to the disclosures now made, do not permit us to doubt that every attempt to revive our Navy has thus far for the most part been misdirected, and all our efforts in that direction have been little better than blind gropings and expensive, aimless follies.

Unquestionably if we are content with the maintenance of a Navy Department simply as a shabby ornament to the Government, a constant watchfulness may prevent some of the scandal and abuse which have found their way into our present organization, and its incurable waste may be reduced to the minimum. But if we desire to build ships for present usefulness instead of naval reminders of the days that are past, we must have a Department organized for the work, supplied with all the talent and ingenuity our country affords, prepared to take advantage of the experience of other nations, systematized so that all effort shall unite and lead in one direction, and fully imbued with the conviction that war vessels, though new, are useless unless they combine all that the ingenuity of man has up to this day brought forth relating to their construction.

I earnestly commend the portion of the Secretary's report devoted to this subject to the attention of Congress, in the hope that his suggestions touching the reorganization of his Department may be adopted as the first step toward the reconstruction of our Navy.

The affairs of the postal service are exhibited by the report of the Postmaster-General, which will be laid before you.

The postal revenue, whose ratio of gain upon the rising prosperity of 1882 and 1883 outstripped the increasing expenses of our growing service, was checked by the reduction in the rate of letter postage which took effect with the beginning of October in the latter year, and it diminished during the two past fiscal years $2,790,000, in about the proportion of $2,270,000 in 1884 to $520,000 in 1885. Natural growth and development have meantime increased expenditure, resulting in a deficiency in the revenue to meet the expenses of the Department of five and a quarter million dollars for the year 1884 and eight and a third million in the last fiscal year. The anticipated and natural revival of the revenue has been oppressed and retarded by the unfavorable business condition of the country, of which the postal service is a faithful indicator. The gratifying fact is shown, however, by the report that our returning prosperity is marked by a gain of $380,000 in the revenue of the latter half of the last year over the corresponding period of the preceding year.

The change in the weight of first-class matter which may be carried for a single rate of postage from a half ounce to an ounce, and the reduction by one-half of the rate of newspaper postage, which, under recent legislation, began with the current year, will operate to restrain the augmentation of receipts which otherwise might have been expected to such a degree that the scale of expense may gain upon the revenue and cause an increased deficiency to be shown at its close. Yet, after no long period of reawakened prosperity, by proper economy it is confidently anticipated that even the present low rates, now as favorable as any country affords, will be adequate to sustain the cost of the service.

The operation of the Post-Office Department is for the convenience and benefit of the people, and the method by which they pay the charges of this useful arm of their public service, so that it be just and impartial, is of less importance to them than the economical expenditure of the means they provide for its maintenance and the due improvement of its agencies, so that they may enjoy its highest usefulness.

A proper attention has been directed to the prevention of waste or extravagance, and good results appear from the report to have already been accomplished.

I approve the recommendation of the Postmaster-General to reduce the charges on domestic money orders of $5 and less from 8 to 5 cents. This change will materially aid those of our people who most of all avail themselves of this instrumentality, but to whom the element of cheapness is of the greatest importance. With this reduction the system would still remain self-supporting.

The free-delivery system has been extended to 19 additional cities during the year, and 178 now enjoy its conveniences. Experience has commended it to those who enjoy its benefits, and further enlargement of its facilities is due to other communities to which it is adapted. In the cities where it has been established, taken together, the local postage exceeds its maintenance by nearly $1,300,000. The limit to which this system is now confined by law has been nearly reached, and the reasons given justify its extension, which is proposed.

It was decided, with my approbation, after a sufficient examination, to be inexpedient for the Post-Office Department to contract for carrying our foreign mails under the additional authority given by the last Congress. The amount limited was inadequate to pay all within the purview of the law the full rate of 50 cents per mile, and it would have been unjust and unwise to have given it to some and denied it to others. Nor could contracts have been let under the law to all at a rate to have brought the aggregate within the appropriation without such practical prearrangement of terms as would have violated it.

The rate of sea and inland postage which was proffered under another statute clearly appears to be a fair compensation for the desired service, being three times the price necessary to secure transportation by other vessels upon any route, and much beyond the charges made to private persons for services not less burdensome.

Some of the steamship companies, upon the refusal of the Postmaster-General to attempt, by the means provided, the distribution of the sum appropriated as an extra compensation, withdrew the services of their vessels and thereby occasioned slight inconvenience, though no considerable injury, the mails having been dispatched by other means.

Whatever may be thought of the policy of subsidizing any line of public conveyance or travel, I am satisfied that it should not be done under cover of an expenditure incident to the administration of a Department, nor should there be any uncertainty as to the recipients of the subsidy or any discretion left to an executive officer as to its distribution. If such gifts of the public money are to be made for the purpose of aiding any enterprise in the supposed interest of the public, I can not but think that the amount to be paid and the beneficiary might better be determined by Congress than in any other way.

The international congress of delegates from the Postal Union countries convened at Lisbon, in Portugal, in February last, and after a session of some weeks the delegates signed a convention amendatory of the present postal-union convention in some particulars designed to advance its purposes. This additional act has had my approval and will be laid before you with the departmental report.

I approve the recommendation of the Postmaster-General that another assistant be provided for his Department. I invite your consideration to the several other recommendations contained in his report.

The report of the Attorney-General contains a history of the conduct of the Department of Justice during the last year and a number of valuable suggestions as to needed legislation, and I invite your careful attention to the same.

The condition of business in the courts of the United States is such that there seems to be an imperative necessity for remedial legislation on the subject. Some of these courts are so overburdened with pending causes that the delays in determining litigation amount often to a denial of justice. Among the plans suggested for relief is one submitted by the Attorney-General. Its main features are: The transfer of all the original jurisdiction of the circuit courts to the district courts and an increase of judges for the latter where necessary; an addition of judges to the circuit courts, and constituting them exclusively courts of appeal, and reasonably limiting appeals thereto; further restrictions of the right to remove causes from the State to Federal courts; permitting appeals to the Supreme Court from the courts of the District of Columbia and the Territories only in the same cases as they are allowed from State courts, and guarding against an unnecessary number of appeals from the circuit courts.

I approve the plan thus outlined, and recommend the legislation necessary for its application to our judicial system.

The present mode of compensating United States marshals and district attorneys should, in my opinion, be changed. They are allowed to charge against the Government certain fees for services, their income being measured by the amount of such fees within a fixed limit as to their annual aggregate. This is a direct inducement for them to make their fees in criminal cases as large as possible in an effort to reach the maximum sum permitted. As an entirely natural consequence, unscrupulous marshals are found encouraging frivolous prosecutions, arresting people on petty charges of crime and transporting them to distant places for examination and trial, for the purpose of earning mileage and other fees; and district attorneys uselessly attend criminal examinations far from their places of residence for the express purpose of swelling their accounts against the Government. The actual expenses incurred in these transactions are also charged against the Government.

Thus the rights and freedom of our citizens are outraged and public expenditures increased for the purpose of furnishing public officers pretexts for increasing the measure of their compensation.

I think marshals and district attorneys should be paid .salaries, adjusted by a rule which will make them commensurate with services fairly rendered.

In connection with this subject I desire to suggest the advisability, if it be found not obnoxious to constitutional objection, of investing United States commissioners with the power to try and determine certain violations of law within the grade of misdemeanors. Such trials might be made to depend upon the option of the accused. The multiplication of small and technical offenses, especially under the provisions of our internal-revenue law, render some change in our present system very desirable in the interests of humanity as well as economy. The district courts are now crowded with petty prosecutions, involving a punishment in case of conviction, of only a slight fine, while the parties accused are harassed by an enforced attendance upon courts held hundreds of miles from their homes. If poor and friendless, they are obliged to remain in jail during months, perhaps, that elapse before a session of the court is held, and are finally brought to trial surrounded by strangers and with but little real opportunity for defense. In the meantime frequently the marshal has charged against the Government his fees for an arrest, the transportation of the accused and the expense of the same, and for summoning witnesses before a commissioner, a grand jury, and a court; the witnesses have been paid from the public funds large fees and traveling expenses, and the commissioner and district attorney have also made their charges against the Government.

This abuse in the administration of our criminal law should be remedied; and if the plan above suggested is not practicable, some other should be devised.

The report of the Secretary of the Interior, containing an account of the operations of this important Department and much interesting information, will be submitted for your consideration.

The most intricate and difficult subject in charge of this Department is the treatment and management of the Indians. I am satisfied that some progress may be noted in their condition as a result of a prudent administration of the present laws and regulations for their control.

But it is submitted that there is lack of a fixed purpose or policy on this subject, which should be supplied. It is useless to dilate upon the wrongs of the Indians, and as useless to indulge in the heartless belief that because their wrongs are revenged in their own atrocious manner, therefore they should be exterminated.

They are within the care of our Government, and their rights are, or should be, protected from invasion by the most solemn obligations. They are properly enough called the wards of the Government; and it should be borne in mind that this guardianship involves on our part efforts for the improvement of their condition and the enforcement of their rights. There seems to be general concurrence in the proposition that the ultimate object of their treatment should be their civilization and citizenship. Fitted by these to keep pace in the march of progress with the advanced civilization about them, they will readily assimilate with the mass of our population, assuming the responsibilities and receiving the protection incident to this condition.

The difficulty appears to be in the selection of the means to be at present employed toward the attainment of this result.

Our Indian population, exclusive of those in Alaska, is reported as numbering 260,000, nearly all being located on lands set apart for their use and occupation, aggregating over 134,000,000 acres. These lands are included in the boundaries of 171 reservations of different dimensions, scattered in 21 States and Territories, presenting great variations in climate and in the kind and quality of their soils. Among the Indians upon these several reservations there exist the most marked differences in natural traits and disposition and in their progress toward civilization. While some are lazy, vicious, and stupid, others are industrious, peaceful, and intelligent; while a portion of them are self-supporting and independent, and have so far advanced in civilization that they make their own laws, administered through officers of their own choice, and educate their children in schools of their own establishment and maintenance, others still retain, in squalor and dependence, almost the savagery of their natural state.

In dealing with this question the desires manifested by the Indians should not be ignored. Here again we find a great diversity. With some the tribal relation is cherished with the utmost tenacity, while its hold upon others is considerably relaxed; the love of home is strong with all, and yet there are those whose attachment to a particular locality is by no means unyielding; the ownership of their lands in severalty is much desired by some, while by others, and sometimes among the most civilized, such a distribution would be bitterly opposed.

The variation of their wants, growing out of and connected with the character of their several locations, should be regarded. Some are upon reservations most fit for grazing, but without flocks or herds; and some, on arable land, have no agricultural implements. While some of the reservations are double the size necessary to maintain the number of Indians now upon them, in a few cases, perhaps, they should be enlarged.

Add to all this the difference in the administration of the agencies. While the same duties are devolved upon all, the disposition of the agents and the manner of their contact with the Indians have much to do with their condition and welfare. The agent who perfunctorily performs his duty and slothfully neglects all opportunity to advance their moral and physical improvement and fails to inspire them with a desire for better things will accomplish nothing in the direction of their civilization, while he who feels the burden of an important trust and has

an interest in his work will, by consistent example, firm yet considerate treatment, and well-directed aid and encouragement, constantly lead
those under his charge toward the light of their enfranchisement.

The history of all the progress which has been made in the civilization of the Indian I think will disclose the fact that the beginning has
been religious teaching, followed by or accompanying secular education.
While the self-sacrificing and pious men and women who have aided in
this good work by their independent endeavor have for their reward the
beneficent results of their labor and the consciousness of Christian duty
well performed, their valuable services should be fully acknowledged by
all who under the law are charged with the control and management of
our Indian wards.

What has been said indicates that in the present condition of the
Indians no attempt should be made to apply a fixed and unyielding
plan of action to their varied and varying needs and circumstances.

The Indian Bureau, burdened as it is with their general oversight
and with the details of the establishment, can hardly possess itself of
the minute phases of the particular cases needing treatment; and thus
the propriety of creating an instrumentality auxiliary to those already
established for the care of the Indians suggests itself.

I recommend the passage of a law authorizing the appointment of six
commissioners, three of whom shall be detailed from the Army, to be
charged with the duty of a careful inspection from time to time of all the
Indians upon our reservations or subject to the care and control of the
Government, with a view of discovering their exact condition and needs
and determining what steps shall be taken on behalf of the Government
to improve their situation in the direction of their self-support and complete civilization; that they ascertain from such inspection what, if any,
of the reservations may be reduced in area, and in such cases what part
not needed for Indian occupation may be purchased by the Government
from the Indians and disposed of for their benefit; what, if any, Indians
may, with their consent, be removed to other reservations, with a view of
their concentration and the sale on their behalf of their abandoned reservations; what Indian lands now held in common should be allotted in
severalty; in what manner and to what extent the Indians upon the reservations can be placed under the protection of our laws and subjected
to their penalties, and which, if any, Indians should be invested with
the right of citizenship. The powers and functions of the commissioners in regard to these subjects should be clearly defined, though they
should, in conjunction with the Secretary of the Interior, be given all
the authority to deal definitely with the questions presented deemed safe
and consistent.

They should be also charged with the duty of ascertaining the Indians who might properly be furnished with implements of agriculture,
and of what kind; in what cases the support of the Government should

be withdrawn; where the present plan of distributing Indian supplies should be changed; where schools may be established and where discontinued; the conduct, methods, and fitness of agents in charge of reservations; the extent to which such reservations are occupied or intruded upon by unauthorized persons, and generally all matters related to the welfare and improvement of the Indian.

They should advise with the Secretary of the Interior concerning these matters of detail in management, and he should be given power to deal with them fully, if he is not now invested with such power.

This plan contemplates the selection of persons for commissioners who are interested in the Indian question and who have practical ideas upon the subject of their treatment.

The expense of the Indian Bureau during the last fiscal year was more than six and a half million dollars. I believe much of this expenditure might be saved under the plan proposed; that its economical effects would be increased with its continuance; that the safety of our frontier settlers would be subserved under its operation, and that the nation would be saved through its results from the imputation of inhumanity, injustice, and mismanagement.

In order to carry out the policy of allotment of Indian lands in severalty, when deemed expedient, it will be necessary to have surveys completed of the reservations, and I hope that provision will be made for the prosecution of this work.

In May of the present year a small portion of the Chiricahua Apaches on the White Mountain Reservation, in Arizona, left the reservation and committed a number of murders and depredations upon settlers in that neighborhood. Though prompt and energetic action was taken by the military, the renegades eluded capture and escaped into Mexico. The formation of the country through which these Indians passed, their thorough acquaintance with the same, the speed of their escape, and the manner in which they scattered and concealed themselves among the mountains near the scene of their outrages put our soldiers at a great disadvantage in their efforts to capture them, though the expectation is still entertained that they will be ultimately taken and punished for their crimes.

The threatening and disorderly conduct of the Cheyennes in the Indian Territory early last summer caused considerable alarm and uneasiness. Investigation proved that their threatening attitude was due in a great measure to the occupation of the land of their reservation by immense herds of cattle, which their owners claimed were rightfully there under certain leases made by the Indians. Such occupation appearing upon examination to be unlawful notwithstanding these leases, the intruders were ordered to remove with their cattle from the lands of the Indians by Executive proclamation. The enforcement of this proclamation had the effect of restoring peace and order among the Indians, and they are now quiet and well behaved.

By an Executive order issued on February 27, 1885, by my predecessor, a portion of the tract of country in the territory known as the
Old Winnebago and Crow Creek reservations was directed to be restored
to the public domain and opened to settlement under the land laws of
the United States, and a large number of persons entered upon those
lands.   This action alarmed the Sioux Indians, who claimed the territory as belonging to their reservation under the treaty of 1868.   This
claim was determined, after careful investigation, to be well founded, and
consequently the Executive order referred to was by proclamation of
April 17, 1885, declared to be inoperative and of no effect, and all persons upon the land were warned to leave.   This warning has been substantially complied with.

The public domain had its origin in cessions of land by the States to
the General Government.   The first cession was made by the State of
New York, and the largest, which in area exceeded all the others, by
the State of Virginia.   The territory the proprietorship of which became
thus vested in the General Government extended from the western line
of Pennsylvania to the Mississippi River.   These patriotic donations of
the States were encumbered with no condition except that they should
be held and used "for the common benefit of the United States."   By
purchase with the common fund of all the people additions were made
to this domain until it extended to the northern line of Mexico, the
Pacific Ocean, and the Polar Sea.   The original trust, "for the common
benefit of the United States," attached to all.   In the execution of that
trust the policy of many homes, rather than large estates, was adopted
by the Government.   That these might be easily obtained, and be the
abode of security and contentment, the laws for their acquisition were
few, easily understood, and general in their character.   But the pressure
of local interests, combined with a speculative spirit, have in many instances procured the passage of laws which marred the harmony of the
general plan and encumbered the system with a multitude of general
and special enactments which render the land laws complicated, subject
the titles to uncertainty, and the purchasers often to oppression and
wrong.   Laws which were intended for the "common benefit" have
been perverted so that large quantities of land are vesting in single
ownerships.   From the multitude and character of the laws, this consequence seems incapable of correction by mere administration.

It is not for the "common benefit of the United States" that a large
area of the public lands should be acquired, directly or through fraud,
in the hands of a single individual.   The nation's strength is in the
people.   The nation's prosperity is in their prosperity.   The nation's
glory is in the equality of her justice.   The nation's perpetuity is in
the patriotism of all her people.   Hence, as far as practicable, the plan
adopted in the disposal of the public lands should have in view the original policy, which encouraged many purchasers of these lands for homes

and discouraged the massing of large areas. Exclusive of Alaska, about three-fifths of the national domain has been sold or subjected to contract or grant. Of the remaining two-fifths a considerable portion is either mountain or desert. A rapidly increasing population creates a growing demand for homes, and the accumulation of wealth inspires an eager competition to obtain the public land for speculative purposes. In the future this collision of interests will be more marked than in the past, and the execution of the nation's trust in behalf of our settlers will be more difficult. I therefore commend to your attention the recommendations contained in the report of the Secretary of the Interior with reference to the repeal and modification of certain of our land laws.

The nation has made princely grants and subsidies to a system of railroads projected as great national highways to connect the Pacific States with the East. It has been charged that these donations from the people have been diverted to private gain and corrupt uses, and thus public indignation has been aroused and suspicion engendered. Our great nation does not begrudge its generosity, but it abhors peculation and fraud; and the favorable regard of our people for the great corporations to which these grants were made can only be revived by a restoration of confidence, to be secured by their constant, unequivocal, and clearly manifested integrity. A faithful application of the undiminished proceeds of the grants to the construction and perfecting of their roads, an honest discharge of their obligations, and entire justice to all the people in the enjoyment of their rights on these highways of travel are all the public asks, and it will be content with no less. To secure these things should be the common purpose of the officers of the Government, as well as of the corporations. With this accomplishment prosperity would be permanently secured to the roads, and national pride would take the place of national complaint.

It appears from the report of the Commissioner of Pensions that there were on the 1st day of July, 1885, 345,125 persons borne upon the pension rolls, who were classified as follows: Army invalids, 241,456; widows, minor children, and dependent relatives of deceased soldiers, 78,841; navy invalids, 2,745; navy widows, minor children, and dependents, 1,926; survivors of the War of 1812, 2,945; and widows of those who served in that war, 17,212. About one man in ten of all those who enlisted in the late war are reported as receiving pensions, exclusive of the dependents of deceased soldiers. On the 1st of July, 1875, the number of pensioners was 234,821, and the increase within the ten years next thereafter was 110,304.

While there is no expenditure of the public funds which the people more cheerfully approve than that made in recognition of the services of our soldiers living and dead, the sentiment underlying the subject should not be vitiated by the introduction of any fraudulent practices. Therefore it is fully as important that the rolls should be cleansed of all those who by fraud have secured a place thereon as that meritorious claims should be speedily examined and adjusted. The reforms in the methods of doing the business of this Bureau which have lately been inaugurated promise better results in both these directions.

The operations of the Patent Office demonstrate the activity of the inventive genius of the country. For the year ended June 30, 1885, the applications for patents, including reissues, and for the registration of trade-marks and labels, numbered 35,688. During the same period there were 22,928 patents granted and reissued and 1,429 trade-marks and labels registered. The number of patents issued in the year 1875 was 14,387. The receipts during the last fiscal year were $1,074,974.35, and the total expenditures, not including contingent expenses, $934,123.11.

There were 9,788 applications for patents pending on the 1st day of July, 1884, and 5,786 on the same date in the year 1885. There has been considerable improvement made in the prompt determination of applications and a consequent relief to expectant inventors.

A number of suggestions and recommendations are contained in the report of the Commissioner of Patents which are well entitled to the consideration of Congress.

In the Territory of Utah the law of the United States passed for the suppression of polygamy has been energetically and faithfully executed during the past year, with measurably good results. A number of convictions have been secured for unlawful cohabitation, and in some cases pleas of guilty have been entered and a slight punishment imposed, upon a promise by the accused that they would not again offend against the law, nor advise, counsel, aid, or abet in any way its violation by others.

The Utah commissioners express the opinion, based upon such information as they are able to obtain, that but few polygamous marriages have taken place in the Territory during the last year. They further report that while there can not be found upon the registration lists of voters the name of a man actually guilty of polygamy, and while none of that class are holding office, yet at the last election in the Territory all the officers elected, except in one county, were men who, though not actually living in the practice of polygamy, subscribe to the doctrine of polygamous marriages as a divine revelation and a law unto all higher and more binding upon the conscience than any human law, local or national. Thus is the strange spectacle presented of a community protected by a republican form of government, to which they owe allegiance, sustaining by their suffrages a principle and a belief which set at naught that obligation of absolute obedience to the law of the land which lies at the foundation of republican institutions.

The strength, the perpetuity, and the destiny of the nation rest upon our homes, established by the law of God, guarded by parental care, regulated by parental authority, and sanctified by parental love.

These are not the homes of polygamy.

The mothers of our land, who rule the nation as they mold the characters and guide the actions of their sons, live according to God's holy ordinances, and each, secure and happy in the exclusive love of the father of her children, sheds the warm light of true womanhood, unperverted and unpolluted, upon all within her pure and wholesome family circle.

These are not the cheerless, crushed, and unwomanly mothers of polygamy.

The fathers of our families are the best citizens of the Republic. Wife and children are the sources of patriotism, and conjugal and parental affection beget devotion to the country. The man who, undefiled with plural marriage, is surrounded in his single home with his wife and children has a stake in the country which inspires him with respect for its laws and courage for its defense.

These are not the fathers of polygamous families.

There is no feature of this practice or the system which sanctions it which is not opposed to all that is of value in our institutions.

There should be no relaxation in the firm but just execution of the law now in operation, and I should be glad to approve such further discreet legislation as will rid the country of this blot upon its fair fame.

Since the people upholding polygamy in our Territories are reenforced by immigration from other lands, I recommend that a law be passed to prevent the importation of Mormons into the country.

The agricultural interest of the country demands just recognition and liberal encouragement. It sustains with certainty and unfailing strength our nation's prosperity by the products of its steady toil, and bears its full share of the burden of taxation without complaint. Our agriculturists have but slight personal representation in the councils of the nation, and are generally content with the humbler duties of citizenship and willing to trust to the bounty of nature for a reward of their labor. But the magnitude and value of this industry are appreciated when the statement is made that of our total annual exports more than three-fourths are the products of agriculture, and of our total population nearly one-half are exclusively engaged in that occupation.

The Department of Agriculture was created for the purpose of acquiring and diffusing among the people useful information respecting the subjects it has in charge, and aiding in the cause of intelligent and progressive farming, by the collection of statistics, by testing the value and usefulness of new seeds and plants, and distributing such as are found desirable among agriculturists. This and other powers and duties with which this Department is invested are of the utmost importance, and if wisely exercised must be of great benefit to the country. The aim of our beneficent Government is the improvement of the people in every station and the amelioration of their condition. Surely our agriculturists should not be neglected. The instrumentality established in aid of the farmers of the land should not only be well equipped for the accomplishment of its purpose, but those for whose benefit it has been adopted should be encouraged to avail themselves fully of its advantages.

The prohibition of the importation into several countries of certain of our animals and their products, based upon the suspicion that health is endangered in their use and consumption, suggests the importance of such precautions for the protection of our stock of all kinds against disease as will disarm suspicion of danger and cause the removal of such an injurious prohibition.

If the laws now in operation are insufficient to accomplish this protection, I recommend their amendment to meet the necessities of the situation; and I commend to the consideration of Congress the suggestions contained in the report of the Commissioner of Agriculture calculated to increase the value and efficiency of this Department.

The report of the Civil Service Commission, which will be submitted, contains an account of the manner in which the civil-service law has been executed during the last year and much valuable information on this important subject.

I am inclined to think that there is no sentiment more general in the minds of the people of our country than a conviction of the correctness of the principle upon which the law enforcing civil-service reform is based. In its present condition the law regulates only a part of the subordinate public positions throughout the country. It applies the test of fitness to applicants for these places by means of a competitive examination, and gives large discretion to the Commissioners as to the character of the examination and many other matters connected with its execution. Thus the rules and regulations adopted by the Commission have much to do with the practical usefulness of the statute and with the results of its application.

The people may well trust the Commission to execute the law with perfect fairness and with as little irritation as is possible. But of course no relaxation of the principle which underlies it and no weakening of the safeguards which surround it can be expected. Experience in its administration will probably suggest amendment of the methods of its execution, but I venture to hope that we shall never again be remitted to the system which distributes public positions purely as rewards for partisan service. Doubts may well be entertained whether our Government could survive the strain of a continuance of this system, which upon every change of Administration inspires an immense army of claimants for office to lay siege to the patronage of Government, engrossing the time of public officers with their importunities, spreading abroad the contagion of their disappointment, and filling the air with the tumult of their discontent.

The allurements of an immense number of offices and places exhibited to the voters of the land, and the promise of their bestowal in recognition of partisan activity, debauch the suffrage and rob political action of its thoughtful and deliberative character. The evil would increase with the multiplication of offices consequent upon our extension, and the mania for office holding, growing from its indulgence, would pervade our population so generally that patriotic purpose, the support of principle, the desire for the public good, and solicitude for the nation's welfare would be nearly banished from the activity of our party contests and cause them to degenerate into ignoble, selfish, and disgraceful struggles for the possession of office and public place.

Civil-service reform enforced by law came none too soon to check the progress of demoralization.

One of its effects, not enough regarded, is the freedom it brings to the political action of those conservative and sober men who, in fear of the confusion and risk attending an arbitrary and sudden change in all the public offices with a change of party rule, cast their ballots against such a chance.

Parties seem to be necessary, and will long continue to exist; nor can it be now denied that there are legitimate advantages, not disconnected with office holding, which follow party supremacy. While partisanship continues bitter and pronounced and supplies so much of motive to sentiment and action, it is not fair to hold public officials in charge of important trusts responsible for the best results in the performance of their duties, and yet insist that they shall rely in confidential and important places upon the work of those not only opposed to them in political affiliation, but so steeped in partisan prejudice and rancor that they have no loyalty to their chiefs and no desire for their success. Civil-service reform does not exact this, nor does it require that those in subordinate positions who fail in yielding their best service or who are incompetent should be retained simply because they are in place. The whining of a clerk discharged for indolence or incompetency, who, though he gained his place by the worst possible operation of the spoils system, suddenly discovers that he is entitled to protection under the sanction of civil-service reform, represents an idea no less absurd than the clamor of the applicant who claims the vacant position as his compensation for the most questionable party work.

The civil-service law does not prevent the discharge of the indolent or incompetent clerk, but it does prevent supplying his place with the unfit party worker. Thus in both these phases is seen benefit to the public service. And the people who desire good government, having secured this statute, will not relinquish its benefits without protest. Nor are they unmindful of the fact that its full advantages can only be gained through the complete good faith of those having its execution in charge. And this they will insist upon.

I recommend that the salaries of the Civil Service Commissioners be increased to a sum more nearly commensurate to their important duties.

It is a source of considerable and not unnatural discontent that no adequate provision has yet been made for accommodating the principal library of the Government. Of the vast collection of books and pamphlets gathered at the Capitol, numbering some 700,000, exclusive of manuscripts, maps, and the products of the graphic arts, also of great volume and value, only about 300,000 volumes, or less than half the collection, are provided with shelf room. The others, which are increasing at the rate of from twenty-five to thirty thousand volumes a year, are not only inaccessible to the public, but are subject to serious damage and deterioration from other causes in their present situation.

A consideration of the facts that the library of the Capitol has twice been destroyed or damaged by fire, its daily increasing value, and its importance as a place of deposit of books under the law relating to copyright makes manifest the necessity of prompt action to insure its proper accommodation and protection.

My attention has been called to a controversy which has arisen from the condition of the law relating to railroad facilities in the city of Washington, which has involved the Commissioners of the District in much annoyance and trouble. I hope this difficulty will be promptly settled by appropriate legislation.

The Commissioners represent that enough of the revenues of the District are now on deposit in the Treasury of the United States to repay the sum advanced by the Government for sewer improvements under the act of June 30, 1884. They desire now an advance of the share which ultimately should be borne by the District of the cost of extensive improvements to the streets of the city. The total expense of these contemplated improvements is estimated at $1,000,000, and they are of the opinion that a considerable sum could be saved if they had all the money in hand, so that contracts for the whole work could be made at the same time. They express confidence that if the advance asked for should be made the Government would be reimbursed the same within a reasonable time. I have no doubt that these improvements could be made much cheaper if undertaken together and prosecuted according to a general plan.

The license law now in force within the District is deficient and uncertain in some of its provisions and ought to be amended. The Commissioners urge, with good reason, the necessity of providing a building for the use of the District government which shall better secure the safety and preservation of its valuable books and records.

The present condition of the law relating to the succession to the Presidency in the event of the death, disability, or removal of both the President and Vice-President is such as to require immediate amendment. This subject has repeatedly been considered by Congress, but no result has been reached. The recent lamentable death of the Vice-President, and vacancies at the same time in all other offices the incumbents of which might immediately exercise the functions of the Presidential office, has caused public anxiety and a just demand that a recurrence of such a condition of affairs should not be permitted.

In conclusion I commend to the wise care and thoughtful attention of Congress the needs, the welfare, and the aspirations of an intelligent and generous nation. To subordinate these to the narrow advantages of partisanship or the accomplishment of selfish aims is to violate the people's trust and betray the people's interests; but an individual sense of responsibility on the part of each of us and a stern determination to perform our duty well must give us place among those who have added in their day and generation to the glory and prosperity of our beloved land.

SECOND ANNUAL MESSAGE.

WASHINGTON, *December 6, 1886.*

To the Congress of the United States:

In discharge of a constitutional duty, and following a well-established precedent in the Executive office, I herewith transmit to the Congress at its reassembling certain information concerning the state of the Union, together with such recommendations for legislative consideration as appear necessary and expedient.

Our Government has consistently maintained its relations of friendship toward all other powers and of neighborly interest toward those whose possessions are contiguous to our own. Few questions have arisen during the past year with other governments, and none of those are beyond the reach of settlement in friendly counsel.

We are as yet without provision for the settlement of claims of citizens of the United States against Chile for injustice during the late war with Peru and Bolivia. The mixed commissions organized under claims conventions concluded by the Chilean Government with certain European States have developed an amount of friction which we trust can be avoided in the convention which our representative at Santiago is authorized to negotiate.

The cruel treatment of inoffensive Chinese has, I regret to say, been repeated in some of the far Western States and Territories, and acts of violence against those people, beyond the power of the local constituted authorities to prevent and difficult to punish, are reported even in distant Alaska. Much of this violence can be traced to race prejudice and competition of labor, which can not, however, justify the oppression of strangers whose safety is guaranteed by our treaty with China equally with the most favored nations.

In opening our vast domain to alien elements the purpose of our law-givers was to invite assimilation, and not to provide an arena for endless antagonism. The paramount duty of maintaining public order and defending the interests of our own people may require the adoption of measures of restriction, but they should not tolerate the oppression of individuals of a special race. I am not without assurance that the Government of China, whose friendly disposition toward us I am most happy to recognize, will meet us halfway in devising a comprehensive remedy by which an effective limitation of Chinese emigration, joined to protection of those Chinese subjects who remain in this country, may be secured.

Legislation is needed to execute the provisions of our Chinese convention of 1880 touching the opium traffic.

While the good will of the Colombian Government toward our country is manifest, the situation of American interests on the Isthmus of Panama has at times excited concern and invited friendly action looking to the performance of the engagements of the two nations concerning the territory embraced in the interoceanic transit. With the subsidence of the Isthmian disturbances and the erection of the State of Panama into a federal district under the direct government of the constitutional administration at Bogota, a new order of things has been inaugurated, which, although as yet somewhat experimental and affording scope for arbitrary exercise of power by the delegates of the national authority, promises much improvement.

The sympathy between the people of the United States and France, born during our colonial struggle for independence and continuing to-day, has received a fresh impulse in the successful completion and dedication of the colossal statue of "Liberty Enlightening the World" in New York Harbor—the gift of Frenchmen to Americans.

A convention between the United States and certain other powers for the protection of submarine cables was signed at Paris on March 14, 1884, and has been duly ratified and proclaimed by this Government. By agreement between the high contracting parties this convention is to go into effect on the 1st of January next, but the legislation required for its execution in the United States has not yet been adopted. I earnestly recommend its enactment.

Cases have continued to occur in Germany giving rise to much correspondence in relation to the privilege of sojourn of our naturalized citizens of German origin revisiting the land of their birth, yet I am happy to state that our relations with that country have lost none of their accustomed cordiality.

The claims for interest upon the amount of tonnage dues illegally exacted from certain German steamship lines were favorably reported in both Houses of Congress at the last session, and I trust will receive final and favorable action at an early day.

The recommendations contained in my last annual message in relation to a mode of settlement of the fishery rights in the waters of British North America, so long a subject of anxious difference between the United States and Great Britain, was met by an adverse vote of the Senate on April 13 last, and thereupon negotiations were instituted to obtain an agreement with Her Britannic Majesty's Government for the promulgation of such joint interpretation and definition of the article of the convention of 1818 relating to the territorial waters and inshore fisheries of the British Provinces as should secure the Canadian rights from encroachment by the United States fishermen and at the same time insure the enjoyment by the latter of the privileges guaranteed to them by such convention.

The questions involved are of long standing, of grave consequence, and from time to time for nearly three-quarters of a century have given rise to earnest international discussions, not unaccompanied by irritation.

Temporary arrangements by treaties have served to allay friction, which, however, has revived as each treaty was terminated. The last arrangement, under the treaty of 1871, was abrogated after due notice by the United States on June 30, 1885, but I was enabled to obtain for our fishermen for the remainder of that season enjoyment of the full privileges accorded by the terminated treaty.

The joint high commission by whom the treaty had been negotiated, although invested with plenary power to make a permanent settlement, were content with a temporary arrangement, after the termination of which the question was relegated to the stipulations of the treaty of 1818, as to the first article of which no construction satisfactory to both countries has ever been agreed upon.

The progress of civilization and growth of population in the British Provinces to which the fisheries in question are contiguous and the expansion of commercial intercourse between them and the United States present to-day a condition of affairs scarcely realizable at the date of the negotiations of 1818.

New and vast interests have been brought into existence; modes of intercourse between the respective countries have been invented and multiplied; the methods of conducting the fisheries have been wholly changed; and all this is necessarily entitled to candid and careful consideration in the adjustment of the terms and conditions of intercourse and commerce between the United States and their neighbors along a frontier of over 3,500 miles.

This propinquity, community of language and occupation, and similarity of political and social institutions indicate the practicability and obvious wisdom of maintaining mutually beneficial and friendly relations.

Whilst I am unfeignedly desirous that such relations should exist between us and the inhabitants of Canada, yet the action of their officials during the past season toward our fishermen has been such as to seriously threaten their continuance.

Although disappointed in my efforts to secure a satisfactory settlement of the fishery question, negotiations are still pending, with reasonable hope that before the close of the present session of Congress announcement may be made that an acceptable conclusion has been reached.

As at an early day there may be laid before Congress the correspondence of the Department of State in relation to this important subject, so that the history of the past fishing season may be fully disclosed and the action and the attitude of the Administration clearly comprehended, a more extended reference is not deemed necessary in this communication.

The recommendation submitted last year that provision be made for a preliminary reconnoissance of the conventional boundary line between Alaska and British Columbia is renewed.

I express my unhesitating conviction that the intimacy of our relations with Hawaii should be emphasized. As a result of the reciprocity treaty of 1875, those islands, on the highway of Oriental and Australasian traffic, are virtually an outpost of American commerce and a stepping-stone to the growing trade of the Pacific. The Polynesian Island groups have been so absorbed by other and more powerful governments that the Hawaiian Islands are left almost alone in the enjoyment of their autonomy, which it is important for us should be preserved. Our treaty is now terminable on one year's notice, but propositions to abrogate it would be, in my judgment, most ill advised. The paramount influence we have there acquired, once relinquished, could only with difficulty be regained, and a valuable ground of vantage for ourselves might be converted into a stronghold for our commercial competitors. I earnestly recommend that the existing treaty stipulations be extended for a further term of seven years. A recently signed treaty to this end is now before the Senate.

The importance of telegraphic communication between those islands and the United States should not be overlooked.

The question of a general revision of the treaties of Japan is again under discussion at Tokyo. As the first to open relations with that Empire, and as the nation in most direct commercial relations with Japan, the United States have lost no opportunity to testify their consistent friendship by supporting the just claims of Japan to autonomy and independence among nations.

A treaty of extradition between the United States and Japan, the first concluded by that Empire, has been lately proclaimed.

The weakness of Liberia and the difficulty of maintaining effective sovereignty over its outlying districts have exposed that Republic to encroachment. It can not be forgotten that this distant community is an offshoot of our own system, owing its origin to the associated benevolence of American citizens, whose praiseworthy efforts to create a nucleus of civilization in the Dark Continent have commanded respect and sympathy everywhere, especially in this country. Although a formal protectorate over Liberia is contrary to our traditional policy, the moral right and duty of the United States to assist in all proper ways in the maintenance of its integrity is obvious, and has been consistently announced during nearly half a century. I recommend that in the reorganization of our Navy a small vessel, no longer found adequate to our needs, be presented to Liberia, to be employed by it in the protection of its coastwise revenues.

The encouraging development of beneficial and intimate relations between the United States and Mexico, which has been so marked within the past few years, is at once the occasion of congratulation and of friendly solicitude. I urgently renew my former representation of the need of speedy legislation by Congress to carry into effect the reciprocity commercial convention of January 20, 1883.

Our commercial treaty of 1831 with Mexico was terminated, according to its provisions, in 1881, upon notification given by Mexico in pursuance of her announced policy of recasting all her commercial treaties. Mexico has since concluded with several foreign governments new treaties of commerce and navigation, defining alien rights of trade, property, and residence, treatment of shipping, consular privileges, and the like. Our yet unexecuted reciprocity convention of 1883 covers none of these points, the settlement of which is so necessary to good relationship. I propose to initiate with Mexico negotiations for a new and enlarged treaty of commerce and navigation.

In compliance with a resolution of the Senate, I communicated to that body on August 2 last, and also to the House of Representatives, the correspondence in the case of A. K. Cutting, an American citizen, then imprisoned in Mexico, charged with the commission of a penal offense in Texas, of which a Mexican citizen was the object.

After demand had been made for his release the charge against him was amended so as to include a violation of Mexican law within Mexican territory.

This joinder of alleged offenses, one within and the other exterior to Mexico, induced me to order a special investigation of the case, pending which Mr. Cutting was released.

The incident has, however, disclosed a claim of jurisdiction by Mexico novel in our history, whereby any offense committed anywhere by a foreigner, penal in the place of its commission, and of which a Mexican is the object, may, if the offender be found in Mexico, be there tried and punished in conformity with Mexican laws.

This jurisdiction was sustained by the courts of Mexico in the Cutting case, and approved by the executive branch of that Government, upon the authority of a Mexican statute. The appellate court in releasing Mr. Cutting decided that the abandonment of the complaint by the Mexican citizen aggrieved by the alleged crime (a libelous publication) removed the basis of further prosecution, and also declared justice to have been satisfied by the enforcement of a small part of the original sentence.

The admission of such a pretension would be attended with serious results, invasive of the jurisdiction of this Government and highly dangerous to our citizens in foreign lands. Therefore I have denied it and protested against its attempted exercise as unwarranted by the principles of law and international usages.

A sovereign has jurisdiction of offenses which take effect within his territory, although concocted or commenced outside of it; but the right is denied of any foreign sovereign to punish a citizen of the United States for an offense consummated on our soil in violation of our laws, even though the offense be against a subject or citizen of such sovereign. The Mexican statute in question makes the claim broadly, and the principle, if conceded, would create a dual responsibility in the citizen and lead to inextricable confusion, destructive of that certainty in the law which is an essential of liberty.

When citizens of the United States voluntarily go into a foreign country, they must abide by the laws there in force, and will not be protected by their own Government from the consequences of an offense against those laws committed in such foreign country; but watchful care and interest of this Government over its citizens are not relinquished because they have gone abroad, and if charged with crime committed in the foreign land a fair and open trial, conducted with decent regard for justice and humanity, will be demanded for them. With less than that this Government will not be content when the life or liberty of its citizens is at stake.

Whatever the degree to which extraterritorial criminal jurisdiction may have been formerly allowed by consent and reciprocal agreement among certain of the European States, no such doctrine or practice was ever known to the laws of this country or of that from which our institutions have mainly been derived.

In the case of Mexico there are reasons especially strong for perfect harmony in the mutual exercise of jurisdiction. Nature has made us irrevocably neighbors, and wisdom and kind feeling should make us friends.

The overflow of capital and enterprise from the United States is a potent factor in assisting the development of the resources of Mexico and in building up the prosperity of both countries.

To assist this good work all grounds of apprehension for the security of person and property should be removed; and I trust that in the interests of good neighborhood the statute referred to will be so modified as to eliminate the present possibilities of danger to the peace of the two countries.

The Government of the Netherlands has exhibited concern in relation to certain features of our tariff laws, which are supposed by them to be aimed at a class of tobacco produced in the Dutch East Indies. Comment would seem unnecessary upon the unwisdom of legislation appearing to have a special national discrimination for its object, which, although unintentional, may give rise to injurious retaliation.

The establishment, less than four years ago, of a legation at Teheran is bearing fruit in the interest exhibited by the Shah's Government in the industrial activity of the United States and the opportunities of beneficial interchanges.

Stable government is now happily restored in Peru by the election of a constitutional President, and a period of rehabilitation is entered upon; but the recovery is necessarily slow from the exhaustion caused by the late war and civil disturbances. A convention to adjust by arbitration claims of our citizens has been proposed and is under consideration.

The naval officer who bore to Siberia the testimonials bestowed by Congress in recognition of the aid given to the *Jeannette* survivors has successfully accomplished his mission. His interesting report will be submitted. It is pleasant to know that this mark of appreciation has been welcomed by the Russian Government and people as befits the traditional friendship of the two countries.

Civil perturbations in the Samoan Islands have during the past few years been a source of considerable embarrassment to the three Governments—Germany, Great Britain, and the United States—whose relations and extraterritorial rights in that important group are guaranteed by treaties. The weakness of the native administration and the conflict of opposing interests in the islands have led King Malietoa to seek alliance or protection in some one quarter, regardless of the distinct engagements whereby no one of the three treaty powers may acquire any paramount or exclusive interest. In May last Malietoa offered to place Samoa under the protection of the United States, and the late consul, without authority, assumed to grant it. The proceeding was promptly disavowed and the overzealous official recalled. Special agents of the three Governments have been deputed to examine the situation in the islands. With a change in the representation of all three powers and a harmonious understanding between them, the peace, prosperity, autonomous administration, and neutrality of Samoa can hardly fail to be secured.

It appearing that the Government of Spain did not extend to the flag of the United States in the Antilles the full measure of reciprocity requisite under our statute for the continuance of the suspension of discriminations against the Spanish flag in our ports, I was constrained in October last* to rescind my predecessor's proclamation of February 14, 1884,† permitting such suspension. An arrangement was, however, speedily reached, and upon notification from the Government of Spain that all differential treatment of our vessels and their cargoes, from the United States or from any foreign country, had been completely and absolutely relinquished, I availed myself of the discretion conferred by

law and issued on the 27th of October my proclamation‡ declaring reciprocal suspension in the United States. It is most gratifying to bear
testimony to the earnest spirit in which the Government of the Queen
Regent has met our efforts to avert the initiation of commercial discriminations and reprisals, which are ever disastrous to the material interests
and the political good will of the countries they may affect.

The profitable development of the large commercial exchanges between the United States and the Spanish Antilles is naturally an object
of solicitude. Lying close at our doors, and finding here their main
markets of supply and demand, the welfare of Cuba and Puerto Rico and
their production and trade are scarcely less important to us than to
Spain. Their commercial and financial movements are so naturally a
part of our system that no obstacle to fuller and freer intercourse should
be permitted to exist. The standing instructions of our representatives
at Madrid and Havana have for years been to leave no effort unessayed
to further these ends, and at no time has the equal good desire of Spain
been more hopefully manifested than now.

The Government of Spain, by removing the consular tonnage fees on
cargoes shipped to the Antilles and by reducing passport fees, has shown
its recognition of the needs of less trammeled intercourse.

An effort has been made during the past year to remove the hindrances
to the proclamation of the treaty of naturalization with the Sublime Porte,
signed in 1874, which has remained inoperative owing to a disagreement
of interpretation of the clauses relative to the effects of the return to and
sojourn of a naturalized citizen in the land of origin. I trust soon to
be able to announce a favorable settlement of the differences as to this
interpretation.

It has been highly satisfactory to note the improved treatment of
American missionaries in Turkey, as has been attested by their acknowledgments to our late minister to that Government of his successful exertions in their behalf.

The exchange of ratifications of the convention of December 5, 1885,
with Venezuela, for the reopening of the awards of the Caracas Commission under the claims convention of 1866, has not yet been effected, owing
to the delay of the Executive of that Republic in ratifying the measure.
I trust that this postponement will be brief; but should it much longer
continue, the delay may well be regarded as a rescission of the compact
and a failure on the part of Venezuela to complete an arrangement so
persistently sought by her during many years and assented to by this
Government in a spirit of international fairness, although to the detriment of holders of *bona fide* awards of the impugned commission.

I renew the recommendation of my last annual message that existing
legislation concerning citizenship and naturalization be revised. We
have treaties with many states providing for the renunciation of citizenship by naturalized aliens, but no statute is found to give effect to such

engagements, nor any which provides a needed central bureau for the registration of naturalized citizens.

Experience suggests that our statutes regulating extradition might be advantageously amended by a provision for the transit across our territory, now a convenient thoroughfare of travel from one foreign country to another, of fugitives surrendered by a foreign government to a third state. Such provisions are not unusual in the legislation of other countries, and tend to prevent the miscarriage of justice. It is also desirable, in order to remove present uncertainties, that authority should be conferred on the Secretary of State to issue a certificate, in case of an arrest for the purpose of extradition, to the officer before whom the proceeding is pending, showing that a requisition for the surrender of the person charged has been duly made. Such a certificate, if required to be received before the prisoner's examination, would prevent a long and expensive judicial inquiry into a charge which the foreign government might not desire to press. I also recommend that express provision be made for the immediate discharge from custody of persons committed for extradition where the President is of opinion that surrender should not be made.

The drift of sentiment in civilized communities toward full recognition of the rights of property in the creations of the human intellect has brought about the adoption by many important nations of an international copyright convention, which was signed at Berne on the 18th of September, 1885.

Inasmuch as the Constitution gives to the Congress the power "to promote the progress of science and useful arts by securing for limited times to authors and inventors the exclusive right to their respective writings and discoveries," this Government did not feel warranted in becoming a signatory pending the action of Congress upon measures of international copyright now before it; but the right of adhesion to the Berne convention hereafter has been reserved. I trust the subject will receive at your hands the attention it deserves, and that the just claims of authors, so urgently pressed, will be duly heeded.

Representations continue to be made to me of the injurious effect upon American artists studying abroad and having free access to the art collections of foreign countries of maintaining a discriminating duty against the introduction of the works of their brother artists of other countries, and I am induced to repeat my recommendation for the abolition of that tax.

Pursuant to a provision of the diplomatic and consular appropriation act approved July 1, 1886, the estimates submitted by the Secretary of State for the maintenance of the consular service have been recast on the basis of salaries for all officers to whom such allowance is deemed advisable. Advantage has been taken of this to redistribute the salaries of the offices now appropriated for, in accordance with the work performed, the importance of the representative duties of the incumbent, and the cost of living at each post. The last consideration has been too often lost sight of in the allowances heretofore made. The compensation which may suffice for the decent maintenance of a worthy and capable officer in a position of onerous and representative trust at a post readily accessible, and where the necessaries of life are abundant and cheap, may prove an inadequate pittance in distant lands, where the better part of a year's pay is consumed in reaching the post of duty, and where the comforts of ordinary civilized existence can only be obtained with difficulty and at exorbitant cost. I trust that in considering the submitted schedules no mistaken theory of economy will perpetuate a system which in the past has virtually closed to deserving talent many offices where capacity and attainments of a high order are indispensable, and in not a few instances has brought discredit on our national character and entailed embarrassment and even suffering on those deputed to uphold our dignity and interests abroad.

In connection with this subject I earnestly reiterate the practical necessity of supplying some mode of trustworthy inspection and report of the manner in which the consulates are conducted. In the absence of such reliable information efficiency can scarcely be rewarded or its opposite corrected.

Increasing competition in trade has directed attention to the value of the consular reports printed by the Department of State, and the efforts of the Government to extend the practical usefulness of these reports have created a wider demand for them at home and a spirit of emulation abroad. Constituting a record of the changes occurring in trade and of the progress of the arts and invention in foreign countries, they are much sought for by all interested in the subjects which they embrace.

The report of the Secretary of the Treasury exhibits in detail the condition of the public finances and of the several branches of the Government related to his Department. I especially direct the attention of the Congress to the recommendations contained in this and the last preceding report of the Secretary touching the simplification and amendment of the laws relating to the collection of our revenues, and in the interest of economy and justice to the Government I hope they may be adopted by appropriate legislation.

The ordinary receipts of the Government for the fiscal year ended June 30, 1886, were $336,439,727.06. Of this amount $192,905,023.41 was received from customs and $116,805,936.48 from internal revenue. The total receipts, as here stated, were $13,749,020.68 greater than for the previous year, but the increase from customs was $11,434,084.10 and from internal revenue $4,407,210.94, making a gain in these items for the last year of $15,841,295.04, a falling off in other resources reducing the total increase to the smaller amount mentioned.

The expense at the different custom-houses of collecting this increased customs revenue was less than the expense attending the collection of such revenue for the preceding year by $490,608, and the increased receipts of internal revenue were collected at a cost to the Internal-Revenue Bureau $155,944.99 less than the expense of such collection for the previous year.

The total ordinary expenses of the Government for the fiscal year ended June 30, 1886, were $242,483,138.50, being less by $17,788,797 than such expenditures for the year preceding, and leaving a surplus in the Treasury at the close of the last fiscal year of $93,956,588.56, as against $63,463,771.27 at the close of the previous year, being an increase in such surplus of $30,492,817.29.

The expenditures are compared with those of the preceding fiscal year and classified as follows:

	Year ending June 30, 1886.	Year ending June 30, 1885.
For civil expenses..	$21,955,604.04	$23,826,942.11
For foreign intercourse...............................	1,332,320.88	5,439,609.11
For Indians	6,099,158.17	6,552,494.63
For pensions	63,404,864.03	56,102,267.49
For the military, including river and harbor improvements and arsenals...................................	34,324,152.74	42,670,578.47
For the Navy, including vessels, machinery, and improvement of navy-yards............................	13,907,887.74	16,021,079.69
For interest on public debt	50,580,145.97	51,386,256.47
For the District of Columbia............................	2,892,321.89	3,499,650.95
Miscellaneous expenditures, including public buildings, light-houses, and collecting the revenue........	47,986,683.04	54,728,056.21

For the current year to end June 30, 1887, the ascertained receipts up to October 1, 1886, with such receipts estimated for the remainder of the year, amount to $356,000,000.

The expenditures ascertained and estimated for the same period are $266,000,000, indicating an anticipated surplus at the close of the year of $90,000,000.

The total value of the exports from the United States to foreign countries during the fiscal year is stated and compared with the preceding year as follows:

	For the year ending June 30, 1886.	For the year ending June 30, 1885.
Domestic merchandise	$665,964,529	$726,682,946
Foreign merchandise......................................	13,560,301	15,506,809
Gold	42,952,191	8,477,892
Silver...	29,511,219	33,753,633

The value of some of our leading exports during the last fiscal year, as compared with the value of the same for the year immediately preceding, is here given, and furnishes information both interesting and suggestive:

	For the year ending June 30, 1886.	For the year ending June 30, 1885.
Cotton and cotton manufactures	$219,045,576	$213,799,049
Tobacco and its manufactures	30,424,908	24,767,305
Breadstuffs	125,846,558	160,370,821
Provisions	90,625,216	107,332,456

Our imports during the last fiscal year, as compared with the previous year, were as follows:

	1886.	1885.
Merchandise	$635,436,136.00	$579,580,053.80
Gold	20,743,349.00	26,691,696.00
Silver	17,850,307.00	16,550,627.00

In my last annual message to the Congress attention was directed to the fact that the revenues of the Government exceeded its actual needs, and it was suggested that legislative action should be taken to relieve the people from the unnecessary burden of taxation thus made apparent.

In view of the pressing importance of the subject I deem it my duty to again urge its consideration.

The income of the Government, by its increased volume and through economies in its collection, is now more than ever in excess of public necessities. The application of the surplus to the payment of such portion of the public debt as is now at our option subject to extinguishment, if continued at the rate which has lately prevailed, would retire that class of indebtedness within less than one year from this date. Thus a continuation of our present revenue system would soon result in the receipt of an annual income much greater than necessary to meet Government expenses, with no indebtedness upon which it could be applied. We should then be confronted with a vast quantity of money, the circulating medium of the people, hoarded in the Treasury when it should be in their hands, or we should be drawn into wasteful public extravagance, with all the corrupting national demoralization which follows in its train.

But it is not the simple existence of this surplus and its threatened attendant evils which furnish the strongest argument against our present scale of Federal taxation. Its worst phase is the exaction of such a surplus through a perversion of the relations between the people and their Government and a dangerous departure from the rules which limit the right of Federal taxation.

Good government, and especially the government of which every American citizen boasts, has for its objects the protection of every person within its care in the greatest liberty consistent with the good order of society and his perfect security in the enjoyment of his earnings with the least possible diminution for public needs. When more of the people's substance is exacted through the form of taxation than is necessary to meet the just obligations of the Government and the expense of its economical administration, such exaction becomes ruthless extortion and a violation of the fundamental principles of a free government.

The indirect manner in which these exactions are made has a tendency to conceal their true character and their extent. But we have arrived at a stage of superfluous revenue which has aroused the people to a realization of the fact that the amount raised professedly for the support of the Government is paid by them as absolutely if added to the price of the things which supply their daily wants as if it was paid at fixed periods into the hand of the taxgatherer.

Those who toil for daily wages are beginning to understand that capital, though sometimes vaunting its importance and clamoring for the protection and favor of the Government, is dull and sluggish till, touched by the magical hand of labor, it springs into activity, furnishing an occasion for Federal taxation and gaining the value which enables it to bear its burden. And the laboring man is thoughtfully inquiring whether in these circumstances, and considering the tribute he constantly pays into the public Treasury as he supplies his daily wants, he receives his fair share of advantages.

There is also a suspicion abroad that the surplus of our revenues indicates abnormal and exceptional business profits, which, under the system which produces such surplus, increase without corresponding benefit to the people at large the vast accumulations of a few among our citizens, whose fortunes, rivaling the wealth of the most favored in antidemocratic nations, are not the natural growth of a steady, plain, and industrious republic.

Our farmers, too, and those engaged directly and indirectly in supplying the products of agriculture, see that day by day, and as often as the daily wants of their households recur, they are forced to pay excessive and needless taxation, while their products struggle in foreign markets with the competition of nations, which, by allowing a freer exchange of productions than we permit, enable their people to sell for prices which distress the American farmer.

As every patriotic citizen rejoices in the constantly increasing pride of our people in American citizenship and in the glory of our national achievements and progress, a sentiment prevails that the leading strings useful to a nation in its infancy may well be to a great extent discarded in the present stage of American ingenuity, courage, and fearless self-reliance; and for the privilege of indulging this sentiment with true American enthusiasm our citizens are quite willing to forego an idle surplus in the public Treasury.

And all the people know that the average rate of Federal taxation upon imports is to-day, in time of peace, but little less, while upon some articles of necessary consumption it is actually more, than was imposed by the grievous burden willingly borne at a time when the Government needed millions to maintain by war the safety and integrity of the Union.

It has been the policy of the Government to collect the principal part of its revenues by a tax upon imports, and no change in this policy is desirable. But the present condition of affairs constrains our people to demand that by a revision of our revenue laws the receipts of the Government shall be reduced to the necessary expense of its economical administration; and this demand should be recognized and obeyed by the people's representatives in the legislative branch of the Government.

In readjusting the burdens of Federal taxation a sound public policy requires that such of our citizens as have built up large and important industries under present conditions should not be suddenly and to their injury deprived of advantages to which they have adapted their business; but if the public good requires it they should be content with such consideration as shall deal fairly and cautiously with their interests, while the just demand of the people for relief from needless taxation is honestly answered.

A reasonable and timely submission to such a demand should certainly be possible without disastrous shock to any interest; and a cheerful concession sometimes averts abrupt and heedless action, often the outgrowth of impatience and delayed justice.

Due regard should be also accorded in any proposed readjustment to the interests of American labor so far as they are involved. We congratulate ourselves that there is among us no laboring class fixed within unyielding bounds and doomed under all conditions to the inexorable fate of daily toil. We recognize in labor a chief factor in the wealth of the Republic, and we treat those who have it in their keeping as citizens entitled to the most careful regard and thoughtful attention. This regard and attention should be awarded them, not only because labor is the capital of our workingmen, justly entitled to its share of Government favor, but for the further and not less important reason that the laboring man, surrounded by his family in his humble home, as a consumer is vitally interested in all that cheapens the cost of living and enables him to bring within his domestic circle additional comforts and advantages.

This relation of the workingman to the revenue laws of the country and the manner in which it palpably influences the question of wages should not be forgotten in the justifiable prominence given to the proper maintenance of the supply and protection of well-paid labor. And these considerations suggest such an arrangement of Government revenues as shall reduce the expense of living, while it does not curtail the opportunity for work nor reduce the compensation of American labor and injuriously affect its condition and the dignified place it holds in the estimation of our people.

But our farmers and agriculturists—those who from the soil produce the things consumed by all—are perhaps more directly and plainly concerned than any other of our citizens in a just and careful system of Federal taxation. Those actually engaged in and more remotely connected with this kind of work number nearly one-half of our population. None labor harder or more continuously than they. No enactments limit their hours of toil and no interposition of the Government enhances to any great extent the value of their products. And yet for many of the necessaries and comforts of life, which the most scrupulous economy enables them to bring into their homes, and for their implements of husbandry, they are obliged to pay a price largely increased by an unnatural profit, which by the action of the Government is given to the more favored manufacturer.

I recommend that, keeping in view all these considerations, the increasing and unnecessary surplus of national income annually accumulating be released to the people by an amendment to our revenue laws which shall cheapen the price of the necessaries of life and give freer entrance to such imported materials as by American labor may be manufactured into marketable commodities.

Nothing can be accomplished, however, in the direction of this much-needed reform unless the subject is approached in a patriotic spirit of devotion to the interests of the entire country and with a willingness to yield something for the public good.

The sum paid upon the public debt during the fiscal year ended June 30, 1886, was $44,551,043.36.

During the twelve months ended October 31, 1886, 3 per cent bonds were called for redemption amounting to $127,283,100, of which $80,643,200 was so called to answer the requirements of the law relating to the sinking fund and $46,639,900 for the purpose of reducing the public debt by application of a part of the surplus in the Treasury to that object. Of the bonds thus called $102,269,450 became subject under such calls to redemption prior to November 1, 1886. The remainder, amounting to $25,013,650, matured under the calls after that date.

In addition to the amount subject to payment and cancellation prior to November 1, there were also paid before that day certain of these bonds, with the interest thereon, amounting to $5,072,350, which were anticipated as to their maturity, of which $2,664,850 had not been called. Thus $107,341,800 had been actually applied prior to the 1st of November, 1886, to the extinguishment of our bonded and interest-bearing debt, leaving on that day still outstanding the sum of $1,153,443,112. Of this amount $86,848,700 were still represented by 3 per cent bonds. They, however, have been since November 1, or will at once be, further reduced by $22,606,150, being bonds which have been called, as already stated, but not redeemed and canceled before the latter date.

During the fiscal year ended June 30, 1886, there were coined, under the compulsory silver-coinage act of 1878, 29,838,905 silver dollars, and the cost of the silver used in such coinage was $23,448,960.01. There had been coined up to the close of the previous fiscal year under the provisions of the law 203,882,554 silver dollars, and on the 1st day of December, 1886, the total amount of such coinage was $247,131,549.

The Director of the Mint reports that at the time of the passage of the law of 1878 directing this coinage the intrinsic value of the dollars thus coined was 94¼ cents each, and that on the 31st day of July, 1886, the price of silver reached the lowest stage ever known, so that the intrinsic or bullion price of our standard silver dollar at that date was less than 72 cents. The price of silver on the 30th day of November last was such as to make these dollars intrinsically worth 78 cents each.

These differences in value of the coins represent the fluctuations in the price of silver, and they certainly do not indicate that compulsory coinage by the Government enhances the price of that commodity or secures uniformity in its value.

Every fair and legal effort has been made by the Treasury Department to distribute this currency among the people. The withdrawal of United States Treasury notes of small denominations and the issuing of small silver certificates have been resorted to in the endeavor to accomplish this result, in obedience to the will and sentiments of the representatives of the people in the Congress. On the 27th day of November, 1886, the people held of these coins, or certificates representing them, the nominal sum of $166,873,041, and we still had $79,464,345 in the Treasury, as against about $142,894,055 so in the hands of the people and $72,865,376 remaining in the Treasury one year ago. The Director of the Mint again urges the necessity of more vault room for the purpose of storing these silver dollars which are not needed for circulation by the people.

I have seen no reason to change the views expressed in my last annual message on the subject of this compulsory coinage, and I again urge its suspension on all the grounds contained in my former recommendation, reenforced by the significant increase of our gold exportations during the last year, as appears by the comparative statement herewith presented, and for the further reasons that the more this currency is distributed among the people the greater becomes our duty to protect it from disaster, that we now have abundance for all our needs, and that there seems but little propriety in building vaults to store such currency when the only pretense for its coinage is the necessity of its use by the people as a circulating medium.

The great number of suits now pending in the United States courts for the southern district of New York growing out of the collection of customs revenue at the port of New York and the number of such suits that are almost daily instituted are certainly worthy the attention of the Congress. These legal controversies, based upon conflicting views by importers and the collector as to the interpretation of our present complex and indefinite revenue laws, might be largely obviated by an amendment of those laws.

But pending such amendment the present condition of this litigation should be relieved. There are now pending about 2,500 of these suits. More than 1,100 have been commenced within the past eighteen months, and many of the others have been at issue for more than twenty-five years. These delays subject the Government to loss of evidence and prevent the preparation necessary to defeat unjust and fictitious claims, while constantly accruing interest threatens to double the demands involved.

In the present condition of the dockets of the courts, well filled with private suits, and of the force allowed the district attorney, no greater than is necessary for the ordinary and current business of his office, these revenue litigations can not be considered.

In default of the adoption by the Congress of a plan for the general reorganization of the Federal courts, as has been heretofore recommended, I urge the propriety of passing a law permitting the appointment of an additional Federal judge in the district where these Government suits have accumulated, so that by continuous sessions of the courts devoted to the trial of these cases they may be determined.

It is entirely plain that a great saving to the Government would be accomplished by such a remedy, and the suitors who have honest claims would not be denied justice through delay.

The report of the Secretary of War gives a detailed account of the administration of his Department and contains sundry recommendations for the improvement of the service, which I fully approve.

The Army consisted at the date of the last consolidated return of 2,103 officers and 24,946 enlisted men.

The expenses of the Department for the last fiscal year were $36,990,-903.38, including $6,294,305.43 for public works and river and harbor improvements.

I especially direct the attention of the Congress to the recommendation that officers be required to submit to an examination as a preliminary to their promotion. I see no objection, but many advantages, in adopting this feature, which has operated so beneficially in our Navy Department, as well as in some branches of the Army.

The subject of coast defenses and fortifications has been fully and carefully treated by the Board on Fortifications, whose report was submitted at the last session of Congress; but no construction work of the kind recommended by the board has been possible during the last year from the lack of appropriations for such purpose.

The defenseless condition of our seacoast and lake frontier is perfectly palpable. The examinations made must convince us all that certain of our cities named in the report of the board should be fortified and that work on the most important of these fortifications should be commenced at once. The work has been thoroughly considered and laid out, the Secretary of War reports, but all is delayed in default of Congressional action.

The absolute necessity, judged by all standards of prudence and foresight, of our preparation for an effectual resistance against the armored ships and steel guns and mortars of modern construction which may threaten the cities on our coasts is so apparent that I hope effective steps will be taken in that direction immediately.

The valuable and suggestive treatment of this question by the Secretary of War is earnestly commended to the consideration of the Congress.

In September and October last the hostile Apaches who, under the leadership of Geronimo, had for eighteen months been on the war path, and during that time had committed many murders and been the cause of constant terror to the settlers of Arizona, surrendered to General Miles, the military commander who succeeded General Crook in the management and direction of their pursuit.

Under the terms of their surrender as then reported, and in view of the understanding which these murderous savages seemed to entertain of the assurances given them, it was considered best to imprison them in such manner as to prevent their ever engaging in such outrages again, instead of trying them for murder. Fort Pickens having been selected as a safe place of confinement, all the adult males were sent thither and will be closely guarded as prisoners. In the meantime the residue of the band, who, though still remaining upon the reservation, were regarded as unsafe and suspected of furnishing aid to those on the war path, had been removed to Fort Marion. The women and larger children of the hostiles were also taken there, and arrangements have been made for putting the children of proper age in Indian schools.

The report of the Secretary of the Navy contains a detailed exhibit of the condition of his Department, with such a statement of the action needed to improve the same as should challenge the earnest attention of the Congress.

The present Navy of the United States, aside from the ships in course of construction, consists of—

First. Fourteen single-turreted monitors, none of which are in commission nor at the present time serviceable. The batteries of these ships are obsolete, and they can only be relied upon as auxiliary ships in harbor defense, and then after such an expenditure upon them as might not be deemed justifiable.

Second. Five fourth-rate vessels of small tonnage, only one of which was designed as a war vessel, and all of which are auxiliary merely.

Third. Twenty-seven cruising ships, three of which are built of iron, of small tonnage, and twenty-four of wood. Of these wooden vessels it is estimated by the Chief Constructor of the Navy that only three will be serviceable beyond a period of six years, at which time it may be said that of the present naval force nothing worthy the name will remain.

All the vessels heretofore authorized are under contract or in course of construction except the armored ships, the torpedo and dynamite boats, and one cruiser. As to the last of these, the bids were in excess of the limit fixed by Congress. The production in the United States of armor and gun steel is a question which it seems necessary to settle at an early day if the armored war vessels are to be completed with those materials of home manufacture. This has been the subject of investigation by two boards and by two special committees of Congress within the last three years. The report of the Gun Foundry Board in 1884, of the Board on Fortifications made in January last, and the reports of the select committees of the two Houses made at the last session of Congress have entirely exhausted the subject, so far as preliminary investigation is involved, and in their recommendations they are substantially agreed.

In the event that the present invitation of the Department for bids to furnish such of this material as is now authorized shall fail to induce domestic manufacturers to undertake the large expenditures required to prepare for this new manufacture, and no other steps are taken by Congress at its coming session, the Secretary contemplates with dissatisfaction the necessity of obtaining abroad the armor and the gun steel for the authorized ships. It would seem desirable that the wants of the Army and the Navy in this regard should be reasonably met, and that by uniting their contracts such inducement might be offered as would result in securing the domestication of these important interests.

The affairs of the postal service show marked and gratifying improvement during the past year. A particular account of its transactions and condition is given in the report of the Postmaster-General, which will be laid before you.

The reduction of the rate of letter postage in 1883, rendering the postal revenues inadequate to sustain the expenditures, and business depression also contributing, resulted in an excess of cost for the fiscal year ended June 30, 1885, of eight and one-third millions of dollars. An additional check upon receipts by doubling the measure of weight in rating sealed correspondence and diminishing one-half the charge for newspaper carriage was imposed by legislation which took effect with the beginning of the past fiscal year, while the constant demand of our territorial development and growing population for the extension and increase of mail facilities and machinery necessitates steady annual advance in outlay, and the careful estimate of a year ago upon the rates of expenditure then existing contemplated the unavoidable augmentation of the deficiency in the last fiscal year by nearly $2,000,000. The anticipated revenue for the last year failed of realization by about $64,000, but proper measures of economy have so satisfactorily limited the growth of expenditure that the total deficiency in fact fell below that of 1885, and at this time the increase of revenue is in a gaining ratio over the increase of

cost, demonstrating the sufficiency of the present rates of postage ultimately to sustain the service.   This is the more pleasing because our
people enjoy now both cheaper postage proportionably to distances and
a vaster and more costly service than any other upon the globe.

Retrenchment has been effected in the cost of supplies, some expenditures unwarranted by law have ceased, and the outlays for mail carriage
have been subjected to beneficial scrutiny.   At the close of the last fiscal
year the expense of transportation on star routes stood at an annual rate
of cost less by over $560,000 than at the close of the previous year and
steamboat and mail-messenger service at nearly $200,000 less.

The service has been in the meantime enlarged and extended by the
establishment of new offices, increase of routes of carriage, expansion of
carrier-delivery conveniences, and additions to the railway mail facilities,
in accordance with the growing exigencies of the country and the long-
established policy of the Government.

The Postmaster-General calls attention to the existing law for compensating railroads and expresses the opinion that a method may be devised
which will prove more just to the carriers and beneficial to the Government; and the subject appears worthy of your early consideration.

The differences which arose during the year with certain of the ocean
steamship companies have terminated by the acquiescence of all in the
policy of the Government approved by the Congress in the postal appropriation at its last session, and the Department now enjoys the utmost
service afforded by all vessels which sail from our ports upon either
ocean—a service generally adequate to the needs of our intercourse.
Petitions have, however, been presented to the Department by numerous
merchants and manufacturers for the establishment of a direct service to
the Argentine Republic and for semimonthly dispatches to the Empire
of Brazil, and the subject is commended to your consideration.   It is an
obvious duty to provide the means of postal communication which our
commerce requires, and with prudent forecast of results the wise extension of it may lead to stimulating intercourse and become the harbinger
of a profitable traffic which will open new avenues for the disposition of
the products of our industry.   The circumstances of the countries at the
far south of our continent are such as to invite our enterprise and afford
the promise of sufficient advantages to justify an unusual effort to bring
about the closer relations which greater freedom of communication would
tend to establish.

I suggest that, as distinguished from a grant or subsidy for the mere
benefit of any line of trade or travel, whatever outlay may be required to
secure additional postal service, necessary and proper and not otherwise
attainable, should be regarded as within the limit of legitimate compensation for such service.

The extension of the free-delivery service as suggested by the Postmaster-General has heretofore received my sanction, and it is to be hoped

a suitable enactment may soon be agreed upon.

The request for an appropriation sufficient to enable the general inspection of fourth-class offices has my approbation.

I renew my approval of the recommendation of the Postmaster-General that another assistant be provided for the Post-Office Department, and I invite your attention to the several other recommendations in his report.

The conduct of the Department of Justice for the last fiscal year is fully detailed in the report of the Attorney-General, and I invite the earnest attention of the Congress to the same and due consideration of the recommendations therein contained.

In the report submitted by this officer to the last session of the Congress he strongly recommended the erection of a penitentiary for the confinement of prisoners convicted and sentenced in the United States courts, and he repeats the recommendation in his report for the last year.

This is a matter of very great importance and should at once receive Congressional action. United States prisoners are now confined in more than thirty different State prisons and penitentiaries scattered in every part of the country. They are subjected to nearly as many different modes of treatment and discipline and are far too much removed from the control and regulation of the Government. So far as they are entitled to humane treatment and an opportunity for improvement and reformation, the Government is responsible to them and society that these things are forthcoming. But this duty can scarcely be discharged without more absolute control and direction than is possible under the present system.

Many of our good citizens have interested themselves, with the most beneficial results, in the question of prison reform. The General Government should be in a situation, since there must be United States prisoners, to furnish important aid in this movement, and should be able to illustrate what may be practically done in the direction of this reform and to present an example in the treatment and improvement of its prisoners worthy of imitation.

With prisons under its own control the Government could deal with the somewhat vexed question of convict labor, so far as its convicts were concerned, according to a plan of its own adoption, and with due regard to the rights and interests of our laboring citizens, instead of sometimes aiding in the operation of a system which causes among them irritation and discontent.

Upon consideration of this subject it might be thought wise to erect more than one of these institutions, located in such places as would best subserve the purposes of convenience and economy in transportation. The considerable cost of maintaining these convicts as at present, in State institutions, would be saved by the adoption of the plan proposed, and by employing them in the manufacture of such articles as were needed for use by the Government quite a large pecuniary benefit would be realized in partial return for our outlay.

I again urge a change in the Federal judicial system to meet the wants of the people and obviate the delays necessarily attending the present condition of affairs in our courts. All are agreed that something should be done, and much favor is shown by those well able to advise to the plan suggested by the Attorney-General at the last session of the Congress and recommended in my last annual message. This recommendation is here renewed, together with another made at the same time, touching a change in the manner of compensating district attorneys and marshals; and the latter subject is commended to the Congress for its action in the interest of economy to the Government, and humanity, fairness, and justice to our people.

The report of the Secretary of the Interior presents a comprehensive summary of the work of the various branches of the public service connected with his Department, and the suggestions and recommendations which it contains for the improvement of the service should receive your careful consideration.

The exhibit made of the condition of our Indian population and the progress of the work for their enlightenment, notwithstanding the many embarrassments which hinder the better administration of this important branch of the service, is a gratifying and hopeful one.

The funds appropriated for the Indian service for the fiscal year just passed, with the available income from Indian land and trust moneys, amounting in all to $7,850,775.12, were ample for the service under the conditions and restrictions of laws regulating their expenditure. There remained a balance on hand on June 30, 1886, of $1,660,023.30, of which $1,337,768.21 are permanent funds for fulfillment of treaties and other like purposes, and the remainder, $322,255.09, is subject to be carried to the surplus fund as required by law.

The estimates presented for appropriations for the ensuing fiscal year amount to $5,608,873.64, or $442,386.20 less than those laid before the Congress last year.

The present system of agencies, while absolutely necessary and well adapted for the management of our Indian affairs and for the ends in view when it was adopted, is in the present stage of Indian management inadequate, standing alone, for the accomplishment of an object which has become pressing in its importance—the more rapid transition from tribal organizations to citizenship of such portions of the Indians as are capable of civilized life.

When the existing system was adopted, the Indian race was outside of the limits of organized States and Territories and beyond the immediate reach and operation of civilization, and all efforts were mainly directed to the maintenance of friendly relations and the preservation of peace and quiet on the frontier. All this is now changed. There is no such thing as the Indian frontier. Civilization, with the busy hum of industry and the influences of Christianity, surrounds these people at every point. None of the tribes are outside of the bounds of organized government and society, except that the Territorial system has not been extended over that portion of the country known as the Indian Territory. As a race the Indians are no longer hostile, but may be considered as submissive to the control of the Government. Few of them only are troublesome. Except the fragments of several bands, all are now gathered upon reservations.

It is no longer possible for them to subsist by the chase and the spontaneous productions of the earth.

With an abundance of land, if furnished with the means and implements for profitable husbandry, their life of entire dependence upon Government rations from day to day is no longer defensible. Their inclination, long fostered by a defective system of control, is to cling to the habits and customs of their ancestors and struggle with persistence against the change of life which their altered circumstances press upon them. But barbarism and civilization can not live together. It is impossible that such incongruous conditions should coexist on the same soil.

They are a portion of our people, are under the authority of our Government, and have a peculiar claim upon and are entitled to the fostering care and protection of the nation. The Government can not relieve itself of this responsibility until they are so far trained and civilized as to be able wholly to manage and care for themselves. The paths in which they should walk must be clearly marked out for them, and they must be led or guided until they are familiar with the way and competent to assume the duties and responsibilities of our citizenship.

Progress in this great work will continue only at the present slow pace and at great expense unless the system and methods of management are improved to meet the changed conditions and urgent demands of the service.

The agents, having general charge and supervision in many cases of more than 5,000 Indians, scattered over large reservations, and burdened with the details of accountability for funds and supplies, have time to look after the industrial training and improvement of a few Indians only. The many are neglected and remain idle and dependent, conditions not favorable for progress and civilization.

The compensation allowed these agents and the conditions of the service are not calculated to secure for the work men who are fitted by ability and skill to properly plan and intelligently direct the methods best adapted to produce the most speedy results and permanent benefits.

Hence the necessity for a supplemental agency or system directed to the end of promoting the general and more rapid transition of the tribes from habits and customs of barbarism to the ways of civilization.

With an anxious desire to devise some plan of operation by which to secure the welfare of the Indians and to relieve the Treasury as far as possible from the support of an idle and dependent population, I recommended in my previous annual message the passage of a law authorizing the appointment of a commission as an instrumentality auxiliary to those already established for the care of the Indians. It was designed that this commission should be composed of six intelligent and capable persons—three to be detailed from the Army—having practical ideas upon the subject of the treatment of Indians and interested in their welfare, and that it should be charged, under the direction of the Secretary of the Interior, with the management of such matters of detail as can not with the present organization be properly and successfully conducted, and which present different phases, as the Indians themselves differ in their progress, needs, disposition, and capacity for improvement or immediate self-support.

By the aid of such a commission much unwise and useless expenditure of money, waste of materials, and unavailing efforts might be avoided; and it is hoped that this or some measure which the wisdom of Congress may better devise to supply the deficiency of the present system may receive your consideration and the appropriate legislation be provided.

The time is ripe for the work of such an agency.

There is less opposition to the education and training of the Indian youth, as shown by the increased attendance upon the schools, and there is a yielding tendency for the individual holding of lands. Development and advancement in these directions are essential, and should have every encouragement. As the rising generation are taught the language of civilization and trained in habits of industry they should assume the duties, privileges, and responsibilities of citizenship.

No obstacle should hinder the location and settlement of any Indian willing to take land in severalty; on the contrary, the inclination to do so should be stimulated at all times when proper and expedient. But there is no authority of law for making allotments on some of the reservations, and on others the allotments provided for are so small that the Indians, though ready and desiring to settle down, are not willing to accept such small areas when their reservations contain ample lands to afford them homesteads of sufficient size to meet their present and future needs.

These inequalities of existing special laws and treaties should be corrected and some general legislation on the subject should be provided, so that the more progressive members of the different tribes may be settled upon homesteads, and by their example lead others to follow, breaking away from tribal customs and substituting therefor the love of home, the interest of the family, and the rule of the state.

The Indian character and nature are such that they are not easily led while brooding over unadjusted wrongs. This is especially so regarding their lands. Matters arising from the construction and operation of railroads across some of the reservations, and claims of title and right of occupancy set up by white persons to some of the best land within other reservations require legislation for their final adjustment.

The settlement of these matters will remove many embarrassments to progress in the work of leading the Indians to the adoption of our institutions and bringing them under the operation, the influence, and the protection of the universal laws of our country.

The recommendations of the Secretary of the Interior and the Commissioner of the General Land Office looking to the better protection of public lands and of the public surveys, the preservation of national forests, the adjudication of grants to States and corporations and of private land claims, and the increased efficiency of the public-land service are commended to the attention of Congress. To secure the widest distribution of public lands in limited quantities among settlers for residence and cultivation, and thus make the greatest number of individual homes, was the primary object of the public-land legislation in the early days of the Republic. This system was a simple one. It commenced with an admirable scheme of public surveys, by which the humblest citizen could identify the tract upon which he wished to establish his home. The price of lands was placed within the reach of all the enterprising, industrious, and honest pioneer citizens of the country. It was soon, however, found that the object of the laws was perverted, under the system of cash sales, from a distribution of land among the people to an accumulation of land capital by wealthy and speculative persons. To check this tendency a preference right of purchase was given to settlers on the land, a plan which culminated in the general preemption act of 1841. The foundation of this system was actual residence and cultivation. Twenty years later the homestead law was devised to more surely place actual homes in the possession of actual cultivators of the soil. The land was given without price, the sole conditions being residence, improvement, and cultivation. Other laws have followed, each designed to encourage the acquirement and use of land in limited individual quantities. But in later years these laws, through vicious administrative methods and under changed conditions of communication and transportation, have been so evaded and violated that their beneficent purpose is threatened with entire defeat. The methods of such evasions and violations are set forth in detail in the reports of the Secretary of the Interior and Commissioner of the General Land Office. The rapid appropriation of our public lands without *bona fide* settlements or cultivation, and not only without intention of residence, but for the purpose of their aggregation in large holdings, in many cases in the hands of foreigners, invites the serious and immediate attention of the Congress.

The energies of the Land Department have been devoted during the present Administration to remedy defects and correct abuses in the public-land service. The results of these efforts are so largely in the nature of reforms in the processes and methods of our land system as to prevent adequate estimate; but it appears by a compilation from the reports of the Commissioner of the General Land Office that the immediate effect in leading cases which have come to a final termination has been the restoration to the mass of public lands of 2,750,000 acres; that 2,370,000 acres are embraced in investigations now pending before the Department or the courts, and that the action of Congress has been asked to effect the restoration of 2,790,000 acres additional; besides which 4,000,000 acres have been withheld from reservation and the rights of entry thereon maintained.

I recommend the repeal of the preemption and timber-culture acts, and that the homestead laws be so amended as to better secure compliance with their requirements of residence, improvement, and cultivation for the period of five years from date of entry, without commutation or provision for speculative relinquishment. I also recommend the repeal of the desert-land laws unless it shall be the pleasure of the Congress to so amend these laws as to render them less liable to abuses. As the chief motive for an evasion of the laws and the principal cause of their result in land accumulation instead of land distribution is the facility with which transfers are made of the right intended to be secured to settlers, it may be deemed advisable to provide by legislation some guards and checks upon the alienation of homestead rights and lands covered thereby until patents issue.

Last year an Executive proclamation was issued directing the removal of fences which inclosed the public domain. Many of these have been removed in obedience to such order, but much of the public land still remains within the lines of these unlawful fences. The ingenious methods resorted to in order to continue these trespasses and the hardihood of the pretenses by which in some cases such inclosures are justified are fully detailed in the report of the Secretary of the Interior.

The removal of the fences still remaining which inclose public lands will be enforced with all the authority and means with which the executive branch of the Government is or shall be invested by the Congress for that purpose.

The report of the Commissioner of Pensions contains a detailed and most satisfactory exhibit of the operations of the Pension Bureau during the last fiscal year. The amount of work done was the largest in any year since the organization of the Bureau, and it has been done at less cost than during the previous year in every division.

On the 30th day of June, 1886, there were 365,783 pensioners on the rolls of the Bureau.

Since 1861 there have been 1,018,735 applications for pensions filed, of which 78,834 were based upon service in the War of 1812. There were 621,754 of these applications allowed, including 60,178 to the soldiers of 1812 and their widows.

The total amount paid for pensions since 1861 is $808,624,811.57.

The number of new pensions allowed during the year ended June 30, 1886, is 40,857, a larger number than has been allowed in any year save one since 1861. The names of 2,229 pensioners which had been previously dropped from the rolls were restored during the year, and after deducting those dropped within the same time for various causes a net increase remains for the year of 20,658 names.

From January 1, 1861, to December 1, 1885, 1,967 private pension acts had been passed. Since the last-mentioned date, and during the last session of the Congress, 644 such acts became laws.

It seems to me that no one can examine our pension establishment and its operations without being convinced that through its instrumentality justice can be very nearly done to all who are entitled under present laws to the pension bounty of the Government.

But it is undeniable that cases exist, well entitled to relief, in which the Pension Bureau is powerless to aid. The really worthy cases of this class are such as only lack by misfortune the kind or quantity of proof which the law and regulations of the Bureau require, or which, though their merit is apparent, for some other reason can not be justly dealt with through general laws. These conditions fully justify application to the Congress and special enactments. But resort to the Congress for a special pension act to overrule the deliberate and careful determination of the Pension Bureau on the merits or to secure favorable action when it could not be expected under the most liberal execution of general laws, it must be admitted opens the door to the allowance of questionable claims and presents to the legislative and executive branches of the Government applications concededly not within the law and plainly devoid of merit, but so surrounded by sentiment and patriotic feeling that they are hard to resist. I suppose it will not be denied that many claims for pension are made without merit and that many have been allowed upon fraudulent representations. This has been declared from the Pension Bureau, not only in this but in prior Administrations.

The usefulness and the justice of any system for the distribution of pensions depend upon the equality and uniformity of its operation.

It will be seen from the report of the Commissioner that there are now paid by the Government 131 different rates of pension.

He estimates from the best information he can obtain that 9,000 of those who have served in the Army and Navy of the United States are now supported, in whole or in part, from public funds or by organized charities, exclusive of those in soldiers' homes under the direction and control of the Government. Only 13 per cent of these are pensioners, while of the entire number of men furnished for the late war something like 20 per cent, including their widows and relatives, have been or now are in receipt of pensions.

The American people, with a patriotic and grateful regard for our ex-soldiers, too broad and too sacred to be monopolized by any special advocates, are not only willing but anxious that equal and exact justice should be done to all honest claimants for pensions. In their sight the friendless and destitute soldier, dependent on public charity, if otherwise entitled, has precisely the same right to share in the provision made for those who fought their country's battles as those better able, through friends and influence, to push their claims. Every pension that is granted under our present plan upon any other grounds than actual service and injury or disease incurred in such service, and every instance of the many in which pensions are increased on other grounds than the merits of the claim, work an injustice to the brave and crippled, but poor and friendless, soldier, who is entirely neglected or who must be content with the smallest sum allowed under general laws.

There are far too many neighborhoods in which are found glaring cases of inequality of treatment in the matter of pensions, and they are largely due to a yielding in the Pension Bureau to importunity on the part of those, other than the pensioner, who are especially interested, or they arise from special acts passed for the benefit of individuals.

The men who fought side by side should stand side by side when they participate in a grateful nation's kind remembrance.

Every consideration of fairness and justice to our ex-soldiers and the protection of the patriotic instinct of our citizens from perversion and violation point to the adoption of a pension system broad and comprehensive enough to cover every contingency, and which shall make unnecessary an objectionable volume of special legislation.

As long as we adhere to the principle of granting pensions for service, and disability as the result of the service, the allowance of pensions should be restricted to cases presenting these features.

Every patriotic heart responds to a tender consideration for those who, having served their country long and well, are reduced to destitution and dependence, not as an incident of their service, but with advancing age or through sickness or misfortune. We are all tempted by the contemplation of such a condition to supply relief, and are often impatient of the limitations of public duty. Yielding to no one in the desire to indulge this feeling of consideration, I can not rid myself of the conviction that if these ex-soldiers are to be relieved they and their cause are entitled to the benefit of an enactment under which relief may be claimed as a right, and that such relief should be granted under the sanction of law, not in evasion of it; nor should such worthy objects of care, all equally entitled, be remitted to the unequal operation of sympathy or the tender mercies of social and political influence, with their unjust discriminations.

The discharged soldiers and sailors of the country are our fellow-citizens, and interested with us in the passage and faithful execution of wholesome laws. They can not be swerved from their duty of citizenship by artful appeals to their spirit of brotherhood born of common peril and suffering, nor will they exact as a test of devotion to their welfare a willingness to neglect public duty in their behalf.

On the 4th of March, 1885, the current business of the Patent Office was, on an average, five and a half months in arrears, and in several divisions more than twelve months behind. At the close of the last fiscal year such current work was but three months in arrears, and it is asserted and believed that in the next few months the delay in obtaining an examination of an application for a patent will be but nominal.

The number of applications for patents during the last fiscal year, including reissues, designs, trade-marks, and labels, equals 40,678, which is considerably in excess of the number received during any preceding year.

The receipts of the Patent Office during the year aggregate $1,205,-167.80, enabling the office to turn into the Treasury a surplus revenue, over and above all expenditures, of about $163,710.30.

The number of patents granted during the last fiscal year, including reissues, trade-marks, designs, and labels, was 25,619, a number also quite largely in excess of that of any preceding year.

The report of the Commissioner shows the office to be in a prosperous condition and constantly increasing in its business. No increase of force is asked for.

The amount estimated for the fiscal year ending June 30, 1886, was $890,760. The amount estimated for the year ending June 30, 1887, was $853,960. The amount estimated for the fiscal year ending June 30, 1888, is $778,770.

The Secretary of the Interior suggests a change in the plan for the payment of the indebtedness of the Pacific subsidized roads to the Government. His suggestion has the unanimous indorsement of the persons selected by the Government to act as directors of these roads and protect the interests of the United States in the board of direction. In considering the plan proposed the sole matters which should be taken into account, in my opinion, are the situation of the Government as a creditor and the surest way to secure the payment of the principal and interest of its debt.

By a recent decision of the Supreme Court of the United States it has been adjudged that the laws of the several States are inoperative to regulate rates of transportation upon railroads if such regulation interferes with the rate of carriage from one State into another. This important field of control and regulation having been thus left entirely unoccupied, the expediency of Federal action upon the subject is worthy of consideration.

The relations of labor to capital and of laboring men to their employers are of the utmost concern to every patriotic citizen. When these are strained and distorted, unjustifiable claims are apt to be insisted upon by both interests, and in the controversy which results the welfare of all and the prosperity of the country are jeopardized. Any intervention of the General Government, within the limits of its constitutional authority, to avert such a condition should be willingly accorded.

In a special message transmitted to the Congress at its last session I suggested the enlargement of our present Labor Bureau and adding to its present functions the power of arbitration in cases where differences arise between employer and employed. When these differences reach such a stage as to result in the interruption of commerce between the States, the application of this remedy by the General Government might be regarded as entirely within its constitutional powers. And I think we might reasonably hope that such arbitrators, if carefully selected and if entitled to the confidence of the parties to be affected, would be voluntarily called to the settlement of controversies of less extent and not necessarily within the domain of Federal regulation.

I am of the opinion that this suggestion is worthy the attention of the Congress.

But after all has been done by the passage of laws, either Federal or State, to relieve a situation full of solicitude, much more remains to be accomplished by the reinstatement and cultivation of a true American sentiment which recognizes the equality of American citizenship. This, in the light of our traditions and in loyalty to the spirit of our institutions, would teach that a hearty cooperation on the part of all interests is the surest path to national greatness and the happiness of all our people; that capital should, in recognition of the brotherhood of our citizenship and in a spirit of American fairness, generously accord to labor its just compensation and consideration, and that contented labor is capital's best protection and faithful ally. It would teach, too, that the diverse situations of our people are inseparable from our civilization; that every citizen should in his sphere be a contributor to the general good; that capital does not necessarily tend to the oppression of labor, and that violent disturbances and disorders alienate from their promoters true American sympathy and kindly feeling.

The Department of Agriculture, representing the oldest and largest of our national industries, is subserving well the purposes of its organization. By the introduction of new subjects of farming enterprise and by opening new sources of agricultural wealth and the dissemination of early information concerning production and prices it has contributed largely to the country's prosperity. Through this agency advanced thought and investigation touching the subjects it has in charge should, among other things, be practically applied to the home production at a low cost of articles of food which are now imported from abroad. Such an innovation will necessarily, of course, in the beginning be within the domain of intelligent experiment, and the subject in every stage should receive all possible encouragement from the Government.

The interests of millions of our citizens engaged in agriculture are involved in an enlargement and improvement of the results of their labor, and a zealous regard for their welfare should be a willing tribute to those whose productive returns are a main source of our progress and power.

The existence of pleuro-pneumonia among the cattle of various States has led to burdensome and in some cases disastrous restrictions in an important branch of our commerce, threatening to affect the quantity and quality of our food supply. This is a matter of such importance and of such far-reaching consequences that I hope it will engage the serious attention of the Congress, to the end that such a remedy may be applied as the limits of a constitutional delegation of power to the General Government will permit.

I commend to the consideration of the Congress the report of the Commissioner and his suggestions concerning the interest intrusted to his care.

The continued operation of the law relating to our civil service has added the most convincing proofs of its necessity and usefulness. It is a fact worthy of note that every public officer who has a just idea of his duty to the people testifies to the value of this reform. Its staunchest friends are found among those who understand it best, and its warmest supporters are those who are restrained and protected by its requirements.

The meaning of such restraint and protection is not appreciated by those who want places under the Government regardless of merit and efficiency, nor by those who insist that the selection of such places should rest upon a proper credential showing active partisan work. They mean to public officers, if not their lives, the only opportunity afforded them to attend to public business, and they mean to the good people of the country the better performance of the work of their Government.

It is exceedingly strange that the scope and nature of this reform are so little understood and that so many things not included within its plan are called by its name. When cavil yields more fully to examination, the system will have large additions to the number of its friends.

Our civil-service reform may be imperfect in some of its details; it may be misunderstood and opposed; it may not always be faithfully applied; its designs may sometimes miscarry through mistake or willful intent; it may sometimes tremble under the assaults of its enemies or languish under the misguided zeal of impracticable friends; but if the people of this country ever submit to the banishment of its underlying principle from the operation of their Government they will abandon the surest guaranty of the safety and success of American institutions.

I invoke for this reform the cheerful and ungrudging support of the Congress. I renew my recommendation made last year that the salaries of the Commissioners be made equal to other officers of the Government having like duties and responsibilities, and I hope that such reasonable appropriations may be made as will enable them to increase the usefulness of the cause they have in charge.

I desire to call the attention of the Congress to a plain duty which the Government owes to the depositors in the Freedman's Savings and Trust Company.

This company was chartered by the Congress for the benefit of the most illiterate and humble of our people, and with the intention of encouraging in them industry and thrift. Most of its branches were presided over by officers holding the commissions and clothed in the uniform of the United States. These and other circumstances reasonably, I think, led these simple people to suppose that the invitation to deposit their hard-earned savings in this institution implied an undertaking on the part of their Government that their money should be safely kept for them.

When this company failed, it was liable in the sum of $2,939,925.22 to 61,131 depositors. Dividends amounting in the aggregate to 62 per cent have been declared, and the sum called for and paid of such dividends seems to be $1,648,181.72. This sum deducted from the entire amount of deposits leaves $1,291,744.50 still unpaid. Past experience has shown that quite a large part of this sum will not be called for. There are assets still on hand amounting to the estimated sum of $16,000.

I think the remaining 38 per cent of such of these deposits as have claimants should be paid by the Government, upon principles of equity and fairness.

The report of the commissioner, soon to be laid before Congress, will give more satisfactory details on this subject.

The control of the affairs of the District of Columbia having been placed in the hands of purely executive officers, while the Congress still retains all legislative authority relating to its government, it becomes my duty to make known the most pressing needs of the District and recommend their consideration.

The laws of the District appear to be in an uncertain and unsatisfactory condition, and their codification or revision is much needed.

During the past year one of the bridges leading from the District to the State of Virginia became unfit for use, and travel upon it was forbidden. This leads me to suggest that the improvement of all the bridges crossing the Potomac and its branches from the city of Washington is worthy the attention of Congress.

The Commissioners of the District represent that the laws regulating the sale of liquor and granting licenses therefor should be at once amended, and that legislation is needed to consolidate, define, and enlarge the scope and powers of charitable and penal institutions within the District.

I suggest that the Commissioners be clothed with the power to make, within fixed limitations, police regulations. I believe this power granted and carefully guarded would tend to subserve the good order of the municipality.

It seems that trouble still exists growing out of the occupation of the streets and avenues by certain railroads having their termini in the city. It is very important that such laws should be enacted upon this subject as will secure to the railroads all the facilities they require for the transaction of their business and at the same time protect citizens from injury to their persons or property.

The Commissioners again complain that the accommodations afforded them for the necessary offices for District business and for the safe-keeping of valuable books and papers are entirely insufficient. I recommend that this condition of affairs be remedied by the Congress, and that suitable quarters be furnished for the needs of the District government.

In conclusion I earnestly invoke such wise action on the part of the people's legislators as will subserve the public good and demonstrate during the remaining days of the Congress as at present organized its ability and inclination to so meet the people's needs that it shall be gratefully remembered by an expectant constituency.

THIRD ANNUAL MESSAGE.

WASHINGTON, *December 6, 1887.*

To the Congress of the United States:

You are confronted at the threshold of your legislative duties with a condition of the national finances which imperatively demands immediate and careful consideration.

The amount of money annually exacted, through the operation of present laws, from the industries and necessities of the people largely exceeds the sum necessary to meet the expenses of the Government.

When we consider that the theory of our institutions guarantees to every citizen the full enjoyment of all the fruits of his industry and enterprise, with only such deduction as may be his share toward the careful and economical maintenance of the Government which protects him, it is plain that the exaction of more than this is indefensible extortion and a culpable betrayal of American fairness and justice. This wrong inflicted upon those who bear the burden of national taxation, like other wrongs, multiplies a brood of evil consequences. The public Treasury, which should only exist as a conduit conveying the people's tribute to its legitimate objects of expenditure, becomes a hoarding place for money needlessly withdrawn from trade and the people's use, thus crippling our national energies, suspending our country's development, preventing investment in productive enterprise, threatening financial disturbance, and inviting schemes of public plunder.

This condition of our Treasury is not altogether new, and it has more than once of late been submitted to the people's representatives in the Congress, who alone can apply a remedy. And yet the situation still continues, with aggravated incidents, more than ever presaging financial convulsion and widespread disaster.

It will not do to neglect this situation because its dangers are not now palpably imminent and apparent. They exist none the less certainly, and await the unforeseen and unexpected occasion when suddenly they will be precipitated upon us.

On the 30th day of June, 1885, the excess of revenues over public expenditures, after complying with the annual requirement of the sinking-fund act, was $17,859,735.84; during the year ended June 30, 1886, such excess amounted to $49,405,545.20, and during the year ended June 30, 1887, it reached the sum of $55,567,849.54.

The annual contributions to the sinking fund during the three years above specified, amounting in the aggregate to $138,058,320.94, and deducted from the surplus as stated, were made by calling in for that purpose outstanding 3 per cent bonds of the Government. During the six months prior to June 30, 1887, the surplus revenue had grown so large by repeated accumulations, and it was feared the withdrawal of this great sum of money needed by the people would so affect the business of the country, that the sum of $79,864,100 of such surplus was applied to the payment of the principal and interest of the 3 per cent bonds still outstanding, and which were then payable at the option of the Government. The precarious condition of financial affairs among the people still needing relief, immediately after the 30th day of June, 1887, the remainder of the 3 per cent bonds then outstanding, amounting with principal and interest to the sum of $18,877,500, were called in and applied to the sinking-fund contribution for the current fiscal year. Notwithstanding these operations of the Treasury Department, representations of distress in business circles not only continued, but increased, and absolute peril seemed at hand. In these circumstances the contribution to the sinking fund for the current fiscal year was at once completed by the expenditure of $27,684,283.55 in the purchase of Government bonds not yet due bearing 4 and 4½ per cent interest, the premium paid thereon averaging about 24 per cent for the former and 8 per cent for the latter. In addition to this, the interest accruing during the current year upon the outstanding bonded indebtedness of the Government was to some extent anticipated, and banks selected as depositories of public money were permitted to somewhat increase their deposits.

While the expedients thus employed to release to the people the money lying idle in the Treasury served to avert immediate danger, our surplus revenues have continued to accumulate, the excess for the present year amounting on the 1st day of December to $55,258,701.19, and estimated to reach the sum of $113,000,000 on the 30th of June next, at which date it is expected that this sum, added to prior accumulations, will swell the surplus in the Treasury to $140,000,000.

There seems to be no assurance that, with such a withdrawal from use of the people's circulating medium, our business community may not in the near future be subjected to the same distress which was quite lately produced from the same cause. And while the functions of our National Treasury should be few and simple, and while its best condition would be reached, I believe, by its entire disconnection with private business interests, yet when, by a perversion of its purposes, it idly holds money uselessly subtracted from the channels of trade, there seems to be reason for the claim that some legitimate means should be devised by the Government to restore in an emergency, without waste or extravagance, such money to its place among the people.

If such an emergency arises, there now exists no clear and undoubted executive power of relief. Heretofore the redemption of 3 per cent bonds, which were payable at the option of the Government, has afforded a means for the disbursement of the excess of our revenues; but these bonds have all been retired, and there are no bonds outstanding the payment of which we have a right to insist upon. The contribution to the sinking fund which furnishes the occasion for expenditure in the purchase of bonds has been already made for the current year, so that there is no outlet in that direction.

In the present state of legislation the only pretense of any existing executive power to restore at this time any part of our surplus revenues to the people by its expenditure consists in the supposition that the Secretary of the Treasury may enter the market and purchase the bonds of the Government not yet due, at a rate of premium to be agreed upon. The only provision of law from which such a power could be derived is found in an appropriation bill passed a number of years ago, and it is subject to the suspicion that it was intended as temporary and limited in its application, instead of conferring a continuing discretion and authority. No condition ought to exist which would justify the grant of power to a single official, upon his judgment of its necessity, to withhold from or release to the business of the people, in an unusual manner, money held in the Treasury, and thus affect at his will the financial situation of the country; and if it is deemed wise to lodge in the Secretary of the Treasury the authority in the present juncture to purchase bonds, it should be plainly vested, and provided, as far as possible, with such checks and limitations as will define this official's right and discretion and at .the same time relieve him from undue responsibility.

In considering the question of purchasing bonds as a means of restoring to circulation the surplus money accumulating in the Treasury, it should be borne in mind that premiums must of course be paid upon such purchase, that there may be a large part of these bonds held as investments which can not be purchased at any price, and that combinations among holders who are willing to sell may unreasonably enhance the cost of such bonds to the Government.

It has been suggested that the present bonded debt might be refunded at a less rate of interest and the difference between the old and new security paid in cash, thus finding use for the surplus in the Treasury. The success of this plan, it is apparent, must depend upon the volition of the holders of the present bonds; and it is not entirely certain that the inducement which must be offered them would result in more financial benefit to the Government than the purchase of bonds, while the latter proposition would reduce the principal of the debt by actual payment instead of extending it.

The proposition to deposit the money held by the Government in banks throughout the country for use by the people is, it seems to me, exceedingly objectionable in principle, as establishing too close a relationship between the operations of the Government Treasury and the business of the country and too extensive a commingling of their money, thus fostering an unnatural reliance in private business upon public funds. If this scheme should be adopted, it should only be done as a temporary expedient to meet an urgent necessity. Legislative and executive effort should generally be in the opposite direction, and should have a tendency to divorce, as much and as fast as can be safely done, the Treasury Department from private enterprise.

Of course it is not expected that unnecessary and extravagant appropriations will be made for the purpose of avoiding the accumulation of an excess of revenue. Such expenditure, besides the demoralization of all just conceptions of public duty which it entails, stimulates a habit of reckless improvidence not in the least consistent with the mission of our people or the high and beneficent purposes of our Government.

I have deemed it my duty to thus bring to the knowledge of my countrymen, as well as to the attention of their representatives charged with the responsibility of legislative relief, the gravity of our financial situation. The failure of the Congress heretofore to provide against the dangers which it was quite evident the very nature of the difficulty must necessarily produce caused a condition of financial distress and apprehension since your last adjournment which taxed to the utmost all the authority and expedients within executive control; and these appear now to be exhausted. If disaster results from the continued inaction of Congress, the responsibility must rest where it belongs.

Though the situation thus far considered is fraught with danger which should be fully realized, and though it presents features of wrong to the people as well as peril to the country, it is but a result growing out of a perfectly palpable and apparent cause, constantly reproducing the same alarming circumstances—a congested National Treasury and a depleted monetary condition in the business of the country. It need hardly be stated that while the present situation demands a remedy, we can only be saved from a like predicament in the future by the removal of its cause.

Our scheme of taxation, by means of which this needless surplus is taken from the people and put into the public Treasury, consists of a tariff or duty levied upon importations from abroad and internal-revenue taxes levied upon the consumption of tobacco and spirituous and malt liquors.   It must be conceded that none of the things subjected to internal-revenue taxation are, strictly speaking, necessaries.   There appears to be no just complaint of this taxation by the consumers of these articles, and there seems to be nothing so well able to bear the burden without hardship to any portion of the people.

But our present tariff laws, the vicious, inequitable, and illogical source of unnecessary taxation, ought to be at once revised and amended.   These laws, as their primary and plain effect, raise the price to consumers of all articles imported and subject to duty by precisely the sum paid for such duties.   Thus the amount of the duty measures the tax paid by those who purchase for use these imported articles.   Many of these things, however, are raised or manufactured in our own country, and the duties now levied upon foreign goods and products are called protection to these home manufactures, because they render it possible for those of our people who are manufacturers to make these taxed articles and sell them for a price equal to that demanded for the imported goods that have paid customs duty.   So it happens that while comparatively a few use the imported articles, millions of our people, who never used and never saw any of the foreign products, purchase and use things of the same kind made in this country, and pay therefor nearly or quite the same enhanced price which the duty adds to the imported articles.   Those who buy imports pay the duty charged thereon into the public Treasury, but the great majority of our citizens, who buy domestic articles of the same class, pay a sum at least approximately equal to this duty to the home manufacturer.   This reference to the operation of our tariff laws is not made by way of instruction, but in order that we may be constantly reminded of the manner in which they impose a burden upon those who consume domestic products as well as those who consume imported articles, and thus create a tax upon all our people.

It is not proposed to entirely relieve the country of this taxation.   It must be extensively continued as the source of the Government's income; and in a readjustment of our tariff the interests of American labor engaged in manufacture should be carefully considered, as well as the preservation of our manufacturers.   It may be called protection or by any other name, but relief from the hardships and dangers of our present tariff laws should be devised with especial precaution against imperiling the existence of our manufacturing interests.   But this existence should not mean a condition which, without regard to the public welfare or a national exigency, must always insure the realization of immense profits instead of moderately profitable returns.   As the volume and diversity of our national activities increase, new recruits are added to those who desire a continuation of the advantages which they conceive the pres-

ent system of tariff taxation directly affords them.   So stubbornly have
all efforts to reform the present condition been resisted by those of our
fellow-citizens thus engaged that they can hardly complain of the suspicion, entertained to a certain extent, that there exists an organized
combination all along the line to maintain their advantage.

We are in the midst of centennial celebrations, and with becoming
pride we rejoice in American skill and ingenuity, in American energy
and enterprise, and in the wonderful natural advantages and resources
developed by a century's national growth.   Yet when an attempt is made
to justify a scheme which permits a tax to be laid upon every consumer
in the land for the benefit of our manufacturers, quite beyond a reasonable demand for governmental regard, it suits the purposes of advocacy
to call our manufactures infant industries still needing the highest and
greatest degree of favor and fostering care that can be wrung from Federal legislation.

It is also said that the increase in the price of domestic manufactures
resulting from the present tariff is necessary in order that higher wages
may be paid to our workingmen employed in manufactories than are paid
for what is called the pauper labor of Europe.   All will acknowledge the
force of an argument which involves the welfare and liberal compensation
of our laboring people.   Our labor is honorable in the eyes of every
American citizen; and as it lies at the foundation of our development
and progress, it is entitled, without affectation or hypocrisy, to the utmost
regard.   The standard of our laborers' life should not be measured by
that of any other country less favored, and they are entitled to their full
share of all our advantages.

By the last census it is made to appear that of the 17,392,099 of our
population engaged in all kinds of industries 7,670,493 are employed in
agriculture, 4,074,238 in professional and personal service (2,934,876 of
whom are domestic servants and laborers), while 1,810,256 are employed
in trade and transportation and 3,837,112 are classed as employed in
manufacturing and mining.

For present purposes, however, the last number given should be considerably reduced.   Without attempting to enumerate all, it will be conceded that there should be deducted from those which it includes 375,143
carpenters and joiners, 285,401 milliners, dressmakers, and seamstresses,
172,726 blacksmiths, 133,756 tailors and tailoresses, 102,473 masons,
76,241 butchers, 41,309 bakers, 22,083 plasterers, and 4,891 engaged in
manufacturing agricultural implements, amounting in the aggregate to
1,214,023, leaving 2,623,089 persons employed in such manufacturing
industries as are claimed to be benefited by a high tariff.

To these the appeal is made to save their employment and maintain
their wages by resisting a change.   There should be no disposition to
answer such suggestions by the allegation that they are in a minority
among those who labor, and therefore should forego an advantage in

the interest of low prices for the majority. Their compensation, as it may be affected by the operation of tariff laws, should at all times be scrupulously kept in view; and yet with slight reflection they will not overlook the fact that they are consumers with the rest; that they too have their own wants and those of their families to supply from their earnings, and that the price of the necessaries of life, as well as the amount of their wages, will regulate the measure of their welfare and comfort.

But the reduction of taxation demanded should be so measured as not to necessitate or justify either the loss of employment by the working-man or the lessening of his wages; and the profits still remaining to the manufacturer after a necessary readjustment should furnish no excuse for the sacrifice of the interests of his employees, either in their oppor-tunity to work or in the diminution of their compensation. Nor can the worker in manufactures fail to understand that while a high tariff is claimed to be necessary to allow the payment of remunerative wages, it certainly results in a very large increase in the price of nearly all sorts of manufactures, which, in almost countless forms, he needs for the use of himself and his family. He receives at the desk of his employer his wages, and perhaps before he reaches his home is obliged, in a purchase for family use of an article which embraces his own labor, to return in the payment of the increase in price which the tariff permits the hard-earned compensation of many days of toil.

The farmer and the agriculturist, who manufacture nothing, but who pay the increased price which the tariff imposes upon every agricultural implement, upon all he wears, and upon all he uses and owns, except the increase of his flocks and herds and such things as his husbandry pro-duces from the soil, is invited to aid in maintaining the present situa-tion; and he is told that a high duty on imported wool is necessary for the benefit of those who have sheep to shear, in order that the price of their wool may be increased. They, of course, are not reminded that the farmer who has no sheep is by this scheme obliged, in his purchases of clothing and woolen goods, to pay a tribute to his fellow-farmer as well as to the manufacturer and merchant, nor is any mention made of the fact that the sheep owners themselves and their households must wear clothing and use other articles manufactured from the wool they sell at tariff prices, and thus as consumers must return their share of this increased price to the tradesman.

I think it may be fairly assumed that a large proportion of the sheep owned by the farmers throughout the country are found in small flocks, numbering from twenty-five to fifty. The duty on the grade of imported wool which these sheep yield is 10 cents each pound if of the value of 30 cents or less and 12 cents if of the value of more than 30 cents. If the liberal estimate of 6 pounds be allowed for each fleece, the duty thereon would be 60 or 72 cents; and this may be taken as the utmost enhancement of its price to the farmer by reason of this duty. Eighteen dollars would thus represent the increased price of the wool from twenty-five sheep and $36 that from the wool of fifty sheep; and at present values this addition would amount to about one-third of its price. If upon its sale the farmer receives this or a less tariff profit, the wool leaves his hands charged with precisely that sum, which in all its changes will adhere to it until it reaches the consumer. When manufactured into cloth and other goods and material for use, its cost is not only increased to the extent of the farmer's tariff profit, but a further sum has been added for the benefit of the manufacturer under the operation of other tariff laws. In the meantime the day arrives when the farmer finds it necessary to purchase woolen goods and material to clothe himself and family for the winter. When he faces the tradesman for that purpose, he discovers that he is obliged not only to return in the way of increased prices his tariff profit on the wool he sold, and which then perhaps lies before him in manufactured form, but that he must add a considerable sum thereto to meet a further increase in cost caused by a tariff duty on the manufacture. Thus in the end he is aroused to the fact that he has paid upon a moderate purchase, as a result of the tariff scheme, which when he sold his wool seemed so profitable, an increase in price more than sufficient to sweep away all the tariff profit he received upon the wool he produced and sold.

When the number of farmers engaged in wool raising is compared with all the farmers in the country and the small proportion they bear to our population is considered; when it is made apparent that in the case of a large part of those who own sheep the benefit of the present tariff on wool is illusory; and, above all, when it must be conceded that the increase of the cost of living caused by such tariff becomes a burden upon those with moderate means and the poor, the employed and unemployed, the sick and well, and the young and old, and that it constitutes a tax which with relentless grasp is fastened upon the clothing of every man, woman, and child in the land, reasons are suggested why the removal or reduction of this duty should be included in a revision of our tariff laws.

In speaking of the increased cost to the consumer of our home manufactures resulting from a duty laid upon imported articles of the same description, the fact is not overlooked that competition among our domestic producers sometimes has the effect of keeping the price of their products below the highest limit allowed by such duty. But it is notorious that this competition is too often strangled by combinations quite prevalent at this time, and frequently called trusts, which have for their object the regulation of the supply and price of commodities made and sold by members of the combination. The people can hardly hope for any consideration in the operation of these selfish schemes.

If, however, in the absence of such combination, a healthy and free competition reduces the price of any particular dutiable article of home production below the limit which it might otherwise reach under our tariff laws, and if with such reduced price its manufacture continues to thrive, it is entirely evident that one thing has been discovered which should be carefully scrutinized in an effort to reduce taxation.

The necessity of combination to maintain the price of any commodity to the tariff point furnishes proof that someone is willing to accept lower prices for such commodity and that such prices are remunerative; and lower prices produced by competition prove the same thing. Thus where either of these conditions exists a case would seem to be presented for an easy reduction of taxation.

The considerations which have been presented touching our tariff laws are intended only to enforce an earnest recommendation that the surplus revenues of the Government be prevented by the reduction of our customs duties, and at the same time to emphasize a suggestion that in accomplishing this purpose we may discharge a double duty to our people by granting to them a measure of relief from tariff taxation in quarters where it is most needed and from sources where it can be most fairly and justly accorded.

Nor can the presentation made of such considerations be with any degree of fairness regarded as evidence of unfriendliness toward our manufacturing interests or of any lack of appreciation of their value and importance.

These interests constitute a leading and most substantial element of our national greatness and furnish the proud proof of our country's progress. But if in the emergency that presses upon us our manufacturers are asked to surrender something for the public good and to avert disaster, their patriotism, as well as a grateful recognition of advantages already afforded, should lead them to willing cooperation. No demand is made that they shall forego all the benefits of governmental regard; but they can not fail to be admonished of their duty, as well as their enlightened self-interest and safety, when they are reminded of the fact that financial panic and collapse, to which the present condition tends, afford no greater shelter or protection to our manufactures than to other important enterprises. Opportunity for safe, careful, and deliberate reform is now offered; and none of us should be unmindful of a time when an abused and irritated people, heedless of those who have resisted timely and reasonable relief, may insist upon a radical and sweeping rectification of their wrongs.

The difficulty attending a wise and fair revision of our tariff laws is not underestimated. It will require on the part of the Congress great labor and care, and especially a broad and national contemplation of the subject and a patriotic disregard of such local and selfish claims as are unreasonable and reckless of the welfare of the entire country.

Under our present laws more than 4,000 articles are subject to duty.

Many of these do not in any way compete with our own manufactures, and many are hardly worth attention as subjects of revenue. A considerable reduction can be made in the aggregate by adding them to the free list. The taxation of luxuries presents no features of hardship; but the necessaries of life used and consumed by all the people, the duty upon which adds to the cost of living in every home, should be greatly cheapened.

The radical reduction of the duties imposed upon raw material used in manufactures, or its free importation, is of course an important factor in any effort to reduce the price of these necessaries. It would not only relieve them from the increased cost caused by the tariff on such material, but the manufactured product being thus cheapened that part of the tariff now laid upon such product, as a compensation to our manufacturers for the present price of raw material, could be accordingly modified. Such reduction or free importation would serve besides to largely reduce the revenue. It is not apparent how such a change can have any injurious effect upon our manufacturers. On the contrary, it would appear to give them a better chance in foreign markets with the manufacturers of other countries, who cheapen their wares by free material. Thus our people might have the opportunity of extending their sales beyond the limits of home consumption, saving them from the depression, interruption in business, and loss caused by a glutted domestic market and affording their employees more certain and steady labor, with its resulting quiet and contentment.

The question thus imperatively presented for solution should be approached in a spirit higher than partisanship and considered in the light of that regard for patriotic duty which should characterize the action of those intrusted with the weal of a confiding people. But the obligation to declared party policy and principle is not wanting to urge prompt and effective action. Both of the great political parties now represented in the Government have by repeated and authoritative declarations condemned the condition of our laws which permit the collection from the people of unnecessary revenue, and have in the most solemn manner promised its correction; and neither as citizens nor partisans are our countrymen in a mood to condone the deliberate violation of these pledges.

Our progress toward a wise conclusion will not be improved by dwelling upon the theories of protection and free trade. This savors too much of bandying epithets. It is a *condition* which confronts us, not a theory. Relief from this condition may involve a slight reduction of the advantages which we award our home productions, but the entire withdrawal of such advantages should not be contemplated. The question of free trade is absolutely irrelevant, and the persistent claim made in certain quarters that all the efforts to relieve the people from unjust and unnecessary taxation are schemes of so-called free traders is mischievous and far removed from any consideration for the public good.

The simple and plain duty which we owe the people is to reduce taxation to the necessary expenses of an economical operation of the Government and to restore to the business of the country the money which we hold in the Treasury through the perversion of governmental powers. These things can and should be done with safety to all our industries, without danger to the opportunity for remunerative labor which our workingmen need, and with benefit to them and all our people by cheapening their means of subsistence and increasing the measure of their comforts.

The Constitution provides that the President "shall from time to time give to the Congress information of the state of the Union." It has been the custom of the Executive, in compliance with this provision, to annually exhibit to the Congress, at the opening of its session, the general condition of the country, and to detail with some particularity the operations of the different Executive Departments. It would be especially agreeable to follow this course at the present time and to call attention to the valuable accomplishments of these Departments during the last fiscal year; but I am so much impressed with the paramount importance of the subject to which this communication has thus far been devoted that I shall forego the addition of any other topic, and only urge upon your immediate consideration the "state of the Union" as shown in the present condition of our Treasury and our general fiscal situation, upon which every element of our safety and prosperity depends.

The reports of the heads of Departments, which will be submitted, contain full and explicit information touching the transaction of the business intrusted to them and such recommendations relating to legislation in the public interest as they deem advisable. I ask for these reports and recommendations the deliberate examination and action of the legislative branch of the Government.

There are other subjects not embraced in the departmental reports demanding legislative consideration, and which I should be glad to submit. Some of them, however, have been earnestly presented in previous messages, and as to them I beg leave to repeat prior recommendations.

As the law makes no provision for any report from the Department of State, a brief history of the transactions of that important Department, together with other matters which it may hereafter be deemed essential to commend to the attention of the Congress, may furnish the occasion for a future communication.

FOURTH ANNUAL MESSAGE.

WASHINGTON, *December 3, 1888.*

To the Congress of the United States:

As you assemble for the discharge of the duties you have assumed as the representatives of a free and generous people, your meeting is marked by an interesting and impressive incident. With the expiration of the present session of the Congress the first century of our constitutional existence as a nation will be completed.

Our survival for one hundred years is not sufficient to assure us that we no longer have dangers to fear in the maintenance, with all its promised blessings, of a government founded upon the freedom of the people. The time rather admonishes us to soberly inquire whether in the past we have always closely kept in the course of safety, and whether we have before us a way plain and clear which leads to happiness and perpetuity.

When the experiment of our Government was undertaken, the chart adopted for our guidance was the Constitution. Departure from the lines there laid down is failure. It is only by a strict adherence to the direction they indicate and by restraint within the limitations they fix that we can furnish proof to the world of the fitness of the American people for self-government.

The equal and exact justice of which we boast as the underlying principle of our institutions should not be confined to the relations of our citizens to each other. The Government itself is under bond to the American people that in the exercise of its functions and powers it will deal with the body of our citizens in a manner scrupulously honest and fair and absolutely just. It has agreed that American citizenship shall be the only credential necessary to justify the claim of equality before the law, and that no condition in life shall give rise to discrimination in the treatment of the people by their Government.

The citizen of our Republic in its early days rigidly insisted upon full compliance with the letter of this bond, and saw stretching out before him a clear field for individual endeavor. His tribute to the support of his Government was measured by the cost of its economical maintenance, and he was secure in the enjoyment of the remaining recompense of his steady and contented toil. In those days the frugality of the people was stamped upon their Government, and was enforced by the free, thoughtful, and intelligent suffrage of the citizen. Combinations, monopolies, and aggregations of capital were either avoided or sternly regulated and restrained. The pomp and glitter of governments less free offered no temptation and presented no delusion to the plain people who, side by side, in friendly competition, wrought for the ennoblement and dignity of man, for the solution of the problem of free government, and for the achievement of the grand destiny awaiting the land which God had given them.

A century has passed. Our cities are the abiding places of wealth and luxury; our manufactories yield fortunes never dreamed of by the fathers of the Republic; our business men are madly striving in the race for riches, and immense aggregations of capital outrun the imagination in the magnitude of their undertakings.

We view with pride and satisfaction this bright picture of our country's growth and prosperity, while only a closer scrutiny develops a somber shading. Upon more careful inspection we find the wealth and luxury of our cities mingled with poverty and wretchedness and unremunerative toil. A crowded and constantly increasing urban population suggests the impoverishment of rural sections and discontent with agricultural pursuits. The farmer's son, not satisfied with his father's simple and laborious life, joins the eager chase for easily acquired wealth.

We discover that the fortunes realized by our manufacturers are no longer solely the reward of sturdy industry and enlightened foresight, but that they result from the discriminating favor of the Government and are largely built upon undue exactions from the masses of our people. The gulf between employers and the employed is constantly widening, and classes are rapidly forming, one comprising the very rich and powerful, while in another are found the toiling poor.

As we view the achievements of aggregated capital, we discover the existence of trusts, combinations, and monopolies, while the citizen is struggling far in the rear or is trampled to death beneath an iron heel. Corporations, which should be the carefully restrained creatures of the law and the servants of the people, are fast becoming the people's masters.

Still congratulating ourselves upon the wealth and prosperity of our country and complacently contemplating every incident of change inseparable from these conditions, it is our duty as patriotic citizens to inquire at the present stage of our progress how the bond of the Government made with the people has been kept and performed.

Instead of limiting the tribute drawn from our citizens to the necessities of its economical administration, the Government persists in exacting from the substance of the people millions which, unapplied and useless, lie dormant in its Treasury. This flagrant injustice and this breach of faith and obligation add to extortion the danger attending the diversion of the currency of the country from the legitimate channels of business.

Under the same laws by which these results are produced the Government permits many millions more to be added to the cost of the living of our people and to be taken from our consumers, which unreasonably swell the profits of a small but powerful minority.

The people must still be taxed for the support of the Government under the operation of tariff laws. But to the extent that the mass of our citizens are inordinately burdened beyond any useful public purpose and for the benefit of a favored few, the Government, under pretext of an exercise of its taxing power, enters gratuitously into partnership with these favorites, to their advantage and to the injury of a vast majority of our people.

This is not equality before the law.

The existing situation is injurious to the health of our entire body politic. It stifles in those for whose benefit it is permitted all patriotic love of country, and substitutes in its place selfish greed and grasping avarice. Devotion to American citizenship for its own sake and for what it should accomplish as a motive to our nation's advancement and the happiness of all our people is displaced by the assumption that the Government, instead of being the embodiment of equality, is but an instrumentality through which especial and individual advantages are to be gained.

The arrogance of this assumption is unconcealed. It appears in the sordid disregard of all but personal interests, in the refusal to abate for the benefit of others one iota of selfish advantage, and in combinations to perpetuate such advantages through efforts to control legislation and improperly influence the suffrages of the people.

The grievances of those not included within the circle of these beneficiaries, when fully realized, will surely arouse irritation and discontent. Our farmers, long suffering and patient, struggling in the race of life with the hardest and most unremitting toil, will not fail to see, in spite of misrepresentations and misleading fallacies, that they are obliged to accept such prices for their products as are fixed in foreign markets where they compete with the farmers of the world; that their lands are declining in value while their debts increase, and that without compensating favor they are forced by the action of the Government to pay for the benefit of others such enhanced prices for the things they need that the scanty returns of their labor fail to furnish their support or leave no margin for accumulation.

Our workingmen, enfranchised from all delusions and no longer frightened by the cry that their wages are endangered by a just revision of our tariff laws, will reasonably demand through such revision steadier employment, cheaper means of living in their homes, freedom for themselves and their children from the doom of perpetual servitude, and an open door to their advancement beyond the limits of a laboring class. Others of our citizens, whose comforts and expenditures are measured by moderate salaries and fixed incomes, will insist upon the fairness and justice of cheapening the cost of necessaries for themselves and their families.

When to the selfishness of the beneficiaries of unjust discrimination under our laws there shall be added the discontent of those who suffer from such discrimination, we will realize the fact that the beneficent purposes of our Government, dependent upon the patriotism and contentment of our people, are endangered.

Communism is a hateful thing and a menace to peace and organized government; but the communism of combined wealth and capital, the outgrowth of overweening cupidity and selfishness, which insidiously undermines the justice and integrity of free institutions, is not less dangerous than the communism of oppressed poverty and toil, which, exasperated by injustice and discontent, attacks with wild disorder the citadel of rule.

He mocks the people who proposes that the Government shall protect the rich and that they in turn will care for the laboring poor. Any intermediary between the people and their Government or the least delegation of the care and protection the Government owes to the humblest citizen in the land makes the boast of free institutions a glittering delusion and the pretended boon of American citizenship a shameless imposition.

A just and sensible revision of our tariff laws should be made for the relief of those of our countrymen who suffer under present conditions. Such a revision should receive the support of all who love that justice and equality due to American citizenship; of all who realize that in this justice and equality our Government finds its strength and its power to protect the citizen and his property; of all who believe that the contented competence and comfort of many accord better with the spirit of our institutions than colossal fortunes unfairly gathered in the hands of a few; of all who appreciate that the forbearance and fraternity among our people, which recognize the value of every American interest, are the surest guaranty of our national progress, and of all who desire to see the products of American skill and ingenuity in every market of the world, with a resulting restoration of American commerce.

The necessity of the reduction of our revenues is so apparent as to be generally conceded, but the means by which this end shall be accomplished and the sum of direct benefit which shall result to our citizens present a controversy of the utmost importance. There should be no scheme accepted as satisfactory by which the burdens of the people are only apparently removed. Extravagant appropriations of public money, with all their demoralizing consequences, should not be tolerated, either as a means of relieving the Treasury of its present surplus or as furnishing pretext for resisting a proper reduction in tariff rates. Existing evils and injustice should be honestly recognized, boldly met, and effectively remedied. There should be no cessation of the struggle until a plan is perfected, fair and conservative toward existing industries, but which will reduce the cost to consumers of the necessaries of life, while it provides for our manufacturers the advantage of freer raw materials and permits no injury to the interests of American labor.

The cause for which the battle is waged is comprised within lines clearly and distinctly defined. It should never be compromised. It is the people's cause.

It can not be denied that the selfish and private interests which are so

persistently heard when efforts are made to deal in a just and comprehensive manner with our tariff laws are related to, if they are not responsible for, the sentiment largely prevailing among the people that the
General Government is the fountain of individual and private aid; that
it may be expected to relieve with paternal care the distress of citizens
and communities, and that from the fullness of its Treasury it should,
upon the slightest possible pretext of promoting the general good, apply
public funds to the benefit of localities and individuals.   Nor can it be
denied that there is a growing assumption that, as against the Government and in favor of private claims and interests, the usual rules and
limitations of business principles and just dealing should be waived.

These ideas have been unhappily much encouraged by legislative acquiescence.   Relief from contracts made with the Government is too easily
accorded in favor of the citizen; the failure to support claims against the
Government by proof is often supplied by no better consideration than
the wealth of the Government and the poverty of the claimant; gratuities
in the form of pensions are granted upon no other real ground than the
needy condition of the applicant, or for reasons less valid; and large sums
are expended for public buildings and other improvements upon representations scarcely claimed to be related to public needs and necessities.

The extent to which the consideration of such matters subordinate and
postpone action upon subjects of great public importance, but involving
no special private or partisan interest, should arrest attention and lead
to reformation.

A few of the numerous illustrations of this condition may be stated.

The crowded condition of the calendar of the Supreme Court, and
the delay to suitors and denial of justice resulting therefrom, has been
strongly urged upon the attention of the Congress, with a plan for the
relief of the situation approved by those well able to judge of its merits.
While this subject remains without effective consideration, many laws
have been passed providing for the holding of terms of inferior courts at
places to suit the convenience of localities, or to lay the foundation of an
application for the erection of a new public building.

Repeated recommendations have been submitted for the amendment
and change of the laws relating to our public lands so that their spoliation and diversion to other uses than as homes for honest settlers might
be prevented.   While a measure to meet this conceded necessity of reform remains awaiting the action of the Congress, many claims to the
public lands and applications for their donation, in favor of States and
individuals, have been allowed.

A plan in aid of Indian management, recommended by those well
informed as containing valuable features in furtherance of the solution
of the Indian problem, has thus far failed of legislative sanction, while
grants of doubtful expediency to railroad corporations, permitting them
to pass through Indian reservations, have greatly multiplied.

The propriety and necessity of the erection of one or more prisons for the confinement of United States convicts, and a post-office building in the national capital, are not disputed. But these needs yet remain unanswered, while scores of public buildings have been erected where their necessity for public purposes is not apparent.

A revision of our pension laws could easily be made which would rest upon just principles and provide for every worthy applicant. But while our general pension laws remain confused and imperfect, hundreds of private pension laws are annually passed, which are the sources of unjust discrimination and popular demoralization.

Appropriation bills for the support of the Government are defaced by items and provisions to meet private ends, and it is freely asserted by responsible and experienced parties that a bill appropriating money for public internal improvement would fail to meet with favor unless it contained items more for local and private advantage than for public benefit.

These statements can be much emphasized by an ascertainment of the proportion of Federal legislation which either bears upon its face its private character or which upon examination develops such a motive power.

And yet the people wait and expect from their chosen representatives such patriotic action as will advance the welfare of the entire country; and this expectation can only be answered by the performance of public duty with unselfish purpose. Our mission among the nations of the earth and our success in accomplishing the work God has given the American people to do require of those intrusted with the making and execution of our laws perfect devotion, above all other things, to the public good.

This devotion will lead us to strongly resist all impatience of constitutional limitations of Federal power and to persistently check the increasing tendency to extend the scope of Federal legislation into the domain of State and local jurisdiction upon the plea of subserving the public welfare. The preservation of the partitions between proper subjects of Federal and local care and regulation is of such importance under the Constitution, which is the law of our very existence, that no consideration of expediency or sentiment should tempt us to enter upon doubtful ground. We have undertaken to discover and proclaim the richest blessings of a free government, with the Constitution as our guide. Let us follow the way it points out; it will not mislead us. And surely no one who has taken upon himself the solemn obligation to support and preserve the Constitution can find justification or solace for disloyalty in the excuse that he wandered and disobeyed in search of a better way to reach the public welfare than the Constitution offers.

What has been said is deemed not inappropriate at a time when, from a century's height, we view the way already trod by the American people and attempt to discover their future path.

The seventh President of the United States—the soldier and statesman and at all times the firm and brave friend of the people—in vindication of his course as the protector of popular rights and the champion of true American citizenship, declared:

The ambition which leads me on is an anxious desire and a fixed determination to restore to the people unimpaired the sacred trust they have confided to my charge; to heal the wounds of the Constitution and to preserve it from further violation; to persuade my countrymen, so far as I may, that it is not in a splendid government supported by powerful monopolies and aristocratical establishments that they will find happiness or their liberties protection, but in a plain system, void of pomp, protecting all and granting favors to none, dispensing its blessings like the dews of heaven, unseen and unfelt save in the freshness and beauty they contribute to produce. It is such a government that the genius of our people requires—such an one only under which our States may remain for ages to come united, prosperous, and free.

In pursuance of a constitutional provision requiring the President from time to time to give to the Congress information of the state of the Union, I have the satisfaction to announce that the close of the year finds the United States in the enjoyment of domestic tranquillity and at peace with all the nations.

Since my last annual message our foreign relations have been strengthened and improved by performance of international good offices and by new and renewed treaties of amity, commerce, and reciprocal extradition of criminals.

Those international questions which still await settlement are all reasonably within the domain of amicable negotiation, and there is no existing subject of dispute between the United States and any foreign power that is not susceptible of satisfactory adjustment by frank diplomatic treatment.

The questions between Great Britain and the United States relating to the rights of American fishermen, under treaty and international comity, in the territorial waters of Canada and Newfoundland, I regret to say, are not yet satisfactorily adjusted.

These matters were fully treated in my message to the Senate of February 20, 1888, together with which a convention, concluded under my authority with Her Majesty's Government on the 15th of February last, for the removal of all causes of misunderstanding, was submitted by me for the approval of the Senate.

This treaty having been rejected by the Senate, I transmitted a message to the Congress on the 23d of August last † reviewing the transactions and submitting for consideration certain recommendations for legislation concerning the important questions involved.

Afterwards, on the 12th of September, in response to a resolution of the Senate, I again communicated fully all the information in my possession as to the action of the government of Canada affecting the commercial relations between the Dominion and the United States, including the treatment of American fishing vessels in the ports and waters of British North America.

These communications have all been published, and therefore opened to the knowledge of both Houses of Congress, although two were addressed to the Senate alone.

Comment upon or repetition of their contents would be superfluous, and I am not aware that anything has since occurred which should be added to the facts therein stated. Therefore I merely repeat, as applicable to the present time, the statement which will be found in my message to the Senate of September 12 last, that—

Since March 3, 1887, no case has been reported to the Department of State wherein complaint was made of unfriendly or unlawful treatment of American fishing vessels on the part of the Canadian authorities in which reparation was not promptly and satisfactorily obtained by the United States consul-general at Halifax.

Having essayed in the discharge of my duty to procure by negotiation the settlement of a long-standing cause of dispute and to remove a constant menace to the good relations of the two countries, and continuing to be of opinion that the treaty of February last, which failed to receive the approval of the Senate, did supply "a satisfactory, practical, and final adjustment, upon a basis honorable and just to both parties, of the difficult and vexed question to which it related," and having subsequently and unavailingly recommended other legislation to Congress which I hoped would suffice to meet the exigency created by the rejection of the treaty, I now again invoke the earnest and immediate attention of the Congress to the condition of this important question as it now stands before them and the country, and for the settlement of which I am deeply solicitous.

Near the close of the month of October last occurrences of a deeply regrettable nature were brought to my knowledge, which made it my painful but imperative duty to obtain with as little delay as possible a new personal channel of diplomatic intercourse in this country with the Government of Great Britain.

The correspondence in relation to this incident will in due course be laid before you, and will disclose the unpardonable conduct of the official referred to in his interference by advice and counsel with the suffrages of American citizens in the very crisis of the Presidential election then near at hand, and also in his subsequent public declarations to justify his action, superadding impugnment of the Executive and Senate of the United States in connection with important questions now pending in controversy between the two Governments.

The offense thus committed was most grave, involving disastrous possibilities to the good relations of the United States and Great Britain, constituting a gross breach of diplomatic privilege and an invasion of the purely domestic affairs and essential sovereignty of the Government to which the envoy was accredited.

Having first fulfilled the just demands of international comity by affording full opportunity for Her Majesty's Government to act in relief of the situation, I considered prolongation of discussion to be unwarranted, and thereupon declined to further recognize the diplomatic character of the person whose continuance in such function would destroy that mutual confidence which is essential to the good understanding of the two Governments and was inconsistent with the welfare and self-respect of the Government of the United States.

The usual interchange of communication has since continued through Her Majesty's legation in this city.

My endeavors to establish by international cooperation measures for the prevention of the extermination of fur seals in Bering Sea have not been relaxed, and I have hopes of being enabled shortly to submit an effective and satisfactory conventional projet with the maritime powers for the approval of the Senate.

The coastal boundary between our Alaskan possessions and British Columbia, I regret to say, has not received the attention demanded by its importance, and which on several occasions heretofore I have had the honor to recommend to the Congress.

The admitted impracticability, if not impossibility, of making an accurate and precise survey and demarcation of the boundary line as it is recited in the treaty with Russia under which Alaska was ceded to the United States renders it absolutely requisite for the prevention of international jurisdictional complications that adequate appropriation for a reconnoissance and survey to obtain proper knowledge of the locality and the geographical features of the boundary should be authorized by Congress with as little delay as possible.

Knowledge to be only thus obtained is an essential prerequisite for negotiation for ascertaining a common boundary, or as preliminary to any other mode of settlement.

It is much to be desired that some agreement should be reached with Her Majesty's Government by which the damages to life and property on the Great Lakes may be alleviated by removing or humanely regulating the obstacles to reciprocal assistance to wrecked or stranded vessels.

The act of June 19, 1878, which offers to Canadian vessels free access to our inland waters in aid of wrecked or disabled vessels, has not yet become effective through concurrent action by Canada.

The due protection of our citizens of French origin or descent from claim of military service in the event of their returning to or visiting France has called forth correspondence which was laid before you at the last session.

In the absence of conventional agreement as to naturalization, which is greatly to be desired, this Government sees no occasion to recede from the sound position it has maintained not only with regard to France, but as to all countries with which the United States have not concluded special treaties.

Twice within the last year has the imperial household of Germany been visited by death; and I have hastened to express the sorrow of this people, and their appreciation of the lofty character of the late aged Emperor William, and their sympathy with the heroism under suffering of his son the late Emperor Frederick.

I renew my recommendation of two years ago for the passage of a bill for the refunding to certain German steamship lines of the interest upon tonnage dues illegally exacted.

On the 12th [2d] of April last   I laid before the House of Representatives full information respecting our interests in Samoa; and in the subsequent correspondence on the same subject, which will be laid before you in due course, the history of events in those islands will be found.

In a message accompanying my approval, on the 1st day of October last, of a bill for the exclusion of Chinese laborers, I laid before Congress full information and all correspondence touching the negotiation of the treaty with China concluded at this capital on the 12th day of March, 1888, and which, having been confirmed by the Senate with certain amendments, was rejected by the Chinese Government.   This message contained a recommendation that a sum of money be appropriated as compensation to Chinese subjects who had suffered injuries at the hands of lawless men within our jurisdiction.   Such appropriation having been duly made, the fund awaits reception by the Chinese Government.

It is sincerely hoped that by the cessation of the influx of this class of Chinese subjects, in accordance with the expressed wish of both Governments, a cause of unkind feeling has been permanently removed.

On the 9th of August, 1887, notification was given by the Japanese minister at this capital of the adjournment of the conference for the revision of the treaties of Japan with foreign powers, owing to the objection of his Government to the provision in the draft jurisdictional convention which required the submission of the criminal code of the Empire to the powers in advance of its becoming operative.   This notification was, however, accompanied with an assurance of Japan's intention to continue the work of revision.

Notwithstanding this temporary interruption of negotiations, it is hoped that improvements may soon be secured in the jurisdictional system as respects foreigners in Japan, and relief afforded to that country from the present undue and oppressive foreign control in matters of commerce.

I earnestly recommend that relief be provided for the injuries accidentally caused to Japanese subjects in the island Ikisima by the target practice of one of our vessels.

A diplomatic mission from Korea has been received, and the formal intercourse between the two countries contemplated by the treaty of 1882 is now established.

Legislative provision is hereby recommended to organize and equip consular courts in Korea.

Persia has established diplomatic representation at this capital, and has evinced very great interest in the enterprise and achievements of our citizens. I am therefore hopeful that beneficial commercial relations between the two countries may be brought about.

I announce with sincere regret that Hayti has again become the theater of insurrection, disorder, and bloodshed. The titular government of President Saloman has been forcibly overthrown and he driven out of the country to France, where he has since died.

The tenure of power has been so unstable amid the war of factions that has ensued since the expulsion of President Saloman that no government constituted by the will of the Haytian people has been recognized as administering responsibly the affairs of that country. Our representative has been instructed to abstain from interference between the warring factions, and a vessel of our Navy has been sent to Haytian waters to sustain our minister and for the protection of the persons and property of American citizens.

Due precautions have been taken to enforce our neutrality laws and prevent our territory from becoming the base of military supplies for either of the warring factions.

Under color of a blockade, of which no reasonable notice had been given, and which does not appear to have been efficiently maintained, a seizure of vessels under the American flag has been reported, and in consequence measures to prevent and redress any molestation of our innocent merchantmen have been adopted.

Proclamation was duly made on the 9th day of November, 1887, of the conventional extensions of the treaty of June 3, 1875, with Hawaii, under which relations of such special and beneficent intercourse have been created.

In the vast field of Oriental commerce now unfolded from our Pacific borders no feature presents stronger recommendations for Congressional action than the establishment of communication by submarine telegraph with Honolulu.

The geographical position of the Hawaiian group in relation to our Pacific States creates a natural interdependency and mutuality of interest which our present treaties were intended to foster, and which make close communication a logical and commercial necessity.

The wisdom of concluding a treaty of commercial reciprocity with Mexico has been heretofore stated in my messages to Congress, and the lapse of time and growth of commerce with that close neighbor and sister Republic confirm the judgment so expressed.

The precise relocation of our boundary line is needful, and adequate appropriation is now recommended.

It is with sincere satisfaction that I am enabled to advert to the spirit of good neighborhood and friendly cooperation and conciliation that has marked the correspondence and action of the Mexican authorities in their share of the task of maintaining law and order about the line of our common boundary.

The long-pending boundary dispute between Costa Rica and Nicaragua was referred to my arbitration, and by an award made on the 22d of March last the question has been finally settled to the expressed satisfaction of both of the parties in interest.

The Empire of Brazil, in abolishing the last vestige of slavery among Christian nations, called forth the earnest congratulations of this Government in expression of the cordial sympathies of our people.

The claims of nearly all other countries against Chile growing out of her late war with Bolivia and Peru have been disposed of, either by arbitration or by a lump settlement. Similar claims of our citizens will continue to be urged upon the Chilean Government, and it is hoped will not be subject to further delays.

A comprehensive treaty of amity and commerce with Peru was proclaimed on November 7 last, and it is expected that under its operation mutual prosperity and good understanding will be promoted.

In pursuance of the policy of arbitration, a treaty to settle the claim of Santos, an American citizen, against Ecuador has been concluded under my authority, and will be duly submitted for the approval of the Senate.

Like disposition of the claim of Carlos Butterfield against Denmark and of Van Bokkelen against Hayti will probably be made, and I trust the principle of such settlements may be extended in practice under the approval of the Senate.

Through unforeseen causes, foreign to the will of both Governments, the ratification of the convention of December 5, 1885, with Venezuela, for the rehearing of claims of citizens of the United States under the treaty of 1866, failed of exchange within the term provided, and a supplementary convention, further extending the time for exchange of ratifications and explanatory of an ambiguous provision of the prior convention, now awaits the advice and consent of the Senate.

Although this matter, in the stage referred to, concerns only the concurrent treaty-making power of one branch of Congress, I advert to it in view of the interest repeatedly and conspicuously shown by you in your legislative capacity in favor of a speedy and equitable adjustment of the questions growing out of the discredited judgments of the previous mixed commission of Caracas. With every desire to do justice to the representations of Venezuela in this regard, the time seems to have come to end this matter, and I trust the prompt confirmation by both parties of the supplementary action referred to will avert the need of legislative or other action to prevent the longer withholding of such rights of actual claimants as may be shown to exist.

As authorized by the Congress, preliminary steps have been taken for the assemblage at this capital during the coming year of the representatives of South and Central American States, together with those of

Mexico, Hayti, and San Domingo, to discuss sundry important monetary and commercial topics.

Excepting in those cases where, from reasons of contiguity of territory and the existence of a common border line incapable of being guarded, reciprocal commercial treaties may be found expedient, it is believed that commercial policies inducing freer mutual exchange of products can be most advantageously arranged by independent but cooperative legislation.

In the mode last mentioned the control of our taxation for revenue will be always retained in our own hands unrestricted by conventional agreements with other governments.

In conformity also with Congressional authority, the maritime powers have been invited to confer in Washington in April next upon the practicability of devising uniform rules and measures for the greater security of life and property at sea. A disposition to accept on the part of a number of the powers has already been manifested, and if the cooperation of the nations chiefly interested shall be secured important results may be confidently anticipated.

The act of June 26, 1884, and the acts amendatory thereof, in relation to tonnage duties, have given rise to extended correspondence with foreign nations with whom we have existing treaties of navigation and commerce, and have caused wide and regrettable divergence of opinion in relation to the imposition of the duties referred to. These questions are important, and I shall make them the subject of a special and more detailed communication at the present session.

With the rapid increase of immigration to our shores and the facilities of modern travel, abuses of the generous privileges afforded by our naturalization laws call for their careful revision.

The easy and unguarded manner in which certificates of American citizenship can now be obtained has induced a class, unfortunately large, to avail themselves of the opportunity to become absolved from allegiance to their native land, and yet by a foreign residence to escape any just duty and contribution of service to the country of their proposed adoption. Thus, while evading the duties of citizenship to the United States, they may make prompt claim for its national protection and demand its intervention in their behalf. International complications of a serious nature arise, and the correspondence of the State Department discloses the great number and complexity of the questions which have been raised.

Our laws regulating the issue of passports should be carefully revised, and the institution of a central bureau of registration at the capital is again strongly recommended. By this means full particulars of each case of naturalization in the United States would be secured and properly indexed and recorded, and thus many cases of spurious citizenship would be detected and unjust responsibilities would be avoided.

The reorganization of the consular service is a matter of serious importance to our national interests. The number of existing principal consular offices is believed to be greater than is at all necessary for the conduct of the public business. It need not be our policy to maintain more than a moderate number of principal offices, each supported by a salary sufficient to enable the incumbent to live in comfort, and so distributed as to secure the convenient supervision, through subordinate agencies, of affairs over a considerable district.

I repeat the recommendations heretofore made by me that the appropriations for the maintenance of our diplomatic and consular service should be recast; that the so-called notarial or unofficial fees, which our representatives abroad are now permitted to treat as personal perquisites, should be forbidden; that a system of consular inspection should be instituted, and that a limited number of secretaries of legation at large should be authorized.

Preparations for the centennial celebration, on April 30, 1889, of the inauguration of George Washington as President of the United States, at the city of New York, have been made by a voluntary organization of the citizens of that locality, and believing that an opportunity should be afforded for the expression of the interest felt throughout the country in this event, I respectfully recommend fitting and cooperative action by Congress on behalf of the people of the United States.

The report of the Secretary of the Treasury exhibits in detail the condition of our national finances and the operations of the several branches of the Government related to his Department.

The total ordinary revenues of the Government for the fiscal year ended June 30, 1888, amounted to $379,266,074.76, of which $219,091,173.63 was received from customs duties and $124,296,871.98 from internal-revenue taxes.

The total receipts from all sources exceeded those for the fiscal year ended June 30, 1887, by $7,862,797.10.

The ordinary expenditures of the Government for the fiscal year ending June 30, 1888, were $259,653,958.67, leaving a surplus of $119,612,-116.09.

The decrease in these expenditures as compared with the fiscal year ended June 30, 1887, was $8,278,221.30, notwithstanding the payment of more than $5,000,000 for pensions in excess of what was paid for that purpose in the latter-mentioned year.

The revenues of the Government for the year ending June 30, 1889, ascertained for the quarter ended September 30, 1888, and estimated for the remainder of the time, amount to $377,000,000, and the actual and estimated ordinary expenditures for the same year are $273,000,000, leaving an estimated surplus of $104,000,000.

The estimated receipts for the year ending June 30, 1890, are $377,-000,000, and the estimated ordinary expenditures for the same time are $275,767,488.34, showing a surplus of $101,232,511.66.

The foregoing statements of surplus do not take into account the sum necessary to be expended to meet the requirements of the sinking-fund act, amounting to more than $47,000,000 annually.

The cost of collecting the customs revenues for the last fiscal year was 2.44 per cent; for the year 1885 it was 3.77 per cent.

The excess of internal-revenue taxes collected during the last fiscal year over those collected for the year ended June 30, 1887, was $5,489,-174.26, and the cost of collecting this revenue decreased from 3.4 per cent in 1887 to less than 3.2 per cent for the last year.   The tax collected on oleomargarine was $723,948.04 for the year ending June 30, 1887, and $864,139.88 for the following year.

The requirements of the sinking-fund act have been met for the year ended June 30, 1888, and for the current year also, by the purchase of bonds.   After complying with this law as positively required, and bonds sufficient for that purpose had been bought at a premium, it was not deemed prudent to further expend the surplus in such purchases until the authority to do so should be more explicit.   A resolution, however, having been passed by both Houses of Congress removing all doubt as to Executive authority, daily purchases of bonds were commenced on the 23d day of April, 1888, and have continued until the present time.   By this plan bonds of the Government not yet due have been purchased up to and including the 30th day of November, 1888, amounting to $94,-700,400, the premium paid thereon amounting to $17,508,613.08.

The premium added to the principal of these bonds represents an investment yielding about 2 per cent interest for the time they still had to run, and the saving to the Government represented by the difference between the amount of interest at 2 per cent upon the sum paid for principal and premium and what it would have paid for interest at the rate specified in the bonds if they had run to their maturity is about $27,165,000.

At first sight this would seem to be a profitable and sensible transaction on the part of the Government, but, as suggested by the Secretary of the Treasury, the surplus thus expended for the purchase of bonds was money drawn from the people in excess of any actual need of the Government and was so expended rather than allow it to remain idle in the Treasury.   If this surplus, under the operation of just and equitable laws, had been left in the hands of the people, it would have been worth in their business at least 6 per cent per annum.   Deducting from the amount of interest upon the principal and premium of these bonds for the time they had to run at the rate of 6 per cent the saving of 2 per cent made for the people by the purchase of such bonds, the loss will appear to be $55,760,000.

This calculation would seem to demonstrate that if excessive and unnecessary taxation is continued and the Government is forced to pursue this policy of purchasing its own bonds at the premiums which it will be necessary to pay, the loss to the people will be hundreds of millions of dollars.

Since the purchase of bonds was undertaken as mentioned nearly all that have been offered were at last accepted. It has been made quite apparent that the Government was in danger of being subjected to combinations to raise their price, as appears by the instance cited by the Secretary of the offering of bonds of the par value of only $326,000 so often that the aggregate of the sums demanded for their purchase amounted to more than $19,700,000.

Notwithstanding the large sums paid out in the purchase of bonds, the surplus in the Treasury on the 30th day of November, 1888, was $52,234,610.01, after deducting about $20,000,000 just drawn out for the payment of pensions.

At the close of the fiscal year ended June 30, 1887, there had been coined under the compulsory silver-coinage act $266,988,280 in silver dollars, $55,504,310 of which were in the hands of the people.

On the 30th day of June, 1888, there had been coined $299,708,790; and of this $55,829,303 was in circulation in coin, and $200,387,376 in silver certificates, for the redemption of which silver dollars to that amount were held by the Government.

On the 30th day of November, 1888, $312,570,990 had been coined, $60,970,990 of the silver dollars were actually in circulation, and $237,-418,346 in certificates.

The Secretary recommends the suspension of the further coinage of silver, and in such recommendation I earnestly concur.

For further valuable information and timely recommendations I ask the careful attention of the Congress to the Secretary's report.

The Secretary of War reports that the Army at the date of the last consolidated returns consisted of 2,189 officers and 24,549 enlisted men.

The actual expenditures of the War Department for the fiscal year ended June 30, 1888, amounted to $41,165,107.07, of which sum $9,158,-516.63 was expended for public works, including river and harbor improvements.

"The Board of Ordnance and Fortifications" provided for under the act approved September 22 last was convened October 30, 1888, and plans and specifications for procuring forgings for 8, 10, and 12 inch guns, under provisions of section 4, and also for procuring 12-inch breech-loading mortars, cast iron, hooped with steel, under the provisions of section 5 of the said act, were submitted to the Secretary of War for reference to the board, by the Ordnance Department, on the same date.

These plans and specifications having been promptly approved by the board and the Secretary of War, the necessary authority to publish advertisements inviting proposals in the newspapers throughout the country was granted by the Secretary on November 12, and on November 13 the advertisements were sent out to the different newspapers designated. The bids for the steel forgings are to be opened on December 20, 1888, and for the mortars on December 15, 1888.

A board of ordnance officers was convened at the Watervliet Arsenal on October 4, 1888, to prepare the necessary plans and specifications for the establishment of an army gun factory at that point. The preliminary report of this board, with estimates for shop buildings and officers' quarters, was approved by the Board of Ordnance and Fortifications November 6 and 8. The specifications and form of advertisement and instructions to bidders have been prepared, and advertisements inviting proposals for the excavations for the shop building and for erecting the two sets of officers' quarters have been published. The detailed drawings and specifications for the gun-factory building are well in hand, and will be finished within three or four months, when bids will be invited for the erection of the building. The list of machines, etc., is made out, and it is expected that the plans for the large lathes, etc., will be completed within about four months, and after approval by the Board of Ordnance and Fortifications bids for furnishing the same will be invited. The machines and other fixtures will be completed as soon as the shop is in readiness to receive them, probably about July, 1890.

Under the provisions of the Army bill for the procurement of pneumatic dynamite guns, the necessary specifications are now being prepared, and advertisements for proposals will issue early in December. The guns will probably be of 15 inches caliber and fire a projectile that will carry a charge each of about 500 pounds of explosive gelatine with full-caliber projectiles. The guns will probably be delivered in from six to ten months from the date of the contract, so that all the guns of this class that can be procured under the provisions of the law will be purchased during the year 1889.

I earnestly request that the recommendations contained in the Secretary's report, all of which are, in my opinion, calculated to increase the usefulness and discipline of the Army, may receive the consideration of the Congress. Among these the proposal that there should be provided a plan for the examination of officers to test their fitness for promotion is of the utmost importance. This reform has been before recommended in the reports of the Secretary, and its expediency is so fully demonstrated by the argument he presents in its favor that its adoption should no longer be neglected.

The death of General Sheridan in August last was a national affliction. The Army then lost the grandest of its chiefs. The country lost a brave and experienced soldier, a wise and discreet counselor, and a modest and sensible man. Those who in any manner came within the range of his personal association will never fail to pay deserved and willing homage to his greatness and the glory of his career, but they will cherish with more tender sensibility the loving memory of his simple, generous, and considerate nature.

The Apache Indians, whose removal from their reservation in Arizona followed the capture of those of their number who engaged in a bloody and murderous raid during a part of the years 1885 and 1886, are now held as prisoners of war at Mount Vernon Barracks, in the State of Alabama. They numbered on the 31st day of October, the date of the last report, 83 men, 170 women, 70 boys, and 59 girls; in all, 382 persons. The commanding officer states that they are in good health and contented, and that they are kept employed as fully as is possible in the circumstances. The children, as they arrive at a suitable age, are sent to the Indian schools at Carlisle and Hampton.

Last summer some charitable and kind people asked permission to send two teachers to these Indians for the purpose of instructing the adults as well as such children as should be found there. Such permission was readily granted, accommodations were provided for the teachers, and some portions of the buildings at the barracks were made available for school purposes. The good work contemplated has been commenced, and the teachers engaged are paid by the ladies with whom the plan originated.

I am not at all in sympathy with those benevolent but injudicious people who are constantly insisting that these Indians should be returned to their reservation. Their removal was an absolute necessity if the lives and property of citizens upon the frontier are to be at all regarded by the Government. Their continued restraint at a distance from the scene of their repeated and cruel murders and outrages is still necessary. It is a mistaken philanthropy, every way injurious, which prompts the desire to see these savages returned to their old haunts. They are in their present location as the result of the best judgment of those having official responsibility in the matter, and who are by no means lacking in kind consideration for the Indians. A number of these prisoners have forfeited their lives to outraged law and humanity. Experience has proved that they are dangerous and can not be trusted. This is true not only of those who on the warpath have heretofore actually been guilty of atrocious murder, but of their kindred and friends, who, while they remained upon their reservation, furnished aid and comfort to those absent with bloody intent.

These prisoners should be treated kindly and kept in restraint far from the locality of their former reservation; they should be subjected to efforts calculated to lead to their improvement and the softening of their savage and cruel instincts, but their return to their old home should be persistently resisted.

The Secretary in his report gives a graphic history of these Indians, and recites with painful vividness their bloody deeds and the unhappy failure of the Government to manage them by peaceful means. It will be amazing if a perusal of this history will allow the survival of a desire for the return of these prisoners to their reservation upon sentimental or any other grounds.

The report of the Secretary of the Navy demonstrates very intelligent management in that important Department, and discloses the most satis-factory progress in the work of reconstructing the Navy made during the past year. Of the ships in course of construction five, viz, the *Charleston*, *Baltimore*, *Yorktown*, *Vesuvius*, and the *Petrel*, have in that time been launched and are rapidly approaching completion; and in addition to the above, the *Philadelphia*, the *San Francisco*, the *Newark*, the *Bennington*, the *Concord*, and the Herreshoff torpedo boat are all under con-tract for delivery to the Department during the next year. The progress already made and being made gives good ground for the expectation that these eleven vessels will be incorporated as part of the American Navy within the next twelve months.

The report shows that notwithstanding the large expenditures for new construction and the additional labor they involve the total ordinary or current expenditures of the Department for the three years ending June 30, 1888, are less by more than 20 per cent than such expenditures for the three years ending June 30, 1884.

The various steps which have been taken to improve the business methods of the Department are reviewed by the Secretary. The purchasing of supplies has been consolidated and placed under a responsible bureau head. This has resulted in the curtailment of open purchases, which in the years 1884 and 1885 amounted to over 50 per cent of all the purchases of the Department, to less than 11 per cent; so that at the present time about 90 per cent of the total departmental purchases are made by contract and after competition. As the expenditures on this account exceed an average of $2,000,000 annually, it is evident that an important improvement in the system has been inaugurated and sub-stantial economies introduced.

The report of the Postmaster-General shows a marked increase of busi-ness in every branch of the postal service.

The number of post-offices on July 1, 1888, was 57,376, an increase of 6,124 in three years and of 2,219 for the last fiscal year. The latter-mentioned increase is classified as follows:

New England States	
Middle States	181
Southern States and Indian Territory (41)	1,406
The States and Territories of the Pacific Coast	190
The ten States and Territories of the West and Northwest	435
District of Columbia	2
Total	2,219

Free-delivery offices have increased from 189 in the fiscal year ended June 30, 1887, to 358 in the year ended June 30, 1888.

In the Railway Mail Service there has been an increase in one year of 168 routes, and in the number of miles traveled per annum an increase of 15,795,917.48. The estimated increase of railroad service for the year was 6,000 miles, but the amount of new railroad service actually put on was 12,764.50 miles.

The volume of business in the Money-Order Division, including trans-actions in postal notes, reached the sum of upward of $143,000,000 for the year.

During the past year parcel-post conventions have been concluded with Barbados, the Bahamas, British Honduras, and Mexico, and are now under negotiation with all the Central and South American States. The increase of correspondence with foreign countries during the past three years is gratifying, and is especially notable and exceptional with the Central and South American States and with Mexico. As the greater part of mail matter exchanged with these countries is commercial in its character, this increase is evidence of the improved business relations with them. The practical operation of the parcel-post conventions, so far as negotiated, has served to fulfill the most favorable predictions as to their benefits. In January last a general postal convention was nego-tiated with the Dominion of Canada, which went into operation on March 1, and which practically makes one postal territory of the United States and Canada. Under it merchandise parcels may now be trans-mitted through the mails at fourth-class rates of postage.

It is not possible here to touch even the leading heads of the great postal establishment to illustrate the enormous and rapid growth of its business and the needs for legislative readjustment of much of its machin-ery that it has outgrown. For these and valuable recommendations of the Postmaster-General attention is earnestly invited to his report.

A Department whose revenues have increased from $19,772,000 in 1870 to $52,700,000 in 1888, despite reductions of postage which have enor-mously reduced rates of revenue while greatly increasing its business, demands the careful consideration of the Congress as to all matters sug-gested by those familiar with its operations, and which are calculated to increase its efficiency and usefulness.

A bill proposed by the Postmaster-General was introduced at the last session of the Congress by which a uniform standard in the amount of gross receipts would fix the right of a community to a public building to be erected by the Government for post-office purposes. It was demon-strated that, aside from the public convenience and the promotion of har-mony among citizens, invariably disturbed by change of leasings and of site, it was a measure of the highest economy and of sound business judgment. It was found that the Government was paying in rents at the rate of from 7 to 10 per cent per annum on what the cost of such public buildings would be. A very great advantage resulting from such a law would be the prevention of a large number of bills constantly intro-duced for the erection of public buildings at places, and involving expend-itures not justified by public necessity. I trust that this measure will become a law at the present session of Congress.

Of the total number of postmasters 54,874 are of the fourth class. These, of course, receive no allowances whatever for expenses in the service, and their compensation is fixed by percentages on receipts at their respective offices. This rate of compensation may have been, and probably was, at some time just, but the standard has remained unchanged through the several reductions in the rates of postage. Such reductions have necessarily cut down the compensation of these officials, while it undoubtedly increased the business performed by them. Simple justice requires attention to this subject, to the end that fourth-class postmasters may receive at least an equivalent to that which the law itself, fixing the rate, intended for them.

Another class of postal employees whose condition seems to demand legislation is that of clerks in post-offices, and I call especial attention to the repeated recommendations of the Postmaster-General for their classification. Proper legislation of this character for the relief of carriers in the free-delivery service has been frequent. Provision is made for their promotion; for substitutes for them on vacation; for substitutes for holidays, and limiting their hours of labor. Seven million dollars has been appropriated for the current year to provide for them, though the total number of offices where they are employed is but 358 for the past fiscal year, with an estimated increase for the current year of but 40, while the total appropriation for all clerks in offices throughout the United States is $5,950,00 .

The legislation affecting the relations of the Government with railroads is in need of revision. While for the most part the railroad companies throughout the country have cordially cooperated with the Post-Office Department in rendering excellent service, yet under the law as it stands, while the compensation to them for carrying the mail is limited and regulated, and although railroads are made post-roads by law, there is no authority reposed anywhere to compel the owner of a railroad to take and carry the United States mails. The only alternative provided by act of Congress in case of refusal is for the Postmaster-General to send mail forward by pony express. This is but an illustration of ill-fitting legislation, reasonable and proper at the time of its enactment, but long since outgrown and requiring readjustment.

It is gratifying to note from the carefully prepared statistics accompanying the Postmaster-General's report that notwithstanding the great expansion of the service the rate of expenditure has been lessened and efficiency has been improved in every branch; that fraud and crime have decreased; that losses from the mails have been reduced, and that the number of complaints of the service made to postmasters and to the Department are far less than ever before.

The transactions of the Department of Justice for the fiscal year ended June 30, 1888, are contained in the report of the Attorney-General, as well as a number of valuable recommendations, the most part of which are repetitions of those previously made, and ought to receive consideration.

It is stated in this report that though judgments in civil suits amounting to $552,021.08 were recovered in favor of the Government during the year, only the sum of $132,934 was collected thereon; and that though fines, penalties, and forfeitures were imposed amounting to $541,808.43, only $109,648.42 of that sum was paid on account thereof. These facts may furnish an illustration of the sentiment which extensively prevails that a debt due the Government should cause no inconvenience to the citizen.

It also appears from this report that though prior to March, 1885, there had been but 6 convictions in the Territories of Utah and Idaho under the laws of 1862 and 1882, punishing polygamy and unlawful cohabitation as crimes, there have been since that date nearly 600 convictions under these laws and the statutes of 1887; and the opinion is expressed that under such a firm and vigilant execution of these laws and the advance of ideas opposed to the forbidden practices polygamy within the United States is virtually at an end.

Suits instituted by the Government under the provisions of the act of March 3, 1887, for the termination of the corporations known as the Perpetual Emigrating Fund Company and the Church of Jesus Christ of Latter-day Saints have resulted in a decree favorable to the Government, declaring the charters of these corporations forfeited and escheating their property. Such property, amounting in value to more than $800,000, is in the hands of a receiver pending further proceedings, an appeal having been taken to the Supreme Court of the United States.

In the report of the Secretary of the Interior, which will be laid before you, the condition of the various branches of our domestic affairs connected with that Department and its operations during the past year are fully exhibited. But a brief reference to some of the subjects discussed in this able and interesting report can here be made; but I commend the entire report to the attention of the Congress, and trust that the sensible and valuable recommendations it contains will secure careful consideration.

I can not too strenuously insist upon the importance of proper measures to insure a right disposition of our public lands, not only as a matter of present justice, but in forecast of the consequences to future generations. The broad, rich acres of our agricultural plains have been long preserved by nature to become her untrammeled gift to a people civilized and free, upon which should rest in well-distributed ownership the numerous homes of enlightened, equal, and fraternal citizens. They came to national possession with the warning example in our eyes of the entail of iniquities in landed proprietorship which other countries have permitted and still suffer. We have no excuse for the violation of principles cogently taught by reason and example, nor for the allowance of pretexts which have sometimes exposed our lands to colossal greed. Laws which open a door to fraudulent acquisition, or administration which permits favor to rapacious seizure by a favored few of expanded areas that many should enjoy, are accessory to offenses against our national welfare and humanity not to be too severely condemned or punished.

It is gratifying to know that something has been done at last to redress the injuries to our people and check the perilous tendency of the reckless waste of the national domain. That over 80,000,000 acres have been arrested from illegal usurpation, improvident grants, and fraudulent entries and claims, to be taken for the homesteads of honest industry—although less than the greater areas thus unjustly lost—must afford a profound gratification to right-feeling citizens, as it is a recompense for the labors and struggles of the recovery. Our dear experience ought sufficiently to urge the speedy enactment of measures of legislation which will confine the future disposition of our remaining agricultural lands to the uses of actual husbandry and genuine homes.

Nor should our vast tracts of so-called desert lands be yielded up to the monopoly of corporations or grasping individuals, as appears to be much the tendency under the existing statute. These lands require but the supply of water to become fertile and productive. It is a problem of great moment how most wisely for the public good that factor shall be furnished. I can not but think it perilous to suffer either these lands or the sources of their irrigation to fall into the hands of monopolies, which by such means may exercise lordship over the areas dependent on their treatment for productiveness. Already steps have been taken to secure accurate and scientific information of the conditions, which is the prime basis of intelligent action. Until this shall be gained the course of wisdom appears clearly to lie in a suspension of further disposal, which only promises to create rights antagonistic to the common interest. No harm can follow this cautionary conduct. The land will remain, and the public good presents no demand for hasty dispossession of national ownership and control.

I commend also the recommendations that appropriate measures be taken to complete the adjustment of the various grants made to the States for internal improvements and of swamp and overflowed lands, as well as to adjudicate and finally determine the validity and extent of the numerous private land claims. All these are elements of great injustice and peril to the settlers upon the localities affected; and now that their existence can not be avoided, no duty is more pressing than to fix as soon as possible their bounds and terminate the threats of trouble which arise from uncertainty.

The condition of our Indian population continues to improve and the proofs multiply that the transforming change, so much to be desired, which shall substitute for barbarism enlightenment and civilizing education, is in favorable progress. Our relations with these people during the year have been disturbed by no serious disorders, but rather marked by a better realization of their true interests and increasing confidence and good will. These conditions testify to the value of the higher tone of consideration and humanity which has governed the later methods of dealing with them, and commend its continued observance.

Allotments in severalty have been made on some reservations until all those entitled to land thereon have had their shares assigned, and the work is still continued. In directing the execution of this duty I have not aimed so much at rapid dispatch as to secure just and fair arrangements which shall best conduce to the objects of the law by producing satisfaction with the results of the allotments made. No measure of general effect has ever been entered on from which more may be fairly hoped if it shall be discreetly administered. It proffers opportunity and inducement to that independence of spirit and life which the Indian peculiarly needs, while at the same time the inalienability of title affords security against the risks his inexperience of affairs or weakness of character may expose him to in dealing with others. Whenever begun upon any reservation it should be made complete, so that all are brought to the same condition, and as soon as possible community in lands should cease by opening such as remain unallotted to settlement. Contact with the ways of industrious and successful farmers will perhaps add a healthy emulation which will both instruct and stimulate.

But no agency for the amelioration of this people appears to me so promising as the extension, urged by the Secretary, of such complete facilities of education as shall at the earliest possible day embrace all teachable Indian youth, of both sexes, and retain them with a kindly and beneficent hold until their characters are formed and their faculties and dispositions trained to the sure pursuit of some form of useful industry. Capacity of the Indian no longer needs demonstration. It is established. It remains to make the most of it, and when that shall be done the curse will be lifted, the Indian race saved, and the sin of their oppression redeemed. The time of its accomplishment depends upon the spirit and justice with which it shall be prosecuted. It can not be too soon for the Indian nor for the interests and good name of the nation.

The average attendance of Indian pupils on the schools increased by over 900 during the year, and the total enrollment reached 15,212. The cost of maintenance was not materially raised. The number of teachable Indian youth is now estimated at 40,000, or nearly three times the enrollment of the schools. It is believed the obstacles in the way of instructing are all surmountable, and that the necessary expenditure would be a measure of economy.

The Sioux tribes on the great reservation of Dakota refused to assent to the act passed by the Congress at its last session for opening a portion of their lands to settlement, notwithstanding modification of the terms was suggested which met most of their objections. Their demand is for immediate payment of the full price of $1.25 per acre for the entire body of land the occupancy of which they are asked to relinquish.

The manner of submission insured their fair understanding of the law, and their action was undoubtedly as thoroughly intelligent as their capacity admitted. It is at least gratifying that no reproach of over-reaching can in any manner lie against the Government, however advisable the favorable completion of the negotiation may have been esteemed.

I concur in the suggestions of the Secretary regarding the Turtle Mountain Indians, the two reservations in California, and the Crees. They should, in my opinion, receive immediate attention.

The number of pensioners added to the rolls during the fiscal year ended June 30, 1888, is 60,252, and increase of pensions was granted in 45,716 cases. The names of 15,730 pensioners were dropped from the rolls during the year from various causes, and at the close of the year the number of persons of all classes receiving pensions was 452,557. Of these there were 806 survivors of the War of 1812, 10,787 widows of those who served in that war, 16,060 soldiers of the Mexican War, and 5,104 widows of said soldiers.

One hundred and two different rates of pensions are paid to these beneficiaries, ranging from $2 to $416.66 per month.

The amount paid for pensions during the fiscal year was $78,775,861.92, being an increase over the preceding year of $5,308,280.22. The expenses attending the maintenance and operation of the Pension Bureau during that period was $3,262,524.67, making the entire expenditures of the Bureau $82,038,386.57, being 21½ per cent of the gross income and nearly 31 per cent of the total expenditures of the Government during the year.

I am thoroughly convinced that our general pension laws should be revised and adjusted to meet as far as possible, in the light of our experience, all meritorious cases. The fact that 102 different rates of pensions are paid can not, in my opinion, be made consistent with justice to the pensioners or to the Government; and the numerous private pension bills that are passed, predicated upon the imperfection of general laws, while they increase in many cases existing inequality and injustice, lend additional force to the recommendation for a revision of the general laws on this subject.

The laxity of ideas prevailing among a large number of our people regarding pensions is becoming every day more marked. The principles upon which they should be granted are in danger of being altogether ignored, and already pensions are often claimed because the applicants are as much entitled as other successful applicants, rather than upon any disability reasonably attributable to military service. If the establishment of vicious precedents be continued, if the granting of pensions be not divorced from partisan and other unworthy and irrelevant considerations, and if the honorable name of veteran unfairly becomes by these means but another term for one who constantly clamors for the aid of the Government, there is danger that injury will be done to the fame and patriotism of many whom our citizens all delight to honor, and that a prejudice will be aroused unjust to meritorious applicants for pensions.

The Department of Agriculture has continued, with a good measure of success, its efforts to develop the processes, enlarge the results, and augment the profits of American husbandry. It has collected and distributed practical information, introduced and tested new plants, checked the spread of contagious diseases of farm animals, resisted the advance of noxious insects and destructive fungous growths, and sought to secure to agricultural labor the highest reward of effort and the fullest immunity from loss. Its records of the year show that the season of 1888 has been one of medium production. A generous supply of the demands of consumption has been assured, and a surplus for exportation, moderate in certain products and bountiful in others, will prove a benefaction alike to buyer and grower.

Four years ago it was found that the great cattle industry of the country was endangered, and those engaged in it were alarmed at the rapid extension of the European lung plague of pleuro-pneumonia. Serious outbreaks existed in Illinois, Missouri, and Kentucky, and in Tennessee animals affected were held in quarantine. Five counties in New York and from one to four counties in each of the States of New Jersey, Pennsylvania, Delaware, and Maryland were almost equally affected.

With this great danger upon us and with the contagion already in the channels of commerce, with the enormous direct and indirect losses already being caused by it, and when only prompt and energetic action could be successful, there were in none of these States any laws authorizing this Department to eradicate the malady or giving the State officials power to cooperate with it for this purpose. The Department even lacked both the requisite appropriation and authority.

By securing State cooperation in connection with authority from Congress the work of eradication has been pressed successfully, and this dreaded disease has been extirpated from the Western States and also from the Eastern States, with the exception of a few restricted areas, which are still under supervision. The danger has thus been removed, and trade and commerce have been freed from the vexatious State restrictions which were deemed necessary for a time.

During the past four years the process of diffusion, as applied to the manufacture of sugar from sorghum and sugar cane, has been introduced into this country and fully perfected by the experiments carried on by the Department of Agriculture. This process is now universally considered to be the most economical one, and it is through it that the sorghum-sugar industry has been established upon a firm basis and the road to its future success opened. The adoption of this diffusion process is also extending in Louisiana and other sugar-producing parts of the country, and will doubtless soon be the only method employed for the extraction of sugar from the cane.

An exhaustive study has also within the same period been undertaken of the subject of food adulteration and the best analytical methods for detecting it. A part of the results of this work has already been published by the Department, which, with the matter in course of preparation, will make the most complete treatise on that subject that has ever been published in any country.

The Department seeks a progressive development. It would combine the discoveries of science with the economics and amelioration of rural practice. A supervision of the endowed experimental-station system recently provided for is a proper function of the Department, and is now in operation. This supervision is very important, and should be wisely and vigilantly directed, to the end that the pecuniary aid of the Government in favor of intelligent agriculture should be so applied as to result in the general good and to the benefit of all our people, thus justifying the appropriations made from the public Treasury.

The adjustment of the relations between the Government and the railroad companies which have received land grants and the guaranty of the public credit in aid of the construction of their roads should receive early attention. The report of a majority of the commissioners appointed to examine the affairs and indebtedness of these roads, in which they favor an extension of the time for the payment of such indebtedness in at least one case where the corporation appears to be able to comply with well-guarded and exact terms of such extension, and the reenforcement of their opinion by gentlemen of undoubted business judgment and experience, appointed to protect the interests of the Government as directors of said corporation, may well lead to the belief that such an extension would be to the advantage of the Government.

The subject should be treated as a business proposition with a view to a final realization of its indebtedness by the Government, rather than as a question to be decided upon prejudice or by way of punishment for previous wrongdoing.

The report of the Commissioners of the District of Columbia, with its accompanying documents, gives in detail the operations of the several departments of the District government, and furnishes evidence that the financial affairs of the District are at present in such satisfactory condition as to justify the Commissioners in submitting to the Congress estimates for desirable and needed improvements.

The Commissioners recommend certain legislation which in their opinion is necessary to advance the interests of the District.

I invite your special attention to their request for such legislation as will enable the Commissioners without delay to collect, digest, and properly arrange the laws by which the District is governed, and which are now embraced in several collections, making them available only with great difficulty and labor. The suggestions they make touching desir-able amendments to the laws relating to licenses granted for carrying on the retail traffic in spirituous liquors, to the observance of Sunday, to the proper assessment and collection of taxes, to the speedy punishment of minor offenders, and to the management and control of the reformatory and charitable institutions supported by Congressional appropriations are commended to careful consideration.

I again call attention to the present inconvenience and the danger to life and property attending the operation of steam railroads through and across the public streets and roads of the District. The propriety of such legislation as will properly guard the use of these railroads and better secure the convenience and safety of citizens is manifest.

The consciousness that I have presented but an imperfect statement of the condition of our country and its wants occasions no fear that any-thing omitted is not known and appreciated by the Congress, upon whom rests the responsibility of intelligent legislation in behalf of a great nation and a confiding people.

As public servants we shall do our duty well if we constantly guard the rectitude of our intentions, maintain unsullied our love of country, and with unselfish purpose strive for the public good.

Benjamin Harrison

March 4, 1889 to March 4, 1893

FIRST ANNUAL MESSAGE.

EXECUTIVE MANSION,
Washington, December 3, 1889.

To the Senate and House of Representatives:

There are few transactions in the administration of the Government that are even temporarily held in the confidence of those charged with the conduct of the public business.   Every step taken is under the observation of an intelligent and watchful people.   The state of the Union is known from day to day, and suggestions as to needed legislation find an earlier voice than that which speaks in these annual communications of the President to Congress.

Good will and cordiality have characterized our relations and correspondence with other governments, and the year just closed leaves few international questions of importance remaining unadjusted.   No obstacle is believed to exist that can long postpone the consideration and adjustment of the still pending questions upon satisfactory and honorable terms.   The dealings of this Government with other states have been and should always be marked by frankness and sincerity, our purposes avowed, and our methods free from intrigue.   This course has borne rich fruit in the past, and it is our duty as a nation to preserve the heritage of good repute which a century of right dealing with foreign governments has secured to us.

It is a matter of high significance and no less of congratulation that the first year of the second century of our constitutional existence finds as honored guests within our borders the representatives of all the independent States of North and South America met together in earnest conference touching the best methods of perpetuating and expanding the relations of mutual interest and friendliness existing among them.   That the opportunity thus afforded for promoting closer international relations and the increased prosperity of the States represented will be used for the mutual good of all I can not permit myself to doubt.   Our people will await with interest and confidence the results to flow from so auspi-cious a meeting of allied and in large part identical interests.

The recommendations of this international conference of enlightened statesmen will doubtless have the considerate attention of Congress and its cooperation in the removal of unnecessary barriers to beneficial intercourse between the nations of America.   But while the commercial results which it is hoped will follow this conference are worthy of pursuit and of the great interests they have excited, it is believed that the crowning benefit will be found in the better securities which may be devised for the maintenance of peace among all American nations and the settlement of all contentions by methods that a Christian civilization can approve.   While viewing with interest our national resources and products, the delegates will, I am sure, find a higher satisfaction in the evidences of unselfish friendship which everywhere attend their intercourse with our people.

Another international conference having great possibilities for good has lately assembled and is now in session in this capital. An invitation was extended by the Government, under the act of Congress of July 9, 1888, to all maritime nations to send delegates to confer touching the revision and amendment of the rules and regulations governing vessels at sea and to adopt a uniform system of marine signals. The response to this invitation has been very general and very cordial. Delegates from twenty-six nations are present in the conference, and they have entered upon their useful work with great zeal and with an evident appreciation of its importance. So far as the agreement to be reached may require legislation to give it effect, the cooperation of Congress is confidently relied upon.

It is an interesting, if not, indeed, an unprecedented, fact that the two international conferences have brought together here the accredited representatives of thirty-three nations.

Bolivia, Ecuador, and Honduras are now represented by resident envoys of the plenipotentiary grade. All the States of the American system now maintain diplomatic representation at this capital.

In this connection it may be noted that all the nations of the Western Hemisphere, with one exception, send to Washington envoys extraordinary and ministers plenipotentiary, being the highest grade accredited to this Government. The United States, on the contrary, sends envoys of lower grades to some of our sister Republics. Our representative in Paraguay and Uruguay is a minister resident, while to Bolivia we send a minister resident and consul-general. In view of the importance of our relations with the States of the American system, our diplomatic agents in those countries should be of the uniform rank of envoy extraordinary and minister plenipotentiary. Certain missions were so elevated by the last Congress with happy effect, and I recommend the completion of the reform thus begun, with the inclusion also of Hawaii and Hayti, in view of their relations to the American system of states.

I also recommend that timely provision be made for extending to Hawaii an invitation to be represented in the international conference now sitting at this capital.

Our relations with China have the attentive consideration which their magnitude and interest demand. The failure of the treaty negotiated under the Administration of my predecessor for the further and more complete restriction of Chinese labor immigration, and with it the legislation of the last session of Congress dependent thereon, leaves some questions open which Congress should now approach in that wise and just spirit which should characterize the relations of two great and friendly powers. While our supreme interests demand the exclusion of a laboring element which experience has shown to be incompatible with our social life, all steps to compass this imperative need should be accompanied with a recognition of the claim of those strangers now lawfully among us to humane and just treatment.

The accession of the young Emperor of China marks, we may hope, an era of progress and prosperity for the great country over which he is called to rule.

The present state of affairs in respect to the Samoan Islands is encouraging. The conference which was held in this city in the summer of 1887 between the representatives of the United States, Germany, and Great Britain having been adjourned because of the persistent divergence of views which was developed in its deliberations, the subsequent course of events in the islands gave rise to questions of a serious character. On the 4th of February last the German minister at this capital, in behalf of his Government, proposed a resumption of the conference at Berlin. This proposition was accepted, as Congress in February last was informed.

Pursuant to the understanding thus reached, commissioners were appointed by me, by and with the advice and consent of the Senate, who proceeded to Berlin, where the conference was renewed. The deliberations extended through several weeks, and resulted in the conclusion of a treaty which will be submitted to the Senate for its approval. I trust that the efforts which have been made to effect an adjustment of this question will be productive of the permanent establishment of law and order in Samoa upon the basis of the maintenance of the rights and interests of the natives as well as of the treaty powers.

The questions which have arisen during the past few years between Great Britain and the United States are in abeyance or in course of amicable adjustment.

On the part of the government of the Dominion of Canada an effort has been apparent during the season just ended to administer the laws and regulations applicable to the fisheries with as little occasion for friction as was possible, and the temperate representations of this Government in respect of cases of undue hardship or of harsh interpretations have been in most cases met with measures of transitory relief. It is trusted that the attainment of our just rights under existing treaties and in virtue of the concurrent legislation of the two contiguous countries will not be long deferred and that all existing causes of difference may be equitably adjusted.

I recommend that provision be made by an international agreement for visibly marking the water boundary between the United States and Canada in the narrow channels that join the Great Lakes. The conventional line therein traced by the northwestern boundary survey years ago is not in all cases readily ascertainable for the settlement of jurisdictional questions.

A just and acceptable enlargement of the list of offenses for which extradition may be claimed and granted is most desirable between this country and Great Britain. The territory of neither should become a secure harbor for the evil doers of the other through any avoidable short-coming in this regard. A new treaty on this subject between the two powers has been recently negotiated and will soon be laid before the Senate.

The importance of the commerce of Cuba and Puerto Rico with the United States, their nearest and principal market, justifies the expectation that the existing relations may be beneficially expanded. The impediments resulting from varying dues on navigation and from the vexatious treatment of our vessels on merely technical grounds of complaint in West India ports should be removed.

The progress toward an adjustment of pending claims between the United States and Spain is not as rapid as could be desired.

Questions affecting American interests in connection with railways constructed and operated by our citizens in Peru have claimed the attention of this Government. It is urged that other governments in pressing Peru to the payment of their claims have disregarded the property rights of American citizens. The matter will be carefully investigated with a view to securing a proper and equitable adjustment.

A similar issue is now pending with Portugal. The Delagoa Bay Railway, in Africa, was constructed under a concession by Portugal to an American citizen. When nearly completed the road was seized by the agents of the Portuguese Government. Formal protest has been made through our minister at Lisbon against this act, and no proper effort will be spared to secure proper relief.

In pursuance of the charter granted by Congress and under the terms of its contract with the Government of Nicaragua the Interoceanic Canal Company has begun the construction of the important waterway between the two oceans which its organization contemplates. Grave complications for a time seemed imminent, in view of a supposed conflict of jurisdiction between Nicaragua and Costa Rica in regard to the accessory privileges to be conceded by the latter Republic toward the construction of works on the San Juan River, of which the right bank is Costa Rican territory. I am happy to learn that a friendly arrangement has been effected between the two nations. This Government has held itself ready to promote in every,proper way the adjustment of all questions that might present obstacles to the completion of a work of such transcendent importance to the commerce of this country, and, indeed, to the commercial interests of the world.

The traditional good feeling between this country and the French Republic has received additional testimony in the participation of our Government and people in the international exposition held at Paris during the past summer. The success of our exhibitors has been gratifying. The report of the commission will be laid before Congress in due season.

This Government has accepted, under proper reserve as to its policy in foreign territories, the invitation of the Government of Belgium to take part in an international congress, which opened at Brussels on the 16th of November, for the purpose of devising measures to promote the abolition of the slave trade in Africa and to prevent the shipment of slaves by sea. Our interest in the extinction of this crime against humanity in the regions where it yet survives has been increased by the results of emancipation within our own borders.

With Germany the most cordial relations continue. The questions arising from the return to the Empire of Germans naturalized in this country are considered and disposed of in a temperate spirit to the entire satisfaction of both Governments.

It is a source of great satisfaction that the internal disturbances of the Republic of Hayti are at last happily ended, and that an apparently stable government has been constituted. It has been duly recognized by the United States.

A mixed commission is now in session in this capital for the settlement of long-standing claims against the Republic of Venezuela, and it is hoped that a satisfactory conclusion will be speedily reached. This Government has not hesitated to express its earnest desire that the boundary dispute now pending between Great Britain and Venezuela may be adjusted amicably and in strict accordance with the historic title of the parties.

The advancement of the Empire of Japan has been evidenced by the recent promulgation of a new constitution, containing valuable guaranties of liberty and providing for a responsible ministry to conduct the Government.

It is earnestly recommended that our judicial rights and processes in Korea be established on a firm basis by providing the machinery necessary to carry out treaty stipulations in that regard.

The friendliness of the Persian Government continues to be shown by its generous treatment of Americans engaged in missionary labors and by the cordial disposition of the Shah to encourage the enterprise of our citizens in the development of Persian resources.

A discussion is in progress touching the jurisdictional treaty rights of the United States in Turkey. An earnest effort will be made to define those rights to the satisfaction of both Governments.

Questions continue to arise in our relations with several countries in respect to the rights of naturalized citizens. Especially is this the case with France, Italy, Russia, and Turkey, and to a less extent with Switzerland. From time to time earnest efforts have been made to regulate this subject by conventions with those countries. An improper use of naturalization should not be permitted, but it is most important that those who have been duly naturalized should everywhere be accorded recognition of the rights pertaining to the citizenship of the country of their adoption. The appropriateness of special conventions for that purpose is recognized in treaties which this Government has concluded with a number of European States, and it is advisable that the difficulties which now arise in our relations with other countries on the same subject should be similarly adjusted.

The recent revolution in Brazil in favor of the establishment of a republican form of government is an event of great interest to the United States. Our minister at Rio de Janeiro was at once instructed to maintain friendly diplomatic relations with the Provisional Government, and the Brazilian representatives at this capital were instructed by the Provisional Government to continue their functions. Our friendly intercourse with Brazil has therefore suffered no interruption.

Our minister has been further instructed to extend on the part of this Government a formal and cordial recognition of the new Republic so soon as the majority of the people of Brazil shall have signified their assent to its establishment and maintenance.

Within our own borders a general condition of prosperity prevails. The harvests of the last summer were exceptionally abundant, and the trade conditions now prevailing seem to promise a successful season to the merchant and the manufacturer and general employment to our working people.

The report of the Secretary of the Treasury for the fiscal year ending June 30, 1889, has been prepared and will be presented to Congress. It presents with clearness the fiscal operations of the Government, and I avail myself of it to obtain some facts for use here.

The aggregate receipts from all sources for the year were $387,050,-058.84, derived as follows:

From customs	$223,832,741.69
From internal revenue	130,881,513.92
From miscellaneous sources	32,335,803.23

The ordinary expenditures for the same period were $281,996,615.60, and the total expenditures, including the sinking fund, were $329,579,-929.25. The excess of receipts over expenditures was, after providing for the sinking fund, $57,470,129.59.

For the current fiscal year the total revenues, actual and estimated are $385,000,000, and the ordinary expenditures, actual and estimated, are $293,000,000, making with the sinking fund a total expenditure of $341,321,116.99, leaving an estimated surplus of $43,678,883.01.

During the fiscal year there was applied to the purchase of bonds, in addition to those for the sinking fund, $90,456,172.35, and during the first quarter of the current year the sum of $37,838,937.77, all of which were credited to the sinking fund. The revenues for the fiscal year ending June 30, 1891, are estimated by the Treasury Department at $385,000,000, and the expenditures for the same period, including the sinking fund, at $341,430,477.70. This shows an estimated surplus for that year of $43,569,522.30, which is more likely to be increased than reduced when the actual transactions are written up.

The existence of so large an actual and anticipated surplus should have he immediate attention of Congress, with a view to reducing the receipts of the Treasury to the needs of the Government as closely as may be. The collection of moneys not needed for public uses imposes an unnecessary burden upon our people, and the presence of so large a surplus in the public vaults is a disturbing element in the conduct of private business. It has called into use expedients for putting it into circulation of very questionable propriety. We should not collect revenue for the purpose of anticipating our bonds beyond the requirements of the sinking fund, but any unappropriated surplus in the Treasury should be so used, as there is no other lawful way of returning the money to circulation, and the profit realized by the Government offers a substantial advantage.

The loaning of public funds to the banks without interest upon the security of Government bonds I regard as an unauthorized and dangerous expedient. It results in a temporary and unnatural increase of the banking capital of favored localities and compels a cautious and gradual recall of the deposits to avoid injury to the commercial interests. It is not to be expected that the banks having these deposits will sell their bonds to the Treasury so long as the present highly beneficial arrangement is continued. They now practically get interest both upon the bonds and their proceeds. No further use should be made of this method of getting the surplus into circulation, and the deposits now outstanding should be gradually withdrawn and applied to the purchase of bonds. It is fortunate that such a use can be made of the existing surplus, and for some time to come of any casual surplus that may exist after Congress has taken the necessary steps for a reduction of the revenue. Such legislation should be promptly but very considerately enacted.

I recommend a revision of our tariff law both in its administrative features and in the schedules. The need of the former is generally conceded, and an agreement upon the evils and inconveniences to be remedied and the best methods for their correction will probably not be difficult. Uniformity of valuation at all our ports is essential, and effective measures should be taken to secure it. It is equally desirable that questions affecting rates and classifications should be promptly decided.

The preparation of a new schedule of customs duties is a matter of great delicacy because of its direct effect upon the business of the country, and of great difficulty by reason of the wide divergence of opinion as to the objects that may properly be promoted by such legislation. Some disturbance of business may perhaps result from the consideration of this subject by Congress, but this temporary ill effect will be reduced to the minimum by prompt action and by the assurance which the country already enjoys that any necessary changes will be so made as not to impair the just and reasonable protection of our home industries. The inequalities of the law should be adjusted, but the protective principle should be maintained and fairly applied to the products of our farms as well as of our shops. These duties necessarily have relation to other things besides the public revenues. We can not limit their effects by fixing our eyes on the public Treasury alone. They have a direct relation to home production, to work, to wages, and to the commercial independence of our country, and the wise and patriotic legislator should enlarge the field of his vision to include all of these. The necessary reduction in our public revenues can, I am sure, be made without making the smaller burden more onerous than the larger by reason of the disabilities and limitations which the process of reduction puts upon both capital and labor. The free list can very safely be extended by placing thereon articles that do not offer injurious competition to such domestic products as our home labor can supply. The removal of the internal tax upon tobacco would relieve an important agricultural product from a burden which was imposed only because our revenue from customs duties was insufficient for the public needs. If safe provision against fraud can be devised, the removal of the tax upon spirits used in the arts and in manufactures would also offer an unobjectionable method of reducing the surplus.

A table presented by the Secretary of the Treasury showing the amount of money of all kinds in circulation each year from 1878 to the present time is of interest. It appears that the amount of national-bank notes in circulation has decreased during that period $114,109,729, of which $37,799,229 is chargeable to the last year. The withdrawal of bank circulation will necessarily continue under existing conditions. It is probable that the adoption of the suggestions made by the Comptroller of the Currency, namely, that the minimum deposit of bonds for the establishment of banks be reduced and that an issue of notes to the par value of the bonds be allowed, would help to maintain the bank circulation. But while this withdrawal of bank notes has been going on there has been a large increase in the amount of gold and silver coin in circulation and in the issues of gold and silver certificates.

The total amount of money of all kinds in circulation on March 1 1878, was $805,793,807, while on October 1, 1889, the total was $1,405,-018,000. There was an increase of $293,417,552 in gold coin, of $57,554,100 in standard silver dollars, of $72,311,249 in gold certificates, of $276,619,715 in silver certificates, and of $14,073,787 in United States notes, making a total of $713,976,403. There was during the same period a decrease of $114,109,729 in bank circulation and of $642,481 in subsidiary silver. The net increase was $599,224,193. The circulation per capita has increased about $5 during the time covered by the table referred to.

The total coinage of silver dollars was on November 1, 1889, $343,-638,001, of which $283,539,521 were in the Treasury vaults and $60,-098,480 were in circulation. Of the amount in the vaults $277,319,944 were represented by outstanding silver certificates, leaving $6,219,577 not in circulation and not represented by certificates.

The law requiring the purchase by the Treasury of $2,000,000 worth of silver bullion each month, to be coined into silver dollars of 412½ grains, has been observed by the Department, but neither the present Secretary nor any of his predecessors has deemed it safe to exercise the discretion given by law to increase the monthly purchases to $4,000,000. When the law was enacted (February 28, 1878) the price of silver in the market was $1.204 per ounce, making the bullion value of the dollar 93 cents. Since that time the price has fallen as low as 91.2 cents per ounce, reducing the bullion value of the dollar to 70.6 cents. Within the last few months the market price has somewhat advanced, and on the 1st day of November last the bullion value of the silver dollar was 72 cents.

The evil anticipations which have accompanied the coinage and use of the silver dollar have not been realized. As a coin it has not had general use, and the public Treasury has been compelled to store it. But this is manifestly owing to the fact that its paper representative is more convenient. The general acceptance and the use of the silver certificate show that silver has not been otherwise discredited. Some favorable conditions have contributed to maintain this practical equality in their commercial use between the gold and silver dollars; but some of these are trade conditions that statutory enactments do not control and of the continuance of which we can not be certain.

I think it is clear that if we should make the coinage of silver at the present ratio free we must expect that the difference in the bullion values of the gold and silver dollars will be taken account of in commercial transactions; and I fear the same result would follow any considerable increase of the present rate of coinage. Such a result would be discreditable to our financial management and disastrous to all business interests. We should not tread the dangerous edge of such a peril. And, indeed, nothing more harmful could happen to the silver interests. Any safe legislation upon this subject must secure the equality of the two coins in their commercial uses.

I have always been an advocate of the use of silver in our currency. We are large producers of that metal, and should not discredit it. To the plan which will be presented by the Secretary of the Treasury for the issuance of notes or certificates upon the deposit of silver bullion at its market value I have been able to give only a hasty examination, owing to the press of other matters and to the fact that it has been so recently formulated. The details of such a law require careful consideration, but the general plan suggested by him seems to satisfy the purpose—to continue the use of silver in connection with our currency and at the same time to obviate the danger of which I have spoken. At a later day I may communicate further with Congress upon this subject.

The enforcement of the Chinese exclusion act has been found to be very difficult on the northwestern frontier. Chinamen landing at Victoria find it easy to pass our border, owing to the impossibility with the force at the command of the customs officers of guarding so long an inland line. The Secretary of the Treasury has authorized the employment of additional officers, who will be assigned to this duty, and every effort will be made to enforce the law. The Dominion exacts a head tax of $50 for each Chinaman landed, and when these persons, in fraud of our law, cross into our territory and are apprehended our officers do not know what to do with them, as the Dominion authorities will not suffer them to be sent back without a second payment of the tax. An effort will be made to reach an understanding that will remove this difficulty.

The proclamation required by section 3 of the act of March 2, 1889, relating to the killing of seals and other fur-bearing animals, was issued by me on the 21st day of March, and a revenue vessel was dispatched to enforce the laws and protect the interests of the United States. The establishment of a refuge station at Point Barrow, as directed by Congress, was successfully accomplished.

Judged by modern standards, we are practically without coast defenses. Many of the structures we have would enhance rather than diminish the perils of their garrisons if subjected to the fire of improved guns, and very few are so located as to give full effect to the greater range of such guns as we are now making for coast-defense uses. This general subject has had consideration in Congress for some years, and the appropriation for the construction of large rifled guns made one year ago was, I am sure, the expression of a purpose to provide suitable works in which these guns might be mounted. An appropriation now made for that purpose would not advance the completion of the works beyond our ability to supply them with fairly effective guns.

The security of our coast cities against foreign attacks should not rest altogether in the friendly disposition of other nations. There should be a second line wholly in our own keeping. I very urgently recommend an appropriation at this session for the construction of such works in our most exposed harbors.

I approve the suggestion of the Secretary of War that provision be made for encamping companies of the National Guard in our coast works for a specified time each year and for their training in the use of heavy guns. His suggestion that an increase of the artillery force of the Army is desirable is also, in this connection, commended to the consideration of Congress.

The improvement of our important rivers and harbors should be promoted by the necessary appropriations. Care should be taken that the Government is not committed to the prosecution of works not of public and general advantage and that the relative usefulness of works of that class is not overlooked. So far as this work can ever be said to be completed, I do not doubt that the end would be sooner and more economically reached if fewer separate works were undertaken at the same time, and those selected for their greater general interest were more rapidly pushed to completion. A work once considerably begun should not be subjected to the risks and deterioration which interrupted or insufficient appropriations necessarily occasion.

The assault made by David S. Terry upon the person of Justice Field, of the Supreme Court of the United States, at Lathrop, Cal., in August last, and the killing of the assailant by a deputy United States marshal who had been deputed to accompany Justice Field and to protect him from anticipated violence at the hands of Terry, in connection with the legal proceedings which have followed, suggest questions which, in my judgment, are worthy of the attention of Congress.

I recommend that more definite provision be made by law not only for the protection of Federal officers, but for a full trial of such cases in the United States courts. In recommending such legislation I do not at all impeach either the general adequacy of the provision made by the State laws for the protection of all citizens or the general good disposition of those charged with the execution of such laws to give protection to the officers of the United States. The duty of protecting its officers, as such, and of punishing those who assault them on account of their official acts should not be devolved expressly or by acquiescence upon the local authorities.

Events which have been brought to my attention happening in other parts of the country have also suggested the propriety of extending by legislation fuller protection to those who may be called as witnesses in the courts of the United States. The law compels those who are supposed to have knowledge of public offenses to attend upon our courts and grand juries and to give evidence. There is a manifest resulting duty that these witnesses shall be protected from injury on account of their testimony. The investigations of criminal offenses are often rendered futile and the punishment of crime impossible by the intimidation of witnesses.

The necessity of providing some more speedy method for disposing of the cases which now come for final adjudication to the Supreme Court becomes every year more apparent and urgent. The plan of providing some intermediate courts having final appellate jurisdiction of certain classes of questions and cases has, I think, received a more general approval from the bench and bar of the country than any other. Without attempting to discuss details, I recommend that provision be made for the establishment of such courts.

The salaries of the judges of the district courts in many of the districts are, in my judgment, inadequate. I recommend that all such salaries now below $5,000 per annum be increased to that amount. It is quite true that the amount of labor performed by these judges is very unequal, but as they can not properly engage in other pursuits to supplement their incomes the salary should be such in all cases as to provide an independent and comfortable support.

Earnest attention should be given by Congress to a consideration of the question how far the restraint of those combinations of capital commonly called "trusts" is matter of Federal jurisdiction. When organized, as they often are, to crush out all healthy competition and to monopolize the production or sale of an article of commerce and general necessity, they are dangerous conspiracies against the public good, and should be made the subject of prohibitory and even penal legislation.

The subject of an international copyright has been frequently commended to the attention of Congress by my predecessors. The enactment of such a law would be eminently wise and just.

Our naturalization laws should be so revised as to make the inquiry into the moral character and good disposition toward our Government of the persons applying for citizenship more thorough. This can only be done by taking fuller control of the examination, by fixing the times for hearing such applications, and by requiring the presence of some one who shall represent the Government in the inquiry. Those who are the avowed enemies of social order or who come to our shores to swell the injurious influence and to extend the evil practices of any association that defies our laws should not only be denied citizenship, but a domicile.

The enactment of a national bankrupt law of a character to be a permanent part of our general legislation is desirable. It should be simple in its methods and inexpensive in its administration.

The report of the Postmaster-General not only exhibits the operations of the Department for the last fiscal year, but contains many valuable suggestions for the improvement and extension of the service, which are commended to your attention. No other branch of the Government has so close a contact with the daily life of the people. Almost everyone uses the service it offers, and every hour gained in the transmission of the great commercial mails has an actual and possible value that only those engaged in trade can understand.

The saving of one day in the transmission of the mails between New York and San Francisco, which has recently been accomplished, is an incident worthy of mention.

The plan suggested of a supervision of the post-offices in separate districts that shall involve instruction and suggestion and a rating of the efficiency of the postmasters would, I have no doubt, greatly improve the service.

A pressing necessity exists for the erection of a building for the joint use of the Department and of the city post-office. The Department was partially relieved by renting outside quarters for a part of its force, but it is again overcrowded. The building used by the city office never was fit for the purpose, and is now inadequate and unwholesome.

The unsatisfactory condition of the law relating to the transmission through the mails of lottery advertisements and remittances is clearly stated by the Postmaster-General, and his suggestion as to amendments should have your favorable consideration.

The report of the Secretary of the Navy shows a reorganization of the bureaus of the Department that will, I do not doubt, promote the efficiency of each.

In general, satisfactory progress has been made in the construction of the new ships of war authorized by Congress. The first vessel of the new Navy, the *Dolphin*, was subjected to very severe trial tests and to very much adverse criticism; but it is gratifying to be able to state that a cruise around the world, from which she has recently returned, has demonstrated that she is a first-class vessel of her rate.

The report of the Secretary shows that while the effective force of the Navy is rapidly increasing by reason of the improved build and armament of the new ships, the number of our ships fit for sea duty grows very slowly. We had on the 4th of March last 37 serviceable ships, and though 4 have since been added to the list, the total has not been increased, because in the meantime 4 have been lost or condemned. Twenty-six additional vessels have been authorized and appropriated for; but it is probable that when they are completed our list will only be increased to 42—a gain of 5. The old wooden ships are disappearing almost as fast as the new vessels are added. These facts carry their own argument. One of the new ships may in fighting strength be equal to two of the old, but it can not do the cruising duty of two. It is important therefore, that we should have a more rapid increase in the number o serviceable ships. I concur in the recommendation of the Secretary that the construction of 8 armored ships, 3 gunboats, and 5 torpedo boats be authorized.

An appalling calamity befell three of our naval vessels on duty at the Samoan Islands, in the harbor of Apia, in March last, involving the loss of 4 officers and 47 seamen, of two vessels, the *Trenton* and the *Vandalia*, and the disabling of a third, the *Nipsic*. Three vessels of the German navy, also in the harbor, shared with our ships the force of the hurricane and suffered even more heavily. While mourning the brave officers and men who died facing with high resolve perils greater than those of battle, it is most gratifying to state that the credit of the American Navy for seamanship, courage, and generosity was magnificently sustained in the storm-beaten harbor of Apia.

The report of the Secretary of the Interior exhibits the transactions of the Government with the Indian tribes. Substantial progress has been made in the education of the children of school age and in the allotment of lands to adult Indians. It is to be regretted that the policy of breaking up the tribal relation and of dealing with the Indian as an individual did not appear earlier in our legislation. Large reservations held in common and the maintenance of the authority of the chiefs and headmen have deprived the individual of every incentive to the exercise of thrift, and the annuity has contributed an affirmative impulse toward a state of confirmed pauperism.

Our treaty stipulations should be observed with fidelity and our legislation should be highly considerate of the best interests of an ignorant and helpless people. The reservations are now generally surrounded by white settlements. We can no longer push the Indian back into the wilderness, and it remains only by every suitable agency to push him upward into the estate of a self-supporting and responsible citizen. For the adult the first step is to locate him upon a farm, and for the child to place him in a school.

School attendance should be promoted by every moral agency, and those failing should be compelled. The national schools for Indians have been very successful and should be multiplied, and as far as possible should be so organized and conducted as to facilitate the transfer of the schools to the States or Territories in which they are located when the Indians in a neighborhood have accepted citizenship and have become otherwise fitted for such a transfer. This condition of things will be attained slowly, but it will be hastened by keeping it in mind; and in the meantime that cooperation between the Government and the mission schools which has wrought much good should be cordially and impartially maintained.

The last Congress enacted two distinct laws relating to negotiations with the Sioux Indians of Dakota for a relinquishment of a portion of their lands to the United States and for dividing the remainder into separate reservations. Both were approved on the same day—March 2. The one submitted to the Indians a specific proposition; the other (section 3 of the Indian appropriation act) authorized the President to appoint three commissioners to negotiate with these Indians for the accomplishment of the same general purpose, and required that any agreements made should be submitted to Congress for ratification.

On the 16th day of April last I appointed Hon. Charles Foster, of Ohio, Hon. William Warner, of Missouri, and Major-General George Crook, of the United States Army, commissioners under the last-named law. They were, however, authorized and directed first to submit to the Indians the definite proposition made to them by the act first mentioned, and only in the event of a failure to secure the assent of the requisite number to that proposition to open negotiations for modified terms under the other act. The work of the commission was prolonged and arduous, but the assent of the requisite number was, it is understood, finally obtained to the proposition made by Congress, though the report of the commission has not yet been submitted. In view of these facts, I shall not, as at present advised, deem it necessary to submit the agreement to Congress for ratification, but it will in due course be submitted for information. This agreement releases to the United States about 9,000,000 acres of land.

The commission provided for by section 14 of the Indian appropriation bill to negotiate with the Cherokee Indians and all other Indians owning or claiming lands lying west of the ninety-sixth degree of longitude for the cession to the United States of all such lands was constituted by the appointment of Hon. Lucius Fairchild, of Wisconsin, Hon. John F. Hartranft, of Pennsylvania, and Hon. Alfred M. Wilson, of Arkansas, and organized on June 29 last. Their first conference with the representatives of the Cherokees was held at Tahlequah July 29, with no definite results. General John F. Hartranft, of Pennsylvania, was prevented by ill health from taking part in the conference. His death, which occurred recently, is justly and generally lamented by a people he had served with conspicuous gallantry in war and with great fidelity in peace. The vacancy thus created was filled by the appointment of Hon. Warren G. Sayre, of Indiana.

A second conference between the commission and the Cherokees was begun November 6, but no results have yet been obtained, nor is it believed that a conclusion can be immediately expected. The cattle syndicate now occupying the lands for grazing purposes is clearly one of the agencies responsible for the obstruction of our negotiations with the Cherokees. The large body of agricultural lands constituting what is known as the "Cherokee Outlet" ought not to be, and, indeed, can not long be, held for grazing and for the advantage of a few against the public interests and the best advantage of the Indians themselves. The United States has now under the treaties certain rights in these lands. These will not be used oppressively, but it can not be allowed that those who by sufferance occupy these lands shall interpose to defeat the wise and beneficent purposes of the Government. I can not but believe that the advantageous character of the offer made by the United States to the Cherokee Nation for a full release of these lands as compared with other suggestions now made to them will yet obtain for it a favorable consideration.

Under the agreement made between the United States and the Muscogee (or Creek) Nation of Indians on the 19th day of January, 1889, an absolute title was secured by the United States to about 3,500,000 acres of land. Section 12 of the general Indian appropriation act approved March 2, 1889, made provision for the purchase by the United States from the Seminole tribe of a certain portion of their lands. The delegates of the Seminole Nation, having first duly evidenced to me their power to act in that behalf, delivered a proper release or conveyance to the United States of all the lands mentioned in the act, which was accepted by me and certified to be in compliance with the statute.

By the terms of both the acts referred to all the lands so purchased were declared to be a part of the public domain and open to settlement under the homestead law. But of the lands embraced in these purchases, being in the aggregate about 5,500,000 acres, 3,500,000 acres had already, under the terms of the treaty of 1866, been acquired by the United States for the purpose of settling other Indian tribes thereon and had been appropriated to that purpose. The land remaining and available for settlement consisted of 1,887,796 acres, surrounded on all sides by lands in the occupancy of Indian tribes. Congress had provided no civil government for the people who were to be invited by my proclamation to settle upon these lands, except as the new court which had been established at Muscogee or the United States courts in some of the adjoining States had power to enforce the general laws of the United States.

In this condition of things I was quite reluctant to open the lands to settlement; but in view of the fact that several thousand persons, many of them with their families, had gathered upon the borders of the Indian Territory with a view to securing homesteads on the ceded lands, and that delay would involve them in much loss and suffering, I did on the 23d day of March last issue a proclamation declaring that the lands therein described would be open to settlement under the provisions of the law on the 22d day of April following at 12 o'clock noon. Two land districts had been established and the offices were opened for the transaction of business when the appointed time arrived.

It is much to the credit of the settlers that they very generally observed the limitation as to the time when they might enter the Territory. Care will be taken that those who entered in violation of the law do not secure the advantage they unfairly sought. There was a good deal of apprehension that the strife for locations would result in much violence and bloodshed, but happily these anticipations were not realized. It is estimated that there are now in the Territory about 60,000 people, and several considerable towns have sprung up, for which temporary municipal governments have been organized. Guthrie is said to have now a population of almost 8,000. Eleven schools and nine churches have been established, and three daily and five weekly newspapers are published in this city, whose charter and ordinances have only the sanction of the voluntary acquiescence of the people from day to day.

Oklahoma City has a population of about 5,000, and is proportionately as well provided as Guthrie with churches, schools, and newspapers. Other towns and villages having populations of from 100 to 1,000 are scattered over the Territory.

In order to secure the peace of this new community in the absence of civil government, I directed General Merritt, commanding the Department of the Missouri, to act in conjunction with the marshals of the United States to preserve the peace, and upon their requisition to use the troops to aid them in executing warrants and in quieting any riots or breaches of the peace that might occur. He was further directed to use his influence to promote good order and to avoid any conflicts between or with the settlers. Believing that the introduction and sale of liquors where no legal restraints or regulations existed would endanger the public peace, and in view of the fact that such liquors must first be introduced into the Indian reservations before reaching the white settlements, I further directed the general commanding to enforce the laws relating to the introduction of ardent spirits into the Indian country.

The presence of the troops has given a sense of security to the well-disposed citizens and has tended to restrain the lawless.　In one instance the officer in immediate command of the troops went further than I deemed justifiable in supporting the *de facto* municipal government of Guthrie, and he was so informed, and directed to limit the interference of the military to the support of the marshals on the lines indicated in the original order.　I very urgently recommend that Congress at once provide a Territorial government for these people.　Serious questions, which may at any time lead to violent outbreaks, are awaiting the institution of courts for their peaceful adjustment.　The American genius for self-government has been well illustrated in Oklahoma; but it is neither safe nor wise to leave these people longer to the expedients which have temporarily served them.

Provision should be made for the acquisition of title to town lots in the towns now established in Alaska, for locating town sites, and for the establishment of municipal governments.　Only the mining laws have been extended to that Territory, and no other form of title to lands can now be obtained.　The general land laws were framed with reference to the disposition of agricultural lands, and it is doubtful if their operation in Alaska would be beneficial.

We have fortunately not extended to Alaska the mistaken policy of establishing reservations for the Indian tribes, and can deal with them from the beginning as individuals with, I am sure, better results; but any disposition of the public lands and any regulations relating to timber and to the fisheries should have a kindly regard to their interests.　Having no power to levy taxes, the people of Alaska are wholly dependent upon the General Government, to whose revenues the seal fisheries make a large annual contribution.　An appropriation for education should neither be overlooked nor stinted.

The smallness of the population and the great distances between the settlements offer serious obstacles to the establishment of the usual Territorial form of government.　Perhaps the organization of several subdistricts with a small municipal council of limited powers for each would be safe and useful.

Attention is called in this connection to the suggestions of the Secretary of the Treasury relating to the establishment of another port of entry in Alaska and of other needed customs facilities and regulations.

In the administration of the land laws the policy of facilitating in every proper way the adjustment of the honest claims of individual settlers upon the public lands has been pursued.　The number of pending cases had during the preceding Administration been greatly increased under the operation of orders for a time suspending final action in a large part of the cases originating in the West and Northwest, and by the subsequent use of unusual methods of examination.　Only those who are familiar with the conditions under which our agricultural lands have been settled can appreciate the serious and often fatal consequences to the settler of a policy that puts his title under suspicion or delays the issuance of his patent.　While care is taken to prevent and to expose fraud, it should not be imputed without reason.

The manifest purpose of the homestead and preemption laws was to promote the settlement of the public domain by persons having a *bona fide* intent to make a home upon the selected lands. Where this intent is well established and the requirements of the law have been substantially complied with, the claimant is entitled to a prompt and friendly consideration of his case; but where there is reason to believe that the claimant is the mere agent of another who is seeking to evade a law intended to promote small holdings and to secure by fraudulent methods large tracts of timber and other lands, both principal and agent should not only be thwarted in their fraudulent purpose, but should be made to feel the full penalties of our criminal statutes. The laws should be so administered as not to confound these two classes and to visit penalties only upon the latter.

The unsettled state of the titles to large bodies of lands in the Territories of New Mexico and Arizona has greatly retarded the development of those Territories. Provision should be made by law for the prompt trial and final adjustment before a judicial tribunal or commission of all claims based upon Mexican grants. It is not just to an intelligent and enterprising people that their peace should be disturbed and their prosperity retarded by these old contentions. I express the hope that differences of opinion as to methods may yield to the urgency of the case.

The law now provides a pension for every soldier and sailor who was mustered into the service of the United States during the Civil War and is now suffering from wounds or disease having an origin in the service and in the line of duty. Two of the three necessary facts, viz, muster and disability, are usually susceptible of easy proof; but the third, origin in the service, is often difficult and in many deserving cases impossible to establish. That very many of those who endured the hardships of our most bloody and arduous campaigns are now disabled from diseases that had a real but not traceable origin in the service I do not doubt. Besides these there is another class composed of men many of whom served an enlistment of three full years and of reenlisted veterans who added a fourth year of service, who escaped the casualties of battle and the assaults of disease, who were always ready for any detail, who were in every battle line of their command, and were mustered out in sound health, and have since the close of the war, while fighting with the same indomitable and independent spirit the contests of civil life, been overcome by disease or casualty.

I am not unaware that the pension roll already involves a very large annual expenditure; neither am I deterred by that fact from recommending that Congress grant a pension to such honorably discharged soldiers and sailors of the Civil War as, having rendered substantial service during the war, are now dependent upon their own labor for a maintenance and by disease or casualty are incapacitated from earning it. Many of the men who would be included in this form of relief are now dependent upon public aid, and it does not, in my judgment, consist with the national honor that they shall continue to subsist upon the local relief given indiscriminately to paupers instead of upon the special and generous provision of the nation they served so gallantly and unselfishly. Our people will, I am sure, very generally approve such legislation. And I am equally sure that the survivors of the Union Army and Navy will feel a grateful sense of relief when this worthy and suffering class of their comrades is fairly cared for.

There are some manifest inequalities in the existing law that should be remedied. To some of these the Secretary of the Interior has called attention.

It is gratifying to be able to state that by the adoption of new and better methods in the War Department the calls of the Pension Office for information as to the military and hospital records of pension claimants are now promptly answered and the injurious and vexatious delays that have heretofore occurred are entirely avoided. This will greatly facilitate the adjustment of all pending claims.

The advent of four new States—South Dakota, North Dakota, Montana, and Washington—into the Union under the Constitution in the same month, and the admission of their duly chosen representatives to our National Congress at the same session, is an event as unexampled as it is interesting.

The certification of the votes cast and of the constitutions adopted in each of the States was filed with me, as required by the eighth section of the act of February 22, 1889, by the governors of said Territories. respectively. Having after a careful examination found that the several constitutions and governments were republican in form and not repugnant to the Constitution of the United States, that all the provisions of the act of Congress had been complied with, and that a majority of the votes cast in each of said proposed States was in favor of the adoption of the constitution submitted therein, I did so declare by a separate proclamation as to each—as to North Dakota and South Dakota on Saturday, November 2;* as to Montana on Friday, November 8,† and as to Washington on Monday, November 11.‡

Each of these States has within it resources the development of which will employ the energies of and yield a comfortable subsistence to a great population. The smallest of these new States, Washington, stands twelfth, and the largest, Montana, third, among the forty-two in area. The people of these States are already well-trained, intelligent, and patriotic American citizens, having common interests and sympathies with those of the older States and a common purpose to defend the integrity and uphold the honor of the nation.

The attention of the Interstate Commerce Commission has been called to the urgent need of Congressional legislation for the better protection of the lives and limbs of those engaged in operating the great interstate freight lines of the country, and especially of the yardmen and brakemen.

A petition signed by nearly 10,000 railway brakemen was presented to the Commission asking that steps might be taken to bring about the use of automatic brakes and couplers on freight cars.

At a meeting of State railroad commissioners and their accredited representatives held at Washington in March last upon the invitation of the Interstate Commerce Commission a resolution was unanimously adopted urging the Commission "to consider what can be done to prevent the loss of life and limb in coupling and uncoupling freight cars and in handling the brakes of such cars." During the year ending June 30, 1888, over 2,000 railroad employees were killed in service and more than 20,000 injured. It is competent, I think, for Congress to require uniformity in the construction of cars used in interstate commerce and the use of improved safety appliances upon such trains. Time will be necessary to make the needed changes, but an earnest and intelligent beginning should be made at once. It is a reproach to our civilization that any class of American workmen should in the pursuit of a necessary and useful vocation be subjected to a peril of life and limb as great as that of a soldier in time of war.

The creation of an Executive Department to be known as the Department of Agriculture by the act of February 9 last was a wise and timely response to a request which had long been respectfully urged by the farmers of the country; but much remains to be done to perfect the organization of the Department so that it may fairly realize the expectations which its creation excited. In this connection attention is called to the suggestions contained in the report of the Secretary, which is herewith submitted. The need of a law officer for the Department such as is provided for the other Executive Departments is manifest. The failure of the last Congress to make the usual provision for the publication of the annual report should be promptly remedied. The public interest in the report and its value to the farming community, I am sure, will not be diminished under the new organization of the Department.

I recommend that the weather service be separated from the War Department and established as a bureau in the Department of Agriculture. This will involve an entire reorganization both of the Weather Bureau and of the Signal Corps, making of the first a purely civil organization and of the other a purely military staff corps. The report of the Chief Signal Officer shows that the work of the corps on its military side has been deteriorating.

The interests of the people of the District of Columbia should not be lost sight of in the pressure for consideration of measures affecting the whole country. Having no legislature of its own, either municipal or general, its people must look to Congress for the regulation of all those concerns that in the States are the subject of local control. Our whole people have an interest that the national capital should be made attractive and beautiful, and, above all, that its repute for social order should be well maintained. The laws regulating the sale of intoxicating drinks in the District should be revised with a view to bringing the traffic under stringent limitations and control.

In execution of the power conferred upon me by the act making appropriations for the expenses of the District of Columbia for the year ending June 30, 1890, I did on the 17th day of August last appoint Rudolph Hering, of New York, Samuel M. Gray, of Rhode Island, and Frederick P. Stearns, of Massachusetts, three eminent sanitary engineers, to examine and report upon the system of sewerage existing in the District of Columbia. Their report, which is not yet completed, will be in due course submitted to Congress.

The report of the Commissioners of the District is herewith transmitted, and the attention of Congress is called to the suggestions contained therein.

The proposition to observe the four hundredth anniversary of the discovery of America by the opening of a world's fair or exposition in some one of our great cities will be presented for the consideration of Congress. The value and interest of such an exposition may well claim the promotion of the General Government.

On the 4th of March last the Civil Service Commission had but a single member. The vacancies were filled on the 7th day of May, and since then the Commissioners have been industriously, though with an inadequate force, engaged in executing the law. They were assured by me that a cordial support would be given them in the faithful and impartial enforcement of the statute and of the rules and regulations adopted in aid of it.

Heretofore the book of eligibles has been closed to everyone, except as certifications were made upon the requisition of the appointing officers. This secrecy was the source of much suspicion and of many charges of favoritism in the administration of the law. What is secret is always suspected; what is open can be judged. The Commission, with the full approval of all its members, has now opened the list of eligibles to the public. The eligible lists for the classified post-offices and custom-houses are now publicly posted in the respective offices, as are also the certifications for appointments. The purpose of the civil-service law was absolutely to exclude any other consideration in connection with appointments under it than that of merit as tested by the examinations. The business proceeds upon the theory that both the examining boards and the appointing officers are absolutely ignorant as to the political views and associations of all persons on the civil-service lists. It is not too much to say, however, that some recent Congressional investigations have somewhat shaken public confidence in the impartiality of the selections for appointment.

The reform of the civil service will make no safe or satisfactory advance until the present law and its equal administration are well established in the confidence of the people. It will be my pleasure, as it is my duty, to see that the law is executed with firmness and impartiality. If some of its provisions have been fraudulently evaded by appointing officers, our resentment should not suggest the repeal of the law, but reform in its administration. We should have one view of the matter, and hold it with a sincerity that is not affected by the consideration that the party to which we belong is for the time in power.

My predecessor, on the 4th day of January, 1889, by an Executive order to take effect March 15, brought the Railway Mail Service under the operation of the civil-service law. Provision was made that the order should take effect sooner in any State where an eligible list was sooner obtained. On the 11th day of March Mr. Lyman, then the only member of the Commission, reported to me in writing that it would not be possible to have the list of eligibles ready before May 1, and requested that the taking effect of the order be postponed until that time, which was done,† subject to the same provision contained in the original order as to States in which an eligible list was sooner obtained.

As a result of the revision of the rules, of the new classification, and of the inclusion of the Railway Mail Service, the work of the Commission has been greatly increased, and the present clerical force is found to be inadequate. I recommend that the additional clerks asked by the Commission be appropriated for.

The duty of appointment is devolved by the Constitution or by the law, and the appointing officers are properly held to a high responsibility in its exercise. The growth of the country and the consequent increase of the civil list have magnified this function of the Executive disproportionally. It can not be denied, however, that the labor connected with this necessary work is increased, often to the point of actual distress, by the sudden and excessive demands that are made upon an incoming Administration for removals and appointments. But, on the other hand, it is not true that incumbency is a conclusive argument for continuance in office. Impartiality, moderation, fidelity to public duty, and a good attainment in the discharge of it must be added before the argument is complete. When those holding administrative offices so conduct themselves as to convince just political opponents that no party consideration or bias affects in any way the discharge of their public duties, we can more easily stay the demand for removals.

I am satisfied that both in and out of the classified service great benefit would accrue from the adoption of some system by which the officer would receive the distinction and benefit that in all private employments comes from exceptional faithfulness and efficiency in the performance of duty.

I have suggested to the heads of the Executive Departments that they consider whether a record might not be kept in each bureau of all those elements that are covered by the terms "faithfulness" and "efficiency," and a rating made showing the relative merits of the clerks of each class, this rating to be regarded as a test of merit in making promotions.

I have also suggested to the Postmaster-General that he adopt some plan by which he can, upon the basis of the reports to the Department and of frequent inspections, indicate the relative merit of postmasters of each class. They will be appropriately indicated in the Official Register and in the report of the Department. That a great stimulus would thus be given to the whole service I do not doubt, and such a record would be the best defense against inconsiderate removals from office.

The interest of the General Government in the education of the people found an early expression, not only in the thoughtful and sometimes warning utterances of our ablest statesmen, but in liberal appropriations from the common resources for the support of education in the new States. No one will deny that it is of the gravest national concern that those who hold the ultimate control of all public affairs should have the necessary intelligence wisely to direct and determine them. National aid to education has heretofore taken the form of land grants, and in that form the constitutional power of Congress to promote the education of the people is not seriously questioned. I do not think it can be successfully questioned when the form is changed to that of a direct grant of money from the public Treasury.

Such aid should be, as it always has been, suggested by some exceptional conditions. The sudden emancipation of the slaves of the South, the bestowal of the suffrage which soon followed, and the impairment of the ability of the States where these new citizens were chiefly found to adequately provide educational facilities presented not only exceptional but unexampled conditions. That the situation has been much ameliorated there is no doubt. The ability and interest of the States have happily increased.

But a great work remains to be done, and I think the General Government should lend its aid. As the suggestion of a national grant in aid of education grows chiefly out of the condition and needs of the emancipated slave and his descendants, the relief should as far as possible, while necessarily proceeding upon some general lines, be applied to the need that suggested it. It is essential, if much good is to be accomplished, that the sympathy and active interest of the people of the States should be enlisted, and that the methods adopted should be such as to stimulate and not to supplant local taxation for school purposes.

As one Congress can not bind a succeeding one in such a case and as the effort must in some degree be experimental, I recommend that any appropriation made for this purpose be so limited in annual amount and as to the time over which it is to extend as will on the one hand give the local school authorities opportunity to make the best use of the first year's allowance, and on the other deliver them from the temptation to unduly postpone the assumption of the whole burden themselves.

The colored people did not intrude themselves upon us. They were brought here in chains and held in the communities where they are now chiefly found by a cruel slave code. Happily for both races, they are now free. They have from a standpoint of ignorance and poverty—which was our shame, not theirs—made remarkable advances in education and in the acquisition of property. They have as a people shown themselves to be friendly and faithful toward the white race under temptations of tremendous strength. They have their representatives in the national cemeteries, where a grateful Government has gathered the ashes of those who died in its defense. They have furnished to our Regular Army regiments that have won high praise from their commanding officers for courage and soldierly qualities and for fidelity to the enlistment oath. In civil life they are now the toilers of their communities, making their full contribution to the widening streams of prosperity which these communities are receiving. Their sudden withdrawal would stop production and bring disorder into the household as well as the shop. Generally they do not desire to quit their homes, and their employers resent the interference of the emigration agents who seek to stimulate such a desire.

But notwithstanding all this, in many parts of our country where the colored population is large the people of that race are by various devices deprived of any effective exercise of their political rights and of many of their civil rights. The wrong does not expend itself upon those whose votes are suppressed. Every constituency in the Union is wronged.

It has been the hope of every patriot that a sense of justice and of respect for the law would work a gradual cure of these flagrant evils. Surely no one supposes that the present can be accepted as a permanent condition. If it is said that these communities must work out this problem for themselves, we have a right to ask whether they are at work upon it. Do they suggest any solution? When and under what conditions is the black man to have a free ballot? When is he in fact to have those full civil rights which have so long been his in law? When is that equality of influence which our form of government was intended to secure to the electors to be restored? This generation should courageously face these grave questions, and not leave them as a heritage of woe to the next. The consultation should proceed with candor, calmness, and great patience, upon the lines of justice and humanity, not of prejudice and cruelty. No question in our country can be at rest except upon the firm base of justice and of the law.

I earnestly invoke the attention of Congress to the consideration of such measures within its well-defined constitutional powers as will secure to all our people a free exercise of the right of suffrage and every other civil right under the Constitution and laws of the United States. No evil, however deplorable, can justify the assumption either on the part of the Executive or of Congress of powers not granted, but both will be highly blamable if all the powers granted are not wisely but firmly used to correct these evils. The power to take the whole direction and control of the election of members of the House of Representatives is clearly given to the General Government. A partial and qualified supervision of these elections is now provided for by law, and in my opinion this law may be so strengthened and extended as to secure on the whole better results than can be attained by a law taking all the processes of such election into Federal control. The colored man should be protected in all of his relations to the Federal Government, whether as litigant, juror, or witness in our courts, as an elector for members of Congress, or as a peaceful traveler upon our interstate railways.

There is nothing more justly humiliating to the national pride and nothing more hurtful to the national prosperity than the inferiority of our merchant marine compared with that of other nations whose general resources, wealth, and seacoast lines do not suggest any reason for their supremacy on the sea. It was not always so, and our people are agreed, I think, that it shall not continue to be so. It is not possible in this communication to discuss the causes of the decay of our shipping interests or the differing methods by which it is proposed to restore them. The statement of a few well-authenticated facts and some general suggestions as to legislation is all that is practicable. That the great steamship lines sailing under the flags of England, France, Germany, Spain, and Italy, and engaged in foreign commerce, were promoted and have since been and now are liberally aided by grants of public money in one form or another is generally known. That the American lines of steamships have been abandoned by us to an unequal contest with the aided lines of other nations until they have been withdrawn, or in the few cases where they are still maintained are subject to serious disadvantages, is matter of common knowledge.

The present situation is such that travelers and merchandise find Liverpool often a necessary intermediate port between New York and some of the South American capitals. The fact that some of the delegates from South American States to the conference of American nations now in session at Washington reached our shores by reversing that line of travel is very conclusive of the need of such a conference and very suggestive as to the first and most necessary step in the direction of fuller and more beneficial intercourse with nations that are now our neighbors upon the lines of latitude, but not upon the lines of established commercial intercourse.

I recommend that such appropriations be made for ocean mail service in American steamships between our ports and those of Central and South America, China, Japan, and the important islands in both of the great oceans as will be liberally remunerative for the service rendered and as will encourage the establishment and in some fair degree equalize the chances of American steamship lines in the competitions which they must meet. That the American States lying south of us will cordially cooperate in establishing and maintaining such lines of steamships to their principal ports I do not doubt.

We should also make provision for a naval reserve to consist of such merchant ships of American construction and of a specified tonnage and speed as the owners will consent to place at the use of the Government in case of need as armed cruisers. England has adopted this policy, and as a result can now upon necessity at once place upon her naval list some of the fastest steamships in the world. A proper supervision of the construction of such vessels would make their conversion into effective ships of war very easy.

I am an advocate of economy in our national expenditures, but it is a misuse of terms to make this word describe a policy that withholds an expenditure for the purpose of extending our foreign commerce. The enlargement and improvement of our merchant marine, the development of a sufficient body of trained American seamen, the promotion of rapid and regular mail communication between the ports of other countries and our own, and the adaptation of large and swift American merchant steamships to naval uses in time of war are public purposes of the highest concern. The enlarged participation of our people in the carrying trade, the new and increased markets that will be opened for the products of our farms and factories, and the fuller and better employment of our mechanics which will result from a liberal promotion of our foreign commerce insure the widest possible diffusion of benefit to all the States and to all our people. Everything is most propitious for the present inauguration of a liberal and progressive policy upon this subject, and we should enter upon it with promptness and decision.

The legislation which I have suggested, it is sincerely believed, will promote the peace and honor of our country and the prosperity and security of the people. I invoke the diligent and serious attention of Congress to the consideration of these and such other measures as may be presented having the same great end in view.

SECOND ANNUAL MESSAGE.

EXECUTIVE MANSION, *December 1, 1890.*

To the Senate and House of Representatives:

The reports of the several Executive Departments, which will be laid before Congress in the usual course, will exhibit in detail the operations of the Government for the last fiscal year. Only the more important incidents and results, and chiefly such as may be the foundation of the recommendations I shall submit, will be referred to in this annual message.

The vast and increasing business of the Government has been transacted by the several Departments during the year with faithfulness, energy, and success.

The revenues, amounting to above $450,000,000, have been collected and disbursed without revealing, so far as I can ascertain, a single case of defalcation or embezzlement. An earnest effort has been made to stimulate a sense of responsibility and public duty in all officers and employees of every grade, and the work done by them has almost wholly escaped unfavorable criticism. I speak of these matters with freedom because the credit of this good work is not mine, but is shared by the heads of the several Departments with the great body of faithful officers and employees who serve under them. The closest scrutiny of Congress is invited to all the methods of administration and to every item of expenditure.

The friendly relations of our country with the nations of Europe and of the East have been undisturbed, while the ties of good will and common interest that bind us to the States of the Western Hemisphere have been notably strengthened by the conference held in this capital to consider measures for the general welfare. Pursuant to the invitation authorized by Congress, the representatives of every independent State of the American continent and of Hayti met in conference in this capital in October, 1889, and continued in session until the 19th of last April. This important convocation marks a most interesting and influential epoch in the history of the Western Hemisphere. It is noteworthy that Brazil, invited while under an imperial form of government, shared as a republic in the deliberations and results of the conference. The recommendations of this conference were all transmitted to Congress at the last session.

The International Marine Conference, which sat at Washington last winter, reached a very gratifying result. The regulations suggested have been brought to the attention of all the Governments represented, and their general adoption is confidently expected. The legislation of Congress at the last session is in conformity with the propositions of the conference, and the proclamation therein provided for will be issued when the other powers have given notice of their adhesion.

The Conference of Brussels, to devise means for suppressing the slave trade in Africa, afforded an opportunity for a new expression of the interest the American people feel in that great work. It soon became evident that the measure proposed would tax the resources of the Kongo Basin beyond the revenues available under the general act of Berlin of 1884. The United States, not being a party to that act, could not share in its revision, but by a separate act the Independent State of the Kongo was freed from the restrictions upon a customs revenue. The demoralizing and destructive traffic in ardent spirits among the tribes also claimed the earnest attention of the conference, and the delegates of the United States were foremost in advocating measures for its repression. An accord was reached the influence of which will be very helpful and extend over a wide region. As soon as these measures shall receive the sanction of the Netherlands, for a time withheld, the general acts will be submitted for ratification by the Senate. Meanwhile negotiations have been opened for a new and completed treaty of friendship, commerce, and navigation between the United States and the Independent State of the Kongo.

Toward the end of the past year the only independent monarchical government on the Western Continent, that of Brazil, ceased to exist, and was succeeded by a republic. Diplomatic relations were at once established with the new Government, but it was not completely recognized until an opportunity had been afforded to ascertain that it had popular approval and support. When the course of events had yielded assurance of this fact, no time was lost in extending to the new Government a full and cordial welcome into the family of American Commonwealths. It is confidently believed that the good relations of the two countries will be preserved and that the future will witness an increased intimacy of intercourse and an expansion of their mutual commerce.

The peace of Central America has again been disturbed through a revolutionary change in Salvador, which was not recognized by other States, and hostilities broke out between Salvador and Guatemala, threatening to involve all Central America in conflict and to undo the progress which had been made toward a union of their interests. The efforts of this Government were promptly and zealously exerted to compose their differences, and through the active efforts of the representative of the United States a provisional treaty of peace was signed August 26, whereby the right of the Republic of Salvador to choose its own rulers was recognized. General Ezeta, the chief of the Provisional Government, has since been confirmed in the Presidency by the Assembly, and diplomatic recognition duly followed.

The killing of General Barrundia on board the Pacific mail steamer *Acapulco*, while anchored in transit in the port of San Jose de Guatemala, demanded careful inquiry. Having failed in a revolutionary attempt to invade Guatemala from Mexican territory, General Barrundia took passage at Acapulco for Panama. The consent of the representatives of the United States was sought to effect his seizure, first at Champerico, where the steamer touched, and afterwards at San Jose. The captain of the steamer refused to give up his passenger without a written order from the United States minister. The latter furnished the desired letter, stipulating as the condition of his action that General Barrundia's life should be spared and that he should be tried only for offenses growing out of his insurrectionary movements. This letter was produced to the captain of the *Acapulco* by the military commander at San Jose as his warrant to take the passenger from the steamer. General Barrundia resisted capture and was killed. It being evident that the minister, Mr. Mizner, had exceeded the bounds of his authority in intervening, in compliance with the demands of the Guatemalan authorities, to authorize and effect, in violation of precedent, the seizure on a vessel of the United States of a passenger in transit charged with political offenses, in order that he might be tried for such offenses under what was described as martial law, I was constrained to disavow Mr. Mizner's act and recall him from his post.

The Nicaragua Canal project, under the control of our citizens, is making most encouraging progress, all the preliminary conditions and initial operations having been accomplished within the prescribed time.

During the past year negotiations have been renewed for the settlement of the claims of American citizens against the Government of Chile, principally growing out of the late war with Peru. The reports from our minister at Santiago warrant the expectation of an early and satisfactory adjustment.

Our relations with China, which have for several years occupied so important a place in our diplomatic history, have called for careful consideration and have been the subject of much correspondence.

The communications of the Chinese minister have brought into view the whole subject of our conventional relations with his country, and at the same time this Government, through its legation at Peking, has sought to arrange various matters and complaints touching the interests and protection of our citizens in China.

In pursuance of the concurrent resolution of October 1, 1890, I have proposed to the Governments of Mexico and Great Britain to consider a conventional regulation of the passage of Chinese laborers across our southern and northern frontiers.

On the 22d day of August last Sir Edmund Monson, the arbitrator selected under the treaty of December 6, 1888, rendered an award to the effect that no compensation was due from the Danish Government to the United States on account of what is commonly known as the Carlos Butterfield claim.

Our relations with the French Republic continue to be cordial. Our representative at that court has very diligently urged the removal of the restrictions imposed upon our meat products, and it is believed that substantial progress has been made toward a just settlement.

The Samoan treaty, signed last year at Berlin by the representatives of the United States, Germany, and Great Britain, after due ratification and exchange, has begun to produce salutary effects. The formation of the government agreed upon will soon replace the disorder of the past by a stable administration alike just to the natives and equitable to the three powers most concerned in trade and intercourse with the Samoan Islands. The chief justice has been chosen by the King of Sweden and Norway on the invitation of the three powers, and will soon be installed. The land commission and the municipal council are in process of organization. A rational and evenly distributed scheme of taxation, both municipal and upon imports, is in operation. Malietoa is respected as King.

The new treaty of extradition with Great Britain, after due ratification, was proclaimed on the 25th of last March. Its beneficial working is already apparent.

The difference between the two Governments touching the fur-seal question in the Bering Sea is not yet adjusted, as will be seen by the correspondence which will soon be laid before the Congress. The offer to submit the question to arbitration, as proposed by Her Majesty's Government, has not been accepted, for the reason that the form of submission proposed is not thought to be calculated to assure a conclusion satisfactory to either party. It is sincerely hoped that before the opening of another sealing season some arrangement may be effected which will assure to the United States a property right derived from Russia, which was not disregarded by any nation for more than eighty years preceding the outbreak of the existing trouble.

In the tariff act a wrong was done to the Kingdom of Hawaii which I am bound to presume was wholly unintentional. Duties were levied on certain commodities which are included in the reciprocity treaty now existing between the United States and the Kingdom of Hawaii, without indicating the necessary exception in favor of that Kingdom. I hope Congress will repair what might otherwise seem to be a breach of faith on the part of this Government.

An award in favor of the United States in the matter of the claim of Mr. Van Bokkelen against Hayti was rendered on the 4th of December 1888, but owing to disorders then and afterwards prevailing in Hayti the terms of payment were not observed. A new agreement as to the time of payment has been approved and is now in force. Other just claims of citizens of the United States for redress of wrongs suffered during the late political conflict in Hayti will, it is hoped, speedily yield to friendly treatment.

Propositions for the amendment of the treaty of extradition between the United States and Italy are now under consideration.

You will be asked to provide the means of accepting the invitation of the Italian Government to take part in an approaching conference to consider the adoption of a universal prime meridian from which to reckon longitude and time. As this proposal follows in the track of the reform sought to be initiated by the Meridian Conference of Washington, held on the invitation of this Government, the United States should manifest a friendly interest in the Italian proposal.

In this connection I may refer with approval to the suggestion of my predecessors that standing provision be made for accepting, whenever deemed advisable, the frequent invitations of foreign governments to share in conferences looking to the advancement of international reforms in regard to science, sanitation, commercial laws and procedure, and other matters affecting the intercourse and progress of modern communities.

In the summer of 1889 an incident occurred which for some time threatened to interrupt the cordiality of our relations with the Government of Portugal. That Government seized the Delagoa Bay Railway, which was constructed under a concession granted to an American citizen, and at the same time annulled the charter. The concessionary, who had embarked his fortune in the enterprise, having exhausted other means of redress, was compelled to invoke the protection of his Government. Our representations, made coincidently with those of the British Government, whose subjects were also largely interested, happily resulted in the recognition by Portugal of the propriety of submitting the claim for indemnity growing out of its action to arbitration. This plan of settlement having been agreed upon, the interested powers readily concurred in the proposal to submit the case to the judgment of three eminent jurists, to be designated by the President of the Swiss Republic, who, upon the joint invitation of the Governments of the United States, Great Britain, and Portugal, has selected persons well qualified for the task before them.

The revision of our treaty relations with the Empire of Japan has continued to be the subject of consideration and of correspondence. The questions involved are both grave and delicate; and while it will be my duty to see that the interests of the United States are not by any changes exposed to undue discrimination, I sincerely hope that such revision as will satisfy the legitimate expectations of the Japanese Government and maintain the present and long-existing friendly relations between Japan and the United States will be effected.

The friendship between our country and Mexico, born of close neighborhood and strengthened by many considerations of intimate intercourse and reciprocal interest, has never been more conspicuous than now nor more hopeful of increased benefit to both nations. The intercourse of the two countries by rail, already great, is making constant growth. The established lines and those recently projected add to the intimacy of traffic and open new channels of access to fresh areas of demand and supply. The importance of the Mexican railway system will be further enhanced to a degree almost impossible to forecast if it should become a link in the projected intercontinental railway. I recommend that our mission in the City of Mexico be raised to the first class.

The cordial character of our relations with Spain warrants the hope that by the continuance of methods of friendly negotiation much may be accomplished in the direction of an adjustment of pending questions and of the increase of our trade. The extent and development of our trade with the island of Cuba invest the commercial relations of the United States and Spain with a peculiar importance. It is not doubted that a special arrangement in regard to commerce, based upon the reciprocity provision of the recent tariff act, would operate most beneficially for both Governments. This subject is now receiving attention.

The restoration of the remains of John Ericsson to Sweden afforded a gratifying occasion to honor the memory of the great inventor, to whose genius our country owes so much, and to bear witness to the unbroken friendship which has existed between the land which bore him and our own, which claimed him as a citizen.

On the 2d of September last the commission appointed to revise the proceedings of the commission under the claims convention between the United States and Venezuela of 1866 brought its labors to a close within the period fixed for that purpose. The proceedings of the late commission were characterized by a spirit of impartiality and a high sense of justice, and an incident which was for many years the subject of discussion between the two Governments has been disposed of in a manner alike honorable and satisfactory to both parties. For the settlement of the claim of the Venezuela Steam Transportation Company, which was the subject of a joint resolution adopted at the last session of Congress, negotiations are still in progress, and their early conclusion is anticipated.

The legislation of the past few years has evinced on the part of Congress a growing realization of the importance of the consular service in fostering our commercial relations abroad and in protecting the domestic revenues. As the scope of operations expands increased provision must be made to keep up the essential standard of efficiency. The necessity of some adequate measure of supervision and inspection has been so often presented that I need only commend the subject to your attention.

The revenues of the Government from all sources for the fiscal year ending June 30, 1890, were $463,963,080.55 and the total expenditures for the same period were $358,618,584.52. The postal receipts have not heretofore been included in the statement of these aggregates, and for the purpose of comparison the sum of $60,882,097.92 should be deducted from both sides of the account. The surplus for the year, including the amount applied to the sinking fund, was $105,344,496.03. The receipts for 1890 were $16,030,923.79 and the expenditures $15,739,871 in excess of those of 1889. The customs receipts increased $5,835,842.88 and the receipts from internal revenue $11,725,191.89, while on the side of expenditures that for pensions was $19,312,075.96 in excess of the preceding year.

The Treasury statement for the current fiscal year, partly actual and partly estimated, is as follows: Receipts from all sources, $406,000,000; total expenditures, $354,000,000, leaving a surplus of $52,000,000, not taking the postal receipts into the account on either side. The loss of revenue from customs for the last quarter is estimated at $25,000,000, but from this is deducted a gain of about $16,000,000 realized during the first four months of the year.

For the year 1892 the total estimated receipts are $373,000,000 and the estimated expenditures $357,852,209.42, leaving an estimated surplus of $15,147,790.58, which, with a cash balance of $52,000,000 at the beginning of the year, will give $67,147,790.58 as the sum available for the redemption of outstanding bonds or other uses. The estimates of receipts and expenditures for the Post-Office Department, being equal, are not included in this statement on either side.

The act "directing the purchase of silver bullion and the issue of Treasury notes thereon," approved July 14, 1890, has been administered by the Secretary of the Treasury with an earnest purpose to get into circulation at the earliest possible dates the full monthly amounts of Treasury notes contemplated by its provisions and at the same time to give to the market for the silver bullion such support as the law contemplates. The recent depreciation in the price of silver has been observed with regret. The rapid rise in price which anticipated and followed the passage of the act was influenced in some degree by speculation, and the recent reaction is in part the result of the same cause and in part of the recent monetary disturbances. Some months of further trial will be necessary to determine the permanent effect of the recent legislation upon silver values, but it is gratifying to know that the increased circulation secured by the act has exerted, and will continue to exert, a most beneficial influence upon business and upon general values.

While it has not been thought best to renew formally the suggestion of an international conference looking to an agreement touching the full use of silver for coinage at a uniform ratio, care has been taken to observe closely any change in the situation abroad, and no favorable opportunity will be lost to promote a result which it is confidently believed would confer very large benefits upon the commerce of the world.

The recent monetary disturbances in England are not unlikely to suggest a reexamination of opinions upon this subject. Our very large supply of gold will, if not lost by impulsive legislation in the supposed interest of silver, give us a position of advantage in promoting a permanent and safe international agreement for the free use of silver as a coin metal.

The efforts of the Secretary to increase the volume of money in circulation by keeping down the Treasury surplus to the lowest practicable limit have been unremitting and in a very high degree successful. The tables presented by him showing the increase of money in circulation during the last two decades, and especially the table showing the increase during the nineteen months he has administered the affairs of the Department, are interesting and instructive. The increase of money in circulation during the nineteen months has been in the aggregate $93,866,813, or about $1.50 per capita, and of this increase only $7,100,000 was due to the recent silver legislation. That this substantial and needed aid given to commerce resulted in an enormous reduction of the public debt and of the annual interest charge is matter of increased satisfaction. There have been purchased and redeemed since March 4, 1889, 4 and 4½ per cent bonds to the amount of $211,832,450, at a cost of $246,620,741, resulting in the reduction of the annual interest charge of $8,967,609 and a total saving of interest of $51,576,706.

I notice with great pleasure the statement of the Secretary that the receipts from internal revenue have increased during the last fiscal year nearly $12,000,000, and that the cost of collecting this larger revenue was less by $90,617 than for the same purpose in the preceding year. The percentage of cost of collecting the customs revenue was less for the last fiscal year than ever before.

The Customs Administration Board, provided for by the act of June 10, 1890, was selected with great care, and is composed in part of men whose previous experience in the administration of the old customs regulations had made them familiar with the evils to be remedied, and in part of men whose legal and judicial acquirements and experience seemed to fit them for the work of interpreting and applying the new statute. The chief aim of the law is to secure honest valuations of all dutiable merchandise and to make these valuations uniform at all our ports of entry. It had been made manifest by a Congressional investigation that a system of undervaluation had been long in use by certain classes of importers, resulting not only in a great loss of revenue, but in a most intolerable discrimination against honesty. It is not seen how this legislation, when it is understood, can be regarded by the citizens of any country having commercial dealings with us as unfriendly. If any duty is supposed to be excessive, let the complaint be lodged there. It will surely not be claimed by any well-disposed people that a remedy may be sought and allowed in a system of quasi smuggling.

The report of the Secretary of War exhibits several gratifying results attained during the year by wise and unostentatious methods. The percentage of desertions from the Army (an evil for which both Congress and the Department have long been seeking a remedy) has been reduced during the past year 24 per cent, and for the months of August and September, during which time the favorable effects of the act of June 16 were felt, 33 per cent, as compared with the same months of 1889.

The results attained by a reorganization and consolidation of the divisions having charge of the hospital and service records of the volunteer soldiers are very remarkable. This change was effected in July, 1889, and at that time there were 40,654 cases awaiting attention, more than half of these being calls from the Pension Office for information necessary to the adjudication of pension claims. On the 30th day of June last, though over 300,000 new calls had come in, there was not a single case that had not been examined and answered.

I concur in the recommendations of the Secretary that adequate and regular appropriations be continued for coast-defense works and ordnance. Plans have been practically agreed upon, and there can be no good reason for delaying the execution of them, while the defenseless state of our great seaports furnishes an urgent reason for wise expedition.

The encouragement that has been extended to the militia of the States, generally and most appropriately designated the "National Guard," should be continued and enlarged. These military organizations constitute in a large sense the Army of the United States, while about five-sixths of the annual cost of their maintenance is defrayed by the States.

The report of the Attorney-General is under the law submitted directly to Congress, but as the Department of Justice is one of the Executive Departments some reference to the work done is appropriate here.

A vigorous and in the main an effective effort has been made to bring to trial and punishment all violators of the law, but at the same time care has been taken that frivolous and technical offenses should not be used to swell the fees of officers or to harass well-disposed citizens. Especial attention is called to the facts connected with the prosecution of violations of the election laws and of offenses against United States officers. The number of convictions secured, very many of them upon pleas of guilty, will, it is hoped, have a salutary restraining influence. There have been several cases where postmasters appointed by me have been subjected to violent interference in the discharge of their official duties and to persecutions and personal violence of the most extreme character. Some of these cases have been dealt with through the Department of Justice, and in some cases the post-offices have been abolished or suspended. I have directed the Postmaster-General to pursue this course in all cases where other efforts failed to secure for any postmaster not himself in fault an opportunity peacefully to exercise the duties of his office. But such action will not supplant the efforts of the Department of Justice to bring the particular offenders to punishment.

The vacation by judicial decrees of fraudulent certificates of naturalization, upon bills in equity filed by the Attorney-General in the circuit court of the United States, is a new application of a familiar equity jurisdiction. Nearly one hundred such decrees have been taken during the year, the evidence disclosing that a very large number of fraudulent certificates of naturalization have been issued. And in this connection I beg to renew my recommendation that the laws be so amended as to require a more full and searching inquiry into all the facts necessary to naturalization before any certificates are granted. It certainly is not too much to require that an application for American citizenship shall be heard with as much care and recorded with as much formality as are given to cases involving the pettiest property right.

At the last session I returned without my approval a bill entitled "An act to prohibit bookmaking and pool selling in the District of Columbia," and stated my objection to be that it did not prohibit but in fact licensed what it purported to prohibit.* An effort will be made under existing laws to suppress this evil, though it is not certain that they will be found adequate.

The report of the Postmaster-General shows the most gratifying progress in the important work committed to his direction. The business methods have been greatly improved. A large economy in expenditures and an increase of four and three-quarters millions in receipts have been realized. The deficiency this year is $5,786,300, as against $6,350,183 last year, notwithstanding the great enlargement of the service. Mail routes have been extended and quickened and greater accuracy and dispatch in distribution and delivery have been attained. The report will be found to be full of interest and suggestion, not only to Congress, but to those thoughtful citizens who may be interested to know what business methods can do for that department of public administration which most nearly touches all our people.

The passage of the act to amend certain sections of the Revised Statutes relating to lotteries, approved September 19, 1890, has been received with great and deserved popular favor. The Post-Office Department and the Department of Justice at once entered upon the enforcement of the law with sympathetic vigor, and already the public mails have been largely freed from the fraudulent and demoralizing appeals and literature emanating from the lottery companies.

The construction and equipment of the new ships for the Navy have made very satisfactory progress. Since March 4, 1889, nine new vessels have been put in commission, and during this winter four more, including one monitor, will be added. The construction of the other vessels authorized is being pushed both in the Government and private yards with energy and watched with the most scrupulous care.

The experiments conducted during the year to test the relative resisting power of armor plates have been so valuable as to attract great attention in Europe. The only part of the work upon the new ships that is threatened by unusual delay is the armor plating, and every effort is being made to reduce that to the minimum. It is a source of congratulation that the anticipated influence of these modern vessels upon the *esprit de corps* of the officers and seamen has been fully realized. Confidence and pride in the ship among the crew are equivalent to a secondary battery. Your favorable consideration is invited to the recommendations of the Secretary.

The report of the Secretary of the Interior exhibits with great fullness and clearness the vast work of that Department and the satisfactory results attained. The suggestions made by him are earnestly commended to the consideration of Congress, though they can not all be given particular mention here.

The several acts of Congress looking to the reduction of the larger Indian reservations, to the more rapid settlement of the Indians upon individual allotments, and the restoration to the public domain of lands in excess of their needs have been largely carried into effect so far as the work was confided to the Executive. Agreements have been concluded since March 4, 1889, involving the cession to the United States of about 14,726,000 acres of land. These contracts have, as required by law, been submitted to Congress for ratification and for the appropriations necessary to carry them into effect. Those with the Sisseton and Wahpeton, Sac and Fox, Iowa, Pottawatomies and Absentee Shawnees, and Cœur d'Alene tribes have not yet received the sanction of Congress. Attention is also called to the fact that the appropriations made in the case of the Sioux Indians have not covered all the stipulated payments. This should be promptly corrected. If an agreement is confirmed, all of its terms should be complied with without delay and full appropriations should be made.

The policy outlined in my last annual message in relation to the patenting of lands to settlers upon the public domain has been carried out in the administration of the Land Office. No general suspicion or imputation of fraud has been allowed to delay the hearing and adjudication of individual cases upon their merits. The purpose has been to perfect the title of honest settlers with such promptness that the value of the entry might not be swallowed up by the expense and extortions to which delay subjected the claimant. The average monthly issue of agricultural patents has been increased about 6,000.

The disability-pension act, which was approved on the 27th of June last, has been put into operation as rapidly as was practicable. The increased clerical force provided was selected and assigned to work, and a considerable part of the force engaged in examinations in the field was recalled and added to the working force of the office. The examination and adjudication of claims have by reason of improved methods been more rapid than ever before. There is no economy to the Government in delay, while there is much hardship and injustice to the soldier. The anticipated expenditure, while very large, will not, it is believed, be in excess of the estimates made before the enactment of the law. This liberal enlargement of the general law should suggest a more careful scrutiny of bills for special relief, both as to the cases where relief is granted and as to the amount allowed.

The increasing numbers and influence of the non-Mormon population of Utah are observed with satisfaction. The recent letter of Wilford Woodruff, president of the Mormon Church, in which he advised his people "to refrain from contracting any marriage forbidden by the laws of the land," has attracted wide attention, and it is hoped that its influence will be highly beneficial in restraining infractions of the laws of the United States. But the fact should not be overlooked that the doctrine or belief of the church that polygamous marriages are rightful and supported by divine revelation remains unchanged. President Woodruff does not renounce the doctrine, but refrains from teaching it, and advises against the practice of it because the law is against it. Now, it is quite true that the law should not attempt to deal with the faith or belief of anyone; but it is quite another thing, and the only safe thing, so to deal with the Territory of Utah as that those who believe polygamy to be rightful shall not have the power to make it lawful.

The admission of the States of Wyoming and Idaho to the Union are events full of interest and congratulation, not only to the people of those States now happily endowed with a full participation in our privileges and responsibilities, but to all our people. Another belt of States stretches from the Atlantic to the Pacific.

The work of the Patent Office has won from all sources very high commendation. The amount accomplished has been very largely increased, and all the results have been such as to secure confidence and consideration for the suggestions of the Commissioner.

The enumeration of the people of the United States under the provisions of the act of March 1, 1889, has been completed, and the result will be at once officially communicated to Congress. The completion of this decennial enumeration devolves upon Congress the duty of making a new apportionment of Representatives "among the several States according to their respective numbers."

At the last session I had occasion to return with my objections several bills making provisions for the erection of public buildings for the reason that the expenditures contemplated were, in my opinion, greatly in excess of any public need. No class of legislation is more liable to abuse or to degenerate into an unseemly scramble about the public Treasury than this. There should be exercised in this matter a wise economy, based upon some responsible and impartial examination and report as to each case, under a general law.

The report of the Secretary of Agriculture deserves especial attention in view of the fact that the year has been marked in a very unusual degree by agitation and organization among the farmers looking to an increase in the profits of their business. It will be found that the efforts of the Department have been intelligently and zealously devoted to the promotion of the interests intrusted to its care.

A very substantial improvement in the market prices of the leading farm products during the year is noticed. The price of wheat advanced from 81 cents in October, 1889, to $1.00¾ in October, 1890; corn from 31 cents to 50¼ cents; oats from 19¼ cents to 43 cents, and barley from 63 cents to 78 cents. Meats showed a substantial but not so large an increase. The export trade in live animals and fowls shows a very large increase. The total value of such exports for the year ending June 30, 1890, was $33,000,000, and the increase over the preceding year was over $15,000,000. Nearly 200,000 more cattle and over 45,000 more hogs were exported than in the preceding year. The export trade in beef and pork products and in dairy products was very largely increased, the increase in the article of butter alone being from 15,504,978 pounds to 29,748,042 pounds, and the total increase in the value of meat and dairy products exported being $34,000,000. This trade, so directly helpful to the farmer, it is believed, will be yet further and very largely increased when the system of inspection and sanitary supervision now provided by law is brought fully into operation.

The efforts of the Secretary to establish the healthfulness of our meats against the disparaging imputations that have been put upon them abroad have resulted in substantial progress. Veterinary surgeons sent out by the Department are now allowed to participate in the inspection of the live cattle from this country landed at the English docks, and during the several months they have been on duty no case of contagious pleuro-pneumonia has been reported. This inspection abroad and the domestic inspection of live animals and pork products provided for by the act of August 30, 1890, will afford as perfect a guaranty for the wholesomeness of our meats offered for foreign consumption as is anywhere given to any food product, and its nonacceptance will quite clearly reveal the real motive of any continued restriction of their use, and that having been made clear the duty of the Executive will be very plain.

The information given by the Secretary of the progress and prospects of the beet-sugar industry is full of interest. It has already passed the experimental stage and is a commercial success. The area over which the sugar beet can be successfully cultivated is very large, and another field crop of great value is offered to the choice of the farmer.

The Secretary of the Treasury concurs in the recommendation of the Secretary of Agriculture that the official supervision provided by the tariff law for sugar of domestic production shall be transferred to the Department of Agriculture.

The law relating to the civil service has, so far as I can learn, been executed by those having the power of appointment in the classified service with fidelity and impartiality, and the service has been increasingly satisfactory. The report of the Commission shows a large amount of good work done during the year with very limited appropriations.

I congratulate the Congress and the country upon the passage at the first session of the Fifty-first Congress of an unusual number of laws of very high importance. That the results of this legislation will be the quickening and enlargement of our manufacturing industries, larger and better markets for our breadstuffs and provisions both at home and abroad, more constant employment and better wages for our working people, and an increased supply of a safe currency for the transaction of business, I do not doubt. Some of these measures were enacted at so late a period that the beneficial effects upon commerce which were in the contemplation of Congress have as yet but partially manifested themselves.

The general trade and industrial conditions throughout the country during the year have shown a marked improvement. For many years prior to 1888 the merchandise balances of foreign trade had been largely in our favor, but during that year and the year following they turned against us. It is very gratifying to know that the last fiscal year again shows a balance in our favor of over $68,000,000. The bank clearings, which furnish a good test of the volume of business transacted, for the first ten months of the year 1890 show as compared with the same months of 1889 an increase for the whole country of about 8.4 per cent, while the increase outside of the city of New York was over 13 per cent. During the month of October the clearings of the whole country showed an increase of 3.1 per cent over October, 1889, while outside of New York the increase was 11.5 per cent. These figures show that the increase in the volume of business was very general throughout the country. That this larger business was being conducted upon a safe and profitable basis is shown by the fact that there were 300 less failures reported in October, 1890, than in the same month of the preceding year, with liabilities diminished by about $5,000,000.

The value of our exports of domestic merchandise during the last year was over $115,000,000 greater than the preceding year, and was only exceeded once in our history. About $100,000,000 of this excess was in agricultural products. The production of pig iron, always a good gauge of general prosperity, is shown by a recent census bulletin to have been 153 per cent greater in 1890 than in 1880, and the production of steel 290 per cent greater. Mining in coal has had no limitation except that resulting from deficient transportation. The general testimony is that labor is everywhere fully employed, and the reports for the last year show a smaller number of employees affected by strikes and lockouts than in any year since 1884. The depression in the prices of agricultural products had been greatly relieved and a buoyant and hopeful tone was beginning to be felt by all our people.

These promising influences have been in some degree checked by the surprising and very unfavorable monetary events which have recently taken place in England. It is gratifying to know that these did not grow in any degree out of the financial relations of London with our people or out of any discredit attached to our securities held in that market. The return of our bonds and stocks was caused by a money stringency in England, not by any loss of value or credit in the securities themselves. We could not, however, wholly escape the ill effects of a foreign monetary agitation accompanied by such extraordinary incidents as characterized this. It is not believed, however, that these evil incidents, which have for the time unfavorably affected values in this country, can long withstand the strong, safe, and wholesome influences which are operating to give to our people profitable returns in all branches of legitimate trade and industry. The apprehension that our tariff may again and at once be subjected to important general changes would undoubtedly add a depressing influence of the most serious character.

The general tariff act has only partially gone into operation, some of its important provisions being limited to take effect at dates yet in the future. The general provisions of the law have been in force less than sixty days. Its permanent effects upon trade and prices still largely stand in conjecture. It is curious to note that the advance in the prices of articles wholly unaffected by the tariff act was by many hastily ascribed to that act.   Notice was not taken of the fact that the general tendency of the markets was upward, from influences wholly apart from the recent tariff legislation. The enlargement of our currency by the silver bill undoubtedly gave an upward tendency to trade and had a marked effect on prices; but this natural and desired effect of the silver legislation was by many erroneously attributed to the tariff act.

There is neither wisdom nor justice in the suggestion that the subject of tariff revision shall be again opened before this law has had a fair trial. It is quite true that every tariff schedule is subject to objections.   No bill was ever framed, I suppose, that in all of its rates and classifications had the full approval even of a party caucus.   Such legislation is always and necessarily the product of compromise as to details, and the present law is no exception.   But in its general scope and effect I think it will justify the support of those who believe that American legislation should conserve and defend American trade and the wages of American workmen.

The misinformation as to the terms of the act which has been so widely disseminated at home and abroad will be corrected by experience, and the evil auguries as to its results confounded by the market reports, the savings banks, international trade balances, and the general prosperity of our people.   Already we begin to hear from abroad and from our custom-houses that the prohibitory effect upon importations imputed to the act is not justified.   The imports at the port of New York for the first three weeks of November were nearly 8 per cent greater than for the same period in 1889 and 29 per cent greater than in the same period of 1888. And so far from being an act to limit exports, I confidently believe that under it we shall secure a larger and more profitable participation in foreign trade than we have ever enjoyed, and that we shall recover a proportionate participation in the ocean carrying trade of the world.

The criticisms of the bill that have come to us from foreign sources may well be rejected for repugnancy.   If these critics really believe that the adoption by us of a free-trade policy, or of tariff rates having reference solely to revenue, would diminish the participation of their own countries in the commerce of the world, their advocacy and promotion, by speech and other forms of organized effort, of this movement among our people is a rare exhibition of unselfishness in trade.   And, on the other hand, if they sincerely believe that the adoption of a protective-tariff policy by this country inures to their profit and our hurt, it is noticeably strange that they should lead the outcry against the authors of a policy so helpful to their countrymen and crown with their favor those who would snatch from them a substantial share of a trade with other lands already inadequate to their necessities.

There is no disposition among any of our people to promote prohibitory or retaliatory legislation.   Our policies are adopted not to the hurt of others, but to secure for ourselves those advantages that fairly grow out of our favored position as a nation. Our form of government, with its incident of universal suffrage, makes it imperative that we shall save our working people from the agitations and distresses which scant work and wages that have no margin for comfort always beget. But after all this is done it will be found that our markets are open to friendly commercial exchanges of enormous value to the other great powers.

From the time of my induction into office the duty of using every power and influence given by law to the executive department for the development of larger markets for our products, especially our farm products, has been kept constantly in mind, and no effort has been or will be spared to promote that end. We are under no disadvantage in any foreign market, except that we pay our workmen and workwomen better wages than are paid elsewhere—better abstractly, better relatively to the cost of the necessaries of life. I do not doubt that a very largely increased foreign trade is accessible to us without bartering for it either our home market for such products of the farm and shop as our own people can supply or the wages of our working people.

In many of the products of wood and iron and in meats and breadstuffs we have advantages that only need better facilities of intercourse and transportation to secure for them large foreign markets. The reciprocity clause of the tariff act wisely and effectively opens the way to secure a large reciprocal trade in exchange for the free admission to our ports of certain products. The right of independent nations to make special reciprocal trade concessions is well established, and does not impair either the comity due to other powers or what is known as the "favored-nation clause," so generally found in commercial treaties. What is given to one for an adequate agreed consideration can not be claimed by another freely. The state of the revenues was such that we could dispense with any import duties upon coffee, tea, hides, and the lower grades of sugar and molasses. That the large advantage resulting to the countries producing and exporting these articles by placing them on the free list entitled us to expect a fair return in the way of customs concessions upon articles exported by us to them was so obvious that to have gratuitously abandoned this opportunity to enlarge our trade would have been an unpardonable error.

There were but two methods of maintaining control of this question open to Congress—to place all of these articles upon the dutiable list, subject to such treaty agreements as could be secured, or to place them all presently upon the free list, but subject to the reimposition of specified duties if the countries from which we received them should refuse to give to us suitable reciprocal benefits. This latter method, I think, possesses great advantages. It expresses in advance the consent of Congress to reciprocity arrangements affecting these products, which must otherwise have been delayed and unascertained until each treaty was ratified by the Senate and the necessary legislation enacted by Congress. Experience has shown that some treaties looking to reciprocal trade have failed to secure a two-thirds vote in the Senate for ratification, and others having passed that stage have for years awaited the concurrence of the House and Senate in such modifications of our revenue laws as were necessary to give effect to their provisions.   We now have the concurrence of both Houses in advance in a distinct and definite offer of free entry to our ports of specific articles.   The Executive is not required to deal in conjecture as to what Congress will accept.   Indeed, this reciprocity provision is more than an offer.   Our part of the bargain is complete; delivery has been made; and when the countries from which we receive sugar, coffee, tea, and hides have placed on their free lists such of our products as shall be agreed upon as an equivalent for our concession, a proclamation of that fact completes the transaction; and in the meantime our own people have free sugar, tea, coffee, and hides.

The indications thus far given are very hopeful of early and favorable action by the countries from which we receive our large imports of coffee and sugar, and it is confidently believed that if steam communication with these countries can be promptly improved and enlarged the next year will show a most gratifying increase in our exports of breadstuffs and provisions, as well as of some important lines of manufactured goods.

In addition to the important bills that became laws before the adjournment of the last session, some other bills of the highest importance were well advanced toward a final vote and now stand upon the calendars of the two Houses in favored positions.   The present session has a fixed limit, and if these measures are not now brought to a final vote all the work that has been done upon them by this Congress is lost.   The proper consideration of these, of an apportionment bill, and of the annual appropriation bills will require not only that no working day of the session shall be lost, but that measures of minor and local interest shall not be allowed to interrupt or retard the progress of those that are of universal interest.   In view of these conditions, I refrain from bringing before you at this time some suggestions that would otherwise be made, and most earnestly invoke your attention to the duty of perfecting the important legislation now well advanced.   To some of these measures, which seem to me most important, I now briefly call your attention.

I desire to repeat with added urgency the recommendations contained in my last annual message in relation to the development of American steamship lines.*   The reciprocity clause of the tariff bill will be largely limited and its benefits retarded and diminished if provision is not contemporaneously made to encourage the establishment of first-class steam communication between our ports and the ports of such nations as may meet our overtures for enlarged commercial exchanges.   The steamship, carrying the mails stately and frequently and offering to passengers a comfortable, safe, and speedy transit, is the first condition of foreign trade.   It carries the order or the buyer, but not all that is ordered or bought.   It gives to the sailing vessels such cargoes as are not urgent or perishable, and, indirectly at least, promotes that important adjunct of commerce. There is now both in this country and in the nations of Central and South America a state of expectation and confidence as to increased trade that will give a double value to your prompt action upon this question.

The present situation of our mail communication with Australia illustrates the importance of early action by Congress. The Oceanic Steamship Company maintains a line of steamers between San Francisco, Sydney, and Auckland consisting of three vessels, two of which are of United States registry and one of foreign registry. For the service done by this line in carrying the mails we pay annually the sum of $46,000, being, as estimated, the full sea and United States inland postage, which is the limit fixed by law. The colonies of New South Wales and New Zealand have been paying annually to these lines £37,000 for carrying the mails from Sydney and Auckland to San Francisco. The contract under which this payment has been made is now about to expire, and those colonies have refused to renew the contract unless the United States shall pay a more equitable proportion of the whole sum necessary to maintain the service.

I am advised by the Postmaster-General that the United States receives for carrying the Australian mails, brought to San Francisco in these steamers, by rail to Vancouver, an estimated annual income of $75,000, while, as I have stated, we are paying out for the support of the steamship line that brings this mail to us only $46,000, leaving an annual surplus resulting from this service of $29,000. The trade of the United States with Australia, which is in a considerable part carried by these steamers, and the whole of which is practically dependent upon the mail communication which they maintain, is largely in our favor. Our total exports of merchandise to Australasian ports during the fiscal year ending June 30, 1890, were $11,266,484, while the total imports of merchandise from these ports were only $4,277,676. If we are not willing to see this important steamship line withdrawn, or continued with Vancouver substituted for San Francisco as the American terminal, Congress should put it in the power of the Postmaster-General to make a liberal increase in the amount now paid for the transportation of this important mail.

The South Atlantic and Gulf ports occupy a very favored position toward the new and important commerce which the reciprocity clause of the tariff act and the postal shipping bill are designed to promote. Steamship lines from these ports to some northern port of South America will almost certainly effect a connection between the railroad systems of the continents long before any continuous line of railroads can be put into operation. The very large appropriation made at the last session for the harbor of Galveston was justified, as it seemed to me, by these considerations. The great Northwest will feel the advantage of trunk lines to the South as well as to the East and of the new markets opened for their surplus food products and for many of their manufactured products.

I had occasion in May last to transmit to Congress a report adopted by the International American Conference upon the subject of the incorporation of an international American bank, with a view to facilitating money exchanges between the States represented in that conference. Such an institution would greatly promote the trade we are seeking to develop.   I renew the recommendation that a careful and well-guarded charter be granted.   I do not think the powers granted should include those ordinarily exercised by trust, guaranty, and safe-deposit companies, or that more branches in the United States should be authorized than are strictly necessary to accomplish the object primarily in view, namely, convenient foreign exchanges.   It is quite important that prompt action should be taken in this matter, in order that any appropriations for better communication with these countries and any agreements that may be made for reciprocal trade may not be hindered by the inconvenience of making exchanges through European money centers or burdened by the tribute which is an incident of that method of business.

The bill for the relief of the Supreme Court has after many years of discussion reached a position where final action is easily attainable, and it is hoped that any differences of opinion may be so harmonized as to save the essential features of this very important measure.   In this connection I earnestly renew my recommendation that the salaries of the judges of the United States district courts be so readjusted that none of them shall receive less than $5,000 per annum.

The subject of the unadjusted Spanish and Mexican land grants and the urgent necessity for providing some commission or tribunal for the trial of questions of title growing out of them were twice brought by me to the attention of Congress at the last session.   Bills have been reported from the proper committees in both Houses upon the subject, and I very earnestly hope that this Congress will put an end to the delay which has attended the settlement of the disputes as to the title between the settlers and the claimants under these grants.   These disputes retard the prosperity and disturb the peace of large and important communities. The governor of New Mexico in his last report to the Secretary of the Interior suggests some modifications of the provisions of the pending bills relating to the small holdings of farm lands.   I commend to your attention the suggestions of the Secretary of the Interior upon this subject.

The enactment of a national bankrupt law I still regard as very desirable.   The Constitution having given to Congress jurisdiction of this subject, it should be exercised and uniform rules provided for the administration of the affairs of insolvent debtors.   The inconveniences resulting from the occasional and temporary exercise of this power by Congress and from the conflicting State codes of insolvency which come into force intermediately should be removed by the enactment of a simple, inexpensive, and permanent national bankrupt law.

I also renew my recommendation in favor of legislation affording just copyright protection to foreign authors on a footing of reciprocal advantage for our authors abroad.

It may still be possible for this Congress to inaugurate by suitable legislation a movement looking to uniformity and increased safety in the use of couplers and brakes upon freight trains engaged in interstate commerce. The chief difficulty in the way is to secure agreement as to the best appliances, simplicity, effectiveness, and cost being considered. This difficulty will only yield to legislation, which should be based upon full inquiry and impartial tests. The purpose should be to secure the cooperation of all well-disposed managers and owners; but the fearful fact that every year's delay involves the sacrifice of 2,000 lives and the maiming of 20,000 young men should plead both with Congress and the managers against any needless delay.

The subject of the conservation and equal distribution of the water supply of the arid regions has had much attention from Congress, but has not as yet been put upon a permanent and satisfactory basis. The urgency of the subject does not grow out of any large present demand for the use of these lands for agriculture, but out of the danger that the water supply and the sites for the necessary catch basins may fall into the hands of individuals or private corporations and be used to render subservient the large areas dependent upon such supply. The owner of the water is the owner of the lands, however the titles may run. All unappropriated natural water sources and all necessary reservoir sites should be held by the Government for the equal use at fair rates of the homestead settlers who will eventually take up these lands. The United States should not, in my opinion, undertake the construction of dams or canals, but should limit its work to such surveys and observations as will determine the water supply, both surface and subterranean, the areas capable of irrigation, and the location and storage capacity of reservoirs. This done, the use of the water and of the reservoir sites might be granted to the respective States or Territories or to individuals or associations upon the condition that the necessary works should be constructed and the water furnished at fair rates without discrimination, the rates to be subject to supervision by the legislatures or by boards of water commissioners duly constituted. The essential thing to be secured is the common and equal use at fair rates of the accumulated water supply. It were almost better that these lands should remain arid than that those who occupy them should become the slaves of unrestrained monopolies controlling the one essential element of land values and crop results.

The use of the telegraph by the Post-Office Department as a means for the rapid transmission of written communications is, I believe, upon proper terms, quite desirable. The Government does not own or operate the railroads, and it should not, I think, own or operate the telegraph lines. It does, however, seem to be quite practicable for the Government to contract with the telegraph companies, as it does with railroad companies, to carry at specified rates such communications as the senders may designate for this method of transmission. I recommend that such legislation be enacted as will enable the Post-Office Department fairly to test by experiment the advantages of such a use of the telegraph.

If any intelligent and loyal company of American citizens were required to catalogue the essential human conditions of national life, I do not doubt that with absolute unanimity they would begin with "free and honest elections." And it is gratifying to know that generally there is a growing and nonpartisan demand for better election laws; but against this sign of hope and progress must be set the depressing and undeniable fact that election laws and methods are sometimes cunningly contrived to secure minority control, while violence completes the shortcomings of fraud.

In my last annual message I suggested that the development of the existing law providing a Federal supervision of Congressional elections offered an effective method of reforming these abuses. The need of such a law has manifested itself in many parts of the country, and its wholesome restraints and penalties will be useful in all. The constitutionality of such legislation has been affirmed by the Supreme Court. Its probable effectiveness is evidenced by the character of the opposition that is made to it. It has been denounced as if it were a new exercise of Federal power and an invasion of the rights of States. Nothing could be further from the truth. Congress has already fixed the time for the election of members of Congress. It has declared that votes for members of Congress must be by written or printed ballot; it has provided for the appointment by the circuit courts in certain cases, and upon the petition of a certain number of citizens, of election supervisors, and made it their duty to supervise the registration of voters conducted by the State officers; to challenge persons offering to register; to personally inspect and scrutinize the registry lists, and to affix their names to the lists for the purpose of identification and the prevention of frauds; to attend at elections and remain with the boxes till they are all cast and counted; to attach to the registry lists and election returns any statement touching the accuracy and fairness of the registry and election, and to take and transmit to the Clerk of the House of Representatives any evidence of fraudulent practices which may be presented to them. The same law provides for the appointment of deputy United States marshals to attend at the polls, support the supervisors in the discharge of their duties, and to arrest persons violating the election laws. The provisions of this familiar title of the Revised Statutes have been put into exercise by both the great political parties, and in the North as well as in the South, by the filing with the court of the petitions required by the law.

It is not, therefore, a question whether we shall have a Federal election law, for we now have one and have had for nearly twenty years, but whether we shall have an effective law. The present law stops just short of effectiveness, for it surrenders to the local authorities all control over the certification which establishes the *prima facie* right to a seat in the House of Representatives. This defect should be cured. Equality of representation and the parity of the electors must be maintained or everything that is valuable in our system of government is lost. The qualifications of an elector must be sought in the law, not in the opinions, prejudices, or fears of any class, however powerful. The path of the elector to the ballot box must be free from the ambush of fear and the enticements of fraud; the count so true and open that none shall gainsay it. Such a law should be absolutely nonpartisan and impartial. It should give the advantage to honesty and the control to majorities. Surely there is nothing sectional about this creed, and if it shall happen that the penalties of laws intended to enforce these rights fall here and not there it is not because the law is sectional, but because, happily, crime is local and not universal. Nor should it be forgotten that every law, whether relating to elections or to any other subject, whether enacted by the State or by the nation, has force behind it; the courts, the marshal or constable, the *posse comitatus*, the prison, are all and always behind the law.

One can not be justly charged with unfriendliness to any section or class who seeks only to restrain violations of law and of personal right. No community will find lawlessness profitable. No community can afford to have it known that the officers who are charged with the preservation of the public peace and the restraint of the criminal classes are themselves the product of fraud or violence. The magistrate is then without respect and the law without sanction. The floods of lawlessness can not be leveed and made to run in one channel. The killing of a United States marshal carrying a writ of arrest for an election offense is full of prompting and suggestion to men who are pursued by a city marshal for a crime against life or property.

But it is said that this legislation will revive race animosities, and some have even suggested that when the peaceful methods of fraud are made impossible they may be supplanted by intimidation and violence. If the proposed law gives to any qualified elector by a hair's weight more than his equal influence or detracts by so much from any other qualified elector, it is fatally impeached. But if the law is equal and the animosities it is to evoke grow out of the fact that some electors have been accustomed to exercise the franchise for others as well as for themselves, then these animosities ought not to be confessed without shame, and can not be given any weight in the discussion without dishonor   No choice is left to me but to enforce with vigor all laws intended to secure to the citizen his constitutional rights and to recommend that the inadequacies of such laws be promptly remedied. If to promote with zeal and ready interest every project for the development of its material interests, its rivers, harbors, mines, and factories, and the intelligence, peace, and security under the law of its communities and its homes is not accepted as sufficient evidence of friendliness to any State or section, I can not add connivance at election practices that not only disturb local results, but rob the electors of other States and sections of their most priceless political rights.

The preparation of the general appropriation bills should be conducted with the greatest care and the closest scrutiny of expenditures. Appropriations should be adequate to the needs of the public service, but they should be absolutely free from prodigality.

I venture again to remind you that the brief time remaining for the consideration of the important legislation now awaiting your attention offers no margin for waste. If the present duty is discharged with diligence, fidelity, and courage, the work of the Fifty-first Congress may be confidently submitted to the considerate judgment of the people.

THIRD ANNUAL MESSAGE.

EXECUTIVE MANSION, *December 9, 1891.*

To the Senate and House of Representatives:

The reports of the heads of the several Executive Departments, required by law to be submitted to me, which are herewith transmitted, and the reports of the Secretary of the Treasury and the Attorney-General, made directly to Congress, furnish a comprehensive view of the administrative work of the last fiscal year relating to internal affairs. It would be of great advantage if these reports could have an attentive perusal by every member of Congress and by all who take an interest in public affairs. Such a perusal could not fail to excite a higher appreciation of the vast labor and conscientious effort which are given to the conduct of our civil administration.

The reports will, I believe, show that every question has been approached, considered, and decided from the standpoint of public duty and upon considerations affecting the public interests alone. Again I invite to every branch of the service the attention and scrutiny of Congress.

The work of the State Department during the last year has been characterized by an unusual number of important negotiations and by diplomatic results of a notable and highly beneficial character. Among these are the reciprocal trade arrangements which have been concluded, in the exercise of the powers conferred by section 3 of the tariff law, with the Republic of Brazil, with Spain for its West India possessions, and with Santo Domingo. Like negotiations with other countries have been much advanced, and it is hoped that before the close of the year further definitive trade arrangements of great value will be concluded.

In view of the reports which had been received as to the diminution of the seal herds in the Bering Sea, I deemed it wise to propose to Her Majesty's Government in February last that an agreement for a closed season should be made pending the negotiations for arbitration, which then seemed to be approaching a favorable conclusion. After much correspondence and delays, for which this Government was not responsible, an agreement was reached and signed on the 15th of June, by which Great Britain undertook from that date and until May 1, 1892, to prohibit the killing by her subjects of seals in the Bering Sea, and the Government of the United States during the same period to enforce its existing prohibition against pelagic sealing and to limit the catch by the fur-seal company upon the islands to 7,500 skins. If this agreement could have been reached earlier in response to the strenuous endeavors of this Government, it would have been more effective; but coming even as late as it did it unquestionably resulted in greatly diminishing the destruction of the seals by the Canadian sealers.

In my last annual message I stated that the basis of arbitration proposed by Her Majesty's Government for the adjustment of the long-pending controversy as to the seal fisheries was not acceptable. I am glad now to be able to announce that terms satisfactory to this Government have been agreed upon and that an agreement as to the arbitrators is all that is necessary to the completion of the convention. In view of the advanced position which this Government has taken upon the subject of international arbitration, this renewed expression of our adherence to this method for the settlement of disputes such as have arisen in the Bering Sea will, I doubt not, meet with the concurrence of Congress.

Provision should be made for a joint demarcation of the frontier line between Canada and the United States wherever required by the increasing border settlements, and especially for the exact location of the water boundary in the straits and rivers.

I should have been glad to announce some favorable disposition of the boundary dispute between Great Britain and Venezuela touching the western frontier of British Guiana, but the friendly efforts of the United States in that direction have thus far been unavailing. This Government will continue to express its concern at any appearance of foreign encroachment on territories long under the administrative control of American States. The determination of a disputed boundary is easily attainable by amicable arbitration where the rights of the respective parties rest, as here, on historic facts readily ascertainable.

The law of the last Congress providing a system of inspection for our meats intended for export, and clothing the President with power to exclude foreign products from our market in case the country sending them should perpetuate unjust discriminations against any product of the

United States, placed this Government in a position to effectively urge the removal of such discriminations against our meats. It is gratifying to be able to state that Germany, Denmark, Italy, Austria, and France, in the order named, have opened their ports to inspected American pork products. The removal of these restrictions in every instance was asked for and given solely upon the ground that we have now provided a meat inspection that should be accepted as adequate to the complete removal of the dangers, real or fancied, which had been previously urged. The State Department, our ministers abroad, and the Secretary of Agriculture have cooperated with unflagging and intelligent zeal for the accomplishment of this great result. The outlines of an agreement have been reached with Germany looking to equitable trade concessions in consideration of the continued free importation of her sugars, but the time has not yet arrived when this correspondence can be submitted to Congress.

The recent political disturbances in the Republic of Brazil have excited regret and solicitude. The information we possessed was too meager to enable us to form a satisfactory judgment of the causes leading to the temporary assumption of supreme power by President Fonseca; but this Government did not fail to express to him its anxious solicitude for the peace of Brazil and for the maintenance of the free political institutions which had recently been established there, nor to offer our advice that great moderation should be observed in the clash of parties and the contest for leadership. These counsels were received in the most friendly spirit, and the latest information is that constitutional government has been reestablished without bloodshed.

The lynching at New Orleans in March last of eleven men of Italian nativity by a mob of citizens was a most deplorable and discreditable incident. It did not, however, have its origin in any general animosity to the Italian people, nor in any disrespect to the Government of Italy, with which our relations were of the most friendly character. The fury of the mob was directed against these men as the supposed participants or accessories in the murder of a city officer. I do not allude to this as mitigating in any degree this offense against law and humanity, but only as affecting the international questions which grew out of it. It was at once represented by the Italian minister that several of those whose lives had been taken by the mob were Italian subjects, and a demand was made for the punishment of the participants and for an indemnity to the families of those who were killed. It is to be regretted that the manner in which these claims were presented was not such as to promote a calm discussion of the questions involved; but this may well be attributed to the excitement and indignation which the crime naturally evoked. The views of this Government as to its obligations to foreigners domiciled here were fully stated in the correspondence, as well as its purpose to make an investigation of the affair with a view to determine whether there were present any circumstances that could under such rules of duty as we had indicated create an obligation upon the United States. The temporary absence of a minister plenipotentiary of Italy at this capital has retarded the further correspondence, but it is not doubted that a friendly conclusion is attainable.

Some suggestions growing out of this unhappy incident are worthy the attention of Congress. It would, I believe, be entirely competent for Congress to make offenses against the treaty rights of foreigners domiciled in the United States cognizable in the Federal courts. This has not, however, been done, and the Federal officers and courts have no power in such cases to intervene, either for the protection of a foreign citizen or for the punishment of his slayers. It seems to me to follow, in this state of the law, that the officers of the State charged with police and judicial powers in such cases must in the consideration of international questions growing out of such incidents be regarded in such sense as Federal agents as to make this Government answerable for their acts in cases where it would be answerable if the United States had used its constitutional power to define and punish crime against treaty rights.

The civil war in Chile, which began in January last, was continued, but fortunately with infrequent and not important armed collisions, until August 28, when the Congressional forces landed near Valparaiso and after a bloody engagement captured that city. President Balmaceda at once recognized that his cause was lost, and a Provisional Government was speedily established by the victorious party. Our minister was promptly directed to recognize and put himself in communication with this Government so soon as it should have established its *de facto* character, which was done. During the pendency of this civil contest frequent indirect appeals were made to this Government to extend belligerent rights to the insurgents and to give audience to their representatives. This was declined, and that policy was pursued throughout which this Government when wrenched by civil war so strenuously insisted upon on the part of European nations. The *Itata*, an armed vessel commanded by a naval officer of the insurgent fleet, manned by its sailors and with soldiers on board, was seized under process of the United States court at San Diego, Cal., for a violation of our neutrality laws. While in the custody of an officer of the court the vessel was forcibly wrested from his control and put to sea. It would have been inconsistent with the dignity and self-respect of this Government not to have insisted that the *Itata* should be returned to San Diego to abide the judgment of the court. This was so clear to the junta of the Congressional party, established at Iquique, that before the arrival of the *Itata* at that port the secretary of foreign relations of the Provisional Government addressed to Rear-Admiral Brown, commanding the United States naval forces, a communication, from which the following is an extract:

The Provisional Government has learned by the cablegrams of the Associated Press that the transport *Itata*, detained in San Diego by order of the United States for taking on board munitions of war, and in possession of the marshal, left the port, carrying on board this official, who was landed at a point near the coast, and then continued her voyage. * * * If this news be correct this Government would deplore the conduct of the *Itata*, and as an evidence that it is not disposed to support or agree to the infraction of the laws of the United States the undersigned takes advantage of the personal relations you have been good enough to maintain with him since your arrival in this port to declare to you that as soon as she is within reach of our orders his Government will put the *Itata*, with the arms and munitions she took on board in San Diego, at the disposition of the United States.

A trial in the district court of the United States for the southern district of California has recently resulted in a decision holding, among other things, that inasmuch as the Congressional party had not been recognized as a belligerent the acts done in its interest could not be a violation of our neutrality laws. From this judgment the United States has appealed, not that the condemnation of the vessel is a matter of importance, but that we may know what the present state of our law is; for if this construction of the statute is correct there is obvious necessity for revision and amendment.

During the progress of the war in Chile this Government tendered its good offices to bring about a peaceful adjustment, and it was at one time hoped that a good result might be reached; but in this we were disappointed.

The instructions to our naval officers and to our minister at Santiago from the first to the last of this struggle enjoined upon them the most impartial treatment and absolute noninterference. I am satisfied that these instructions were observed and that our representatives were always watchful to use their influence impartially in the interest of humanity, and on more than one occasion did so effectively. We could not forget, however, that this Government was in diplomatic relations with the then established Government of Chile, as it is now in such relations with the successor of that Government. I am quite sure that President Montt, who has, under circumstances of promise for the peace of Chile, been installed as President of that Republic, will not desire that in the unfortunate event of any revolt against his authority the policy of this Government should be other than that which we have recently observed. No official complaint of the conduct of our minister or of our naval officers during the struggle has been presented to this Government, and it is a matter of regret that so many of our own people should have given ear to unofficial charges and complaints that manifestly had their origin in rival interests and in a wish to pervert the relations of the United States with Chile.

The collapse of the Government of Balmaceda brought about a condition which is unfortunately too familiar in the history of the Central and South American States. With the overthrow of the Balmaceda Government he and many of his councilors and officers became at once fugitives for their lives, and appealed to the commanding officers of the foreign naval vessels in the harbor of Valparaiso and to the resident foreign ministers at Santiago for asylum. This asylum was freely given, according to my information, by the naval vessels of several foreign powers and by several of the legations at Santiago. The American minister as well as his colleagues, acting upon the impulse of humanity, extended asylum to political refugees whose lives were in peril. I have not been willing to direct the surrender of such of these persons as are still in the American legation without suitable conditions.

It is believed that the Government of Chile is not in a position, in view of the precedents with which it has been connected, to broadly deny the right of asylum, and the correspondence has not thus far presented any such denial. The treatment of our minister for a time was such as to call for a decided protest, and it was very gratifying to observe that unfriendly measures, which were undoubtedly the result of the prevailing excitement, were at once rescinded or suitably relaxed.

On the 16th of October an event occurred in Valparaiso so serious and tragic in its circumstances and results as to very justly excite the indignation of our people and to call for prompt and decided action on the part of this Government. A considerable number of the sailors of the United States steamship *Baltimore*, then in the harbor at Valparaiso, being upon shore leave and unarmed, were assaulted by armed men nearly simultaneously in different localities in the city. One petty officer was killed outright and seven or eight seamen were seriously wounded, one of whom has since died. So savage and brutal was the assault that several of our sailors received more than two and one as many as eighteen stab wounds. An investigation of the affair was promptly made by a board of officers of the *Baltimore*, and their report shows that these assaults were unprovoked, that our men were conducting themselves in a peaceable and orderly manner, and that some of the police of the city took part in the assault and used their weapons with fatal effect, while a few others, with some well-disposed citizens, endeavored to protect our men. Thirty-six of our sailors were arrested, and some of them while being taken to prison were cruelly beaten and maltreated. The fact that they were all discharged, no criminal charge being lodged against any one of them, shows very clearly that they were innocent of any breach of the peace.

So far as I have yet been able to learn no other explanation of this bloody work has been suggested than that it had its origin in hostility to those men as sailors of the United States, wearing the uniform of their Government, and not in any individual act or personal animosity. The attention of the Chilean Government was at once called to this affair, and a statement of the facts obtained by the investigation we had conducted was submitted, accompanied by a request to be advised of any other or qualifying facts in the possession of the Chilean Government that might tend to relieve this affair of the appearance of an insult to this Government. The Chilean Government was also advised that if such qualifying facts did not exist this Government would confidently expect full and prompt reparation.

It is to be regretted that the reply of the secretary for foreign affairs of the Provisional Government was couched in an offensive tone. To this no response has been made. This Government is now awaiting the result of an investigation which has been conducted by the criminal court at Valparaiso. It is reported unofficially that the investigation is about completed, and it is expected that the result will soon be communicated to this Government, together with some adequate and satisfactory response to the note by which the attention of Chile was called to this incident. If these just expectations should be disappointed or further needless delay intervene, I will by a special message bring this matter again to the attention of Congress for such action as may be necessary. The entire correspondence with the Government of Chile will at an early day be submitted to Congress.

I renew the recommendation of my special message dated January 16, 1890, for the adoption of the necessary legislation to enable this Government to apply in the case of Sweden and Norway the same rule in respect to the levying of tonnage dues as was claimed and secured to the shipping of the United States in 1828 under Article VIII of the treaty of 1827.

The adjournment of the Senate without action on the pending acts for the suppression of the slave traffic in Africa and for the reform of the revenue tariff of the Independent State of the Kongo left this Government unable to exchange those acts on the date fixed, July 2, 1891. A *modus vivendi* has been concluded by which the power of the Kongo State to levy duties on imports is left unimpaired, and by agreement of all the signatories to the general slave-trade act the time for the exchange of ratifications on the part of the United States has been extended to February 2, 1892.

The late outbreak against foreigners in various parts of the Chinese Empire has been a cause of deep concern in view of the numerous establishments of our citizens in the interior of that country. This Government can do no less than insist upon a continuance of the protective and punitory measures which the Chinese Government has heretofore applied. No effort will be omitted to protect our citizens peaceably sojourning in China, but recent unofficial information indicates that what was at first regarded as an outbreak of mob violence against foreigners has assumed the larger form of an insurrection against public order.

The Chinese Government has declined to receive Mr. Blair as the minister of the United States on the ground that as a participant while a Senator in the enactment of the existing legislation against the introduction of Chinese laborers he has become unfriendly and objectionable to China. I have felt constrained to point out to the Chinese Government the untenableness of this position, which seems to rest as much on the unacceptability of our legislation as on that of the person chosen, and which if admitted would practically debar the selection of any representative so long as the existing laws remain in force.

You will be called upon to consider the expediency of making special provision by law for the temporary admission of some Chinese artisans and laborers in connection with the exhibit of Chinese industries at the approaching Columbian Exposition. I regard it as desirable that the Chinese exhibit be facilitated in every proper way.

A question has arisen with the Government of Spain touching the rights of American citizens in the Caroline Islands. Our citizens there long prior to the confirmation of Spain's claim to the islands had secured by settlement and purchase certain rights to the recognition and maintenance of which the faith of Spain was pledged. I have had reason within the past year very strongly to protest against the failure to carry out this pledge on the part of His Majesty's ministers, which has resulted in great injustice and injury to the American residents.

The Government and people of Spain propose to celebrate the four hundredth anniversary of the discovery of America by holding an exposition at Madrid, which will open on the 12th of September and continue until the 31st of December, 1892. A cordial invitation has been extended to the United States to take part in this commemoration, and as Spain was one of the first nations to express the intention to participate in the World's Columbian Exposition at Chicago, it would be very appropriate for this Government to give this invitation its friendly promotion.

Surveys for the connecting links of the projected intercontinental railway are in progress, not only in Mexico, but at various points along the course mapped out. Three surveying parties are now in the field under the direction of the commission. Nearly 1,000 miles of the proposed road have been surveyed, including the most difficult part, that through Ecuador and the southern part of Colombia. The reports of the engineers are very satisfactory, and show that no insurmountable obstacles have been met with.

On November 12, 1884, a treaty was concluded with Mexico reaffirming the boundary between the two countries as described in the treaties of February 2, 1848, and December 30, 1853. March 1, 1889, a further treaty was negotiated to facilitate the carrying out of the principles of the treaty of 1884 and to avoid the difficulties occasioned by reason of the changes and alterations that take place from natural causes in the Rio Grande and Colorado rivers in the portions thereof constituting the boundary line between the two Republics. The International Boundary Commission provided for by the treaty of 1889 to have exclusive jurisdiction of any question that may arise has been named by the Mexican Government. An appropriation is necessary to enable the United States to fulfill its treaty obligations in this respect.

The death of King Kalakaua in the United States afforded occasion to testify our friendship for Hawaii by conveying the King's body to his own land in a naval vessel with all due honors.   The Government of his successor, Queen Liliuokolani is seeking to promote closer commercial relations with the United States.   Surveys for the much-needed submarine cable from our Pacific coast to Honolulu are in progress, and this enterprise should have the suitable promotion of the two Governments.   I strongly recommend that provision be made for improving the harbor of Pearl River and equipping it as a naval station.

The arbitration treaty formulated by the International American Conference lapsed by reason of the failure to exchange ratifications fully within the limit of time provided; but several of the Governments concerned have expressed a desire to save this important result of the conference by an extension of the period.   It is, in my judgment, incumbent upon the United States to conserve the influential initiative it has taken in this measure by ratifying the instrument and by advocating the proposed extension of the time for exchange.   These views have been made known to the other signatories.

This Government has found occasion to express in a friendly spirit, but with much earnestness, to the Government of the Czar its serious concern because of the harsh measures now being enforced against the Hebrews in Russia.   By the revival of antisemitic laws, long in abeyance, great numbers of those unfortunate people have been constrained to abandon their homes and leave the Empire by reason of the impossibility of finding subsistence within the pale to which it is sought to confine them.   The immigration of these people to the United States—many other countries being closed to them—is largely increasing and is likely to assume proportions which may make it difficult to find homes and employment for them here and to seriously affect the labor market.   It is estimated that over 1,000,000 will be forced from Russia within a few years.   The Hebrew is never a beggar; he has always kept the law—life by toil—often under severe and oppressive civil restrictions.   It is also true that no race, sect, or class has more fully cared for its own than the Hebrew race.   But the sudden transfer of such a multitude under conditions that tend to strip them of their small accumulations and to depress their energies and courage is neither good for them nor for us.

The banishment, whether by direct decree or by not less certain indirect methods, of so large a number of men and women is not a local question.   A decree to leave one country is in the nature of things an order to enter another—some other.   This consideration, as well as the suggestion of humanity, furnishes ample ground for the remonstrances which we have presented to Russia, while our historic friendship for that Government can not fail to give the assurance that our representations are those of a sincere wellwisher.

The annual report or the Maritime Canal Company of Nicaragua shows that much costly and necessary preparatory work has been done during the year in the construction of shops, railroad tracks, and harbor piers and breakwaters, and that the work of canal construction has made some progress.

I deem it to be a matter of the highest concern to the United States that this canal, connecting the waters of the Atlantic and Pacific oceans and giving to us a short water communication between our ports upon those two great seas, should be speedily constructed and at the smallest practicable limit of cost. The gain in freights to the people and the direct saving to the Government of the United States in the use of its naval vessels would pay the entire cost of this work within a short series of years. The report of the Secretary of the Navy shows the saving in our naval expenditures which would result.

The Senator from Alabama (Mr. Morgan) in his argument upon this subject before the Senate at the last session did not overestimate the importance of this work when he said that "the canal is the most important subject now connected with the commercial growth and progress of the United States."

If this work is to be promoted by the usual financial methods and without the aid of this Government, the expenditures in its interest-bearing securities and stock will probably be twice the actual cost. This will necessitate higher tolls and constitute a heavy and altogether needless burden upon our commerce and that of the world. Every dollar of the bonds and stock of the company should represent a dollar expended in the legitimate and economical prosecution of the work. This is only possible by giving to the bonds the guaranty of the United States Government. Such a guaranty would secure the ready sale at par of a 3 per cent bond from time to time as the money was needed. I do not doubt that built upon these business methods the canal would when fully inaugurated earn its fixed charges and operating expenses. But if its bonds are to be marketed at heavy discounts and every bond sold is to be accompanied by a gift of stock, as has come to be expected by investors in such enterprises, the traffic will be seriously burdened to pay interest and dividends. I am quite willing to recommend Government promotion in the prosecution of a work which, if no other means offered for securing its completion, is of such transcendent interest that the Government should, in my opinion, secure it by direct appropriations from its Treasury.

A guaranty of the bonds of the canal company to an amount necessary to the completion of the canal could, I think, be so given as not to involve any serious risk of ultimate loss. The things to be carefully guarded are the completion of the work within the limits of the guaranty, the subrogation of the United States to the rights of the first-mortgage bondholders for any amounts it may have to pay, and in the meantime a control of the stock of the company as a security against mismanagement and loss. I most sincerely hope that neither party nor sectional lines will be drawn upon this great American project, so full of interest to the people of all our States and so influential in its effects upon the prestige and prosperity of our common country.

The island of Navassa, in the West Indian group, has, under the provisions of Title VII of the Revised Statutes, been recognized by the President as appertaining to the United States. It contains guano deposits, is owned by the Navassa Phosphate Company, and is occupied solely by its employees. In September, 1889, a revolt took place among these laborers, resulting in the killing of some of the agents of the company, caused, as the laborers claimed, by cruel treatment. These men were arrested and tried in the United States court at Baltimore, under section 5576 of the statute referred to, as if the offenses had been committed on board a merchant vessel of the United States on the high seas. There appeared on the trial and otherwise came to me such evidences of the bad treatment of the men that in consideration of this and of the fact that the men had no access to any public officer or tribunal for protection or the redress of their wrongs I commuted the death sentences that had been passed by the court upon three of them. In April last my attention was again called to this island and to the unregulated condition of things there by a letter from a colored laborer, who complained that he was wrongfully detained upon the island by the phosphate company after the expiration of his contract of service. A naval vessel was sent to examine into the case of this man and generally into the condition of things on the island. It was found that the laborer referred to had been detained beyond the contract limit and that a condition of revolt again existed among the laborers. A board of naval officers reported, among other things, as follows:

We would desire to state further that the discipline maintained on the island seems to be that of a convict establishment without its comforts and cleanliness, and that until more attention is paid to the shipping of laborers by placing it under Government supervision to prevent misunderstanding and misrepresentation, and until some amelioration is shown in the treatment of the laborers, these disorders will be of constant occurrence.

I recommend legislation that shall place labor contracts upon this and other islands having the relation that Navassa has to the United States under the supervision of a court commissioner, and that shall provide at the expense of the owners an officer to reside upon the island, with power to judge and adjust disputes and to enforce a just and humane treatment of the employees. It is inexcusable that American laborers should be left within our own jurisdiction without access to any Government officer or tribunal for their protection and the redress of their wrongs.

International copyright has been secured, in accordance with the conditions of the act of March 3, 1891, with Belgium, France, Great Britain and the British possessions, and Switzerland, the laws of those countries permitting to our citizens the benefit of copyright on substantially the same basis as to their own citizens or subjects.

With Germany a special convention has been negotiated upon this subject which will bring that country within the reciprocal benefits of our legislation.

The general interest in the operations of the Treasury Department has been much augmented during the last year by reason of the conflicting predictions, which accompanied and followed the tariff and other legislation of the last Congress affecting the revenues, as to the results of this legislation upon the Treasury and upon the country. On the one hand it was contended that imports would so fall off as to leave the Treasury bankrupt and that the prices of articles entering into the living of the people would be so enhanced as to disastrously affect their comfort and happiness, while on the other it was argued that the loss to the revenue, largely the result of placing sugar on the free list, would be a direct gain to the people; that the prices of the necessaries of life, including those most highly protected, would not be enhanced; that labor would have a larger market and the products of the farm advanced prices, while the Treasury surplus and receipts would be adequate to meet the appropriations, including the large exceptional expenditures for the refunding to the States of the direct tax and the redemption of the 4½ per cent bonds.

It is not my purpose to enter at any length into a discussion of the effects of the legislation to which I have referred; but a brief examination of the statistics of the Treasury and a general glance at the state of business throughout the country will, I think, satisfy any impartial inquirer that its results have disappointed the evil prophecies of its opponents and in a large measure realized the hopeful predictions of its friends. Rarely, if ever before, in the history of the country has there been a time when the proceeds of one day's labor or the product of one farmed acre would purchase so large an amount of those things that enter into the living of the masses of the people. I believe that a full test will develop the fact that the tariff act of the Fifty-first Congress is very favorable in its average effect upon the prices of articles entering into common use.

During the twelve months from October 1, 1890, to September 30, 1891, the total value of our foreign commerce (imports and exports combined) was $1,747,806,406, which was the largest of any year in the history of the United States. The largest in any previous year was in 1890, when our commerce amounted to $1,647,139,093, and the last year exceeds this enormous aggregate by over one hundred millions. It is interesting, and to some will be surprising, to know that during the year ending September 30, 1891, our imports of merchandise amounted to $824,715,270, which was an increase of more than $11,000,000 over the value of the imports of the corresponding months of the preceding year, when the imports of merchandise were unusually large in anticipation of the tariff legislation then pending. The average annual value of the imports of merchandise for the ten years from 1881 to 1890 was $692,186,522, and during the year ending September 30, 1891, this annual average was exceeded by $132,528,469.

The value of free imports during the twelve months ending September 30, 1891, was $118,092,387 more than the value of free imports during the corresponding twelve months of the preceding year, and there was during the same period a decrease of $106,846,508 in the value of imports of dutiable merchandise. The percentage of merchandise admitted free of duty during the year to which I have referred, the first under the new tariff, was 48.18, while during the preceding twelve months, under the old tariff, the percentage was 34.27, an increase of 13.91 per cent. If we take the six months ending September 30 last, which covers the time during which sugars have been admitted free of duty, the per cent of value of merchandise imported free of duty is found to be 55.37, which is a larger percentage of free imports than during any prior fiscal year in the history of the Government.

If we turn to exports of merchandise, the statistics are full of gratification. The value of such exports of merchandise for the twelve months ending September 30, 1891, was $923,091,136, while for the corresponding previous twelve months it was $860,177,115, an increase of $62,914,021, which is nearly three times the average annual increase of exports of merchandise for the preceding twenty years. This exceeds in amount and value the exports of merchandise during any year in the history of the Government. The increase in the value of exports of agricultural products during the year referred to over the corresponding twelve months of the prior year was $45,846,197, while the increase in the value of exports of manufactured products was $16,838,240.

There is certainly nothing in the condition of trade, foreign or domestic, there is certainly nothing in the condition of our people of any class, to suggest that the existing tariff and revenue legislation bears oppressively upon the people or retards the commercial development of the nation. It may be argued that our condition would be better if tariff legislation were upon a free-trade basis; but it can not be denied that all the conditions of prosperity and of general contentment are present in a larger degree than ever before in our history, and that, too, just when it was prophesied they would be in the worst state. Agitation for radical changes in tariff and financial legislation can not help but may seriously impede business, to the prosperity of which some degree of stability in legislation is essential.

I think there are conclusive evidences that the new tariff has created several great industries, which will within a few years give employment to several hundred thousand American working men and women. In view of the somewhat overcrowded condition of the labor market of the United States, every patriotic citizen should rejoice at such a result.

The report of the Secretary of the Treasury shows that the total receipts of the Government from all sources for the fiscal year ending June 30, 1891, were $458,544,233.03, while the expenditures for the same period were $421,304,470.46, leaving a surplus of $37,239,762.57.

The receipts of the fiscal year ending June 30, 1892, actual and estimated, are $433,000,000 and the expenditures $409,000,000. For the fiscal year ending June 30, 1893, the estimated receipts are $455,336,350 and the expenditures $441,300,093.

Under the law of July 14, 1890, the Secretary of the Treasury has purchased (since August 13) during the fiscal year 48,393,113 ounces of silver bullion at an average cost of $1.045 per ounce. The highest price paid during the year was $1.2025 and the lowest $0.9636. In exchange for this silver bullion there have been issued $50,577,498 of the Treasury notes authorized by the act. The lowest price of silver reached during the fiscal year was $0.9636 on April 22, 1891; but on November 1 the market price was only $0.96, which would give to the silver dollar a bullion value of 74¼ cents.

Before the influence of the prospective silver legislation was felt in the market silver was worth in New York about $0.955 per ounce. The ablest advocates of free coinage in the last Congress were most confident in their predictions that the purchases by the Government required by the law would at once bring the price of silver to $1.2929 per ounce, which would make the bullion value of a dollar 100 cents and hold it there. The prophecies of the antisilver men of disasters to result from the coinage of $2,000,000 per month were not wider of the mark. The friends of free silver are not agreed, I think, as to the causes that brought their hopeful predictions to naught. Some facts are known. The exports of silver from London to India during the first nine months of this calendar year fell off over 50 per cent, or $17,202,730, compared with the same months of the preceding year. The exports of domestic silver bullion from this country, which had averaged for the last ten years over $17,000,000, fell in the last fiscal year to $13,797,391, while for the first time in recent years the imports of silver into this country exceeded the exports by the sum of $2,745,365. In the previous year the net exports of silver from the United States amounted to $8,545,455. The production of the United States increased from 50,000,000 ounces in 1889 to 54,500,000 in 1890. The Government is now buying and putting aside annually 54,000,000 ounces, which, allowing for 7,140,000 ounces of new bullion used in the arts, is 6,640,000 more than our domestic products available for coinage.

I hope the depression in the price of silver is temporary and that a further trial of this legislation will more favorably affect it. That the increased volume of currency thus supplied for the use of the people was needed and that beneficial results upon trade and prices have followed this legislation I think must be very clear to everyone. Nor should it be forgotten that for every dollar of these notes issued a full dollar's worth of silver bullion is at the time deposited in the Treasury as a security for its redemption. Upon this subject, as upon the tariff, my recommendation is that the existing laws be given a full trial and that our business interests be spared the distressing influence which threats of radical changes always impart. Under existing legislation it is in the power of the Treasury Department to maintain that essential condition of national finance as well as of commercial prosperity—the parity in use of the coined dollars and their paper representatives. The assurance that these powers would be freely and unhesitatingly used has done much to produce and sustain the present favorable business conditions.

I am still of the opinion that the free coinage of silver under existing conditions would disastrously affect our business interests at home and abroad. We could not hope to maintain an equality in the purchasing power of the gold and silver dollar in our own markets, and in foreign trade the stamp gives no added value to the bullion contained in coins. The producers of the country, its farmers and laborers, have the highest interest that every dollar, paper or coin, issued by the Government shall be as good as any other. If there is one less valuable than another, its sure and constant errand will be to pay them for their toil and for their crops. The money lender will protect himself by stipulating for payment in gold, but the laborer has never been able to do that. To place business upon a silver basis would mean a sudden and severe contraction of the currency by the withdrawal of gold and gold notes and such an unsettling of all values as would produce a commercial panic. I can not believe that a people so strong and prosperous as ours will promote such a policy.

The producers of silver are entitled to just consideration, but they should not forget that the Government is now buying and putting out of the market what is the equivalent of the entire product of our silver mines. This is more than they themselves thought of asking two years ago. I believe it is the earnest desire of a great majority of the people, as it is mine, that a full coin use shall be made of silver just as soon as the cooperation of other nations can be secured and a ratio fixed that will give circulation equally to gold and silver. The business of the world requires the use of both metals; but I do not see any prospect of gain, but much of loss, by giving up the present system, in which a full use is made of gold and a large use of silver, for one in which silver alone will circulate. Such an event would be at once fatal to the further progress of the silver movement. Bimetallism is the desired end, and the true friends of silver will be careful not to overrun the goal and bring in silver monometallism with its necessary attendants—the loss of our gold to Europe and the relief of the pressure there for a larger currency. I have endeavored by the use of official and unofficial agencies to keep a close observation of the state of public sentiment in Europe upon this

question and have not found it to be such as to justify me in proposing
an international conference. There is, however, I am sure, a growing
sentiment in Europe in favor of a larger use of silver, and I know of no
more effectual way of promoting this sentiment than by accumulating
gold here. A scarcity of gold in the European reserves will be the most
persuasive argument for the use of silver.

The exports of gold to Europe, which began in February last and continued until the close of July, aggregated over $70,000,000. The net
loss of gold during the fiscal year was nearly $68,000,000. That no seri-
ous monetary disturbance resulted was most gratifying and gave to
Europe fresh evidence of the strength and stability of our financial institutions. With the movement of crops the outflow of gold was speedily
stopped and a return set in. Up to December 1 we had recovered of our
gold lost at the port of New York $27,854,000, and it is confidently be-
lieved that during the winter and spring this aggregate will be steadily
and largely increased.

The presence of a large cash surplus in the Treasury has for many
years been the subject of much unfavorable criticism, and has furnished
an argument to those who have desired to place the tariff upon a purely
revenue basis. It was agreed by all that the withdrawal from circulation
of so large an amount of money was an embarrassment to the business
of the country and made necessary the intervention of the Department
at frequent intervals to relieve threatened monetary panics. The surplus on March 1, 1889, was $183,827,190.29. The policy of applying
this surplus to the redemption of the interest-bearing securities of the
United States was thought to be preferable to that of depositing it without interest in selected national banks. There have been redeemed
since the date last mentioned of interest-bearing securities $259,079,350,
resulting in a reduction of the annual interest charge of $11,684,675.
The money which had been deposited in banks without interest has been
gradually withdrawn and used in the redemption of bonds.

The result of this policy, of the silver legislation, and of the refunding
of the 4½ per cent bonds has been a large increase of the money in circulation. At the date last named the circulation was $1,404,205,896,
or $23.03 per capita, while on the 1st day of December, 1891, it had
increased to $1,577,262,070, or $24.38 per capita. The offer of the Secretary of the Treasury to the holders of the 4½ per cent bonds to extend
the time of redemption, at the option of the Government, at an interest
of 2 per cent, was accepted by the holders of about one-half the amount,
and the unextended bonds are being redeemed on presentation.

The report of the Secretary of War exhibits the results of an intelligent, progressive, and businesslike administration of a Department
which has been too much regarded as one of mere routine. The separation of Secretary Proctor from the Department by reason of his appointment as a Senator from the State of Vermont is a source of great regret

to me and to his colleagues in the Cabinet, as I am sure it will be to all those who have had business with the Department while under his charge.

In the administration of army affairs some especially good work has been accomplished. The efforts of the Secretary to reduce the percentage of desertions by removing the causes that promoted it have been so successful as to enable him to report for the last year a lower percentage of desertion than has been before reached in the history of the Army. The resulting money saving is considerable, but the improvement in the morale of the enlisted men is the most valuable incident of the reforms which have brought about this result.

The work of securing sites for shore batteries for harbor defense and the manufacture of mortars and guns of high power to equip them have made good progress during the year. The preliminary work of tests and plans which so long delayed a start is now out of the way. Some guns have been completed, and with an enlarged shop and a more complete equipment at Watervliet the Army will soon be abreast of the Navy in gun construction. Whatever unavoidable causes of delay may arise, there should be none from delayed or insufficient appropriations. We shall be greatly embarrassed in the proper distribution and use of naval vessels until adequate shore defenses are provided for our harbors.

I concur in the recommendation of the Secretary that the three-battalion organization be adopted for the infantry. The adoption of a smokeless powder and of a modern rifle equal in range, precision, and rapidity of fire to the best now in use will, I hope, not be longer delayed.

The project of enlisting Indians and organizing them into separate companies upon the same basis as other soldiers was made the subject of very careful study by the Secretary and received my approval. Seven companies have been completely organized and seven more are in process of organization. The results of six months' training have more than realized the highest anticipations. The men are readily brought under discipline, acquire the drill with facility, and show great pride in the right discharge of their duty and perfect loyalty to their officers, who declare that they would take them into action with confidence. The discipline, order, and cleanliness of the military posts will have a wholesome and elevating influence upon the men enlisted, and through them upon their tribes, while a friendly feeling for the whites and a greater respect for the Government will certainly be promoted.

The great work done in the Record and Pension Division of the War Department by Major Ainsworth, of the Medical Corps, and the clerks under him is entitled to honorable mention. Taking up the work with nearly 41,000 cases behind, he closed the last fiscal year without a single case left over, though the new cases had increased 52 per cent in number over the previous year by reason of the pension legislation of the last Congress.

I concur in the recommendation of the Attorney-General that the right in felony cases to a review by the Supreme Court be limited. It would seem that personal liberty would have a safe guaranty if the right of review in cases involving only fine and imprisonment were limited to the circuit court of appeals, unless a constitutional question should in some way be involved.

The judges of the Court of Private Land Claims, provided for by the act of March 3, 1891, have been appointed and the court organized. It is now possible to give early relief to communities long repressed in their development by unsettled land titles and to establish the possession and right of settlers whose lands have been rendered valueless by adverse and unfounded claims.

The act of July 9, 1888, provided for the incorporation and management of a reform school for girls in the District of Columbia; but it has remained inoperative for the reason that no appropriation has been made for construction or maintenance. The need of such an institution is very urgent. Many girls could be saved from depraved lives by the wholesome influences and restraints of such a school. I recommend that the necessary appropriation be made for a site and for construction.

The enforcement by the Treasury Department of the law prohibiting the coming of Chinese to the United States has been effective as to such as seek to land from vessels entering our ports. The result has been to divert the travel to vessels entering the ports of British Columbia, whence passage into the United States at obscure points along the Dominion boundary is easy. A very considerable number of Chinese laborers have during the past year entered the United States from Canada and Mexico.

The officers of the Treasury Department and of the Department of Justice have used every means at their command to intercept this immigration; but the impossibility of perfectly guarding our extended frontier is apparent. The Dominion government collects a head tax of $50 from every Chinaman entering Canada, and thus derives a considerable revenue from those who only use its ports to reach a position of advantage to evade our exclusion laws. There seems to be satisfactory evidence that the business of passing Chinamen through Canada to the United States is organized and quite active. The Department of Justice has construed the laws to require the return of any Chinaman found to be unlawfully in this country to China as the country from which he came, notwithstanding the fact that he came by way of Canada; but several of the district courts have in cases brought before them overruled this view of the law and decided that such persons must be returned to Canada. This construction robs the law of all effectiveness, even if the decrees could be executed, for the men returned can the next day recross our border. But the only appropriation made is for sending them back to China, and the Canadian officials refuse to allow them to reenter

Canada without the payment of the fifty-dollar head tax. I recommend such legislation as will remedy these defects in the law.

In previous messages I have called the attention of Congress to the necessity of so extending the jurisdiction of the United States courts as to make triable therein any felony committed while in the act of violating a law of the United States. These courts can not have that independence and effectiveness which the Constitution contemplates so long as the felonious killing of court officers, jurors, and witnesses in the discharge of their duties or by reason of their acts as such is only cognizable in the State courts. The work done by the Attorney-General and the officers of his Department, even under the present inadequate legislation, has produced some notable results in the interest of law and order.

The Attorney-General and also the Commissioners of the District of Columbia call attention to the defectiveness and inadequacy of the laws relating to crimes against chastity in the District of Columbia. A stringent code upon this subject has been provided by Congress for Utah, and it is a matter of surprise that the needs of this District should have been so long overlooked.

In the report of the Postmaster-General some very gratifying results are exhibited and many betterments of the service suggested. A perusal of the report gives abundant evidence that the supervision and direction of the postal system have been characterized by an intelligent and conscientious desire to improve the service. The revenues of the Department show an increase of over $5,000,000, with a deficiency for the year 1892 of less than $4,000,000, while the estimate for the year 1893 shows a surplus of receipts over expenditures.

Ocean mail post-offices have been established upon the steamers of the North German Lloyd and Hamburg lines, saving by the distribution on shipboard from two to fourteen hours' time in the delivery of mail at the port of entry and often much more than this in the delivery at interior places. So thoroughly has this system, initiated by Germany and the United States, evidenced its usefulness that it can not be long before it is installed upon all the great ocean mail-carrying steamships.

Eight thousand miles of new postal service has been established upon railroads, the car distribution to substations in the great cities has been increased about 12 per cent, while the percentage of errors in distribution has during the past year been reduced over one-half. An appropriation was given by the last Congress for the purpose of making some experiments in free delivery in the smaller cities and towns. The results of these experiments have been so satisfactory that the Postmaster-General recommends, and I concur in the recommendation, that the free-delivery system be at once extended to towns of 5,000 population. His discussion of the inadequate facilities extended under our present system to rural communities and his suggestions with a view to give these communities a fuller participation in the benefits of the postal service are worthy of your careful consideration. It is not just that the farmer, who receives his mail at a neighboring town, should not only be compelled to send to the post-office for it, but to pay a considerable rent for a box in which to place it or to wait his turn at a general-delivery window, while the city resident has his mail brought to his door. It is stated that over 54,000 neighborhoods are under the present system receiving mail at post-offices where money orders and postal notes are not issued. The extension of this system to these communities is especially desirable, as the patrons of such offices are not possessed of the other facilities offered in more populous communities for the transmission of small sums of money.

I have in a message to the preceding Congress expressed my views as to a modified use of the telegraph in connection with the postal service. In pursuance of the ocean mail law of March 3, 1891, and after a most careful study of the whole subject and frequent conferences with ship-owners, boards of trade, and others, advertisements were issued by the Postmaster-General for 53 lines of ocean mail service—10 to Great Britain and the Continent, 27 to South America, 3 to China and Japan, 4 to Australia and the Pacific islands, 7 to the West Indies, and 2 to Mexico. It was not, of course, expected that bids for all these lines would be received or that service upon them all would be contracted for. It was intended, in furtherance of the act, to secure as many new lines as possible, while including in the list most or all of the foreign lines now occupied by American ships. It was hoped that a line to England and perhaps one to the Continent would be secured; but the outlay required to equip such lines wholly with new ships of the first class and the difficulty of establishing new lines in competition with those already established deterred bidders whose interest had been enlisted. It is hoped that a way may yet be found of overcoming these difficulties.

The Brazil Steamship Company, by reason of a miscalculation as to the speed of its vessels, was not able to bid under the terms of the advertisement. The policy of the Department was to secure from the established lines an improved service as a condition of giving to them the benefits of the law. This in all instances has been attained. The Postmaster-General estimates that an expenditure in American shipyards of about $10,000,000 will be necessary to enable the bidders to construct the ships called for by the service which they have accepted. I do not think there is any reason for discouragement or for any turning back from the policy of this legislation. Indeed, a good beginning has been made, and as the subject is further considered and understood by capitalists and shipping people new lines will be ready to meet future proposals, and we may date from the passage of this law the revival of American shipping interests and the recovery of a fair share of the carrying trade of the world. We were receiving for foreign postage nearly $2,000,000 under the old system, and the outlay for ocean mail service did not exceed $600,000 per annum. It is estimated by the Postmaster-General that if all the contracts proposed are completed it will require $247,354 for this year in addition to the appropriation for sea and inland postage already in the estimates, and that for the next fiscal year, ending June 30, 1893, there would probably be needed about $560,000.

The report of the Secretary of the Navy shows a gratifying increase of new naval vessels in commission. The *Newark, Concord, Bennington,* and *Miantonomoh* have been added during the year, with an aggregate of something more than 11,000 tons. Twenty-four warships of all classes are now under construction in the navy-yards and private shops; but while the work upon them is going forward satisfactorily, the completion of the more important vessels will yet require about a year's time. Some of the vessels now under construction, it is believed, will be triumphs of naval engineering. When it is recollected that the work of building a modern navy was only initiated in the year 1883, that our naval constructors and shipbuilders were practically without experience in the construction of large iron or steel ships, that our engine shops were unfamiliar with great marine engines, and that the manufacture of steel forgings for guns and plates was almost wholly a foreign industry, the progress that has been made is not only highly satisfactory, but furnishes the assurance that the United States will before long attain in the construction of such vessels, with their engines and armaments, the same preeminence which it attained when the best instrument of ocean commerce was the clipper ship and the most impressive exhibit of naval power the old wooden three-decker man-of-war. The officers of the Navy and the proprietors and engineers of our great private shops have responded with wonderful intelligence and professional zeal to the confidence expressed by Congress in its liberal legislation. We have now at Washington a gun shop, organized and conducted by naval officers, that in its system, economy, and product is unexcelled. Experiments with armor plate have been conducted during the year with most important results. It is now believed that a plate of higher resisting power than any in use has been found and that the tests have demonstrated that cheaper methods of manufacture than those heretofore thought necessary can be used.

I commend to your favorable consideration the recommendations of the Secretary, who has, I am sure, given to them the most conscientious study. There should be no hesitation in promptly completing a navy of the best modern type large enough to enable this country to display its flag in all seas for the protection of its citizens and of its extending commerce. The world needs no assurance of the peaceful purposes of the United States, but we shall probably be in the future more largely a competitor in the commerce of the world, and it is essential to the dignity of this nation and to that peaceful influence which it should exercise on this hemisphere that its Navy should be adequate both upon the shores of the Atlantic and of the Pacific.

The report of the Secretary of the Interior shows that a very gratifying progress has been made in all of the bureaus which make up that complex and difficult Department.

The work in the Bureau of Indian Affairs was perhaps never so large as now, by reason of the numerous negotiations which have been proceeding with the tribes for a reduction of the reservations, with the incident labor of making allotments, and was never more carefully conducted. The provision of adequate school facilities for Indian children and the locating of adult Indians upon farms involve the solution of the "Indian question." Everything else—rations, annuities, and tribal negotiations, with the agents, inspectors, and commissioners who distribute and conduct them—must pass away when the Indian has become a citizen, secure in the individual ownership of a farm from which he derives his subsistence by his own labor, protected by and subordinate to the laws which govern the white man, and provided by the General Government or by the local communities in which he lives with the means of educating his children. When an Indian becomes a citizen in an organized State or Territory, his relation to the General Government ceases in great measure to be that of a ward; but the General Government ought not at once to put upon the State or Territory the burden of the education of his children.

It has been my thought that the Government schools and school buildings upon the reservations would be absorbed by the school systems of the States and Territories; but as it has been found necessary to protect the Indian against the compulsory alienation of his land by exempting him from taxation for a period of twenty-five years, it would seem to be right that the General Government, certainly where there are tribal funds in its possession, should pay to the school fund of the State what would be equivalent to the local school tax upon the property of the Indian. It will be noticed from the report of the Commissioner of Indian Affairs that already some contracts have been made with district schools for the education of Indian children. There is great advantage, I think, in bringing the Indian children into mixed schools. This process will be gradual, and in the meantime the present educational provisions and arrangements, the result of the best experience of those who have been charged with this work, should be continued. This will enable those religious bodies that have undertaken the work of Indian education with so much zeal and with results so restraining and beneficent to place their institutions in new and useful relations to the Indian and to his white neighbors.

The outbreak among the Sioux which occurred in December last is as to its causes and incidents fully reported upon by the War Department and the Department of the Interior. That these Indians had some just complaints, especially in the matter of the reduction of the appropriation for rations and in the delays attending the enactment of laws to enable the Department to perform the engagements entered into with them, is probably true; but the Sioux tribes are naturally warlike and turbulent, and their warriors were excited by their medicine men and chiefs, who preached the coming of an Indian messiah who was to give them power to destroy their enemies. In view of the alarm that prevailed among the white settlers near the reservation and of the fatal consequences that would have resulted from an Indian incursion, I placed at the disposal of General Miles, commanding the Division of the Missouri, all such forces as were thought by him to be required. He is entitled to the credit of having given thorough protection to the settlers and of bringing the hostiles into subjection with the least possible loss of life.

The appropriation of $2,991,450 for the Choctaws and Chickasaws contained in the general Indian appropriation bill of March 3, 1891, has not been expended, for the reason that I have not yet approved a release (to the Government) of the Indian claim to the lands mentioned. This matter will be made the subject of a special message, placing before Congress all the facts which have come to my knowledge.

The relation of the Five Civilized Tribes now occupying the Indian Territory to the United States is not, I believe, that best calculated to promote the highest advancement of these Indians. That there should be within our borders five independent states having no relations, except those growing out of treaties, with the Government of the United States, no representation in the National Legislature, its people not citizens, is a startling anomaly.

It seems to me to be inevitable that there shall be before long some organic changes in the relation of these people to the United States. What form these changes should take I do not think it desirable now to suggest, even if they were well defined in my own mind. They should certainly involve the acceptance of citizenship by the Indians and a representation in Congress. These Indians should have opportunity to present their claims and grievances upon the floor rather than, as now, in the lobby. If a commission could be appointed to visit these tribes to confer with them in a friendly spirit upon this whole subject, even if no agreement were presently reached the feeling of the tribes upon this question would be developed, and discussion would prepare the way for changes which must come sooner or later.

The good work of reducing the larger Indian reservations by allotments in severalty to the Indians and the cession of the remaining lands to the United States for disposition under the homestead law has been prosecuted during the year with energy and success. In September last I was enabled to open to settlement in the Territory of Oklahoma 900,000 acres of land, all of which was taken up by settlers in a single.

day. The rush for these lands was accompanied by a great deal of excitement, but was happily free from incidents of violence.

It was a source of great regret that I was not able to open at the same time the surplus lands of the Cheyenne and Arapahoe Reservation, amounting to about 3,000,000 acres, by reason of the insufficiency of the appropriation for making the allotments. Deserving and impatient settlers are waiting to occupy these lands, and I urgently recommend that a special deficiency appropriation be promptly made of the small amount needed, so that the allotments may be completed and the surplus lands opened in time to permit the settlers to get upon their homesteads in the early spring.

During the past summer the Cherokee Commission have completed arrangements with the Wichita, Kickapoo, and Tonkawa tribes whereby, if the agreements are ratified by Congress, over 800,000 additional acres will be opened to settlement in Oklahoma.

The negotiations for the release by the Cherokees of their claim to the Cherokee Strip have made no substantial progress so far as the Department is officially advised, but it is still hoped that the cession of this large and valuable tract may be secured. The price which the commission was authorized to offer—$1.25 per acre—is, in my judgment, when all the circumstances as to title and the character of the lands are considered, a fair and adequate one, and should have been accepted by the Indians.

Since March 4, 1889, about 23,000,000 acres have been separated from Indian reservations and added to the public domain for the use of those who desired to secure free homes under our beneficent laws. It is difficult to estimate the increase of wealth which will result from the conversion of these waste lands into farms, but it is more difficult to estimate the betterment which will result to the families that have found renewed hope and courage in the ownership of a home and the assurance of a comfortable subsistence under free and healthful conditions. It is also gratifying to be able to feel, as we may, that this work has proceeded upon lines of justice toward the Indian, and that he may now, if he will, secure to himself the good influences of a settled habitation, the fruits of industry, and the security of citizenship.

Early in this Administration a special effort was begun to bring up the work of the General Land Office. By faithful work the arrearages have been rapidly reduced. At the end of the last fiscal year only 84,172 final agricultural entries remained undisposed of, and the Commissioner reports that with the present force the work can be fully brought up by the end of the next fiscal year.

Your attention is called to the difficulty presented by the Secretary of the Interior as to the administration of the law of March 3, 1891, establishing a Court of Private Land Claims. The small holdings intended to be protected by the law are estimated to be more than 15,000 in number. The claimants are a most deserving class and their titles are supported by the strongest equities. The difficulty grows out of the fact that the lands have largely been surveyed according to our methods, while the holdings, many of which have been in the same family for generations, are laid out in narrow strips a few rods wide upon a stream and running back to the hills for pasturage and timber. Provision should be made for numbering these tracts as lots and for patenting them by such numbers and without reference to section lines.

The administration of the Pension Bureau has been characterized during the year by great diligence. The total number of pensioners upon the roll on the 30th day of June, 1891, was 676,160. There were allowed during the fiscal year ending at that time 250,565 cases. Of this number 102,387 were allowed under the law of June 27, 1890. The issuing of certificates has been proceeding at the rate of about 30,000 per month, about 75 per cent of these being cases under the new law. The Commissioner expresses the opinion that he will be able to carefully adjudicate and allow 350,000 claims during the present fiscal year. The appropriation for the payment of pensions for the fiscal year 1890–91 was $127,685,793.89 and the amount expended $118,530,649.25, leaving an unexpended surplus of $9,155,144.64.

The Commissioner is quite confident that there will be no call this year for a deficiency appropriation, notwithstanding the rapidity with which the work is being pushed. The mistake which has been made by many in their exaggerated estimates of the cost of pensions is in not taking account of the diminished value of first payments under the recent legislation. These payments under the general law have been for many years very large, as the pensions when allowed dated from the time of filing the claim, and most of these claims had been pending for years. The first payments under the law of June, 1890, are relatively small, and as the per cent of these cases increases and that of the old cases diminishes the annual aggregate of first payments is largely reduced. The Commissioner, under date of November 13, furnishes me with the statement that during the last four months 113,175 certificates were issued, 27,893 under the general law and 85,282 under the act of June 27, 1890. The average first payment during these four months was $131.85, while the average first payment upon cases allowed during the year ending June 30, 1891, was $239.33, being a reduction in the average first payments during these four months of $107.48.

The estimate for pension expenditures for the fiscal year ending June 30, 1893, is $144,956,000, which, after a careful examination of the subject, the Commissioner is of the opinion will be sufficient. While these disbursements to the disabled soldiers of the great Civil War are large, they do not realize the exaggerated estimates of those who oppose this beneficent legislation. The Secretary of the Interior shows with great fullness the care that is taken to exclude fraudulent claims, and also the gratifying fact that the persons to whom these pensions are going are men who rendered not slight but substantial war service.

The report of the Commissioner of Railroads shows that the total debt of the subsidized railroads to the United States was on December 31, 1890, $112,512,613.06. A large part of this debt is now fast approaching maturity, with no adequate provision for its payment. Some policy for dealing with this debt with a view to its ultimate collection should be at once adopted. It is very difficult, well-nigh impossible, for so large a body as the Congress to conduct the necessary negotiations and investigations. I therefore recommend that provision be made for the appointment of a commission to agree upon and report a plan for dealing with this debt.

The work of the Census Bureau is now far in advance and the great bulk of the enormous labor involved completed. It will be more strictly a statistical exhibit and less encumbered by essays than its immediate predecessors. The methods pursued have been fair, careful, and intelligent, and have secured the approval of the statisticians who have followed them with a scientific and nonpartisan interest. The appropriations necessary to the early completion and publication of the authorized volumes should be given in time to secure against delays, which increase the cost and at the same time diminish the value of the work.

The report of the Secretary exhibits with interesting fullness the condition of the Territories. They have shared with the States the great increase in farm products, and are bringing yearly large areas into cultivation by extending their irrigating canals. This work is being done by individuals or local corporations and without that system which a full preliminary survey of the water supply and of the irrigable lands would enable them to adopt. The future of the Territories of New Mexico, Arizona, and Utah in their material growth and in the increase, independence, and happiness of their people is very largely dependent upon wise and timely legislation, either by Congress or their own legislatures, regulating the distribution of the water supply furnished by their streams. If this matter is much longer neglected, private corporations will have unrestricted control of one of the elements of life and the patentees of the arid lands will be tenants at will of the water companies.

The United States should part with its ownership of the water sources and the sites for reservoirs, whether to the States and Territories or to individuals or corporations, only upon conditions that will insure to the settlers their proper water supply upon equal and reasonable terms. In the Territories this whole subject is under the full control of Congress, and in the States it is practically so as long as the Government holds the title to the reservoir sites and water sources and can grant them upon such conditions as it chooses to impose. The improvident granting of franchises of enormous value without recompense to the State or municipality from which they proceed and without proper protection of the public interests is the most noticeable and flagrant evil of modern legislation. This fault should not be committed in dealing with a subject that will before many years affect so vitally thousands of our people.

The legislation of Congress for the repression of polygamy has, after years of resistance on the part of the Mormons, at last brought them to the conclusion that resistance is unprofitable and unavailing. The power of Congress over this subject should not be surrendered until we have satisfactory evidence that the people of the State to be created would exercise the exclusive power of the State over this subject in the same way. The question is not whether these people now obey the laws of Congress against polygamy, but rather would they make, enforce, and maintain such laws themselves if absolutely free to regulate the subject? We can not afford to experiment with this subject, for when a State is once constituted the act is final and any mistake irretrievable. No compact in the enabling act could, in my opinion, be binding or effective.

I recommend that provision be made for the organization of a simple form of town government in Alaska, with power to regulate such matters as are usually in the States under municipal control. These local civil organizations will give better protection in some matters than the present skeleton Territorial organization. Proper restrictions as to the power to levy taxes and to create debt should be imposed.

If the establishment of the Department of Agriculture was regarded by anyone as a mere concession to the unenlightened demand of a worthy class of people, that impression has been most effectually removed by the great results already attained. Its home influence has been very great in disseminating agricultural and horticultural information, in stimulating and directing a further diversification of crops, in detecting and eradicating diseases of domestic animals, and, more than all, in the close and informal contact which it has established and maintains with the farmers and stock raisers of the whole country. Every request for information has had prompt attention and every suggestion merited consideration. The scientific corps of the Department is of a high order and is pushing its investigations with method and enthusiasm.

The inspection by this Department of cattle and pork products intended for shipment abroad has been the basis of the success which has attended our efforts to secure the removal of the restrictions maintained by the European Governments.

For ten years protests and petitions upon this subject from the packers and stock raisers of the United States have been directed against these restrictions, which so seriously limited our markets and curtailed the profits of the farm. It is a source of general congratulation that success has at last been attained, for the effects of an enlarged foreign market for these meats will be felt not only by the farmer, but in our public finances and in every branch of trade. It is particularly fortunate that the increased demand for food products resulting from the removal of the restrictions upon our meats and from the reciprocal trade arrangements to which I have referred should have come at a time when the agricultural surplus is so large. Without the help thus derived lower prices would have prevailed. The Secretary of Agriculture estimates that the restrictions upon the importation of our pork products into Europe lost us a market for $20,000,000 worth of these products annually.

The grain crop of this year was the largest in our history—50 per cent greater than that of last year—and yet the new markets that have been opened and the larger demand resulting from short crops in Europe have sustained prices to such an extent that the enormous surplus of meats and breadstuffs will be marketed at good prices, bringing relief and prosperity to an industry that was much depressed. The value of the grain crop of the United States is estimated by the Secretary to be this year $500,000,000 more than last; of meats $150,000,000 more, and of all products of the farm $700,000,000 more. It is not inappropriate, I think, here to suggest that our satisfaction in the contemplation of this marvelous addition to the national wealth is unclouded by any suspicion of the currency by which it is measured and in which the farmer is paid for the products of his fields.

The report of the Civil Service Commission should receive the careful attention of the opponents as well as the friends of this reform. The Commission invites a personal inspection by Senators and Representatives of its records and methods, and every fair critic will feel that such an examination should precede a judgment of condemnation either of the system or its administration. It is not claimed that either is perfect, but I believe that the law is being executed with impartiality and that the system is incomparably better and fairer than that of appointments upon favor. I have during the year extended the classified service to include superintendents, teachers, matrons, and physicians in the Indian service. This branch of the service is largely related to educational and philanthropic work and will obviously be the better for the change.

The heads of the several Executive Departments have been directed to establish at once an efficiency record as the basis of a comparative rating of the clerks within the classified service, with a view to placing promotions therein upon the basis of merit. I am confident that such a record, fairly kept and open to the inspection of those interested, will powerfully stimulate the work of the Departments and will be accepted by all as placing the troublesome matter of promotions upon a just basis.

I recommend that the appropriation for the Civil Service Commission be made adequate to the increased work of the next fiscal year.

I have twice before urgently called the attention of Congress to the necessity of legislation for the protection of the lives of railroad employees, but nothing has yet been done. During the year ending June 30, 1890, 369 brakemen were killed and 7,841 maimed while engaged in coupling cars. The total number of railroad employees killed during the year was 2,451 and the number injured 22,390. This is a cruel and largely needless sacrifice. The Government is spending nearly $1,000,000 annually to save the lives of shipwrecked seamen; every steam vessel is rigidly inspected and required to adopt the most approved safety appliances. All this is good. But how shall we excuse the lack of interest and effort in behalf of this army of brave young men who in our land commerce are being sacrificed every year by the continued use of antiquated and dangerous appliances? A law requiring of every railroad engaged in interstate commerce the equipment each year of a given per cent of its freight cars with automatic couplers and air brakes would compel an agreement between the roads as to the kind of brakes and couplers to be used, and would very soon and very greatly reduce the present fearful death rate among railroad employees.

The method of appointment by the States of electors of President and Vice-President has recently attracted renewed interest by reason of a departure by the State of Michigan from the method which had become uniform in all the States. Prior to 1832 various methods had been used by the different States, and even by the same State. In some the choice was made by the legislature; in others electors were chosen by districts, but more generally by the voters of the whole State upon a general ticket. The movement toward the adoption of the last-named method had an early beginning and went steadily forward among the States until in 1832 there remained but a single State (South Carolina) that had not adopted it. That State until the Civil War continued to choose its electors by a vote of the legislature, but after the war changed its method and conformed to the practice of the other States. For nearly sixty years all the States save one have appointed their electors by a popular vote upon a general ticket, and for nearly thirty years this method was universal.

After a full test of other methods, without important division or dissent in any State and without any purpose of party advantage, as we must believe, but solely upon the considerations that uniformity was desirable and that a general election in territorial divisions not subject to change was most consistent with the popular character of our institutions, best preserved the equality of the voters, and perfectly removed the choice of President from the baneful influence of the "gerrymander," the practice of all the States was brought into harmony. That this concurrence should now be broken is, I think, an unfortunate and even a threatening episode, and one that may well suggest whether the States that still give their approval to the old and prevailing method ought not to secure by a constitutional amendment a practice which has had the approval of all. The recent Michigan legislation provides for choosing what are popularly known as the Congressional electors for President by Congressional districts and the two Senatorial electors by districts created for that purpose. This legislation was, of course, accompanied by a new Congressional apportionment, and the two statutes bring the electoral vote of the State under the influence of the "gerrymander."

These gerrymanders for Congressional purposes are in most cases buttressed by a gerrymander of the legislative districts, thus making it impossible for a majority of the legal voters of the State to correct the apportionment and equalize the Congressional districts. A minority rule is established that only a political convulsion can overthrow. I have recently been advised that in one county of a certain State three districts for the election of members of the legislature are constituted as follows: One has 65,000 population, one 15,000, and one 10,000, while in another county detached, noncontiguous sections have been united to make a legislative district. These methods have already found effective application to the choice of Senators and Representatives in Congress, and now an evil start has been made in the direction of applying them to the choice by the States of electors of President and Vice-President. If this is accomplished, we shall then have the three great departments of the Government in the grasp of the "gerrymander," the legislative and executive directly and the judiciary indirectly through the power of appointment.

An election implies a body of electors having prescribed qualifications, each one of whom has an equal value and influence in determining the result. So when the Constitution provides that "each State shall appoint" (elect), "in such manner as the legislature thereof may direct, a number of electors," etc., an unrestricted power was not given to the legislatures in the selection of the methods to be used. "A republican form of government" is guaranteed by the Constitution to each State, and the power given by the same instrument to the legislatures of the States to prescribe methods for the choice by the State of electors must be exercised under that limitation. The essential features of such a government are the right of the people to choose their own officers and the nearest practicable equality of value in the suffrages given in determining that choice.

It will not be claimed that the power given to the legislature would support a law providing that the persons receiving the smallest vote should be the electors or a law that all the electors should be chosen by the voters of a single Congressional district. The State is to choose, and under the pretense of regulating methods the legislature can neither vest the right of choice elsewhere nor adopt methods not conformable to republican institutions. It is not my purpose here to discuss the question whether a choice by the legislature or by the voters of equal single districts is a choice by the State, but only to recommend such regulation of this matter by constitutional amendment as will secure uniformity and prevent that disgraceful partisan jugglery to which such a liberty of choice, if it exists, offers a temptation.

Nothing just now is more important than to provide every guaranty for the absolutely fair and free choice by an equal suffrage within the respective States of all the officers of the National Government, whether that suffrage is applied directly, as in the choice of members of the House of Representatives, or indirectly, as in the choice of Senators and electors of President. Respect for public officers and obedience to law will not cease to be the characteristics of our people until our elections cease to declare the will of majorities fairly ascertained without fraud, suppression, or gerrymander. If I were called upon to declare wherein our chief national danger lies, I should say without hesitation in the overthrow of majority control by the suppression or perversion of the popular suffrage. That there is a real danger here all must agree; but the energies of those who see it have been chiefly expended in trying to fix responsibility upon the opposite party rather than in efforts to make such practices impossible by either party.

Is it not possible now to adjourn that interminable and inconclusive debate while we take by consent one step in the direction of reform by eliminating the gerrymander, which has been denounced by all parties as an influence in the selection of electors of President and members of Congress? All the States have, acting freely and separately, determined that the choice of electors by a general ticket is the wisest and safest method, and it would seem there could be no objection to a constitutional amendment making that method permanent. If a legislature chosen in one year upon purely local questions should, pending a Presidential contest, meet, rescind the law for a choice upon a general ticket, and provide for the choice of electors by the legislature, and this trick should determine the result, it is not too much to say that the public peace might be seriously and widely endangered.

I have alluded to the "gerrymander" as affecting the method of selecting electors of President by Congressional districts, but the primary intent and effect of this form of political robbery have relation to the selection of members of the House of Representatives. The power of Congress is ample to deal with this threatening and intolerable abuse. The unfailing test of sincerity in election reform will be found in a willingness to confer as to remedies and to put into force such measures as will most effectually preserve the right of the people to free and equal representation.

An attempt was made in the last Congress to bring to bear the constitutional powers of the General Government for the correction of fraud against the suffrage. It is important to know whether the opposition to such measures is really rested in particular features supposed to be objectionable or includes any proposition to give to the election laws of the United States adequacy to the correction of grave and acknowledged evils. I must yet entertain the hope that it is possible to secure a calm, patriotic consideration of such constitutional or statutory changes as may be necessary to secure the choice of the officers of the Government to the people by fair apportionments and free elections.

I believe it would be possible to constitute a commission, nonpartisan in its membership and composed of patriotic, wise, and impartial men, to whom a consideration of the question of the evils connected with our election system and methods might be committed with a good prospect of securing unanimity in some plan for removing or mitigating those evils. The Constitution would permit the selection of the commission to be vested in the Supreme Court if that method would give the best guaranty of impartiality. This commission should be charged with the duty of inquiring into the whole subject of the law of elections as related to the choice of officers of the National Government, with a view to securing to every elector a free and unmolested exercise of the suffrage and as near an approach to an equality of value in each ballot cast as is attainable.

While the policies of the General Government upon the tariff, upon the restoration of our merchant marine, upon river and harbor improvements, and other such matters of grave and general concern are liable to be turned this way or that by the results of Congressional elections and administrative policies, sometimes involving issues that tend to peace or war, to be turned this way or that by the results of a Presidential election, there is a rightful interest in all the States and in every Congressional district that will not be deceived or silenced by the audacious pretense that the question of the right of any body of legal voters in any State or in any Congressional district to give their suffrages freely upon these general questions is a matter only of local concern or control. The demand that the limitations of suffrage shall be found in the law, and only there, is a just demand, and no just man should resent or resist it. My appeal is and must continue to be for a consultation that shall "proceed with candor, calmness, and patience upon the lines of justice and humanity, not of prejudice and cruelty."

To the consideration of these very grave questions I invite not only the attention of Congress, but that of all patriotic citizens. We must not entertain the delusion that our people have ceased to regard a free ballot and equal representation as the price of their allegiance to laws and to civil magistrates.

I have been greatly rejoiced to notice many evidences of the increased unification of our people and of a revived national spirit. The vista that now opens to us is wider and more glorious than ever before. Gratification and amazement struggle for supremacy as we contemplate the population, wealth, and moral strength of our country. A trust momentous in its influence upon our people and upon the world is for a brief time committed to us, and we must not be faithless to its first condition—the defense of the free and equal influence of the people in the choice of public officers and in the control of public affairs.

FOURTH ANNUAL MESSAGE.

EXECUTIVE MANSION, *December 6, 1892.*

To the Senate and House of Representatives:

In submitting my annual message to Congress I have great satisfaction in being able to say that the general conditions affecting the commercial and industrial interests of the United States are in the highest degree favorable. A comparison of the existing conditions with those of the most favored period in the history of the country will, I believe, show that so high a degree of prosperity and so general a diffusion of the comforts of life were never before enjoyed by our people.

The total wealth of the country in 1860 was $16,159,616,068. In 1890 it amounted to $62,610,000,000, an increase of 287 per cent.

The total mileage of railways in the United States in 1860 was 30,626. In 1890 it was 167,741, an increase of 448 per cent; and it is estimated that there will be about 4,000 miles of track added by the close of the year 1892.

The official returns of the Eleventh Census and those of the Tenth Census for seventy-five leading cities furnish the basis for the following comparisons:

In 1880 the capital invested in manufacturing was $1,232,839,670.

In 1890 the capital invested in manufacturing was $2,900,735,884.

In 1880 the number of employees was 1,301,388.

In 1890 the number of employees was 2,251,134.

In 1880 the wages earned were $501,965,778.

In 1890 the wages earned were $1,221,170,454.

In 1880 the value of the product was $2,711,579,899.

In 1890 the value of the product was $4,860,286,837.

I am informed by the Superintendent of the Census that the omission of certain industries in 1880 which were included in 1890 accounts in part for the remarkable increase thus shown, but after making full allowance for differences of method and deducting the returns for all industries not included in the census of 1880 there remain in the reports from these seventy-five cities an increase in the capital employed of $1,522,-745,604, in the value of the product of $2,024,236,166, in wages earned of $677,943,929, and in the number of wage earners employed of 856,029. The wage earnings not only show an increased aggregate, but an increase per capita from $386 in 1880 to $547 in 1890, or 41.71 per cent.

The new industrial plants established since October 6, 1890, and up to October 22, 1892, as partially reported in the American Economist, number 345, and the extension of existing plants 108; the new capital invested amounts to $40,449,050, and the number of additional employees to 37,285.

The Textile World for July, 1892, states that during the first six months of the present calendar year 135 new factories were built, of which 40 are cotton mills, 48 knitting mills, 26 woolen mills, 15 silk mills, 4 plush mills, and 2 linen mills. Of the 40 cotton mills 21 have been built in the Southern States. Mr. A. B. Shepperson, of the New York Cotton Exchange, estimates the number of working spindles in the United States on September 1, 1892, at 15,200,000, an increase of 660,000 over the year 1891. The consumption of cotton by American mills in 1891 was 2,396,-000 bales, and in 1892 2,584,000 bales, an increase of 188,000 bales. From the year 1869 to 1892, inclusive, there has been an increase in the consumption of cotton in Europe of 92 per cent, while during the same period the increased consumption in the United States has been about 150 per cent.

The report of Ira Ayer, special agent of the Treasury Department, shows that at the date of September 30, 1892, there were 32 companies manufacturing tin and terne plate in the United States and 14 companies building new works for such manufacture. The estimated investment in buildings and plants at the close of the fiscal year June 30, 1893, if existing conditions were to be continued, was $5,000,000 and the estimated rate of production 200,000,000 pounds per annum. The actual production for the quarter ending September 30, 1892, was 10,952,725 pounds.

The report of Labor Commissioner Peck, of New York, shows that during the year 1891, in about 6,000 manufacturing establishments in that State embraced within the special inquiry made by him, and representing 67 different industries, there was a net increase over the year 1890 of $31,315,130.68 in the value of the product and of $6,377,925.09 in the amount of wages paid. The report of the commissioner of labor for the State of Massachusetts shows that 3,745 industries in that State paid $129,416,248 in wages during the year 1891, against $126,030,303 in 1890, an increase of $3,335,945, and that there was an increase of $9,932,490 in the amount of capital and of 7,346 in the number of persons employed in the same period.

During the last six months of the year 1891 and the first six months of 1892 the total production of pig iron was 9,710,819 tons, as against 9,202,703 tons in the year 1890, which was the largest annual production ever attained. For the same twelve months of 1891–92 the production of Bessemer ingots was 3,878,581 tons, an increase of 189,710 gross tons over the previously unprecedented yearly production of 3,688,871 gross tons in 1890. The production of Bessemer steel rails for the first six months of 1892 was 772,436 gross tons, as against 702,080 gross tons during the last six months of the year 1891.

The total value of our foreign trade (exports and imports of merchandise) during the last fiscal year was $1,857,680,610, an increase of $128,-283,604 over the previous fiscal year. The average annual value of our imports and exports of merchandise for the ten fiscal years prior to 1891 was $1,457,322,019.   It will be observed that our foreign trade for 1892 exceeded this annual average value by $400,358,591, an increase of 27.47 per cent.   The significance and value of this increase are shown by the fact that the excess in the trade of 1892 over 1891 was wholly in the value of exports, for there was a decrease in the value of imports of $17,513,754.

The value of our exports during the fiscal year 1892 reached the highest figure in the history of the Government, amounting to $1,030,278,148, exceeding by $145,797,338 the exports of 1891 and exceeding the value of the imports by $202,875,686.   A comparison of the value of our exports for 1892 with the annual average for the ten years prior to 1891 shows an excess of $265,142,651, or of 34.65 per cent.   The value of our imports of merchandise for 1892, which was $829,402,462, also exceeded the annual average value of the ten years prior to 1891 by $135,-215,940.   During the fiscal year 1892 the value of imports free of duty amounted to $457,999,658, the largest aggregate in the history of our commerce.   The value of the imports of merchandise entered free of duty in 1892 was 55.35 per cent of the total value of imports, as compared with 43.35 per cent in 1891 and 33.66 per cent in 1890.

In our coastwise trade a most encouraging development is in progress, there having been in the last four years an increase of 16 per cent.   In internal commerce the statistics show that no such period of prosperity has ever before existed.   The freight carried in the coastwise trade of the Great Lakes in 1890 aggregated 28,295,959 tons.   On the Mississippi, Missouri, and Ohio rivers and tributaries in the same year the traffic aggregated 29,405,046 tons, and the total vessel tonnage passing through the Detroit River during that year was 21,684,000 tons.   The vessel tonnage entered and cleared in the foreign trade of London during 1890 amounted to 13,480,767 tons, and of Liverpool 10,941,800 tons, a total for these two great shipping ports of 24,422,568 tons, only slightly in excess of the vessel tonnage passing through the Detroit River.   And it should be said that the season for the Detroit River was but 228 days, while of course in London and Liverpool the season was for the entire year.   The vessel tonnage passing through the St. Marys Canal for the fiscal year 1892 amounted to 9,828,874 tons, and the freight tonnage of the Detroit River is estimated for that year at 25,000,000 tons, against 23,209,619 tons in 1891.   The aggregate traffic on our railroads for the year 1891 amounted to 704,398,609 tons of freight, compared with 691,344,437 tons in 1890, an increase of 13,054,172 tons.

Another indication of the general prosperity of the country is found in the fact that the number of depositors in savings banks increased from 693,870 in 1860 to 4,258,893 in 1890, an increase of 513 per cent, and the amount of deposits from $149,277,504 in 1860 to $1,524,844,506 in 1890, an increase of 921 per cent.   In 1891 the amount of deposits in savings banks was $1,623,079,749.   It is estimated that 90 per cent of these deposits represent the savings of wage earners. The bank clearances for nine months ending September 30, 1891, amounted to $41,049,390,808. For the same months in 1892 they amounted to $45,189,601,947, an excess for the nine months of $4,140,211,139.

There never has been a time in our history when work was so abundant or when wages were as high, whether measured by the currency in which they are paid or by their power to supply the necessaries and comforts of life. It is true that the market prices of cotton and wheat have been low. It is one of the unfavorable incidents of agriculture that the farmer can not produce upon orders. He must sow and reap in ignorance of the aggregate production of the year, and is peculiarly subject to the depreciation which follows overproduction. But while the fact I have stated is true as to the crops mentioned, the general average of prices has been such as to give to agriculture a fair participation in the general prosperity. The value of our total farm products has increased from $1,363,-646,866 in 1860 to $4,500,000,000 in 1891, as estimated by statisticians, an increase of 230 per cent. The number of hogs January 1, 1891, was 50,625,106 and their value $210,193,925; on January 1, 1892, the number was 52,398,019 and the value $241,031,415. On January 1, 1891, the number of cattle was 36,875,648 and the value $544,127,908; on January 1, 1892, the number was 37,651,239 and the value $570,749,155.

If any are discontented with their state here, if any believe that wages or prices, the returns for honest toil, are inadequate, they should not fail to remember that there is no other country in the world where the conditions that seem to them hard would not be accepted as highly prosperous. The English agriculturist would be glad to exchange the returns of his labor for those of the American farmer and the Manchester workmen their wages for those of their fellows at Fall River.

I believe that the protective system, which has now for something more than thirty years continuously prevailed in our legislation, has been a mighty instrument for the development of our national wealth and a most powerful agency in protecting the homes of our workingmen from the invasion of want. I have felt a most solicitous interest to preserve to our working people rates of wages that would not only give daily bread, but supply a comfortable margin for those home attractions and family comforts and enjoyments without which life is neither hopeful nor sweet. They are American citizens—a part of the great people for whom our Constitution and Government were framed and instituted—and it can not be a perversion of that Constitution to so legislate as to preserve in their homes the comfort, independence, loyalty, and sense of interest in the Government which are essential to good citizenship in peace, and which will bring this stalwart throng, as in 1861, to the defense of the flag when it is assailed.

It is not my purpose to renew here the argument in favor of a protective tariff. The result of the recent election must be accepted as having

introduced a new policy.   We must assume that the present tariff, constructed upon the lines of protection, is to be repealed and that there is
to be substituted for it a tariff law constructed solely with reference to
revenue; that no duty is to be higher because the increase will keep open
an American mill or keep up the wages of an American workman, but
that in every case such a rate of duty is to be imposed as will bring to
the Treasury of the United States the largest returns of revenue.   The
contention has not been between schedules, but between principles, and it
would be offensive to suggest that the prevailing party will not carry into
legislation the principles advocated by it and the pledges given to the
people.   The tariff bills passed by the House of Representatives at the last
session were, as I suppose, even in the opinion of their promoters, inadequate, and justified only by the fact that the Senate and House of Representatives were not in accord and that a general revision could not
therefore be undertaken.

I recommend that the whole subject of tariff revision be left to the
incoming Congress.   It is matter of regret that this work must be delayed for at least three months, for the threat of great tariff changes
introduces so much uncertainty that an amount, not easily estimated, of
business inaction and of diminished production will necessarily result.
It is possible also that this uncertainty may result in decreased revenues
from customs duties, for our merchants will make cautious orders for
foreign goods in view of the prospect of tariff reductions and the uncertainty as to when they will take effect.   Those who have advocated a
protective tariff can well afford to have their disastrous forecasts of a
change of policy disappointed.   If a system of customs duties can be
framed that will set the idle wheels and looms of Europe in motion and
crowd our warehouses with foreign-made goods and at the same time
keep our own mills busy; that will give us an increased participation in
the "markets of the world" of greater value than the home market we
surrender; that will give increased work to foreign workmen upon products to be consumed by our people without diminishing the amount of
work to be done here; that will enable the American manufacturer to
pay to his workmen from 50 to 100 per cent more in wages than is paid
in the foreign mill, and yet to compete in our market and in foreign
markets with the foreign producer; that will further reduce the cost of
articles of wear and food without reducing the wages of those who produce them; that can be celebrated, after its effects have been realized, as
its expectation has been in European as well as in American cities, the
authors and promoters of it will be entitled to the highest praise.   We
have had in our history several experiences of the contrasted effects of a
revenue and of a protective tariff, but this generation has not felt them,
and the experience of one generation is not highly instructive to the next.
The friends of the protective system with undiminished confidence in
the principles they have advocated will await the results of the new
experiment.

The strained and too often disturbed relations existing between the employees and the employers in our great manufacturing establishments have not been favorable to a calm consideration by the wage earner of the effect upon wages of the protective system. The facts that his wages were the highest paid in like callings in the world and that a maintenance of this rate of wages in the absence of protective duties upon the product of his labor was impossible were obscured by the passion evoked by these contests. He may now be able to review the question in the light of his personal experience under the operation of a tariff for revenue only. If that experience shall demonstrate that present rates of wages are thereby maintained or increased, either absolutely or in their purchasing power, and that the aggregate volume of work to be done in this country is increased or even maintained, so that there are more or as many days' work in a year, at as good or better wages, for the American workmen as has been the case under the protective system, everyone will rejoice. A general process of wage reduction can not be contemplated by any patriotic citizen without the gravest apprehension. It may be, indeed I believe is, possible for the American manufacturer to compete successfully with his foreign rival in many branches of production without the defense of protective duties if the pay rolls are equalized; but the conflict that stands between the producer and that result and the distress of our working people when it is attained are not pleasant to contemplate. The Society of the Unemployed, now holding its frequent and threatening parades in the streets of foreign cities, should not be allowed to acquire an American domicile.

The reports of the heads of the several Executive Departments, which are herewith submitted, have very naturally included a résumé of the whole work of the Administration with the transactions of the last fiscal year. The attention not only of Congress but of the country is again invited to the methods of administration which have been pursued and to the results which have been attained. Public revenues amounting to $1,414,079,292.28 have been collected and disbursed without loss from misappropriation, without a single defalcation of such importance as to attract the public attention, and at a diminished per cent of cost for collection. The public business has been transacted not only with fidelity, but progressively and with a view to giving to the people in the fullest possible degree the benefits of a service established and maintained for their protection and comfort.

Our relations with other nations are now undisturbed by any serious controversy. The complicated and threatening differences with Germany and England relating to Samoan affairs, with England in relation to the seal fisheries in the Bering Sea, and with Chile growing out of the *Baltimore* affair have been adjusted.

There have been negotiated and concluded, under section 3 of the tariff law, commercial agreements relating to reciprocal trade with the following countries: Brazil, Dominican Republic, Spain for Cuba and Puerto Rico, Guatemala, Salvador, the German Empire, Great Britain for certain West Indian colonies and British Guiana, Nicaragua, Honduras, and Austria-Hungary.

Of these, those with Guatemala, Salvador, the German Empire, Great Britain, Nicaragua, Honduras, and Austria-Hungary have been concluded since my last annual message.   Under these trade arrangements a free or favored admission has been secured in every case for an important list of American products.   Especial care has been taken to secure markets for farm products, in order to relieve that great underlying industry of the depression which the lack of an adequate foreign market for our surplus often brings.   An opening has also been made for manufactured products that will undoubtedly, if this policy is maintained, greatly augment our export trade.   The full benefits of these arrangements can not be realized instantly.   New lines of trade are to be opened.   The commercial traveler must survey the field.   The manufacturer must adapt his goods to the new markets and facilities for exchange must be established.   This work has been well begun, our merchants and manufacturers having entered the new fields with courage and enterprise.   In the case of food products, and especially with Cuba, the trade did not need to wait, and the immediate results have been most gratifying.   If this policy and these trade arrangements can be continued in force and aided by the establishment of American steamship lines, I do not doubt that we shall within a short period secure fully one-third of the total trade of the countries of Central and South America, which now amounts to about $600,-000,000 annually.   In 1885 we had only 8 per cent of this trade.

The following statistics show the increase in our trade with the countries with which we have reciprocal trade agreements from the date when such agreements went into effect up to September 30, 1892, the increase being in some almost wholly and in others in an important degree the result of these agreements:

The domestic exports to Germany and Austria-Hungary have increased in value from $47,673,756 to $57,993,064, an increase of $10,-319,308, or 21.63 per cent.   With American countries the value of our exports has increased from $44,160,285 to $54,613,598, an increase of $10,453,313, or 23.67 per cent.   The total increase in the value of exports to all the countries with which we have reciprocity agreements has been $20,772,621.   This increase is chiefly in wheat, flour, meat, and dairy products and in manufactures of iron and steel and lumber. There has been a large increase in the value of imports from all these countries since the commercial agreements went into effect, amounting to $74,294,525, but it has been entirely in imports from the American countries, consisting mostly of sugar, coffee, india rubber, and crude drugs.   The alarmed attention of our European competitors for the South American market has been attracted to this new American policy and to our acquisition and their loss of South American trade.

A treaty providing for the arbitration of the dispute between Great Britain and the United States as to the killing of seals in the Bering Sea was concluded on the 29th of February last. This treaty was accompanied by an agreement prohibiting pelagic sealing pending the arbitration, and a vigorous effort was made during this season to drive out all poaching sealers from the Bering Sea. Six naval vessels, three revenue cutters, and one vessel from the Fish Commission, all under the command of Commander Evans, of the Navy, were sent into the sea, which was systematically patrolled. Some seizures were made, and it is believed that the catch in the Bering Sea by poachers amounted to less than 500 seals. It is true, however, that in the North Pacific, while the seal herds were on their way to the passes between the Aleutian Islands, a very large number, probably 35,000, were taken. The existing statutes of the United States do not restrain our citizens from taking seals in the Pacific Ocean, and perhaps should not unless the prohibition can be extended to the citizens of other nations. I recommend that power be given to the President by proclamation to prohibit the taking of seals in the North Pacific by American vessels in case, either as the result of the findings of the Tribunal of Arbitration or otherwise, the restraints can be applied to the vessels of all countries. The case of the United States for the Tribunal of Arbitration has been prepared with great care and industry by the Hon. John W. Foster, and the counsel who represent this Government express confidence that a result substantially establishing our claims and preserving this great industry for the benefit of all nations will be attained.

During the past year a suggestion was received through the British minister that the Canadian government would like to confer as to the possibility of enlarging upon terms of mutual advantage the commercial exchanges of Canada and of the United States, and a conference was held at Washington, with Mr. Blaine acting for this Government and the British minister at this capital and three members of the Dominion cabinet acting as commissioners on the part of Great Britain. The conference developed the fact that the Canadian government was only prepared to offer to the United States in exchange for the concessions asked the admission of natural products. The statement was frankly made that favored rates could not be given to the United States as against the mother country. This admission, which was foreseen, necessarily terminated the conference upon this question. The benefits of an exchange of natural products would be almost wholly with the people of Canada. Some other topics of interest were considered in the conference, and have resulted in the making of a convention for examining the Alaskan boundary and the waters of Passamaquoddy Bay adjacent to Eastport, Me., and in the initiation of an arrangement for the protection of fish life in the coterminous and neighboring waters of our northern border.

The controversy as to tolls upon the Welland Canal, which was presented to Congress at the last session by special message,* having failed of adjustment, I felt constrained to exercise the authority conferred by the act of July 26, 1892, and to proclaim a suspension of the free use of St. Marys Falls Canal to cargoes in transit to ports in Canada.† The Secretary of the Treasury established such tolls as were thought to be equivalent to the exactions unjustly levied upon our commerce in the Canadian canals.

If, as we must suppose, the political relations of Canada and the disposition of the Canadian government are to remain unchanged, a somewhat radical revision of our trade relations should, I think, be made. Our relations must continue to be intimate, and they should be friendly. I regret to say, however, that in many of the controversies, notably those as to the fisheries on the Atlantic, the sealing interests on the Pacific, and the canal tolls, our negotiations with Great Britain have continuously been thwarted or retarded by unreasonable and unfriendly objections and protests from Canada. In the matter of the canal tolls our treaty rights were flagrantly disregarded. It is hardly too much to say that the Canadian Pacific and other railway lines which parallel our northern boundary are sustained by commerce having either its origin or terminus, or both, in the United States. Canadian railroads compete with those of the United States for our traffic, and without the restraints of our interstate-commerce act. Their cars pass almost without detention into and out of our territory.

The Canadian Pacific Railway brought into the United States from China and Japan via British Columbia during the year ended June 30, 1892, 23,239,689 pounds of freight, and it carried from the United States, to be shipped to China and Japan via British Columbia, 24,068,346 pounds of freight. There were also shipped from the United States over this road from Eastern ports of the United States to our Pacific ports during the same year 13,912,073 pounds of freight, and there were received over this road at the United States Eastern ports from ports on the Pacific Coast 13,293,315 pounds of freight. Mr. Joseph Nimmo, jr., former chief of the Bureau of Statistics, when before the Senate Select Committee on Relations with Canada, April 26, 1890, said that "the value of goods thus transported between different points in the United States across Canadian territory probably amounts to $100,000,000 a year."

There is no disposition on the part of the people or Government of the United States to interfere in the smallest degree with the political relations of Canada. That question is wholly with her own people. It is time for us, however, to consider whether, if the present state of things and trend of things is to continue, our interchanges upon lines of land transportation should not be put upon a different basis and our entire independence of Canadian canals and of the St. Lawrence as an outlet to the sea secured by the construction of an American canal around the Falls of Niagara and the opening of ship communication between the Great

Lakes and one of our own seaports. We should not hesitate to avail ourselves of our great natural trade advantages. We should withdraw the support which is given to the railroads and steamship lines of Canada by a traffic that properly belongs to us and no longer furnish the earnings which lighten the otherwise crushing weight of the enormous public subsidies that have been given to them. The subject of the power of the Treasury to deal with this matter without further legislation has been under consideration, but circumstances have postponed a conclusion. It is probable that a consideration of the propriety of a modification or abrogation of the article of the treaty of Washington relating to the transit of goods in bond is involved in any complete solution of the question.

Congress at the last session was kept advised of the progress of the serious and for a time threatening difference between the United States and Chile. It gives me now great gratification to report that the Chilean Government in a most friendly and honorable spirit has tendered and paid as an indemnity to the families of the sailors of the *Baltimore* who were killed and to those who were injured in the outbreak in the city of Valparaiso the sum of $75,000. This has been accepted not only as an indemnity for a wrong done, but as a most gratifying evidence that the Government of Chile rightly appreciates the disposition of this Government to act in a spirit of the most absolute fairness and friendliness in our intercourse with that brave people. A further and conclusive evidence of the mutual respect and confidence now existing is furnished by the fact that a convention submitting to arbitration the mutual claims of the citizens of the respective Governments has been agreed upon. Some of these claims have been pending for many years and have been the occasion of much unsatisfactory diplomatic correspondence.

I have endeavored in every way to assure our sister Republics of Central and South America that the United States Government and its people have only the most friendly disposition toward them all. We do not covet their territory. We have no disposition to be oppressive or exacting in our dealings with any of them, even the weakest. Our interests and our hopes for them all lie in the direction of stable governments by their people and of the largest development of their great commercial resources. The mutual benefits of enlarged commercial exchanges and of a more familiar and friendly intercourse between our peoples we do desire, and in this have sought their friendly cooperation.

I have believed, however, while holding these sentiments in the greatest sincerity, that we must insist upon a just responsibility for any injuries inflicted upon our official representatives or upon our citizens. This insistence, kindly and justly but firmly made, will, I believe, promote peace and mutual respect.

Our relations with Hawaii have been such as to attract an increased interest, and must continue to do so. I deem it of great importance that the projected submarine cable, a survey for which has been made, should be promoted.   Both for naval and commercial uses we should have quick communication with Honolulu.   We should before this have availed ourselves of the concession made many years ago to this Government for a harbor and naval station at Pearl River.   Many evidences of the friendliness of the Hawaiian Government have been given in the past, and it is gratifying to believe that the advantage and necessity of a continuance of very close relations is appreciated.

The friendly act of this Government in expressing to the Government of Italy its reprobation and abhorrence of the lynching of Italian subjects in New Orleans by the payment of 125,000 francs, or $24,330.90, was accepted by the King of Italy with every manifestation of gracious appreciation, and the incident has been highly promotive of mutual respect and good will.

In consequence of the action of the French Government in proclaiming a protectorate over certain tribal districts of the west coast of Africa eastward of the San Pedro River, which has long been regarded as the southeastern boundary of Liberia, I have felt constrained to make protest against this encroachment upon the territory of a Republic which was founded by citizens of the United States and toward which this country has for many years held the intimate relation of a friendly counselor.

The recent disturbances of the public peace by lawless foreign marauders on the Mexican frontier have afforded this Government an opportunity to testify its good will for Mexico and its earnest purpose to fulfill the obligations of international friendship by pursuing and dispersing the evil doers.   The work of relocating the boundary of the treaty of Guadalupe Hidalgo westward from El Paso is progressing favorably.

Our intercourse with Spain continues on a friendly footing.   I regret, however, not to be able to report as yet the adjustment of the claims of the American missionaries arising from the disorders at Ponape, in the Caroline Islands, but I anticipate a satisfactory adjustment in view of renewed and urgent representations to the Government at Madrid.

The treatment of the religious and educational establishments of American citizens in Turkey has of late called for a more than usual share of attention.   A tendency to curtail the toleration which has so beneficially prevailed is discernible and has called forth the earnest remonstrance of this Government.   Harassing regulations in regard to schools and churches have been attempted in certain localities, but not without due protest and the assertion of the inherent and conventional rights of our countrymen.   Violations of domicile and search of the persons and effects of citizens of the United States by apparently irresponsible officials in the Asiatic *vilayets* have from time to time been reported.   An aggravated instance of injury to the property of an American missionary at Bourdour, in the Province of Konia, called forth an urgent claim for reparation, which I am pleased to say was promptly heeded by the Government of the Porte.   Interference with the trading ventures of our citizens in Asia Minor is also reported, and the lack of consular representation in that region is a serious drawback to instant and effective protection. I can not believe that these incidents represent a settled policy, and shall not cease to urge the adoption of proper remedies.

International copyright has been extended to Italy by proclamation in conformity with the act of March 3, 1891, upon assurance being given that Italian law permits to citizens of the United States the benefit of copyright on substantially the same basis as to subjects of Italy. By a special convention proclaimed January 15, 1892, reciprocal provisions of copyright have been applied between the United States and Germany. Negotiations are in progress with other countries to the same end.

I repeat with great earnestness the recommendation which I have made in several previous messages that prompt and adequate support be given to the American company engaged in the construction of the Nicaragua ship canal. It is impossible to overstate the value from every standpoint of this great enterprise, and I hope that there may be time, even in this Congress, to give to it an impetus that will insure the early completion of the canal and secure to the United States its proper relation to it when completed.

The Congress has been already advised that the invitations of this Government for the assembling of an international monetary conference to consider the question of an enlarged use of silver were accepted by the nations to which they were addressed. The conference assembled at Brussels on the 22d of November, and has entered upon the consideration of this great question. I have not doubted, and have taken occasion to express that belief as well in the invitations issued for this conference as in my public messages, that the free coinage of silver upon an agreed international ratio would greatly promote the interests of our people and equally those of other nations. It is too early to predict what results may be accomplished by the conference. If any temporary check or delay intervenes, I believe that very soon commercial conditions will compel the now reluctant governments to unite with us in this movement to secure the enlargement of the volume of coined money needed for the transaction of the business of the world.

The report of the Secretary of the Treasury will attract especial interest in view of the many misleading statements that have been made as to the state of the public revenues. Three preliminary facts should not only be stated but emphasized before looking into details: First, that the public debt has been reduced since March 4, 1889, $259,074,200, and the annual interest charge $11,684,469; second, that there have been paid out for pensions during this Administration up to November 1, 1892, $432,564,178.70, an excess of $114,466,386.09 over the sum expended during the period from March 1, 1885, to March 1, 1889; and, third, that under the existing tariff up to December 1 about $93,000,000 of revenue which would have been collected upon imported sugars if the duty had been maintained has gone into the pockets of the people, and not into the public Treasury, as before. If there are any who still think that the surplus should have been kept out of circulation by hoarding it in the Treasury, or deposited in favored banks without interest while the Government continued to pay to these very banks interest upon the bonds deposited as security for the deposits, or who think that the extended pension legislation was a public robbery, or that the duties upon sugar should have been maintained, I am content to leave the argument where it now rests while we wait to see whether these criticisms will take the form of legislation.

The revenues for the fiscal year ending June 30, 1892, from all sources were $425,868,260.22, and the expenditures for all purposes were $415,-953,806.56, leaving a balance of $9,914,453.66. There were paid during the year upon the public debt $40,570,467.98. The surplus in the Treasury and the bank redemption fund passed by the act of July 14, 1890, to the general fund furnished in large part the cash available and used for the payments made upon the public debt. Compared with the year 1891, our receipts from customs duties fell off $42,069,241.08, while our receipts from internal revenue increased $8,284,823.13, leaving the net loss of revenue from these principal sources $33,784,417.95. The net loss of revenue from all sources was $32,675,972.81.

The revenues, estimated and actual, for the fiscal year ending June 30, 1893, are placed by the Secretary at $463,336,350.44, and the expenditures at $461,336,350.44, showing a surplus of receipts over expenditures of $2,000,000. The cash balance in the Treasury at the end of the fiscal year it is estimated will be $20,992,377.03. So far as these figures are based upon estimates of receipts and expenditures for the remaining months of the current fiscal year, there are not only the usual elements of uncertainty, but some added elements. New revenue legislation, or even the expectation of it, may seriously reduce the public revenues during the period of uncertainty and during the process of business adjustment to the new conditions when they become known. But the Secretary has very wisely refrained from guessing as to the effect of possible changes in our revenue laws, since the scope of those changes and the time of their taking effect can not in any degree be forecast or foretold by him. His estimates must be based upon existing laws and upon a continuance of existing business conditions, except so far as these conditions may be affected by causes other than new legislation.

The estimated receipts for the fiscal year ending June 30, 1894, are $490,121,365.38, and the estimated appropriations $457,261,335.33, leaving an estimated surplus of receipts over expenditures of $32,860,-030.05. This does not include any payment to the sinking fund. In the recommendation of the Secretary that the sinking-fund law be repealed I concur. The redemption of bonds since the passage of the law to June 30, 1892, has already exceeded the requirements by the sum of

$990,510,681.49. The retirement of bonds in the future before maturity should be a matter of convenience, not of compulsion. We should not collect revenue for that purpose, but only use any casual surplus. To the balance of $32,860,030.05 of receipts over expenditures for the year 1894 should be added the estimated surplus at the beginning of the year, $20,992,377.03, and from this aggregate there must be deducted, as stated by the Secretary, about $44,000,000 of estimated unexpended appropriations.

The public confidence in the purpose and ability of the Government to maintain the parity of all of our money issues, whether coin or paper, must remain unshaken. The demand for gold in Europe and the consequent calls upon us are in a considerable degree the result of the efforts of some of the European Governments to increase their gold reserves, and these efforts should be met by appropriate legislation on our part. The conditions that have created this drain of the Treasury gold are in an important degree political, and not commercial. In view of the fact that a general revision of our revenue laws in the near future seems to be probable, it would be better that any changes should be a part of that revision rather than of a temporary nature.

During the last fiscal year the Secretary purchased under the act of July 14, 1890, 54,355,748 ounces of silver and issued in payment therefor $51,106,608 in notes. The total purchases since the passage of the act have been 120,479,981 ounces and the aggregate of notes issued $116,-783,590. The average price paid for silver during the year was 94 cents per ounce, the highest price being $1.02¾ July 1, 1891, and the lowest 83 cents March 21, 1892. In view of the fact that the monetary conference is now sitting and that no conclusion has yet been reached, I withhold any recommendation as to legislation upon this subject.

The report of the Secretary of War brings again to the attention of Congress some important suggestions as to the reorganization of the infantry and artillery arms of the service, which his predecessors have before urgently presented. Our Army is small, but its organization should all the more be put upon the most approved modern basis. The conditions upon what we have called the "frontier" have heretofore required the maintenance of many small posts, but now the policy of concentration is obviously the right one. The new posts should have the proper strategic relations to the only "frontiers" we now have—those of the seacoast and of our northern and part of our southern boundary. I do not think that any question of advantage to localities or to States should determine the location of the new posts. The reorganization and enlargement of the Bureau of Military Information which the Secretary has effected is a work the usefulness of which will become every year more apparent. The work of building heavy guns and the construction of coast defenses has been well begun and should be carried on without check.

The report of the Attorney-General is by law submitted directly to Congress, but I can not refrain from saying that he has conducted the increasing work of the Department of Justice with great professional skill. He has in several directions secured from the courts decisions giving increased protection to the officers of the United States and bringing some classes of crime that escaped local cognizance and punishment into the tribunals of the United States, where they could be tried with impartiality.

The numerous applications for Executive clemency presented in behalf of persons convicted in United States courts and given penitentiary sentences have called my attention to a fact referred to by the Attorney-General in his report, namely, that a time allowance for good behavior for such prisoners is prescribed by the Federal statutes only where the State in which the penitentiary is located has made no such provision. Prisoners are given the benefit of the provisions of the State law regulating the penitentiary to which they may be sent. These are various, some perhaps too liberal and some perhaps too illiberal. The result is that a sentence for five years means one thing if the prisoner is sent to one State for confinement and quite a different thing if he is sent to another. I recommend that a uniform credit for good behavior be prescribed by Congress.

I have before expressed my concurrence in the recommendation of the Attorney-General that degrees of murder should be recognized in the Federal statutes, as they are, I believe, in all the States. These grades are founded on correct distinctions in crime. The recognition of them would enable the courts to exercise some discretion in apportioning punishment and would greatly relieve the Executive of what is coming to be a very heavy burden—the examination of these cases on application for commutation.

The aggregate of claims pending against the Government in the Court of Claims is enormous. Claims to the amount of nearly $400,000,000 for the taking of or injury to the property of persons claiming to be loyal during the war are now before that court for examination. When to these are added the Indian depredation claims and the French spoliation claims, an aggregate is reached that is indeed startling. In the defense of all these cases the Government is at great disadvantage. The claimants have preserved their evidence, whereas the agents of the Government are sent into the field to rummage for what they can find. This difficulty is peculiarly great where the fact to be established is the disloyalty of the claimant during the war. If this great threat against our revenues is to have no other check, certainly Congress should supply the Department of Justice with appropriations sufficiently liberal to secure the best legal talent in the defense of these claims and to pursue its vague search for evidence effectively.

The report of the Postmaster-General shows a most gratifying increase and a most efficient and progressive management of the great business of that Department. The remarkable increase in revenues, in the number of post-offices, and in the miles of mail carriage furnishes further evidence of the high state of prosperity which our people are enjoying. New offices mean new hamlets and towns, new routes mean the extension of our border settlements, and increased revenues mean an active commerce. The Postmaster-General reviews the whole period of his administration of the office and brings some of his statistics down to the month of November last. The postal revenues have increased during the last year nearly $5,000,000. The deficit for the year ending June 30, 1892, is $848,341 less than the deficiency of the preceding year. The deficiency of the present fiscal year it is estimated will be reduced to $1,552,423, which will not only be extinguished during the next fiscal year, but a surplus of nearly $1,000,000 should then be shown. In these calculations the payments to be made under the contracts for ocean mail service have not been included. There have been added 1,590 new mail routes during the year, with a mileage of 8,563 miles, and the total number of new miles of mail trips added during the year is nearly 17,000,000. The number of miles of mail journeys added during the last four years is about 76,000,000, this addition being 21,000,000 miles more than were in operation in the whole country in 1861.

The number of post-offices has been increased by 2,790 during the year, and during the past four years, and up to October 29 last, the total increase in the number of offices has been nearly 9,000. The number of free-delivery offices has been nearly doubled in the last four years, and the number of money-order offices more than doubled within that time.

For the three years ending June 30, 1892, the postal revenue amounted to $197,744,359, which was an increase of $52,263,150 over the revenue for the three years ending June 30, 1888, the increase during the last three years being more than three and a half times as great as the increase during the three years ending June 30, 1888. No such increase as that shown for these three years has ever previously appeared in the revenues of the Department. The Postmaster-General has extended to the post-offices in the larger cities the merit system of promotion introduced by my direction into the Departments here, and it has resulted there, as in the Departments, in a larger volume of work and that better done.

Ever since our merchant marine was driven from the sea by the rebel cruisers during the War of the Rebellion the United States has been paying an enormous annual tribute to foreign countries in the shape of freight and passage moneys. Our grain and meats have been taken at our own docks and our large imports there laid down by foreign shipmasters. An increasing torrent of American travel to Europe has contributed a vast sum annually to the dividends of foreign shipowners. The balance of trade shown by the books of our custom-houses has been very largely reduced and in many years altogether extinguished by this constant drain.   In the year 1892 only 12.3 per cent of our imports were brought in American vessels.   These great foreign steamships maintained by our traffic are many of them under contracts with their respective Governments by which in time of war they will become a part of their armed naval establishments.   Profiting by our commerce in peace, they will become the most formidable destroyers of our commerce in time of war. I have felt, and have before expressed the feeling, that this condition of things was both intolerable and disgraceful.   A wholesome change of policy, and one having in it much promise, as it seems to me, was begun by the law of March 3, 1891.   Under this law contracts have been made by the Postmaster-General for eleven mail routes.   The expenditure involved by these contracts for the next fiscal year approximates $954,-123.33.   As one of the results already reached sixteen American steamships, of an aggregate tonnage of 57,400 tons, costing $7,400,000, have been built or contracted to be built in American shipyards.

The estimated tonnage of all steamships required under existing contracts is 165,802, and when the full service required by these contracts is established there will be forty-one mail steamers under the American flag, with the probability of further necessary additions in the Brazilian and Argentine service.   The contracts recently let for transatlantic service will result in the construction of five ships of 10,000 tons each, costing $9,000,000 to $10,000,000, and will add, with the *City of New York* and *City of Paris*, to which the Treasury Department was authorized by legislation at the last session to give American registry, seven of the swiftest vessels upon the sea to our naval reserve.   The contracts made with the lines sailing to Central and South American ports have increased the frequency and shortened the time of the trips, added new ports of call, and sustained some lines that otherwise would almost certainly have been withdrawn.   The service to Buenos Ayres is the first to the Argentine Republic under the American flag.   The service to Southampton, Boulogne, and Antwerp is also new, and is to be begun with the steamships *City of New York* and *City of Paris* in February next.

I earnestly urge the continuance of the policy inaugurated by this legislation, and that the appropriations required to meet the obligations of the Government under the contracts may be made promptly, so that the lines that have entered into these engagements may not be embarrassed. We have had, by reason of connections with the transcontinental railway lines constructed through our own territory, some advantages in the ocean trade of the Pacific that we did not possess on the Atlantic.   The construction of the Canadian Pacific Railway and the establishment under large subventions from Canada and England of fast steamship service from Vancouver with Japan and China seriously threaten our shipping interests in the Pacific.   This line of English steamers receives, as is stated by the Commissioner of Navigation, a direct subsidy of $400,000 annually, or $30,767 per trip for thirteen voyages, in addition to some further aid from the Admiralty in connection with contracts under which the vessels may be used for naval purposes. The competing American Pacific mail line under the act of March 3, 1891, receives only $6,389 per round trip.

Efforts have been making within the last year, as I am informed, to establish under similar conditions a line between Vancouver and some Australian port, with a view of seizing there a trade in which we have had a large interest. The Commissioner of Navigation states that a very large per cent of our imports from Asia are now brought to us by English steamships and their connecting railways in Canada. With a view of promoting this trade, especially in tea, Canada has imposed a discriminating duty of 10 per cent upon tea and coffee brought into the Dominion from the United States. If this unequal contest between American lines without subsidy, or with diminished subsidies, and the English Canadian line to which I have referred is to continue, I think we should at least see that the facilities for customs entry and transportation across our territory are not such as to make the Canadian route a favored one, and that the discrimination as to duties to which I have referred is met by a like discrimination as to the importation of these articles from Canada.

No subject, I think, more nearly touches the pride, the power, and the prosperity of our country than this of the development of our merchant marine upon the sea. If we could enter into conference with other competitors and all would agree to withhold government aid, we could perhaps take our chances with the rest; but our great competitors have established and maintained their lines by government subsidies until they now have practically excluded us from participation. In my opinion no choice is left to us but to pursue, moderately at least, the same lines.

The report of the Secretary of the Navy exhibits great progress in the construction of our new Navy. When the present Secretary entered upon his duties, only 3 modern steel vessels were in commission. The vessels since put in commission and to be put in commission during the winter will make a total of 19 during his administration of the Department. During the current year 10 war vessels and 3 navy tugs have been launched, and during the four years 25 vessels will have been launched. Two other large ships and a torpedo boat are under contract and the work upon them well advanced, and the 4 monitors are awaiting only the arrival of their armor, which has been unexpectedly delayed, or they would have been before this in commission.

Contracts have been let during this Administration, under the appropriations for the increase of the Navy, including new vessels and their appurtenances, to the amount of $35,000,000, and there has been expended during the same period for labor at navy-yards upon similar work $8,000,000 without the smallest scandal or charge of fraud or partiality. The enthusiasm and interest of our naval officers, both of the staff and line, have been greatly kindled. They have responded magnificently to the confidence of Congress and have demonstrated to the world an unexcelled capacity in construction, in ordnance, and in everything involved in the building, equipping, and sailing of great war ships.

At the beginning of Secretary Tracy's administration several difficult problems remained to be grappled with and solved before the efficiency in action of our ships could be secured. It is believed that as the result of new processes in the construction of armor plate our later ships will be clothed with defensive plates of higher resisting power than are found on any war vessels afloat. We were without torpedoes. Tests have been made to ascertain the relative efficiency of different constructions, a torpedo has been adopted, and the work of construction is now being carried on successfully. We were without armor-piercing shells and without a shop instructed and equipped for the construction of them. We are now making what is believed to be a projectile superior to any before in use. A smokeless powder has been developed and a slow-burning powder for guns of large caliber. A high explosive capable of use in shells fired from service guns has been found, and the manufacture of gun cotton has been developed so that the question of supply is no longer in doubt.

The development of a naval militia, which has been organized in eight States and brought into cordial and cooperative relations with the Navy, is another important achievement. There are now enlisted in these organizations 1,800 men, and they are likely to be greatly extended. I recommend such legislation and appropriations as will encourage and develop this movement. The recommendations of the Secretary will, I do not doubt, receive the friendly consideration of Congress, for he has enjoyed, as he has deserved, the confidence of all those interested in the development of our Navy, without any division upon partisan lines. I earnestly express the hope that a work which has made such noble progress may not now be stayed. The wholesome influence for peace and the increased sense of security which our citizens domiciled in other lands feel when these magnificent ships under the American flag appear is already most gratefully apparent. The ships from our Navy which will appear in the great naval parade next April in the harbor of New York will be a convincing demonstration to the world that the United States is again a naval power.

The work of the Interior Department, always very burdensome, has been larger than ever before during the administration of Secretary Noble. The disability-pension law, the taking of the Eleventh Census, the opening of vast areas of Indian lands to settlement, the organization of Oklahoma, and the negotiations for the cession of Indian lands furnish some of the particulars of the increased work, and the results achieved testify to the ability, fidelity, and industry of the head of the Department and his efficient assistants.

Several important agreements for the cession of Indian lands negotiated by the commission appointed under the act of March 2, 1889, are awaiting the action of Congress. Perhaps the most important of these is that for the cession of the Cherokee Strip. This region has been the source of great vexation to the executive department and of great friction and unrest between the settlers who desire to occupy it and the Indians who assert title. The agreement which has been made by the commission is perhaps the most satisfactory that could have been reached. It will be noticed that it is conditioned upon its ratification by Congress before March 4, 1893. The Secretary of the Interior, who has given the subject very careful thought, recommends the ratification of the agreement, and I am inclined to follow his recommendation. Certain it is that some action by which this controversy shall be brought to an end and these lands opened to settlement is urgent.

The form of government provided by Congress on May 17, 1884, for Alaska was in its frame and purpose temporary. The increase of population and the development of some important mining and commercial interests make it imperative that the law should be revised and better provision made for the arrest and punishment of criminals.

The report of the Secretary shows a very gratifying state of facts as to the condition of the General Land Office. The work of issuing agricultural patents, which seemed to be hopelessly in arrear when the present Secretary undertook the duties of his office, has been so expedited that the bureau is now upon current business. The relief thus afforded to honest and worthy settlers upon the public lands by giving to them an assured title to their entries has been of incalculable benefit in developing the new States and the Territories.

The Court of Private Land Claims, established by Congress for the promotion of this policy of speedily settling contested land titles, is making satisfactory progress in its work, and when the work is completed a great impetus will be given to the development of those regions where unsettled claims under Mexican grants have so long exercised their repressive influence. When to these results are added the enormous cessions of Indian lands which have been opened to settlement, aggregating during this Administration nearly 26,000,000 acres, and the agreements negotiated and now pending in Congress for ratification by which about 10,000,000 additional acres will be opened to settlement, it will be seen how much has been accomplished.

The work in the Indian Bureau in the execution of the policy of recent legislation has been largely directed to two chief purposes: First, the allotment of lands in severalty to the Indians and the cession to the United States of the surplus lands, and, secondly, to the work of educating the Indian for his own protection in his closer contact with the white man and for the intelligent exercise of his new citizenship. Allotments have been made and patents issued to 5,900 Indians under the present

Secretary and Commissioner, and 7,600 additional allotments have been made for which patents are now in process of preparation. The school attendance of Indian children has been increased during that time over 13 per cent, the enrollment for 1892 being nearly 20,000. A uniform system of school text-books and of study has been adopted and the work in these national schools brought as near as may be to the basis of the free common schools of the States. These schools can be transferred and merged into the common-school systems of the States when the Indian has fully assumed his new relation to the organized civil community in which he resides and the new States are able to assume the burden. I have several times been called upon to remove Indian agents appointed by me, and have done so promptly upon every sustained complaint of unfitness or misconduct. I believe, however, that the Indian service at the agencies has been improved and is now administered on the whole with a good degree of efficiency. If any legislation is possible by which the selection of Indian agents can be wholly removed from all partisan suggestions or considerations, I am sure it would be a great relief to the Executive and a great benefit to the service. The appropriation for the subsistence of the Cheyenne and Arapahoe Indians made at the last session of Congress was inadequate. This smaller appropriation was estimated for by the Commissioner upon the theory that the large fund belonging to the tribe in the public Treasury could be and ought to be used for their support. In view, however, of the pending depredation claims against this fund and other considerations, the Secretary of the Interior on the 12th of April last submitted a supplemental estimate for $50,000. This appropriation was not made, as it should have been, and the oversight ought to be remedied at the earliest possible date.

In a special message to this Congress at the last session I stated the reasons why I had not approved the deed for the release to the United States by the Choctaws and Chickasaws of the lands formerly embraced in the Cheyenne and Arapahoe Reservation and remaining after allotments to that tribe. A resolution of the Senate expressing the opinion of that body that notwithstanding the facts stated in my special message the deed should be approved and the money, $2,991,450, paid over was presented to me May 10, 1892. My special message was intended to call the attention of Congress to the subject, and in view of the fact that it is conceded that the appropriation proceeded upon a false basis as to the amount of lands to be paid for and is by $50,000 in excess of the amount they are entitled to (even if their claim to the land is given full recognition at the rate agreed upon), I have not felt willing to approve the deed, and shall not do so, at least until both Houses of Congress have acted upon the subject. It has been informally proposed by the claimants to release this sum of $50,000, but I have no power to demand or accept such a release, and such an agreement would be without consideration and void.

I desire further to call the attention of Congress to the fact that the recent agreement concluded with the Kiowas and Comanches relates to lands which were a part of the "leased district," and to which the claim of the Choctaws and Chickasaws is precisely that recognized by Congress in the legislation I have referred to. The surplus lands to which this claim would attach in the Kiowa and Comanche Reservation is 2,500,000 acres, and at the same rate the Government will be called upon to pay to the Choctaws and Chickasaws for these lands $3,125,000. This sum will be further augmented, especially if the title of the Indians to the tract now Greer County, Tex., is established. The duty devolved upon me in this connection was simply to pass upon the form of the deed; but as in my opinion the facts mentioned in my special message were not adequately brought to the attention of Congress in connection with the legislation, I have felt that I would not be justified in acting without some new expression of the legislative will.

The report of the Commissioner of Pensions, to which extended notice is given by the Secretary of the Interior in his report, will attract great attention. Judged by the aggregate amount of work done, the last year has been the greatest in the history of the office. I believe that the organization of the office is efficient and that the work has been done with fidelity. The passage of what is known as the disability bill has, as was foreseen, very largely increased the annual disbursements to the disabled veterans of the Civil War. The estimate for this fiscal year was $144,956,000, and that amount was appropriated. A deficiency amounting to $10,508,621 must be provided for at this session. The estimate for pensions for the fiscal year ending June 30, 1894, is $165,000,000. The Commissioner of Pensions believes that if the present legislation and methods are maintained and further additions to the pension laws are not made the maximum expenditure for pensions will be reached June 30, 1894, and will be at the highest point $188,000,000 per annum.

I adhere to the views expressed in previous messages that the care of the disabled soldiers of the War of the Rebellion is a matter of national concern and duty. Perhaps no emotion cools sooner than that of gratitude, but I can not believe that this process has yet reached a point with our people that would sustain the policy of remitting the care of these disabled veterans to the inadequate agencies provided by local laws. The parade on the 20th of September last upon the streets of this capital of 60,000 of the surviving Union veterans of the War of the Rebellion was a most touching and thrilling episode, and the rich and gracious welcome extended to them by the District of Columbia and the applause that greeted their progress from tens of thousands of people from all the States did much to revive the glorious recollections of the Grand Review when these men and many thousand others now in their graves were welcomed with grateful joy as victors in a struggle in which the national unity, honor, and wealth were all at issue.

In my last annual message I called attention to the fact that some legislative action was necessary in order to protect the interests of the

Government in its relations with the Union Pacific Railway. The Commissioner of Railroads has submitted a very full report, giving exact information as to the debt, the liens upon the company's property, and its resources. We must deal with the question as we find it and take that course which will under existing conditions best secure the interests of the United States. I recommended in my last annual message that a commission be appointed to deal with this question, and I renew that recommendation and suggest that the commission be given full power.

The report of the Secretary of Agriculture contains not only a most interesting statement of the progressive and valuable work done under the administration of Secretary Rusk, but many suggestions for the enlarged usefulness of this important Department. In the successful efforts to break down the restrictions to the free introduction of our meat products in the countries of Europe the Secretary has been untiring from the first, stimulating and aiding all other Government officers at home and abroad whose official duties enabled them to participate in the work. The total trade in hog products with Europe in May, 1892, amounted to 82,000,000 pounds, against 46,900,000 in the same month of 1891; in June, 1892, the export aggregated 85,700,000 pounds, against 46,500,000 pounds in the same month of the previous year; in July there was an increase of 41 per cent and in August of 55 per cent over the corresponding months of 1891. Over 40,000,000 pounds of inspected pork have been exported since the law was put into operation, and a comparison of the four months of May, June, July, and August, 1892, with the same months of 1891 shows an increase in the number of pounds of our export of pork products of 62 per cent and an increase in value of 66½ per cent. The exports of dressed beef increased from 137,900,000 pounds in 1889 to 220,500,000 pounds in 1892, or about 60 per cent. During the past year there have been exported 394,607 head of live cattle, as against 205,786 exported in 1889. This increased exportation has been largely promoted by the inspection authorized by law and the faithful efforts of the Secretary and his efficient subordinates to make that inspection thorough and to carefully exclude from all cargoes diseased or suspected cattle. The requirement of the English regulations that live cattle arriving from the United States must be slaughtered at the docks had its origin in the claim that pleuro-pneumonia existed among American cattle and that the existence of the disease could only certainly be determined by a *post mortem* inspection.

The Department of Agriculture has labored with great energy and faithfulness to extirpate this disease, and on the 26th day of September last a public announcement was made by the Secretary that the disease no longer existed anywhere within the United States. He is entirely satisfied after the most searching inquiry that this statement was justified, and that by a continuance of the inspection and quarantine now required of cattle brought into this country the disease can be prevented from again getting any foothold. The value to the cattle industry of the

United States of this achievement can hardly be estimated. We can not, perhaps, at once insist that this evidence shall be accepted as satisfactory by other countries; but if the present exemption from the disease is maintained and the inspection of our cattle arriving at foreign ports, in which our own veterinarians participate, confirms it, we may justly expect that the requirement that our cattle shall be slaughtered at the docks will be revoked, as the sanitary restrictions upon our pork products have been. If our cattle can be taken alive to the interior, the trade will be enormously increased.

Agricultural products constituted 78.1 per cent of our unprecedented exports for the fiscal year which closed June 30, 1892, the total exports being $1,030,278,030 and the value of the agricultural products $793,-717,676, which exceeds by more than $150,000,000 the shipment of agricultural products in any previous year.

An interesting and a promising work for the benefit of the American farmer has been begun through agents of the Agricultural Department in Europe, and consists in efforts to introduce the various products of Indian corn as articles of human food. The high price of rye offered a favorable opportunity for the experiment in Germany of combining corn meal with rye to produce a cheaper bread. A fair degree of success has been attained, and some mills for grinding corn for food have been introduced. The Secretary is of the opinion that this new use of the products of corn has already stimulated exportations, and that if diligently prosecuted large and important markets can presently be opened for this great American product.

The suggestions of the Secretary for an enlargement of the work of the Department are commended to your favorable consideration. It may, I think, be said without challenge that in no corresponding period has so much been done as during the last four years for the benefit of American agriculture.

The subject of quarantine regulations, inspection, and control was brought suddenly to my attention by the arrival at our ports in August last of vessels infected with cholera. Quarantine regulations should be uniform at all our ports. Under the Constitution they are plainly within the exclusive Federal jurisdiction when and so far as Congress shall legislate. In my opinion the whole subject should be taken into national control and adequate power given to the Executive to protect our people against plague invasions. On the 1st of September last I approved regulations establishing a twenty-day quarantine for all vessels bringing immigrants from foreign ports. This order will be continued in force. Some loss and suffering have resulted to passengers, but a due care for the homes of our people justifies in such cases the utmost precaution. There is danger that with the coming of spring cholera will again appear, and a liberal appropriation should be made at this session to enable our quarantine and port officers to exclude the deadly plague.

But the most careful and stringent quarantine regulations may not be sufficient absolutely to exclude the disease. The progress of medical and sanitary science has been such, however, that if approved precautions are taken at once to put all of our cities and towns in the best sanitary condition, and provision is made for isolating any sporadic cases and for a thorough disinfection, an epidemic can, I am sure, be avoided. This work appertains to the local authorities, and the responsibility and the penalty will be appalling if it is neglected or unduly delayed.

We are peculiarly subject in our great ports to the spread of infectious diseases by reason of the fact that unrestricted immigration brings to us out of European cities, in the overcrowded steerages of great steamships, a large number of persons whose surroundings make them the easy victims of the plague. This consideration, as well as those affecting the political, moral, and industrial interests of our country, leads me to renew the suggestion that admission to our country and to the high privileges of its citizenship should be more restricted and more careful. We have, I think, a right and owe a duty to our own people, and especially to our working people, not only to keep out the vicious, the ignorant, the civil disturber, the pauper, and the contract laborer, but to check the too great flow of immigration now coming by further limitations.

The report of the World's Columbian Exposition has not yet been submitted. That of the board of management of the Government exhibit has been received and is herewith transmitted. The work of construction and of preparation for the opening of the exposition in May next has progressed most satisfactorily and upon a scale of liberality and magnificence that will worthily sustain the honor of the United States.

The District of Columbia is left by a decision of the supreme court of the District without any law regulating the liquor traffic. An old statute of the legislature of the District relating to the licensing of various vocations has hitherto been treated by the Commissioners as giving them power to grant or refuse licenses to sell intoxicating liquors and as subjecting those who sold without licenses to penalties; but in May last the supreme court of the District held against this view of the powers of the Commissioners. It is of urgent importance, therefore, that Congress should supply, either by direct enactment or by conferring discretionary powers upon the Commissioners, proper limitations and restraints upon the liquor traffic in the District. The District has suffered in its reputation by many crimes of violence, a large per cent of them resulting from drunkenness and the liquor traffic. The capital of the nation should be freed from this reproach by the enactment of stringent restrictions and limitations upon the traffic.

In renewing the recommendation which I have made in three preceding annual messages that Congress should legislate for the protection of railroad employees against the dangers incident to the old and inadequate methods of braking and coupling which are still in use upon freight trains, I do so with the hope that this Congress may take action upon the subject. Statistics furnished by the Interstate Commerce Commission show that during the year ending June 30, 1891, there were forty-seven different styles of car couplers reported to be in use, and that during the same period there were 2,660 employees killed and 26,140 injured. Nearly 16 per cent of the deaths occurred in the coupling and uncoupling of cars and over 36 per cent of the injuries had the same origin.

The Civil Service Commission ask for an increased appropriation for needed clerical assistance, which I think should be given. I extended the classified service March 1, 1892, to include physicians, superintendents, assistant superintendents, school-teachers, and matrons in the Indian service, and have had under consideration the subject of some further extensions, but have not as yet fully determined the lines upon which extensions can most properly and usefully be made.

I have in each of the three annual messages which it has been my duty to submit to Congress called attention to the evils and dangers connected with our election methods and practices as they are related to the choice of officers of the National Government. In my last annual message I endeavored to invoke serious attention to the evils of unfair apportionments for Congress. I can not close this message without again calling attention to these grave and threatening evils. I had hoped that it was possible to secure a nonpartisan inquiry by means of a commission into evils the existence of which is known to all, and that out of this might grow legislation from which all thought of partisan advantage should be eliminated and only the higher thought appear of maintaining the freedom and purity of the ballot and the equality of the elector, without the guaranty of which the Government could never have been formed and without the continuance of which it can not continue to exist in peace and prosperity.

It is time that mutual charges of unfairness and fraud between the great parties should cease and that the sincerity of those who profess a desire for pure and honest elections should be brought to the test of their willingness to free our legislation and our election methods from everything that tends to impair the public confidence in the announced result. The necessity for an inquiry and for legislation by Congress upon this subject is emphasized by the fact that the tendency of the legislation in some States in recent years has in some important particulars been away from and not toward free and fair elections and equal apportionments. Is it not time that we should come together upon the high plane of patriotism while we devise methods that shall secure the right of every man qualified by law to cast a free ballot and give to every such ballot an equal value in choosing our public officers and in directing the policy of the Government?

Lawlessness is not less such, but more, where it usurps the functions

of the peace officer and of the courts. The frequent lynching of colored
people accused of crime is without the excuse, which has sometimes
been urged by mobs for a failure to pursue the appointed methods for
the punishment of crime, that the accused have an undue influence over
courts and juries. Such acts are a reproach to the community where
they occur, and so far as they can be made the subject of Federal jurisdiction the strongest repressive legislation is demanded. A public sentiment that will sustain the officers of the law in resisting mobs and in
protecting accused persons in their custody should be promoted by every
possible means. The officer who gives his life in the brave discharge of
this duty is worthy of special honor. No lesson needs to be so urgently
impressed upon our people as this, that no worthy end or cause can be
promoted by lawlessness.

This exhibit of the work of the Executive Departments is submitted
to Congress and to the public in the hope that there will be found in it a
due sense of responsibility and an earnest purpose to maintain the national
honor and to promote the happiness and prosperity of all our people,
and this brief exhibit of the growth and prosperity of the country will
give us a level from which to note the increase or decadence that new
legislative policies may bring to us. There is no reason why the national
influence, power, and prosperity should not observe the same rates of increase that have characterized the past thirty years. We carry the great
impulse and increase of these years into the future. There is no reason
why in many lines of production we should not surpass all other nations,
as we have already done in some. There are no near frontiers to our
possible development. Retrogression would be a crime.

Grover Cleveland

March 4, 1893 to March 4, 1897

FIRST ANNUAL MESSAGE.

EXECUTIVE MANSION,
Washington, December 4, 1893.

To the Congress of the United States:

The constitutional duty which requires the President from time to time to give to the Congress information of the state of the Union and recommend to their consideration such measures as he shall judge necessary and expedient is fittingly entered upon by commending to the Congress a careful examination of the detailed statements and well-supported recommendations contained in the reports of the heads of Departments, who are chiefly charged with the executive work of the Government. In an effort to abridge this communication as much as is consistent with its purpose I shall supplement a brief reference to the contents of these departmental reports by the mention of such executive business and incidents as are not embraced therein and by such recommendations as appear to be at this particular time appropriate.

While our foreign relations have not at all times during the past year been entirely free from perplexity, no embarrassing situation remains that will not yield to the spirit of fairness and love of justice which, joined with consistent firmness, characterize a truly American foreign policy.

My predecessor having accepted the office of arbitrator of the long-standing Missions boundary dispute, tendered to the President by the Argentine Republic and Brazil, it has been my agreeable duty to receive the special envoys commissioned by those States to lay before me evidence and arguments in behalf of their respective Governments.

The outbreak of domestic hostilities in the Republic of Brazil found the United States alert to watch the interests of our citizens in that country, with which we carry on important commerce. Several vessels of our new Navy are now and for some time have been stationed at Rio de Janeiro. The struggle being between the established Government, which controls the machinery of administration, and with which we maintain friendly relations, and certain officers of the navy employing the vessels of their command in an attack upon the national capital and chief seaport, and lacking as it does the elements of divided administration, I have failed to see that the insurgents can reasonably claim recognition as belligerents.

Thus far the position of our Government has been that of an attentive but impartial observer of the unfortunate conflict. Emphasizing our fixed policy of impartial neutrality in such a condition of affairs as now exists, I deemed it necessary to disavow in a manner not to be misunderstood the unauthorized action of our late naval commander in those waters in saluting the revolted Brazilian admiral, being indisposed to countenance an act calculated to give gratuitous sanction to the local insurrection.

The convention between our Government and Chile having for its object the settlement and adjustment of the demand of the two countries against each other has been made effective by he organization of the claims commission provided for. The two Governments failing to agree upon the third member of the commission, the good offices of the President of the Swiss Republic were invoked, as provided in the treaty, and the selection of the Swiss representative in this country to complete the organization was gratifying alike to the United States and Chile.

The vexatious question of so-called legation asylum for offenders against the state and its laws was presented anew in Chile by the unauthorized action of the late United States minister in receiving into his official residence two persons who had just failed in an attempt at revolution and against whom criminal charges were pending growing out of a former abortive disturbance. The doctrine of asylum as applied to this case is not sanctioned by the best precedents, and when allowed tends to encourage sedition and strife. Under no circumstances can the representatives of this Government be permitted, under the ill-defined fiction of extraterritoriality, to interrupt the administration of criminal justice in the countries to which they are accredited. A temperate demand having been made by the Chilean Government for the correction of this conduct in the instance mentioned, the minister was instructed no longer to harbor the offenders.

The legislation of last year known as the Geary law, requiring the registration of all Chinese laborers entitled to residence in the United States and the deportation of all not complying with the provisions of the act within the time prescribed, met with much opposition from Chinamen in this country. Acting upon the advice of eminent counsel that the law was unconstitutional, the great mass of Chinese laborers, pending judicial inquiry as to its validity, in good faith declined to apply for the certificates required by its provisions. A test case upon proceeding by *habeas corpus* was brought before the Supreme Court, and on May 15, 1893, a decision was made by that tribunal sustaining the law.

It is believed that under the recent amendment of the act extending the time for registration the Chinese laborers thereto entitled who desire to reside in this country will now avail themselves of the renewed privilege thus afforded of establishing by lawful procedure their right to remain, and that thereby the necessity of enforced deportation may to a great degree be avoided.

It has devolved upon the United States minister at Peking, as dean of the diplomatic body, and in the absence of a representative of Sweden and Norway, to press upon the Chinese Government reparation for the recent murder of Swedish missionaries at Sung-pu. This question is of vital interest to all countries whose citizens engage in missionary work in the interior.

By Article XII of the general act of Brussels, signed July 2, 1890, for the suppression of the slave trade and the restriction of certain injurious commerce in the Independent State of the Kongo and in the adjacent zone of central Africa, the United States and the other signatory powers agreed to adopt appropriate means for the punishment of persons selling arms and ammunition to the natives and for the confiscation of the inhibited articles. It being the plain duty of this Government to aid in sup· pressing the nefarious traffic, impairing as it does the praiseworthy and civilizing efforts now in progress in that region, I recommend that an act be passed prohibiting the sale of arms and intoxicants to natives in the regulated zone by our citizens.

Costa Rica has lately testified its friendliness by surrendering to the United States, in the absence of a convention of extradition, but upon duly submitted evidence of criminality, a noted fugitive from justice. It is trusted that the negotiation of a treaty with that country to meet recurring cases of this kind will soon be accomplished. In my opinion treaties for reciprocal extradition should be concluded with all those countries with which the United States has not already conventional arrangements of that character.

I have deemed it fitting to express to the Governments of Costa Rica and Colombia the kindly desire of the United States to see their pending boundary dispute finally closed by arbitration in conformity with the spirit of the treaty concluded between them some years ago.

Our relations with the French Republic continue to be intimate and cordial. I sincerely hope that the extradition treaty with that country, as amended by the Senate, will soon be operative.

While occasional questions affecting our naturalized citizens returning to the land of their birth have arisen in our intercourse with Germany, our relations with that country continue satisfactory.

The questions affecting our relations with Great Britain have been treated in a spirit of friendliness.

Negotiations are in progress between the two Governments with a view to such concurrent action as will make the award and regulations agreed upon by the Bering Sea Tribunal of Arbitration practically effective, and it is not doubted that Great Britain will cooperate freely with this country for the accomplishment of that purpose.

The dispute growing out of the discriminating tolls imposed in the Welland Canal upon cargoes of cereals bound to and from the lake ports of the United States was adjusted by the substitution of a more equitable schedule of charges, and my predecessor thereupon suspended his proclamation imposing discriminating tolls upon British transit through our canals.

A request for additions to the list of extraditable offenses covered by the existing treaty between the two countries is under consideration.

During the past year an American citizen employed in a subordinate commercial position in Hayti, after suffering a protracted imprisonment on an unfounded charge of smuggling, was finally liberated on judicial examination. Upon urgent representation to the Haytian Government a suitable indemnity was paid to the sufferer.

By a law of Hayti a sailing vessel, having discharged her cargo, is refused clearance until the duties on such cargo have been paid. The hardship of this measure upon American shipowners, who conduct the bulk of the carrying trade of that country, has been insisted on with a view of securing the removal of this cause of complaint.

Upon receiving authentic information of the firing upon an American mail steamer touching at the port of Amapala because her captain refused to deliver up a passenger in transit from Nicaragua to Guatemala upon demand of the military authorities of Honduras, our minister to that country, under instructions, protested against the wanton act and demanded satisfaction. The Government of Honduras, actuated by a sense of justice and in a spirit of the utmost friendship, promptly disavowed the illegal conduct of its officers and expressed sincere regret for the occurrence.

It is confidently anticipated that a satisfactory adjustment will soon be reached of the questions arising out of the seizure and use of American vessels by insurgents in Honduras and the subsequent denial by the successful Government of commercial privileges to those vessels on that account.

A notable part of the southeasterly coast of Liberia between the Cavally and San Pedro rivers, which for nearly half a century has been generally recognized as belonging to that Republic by cession and purchase, has been claimed to be under the protectorate of France in virtue of agreements entered into by the native tribes, over whom Liberia's control has not been well maintained.

More recently negotiations between the Liberian representative and the French Government resulted in the signature at Paris of a treaty whereby as an adjustment certain Liberian territory is ceded to France. This convention at last advices had not been ratified by the Liberian Legislature and Executive.

Feeling a sympathetic interest in the fortunes of the little Commonwealth, the establishment and development of which were largely aided by the benevolence of our countrymen, and which constitutes the only independently sovereign state on the west coast of Africa, this Government has suggested to the French Government its earnest concern lest territorial impairment in Liberia should take place without her unconstrained consent.

Our relations with Mexico continue to be of that close and friendly nature which should always characterize the intercourse of two neighboring republics.

The work of relocating the monuments marking the boundary between the two countries from Paso del Norte to the Pacific is now nearly completed.

The commission recently organized under the conventions of 1884 and 1889 it is expected will speedily settle disputes growing out of the shifting currents of the Rio Grande River east of El Paso.

Nicaragua has recently passed through two revolutions, the party at first successful having in turn been displaced by another. Our newly appointed minister by his timely good offices aided in a peaceful adjustment of the controversy involved in the first conflict. The large American interests established in that country in connection with the Nicaragua Canal were not molested.

The canal company has unfortunately become financially seriously embarrassed, but a generous treatment had been extended to it by the Government of Nicaragua. The United States are especially interested in the successful achievement of the vast undertaking this company has in charge. That it should be accomplished under distinctively American auspices, and its enjoyment assured not only to the vessels of this country as a channel of communication between our Atlantic and Pacific seaboards, but to the ships of the world in the interests of civilization, is a proposition which, in my judgment, does not admit of question.

Guatemala has also been visited by the political vicissitudes which have afflicted her Central American neighbors, but the dissolution of its Legislature and the proclamation of a dictatorship have been unattended with civil war.

An extradition treaty with Norway has recently been exchanged and proclaimed.

The extradition treaty with Russia signed in March, 1887, and amended and confirmed by the Senate in February last, was duly proclaimed last June.

Led by a desire to compose differences and contribute to the restoration of order in Samoa, which for some years previous had been the scene of conflicting foreign pretensions and native strife, the United States, departing from its policy consecrated by a century of observance, entered four years ago into the treaty of Berlin, thereby becoming jointly bound with England and Germany to establish and maintain Malietoa Laupepa as King of Samoa. The treaty provided for a foreign court of justice; a municipal council for the district of Apia, with a foreign president thereof, authorized to advise the King; a tribunal for the settlement of native and foreign land titles, and a revenue system for the Kingdom. It entailed upon the three powers that part of the cost of the new Government not met by the revenue of the islands.

Early in the life of this triple protectorate the native dissensions it was designed to quell revived. Rivals defied the authority of the new King, refusing to pay taxes and demanding the election of a ruler by native suffrage. Mataafa, an aspirant to the throne, and a large number of his native adherents were in open rebellion on one of the islands. Quite lately, at the request of the other powers and in fulfillment of its treaty obligation, this Government agreed to unite in a joint military movement of such dimensions as would probably secure the surrender of the insurgents without bloodshed.

The war ship *Philadelphia* was accordingly put under orders for Samoa, but before she arrived the threatened conflict was precipitated by King Malietoa's attack upon the insurgent camp. Mataafa was defeated and a number of his men killed. The British and German naval vessels present subsequently secured the surrender of Mataafa and his adherents. The defeated chief and ten of his principal supporters were deported to a German island of the Marshall group, where they are held as prisoners under the joint responsibility and cost of the three powers.

This incident and the events leading up to it signally illustrate the impolicy of entangling alliances with foreign powers.

More than fifteen years ago this Government preferred a claim against Spain in behalf of one of our citizens for property seized and confiscated in Cuba. In 1886 the claim was adjusted, Spain agreeing to pay unconditionally, as a fair indemnity, $1,500,000. A respectful but earnest note was recently addressed to the Spanish Government insisting upon prompt fulfillment of its long-neglected obligation.

Other claims preferred by the United States against Spain in behalf of American citizens for property confiscated in Cuba have been pending for many years.

At the time Spain's title to the Caroline Islands was confirmed by arbitration that Government agreed that the rights which had been acquired there by American missionaries should be recognized and respected. It is sincerely hoped that this pledge will be observed by allowing our missionaries, who were removed from Ponape to a place of safety by a United States war ship during the late troubles between the Spanish garrison and the natives, to return to their field of usefulness.

The reproduced caravel *Santa Maria*, built by Spain and sent to the Columbian Exposition, has been presented to the United States in token of amity and in commemoration of the event it was designed to celebrate. I recommend that in accepting this gift Congress make grateful recognition of the sincere friendship which prompted it.

Important matters have demanded attention in our relations with the Ottoman Porte.

The firing and partial destruction by an unrestrained mob of one of the school buildings of Anatolia College, established by citizens of the United States at Marsovan, and the apparent indifference of the Turkish Government to the outrage, notwithstanding the complicity of some of its officials, called for earnest remonstrance, which was followed by promise of reparation and punishment of the offenders.

Indemnity for the injury to the buildings has already been paid, permission to rebuild given, registration of the school property in the name of the American owners secured, and efficient protection guaranteed.

Information received of maltreatment suffered by an inoffensive American woman engaged in missionary work in Turkish Koordistan was followed by such representations to the Porte as resulted in the issuance of orders for the punishment of her assailants, the removal of a delinquent official, and the adoption of measures for the protection of our citizens engaged in mission and other lawful work in that quarter.

Turkey complains that her Armenian subjects obtain citizenship in this country not to identify themselves in good faith with our people, but with the intention of returning to the land of their birth and there engaging in sedition. This complaint is not wholly without foundation. A journal published in this country in the Armenian language openly counsels its readers to arm, organize, and participate in movements for the subversion of Turkish authority in the Asiatic provinces. The Ottoman Government has announced its intention ·to expel from its dominions Armenians who have obtained naturalization in the United States since 1868.

The right to exclude any or all classes of aliens is an attribute of sovereignty. It is a right asserted and, to a limited extent, enforced by the United States, with the sanction of our highest court. There being no naturalization treaty between the United States and Turkey, our minister at Constantinople has been instructed that, while recognizing the right of that Government to enforce its declared policy against naturalized Armenians, he is expected to protect them from unnecessary harshness of treatment.

In view of the impaired financial resources of Venezuela consequent upon the recent revolution there, a modified arrangement for the satisfaction of the awards of the late revisory claims commission, in progressive installments, has been assented to, and payments are being regularly made thereunder.

The boundary dispute between Venezuela and British Guiana is yet unadjusted. A restoration of diplomatic intercourse between that Republic and Great Britain and reference of the question to impartial arbitration would be a most gratifying consummation.

The ratification by Venezuela of the convention for the arbitration of the long-deferred claim of the Venezuelan Transportation Company is awaited.

It is hardly necessary for me to state that the questions arising from our relations with Hawaii have caused serious embarrassment. Just prior to the installation of the present Administration the existing Government of Hawaii had been suddenly overthrown and a treaty of annexation had been negotiated between the Provisional Government of the islands and the United States and submitted to the Senate for ratification. This treaty I withdrew for examination and dispatched Hon. James H. Blount, of Georgia, to Honolulu as a special commissioner to make an impartial investigation of the circumstances attending the change of government and of all the conditions bearing upon the subject of the treaty. After a thorough and exhaustive examination Mr. Blount submitted to me his report, showing beyond all question that the constitutional Government of Hawaii had been subverted with the active aid of our representative to that Government and through the intimidation caused by the presence of an armed naval force of the United States, which was landed for that purpose at the instance of our minister. Upon the facts developed it seemed to me the only honorable course for our Government to pursue was to undo the wrong that had been done by those representing us and to restore as far as practicable the status existing at the time of our forcible intervention. With a view of accomplishing this result within the constitutional limits of executive power, and recognizing all our obligations and responsibilities growing out of any changed conditions brought about by our unjustifiable interference, our present minister at Honolulu has received appropriate instructions to that end. Thus far no information of the accomplishment of any definite results has been received from him.

Additional advices are soon expected. When received they will be promptly sent to the Congress, together with all other information at hand, accompanied by a special Executive message fully detailing all the facts necessary to a complete understanding of the case and presenting a history of all the material events leading up to the present situation.

By a concurrent resolution passed by the Senate February 14, 1890, and by the House of Representatives on the 3d of April following the President was requested to "invite from time to time, as fit occasions may arise, negotiations with any government with which the United States has or may have diplomatic relations, to the end that any differences or disputes arising between the two governments which can not be adjusted by diplomatic agency may be referred to arbitration and be peaceably adjusted by such means." April 18, 1890, the International American Conference of Washington by resolution expressed the wish that all controversies between the republics of America and the nations of Europe might be settled by arbitration, and recommended that the government of each nation represented in that conference should communicate this wish to all friendly powers. A favorable response has been received from Great Britain in the shape of a resolution adopted by Parliament July 16 last, cordially sympathizing with the purpose in view and expressing the hope that Her Majesty's Government will lend ready cooperation to the Government of the United States upon the basis of the concurrent resolution above quoted.

It affords me signal pleasure to lay this parliamentary resolution before the Congress and to express my sincere gratification that the sentiment of two great and kindred nations is thus authoritatively manifested in favor of the rational and peaceable settlement of international quarrels by honorable resort to arbitration.

Since the passage of the act of March 3, 1893, authorizing the President to raise the grade of our envoys to correspond with the rank in which foreign countries accredit their agents here, Great Britain, France, Italy, and Germany have conferred upon their representatives at this capital the title of ambassador, and I have responded by accrediting the agents of the United States in those countries with the same title. A like elevation of mission is announced by Russia, and when made will be similarly met. This step fittingly comports with the position the United States hold in the family of nations.

During my former Administration I took occasion to recommend a recast of the laws relating to the consular service, in order that it might become a more efficient agency in the promotion of the interests it was intended to subserve. The duties and powers of consuls have been expanded with the growing requirements of our foreign trade. Discharging important duties affecting our commerce and American citizens abroad, and in certain countries exercising judicial functions, these officers should be men of character, intelligence, and ability.

Upon proof that the legislation of Denmark secures copyright to American citizens on equal footing with its own, the privileges of our copyright laws have been extended by proclamation to subjects of that country.

The Secretary of the Treasury reports that the receipts of the Government from all sources during the fiscal year ended June 30, 1893, amounted to $461,716,561.94 and its expenditures to $459,374,674.29. There was collected from customs $205,355,016.73 and from internal revenue $161,027,623.93. Our dutiable imports amounted to $421,856,711, an increase of $52,453,907 over the preceding year, and importations free of duty amounted to $444,544,211, a decrease from the preceding year of $13,455,447. Internal-revenue receipts exceeded those of the preceding year by $7,147,445.32. The total tax collected on distilled spirits was $94,720,260.55, on manufactured tobacco $31,889,711.74, and on fermented liquors $32,548,983.07. We exported merchandise during the year amounting to $847,665,194, a decrease of $182,612,954 from the preceding year. The amount of gold exported was larger than any previous year in the history of the Government, amounting to $108,680,844, and exceeding the amount exported during the preceding year by $58,485,517.

The sum paid from the Treasury for sugar bounty was $9,375,130.88, an increase over the preceding year of $2,033,053.09.

It is estimated upon the basis of present revenue laws that the receipts of the Government for the year ending June 30, 1894, will be $430,121,365.38 and its expenditures $458,121,365.28, resulting in a deficiency of $28,000,000.

On the 1st day of November, 1893, the amount of money of all kinds in circulation, or not included in Treasury holdings, was $1,718,544,682.

an increase for the year of $112,404,947. Estimating our population at 67,426,000 at the time mentioned, the per capita circulation was $25.49. On the same date there was in the Treasury gold bullion amounting to $96,657,273 and silver bullion which was purchased at a cost of $126,261,553.

The purchases of silver under the law of July 14, 1890, during the last fiscal year aggregated 54,008,162.59 fine ounces, which cost $45,531,-374.53. The total amount of silver purchased from the time that law became operative until the repeal of its purchasing clause, on the 1st day of November, 1893, was 168,674,590.46 fine ounces, which cost $155,-930,940.84. Between the 1st day of March, 1873, and the 1st day of November, 1893, the Government purchased under all laws 503,003,717 fine ounces of silver, at a cost of $516,622,948. The silver dollars that have been coined under the act of July 14, 1890, number 36,087,285. The seigniorage arising from such coinage was $6,977,098.39, leaving on hand in the mints 140,699,760 fine ounces of silver, which cost $126,-758,218.

Our total coinage of all metals during the last fiscal year consisted of 97,280,875 pieces, valued at $43,685,178.80, of which there was $30,-038,140 in gold coin, $5,343,715 in silver dollars, $7,217,220.90 in subsidiary silver coin, and $1,086,102.90 in minor coins.

During the calendar year 1892 the production of precious metals in the United States was estimated to be 1,596,375 fine ounces of gold of the commercial and coinage value of $33,000,000 and 58,000,000 fine ounces of silver of the bullion or market value of $50,750,000 and of the coinage value of $74,989,900.

It is estimated that on the 1st day of July, 1893, the metallic stock of money in the United States, consisting of coin and bullion, amounted to $1,213,559,169, of which $597,697,685 was gold and $615,861,484 was silver.

One hundred and nineteen national banks were organized during the year ending October 31, 1893, with a capital of $11,230,000. Forty-six went into voluntary liquidation and 158 suspended. Sixty-five of the suspended banks were insolvent, 86 resumed business, and 7 remain in the hands of the bank examiners, with prospects of speedy resumption. Of the new banks organized, 44 were located in the Eastern States, 41 west of the Mississippi River, and 34 in the Central and Southern States. The total number of national banks in existence on October 31, 1893, was 3,796, having an aggregate capital of $695,558,120. The net increase in the circulation of these banks during the year was $36,886,972.

The recent repeal of the provision of law requiring the purchase of silver bullion by the Government as a feature of our monetary scheme has made an entire change in the complexion of our currency affairs. I do not doubt that the ultimate result of this action will be most salutary and far-reaching. In the nature of things, however, it is impossible to know at this time precisely what conditions will be brought about by the change, or what, if any, supplementary legislation may in the light of such conditions appear to be essential or expedient. Of course, after the recent financial perturbation, time is necessary for the reestablishment of business confidence. When, however, through this restored confidence, the money which has been frightened into hoarding places is returned to trade and enterprise, a survey of the situation will probably disclose a safe path leading to a permanently sound currency, abundantly sufficient to meet every requirement of our increasing population and business.

In the pursuit of this object we should resolutely turn away from alluring and temporary expedients, determined to be content with nothing less than a lasting and comprehensive financial plan. In these circumstances I am convinced that a reasonable delay in dealing with this subject, instead of being injurious, will increase the probability of wise action.

The monetary conference which assembled at Brussels upon our invitation was adjourned to the 30th day of November of the present year. The considerations just stated and the fact that a definite proposition from us seemed to be expected upon the reassembling of the conference led me to express a willingness to have the meeting still further postponed.

It seems to me that it would be wise to give general authority to the President to invite other nations to such a conference at any time when there should be a fair prospect of accomplishing an international agreement on the subject of coinage.

I desire also to earnestly suggest the wisdom of amending the existing statutes in regard to the issuance of Government bonds. The authority now vested in the Secretary of the Treasury to issue bonds is not as clear as it should be, and the bonds authorized are disadvantageous to the Government both as to the time of their maturity and rate of interest.

The Superintendent of Immigration, through the Secretary of the Treasury, reports that during the last fiscal year there arrived at our ports 440,793 immigrants. Of these, 1,063 were not permitted to land under the limitations of the law and 577 were returned to the countries from whence they came by reason of their having become public charges. The total arrivals were 141,034 less than for the previous year.

The Secretary in his report gives an account of the operation of the Marine-Hospital Service and of the good work done under its supervision in preventing the entrance and spread of contagious diseases.

The admonitions of the last two years touching our public health and the demonstrated danger of the introduction of contagious diseases from foreign ports have invested the subject of national quarantine with increased interest. A more general and harmonious system than now exists, acting promptly and directly everywhere and constantly operating by preventive means to shield our country from the invasion of disease, and at the same time having due regard to the rights and duties of local agencies, would, I believe, add greatly to the safety of our people.

The Secretary of War reports that the strength of the Army on the 30th day of September last was 25,778 enlisted men and 2,144 officers.

The total expenditures of the Department for the year ending June 30, 1893, amounted to $51,966,074.89. Of this sum $1,992,581.95 was for salaries and contingent expenses, $23,377,828.35 for the support of the military establishment, $6,077,033.18 for miscellaneous objects, and $20,-518,631.41 for public works. This latter sum includes $15,296,876.46 for river and harbor improvements and $3,266,141.20 for fortifications and other works of defense.

The total enrollment of the militia of the several States was on the 31st of October of the current year 112,597 officers and enlisted men. The officers of the Army detailed for the inspection and instruction of this reserve of our military force report that increased interest and marked progress are apparent in the discipline and efficiency of the organization.

Neither Indian outbreaks nor domestic violence have called the Army into service during the year, and the only active military duty required of it has been in the Department of Texas, where violations of the neutrality laws of the United States and Mexico were promptly and efficiently dealt with by the troops, eliciting the warm approval of the civil and military authorities of both countries.

The operation of wise laws and the influences of civilization constantly tending to relieve the country from the dangers of Indian hostilities, together with the increasing ability of the States, through the efficiency of the National Guard organizations, to protect their citizens from domestic violence, lead to the suggestion that the time is fast approaching when there should be a reorganization of our Army on the lines of the present necessities of the country. This change contemplates neither increase in number nor added expense, but a redistribution of the force and an encouragement of measures tending to greater efficiency among the men and improvement of the service.

The adoption of battalion formations for infantry regiments, the strengthening of the artillery force, the abandonment of smaller and unnecessary posts, and the massing of the troops at important and accessible stations all promise to promote the usefulness of the Army. In the judgment of army officers, with but few exceptions, the operation of the law forbidding the reenlistment of men after ten years' service has not proved its wisdom, and while the arguments that led to its adoption were not without merit the experience of the year constrains me to join in the recommendation for its repeal.

It is gratifying to note that we have begun to attain completed results in the comprehensive scheme of seacoast defense and fortification entered upon eight years ago. A large sum has been already expended, but the cost of maintenance will be inconsiderable as compared with the expense

of construction and ordnance.   At the end of the current calendar year
the War Department will have nine 12-inch guns, twenty 10-inch, and
thirty-four 8-inch guns ready to be mounted on gun lifts and carriages,
and seventy-five 12-inch mortars.   In addition to the product of the
Army Gun Factory, now completed at Watervliet, the Government has
contracted with private parties for the purchase of one hundred guns of
these calibers, the first of which should be delivered to the Department
for test before July 1, 1894.

The manufacture of heavy ordnance keeps pace with current needs,
but to render these guns available for the purposes they are designed to
meet emplacements must be prepared for them.   Progress has been made
in this direction, and it is desirable that Congress by adequate appropriations should provide for the uninterrupted prosecution of this necessary
work.

After much preliminary work and exhaustive examination in accordance with the requirements of the law, the board appointed to select a
magazine rifle of modern type with which to replace the obsolete Springfield rifle of the infantry service completed its labors during the last
year, and the work of manufacture is now in progress at the national
armory at Springfield.   It is confidently expected that by the end of the
current year our infantry will be supplied with a weapon equal to that
of the most progressive armies of the world.

The work on the projected Chickamauga and Chattanooga National
Military Park has been prosecuted with zeal and judgment, and its opening will be celebrated during the coming year.   Over 9 square miles of the
Chickamauga battlefield have been acquired, 25 miles of roadway have
been constructed, and permanent tablets have been placed at many historical points, while the invitation to the States to mark the positions of
their troops participating in the battle has been very generally accepted.

The work of locating and preserving the lines of battle at the Gettys-
burg battlefield is making satisfactory progress on the plans directed by
the last Congress.

The reports of the Military Academy at West Point and the several
schools for special instruction of officers show marked advance in the
education of the Army and a commendable ambition among its officers
to excel in the military profession and to fit themselves for the highest
service to the country.

Under the supervision of Adjutant-General Robert Williams, lately
retired, the Bureau of Military Information has become well established
and is performing a service that will put in possession of the Government
in time of war most valuable information, and at all times serve a purpose of great utility in keeping the Army advised of the world's progress in all matters pertaining to the art of war.

The report of the Attorney-General contains the usual summary of the
affairs and proceedings of the Department of Justice for the past year,

together with certain recommendations as to needed legislation on various subjects. I can not too heartily indorse the proposition that the fee system as applicable to the compensation of United States attorneys, marshals, clerks of Federal courts, and United States commissioners should be abolished with as little delay as possible. It is clearly in the interest of the community that the business of the courts, both civil and criminal, shall be as small and as inexpensively transacted as the ends of justice will allow.

The system is therefore thoroughly vicious which makes the compensation of court officials depend upon the volume of such business, and thus creates a conflict between a proper execution of the law and private gain, which can not fail to be dangerous to the rights and freedom of the citizen and an irresistible temptation to the unjustifiable expenditure of public funds. If in addition to this reform another was inaugurated which would give to United States commissioners the final disposition of petty offenses within the grade of misdemeanors, especially those coming under the internal-revenue laws, a great advance would be made toward a more decent administration of the criminal law.

In my first message to Congress, dated December 8, 1885, I strongly recommended these changes and referred somewhat at length to the evils of the present system. Since that time the criminal business of the Federal courts and the expense attending it have enormously increased. The number of criminal prosecutions pending in the circuit and district courts of the United States on the 1st day of July, 1885, was 3,808, of which 1,884 were for violations of the internal-revenue laws, while the number of such prosecutions pending on the 1st day of July, 1893, was 9,500, of which 4,200 were for violations of the internal-revenue laws. The expense of the United States courts, exclusive of judges' salaries, for the year ending July 1, 1885, was $2,874,733.11 and for the year ending July 1, 1893, $4,528,676.87.

It is therefore apparent that the reasons given in 1885 for a change in the manner of enforcing the Federal criminal law have gained cogency and strength by lapse of time.

I also heartily join the Attorney-General in recommending legislation fixing degrees of the crime of murder within Federal jurisdiction, as has been done in many of the States; authorizing writs of error on behalf of the Government in cases where final judgment is rendered against the sufficiency of an indictment or against the Government upon any other question arising before actual trial; limiting the right of review in cases of felony punishable only by fine and imprisonment to the circuit court of appeals, and making speedy provision for the construction of such prisons and reformatories as may be necessary for the confinement of United States convicts.

The report of the Postmaster-General contains a detailed statement of the operations of the Post-Office Department during the last fiscal year and much interesting information touching this important branch of the public service.

The business of the mails indicates with absolute certainty the condition of the business of the country, and depression in financial affairs inevitably and quickly reduces the postal revenues. Therefore a larger discrepancy than usual between the post-office receipts and expenditures is the expected and unavoidable result of the distressing stringency which has prevailed throughout the country during much of the time covered by the Postmaster-General's report. At a date when better times were anticipated it was estimated by his predecessor that the deficiency on the 30th day of June, 1893, would be but a little over a million and a half dollars. It amounted, however, to more than five millions. At the same time and under the influence of like anticipations estimates were made for the current fiscal year, ending June 30, 1894, which exhibited a surplus of revenue over expenditures of $872,245.71; but now, in view of the actual receipts and expenditures during that part of the current fiscal year already expired, the present Postmaster-General estimates that at its close instead of a surplus there will be a deficiency of nearly $8,000,000.

The post-office receipts for the last fiscal year amounted to $75,896,-933.16 and its expenditures to $81,074,104.90. This post-office deficiency would disappear or be immensely decreased if less matter were carried free through the mails, an item of which is upward of 300 tons of seeds and grain from the Agricultural Department.

The total number of post-offices in the United States on the 30th day of June, 1893, was 68,403, an increase of 1,284 over the preceding year. Of these, 3,360 were Presidential, an increase in that class of 204 over the preceding year.

Forty-two free-delivery offices were added during the year to those already existing, making a total of 610 cities and towns provided with free delivery on June 30, 1893. Ninety-three other cities and towns are now entitled to this service under the law, but it has not been accorded them on account of insufficient funds to meet the expenses of its establishment.

I am decidedly of the opinion that the provisions of the present law permit as general an introduction of this feature of mail service as is necessary or justifiable, and that it ought not to be extended to smaller communities than are now designated.

The expenses of free delivery for the fiscal year ending June 30, 1894, will be more than $11,000,000, and under legislation now existing there must be a constant increase in this item of expenditure.

There were 6,401 additions to the domestic money-order offices during the last fiscal year, being the largest increase in any year since the inauguration of the system. The total number of these offices at the close of the year was 18,434. There were 13,309,735 money orders issued from these offices, being an increase over the preceding year of 1,240,293, and the value of these orders amounted to $127,576,433.65, an increase of $7,509,632.58. There were also issued during the year postal notes amounting to $12,903,076.73.

During the year 195 international money-order offices were added to those already provided, making a total of 2,407 in operation on June 30, 1893. The number of international money orders issued during the year was 1,055,999, an increase over the preceding year of 72,525, and their value was $16,341,837.86, an increase of $1,221,506.31. The number of orders paid was 300,917, an increase over the preceding year of 13,503, and their value was $5,283,375.70, an increase of $94,094.83.

From the foregoing statements it appears that the total issue of money orders and postal notes for the year amounted to $156,821,348.24.

The number of letters and packages mailed during the year for special delivery was 3,375,693, an increase over the preceding year of nearly 22 per cent. The special-delivery stamps used upon these letters and packages amounted to $337,569.30, and the messengers' fees paid for their delivery amounted to $256,592.71, leaving a profit to the Government of $80,976.59.

The Railway Mail Service not only adds to the promptness of mail delivery at all offices, but it is the especial instrumentality which puts the smaller and way places in the service on an equality in that regard with the larger and terminal offices. This branch of the postal service has therefore received much attention from the Postmaster-General, and though it is gratifying to know that it is in a condition of high efficiency and great usefulness, I am led to agree with the Postmaster-General that there is room for its further improvement.

There are now connected to the Post-Office establishment 28,324 employees who are in the classified service. The head of this great Department gives conclusive evidence of the value of civil-service reform when, after an experience that renders his judgment on the subject absolutely reliable, he expresses the opinion that without the benefit of this system it would be impossible to conduct the vast business intrusted to him.

I desire to commend as especially worthy of prompt attention the suggestions of the Postmaster-General relating to a more sensible and businesslike organization and a better distribution of responsibility in his Department.

The report of the Secretary of the Navy contains a history of the operations of his Department during the past year and exhibits a most gratifying condition of the personnel of our Navy. He presents a satisfactory account of the progress which has been made in the construction of vessels and makes a number of recommendations to which attention is especially invited.

During the past six months the demands for cruising vessels have been many and urgent. There have been revolutions calling for vessels to protect American interests in Nicaragua, Guatemala, Costa Rica, Honduras, Argentina, and Brazil, while the condition of affairs in Honolulu has required the constant presence of one or more ships. With all these calls upon our Navy it became necessary, in order to make up a sufficient fleet to patrol the Bering Sea under the *modus vivendi* agreed upon with Great Britain, to detail to that service one vessel from the Fish Commission and three from the Revenue Marine.

Progress in the construction of new vessels has not been as rapid as was anticipated. There have been delays in the completion of unarmored vessels, but for the most part they have been such as are constantly occurring even in countries having the largest experience in naval shipbuilding. The most serious delays, however, have been in the work upon armored ships. The trouble has been the failure of contractors to deliver armor as agreed. The difficulties seem now, however, to have been all overcome, and armor is being delivered with satisfactory promptness. As a result of the experience acquired by shipbuilders and designers and material men, it is believed that the dates when vessels will be completed can now be estimated with reasonable accuracy. Great guns, rapid-fire guns, torpedoes, and powder are being promptly supplied.

The following vessels of the new Navy have been completed and are now ready for service: The double-turreted coast-defense monitor *Miantonomoh*, the double-turreted coast-defense monitor *Monterey*, the armored cruiser *New York*, the protected cruisers *Baltimore, Chicago, Philadelphia, Newark, San Francisco, Charleston, Atlanta*, and *Boston*, the cruiser *Detroit*, the gunboats *Yorktown, Concord, Bennington, Machias, Castine*, and *Petrel*, the dispatch vessel *Dolphin*, the practice vessel *Bancroft*, and the dynamite gunboat *Vesuvius*. Of these the *Bancroft, Machias, Detroit*, and *Castine* have been placed in commission during the current calendar year.

The following vessels are in process of construction: The second-class battle ships *Maine* and *Texas*, the cruisers *Montgomery* and *Marblehead*, and the coast-defense monitors *Terror, Puritan, Amphitrite*, and *Monadnock*, all of which will be completed within one year; the harbor-defense ram *Katahdin* and the protected cruisers *Columbia, Minneapolis, Olympia, Cincinnati*, and *Raleigh*, all of which will be completed prior to July 1, 1895; the first-class battle ships *Iowa, Indiana, Massachusetts*, and *Oregon*, which will be completed February 1, 1896, and the armored cruiser *Brooklyn*, which will be completed by August 1 of that year. It is also expected that the three gunboats authorized by the last Congress will be completed in less than two years.

Since 1886 Congress has at each session authorized the building of one or more vessels, and the Secretary of the Navy presents an earnest plea for the continuance of this plan. He recommends the authorization of at least one battle ship and six torpedo boats.

While I am distinctly in favor of consistently pursuing the policy we have inaugurated of building up a thorough and efficient Navy, I can not refrain from the suggestion that the Congress should carefully take into account the number of unfinished vessels on our hands and the depleted condition of our Treasury in considering the propriety of an appropriation at this time to begin new work.

The method of employing mechanical labor at navy-yards through boards of labor and making efficiency the sole test by which laborers are employed and continued is producing the best results, and the Secretary is earnestly devoting himself to its development. Attention is invited to the statements of his report in regard to the workings of the system.

The Secretary of the Interior has the supervision of so many important subjects that his report is of especial value and interest.

On the 30th day of June, 1893, there were on the pension rolls 966,012 names, an increase of 89,944 over the number on the rolls June 30, 1892. Of these there were 17 widows and daughters of Revolutionary soldiers, 86 survivors of the War of 1812, 5,425 widows of soldiers of that war, 21,518 survivors and widows of the Mexican War, 3,882 survivors and widows of Indian wars, 284 army nurses, and 475,645 survivors and widows and children of deceased soldiers and sailors of the War of the Rebellion. The latter number represents those pensioned on account of disabilities or death resulting from army and navy service. The number of persons remaining on the rolls June 30, 1893, who were pensioned under the act of June 27, 1890, which allows pensions on account of death and disability not chargeable to army service, was 459,155.

The number added to the rolls during the year was 123,634 and the number dropped was 33,690. The first payments on pensions allowed during the year amounted to $33,756,549.98. This includes arrears, or the accumulation between the time from which the allowance of pension dates and the time of actually granting the certificate.

Although the law of 1890 permits pensions for disabilities not related to military service, yet as a requisite to its benefits a disability must exist incapacitating applicants "from the performance of manual labor to such a degree as to render them unable to earn a support." The execution of this law in its early stages does not seem to have been in accord with its true intention, but toward the close of the last Administration an authoritative construction was given to the statute, and since that time this construction has been followed. This has had the effect of limiting the operation of the law to its intended purpose. The discovery having been made that many names had been put upon the pension roll by means of wholesale and gigantic frauds, the Commissioner suspended payments upon a number of pensions which seemed to be fraudulent or unauthorized pending a complete examination, giving notice to the pensioners, in order that they might have an opportunity to establish, if possible, the justice of their claims notwithstanding apparent invalidity.

This, I understand, is the practice which has for a long time prevailed in the Pension Bureau; but after entering upon these recent investigations the Commissioner modified this rule so as not to allow until after a complete examination interference with the payment of a pension apparently not altogether void, but which merely had been fixed at a rate higher than that authorized by law.

I am unable to understand why frauds in the pension rolls should not be exposed and corrected with thoroughness and vigor. Every name fraudulently put upon these rolls is a wicked imposition upon the kindly sentiment in which pensions have their origin; every fraudulent pensioner has become a bad citizen; every false oath in support of a pension has made perjury more common, and false and undeserving pensioners rob the people not only of their money, but of the patriotic sentiment which the survivors of a war fought for the preservation of the Union ought to inspire. Thousands of neighborhoods have their well-known fraudulent pensioners, and recent developments by the Bureau establish appalling conspiracies to accomplish pension frauds. By no means the least wrong done is to brave and deserving pensioners, who certainly ought not to be condemned to such association.

Those who attempt in the line of duty to rectify these wrongs should not be accused of enmity or indifference to the claims of honest veterans.

The sum expended on account of pensions for the year ending June 30, 1893, was $156,740,467.14.

The Commissioner estimates that $165,000,000 will be required to pay pensions during the year ending June 30, 1894.

The condition of the Indians and their ultimate fate are subjects which are related to a sacred duty of the Government and which strongly appeal to the sense of justice and the sympathy of our people.

Our Indians number about 248,000. Most of them are located on 161 reservations, containing 86,116,531 acres of land. About 110,000 of these Indians have to a large degree adopted civilized customs. Lands in severalty have been allotted to many of them. Such allotments have been made to 10,000 individuals during the last fiscal year, embracing about 1,000,000 acres. The number of Indian Government schools opened during the year was 195, an increase of 12 over the preceding year. Of this total 170 were on reservations, of which 73 were boarding schools and 97 were day schools. Twenty boarding schools and 5 day schools supported by the Government were not located on reservations. The total number of Indian children enrolled during the year as attendants of all schools was 21,138, an increase of 1,231 over the enrollment for the previous year.

I am sure that secular education and moral and religious teaching must be important factors in any effort to save the Indian and lead him to civilization. I believe, too, that the relinquishment of tribal relations and the holding of land in severalty may in favorable conditions aid this consummation. It seems to me, however, that allotments of land in severalty ought to be made with great care and circumspection. If hastily ⌐one, before the Indian knows its meaning, while yet he has little or no idea of tilling a farm and no conception of thrift, there is great danger that a reservation life in tribal relations may be exchanged for the pauperism of civilization instead of its independence and elevation.

The solution of the Indian problem depends very largely upon good administration. The personal fitness of agents and their adaptability to the peculiar duty of caring for their wards are of the utmost importance.

The law providing that, except in special cases, army officers shall be detailed as Indian agents it is hoped will prove a successful experiment.

There is danger of great abuses creeping into the prosecution of claims for Indian depredations, and I recommend that every possible safeguard be provided against the enforcement of unjust and fictitious claims of this description.

The appropriations on account of the Indian Bureau for the year ending June 30, 1894, amount to $7,954,962.99, a decrease as compared with the year preceding it of $387,131.95.

The vast area of land which but a short time ago constituted the public domain is rapidly falling into private hands. It is certain that in the transfer the beneficent intention of the Government to supply from its domain homes to the industrious and worthy home seekers is often frustrated. Though the speculator, who stands with extortionate purpose between the land office and those who, with their families, are invited by the Government to settle on the public lands, is a despicable character who ought not to be tolerated, yet it is difficult to thwart his schemes. The recent opening to settlement of the lands in the Cherokee Outlet, embracing an area of 6,500,000 acres, notwithstanding the utmost care in framing the regulations governing the selection of locations and notwithstanding the presence of United States troops, furnished an exhibition, though perhaps in a modified degree, of the mad scramble, the violence, and the fraudulent occupation which have accompanied previous openings of public land.

I concur with the Secretary in the belief that these outrageous incidents can not be entirely prevented without a change in the laws on the subject, and I hope his recommendations in that direction will be favorably considered.

I especially commend to the attention of the Congress the statements contained in the Secretary's report concerning forestry. The time has come when efficient measures should be taken for the preservation of our forests from indiscriminate and remediless destruction.

The report of the Secretary of Agriculture will be found exceedingly interesting, especially to that large part of our citizens intimately concerned in agricultural occupations.

On the 7th day of March, 1893, there were upon its pay rolls 2,430 employees. This number has been reduced to 1,850 persons. In view of a depleted public Treasury and the imperative demand of the people for economy in the administration of their Government, the Secretary has entered upon the task of rationally reducing expenditures by the elimination from the pay rolls of all persons not needed for an efficient conduct of the affairs of the Department.

During the first quarter of the present year the expenses of the Department aggregated $345,876.76, as against $402,012.42 for the corresponding period of the fiscal year ending June 30, 1893. The Secretary makes apparent his intention to continue this rate of reduction by submitting estimates for the next fiscal year less by $994,280 than those for the present year.

Among the heads of divisions in this Department the changes have been exceedingly few. Three vacancies occurring from death and resignations have been filled by the promotion of assistants in the same divisions.

These promotions of experienced and faithful assistants have not only been in the interest of efficient work, but have suggested to those in the Department who look for retention and promotion that merit and devotion to duty are their best reliance.

The amount appropriated for the Bureau of Animal Industry for the current fiscal year is $850,000. The estimate for the ensuing year is $700,000.

The regulations of 1892 concerning Texas fever have been enforced during the last year and the large stock yards of the country have been kept free from infection. Occasional local outbreaks have been largely such as could have been effectually guarded against by the owners of the affected cattle.

While contagious pleuro-pneumonia in cattle has been eradicated, animal tuberculosis, a disease widespread and more dangerous to human life than pleuro-pneumonia, is still prevalent. Investigations have been made during the past year as to the means of its communication and the method of its correct diagnosis. Much progress has been made in this direction by the studies of the division of animal pathology, but work ought to be extended, in cooperation with local authorities, until the danger to human life arising from this cause is reduced to a minimum.

The number of animals arriving from Canada during the year and inspected by Bureau officers was 462,092, and the number from transatlantic countries was 1,297. No contagious diseases were found among the imported animals.

The total number of inspections of cattle for export during the past fiscal year was 611,542. The exports show a falling off of about 25 per cent from the preceding year, the decrease occurring entirely in the last half of the year. This suggests that the falling off may have been largely due to an increase in the price of American export cattle.

During the year ending June 30, 1893, exports of inspected pork aggregated 20,677,410 pounds, as against 38,152,874 pounds for the preceding year. The falling off in this export was not confined, however, to inspected pork, the total quantity exported for 1892 being 665,490,616 pounds, while in 1893 it was only 527,308,695 pounds.

I join the Secretary in recommending that hereafter each applicant for the position of inspector or assistant inspector in the Bureau of Animal Industry be required, as a condition precedent to his appointment, to exhibit to the United States Civil Service Commission his diploma from an established, regular, and reputable veterinary college, and that this be supplemented by such an examination in veterinary science as the Commission may prescribe.

The exports of agricultural products from the United States for the fiscal year ending June 30, 1892, attained the enormous figure of $800,-000,000, in round numbers, being 78.7 per cent of our total exports. In the last fiscal year this aggregate was greatly reduced, but nevertheless reached 615,000,000, being 75.1 per cent of all American commodities exported.

A review of our agricultural exports with special reference to their destination will show that in almost every line the United Kingdom of Great Britain and Ireland absorbs by far the largest proportion. Of cattle the total exports aggregated in value for the fiscal year ending June 30, 1893, $26,000,000, of which Great Britain took considerably over $25,000,000. Of beef products of all kinds our total exports were $28,000,000, of which Great Britain took $24,000,000. Of pork products the total exports were $84,000,000, of which Great Britain took $53,000,000. In breadstuffs, cotton, and minor products like proportions sent to the same destination are shown.

The work of the statistical division of the Department of Agriculture deals with all that relates to the economics of farming.

The main purpose of its monthly reports is to keep the farmers informed as fully as possible of all matters having any influence upon the world's markets, in which their products find sale. Its publications relate especially to the commercial side of farming.

It is therefore of profound importance and vital concern to the farmers of the United States, who represent nearly one-half of our population, and also of direct interest to the whole country, that the work of this division be efficiently performed and that the information it has gathered be promptly diffused.

It is a matter for congratulation to know that the Secretary will not spare any effort to make this part of his work thoroughly useful.

In the year 1839 the Congress appropriated $1,000, to be taken from the Patent Office funds, for the purpose of collecting and distributing rare and improved varieties of seeds and for prosecuting agricultural investigations and procuring agricultural statistics. From this small beginning the seed division of the Department of Agriculture has grown to its present unwieldy and unjustifiably extravagant proportions.

During the last fiscal year the cost of seeds purchased was $66,548.61. The remainder of an appropriation of $135,000 was expended in putting them up and distributing them. It surely never could have entered the minds of those who first sanctioned appropriations of public money for the purchase of new and improved varieties of seeds for gratuitous distribution that from this would grow large appropriations for the purchase and distribution by members of Congress of ordinary seeds, bulbs, and cuttings which are common in all the States and Territories and everywhere easily obtainable at low prices.

In each State and Territory an agricultural experiment station has been established. These stations, by their very character and name, are the proper agencies to experiment with and test new varieties of seeds; and yet this indiscriminate and wasteful distribution by legislation and legislators continues, answering no purpose unless it be to remind constituents that their representatives are willing to remember them with gratuities at public cost.

Under the sanction of existing legislation there was sent out from the Agricultural Department during the last fiscal year enough of cabbage seed to plant 19,200 acres of land, a sufficient quantity of beans to plant 4,000 acres, beet seed enough to plant 2,500 acres, sweet corn enough to plant 7,800 acres, sufficient cucumber seed to cover 2,025 acres with vines, and enough muskmelon and watermelon seeds to plant 2,675 acres. The total quantity of flower and vegetable seeds thus distributed was contained in more than 9,000,000 packages, and they were sufficient if planted to cover 89,596 acres of land.

In view of these facts this enormous expenditure without legitimate returns of benefit ought to be abolished. Anticipating a consummation so manifestly in the interest of good administration, more than $100,000 has been stricken from the estimate made to cover this object for the year ending June 30, 1895; and the Secretary recommends that the remaining $35,000 of the estimate be confined strictly to the purchase of new and improved varieties of seeds, and that these be distributed through experiment stations.

Thus the seed will be tested, and after the test has been completed by the experiment station the propagation of the useful varieties and the rejection of the valueless may safely be left to the common sense of the people.

The continued intelligent execution of the civil-service law and the increasing approval by the people of its operation are most gratifying. The recent extension of its limitations and regulations to the employees at free-delivery post-offices, which has been honestly and promptly accomplished by the Commission, with the hearty cooperation of the Postmaster-General, is an immensely important advance in the usefulness of the system.

I am, if possible, more than ever convinced of the incalculable benefits conferred by the civil-service law, not only in its effect upon the public service, but also, what is even more important, in its effect in elevating the tone of political life generally.

The course of civil-service reform in this country instructively and interestingly illustrates how strong a hold a movement gains upon our people which has underlying it a sentiment of justice and right and which at the same time promises better administration of their Government.

The law embodying this reform found its way to our statute book more from fear of the popular sentiment existing in its favor than from any love for the reform itself on the part of legislators, and it has lived and grown and flourished in spite of the covert as well as open hostility of spoilsmen and notwithstanding the querulous impracticability of many self-constituted guardians. Beneath all the vagaries and sublimated theories which are attracted to it there underlies this reform a sturdy common-sense principle not only suited to this mundane sphere, but whose application our people are more and more recognizing to be absolutely essential to the most successful operation of their Government, if not to its perpetuity.

It seems to me to be entirely inconsistent with the character of this reform, as well as with its best enforcement, to oblige the Commission to rely for clerical assistance upon clerks detailed from other Departments. There ought not to be such a condition in any Department that clerks hired to do work there can be spared to habitually work at another place, and it does not accord with a sensible view of civil-service reform that persons should be employed on the theory that their labor is necessary in one Department when in point of fact their services are devoted to entirely different work in another Department.

I earnestly urge that the clerks necessary to carry on the work of the Commission be regularly put upon its roster and that the system of obliging the Commissioners to rely upon the services of clerks belonging to other Departments be discontinued. This ought not to increase the expense to the Government, while it would certainly be more consistent and add greatly to the efficiency of the Commission.

Economy in public expenditure is a duty that can not innocently be neglected by those intrusted with the control of money drawn from the people for public uses. It must be confessed that our apparently endless resources, the familiarity of our people with immense accumulations of wealth, the growing sentiment among them that the expenditure of public money should in some manner be to their immediate and personal advantage, the indirect and almost stealthy manner in which a large part of our taxes is exacted, and a degenerated sense of official accountability have led to growing extravagance in governmental appropriations.

At this time, when a depleted public Treasury confronts us, when many of our people are engaged in a hard struggle for the necessaries of life, and when enforced economy is pressing upon the great mass of our countrymen, I desire to urge with all the earnestness at my command that Congressional legislation be so limited by strict economy as to exhibit an appreciation of the condition of the Treasury and a sympathy with the straitened circumstances of our fellow-citizens.

The duty of public economy is also of immense importance in its intimate and necessary relation to the task now in hand of providing revenue to meet Government expenditures and yet reducing the people's burden of Federal taxation.

After a hard struggle tariff reform is directly before us. Nothing so important claims our attention and nothing so clearly presents itself as both an opportunity and a duty—an opportunity to deserve the gratitude of our fellow-citizens and a duty imposed upon us by our oft-repeated professions and by the emphatic mandate of the people. After full discussion our countrymen have spoken in favor of this reform, and they have confided the work of its accomplishment to the hands of those who are solemnly pledged to it.

If there is anything in the theory of a representation in public places of the people and their desires, if public officers are really the servants of the people, and if political promises and professions have any binding force, our failure to give the relief so long awaited will be sheer recreancy. Nothing should intervene to distract our attention or disturb our effort until this reform is accomplished by wise and careful legislation.

While we should stanchly adhere to the principle that only the necessity of revenue justifies the imposition of tariff duties and other Federal taxation and that they should be limited by strict economy, we can not close our eyes to the fact that conditions have grown up among us which in justice and fairness call for discriminating care in the distribution of such duties and taxation as the emergencies of our Government actually demand.

Manifestly if we are to aid the people directly through tariff reform, one of its most obvious features should be a reduction in present tariff charges upon the necessaries of life. The benefits of such a reduction would be palpable and substantial, seen and felt by thousands who would be better fed and better clothed and better sheltered. These gifts should be the willing benefactions of a Government whose highest function is the promotion of the welfare of the people.

Not less closely related to our people's prosperity and well-being is the removal of restrictions upon the importation of the raw materials necessary to our manufactures. The world should be open to our national ingenuity and enterprise. This can not be while Federal legislation through the imposition of high tariff forbids to American manufacturers as cheap materials as those used by their competitors. It is quite obvious that the enhancement of the price of our manufactured products resulting from this policy not only confines the market for these products within our own borders, to the direct disadvantage of our manufacturers, but also increases their cost to our citizens.

The interests of labor are certainly, though indirectly, involved in this feature of our tariff system. The sharp competition and active struggle among our manufacturers to supply the limited demand for their goods soon fill the narrow market to which they are confined. Then follows a suspension of work in mills and factories, a discharge of employees, and distress in the homes of our workingmen.

Even if the often-disproved assertion could be made good that a lower rate of wages would result from free raw materials and low tariff duties, the intelligence of our workmen leads them quickly to discover that their steady employment, permitted by free raw materials, is the most important factor in their relation to tariff legislation.

A measure has been prepared by the appropriate Congressional committee embodying tariff reform on the lines herein suggested, which will be promptly submitted for legislative action. It is the result of much patriotic and unselfish work, and I believe it deals with its subject consistently and as thoroughly as existing conditions permit.

I am satisfied that the reduced tariff duties provided for in the proposed legislation, added to existing internal-revenue taxation, will in the near future, though perhaps not immediately, produce sufficient revenue to meet the needs of the Government.

The committee, after full consideration and to provide against a temporary deficiency which may exist before the business of the country adjusts itself to the new tariff schedules, have wisely embraced in their plan a few additional internal-revenue taxes, including a small tax upon incomes derived from certain corporate investments.

These new adjustments are not only absolutely just and easily borne, but they have the further merit of being such as can be remitted without unfavorable business disturbance whenever the necessity of their imposition no longer exists.

In my great desire for the success of this measure I can not restrain the suggestion that its success can only be attained by means of unselfish counsel on the part of the friends of tariff reform and as a result of their willingness to subordinate personal desires and ambitions to the general good. The local interests affected by the proposed reform are so numerous and so varied that if all are insisted upon the legislation embodying the reform must inevitably fail.

In conclusion my intense feeling of responsibility impels me to invoke for the manifold interests of a generous and confiding people the most scrupulous care and to pledge my willing support to every legislative effort for the advancement of the greatness and prosperity of our beloved country.

SECOND ANNUAL MESSAGE.

EXECUTIVE MANSION, *December 3, 1894.*

To the Congress of the United States:

The assemblage within the nation's legislative halls of those charged with the duty of making laws for the benefit of a generous and free people impressively suggests the exacting obligation and inexorable responsibility involved in their task.   At the threshold of such labor now to be undertaken by the Congress of the United States, and in the discharge of an executive duty enjoined by the Constitution, I submit this communication, containing a brief statement of the condition of our national affairs and recommending such legislation as seems to me necessary and expedient.

The history of our recent dealings with other nations and our peaceful relations with them at this time additionally demonstrate the advantage of consistently adhering to a firm but just foreign policy, free from envious or ambitious national schemes and characterized by entire honesty and sincerity.

During the past year, pursuant to a law of Congress, commissioners were appointed to the Antwerp Industrial Exposition.   Though the participation of American exhibitors fell far short of completely illustrating our national ingenuity and industrial achievements, yet it was quite creditable in view of the brief time allowed for preparation.

I have endeavored to impress upon the Belgian Government the needlessness and positive harmfulness of its restrictions upon the importation of certain of our food products, and have strongly urged that the rigid supervision and inspection under our laws are amply sufficient to prevent the exportation from this country of diseased cattle and unwholesome meat.

The termination of the civil war in Brazil has been followed by the general prevalence of peace and order.   It appearing at an early stage of the insurrection that its course would call for unusual watchfulness on the part of this Government, our naval force in the harbor of Rio de Janeiro was strengthened.   This precaution, I am satisfied, tended to restrict the issue to a simple trial of strength between the Brazilian Government and the insurgents and to avert complications which at times seemed imminent.   Our firm attitude of neutrality was maintained to the end.   The insurgents received no encouragement of eventual asylum from our commanders, and such opposition as they encountered was for the protection of our commerce and was clearly justified by public law.

A serious tension of relations having arisen at the close of the war between Brazil and Portugal by reason of the escape of the insurgent admiral Da Gama and his followers, the friendly offices of our representatives to those countries were exerted for the protection of the subjects of either within the territory of the other.

Although the Government of Brazil was duly notified that the commercial arrangement existing between the United States and that country based on the third section of the tariff act of 1890 was abrogated on August 28, 1894, by the taking effect of the tariff law now in force, that Government subsequently notified us of its intention to terminate such arrangement on the 1st day of January, 1895, in the exercise of the right reserved in the agreement between the two countries. I invite attention to the correspondence between the Secretary of State and the Brazilian minister on this subject.

The commission organized under the convention which we had entered into with Chile for the settlement of the outstanding claims of each Government against the other adjourned at the end of the period stipulated for its continuance leaving undetermined a number of American cases which had been duly presented. These claims are not barred, and negotiations are in progress for their submission to a new tribunal.

On the 17th of March last a new treaty with China in further regulation of emigration was signed at Washington, and on August 13 it received the sanction of the Senate. Ratification on the part of China and formal exchange are awaited to give effect to this mutually beneficial convention.

A gratifying recognition of the uniform impartiality of this country toward all foreign states was manifested by the coincident request of the Chinese and Japanese Governments that the agents of the United States should within proper limits afford protection to the subjects of the other during the suspension of diplomatic relations due to a state of war. This delicate office was accepted, and a misapprehension which gave rise to the belief that in affording this kindly unofficial protection our agents would exercise the same authority which the withdrawn agents of the belligerents had exercised was promptly corrected. Although the war between China and Japan endangers no policy of the United States, it deserves our gravest consideration by reason of its disturbance of our growing commercial interests in the two countries and the increased dangers which may result to our citizens domiciled or sojourning in the interior of China.

Acting under a stipulation in our treaty with Korea (the first concluded with a western power), I felt constrained at the beginning of the controversy to tender our good offices to induce an amicable arrangement of the initial difficulty growing out of the Japanese demands for administrative reforms in Korea, but the unhappy precipitation of actual hostilities defeated this kindly purpose.

Deploring the destructive war between the two most powerful of the eastern nations and anxious that our commercial interests in those countries may be preserved and that the safety of our citizens there shall not be jeopardized, I would not hesitate to heed any intimation that our friendly aid for the honorable termination of hostilities would be acceptable to both belligerents.

A convention has been finally concluded for the settlement by arbitration of the prolonged dispute with Ecuador growing out of the proceedings against Emilio Santos, a naturalized citizen of the United States.

Our relations with the Republic of France continue to be such as should exist between nations so long bound together by friendly sympathy and similarity in their form of government.

The recent cruel assassination of the President of this sister Republic called forth such universal expressions of sorrow and condolence from our people and Government as to leave no doubt of the depth and sincerity of our attachment. The resolutions passed by the Senate and House of Representatives on the occasion have been communicated to the widow of President Carnot.

Acting upon the reported discovery of Texas fever in cargoes of American cattle, the German prohibition against importations of live stock and fresh meats from this country has been revived. It is hoped that Germany will soon become convinced that the inhibition is as needless as it is harmful to mutual interests.

The German Government has protested against that provision of the customs tariff act which imposes a discriminating duty of one-tenth of 1 cent a pound on sugars coming from countries paying an export bounty thereon, claiming that the exaction of such duty is in contravention of Articles V and IX of the treaty of 1828 with Prussia.

In the interests of the commerce of both countries and to avoid even the accusation of treaty violation, I recommend the repeal of so much of the statute as imposes that duty, and I invite attention to the accompanying report of the Secretary of State, containing a discussion of the questions raised by the German protests.

Early in the present year an agreement was reached with Great Britain concerning instructions to be given to the naval commanders of the two Governments in Bering Sea and the contiguous North Pacific Ocean for their guidance in the execution of the award of the Paris Tribunal of Arbitration and the enforcement of the regulations therein prescribed for the protection of seal life in the waters mentioned. An understanding has also been reached for the payment by the United States of $425,000 in full satisfaction of all claims which may be made by Great Britain for damages growing out of the controversy as to fur seals in Bering Sea or the seizure of British vessels engaged in taking seal in those waters. The award and findings of the Paris Tribunal to a great extent determined the facts and principles upon which these claims should be adjusted, and they have been subjected by both Governments to a thorough examination upon the principles as well as the facts which they involve. I am convinced that a settlement upon the terms mentioned would be an equitable and advantageous one, and I recommend that provision be made for the prompt payment of the stated sum.

Thus far only France and Portugal have signified their willingness to adhere to the regulations established under the award of the Paris Tribunal of Arbitration.

Preliminary surveys of the Alaskan boundary and a preparatory examination of the question of protection of food fish in the contiguous waters of the United States and the Dominion of Canada are in progress.

The boundary of British Guiana still remains in dispute between Great Britain and Venezuela. Believing that its early settlement on some just basis alike honorable to both parties is in the line of our established policy to remove from this hemisphere all causes of difference with powers beyond the sea, I shall renew the efforts heretofore made to bring about a restoration of diplomatic relations between the disputants and to induce a reference to arbitration—a resort which Great Britain so conspicuously favors in principle and respects in practice and which is earnestly sought by her weaker adversary.

Since communicating the voluminous correspondence in regard to Hawaii and the action taken by the Senate and House of Representatives on certain questions submitted to the judgment and wider discretion of Congress the organization of a government in place of the provisional arrangement which followed the deposition of the Queen has been announced, with evidence of its effective operation. The recognition usual in such cases has been accorded the new Government.

Under our present treaties of extradition with Italy miscarriages of justice have occurred owing to the refusal of that Government to surrender its own subjects. Thus far our efforts to negotiate an amended convention obviating this difficulty have been unavailing.

Apart from the war in which the Island Empire is engaged, Japan attracts increasing attention in this country by her evident desire to cultivate more liberal intercourse with us and to seek our kindly aid in furtherance of her laudable desire for complete autonomy in her domestic affairs and full equality in the family of nations. The Japanese Empire of to-day is no longer the Japan of the past, and our relations with this progressive nation should not be less broad and liberal than those with other powers.

Good will, fostered by many interests in common, has marked our relations with our nearest southern neighbor. Peace being restored along her northern frontier, Mexico has asked the punishment of the late disturbers of her tranquillity. There ought to be a new treaty of commerce and navigation with that country to take the place of the one which terminated thirteen years ago. The friendliness of the intercourse between the two countries is attested by the fact that during this long period the commerce of each has steadily increased under the rule of mutual consideration, being neither stimulated by conventional arrangements nor retarded by jealous rivalries or selfish distrust.

An indemnity tendered by Mexico as a gracious act for the murder in 1887 of Leon Baldwin, an American citizen, by a band of marauders in Durango has been accepted and is being paid in installments.

The problem of the storage and use of the waters of the Rio Grande for irrigation should be solved by appropriate concurrent action of the two interested countries. Rising in the Colorado heights, the stream flows intermittently, yielding little water during the dry months to the irriga· tion channels already constructed along its course. This scarcity is often severely felt in the regions where the river forms a common boundary. Moreover, the frequent changes in its course through level sands often raise embarrassing questions of territorial jurisdiction.

Prominent among the questions of the year was the Bluefields incident, in what is known as the Mosquito Indian Strip, bordering on the Atlantic Ocean and within the jurisdiction of Nicaragua. By .he treaty of 1860 between Great Britain and Nicaragua the former Government expressly recognized the sovereignty of the latter over the strip, and a limited form of self-government was guaranteed to the Mosquito Indians, to be exercised according to their customs, for themselves and other dwellers within its limits. The so-called native government, which grew to be largely made up of aliens, for many years disputed the sovereignty of Nicaragua over the strip and claimed the right to maintain therein a practically independent municipal government. Early in the past year efforts of Nicaragua to maintain sovereignty over the Mosquito territory led to serious disturbances, culminating in the suppression of the native government and the attempted substitution of an impracticable composite administration in which Nicaragua and alien residents were to participate. Failure was followed by an insurrection, which for a time subverted Nicaraguan rule, expelling her officers and restoring the old organization. This in turn gave place to the existing local government established and upheld by Nicaragua.

Although the alien interests arrayed against Nicaragua in these transactions have been largely American and the commerce of that region for some time has been and still is chiefly controlled by our citizens, we can not for that reason challenge the rightful sovereignty of Nicaragua over this important part of her domain.

For some months one, and during part of the time two, of our naval ships have been stationed at Bluefields for the protection of all legitimate interests of our citizens. In September last the Government at Managua expelled from its territory twelve or more foreigners, including two Americans, for alleged participation in the seditious or revolutionary movements against the Republic at Bluefields already mentioned; but through the earnest remonstrance of this Government the two Americans have been permitted to return to the peaceful management of their business. Our naval commanders at the scene of these disturbances by their constant exhibition of firmness and good judgment contributed largely to the prevention of more serious consequences and to the restoration of quiet and order. I regret that in the midst of these occurrences there happened a most grave and irritating failure of Nicaraguan justice. An American citizen named Wilson, residing at Rama, in the Mosquito territory, was murdered by one Argüello, the acting governor of the town. After some delay the murderer was arrested, but so insecurely confined or guarded that he escaped, and notwithstanding our repeated demands it is claimed that his recapture has been impossible by reason of his flight beyond Nicaraguan jurisdiction.

The Nicaraguan authorities, having given notice of forfeiture of their concession to the canal company on grounds purely technical and not embraced in the contract, have receded from that position.

Peru, I regret to say, shows symptoms of domestic disturbance, due probably to the slowness of her recuperation from the distresses of the war of 1881. Weakened in resources, her difficulties in facing international obligations invite our kindly sympathy and justify our forbearance in pressing long-pending claims. I have felt constrained to testify this sympathy in connection with certain demands urgently preferred by other powers.

The recent death of the Czar of Russia called forth appropriate expressions of sorrow and sympathy on the part of our Government with his bereaved family and the Russian people. As a further demonstration of respect and friendship our minister at St. Petersburg was directed to represent our Government at the funeral ceremonies.

The sealing interests of Russia in Bering Sea are second only to our own. A *modus vivendi* has therefore been concluded with the Imperial Government restrictive of poaching on the Russian rookeries and of sealing in waters which were not comprehended in the protected area defined in the Paris award.

Occasion has been found to urge upon the Russian Government equality of treatment for our great life-insurance companies whose operations have been extended throughout Europe. Admitting as we do foreign corporations to transact business in the United States, we naturally expect no less tolerance for our own in the ample fields of competition abroad.

But few cases of interference with naturalized citizens returning to Russia have been reported during the current year. One Krzeminski was arrested last summer in a Polish province on a reported charge of unpermitted renunciation of Russian allegiance, but it transpired that the proceedings originated in alleged malfeasance committed by Krzeminski while an imperial official a number of years ago. Efforts for his release, which promised to be successful, were in progress when his death was reported.

The Government of Salvador having been overthrown by an abrupt popular outbreak, certain of its military and civil officers, while hotly pursued by infuriated insurgents, sought refuge on board the United States war ship *Bennington*, then lying in a Salvadorean port. Although the practice of asylum is not favored by this Government, yet in view of the imminent peril which threatened the fugitives and solely from considerations of humanity they were afforded shelter by our naval commander, and when afterwards demanded under our treaty of extradition with Salvador for trial on charges of murder, arson, and robbery I directed that such of them as had not voluntarily left the ship be conveyed to one of our nearest ports where a hearing could be had before a judicial officer, in compliance with the terms of the treaty.   On their arrival at San Francisco such a proceeding was promptly instituted before the United States district judge, who held that the acts constituting the alleged offenses were political and discharged all the accused except one Cienfuegos, who was held for an attempt to murder.   Thereupon I was constrained to direct his release for the reason that an attempt to murder was not one of the crimes charged against him and upon which his surrender to the Salvadorean authorities had been demanded.

Unreasonable and unjust fines imposed by Spain on the vessels and commerce of the United States have demanded from time to time during the last twenty years earnest remonstrance on the part of our Government.   In the immediate past exorbitant penalties have been imposed upon our vessels and goods by customs authorities of Cuba and Puerto Rico for clerical errors of the most trivial character in the manifests of bills of lading.   In some cases fines amounting to thousands of dollars have been levied upon cargoes or the carrying vessels when the goods in question were entitled to free entry.   Fines have been exacted even when the error had been detected and the Spanish authorities notified before the arrival of the goods in port.

This conduct is in strange contrast with the considerate and liberal treatment extended to Spanish vessels and cargoes in our ports in like cases.   No satisfactory settlement of these vexatious questions has yet been reached.

The Mora case, referred to in my last annual message, remains unsettled.   From the diplomatic correspondence on this subject which has been laid before the Senate it will be seen that this Government has offered to conclude a convention with Spain for disposal by arbitration of outstanding claims between the two countries, except the Mora claim, which, having been long ago adjusted, now only awaits payment as stipulated, and of course it could not be included in the proposed convention. It was hoped that this offer would remove parliamentary obstacles encountered by the Spanish Government in providing payment of the Mora indemnity.   I regret to say that no definite reply to this offer has yet been made and all efforts to secure payment of this settled claim have been unavailing.

In my last annual message I adverted to the claim on the part of Turkey of the right to expel as persons undesirable and dangerous Armenians naturalized in the United States and returning to Turkish jurisdiction.   Numerous questions in this relation have arisen.   While this Government acquiesces in the asserted right of expulsion, it will not consent that Armenians may be imprisoned or otherwise punished for no other reason than having acquired without imperial consent American citizenship.

Three of the assailants of Miss Melton, an American teacher in Mosul, have been convicted by the Ottoman courts, and I am advised that an appeal against the acquittal of the remaining five has been taken by the Turkish prosecuting officer.

A convention has been concluded with Venezuela for the arbitration of a long-disputed claim growing out of the seizure of certain vessels the property of citizens of the United States. Although signed, the treaty of extradition with Venezuela is not yet in force, owing to the insistence of that Government that when surrendered its citizens shall in no case be liable to capital punishment.

The rules for the prevention of collisions at sea which were framed by the maritime conference held in this city in 1889, having been concurrently incorporated in the statutes of the United States and Great Britain, have been announced to take effect March 1, 1895, and invitations have been extended to all maritime nations to adhere to them. Favorable responses have thus far been received from Austria, France, Portugal, Spain, and Sweden.

In my last annual message I referred briefly to the unsatisfactory state of affairs in Samoa under the operation of the Berlin treaty as signally illustrating the impolicy of entangling alliances with foreign powers, and on May 9, 1894, in response to a resolution of the Senate, I sent a special message and documents to that body on the same subject, which emphasized my previously expressed opinions. Later occurrences, the correspondence in regard to which will be laid before the Congress, further demonstrate that the Government which was devised by the three powers and forced upon the Samoans against their inveterate hostility can be maintained only by the continued presence of foreign military force and at no small sacrifice of life and treasure.

The suppression of the Mataafa insurrection by the powers and the subsequent banishment of the leader and eleven other chiefs, as recited in my last message, did not bring lasting peace to the islands. Formidable uprisings continued, and finally a rebellion broke out in the capital island, Upolu, headed in Aana, the western district, by the younger Tamasese, and in Atua, the eastern district, by other leaders. The insurgents ravaged the country and fought the Government's troops up to the very doors of Apia. The King again appealed to the powers for help, ar d the combined British and German naval forces reduced the Atuans to apparent subjection, not, however, without considerable loss to the natives. A few days later Tamasese and his adherents, fearing the ships and the marines, professed submission.

Reports received from our agents at Apia do not justify the belief that the peace thus brought about will be of long duration. It is their conviction that the natives are at heart hostile to the present Government, that such of them as profess loyalty to it do so from fear of the powers, and that it would speedily go to pieces if the war ships were withdrawn. In reporting to his Government on the unsatisfactory situation since the suppression of the late revolt by foreign armed forces, the German consul at Apia stated:

That peace will be lasting is hardly to be presumed. The lesson given by firing on Atua was not sufficiently sharp and incisive to leave a lasting impression on the forgetful Samoan temperament. In fact, conditions are existing which show that peace will not last and is not seriously intended. Malietoa, the King, and his chiefs are convinced that the departure of the war ships will be a signal for a renewal of war. The circumstance that the representatives of the villages of all the districts which were opposed to the Government have already withdrawn to Atua to hold meetings, and that both Atua and Aana have forbidden inhabitants of those districts which fought on the side of the Government to return to their villages, and have already partly burned down the latter, indicates that a real conciliation of the parties is still far off.

And in a note of the 10th ultimo, inclosing a copy of that report for the information of this Government, the German ambassador said:

The contents of the report awakened the Imperial Government's apprehension that under existing circumstances the peace concluded with the rebels will afford no assurance of the lasting restoration of tranquillity in the islands.

The present Government has utterly failed to correct, if indeed it has not aggravated, the very evils it was intended to prevent. It has not stimulated our commerce with the islands. Our participation in its establishment against the wishes of the natives was in plain defiance of the conservative teachings and warnings of the wise and patriotic men who laid the foundations of our free institutions, and I invite an expression of the judgment of Congress on the propriety of steps being taken by this Government looking to the withdrawal from its engagements with the other powers on some reasonable terms not prejudicial to any of our existing rights.

The Secretary of the Treasury reports that the receipts of the Government from all sources of revenue during the fiscal year ending June 30, 1894, amounted to $372,802,498.29 and its expenditures to $442,605,-758.87, leaving a deficit of $69,803,260.58. There was a decrease of $15,952,674.66 in the ordinary expense of the Government as compared with the fiscal year 1893.

There was collected from customs $131,818,530.62 and from internal revenue $147,168,449.70. The balance of the income for the year, amounting to $93,815,517.97, was derived from the sales of lands and other sources.

The value of our total dutiable imports amounted to $275,199,086, being $146,657,625 less than during the preceding year, and the importations free of duty amounted to $379,795,536, being $64,748,675 less than during the preceding year. The receipts from customs were

$73,536,486.11 less and from internal revenue $13,836,539.97 less than in 1893.

The total tax collected from distilled spirits was $85,259,250.25, on manufactured tobacco $28,617,898.62, and on fermented liquors $31,414,-788.04.

Our exports of merchandise, domestic and foreign, amounted during the year to $892,140,572, being an increase over the preceding year of $44,495,378.

The total amount of gold exported during the fiscal year was $76,898,-061, as against $108,680,444 during the fiscal year 1893. The amount imported was $72,449,119, as against $21,174,381 during the previous year.

The imports of silver were $13,286,552 and the exports were $50,-451,265.

The total bounty paid upon the production of sugar in the United States for the fiscal year was $12,100,208.89, being an increase of $2,725,078.01 over the payments made during the preceding year. The amount of bounty paid from July 1, 1894, to August 28, 1894, the time when further payments ceased by operation of law, was $966,185.84. The total expenses incurred in the payment of the bounty upon sugar during the fiscal year was $130,140.85.

It is estimated that upon the basis of the present revenue laws the receipts of the Government during the current fiscal year, ending June 30, 1895, will be $424,427,748.44 and its expenditures $444,427,748.44, resulting in a deficit of $20,000,000.

On the 1st day of November, 1894, the total stock of money of all kinds in the country was $2,240,773,888, as against $2,204,651,000 on the 1st day of November, 1893, and the money of all kinds in circulation, or not included in the Treasury holdings, was $1,672,093,422, or $24.27 per capita upon an estimated population of 68,887,000. At the same date there was held in the Treasury gold bullion amounting to $44,615,-177.55 and silver bullion which was purchased at a cost of $127,772,988. The purchase of silver bullion under the act of July 14, 1890, ceased on the 1st day of November, 1893, and up to that time there had been purchased during the fiscal year 11,917,658.78 fine ounces, at a cost of $8,715,-521.32, an average cost of $0.7313 per fine ounce. The total amount of silver purchased from the time that law took effect until the repeal of its purchasing clause, on the date last mentioned, was 168,674,682.53 fine ounces, which cost $155,931,002.25, the average price per fine ounce being $0.9244.

The total amount of standard silver dollars coined at the mints of the United States since the passage of the act of February 28, 1878, is $421,-776,408, of which $378,166,793 were coined under the provisions of that act, $38,531,143 under the provisions of the act of July 14, 1890, and $5,078,472 under the act providing for the coinage of trade-dollar bullion.

The total coinage of all metals at our mints during the last fiscal year consisted of 63,485,220 pieces, valued at $106,216,730.06, of which there were $99,474,912.50 in gold coined, $758 in standard silver dollars, $6,024,140.30 in subsidiary silver coin, and $716,919.26 in minor coin.

During the calendar year 1893 the production of precious metals in the United States was estimated at 1,739,323 fine ounces of gold of the commercial and coinage value of $35,955,000 and 60,000,000 fine ounces of silver of the bullion or market value of $46,800,000 and of the coinage value of $77,576,000. It is estimated that on the 1st day of July, 1894, the stock of metallic money in the United States, consisting of coin and bullion, amounted to $1,251,640,958, of which $627,923,201 was gold and $624,347,757 was silver.

Fifty national banks were organized during the year ending October 31, 1894, with a capital of $5,285,000, and 79, with a capital of $10,475,-000, went into voluntary liquidation. Twenty-one banks, with a capital of $2,770,000, were placed in the hands of receivers. The total number of national banks in existence on the 31st day of October last was 3,756, being 40 less than on the 31st day of October, 1893. The capital stock paid in was $672,671,365, being $9,678,491 less than at the same time in the previous year, and the surplus fund and individual profits, less expenses and taxes paid, amounted to $334,121,082.10, which was $16,-089,780 less than on October 31, 1893. The circulation was decreased $1,741,563. The obligations of the banks to each other were increased $117,268,334 and the individual deposits were $277,294,489 less than at the corresponding date in the previous year. Loans and discounts were $161,206,923 more than at the same time the previous year, and checks and other cash items were $90,349,963 more. The total resources of the banks at the date mentioned amounted to $3,473,922,055, as against $3,109,563,284.36 in 1893.

From the report of the Secretary of War it appears that the strength of the Army on September 30, 1894, was 2,135 officers and 25,765 enlisted men. Although this is apparently a very slight decrease compared with the previous year, the actual effective force has been increased to the equivalent of nearly two regiments through the reorganization of the system of recruiting and the consequent release to regimental duty of the large force of men hitherto serving at the recruiting depots. The abolition of these depots, it is predicted, will furthermore effect an annual reduction approximating $250,000 in the direct expenditures, besides promoting generally the health, morale, and discipline of the troops.

The execution of the policy of concentrating the Army at important centers of population and transportation, foreshadowed in the last annual report of the Secretary, has resulted in the abandonment of fifteen of the smaller posts, which was effected under a plan which assembles organizations of the same regiments hitherto widely separated. This renders our small forces more readily effective for any service which they may be called upon to perform, increases the extent of the territory under protection without diminishing the security heretofore afforded to any locality, improves the discipline, training, and *esprit de corps* of the Army, besides considerably decreasing the cost of its maintenance.

Though the forces of the Department of the East have been somewhat increased, more than three-fourths of the Army is still stationed west of the Mississippi. This carefully matured policy, which secures the best and greatest service in the interests of the general welfare from the small force comprising our Regular Army, should not be thoughtlessly embarrassed by the creation of new and unnecessary posts through acts of Congress to gratify the ambitions or interests of localities.

While the maximum legal strength of the Army is 25,000 men, the effective strength, through various causes, is but little over 20,000 men. The purpose of Congress does not, therefore, seem to be fully attained by the existing condition. While no considerable increase in the Army is, in my judgment, demanded by recent events, the policy of seacoast fortification, in the prosecution of which we have been steadily engaged for some years, has so far developed as to suggest that the effective strength of the Army be now made at least equal to the legal strength. Measures taken by the Department during the year, as indicated, have already considerably augmented the effective force, and the Secretary of War presents a plan, which I recommend to the consideration of Congress, to attain the desired end. Economies effected in the Department in other lines of its work will offset to a great extent the expenditure involved in the proposition submitted. Among other things this contemplates the adoption of the three-battalion formation of regiments, which for several years has been indorsed by the Secretaries of War and the Generals Commanding the Army. Compact in itself, it provides a skeleton organization, ready to be filled out in the event of war, which is peculiarly adapted to our strength and requirements; and the fact that every other nation, with a single exception, has adopted this formation to meet the conditions of modern warfare should alone secure for the recommendation an early consideration.

It is hardly necessary to recall the fact that in obedience to the commands of the Constitution and the laws, and for the purpose of protecting the property of the United States, aiding the process of Federal courts, and removing lawless obstructions to the performance by the Government of its legitimate functions, it became necessary in various localities during the year to employ a considerable portion of the regular troops. The duty was discharged promptly, courageously, and with marked discretion by the officers and men, and the most gratifying proof was thus afforded that the Army deserves that complete confidence in its efficiency and discipline which the country has at all times manifested.

The year has been free from disturbances by Indians, and the chances of further depredations on their part are constantly becoming more remote and improbable.

The total expenditures for the War Department for the year ended June 30, 1894, amounted to $56,039,009.34. Of this sum $2,000,614.99 was for salaries and contingent expenses, $23,665,156.16 for the support of the military establishment, $5,001,682.23 for miscellaneous objects, and $25,371,555.96 for public works. This latter sum includes $19,-494,037.49 for river and harbor improvements and $3,947,863.56 for fortifications and other works of defense. The appropriations for the current year aggregate $52,429,112.78, and the estimates submitted by the Secretary of War for the next fiscal year call for appropriations amounting to $52,318,629.55.

The skill and industry of our ordnance officers and inventors have, it is believed, overcome the mechanical obstacles which have heretofore delayed the armament of our coasts, and this great national undertaking upon which we have entered may now proceed as rapidly as Congress shall determine. With a supply of finished guns of large caliber already on hand, to which additions should now rapidly follow, the wisdom of providing carriages and emplacements for their mount can not be too strongly urged.

The total enrollment of the militia of the several States is 117,533 officers and enlisted men, an increase of 5,343 over the number reported at the close of the previous year. The reports of militia inspections by Regular Army officers show a marked increase in interest and efficiency among the State organizations, and I strongly recommend a continuance of the policy of affording every practical encouragement possible to this important auxiliary of our military establishment.

The condition of the Apache Indians held as prisoners by the Government for eight years at a cost of half a million dollars has been changed during the year from captivity to one which gives them an opportunity to demonstrate their capacity for self-support and at least partial civilization. Legislation enacted at the late session of Congress gave the War Department authority to transfer the survivors, numbering 346, from Mount Vernon Barracks, in Alabama, to any suitable reservation. The Department selected as their future home the military lands near Fort Sill, Ind. T., where, under military surveillance, the former prisoners have been established in agriculture under conditions favorable to their advancement.

In recognition of the long and distinguished military services and faithful discharge of delicate and responsible civil duties by Major-General John M. Schofield, now the General Commanding the Army, it is suggested to Congress that the temporary revival of the grade of lieutenant-general in his behalf would be a just and gracious act and would permit his retirement, now near at hand, with rank befitting his merits.

The report of the Attorney-General notes the gratifying progress made by the Supreme Court in overcoming the arrears of its business and in reaching a condition in which it will be able to dispose of cases as they arise without any unreasonable delay. This result is of course very largely due to the successful working of the plan inaugurating circuit courts of appeals. In respect to these tribunals the suggestion is made in quarters entitled to the highest consideration that an additional circuit judge for each circuit would greatly strengthen these courts and the confidence reposed in their adjudications, and that such an addition would not create a greater force of judges than the increasing business of such courts requires. I commend the suggestion to the careful consideration of the Congress. Other important topics are adverted to in the report, accompanied by recommendations, many of which have been treated at large in previous messages, and at this time, therefore, need only be named. I refer to the abolition of the fee system as a measure of compensation to Federal officers; the enlargement of the powers of United States commissioners, at least in the Territories; the allowance of writs of error in criminal cases on behalf of the United States, and the establishment of degrees in the crime of murder. A topic dealt with by the Attorney-General of much importance is the condition of the administration of justice in the Indian Territory. The permanent solution of what is called the Indian problem is probably not to be expected at once, but meanwhile such ameliorations of present conditions as the existing system will admit of ought not to be neglected. I am satisfied there should be a Federal court established for the Territory, with sufficient judges, and that this court should sit within the Territory and have the same jurisdiction as to Territorial affairs as is now vested in the Federal courts sitting in Arkansas and Texas.

Another subject of pressing moment referred to by the Attorney-General is the reorganization of the Union Pacific Railway Company on a basis equitable as regards all private interests and as favorable to the Government as existing conditions will permit. The operation of a railroad by a court through a receiver is an anomalous state of things which should be terminated on all grounds, public and private, at the earliest possible moment. Besides, not to enact the needed enabling legislation at the present session postpones the whole matter until the assembling of a new Congress and inevitably increases all the complications of the situation, and could not but be regarded as a signal failure to solve a problem which has practically been before the present Congress ever since its organization.

Eight years ago in my annual message I urged upon the Congress as strongly as I could the location and construction of two prisons for the confinement of United States prisoners. A similar recommendation has been made from time to time since, and a few years ago a law was passed providing for the selection of sites for three such institutions. No appropriation has, however, been made to carry the act into effect, and the old and discreditable condition still exists.

It is not my purpose at this time to repeat the considerations which make an impregnable case in favor of the ownership and management by the Government of the penal institutions in which Federal prisoners are confined. I simply desire to again urge former recommendations on the subject and to particularly call the attention of the Congress to that part of the report of the Secretary of War in which he states that the military prison at Fort Leavenworth, Kans., can be turned over to the Government as a prison for Federal convicts without the least difficulty and with an actual saving of money from every point of view.

Pending a more complete reform, I hope that by the adoption of the suggestion of the Secretary of War this easy step may be taken in the direction of the proper care of its convicts by the Government of the United States.

The report of the Postmaster-General presents a comprehensive statement of the operations of the Post-Office Department for the last fiscal year.

The receipts of the Department during the year amounted to $75,-080,479.04 and the expenditures to $84,324,414.15.

The transactions of the postal service indicate with barometric certainty the fluctuations in the business of the country. Inasmuch, therefore, as business complications continued to exist throughout the last year to an unforeseen extent, it is not surprising that the deficiency of revenue to meet the expenditures of the Post-Office Department, which was estimated in advance at about $8,000,000, should be exceeded by nearly $1,225,000. The ascertained revenues of the last year, which were the basis of calculation for the current year, being less than estimated, the deficiency for the current year will be correspondingly greater, though the Postmaster-General states that the latest indications are so favorable that he confidently predicts an increase of at least 8 per cent in the revenues of the current year over those of the last year.

The expenditures increase steadily and necessarily with the growth and needs of the country, so that the deficiency is greater or less in any year, depending upon the volume of receipts.

The Postmaster-General states that this deficiency is unnecessary and might be obviated at once if the law regulating rates upon mail matter of the second class was modified. The rate received for the transmission of this second-class matter is 1 cent per pound, while the cost of such transmission to the Government is eight times that amount. In the general terms of the law this rate covers newspapers and periodicals. The extensions of the meaning of these terms from time to time have admitted to the privileges intended for legitimate newspapers and periodicals a surprising range of publications and created abuses the cost of which amounts in the aggregate to the total deficiency of the Post-Office Department. Pretended newspapers are started by business houses for the mere purpose of advertising goods, complying with the law in form only and discontinuing the publications as soon as the period of advertising is over. "Sample copies" of pretended newspapers are issued in great numbers for a like purpose only. The result is a great loss of revenue to the Government, besides its humiliating use as an agency to aid in carrying out the scheme of a business house to advertise its goods by means of a trick upon both its rival houses and the regular and legitimate newspapers. Paper-covered literature, consisting mainly of trashy novels, to the extent of many thousands of tons is sent through the mails at 1 cent per pound, while the publishers of standard works are required to pay eight times that amount in sending their publications. Another abuse consists in the free carriage through the mails of hundreds of tons of seed and grain uselessly distributed through the Department of Agriculture. The Postmaster-General predicts that if the law be so amended as to eradicate these abuses not only will the Post-Office Department show no deficiency, but he believes that in the near future all legitimate newspapers and periodical magazines might be properly transmitted through the mails to their subscribers free of cost. I invite your prompt consideration of this subject and fully indorse the views of the Postmaster-General.

The total number of post-offices in the United States on the 30th day of June, 1894, was 69,805, an increase of 1,403 over the preceding year. Of these, 3,428 were Presidential, an increase in that class of 68 over the preceding year.

Six hundred and ten cities and towns are provided with free delivery. Ninety-three other cities and towns entitled to this service under the law have not been accorded it on account of insufficient funds. The expense of free delivery for the current fiscal year will be more than $12,300,000, and under existing legislation this item of expenditure is subject to constant increase. The estimated cost of rural free delivery generally is so very large that it ought not to be considered in the present condition of affairs.

During the year 830 additional domestic money-order offices were established. The total number of these offices at the close of the year was 19,264. There were 14,304,041 money orders issued during the year, being an increase over the preceding year of 994,306. The value of these orders amounted to $138,793,579.49, an increase of $11,217,145.84. There were also issued during the year postal notes amounting to $12,-649,094.55.

During the year 218 international money-order offices were added to those already established, making a total of 2,625 such offices in operation June 30, 1894. The number of international money orders issued during the year was 917,823, a decrease in number of 138,176, and their value was $13,792,455.31, a decrease in amount of $2,549,382.55. The number of orders paid was 361,180, an increase over the preceding year of 60,263, and their value was $6,568,493.78, an increase of $1,285,118.08.

From the foregoing statements it appears that the total issue of money orders and postal notes for the year amounted to $165,235,129.35.

The number of letters and packages mailed during the year for special delivery was 3,436,970. The special-delivery stamps used upon these letters and packages amounted to $343,697. The messengers fees paid for their delivery amounted to $261,209.70, leaving a balance in favor of the Government of $82,487.30.

The report shows most gratifying results in the way of economies worked out without affecting the efficiency of the postal service. These consist in the abrogation of steamship subsidy contracts, reletting of mail transportation contracts, and in the cost and amount of supplies used in the service, amounting in all to $16,619,047.42.

This report also contains a valuable contribution to the history of the Universal Postal Union, an arrangement which amounts practically to the establishment of one postal system for the entire civilized world. Special attention is directed to this subject at this time in view of the fact that the next congress of the union will meet in Washington in 1897, and it is hoped that timely action will be taken in the direction of perfecting preparations for that event.

The Postmaster-General renews the suggestion made in a previous report that the Department organization be increased to the extent of creating a direct district supervision of all postal affairs, and in this suggestion I fully concur.

There are now connected with the Post-Office establishment 32,661 employees who are in the classified service. This includes many who have been classified upon the suggestion of the Postmaster-General. He states that another year's experience at the head of the Department serves only to strengthen the conviction as to the excellent working of the civil-service law in this branch of the public service.

Attention is called to the report of the Secretary of the Navy, which shows very gratifying progress in the construction of ships for our new Navy. All the vessels now building, including the three torpedo boats authorized at the last session of Congress and excepting the first-class battle ship *Iowa*, will probably be completed during the coming fiscal year.

The estimates for the increase of the Navy for the year ending June 30, 1896, are large, but they include practically the entire sum necessary to complete and equip all the new ships not now in commission, so that unless new ships are authorized the appropriations for the naval service for the fiscal year ending June 30, 1897, should fall below the estimates for the coming year by at least $12,000,000.

The Secretary presents with much earnestness a plea for the authorization of three additional battle ships and ten or twelve torpedo boats. While the unarmored vessels heretofore authorized, including those now nearing completion, will constitute a fleet which it is believed is sufficient for ordinary cruising purposes in time of peace, we have now completed and in process of construction but four first-class battle ships and but few torpedo boats. If we are to have a navy for warlike operations, offensive and defensive, we certainly ought to increase both the number of battle ships and torpedo boats.

The manufacture of armor requires expensive plants and the aggregation of many skilled workmen. All the armor necessary to complete the vessels now building will be delivered before the 1st of June next. If no new contracts are given out, contractors must disband their workmen and their plants must lie idle. Battle ships authorized at this time would not be well under way until late in the coming fiscal year, and at least three years and a half from the date of the contract would be required for their completion. The Secretary states that not more than 15 per cent of the cost of such ships need be included in the appropriations for the coming year.

I recommend that provision be made for the construction of additional battle ships and torpedo boats.

The Secretary recommends the manufacture not only of a reserve supply of ordnance and ordnance material for ships of the Navy, but also a supply for the auxiliary fleet. Guns and their appurtenances should be provided and kept on hand for both these purposes. We have not to-day a single gun that could be put upon the ships *Paris* or *New York* of the International Navigation Company or any other ship of our reserve Navy.

The manufacture of guns at the Washington Navy-Yard is proceeding satisfactorily, and none of our new ships will be required to wait for their guns or ordnance equipment.

An important order has been issued by the Secretary of the Navy coordinating the duties of the several bureaus concerned in the construction of ships. This order, it is believed, will secure to a greater extent than has heretofore been possible the harmonious action of these several bureaus and make the attainment of the best results more certain.

During the past fiscal year there has been an unusual and pressing demand in many quarters of the world for the presence of vessels to guard American interests.

In January last, during the Brazilian insurrection, a large fleet was concentrated in the harbor of Rio de Janeiro. The vigorous action of Rear-Admiral Benham in protecting the personal and commercial rights of our citizens during the disturbed conditions afforded results which will, it is believed, have a far-reaching and wholesome influence whenever in like circumstances it may become necessary for our naval commanders to interfere on behalf of our people in foreign ports.

The war now in progress between China and Japan has rendered it necessary or expedient to dispatch eight vessels to those waters.

Both the Secretary of the Navy and the Secretary of the Treasury recommend the transfer of the work of the Coast Survey proper to the Navy Department. I heartily concur in this recommendation. Excluding Alaska and a very small area besides, all the work of mapping and charting our coasts has been completed. The hydrographic work, which must be done over and over again by reason of the shifting and varying depths of water consequent upon the action of streams and tides, has heretofore been done under the direction of naval officers in subordination to the Superintendent of the Coast Survey. There seems to be no good reason why the Navy should not have entire charge hereafter of such work, especially as the Hydrographic Office of the Navy Department is now and has been for many years engaged in making efficient maps entirely similar to those prepared by the Coast Survey.

I feel it my imperative duty to call attention to the recommendation of the Secretary in regard to the personnel of the line of the Navy. The stagnation of promotion in this the vital branch of the service is so great as to seriously impair its efficiency.

I consider it of the utmost importance that the young and middle-aged officers should before the eve of retirement be permitted to reach a grade entitling them to active and important duty.

The system adopted a few years ago regulating the employment of labor at the navy-yards is rigidly upheld and has fully demonstrated its usefulness and expediency. It is within the domain of civil-service reform inasmuch as workmen are employed through a board of labor selected at each navy-yard and are given work without reference to politics and in the order of their application, preference, however, being given to Army and Navy veterans and those having former navy-yard experience.

Amendments suggested by experience have been made to the rules regulating the system. Through its operation the work at our navy-yards has been vastly improved in efficiency and the opportunity to work has been honestly and fairly awarded to willing and competent applicants.

It is hoped that if this system continues to be strictly adhered to there will soon be as a natural consequence such an equalization of party benefit as will remove all temptation to relax or abandon it.

The report of the Secretary of the Interior exhibits the situation of the numerous and interesting branches of the public service connected with his Department. I commend this report and the valuable recommendations of the Secretary to the careful attention of the Congress.

The public land disposed of during the year amounted to 10,406,100.77 acres, including 28,876.05 of Indian lands.

It is estimated that the public domain still remaining amounts to a little more than 600,000,000 acres, including, however, about 360,000,000 acres in Alaska, as well as military reservations and railroad and other selections of lands yet unadjudicated.

The total cash receipts from sale of lands amounted to $2,674,285.79, including $91,981.03 received for Indian lands.

Thirty-five thousand patents were issued for agricultural lands, and 3,100 patents were issued to Indians on allotments of their holdings in severalty, the land so allotted being inalienable by the Indian allottees for a period of twenty-five years after patent.

There were certified and patented on account of railroad and wagon-road grants during the year 865,556.45 acres of land, and at the close of the year 29,000,000 acres were embraced in the lists of selections made by railroad and wagon-road companies and awaited settlement.

The selections of swamp lands and that taken as indemnity therefor since the passage of the act providing for the same in 1849 amount to nearly or quite 80,500,000 acres, of which 58,000,000 have been patented to States. About 138,000 acres were patented during the last year. Nearly 820,000 acres of school and education grants were approved during the year, and at its close 1,250,363.81 acres remained unadjusted.

It appears that the appropriation for the current year on account of special service for the protection of the public lands and the timber thereon is much less than those for previous years, and inadequate for an efficient performance of the work. A larger sum of money than has been appropriated during a number of years past on this account has been returned to the Government as a result of the labors of those employed in the particular service mentioned, and I hope it will not be crippled by insufficient appropriation.

I fully indorse the recommendation of the Secretary that adequate protection be provided for our forest reserves and that a comprehensive forestry system be inaugurated. Such keepers and superintendents as are necessary to protect the forests already reserved should be provided. I am of the opinion that there should be an abandonment of the policy sanctioned by present laws under which the Government, for a very small consideration, is rapidly losing title to immense tracts of land covered with timber, which should be properly reserved as permanent sources of timber supply.

The suggestion that a change be made in the manner of securing surveys of the public lands is especially worthy of consideration. I am satisfied that these surveys should be made by a corps of competent surveyors under the immediate control and direction of the Commissioner of the General Land Office.

An exceedingly important recommendation of the Secretary relates to the manner in which contests and litigated cases growing out of efforts to obtain Government land are determined. The entire testimony upon which these controversies depend in all their stages is taken before the local registers and receivers, and yet these officers have no power to subpoena witnesses or to enforce their attendance to testify. These cases, numbering three or four thousand annually, are sent by the local officers to the Commissioner of the General Land Office for his action. The exigencies of his other duties oblige him to act upon the decisions of the registers and receivers without an opportunity of thorough personal examination. Nearly 2,000 of these cases are appealed annually from the Commissioner to the Secretary of the Interior. Burdened with other important administrative duties, his determination of these appeals must be almost perfunctory and based upon the examination of others, though this determination of the Secretary operates as a final adjudication upon rights of very great importance.

I concur in the opinion that the Commissioner of the General Land Office should be relieved from the duty of deciding litigated land cases, that a nonpartisan court should be created to pass on such cases, and that the decisions of this court should be final, at least so far as the decisions of the Department are now final. The proposed court might be given authority to certify questions of law in matters of especial importance to the Supreme Court of the United States or the court of appeals for the District of Columbia for decision. The creation of such a tribunal would expedite the disposal of cases and insure decisions of a more satisfactory character. The registers and receivers who originally hear and decide these disputes should be invested with authority to compel witnesses to attend and testify before them.

Though the condition of the Indians shows a steady and healthy progress, their situation is not satisfactory at all points. Some of them to whom allotments of land have been made are found to be unable or disinclined to follow agricultural pursuits or to otherwise beneficially manage their land. This is especially true of the Cheyennes and Arapahoes, who, as it appears by reports of their agent, have in many instances never been located upon their allotments, and in some cases do not even know where their allotments are. Their condition has deteriorated. They are not self-supporting and they live in camps and spend their time in idleness.

I have always believed that allotments of reservation lands to Indians in severalty should be made sparingly, or at least slowly, and with the utmost caution. In these days, when white agriculturists and stock raisers of experience and intelligence find their lot a hard one, we ought not to expect Indians, unless far advanced in civilization and habits of industry, to support themselves on the small tracts of land usually allotted to them.

If the self-supporting scheme by allotment fails, the wretched pauperism of the allottees which results is worse than their original condition of regulated dependence. It is evident that the evil consequences of ill-advised allotment are intensified in cases where the false step can not be retraced on account of the purchase by the Government of reservation lands remaining after allotments are made and the disposition of such remaining lands to settlers or purchasers from the Government.

I am convinced that the proper solution of the Indian problem and the success of every step taken in that direction depend to a very large extent upon the intelligence and honesty of the reservation agents and the interest they have in their work. An agent fitted for his place can do much toward preparing the Indians under his charge for citizenship and allotment of their lands, and his advice as to any matter concerning their welfare will not mislead.   An unfit agent will make no effort to advance the Indians on his reservation toward civilization or preparation for allotment of lands in severalty, and his opinion as to their condition in this and other regards is heedless and valueless.

The indications are that the detail of army officers as Indian agents will result in improved management on the reservations.

Whenever allotments are made and any Indian on the reservation has previously settled upon a lot and cultivated it or shown a disposition to improve it in any way, such lot should certainly be allotted to him, and this should be made plainly obligatory by statute.

In the light of experience and considering the uncertainty of the Indian situation and its exigencies in the future, I am not only disposed to be very cautious in making allotments, but I incline to agree with the Secretary of the Interior in the opinion that when allotments are made the balance of reservation land remaining after allotment, instead of being bought by the Government from the Indians and opened for settlement with such scandals and unfair practices as seem unavoidable, should remain for a time at least as common land or be sold by the Government on behalf of the Indians in an orderly way and at fixed prices, to be determined by its location and desirability, and that the proceeds, less expenses, should be held in trust for the benefit of the Indian proprietors.

The intelligent Indian-school management of the past year has been followed by gratifying results.   Efforts have been made to advance the work in a sound and practical manner.   Five institutes of Indian teachers have been held during the year, and have proved very beneficial through the views exchanged and methods discussed particularly applicable to Indian education.

Efforts are being made in the direction of a gradual reduction of the number of Indian contract schools, so that in a comparatively short time they may give way altogether to Government schools, and it is hoped that the change may be so gradual as to be perfected without too great expense to the Government or undue disregard of investments made by those who have established and are maintaining such contract schools.

The appropriation for the current year, ending June 30, 1895, applicable to the ordinary expenses of the Indian service amounts to $6,733,-003.18, being less by $663,240.64 than the sum appropriated on the same account for the previous year.

At the close of the last fiscal year, on the 30th day of June, 1894, there were 969,544 persons on our pension rolls, being a net increase of 3,532 over the number reported at the end of the previous year.

These pensioners may be classified as follows: Soldiers and sailors survivors of all wars, 753,968; widows and relatives of deceased soldiers, 215,162; army nurses in the War of the Rebellion, 414.   Of these pensioners 32,039 are surviving soldiers of Indian and other wars prior to the late Civil War and the widows or relatives of such soldiers.

The remainder, numbering 937,505, are receiving pensions on account of the rebellion, and of these 469,344 are on the rolls under the authority of the act of June 27, 1890, sometimes called the dependent-pension law.

The total amount expended for pensions during the year was $139,-804,461.05, leaving an unexpended balance from the sum appropriated of $25,205,712.65.

The sum necessary to meet pension expenditures for the year ending June 30, 1896, is estimated at $140,000,000.

The Commissioner of Pensions is of the opinion that the year 1895, being the thirtieth after the close of the War of the Rebellion, must, according to all sensible human calculation, see the highest limit of the pension roll, and that after that year it must begin to decline.

The claims pending in the Bureau have decreased more than 90,000 during the year. A large proportion of the new claims filed are for increase of pension by those now on the rolls.

The number of certificates issued was 80,213.

The names dropped from the rolls for all causes during the year numbered 37,951.

Among our pensioners are 9 widows and 3 daughters of soldiers of the Revolution and 45 survivors of the War of 1812.

The barefaced and extensive pension frauds exposed under the direction of the courageous and generous veteran soldier now at the head of the Bureau leave no room for the claim that no purgation of our pension rolls was needed or that continued vigilance and prompt action are not necessary to the same end.

The accusation that an effort to detect pension frauds is evidence of unfriendliness toward our worthy veterans and a denial of their claims to the generosity of the Government suggests an unfortunate indifference to the commission of any offense which has for its motive the securing of a pension and indicates a willingness to be blind to the existence of mean and treacherous crimes which play upon demagogic fears and make sport of the patriotic impulse of a grateful people.

The completion of the Eleventh Census is now in charge of the Commissioner of Labor. The total disbursements on account of the work for the fiscal year ending June 30, 1894, amounted to $10,365,676.81. At the close of the year the number of persons employed in the Census Office was 679; at present there are about 400. The whole number of volumes necessary to comprehend the Eleventh Census will be 25, and they will contain 22,270 printed pages. The assurance is confidently made that before the close of the present calendar year the material still incomplete will be practically in hand, and the census can certainly be closed by the 4th of March, 1895. After that the revision and proof reading necessary to bring out the volumes will still be required.

The text of the census volumes has been limited as far as possible to the analysis of the statistics presented. This method, which is in accordance with law, has caused more or less friction and in some instances individual disappointment, for when the Commissioner of Labor took charge of the work he found much matter on hand which according to this rule he was compelled to discard. The census is being prepared according to the theory that it is designed to collect facts and certify them to the public not to elaborate arguments or to present personal views.

The Secretary of Agriculture in his report reviews the operations of his Department for the last fiscal year and makes recommendations for the further extension of its usefulness. He reports a saving in expenditures during the year of $600,000, which is covered back into the Treasury. This sum is 23 per cent of the entire appropriation.

A special study has been made of the demand for American farm products in all foreign markets, especially Great Britain. That country received from the United States during the nine months ending September 30, 1894, 305,910 live beef cattle, valued at $26,500,000, as against 182,-611 cattle, valued at $16,634,000, during the same period for 1893.

During the first six months of 1894 the United Kingdom took also 112,000,000 pounds of dressed beef from the United States, valued at nearly $10,000,000.

The report shows that during the nine months immediately preceding September 30, 1894, the United States exported to Great Britain 222,-676,000 pounds of pork; of apples, 1,900,000 bushels, valued at $2,500,-000, and of horses 2,811, at an average value of $139 per head. There was a falling off in American wheat exports of 13,500,000 bushels, and the Secretary is inclined to believe that wheat may not in the future be the staple export cereal product of our country, but that corn will continue to advance in importance as an export on account of the new uses to which it is constantly being appropriated.

The exports of agricultural products from the United States for the fiscal year ending June 30, 1894, amounted to $628,363,038, being 72.28 per cent of American exports of every description, and the United Kingdom of Great Britain took more than 54 per cent of all farm products finding foreign markets.

The Department of Agriculture has undertaken during the year two new and important lines of research. The first relates to grasses and forage plants, with the purpose of instructing and familiarizing the people as to the distinctive grasses of the United States and teaching them how to introduce valuable foreign forage plants which may be adapted to this country. The second relates to agricultural soils and crop production, involving the analyses of samples of soils from all sections of the American Union, to demonstrate their adaptability to particular plants and crops. Mechanical analyses of soils may be of such inestimable utility that it is foremost in the new lines of agricultural research, and the Secretary therefore recommends that a division having it in charge be permanently established in the Department.

The amount appropriated for the Weather Bureau was $951,100. Of that sum $138,500, or 14 per cent, has been saved and is returned to the Treasury.

As illustrating the usefulness of this service it may be here stated that the warnings which were very generally given of two tropical storms occurring in September and October of the present year resulted in detaining safely in port 2,305 vessels, valued at $36,283,913, laden with cargoes of probably still greater value. What is much more important and gratifying, many human lives on these ships were also undoubtedly saved.

The appropriation to the Bureau of Animal Industry was $850,000, and the expenditures for the year were only $495,429.24, thus leaving unexpended $354,570.76. The inspection of beef animals for export and interstate trade has been continued, and 12,944,056 head were inspected during the year, at a cost of 1¾ cents per head, against 4¾ cents for 1893. The amount of pork microscopically examined was 35,437,937 pounds, against 20,677,410 pounds in the preceding year. The cost of this inspection has been diminished from 8¾ cents per head in 1893 to 6½ cents in 1894.

The expense of inspecting the pork sold in 1894 to Germany and France by the United States was $88,922.10. The quantity inspected was greater by 15,000,000 pounds than during the preceding year, when the cost of such inspection was $172,367.08. The Secretary of Agriculture recommends that the law providing for the microscopic inspection of export and interstate meat be so amended as to compel owners of the meat inspected to pay the cost of such inspection, and I call attention to the arguments presented in his report in support of this recommendation.

The live beef cattle exported and tagged during the year numbered 353,535. This is an increase of 69,533 head over the previous year.

The sanitary inspection of cattle shipped to Europe has cost an average of 10¾ cents for each animal, and the cost of inspecting Southern cattle and the disinfection of cars and stock yards averages 2.7 cents per animal.

The scientific inquiries of the Bureau of Animal Industry have progressed steadily during the year. Much tuberculin and mallein have been furnished to State authorities for use in the agricultural colleges and experiment stations for the treatment of tuberculosis and glanders.

Quite recently this Department has published the results of its investigations of bovine tuberculosis, and its researches will be vigorously continued. Certain herds in the District of Columbia will be thoroughly inspected and will probably supply adequate scope for the Department to intelligently prosecute its scientific work and furnish sufficient material for purposes of illustration, description, and definition.

The sterilization of milk suspected of containing the bacilli of tuberculosis has been during the year very thoroughly explained in a leaflet by

Dr. D. E. Salmon, the Chief of the Bureau, and given general circulation throughout the country.

The Office of Experiment Stations, which is a part of the United States Department of Agriculture, has during the past year engaged itself almost wholly in preparing for publication works based upon the reports of agricultural experiment stations and other institutions for agricultural inquiry in the United States and foreign countries.

The Secretary in his report for 1893 called attention to the fact that the appropriations made for the support of the experiment stations throughout the Union were the only moneys taken out of the National Treasury by act of Congress for which no accounting to Federal authorities was required. Responding to this suggestion, the Fifty-third Congress, in making the appropriation for the Department for the present fiscal year, provided that—

The Secretary of Agriculture shall prescribe the form of annual financial state· ment required by section 3 of said act of March 2, 1887; shall ascertain whether the expenditures under the appropriation hereby made are in accordance with the provisions of said act, and shall make report thereon to Congress.

In obedience to this law the Department of Agriculture immediately sent out blank forms of expense accounts to each station, and proposes in addition to make, through trusted experts, systematic examination of the several stations during each year for the purpose of acquiring by personal investigation the detailed information necessary to enable the Secretary of Agriculture to make, as the statute provides, a satisfactory report to Congress. The boards of management of the several stations with great alacrity and cordiality have approved the amendment to the law providing this supervision of their expenditures, anticipating that it will increase the efficiency of the stations and protect their directors and managers from loose charges concerning their use of public funds, besides bringing the Department of Agriculture into closer and more confidential relations with the experimental stations, and through their joint service largely increasing their usefulness to the agriculture of the country.

Acting upon a recommendation contained in the report of 1893, Congress appropriated $10,000 "to enable the Secretary of Agriculture to investigate and report upon the nutritive value of the various articles and commodities used for human food, with special suggestions of full, wholesome, and edible rations less wasteful and more economical than those in common use."

Under this appropriation the Department has prepared and now has nearly ready for distribution an elementary discussion of the nutritive value and pecuniary economy of food. When we consider that fully one-half of all the money earned by the wage earners of the civilized world is expended by them for food, the importance and utility of such an investigation is apparent.

The Department expended in the fiscal year 1893 $2,354,809.56, and out of that sum the total amount expended in scientific research was 45.6 per cent. But in the year ending June 30, 1894, out of a total expenditure of $1,948,988.38, the Department applied 51.8 per cent of that sum to scientific work and investigation. It is therefore very plainly observable that the economies which have been practiced in the administration of the Department have not been at the expense of scientific research.

The recommendation contained in the report of the Secretary for 1893 that the vicious system of promiscuous free distribution of its departmental documents be abandoned is again urged. These publications may well be furnished without cost to public libraries, educational institutions, and the officers and libraries of States and of the Federal Government; but from all individuals applying for them a price covering the cost of the document asked for should be required. Thus the publications and documents would be secured by those who really desire them for proper purposes. Half a million of copies of the report of the Secretary of Agriculture are printed for distribution, at an annual cost of about $300,000. Large numbers of them are cumbering storerooms at the Capitol and the shelves of secondhand-book stores throughout the country. All this labor and waste might be avoided if the recommendations of the Secretary were adopted.

The Secretary also again recommends that the gratuitous distribution of seeds cease and that no money be appropriated for that purpose except to experiment stations. He reiterates the reasons given in his report for 1893 for discontinuing this unjustifiable gratuity, and I fully concur in the conclusions which he has reached.

The best service of the statistician of the Department of Agriculture is the ascertainment, by diligence and care, of the actual and real conditions, favorable or unfavorable, of the farmers and farms of the country, and to seek the causes which produce these conditions, to the end that the facts ascertained may guide their intelligent treatment.

A further important utility in agricultural statistics is found in their elucidation of the relation of the supply of farm products to the demand for them in the markets of the United States and of the world.

It is deemed possible that an agricultural census may be taken each year through the agents of the statistical division of the Department. Such a course is commended for trial by the chief of that division. Its scope would be:

(1) The area under each of the more important crops.

(2) The aggregate products of each of such crops.

(3) The quantity of wheat and corn in the hands of farmers at a date after the spring sowings and plantings and before the beginning of harvest, and also the quantity of cotton and tobacco remaining in the hands of planters, either at the same date or at some other designated time.

The cost of the work is estimated at $500,000.

Owing to the peculiar quality of the statistician's work and the natural and acquired fitness necessary to its successful prosecution, the Secretary of Agriculture expresses the opinion that every person employed in gathering statistics under the chief of that division should be admitted to that service only after a thorough, exhaustive, and successful examination at the hands of the United States Civil Service Commission. This has led him to call for such examination of candidates for the position of assistant statisticians, and also of candidates for chiefs of sections in that division.

The work done by the Department of Agriculture is very superficially dealt with in this communication, and I commend the report of the Secretary and the very important interests with which it deals to the careful attention of the Congress.

The advantages to the public service of an adherence to the principles of civil-service reform are constantly more apparent, and nothing is so encouraging to those in official life who honestly desire good government as the increasing appreciation by our people of these advantages. A vast majority of the voters of the land are ready to insist that the time and attention of those they select to perform for them important public duties should not be distracted by doling out minor offices, and they are growing to be unanimous in regarding party organization as something that should be used in establishing party principles instead of dictating the distribution of public places as rewards of partisan activity.

Numerous additional offices and places have lately been brought within civil-service rules and regulations, and some others will probably soon be included.

The report of the Commissioners will be submitted to the Congress, and I invite careful attention to the recommendations it contains.

I am entirely convinced that we ought not to be longer without a national board of health or national health officer charged with no other duties than such as pertain to the protection of our country from the invasion of pestilence and disease. This would involve the establishment by such board or officer of proper quarantine precautions, or the necessary aid and counsel to local authorities on the subject; prompt advice and assistance to local boards of health or health officers in the suppression of contagious disease, and in cases where there are no such local boards or officers the immediate direction by the national board or officer of measures of suppression; constant and authentic information concerning the health of foreign countries and all parts of our own country as related to contagious diseases, and consideration of regulations to be enforced in foreign ports to prevent the introduction of contagion into our cities and the measures which should be adopted to secure their enforcement.

There seems to be at this time a decided inclination to discuss measures of protection against contagious diseases in international conference, with a view of adopting means of mutual assistance. The creation of such a national health establishment would greatly aid our standing in such conferences and improve our opportunities to avail ourselves of their benefits.

I earnestly recommend the inauguration of a national board of health or similar national instrumentality, believing the same to be a needed precaution against contagious disease and in the interest of the safety and health of our people.

By virtue of a statute of the United States passed in 1888 I appointed in July last Hon. John D. Kernan, of the State of New York, and Hon. Nicholas E. Worthington, of the State of Illinois, to form, with Hon. Carroll D. Wright, Commissioner of Labor, who was designated by said statute, a commission for the purpose of making careful inquiry into the causes of the controversies between certain railroads and their employees which had resulted in an extensive and destructive strike, accompanied by much violence and dangerous disturbance, with considerable loss of life and great destruction of property.

The report of the commissioners has been submitted to me and will be transmitted to the Congress with the evidence taken upon their investigation.

Their work has been well done, and their standing and intelligence give assurance that the report and suggestions they make are worthy of careful consideration.

The tariff act passed at the last session of the Congress needs important amendments if it is to be executed effectively and with certainty. In addition to such necessary amendments as will not change rates of duty, I am still very decidedly in favor of putting coal and iron upon the free list.

So far as the sugar schedule is concerned, I would be glad, under existing aggravations, to see every particle of differential duty in favor of refined sugar stricken out of our tariff law. If with all the favor now accorded the sugar-refining interest in our tariff laws it still languishes to the extent of closed refineries and thousands of discharged workmen, it would seem to present a hopeless case for reasonable legislative aid. Whatever else is done or omitted, I earnestly repeat here the recommendation I have made in another portion of this communication, that the additional duty of one-tenth of a cent per pound laid upon sugar imported from countries paying a bounty on its export be abrogated. It seems to me that exceedingly important considerations point to the propriety of this amendment.

With the advent of a new tariff policy not only calculated to relieve the consumers of our land in the cost of their daily life, but to invite a better development of American thrift and create for us closer and more profitable commercial relations with the rest of the world, it follows as a logical and imperative necessity that we should at once remove the chief if not the only obstacle which has so long prevented our participation in the foreign carrying trade of the sea. A tariff built upon the theory that it is well to check imports and that a home market should bound the industry and effort of American producers was fitly supplemented by a refusal to allow American registry to vessels built abroad, though owned and navigated by our people, thus exhibiting a willingness to abandon all contest for the advantages of American transoceanic carriage. Our new tariff policy, built upon the theory that it is well to encourage such importations as our people need, and that our products and manufactures should find markets in every part of the habitable globe, is consistently supplemented by the greatest possible liberty to our citizens in the ownership and navigation of ships in which our products and manufactures may be transported. The millions now paid to foreigners for carrying American passengers and products across the sea should be turned into American hands. Shipbuilding, which has been protected to strangulation, should be revived by the prospect of profitable employment for ships when built, and the American sailor should be resurrected and again take his place—a sturdy and industrious citizen in time of peace and a patriotic and safe defender of American interests in the day of conflict.

The ancient provision of our law denying American registry to ships built abroad and owned by Americans appears in the light of present conditions not only to be a failure for good at every point, but to be nearer a relic of barbarism than anything that exists under the permission of a statute of the United States. I earnestly recommend its prompt repeal.

During the last month the gold reserved in the Treasury for the purpose of redeeming the notes of the Government circulating as money in the hands of the people became so reduced and its further depletion in the near future seemed so certain that in the exercise of proper care for the public welfare it became necessary to replenish this reserve and thus maintain popular faith in the ability and determination of the Government to meet as agreed its pecuniary obligations.

It would have been well if in this emergency authority had existed to issue the bonds of the Government bearing a low rate of interest and maturing within a short period; but the Congress having failed to confer such authority, resort was necessarily had to the resumption act of 1875, and pursuant to its provisions bonds were issued drawing interest at the rate of 5 per cent per annum and maturing ten years after their issue, that being the shortest time authorized by the act. I am glad to say, however, that on the sale of these bonds the premium received operated to reduce the rate of interest to be paid by the Government to less than 3 per cent.

Nothing could be worse or further removed from sensible finance than the relations existing between the currency the Government has issued, the gold held for its redemption, and the means which must be resorted to for the purpose of replenishing such redemption fund when impaired. Even if the claims upon this fund were confined to the obligations originally intended and if the redemption of these obligations meant their cancellation, the fund would be very small. But these obligations when received and redeemed in gold are not canceled, but are reissued and may do duty many times by way of drawing gold from the Treasury. Thus we have an endless chain in operation constantly depleting the Treasury's gold and never near a final rest. As if this was not bad enough, we have, by a statutory declaration that it is the policy of the Government to maintain the parity between gold and silver, aided the force and momentum of this exhausting process and added largely to the currency obligations claiming this peculiar gold redemption. Our small gold reserve is thus subject to drain from every side. The demands that increase our danger also increase the necessity of protecting this reserve against depletion, and it is most unsatisfactory to know that the protection afforded is only a temporary palliation.

It is perfectly and palpably plain that the only way under present conditions by which this reserve when dangerously depleted can be replenished is through the issue and sale of the bonds of the Government for gold, and yet Congress has not only thus far declined to authorize the issue of bonds best suited to such a purpose, but there seems a disposition in some quarters to deny both the necessity and power for the issue of bonds at all.

I can not for a moment believe that any of our citizens are deliberately willing that their Government should default in its pecuniary obligations or that its financial operations should be reduced to a silver basis. At any rate, I should not feel that my duty was done if I omitted any effort I could make to avert such a calamity. As long, therefore, as no provision is made for the final redemption or the putting aside of the currency obligation now used to repeatedly and constantly draw from the Government its gold, and as long as no better authority for bond issues is allowed than at present exists, such authority will be utilized whenever and as often as it becomes necessary to maintain a sufficient gold reserve, and in abundant time to save the credit of our country and make good the financial declarations of our Government.

Questions relating to our banks and currency are closely connected with the subject just referred to, and they also present some unsatisfactory features. Prominent among them are the lack of elasticity in our currency circulation and its frequent concentration in financial centers when it is most needed in other parts of the country.

The absolute divorcement of the Government from the business of banking is the ideal relationship of the Government to the circulation of the currency of the country.

This condition can not be immediately reached, but as a step in that direction and as a means of securing a more elastic currency and obviating other objections to the present arrangement of bank circulation the Secretary of the Treasury presents in his report a scheme modifying present banking laws and providing for the issue of circulating notes by State banks free from taxation under certain limitations.

The Secretary explains his plan so plainly and its advantages are developed by him with such remarkable clearness that any effort on my part to present argument in its support would be superfluous. I shall therefore content myself with an unqualified indorsement of the Secretary's proposed changes in the law and a brief and imperfect statement of their prominent features.

It is proposed to repeal all laws providing for the deposit of United States bonds as security for circulation; to permit national banks to issue circulating notes not exceeding in amount 75 per cent of their paid-up and unimpaired capital, provided they deposit with the Government as a guaranty fund, in United States legal-tender notes, including Treasury notes of 1890, a sum equal in amount to 30 per cent of the notes they desire to issue, this deposit to be maintained at all times, but whenever any bank retires any part of its circulation a proportional part of its guaranty fund shall be returned to it; to permit the Secretary of the Treasury to prepare and keep on hand ready for issue in case an increase in circulation is desired blank national-bank notes for each bank having circulation and to repeal the provisions of the present law imposing limitations and restrictions upon banks desiring to reduce or increase their circulation, thus permitting such increase or reduction within the limit of 75 per cent of capital to be quickly made as emergencies arise.

In addition to the guaranty fund required, it is proposed to provide a safety fund for the immediate redemption of the circulating notes of failed banks by imposing a small annual tax, say one-half of 1 per cent, upon the average circulation of each bank until the fund amounts to 5 per cent of the total circulation outstanding. When a bank fails its guaranty fund is to be paid into this safety fund and its notes are to be redeemed in the first instance from such safety fund thus augmented, any impairment of such fund caused thereby to be made good from the immediately available cash assets of said bank, and if these should be insufficient such impairment to be made good by *pro rata* assessment among the other banks, their contributions constituting a first lien upon the assets of the failed bank in favor of the contributing banks. As a further security it is contemplated that the existing provision fixing the individual liability of stockholders is to be retained and the bank's indebtedness on account of its circulating notes is to be made a first lien on all its assets.

For the purpose of meeting the expense of printing notes, official supervision, cancellation, and other like charges there shall be imposed a tax of say one-half of 1 per cent per annum upon the average amount of notes in circulation.

It is further provided that there shall be no national-bank notes issued of a less denomination than $10; that each national bank, except in case of a failed bank, shall redeem or retire its notes in the first instance at its own office or at agencies to be designated by it. and that no fixed reserve need be maintained on account of deposits.

Another very important feature of this plan is the exemption of State banks from taxation by the United States in cases where it is shown to the satisfaction of the Secretary of the Treasury and Comptroller of the Currency by banks claiming such exemption that they have not had outstanding their circulating notes exceeding 75 per cent of their paid-up and unimpaired capital; that their stockholders are individually liable for the redemption of their circulating notes to the full extent of their ownership of stock; that the liability of said banks upon their circulating notes constitutes under their State law a first lien upon their assets; that such banks have kept and maintained a guaranty fund in United States legal-tender notes, including Treasury notes of 1890, equal to 30 per cent of their outstanding circulating notes, and that such banks have promptly redeemed their circulating notes when presented at their principal or branch offices.

It is quite likely that this scheme may be usefully amended in some of its details, but I am satisfied it furnishes a basis for a very great improvement in our present banking and currency system.

I conclude this communication fully appreciating that the responsibility for all legislation affecting the people of the United States rests upon their representatives in the Congress, and assuring them that, whether in accordance with recommendations I have made or not, I shall be glad to cooperate in perfecting any legislation that tends to the prosperity and welfare of our country.

THIRD ANNUAL MESSAGE.

EXECUTIVE MANSION, *December 2, 1895.*

To the Congress of the United States:

The present assemblage of the legislative branch of our Government occurs at a time when the interests of our people and the needs of the country give especial prominence to the condition of our foreign relations and the exigencies of our national finances. The reports of the heads of the several administrative Departments of the Government fully and plainly exhibit what has been accomplished within the scope of their respective duties and present such recommendations for the betterment of our country's condition as patriotic and intelligent labor and observation suggest.

I therefore deem my executive duty adequately performed at this time by presenting to the Congress the important phases of our situation as related to our intercourse with foreign nations and a statement of the financial problems which confront us, omitting, except as they are related to these topics, any reference to departmental operations.

I earnestly invite, however, not only the careful consideration but the severely critical scrutiny of the Congress and my fellow-countrymen to the reports concerning these departmental operations. If justly and fairly examined, they will furnish proof of assiduous and painstaking care for the public welfare. I press the recommendations they contain upon the respectful attention of those charged with the duty of legislation, because I believe their adoption would promote the people's good.

By amendatory tariff legislation in January last the Argentine Republic, recognizing the value of the large market opened to the free importation of its wools under our last tariff act, has admitted certain products of the United States to entry at reduced duties. It is pleasing to note that the efforts we have made to enlarge the exchanges of trade on a sound basis of mutual benefit are in this instance appreciated by the country from which our woolen factories draw their needful supply of raw material.

The Missions boundary dispute between the Argentine Republic and Brazil, referred to the President of the United States as arbitrator during the term of my predecessor, and which was submitted to me for determination, resulted in an award in favor of Brazil upon the historical and documentary evidence presented, thus ending a long-protracted controversy and again demonstrating the wisdom and desirability of settling international boundary disputes by recourse to friendly arbitration.

Negotiations are progressing for a revival of the United States and Chilean Claims Commission, whose work was abruptly terminated last year by the expiration of the stipulated time within which awards could be made.

The resumption of specie payments by Chile is a step of great interest and importance both in its direct consequences upon her own welfare and as evincing the ascendency of sound financial principles in one of the most influential of the South American Republics.

The close of the momentous struggle between China and Japan, while relieving the diplomatic agents of this Government from the delicate duty they undertook at the request of both countries of rendering such service to the subjects of either belligerent within the territorial limits of the other as our neutral position permitted, developed a domestic condition in the Chinese Empire which has caused much anxiety and called for prompt and careful attention. Either as a result of a weak control by the central Government over the provincial administrations, following a diminution of traditional governmental authority under the stress of an overwhelming national disaster, or as a manifestation upon good opportunity of the aversion of the Chinese population to all foreign ways and undertakings, there have occurred in widely separated provinces of China serious outbreaks of the old fanatical spirit against foreigners, which, unchecked by the local authorities, if not actually connived at by them, have culminated in mob attacks on foreign missionary stations, causing much destruction of property and attended with personal injuries as well as loss of life.

Although but one American citizen was reported to have been actu-ally wounded, and although the destruction of property may have fallen more heavily upon the missionaries of other nationalities than our own, it plainly behooved this Government to take the most prompt and decided action to guard against similar or perhaps more dreadful calamities befalling the hundreds of American mission stations which have grown up throughout the interior of China under the temperate rule of toleration, custom, and imperial edict. The demands of the United States and other powers for the degradation and punishment of the responsible officials of the respective cities and provinces who by neglect or otherwise had permitted uprisings, and for the adoption of stern measures by the Emperor's Government for the protection of the life and property of foreigners, were followed by the disgrace and dismissal of certain provincial officials found derelict in duty and the punishment by death of a number of those adjudged guilty of actual participation in the outrages.

This Government also insisted that a special American commission should visit the province where the first disturbances occurred for the purpose of investigation. The latter commission, formed after much opposition, has gone overland from Tientsin, accompanied by a suitable Chinese escort, and by its demonstration of the readiness and ability of our Government to protect its citizens will act, it is believed, as a most influential deterrent of any similar outbreaks.

The energetic steps we have thus taken are all the more likely to result in future safety to our citizens in China because the Imperial Government is, I am persuaded, entirely convinced that we desire only the liberty and protection of our own citizens and redress for any wrongs they may have suffered, and that we have no ulterior designs or objects, political or otherwise. China will not forget either our kindly service to her citizens during her late war nor the further fact that, while furnishing all the facilities at our command to further the negotiation of a peace between her and Japan, we sought no advantages and interposed no counsel.

The Governments of both China and Japan have, in special dispatches transmitted through their respective diplomatic representatives, expressed in a most pleasing manner their grateful appreciation of our assistance to their citizens during the unhappy struggle and of the value of our aid in paving the way to their resumption of peaceful relations.

The customary cordial relations between this country and France have been undisturbed, with the exception that a full explanation of the treatment of John L. Waller by the expeditionary military authorities of France still remains to be given. Mr. Waller, formerly United States consul at Tamatav, remained in Madagascar after his term of office expired, and was apparently successful in procuring business concessions from the Hovas of greater or less value. After the occupation of Tamatav and the declaration of martial law by the French he was arrested upon various charges, among them that of communicating military information to the enemies of France, was tried and convicted by a military tribunal, and sentenced to twenty years' imprisonment.

Following the course justified by abundant precedents, this Government requested from that of France the record of the proceedings of the French tribunal which resulted in Mr. Waller's condemnation. This request has been complied with to the extent of supplying a copy of the official record, from which appear the constitution and organization of the court, the charges as formulated, and the general course and result of the trial, and by which it is shown that the accused was tried in open court and was defended by counsel; but the evidence adduced in support of the charges, which was not received by the French minister for foreign affairs till the first week in October, has thus far been withheld, the French Government taking the ground that its production in response to our demand would establish a bad precedent. The efforts of our ambassador to procure it, however, though impeded by recent changes in the French ministry, have not been relaxed, and it is confidently expected that some satisfactory solution of the matter will shortly be reached. Meanwhile it appears that Mr. Waller's confinement has every alleviation which the state of his health and all the other circumstances of the case demand or permit.

In agreeable contrast to the difference above noted respecting a matter of common concern, where nothing is sought except such a mutually satisfactory outcome as the true merits of the case require, is the recent resolution of the French Chambers favoring the conclusion of a permanent treaty of arbitration between the two countries.

An invitation has been extended by France to the Government and people of the United States to participate in a great international exposition at Paris in 1900 as a suitable commemoration of the close of this the world's marvelous century of progress. I heartily recommend its acceptance, together with such legislation as will adequately provide for a due representation of this Government and its people on the occasion.

Our relations with the States of the German Empire are in some aspects typical of a condition of things elsewhere found in countries whose productions and trade are similar to our own. The close rivalries of competing industries; the influence of the delusive doctrine that the internal development of a nation is promoted and its wealth increased by a policy which, in undertaking to reserve its home markets for the exclusive use of its own producers, necessarily obstructs their sales in foreign markets and prevents free access to the products of the world; the desire to retain trade in time-worn ruts, regardless of the inexorable laws of new needs and changed conditions of demand and supply, and our own halting tardiness in inviting a freer exchange of commodities, and by this means imperiling our footing in the external markets naturally open to us, have created a situation somewhat injurious to American export interests, not only in Germany, where they are perhaps most noticeable, but in adjacent countries. The exports affected are largely American cattle and other food products, the reason assigned for unfavorable discrimination being that their consumption is deleterious to the public health. This is all the more irritating in view of the fact that no European state is as jealous of the excellence and wholesomeness of its exported food supplies as the United States, nor so easily able, on account of inherent soundness, to guarantee those qualities.

Nor are these difficulties confined to our food products designed for exportation. Our great insurance companies, for example, having built up a vast business abroad and invested a large share of their gains in foreign countries in compliance with the local laws and regulations then existing, now find themselves within a narrowing circle of onerous and unforeseen conditions, and are confronted by the necessity of retirement from a field thus made unprofitable, if, indeed, they are not summarily expelled, as some of them have lately been from Prussia.

It is not to be forgotten that international trade can not be one-sided. Its currents are alternating, and its movements should be honestly reciprocal. Without this it almost necessarily degenerates into a device to gain advantage or a contrivance to secure benefits with only the semblance of a return. In our dealings with other nations we ought to be open-handed and scrupulously fair. This should be our policy as a producing nation, and it plainly becomes us as a people who love generosity and the moral aspects of national good faith and reciprocal forbearance.

These considerations should not, however, constrain us to submit to unfair discrimination nor to silently acquiesce in vexatious hindrances to the enjoyment of our share of the legitimate advantages of proper trade relations If an examination of the situation suggests such measures on our part as would involve restrictions similar to those from which we suffer, the way to such a course is easy. It should, however, by no means be lightly entered upon, since the necessity for the inauguration of such a policy would be regretted by the best sentiment of our people and because it naturally and logically might lead to consequences of the gravest character.

I take pleasure in calling to your attention the encomiums bestowed on those vessels of our new Navy which took part in the notable ceremony of the opening of the Kiel Canal. It was fitting that this extraordinary achievement of the newer German nationality should be celebrated in the presence of America's exposition of the latest developments of the world's naval energy.

Our relations with Great Britain, always intimate and important, have demanded during the past year even a greater share of consideration than is usual.

Several vexatious questions were left undetermined by the decision of the Bering Sea Arbitration Tribunal. The application of the principles laid down by that august body has not been followed by the results they were intended to accomplish, either because the principles themselves lacked in breadth and definiteness or because their execution has been more or less imperfect. Much correspondence has been exchanged between the two Governments on the subject of preventing the exterminating slaughter of seals. The insufficiency of the British patrol of Bering Sea under the regulations agreed on by the two Governments has been pointed out, and yet only two British ships have been on police duty during this season in those waters.

The need of a more effective enforcement of existing regulations as well as the adoption of such additional regulations as experience has shown to be absolutely necessary to carry out the intent of the award have been earnestly urged upon the British Government, but thus far without effective results. In the meantime the depletion of the seal herds by means of pelagic hunting has so alarmingly progressed that unless their slaughter is at once effectively checked their extinction within a few years seems to be a matter of absolute certainty.

The understanding by which the United States was to pay and Great Britain to receive a lump sum of $425,000 in full settlement of all British claims for damages arising from our seizure of British sealing vessels unauthorized under the award of the Paris Tribunal of Arbitration was not confirmed by the last Congress, which declined to make the necessary appropriation. I am still of the opinion that this arrangement was a judicious and advantageous one for the Government, and I earnestly recommend that it be again considered and sanctioned. If, however, this does not meet with the favor of Congress, it certainly will hardly dissent from the proposition that the Government is bound by every consideration of honor and good faith to provide for the speedy adjustment of these claims by arbitration as the only other alternative. A treaty of arbitration has therefore been agreed upon, and will be immediately laid before the Senate, so that in one of the modes suggested a final settlement may be reached.

Notwithstanding that Great Britain originated the proposal to enforce international rules for the prevention of collisions at sea, based on the recommendations of the Maritime Conference of Washington, and concurred in, suggesting March 11, 1895, as the date to be set by proclamation for carrying these rules into general effect, Her Majesty's Government, having encountered opposition on the part of British shipping interests, announced its inability to accept that date, which was consequently canceled. The entire matter is still in abeyance, without prospect of a better condition in the near future.

The commissioners appointed to mark the international boundary in Passamaquoddy Bay according to the description of the treaty of Ghent have not yet fully agreed.

The completion of the preliminary survey of that Alaskan boundary which follows the contour of the coast from the southernmost point of Prince of Wales Island until it strikes the one hundred and forty-first meridian at or near the summit of Mount St. Elias awaits further necessary appropriation, which is urgently recommended. This survey was undertaken under the provisions of the convention entered into by this country and Great Britain July 22, 1892, and the supplementary convention of February 3, 1894.

As to the remaining section of the Alaskan boundary, which follows the one hundred and forty-first meridian northwardly from Mount St. Elias to the Frozen Ocean, the settlement of which involves the physical location of the meridian mentioned, no conventional agreement has yet been made. The ascertainment of a given meridian at a particular point is a work requiring much time and careful observations and surveys. Such observations and surveys were undertaken by the United States Coast and Geodetic Survey in 1890 and 1891, while similar work in the same quarters, under British auspices, is believed to give nearly coincident results; but these surveys have been independently conducted, and no international agreement to mark those or any other parts of the one hundred and forty-first meridian by permanent monuments has yet been made. In the meantime the valley of the Yukon is becoming a highway through the hitherto unexplored wilds of Alaska, and abundant mineral wealth has been discovered in that region, especially at or near the junction of the boundary meridian with the Yukon and its tributaries. In these circumstances it is expedient, and, indeed, imperative, that the jurisdictional limits of the respective Governments in this new region be speedily determined. Her Britannic Majesty's Government has proposed a joint delimitation of the one hundred and forty-first meridian by an international commission of experts, which, if Congress will authorize it and make due provision therefor, can be accomplished with no unreasonable delay. It is impossible to overlook the vital importance of continuing the work already entered upon and supplementing it by further effective measures looking to the exact location of this entire boundary line.

I call attention to the unsatisfactory delimitation of the respective jurisdictions of the United States and the Dominion of Canada in the Great Lakes at the approaches to the narrow waters that connect them. The waters in question are frequented by fishermen of both nationalities and their nets are there used. Owing to the uncertainty and ignorance as to the true boundary, vexatious disputes and injurious seizures of boats and nets by Canadian cruisers often occur, while any positive settlement thereof by an accepted standard is not easily to be reached. A joint commission to determine the line in those quarters on a practical basis, by measured courses following range marks on shore, is a necessity for which immediate provision should be made.

It being apparent that the boundary dispute between Great Britain and the Republic of Venezuela concerning the limits of British Guiana was approaching an acute stage, a definite statement of the interest and policy of the United States as regards the controversy seemed to be required both on its own account and in view of its relations with the friendly powers directly concerned. In July last, therefore, a dispatch was addressed to our ambassador at London for communication to the British Government in which the attitude of the United States was fully and distinctly set forth. The general conclusions therein reached and formulated are in substance that the traditional and established policy of this Government is firmly opposed to a forcible increase by any European power of its territorial possessions on this continent; that this policy is as well founded in principle as it is strongly supported by numerous precedents; that as a consequence the United States is bound to protest against the enlargement of the area of British Guiana in derogation of the rights and against the will of Venezuela; that considering the disparity in strength of Great Britain and Venezuela the territorial dispute between them can be reasonably settled only by friendly and impartial arbitration, and that the resort to such arbitration should include the whole controversy, and is not satisfied if one of the powers concerned is permitted to draw an arbitrary line through the territory in debate and to declare that it will submit to arbitration only the portion lying on one side of it. In view of these conclusions, the dispatch in question called upon the British Government for a definite answer to the question whether it would or would not submit the territorial controversy between itself and Venezuela in its entirety to impartial arbitration. The answer of the British Government has not yet been received, but is expected shortly, when further communication on the subject will probably be made to the Congress.

Early in January last an uprising against the Government of Hawaii was promptly suppressed. Martial law was forthwith proclaimed and numerous arrests were made of persons suspected of being in sympathy with the Royalist party. Among these were several citizens of the United States, who were either convicted by a military court and sentenced to death, imprisonment, or fine or were deported without trial. The United States, while denying protection to such as had taken the Hawaiian oath of allegiance, insisted that martial law, though altering the forms of justice, could not supersede justice itself, and demanded stay of execution until the proceedings had been submitted to this Government and knowledge obtained therefrom that our citizens had received fair trial. The death sentences were subsequently commuted or were remitted on condition of leaving the islands. The cases of certain Americans arrested and expelled by arbitrary order without formal charge or trial have had attention, and in some instances have been found to justify remonstrance and a claim for indemnity, which Hawaii has not thus far conceded.

Mr. Thurston, the Hawaiian minister, having furnished this Government abundant reason for asking that he be recalled, that course was pursued, and his successor has lately been received.

The deplorable lynching of several Italian laborers in Colorado was naturally followed by international representations, and I am happy to say that the best efforts of the State in which the outrages occurred have been put forth to discover and punish the authors of this atrocious crime. The dependent families of some of the unfortunate victims invite by their deplorable condition gracious provision for their needs.

These manifestations against helpless aliens may be traced through successive stages to the vicious *padroni* system, which, unchecked by our immigration and contract-labor statutes, controls these workers from the moment of landing on our shores and farms them out in distant and often rude regions, where their cheapening competition in the fields of bread-winning toil brings them into collision with other labor interests. While welcoming, as we should, those who seek our shores to merge themselves in our body politic and win personal competence by honest effort, we can not regard such assemblages of distinctively alien laborers, hired out in the mass to the profit of alien speculators and shipped hither and thither as the prospect of gain may dictate, as otherwise than repugnant to the spirit of our civilization, deterrent to individual advancement, and hindrances to the building up of stable communities resting upon the wholesome ambitions of the citizen and constituting the prime factor in the prosperity and progress of our nation.   If legislation can reach this growing evil, it certainly should be attempted.

Japan has furnished abundant evidence of her vast gain in every trait and characteristic that constitutes a nation's greatness.   We have reason for congratulation in the fact that the Government of the United States, by the exchange of liberal treaty stipulations with the new Japan, was the first to recognize her wonderful advance and to extend to her the consideration and confidence due to her national enlightenment and progressive character.

The boundary dispute which lately threatened to embroil Guatemala and Mexico has happily yielded to pacific counsels, and its determination has, by the joint agreement of the parties, been submitted to the sole arbitration of the United States minister to Mexico.

The commission appointed under the convention of February 18, 1889, to set new monuments along the boundary between the United States and Mexico has completed its task.

As a sequel to the failure of a scheme for the colonization in Mexico of negroes, mostly immigrants from Alabama under contract, a great number of these helpless and suffering people, starving and smitten with contagious disease, made their way or were assisted to the frontier, where, in wretched plight, they were quarantined by the Texas authorities. Learning of their destitute condition, I directed rations to be temporarily furnished them through the War Department.   At the expiration of their quarantine they were conveyed by the railway companies at comparatively nominal rates to their homes in Alabama, upon my assurance, in the absence of any fund available for the cost of their transportation, that I would recommend to Congress an appropriation for its payment. I now strongly urge upon Congress the propriety of making such an appropriation. It should be remembered that the measures taken were dictated not only by sympathy and humanity, but by a conviction that it was not compatible with the dignity of this Government that so large a body of our dependent citizens should be thrown for relief upon the charity of a neighboring state.

In last year's message I narrated at some length the jurisdictional questions then freshly arisen in the Mosquito Indian Strip of Nicaragua. Since that time, by the voluntary act of the Mosquito Nation, the territory reserved to them has been incorporated with Nicaragua, the Indians formally subjecting themselves to be governed by the general laws and regulations of the Republic instead of by their own customs and regulations, and thus availing themselves of a privilege secured to them by the treaty between Nicaragua and Great Britain of January 28, 1860.

After this extension of uniform Nicaraguan administration to the Mosquito Strip, the case of the British vice-consul, Hatch, and of several of his countrymen who had been summarily expelled from Nicaragua and treated with considerable indignity provoked a claim by Great Britain upon Nicaragua for pecuniary indemnity, which, upon Nicaragua's refusal to admit liability, was enforced by Great Britain. While the sovereignty and jurisdiction of Nicaragua was in no way questioned by Great Britain, the former's arbitrary conduct in regard to British subjects furnished the ground for this proceeding.

A British naval force occupied without resistance the Pacific seaport of Corinto, but was soon after withdrawn upon the promise that the sum demanded would be paid. Throughout this incident the kindly offices of the United States were invoked and were employed in favor of as peaceful a settlement and as much consideration and indulgence toward Nicaragua as were consistent with the nature of the case. Our efforts have since been made the subject of appreciative and grateful recognition by Nicaragua.

The coronation of the Czar of Russia at Moscow in May next invites the ceremonial participation of the United States, and in accordance with usage and diplomatic propriety our minister to the imperial court has been directed to represent our Government on the occasion.

Correspondence is on foot touching the practice of Russian consuls within the jurisdiction of the United States to interrogate citizens as to their race and religious faith, and upon ascertainment thereof to deny to Jews authentication of passports or legal documents for use in Russia. Inasmuch as such a proceeding imposes a disability which in the case of succession to property in Russia may be found to infringe the treaty rights of our citizens, and which is an obnoxious invasion of our territorial jurisdiction, it has elicited fitting remonstrance, the result of which, it is hoped, will remove the cause of complaint.   The pending claims of sealing vessels of the United States seized in Russian waters remain unadjusted.   Our recent convention with Russia establishing a *modus vivendi* as to imperial jurisdiction in such cases has prevented further difficulty of this nature.

The Russian Government has welcomed in principle our suggestion for a *modus vivendi*, to embrace Great Britain and Japan, looking to the better preservation of seal life in the North Pacific and Bering Sea and the extension of the protected area defined by the Paris Tribunal to all Pacific waters north of the thirty-fifth parallel.   It is especially noticeable that Russia favors prohibition of the use of firearms in seal hunting throughout the proposed area and a longer closed season for pelagic sealing.

In my last two annual messages I called the attention of the Congress to the position we occupied as one of the parties to a treaty or agreement by which we became jointly bound with England and Germany to so interfere with the government and control of Samoa as in effect to assume the management of its affairs.   On the 9th day of May, 1894, I transmitted to the Senate a special message, with accompanying documents, giving information on the subject and emphasizing the opinion I have at all times entertained, that our situation in this matter was inconsistent with the mission and traditions of our Government, in violation of the principles we profess, and in all its phases mischievous and vexatious.

I again press this subject upon the attention of the Congress and ask for such legislative action or expression as will lead the way to our relief from obligations both irksome and unnatural.

Cuba is again gravely disturbed.   An insurrection in some respects more active than the last preceding revolt, which continued from 1868 to 1878, now exists in a large part of the eastern interior of the island, menacing even some populations on the coast.   Besides deranging the commercial exchanges of the island, of which our country takes the predominant share, this flagrant condition of hostilities, by arousing sentimental sympathy and inciting adventurous support among our people, has entailed earnest effort on the part of this Government to enforce obedience to our neutrality laws and to prevent the territory of the United States from being abused as a vantage ground from which to aid those in arms against Spanish sovereignty.

Whatever may be the traditional sympathy of our countrymen as individuals with a people who seem to be struggling for larger autonomy and greater freedom, deepened, as such sympathy naturally must be, in behalf of our neighbors, yet the plain duty of their Government is to observe in good faith the recognized obligations of international relationship.   The performance of this duty should not be made more difficult by a disregard on the part of our citizens of the obligations growing out of their allegiance to their country, which should restrain them from violating as individuals the neutrality which the nation of which they are members is bound to observe in its relations to friendly sovereign states. Though neither the warmth of our people's sympathy with the Cuban insurgents, nor our loss and material damage consequent upon the futile endeavors thus far made to restore peace and order, nor any shock our humane sensibilities may have received from the cruelties which appear to especially characterize this sanguinary and fiercely conducted war, have in the least shaken the determination of the Government to honestly fulfill every international obligation, yet it is to be earnestly hoped on every ground that the devastation of armed conflict may speedily be stayed and order and quiet restored to the distracted island, bringing in their train the activity and thrift of peaceful pursuits.

One notable instance of interference by Spain with passing American ships has occurred. On March 8 last the *Allianca*, while bound from Colon to New York, and following the customary track for vessels near the Cuban shore, but outside the 3-mile limit, was fired upon by a Spanish gunboat. Protest was promptly made by the United States against this act as not being justified by a state of war, nor permissible in respect of vessels on the usual paths of commerce, nor tolerable in view of the wanton peril occasioned to innocent life and property. The act was disavowed, with full expression of regret and assurance of nonrecurrence of such just cause of complaint, while the offending officer was relieved of his command. Military arrests of citizens of the United States in Cuba have occasioned frequent reclamations. Where held on criminal charges their delivery to the ordinary civil jurisdiction for trial has been demanded and obtained in conformity with treaty provisions, and where merely detained by way of military precaution under a proclaimed state of siege, without formulated accusation, their release or trial has been insisted upon. The right of American consular officers in the island to prefer protests and demands in such cases having been questioned by the insular authority, their enjoyment of the privilege stipulated by treaty for the consuls of Germany was claimed under the most-favored-nation provision of our own convention and was promptly recognized.

The long-standing demand of Antonio Maximo Mora against Spain has at last been settled by the payment, on the 14th of September last, of the sum originally agreed upon in liquidation of the claim. Its distribution among the parties entitled to receive it has proceeded as rapidly as the rights of those claiming the fund could be safely determined.

The enforcement of differential duties against products of this country exported to Cuba and Puerto Rico prompted the immediate claim on our part to the benefit of the minimum tariff of Spain in return for the most favorable treatment permitted by our laws as regards the production of Spanish territories. A commercial arrangement was concluded in January last securing the treatment so claimed.

Vigorous protests against excessive fines imposed on our ships and merchandise by the customs officers of these islands for trivial errors have resulted in the remission of such fines in instances where the equity of the complaint was apparent, though the vexatious practice has not been wholly discontinued.

Occurrences in Turkey have continued to excite concern. The reported massacres of Christians in Armenia and the development there and in other districts of a spirit of fanatic hostility to Christian influences naturally excited apprehension for the safety of the devoted men and women who, as dependents of the foreign missionary societies in the United States, reside in Turkey under the guaranty of law and usage and in the legitimate performance of their educational and religious mission. No efforts have been spared in their behalf, and their protection in person and property has been earnestly and vigorously enforced by every means within our power.

I regret, however, that an attempt on our part to obtain better information concerning the true condition of affairs in the disturbed quarter of the Ottoman Empire by sending thither the United States consul at Sivas to make investigation and report was thwarted by the objections of the Turkish Government. This movement on our part was in no sense meant as a gratuitous entanglement of the United States in the so-called Eastern question nor as an officious interference with the right and duty which belong by treaty to certain great European powers calling for their intervention in political matters affecting the good government and religious freedom of the non-Mussulman subjects of the Sultan, but it arose solely from our desire to have an accurate knowledge of the conditions in our efforts to care for those entitled to our protection.

The presence of our naval vessels which are now in the vicinity of the disturbed localities affords opportunities to acquire a measure of familiarity with the condition of affairs and will enable us to take suitable steps for the protection of any interests of our countrymen within reach of our ships that might be found imperiled.

The Ottoman Government has lately issued an imperial *irade* exempting forever from taxation an American college for girls at Scutari. Repeated assurances have also been obtained by our envoy at Constantinople that similar institutions maintained and administered by our countrymen shall be secured in the enjoyment of all rights and that our citizens throughout the Empire shall be protected.

The Government, however, in view of existing facts, is far from relying upon such assurances as the limit of its duty. Our minister has been vigilant and alert in affording all possible protection in individual cases where danger threatened or safety was imperiled. We have sent ships as far toward the points of actual disturbance as it is possible for them to go, where they offer refuge to those obliged to flee, and we have the promise of other powers which have ships in the neighborhood that our citizens as well as theirs will be received and protected on board those ships. On the demand of our minister orders have been issued by the Sultan that Turkish soldiers shall guard and escort to the coast American refugees.

These orders have been carried out, and our latest intelligence gives assurance of the present personal safety of our citizens and missionaries. Though thus far no lives of American citizens have been sacrificed, there can be no doubt that serious loss and destruction of mission property have resulted from riotous conflicts and outrageous attacks.

By treaty several of the most powerful European powers have secured a right and have assumed a duty not only in behalf of their own citizens and in furtherance of their own interests, but as agents of the Christian world. Their right is to enforce such conduct of Turkish government as will restrain fanatical brutality, and if this fails their duty is to so interfere as to insure against such dreadful occurrences in Turkey as have lately shocked civilization. The powers declare this right and this duty to be theirs alone, and it is earnestly hoped that prompt and effective action on their part will not be delayed.

The new consulates at Erzerum and Harpoot, for which appropriation was made last session, have been provisionally filled by trusted employees of the Department of State. These appointees, though now in Turkey, have not yet received their exequaturs.

The arbitration of the claim of the Venezuela Steam Transportation Company under the treaty of January 19, 1892, between the United States and Venezuela, resulted in an award in favor of the claimant.

The Government has used its good offices toward composing the differences between Venezuela on the one hand and France and Belgium on the other growing out of the dismissal of the representatives of those powers on the ground of a publication deemed offensive to Venezuela. Although that dismissal was coupled with a cordial request that other more personally agreeable envoys be sent in their stead, a rupture of intercourse ensued and still continues.

In view of the growth of our interests in foreign countries and the encouraging prospects for a general expansion of our commerce, the question of an improvement in the consular service has increased in importance and urgency. Though there is no doubt that the great body of consular officers are rendering valuable services to the trade and industries of the country, the need of some plan of appointment and control which would tend to secure a higher average of efficiency can not be denied.

The importance of the subject has led the Executive to consider what steps might properly be taken without additional legislation to answer the need of a better system of consular appointments. The matter having been committed to the consideration of the Secretary of State, in pursuance of his recommendations an Executive order was issued on the 20th of September, 1895, by the terms of which it is provided that after that date any vacancy in a consulate or commercial agency with an annual

salary or compensation from official fees of not more than $2,500 or less
than $1,000 should be filled either by transfer or promotion from some
other position under the Department of State of a character tending to
qualify the incumbent for the position to be filled, or by the appointment
of a person not under the Department of State, but having previously
served thereunder and shown his capacity and fitness for consular duty,
or by the appointment of a person who, having been selected by the President and sent to a board for examination, is found upon such examination to be qualified for the position.   Posts which pay less than $1,000
being usually, on account of their small compensation, filled by selection
from residents of the locality, it was not deemed practicable to put them
under the new system.

The compensation of $2,500 was adopted as the maximum limit in the
classification for the reason that consular officers receiving more than
that sum are often charged with functions and duties scarcely inferior in
dignity and importance to those of diplomatic agents, and it was therefore
thought best to continue their selection in the discretion of the Executive without subjecting them to examination before a board.   Excluding
71 places with compensation at present less than $1,000 and 53 places
above the maximum in compensation, the number of positions remaining
within the scope of the order is 196.   This number will undoubtedly be
increased by the inclusion of consular officers whose remuneration in fees,
now less than $1,000, will be augmented with the growth of our foreign
commerce and a return to more favorable business conditions.

In execution of the Executive order referred to the Secretary of State
has designated as a board to conduct the prescribed examinations the
Third Assistant Secretary of State, the Solicitor of the Department of
State, and the Chief of the Consular Bureau, and has specified the subjects to which such examinations shall relate.

It is not assumed that this system will prove a full measure of consular
reform.   It is quite probable that actual experience will show particulars
in which the order already issued may be amended and demonstrate that
for the best results appropriate legislation by Congress is imperatively
required.

In any event, these efforts to improve the consular service ought to be
immediately supplemented by legislation providing for consular inspection.   This has frequently been a subject of Executive recommendation,
and I again urge such action by Congress as will permit the frequent and
thorough inspection of consulates by officers appointed for that purpose
or by persons already in the diplomatic or consular service.   The expense
attending such a plan would be insignificant compared with its usefulness, and I hope the legislation necessary to set it on foot will be speedily
forthcoming.

I am thoroughly convinced that in addition to their salaries our ambassadors and ministers at foreign courts should be provided by the

Government with official residences. The salaries of these officers are comparatively small and in most cases insufficient to pay, with other necessary expenses, the cost of maintaining household establishments in keeping with their important and delicate functions. The usefulness of a nation's diplomatic representative undeniably depends much upon the appropriateness of his surroundings, and a country like ours, while avoiding unnecessary glitter and show, should be certain that it does not suffer in its relations with foreign nations through parsimony and shabbiness in its diplomatic outfit. These considerations and the other advantages of having fixed and somewhat permanent locations for our embassies would abundantly justify the moderate expenditure necessary to carry out this suggestion.

As we turn from a review of our foreign relations to the contemplation of our national financial situation we are immediately aware that we approach a subject of domestic concern more important than any other that can engage our attention, and one at present in such a perplexing and delicate predicament as to require prompt and wise treatment.

We may well be encouraged to earnest effort in this direction when we recall the steps already taken toward improving our economic and financial situation and when we appreciate how well the way has been prepared for further progress by an aroused and intelligent popular interest in these subjects.

By command of the people a customs-revenue system designed for the protection and benefit of favored classes at the expense of the great mass of our countrymen, and which, while inefficient for the purpose of revenue, curtailed our trade relations and impeded our entrance to the markets of the world, has been superseded by a tariff policy which in principle is based upon a denial of the right of the Government to obstruct the avenues to our people's cheap living or lessen their comfort and contentment for the sake of according especial advantages to favorites, and which, while encouraging our intercourse and trade with other nations, recognizes the fact that American self-reliance, thrift, and ingenuity can build up our country's industries and develop its resources more surely than enervating paternalism.

The compulsory purchase and coinage of silver by the Government, unchecked and unregulated by business conditions and heedless of our currency needs, which for more than fifteen years diluted our circulating medium, undermined confidence abroad in our financial ability, and at last culminated in distress and panic at home, has been recently stopped by the repeal of the laws which forced this reckless scheme upon the country.

The things thus accomplished, notwithstanding their extreme importance and beneficent effects, fall far short of curing the monetary evils from which we suffer as a result of long indulgence in ill-advised financial expedients.

The currency denominated United States notes and commonly known as greenbacks was issued in large volume during the late Civil War and was intended originally to meet the exigencies of that period. It will be seen by a reference to the debates in Congress at the time the laws were passed authorizing the issue of these notes that their advocates declared they were intended for only temporary use and to meet the emergency of war. In almost if not all the laws relating to them some provision was made contemplating their voluntary or compulsory retirement. A large quantity of them, however, were kept on foot and mingled with the currency of the country, so that at the close of the year 1874 they amounted to $381,999,073.

Immediately after that date, and in January, 1875, a law was passed providing for the resumption of specie payments, by which the Secretary of the Treasury was required whenever additional circulation was issued to national banks to retire United States notes equal in amount to 80 per cent of such additional national-bank circulation until such notes were reduced to $300,000,000. This law further provided that on and after the 1st day of January, 1879, the United States notes then outstanding should be redeemed in coin, and in order to provide and prepare for such redemption the Secretary of the Treasury was authorized not only to use any surplus revenues of the Government, but to issue bonds of the United States and dispose of them for coin and to use the proceeds for the purposes contemplated by the statute.

In May, 1878, and before the date thus appointed for the redemption and retirement of these notes, another statute was passed forbidding their further cancellation and retirement. Some of them had, however, been previously redeemed and canceled upon the issue of additional national-bank circulation, as permitted by the law of 1875, so that the amount outstanding at the time of the passage of the act forbidding their further retirement was $346,681,016.

The law of 1878 did not stop at distinct prohibition, but contained in addition the following express provision:

And when any of said notes may be redeemed or be received into the Treasury under any law from any source whatever, and shall belong to the United States, they shall not be retired, canceled, or destroyed, but they shall be reissued and paid out again and kept in circulation.

This was the condition of affairs on the 1st day of January, 1879, which had been fixed upon four years before as the date for entering upon the redemption and retirement of all these notes, and for which such abundant means had been provided.

The Government was put in the anomalous situation of owing to the holders of its notes debts payable in gold on demand which could neither be retired by receiving such notes in discharge of obligations due the Government nor canceled by actual payment in gold. It was forced to redeem without redemption and to pay without acquittance.

There had been issued and sold $95,500,000 of the bonds authorized by the resumption act of 1875, the proceeds of which, together with other gold in the Treasury, created a gold fund deemed sufficient to meet the demands which might be made upon it for the redemption of the outstanding United States notes. This fund, together with such other gold as might be from time to time in the Treasury available for the same purpose, has been since called our gold reserve, and $100,000,000 has been regarded as an adequate amount to accomplish its object. This fund amounted on the 1st day of January, 1879, to $114,193,360, and though thereafter constantly fluctuating it did not fall below that sum until July, 1892. In April, 1893, for the first time since its establishment, this reserve amounted to less than $100,000,000, containing at that date only $97,011,330.

In the meantime, and in July, 1890, an act had been passed directing larger governmental monthly purchases of silver than had been required under previous laws, and providing that in payment for such silver Treasury notes of the United States should be issued payable on demand in gold or silver coin, at the discretion of the Secretary of the Treasury. It was, however, declared in the act to be "the established policy of the United States to maintain the two metals on a parity with each other upon the present legal ratio or such ratio as may be provided by law." In view of this declaration it was not deemed permissible for the Secretary of the Treasury to exercise the discretion in terms conferred on him by refusing to pay gold on these notes when demanded, because by such discrimination in favor of the gold dollar the so-called parity of the two metals would be destroyed and grave and dangerous consequences would be precipitated by affirming or accentuating the constantly widening disparity between their actual values under the existing ratio.

It thus resulted that the Treasury notes issued in payment of silver purchases under the law of 1890 were necessarily treated as gold obligations at the option of the holder. These notes on the 1st day of November, 1893, when the law compelling the monthly purchase of silver was repealed, amounted to more than $155,000,000. The notes of this description now outstanding added to the United States notes still undiminished by redemption or cancellation constitute a volume of gold obligations amounting to nearly $500,000,000.

These obligations are the instruments which ever since we had a gold reserve have been used to deplete it.

This reserve, as has been stated, had fallen in April, 1893, to $97,011,330. It has from that time to the present, with very few and unimportant upward movements, steadily decreased, except as it has been temporarily replenished by the sale of bonds.

Among the causes for this constant and uniform shrinkage in this fund may be mentioned the great falling off of exports under the operation of the tariff law until recently in force, which crippled our exchange of commodities with foreign nations and necessitated to some extent the payment of our balances in gold; the unnatural infusion of silver into our currency and the increasing agitation for its free and unlimited coinage, which have created apprehension as to our disposition or ability to continue gold payments; the consequent hoarding of gold at home and the stoppage of investments of foreign capital, as well as the return of our securities already sold abroad; and the high rate of foreign exchange, which induced the shipment of our gold to be drawn against as a matter of speculation.

In consequence of these conditions the gold reserve on the 1st day of February, 1894, was reduced to $65,438,377, having lost more than $31,-000,000 during the preceding nine months, or since April, 1893. Its replenishment being necessary and no other manner of accomplishing it being possible, resort was had to the issue and sale of bonds provided for by the resumption act of 1875. Fifty millions of these bonds were sold, yielding $58,633,295.71, which was added to the reserve fund of gold then on hand. As a result of this operation this reserve, which had suffered constant and large withdrawals in the meantime, stood on the 6th day of March, 1894, at the sum of $107,446,802. Its depletion was, however, immediately thereafter so accelerated that on the 30th day of June, 1894, it had fallen to $64,873,025, thus losing by withdrawals more than $42,000,000 in five months and dropping slightly below its situation when the sale of $50,000,000 in bonds was effected for its replenishment.

This depressed condition grew worse, and on the 24th day of November, 1894, our gold reserve being reduced to $57,669,701, it became necessary to again strengthen it.

This was done by another sale of bonds amounting to $50,000,000, from which there was realized $58,538,500, with which the fund was increased to $111,142,021 on the 4th day of December, 1894.

Again disappointment awaited the anxious hope for relief. There was not even a lull in the exasperating withdrawals of gold. On the contrary, they grew larger and more persistent than ever. Between the 4th day of December, 1894, and early in February, 1895, a period of scarcely more than two months after the second reenforcement of our gold reserve by the sale of bonds, it had lost by such withdrawals more than $69,000,000 and had fallen to $41,340,181. Nearly $43,000,000 had been withdrawn within the month immediately preceding this situation.

In anticipation of impending trouble I had on the 28th day of January, 1895, addressed a communication* to the Congress fully setting forth our difficulties and dangerous position and earnestly recommending that authority be given the Secretary of the Treasury to issue bonds bearing a low rate of interest, payable by their terms in gold, for the purpose of maintaining a sufficient gold reserve and also for the redemption and cancellation of outstanding United States notes and the Treasury notes issued for the purchase of silver under the law of 1890. This recommendation did not, however, meet with legislative approval.

In February, 1895, therefore, the situation was exceedingly critical. With a reserve perilously low and a refusal of Congressional aid, everything indicated that the end of gold payments by the Government was imminent. The results of prior bond issues had been exceedingly unsatisfactory, and the large withdrawals of gold immediately succeeding their public sale in open market gave rise to a reasonable suspicion that a large part of the gold paid into the Treasury upon such sales was promptly drawn out again by the presentation of United States notes or Treasury notes, and found its way to the hands of those who had only temporarily parted with it in the purchase of bonds.

In this emergency, and in view of its surrounding perplexities, it became entirely apparent to those upon whom the struggle for safety was devolved not only that our gold reserve must, for the third time in less than thirteen months, be restored by another issue and sale of bonds bearing a high rate of interest and badly suited to the purpose, but that a plan must be adopted for their disposition promising better results than those realized on previous sales. An agreement was therefore made with a number of financiers and bankers whereby it was stipulated that bonds described in the resumption act of 1875, payable in coin thirty years after their date, bearing interest at the rate of 4 per cent per annum, and amounting to about $62,000,000, should be exchanged for gold, receivable by weight, amounting to a little more than $65,000,000.

This gold was to be delivered in such installments as would complete its delivery within about six months from the date of the contract, and at least one-half of the amount was to be furnished from abroad. It was also agreed by those supplying this gold that during the continuance of the contract they would by every means in their power protect the Government against gold withdrawals. The contract also provided that if Congress would authorize their issue bonds payable by their terms in gold and bearing interest at the rate of 3 per cent per annum might within ten days be substituted at par for the 4 per cent bonds described in the agreement.

On the day this contract was made its terms were communicated to Congress by a special Executive message,* in which it was stated that more than $16,000,000 would be saved to the Government if gold bonds bearing 3 per cent interest were authorized to be substituted for those mentioned in the contract.

The Congress having declined to grant the necessary authority to secure this saving, the contract, unmodified, was carried out, resulting in a gold reserve amounting to $107,571,230 on the 8th day of July, 1895. The performance of this contract not only restored the reserve, but checked for a time the withdrawals of gold and brought on a period of restored confidence and such peace and quiet in business circles as were of the greatest possible value to every interest that affects our people. I have never had the slightest misgiving concerning the wisdom or propriety of this arrangement, and am quite willing to answer for my full share of responsibility for its promotion. I believe it averted a disaster the imminence of which was, fortunately, not at the time generally understood by our people.

Though the contract mentioned stayed for a time the tide of gold withdrawal, its good results could not be permanent. Recent withdrawals have reduced the reserve from $107,571,230 on the 8th day of July, 1895, to $79,333,966. How long it will remain large enough to render its increase unnecessary is only matter of conjecture, though quite large withdrawals for shipment in the immediate future are predicted in well-informed quarters. About $16,000,000 has been withdrawn during the month of November.

The foregoing statement of events and conditions develops the fact that after increasing our interest-bearing bonded indebtedness more than $162,000,000 to save our gold reserve we are nearly where we started, having now in such reserve $79,333,966, as against $65,438,377 in February, 1894, when the first bonds were issued.

Though the amount of gold drawn from the Treasury appears to be very large as gathered from the facts and figures herein presented, it actually was much larger, considerable sums having been acquired by the Treasury within the several periods stated without the issue of bonds. On the 28th of January, 1895, it was reported by the Secretary of the Treasury that more than $172,000,000 of gold had been withdrawn for hoarding or shipment during the year preceding. He now reports that from January 1, 1879, to July 14, 1890, a period of more than eleven years, only a little over $28,000,000 was withdrawn, and that between July 14, 1890, the date of the passage of the law for an increased purchase of silver, and the 1st day of December, 1895, or within less than five and a half years, there was withdrawn nearly $375,000,000, making a total of more than $403,000,000 drawn from the Treasury in gold since January 1, 1879, the date fixed in 1875 for the retirement of the United States notes.

Nearly $327,000,000 of the gold thus withdrawn has been paid out on these United States notes, and yet every one of the $346,000,000 is still uncanceled and ready to do service in future gold depletions.

More than $76,000,000 in gold has since their creation in 1890 been paid out from the Treasury upon the notes given on the purchase of silver by the Government, and yet the whole, amounting to $155,000,000, except a little more than $16,000,000 which has been retired by exchanges for silver at the request of the holders, remains outstanding and prepared to join their older and more experienced allies in future raids upon the Treasury's gold reserve.

In other words, the Government has paid in gold more than nine-tenths of its United States notes and still owes them all. It has paid in gold about one-half of its notes given for silver purchases without extinguishing by such payment one dollar of these notes.

When, added to all this, we are reminded that to carry on this astounding financial scheme the Government has incurred a bonded indebtedness of $95,500,000 in establishing a gold reserve and of $162,315,400 in efforts to maintain it; that the annual interest charge on such bonded indebtedness is more than $11,000,000; that a continuance of our present course may result in further bond issues, and that we have suffered or are threatened with all this for the sake of supplying gold for foreign shipment or facilitating its hoarding at home, a situation is exhibited which certainly ought to arrest attention and provoke immediate legislative relief.

I am convinced the only thorough and practicable remedy for our troubles is found in the retirement and cancellation of our United States notes, commonly called greenbacks, and the outstanding Treasury notes issued by the Government in payment of silver purchases under the act of 1890.

I believe this could be quite readily accomplished by the exchange of these notes for United States bonds, of small as well as large denominations, bearing a low rate of interest. They should be long-term bonds, thus increasing their desirability as investments, and because their payment could be well postponed to a period far removed from present financial burdens and perplexities, when with increased prosperity and resources they would be more easily met.

To further insure the cancellation of these notes and also provide a way by which gold may be added to our currency in lieu of them, a feature in the plan should be an authority given to the Secretary of the Treasury to dispose of the bonds abroad for gold if necessary to complete the contemplated redemption and cancellation, permitting him to use the proceeds of such bonds to take up and cancel any of the notes that may be in the Treasury or that may be received by the Government on any account.

The increase of our bonded debt involved in this plan would be amply compensated by renewed activity and enterprise in all business circles, the restored confidence at home, the reinstated faith in our monetary strength abroad, and the stimulation of every interest and industry that would follow the cancellation of the gold-demand obligations now afflicting us. In any event, the bonds proposed would stand for the extinguishment of a troublesome indebtedness, while in the path we now follow there lurks the menace of unending bonds, with our indebtedness still undischarged and aggravated in every feature. The obligations necessary to fund this indebtedness would not equal in amount those from which we have been relieved since 1884 by anticipation and payment beyond the requirements of the sinking fund out of our surplus revenues.

The currency withdrawn by the retirement of the United States notes and Treasury notes, amounting to probably less than $486,000,000, might be supplied by such gold as would be used on their retirement or by an increase in the circulation of our national banks. Though the aggregate capital of those now in existence amounts to more than $664,000,000, their outstanding circulation based on bond security amounts to only about $190,000,000. They are authorized to issue notes amounting to 90 per cent of the bonds deposited to secure their circulation, but in no event beyond the amount of their capital stock, and they are obliged to pay 1 per cent tax on the circulation they issue.

I think they should be allowed to issue circulation equal to the par value of the bonds they deposit to secure it, and that the tax on their circulation should be reduced to one-fourth of 1 per cent, which would undoubtedly meet all the expense the Government incurs on their account. In addition they should be allowed to substitute or deposit in lieu of the bonds now required as security for their circulation those which would be issued for the purpose of retiring the United States notes and Treasury notes.

The banks already existing, if they desired to avail themselves of the provisions of law thus modified, could issue circulation, in addition to that already outstanding, amounting to $478,000,000, which would nearly or quite equal the currency proposed to be canceled. At any rate, I should confidently expect to see the existing national banks or others to be organized avail themselves of the proposed encouragements to issue circulation and promptly fill any vacuum and supply every currency need.

It has always seemed to me that the provisions of law regarding the capital of national banks, which operate as a limitation to their location, fail to make proper compensation for the suppression of State banks, which came near to the people in all sections of the country and readily furnished them with banking accommodations and facilities. Any inconvenience or embarrassment arising from these restrictions on the location of national banks might well be remedied by better adapting the present system to the creation of banks in smaller communities or by permitting banks of large capital to establish branches in such localities as would serve the people, so regulated and restrained as to secure their safe and conservative control and management.

But there might not be the necessity for such an addition to the currency by new issues of bank circulation as at first glance is indicated. If we should be relieved from maintaining a gold reserve under conditions that constitute it the barometer of our solvency, and if our Treasury should no longer be the foolish purveyor of gold for nations abroad or for speculation and hoarding by our citizens at home, I should expect to see gold resume its natural and normal functions in the business affairs of the country and cease to be an object attracting the timid watch of our people and exciting their sensitive imaginations.

I do not overlook the fact that the cancellation of the Treasury notes issued under the silver-purchasing act of 1890 would leave the Treasury in the actual ownership of sufficient silver, including seigniorage, to coin nearly $178,000,000 in standard dollars. It is worthy of consideration whether this might not from time to time be converted into dollars or fractional coin and slowly put into circulation, as in the judgment of the Secretary of the Treasury the necessities of the country should require.

Whatever is attempted should be entered upon fully appreciating the fact that by careless, easy descent we have reached a dangerous depth, and that our ascent will not be accomplished without laborious toil and struggle. We shall be wise if we realize that we are financially ill and that our restoration to health may require heroic treatment and unpleasant remedies.

In the present stage of our difficulty it is not easy to understand how the amount of our revenue receipts directly affects it. The important question is not the quantity of money received in revenue payments, but the kind of money we maintain and our ability to continue in sound financial condition. We are considering the Government's holdings of gold as related to the soundness of our money and as affecting our national credit and monetary strength.

If our gold reserve had never been impaired; if no bonds had ever been issued to replenish it; if there had been no fear and timidity concern·ing our ability to continue gold payments; if any part of our revenues were now paid in gold, and if we could look to our gold receipts as a means of maintaining a safe reserve, the amount of our revenues would be an influential factor in the problem. But, unfortunately, all the circumstances that might lend weight to this consideration are entirely lacking.

In our present predicament no gold is received by the Government in payment of revenue charges, nor would there be if the revenues were increased. The receipts of the Treasury, when not in silver certificates, consist of United States notes and Treasury notes issued for silver purchases. These forms of money are only useful to the Government in paying its current ordinary expenses, and its quantity in Government possession does not in the least contribute toward giving us that kind of safe financial standing or condition which is built on gold alone.

If it is said that these notes if held by the Government can be used to obtain gold for our reserve, the answer is easy. The people draw gold from the Treasury on demand upon United States notes and Treasury notes, but the proposition that the Treasury can on demand draw gold from the people upon them would be regarded in these days with wonder and amusement; and even if this could be done there is nothing to prevent those thus parting with their gold from regaining it the next day or the next hour by the presentation of the notes they received in exchange for it.

The Secretary of the Treasury might use such notes taken from a surplus revenue to buy gold in the market. Of course he could not do this without paying a premium.   Private holders of gold, unlike the Government, having no parity to maintain, would not be restrained from making the best bargain possible when they furnished gold to the Treasury; but the moment the Secretary of the Treasury bought gold on any terms above par he would establish a general and universal premium upon it, thus breaking down the parity between gold and silver, which the Government is pledged to maintain, and opening the way to new and serious complications.   In the meantime the premium would not remain stationary, and the absurd spectacle might be presented of a dealer selling gold to the Government and with United States notes or Treasury notes in his hand immediately clamoring for its return and a resale at a higher premium.

It may be claimed that a large revenue and redundant receipts might favorably affect the situation under discussion by affording an opportunity of retaining these notes in the Treasury when received, and thus preventing their presentation for gold.   Such retention to be useful ought to be at least measurably permanent; and this is precisely what is prohibited, so far as United States notes are concerned, by the law of 1878, forbidding their further retirement.   That statute in so many words provides that these notes when received into the Treasury and belonging to the United States shall be "paid out again and kept in circulation."

It will, moreover, be readily seen that the Government could not refuse to pay out United States notes and Treasury notes in current transactions when demanded, and insist on paying out silver alone, and still maintain the parity between that metal and the currency representing gold.   Besides, the accumulation in the Treasury of currency of any kind exacted from the people through taxation is justly regarded as an evil, and it can not proceed far without vigorous protest against an unjustifiable retention of money from the business of the country and a denunciation of a scheme of taxation which proves itself to be unjust when it takes from the earnings and income of the citizen money so much in excess of the needs of Government support that large sums can be gathered and kept in the Treasury.   Such a condition has heretofore in times of surplus revenue led the Government to restore currency to the people by the purchase of its unmatured bonds at a large premium and by a large increase of its deposits in national banks, and we easily remember that the abuse of Treasury accumulation has furnished a most persuasive argument in favor of legislation radically reducing our tariff taxation.

Perhaps it is supposed that sufficient revenue receipts would in a sentimental way improve the situation by inspiring confidence in our solvency and allaying the fear of pecuniary exhaustion.   And yet through all our struggles to maintain our gold reserve there never has been any apprehension as to our ready ability to pay our way with such money as we had, and the question whether or not our current receipts met our current expenses has not entered into the estimate of our solvency. Of course the general state of our funds, exclusive of gold, was entirely immaterial to the foreign creditor and investor. His debt could only be paid in gold, and his only concern was our ability to keep on hand that kind of money.

On July 1, 1892, more than a year and a half before the first bonds were issued to replenish the gold reserve, there was a net balance in the Treasury, exclusive of such reserve, of less than $13,000,000, but the gold reserve amounted to more than $114,000,000, which was the quieting feature of the situation. It was when the stock of gold began rapidly to fall that fright supervened and our securities held abroad were returned for sale and debts owed abroad were pressed for payment. In the meantime extensive shipments of gold and other unfavorable indications caused restlessness and fright among our people at home. Thereupon the general state of our funds, exclusive of gold, became also immaterial to them, and they too drew gold from the Treasury for hoarding against all contingencies. This is plainly shown by the large increase in the proportion of gold withdrawn which was retained by our own people as time and threatening incidents progressed. During the fiscal year ending June 30, 1894, nearly $85,000,000 in gold was withdrawn from the Treasury and about $77,000,000 was sent abroad, while during the fiscal year ending June 30, 1895, over $117,000,000 was drawn out, of which only about $66,000,000 was shipped, leaving the large balance of such withdrawals to be accounted for by domestic hoarding.

Inasmuch as the withdrawal of our gold has resulted largely from fright, there is nothing apparent that will prevent its continuance or recurrence, with its natural consequences, except such a change in our financial methods as will reassure the frightened and make the desire for gold less intense. It is not clear how an increase in revenue, unless it be in gold, can satisfy those whose only anxiety is to gain gold from the Government's store.

It can not, therefore, be safe to rely upon increased revenues as a cure for our present troubles.

It is possible that the suggestion of increased revenue as a remedy for the difficulties we are considering may have originated in an intimation or distinct allegation that the bonds which have been issued ostensibly to replenish our gold reserve were really issued to supply insufficient revenue. Nothing can be further from the truth. Bonds were issued to obtain gold for the maintenance of our national credit. As has been shown, the gold thus obtained has been drawn again from the Treasury upon United States notes and Treasury notes. This operation would have been promptly prevented if possible; but these notes having thus been passed to the Treasury, they became the money of the Government, like any other ordinary Government funds, and there was nothing to do but to use them in paying Government expenses when needed.

At no time when bonds have been issued has there been any consideration of the question of paying the expenses of Government with their proceeds. There was no necessity to consider that question. At the time of each bond issue we had a safe surplus in the Treasury for ordinary operations, exclusive of the gold in our reserve. In February, 1894, when the first issue of bonds was made, such surplus amounted to over $18,000,000; in November, when the second issue was made, it amounted to more than $42,000,000, and in February, 1895, when bonds for the third time were issued, such surplus amounted to more than $100,000,000. It now amounts to $98,072,420.30.

Besides all this, the Secretary of the Treasury had no authority whatever to issue bonds to increase the ordinary revenues or pay current expenses.

I can not but think there has been some confusion of ideas regarding the effects of the issue of bonds and the results of the withdrawal of gold. It was the latter process, and not the former, that, by substituting in the Treasury United States notes and Treasury notes for gold, increased by their amount the money which was in the first instance subject to ordinary Government expenditure.

Although the law compelling an increased purchase of silver by the Government was passed on the 14th day of July, 1890, withdrawals of gold from the Treasury upon the notes given in payment on such purchases did not begin until October, 1891. Immediately following that date the withdrawals upon both these notes and United States notes increased very largely, and have continued to such an extent that since the passage of that law there has been more than thirteen times as much gold taken out of the Treasury upon United States notes and Treasury notes issued for silver purchases as was thus withdrawn during the eleven and a half years immediately prior thereto and after the 1st day of January, 1879, when specie payments were resumed.

It is neither unfair nor unjust to charge a large share of our present financial perplexities and dangers to the operation of the laws of 1878 and 1890 compelling the purchase of silver by the Government, which not only furnished a new Treasury obligation upon which its gold could be withdrawn, but so increased the fear of an overwhelming flood of silver and a forced descent to silver payments that even the repeal of these laws did not entirely cure the evils of their existence.

While I have endeavored to make a plain statement of the disordered condition of our currency and the present dangers menacing our prosperity and to suggest a way which leads to a safer financial system, I have constantly had in mind the fact that many of my countrymen, whose sincerity I do not doubt, insist that the cure for the ills now threatening us may be found in the single and simple remedy of the free coinage of silver. They contend that our mints shall be at once thrown open to the free, unlimited, and independent coinage of both gold and silver dollars of full legal-tender quality, regardless of the action of any other government and in full view of the fact that the ratio between the metals which they suggest calls for 100 cents' worth of gold in the gold dollar at the present standard and only 50 cents in intrinsic worth of silver in the silver dollar.

Were there infinitely stronger reasons than can be adduced for hoping that such action would secure for us a bimetallic currency moving on lines of parity, an experiment so novel and hazardous as that proposed might well stagger those who believe that stability is an imperative condition of sound money.

No government, no human contrivance or act of legislation, has ever been able to hold the two metals together in free coinage at a ratio appreciably different from that which is established in the markets of the world.

Those who believe that our independent free coinage of silver at an artificial ratio with gold of 16 to 1 would restore the parity between the metals, and consequently between the coins, oppose an unsupported and improbable theory to the general belief and practice of other nations and to the teaching of the wisest statesmen and economists of the world, both in the past and present, and, what is far more conclusive, they run counter to our own actual experiences.

Twice in our earlier history our lawmakers, in attempting to establish a bimetallic currency, undertook free coinage upon a ratio which accidentally varied from the actual relative values of the two metals not more than 3 per cent. In both cases, notwithstanding greater difficulties and cost of transportation than now exist, the coins whose intrinsic worth was undervalued in the ratio gradually and surely disappeared from our circulation and went to other countries where their real value was better recognized.

Acts of Congress were impotent to create equality where natural causes decreed even a slight inequality.

Twice in our recent history we have signally failed to raise by legislation the value of silver. Under an act of Congress passed in 1878 the Government was required for more than twelve years to expend annually at least $24,000,000 in the purchase of silver bullion for coinage. The act of July 14, 1890, in a still bolder effort, increased the amount of silver the Government was compelled to purchase and forced it to become the buyer annually of 54,000,000 ounces, or practically the entire product of our mines. Under both laws silver rapidly and steadily declined in value. The prophecy and the expressed hope and expectation of those in the Congress who led in the passage of the last-mentioned act that it would reestablish and maintain the former parity between the two metals are still fresh in our memory.

In the light of these experiences, which accord with the experiences of other nations, there is certainly no secure ground for the belief that an act of Congress could now bridge an inequality of 50 per cent between gold and silver at our present ratio, nor is there the least possibility that our country, which has less than one-seventh of the silver money in the world, could by its action alone raise not only our own but all silver to its lost ratio with gold. Our attempt to accomplish this by the free coinage of silver at a ratio differing widely from actual relative values would be the signal for the complete departure of gold from our circulation, the immediate and large contraction of our circulating medium, and a shrinkage in the real value and monetary efficiency of all other forms of currency as they settled to the level of silver monometallism. Everyone who receives a fixed salary and every worker for wages would find the dollar in his hand ruthlessly scaled down to the point of bitter disappointment, if not to pinching privation.

A change in our standard to silver monometallism would also bring on a collapse of the entire system of credit, which, when based on a standard which is recognized and adopted by the world of business, is many times more potent and useful than the entire volume of currency and is safely capable of almost indefinite expansion to meet the growth of trade and enterprise. In a self-invited struggle through darkness and uncertainty our humiliation would be increased by the consciousness that we had parted company with all the enlightened and progressive nations of the world and were desperately and hopelessly striving to meet the stress of modern commerce and competition with a debased and unsuitable currency and in association with the few weak and laggard nations which have silver alone as their standard of value.

All history warns us against rash experiments which threaten violent changes in our monetary standard and the degradation of our currency. The past is full of lessons teaching not only the economic dangers but the national immorality that follow in the train of such experiments. I will not believe that the American people can be persuaded after sober deliberation to jeopardize their nation's prestige and proud standing by encouraging financial nostrums, nor that they will yield to the false allurements of cheap money when they realize that it must result in the weakening of that financial integrity and rectitude which thus far in our history has been so devotedly cherished as one of the traits of true Americanism.

Our country's indebtedness, whether owing by the Government or existing between individuals, has been contracted with reference to our present standard. To decree by act of Congress that these debts shall be payable in less valuable dollars than those within the contemplation and intention of the parties when contracted would operate to transfer by the fiat of law and without compensation an amount of property and a volume of rights and interests almost incalculable.

Those who advocate a blind and headlong plunge to free coinage in the name of bimetallism, and professing the belief, contrary to all experience, that we could thus establish a double standard and a concurrent circulation of both metals in our coinage, are certainly reckoning from a cloudy standpoint. Our present standard of value is the standard of the civilized world and permits the only bimetallism now possible, or at least that is within the independent reach of any single nation, however powerful that nation may be. While the value of gold as a standard is steadied by almost universal commercial and business use, it does not despise silver nor seek its banishment. Wherever this standard is maintained there is at its side in free and unquestioned circulation a volume of silver currency sometimes equaling and sometimes even exceeding it in amount both maintained at a parity notwithstanding a depreciation or fluctuation in the intrinsic value of silver.

There is a vast difference between a standard of value and a currency for monetary use. The standard must necessarily be fixed and certain. The currency may be in divers forms and of various kinds. No silver-standard country has a gold currency in circulation, but an enlightened and wise system of finance secures the benefits of both gold and silver as currency and circulating medium by keeping the standard stable and all other currency at par with it. Such a system and such a standard also give free scope for the use and expansion of safe and conservative credit, so indispensable to broad and growing commercial transactions and so well substituted for the actual use of money. If a fixed and stable standard is maintained, such as the magnitude and safety of our commercial transactions and business require, the use of money itself is conveniently minimized.

Every dollar of fixed and stable value has through the agency of confident credit an astonishing capacity of multiplying itself in financial work. Every unstable and fluctuating dollar fails as a basis of credit, and in its use begets gambling speculation and undermines the foundations of honest enterprise.

I have ventured to express myself on this subject with earnestness and plainness of speech because I can not rid myself of the belief that there lurk in the proposition for the free coinage of silver, so strongly approved and so enthusiastically advocated by a multitude of my countrymen, a serious menace to our prosperity and an insidious temptation of our people to wander from the allegiance they owe to public and private integrity. It is because I do not distrust the good faith and sincerity of those who press this scheme that I have imperfectly but with zeal submitted my thoughts upon this momentous subject. I can not refrain from begging them to reexamine their views and beliefs in the light of patriotic reason and familiar experience and to weigh again and again the consequences of such legislation as their efforts have invited. Even the continued agitation of the subject adds greatly to the difficulties of a dangerous financial situation already forced upon us.

In conclusion I especially entreat the people's representatives in the Congress, who are charged with the responsibility of inaugurating measures for the safety and prosperity of our common country, to promptly

and effectively consider the ills of our critical financial plight.   I have
suggested a remedy which my judgment approves.   I desire, however,
to assure the Congress that I am prepared to cooperate with them in perfecting any other measure promising thorough and practical relief, and
that I will gladly labor with them in every patriotic endeavor to further
the interests and guard the welfare of our countrymen, whom in our respective places of duty we have undertaken to serve.

FOURTH ANNUAL MESSAGE.

EXECUTIVE MANSION, *December 7, 1896.*

To the Congress of the United States:

As representatives of the people in the legislative branch of their Government, you have assembled at a time when the strength and excellence
of our free institutions and the fitness of our citizens to enjoy popular
rule have been again made manifest.   A political contest involving momentous consequences, fraught with feverish apprehension, and creating
aggressiveness so intense as to approach bitterness and passion has been
waged throughout our land and determined by the decree of free and
independent suffrage without disturbance of our tranquillity or the least
sign of weakness in our national structure.

When we consider these incidents and contemplate the peaceful obedience and manly submission which have succeeded a heated clash of political opinions, we discover abundant evidence of a determination on the
part of our countrymen to abide by every verdict of the popular will and
to be controlled at all times by an abiding faith in the agencies established for the direction of the affairs of their Government.

Thus our people exhibit a patriotic disposition which entitles them to
demand of those who undertake to make and execute their laws such
faithful and unselfish service in their behalf as can only be prompted by
a serious appreciation of the trust and confidence which the acceptance
of public duty invites.

In obedience to a constitutional requirement I herein submit to the
Congress certain information concerning national affairs, with the sug-
gestion of such legislation as in my judgment is necessary and expedient.
To secure brevity and avoid tiresome narration I shall omit many details

concerning matters within Federal control which, though by no means unimportant, are more profitably discussed in departmental reports. I shall also further curtail this communication by omitting a minute recital of many minor incidents connected with our foreign relations which have heretofore found a place in Executive messages, but are now contained in a report of the Secretary of State, which is herewith submitted.

At the outset of a reference to the more important matters affecting our relations with foreign powers it would afford me satisfaction if I could assure the Congress that the disturbed condition in Asiatic Turkey had during the past year assumed a less hideous and bloody aspect and that, either as a consequence of the awakening of the Turkish Government to the demands of humane civilization or as the result of decisive action on the part of the great nations having the right by treaty to interfere for the protection of those exposed to the rage of mad bigotry and cruel fanaticism, the shocking features of the situation had been mitigated. Instead, however, of welcoming a softened disposition or protective intervention, we have been afflicted by continued and not unfrequent reports of the wanton destruction of homes and the bloody butchery of men, women, and children, made martyrs to their profession of Christian faith.

While none of our citizens in Turkey have thus far been killed or wounded, though often in the midst of dreadful scenes of danger, their safety in the future is by no means assured. Our Government at home and our minister at Constantinople have left nothing undone to protect our missionaries in Ottoman territory, who constitute nearly all the individuals residing there who have a right to claim our protection on the score of American citizenship. Our efforts in this direction will not be relaxed; but the deep feeling and sympathy that have been aroused among our people ought not to so far blind their reason and judgment as to lead them to demand impossible things. The outbreaks of blind fury which lead to murder and pillage in Turkey occur suddenly and without notice, and an attempt on our part to force such a hostile presence there as might be effective for prevention or protection would not only be resisted by the Ottoman Government, but would be regarded as an interruption of their plans by the great nations who assert their exclusive right to intervene in their own time and method for the security of life and property in Turkey.

Several naval vessels are stationed in the Mediterranean as a measure of caution and to furnish all possible relief and refuge in case of emergency.

We have made claims against the Turkish Government for the pillage and destruction of missionary property at Harpoot and Marash during uprisings at those places. Thus far the validity of these demands has not been admitted, though our minister, prior to such outrages and in anticipation of danger, demanded protection for the persons and property of our missionary citizens in the localities mentioned and notwithstanding that strong evidence exists of actual complicity of Turkish soldiers in the work of destruction and robbery.

The facts as they now appear do not permit us to doubt the justice of these claims, and nothing will be omitted to bring about their prompt settlement.

A number of Armenian refugees having arrived at our ports, an order has lately been obtained from the Turkish Government permitting the wives and children of such refugees to join them here. It is hoped that hereafter no obstacle will be interposed to prevent the escape of all those who seek to avoid the perils which threaten them in Turkish dominions.

Our recently appointed consul to Erzerum is at his post and discharging the duties of his office, though for some unaccountable reason his formal exequatur from the Sultan has not been issued.

I do not believe that the present somber prospect in Turkey will be long permitted to offend the sight of Christendom. It so mars the humane and enlightened civilization that belongs to the close of the nineteenth century that it seems hardly possible that the earnest demand of good people throughout the Christian world for its corrective treatment will remain unanswered.

The insurrection in Cuba still continues with all its perplexities. It is difficult to perceive that any progress has thus far been made toward the pacification of the island or that the situation of affairs as depicted in my last annual message has in the least improved. If Spain still holds Havana and the seaports and all the considerable towns, the insurgents still roam at will over at least two-thirds of the inland country. If the determination of Spain to put down the insurrection seems but to strengthen with the lapse of time and is evinced by her unhesitating devotion of largely increased military and naval forces to the task, there is much reason to believe that the insurgents have gained in point of numbers and character and resources and are none the less inflexible in their resolve not to succumb without practically securing the great objects for which they took up arms. If Spain has not yet reestablished her authority, neither have the insurgents yet made good their title to be regarded as an independent state. Indeed, as the contest has gone on the pretense that civil government exists on the island, except so far as Spain is able to maintain it, has been practically abandoned. Spain does keep on foot such a government, more or less imperfectly, in the large towns and their immediate suburbs; but that exception being made, the entire country is either given over to anarchy or is subject to the military occupation of one or the other party. It is reported, indeed, on reliable authority that at the demand of the commander in chief of the insurgent army the putative Cuban government has now given up all attempt to exercise its functions, leaving that government confessedly (what there is the best reason for supposing it always to have been in fact) a government merely on paper.

Were the Spanish armies able to meet their antagonists in the open or in pitched battle, prompt and decisive results might be looked for, and the immense superiority of the Spanish forces in numbers, discipline, and equipment could hardly fail to tell greatly to their advantage. But they are called upon to face a foe that shuns general engagements, that can choose and does choose its own ground, that from the nature of the country is visible or invisible at pleasure, and that fights only from ambuscade and when all the advantages of position and numbers are on its side. In a country where all that is indispensable to life in the way of food, clothing, and shelter is so easily obtainable, especially by those born and bred on the soil, it is obvious that there is hardly a limit to the time during which hostilities of this sort may be prolonged. Meanwhile, as in all cases of protracted civil strife, the passions of the combatants grow more and more inflamed and excesses on both sides become more frequent and more deplorable. They are also participated in by bands of marauders, who, now in the name of one party and now in the name of the other, as may best suit the occasion, harry the country at will and plunder its wretched inhabitants for their own advantage. Such a condition of things would inevitably entail immense destruction of property, even if it were the policy of both parties to prevent it as far as practicable; but while such seemed to be the original policy of the Spanish Government, it has now apparently abandoned it and is acting upon the same theory as the insurgents, namely, that the exigencies of the contest require the wholesale annihilation of property that it may not prove of use and advantage to the enemy.

It is to the same end that, in pursuance of general orders, Spanish garrisons are now being withdrawn from plantations and the rural population required to concentrate itself in the towns. The sure result would seem to be that the industrial value of the island is fast diminishing and that unless there is a speedy and radical change in existing conditions it will soon disappear altogether. That value consists very largely, of course, in its capacity to produce sugar—a capacity already much reduced by the interruptions to tillage which have taken place during the last two years. It is reliably asserted that should these interruptions continue during the current year, and practically extend, as is now threatened, to the entire sugar-producing territory of the island, so much time and so much money will be required to restore the land to its normal productiveness that it is extremely doubtful if capital can be induced to even make the attempt.

The spectacle of the utter ruin of an adjoining country, by nature one of the most fertile and charming on the globe, would engage the serious attention of the Government and people of the United States in any circumstances. In point of fact, they have a concern with it which is by no means of a wholly sentimental or philanthropic character. It lies so near to us as to be hardly separated from our territory. Our actual pecuniary interest in it is second only to that of the people and Government of Spain.   It is reasonably estimated that at least from $30,000,000 to $50,000,000 of American capital are invested in plantations and in rail-road, mining, and other business enterprises on the island.   The volume of trade between the United States and Cuba, which in 1889 amounted to about $64,000,000, rose in 1893 to about $103,000,000, and in 1894, the year before the present insurrection broke out, amounted to nearly $96,000,000.   Besides this large pecuniary stake in the fortunes of Cuba, the United States finds itself inextricably involved in the present contest in other ways, both vexatious and costly.

Many Cubans reside in this country, and indirectly promote the in-surrection through the press, by public meetings, by the purchase and shipment of arms, by the raising of funds, and by other means which the spirit of our institutions and the tenor of our laws do not permit to be made the subject of criminal prosecutions.   Some of them, though Cubans at heart and in all their feelings and interests, have taken out papers as naturalized citizens of the United States—a proceeding resorted to with a view to possible protection by this Government, and not un-naturally regarded with much indignation by the country of their origin. The insurgents are undoubtedly encouraged and supported by the wide-spread sympathy the people of this country always and instinctively feel for every struggle for better and freer government, and which, in the case of the more adventurous and restless elements of our population, leads in only too many instances to active and personal participation in the contest.   The result is that this Government is constantly called upon to protect American citizens, to claim damages for injuries to per-sons and property, now estimated at many millions of dollars, and to ask explanations and apologies for the acts of Spanish officials whose zeal for the repression of rebellion sometimes blinds them to the immunities belonging to the unoffending citizens of a friendly power.   It follows from the same causes that the United States is compelled to actively police a long line of seacoast against unlawful expeditions, the escape of which the utmost vigilance will not always suffice to prevent.

These inevitable entanglements of the United States with the rebellion in Cuba, the large American property interests affected, and considera-tions of philanthropy and humanity in general have led to a vehement demand in various quarters for some sort of positive intervention on the part of the United States.   It was at first proposed that belligerent rights should be accorded to the insurgents—a proposition no longer urged be-cause untimely and in practical operation clearly perilous and injurious to our own interests.   It has since been and is now sometimes contended that the independence of the insurgents should be recognized; but imper-fect and restricted as the Spanish government of the island may be, no other exists there, unless the will of the military officer in temporary command of a particular district can be dignified as a species of govern-ment.   It is now also suggested that the United States should buy the island—a suggestion possibly worthy of consideration if there were any evidence of a desire or willingness on the part of Spain to entertain such a proposal. It is urged finally that, all other methods failing, the existing internecine strife in Cuba should be terminated by our intervention, even at the cost of a war between the United States and Spain—a war which its advocates confidently prophesy could neither be large in its proportions nor doubtful in its issue.

The correctness of this forecast need be neither affirmed nor denied. The United States has, nevertheless, a character to maintain as a nation, which plainly dictates that right and not might should be the rule of its conduct. Further, though the United States is not a nation to which peace is a necessity, it is in truth the most pacific of powers and desires nothing so much as to live in amity with all the world. Its own ample and diversified domains satisfy all possible longings for territory, preclude all dreams of conquest, and prevent any casting of covetous eyes upon neighboring regions, however attractive. That our conduct toward Spain and her dominions has constituted no exception to this national disposition is made manifest by the course of our Government, not only thus far during the present insurrection, but during the ten years that followed the rising at Yara in 1868. No other great power, it may safely be said, under circumstances of similar perplexity, would have manifested the same restraint and the same patient endurance. It may also be said that this persistent attitude of the United States toward Spain in connection with Cuba unquestionably evinces no slight respect and regard for Spain on the part of the American people. They in truth do not forget her connection with the discovery of the Western Hemisphere, nor do they underestimate the great qualities of the Spanish people nor fail to fully recognize their splendid patriotism and their chivalrous devotion to the national honor.

They view with wonder and admiration the cheerful resolution with which vast bodies of men are sent across thousands of miles of ocean and an enormous debt accumulated that the costly possession of the gem of the Antilles may still hold its place in the Spanish crown. And yet neither the Government nor the people of the United States have shut their eyes to the course of events in Cuba or have failed to realize the existence of conceded grievances which have led to the present revolt from the authority of Spain—grievances recognized by the Queen Regent and by the Cortes, voiced by the most patriotic and enlightened of Spanish statesmen, without regard to party, and demonstrated by reforms proposed by the executive and approved by the legislative branch of the Spanish Government. It is in the assumed temper and disposition of the Spanish Government to remedy these grievances, fortified by indications of influential public opinion in Spain, that this Government has hoped to discover the most promising and effective means of composing the present strife with honor and advantage to Spain and with the achievement of all the reasonable objects of the insurrection.

It would seem that if Spain should offer to Cuba genuine autonomy—a measure of home rule which, while preserving the sovereignty of Spain, would satisfy all rational requirements of her Spanish subjects—there should be no just reason why the pacification of the island might not be effected on that basis. Such a result would appear to be in the true interest of all concerned. It would at once stop the conflict which is now consuming the resources of the island and making it worthless for whichever party may ultimately prevail. It would keep intact the possessions of Spain without touching her honor, which will be consulted rather than impugned by the adequate redress of admitted grievances. It would put the prosperity of the island and the fortunes of its inhabitants within their own control without severing the natural and ancient ties which bind them to the mother country, and would yet enable them to test their capacity for self-government under the most favorable conditions. It has been objected on the one side that Spain should not promise autonomy until her insurgent subjects lay down their arms; on the other side, that promised autonomy, however liberal, is insufficient, because without assurance of the promise being fulfilled.

But the reasonableness of a requirement by Spain of unconditional surrender on the part of the insurgent Cubans before their autonomy is conceded is not altogether apparent. It ignores important features of the situation—the stability two years' duration has given to the insurrection; the feasibility of its indefinite prolongation in the nature of things, and, as shown by past experience, the utter and imminent ruin of the island unless the present strife is speedily composed; above all, the rank abuses which all parties in Spain, all branches of her Government, and all her leading public men concede to exist and profess a desire to remove. Facing such circumstances, to withhold the proffer of needed reforms until the parties demanding them put themselves at mercy by throwing down their arms has the appearance of neglecting the gravest of perils and inviting suspicion as to the sincerity of any professed willingness to grant reforms The objection on behalf of the insurgents that promised reforms can not be relied upon must of course be considered, though we have no right to assume and no reason for assuming that anything Spain undertakes to do for the relief of Cuba will not be done according to both the spirit and the letter of the undertaking.

Nevertheless, realizing that suspicions and precautions on the part of the weaker of two combatants are always natural and not always unjustifiable, being sincerely desirous in the interest of both as well as on its own account that the Cuban problem should be solved with the least possible delay, it was intimated by this Government to the Government of Spain some months ago that if a satisfactory measure of home rule were tendered the Cuban insurgents and would be accepted by them upon a guaranty of its execution the United States would endeavor to find a way not objectionable to Spain of furnishing such guaranty. While no definite response to this intimation has yet been received from the Spanish Government, it is believed to be not altogether unwelcome, while, as already suggested, no reason is perceived why it should not be approved by the insurgents. Neither party can fail to see the importance of early action, and both must realize that to prolong the present state of things for even a short period will add enormously to the time and labor and expenditure necessary to bring about the industrial recuperation of the island. It is therefore fervently hoped on all grounds that earnest efforts for healing the breach between Spain and the insurgent Cubans upon the lines above indicated may be at once inaugurated and pushed to an immediate and successful issue. The friendly offices of the United States, either in the manner above outlined or in any other way consistent with our Constitution and laws, will always be at the disposal of either party.

Whatever circumstances may arise, our policy and our interests would constrain us to object to the acquisition of the island or an interference with its control by any other power.

It should be added that it can not be reasonably assumed that the hitherto expectant attitude of the United States will be indefinitely maintained. While we are anxious to accord all due respect to the sovereignty of Spain, we can not view the pending conflict in all its features and properly apprehend our inevitably close relations to it and its possible results without considering that by the course of events we may be drawn into such an unusual and unprecedented condition as will fix a limit to our patient waiting for Spain to end the contest, either alone and in her own way or with our friendly cooperation.

When the inability of Spain to deal successfully with the insurrection has become manifest and it is demonstrated that her sovereignty is extinct in Cuba for all purposes of its rightful existence, and when a hopeless struggle for its reestablishment has degenerated into a strife which means nothing more than the useless sacrifice of human life and the utter destruction of the very subject-matter of the conflict, a situation will be presented in which our obligations to the sovereignty of Spain will be superseded by higher obligations, which we can hardly hesitate to recognize and discharge. Deferring the choice of ways and methods until the time for action arrives, we should make them depend upon the precise conditions then existing; and they should not be determined upon without giving careful heed to every consideration involving our honor and interest or the international duty we owe to Spain. Until we face the contingencies suggested or the situation is by other incidents imperatively changed we should continue in the line of conduct heretofore pursued, thus in all circumstances exhibiting our obedience to the requirements of public law and our regard for the duty enjoined upon us by the position we occupy in the family of nations.

A contemplation of emergencies that may arise should plainly lead us to avoid their creation, either through a careless disregard of present duty or even an undue stimulation and ill-timed expression of feeling. But I have deemed it not amiss to remind the Congress that a time may arrive when a correct policy and care for our interests, as well as a regard for the interests of other nations and their citizens, joined by considerations of humanity and a desire to see a rich and fertile country intimately related to us saved from complete devastation, will constrain our Government to such action as will subserve the interests thus involved and at the same time promise to Cuba and its inhabitants an opportunity to enjoy the blessings of peace.

The Venezuelan boundary question has ceased to be a matter of difference between Great Britain and the United States, their respective Governments having agreed upon the substantial provisions of a treaty between Great Britain and Venezuela submitting the whole controversy to arbitration. The provisions of the treaty are so eminently just and fair that the assent of Venezuela thereto may confidently be anticipated.

Negotiations for a treaty of general arbitration for all differences between Great Britain and the United States are far advanced and promise to reach a successful consummation at an early date.

The scheme of examining applicants for certain consular positions to test their competency and fitness, adopted under an Executive order issued on the 20th of September, 1895, has fully demonstrated the usefulness of this innovation. In connection with this plan of examination promotions and transfers of deserving incumbents have been quite extensively made, with excellent results.

During the past year 35 appointments have been made in the consular service, 27 of which were made to fill vacancies caused by death or resignation or to supply newly created posts, 2 to succeed incumbents removed for cause, 2 for the purpose of displacing alien consular officials by American citizens, and 4 merely changing the official title of incumbent from commercial agent to consul. Twelve of these appointments were transfers or promotions from other positions under the Department of State, 4 of those appointed had rendered previous service under the Department, 8 were made of persons who passed a satisfactory examination, 7 were appointed to places not included in the order of September 20, 1895, and 4 appointments, as above stated, involved no change of incumbency.

The inspection of consular offices provided for by an appropriation for that purpose at the last session of the Congress has been productive of such wholesome effects that I hope this important work will in the future be continued. I know of nothing that can be done with the same slight expense so improving to the service.

I desire to repeat the recommendation contained in my last annual message in favor of providing at public expense official residences for our ambassadors and ministers at foreign capitals. The reasons supporting this recommendation are strongly stated in the report of the Secretary of State, and the subject seems of such importance that I hope it may receive the early attention of the Congress.

We have during the last year labored faithfully and against unfavorable conditions to secure better preservation of seal life in the Bering Sea. Both the United States and Great Britain have lately dispatched commissioners to these waters to study the habits and condition of the seal herd and the causes of their rapid decrease. Upon the reports of these commissioners, soon to be submitted, and with the exercise of patience and good sense on the part of all interested parties, it is earnestly hoped that hearty cooperation may be secured for the protection against threatened extinction of seal life in the Northern Pacific and Bering Sea.

The Secretary of the Treasury reports that during the fiscal year ended June 30, 1896, the receipts of the Government from all sources amounted to $409,475,408.78. During the same period its expenditures were $434,678,654.48, the excess of expenditures over receipts thus amounting to $25,203,245.70. The ordinary expenditures during the year were $4,015,852.21 less than during the preceding fiscal year. Of the receipts mentioned there was derived from customs the sum of $160,021,751.67 and from internal revenue $146,830,615.66. The receipts from customs show an increase of $7,863,134.22 over those from the same source for the fiscal year ended June 30, 1895, and the receipts from internal revenue an increase of $3,584,537.91.

The value of our imported dutiable merchandise during the last fiscal year was $369,757,470 and the value of free goods imported $409,967,-470, being an increase of $6,523,675 in the value of dutiable goods and $41,231,034 in the value of free goods over the preceding year. Our exports of merchandise, foreign and domestic, amounted in value to $882,606,938, being an increase over the preceding year of $75,068,773. The average *ad valorem* duty paid on dutiable goods imported during the year was 39.94 per cent and on free and dutiable goods taken together 20.55 per cent.

The cost of collecting our internal revenue was 2.78 per cent, as against 2.81 per cent for the fiscal year ending June 30, 1895. The total production of distilled spirits, exclusive of fruit brandies, was 86,588,703 taxable gallons, being an increase of 6,639,108 gallons over the preceding year. There was also an increase of 1,443,676 gallons of spirits produced from fruit as compared with the preceding year. The number of barrels of beer produced was 35,859,250, as against 33,589,784 produced in the preceding fiscal year, being an increase of 2,269,466 barrels.

The total amount of gold exported during the last fiscal year was $112,-409,947 and of silver $60,541,670, being an increase of $45,941,466 of gold and $13,246,384 of silver over the exportations of the preceding fiscal year. The imports of gold were $33,525,065 and of silver $28,-777,186, being $2,859,695 less of gold and $8,566,007 more of silver than during the preceding year.

The total stock of metallic money in the United States at the close of the last fiscal year, ended on the 30th day of June, 1896, was $1,228,-326,035, of which $599,597,964 was in gold and $628,728,071 in silver.

On the 1st day of November, 1896, the total stock of money of all kinds in the country was $2,285,410,590, and the amount in circulation, not including that in the Treasury holdings, was $1,627,055,641, being $22.63 per capita upon an estimated population of 71,902,000.

The production of the precious metals in the United States during the calendar year 1895 is estimated to have been 2,254,760 fine ounces of gold, of the value of $46,610,000, and 55,727,000 fine ounces of silver, of the commercial value of $36,445,000 and the coinage value of $72,051,-000. The estimated production of these metals throughout the world during the same period was 9,688,821 fine ounces of gold, amounting to $200,285,700 in value, and 169,189,249 fine ounces of silver, of the commercial value of $110,654,000 and of the coinage value of $218,738,100 according to our ratio.

The coinage of these metals in the various countries of the world during the same calendar year amounted to $232,701,438 in gold and $121,996,219 in silver.

The total coinage at the mints of the United States during the fiscal year ended June 30, 1896, amounted to $71,188,468.52, of which $58,-878,490 was in gold coins and $12,309,978.52 in standard silver dollars, subsidiary coins, and minor coins.

The number of national banks organized from the time the law authorizing their creation was passed up to October 31, 1896, was 5,051, and of this number 3,679 were at the date last mentioned in active operation, having authorized capital stock of $650,014,895, held by 288,902 shareholders, and circulating notes amounting to $211,412,620.

The total outstanding circulating notes of all national banks on the 31st day of October, 1896, amounted to $234,553,807, including unredeemed but fully secured notes of banks insolvent and in process of liquidation. The increase in national-bank circulation during the year ending on that day was $21,099,429. On October 6, 1896, when the condition of national banks was last reported, the total resources of the 3,679 active institutions were $3,263,685,313.83, which included $1,893,268,839.31 in loans and discounts and $362,165,733.85 in money of all kinds on hand. Of their liabilities $1,597,891,058.03 was due to individual depositors and $209,944,019 consisted of outstanding circulating notes.

There were organized during the year preceding the date last mentioned 28 national banks, located in 15 States, of which 12 were organized in the Eastern States, with a capital of $1,180,000, 6 in the Western States, with a capital of $875,000, and 10 in the Southern States, with a capital of $1,190,000. During the year, however, 37 banks voluntarily abandoned their franchises under the national law, and in the case of 27 others it was found necessary to appoint receivers. Therefore, as compared with the year preceding, there was a decrease of 36 in the number of active banks.

The number of existing banks organized under State laws is 5,708.

The number of immigrants arriving in the United States during the fiscal year was 343,267, of whom 340,468 were permitted to land and 2,799 were debarred on various grounds prescribed by law and returned to the countries whence they came at the expense of the steamship companies by which they were brought in. The increase in immigration over the preceding year amounted to 84,731. It is reported that with some exceptions the immigrants of the past year were of a hardy laboring class, accustomed and able to earn a support for themselves, and it is estimated that the money brought with them amounted to at least $5,000,-000, though it was probably much in excess of that sum, since only those having less than $30 are required to disclose the exact amount, and it is known that many brought considerable sums of money to buy land and build homes. Including all the immigrants arriving who were over 14 years of age, 28.63 per cent were illiterate, as against 20.37 per cent of those of that age arriving during the preceding fiscal year. The number of immigrants over 14 years old, the countries from which they came, and the percentage of illiterates among them were as follows: Italy, 57,515, with 54.59 per cent; Ireland, 37,496, with 7 per cent; Russia, 35,188, with 41.14 per cent; Austria-Hungary and provinces, 57,053, with 38.92 per cent; Germany, 25,334, with 2.96 per cent; Sweden, 18,821, with 1.16 per cent; while from Portugal there came 2,067, of whom 77.69 per cent were illiterate. There arrived from Japan during the year only 1,110 immigrants, and it is the opinion of the immigration authorities that the apprehension heretofore existing to some extent of a large immigration from Japan to the United States is without any substantial foundation.

From the Life-Saving Service it is reported that the number of disasters to documented vessels within the limits of its operations during the year was 437. These vessels had on board 4,608 persons, of whom 4,595 were saved and 13 lost. The value of such vessels is estimated at $8,880,140 and of their cargoes $3,846,380, making the total value of property imperiled $12,726,520. Of this amount $11,292,707 was saved and $1,432,750 was lost. Sixty-seven of the vessels were totally wrecked. There were besides 243 casualties to small undocumented craft, on board of which there were 594 persons, of whom 587 were saved and 7 were lost. The value of the property involved in these latter casualties is estimated at $119,265, of which $114,915 was saved and $4,350 was lost. The life-saving crews during the year also rescued or assisted numerous other vessels and warned many from danger by signals, both by day and night. The number of disasters during the year exceeded that of any previous year in the history of the service, but the saving of both life and property was greater than ever before in proportion to the value of the property involved and to the number of persons imperiled.

The operations of the Marine-Hospital Service, the Revenue-Cutter Service, the Steamboat-Inspection Service, the Light-House Service, the Bureau of Navigation, and other branches of public work attached to the Treasury Department, together with various recommendations concerning their support and improvement, are fully stated in the report of the Secretary of the Treasury, to which the attention of the Congress is especially invited.

The report of the Secretary of War exhibits satisfactory conditions in the several branches of the public service intrusted to his charge.

The limit of our military force as fixed by law is constantly and readily maintained. The present discipline and morale of our Army are excellent, and marked progress and efficiency are apparent throughout its entire organization.

With the exception of delicate duties in the suppression of slight Indian disturbances along our southwestern boundary, in which the Mexican troops cooperated, and the compulsory but peaceful return, with the consent of Great Britain, of a band of Cree Indians from Montana to the British possessions, no active operations have been required of the Army during the year past.

Changes in methods of administration, the abandonment of unnecessary posts and consequent concentration of troops, and the exercise of care and vigilance by the various officers charged with the responsibility in the expenditure of the appropriations have resulted in reducing to a minimum the cost of maintenance of our military establishment.

During the past year the work of constructing permanent infantry and cavalry posts has been continued at the places heretofore designated. The Secretary of War repeats his recommendation that appropriations for barracks and quarters should more strictly conform to the needs of the service as judged by the Department rather than respond to the wishes and importunities of localities. It is imperative that much of the money provided for such construction should now be allotted to the erection of necessary quarters for the garrisons assigned to the coast defenses, where many men will be needed to properly care for and operate modern guns. It is essential, too, that early provision be made to supply the necessary force of artillery to meet the demands of this service.

The entire Army has now been equipped with the new magazine arms, and wise policy demands that all available public and private resources should be so employed as to provide within a reasonable time a sufficient number to supply the State militia with these modern weapons and provide an ample reserve for any emergency.

The organized militia numbers 112,879 men. The appropriations for its support by the several States approximate $2,800,000 annually, and $400,000 is contributed by the General Government. Investigation shows these troops to be usually well drilled and inspired with much military interest, but in many instances they are so deficient in proper arms and equipment that a sudden call to active duty would find them inadequately prepared for field service. I therefore recommend that prompt measures be taken to remedy this condition and that every encouragement be given to this deserving body of unpaid and voluntary citizen soldiers, upon whose assistance we must largely rely in time of trouble.

During the past year rapid progress has been made toward the completion of the scheme adopted for the erection and armament of fortifications along our seacoast, while equal progress has been made in providing the material for submarine defense in connection with these works.

It is peculiarly gratifying at this time to note the great advance that has been made in this important undertaking since the date of my annual message to the Fifty-third Congress at the opening of its second session, in December, 1893. At that time I informed the Congress of the approaching completion of nine 12-inch, twenty 10-inch, and thirty-four 8-inch high-power steel guns and seventy-five 12-inch rifled mortars.

This total then seemed insignificant when compared with the great work remaining to be done. Yet it was none the less a source of satisfaction to every citizen when he reflected that it represented the first installment of the new ordnance of American design and American manufacture and demonstrated our ability to supply from our own resources guns of unexcelled power and accuracy.

At that date, however, there were practically no carriages upon which to mount these guns and only thirty-one emplacements for guns and sixty-four for mortars. Nor were all these emplacements in condition to receive their armament. Only one high-power gun was at that time in position for the defense of the entire coast.

Since that time the number of guns actually completed has been increased to a total of twenty-one 12-inch, fifty-six 10-inch, sixty-one 8-inch high-power breech-loading steel guns, ten rapid-fire guns, and eighty 12-inch rifled mortars. In addition there are in process of construction one 16-inch-type gun, fifty 12-inch, fifty-six 10-inch, twenty-seven 8-inch high-power guns, and sixty-six 12-inch rifled mortars; in all, four hundred and twenty-eight guns and mortars.

During the same year, immediately preceding the message referred to, the first modern gun carriage had been completed and eleven more were in process of construction. All but one were of the nondisappearing type. These, however, were not such as to secure necessary cover for the artillery gunners against the intense fire of modern machine rapid-fire and high-power guns.

The inventive genius of ordnance and civilian experts has been taxed in designing carriages that would obviate this fault, resulting, it is believed, in the solution of this difficult problem. Since 1893 the number of gun carriages constructed or building has been raised to a total of 129, of which 90 are on the disappearing principle, and the number of mortar carriages to 152, while the 95 emplacements which were provided for prior to that time have been increased to 280 built and building.

This improved situation is largely due to the recent generous response of Congress to the recommendations of the War Department.

Thus we shall soon have complete about one-fifth of the comprehensive system the first step in which was noted in my message to the Congress of December 4, 1893.

When it is understood that a masonry emplacement not only furnishes a platform for the heavy modern high-power gun, but also in every particular serves the purpose and takes the place of the fort of former days, the importance of the work accomplished is better comprehended.

In the hope that the work will be prosecuted with no less vigor in the future, the Secretary of War has submitted an estimate by which, if allowed, there will be provided and either built or building by the end of the next fiscal year such additional guns, mortars, gun carriages, and emplacements as will represent not far from one-third of the total work to be done under the plan adopted for our coast defenses, thus affording a prospect that the entire work will be substantially completed within six years. In less time than that, however, we shall have attained a marked degree of security.

The experience and results of the past year demonstrate that with a continuation of present careful methods the cost of the remaining work will be much less than the original estimate.

We should always keep in mind that of all forms of military preparation coast defense alone is essentially pacific in its nature. While it gives the sense of security due to a consciousness of strength, it is neither the **purpose nor the effect of such permanent fortifications to involve us in** foreign complications, but rather to guarantee us against them. They are not temptation to war, but security against it. Thus they are thoroughly in accord with all the traditions of our national diplomacy.

The Attorney-General presents a detailed and interesting statement of the important work done under his supervision during the last fiscal year.

The ownership and management by the Government of penitentiaries for the confinement of those convicted in United States courts of violations of Federal laws, which for many years has been a subject of Executive recommendation, have at last to a slight extent been realized by the utilization of the abandoned military prison at Fort Leavenworth as a United States penitentiary.

This is certainly a movement in the right direction, but it ought to be at once supplemented by the rebuilding or extensive enlargement of this improvised prison and the construction of at least one more, to be located in the Southern States. The capacity of the Leavenworth Penitentiary is so limited that the expense of its maintenance, calculated at a per capita rate upon the number of prisoners it can accommodate, does not make as economical an exhibit as it would if it were larger and better adapted to prison purposes; but I am thoroughly convinced that economy, humanity, and a proper sense of responsibility and duty toward those whom we punish for violations of Federal law dictate that the Federal Government should have the entire control and management of the penitentiaries where convicted violators are confined.

It appears that since the transfer of the Fort Leavenworth Military Prison to its new uses the work previously done by prisoners confined there, and for which expensive machinery has been provided, has been discontinued. This work consisted of the manufacture of articles for army use, now done elsewhere. On all grounds it is exceedingly desirable that the convicts confined in this penitentiary be allowed to resume work of this description.

It is most gratifying to note the satisfactory results that have followed the inauguration of the new system provided for by the act of May 28, 1896, under which certain Federal officials are compensated by salaries instead of fees. The new plan was put in operation on the 1st day of July, 1896, and already the great economy it enforces, its prevention of abuses, and its tendency to a better enforcement of the laws are strikingly apparent. Detailed evidence of the usefulness of this long-delayed but now happily accomplished reform will be found clearly set forth in the Attorney-General's report.

Our Post-Office Department is in good condition, and the exhibit made of its operations during the fiscal year ended June 30, 1896, if allowance is made for imperfections in the laws applicable to it, is very satisfactory. The total receipts during the year were $82,499,208.40. The total expenditures were $90,626,296.84, exclusive of the $1,559,898.27 which was earned by the Pacific Railroad for transportation and credited on their debt to the Government. There was an increase of receipts over the previous year of $5,516,080.21, or 7.1 per cent, and an increase of expenditures of $3,836,124.02, or 4.42 per cent. The deficit was $1,679,- 956.19 less than that of the preceding year. The chief expenditures of the postal service are regulated by law and are not in the control of the Postmaster-General. All that he can accomplish by the most watchful administration and economy is to enforce prompt and thorough collection and accounting for public moneys and such minor savings in small expenditures and in letting those contracts, for post-office supplies and star service, which are not regulated by statute.

An effective cooperation between the Auditor's Office and the Post-Office Department and the making and enforcement of orders by the Department requiring immediate notification to their sureties of all delinquencies on the part of postmasters, and compelling such postmasters to make more frequent deposits of postal funds, have resulted in a prompter auditing of their accounts and much less default to the Government than heretofore.

The year's report shows large extensions of both star-route service and railway mail service, with increased postal facilities. Much higher accuracy in handling mails has also been reached, as appears by the decrease of errors in the railway mail service and the reduction of mail matter returned to the Dead-Letter Office.

The deficit for the last year, although much less than that of the last and preceding years, emphasizes the necessity for legislation to correct the growing abuse of second-class rates, to which the deficiency is mainly attributable. The transmission at the rate of 1 cent a pound of serial libraries, advertising sheets, "house organs" (periodicals advertising some particular "house" or institution), sample copies, and the like ought certainly to be discontinued. A glance at the revenues received for the work done last year will show more plainly than any other statement the gross abuse of the postal service and the growing waste of its earnings.

The free matter carried in the mails for the Departments, offices, etc., of the Government and for Congress, in pounds, amounted to 94,480,189.

If this is offset against buildings for post-offices and stations, the rental of which would more than compensate for such free postal service, we have this exhibit:

Weight of mail matter (other than above) transmitted through the mails for the year ending June 30, 1896.

Class.	Weight.	Revenue.
	Pounds.	
1. Domestic and foreign letters and postal cards, etc......	65,337,343	$60,624,464
2. Newspapers and periodicals, 1 cent per pound..........	348,988,648	2,996,403
3. Books, seeds, etc., 8 cents a pound......................	78,701,148	10,324,069
4. Parcels, etc., 16 cents a pound...........................	19,950,187	3,129,321
Total	512,977,326	77,044,257

The remainder of our postal revenue, amounting to something more than $5,000,000, was derived from box rents, registry fees, money-order business, and other similar items.

The entire expenditures of the Department, including pay for transportation credited to the Pacific railroads, were $92,186,195.11, which may be considered as the cost of receiving, carrying, and delivering the above mail matter. It thus appears that though the second-class matter constituted more than two-thirds of the total that was carried, the revenue derived from it was less than one-thirtieth of the total expense.

The average revenue was—
From each pound of first-class matter ....cents.. 93.0
From each pound of second class* ....mills.. 8.5
From each pound of third class ....cents.. 13.1
From each pound of fourth class...do... 15.6

The growth in weight of second-class matter has been from 299,000,000 pounds in 1894 to 312,000,000 in 1895 and to almost 349,000,000 in 1896, and it is quite evident this increasing drawback is far outstripping any possible growth of postal revenues.

Our mail service should of course be such as to meet the wants and even the conveniences of our people at a direct charge upon them so light as perhaps to exclude the idea of our Post-Office Department being a money-making concern; but in the face of a constantly recurring deficiency in its revenues and in view of the fact that we supply the best mail service in the world it seems to me it is quite time to correct the abuses that swell enormously our annual deficit. If we concede the public policy of carrying weekly newspapers free in the county of publication, and even the policy of carrying at less than one-tenth of their cost other *bona fide* newspapers and periodicals, there can be no excuse for subjecting the service to the further immense and increasing loss involved in carrying at the nominal rate of 1 cent a pound the serial libraries, sometimes including trashy and even harmful literature, and other matter which under the loose interpretation of a loose statute have been gradually given second-class rates, thus absorbing all profitable returns derived from first-class matter, which pays three or four times more than its cost, and producing a large annual loss to be paid by general taxation. If such second-class matter paid merely the cost of its handling, our deficit would disappear and a surplus result which might be used to give the people still better mail facilities or cheaper rates of letter postage. I recommend that legislation be at once enacted to correct these abuses and introduce better business ideas in the regulation of our postal rates.

Experience and observation have demonstrated that certain improvements in the organization of the Post-Office Department must be secured before we can gain the full benefit of the immense sums expended in its administration. This involves the following reforms, which I earnestly recommend:

There should be a small addition to the existing inspector service, to be employed in the supervision of the carrier force, which now numbers 13,000 men and performs its service practically without the surveillance exercised over all other branches of the postal or public service. Of course such a lack of supervision and freedom from wholesome disciplinary restraints must inevitably lead to imperfect service. There should also be appointed a few inspectors who could assist the central office in necessary investigation concerning matters of post-office leases, post-office sites, allowances for rent, fuel, and lights, and in organizing and securing the best results from the work of the 14,000 clerks now employed in first and second class offices.

I am convinced that the small expense attending the inauguration of these reforms would actually be a profitable investment.

I especially recommend such a recasting of the appropriations by Congress for the Post-Office Department as will permit the Postmaster-General to proceed with the work of consolidating post-offices. This work has already been entered upon sufficiently to fully demonstrate by experiment and experience that such consolidation is productive of better service, larger revenues, and less expenditures, to say nothing of the further advantage of gradually withdrawing post-offices from the spoils system.

The Universal Postal Union, which now embraces all the civilized world and whose delegates will represent 1,000,000,000 people, will hold its fifth congress in the city of Washington in May, 1897. The United States may be said to have taken the initiative which led to the first meeting of this congress, at Berne in 1874, and the formation of the

Universal Postal Union, which brings the postal service of all countries to every man's neighborhood and has wrought marvels in cheapening postal rates and securing absolutely safe mail communication throughout the world. Previous congresses have met in Berne, Paris, Lisbon, and Vienna, and the respective countries in which they have assembled have made generous provision for their accommodation and for the reception and entertainment of the delegates.

In view of the importance of this assemblage and of its deliberations and of the honors and hospitalities accorded to our representatives by other countries on similar occasions, I earnestly hope that such an appropriation will be made for the expenses necessarily attendant upon the coming meeting in our capital city as will be worthy of our national hospitality and indicative of our appreciation of the event.

The work of the Navy Department and its present condition are fully exhibited in the report of the Secretary.

The construction of vessels for our new Navy has been energetically prosecuted by the present Administration upon the general lines previously adopted, the Department having seen no necessity for radical changes in prior methods, under which the work was found to be progressing in a manner highly satisfactory. It has been decided, however, to provide in every shipbuilding contract that the builder should pay all trial expenses, and it has also been determined to pay no speed premiums in future contracts. The premiums recently earned and some yet to be decided are features of the contracts made before this conclusion was reached.

On March 4, 1893, there were in commission but two armored vessels—the double-turreted monitors *Miantonomoh* and *Monterey*. Since that date, of vessels theretofore authorized, there have been placed in their first commission 3 first-class and 2 second-class battle ships, 2 armored cruisers, 1 harbor-defense ram, and 5 double-turreted monitors, including the *Maine* and the *Puritan*, just completed. Eight new unarmored cruisers and 2 new gunboats have also been commissioned. The *Iowa*, another battle ship, will be completed about March 1, and at least 4 more gunboats will be ready for sea in the early spring.

It is gratifying to state that our ships and their outfits are believed to be equal to the best that can be manufactured elsewhere, and that such notable reductions have been made in their cost as to justify the statement that quite a number of vessels are now being constructed at rates as low as those that prevail in European shipyards.

Our manufacturing facilities are at this time ample for all possible naval contingencies. Three of our Government navy-yards—those at Mare Island, Cal., Norfolk, Va., and Brooklyn, N. Y.—are equipped for shipbuilding, our ordnance plant in Washington is equal to any in the world, and at the torpedo station we are successfully making the highest grades of smokeless powder. The first-class private shipyards at Newport News, Philadelphia, and San Francisco are building battle ships; eleven contractors, situated in the States of Maine, Rhode Island, Pennsylvania, New Jersey, Maryland, Virginia, and the State of Washington, are constructing gunboats or torpedo boats; two plants are manufacturing large quantities of first-class armor, and American factories are producing automobile torpedoes, powder, projectiles, rapid-fire guns, and everything else necessary for the complete outfit of naval vessels.

There have been authorized by Congress since March, 1893, 5 battle ships, 6 light-draft gunboats, 16 torpedo boats, and 1 submarine torpedo boat. Contracts for the building of all of them have been let. The Secretary expresses the opinion that we have for the present a sufficient supply of cruisers and gunboats, and that hereafter the construction of battle ships and torpedo boats will supply our needs.

Much attention has been given to the methods of carrying on departmental business. Important modifications in the regulations have been made, tending to unify the control of shipbuilding as far as may be under the Bureau of Construction and Repair, and also to improve the mode of purchasing supplies for the Navy by the Bureau of Supplies and Accounts. The establishment under recent acts of Congress of a supply fund with which to purchase these supplies in large quantities and other modifications of methods have tended materially to their cheapening and better quality.

The War College has developed into an institution which it is believed will be of great value to the Navy in teaching the science of war, as well as in stimulating professional zeal in the Navy, and it will be especially useful in the devising of plans for the utilization in case of necessity of all the naval resources of the United States.

The Secretary has persistently adhered to the plan he found in operation for securing labor at navy-yards through boards of labor employment, and has done much to make it more complete and efficient. The naval officers who are familiar with this system and its operation express the decided opinion that its results have been to vastly improve the character of the work done at our yards and greatly reduce its cost.

Discipline among the officers and men of the Navy has been maintained to a high standard and the percentage of American citizens enlisted has been very much increased.

The Secretary is considering and will formulate during the coming winter a plan for laying up ships in reserve, thereby largely reducing the cost of maintaining our vessels afloat. This plan contemplates that battle ships, torpedo boats, and such of the cruisers as are not needed for active service at sea shall be kept in reserve with skeleton crews on board to keep them in condition, cruising only enough to insure the efficiency of the ships and their crews in time of activity.

The economy to result from this system is too obvious to need comment.

The Naval Militia, which was authorized a few years ago as an experiment, has now developed into a body of enterprising young men, active and energetic in the discharge of their duties and promising great usefulness. This establishment has nearly the same relation to our Navy as the National Guard in the different States bears to our Army, and it constitutes a source of supply for our naval forces the importance of which is immediately apparent.

The report of the Secretary of the Interior presents a comprehensive and interesting exhibit of the numerous and important affairs committed to his supervision. It is impossible in this communication to do more than briefly refer to a few of the subjects concerning which the Secretary gives full and instructive information.

The money appropriated on account of this Department and for its disbursement for the fiscal year ended June 30, 1896, amounted to more than $157,000,000, or a greater sum than was appropriated for the entire maintenance of the Government for the two fiscal years ended June 30, 1861.

Our public lands, originally amounting to 1,840,000,000 acres, have been so reduced that only about 600,000,000 acres still remain in Government control, excluding Alaska. The balance, being by far the most valuable portion, has been given away to settlers, to new States, and to railroads or sold at a comparatively nominal sum. The patenting of land in execution of railroad grants has progressed rapidly during the year, and since the 4th day of March, 1893, about 25,000,000 acres have thus been conveyed to these corporations.

I agree with the Secretary that the remainder of our public lands should be more carefully dealt with and their alienation guarded by better economy and greater prudence.

The commission appointed from the membership of the National Academy of Sciences, provided for by an act of Congress, to formulate plans for a national forestry system will, it is hoped, soon be prepared to present the result of thorough and intelligent examination of this important subject.

The total Indian population of the United States is 177,235, according to a census made in 1895, exclusive of those within the State of New York and those comprising the Five Civilized Tribes. Of this number there are approximately 38,000 children of school age. During the year 23,393 of these were enrolled in schools. The progress which has attended recent efforts to extend Indian-school facilities and the anticipation of continued liberal appropriations to that end can not fail to afford the utmost satisfaction to those who believe that the education of Indian children is a prime factor in the accomplishment of Indian civilization.

It may be said in general terms that in every particular the improvement of the Indians under Government care has been most marked and encouraging.

The Secretary, the Commissioner of Indian Affairs, and the agents having charge of Indians to whom allotments have been made strongly urge the passage of a law prohibiting the sale of liquor to allottees who have taken their lands in severalty. I earnestly join in this recommendation and venture to express the hope that the Indian may be speedily protected against this greatest of all obstacles to his well-being and advancement.

The condition of affairs among the Five Civilized Tribes, who occupy large tracts of land in the Indian Territory and who have governments of their own, has assumed such an aspect as to render it almost indispensable that there should be an entire change in the relations of these Indians to the General Government. This seems to be necessary in furtherance of their own interests, as well as for the protection of non-Indian residents in their territory. A commission organized and empowered under several recent laws is now negotiating with these Indians for the relinquishment of their courts and the division of their common lands in severalty and are aiding in the settlement of the troublesome question of tribal membership. The reception of their first proffers of negotiation was not encouraging, but through patience and such conduct on their part as demonstrated that their intentions were friendly and in the interest of the tribes the prospect of success has become more promising. The effort should be to save these Indians from the consequences of their own mistakes and improvidence and to secure to the real Indian his rights as against intruders and professed friends who profit by his retrogression. A change is also needed to protect life and property through the operation of courts conducted according to strict justice and strong enough to enforce their mandates.

As a sincere friend of the Indian, I am exceedingly anxious that these reforms should be accomplished with the consent and aid of the tribes and that no necessity may be presented for radical or drastic legislation. I hope, therefore, that the commission now conducting negotiations will soon be able to report that progress has been made toward a friendly adjustment of existing difficulties.

It appears that a very valuable deposit of gilsonite or asphaltum has been found on the reservation in Utah occupied by the Uncompahgre Ute Indians. Every consideration of care for the public interest and every sensible business reason dictate such management or disposal of this important source of public revenue as will except it from the general rules and incidents attending the ordinary disposition of public lands and secure to the Government a fair share at least of its advantages in place of its transfer for a nominal sum to interested individuals.

I indorse the recommendation made by the present Secretary of the Interior, as well as his predecessor, that a permanent commission, consisting of three members, one of whom shall be an army officer, be created to perform the duties now devolving upon the Commissioner and Assistant Commissioner of Indian Affairs. The management of the Bureau involves such numerous and diverse details and the advantages of an uninterrupted policy are so apparent that I hope the change suggested will meet the approval of the Congress.

The diminution of our enormous pension roll and the decrease of pension expenditure, which have been so often confidently foretold, still fail in material realization. The number of pensioners on the rolls at the close of the fiscal year ended June 30, 1896, was 970,678. This is the largest number ever reported. The amount paid exclusively for pensions during the year was $138,214,761.94, a slight decrease from that of the preceding year, while the total expenditures on account of pensions, including the cost of maintaining the Department and expenses attending pension distribution, amounted to $142,206,550.59, or within a very small fraction of one-third of the entire expense of supporting the Government during the same year. The number of new pension certificates issued was 90,640. Of these, 40,374 represent original allowances of claims and 15,878 increases of existing pensions.

The number of persons receiving pensions from the United States, but residing in foreign countries, at the close of the last fiscal year was 3,781, and the amount paid to them during the year was $582,735.38.

The sum appropriated for the payment of pensions for the current fiscal year, ending June 30, 1897, is $140,000,000, and for the succeeding year it is estimated that the same amount will be necessary.

The Commissioner of Pensions reports that during the last fiscal year 339 indictments were found against violators of the pension laws. Upon these indictments 167 convictions resulted.

In my opinion, based upon such statements as these and much other information and observation, the abuses which have been allowed to creep into our pension system have done incalculable harm in demoralizing our people and undermining good citizenship. I have endeavored within my sphere of official duty to protect our pension roll and make it what it should be, a roll of honor, containing the names of those disabled in their country's service and worthy of their country's affectionate remembrance. When I have seen those who pose as the soldiers' friends active and alert in urging greater laxity and more reckless pension expenditure, while nursing selfish schemes, I have deprecated the approach of a situation when necessary retrenchment and enforced economy may lead to an attack upon pension abuses so determined as to overlook the discrimination due to those who, worthy of a nation's care, ought to live and die under the protection of a nation's gratitude.

The Secretary calls attention to the public interests involved in an adjustment of the obligations of the Pacific railroads to the Government. I deem it to be an important duty to especially present this subject to the consideration of the Congress.

On January 1, 1897, with the amount already matured, more than $13,000,000 of the principal of the subsidy bonds issued by the United

States in aid of the construction of the Union Pacific Railway, including its Kansas line, and more than $6,000,000 of like bonds issued in aid of the Central Pacific Railroad, including those issued to the Western Pacific Railroad Company, will have fallen due and been paid or must on that day be paid by the Government. Without any reference to the application of the sinking fund now in the Treasury, this will create such a default on the part of these companies to the Government as will give it the right to at once institute proceedings to foreclose its mortgage lien. In addition to this indebtedness, which will be due January 1, 1897, there will mature between that date and January 1, 1899, the remaining principal of such subsidy bonds, which must also be met by the Government. These amount to more than $20,000,000 on account of the Union Pacific lines and exceed $21,000,000 on account of the Central Pacific lines.

The situation of these roads and the condition of their indebtedness to the Government have been fully set forth in the reports of various committees to the present and prior Congresses, and as early as 1887 they were thoroughly examined by a special commission appointed pursuant to an act of Congress. The considerations requiring an adjustment of the Government's relations to the companies have been clearly presented and the conclusion reached with practical uniformity that if these relations are not terminated they should be revised upon a basis securing their safe continuance.

Under section 4 of the act of Congress passed March 3, 1887, the President is charged with the duty, in the event that any mortgage or other incumbrance paramount to the interest of the United States in the property of the Pacific railroads should exist and be lawfully liable to be enforced, to direct the action of the Departments of Treasury and of Justice in the protection of the interest of the United States by redemption or through judicial proceedings, including foreclosures of the Government liens.

In view of the fact that the Congress has for a number of years almost constantly had under consideration various plans for dealing with the conditions existing between these roads and the Government, I have thus far felt justified in withholding action under the statute above mentioned.

In the case of the Union Pacific Company, however, the situation has become especially and immediately urgent. Proceedings have been instituted to foreclose a first mortgage upon those aided parts of the main lines upon which the Government holds a second and subordinate mortgage lien. In consequence of those proceedings and increasing complications, added to the default occurring on the 1st day of January, 1897, a condition will be presented at that date, so far as this company is concerned, that must emphasize the mandate of the act of 1887 and give to Executive duty under its provisions a more imperative aspect. Therefore, unless Congress shall otherwise direct or shall have previously determined upon a different solution of the problem, there will hardly appear to exist any reason for delaying beyond the date of the default above mentioned such Executive action as will promise to subserve the public interests and save the Government from the loss threatened by further inaction.

The Department of Agriculture is so intimately related to the welfare of our people and the prosperity of our nation that it should constantly receive the care and encouragement of the Government. From small beginnings it has grown to be the center of agricultural intelligence and the source of aid and encouragement to agricultural efforts. Large sums of money are annually appropriated for the maintenance of this Department, and it must be confessed that the legislation relating to it has not always been directly in the interest of practical farming or properly guarded against waste and extravagance. So far, however, as public money has been appropriated fairly and sensibly to help those who actually till the soil, no expenditure has been more profitably made or more generally approved by the people.

Under the present management of the Department its usefulness has been enhanced in every direction, and at the same time strict economy has been enforced to the utmost extent permitted by Congressional action. From the report of the Secretary it appears that through careful and prudent financial management he has annually saved a large sum from his appropriations, aggregating during his incumbency and up to the close of the present fiscal year nearly one-fifth of the entire amount appropriated. These results have been accomplished by a conscientious study of the real needs of the farmer and such a regard for economy as the genuine farmer ought to appreciate, supplemented by a rigid adherence to civil-service methods in a Department which should be conducted in the interest of agriculture instead of partisan politics.

The Secretary reports that the value of our exports of farm products during the last fiscal year amounted to $570,000,000, an increase of $17,-000,000 over those of the year immediately preceding. This statement is not the less welcome because of the fact that, notwithstanding such increase, the proportion of exported agricultural products to our total exports of all descriptions fell off during the year. The benefits of an increase in agricultural exports being assured, the decrease in its proportion to our total exports is the more gratifying when we consider that it is owing to the fact that such total exports for the year increased more than $75,000,000.

The large and increasing exportation of our agricultural products suggests the great usefulness of the organization lately established in the Department for the purpose of giving to those engaged in farming pursuits reliable information concerning the condition, needs, and advantages of different foreign markets. Inasmuch as the success of the farmer depends upon the advantageous sale of his products, and inasmuch as foreign markets must largely be the destination of such products, it is quite apparent that a knowledge of the conditions and wants that affect those markets ought to result in sowing more intelligently and reaping with a better promise of profit. Such information points out the way to a prudent foresight in the selection and cultivation of crops and to a release from the bondage of unreasoning monotony of production, a glutted and depressed market, and constantly recurring unprofitable toil.

In my opinion the gratuitous distribution of seeds by the Department as at present conducted ought to be discontinued. No one can read the statement of the Secretary on this subject and doubt the extravagance and questionable results of this practice. The professed friends of the farmer, and certainly the farmers themselves, are naturally expected to be willing to rid a Department devoted to the promotion of farming interests of a feature which tends so much to its discredit.

The Weather Bureau, now attached to the Department of Agriculture, has continued to extend its sphere of usefulness, and by an uninterrupted improvement in the accuracy of its forecasts has greatly increased its efficiency as an aid and protection to all whose occupations are related to weather conditions.

Omitting further reference to the operations of the Department, I commend the Secretary's report and the suggestions it contains to the careful consideration of the Congress.

The progress made in civil-service reform furnishes a cause for the utmost congratulation. It has survived the doubts of its friends as well as the rancor of its enemies and has gained a permanent place among the agencies destined to cleanse our politics and to improve, economize, and elevate the public service.

There are now in the competitive classified service upward of 84,000 places, more than half of these having been included from time to time since March 4, 1893. A most radical and sweeping extension was made by Executive order dated the 6th day of May, 1896, and if fourth-class postmasterships are not included in the statement it may be said that practically all positions contemplated by the civil-service law are now classified. Abundant reasons exist for including these postmasterships, based upon economy, improved service, and the peace and quiet of neighborhoods. If, however, obstacles prevent such action at present, I earnestly hope that Congress will, without increasing post-office appropriations, so adjust them as to permit in proper cases a consolidation of these post-offices, to the end that through this process the result desired may to a limited extent be accomplished.

The civil-service rules as amended during the last year provide for a sensible and uniform method of promotion, basing eligibility to better positions upon demonstrated efficiency and faithfulness. The absence of fixed rules on this subject has been an infirmity in the system more and more apparent as its other benefits have been better appreciated.

The advantages of civil-service methods in their business aspects are

too well understood to require argument.   Their application has become
a necessity to the executive work of the Government.   But those who
gain positions through the operation of these methods should be made
to understand that the nonpartisan scheme through which they receive
their appointments demands from them by way of reciprocity nonpartisan and faithful performance of duty under every Administration and
cheerful fidelity to every chief.   While they should be encouraged to de-
cently exercise their rights of citizenship and to support through their
suffrages the political beliefs they honestly profess, the noisy, pestilent,
and partisan employee, who loves political turmoil and contention or who
renders lax and grudging service to an Administration not representing
his political views, should be promptly and fearlessly dealt with in such
a way as to furnish a warning to others who may be likewise disposed.

The annual report of the Commissioners will be duly transmitted, anu
I commend the important matter they have in charge to the careful consideration of the Congress.

The Interstate Commerce Commission has during the last year supplied abundant evidence of its usefulness and the importance of the work
committed to its charge.

Public transportation is a universal necessity, and the question of just
and reasonable charges therefor has become of vital importance not only
to shippers and carriers, but also to the vast multitude of producers and
consumers.   The justice and equity of the principles embodied in the
existing law passed for the purpose of regulating these charges are everywhere conceded, and there appears to be no question that the policy thus
entered upon has a permanent place in our legislation.

As the present statute when enacted was in the nature of the case more
or less tentative and experimental, it was hardly expected to supply a
complete and adequate system.   While its wholesome effects are manifest and have amply justified its enactment, it is evident that all desired
reforms in transportation methods have not been fully accomplished.   In
view of the judicial interpretation which some provisions of this statute
have received and the defects disclosed by the efforts made for its enforcement, its revision and amendment appear to be essential, to the end that it
may more effectually reach the evils designed to be corrected.   I hope the
recommendations of the Commission upon this subject will be promptly
and favorably considered by the Congress.

I desire to recur to the statements elsewhere made concerning the Government's receipts and expenditures for the purpose of venturing upon
some suggestions touching our present tariff law and its operation.

This statute took effect on the 28th day of August, 1894.   Whatever
may be its shortcomings as a complete measure of tariff reform, it must
be conceded that it has opened the way to a freer and greater exchange
of commodities between us and other countries, and thus furnished a
wider market for our products and manufactures.

The only entire fiscal year during which this law has been in force ended on the 30th day of June, 1896. In that year our imports increased over those of the previous year more than $6,500,000, while the value of the domestic products we exported and which found markets abroad was nearly $70,000,000 more than during the preceding year.

Those who insist that the cost to our people of articles coming to them from abroad for their needful use should only be increased through tariff charges to an extent necessary to meet the expenses of the Government, as well as those who claim that tariff charges may be laid upon such articles beyond the necessities of Government revenue and with the additional purpose of so increasing their price in our markets as to give American manufacturers and producers better and more profitable opportunities, must agree that our tariff laws are only primarily justified as sources of revenue to enable the Government to meet the necessary expenses of its maintenance. Considered as to its efficiency in this aspect, the present law can by no means fall under just condemnation. During the only complete fiscal year of its operation it has yielded nearly $8,000,000 more revenue than was received from tariff duties in the preceding year. There was, nevertheless, a deficit between our receipts and expenditures of a little more than $25,000,000. This, however, was not unexpected.

The situation was such in December last, seven months before the close of the fiscal year, that the Secretary of the Treasury foretold a deficiency of $17,000,000. The great and increasing apprehension and timidity in business circles and the depression in all activities intervening since that time, resulting from causes perfectly well understood and entirely disconnected with our tariff law or its operation, seriously checked the imports we would have otherwise received and readily account for the difference between this estimate of the Secretary and the actual deficiency, as well as for a continued deficit. Indeed, it must be confessed that we could hardly have had a more unfavorable period than the last two years for the collection of tariff revenue. We can not reasonably hope that our recuperation from this business depression will be sudden, but it has already set in with a promise of acceleration and continuance.

I believe our present tariff law, if allowed a fair opportunity, will in the near future yield a revenue which, with reasonably economical expenditures, will overcome all deficiencies. In the meantime no deficit that has occurred or may occur need excite or disturb us. To meet any such deficit we have in the Treasury in addition to a gold reserve of one hundred millions a surplus of more than $128,000,000 applicable to the payment of the expenses of the Government, and which must, unless expended for that purpose, remain a useless hoard, or, if not extravagantly wasted, must in any event be perverted from the purpose of its exaction from our people. The payment, therefore, of any deficiency in the revenue from this fund is nothing more than its proper and legitimate use.

The Government thus applying a surplus fortunately in its Treasury to the payment of expenses not met by its current revenues is not at all to be likened to a man living beyond his income and thus incurring debt or encroaching on his principal.

It is not one of the functions of our Government to accumulate and make additions to a fund not needed for immediate expenditure. With individuals it is the chief object of struggle and effort. The application of an accumulated fund by the Government to the payment of its running expenses is a duty. An individual living beyond his income and embarrassing himself with debt or drawing upon his accumulated fund of principal is either unfortunate or improvident. The distinction is between a government charged with the duty of expending for the benefit of the people and for proper purposes all the money it receives from any source, and the individual, who is expected to manifest a natural desire to avoid debt or to accumulate as much as possible and to live within the income derived from such accumulations, to the end that they may be increased or at least remain unimpaired for the future use and enjoyment of himself or the objects of his love and affection who may survive him.

It is immeasurably better to appropriate our surplus to the payment of justifiable expenses than to allow it to become an invitation to reckless appropriations and extravagant expenditures.

I suppose it will not be denied that under the present law our people obtain the necessaries of a comfortable existence at a cheaper rate than formerly. This is a matter of supreme importance, since it is the palpable duty of every just government to make the burdens of taxation as light as possible. The people should not be required to relinquish this privilege of cheaper living except under the stress of their Government's necessity made plainly manifest.

This reference to the condition and prospects of our revenues naturally suggests an allusion to the weakness and vices of our financial methods. They have been frequently pressed upon the attention of Congress in previous Executive communications and the inevitable danger of their continued toleration pointed out. Without now repeating these details, I can not refrain from again earnestly presenting the necessity of the prompt reform of a system opposed to every rule of sound finance and shown by experience to be fraught with the gravest peril and perplexity. The terrible Civil War, which shook the foundations of our Government more than thirty years ago, brought in its train the destruction of property, the wasting of our country's substance, and the estrangement of brethren. These are now past and forgotten. Even the distressing loss of life the conflict entailed is but a sacred memory which fosters patriotic sentiment and keeps alive a tender regard for those who nobly died. And yet there remains with us to-day in full strength and activity, as an incident of that tremendous struggle, a feature of its financial necessities not only unsuited to our present circumstances, but manifestly a disturbing menace to business security and an ever-present agent of monetary distress.

Because we may be enjoying a temporary relief from its depressing influence, this should not lull us into a false security nor lead us to forget the suddenness of past visitations.

I am more convinced than ever that we can have no assured financial peace and safety until the Government currency obligations upon which gold may be demanded from the Treasury are withdrawn from circulation and canceled. This might be done, as has been heretofore recommended, by their exchange for long-term bonds bearing a low rate of interest or by their redemption with the proceeds of such bonds. Even if only the United States notes known as greenbacks were thus retired it is probable that the Treasury notes issued in payment of silver purchases under the act of July 14, 1890, now paid in gold when demanded, would not create much disturbance, as they might from time to time, when received in the Treasury by redemption in gold or otherwise, be gradually and prudently replaced by silver coin.

This plan of issuing bonds for the purpose of redemption certainly appears to be the most effective and direct path to the needed reform. In default of this, however, it would be a step in the right direction if currency obligations redeemable in gold whenever so redeemed should be canceled instead of being reissued. This operation would be a slow remedy, but it would improve present conditions.

National banks should redeem their own notes. They should be allowed to issue circulation to the par value of bonds deposited as security for its redemption and the tax on their circulation should be reduced to one-fourth of 1 per cent.

In considering projects for the retirement of United States notes and Treasury notes issued under the law of 1890, I am of the opinion that we have placed too much stress upon the danger of contracting the currency and have calculated too little upon the gold that would be added to our circulation if invited to us by better and safer financial methods. It is not so much a contraction of our currency that should be avoided as its unequal distribution.

This might be obviated and any fear of harmful contraction at the same time removed by allowing the organization of smaller banks and in less populous communities than are now permitted, and also authorizing existing banks to establish branches in small communities under proper restrictions.

The entire case may be presented by the statement that the day of sensible and sound financial methods will not dawn upon us until our Government abandons the banking business and the accumulation of funds and confines its monetary operations to the receipt of the money contributed by the people for its support and to the expenditure of such money for the people's benefit.

Our business interests and all good citizens long for rest from feverish agitation and the inauguration by the Government of a reformed financial policy which will encourage enterprise and make certain the rewards of labor and industry.

Another topic in which our people rightfully take a deep interest may be here briefly considered. I refer to the existence of trusts and other huge aggregations of capital the object of which is to secure the monopoly of some particular branch of trade, industry, or commerce and to stifle wholesome competition. When these are defended, it is usually on the ground that though they increase profits they also reduce prices, and thus may benefit the public. It must be remembered, however, that a reduction of prices to the people is not one of the real objects of these organizations, nor is their tendency necessarily in that direction. If it occurs in a particular case it is only because it accords with the purposes or interests of those managing the scheme.

Such occasional results fall far short of compensating the palpable evils charged to the account of trusts and monopolies. Their tendency is to crush out individual independence and to hinder or prevent the free use of human faculties and the full development of human character. Through them the farmer, the artisan, and the small trader is in danger of dislodgment from the proud position of being his own master, watchful of all that touches his country's prosperity, in which he has an individual lot, and interested in all that affects the advantages of business of which he is a factor, to be relegated to the level of a mere appurtenance to a great machine, with little free will, with no duty but that of passive obedience, and with little hope or opportunity of rising in the scale of responsible and helpful citizenship.

To the instinctive belief that such is the inevitable trend of trusts and monopolies is due the widespread and deep-seated popular aversion in which they are held and the not unreasonable insistence that, whatever may be their incidental economic advantages, their general effect upon personal character, prospects, and usefulness can not be otherwise than injurious.

Though Congress has attempted to deal with this matter by legislation, the laws passed for that purpose thus far have proved ineffective, not because of any lack of disposition or attempt to enforce them, but simply because the laws themselves as interpreted by the courts do not reach the difficulty. If the insufficiencies of existing laws can be remedied by further legislation, it should be done. The fact must be recognized, however, that all Federal legislation on this subject may fall short of its purpose because of inherent obstacles and also because of the complex character of our governmental system, which, while making the Federal authority supreme within its sphere, has carefully limited that sphere by metes and bounds that can not be transgressed. The decision of our highest court on this precise question renders it quite doubtful whether the evils of trusts and monopolies can be adequately treated through Federal action unless they seek directly and purposely to include in their objects transportation or intercourse between States or between the United States and foreign countries.

It does not follow, however, that this is the limit of the remedy that may be applied. Even though it may be found that Federal authority is not broad enough to fully reach the case, there can be no doubt of the power of the several States to act effectively in the premises, and there should be no reason to doubt their willingness to judiciously exercise such power.

In concluding this communication its last words shall be an appeal to the Congress for the most rigid economy in the expenditure of the money it holds in trust for the people. The way to perplexing extravagance is easy, but a return to frugality is difficult. When, however, it is considered that those who bear the burdens of taxation have no guaranty of honest care save in the fidelity of their public servants, the duty of all possible retrenchment is plainly manifest.

When our differences are forgotten and our contests of political opinion are no longer remembered, nothing in the retrospect of our public service will be as fortunate and comforting as the recollection of official duty well performed and the memory of a constant devotion to the interests of our confiding fellow-countrymen.

William McKinley

March 4, 1897 to September 14, 1901

FIRST ANNUAL MESSAGE.

EXECUTIVE MANSION, *December 6, 1897.*

To the Senate and House of Representatives:

It gives me pleasure to extend greeting to the Fifty-fifth Congress, assembled in regular session at the seat of Government, with many of whose Senators and Representatives I have been associated in the legislative service. Their meeting occurs under felicitous conditions, justifying sincere congratulation and calling for our grateful acknowledgment to a beneficent Providence which has so signally blessed and prospered us as a nation. Peace and good will with all the nations of the earth continue unbroken.

A matter of genuine satisfaction is the growing feeling of fraternal regard and unification of all sections of our country, the incompleteness of which has too long delayed realization of the highest blessings of the Union. The spirit of patriotism is universal and is ever increasing in fervor. The public questions which now most engross us are lifted far above either partisanship, prejudice, or former sectional differences. They affect every part of our common country alike and permit of no division on ancient lines. Questions of foreign policy, of revenue, the soundness of the currency, the inviolability of national obligations, the improvement of the public service, appeal to the individual conscience of every earnest citizen to whatever party he belongs or in whatever section of the country he may reside.

The extra session of this Congress which closed during July last enacted important legislation, and while its full effect has not yet been realized, what it has already accomplished assures us of its timeliness and wisdom. To test its permanent value further time will be required, and the people, satisfied with its operation and results thus far, are in no mind to withhold from it a fair trial.

Tariff legislation having been settled by the extra session of Congress, the question next pressing for consideration is that of the currency.

The work of putting our finances upon a sound basis, difficult as it may seem, will appear easier when we recall the financial operations of the Government since 1866. On the 30th day of June of that year we had outstanding demand liabilities in the sum of $728,868,447.41. On the 1st of January, 1879, these liabilities had been reduced to $443,889,495.88. Of our interest-bearing obligations, the figures are even more striking. On July 1, 1866, the principal of the interest-bearing debt of the Government was $2,332,331,208. On the 1st day of July, 1893, this sum had been reduced to $585,037,100, or an aggregate reduction of $1,747,294,108. The interest-bearing debt of the United States on the 1st day of December, 1897, was $847,365,620. The Government money now outstanding (December 1) consists of $346,681,016 of United States notes, $107,793,280 of Treasury notes issued by authority of the law of 1890, $384,963,504 of silver certificates, and $61,-280,761 of standard silver dollars.

With the great resources of the Government, and with the honorable example of the past before us, we ought not to hesitate to enter upon a currency revision which will make our demand obligations less onerous to the Government and relieve our financial laws from ambiguity and doubt.

The brief review of what was accomplished from the close of the war to 1893, makes unreasonable and groundless any distrust either of our financial ability or soundness; while the situation from 1893 to 1897 must admonish Congress of the immediate necessity of so legislating as to make the return of the conditions then prevailing impossible.

There are many plans proposed as a remedy for the evil. Before we can find the true remedy we must appreciate the real evil. It is not that our currency of every kind is not good, for every dollar of it is good; good because the Government's pledge is out to keep it so, and that pledge will not be broken. However, the guaranty of our purpose to keep the pledge will be best shown by advancing toward its fulfillment.

The evil of the present system is found in the great cost to the Government of maintaining the parity of our different forms of money, that is, keeping all of them at par with gold. We surely cannot be longer heedless of the burden this imposes upon the people, even under fairly prosperous conditions, while the past four years have demonstrated that it is not only an expensive charge upon the Government, but a dangerous menace to the National credit.

It is manifest that we must devise some plan to protect the Government against bond issues for repeated redemptions. We must either curtail the opportunity for speculation, made easy by the multiplied redemptions of our demand obligations, or increase the gold reserve for their redemption. We have $900,000,000 of currency which the Government by solemn enactment has undertaken to keep at par with gold. Nobody is obliged to redeem in gold but the Government. The banks are not required to redeem in gold. The Government is obliged to keep equal with gold all its outstanding currency and coin obligations, while its receipts are not required to be paid in gold. They are paid in every kind of money but gold, and the only means by which the Government can with certainty get gold is by borrowing. It can get it in no other way when it most needs it. The Government without any fixed gold revenue is pledged to maintain gold redemption, which it has steadily and faithfully done, and which, under the authority now given, it will continue to do.

The law which requires the Government, after having redeemed its United States notes, to pay them out again as current funds, demands a constant replenishment of the gold reserve. This is especially so in times of business panic and when the revenues are insufficient to meet the expenses of the Government. At such times the Government has no other way to supply its deficit and maintain redemption but through the increase of its bonded debt, as during the Administration of my predecessor, when $262,315,400 of four-and-a-half per cent bonds were issued and sold and the proceeds used to pay the expenses of the Government in excess of the revenues and sustain the gold reserve. While it is true that the greater part of the proceeds of these bonds were used to supply deficient revenues, a considerable portion was required to maintain the gold reserve.

With our revenues equal to our expenses, there would be no deficit requiring the issuance of bonds. But if the gold reserve falls below $100,000,000, how will it be replenished except by selling more bonds? Is there any other way practicable under existing law? The serious question then is, Shall we continue the policy that has been pursued in the past; that is, when the gold reserve reaches the point of danger, issue more bonds and supply the needed gold, or shall we provide other means to prevent these recurring drains upon the gold reserve? If no further legislation is had and the policy of selling bonds is to be continued, then Congress should give the Secretary of the Treasury authority to sell bonds at long or short periods, bearing a less rate of interest than is now authorized by law.

I earnestly recommend, as soon as the receipts of the Government are quite sufficient to pay all the expenses of the Government, that when any of the United States notes are presented for redemption in gold and are redeemed in gold, such notes shall be kept and set apart, and only paid out in exchange for gold. This is an obvious duty. If the holder of the United States note prefers the gold and gets it from the Government, he should not receive back from the Government a United States note without paying gold in exchange for it. The reason for this is made all the more apparent when the Government issues an interest-bearing debt to provide gold for the redemption of United States notes—a non-interest-bearing debt. Surely it should not pay them out again except on demand and for gold. If they are put out in any other way, they may return again to be followed by another bond issue to redeem them—another interest-bearing debt to redeem a non-interest-bearing debt.

In my view, it is of the utmost importance that the Government should be relieved from the burden of providing all the gold required for exchanges and export. This responsibility is alone borne by the Government, without any of the usual and necessary banking powers to help itself. The banks do not feel the strain of gold redemption. The whole strain rests upon the Government, and the size of the gold reserve in the Treasury has come to be, with or without reason, the signal of danger or of security. This ought to be stopped.

If we are to have an era of prosperity in the country, with sufficient receipts for the expenses of the Government, we may feel no immediate embarrassment from our present currency; but the danger still exists, and will be ever present, menacing us so long as the existing system continues. And, besides, it is in times of adequate revenues and business tranquillity that the Government should prepare for the worst. We cannot avoid, without serious consequences, the wise consideration and prompt solution of this question.

The Secretary of the Treasury has outlined a plan, in great detail, for the purpose of removing the threatened recurrence of a depleted gold reserve and save us from future embarrassment on that account. To this plan I invite your careful consideration.

I concur with the Secretary of the Treasury in his recommendation that National banks be allowed to issue notes to the face value of the bonds which they have deposited for circulation, and that the tax on circulating notes secured by deposit of such bonds be reduced to one-half of one per cent per annum. I also join him in recommending that authority be given for the establishment of National banks with a minimum capital of $25,000. This will enable the smaller villages and agricultural regions of the country to be supplied with currency to meet their needs.

I recommend that the issue of National bank notes be restricted to the denomination of ten dollars and upwards. If the suggestions I have herein made shall have the approval of Congress, then I would recommend that National banks be required to redeem their notes in gold.

The most important problem with which this Government is now called upon to deal pertaining to its foreign relations concerns its duty toward Spain and the Cuban insurrection. Problems and conditions more or less in common with those now existing have confronted this Government at various times in the past. The story of Cuba for many years has been one of unrest, growing discontent, an effort toward a larger enjoyment of liberty and self-control, of organized resistance to the mother country, of depression after distress and warfare, and of ineffectual settlement to be followed by renewed revolt. For no enduring period since the enfranchisement of the continental possessions of Spain in the Western Continent has the condition of Cuba or the policy of Spain toward Cuba not caused concern to the United States.

The prospect from time to time that the weakness of Spain's hold upon the island and the political vicissitudes and embarrassments of the home Government might lead to the transfer of Cuba to a continental power called forth between 1823 and 1860 various emphatic declarations of the policy of the United States to permit no disturbance of Cuba's connection with Spain unless in the direction of independence or acquisition by us through purchase, nor has there been any change of this declared policy since upon the part of the Government.

The revolution which began in 1868 lasted for ten years despite the strenuous efforts of the successive peninsular governments to suppress it. Then as now the Government of the United States testified its grave concern and offered its aid to put an end to bloodshed in Cuba. The overtures made by General Grant were refused and the war dragged on, entailing great loss of life and treasure and increased injury to American interests, besides throwing enhanced burdens of neutrality upon this Government. In 1878 peace was brought about by the truce of Zanjon, obtained by negotiations between the Spanish commander, Martinez de Campos, and the insurgent leaders.

The present insurrection broke out in February, 1895. It is not my purpose at this time to recall its remarkable increase or to characterize its tenacious resistance against the enormous forces massed against it by Spain. The revolt and the efforts to subdue it carried destruction to every quarter of the island, developing wide proportions and defying the efforts of Spain for its suppression. The civilized code of war has been disregarded, no less so by the Spaniards than by the Cubans.

The existing conditions can not but fill this Government and the American people with the gravest apprehension. There is no desire on the part of our people to profit by the misfortunes of Spain. We have only the desire to see the Cubans prosperous and contented, enjoying that measure of self-control which is the inalienable right of man, protected in their right to reap the benefit of the exhaustless treasures of their country.

The offer made by my predecessor in April, 1896, tendering the friendly offices of this Government, failed. Any mediation on our part was not accepted. In brief, the answer read: "There is no effectual way to pacify Cuba unless it begins with the actual submission of the rebels to the mother country." Then only could Spain act in the promised direction, of her own motion and after her own plans.

The cruel policy of concentration was initiated February 16, 1896. The productive districts controlled by the Spanish armies were depopulated. The agricultural inhabitants were herded in and about the garrison towns, their lands laid waste and their dwellings destroyed. This policy the late cabinet of Spain justified as a necessary measure of war and as a means of cutting off supplies from the insurgents. It has utterly failed as a war measure. It was not civilized warfare. It was extermination.

Against this abuse of the rights of war I have felt constrained on repeated occasions to enter the firm and earnest protest of this Government. There was much of public condemnation of the treatment of American citizens by alleged illegal arrests and long imprisonment awaiting trial or pending protracted judicial proceedings. I felt it my first duty to make instant demand for the release or speedy trial of all American citizens under arrest. Before the change of the Spanish cabinet in October last twenty-two prisoners, citizens of the United States, had been given their freedom.

For the relief of our own citizens suffering because of the conflict the aid of Congress was sought in a special message, and under the appropriation of May 24, 1897, effective aid has been given to American citizens in Cuba, many of them at their own request having been returned to the United States.

The instructions given to our new minister to Spain before his departure for his post directed him to impress upon that Government the sincere wish of the United States to lend its aid toward the ending of the war in Cuba by reaching a peaceful and lasting result, just and honorable alike to Spain and to the Cuban people. These instructions recited the character and duration of the contest, the widespread losses it entails, the burdens and restraints it imposes upon us, with constant disturbance of national interests, and the injury resulting from an indefinite continuance of this state of things. It was stated that at this juncture our Government was constrained to seriously inquire if the time was not ripe when Spain of her own volition, moved by her own interests and every sentiment of humanity, should put a stop to this destructive war and make proposals of settlement honorable to herself and just to her Cuban colony. It was urged that as a neighboring nation, with large interests in Cuba, we could be required to wait only a reasonable time for the mother country to establish its authority and restore peace and order within the borders of the island; that we could not contemplate an indefinite period for the accomplishment of this result.

No solution was proposed to which the slightest idea of humiliation to Spain could attach, and, indeed, precise proposals were withheld to avoid embarrassment to that Government. All that was asked or expected was that some safe way might be speedily provided and permanent peace restored. It so chanced that the consideration of this offer, addressed to the same Spanish administration which had declined the tenders of my predecessor, and which for more than two years had poured men and treasure into Cuba in the fruitless effort to suppress the revolt, fell to others. Between the departure of General Woodford, the new envoy, and his arrival in Spain the statesman who had shaped the policy of his country fell by the hand of an assassin, and although the cabinet of the late premier still held office and received from our envoy the proposals he bore, that cabinet gave place within a few days thereafter to a new administration, under the leadership of Sagasta.

The reply to our note was received on the 23d day of October. It is in the direction of a better understanding. It appreciates the friendly purposes of this Government. It admits that our country is deeply affected by the war in Cuba and that its desires for peace are just. It declares that the present Spanish government is bound by every consideration to a change of policy that should satisfy the United States and pacify Cuba within a reasonable time. To this end Spain has decided to put into effect the political reforms heretofore advocated by the present premier, without halting for any consideration in the path which in its judgment leads to peace. The military operations, it is said, will continue, but will be humane and conducted with all regard for private rights, being accompanied by political action leading to the autonomy of Cuba while guarding Spanish sovereignty. This, it is claimed, will result in investing Cuba with a distinct personality, the island to be governed by an executive and by a local council or chamber, reserving to Spain the control of the foreign relations, the army and navy, and the judicial administration. To accomplish this the present government proposes to modify existing legislation by decree, leaving the Spanish Cortes, with the aid of Cuban senators and deputies, to solve the economic problem and properly distribute the existing debt.

In the absence of a declaration of the measures that this Government proposes to take in carrying out its proffer of good offices, it suggests that Spain be left free to conduct military operations and grant political reforms, while the United States for its part shall enforce its neutral obligations and cut off the assistance which it is asserted the insurgents receive from this country. The supposition of an indefinite prolongation of the war is denied. It is asserted that the western provinces are already well-nigh reclaimed, that the planting of cane and tobacco therein has been resumed, and that by force of arms and new and ample reforms very early and complete pacification is hoped for.

The immediate amelioration of existing conditions under the new administration of Cuban affairs is predicted, and therewithal the disturbance and all occasion for any change of attitude on the part of the United States. Discussion of the question of the international duties and responsibilities of the United States as Spain understands them is presented, with an apparent disposition to charge us with failure in this regard. This charge is without any basis in fact. It could not have been made if Spain had been cognizant of the constant efforts this Government has made, at the cost of millions and by the employment of the administrative machinery of the nation at command, to perform its full duty according to the law of nations. That it has successfully prevented the departure of a single military expedition or armed vessel from our shores in violation of our laws would seem to be a sufficient answer. But of this aspect of the Spanish note it is not necessary to speak further now. Firm in the conviction of a wholly performed obligation, due response to this charge has been made in diplomatic course.

Throughout all these horrors and dangers to our own peace this Government has never in any way abrogated its sovereign prerogative of reserving to itself the determination of its policy and course according to its own high sense of right and in consonance with the dearest interests and convictions of our own people should the prolongation of the strife so demand.

Of the untried measures there remain only: Recognition of the insurgents as belligerents; recognition of the independence of Cuba; neutral intervention to end the war by imposing a rational compromise between the contestants, and intervention in favor of one or the other party. I speak not of forcible annexation, for that can not be thought of. That, by our code of morality, would be criminal aggression.

Recognition of the belligerency of the Cuban insurgents has often been canvassed as a possible, if not inevitable, step both in regard to the previous ten years' struggle and during the present war. I am not unmindful that the two Houses of Congress in the spring of 1896 expressed the opinion by concurrent resolution that a condition of public war existed requiring or justifying the recognition of a state of belligerency in Cuba, and during the extra session the Senate voted a joint resolution of like import, which, however, was not brought to a vote in the House of Representatives. In the presence of these significant expressions of the sentiment of the legislative branch it behooves the Executive to soberly consider the conditions under which so important a measure must needs rest for justification. It is to be seriously considered whether the Cuban insurrection possesses beyond dispute the attributes of statehood, which alone can demand the recognition of belligerency in its favor. Possession, in short, of the essential qualifications of sovereignty by the insurgents and the conduct of the war by them according to the received code of war are no less important factors toward the determination of the problem of belligerency than are the influences and consequences of the struggle upon the internal polity of the recognizing state.

The wise utterances of President Grant in his memorable message of December 7, 1875, are signally relevant to the present situation in Cuba, and it may be wholesome now to recall them. At that time a ruinous conflict had for seven years wasted the neighboring island. During all those years an utter disregard of the laws of civilized warfare and of the just demands of humanity, which called forth expressions of condemnation from the nations of Christendom, continued unabated. Desolation and ruin pervaded that productive region, enormously affecting the commerce of all commercial nations, but that of the United States more than any other by reason of proximity and larger trade and intercourse. At that juncture General Grant uttered these words, which now, as then, sum up the elements of the problem:

A recognition of the independence of Cuba being, in my opinion, impracticable and indefensible, the question which next presents itself is that of the recognition of belligerent rights in the parties to the contest.

In a former message to Congress I had occasion to consider this question, and reached the conclusion that the conflict in Cuba, dreadful and devastating as were its incidents, did not rise to the fearful dignity of war. * * * It is possible that the acts of foreign powers, and even acts of Spain herself, of this very nature, might be pointed to in defense of such recognition. But now, as in its past history, the United States should carefully avoid the false lights which might lead it into the mazes of doubtful law and of questionable propriety, and adhere rigidly and sternly to the rule, which has been its guide, of doing only that which is right and honest and of good report. The question of according or of withholding rights of belligerency must be judged in every case in view of the particular attending facts. Unless justified by necessity, it is always, and justly, regarded as an unfriendly act and a gratuitous demonstration of moral support to the rebellion. It is necessary, and it is required, when the interests and rights of another government or of its people are so far affected by a pending civil conflict as to require a definition of its relations to the parties thereto. But this conflict must be one which will be recognized in the sense of international law as war. Belligerence, too, is a fact. The mere existence of contending armed bodies and their occasional conflicts do not constitute war in the sense referred to. Applying to the existing condition of affairs in Cuba the tests recognized by publicists and writers on international law, and which have been observed by nations of dignity, honesty, and power when free from sensitive or selfish and unworthy motives, I fail to find in the insurrection the existence of such a substantial political organization, real, palpable, and manifest to the world, having the forms and capable of the ordinary functions of government toward its own people and to other states, with courts for the administration of justice, with a local habitation, possessing such organization of force, such material, such occupation of territory, as to take the contest out of the category of a mere rebellious insurrection or occasional skirmishes and place it on the terrible footing of war, to which a recognition of belligerency would aim to elevate it. The contest, moreover, is solely on land; the insurrection has not possessed itself of a single seaport whence it may send forth its flag, nor has it any means of communication with foreign powers except through the military lines of its adversaries. No apprehension of any of those sudden and difficult complications which a war upon the ocean is apt to precipitate upon the vessels, both commercial and national, and upon the consular officers of other powers calls for the definition of their relations to the parties to the contest. Considered as a question of expediency, I regard the accordance of belligerent rights still to be as unwise and premature as I regard it to be, at present, indefensible as a measure of right. Such recognition entails upon the country according the rights which flow from it difficult and complicated duties, and requires the exaction from the contending parties of the strict observance of their rights and obligations. It confers the right of search upon the high seas by vessels of both parties; it would subject the carrying of arms and munitions of war, which now may be transported freely and without interruption in the vessels of the United States, to detention and to possible seizure; it would give rise to countless vexatious questions, would release the parent Government from responsibility for acts done by the insurgents, and would invest Spain with the right to exercise the supervision recognized by our treaty of 1795 over our commerce on the high seas, a very large part of which, in its traffic between the Atlantic and the Gulf States and between all of them and the States on the Pacific, passes through the waters which wash the shores of Cuba. The exercise of this supervision could scarce fail to lead, if not to abuses, certainly to collisions perilous to the peaceful relations of the two States. There can be little doubt to what result such supervision would before long draw this nation. It would be unworthy of the United States to inaugurate the possibilities of such result by measures of questionable right or expediency or by any indirection.

Turning to the practical aspects of a recognition of belligerency and reviewing its inconveniences and positive dangers, still further pertinent considerations appear. In the code of nations there is no such thing as a naked recognition of belligerency, unaccompanied by the assumption of international neutrality. Such recognition, without more, will not confer upon either party to a domestic conflict a status not theretofore actually possessed or affect the relation of either party to other states. The act of recognition usually takes the form of a solemn proclamation of neutrality, which recites the *de facto* condition of belligerency as its motive. It announces a domestic law of neutrality in the declaring state.   It assumes the international obligations of a neutral in the presence of a public state of war.   It warns all citizens and others within the jurisdiction of the proclaimant that they violate those rigorous obligations at their own peril and can not expect to be shielded from the consequences.   The right of visit and search on the seas and seizure of vessels and cargoes and contraband of war and good prize under admiralty law must under international law be admitted as a legitimate consequence of a proclamation of belligerency.   While according the equal belligerent rights defined by public law to each party in our ports disfavors would be imposed on both, which, while nominally equal, would weigh heavily in behalf of Spain herself. Possessing a navy and controlling the ports of Cuba, her maritime rights could be asserted not only for the military investment of the island, but up to the margin of our own territorial waters, and a condition of things would exist for which the Cubans within their own domain could not hope to create a parallel, while its creation through aid or sympathy from within our domain would be even more impossible than now, with the additional obligations of international neutrality we would perforce assume.

The enforcement of this enlarged and onerous code of neutrality would only be influential within our own jurisdiction by land and sea and applicable by our own instrumentalities.   It could impart to the United States no jurisdiction between Spain and the insurgents.   It would give the United States no right of intervention to enforce the conduct of the strife within the paramount authority of Spain according to the international code of war.

For these reasons I regard the recognition of the belligerency of the Cuban insurgents as now unwise, and therefore inadmissible.   Should that step hereafter be deemed wise as a measure of right and duty, the Executive will take it.

Intervention upon humanitarian grounds has been frequently suggested and has not failed to receive my most anxious and earnest consideration. But should such a step be now taken, when it is apparent that a hopeful change has supervened in the policy of Spain toward Cuba?   A new government has taken office in the mother country.   It is pledged in advance to the declaration that all the effort in the world can not suffice to maintain peace in Cuba by the bayonet; that vague promises of reform after subjugation afford no solution of the insular problem; that with a substitution of commanders must come a change of the past system of warfare for one in harmony with a new policy, which shall no longer aim to drive the Cubans to the "horrible alternative of taking to the thicket or succumbing in misery;" that reforms must be instituted in accordance with the needs and circumstances of the time, and that these reforms, while designed to give full autonomy to the colony and to create a virtual entity and self-controlled administration, shall yet conserve and affirm the sovereignty of Spain by a just distribution of powers and burdens upon a basis of mutual interest untainted by methods of selfish expediency.

The first acts of the new government lie in these honorable paths. The policy of cruel rapine and extermination that so long shocked the universal sentiment of humanity has been reversed. Under the new military commander a broad clemency is proffered. Measures have already been set on foot to relieve the horrors of starvation. The power of the Spanish armies, it is asserted, is to be used not to spread ruin and desolation, but to protect the resumption of peaceful agricultural pursuits and productive industries. That past methods are futile to force a peace by subjugation is freely admitted, and that ruin without conciliation must inevitably fail to win for Spain the fidelity of a contented dependency.

Decrees in application of the foreshadowed reforms have already been promulgated. The full text of these decrees has not been received, but as furnished in a telegraphic summary from our minister are: All civil and electoral rights of peninsular Spaniards are, in virtue of existing constitutional authority, forthwith extended to colonial Spaniards. A scheme of autonomy has been proclaimed by decree, to become effective upon ratification by the Cortes. It creates a Cuban parliament, which, with the insular executive, can consider and vote upon all subjects affecting local order and interests, possessing unlimited powers save as to matters of state, war, and the navy, as to which the Governor-General acts by his own authority as the delegate of the central Government. This parliament receives the oath of the Governor-General to preserve faithfully the liberties and privileges of the colony, and to it the colonial secretaries are responsible. It has the right to propose to the central Government, through the Governor-General, modifications of the national charter and to invite new projects of law or executive measures in the interest of the colony.

Besides its local powers, it is competent, first, to regulate electoral registration and procedure and prescribe the qualifications of electors and the manner of exercising suffrage; second, to organize courts of justice with native judges from members of the local bar; third, to frame the insular budget, both as to expenditures and revenues, without limitation of any kind, and to set apart the revenues to meet the Cuban share of the national budget, which latter will be voted by the national Cortes with the assistance of Cuban senators and deputies; fourth, to initiate or take part in the negotiations of the national Government for commercial treaties which may affect Cuban interests; fifth, to accept or reject commercial treaties which the national Government may have concluded without the participation of the Cuban government; sixth, to frame the colonial tariff, acting in accord with the peninsular Government in scheduling articles of mutual commerce between the mother country and the colonies. Before introducing or voting upon a bill the Cuban government or the chambers will lay the project before the central Government and hear its opinion thereon, all the correspondence in such regard being made public. Finally, all conflicts of jurisdiction arising between the different municipal, provincial, and insular assemblies, or between the latter and the insular executive power, and which from their nature may not be referable to the central Government for decision, shall be submitted to the courts.

That the government of Sagasta has entered upon a course from which recession with honor is impossible can hardly be questioned; that in the few weeks it has existed it has made earnest of the sincerity of its professions is undeniable. I shall not impugn its sincerity, nor should impatience be suffered to embarrass it in the task it has undertaken. It is honestly due to Spain and to our friendly relations with Spain that she should be given a reasonable chance to realize her expectations and to prove the asserted efficacy of the new order of things to which she stands irrevocably committed. She has recalled the commander whose brutal orders inflamed the American mind and shocked the civilized world. She has modified the horrible order of concentration and has undertaken to care for the helpless and permit those who desire to resume the cultivation of their fields to do so, and assures them of the protection of the Spanish Government in their lawful occupations. She has just released the *Competitor* prisoners, heretofore sentenced to death, and who have been the subject of repeated diplomatic correspondence during both this and the preceding Administration.

Not a single American citizen is now in arrest or confinement in Cuba of whom this Government has any knowledge. The near future will demonstrate whether the indispensable condition of a righteous peace, just alike to the Cubans and to Spain as well as equitable to all our interests so intimately involved in the welfare of Cuba, is likely to be attained. If not, the exigency of further and other action by the United States will remain to be taken. When that time comes that action will be determined in the line of indisputable right and duty. It will be faced, without misgiving or hesitancy in the light of the obligation this Government owes to itself, to the people who have confided to it the protection of their interests and honor, and to humanity.

Sure of the right, keeping free from all offense ourselves, actuated only by upright and patriotic considerations, moved neither by passion nor selfishness, the Government will continue its watchful care over the rights and property of American citizens and will abate none of its efforts to bring about by peaceful agencies a peace which shall be honorable and enduring. If it shall hereafter appear to be a duty imposed by our obligations to ourselves, to civilization and humanity to intervene with force, it shall be without fault on our part and only because the necessity for such action will be so clear as to command the support and approval of the civilized world.

By a special message dated the 16th day of June last, I laid before the Senate a treaty signed that day by the plenipotentiaries of the United States and of the Republic of Hawaii, having for its purpose the incorporation of the Hawaiian Islands as an integral part of the United States and under its sovereignty. The Senate having removed the injunction of secrecy, although the treaty is still pending before that body, the subject may be properly referred to in this Message because the necessary action of the Congress is required to determine by legislation many details of the eventual union should the fact of annexation be accomplished, as I believe it should be.

While consistently disavowing from a very early period any aggressive policy of absorption in regard to the Hawaiian group, a long series of declarations through three-quarters of a century has proclaimed the vital interest of the United States in the independent life of the Islands and their intimate commercial dependence upon this country. At the same time it has been repeatedly asserted that in no event could the entity of Hawaiian statehood cease by the passage of the Islands under the domination or influence of another power than the United States. Under these circumstances, the logic of events required that annexation, heretofore offered but declined, should in the ripeness of time come about as the natural result of the strengthening ties that bind us to those Islands, and be realized by the free will of the Hawaiian State.

That treaty was unanimously ratified without amendment by the Senate and President of the Republic of Hawaii on the 10th of September last, and only awaits the favorable action of the American Senate to effect the complete absorption of the Islands into the domain of the United States. What the conditions of such a union shall be, the political relation thereof to the United States, the character of the local administration, the quality and degree of the elective franchise of the inhabitants, the extension of the federal laws to the territory or the enactment of special laws to fit the peculiar condition thereof, the regulation if need be of the labor system therein, are all matters which the treaty has wisely relegated to the Congress.

If the treaty is confirmed as every consideration of dignity and honor requires, the wisdom of Congress will see to it that, avoiding abrupt assimilation of elements perhaps hardly yet fitted to share in the highest franchises of citizenship, and having due regard to the geographical conditions, the most just provisions for self-rule in local matters with the largest political liberties as an integral part of our Nation will be accorded to the Hawaiians. No less is due to a people who, after nearly five years of demonstrated capacity to fulfill the obligations of self-governing statehood, come of their free will to merge their destinies in our body-politic.

The questions which have arisen between Japan and Hawaii by reason of the treatment of Japanese laborers emigrating to the Islands under the Hawaiian-Japanese convention of 1888, are in a satisfactory stage of settlement by negotiation. This Government has not been invited to mediate, and on the other hand has sought no intervention in that matter, further than to evince its kindliest disposition toward such a speedy and direct adjustment by the two sovereign States in interest as shall comport with equity and honor. It is gratifying to learn that the apprehensions at first displayed on the part of Japan lest the cessation of Hawaii's national life through annexation might impair privileges to which Japan honorably laid claim, have given place to confidence in the uprightness of this Government, and in the sincerity of its purpose to deal with all possible ulterior questions in the broadest spirit of friendliness.

As to the representation of this Government to Nicaragua, Salvador, and Costa Rica, I have concluded that Mr. William L. Merry, confirmed as minister of the United States to the States of Nicaragua, Salvador and Costa Rica, shall proceed to San José, Costa Rica, and there temporarily establish the headquarters of the United States to those three States. I took this action for what I regarded as the paramount interests of this country. It was developed upon an investigation by the Secretary of State that the Government of Nicaragua, while not unwilling to receive Mr. Merry in his diplomatic quality, was unable to do so because of the compact concluded June 20, 1895, whereby that Republic and those of Salvador and Honduras, forming what is known as the Greater Republic of Central America, had surrendered to the representative Diet thereof their right to receive and send diplomatic agents. The Diet was not willing to accept him because he was not accredited to that body. I could not accredit him to that body because the appropriation law of Congress did not permit it. Mr. Baker, the present minister at Managua, has been directed to present his letters of recall.

Mr. W. Godfrey Hunter has likewise been accredited to the Governments of Guatemala and Honduras, the same as his predecessor Guatemala is not a member of the Greater Republic of Central America, but Honduras is. Should this latter Government decline to receive him, he has been instructed to report this fact to his Government and await its further instructions.

A subject of large importance to our country, and increasing appreciation on the part of the people, is the completion of the great highway of trade between the Atlantic and Pacific, known as the Nicaragua Canal. Its utility and value to American commerce is universally admitted. The Commission appointed under date of July 24 last "to continue the surveys and examinations authorized by the act approved March 2, 1895," in regard to "the proper route, feasibility, and cost of construction of the Nicaragua Canal, with a view of making complete plans for the entire work of construction of such canal," is now employed in the undertaking. In the future I shall take occasion to transmit to Congress the report of this Commission, making at the same time such further suggestions as may then seem advisable.

Under the provisions of the act of Congress approved March 3, 1897, for the promotion of an international agreement respecting bimetallism, I appointed on the 14th day of April, 1897, Hon. Edward O. Wolcott of Colorado, Hon. Adlai E. Stevenson of Illinois, and Hon. Charles J. Paine of Massachusetts, as special envoys to represent the United States. They have been diligent in their efforts to secure the concurrence and cooperation of European countries in the international settlement of the question, but up to this time have not been able to secure an agreement contemplated by their mission.

The gratifying action of our great sister Republic of France in joining this country in the attempt to bring about an agreement among the principal commercial nations of Europe, whereby a fixed and relative value between gold and silver shall be secured, furnishes assurance that we are not alone among the larger nations of the world in realizing the international character of the problem and in the desire of reaching some wise and practical solution of it. The British Government has published a *résumé* of the steps taken jointly by the French ambassador in London and the special envoys of the United States, with whom our ambassador at London actively co-operated in the presentation of this subject to Her Majesty's Government. This will be laid before Congress.

Our special envoys have not made their final report, as further negotiations between the representatives of this Government and the Governments of other countries are pending and in contemplation. They believe that doubts which have been raised in certain quarters respecting the position of maintaining the stability of the parity between the metals and kindred questions may yet be solved by further negotiations.

Meanwhile it gives me satisfaction to state that the special envoys have already demonstrated their ability and fitness to deal with the subject, and it is to be earnestly hoped that their labors may result in an international agreement which will bring about recognition of both gold and silver as money upon such terms, and with such safeguards as will secure the use of both metals upon a basis which shall work no injustice to any class of our citizens.

In order to execute as early as possible the provisions of the third and fourth sections of the Revenue Act, approved July 24, 1897, I appointed the Hon. John A. Kasson of Iowa, a special commissioner plenipotentiary to undertake the requisite negotiations with foreign countries desiring to avail themselves of these provisions. The negotiations are now proceeding with several Governments, both European and American. It is believed that by a careful exercise of the powers conferred by that Act some grievances of our own and of other countries in our mutual trade relations may be either removed, or largely alleviated, and that the volume of our commercial exchanges may be enlarged, with advantage to both contracting parties.

Most desirable from every standpoint of national interest and patriotism is the effort to extend our foreign commerce. To this end our merchant marine should be improved and enlarged. We should do our full share of the carrying trade of the world. We do not do it now. We should be the laggard no longer. The inferiority of our merchant marine is justly humiliating to the national pride. The Government by every proper constitutional means, should aid in making our ships familiar visitors at every commercial port of the world, thus opening up new and valuable markets to the surplus products of the farm and the factory.

The efforts which had been made during the two previous years by my predecessor to secure better protection to the fur seals in the North Pacific Ocean and Bering Sea, were renewed at an early date by this Administration, and have been pursued with earnestness. Upon my invitation, the Governments of Japan and Russia sent delegates to Washington, and an international conference was held during the months of October and November last, wherein it was unanimously agreed that under the existing regulations this species of useful animals was threatened with extinction, and that an international agreement of all the interested powers was necessary for their adequate protection.

The Government of Great Britain did not see proper to be represented at this conference, but subsequently sent to Washington, as delegates, the expert commissioners of Great Britain and Canada who had, during the past two years, visited the Pribilof Islands, and who met in conference similar commissioners on the part of the United States. The result of this conference was an agreement on important facts connected with the condition of the seal herd, heretofore in dispute, which should place beyond controversy the duty of the Governments concerned to adopt measures without delay for the preservation and restoration of the herd. Negotiations to this end are now in progress, the result of which I hope to be able to report to Congress at an early day.

International arbitration cannot be omitted from the list of subjects claiming our consideration. Events have only served to strengthen the general views on this question expressed in my inaugural address. The best sentiment of the civilized world is moving toward the settlement of differences between nations without resorting to the horrors of war. Treaties embodying these humane principles on broad lines, without in any way imperiling our interests or our honor, shall have my constant encouragement.

The acceptance by this Government of the invitation of the Republic of France to participate in the Universal Exposition of 1900, at Paris, was immediately followed by the appointment of a special commissioner to represent the United States in the proposed exposition, with special reference to the securing of space for an adequate exhibit on behalf of the United States.

The special commissioner delayed his departure for Paris long enough to ascertain the probable demand for space by American exhibitors. His inquiries developed an almost unprecedented interest in the proposed exposition, and the information thus acquired enabled him to justify an application for a much larger allotment of space for the American section than had been reserved by the exposition authorities. The result was particularly gratifying, in view of the fact that the United States was one of the last countries to accept the invitation of France.

The reception accorded our special commissioner was most cordial, and he was given every reasonable assurance that the United States would receive a consideration commensurate with the proportions of our exhibit. The report of the special commissioner as to the magnitude and importance of the coming exposition, and the great demand for space by American exhibitors, supplies new arguments for a liberal and judicious appropriation by Congress, to the end that an exhibit fairly representative of the industries and resources of our country may be made in an exposition which will illustrate the world's progress during the nineteenth century. That exposition is intended to be the most important and comprehensive of the long series of international exhibitions, of which our own at Chicago was a brilliant example, and it is desirable that the United States should make a worthy exhibit of American genius and skill and their unrivaled achievements in every branch of industry.

The present immediately effective force of the Navy consists of four battle ships of the first class, two of the second, and forty-eight other vessels, ranging from armored cruisers to torpedo boats. There are under construction five battle ships of the first class, sixteen torpedo boats, and one submarine boat. No provision has yet been made for the armor of three of the five battle ships, as it has been impossible to obtain it at the price fixed by Congress. It is of great importance that Congress provide this armor, as until then the ships are of no fighting value.

The present naval force, especially in view of its increase by the ships now under construction, while not as large as that of a few other powers, is a formidable force ; its vessels are the very best of each type; and with the increase that should be made to it from time to time in the future, and careful attention to keeping it in a high state of efficiency and repair, it is well adapted to the necessities of the country.

The great increase of the Navy which has taken place in recent years was justified by the requirements for national defense, and has received public approbation. The time has now arrived, however, when this increase, to which the country is committed, should, for a time, take the form of increased facilities commensurate with the increase of our naval vessels. It is an unfortunate fact that there is only one dock on the Pacific Coast capable of docking our largest ships, and only one on the Atlantic Coast, and that the latter has for the last six or seven months been under repair and therefore incapable of use. Immediate steps should be taken to provide three or four docks of this capacity on the Atlantic Coast, at least one on the Pacific Coast, and a floating dock in the Gulf. This is the recommendation of a very competent Board, appointed to investigate the subject. There should also be ample provision made for powder and projectiles, and other munitions of war, and for an increased number of officers and enlisted men. Some additions are also necessary to our navy-yards, for the repair and care of our large number of vessels. As there are now on the stocks five battle ships of the largest class, which cannot be completed for a year or two, I concur with the recommendation of the Secretary of the Navy for an appropriation authorizing the construction of one battle ship for the Pacific Coast, where, at present, there is only one in commission and one under construction, while on the Atlantic Coast there are three in commission and four under construction; and also that several torpedo boats be authorized in connection with our general system of coast defense.

The Territory of Alaska requires the prompt and early attention of Congress. The conditions now existing demand material changes in the laws relating to the Territory. The great influx of population during the past summer and fall and the prospect of a still larger immigration in the spring will not permit us to longer neglect the extension of civil authority within the Territory or postpone the establishment of a more thorough government.

A general system of public surveys has not yet been extended to Alaska and all entries thus far made in that district are upon special surveys. The act of Congress extending to Alaska the mining laws of the United States contained the reservation that it should not be construed to put in force the general land laws of the country. By act approved March 3, 1891, authority was given for entry of lands for town-site purposes and also for the purchase of not exceeding one hundred and sixty acres then or thereafter occupied for purposes of trade and manufacture. The purpose of Congress as thus far expressed has been that only such rights should apply to that Territory as should be specifically named.

It will be seen how much remains to be done for that vast and remote and yet promising portion of our country. Special authority was given to the President by the Act of Congress approved July 24, 1897, to divide that Territory into two land districts and to designate the boundaries thereof and to appoint registers and receivers of said land offices, and the President was also authorized to appoint a surveyor-general for the entire district. Pursuant to this authority, a surveyor-general and receiver have been appointed, with offices at Sitka. If in the ensuing year the conditions justify it, the additional land district authorized by law will be established, with an office at some point in the Yukon Valley. No appropriation, however, was made for this purpose, and that is now necessary to be done for the two land districts into which the Territory is to be divided.

I concur with the Secretary of War in his suggestions as to the necessity for a military force in the Territory of Alaska for the protection of persons and property. Already a small force, consisting of twenty-five men, with two officers, under command of Lieutenant-Colonel Randall, of the Eighth Infantry, has been sent to St. Michael to establish a military post.

As it is to the interest of the Government to encourage the development and settlement of the country and its duty to follow up its citizens there with the benefits of legal machinery, I earnestly urge upon Congress the establishment of a system of government with such flexibility as will enable it to adjust itself to the future areas of greatest population.

The startling though possibly exaggerated reports from the Yukon River country, of the probable shortage of food for the large number of people who are wintering there without the means of leaving the country are confirmed in such measure as to justify bringing the matter to the attention of Congress. Access to that country in winter can be had only by the passes from Dyea and vicinity, which is a most difficult and perhaps an impossible task. However, should these reports of the suffering of our fellow-citizens be further verified, every effort at any cost should be made to carry them relief.

For a number of years past it has been apparent that the conditions under which the Five Civilized Tribes were established in the Indian Territory under treaty provisions with the United States, with the right of self-government and the exclusion of all white persons from within their borders, have undergone so complete a change as to render the continuance of the system thus inaugurated practically impossible. The total number of the Five Civilized Tribes, as shown by the last census, is 45,494, and this number has not materially increased; while the white population is estimated at from 200,000 to 250,000 which, by permission of the Indian Government has settled in the Territory. The present area of the Indian Territory contains 25,694,564 acres, much of which is very fertile land. The United States citizens residing in the Territory, most of whom have gone there by invitation or with the consent of the tribal authorities, have made permanent homes for themselves. Numerous towns have been built in which from 500 to 5,000 white people now reside. Valuable residences and business houses have been erected in many of them. Large business enterprises are carried on in which vast sums of money are employed, and yet these people, who have invested their capital in the development of the productive resources of the country, are without title to the land they occupy, and have no voice whatever in the government either of the Nations or Tribes. Thousands of their children who were born in the Territory are of school age, but the doors of the schools of the Nations are shut against them, and what education they get is by private contribution. No provision for the protection of the life or property of these white citizens is made by the Tribal Governments and Courts.

The Secretary of the Interior reports that leading Indians have absorbed great tracts of land to the exclusion of the common people, and government by an Indian aristocracy has been practically established, to the detriment of the people. It has been found impossible for the United States to keep its citizens out of the Territory, and the executory conditions contained in the treaties with these Nations have for the most part become impossible of execution. Nor has it been possible for the Tribal Governments to secure to each individual Indian his full enjoyment in common with other Indians of the common property of the Nations. Friends of the Indians have long believed that the best interests of the Indians of the Five Civilized Tribes would be found in American citizenship, with all the rights and privileges which belong to that condition.

By section 16, of the act of March 3, 1893, the President was authorized to appoint three commissioners to enter into negotiations with the Cherokee, Choctaw, Chickasaw, Muscogee (or Creek), and Seminole Nations, commonly known as the Five Civilized Tribes in the Indian Territory. Briefly, the purposes of the negotiations were to be: The extinguishment of Tribal titles to any lands within that Territory now held by any and all such Nations or Tribes, either by cession of the same or some part thereof to the United States, or by allotment and division of the same in severalty among the Indians of such Nations or Tribes respectively as may be entitled to the same, or by such other method as may be agreed upon between the several Nations and Tribes aforesaid, or each of them, with the United States, with a view to such an adjustment upon the basis of justice and equity as may, with the consent of the said Nations of Indians so far as may be necessary, be requisite and suitable to enable the ultimate creation of a State or States of the Union which shall embrace the lands within said Indian Territory.

The Commission met much opposition from the beginning. The Indians were very slow to act, and those in control manifested a decided disinclination to meet with favor the propositions submitted to them. A little more than three years after this organization the Commission effected an agreement with the Choctaw Nation alone. The Chickasaws, however, refused to agree to its terms, and as they have a common interest with the Choctaws in the lands of said Nations, the agreement with the latter Nation could have no effect without the consent of the former.   On April 23, 1897, the Commission effected an agreement with both tribes — the Choctaws and Chickasaws.   This agreement, it is understood, has been ratified by the constituted authorities of the respective Tribes or Nations parties thereto, and only requires ratification by Congress to make it binding.

On the 27th of September, 1897, an agreement was effected with the Creek Nation, but it is understood that the National Council of said Nation has refused to ratify the same.   Negotiations are yet to be had with the Cherokees, the most populous of the Five Civilized Tribes, and with the Seminoles, the smallest in point of numbers and territory.

The provision in the Indian Appropriation Act, approved June 10, 1896, makes it the duty of the Commission to investigate and determine the rights of applicants for citizenship in the Five Civilized Tribes, and to make complete census rolls of the citizens of said Tribes. The Commission is at present engaged in this work among the Creeks, and has made appointments for taking the census of these people up to and including the 30th of the present month.

Should the agreement between the Choctaws and Chickasaws be ratified by Congress and should the other Tribes fail to make an agreement with the Commission, then it will be necessary that some legislation shall be had by Congress, which, while just and honorable to the Indians, shall be equitable to the white people who have settled upon these lands by invitation of the Tribal Nations.

Hon. Henry L. Dawes, Chairman of the Commission, in a letter to the Secretary of the Interior, under date of October 11, 1897, says: "Individual ownership is, in their (the Commission's) opinion, absolutely essential to any permanent improvement in present conditions, and the lack of it is the root of nearly all the evils which so grievously afflict these people.   Allotment by agreement is the only possible method, unless the United States Courts are clothed with the authority to apportion the lands among the citizen Indians for whose use it was originally granted."

I concur with the Secretary of the Interior that there can be no cure for the evils engendered by the perversion of these great trusts, excepting by their resumption by the Government which created them.

The recent prevalence of yellow fever in a number of cities and towns throughout the South has resulted in much disturbance of commerce, and demonstrated the necessity of such amendments to our quarantine laws as will make the regulations of the national quarantine authorities paramount.   The Secretary of the Treasury, in the portion of his report relating to the operation of the Marine Hospital Service, calls attention to the defects in the present quarantine laws, and recommends amendments thereto which will give the Treasury Department the requisite authority to prevent the invasion of epidemic diseases from foreign countries, and in times of emergency, like that of the past summer, will add to the efficiency of the sanitary measures for the protection of the people, and at the same time prevent unnecessary restriction of commerce. I concur in his recommendation.

In further effort to prevent the invasion of the United States by yellow fever, the importance of the discovery of the exact cause of the disease, which up to the present time has been undetermined, is obvious, and to this end a systematic bacteriological investigation should be made. I therefore recommend that Congress authorize the appointment of a commission by the President, to consist of four expert bacteriologists, one to be selected from the medical officers of the Marine Hospital Service, one to be appointed from civil life, one to be detailed from the medical officers of the Army, and one from the medical officers of the Navy.

The Union Pacific Railway, Main Line, was sold under the decree of the United States Court for the District of Nebraska, on the 1st and 2d of November of this year. The amount due the Government consisted of the principal of the subsidy bonds, $27,236,512, and the accrued interest thereon, $31,211,711.75, making the total indebtedness, $58,-448,223.75. The bid at the sale covered the first mortgage lien and the entire mortgage claim of the Government, principal and interest.

The sale of the subsidized portion of the Kansas Pacific Line, upon which the Government holds a second mortgage lien, has been postponed at the instance of the Government to December 16, 1897. The debt of this division of the Union Pacific Railway to the Government on November 1, 1897, was the principal of the subsidy bonds, $6,303,000, and the unpaid and accrued interest thereon, $6,626,-690.33, making a total of $12,929,690.33.

The sale of this road was originally advertised for November 4, but for the purpose of securing the utmost public notice of the event it was postponed until December 16, and a second advertisement of the sale was made. By the decree of the Court, the upset price on the sale of the Kansas Pacific will yield to the Government the sum of $2,500,000 over all prior liens, costs, and charges. If no other or better bid is made, this sum is all that the Government will receive on its claim of nearly $13,000,000. The Government has no information as to whether there will be other bidders or a better bid than the minimum amount herein stated. The question presented therefore is: Whether the Government shall, under the authority given it by the act of March 3, 1887, purchase or redeem the road in the event that a bid is not made by private parties covering the entire Government claim. To qualify the Government to bid at the sales will require a deposit of $900,000, as follows: In the Government cause $500,000 and in each of the first mortgage causes $200,000, and in the latter the deposit must be in cash. Payments at the sale are as follows : Upon the acceptance of the bid a sum which with the amount already deposited shall equal fifteen per cent of the bid ; the balance in installments of twenty-five per cent thirty, forty, and fifty days after the confirmation of the sale. The lien on the Kansas Pacific prior to that of the Government on the 30th July, 1897, principal and interest, amounted to $7,281,048.11. The Government, therefore, should it become the highest bidder, will have to pay the amount of the first mortgage lien.

I believe that under the act of 1887 it has the authority to do this and in absence of any action by Congress I shall direct the Secretary of the Treasury to make the necessary deposit as required by the Court's decree to qualify as a bidder and to bid at the sale a sum which will at least equal the principal of the debt due to the Government ; but suggest in order to remove all controversy that an amendment of the law be immediately passed explicitly giving such powers and appropriating in general terms whatever sum is sufficient therefor.

In so important a matter as the Government becoming the possible owner of railroad property which it perforce must conduct and operate, I feel constrained to lay before Congress these facts for its consideration and action before the consummation of the sale. It is clear to my mind that the Government should not permit the property to be sold at a price which will yield less than one-half of the principal of its debt and less than one-fifth of its entire debt, principal and interest. But whether the Government, rather than accept less than its claim, should become a bidder and thereby the owner of the property, I submit to the Congress for action.

The Library building provided for by the act of Congress approved April 15, 1886, has been completed and opened to the public. It should be a matter of congratulation that through the foresight and munificence of Congress the nation possesses this noble treasure-house of knowledge. It is earnestly to be hoped that having done so much toward the cause of education, Congress will continue to develop the Library in every phase of research to the end that it may be not only one of the most magnificent but among the richest and most useful libraries in the world.

The important branch of our Government known as the Civil Service, the practical improvement of which has long been a subject of earnest discussion, has of late years received increased legislative and Executive approval. During the past few months the service has been placed upon a still firmer basis of business methods and personal merit. While the right of our veteran soldiers to reinstatement in deserving cases has been asserted, dismissals for merely political reasons have been carefully guarded against, the examinations for admittance to the service enlarged and at the same time rendered less technical and more practical ; and a distinct advance has been made by giving a hearing before dismissal upon all cases where incompetency is charged or demand made for the removal of officials in any of the Departments. This order has been made to give to the accused his right to be heard but without in any way impairing the power of removal, which should always be exercised in cases of inefficiency and incompetency, and which is one of the vital safeguards of the civil service reform system, preventing stagnation and deadwood and keeping every employee keenly alive to the fact that the security of his tenure depends not on favor but on his own tested and carefully watched record of service.

Much of course still remains to be accomplished before the system can be made reasonably perfect for our needs. There are places now in the classified service which ought to be exempted and others not classified may properly be included. I shall not hesitate to exempt cases which I think have been improperly included in the classified service or include those which in my judgment will best promote the public service. The system has the approval of the people and it will be my endeavor to uphold and extend it.

I am forced by the length of this Message to omit many important references to affairs of the Government with which Congress will have to deal at the present session. They are fully discussed in the departmental reports, to all of which I invite your earnest attention.

The estimates of the expenses of the Government by the several Departments will, I am sure, have your careful scrutiny. While the Congress may not find it an easy task to reduce the expenses of the Government, it should not encourage their increase. These expenses will in my judgment admit of a decrease in many branches of the Government without injury to the public service. It is a commanding duty to keep the appropriations within the receipts of the Government, and thus avoid a deficit.

SECOND ANNUAL MESSAGE.

EXECUTIVE MANSION, *December 5, 1898.*

To the Senate and House of Representatives:

Notwithstanding the added burdens rendered necessary by the war, our people rejoice in a very satisfactory and steadily increasing degree of prosperity, evidenced by the largest volume of business ever recorded. Manufacture has been productive, agricultural pursuits have yielded abundant returns, labor in all fields of industry is better rewarded, revenue legislation passed by the present Congress has increased the Treasury's receipts to the amount estimated by its authors, the finances of the

Government have been successfully administered and its credit advanced to the first rank, while its currency has been maintained at the world's highest standard. Military service under a common flag and for a right-eous cause has strengthened the national spirit and served to cement more closely than ever the fraternal bonds between every section of the country.

A review of the relation of the United States to other powers, always appropriate, is this year of primary importance in view of the momentous issues which have arisen, demanding in one instance the ultimate deter-mination by arms and involving far-reaching consequences which will require the earnest attention of the Congress.

In my last annual message very full consideration was given to the question of the duty of the Government of the United States toward Spain and the Cuban insurrection as being by far the most important problem with which we were then called upon to deal. The considera-tions then advanced and the exposition of the views therein expressed disclosed my sense of the extreme gravity of the situation. Setting aside as logically unfounded or practically inadmissible the recognition of the Cuban insurgents as belligerents, the recognition of the independence of Cuba, neutral intervention to end the war by imposing a rational compro-mise between the contestants, intervention in favor of one or the other party, and forcible annexation of the island, I concluded it was honestly due to our friendly relations with Spain that she should be given a rea-sonable chance to realize her expectations of reform to which she had become irrevocably committed. Within a few weeks previously she had announced comprehensive plans which it was confidently asserted would be efficacious to remedy the evils so deeply affecting our own country, so injurious to the true interests of the mother country as well as to those of Cuba, and so repugnant to the universal sentiment of humanity.

The ensuing month brought little sign of real progress toward the pacification of Cuba. The autonomous administrations set up in the capital and some of the principal cities appeared not to gain the favor of the inhabitants nor to be able to extend their influence to the large ex-tent of territory held by the insurgents, while the military arm, obviously unable to cope with the still active rebellion, continued many of the most objectionable and offensive policies of the government that had preceded it. No tangible relief was afforded the vast numbers of unhappy recon-centrados, despite the reiterated professions made in that regard and the amount appropriated by Spain to that end. The proffered expedient of zones of cultivation proved illusory. Indeed no less practical nor more delusive promises of succor could well have been tendered to the ex-hausted and destitute people, stripped of all that made life and home dear and herded in a strange region among unsympathetic strangers hardly less necessitous than themselves.

By the end of December the mortality among them had frightfully in-creased. Conservative estimates from Spanish sources placed the deaths among these distressed people at over 40 per cent from the time General Weyler's decree of reconcentration was enforced. With the acquiescence of the Spanish authorities, a scheme was adopted for relief by charitable contributions raised in this country and distributed, under the direction of the consul-general and the several consuls, by noble and earnest individual effort through the organized agencies of the American Red Cross. Thousands of lives were thus saved, but many thousands more were inaccessible to such forms of aid.

The war continued on the old footing, without comprehensive plan, developing only the same spasmodic encounters, barren of strategic result, that had marked the course of the earlier ten years' rebellion as well as the present insurrection from its start. No alternative save physical exhaustion of either combatant, and therewithal the practical ruin of the island, lay in sight, but how far distant no one could venture to conjecture.

At this juncture, on the 15th of February last, occurred the destruction of the battle ship *Maine* while rightfully lying in the harbor of Havana on a mission of international courtesy and good will—a catastrophe the suspicious nature and horror of which stirred the nation's heart profoundly. It is a striking evidence of the poise and sturdy good sense distinguishing our national character that this shocking blow, falling upon a generous people already deeply touched by preceding events in Cuba, did not move them to an instant desperate resolve to tolerate no longer the existence of a condition of danger and disorder at our doors that made possible such a deed, by whomsoever wrought. Yet the instinct of justice prevailed, and the nation anxiously awaited the result of the searching investigation at once set on foot. The finding of the naval board of inquiry established that the origin of the explosion was external, by a submarine mine, and only halted through lack of positive testimony to fix the responsibility of its authorship.

All these things carried conviction to the most thoughtful, even before the finding of the naval court, that a crisis in our relations with Spain and toward Cuba was at hand. So strong was this belief that it needed but a brief Executive suggestion to the Congress to receive immediate answer to the duty of making instant provision for the possible and perhaps speedily probable emergency of war, and the remarkable, almost unique, spectacle was presented of a unanimous vote of both Houses, on the 9th of March, appropriating $50,000,000 "for the national defense and for each and every purpose connected therewith, to be expended at the discretion of the President." That this act of prevision came none too soon was disclosed when the application of the fund was undertaken. Our coasts were practically undefended. Our Navy needed large provision for increased ammunition and supplies, and even numbers to cope with any sudden attack from the navy of Spain, which comprised modern vessels of the highest type of continental perfection. Our Army also required enlargement of men and munitions. The details of the hurried preparation for the dreaded contingency are told in the reports of the Secretaries of War and of the Navy, and need not be repeated here. It is sufficient to say that the outbreak of war when it did come found our nation not unprepared to meet the conflict.

Nor was the apprehension of coming strife confined to our own country. It was felt by the continental powers, which on April 6, through their ambassadors and envoys, addressed to the Executive an expression of hope that humanity and moderation might mark the course of this Government and people, and that further negotiations would lead to an agreement which, while securing the maintenance of peace, would afford all necessary guaranties for the reestablishment of order in Cuba. In responding to that representation I said I shared the hope the envoys had expressed that peace might be preserved in a manner to terminate the chronic condition of disturbance in Cuba, so injurious and menacing to our interests and tranquillity, as well as shocking to our sentiments of humanity; and while appreciating the humanitarian and disinterested character of the communication they had made on behalf of the powers, I stated the confidence of this Government, for its part, that equal appreciation would be shown for its own earnest and unselfish endeavors to fulfill a duty to humanity by ending a situation the indefinite prolongation of which had become insufferable.

Still animated by the hope of a peaceful solution and obeying the dictates of duty, no effort was relaxed to bring about a speedy ending of the Cuban struggle. Negotiations to this object continued actively with the Government of Spain, looking to the immediate conclusion of a six months' armistice in Cuba, with a view to effect the recognition of her people's right to independence. Besides this, the instant revocation of the order of reconcentration was asked, so that the sufferers, returning to their homes and aided by united American and Spanish effort, might be put in a way to support themselves and, by orderly resumption of the well-nigh destroyed productive energies of the island, contribute to the restoration of its tranquillity and well-being. Negotiations continued for some little time at Madrid, resulting in offers by the Spanish Government which could not but be regarded as inadequate. It was proposed to confide the preparation of peace to the insular parliament, yet to be convened under the autonomous decrees of November, 1897, but without impairment in any wise of the constitutional powers of the Madrid Government, which to that end would grant an armistice, if solicited by the insurgents, for such time as the general in chief might see fit to fix. How and with what scope of discretionary powers the insular parliament was expected to set about the "preparation" of peace did not appear. If it were to be by negotiation with the insurgents, the issue seemed to rest on the one side with a body chosen by a fraction of the electors in the districts under Spanish control, and on the other with the insurgent population holding the interior country, unrepresented in the so-called parliament and defiant at the suggestion of suing for peace.

Grieved and disappointed at this barren outcome of my sincere endeavors to reach a practicable solution, I felt it my duty to remit the whole question to the Congress. In the message of April 11, 1898, I announced that with this last overture in the direction of immediate peace in Cuba and its disappointing reception by Spain the effort of the Executive was brought to an end. I again reviewed the alternative courses of action which had been proposed, concluding that the only one consonant with international policy and compatible with our firm-set historical traditions was intervention as a neutral to stop the war and check the hopeless sacrifice of life, even though that resort involved "hostile constraint upon both the parties to the contest, as well to enforce a truce as to guide the eventual settlement." The grounds justifying that step were the interests of humanity, the duty to protect the life and property of our citizens in Cuba, the right to check injury to our commerce and people through the devastation of the island, and, most important, the need of removing at once and forever the constant menace and the burdens entailed upon our Government by the uncertainties and perils of the situation caused by the unendurable disturbance in Cuba. I said:

The long trial has proved that the object for which Spain has waged the war can not be attained. The fire of insurrection may flame or may smolder with varying seasons, but it has not been and it is plain that it can not be extinguished by present methods. The only hope of relief and repose from a condition which can no longer be endured is the enforced pacification of Cuba. In the name of humanity, in the name of civilization, in behalf of endangered American interests which give us the right and the duty to speak and to act, the war in Cuba must stop.

In view of all this the Congress was asked to authorize and empower the President to take measures to secure a full and final termination of hostilities between Spain and the people of Cuba and to secure in the island the establishment of a stable government, capable of maintaining order and observing its international obligations, insuring peace and tranquillity and the security of its citizens as well as our own, and for the accomplishment of those ends to use the military and naval forces of the United States as might be necessary, with added authority to continue generous relief to the starving people of Cuba.

The response of the Congress, after nine days of earnest deliberation, during which the almost unanimous sentiment of your body was developed on every point save as to the expediency of coupling the proposed action with a formal recognition of the Republic of Cuba as the true and lawful government of that island—a proposition which failed of adoption—the Congress, after conference, on the 19th of April, by a vote of 42 to 35 in the Senate and 311 to 6 in the House of Representatives, passed the memorable joint resolution declaring—

First. That the people of the island of Cuba are, and of right ought to be, free and independent.

Second. That it is the duty of the United States to demand, and the Government of the United States does hereby demand, that the Government of Spain at once relinquish its authority and government in the island of Cuba and withdraw its land and naval forces from Cuba and Cuban waters.

Third. That the President of the United States be, and he hereby is, directed and empowered to use the entire land and naval forces of the United States and to call into the actual service of the United States the militia of the several States to such extent as may be necessary to carry these resolutions into effect.

Fourth. That the United States hereby disclaims any disposition or intention to exercise sovereignty, jurisdiction, or control over said island except for the pacification thereof, and asserts its determination when that is accomplished to leave the government and control of the island to its people.

This resolution was approved by the Executive on the next day, April 20. A copy was at once communicated to the Spanish minister at this capital, who forthwith announced that his continuance in Washington had thereby become impossible, and asked for his passports, which were given him. He thereupon withdrew from Washington, leaving the protection of Spanish interests in the United States to the French ambassador and the Austro-Hungarian minister. Simultaneously with its communication to the Spanish minister here, General Woodford, the American minister at Madrid, was telegraphed confirmation of the text of the joint resolution and directed to communicate it to the Government of Spain with the formal demand that it at once relinquish its authority and government in the island of Cuba and withdraw its forces therefrom, coupling this demand with announcement of the intentions of this Government as to the future of the island, in conformity with the fourth clause of the resolution, and giving Spain until noon of April 23 to reply.

That demand, although, as above shown, officially made known to the Spanish envoy here, was not delivered at Madrid. After the instruction reached General Woodford on the morning of April 21, but before he could present it, the Spanish minister of state notified him that upon the President's approval of the joint resolution the Madrid Government, regarding the act as "equivalent to an evident declaration of war," had ordered its minister in Washington to withdraw, thereby breaking off diplomatic relations between the two countries and ceasing all official communication between their respective representatives. General Woodford thereupon demanded his passports and quitted Madrid the same day.

Spain having thus denied the demand of the United States and initiated that complete form of rupture of relations which attends a state of war, the executive powers authorized by the resolution were at once used by me to meet the enlarged contingency of actual war between sovereign states. On April 22 I proclaimed a blockade of the north coast of Cuba, including ports on said coast between Cardenas and Bahia Honda, and the port of Cienfuegos, on the south coast of Cuba, and on the 23d I called for volunteers to execute the purpose of the resolution. By my message of April 25 the Congress was informed of the situation, and I recommended formal declaration of the existence of a state of war between the

United States and Spain. The Congress accordingly voted on the same day the act approved April 25, 1898, declaring the existence of such war from and including the 21st day of April, and reenacted the provision of the resolution of April 20 directing the President to use all the armed forces of the nation to carry that act into effect. Due notification of the existence of war as aforesaid was given April 25 by telegraph to all the governments with which the United States maintain relations, in order that their neutrality might be assured during the war. The various governments responded with proclamations of neutrality, each after its own methods. It is not among the least gratifying incidents of the struggle that the obligations of neutrality were impartially discharged by all, often under delicate and difficult circumstances.

In further fulfillment of international duty I issued, April 26, 1898, a proclamation announcing the treatment proposed to be accorded to vessels and their cargoes as to blockade, contraband, the exercise of the right of search, and the immunity of neutral flags and neutral goods under enemy's flag. A similar proclamation was made by the Spanish Government. In the conduct of hostilities the rules of the Declaration of Paris, including abstention from resort to privateering, have accordingly been observed by both belligerents, although neither was a party to that declaration.

Our country thus, after an interval of half a century of peace with all nations, found itself engaged in deadly conflict with a foreign enemy. Every nerve was strained to meet the emergency. The response to the initial call for 125,000 volunteers was instant and complete, as was also the result of the second call, of May 25, for 75,000 additional volunteers. The ranks of the Regular Army were increased to the limits provided by the act of April 26, 1898.

The enlisted force of the Navy on the 15th day of August, when it reached its maximum, numbered 24,123 men and apprentices. One hundred and three vessels were added to the Navy by purchase, 1 was presented to the Government, 1 leased, and the 4 vessels of the International Navigation Company—the *St. Paul, St. Louis, New York,* and *Paris*—were chartered. In addition to these the revenue cutters and lighthouse tenders were turned over to the Navy Department and became temporarily a part of the auxiliary Navy.

The maximum effective fighting force of the Navy during the war, separated into classes, was as follows:

Four battle ships of the first class, 1 battle ship of the second class, 2 armored cruisers, 6 coast-defense monitors, 1 armored ram, 12 protected cruisers, 3 unprotected cruisers, 18 gunboats, 1 dynamite cruiser, 11 torpedo boats; vessels of the old Navy, including monitors, 14. Auxiliary Navy: 11 auxiliary cruisers, 28 converted yachts, 27 converted tugs, 19 converted colliers, 15 revenue cutters, 4 light-house tenders, and 19 miscellaneous vessels.

Much alarm was felt along our entire Atlantic seaboard lest some attack might be made by the enemy. Every precaution was taken to prevent possible injury to our great cities lying along the coast. Temporary garrisons were provided, drawn from the State militia; infantry and light batteries were drawn from the volunteer force. About 12,000 troops were thus employed. The coast signal service was established for observing the approach of an enemy's ships to the coast of the United States, and the Life-Saving and Light-House services cooperated, which enabled the Navy Department to have all portions of the Atlantic coast, from Maine to Texas, under observation.

The auxiliary Navy was created under the authority of Congress and was officered and manned by the Naval Militia of the several States. This organization patrolled the coast and performed the duty of a second line of defense.

Under the direction of the Chief of Engineers submarine mines were placed at the most exposed points. Before the outbreak of the war permanent mining casemates and cable galleries had been constructed at nearly all important harbors. Most of the torpedo material was not to be found in the market, and had to be specially manufactured. Under date of April 19 district officers were directed to take all preliminary measures short of the actual attaching of the loaded mines to the cables, and on April 22 telegraphic orders were issued to place the loaded mines in position.

The aggregate number of mines placed was 1,535, at the principal harbors from Maine to California. Preparations were also made for the planting of mines at certain other harbors, but owing to the early destruction of the Spanish fleet these mines were not placed.

The Signal Corps was promptly organized, and performed service of the most difficult and important character. Its operations during the war covered the electrical connection of all coast fortifications, the establishment of telephonic and telegraphic facilities for the camps at Manila, Santiago, and in Puerto Rico. There were constructed 300 miles of line at ten great camps, thus facilitating military movements from those points in a manner heretofore unknown in military administration. Field telegraph lines were established and maintained under the enemy's fire at Manila, and later the Manila-Hongkong cable was reopened.

In Puerto Rico cable communications were opened over a discontinued route, and on land the headquarters of the commanding officer was kept in telegraphic or telephonic communication with the division commanders on four different lines of operations.

There was placed in Cuban waters a completely outfitted cable ship, with war cables and cable gear, suitable both for the destruction of communications belonging to the enemy and the establishment of our own. Two ocean cables were destroyed under the enemy's batteries at Santiago. The day previous to the landing of General Shafter's corps, at Caimanera, within 20 miles of the landing place, cable communications were established and a cable station opened giving direct communication with the Government at Washington. This service was invaluable to the Executive in directing the operations of the Army and Navy. With a total force of over 1,300, the loss was by disease in camp and field, officers and men included, only 5.

The national-defense fund of $50,000,000 was expended in large part by the Army and Navy, and the objects for which it was used are fully shown in the reports of the several Secretaries. It was a most timely appropriation, enabling the Government to strengthen its defenses and make preparations greatly needed in case of war.

This fund being inadequate to the requirements of equipment and for the conduct of the war, the patriotism of the Congress provided the means in the war-revenue act of June 13 by authorizing a 3 per cent popular loan not to exceed $400,000,000 and by levying additional imposts and taxes. Of the authorized loan $200,000,000 were offered and promptly taken, the subscriptions so far exceeding the call as to cover it many times over, while, preference being given to the smaller bids, no single allotment exceeded $5,000. This was a most encouraging and significant result, showing the vast resources of the nation and the determination of the people to uphold their country's honor.

It is not within the province of this message to narrate the history of the extraordinary war that followed the Spanish declaration of April 21, but a brief recital of its more salient features is appropriate.

The first encounter of the war in point of date took place April 27, when a detachment of the blockading squadron made a reconnoissance in force at Matanzas, shelled the harbor forts, and demolished several new works in construction.

The next engagement was destined to mark a memorable epoch in maritime warfare. The Pacific fleet, under Commodore George Dewey, had lain for some weeks at Hongkong. Upon the colonial proclamation of neutrality being issued and the customary twenty-four hours' notice being given, it repaired to Mirs Bay, near Hongkong, whence it proceeded to the Philippine Islands under telegraphed orders to capture or destroy the formidable Spanish fleet then assembled at Manila. At daybreak on the 1st of May the American force entered Manila Bay, and after a few hours' engagement effected the total destruction of the Spanish fleet, consisting of ten war ships and a transport, besides capturing the naval station and forts at Cavite, thus annihilating the Spanish naval power in the Pacific Ocean and completely controlling the bay of Manila, with the ability to take the city at will. Not a life was lost on our ships, the wounded only numbering seven, while not a vessel was materially injured. For this gallant achievement the Congress, upon my recommendation, fitly bestowed upon the actors preferment and substantial reward.

The effect of this remarkable victory upon the spirit of our people and upon the fortunes of the war was instant. A prestige of invincibility thereby attached to our arms which continued throughout the struggle. Reenforcements were hurried to Manila under the command of Major-General Merritt and firmly established within sight of the capital, which lay helpless before our guns.

On the 7th day of May the Government was advised officially of the victory at Manila, and at once inquired of the commander of our fleet what troops would be required. The information was received on the 15th day of May, and the first army expedition sailed May 25 and arrived off Manila June 30. Other expeditions soon followed, the total force consisting of 641 officers and 15,058 enlisted men.

Only reluctance to cause needless loss of life and property prevented the early storming and capture of the city, and therewith the absolute military occupancy of the whole group. The insurgents meanwhile had resumed the active hostilities suspended by the uncompleted truce of December, 1897. Their forces invested Manila from the northern and eastern sides, but were constrained by Admiral Dewey and General Merritt from attempting an assault. It was fitting that whatever was to be done in the way of decisive operations in that quarter should be accomplished by the strong arm of the United States alone. Obeying the stern precept of war which enjoins the overcoming of the adversary and the extinction of his power wherever assailable as the speedy and sure means to win a peace, divided victory was not permissible, for no partition of the rights and responsibilities attending the enforcement of a just and advantageous peace could be thought of.

Following the comprehensive scheme of general attack, powerful forces were assembled at various points on our coast to invade Cuba and Puerto Rico Meanwhile naval demonstrations were made at several exposed points. On May 11 the cruiser *Wilmington* and torpedo boat *Winslow* were unsuccessful in an attempt to silence the batteries at Cardenas, a gallant ensign, Worth Bagley, and four seamen falling. These grievous fatalities were, strangely enough, among the very few which occurred during our naval operations in this extraordinary conflict.

Meanwhile the Spanish naval preparations had been pushed with great vigor. A powerful squadron under Admiral Cervera, which had assembled at the Cape Verde Islands before the outbreak of hostilities, had crossed the ocean, and by its erratic movements in the Caribbean Sea delayed our military plans while baffling the pursuit of our fleets. For a time fears were felt lest the *Oregon* and *Marietta*, then nearing home after their long voyage from San Francisco of over 15,000 miles, might be surprised by Admiral Cervera's fleet, but their fortunate arrival dispelled these apprehensions and lent much-needed reenforcement. Not until Admiral Cervera took refuge in the harbor of Santiago de Cuba, about May 19. was it practicable to plan a systematic naval and military attack upon the Antillean possessions of Spain.

Several demonstrations occurred on the coasts of Cuba and Puerto Rico in preparation for the larger event. On May 13 the North Atlantic Squadron shelled San Juan de Puerto Rico. On May 30 Commodore Schley's squadron bombarded the forts guarding the mouth of Santiago Harbor. Neither attack had any material result. It was evident that well-ordered land operations were indispensable to achieve a decisive advantage.

The next act in the war thrilled not alone the hearts of our countrymen but the world by its exceptional heroism. On the night of June 3 Lieutenant Hobson, aided by seven devoted volunteers, blocked the narrow outlet from Santiago Harbor by sinking the collier *Merrimac* in the channel, under a fierce fire from the shore batteries, escaping with their lives as by a miracle, but falling into the hands of the Spaniards. It is a most gratifying incident of the war that the bravery of this little band of heroes was cordially appreciated by the Spanish admiral, who sent a flag of truce to notify Admiral Sampson of their safety and to compliment them on their daring act. They were subsequently exchanged July 7.

By June 7 the cutting of the last Cuban cable isolated the island. Thereafter the invasion was vigorously prosecuted. On June 10, under a heavy protecting fire, a landing of 600 marines from the *Oregon, Marblehead,* and *Yankee* was effected in Guantanamo Bay, where it had been determined to establish a naval station.

This important and essential port was taken from the enemy, after severe fighting, by the marines, who were the first organized force of the United States to land in Cuba.

The position so won was held despite desperate attempts to dislodge our forces. By June 16 additional forces were landed and strongly intrenched. On June 22 the advance of the invading army under Major-General Shafter landed at Daiquiri, about 15 miles east of Santiago. This was accomplished under great difficulties, but with marvelous dispatch. On June 23 the movement against Santiago was begun. On the 24th the first serious engagement took place, in which the First and Tenth Cavalry and the First United States Volunteer Cavalry, General Young's brigade of General Wheeler's division, participated, losing heavily. By nightfall, however, ground within 5 miles of Santiago was won. The advantage was steadily increased. On July 1 a severe battle took place, our forces gaining the outworks of Santiago; on the 2d El Caney and San Juan were taken after a desperate charge, and the investment of the city was completed. The Navy cooperated by shelling the town and the coast forts.

On the day following this brilliant achievement of our land forces, the 3d of July, occurred the decisive naval combat of the war. The Spanish fleet, attempting to leave the harbor, was met by the American squadron under command of Commodore Sampson. In less than three hours all the Spanish ships were destroyed, the two torpedo boats being sunk and the *María Teresa, Almirante Oquendo, Vizcaya*, and *Cristóbal Colón* driven ashore. The Spanish admiral and over 1,300 men were taken prisoners. While the enemy's loss of life was deplorably large, some 600 perishing, on our side but one man was killed, on the *Brooklyn*, and one man seriously wounded. Although our ships were repeatedly struck, not one was seriously injured. Where all so conspicuously distinguished themselves, from the commanders to the gunners and the unnamed heroes in the boiler rooms, each and all contributing toward the achievement of this astounding victory, for which neither ancient nor modern history affords a parallel in the completeness of the event and the marvelous disproportion of casualties, it would be invidious to single out any for especial honor. Deserved promotion has rewarded the more conspicuous actors. The nation's profoundest gratitude is due to all of these brave men who by their skill and devotion in a few short hours crushed the sea power of Spain and wrought a triumph whose decisiveness and far-reaching consequences can scarcely be measured. Nor can we be unmindful of the achievements of our builders, mechanics, and artisans for their skill in the construction of our war ships.

With the catastrophe of Santiago Spain's effort upon the ocean virtually ceased. A spasmodic effort toward the end of June to send her Mediterranean fleet, under Admiral Camara, to relieve Manila was abandoned, the expedition being recalled after it had passed through the Suez Canal.

The capitulation of Santiago followed. The city was closely besieged by land, while the entrance of our ships into the harbor cut off all relief on that side. After a truce to allow of the removal of noncombatants protracted negotiations continued from July 3 until July 15, when, under menace of immediate assault, the preliminaries of surrender were agreed upon. On the 17th General Shafter occupied the city. The capitulation embraced the entire eastern end of Cuba. The number of Spanish soldiers surrendering was 22,000, all of whom were subsequently conveyed to Spain at the charge of the United States. The story of this successful campaign is told in the report of the Secretary of War, which will be laid before you. The individual valor of officers and soldiers was never more strikingly shown than in the several engagements leading to the surrender of Santiago, while the prompt movements and successive victories won instant and universal applause. To those who gained this complete triumph, which established the ascendency of the United States upon land as the fight off Santiago had fixed our supremacy on the seas, the earnest and lasting gratitude of the nation is unsparingly due. Nor should we alone remember the gallantry of the living; the dead claim our tears, and our losses by battle and disease must cloud any exultation at the result and teach us to weigh the awful cost of war, however rightful the cause or signal the victory.

With the fall of Santiago the occupation of Puerto Rico became the next strategic necessity. General Miles had previously been assigned to organize an expedition for that purpose. Fortunately he was already at Santiago, where he had arrived on the 11th of July with reenforcements for General Shafter's army.

With these troops, consisting of 3,415 infantry and artillery, two companies of engineers, and one company of the Signal Corps, General Miles left Guantanamo on July 21, having nine transports convoyed by the fleet under Captain Higginson with the *Massachusetts* (flagship), *Dixie*, *Gloucester*, *Columbia*, and *Yale*, the two latter carrying troops. The expedition landed at Guanica July 25, which port was entered with little opposition. Here the fleet was joined by the *Annapolis* and the *Wasp*, while the *Puritan* and *Amphitrite* went to San Juan and joined the *New Orleans*, which was engaged in blockading that port. The Major-General Commanding was subsequently reenforced by General Schwan's brigade of the Third Army Corps, by General Wilson with a part of his division, and also by General Brooke with a part of his corps, numbering in all 16,973 officers and men.

On July 27 he entered Ponce, one of the most important ports in the island, from which he thereafter directed operations for the capture of the island.

With the exception of encounters with the enemy at Guayama, Hormigueros, Coamo, and Yauco and an attack on a force landed at Cape San Juan, there was no serious resistance. The campaign was prosecuted with great vigor, and by the 12th of August much of the island was in our possession and the acquisition of the remainder was only a matter of a short time. At most of the points in the island our troops were enthusiastically welcomed. Protestations of loyalty to the flag and gratitude for delivery from Spanish rule met our commanders at every stage. As a potent influence toward peace the outcome of the Puerto Rican expedition was of great consequence, and generous commendation is due to those who participated in it.

The last scene of the war was enacted at Manila, its starting place. On August 15, after a brief assault upon the works by the land forces, in which the squadron assisted, the capital surrendered unconditionally. The casualties were comparatively few. By this the conquest of the Philippine Islands, virtually accomplished when the Spanish capacity for resistance was destroyed by Admiral Dewey's victory of the 1st of May, was formally sealed. To General Merritt, his officers and men, for their uncomplaining and devoted service and for their gallantry in action, the nation is sincerely grateful. Their long voyage was made with singular success, and the soldierly conduct of the men, most of whom were without previous experience in the military service, deserves unmeasured praise.

The total casualties in killed and wounded in the Army during the war with Spain were: Officers killed, 23; enlisted men killed, 257; total,

280; officers wounded, 113; enlisted men wounded, 1,464; total, 1,577. Of the Navy: Killed, 17; wounded, 67; died as result of wounds, 1; invalided from service, 6; total, 91.

It will be observed that while our Navy was engaged in two great battles and in numerous perilous undertakings in blockade and bombardment, and more than 50,000 of our troops were transported to distant lands and were engaged in assault and siege and battle and many skirmishes in unfamiliar territory, we lost in both arms of the service a total of 1,668 killed and wounded; and in the entire campaign by land and sea we did not lose a gun or a flag or a transport or a ship, and, with the exception of the crew of the *Merrimac,* not a soldier or sailor was taken prisoner.

On August 7, forty-six days from the date of the landing of General Shafter's army in Cuba and twenty-one days from the surrender of Santiago, the United States troops commenced embarkation for home, and our entire force was returned to the United States as early as August 24. They were absent from the United States only two months.

It is fitting that I should bear testimony to the patriotism and devotion of that large portion of our Army which, although eager to be ordered to the post of greatest exposure, fortunately was not required outside of the United States. They did their whole duty, and, like their comrades at the front, have earned the gratitude of the nation. In like manner, the officers and men of the Army and of the Navy who remained in their departments and stations faithfully performing most important duties connected with the war, and whose requests for assignment in the field and at sea I was compelled to refuse because their services were indispensable here, are entitled to the highest commendation. It is my regret that there seems to be no provision for their suitable recognition.

In this connection it is a pleasure for me to mention in terms of cordial appreciation the timely and useful work of the American National Red Cross, both in relief measures preparatory to the campaigns, in sanitary assistance at several of the camps of assemblage, and later, under the able and experienced leadership of the president of the society, Miss Clara Barton, on the fields of battle and in the hospitals at the front in Cuba. Working in conjunction with the governmental authorities and under their sanction and approval, and with the enthusiastic cooperation of many patriotic women and societies in the various States, the Red Cross has fully maintained its already high reputation for intense earnestness and ability to exercise the noble purposes of its international organization, thus justifying the confidence and support which it has received at the hands of the American people. To the members and officers of this society and all who aided them in their philanthropic work the sincere and lasting gratitude of the soldiers and the public is due and is freely accorded.

In tracing these events we are constantly reminded of our obligations to the Divine Master for His watchful care over us and His safe guidance, for which the nation makes reverent acknowledgment and offers humble prayer for the continuance of His favor.

The annihilation of Admiral Cervera's fleet, followed by the capitulation of Santiago, having brought to the Spanish Government a realizing sense of the hopelessness of continuing a struggle now become wholly unequal, it made overtures of peace through the French ambassador, who, with the assent of his Government, had acted as the friendly representative of Spanish interests during the war. On the 26th of July M. Cambon presented a communication signed by the Duke of Almodóvar, the Spanish minister of state, inviting the United States to state the terms upon which it would be willing to make peace. On the 30th of July, by a communication addressed to the Duke of Almodóvar and handed to M. Cambon, the terms of this Government were announced substantially as in the protocol afterwards signed. On the 19th of August the Spanish reply, dated August 7, was handed by M. Cambon to the Secretary of State. It accepted unconditionally the terms imposed as to Cuba, Puerto Rico, and an island of the Ladrones group, but appeared to seek to introduce inadmissible reservations in regard to our demand as to the Philippine Islands. Conceiving that discussion on this point could neither be practical nor profitable, I directed that in order to avoid misunderstanding the matter should be forthwith closed by proposing the embodiment in a formal protocol of the terms upon which the negotiations for peace were to be undertaken. The vague and inexplicit suggestions of the Spanish note could not be accepted, the only reply being to present as a virtual ultimatum a draft of protocol embodying the precise terms tendered to Spain in our note of July 30, with added stipulations of detail as to the appointment of commissioners to arrange for the evacuation of the Spanish Antilles. On August 12 M. Cambon announced his receipt of full powers to sign the protocol so submitted. Accordingly, on the afternoon of August 12, M. Cambon, as the plenipotentiary of Spain, and the Secretary of State, as the plenipotentiary of the United States, signed a protocol providing—

ARTICLE I. Spain will relinquish all claim of sovereignty over and title to Cuba.

ART. II. Spain will cede to the United States the island of Puerto Rico and other islands now under Spanish sovereignty in the West Indies, and also an island in the Ladrones to be selected by the United States.

ART. III. The United States will occupy and hold the city, bay, and harbor of Manila pending the conclusion of a treaty of peace which shall determine the control, disposition, and government of the Philippines.

The fourth article provided for the appointment of joint commissions on the part of the United States and Spain, to meet in Havana and San Juan, respectively, for the purpose of arranging and carrying out the details of the stipulated evacuation of Cuba, Puerto Rico, and other Spanish islands in the West Indies.

The fifth article provided for the appointment of not more than five commissioners on each side, to meet at Paris not later than October 1 and to proceed to the negotiation and conclusion of a treaty of peace, subject to ratification according to the respective constitutional forms of the two countries.

The sixth and last article provided that upon the signature of the protocol hostilities between the two countries should be suspended and that notice to that effect should be given as soon as possible by each Government to the commanders of its military and naval forces.

Immediately upon the conclusion of the protocol I issued a proclamation, of August 12, suspending hostilities on the part of the United States. The necessary orders to that end were at once given by telegraph. The blockade of the ports of Cuba and San Juan de Puerto Rico was in like manner raised. On the 18th of August the muster out of 100,000 volunteers, or as near that number as was found to be practicable, was ordered.

On the 1st of December 101,165 officers and men had been mustered out and discharged from the service, and 9,002 more will be mustered out by the 10th of this month; also a corresponding number of general and general staff officers have been honorably discharged the service.

The military commissions to superintend the evacuation of Cuba, Puerto Rico, and the adjacent islands were forthwith appointed—for Cuba, Major-General James F. Wade, Rear-Admiral William T. Sampson, Major-General Matthew C. Butler; for Puerto Rico, Major-General John R. Brooke, Rear-Admiral Winfield S. Schley, Brigadier-General William W. Gordon—who soon afterwards met the Spanish commissioners at Havana and San Juan, respectively. The Puerto Rican Joint Commission speedily accomplished its task, and by the 18th of October the evacuation of the island was completed. The United States flag was raised over the island at noon on that day. The administration of its affairs has been provisionally intrusted to a military governor until the Congress shall otherwise provide. The Cuban Joint Commission has not yet terminated its labors. Owing to the difficulties in the way of removing the large numbers of Spanish troops still in Cuba, the evacuation can not be completed before the 1st of January next.

Pursuant to the fifth article of the protocol, I appointed William R. Day, lately Secretary of State; Cushman K. Davis, William P. Frye, and George Gray, Senators of the United States, and Whitelaw Reid to be the peace commissioners on the part of the United States. Proceeding in due season to Paris, they there met on the 1st of October five commissioners similarly appointed on the part of Spain. Their negotiations have made hopeful progress, so that I trust soon to be able to lay a definitive treaty of peace before the Senate, with a review of the steps leading to its signature.

I do not discuss at this time the government or the future of the new possessions which will come to us as the result of the war with Spain. Such discussion will be appropriate after the treaty of peace shall be ratified. In the meantime and until the Congress has legislated otherwise it will be my duty to continue the military governments which have existed since our occupation and give to the people security in life and property and encouragement under a just and beneficent rule.

As soon as we are in possession of Cuba and have pacified the island it will be necessary to give aid and direction to its people to form a government for themselves. This should be undertaken at the earliest moment consistent with safety and assured success. It is important that our relations with this people shall be of the most friendly character and our commercial relations close and reciprocal. It should be our duty to assist in every proper way to build up the waste places of the island, encourage the industry of the people, and assist them to form a government which shall be free and independent, thus realizing the best aspirations of the Cuban people.

Spanish rule must be replaced by a just, benevolent, and humane government, created by the people of Cuba, capable of performing all international obligations, and which shall encourage thrift, industry, and prosperity and promote peace and good will among all of the inhabitants, whatever may have been their relations in the past. Neither revenge nor passion should have a place in the new government. Until there is complete tranquillity in the island and a stable government inaugurated military occupation will be continued.

With the one exception of the rupture with Spain, the intercourse of the United States with the great family of nations has been marked with cordiality, and the close of the eventful year finds most of the issues that necessarily arise in the complex relations of sovereign states adjusted or presenting no serious obstacle to a just and honorable solution by amicable agreement.

A long unsettled dispute as to the extended boundary between the Argentine Republic and Chile, stretching along the Andean crests from the southern border of the Atacama Desert to Magellan Straits, nearly a third of the length of the South American continent, assumed an acute stage in the early part of the year, and afforded to this Government occasion to express the hope that the resort to arbitration, already contemplated by existing conventions between the parties, might prevail despite the grave difficulties arising in its application. I am happy to say that arrangements to this end have been perfected, the questions of fact upon which the respective commissioners were unable to agree being in course of reference to Her Britannic Majesty for determination. A residual difference touching the northern boundary line across the Atacama Desert, for which existing treaties provided no adequate adjustment, bids fair to be settled in like manner by a joint commission, upon which the United States minister at Buenos Ayres has been invited to serve as umpire in the last resort.

I have found occasion to approach the Argentine Government with a view to removing differences of rate charges imposed upon the cables of an American corporation in the transmission between Buenos Ayres and the cities of Uruguay and Brazil of through messages passing from and to the United States. Although the matter is complicated by exclusive concessions by Uruguay and Brazil to foreign companies, there is strong hope that a good understanding will be reached and that the important channels of commercial communication between the United States and the Atlantic cities of South America may be freed from an almost prohibitory discrimination.

In this relation I may be permitted to express my sense of the fitness of an international agreement whereby the interchange of messages over connecting cables may be regulated on a fair basis of uniformity. The world has seen the postal system developed from a congeries of independent and exclusive services into a well-ordered union, of which all countries enjoy the manifold benefits. It would be strange were the nations not in time brought to realize that modern civilization, which owes so much of its progress to the annihilation of space by the electric force, demands that this all-important means of communication be a heritage of all peoples, to be administered and regulated in their common behoof. A step in this direction was taken when the international convention of 1884 for the protection of submarine cables was signed, and the day is, I trust, not far distant when this medium for the transmission of thought from land to land may be brought within the domain of international concert as completely as is the material carriage of commerce and correspondence upon the face of the waters that divide them.

The claim of Thomas Jefferson Page against Argentina, which has been pending many years, has been adjusted. The sum awarded by the Congress of Argentina was $4,242.35.

The sympathy of the American people has justly been offered to the ruler and the people of Austria-Hungary by reason of the affliction that has lately befallen them in the assassination of the Empress-Queen of that historic realm.

On the 10th of September, 1897, a conflict took place at Lattimer, Pa., between a body of striking miners and the sheriff of Luzerne County and his deputies, in which 22 miners were killed and 44 wounded, of whom 10 of the killed and 12 of the wounded were Austrian and Hungarian subjects. This deplorable event naturally aroused the solicitude of the Austro-Hungarian Government, which, on the assumption that the killing and wounding involved the unjustifiable misuse of authority, claimed reparation for the sufferers. Apart from the searching investigation and peremptory action of the authorities of Pennsylvania, the Federal Executive took appropriate steps to learn the merits of the case, in order to be in a position to meet the urgent complaint of a friendly power. The sheriff and his deputies, having been indicted for murder, were tried, and acquitted, after protracted proceedings and the hearing of hundreds of witnesses, on the ground that the killing was in the line of their official duty to uphold law and preserve public order in the State. A representative of the Department of Justice attended the trial and reported its course fully. With all the facts in its possession, this Government expects to reach a harmonious understanding on the subject with that of Austria-Hungary, notwithstanding the renewed claim of the latter, after learning the result of the trial, for indemnity for its injured subjects.

Despite the brief time allotted for preparation, the exhibits of this country at the Universal Exposition at Brussels in 1897 enjoyed the singular distinction of a larger proportion of awards, having regard to the number and classes of articles entered than those of other countries. The worth of such a result in making known our national capacity to supply the world's markets is obvious.

Exhibitions of this international character are becoming more frequent as the exchanges of commercial countries grow more intimate and varied. Hardly a year passes that this Government is not invited to national participation at some important foreign center, but often on too short notice to permit of recourse to Congress for the power and means to do so. My predecessors have suggested the advisability of providing by a general enactment and a standing appropriation for accepting such invitations and for representation of this country by a commission. This plan has my cordial approval.

I trust that the Belgian restrictions on the importation of cattle from the United States, originally adopted as a sanitary precaution, will at an early day be relaxed as to their present features of hardship and discrimination, so as to admit live cattle under due regulation of their slaughter after landing. I am hopeful, too, of favorable change in the Belgian treatment of our preserved and salted meats. The growth of direct trade between the two countries, not alone for Belgian consumption and Belgian products, but by way of transit from and to other continental states, has been both encouraging and beneficial. No effort will be spared to enlarge its advantages by seeking the removal of needless impediments and by arrangements for increased commercial exchanges.

The year's events in Central America deserve more than passing mention.

A menacing rupture between Costa Rica and Nicaragua was happily composed by the signature of a convention between the parties, with the concurrence of the Guatemalan representative as a mediator, the act being negotiated and signed on board the United States steamer *Alert*, then lying in Central American waters. It is believed that the good offices of our envoy and of the commander of that vessel contributed toward this gratifying outcome.

In my last annual message the situation was presented with respect to the diplomatic representation of this Government in Central America created by the association of Nicaragua, Honduras, and Salvador under the title of the Greater Republic of Central America, and the delegation of their international functions to the Diet thereof. While the representative character of the Diet was recognized by my predecessor and has been confirmed during my Administration by receiving its accredited envoy and granting exequaturs to consuls commissioned under its authority, that recognition was qualified by the distinct understanding that the responsibility of each of the component sovereign Republics toward the United States remained wholly unaffected.

This proviso was needful inasmuch as the compact of the three Republics was at the outset an association whereby certain representative functions were delegated to a tripartite commission rather than a federation possessing centralized powers of government and administration. In this view of their relation and of the relation of the United States to the several Republics, a change in the representation of this country in Central America was neither recommended by the Executive nor initiated by Congress, thus leaving one of our envoys accredited, as heretofore, separately to two States of the Greater Republic, Nicaragua and Salvador, and to a third State, Costa Rica, which was not a party to the compact, while our other envoy was similarly accredited to a union State, Honduras, and a nonunion State, Guatemala. The result has been that the one has presented credentials only to the President of Costa Rica, the other having been received only by the Government of Guatemala.

Subsequently the three associated Republics entered into negotiations for taking the steps forecast in the original compact. A convention of their delegates framed for them a federal constitution under the name of the United States of Central America, and provided for a central federal government and legislature. Upon ratification by the constituent States, the 1st of November last was fixed for the new system to go into operation. Within a few weeks thereafter the plan was severely tested by revolutionary movements arising, with a consequent demand for unity of action on the part of the military power of the federal States to suppress them. Under this strain the new union seems to have been weakened through the withdrawal of its more important members. This Government was not officially advised of the installation of the federation and has maintained an attitude of friendly expectancy, while in no wise relinquishing the position held from the outset that the responsibilities of the several States toward us remained unaltered by their tentative relations among themselves.

The Nicaragua Canal Commission, under the chairmanship of Rear-Admiral John G. Walker, appointed July 24, 1897, under the authority of a provision in the sundry civil act of June 4 of that year, has nearly completed its labors, and the results of its exhaustive inquiry into the proper route, the feasibility, and the cost of construction of an interoceanic canal by a Nicaraguan route will be laid before you. In the performance of its task the commission received all possible courtesy and assistance from the Governments of Nicaragua and Costa Rica, which thus testified their appreciation of the importance of giving a speedy and practical outcome to the great project that has for so many years engrossed the attention of the respective countries.

As the scope of the recent inquiry embraced the whole subject, with the aim of making plans and surveys for a canal by the most convenient route, it necessarily included a review of the results of previous surveys and plans, and in particular those adopted by the Maritime Canal Company under its existing concessions from Nicaragua and Costa Rica, so that to this extent those grants necessarily hold as essential a part in the deliberations and conclusions of the Canal Commission as they have held and must needs hold in the discussion of the matter by the Congress. Under these circumstances and in view of overtures made to the Governments of Nicaragua and Costa Rica by other parties for a new canal concession predicated on the assumed approaching lapse of the contracts of the Maritime Canal Company with those States, I have not hesitated to express my conviction that considerations of expediency and international policy as between the several governments interested in the construction and control of an interoceanic canal by this route require the maintenance of the *status quo* until the Canal Commission shall have reported and the United States Congress shall have had the opportunity to pass finally upon the whole matter during the present session, without prejudice by reason of any change in the existing conditions.

Nevertheless, it appears that the Government of Nicaragua, as one of its last sovereign acts before merging its powers in those of the newly formed United States of Central America, has granted an optional concession to another association, to become effective on the expiration of the present grant. It does not appear what surveys have been made or what route is proposed under this contingent grant, so that an examination of the feasibility of its plans is necessarily not embraced in the report of the Canal Commission. All these circumstances suggest the urgency of some definite action by the Congress at this session if the labors of the past are to be utilized and the linking of the Atlantic and Pacific oceans by a practical waterway is to be realized. That the construction of such a maritime highway is now more than ever indispensable to that intimate and ready intercommunication between our eastern and western seaboards demanded by the annexation of the Hawaiian Islands and the prospective expansion of our influence and commerce in the Pacific, and that our national policy now more imperatively than ever calls for its control by this Government, are propositions which I doubt not the Congress will duly appreciate and wisely act upon.

A convention providing for the revival of the late United States and Chilean Claims Commission and the consideration of claims which were duly presented to the late commission, but not considered because of the expiration of the time limited for the duration of the commission, was signed May 24, 1897, and has remained unacted upon by the Senate. The term therein fixed for effecting the exchange of ratifications having elapsed, the convention falls unless the time be extended by amendment, which I am endeavoring to bring about, with the friendly concurrence of the Chilean Government.

The United States has not been an indifferent spectator of the extraordinary events transpiring in the Chinese Empire, whereby portions of its maritime provinces are passing under the control of various European powers; but the prospect that the vast commerce which the energy of our citizens and the necessity of our staple productions for Chinese uses has built up in those regions may not be prejudiced through any exclusive treatment by the new occupants has obviated the need of our country becoming an actor in the scene. Our position among nations, having a large Pacific coast and a constantly expanding direct trade with the farther Orient, gives us the equitable claim to consideration and friendly treatment in this regard, and it will be my aim to subserve our large interests in that quarter by all means appropriate to the constant policy of our Government. The territories of Kiao-chow, of Wei-hai-wei, and of Port Arthur and Talienwan, leased to Germany, Great Britain, and Russia, respectively, for terms of years, will, it is announced, be open to international commerce during such alien occupation; and if no discriminating treatment of American citizens and their trade be found to exist or be hereafter developed, the desire of this Government would appear to be realized.

In this relation, as showing the volume and value of our exchanges with China and the peculiarly favorable conditions which exist for their expansion in the normal course of trade, I refer to the communication addressed to the Speaker of the House of Representatives by the Secretary of the Treasury on the 14th of last June, with its accompanying letter of the Secretary of State, recommending an appropriation for a commission to study the commercial and industrial conditions in the Chinese Empire and report as to the opportunities for and obstacles to the enlargement of markets in China for the raw products and manufactures of the United States. Action was not taken thereon during the late session. I cordially urge that the recommendation receive at your hands the consideration which its importance and timeliness merit.

Meanwhile there may be just ground for disquietude in view of the unrest and revival of the old sentiment of opposition and prejudice to alien people which pervades certain of the Chinese provinces. As in the case of the attacks upon our citizens in Szechuen and at Kutien in 1895, the United States minister has been instructed to secure the fullest measure of protection, both local and imperial, for any menaced American interests, and to demand, in case of lawless injury to person or property, instant reparation appropriate to the case. War ships have been stationed at Tientsin for more ready observation of the disorders which have invaded even the Chinese capital, so as to be in a position to act should need arise, while a guard of marines has been sent to Peking to afford the minister the same measure of authoritative protection as the representatives of other nations have been constrained to employ.

Following close upon the rendition of the award of my predecessor as arbitrator of the claim of the Italian subject Cerruti against the Republic of Colombia, differences arose between the parties to the arbitration in regard to the scope and extension of the award, of which certain articles were contested by Colombia, while Italy claimed their literal fulfillment. The award having been made by the President of the United States, as an act of friendly consideration and with the sole view to an impartial composition of the matter in dispute, I could not but feel deep concern at such a miscarriage, and while unable to accept the Colombian theory that I, in my official capacity, possessed continuing functions as arbitrator, with power to interpret or revise the terms of the award, my best efforts were lent to bring the parties to a harmonious agreement as to the execution of its provisions.

A naval demonstration by Italy resulted in an engagement to pay the liabilities claimed upon their ascertainment; but this apparent disposition of the controversy was followed by a rupture of diplomatic intercourse between Colombia and Italy, which still continues, although, fortunately, without acute symptoms having supervened. Notwithstanding this, efforts are reported to be continuing for the ascertainment of Colombia's contingent liability on account of Cerruti's debts under the fifth article of the award.

A claim of an American citizen against the Dominican Republic for a public bridge over the Ozama River, which has been in diplomatic controversy for several years, has been settled by expert arbitration and an award in favor of the claimant amounting to about $90,000. It, however, remains unpaid, despite urgent demands for its settlement according to the terms of the compact.

There is now every prospect that the participation of the United States in the Universal Exposition to be held in Paris in 1900 will be on a scale commensurate with the advanced position held by our products and industries in the world's chief marts.

The preliminary report of Mr. Moses P. Handy, who, under the act approved July 19, 1897, was appointed special commissioner with a view to securing all attainable information necessary to a full and complete understanding by Congress in regard to the participation of this Government in the Paris Exposition, was laid before you by my message of December 6, 1897, and showed the large opportunities opened to make known our national progress in arts, science, and manufactures, as well as the urgent need of immediate and adequate provision to enable due advantage thereof to be taken.   Mr. Handy's death soon afterwards rendered it necessary for another to take up and complete his unfinished work, and on January 11 last Mr. Thomas W. Cridler, Third Assistant Secretary of State, was designated to fulfill that task.   His report was laid before you by my message of June 14, 1898, with the gratifying result of awakening renewed interest in the projected display.   By a provision in the sundry civil appropriation act of July 1, 1898, a sum not to exceed $650,000 was allotted for the organization of a commission to care for the proper preparation and installation of American exhib-its and for the display of suitable exhibits by the several Executive Departments, particularly by the Department of Agriculture, the Fish Commission, and the Smithsonian Institution, in representation of the Government of the United States.

Pursuant to that enactment I appointed Mr. Ferdinand W. Peck, of Chicago, commissioner-general, with an assistant commissioner-general and a secretary.   Mr. Peck at once proceeded to Paris, where his success in enlarging the scope and variety of the United States exhibit has been most gratifying.   Notwithstanding the comparatively limited area of the exposition site—less than one-half that of the World's Fair at Chicago—the space assigned to the United States has been increased from the absolute allotment of 157,403 square feet reported by Mr. Handy to some 202,000 square feet, with corresponding augmentation of the field for a truly characteristic representation of the various important branches of our country's development.   Mr. Peck's report will be laid before you. In my judgment its recommendations will call for your early considera-tion, especially as regards an increase of the appropriation to at least one million dollars in all, so that not only may the assigned space be fully taken up by the best possible exhibits in every class, but the preparation and installation be on so perfect a scale as to rank among the first in that unparalleled competition of artistic and inventive production, and thus counterbalance the disadvantage with which we start as compared with other countries whose appropriations are on a more generous scale and whose preparations are in a state of much greater forwardness than our own.

Where our artisans have the admitted capacity to excel, where our inventive genius has initiated many of the grandest discoveries of these later days of the century, and where the native resources of our land are as limitless as they are valuable to supply the world's needs, it is our province, as it should be our earnest care, to lead in the march of human progress, and not rest content with any secondary place.   Moreover, if this be due to ourselves, it is no less due to the great French nation whose guests we become, and which has in so many ways testified its wish and hope that our participation shall befit the place the two peoples have won in the field of universal development.

The commercial arrangement made with France on the 28th of May,

1898, under the provisions of section 3 of the tariff act of 1897, went into effect on the 1st day of June following. It has relieved a portion of our export trade from serious embarrassment. Further negotiations are now pending under section 4 of the same act with a view to the increase of trade between the two countries to their mutual advantage. Negotiations with other governments, in part interrupted by the war with Spain, are in progress under both sections of the tariff act. I hope to be able to announce some of the results of these negotiations during the present session of Congress.

Negotiations to the same end with Germany have been set on foot. Meanwhile no effort has been relaxed to convince the Imperial Government of the thoroughness of our inspection of pork products for exportation, and it is trusted that the efficient administration of this measure by the Department of Agriculture will be recognized as a guaranty of the healthfulness of the food staples we send abroad to countries where their use is large and necessary.

I transmitted to the Senate on the 10th of February last information touching the prohibition against the importation of fresh fruits from this country, which had then recently been decreed by Germany on the ground of danger of disseminating the San José scale insect. This precautionary measure was justified by Germany on the score of the drastic steps taken in several States of the Union against the spread of the pest, the elaborate reports of the Department of Agriculture being put in evidence to show the danger to German fruit-growing interests should the scale obtain a lodgment in that country. Temporary relief was afforded in the case of large consignments of fruit then on the way by inspection and admission when found noninfected. Later the prohibition was extended to dried fruits of every kind, but was relaxed so as to apply only to unpeeled fruit and fruit waste. As was to be expected, the alarm reached to other countries, and Switzerland has adopted a similar inhibition. Efforts are in progress to induce the German and Swiss Governments to relax the prohibition in favor of dried fruits shown to have been cured under circumstances rendering the existence of animal life impossible.

Our relations with Great Britain have continued on the most friendly footing. Assenting to our request, the protection of Americans and their interests in Spanish jurisdiction was assumed by the diplomatic and consular representatives of Great Britain, who fulfilled their delicate and arduous trust with tact and zeal, eliciting high commendation. I may be allowed to make fitting allusion to the instance of Mr. Ramsden, Her Majesty's consul at Santiago de Cuba, whose untimely death after distinguished service and untiring effort during the siege of that city was sincerely lamented.

In the early part of April last, pursuant to a request made at the instance of the Secretary of State by the British ambassador at this capital, the

Canadian government granted facilities for the passage of four United States revenue cutters from the Great Lakes to the Atlantic coast by way of the Canadian canals and the St. Lawrence River. The vessels had reached Lake Ontario and were there awaiting the opening of navigation when war was declared between the United States and Spain. Her Majesty's Government thereupon, by a communication of the latter part of April, stated that the permission granted before the outbreak of hostilities would not be withdrawn provided the United States Govern. ment gave assurance that the vessels in question would proceed direct to a United States port without engaging in any hostile operation. This Government promptly agreed to the stipulated condition, it being understood that the vessels would not be prohibited from resisting any hostile attack.

It will give me especial satisfaction if I shall be authorized to communicate to you a favorable conclusion of the pending negotiations with Great Britain in respect to the Dominion of Canada. It is the earnest wish of this Government to remove all sources of discord and irritation in our relations with the neighboring Dominion. The trade between the two countries is constantly increasing, and it is important to both countries that all reasonable facilities should be granted for its development.

The Government of Greece strongly urges the onerousness of the duty here imposed upon the currants of that country, amounting to 100 per cent or more of their market value. This fruit is stated to be exclusively a Greek product, not coming into competition with any domestic product. The question of reciprocal commercial relations with Greece, including the restoration of currants to the free list, is under consideration.

The long-standing claim of Bernard Campbell for damages for injuries sustained from a violent assault committed against him by military authorities in the island of Haiti has been settled by the agreement of that Republic to pay him $10,000 in American gold. Of this sum $5,000 has already been paid. It is hoped that other pending claims of American citizens against that Republic may be amicably adjusted.

Pending the consideration by the Senate of the treaty signed June 16, 1897, by the plenipotentiaries of the United States and of the Republic of Hawaii, providing for the annexation of the islands, a joint resolution to accomplish the same purpose by accepting the offered cession and incorporating the ceded territory into the Union was adopted by the Congress and approved July 7, 1898. I thereupon directed the United States steamship *Philadelphia* to convey Rear-Admiral Miller to Honolulu, and intrusted to his hands this important legislative act, to be delivered to the President of the Republic of Hawaii, with whom the Admiral and the United States minister were authorized to make appropriate arrangements for transferring the sovereignty of the islands to the United States. This was simply but impressively accomplished on the 12th of August last by the delivery of a certified copy of the resolution to President Dole, who thereupon yielded up to the representative of the Government of the United States the sovereignty and public property of the Hawaiian Islands.

Pursuant to the terms of the joint resolution and in exercise of the authority thereby conferred upon me, I directed that the civil, judicial, and military powers theretofore exercised by the officers of the Government of the Republic of Hawaii should continue to be exercised by those officers until Congress shall provide a government for the incorporated territory, subject to my power to remove such officers and to fill vacancies. The President, officers, and troops of the Republic thereupon took the oath of allegiance to the United States, thus providing for the uninterrupted continuance of all the administrative and municipal functions of the annexed territory until Congress shall otherwise enact.

Following the further provision of the joint resolution, I appointed the Hons. Shelby M. Cullom, of Illinois, John T. Morgan, of Alabama, Robert R. Hitt, of Illinois, Sanford B. Dole, of Hawaii, and Walter F. Frear, of Hawaii, as commissioners to confer and recommend to Congress such legislation concerning the Hawaiian Islands as they should deem necessary or proper. The commissioners having fulfilled the mission confided to them, their report will be laid before you at an early day. It is believed that their recommendations will have the earnest consideration due to the magnitude of the responsibility resting upon you to give such shape to the relationship of those mid-Pacific lands to our home Union as will benefit both in the highest degree, realizing the aspirations of the community that has cast its lot with us and elected to share our political heritage, while at the same time justifying the foresight of those who for three-quarters of a century have looked to the assimilation of Hawaii as a natural and inevitable consummation, in harmony with our needs and in fulfillment of our cherished traditions.

The questions heretofore pending between Hawaii and Japan growing out of the alleged mistreatment of Japanese treaty immigrants were, I am pleased to say, adjusted before the act of transfer by the payment of a reasonable indemnity to the Government of Japan.

Under the provisions of the joint resolution, the existing customs relations of the Hawaiian Islands with the United States and with other countries remain unchanged until legislation shall otherwise provide. The consuls of Hawaii here and in foreign countries continue to fulfill their commercial agencies, while the United States consulate at Honolulu is maintained for all appropriate services pertaining to trade and the revenue. It would be desirable that all foreign consuls in the Hawaiian Islands should receive new exequaturs from this Government.

The attention of Congress is called to the fact that, our consular offices having ceased to exist in Hawaii and being about to cease in other countries coming under the sovereignty of the United States, the provisions for the relief and transportation of destitute American seamen in

these countries under our consular regulations will in consequence terminate. It is proper, therefore, that new legislation should be enacted
upon this subject in order to meet the changed conditions.

The interpretation of certain provisions of the extradition convention
of December 11, 1861, has been at various times the occasion of controversy with the Government of Mexico. An acute difference arose in the
case of the Mexican demand for the delivery of Jesús Guerra, who, having led a marauding expedition near the border with the proclaimed
purpose of initiating an insurrection against President Diaz, escaped into
Texas. Extradition was refused on the ground that the alleged offense
was political in its character, and therefore came within the treaty proviso of nonsurrender. The Mexican contention was that the exception only related to purely political offenses, and that as Guerra's acts
were admixed with the common crime of murder, arson, kidnaping, and
robbery, the option of nondelivery became void, a position which this
Government was unable to admit in view of the received international
doctrine and practice in the matter. The Mexican Government, in view
of this, gave notice January 24, 1898, of the termination of the convention, to take effect twelve months from that date, at the same time inviting the conclusion of a new convention, toward which negotiations are
on foot.

In this relation I may refer to the necessity of some amendment of our
existing extradition statute. It is a common stipulation of such treaties
that neither party shall be bound to give up its own citizens, with the
added proviso in one of our treaties, that with Japan, that it may surrender if it see fit. It is held in this country by an almost uniform course
of decisions that where a treaty negatives the obligation to surrender the
President is not invested with legal authority to act. The conferment of
such authority would be in the line of that sound morality which shrinks
from affording secure asylum to the author of a heinous crime. Again,
statutory provision might well be made for what is styled extradition by
way of transit, whereby a fugitive surrendered by one foreign government
to another may be conveyed across the territory of the United States to
the jurisdiction of the demanding state. A recommendation in this behalf made in the President's message of 1886 was not acted upon. The
matter is presented for your consideration.

The problem of the Mexican free zone has been often discussed with
regard to its inconvenience as a provocative of smuggling into the United
States along an extensive and thinly guarded land border. The effort
made by the joint resolution of March 1, 1895, to remedy the abuse charged
by suspending the privilege of free transportation in bond across the territory of the United States to Mexico failed of good result, as is stated
in Report No. 702 of the House of Representatives, submitted in the last
session, March 11, 1898. As the question is one to be conveniently met
by wise concurrent legislation of the two countries looking to the protec-

tion of the revenues by harmonious measures operating equally on either side of the boundary, rather than by conventional arrangements, I suggest that Congress consider the advisability of authorizing and inviting a conference of representatives of the Treasury Departments of the United States and Mexico to consider the subject in all its complex bearings, and make report with pertinent recommendations to the respective Governments for the information and consideration of their Congresses.

The Mexican Water Boundary Commission has adjusted all matters submitted to it to the satisfaction of both Governments save in three important cases—that of the "Chamizal" at El Paso, Tex., where the two commissioners failed to agree, and wherein, for this case only, this Government has proposed to Mexico the addition of a third member; the proposed elimination of what are known as "Bancos," small isolated islands formed by the cutting off of bends in the Rio Grande, from the operation of the treaties of 1884 and 1889, recommended by the commissioners and approved by this Government, but still under consideration by Mexico; and the subject of the "Equitable distribution of the waters of the Rio Grande," for which the commissioners recommended an international dam and reservoir, approved by Mexico, but still under consideration by this Government. Pending these questions it is necessary to extend the life of the commission, which expires December 23 next.

The coronation of the young Queen of the Netherlands was made the occasion of fitting congratulations.

The claim of Victor H. McCord against Peru, which for a number of years has been pressed by this Government and has on several occasions attracted the attention of the Congress, has been satisfactorily adjusted. A protocol was signed May 17, 1898, whereby, the fact of liability being admitted, the question of the amount to be awarded was submitted to the chief justice of Canada as sole arbitrator. His award sets the indemnity due the claimant at $40,000.

The Government of Peru has given the prescribed notification of its intention to abrogate the treaty of friendship, commerce, and navigation concluded with this country August 31, 1887. As that treaty contains many important provisions necessary to the maintenance of commerce and good relations, which could with difficulty be replaced by the negotiation of renewed provisions within the brief twelve months intervening before the treaty terminates, I have invited suggestions by Peru as to the particular provisions it is desired to annul, in the hope of reaching an arrangement whereby the remaining articles may be provisionally saved.

His Majesty the Czar having announced his purpose to raise the Imperial Russian mission at this capital to the rank of an embassy, I responded, under the authority conferred by the act of March 3, 1893, by commissioning and accrediting the actual representative at St. Petersburg in the capacity of ambassador extraordinary and plenipotentiary.   The Russian ambassador to this country has since presented his credentials.

The proposal of the Czar for a general reduction of the vast military establishments that weigh so heavily upon many peoples in time of peace was communicated to this Government with an earnest invitation to be represented in the conference which it is contemplated to assemble with a view to discussing the means of accomplishing so desirable a result. His Majesty was at once informed of the cordial sympathy of this Government with the principle involved in his exalted proposal and of the readiness of the United States to take part in the conference.   The active military force of the United States, as measured by our population, territorial area, and taxable wealth, is, and under any conceivable prospective conditions must continue to be, in time of peace so conspicuously less than that of the armed powers to whom the Czar's appeal is especially addressed that the question can have for us no practical importance save as marking an auspicious step toward the betterment of the condition of the modern peoples and the cultivation of peace and good will among them; but in this view it behooves us as a nation to lend countenance and aid to the beneficent project.

The claims of owners of American sealing vessels for seizure by Russian cruisers in Bering Sea are being pressed to a settlement.   The equities of the cases justify the expectation that a measure of reparation will eventually be accorded in harmony with precedent and in the light of the proven facts.

The recommendation made in my special message of April 27 last is renewed, that appropriation be made to reimburse the master and owners of the Russian bark *Hans* for wrongful arrest of the master and detention of the vessel in February, 1896, by officers of the United States district court for the southern district of Mississippi.   The papers accompanying my said message make out a most meritorious claim and justify the urgency with which it has been presented by the Government of Russia.

Malietoa Laupepa, King of Samoa, died on August 22 last.   According to Article I of the general act of Berlin, "his successor shall be duly elected according to the laws and customs of Samoa."

Arrangements having been agreed upon between the signatories of the general act for the return of Mataafa and the other exiled Samoan chiefs, they were brought from Jaluit by a German war vessel and landed at Apia on September 18 last.

Whether the death of Malietoa and the return of his old-time rival Mataafa will add to the undesirable complications which the execution of the tripartite general act has heretofore developed remains to be seen. The efforts of this Government will, as heretofore, be addressed toward a harmonious and exact fulfillment of the terms of the international engagement to which the United States became a party in 1889.

The Cheek claim against Siam, after some five years of controversy, has been adjusted by arbitration under an agreement signed July 6, 1897, an award of 706,721 ticals (about $187,987.78), with release of the Cheek estate from mortgage claims, having been rendered March 21, 1898, in favor of the claimant by the arbitrator, Sir Nicholas John Hannen, British chief justice for China and Japan.

An envoy from Siam has been accredited to this Government and has presented his credentials.

Immediately upon the outbreak of the war with Spain the Swiss Government, fulfilling the high mission it has deservedly assumed as the patron of the International Red Cross, proposed to the United States and Spain that they should severally recognize and carry into execution, as a *modus vivendi*, during the continuance of hostilities, the additional articles proposed by the international conference of Geneva, October 20, 1868, extending the effects of the existing Red Cross convention of 1864 to the conduct of naval war. Following the example set by France and Germany in 1870 in adopting such a *modus vivendi*, and in view of the accession of the United States to those additional articles in 1882, although the exchange of ratifications thereof still remained uneffected, the Swiss proposal was promptly and cordially accepted by us, and simultaneously by Spain.

This Government feels a keen satisfaction in having thus been enabled to testify its adherence to the broadest principles of humanity even amidst the clash of war, and it is to be hoped that the extension of the Red Cross compact to hostilities by sea as well as on land may soon become an accomplished fact through the general promulgation of the additional naval Red Cross articles by the maritime powers now parties to the convention of 1864.

The important question of the claim of Switzerland to the perpetual cantonal allegiance of American citizens of Swiss origin has not made hopeful progress toward a solution, and controversies in this regard still continue.

The newly accredited envoy of the United States to the Ottoman Porte carries instructions looking to the disposal of matters in controversy with Turkey for a number of years. He is especially charged to press for a just settlement of our claims for indemnity by reason of the destruction of the property of American missionaries resident in that country during the Armenian troubles of 1895, as well as for the recognition of older claims of equal justness.

He is also instructed to seek an adjustment of the dispute growing out of the refusal of Turkey to recognize the acquired citizenship of Ottoman-born persons naturalized in the United States since 1869 without prior imperial consent, and in the same general relation he is directed to endeavor to bring about a solution of the question which has more or less acutely existed since 1869 concerning the jurisdictional rights of the

United States in matters of criminal procedure and punishment under Article IV of the treaty of 1830. This latter difficulty grows out of a verbal difference, claimed by Turkey to be essential, between the original Turkish text and the promulgated translation.

After more than two years from the appointment of a consul of this country to Erzerum, he has received his exequatur.

The arbitral tribunal appointed under the treaty of February 2, 1897, between Great Britain and Venezuela, to determine the boundary line between the latter and the colony of British Guiana, is to convene at Paris during the present month. It is a source of much gratification to this Government to see the friendly resort of arbitration applied to the settlement of this controversy, not alone because of the earnest part we have had in bringing about the result, but also because the two members named on behalf of Venezuela, Mr. Chief Justice Fuller and Mr. Justice Brewer, chosen from our highest court, appropriately testify the continuing interest we feel in the definitive adjustment of the question according to the strictest rules of justice. The British members, Lord Herschell and Sir Richard Collins, are jurists of no less exalted repute, while the fifth member and president of the tribunal, M. F. De Martens, has earned a world-wide reputation as an authority upon international law.

The claim of Felipe Scandella against Venezuela for arbitrary expulsion and injury to his business has been adjusted by the revocation of the order of expulsion and by the payment of the sum of $16,000.

I have the satisfaction of being able to state that the Bureau of the American Republics, created in 1890 as the organ for promoting commercial intercourse and fraternal relations among the countries of the Western Hemisphere, has become a more efficient instrument of the wise purposes of its founders, and is receiving the cordial support of the contributing members of the international union which are actually represented in its board of management. A commercial directory, in two volumes, containing a mass of statistical matter descriptive of the industrial and commercial interests of the various countries, has been printed in English, Spanish, Portuguese, and French, and a monthly bulletin published in these four languages and distributed in the Latin-American countries as well as in the United States has proved to be a valuable medium for disseminating information and furthering the varied interests of the international union.

During the past year the important work of collecting information of practical benefit to American industries and trade through the agency of the diplomatic and consular officers has been steadily advanced, and in order to lay such data before the public with the least delay the practice was begun in January, 1898, of issuing the commercial reports from day to day as they are received by the Department of State. It is believed that for promptitude as well as fullness of information the service thus supplied to our merchants and manufacturers will be found to show sensible improvement and to merit the liberal support of Congress.

The experiences of the last year bring forcibly home to us a sense of the burdens and the waste of war. We desire, in common with most civilized nations, to reduce to the lowest possible point the damage sustained in time of war by peaceable trade and commerce. It is true we may suffer in such cases less than other communities, but all nations are damaged more or less by the state of uneasiness and apprehension into which an outbreak of hostilities throws the entire commercial world. It should be our object, therefore, to minimize, so far as practicable, this inevitable loss and disturbance. This purpose can probably best be accomplished by an international agreement to regard all private property at sea as exempt from capture or destruction by the forces of belligerent powers. The United States Government has for many years advocated this humane and beneficent principle, and is now in position to recommend it to other powers without the imputation of selfish motives. I therefore suggest for your consideration that the Executive be authorized to correspond with the governments of the principal maritime powers with a view of incorporating into the permanent law of civilized nations the principle of the exemption of all private property at sea, not contraband of war, from capture or destruction by belligerent powers.

The Secretary of the Treasury reports that the receipts of the Government from all sources during the fiscal year ended June 30, 1898, including $64,751,223 received from sale of Pacific railroads, amounted to $405,321,335, and its expenditures to $443,368,582. There was collected from customs $149,575,062 and from internal revenue $170,900,641. Our dutiable imports amounted to $324,635,479, a decrease of $58,156,690 over the preceding year, and importations free of duty amounted to $291,-414,175, a decrease from the preceding year of $90,524,068. Internal-revenue receipts exceeded those of the preceding year by $24,212,067.

The total tax collected on distilled spirits was $92,546,999; on manufactured tobacco, $36,230,522, and on fermented liquors, $39,515,421. We exported merchandise during the year amounting to $1,231,482,330, an increase of $180,488,774 from the preceding year.

It is estimated upon the basis of present revenue laws that the receipts of the Government for the year ending June 30, 1899, will be $577,-874,647, and its expenditures $689,874,647, resulting in a deficiency of $112,000,000.

On the 1st of December, 1898, there was held in the Treasury gold coin amounting to $138,441,547, gold bullion amounting to $138,502,545, silver bullion amounting to $93,359,250, and other forms of money amounting to $451,963,981.

On the same date the amount of money of all kinds in circulation, or not included in Treasury holdings, was $1,886,879,504, an increase for the year of $165,794,966. Estimating our population at 75,194,000 at the time mentioned, the per capita circulation was $25.09. On the same date there was in the Treasury gold bullion amounting to $138,502,545.

The provisions made for strengthening the resources of the Treasury in connection with the war have given increased confidence in the purpose and power of the Government to maintain the present standard, and have established more firmly than ever the national credit at home and abroad. A marked evidence of this is found in the inflow of gold to the Treasury. Its net gold holdings on November 1, 1898, were $239,885,162 as compared with $153,573,147 on November 1, 1897, and an increase of net cash of $207,756,100, November 1, 1897, to $300,238,275, November 1, 1898. The present ratio of net Treasury gold to outstanding Government liabilities, including United States notes, Treasury notes of 1890, silver certificates, currency certificates, standard silver dollars, and fractional silver coin, November 1, 1898, was 25.35 per cent, as compared with 16.96 per cent, November 1, 1897.

I renew so much of my recommendation of December, 1897, as follows:

That when any of the United States notes are presented for redemption in gold and are redeemed in gold, such notes shall be kept and set apart and only paid out in exchange for gold. This is an obvious duty. If the holder of the United States note prefers the gold and gets it from the Government, he should not receive back from the Government a United States note without paying gold in exchange for it. The reason for this is made all the more apparent when the Government issues an interest-bearing debt to provide gold for the redemption of United States notes—a non-interest-bearing debt. Surely it should not pay them out again except on demand and for gold. If they are put out in any other way, they may return again, to be followed by another bond issue to redeem them—another interest-bearing debt to redeem a non-interest-bearing debt.

This recommendation was made in the belief that such provisions of law would insure to a greater degree the safety of the present standard, and better protect our currency from the dangers to which it is subjected from a disturbance in the general business conditions of the country.

In my judgment the present condition of the Treasury amply justifies the immediate enactment of the legislation recommended one year ago, under which a portion of the gold holdings should be placed in a trust fund from which greenbacks should be redeemed upon presentation, but when once redeemed should not thereafter be paid out except for gold.

It is not to be inferred that other legislation relating to our currency is not required; on the contrary, there is an obvious demand for it.

The importance of adequate provision which will insure to our future a money standard related as our money standard now is to that of our commercial rivals is generally recognized.

The companion proposition that our domestic paper currency shall be kept safe and yet be so related to the needs of our industries and internal commerce as to be adequate and responsive to such needs is a proposition scarcely less important. The subject, in all its parts, is commended to the wise consideration of the Congress.

The annexation of Hawaii and the changed relations of the United States to Cuba, Puerto Rico, and the Philippines resulting from the war, compel the prompt adoption of a maritime policy by the United States. There should be established regular and frequent steamship communication, encouraged by the United States, under the American flag, with the newly acquired islands. Spain furnished to its colonies, at an annual cost of about $2,000,000, steamship lines communicating with a portion of the world's markets, as well as with trade centers of the home Government. The United States will not undertake to do less. It is our duty to furnish the people of Hawaii with facilities, under national control, for their export and import trade. It will be conceded that the present situation calls for legislation which shall be prompt, durable, and liberal.

The part which American merchant vessels and their seamen performed in the war with Spain demonstrates that this service, furnishing both pickets and the second line of defense, is a national necessity, and should be encouraged in every constitutional way. Details and methods for the accomplishment of this purpose are discussed in the report of the Secretary of the Treasury, to which the attention of Congress is respectfully invited.

In my last annual message I recommended that Congress authorize the appointment of a commission for the purpose of making systematic investigations with reference to the cause and prevention of yellow fever. This matter has acquired an increased importance as a result of the military occupation of the island of Cuba and the commercial intercourse between this island and the United States which we have every reason to expect. The sanitary problems connected with our new relations with the island of Cuba and the acquisition of Puerto Rico are no less important than those relating to finance, commerce, and administration. It is my earnest desire that these problems may be considered by competent experts and that everything may be done which the most recent advances in sanitary science can offer for the protection of the health of our soldiers in those islands and of our citizens who are exposed to the dangers of infection from the importation of yellow fever. I therefore renew my recommendation that the authority of Congress may be given and a suitable appropriation made to provide for a commission of experts to be appointed for the purpose indicated.

Under the act of Congress approved April 26, 1898, authorizing the President in his discretion, "upon a declaration of war by Congress, or a declaration by Congress that war exists," I directed the increase of the Regular Army to the maximum of 62,000, authorized in said act.

There are now in the Regular Army 57,862 officers and men. In said act it was provided—

That at the end of any war in which the United States may become involved the

Army shall be reduced to a peace basis by the transfer in the same arm of the service or absorption by promotion or honorable discharge, under such regulations as the Secretary of War may establish, of supernumerary commissioned officers and the honorable discharge or transfer of supernumerary enlisted men; and nothing contained in this act shall be construed as authorizing the permanent increase of the commissioned or enlisted force of the Regular Army beyond that now provided by the law in force prior to the passage of this act, except as to the increase of twenty-five majors provided for in section 1 hereof.

The importance of legislation for the permanent increase of the Army is therefore manifest, and the recommendation of the Secretary of War for that purpose has my unqualified approval. There can be no question that at this time, and probably for some time in the future, 100,000 men will be none too many to meet the necessities of the situation. At all events, whether that number shall be required permanently or not, the power should be given to the President to enlist that force if in his discretion it should be necessary; and the further discretion should be given him to recruit for the Army within the above limit from the inhabitants of the islands with the government of which we are charged. It is my purpose to muster out the entire Volunteer Army as soon as the Congress shall provide for the increase of the regular establishment. This will be only an act of justice and will be much appreciated by the brave men who left their homes and employments to help the country in its emergency.

In my last annual message I stated:

The Union Pacific Railway, main line, was sold under the decree of the United States court for the district of Nebraska on the 1st and 2d of November of this year. The amount due the Government consisted of the principal of the subsidy bonds, $27,236,-512, and the accrued interest thereon, $31,211,711.75, making the total indebtedness $58,448,223.75. The bid at the sale covered the first-mortgage lien and the entire mortgage claim of the Government, principal and interest.

This left the Kansas Pacific case unconcluded. By a decree of the court in that case an upset price for the property was fixed at a sum which would yield to the Government only $2,500,000 upon its lien. The sale, at the instance of the Government, was postponed first to December 15, 1897, and later, upon the application of the United States, was postponed to the 16th day of February, 1898.

Having satisfied myself that the interests of the Government required that an effort should be made to obtain a larger sum, I directed the Secretary of the Treasury, under the act passed March 3, 1887, to pay out of the Treasury to the persons entitled to receive the same the amounts due upon all prior mortgages upon the Eastern and Middle divisions of said railroad out of any money in the Treasury not otherwise appropriated, whereupon the Attorney-General prepared a petition to be presented to the court, offering to redeem said prior liens in such manner as the court might direct, and praying that thereupon the United States might be held to be subrogated to all the rights of said prior lien holders and that a receiver might be appointed to take possession of the mortgaged premises and maintain and operate the same until the court or Congress otherwise directed. Thereupon the reorganization committee agreed that if said petition was withdrawn and the sale allowed to proceed on the 16th of February, 1898, they would bid a sum at the sale which would realize to the Government the entire principal of its debt, $6,303,000.

Believing that no better price could be obtained and appreciating the difficulties under which the Government would labor if it should become the purchaser of the road at the sale, in the absence of any authority by Congress to take charge of and operate the road I directed that upon the guaranty of a minimum bid which should give the Government the principal of its debt the sale should proceed. By this transaction the Government secured an advance of $3,803,000 over and above the sum which the court had fixed as the upset price, and which the reorganization committee had declared was the maximum which they would pay for the property.

It is a gratifying fact that the result of these proceedings against the Union Pacific system and the Kansas Pacific line is that the Government has received on account of its subsidy claim the sum of $64,751,223.75, an increase of $18,997,163.76 over the sum which the reorganization committee originally agreed to bid for the joint property, the Government receiving its whole claim, principal and interest, on the Union Pacific, and the principal of its debt on the Kansas Pacific Railroad.

Steps had been taken to foreclose the Government's lien upon the Central Pacific Railroad Company, but before action was commenced Congress passed an act, approved July 7, 1898, creating a commission consisting of the Secretary of the Treasury, the Attorney-General, and the Secretary of the Interior, and their successors in office, with full power to settle the indebtedness to the Government growing out of the issue of bonds in aid of the construction of the Central Pacific and Western Pacific bond-aided railroads, subject to the approval of the President.

No report has yet been made to me by the commission thus created. Whatever action is had looking to a settlement of the indebtedness in accordance with the act referred to will be duly submitted to the Congress.

I deem it my duty to call to the attention of Congress the condition of the present building occupied by the Department of Justice. The business of that Department has increased very greatly since it was established in its present quarters. The building now occupied by it is neither large enough nor of suitable arrangement for the proper accommodation of the business of the Department. The Supervising Architect has pronounced it unsafe and unsuited for the use to which it is put. The Attorney-General in his report states that the library of the Department is upon the fourth floor, and that all the space allotted to it is so crowded with books as to dangerously overload the structure. The first floor is occupied by the Court of Claims. The building is of an old and dilapidated appearance, unsuited to the dignity which should attach to this important Department.

A proper regard for the safety, comfort, and convenience of the officers and employees would justify the expenditure of a liberal sum of money in the erection of a new building of commodious proportions and handsome appearance upon the very advantageous site already secured for that purpose, including the ground occupied by the present structure and adjoining vacant lot, comprising in all a frontage of 201 feet on Pennsylvania avenue and a depth of 136 feet.

In this connection I may likewise refer to the inadequate accommodations provided for the Supreme Court in the Capitol, and suggest the wisdom of making provision for the erection of a separate building for the court and its officers and library upon available ground near the Capitol.

The postal service of the country advances with extraordinary growth. Within twenty years both the revenues and the expenditures of the Post-Office Department have multiplied threefold. In the last ten years they have nearly doubled. Our postal business grows much more rapidly than our population. It now involves an expenditure of $100,000,000 a year, numbers 73,000 post-offices, and enrolls 200,000 employees. This remarkable extension of a service which is an accurate index of the public conditions presents gratifying evidence of the advancement of education, of the increase of communication and business activity, and of the improvement of mail facilities leading to their constantly augmenting use.

The war with Spain laid new and exceptional labors on the Post-Office Department. The mustering of the military and naval forces of the United States required special mail arrangements for every camp and every campaign. The communication between home and camp was naturally eager and expectant. In some of the larger places of rendezvous as many as 50,000 letters a day required handling. This necessity was met by the prompt detail and dispatch of experienced men from the established force and by directing all the instrumentalities of the railway mail and post-office service, so far as necessary, to this new need. Congress passed an act empowering the Postmaster-General to establish offices or branches at every military camp or station, and under this authority the postal machinery was speedily put into effective operation.

Under the same authority, when our forces moved upon Cuba, Puerto Rico, and the Philippines they were attended and followed by the postal service. Though the act of Congress authorized the appointment of postmasters where necessary, it was early determined that the public interests would best be subserved, not by new designations, but by the detail of experienced men familiar with every branch of the service, and this policy was steadily followed. When the territory which was the theater of conflict came into our possession, it became necessary to reestablish mail facilities for the resident population as well as to provide them for our forces of occupation, and the former requirement was met through the extension and application of the latter obligation. I gave the requisite authority, and the same general principle was applied to this as to other branches of civil administration under military occupation. The details are more particularly given in the report of the Postmaster-General, and, while the work is only just begun, it is pleasing to be able to say that the service in the territory which has come under our control is already materially improved.

The following recommendations of the Secretary of the Navy relative to the increase of the Navy have my earnest approval:

1. **Three seagoing** sheathed and coppered battle ships of about 13,500 **tons trial displacement,** carrying the heaviest armor and most powerful ordnance for vessels of their class, and to have the highest practicable speed and great radius of action. Estimated cost, exclusive of armor and armament, $3,600,000 each.

2. Three sheathed and coppered armored cruisers of about 12,000 tons trial displacement, carrying the heaviest armor and most powerful ordnance for vessels of their class, and to have the highest practicable speed and great radius of action. Estimated cost, exclusive of armor and armament, $4,000,000 each.

3. Three sheathed and coppered protected cruisers of about 6,000 tons trial displacement, to have the highest practicable speed and great radius of action, and to carry the most powerful ordnance suitable for vessels of their class. Estimated cost, exclusive of armor and armament, $2,150,000 each.

4. Six sheathed and coppered cruisers of about 2,500 tons trial displacement, to have the highest speed compatible with good cruising qualities, great radius of action, and to carry the most powerful ordnance suited to vessels of their class. Estimated cost, exclusive of armament, $1,141,800 each.

I join with the Secretary of the Navy in recommending that the grades of admiral and vice-admiral be temporarily revived, to be filled by officers who have specially distinguished themselves in the war with Spain.

I earnestly urge upon Congress the importance of early legislation providing for the taking of the Twelfth Census. This is necessary in view of the large amount of work which must be performed in the preparation of the schedules preparatory to the enumeration of the population.

There were on the pension rolls on June 30, 1898, 993,714 names, an increase of nearly 18,000 over the number on the rolls on the same day of the preceding year. The amount appropriated by the act of December 22, 1896, for the payment of pensions for the fiscal year of 1898 was $140,000,000. Eight million seventy thousand eight hundred and seventy-two dollars and forty-six cents was appropriated by the act of March

31, 1898, to cover deficiencies in army pensions, and repayments in the sum of $12,020.33, making a total of $148,082,892.79 available for the payment of pensions during the fiscal year 1898. The amount disbursed from that sum was $144,651,879.80, leaving a balance of $3,431,012.99 unexpended on the 30th of June, 1898, which was covered into the Treasury. There were 389 names added to the rolls during the year by special acts passed at the second session of the Fifty-fifth Congress, making a total of 6,486 pensioners by Congressional enactments since 1861.

The total receipts of the Patent Office during the past year were $1,253,948.44. The expenditures were $1,081,633.79, leaving a surplus of $172,314.65.

The public lands disposed of by the Government during the year reached 8,453,896.92 acres, an increase of 614,780.26 acres over the previous year. The total receipts from public lands during the fiscal year amounted to $2,277,995.18, an increase of $190,063.90 over the preceding year. The lands embraced in the eleven forest reservations which were suspended by the act of June 4, 1897, again became subject to the operations of the proclamations of February 22, 1897, creating them, which added an estimated amount of 19,951,360 acres to the area embraced in the reserves previously created. In addition thereto two new reserves were created during the year—the Pine Mountain and Zaca Lake Reserve, in California, embracing 1,644,594 acres, and the Prescott Reserve, in Arizona, embracing 10,240 acres—while the Pecos River Reserve, in New Mexico, has been changed and enlarged to include 120,000 additional acres.

At the close of the year thirty forest reservations, not including those of the Afognak Forest and the Fish-Culture Reserve, in Alaska, had been created by Executive proclamations under section 24 of the act of March 3, 1891, embracing an estimated area of 40,719,474 acres.

The Department of the Interior has inaugurated a forest system, made possible by the act of July, 1898, for a graded force of officers in control of the reserves. This system has only been in full operation since August, but good results have already been secured in many sections. The reports received indicate that the system of patrol has not only prevented destructive fires from gaining headway, but has diminished the number of fires.

The special attention of the Congress is called to that part of the report of the Secretary of the Interior in relation to the Five Civilized Tribes. It is noteworthy that the general condition of the Indians shows marked progress. But one outbreak of a serious character occurred during the year, and that among the Chippewa Indians of Minnesota, which happily has been suppressed.

While it has not yet been practicable to enforce all the provisions of the act of June 28, 1898, "for the protection of the people of the Indian Territory, and for other purposes," it is having a salutary effect upon the nations composing the five tribes. The Dawes Commission reports that the most gratifying results and greater advance toward the attainment of the objects of the Government have been secured in the past year than in any previous year. I can not too strongly indorse the recommendation of the commission and of the Secretary of the Interior for the necessity of providing for the education of the 30,000 white children resident in the Indian Territory.

The Department of Agriculture has been active in the past year. Explorers have been sent to many of the countries of the Eastern and Western hemispheres for seeds and plants that may be useful to the United States, and with the further view of opening up markets for our surplus products. The Forestry Division of the Department is giving special attention to the treeless regions of our country and is introducing species specially adapted to semiarid regions. Forest fires, which seriously interfere with production, especially in irrigated regions, are being studied, that losses from this cause may be avoided. The Department is inquiring into the use and abuse of water in many States of the West, and collating information regarding the laws of the States, the decisions of the courts, and the customs of the people in this regard, so that uniformity may be secured. Experiment stations are becoming more effective every year. The annual appropriation of $720,000 by Congress is supplemented by $400,000 from the States. Nation-wide experiments have been conducted to ascertain the suitableness as to soil and climate and States for growing sugar beets. The number of sugar factories has been doubled in the past two years, and the ability of the United States to produce its own sugar from this source has been clearly demonstrated.

The Weather Bureau forecast and observation stations have been extended around the Caribbean Sea, to give early warning of the approach of hurricanes from the south seas to our fleets and merchant marine.

In the year 1900 will occur the centennial anniversary of the founding of the city of Washington for the permanent capital of the Government of the United States by authority of an act of Congress approved July 16, 1790. In May, 1800, the archives and general offices of the Federal Government were removed to this place. On the 17th of November, 1800, the National Congress met here for the first time and assumed exclusive control of the Federal district and city. This interesting event assumes all the more significance when we recall the circumstances attending the choosing of the site, the naming of the capital in honor of the Father of his Country, and the interest taken by him in the adoption of plans for its future development on a magnificent scale.

These original plans have been wrought out with a constant progress and a signal success even beyond anything their framers could have foreseen. The people of the country are justly proud of the distinctive beauty and government of the capital and of the rare instruments of science and education which here find their natural home.

A movement lately inaugurated by the citizens to have the anniversary celebrated with fitting ceremonies, including, perhaps, the establishment of a handsome permanent memorial to mark so historical an occasion and to give it more than local recognition, has met with general favor on the part of the public.

I recommend to the Congress the granting of an appropriation for this purpose and the appointment of a committee from its respective bodies. It might also be advisable to authorize the President to appoint a committee from the country at large, which, acting with the Congressional and District of Columbia committees, can complete the plans for an appropriate national celebration.

The alien contract law is shown by experience to need some amendment; a measure providing better protection for seamen is proposed; the rightful application of the eight-hour law for the benefit of labor and of the principle of arbitration are suggested for consideration; and I commend these subjects to the careful attention of the Congress.

The several departmental reports will be laid before you. They give in great detail the conduct of the affairs of the Government during the past year and discuss many questions upon which the Congress may feel called upon to act.

THIRD ANNUAL MESSAGE.

EXECUTIVE MANSION, *December 5, 1899.*
To the Senate and House of Representatives:

At the threshold of your deliberations you are called to mourn with your countrymen the death of Vice-President Hobart, who passed from this life on the morning of November 21 last. His great soul now rests in eternal peace. His private life was pure and elevated. while his public career was ever distinguished by large capacity, stainless integrity, and exalted motives. He has been removed from the high office which he honored and dignified, but his lofty character, his devotion to duty, his honesty of purpose, and noble virtues remain with us as a priceless legacy and example.

The Fifty-sixth Congress convenes in its first regular session with the country in a condition of unusual prosperity, of universal good will among the people at home, and in relations of peace and friendship with every government of the world. Our foreign commerce has shown great increase in volume and value. The combined imports and exports for the year are the largest ever shown by a single year in all our history. Our exports for 1899 alone exceeded by more than a billion dollars our imports and exports combined in 1870. The imports per capita are 20 per cent less than in 1870, while the exports per capita are 58 per cent more than in 1870, showing the enlarged capacity of the United States to satisfy the wants of its own increasing population, as well as to contribute to those of the peoples of other nations.

Exports of agricultural products were $784,776,142. Of manufactured products we exported in value $339,592,146, being larger than any previous year. It is a noteworthy fact that the only years in all our history when the products of our manufactories sold abroad exceeded those bought abroad were 1898 and 1899.

Government receipts from all sources for the fiscal year ended June 30, 1899, including $11,798,314.14, part payment of the Central Pacific Railroad indebtedness, aggregated $610,982,004.35. Customs receipts were $206,128,481.75, and those from internal revenue $273,437,161.51.

For the fiscal year the expenditures were $700,093,564.02, leaving a deficit of $89,111,559.67.

The Secretary of the Treasury estimates that the receipts for the current fiscal year will aggregate $640,958,112, and upon the basis of present appropriations the expenditures will aggregate $600,958,112, leaving a surplus of $40,000,000.

For the fiscal year ended June 30, 1899, the internal-revenue receipts were increased about $100,000,000.

The present gratifying strength of the Treasury is shown by the fact that on December 1, 1899, the available cash balance was $278,004,837.72, of which $239,744,905.36 was in gold coin and bullion. The conditions of confidence which prevail throughout the country have brought gold into more general use and customs receipts are now almost entirely paid in that coin.

The strong position of the Treasury with respect to cash on hand and the favorable showing made by the revenues have made it possible for the Secretary of the Treasury to take action under the provisions of section 3694, Revised Statutes, relating to the sinking fund. Receipts exceeded expenditures for the first five months of the current fiscal year by $13,413,389.91, and, as mentioned above, the Secretary of the Treasury estimates that there will be a surplus of approximately $40,000,000 at the end of the year. Under such conditions it was deemed advisable and proper to resume compliance with the provisions of the sinking-fund law, which for eight years has not been done because of deficiencies in the revenues. The Treasury Department therefore offered to purchase during November $25,000,000 of the 5 per cent loan of 1904, or the 4 per cent funded loan of 1907, at the current market price. The amount offered and purchased during November was $18,408,600. The premium paid by the Government on such purchases was $2,263,521 and the net saving in interest was about $2,885,000. The success of this operation was sufficient to induce the Government to continue the offer to purchase bonds to and including the 23d day of December, instant, unless the remainder of the $25,000,000 called for should be presented in the meantime for redemption.

Increased activity in industry, with its welcome attendant—a larger employment for labor at higher wages—gives to the body of the people a larger power to absorb the circulating medium. It is further true that year by year, with larger areas of land under cultivation, the increasing volume of agricultural products, cotton, corn, and wheat, calls for a larger volume of money supply. This is especially noticeable at the crop-harvesting and crop-moving period.

In its earlier history the National Banking Act seemed to prove a reasonable avenue through which needful additions to the circulation could from time to time be made. Changing conditions have apparently rendered it now inoperative to that end. The high margin in bond securities required, resulting from large premiums which Government bonds command in the market, or the tax on note issues, or both operating together, appear to be the influences which impair its public utility.

The attention of Congress is respectfully invited to this important matter, with the view of ascertaining whether or not such reasonable modifications can be made in the National Banking Act as will render its service in the particulars here referred to more responsive to the people's needs. I again urge that national banks be authorized to organize with a capital of $25,000.

I urgently recommend that to support the existing gold standard, and to maintain "the parity in value of the coins of the two metals (gold and silver) and the equal power of every dollar at all times in the market and in the payment of debts," the Secretary of the Treasury be given additional power and charged with the duty to sell United States bonds and to employ such other effective means as may be necessary to these ends. The authority should include the power to sell bonds on long and short time, as conditions may require, and should provide for a rate of interest lower than that fixed by the act of January 14, 1875. While there is now no commercial fright which withdraws gold from the Government, but, on the contrary, such widespread confidence that gold seeks the Treasury demanding paper money in exchange, yet the very situation points to the present as the most fitting time to make adequate provision to insure the continuance of the gold standard and of public confidence in the ability and purpose of the Government to meet all its obligations in the money which the civilized world recognizes as the best. The financial transactions of the Government are conducted upon a gold basis. We receive gold when we sell United States bonds and use gold for their payment. We are maintaining the parity of all the money issued or coined by authority of the Government. We are doing these things with the means at hand. Happily at the present time we are not compelled to resort to loans to supply gold. It has been done in the past, however, and may have to be done in the future. It behooves us, therefore, to provide at once the best means to meet the emergency when it arises, and the best means are those which are the most certain and economical. Those now authorized have the virtue neither of directness nor economy. We have already eliminated one of the causes of our financial plight and embarrassment during the years 1893, 1894, 1895, and 1896. Our receipts now equal our expenditures; deficient revenues no longer create alarm Let us remove the only remaining cause by conferring the full and necessary power on the Secretary of the Treasury and impose upon him the duty to uphold the present gold standard and preserve the coins of the two metals on a parity with each other, which is the repeatedly declared policy of the United States.

In this connection I repeat my former recommendations that a portion of the gold holdings shall be placed in a trust fund from which greenbacks shall be redeemed upon presentation, but when once redeemed shall not thereafter be paid out except for gold.

The value of an American merchant marine to the extension of our commercial trade and the strengthening of our power upon the sea invites the immediate action of the Congress. Our national development will be one-sided and unsatisfactory so long as the remarkable growth of our inland industries remains unaccompanied by progress on the seas. There is no lack of constitutional authority for legislation which shall give to the country maritime strength commensurate with its industrial achievements and with its rank among the nations of the earth.

The past year has recorded exceptional activity in our shipyards. and the promises of continual prosperity in shipbuilding are abundant. Advanced legislation for the protection of our seamen has been enacted. Our coast trade, under regulations wisely framed at the beginning of the Government and since, shows results for the past fiscal year unequaled in our records or those of any other power. We shall fail to realize our opportunities, however, if we complacently regard only matters at home and blind ourselves to the necessity of securing our share in the valuable carrying trade of the world.

Last year American vessels transported a smaller share of our exports and imports than during any former year in all our history, and the measure of our dependence upon foreign shipping was painfully manifested to our people. Without any choice of our own, but from necessity, the Departments of the Government charged with military and naval operations in the East and West Indies had to obtain from foreign flags merchant vessels essential for those operations.

The other great nations have not hesitated to adopt the required means to develop their shipping as a factor in national defense and as one of the surest and speediest means of obtaining for their producers a share in foreign markets. Like vigilance and effort on our part cannot fail to improve our situation, which is regarded with humiliation at home and with surprise abroad. Even the seeming sacrifices, which at the beginning may be involved, will be offset later by more than equivalent gains.

The expense is as nothing compared to the advantage to be achieved. The reestablishment of our merchant marine involves in a large measure our continued industrial progress and the extension of our commercial triumphs. I am satisfied the judgment of the country favors the policy of aid to our merchant marine, which will broaden our commerce and markets and upbuild our sea-carrying capacity for the products of agriculture and manufacture; which, with the increase of our Navy, mean more work and wages to our countrymen, as well as a safeguard to American interests in every part of the world.

Combinations of capital organized into trusts to control the conditions of trade among our citizens, to stifle competition, limit production, and determine the prices of products used and consumed by the people, are justly provoking public discussion, and should early claim the attention of the Congress.

The Industrial Commission, created by the act of the Congress of June 18, 1898, has been engaged in extended hearings upon the disputed questions involved in the subject of combinations in restraint of trade and competition. They have not yet completed their investigation of this subject, and the conclusions and recommendations at which they may arrive are undetermined.

The subject is one giving rise to many divergent views as to the nature and variety or cause and extent of the injuries to the public which may result from large combinations concentrating more or less numerous enterprises and establishments, which previously to the formation of the combination were carried on separately.

It is universally conceded that combinations which engross or control the market of any particular kind of merchandise or commodity necessary to the general community, by suppressing natural and ordinary competition, whereby prices are unduly enhanced to the general consumer, are obnoxious not only to the common law but also to the public welfare. There must be a remedy for the evils involved in such organizations. If the present law can be extended more certainly to control or check these monopolies or trusts, it should be done without delay. Whatever power the Congress possesses over this most important subject should be promptly ascertained and asserted.

President Harrison in his annual message of December 3, 1889, says:

Earnest attention should be given by Congress to a consideration of the question how far the restraint of those combinations of capital commonly called "trusts" is matter of Federal jurisdiction. When organized, as they often are, to crush out all healthy competition and to monopolize the production or sale of an article of commerce and general necessity they are dangerous conspiracies against the public good, and should be made the subject of prohibitory and even penal legislation.

An act to protect trade and commerce against unlawful restraints and monopolies was passed by Congress on the 2d of July, 1890. The provisions of this statute are comprehensive and stringent. It declares every contract or combination, in the form of a trust or otherwise, or conspiracy in the restraint of trade or commerce among the several States or with foreign nations, to be unlawful. It denominates as a criminal every person who makes any such contract or engages in any such combination or conspiracy, and provides a punishment by fine or imprisonment. It invests the several circuit courts of the United States with jurisdiction to prevent and restrain violations of the act, and makes it the duty of the several United States district attorneys, under the direction of the Attorney-General, to institute proceedings in equity to prevent and restrain such violations. It further confers upon any person who shall be injured in his business or property by any other person or corporation by reason of anything forbidden or declared to be unlawful by the act, the power to sue therefor in any circuit court of the United States without respect to the amount in controversy, and to recover threefold the damages by him sustained and the costs of the suit, including reasonable attorney fees. It will be perceived that the act is aimed at every kind of combination in the nature of a trust or monopoly in restraint of interstate or international commerce.

The prosecution by the United States of offenses under the act of 1890 has been frequently resorted to in the Federal courts, and notable efforts in the restraint of interstate commerce, such as the Trans-

Missouri Freight Association and the Joint Traffic Association, have been successfully opposed and suppressed.

President Cleveland in his annual message of December 7, 1896 — more than six years subsequent to the enactment of this law — after stating the evils of these trust combinations, says:

Though Congress has attempted to deal with this matter by legislation, the laws passed for that purpose thus far have proved ineffective, not because of any lack of disposition or attempt to enforce them, but simply because the laws themselves as interpreted by the courts do not reach the difficulty. If the insufficiencies of existing laws can be remedied by further legislation, it should be done. The fact must be recognized, however, that all Federal legislation on this subject may fall short of its purpose because of inherent obstacles, and also because of the complex character of our governmental system, which, while making the Federal authority supreme within its sphere, has carefully limited that sphere by metes and bounds which cannot be transgressed. The decision of our highest court on this precise question renders it quite doubtful whether the evils of trusts and monopolies can be adequately treated through Federal action, unless they seek directly and purposely to include in their objects transportation or intercourse between States or between the United States and foreign countries.

It does not follow, however, that this is the limit of the remedy that may be applied. Even though it may be found that Federal authority is not broad enough to fully reach the case, there can be no doubt of the power of the several States to act effectively in the premises, and there should be no reason to doubt their willingness to judiciously exercise such power.

The State legislation to which President Cleveland looked for relief from the evils of trusts has failed to accomplish fully that object. This is probably due to a great extent to the fact that different States take different views as to the proper way to discriminate between evil and injurious combinations and those associations which are beneficial and necessary to the business prosperity of the country. The great diversity of treatment in different States arising from this cause and the intimate relations of all parts of the country to each other without regarding State lines in the conduct of business have made the enforcement of State laws difficult.

It is apparent that uniformity of legislation upon this subject in the several States is much to be desired. It is to be hoped that such uniformity founded in a wise and just discrimination between what is injurious and what is useful and necessary in business operations may be obtained and that means may be found for the Congress within the limitations of its constitutional power so to supplement an effective code of State legislation as to make a complete system of laws throughout the United States adequate to compel a general observance of the salutary rules to which I have referred.

The whole question is so important and far-reaching that I am sure no part of it will be lightly considered, but every phase of it will have the studied deliberation of the Congress, resulting in wise and judicious action.

A review of our relations with foreign States is presented with such recommendations as are deemed appropriate.

The long-pending boundary dispute between the Argentine Republic and Chile was settled in March last by the award of an arbitral commission, on which the United States minister at Buenos Ayres served as umpire.

Progress has been made toward the conclusion of a convention of extradition with the Argentine Republic. Having been advised and consented to by the United States Senate and ratified by Argentina, it only awaits the adjustment of some slight changes in the text before exchange.

In my last annual message I adverted to the claim of the Austro-Hungarian Government for indemnity for the killing of certain Austrian and Hungarian subjects by the authorities of the State of Pennsylvania, at Lattimer, while suppressing an unlawful tumult of miners, September 10, 1897. In view of the verdict of acquittal rendered by the court before which the sheriff and his deputies were tried for murder, and following the established doctrine that the Government may not be held accountable for injuries suffered by individuals at the hands of the public authorities while acting in the line of duty in suppressing disturbance of the public peace, this Government, after due consideration of the claim advanced by the Austro-Hungarian Government, was constrained to decline liability to indemnify the sufferers.

It is gratifying to be able to announce that the Belgian Government has mitigated the restrictions on the importation of cattle from the United States, to which I referred in my last annual message.

Having been invited by Belgium to participate in a congress, held at Brussels, to revise the provisions of the general act of July 2, 1890, for the repression of the African slave trade, to which the United States was a signatory party, this Government preferred not to be represented by a plenipotentiary, but reserved the right of accession to the result. Notable changes were made, those especially concerning this country being in the line of the increased restriction of the deleterious trade in spirituous liquors with the native tribes, which this Government has from the outset urgently advocated. The amended general act will be laid before the Senate, with a view to its advice and consent.

Early in the year the peace of Bolivia was disturbed by a successful insurrection. The United States minister remained at his post, attending to the American interests in that quarter, and using besides his good offices for the protection of the interests of British subjects in the absence of their national representative. On the establishment of the new Government, our minister was directed to enter into relations therewith.

General Pando was elected President of Bolivia on October 23.

Our representative has been instructed to use all permissible friendly endeavors to induce the Government of Bolivia to amend its marriage laws so as to give legal status to the non-Catholic and civil marriages of aliens within its jurisdiction, and strong hopes are entertained that the Bolivian law in this regard will be brought, as was that of Peru some years ago, into harmony with the general practice of modern States.

A convention of extradition with Brazil, signed May 14, 1897, has been ratified by the Brazilian Legislature.

During the past summer two national ships of the United States have visited Brazilian ports on a friendly mission and been cordially received. The voyage of the *Wilmington* up the Amazon River gave rise to a passing misunderstanding, owing to confusion in obtaining permission to visit the interior and make surveys in the general interest of navigation, but the incident found a ready adjustment in harmony with the close relations of amity which this Government has always sedulously sought to cultivate with the commonwealths of the Western Continent.

The claim growing out of the seizure of the American-owned newspaper "The Panama Star and Herald" by the authorities of Colombia has been settled, after a controversy of several years, by an agreement assessing at $30,000 the indemnity to be paid by the Colombian Government, in three installments of $10,000 each.

The good will of Colombia toward our country has been testified anew by the cordial extension of facilities to the Nicaraguan Canal Commission in their approaching investigation of the Panama Canal and other projected routes across the Isthmus of Darien.

Toward the end of October an insurrectionary disturbance developed in the Colombian Republic. This movement has thus far not attained any decisive result and is still in progress.

Discussion of the questions raised by the action of Denmark in imposing restrictions on the importation of American meats has continued without substantial result in our favor.

The neighboring island Republic of Santo Domingo has lately been the scene of revolution, following a long period of tranquillity. It began with the killing of President Heureaux in July last, and culminated in the relinquishment by the succeeding Vice-President of the reins of government to the insurgents. The first act of the provisional government was the calling of a presidential and constituent election. Juan Isidro Jimenez, having been elected President, was inaugurated on the 14th of November. Relations have been entered into with the newly established Government.

The experimental association of Nicaragua, Honduras, and Salvador, under the title of the Greater Republic of Central America, when apparently on the threshold of a complete federal organization by the adoption of a constitution and the formation of a national legislature, was disrupted in the last days of November, 1898, by the withdrawal of Salvador. Thereupon Nicaragua and Honduras abandoned the joint compact, each resuming its former independent sovereignty. This was followed by the reception of Minister Merry by the Republics of Nicaragua and Salvador, while Minister Hunter in turn presented his credentials to the Government of Honduras, thus reverting to the old distribution of the diplomatic agencies of the United States in Central America for which our existing statutes provide. A Nicaraguan envoy has been accredited to the United States.

An insurrectionary movement, under General Reyes, broke out at Bluefields in February last, and for a time exercised actual control in the Mosquito Territory. The *Detroit* was promptly sent thither for the protection of American interests. After a few weeks the Reyes government renounced the conflict, giving place to the restored supremacy of Nicaragua. During the interregnum certain public dues accruing under Nicaraguan law were collected from American merchants by the authorities for the time being in effective administrative control. Upon the titular government regaining power, a second payment of these dues was demanded. Controversy arose touching the validity of the original payment of the debt to the *de facto* regent of the territory. An arrangement was effected in April last by the United States minister and the foreign secretary of Nicaragua whereby the amounts of the duplicate payments were deposited with the British consul pending an adjustment of the matter by direct agreement between the Governments of the United States and Nicaragua. The controversy is still unsettled.

The contract of the Maritime Canal Company of Nicaragua was declared forfeited by the Nicaraguan Government on the 10th of October, on the ground of nonfulfillment within the ten years' term stipulated in the contract. The Maritime Canal Company has lodged a protest against this action, alleging rights in the premises which appear worthy of consideration. This Government expects that Nicaragua will afford the protestants a full and fair hearing upon the merits of the case.

The Nicaragua Canal Commission, which had been engaged upon the work of examination and survey for a ship-canal route across Nicaragua, having completed its labors and made its report, was dissolved on May 31, and on June 10 a new commission, known as the Isthmian Canal Commission, was organized under the terms of the act approved March 3, 1899, for the purpose of examining the American Isthmus with a view to determining the most practicable and feasible route for a ship canal across that Isthmus, with its probable cost, and other essential details.

This Commission, under the presidency of Rear-Admiral John G. Walker, U. S. N. (retired), entered promptly upon the work intrusted to it, and is now carrying on examinations in Nicaragua along the route of the Panama Canal, and in Darien from the Atlantic, in the neighborhood of the Atrato River, to the Bay of Panama, on the Pacific side. Good progress has been made, but under the law a comprehensive and complete investigation is called for, which will require much labor and considerable time for its accomplishment. The work will be prosecuted as expeditiously as possible and a report made at the earliest practicable date.

The great importance of this work cannot be too often or too strongly pressed upon the attention of the Congress. In my message of a year ago I expressed my views of the necessity of a canal which would link the two great oceans, to which I again invite your consideration. The reasons then presented for early action are even stronger now.

A pleasing incident in the relations of this Government with that of Chile occurred in the generous assistance given to the war ship *Newark* when in distress in Chilean waters. Not alone in this way has the friendly disposition of Chile found expression. That country has acceded to the convention for the establishment of the Bureau of the American Republics, in which organization every independent State of the continent now shares.

The exchange of ratifications of a convention for the revival of the United States and Chilean Claims Commission and for the adjudication of claims heretofore presented but not determined during the life of the previous Commission has been delayed by reason of the necessity for fresh action by the Chilean Senate upon the amendments attached to the ratification of the treaty by the United States Senate. This formality is soon to be accomplished.

In view of disturbances in the populous provinces of northern China, where are many of our citizens, and of the imminence of disorder near the capital and toward the seaboard, a guard of marines was landed from the *Boston* and stationed during last winter in the legation compound at Peking. With the restoration of order this protection was withdrawn.

The interests of our citizens in that vast Empire have not been neglected during the past year. Adequate protection has been secured for our missionaries and some injuries to their property have been redressed.

American capital has sought and found various opportunities of competing to carry out the internal improvements which the Imperial Government is wisely encouraging, and to develop the natural resources of the Empire. Our trade with China has continued to grow, and our commercial rights under existing treaties have been everywhere maintained during the past year, as they will be in the future.

The extension of the area open to international foreign settlement at Shanghai and the opening of the ports of Nanking, Tsing-tao (Kiao chao), and Ta-lien-wan to foreign trade and settlement will doubtless afford American enterprise additional facilities and new fields, of which it will not be slow to take advantage.

In my message to Congress of December 5, 1898, I urged that the recommendation which had been made to the Speaker of the House of Representatives by the Secretary of the Treasury on the 14th of June, 1898, for an appropriation for a commission to study the commercial and industrial conditions in the Chinese Empire and report as to the opportunities for, and obstacles to, the enlargement of markets in China for the raw products and manufactures of the United States, should receive at your hands the consideration which its importance and timeliness merited, but the Congress failed to take action.

I now renew this recommendation, as the importance of the subject has steadily grown since it was first submitted to you, and no time should be lost in studying for ourselves the resources of this great field for American trade and enterprise.

The death of President Faure in February last called forth those sincere expressions of sympathy which befit the relations of two Republics as closely allied by unbroken historic ties as are the United States and France.

Preparations for the representation of the industries, arts, and products of the United States at the World's Exposition to be held in Paris next year continue on an elaborate and comprehensive scale, thanks to the generous appropriation provided by Congress and to the friendly interest the French Government has shown in furthering a typical exhibit of American progress.

There has been allotted to the United States a considerable addition of space, which, while placing our country in the first rank among exhibitors, does not suffice to meet the increasingly urgent demands of our manufacturers. The efforts of the Commissioner-General are ably directed toward a strictly representative display of all that most characteristically marks American achievement in the inventive arts, and most adequately shows the excellence of our natural productions.

In this age of keen rivalry among nations for mastery in commerce, the doctrine of evolution and the rule of the survival of the fittest must be as inexorable in their operation as they are positive in the results they bring about. The place won in the struggle by an industrial people can only be held by unrelaxed endeavor and constant advance in achievement. The present extraordinary impetus in every line of American exportation and the astounding increase in the volume and value of our share in the world's markets may not be attributed to accidental conditions.

The reasons are not far to seek. They lie deep in our national character and find expression year by year in every branch of handicraft, in every new device whereby the materials we so abundantly produce are subdued to the artisan's will and made to yield the largest, most practical, and most beneficial return. The American exhibit at Paris should, and I am confident will, be an open volume, whose lessons of skillfully directed endeavor, unfaltering energy, and consummate performance may be read by all on every page, thus spreading abroad a clearer knowledge of the worth of our productions and the justice of our claim to an important place in the marts of the world. To accomplish this by judicious selection, by recognition of paramount merit in whatever walk of trade or manufacture it may appear, and by orderly classification and attractive installation is the task of our Commission.

The United States Government building·is approaching completion, and no effort will be spared to make it worthy, in beauty of architectural plan and in completeness of display, to represent our nation. It has been suggested that a permanent building of similar or appropriate design be erected on a convenient site, already given by the municipality, near the exposition grounds, to serve in commemoration of the part taken by this country in this great enterprise, as an American National Institute, for our countrymen resorting to Paris for study.

I am informed by our Commissioner-General that we shall have in the American sections at Paris over 7,000 exhibitors, from every State in our country, a number ten times as great as those which were represented at Vienna in 1873, six times as many as those in Paris in 1878, and four times as many as those who exhibited in Paris in 1889. This statement does not include the exhibits from either Cuba, Puerto Rico, or Hawaii, for which arrangements have been made.

A number of important international congresses on special topics affecting public interests are proposed to be held in Paris next summer in connection with the exposition. Effort will be made to have the several technical branches of our administration efficiently represented at those conferences, each in its special line, and to procure the largest possible concourse of State representatives, particularly at the Congresses of Public Charity and Medicine.

Our relations with Germany continue to be most cordial. The increasing intimacy of direct association has been marked during the year by the granting permission in April for the landing on our shores of a cable from Borkum Emden, on the North Sea, by way of the Azores, and also by the conclusion on September 2 of a Parcels

Post Convention with the German Empire. In all that promises closer relations of intercourse and commerce and a better understanding between two races having so many traits in common, Germany can be assured of the most cordial cooperation of this Government and people. We may be rivals in many material paths, but our rivalry should be generous and open, ever aiming toward the attainment of larger results and the mutually beneficial advancement of each in the line of its especial adaptabilities.

The several governments of the Empire seem reluctant to admit the natural excellence of our food productions and to accept the evidence we constantly tender of the care with which their purity is guarded by rigid inspection from the farm, through the slaughterhouse and the packing establishments, to the port of shipment. Our system of control over exported food staples invites examination from any quarter and challenges respect by its efficient thoroughness.

It is to be hoped that in time the two Governments will act in common accord toward the realization of their common purpose to safeguard the public health and to insure the purity and wholesomeness of all food products imported by either country from the other. Were the Congress to authorize an invitation to Germany, in connection with the pending repiprocity negotiations, for the constitution of a joint commission of scientific experts and practical men of affairs to conduct a searching investigation of food production and exportation in both countries and report to their respective legislatures for the adoption of such remedial measures as they might recommend for either, the way might be opened for the desirable result indicated.

Efforts to obtain for American life insurance companies a full hearing as to their business operations in Prussia have, after several years of patient representation, happily succeeded, and one of the most important American companies has been granted a concession to continue business in that Kingdom.

I am also glad to announce that the German insurance companies have been readmitted by the superintendent of insurance to do business in the State of New York.

Subsequent to the exchange of our peace treaty with Spain, Germany acquired the Caroline Islands by purchase, paying therefor $5,000,000. Assurances have been received from the German Government that the rights of American missionaries and traders there will be considerately observed.

In my last annual message I referred to the pending negotiations with Great Britain in respect to the Dominion of Canada. By means of an executive agreement, a Joint High Commission had been created for the purpose of adjusting all unsettled questions between the United States and Canada, embracing twelve subjects, among which were the questions of the fur seals, the fisheries of the coast and contiguous inland waters, the Alaskan boundary, the transit of merchandise in bond, the alien labor laws, mining rights, reciprocity in trade, revision of the agreement respecting naval vessels in the Great Lakes, a more complete marking of parts of the boundary, provision for the conveyance of criminals, and for wrecking and salvage.

Much progress had been made by the Commission toward the adjustment of many of these questions, when it became apparent that an irreconcilable difference of views was entertained respecting the delimitation of the Alaskan boundary. In the failure of an agreement as to the meaning of Articles III and IV of the treaty of 1825 between Russia and Great Britain, which defined the boundary between Alaska and Canada, the American Commissioners proposed that the subject of the boundary be laid aside, and that the remaining questions of difference be proceeded with, some of which were so far advanced as to assure the probability of a settlement. This being declined by the British Commissioners, an adjournment was taken until the boundary should be adjusted by the two Governments. The subject has been receiving the careful attention which its importance demands, with the result that a *modus vivendi* for provisional demarcations in the region about the head of Lynn Canal has been agreed upon; and it is hoped that the negotiations now in progress between the two Governments will end in an agreement for the establishment and delimitation of a permanent boundary.

Apart from these questions growing out of our relationship with our northern neighbor, the most friendly disposition and ready agreement have marked the discussion of numerous matters arising in the vast and intimate intercourse of the United States with Great Britain.

This Government has maintained an attitude of neutrality in the unfortunate contest between Great Britain and the Boer States of Africa. We have remained faithful to the precept of avoiding entangling alliances as to affairs not of our direct concern. Had circumstances suggested that the parties to the quarrel would have welcomed any kindly expression of the hope of the American people that war might be averted, good offices would have been gladly tendered. The United States representative at Pretoria was early instructed to see that all neutral American interests be respected by the combatants. This has been an easy task in view of the positive declarations of both British and Boer authorities that the personal and property rights of our citizens should be observed.

Upon the withdrawal of the British agent from Pretoria the United States consul was authorized, upon the request of the British Government and with the assent of the South African and Orange Free

State Governments, to exercise the customary good offices of a neutral for the care of British interests. In the discharge of this function, I am happy to say that abundant opportunity has been afforded to show the impartiality of this Government toward both the combatants.

For the fourth time in the present decade, question has arisen with the Government of Italy in regard to the lynching of Italian subjects. The latest of these deplorable events occurred at Tallulah, Louisiana, whereby five unfortunates of Italian origin were taken from jail and hanged.

The authorities of the State and a representative of the Italian Embassy having separately investigated the occurrence, with discrepant results, particularly as to the alleged citizenship of the victims, and it not appearing that the State had been able to discover and punish the violators of the law, an independent investigation has been set on foot, through the agency of the Department of State, and is still in progress. The result will enable the Executive to treat the question with the Government of Italy in a spirit of fairness and justice. A satisfactory solution will doubtless be reached.

The recurrence of these distressing manifestations of blind mob fury directed at dependents or natives of a foreign country suggests that the contingency has arisen for action by Congress in the direction of conferring upon the Federal courts jurisdiction in this class of international cases where the ultimate responsibility of the Federal Government may be involved. The suggestion is not new. In his annual message of December 9, 1891, my predecessor, President Harrison, said:

It would, I believe, be entirely competent for Congress to make offenses against the treaty rights of foreigners domiciled in the United States cognizable in the Federal courts. This has not, however, been done, and the Federal officers and courts have no power in such cases to intervene either for the protection of a foreign citizen or for the punishment of his slayers. It seems to me to follow, in this state of the law, that the officers of the State charged with police and judicial powers in such cases must, in the consideration of international questions growing out of such incidents, be regarded in such sense as Federal agents as to make this Government answerable for their acts in cases where it would be answerable if the United States had used its constitutional power to define and punish crimes against treaty rights.

A bill to provide for the punishment of violations of treaty rights of aliens was introduced in the Senate March 1, 1892, and reported favorably March 30. Having doubtless in view the language of that part of Article III of the treaty of February 26, 1871, between the United States and Italy, which stipulates that "The citizens of each of the high contracting parties shall receive, in the States and Territories of the other, most constant protection and security for their persons and property, and shall enjoy in this respect the same rights and privileges as are or shall be granted to the natives, on their submitting themselves to the conditions imposed upon the natives," the bill so introduced and reported provided that any act committed in any State or Territory of the United States in violation of the rights of a citizen or subject of a foreign country secured to such citizen or subject by treaty between the United States and such foreign country and constituting a crime under the laws of the State or Territory shall constitute a like crime against the United States and be cognizable in the Federal courts. No action was taken by Congress in the matter.

I earnestly recommend that the subject be taken up anew and acted upon during the present session. The necessity for some such provision abundantly appears. Precedent for constituting a Federal jurisdiction in criminal cases where aliens are sufferers is rationally deducible from the existing statute, which gives to the district and circuit courts of the United States jurisdiction of civil suits brought by aliens where the amount involved exceeds a certain sum. If such jealous solicitude be shown for alien rights in cases of merely civil and pecuniary import, how much greater should be the public duty to take cognizance of matters affecting the lives and the rights of aliens under the settled principles of international law no less than under treaty stipulation, in cases of such transcendent wrong-doing as mob murder, especially when experience has shown that local justice is too often helpless to punish the offenders.

After many years of endeavor on the part of this Government to that end the Italian Government has consented to enter into negotiations for a naturalization convention, having for one of its objects the regulation of the status of Italians (except those of an age for active military service) who, having been naturalized in the United States, may revisit Italy. It is hoped that with the mutually conciliatory spirit displayed a successful conclusion will be reached.

The treaty of commerce and navigation between the United States and Japan on November 22, 1894, took effect in accordance with the terms of its XIXth Article on the 17th of July last, simultaneously with the enforcement of like treaties with the other powers, except France, whose convention did not go into operation until August 4, the United States being, however, granted up to that date all the privileges and rights accorded to French citizens under the old French treaty. By this notable conventional reform Japan's position as a fully independent sovereign power is assured, control being gained of taxation, customs revenues, judicial administration, coasting trade, and all other domestic functions of government, and foreign extra-territorial rights being renounced.

Comprehensive codes of civil and criminal procedure according to western methods, public instruction, patents and copyrights, municipal administration, including jurisdiction over the former foreign settlements, customs tariffs and procedure, public health, and other administrative measures have been proclaimed. The working of the new system has given rise to no material complaints on the part of the American citizens or interests, a circumstance which attests the ripe consideration with which the change has been prepared.

Valuable assistance was rendered by the Japanese authorities to the United States transport ship *Morgan City* while stranded at Kobe. Permission has been granted to land and pasture army horses at Japanese ports of call on the way to the Philippine Islands. These kindly evidences of good will are highly appreciated.

The Japanese Government has shown a lively interest in the proposition of the Pacific Cable Company to add to its projected cable lines to Hawaii, Guam, and the Philippines a branch connection with the coast of Japan. It would be a gratifying consummation were the utility of the contemplated scheme enhanced by bringing Japan and the United States into direct telegraphic relation.

Without repeating the observations of my special message of February 10, 1899, concerning the necessity of a cable to Manila, I respectfully invite attention to it.

I recommend that, in case the Congress should not take measures to bring about this result by direct action of the Government, the Postmaster-General be authorized to invite competitive bids for the establishment of a cable; the company making the best responsible bid to be awarded the contract; the successful company to give ample bonds to insure the completion of the work within a reasonable time.

The year has been marked by constant increase in the intimacy of our relations with Mexico and in the magnitude of mutually advantageous interchanges. This Government has omitted no opportunity to show its strong desire to develop and perpetuate the ties of cordiality now so long happily unbroken.

Following the termination on January 20, 1899, by Mexico of the convention of extradition of December 11, 1861, a new treaty more in accordance with the ascertained needs of both countries was signed February 22, 1899, and exchanged in the City of Mexico on the 22d of April last. Its operation thus far has been effective and satisfactory. A recent case has served to test the application of its IVth Article, which provides that neither party shall be bound to deliver up its own citizens, but that the executive authority of each shall have the power to deliver them up if in its discretion it be deemed proper to do so.

The extradition of Mrs. Mattie Rich, a citizen of the United States, charged with homicide committed in Mexico, was after mature consideration directed by me in the conviction that the ends of justice would be thereby subserved.   Similar action, on appropriate occasion, by the Mexican Executive will not only tend to accomplish the desire of both Governments that grave crimes go not unpunished, but also to repress lawlessness along the border of the two countries. The new treaty stipulates that neither Government shall assume jurisdiction in the punishment of crimes committed exclusively within the territory of the other.   This will obviate in future the embarrassing controversies which have heretofore arisen through Mexico's assertion of a claim to try and punish an American citizen for an offense committed within the jurisdiction of the United States.

The International Water Boundary Commission, organized by the convention of March 1, 1889, for the adjustment of questions affecting the Rio Grande frontier, has not yet completed its labors.   A further extension of its term for one year, until December 24, 1899, was effected by a convention signed December 2, 1898, and exchanged and proclaimed in February last.

An invitation extended to the President of Mexico to visit Chicago in October, on the occasion of laying the corner stone of the United States Government building in that city, was cordially accepted by him, with the necessary consent of the Mexican Congress, but the illness of a member of his family prevented his attendance.   The Minister of Foreign Relations, however, came as the personal representative of President Diaz, and in that high character was duly honored.

Claims growing out of the seizure of American sealing vessels in Bering Sea have been under discussion with the Government of Russia for several years, with the recent happy result of an agreement to submit them to the decision of a single arbitrator.   By this act Russia affords proof of her adherence to the beneficent principle of arbitration which her plenipotentiaries conspicuously favored at The Hague Disarmament Conference when it was advocated by the representatives of the United States.

A suggestion for a permanent exposition of our products and manufactures in Russia, although not yet fully shaped, has been so cordially welcomed by the Imperial Government that it may not inaptly take a fitting place in whatever legislation the Congress may adopt looking to enlargement of our commercial opportunities abroad.

Important events have occurred in the Samoan Islands.   The election, according to the laws and customs of Samoa, of a successor to the late King, Malietoa Laupepa, developed a contest as to the validity of the result, which issue, by the terms of the General Act, was to be decided by the Chief Justice.   Upon his rendering a judgment in favor of Malietoa Tanu, the rival chief, Mataafa, took up arms. The active intervention of American and British war ships became imperative to restore order, at the cost of sanguinary encounters.

In this emergency a joint commission of representatives of the United States, Germany, and Great Britain was sent to Samoa to investigate the situation and provide a temporary remedy. By its active efforts a peaceful solution was reached for the time being, the kingship being abolished and a provisional government established. Recommendations unanimously made by the commission for a permanent adjustment of the Samoan question were taken under consideration by the three powers parties to the General Act. But the more they were examined the more evident it became that a radical change was necessary in the relations of the powers to Samoa.

The inconveniences and possible perils of the tripartite scheme of supervision and control in the Samoan group by powers having little interest in common in that quarter beyond commercial rivalry had been once more emphasized by the recent events. The suggested remedy of the Joint Commission, like the scheme it aimed to replace. amounted to what has been styled a *tridominium*, being the exercise of the functions of sovereignty by an unanimous agreement of three powers. The situation had become far more intricate and embar. rassing from every point of view than it was when my predecessor, in 1894, summed up its perplexities and condemned the participation in it of the United States.

The arrangement under which Samoa was administered had proved impracticable and unacceptable to all the powers concerned. To withdraw from the agreement and abandon the islands to Germany and Great Britain would not be compatible with our interests in the archipelago. To relinquish our rights in the harbor of Pago Pago, the best anchorage in the Pacific, the occupancy of which had been leased to the United States in 1878 by the first foreign treaty ever concluded by Samoa, was not to be thought of either as regards the needs of our Navy or the interests of our growing commerce with the East. We could not have considered any proposition for the abrogation of the tripartite control which did not confirm us in all our rights and safeguard all our national interests in the islands.

Our views commended themselves to the other powers. A satisfactory arrangement was concluded between the Governments of Germany and of England, by virtue of which England retired from Samoa in view of compensations in other directions, and both powers renounced in favor of the United States all their rights and claims over and in respect to that portion of the group lying to the east of the one hundred and seventy-first degree of west longitude, embracing the islands of Tutuila, Ofoo, Olosenga, and Manua. I transmit to the Senate, for its constitutional action thereon, a convention, which besides the provisions above mentioned also guarantees us the same privileges and conditions in respect to commerce and commercial vessels in all of the islands of Samoa as those possessed by Germany.

Claims have been preferred by white residents of Samoa on account of injuries alleged to have been suffered through the acts of the treaty Governments in putting down the late disturbances. A convention has been made between the three powers for the investigation and settlement of these claims by a neutral arbitrator, to which the attention of the Senate will be invited.

My annual message of last year was necessarily devoted in great part to a consideration of the Spanish War and of the results it wrought and the conditions it imposed for the future. I am gratified to announce that the treaty of peace has restored friendly relations between the two powers. Effect has been given to its most important provisions. The evacuation of Puerto Rico having already been accomplished on the 18th of October, 1898, nothing remained necessary there but to continue the provisional military control of the island until the Congress should enact a suitable government for the ceded territory. Of the character and scope of the measures to that end I shall treat in another part of this message.

The withdrawal of the authority of Spain from the island of Cuba was effected by the 1st of January, so that the full re-establishment of peace found the relinquished territory held by us in trust for the inhabitants, maintaining, under the direction of the Executive, such government and control therein as should conserve public order, restore the productive conditions of peace so long disturbed by the instability and disorder which prevailed for the greater part of the preceding three decades, and build up that tranquil development of the domestic state whereby alone can be realized the high purpose, as proclaimed in the joint resolution adopted by the Congress on the 19th of April, 1898, by which the United States disclaimed any disposition or intention to exercise sovereignty, jurisdiction, or control over Cuba, except for the pacification thereof, and asserted its determination when that was accomplished to leave the government and control of the island to its people. The pledge contained in this resolution is of the highest honorable obligation and must be sacredly kept.

I believe that substantial progress has been made in this direction. All the administrative measures adopted in Cuba have aimed to fit it for a regenerated existence by enforcing the supremacy of law and justice; by placing wherever practicable the machinery of administration in the hands of the inhabitants; by instituting needed sanitary reforms; by spreading education; by fostering industry and trade; by inculcating public morality, and, in short, by taking every rational step to aid the Cuban people to attain to that plane of self-conscious respect and self-reliant unity which fits an enlightened community for self-government within its own sphere, while enabling it to fulfill all outward obligation.

This nation has assumed before the world a grave responsibility for the future good government of Cuba. We have accepted a trust the fulfillment of which calls for the sternest integrity of purpose and the exercise of the highest wisdom. The new Cuba yet to arise from the ashes of the past must needs be bound to us by ties of singular intimacy and strength if its enduring welfare is to be assured. Whether those ties shall be organic or conventional, the destinies of Cuba are in some rightful form and manner irrevocably linked with our own, but how and how far is for the future to determine in the ripeness of events. Whatever be the outcome, we must see to it that free Cuba be a reality, not a name, a perfect entity, not a hasty experiment bearing within itself the elements of failure. Our mission, to accomplish which we took up the wager of battle, is not to be fulfilled by turning adrift any loosely framed commonwealth to face the vicissitudes which too often attend weaker States whose natural wealth and abundant resources are offset by the incongruities of their political organization and the recurring occasions for internal rivalries to sap their strength and dissipate their energies. The greatest blessing which can come to Cuba is the restoration of her agricultural and industrial prosperity, which will give employment to idle men and re-establish the pursuits of peace. This is her chief and immediate need.

On the 19th of August last an order was made for the taking of the census in the island, to be completed on the 30th of November. By the treaty of peace the Spanish people on the island have until April 11, 1900, to elect whether they will remain citizens of Spain or become citizens of Cuba. Until then it cannot be definitely ascertained who shall be entitled to participate in the formation of the government of Cuba. By that time the results of the census will have been tabulated and we shall proceed to provide for elections which will commit the municipal governments of the island to the officers elected by the people. The experience thus acquired will prove of great value in the formation of a representative convention of the people to draft a constitution and establish a general system of independent government for the island. In the meantime and so long as we exercise control over the island the products of Cuba should have a market in the United States on as good terms and with as favorable rates of duty as are given to the West India Islands under treaties of reciprocity which shall be made.

For the relief of the distressed in the island of Cuba the War Department has issued supplies to destitute persons through the officers of the Army, which have amounted to 5,493,000 rations, at a cost of $1,417,554.07.

To promote the disarmament of the Cuban volunteer army, and in the interest of public peace and the welfare of the people, the sum of $75 was paid to each Cuban soldier borne upon the authenticated rolls, on condition that he should deposit his arms with the authorities designated by the United States. The sum thus disbursed aggregated $2,547,750, which was paid from the emergency fund provided by the act of January 5, 1899, for that purpose.

Out of the Cuban island revenues during the six months ending June 30, 1899, $1,712,014.20 was expended for sanitation, $293,881.70 for charities and hospitals, and $88,944.03 for aid to the destitute.

Following the exchange of ratifications of the treaty of peace the two Governments accredited ministers to each other, Spain sending to Washington the Duke of Arcos, an eminent diplomatist, previously stationed in Mexico, while the United States transferred to Madrid Hon. Bellamy Storer, its minister at Brussels. This was followed by the respective appointment of consuls, thereby fully resuming the relations interrupted by the war. In addition to its consular representation in the United States, the Spanish Government has appointed consuls for Cuba, who have been provisionally recognized during the military administration of the affairs of that island.

Judicial intercourse between the courts of Cuba and Puerto Rico and of Spain has been established, as provided by the treaty of peace. The Cuban political prisoners in Spanish penal stations have been and are being released and returned to their homes, in accordance with Article VI of the treaty. Negotiations are about to be had for defining the conventional relations between the two countries, which fell into abeyance by reason of the war. I trust that these will include a favorable arrangement for commercial reciprocity under the terms of sections 3 and 4 of the current tariff act. In these, as in all matters of international concern, no effort will be spared to respond to the good disposition of Spain, and to cultivate in all practicable ways the intimacy which should prevail between two nations whose past history has so often and in so many ways been marked by sincere friendship and by community of interests.

I would recommend appropriate legislation in order to carry into execution Article VII of the Treaty of Peace with Spain, by which the United States assured the payment of certain claims for indemnity of its citizens against Spain.

The United States minister to Turkey continues, under instructions, to press for a money payment in satisfaction of the just claims for injuries suffered by American citizens in the disorders of several years past and for wrongs done to them by the Ottoman authorities. Some of these claims are of many years' standing. This Government is hopeful of a general agreement in this regard.

In the Turkish Empire the situation of our citizens remains unsatisfactory. Our efforts during nearly forty years to bring about a convention of naturalization seem to be on the brink of final failure through the announced policy of the Ottoman Porte to refuse recognition of the alien status of native Turkish subjects naturalized abroad since 1867. Our statutes do not allow this Government to admit any distinction between the treatment of native and naturalized Americans abroad, so that ceaseless controversy arises in cases where persons owing in the eye of international law a dual allegiance are prevented from entering Turkey or are expelled after entrance. Our law in this regard contrasts with that of the European States. The British act, for instance, does not claim effect for the naturalization of an alien in the event of his return to his native country, unless the change be recognized by the law of that country or stipulated by treaty between it and the naturalizing State.

The arbitrary treatment, in some instances, of American productions in Turkey has attracted attention of late, notably in regard to our flour. Large shipments by the recently opened direct steamship line to Turkish ports have been denied entrance on the score that, although of standard composition and unquestioned purity, the flour was pernicious to health because of deficient "elasticity" as indicated by antiquated and untrustworthy tests. Upon due protest by the American minister, and it appearing that the act was a virtual discrimination against our product, the shipments in question were admitted. In these, as in all instances, wherever occurring, when American products may be subjected in a foreign country, upon specious pretexts, to discrimination compared with the like products of another country, this Government will use its earnest efforts to secure fair and equal treatment for its citizens and their goods. Failing this, it will not hesitate to apply whatever corrective may be provided by the statutes.

The International Commission of Arbitration, appointed under the Anglo-Venezuelan treaty of 1897, rendered an award on October 3 last, whereby the boundary line between Venezuela and British Guiana is determined, thus ending a controversy which has existed for the greater part of the century. The award, as to which the arbitrators were unanimous, while not meeting the extreme contention of either party, gives to Great Britain a large share of the interior territory in dispute and to Venezuela the entire mouth of the Orinoco, including Barima Point and the Caribbean littoral for some distance to the eastward. The decision appears to be equally satisfactory to both parties.

Venezuela has once more undergone a revolution. The insurgents, under General Castro, after a sanguinary engagement in which they suffered much loss, rallied in the mountainous interior and advanced toward the capital. The bulk of the army having sided with the movement, President Andrade quitted Caracas, where General Castro set up a provisional government with which our minister and the representatives of other powers entered into diplomatic relations on the 20th of November, 1899.

The fourth section of the Tariff Act approved July 24, 1897, appears to provide only for commercial treaties which should be entered into by the President and also ratified by the Senate within two years from its passage. Owing to delays inevitable in negotiations of this nature, none of the treaties initiated under that section could be concluded in time for ratification by the Senate prior to its adjournment on the 4th of March last. Some of the pending negotiations, however, were near conclusion at that time, and the resulting conventions have since been signed by the plenipotentiaries. Others, within both the third and fourth sections of the act, are still under consideration. Acting under the constitutional power of the Executive in respect to treaties, I have deemed it my duty, while observing the limitations of concession provided by the fourth section, to bring to a conclusion all pending negotiations, and submit them to the Senate for its advice and consent.

Conventions of reciprocity have been signed during the Congressional recess with Great Britain for the respective colonies of British Guiana, Barbados, Bermuda, Jamaica, and Turks and Caicos Islands, and with the Republic of Nicaragua.

Important reciprocal conventions have also been concluded with France and with the Argentine Republic.

In my last annual message the progress noted in the work of the diplomatic and consular officers in collecting information as to the industries and commerce of other countries, and in the care and promptitude with which their reports are printed and distributed, has continued during the past year, with increasingly valuable results in suggesting new sources of demand for American products and in pointing out the obstacles still to be overcome in facilitating the remarkable expansion of our foreign trade. It will doubtless be gratifying to Congress to learn that the various agencies of the Department of State are co-operating in these endeavors with a zeal and effectiveness which are not only receiving the cordial recognition of our business interests, but are exciting the emulation of other Governments. In any rearrangement of the great and complicated work of obtaining official data of an economic character which Congress may undertake it is most important, in my judgment, that the results already secured by the efforts of the Department of State should be carefully considered with a view to a judicious development and increased utility to our export trade.

The interest taken by the various States forming the International Union of American Republics in the work of its organic bureau is evidenced by the fact that for the first time since its creation in 1890 all the Republics of South and Central America are now represented in it.

The unanimous recommendation of the International American Conference, providing for the International Union of American Republics, stated that it should continue in force during a term of ten years from the date of its organization, and no country becoming a member of the union should cease to be a member until the end of said period of ten years, and unless twelve months before the expira- tion of said period a majority of the members of the union had given to the Secretary of State of the United States official notice of their wish to terminate the union at the end of its first period, that the union should continue to be maintained for another period of ten years, and thereafter, under the same conditions, for successive periods of ten years each.

The period for notification expired on July 14, 1899, without any of the members having given the necessary notice of withdrawal. Its maintenance is therefore assured for the next ten years. In view of this fact and of the numerous questions of general interest and common benefit to all of the Republics of America, some of which were considered by the first International American Conference, but not finally settled, and others which have since then grown to im- portance, it would seem expedient that the various Republics con- stituting the Union should be invited to hold at an early date another conference in the capital of one of the countries other than the United States, which has already enjoyed this honor.

The purely international character of the work being done by the bureau and the appreciation of its value are further emphasized by the active co-operation which the various Governments of the Latin- American Republics and their diplomatic representatives in this capital are now exhibiting and the zealous endeavors they are mak- ing to extend its field of usefulness, to promote through it commer- cial intercourse, and strengthen the bonds of amity and confidence between its various members and the nations of this continent.

The act to encourage the holding of the Pan-American Exposition on the Niagara frontier, within the county of Erie or Niagara, in the State of New York, in the year 1901, was approved on March 3, 1899.

This exposition, which will be held in the city of Buffalo, in the near vicinity of the great Niagara cataract, and within a day's jour- ney of which reside 40,000,000 of our people, will be confined entirely to the Western Hemisphere. Satisfactory assurances have already been given by the diplomatic representatives of Great Britain, Mexico, the Central and South American Republics, and most of the States of the United States that these countries and States will make an unique, interesting, and instructive exhibit, peculiarly illustrative of their material progress during the century which is about to close.

The law provides an appropriation of $500,000 for the purpose of making an exhibit at the exposition by the Government of the United States from its Executive Departments and from the Smithsonian Institution and National Museum, the United States Commission of Fish and Fisheries, the Department of Labor, and the Bureau of the American Republics. To secure a complete and harmonious arrangement of this Government exhibit a board of management has already been created, and charged with the selection, purchase, preparation, transportation, arrangement, and safe-keeping of the articles and materials to be exhibited. This board has been organized and has already entered upon the performance of its duties, as provided for by the law

I have every reason to hope and believe that this exposition will tend more firmly to cement the cordial relations between the nations on this continent.

In accordance with an act of Congress approved December 21, 1898, and under the auspices of the Philadelphia Commercial Museum, a most interesting and valuable exposition of products and manufactures especially adapted to export trade was held in Philadelphia from the 14th of September to the 1st of December, 1899. The representative character of the exhibits and the widespread interest manifested in the special objects of the undertaking afford renewed encouragement to those who look confidently to the steady growth of our enlarged exportation of manufactured goods, which has been the most remarkable fact in the economic development of the United States in recent years. A feature of this exposition which is likely to become of permanent and increasing utility to our industries is the collection of samples of merchandise produced in various countries with special reference to particular markets, providing practical object lessons to United States manufacturers as to qualities, styles, and prices of goods such as meet the special demands of consumers and may be exported with advantage.

In connection with the exposition an International Commercial Congress was held, upon the invitation of the Philadelphia Commercial Museum, transmitted by the Department of State to the various foreign Governments, for an exchange of information and opinions with the view to the promotion of international trade. This invitation met with general and cordial acceptance, and the Congress, which began its sessions at the exposition on the 13th of October proved to be of great practical importance, from the fact that it developed a general recognition of the interdependence of nations in trade and a most gratifying spirit of accommodation with reference to the gradual removal of existing impediments to reciprocal relations, without injury to the industrial interests of either party.

In response to the invitation of His Majesty, the Emperor of Russia, delegates from twenty-six countries were assembled at The

Hague on the 18th of May, as members of a conference in the interest of peace. The commission from the United States consisted of
the Hon. Andrew D. White, the Hon. Seth Low, the Hon. Stanford
Newel, Captain Alfred T. Mahan, of the United States Navy, Captain William Crozier, of the United States Army, and the Hon.
Frederick W. Holls, secretary. The occasion seemed to be oppor-
tune for the serious consideration of a plan for the pacific adjustment
of international differences, a subject in which the American people
have been deeply interested for many years, and a definite project for
a permanent international tribunal was included in the instructions
to the delegates of the United States.

The final act of the conference includes conventions upon the
amelioration of the laws and customs of war on land, the adaptation
to maritime warfare of the principles of the Geneva Convention of
1864, and the extension of judicial methods to international cases.
The Convention for the Pacific Settlement of International Conflicts
embodies the leading features of the American plan, with such modifications as were rendered necessary by the great diversity of views
and interests represented by the delegates. The four titles of the
convention provide for the maintenance of general peace, the exercise of good offices and mediation, the formation of commissions of
inquiry, and international arbitration.

The mediation provided for by the convention is purely voluntary
and advisory, and is intended to avoid any invasion or limitation of
the sovereign rights of the adhering States. The commissions of
inquiry proposed consists of delegations to be specifically constituted
for particular purposes by means of conventions between the contesting parties, having for their object the clear understanding of
international differences before resorting to the use of force. The
provision for arbitration contemplates the formation of a permanent
tribunal before which disputed cases may be brought for settlement
by the mutual consent of the litigants in each separate case. The
advantages of such a permanent tribunal over impromptu commissions of arbitration are conceived to be the actual existence of a
competent court, prepared to administer justice, the greater economy
resulting from a well-devised system, and the accumulated judicial
skill and experience which such a tribunal would soon possess.

While earnestly promoting the idea of establishing a permanent
international tribunal, the delegation of the United States was not
unmindful of the inconveniences which might arise from an obtru-
sive exercise of mediation, and in signing the convention carefully
guarded the historic position of the United States by the following
declaration:

Nothing contained in this convention shall be so construed as to require the
United States of America to depart from its traditional policy of not intruding upon,

interfering with, or entangling itself in the political questions or policy or internal administration of any foreign state ; nor shall anything contained in the said convention be construed to imply a relinquishment by the United States of America of its traditional attitude toward purely American questions.

Thus interpreted, the Convention for the Pacific Settlement of International Conflicts may be regarded as realizing the earnest desire of great numbers of American citizens, whose deep sense of justice, expressed in numerous resolutions and memorials, has urged them to labor for this noble achievement. The general character of this convention, already signed by the delegates of more than twenty sovereign States, further commends it to the favorable action of the Senate of the United States, whose ratification it still awaits.

Since my last annual message, and in obedience to the acts of the Congress of April 22 and 26, 1898, the remaining volunteer force enlisted for the Spanish War, consisting of 34,834 regulars and 110, 202 volunteers, with over 5,000 volunteer officers, has been discharged from the military service. Of the volunteers, 667 officers and 14,831 men were serving in the Philippines, and 1,650 of the regulars, who were entitled to be mustered out after the ratification of the treaty of peace. They voluntarily remained at the front until their places could be filled by new troops. They were returned home in the order in which they went to Manila, and are now all of them out of the service and in the ranks of citizenship. I recommend that the Congress provide a special medal of honor for the volunteers, regulars, sailors, and marines on duty in the Philippines who voluntarily remained in the service after their terms of enlistment had expired.

By the act of March 2, 1899, Congress gave authority to increase the Regular Army to a maximum not exceeding 65,000 enlisted men, and to enlist a force of 35,000 volunteers, to be recruited from the country at large. By virtue of this authority the Regular Army has been increased to the number of 61,999 enlisted men and 2,248 officers, and new volunteer regiments have been organized aggregating 33,050 enlisted men and 1,524 officers. Two of these volunteer regiments are made up of colored men, with colored line officers. The new troops to take the places of those returning from the Philippines have been transported to Manila to the number of 581 officers and 26,322 enlisted men of the Regular Army and 594 officers and 15,388 enlisted men of the new volunteer force, while 504 officers and 14,119 men of the volunteer force are on the ocean *en route* to Manila.

The force now in Manila consists of 905 officers and 30,578 regulars, and 594 officers and 15,388 of the volunteers, making an aggregate of 1,499 officers and 45,966 men. When the troops now under orders shall reach Manila the force in the archipelago will comprise

2,051 officers and 63,483 men. The muster out of the great volunteer army organized for the Spanish War and the creation of a new army, the transportation from Manila to San Francisco of those entitled to discharge and the transportation of the new troops to take their places have been a work of great magnitude well and ably done, for which too much credit cannot be given the War Department.

During the past year we have reduced our force in Cuba and Puerto Rico. In Cuba we now have 334 officers and 10,796 enlisted men; in Puerto Rico, 87 officers and 2,855 enlisted men and a battalion of 400 men composed of native Puerto Ricans; while stationed throughout the United States are 910 officers and 17,317 men, and in Hawaii 12 officers and 453 enlisted men.

The operations of the Army are fully presented in the report of the Secretary of War. I cannot withhold from officers and men the highest commendation for their soldierly conduct in trying situations, their willing sacrifices for their country, and the integrity and ability with which they have performed unusual and difficult duties in our island possessions.

In the organization of the volunteer regiments authorized by the act of March 2, 1899, it was found that no provision had been made for chaplains. This omission was doubtless from inadvertence. I recommend the early authorization for the appointment of one chaplain for each of said regiments. These regiments are now in the Philippines, and it is important that immediate action be had.

In restoring peaceful conditions, orderly rule, and civic progress in Cuba, Puerto Rico, and, so far as practicable, in the Philippines, the rehabilitation of the postal service has been an essential and important part of the work. It became necessary to provide mail facilities both for our forces of occupation and for the native population. To meet this requirement has involved a substantial reconstruction. The existing systems were so fragmentary, defective, and inadequate that a new and comprehensive organization had to be created. American trained officials have been assigned to the directing and executive positions, while natives have been chiefly employed in making up the body of the force. In working out this plan the merit rule has been rigorously and faithfully applied.

The appointment of Director-General of Posts of Cuba was given to an expert who had been Chief Post-Office Inspector and Assistant Postmaster-General, and who united large experience with administrative capacity. For the postmastership at Havana the range of skilled and available men was scanned, and the choice fell upon one who had been twenty years in the service as deputy postmaster and postmaster of a large city. This principle governed and determined the selection of the American officials sent not only to Cuba, but to Puerto Rico and the Philippines, and they were instructed to apply it so far as practicable in the employment of the natives as minor postmasters and clerks.   The postal system in Cuba, though remaining under the general guidance of the Postmaster-General, was made essentially independent.   It was felt that it should not be a burden upon the postal service of the United States, and provision was made that any deficit in the postal revenue should be a charge upon the general revenues of the island.

Though Puerto Rico and the Philippines hold a different relation to the United States, yet, for convenience of administration, the same principle of an autonomous system has been extended to them. The development of the service in all of the islands has been rapid and successful.   It has moved forward on American lines, with free delivery, money order, and registry systems, and has given the people mail facilities far greater and more reliable than any they have ever before enjoyed.   It is thus not only a vital agency of industrial, social, and business progress, but an important influence in diffusing a just understanding of the true spirit and character of American administration.

The domestic postal service continues to grow with extraordinary rapidity.   The expenditures and the revenues will each exceed $100,000,000 during the current year.   Fortunately, since the revival of prosperous times the revenues have grown much faster than the expenditures, and there is every indication that a short period will witness the obliteration of the annual deficit.   In this connection the report of the Postmaster-General embodies a statement of some evils which have grown up outside of the contemplation of law in the treatment of some classes of mail matter which wrongly exercise the privilege of the pound rate, and shows that if this matter had been properly classified and had paid the rate which it should have paid, instead of a postal deficit for the last fiscal year of $6,610,000, there would have been on one basis a surplus of $17,637,570, and on another of $5,733,836.   The reform thus suggested, in the opinion of the Postmaster-General, would not only put the postal service at once on a self-sustaining basis, but would permit great and valuable improvements, and I commend the subject to the consideration of the Congress.

The Navy has maintained the spirit and high efficiency which have always characterized that service, and has lost none of the gallantry in heroic action which has signalized its brilliant and glorious past. The Nation has equal pride in its early and later achievements.   Its habitual readiness for every emergency has won the confidence and admiration of the country.   The people are interested in the continued preparation and prestige of the Navy and will justify liberal appropriations for its maintenance and improvement. The officers have shown peculiar adaptation for the performance of new and delicate duties which our recent war has imposed.

It cannot be doubted that Congress will at once make necessary provision for the armor plate for the vessels now under contract and building. Its attention is respectfully called to the report of the Secretary of the Navy, in which the subject is fully presented. I unite in his recommendation that the Congress enact such special legislation as may be necessary to enable the Department to make contracts early in the coming year for armor of the best quality that can be obtained in this country for the *Maine*, *Ohio*, and *Missouri*, and that the provision of the act of March 3, 1899, limiting the price of armor to $300 per ton be removed.

In the matter of naval construction Italy and Japan, of the great powers, laid down less tonnage in the year 1899 than this country, and Italy alone has less tonnage under construction. I heartily concur in the recommendations for the increase of the Navy, as suggested by the Secretary.

Our future progress and prosperity depend upon our ability to equal, if not surpass, other nations in the enlargement and advance of science, industry, and commerce. To invention we must turn as one of the most powerful aids to the accomplishment of such a result. The attention of the Congress is directed to the report of the Commissioner of Patents, in which will be found valuable suggestions and recommendations.

On the 30th of June, 1899, the pension roll of the United States numbered 991,519. These include the pensioners of the Army and Navy in all our wars. The number added to the rolls during the year was 40,991. The number dropped by reason of death, remarriage, minors by legal limitation, failure to claim within three years, and other causes, was 43,186, and the number of claims disallowed was 107,919. During the year 89,054 pension certificates were issued, of which 37,077 were for new or original pensions. The amount disbursed for army and navy pensions during the year was $138,355,052.95, which was $1,651,461.61 less than the sum of the appropriations.

The Grand Army of the Republic at its recent national encampment held in Philadelphia has brought to my attention and to that of the Congress the wisdom and justice of a modification of the third section of the act of June 27, 1890, which provides pensions for the widows of officers and enlisted men who served ninety days or more during the War of the Rebellion and were honorably discharged, provided that such widows are without other means of support than their daily labor and were married to the soldier, sailor, or marine on account of whose service they claim pension prior to the date of the act.

The present holding of the Department is that if the widow's income aside from ner aaily labor does not exceed in amount what her
pension would be, to wit, $96 per annum, she would be deemed to
be without other means of support than her daily labor, and would
be entitled to a pension under this act; while if the widow's income
independent or the amount received by her as the result of her daily
labor exceeds $96, she would not be pensionable under the act. i
am advised by the Commissioner of Pensions that the amount of the
income allowed before title to pension would be barred has varied
widely under different administrations of the Pension Office, as well
as during different periods of the same administration, and has been
the cause of just complaint and criticism.

With the approval of the Secretary of the Interior the Commissioner of Pensions recommends that, in order to make the practice
at all times uniform and to do justice to the dependent widow, the
amount of income allowed independent of the proceeds of her daily
labor should be not less than $250 per annum, and he urges that the
Congress shall so amend the act as to permit the Pension Office to
grant pensionable status to widows under the terms of the third section of the act of June 27, 1890, whose income aside from the proceeds of daily labor is not in excess of $250 per annum. I believe
this to be a simple act of justice and heartily recommend it.

The Dawes Commission reports that gratifying progress has been
made in its work during the preceding year. The field-work of enrollment of four of the nations has been completed. I recommend
that Congress at an early day make liberal appropriation for educational purposes in the Indian Territory.

In accordance with the act of Congress approved March 3, 1899.
the preliminary work in connection with the Twelfth Census is now
fully under way. The officers required for the proper administration
of the duties imposed have been selected. The provision for securing a proper enumeration of the population, as well as to secure
evidence of the industrial growth of the Nation, is broader and more
comprehensive than any similar legislation in the past. The Director
advises that every needful effort is being made to push this great
work to completion in the time limited by the statute. It is believed
that the Twelfth Census will emphasize our remarkable advance in
all that pertains to national progress.

Under the authority of the act of Congress approved July 7, 1898,
the commission consisting of the Secretary of the Treasury, the
Attorney-General, and the Secretary of the Interior has made an
agreement of settlement, which has had my approval, of the indebtedness to the Government growing out of the issue of bonds to aid
in the construction of the Central Pacific and Western Pacific railroads. The agreement secures to the Government the principal and

interest of said bonds, amounting to $58,812,715.48. There has been paid thereon $11,762,543.12, which has been covered into the Treasury, and the remainder, payable within ten years, with interest at the rate of 3 per cent per annum, payable semiannually, is secured by the deposit of an equal amount of first-mortgage bonds of the Pacific Railway companies. The amounts paid and secured to be paid to the Government on account of the Pacific Railroad subsidy claims are:

Union Pacific, cash	$58,448,223.75
Kansas Pacific, cash	6,303,000.00
Central and Western Pacific, cash	11,798,314.14
Notes, secured	47,050,172.36
Kansas Pacific — dividends for deficiency due United States, cash	821,897.70
Making a total of	124,421,607.95

The whole indebtedness was about $130,000,000, more than half of which consisted of accrued interest, for which sum the Government has realized the entire amount less about $6,000,000 within a period of two years.

On June 30, 1898, there were thirty forest reservations (exclusive of the Afognak Forest and Fish Culture Reserve in Alaska), embracing an estimated area of 40,719,474 acres. During the past year two of the existing forest reserves, the Trabuco Canyon (California) and Black Hills (South Dakota and Wyoming), have been considerably enlarged, the area of the Mount Rainier Reserve, in the State of Washington, has been somewhat reduced, and six additional reserves have been established, namely, the San Francisco Mountains (Arizona), the Black Mesa (Arizona), Lake Tahoe (California), Gallatin (Montana), Gila River (New Mexico), and Fish Lake (Utah), the total estimated area of which is 5,205,775 acres. This makes at the present time a total of thirty-six forest reservations, embracing an estimated area of 46,021,899 acres. This estimated area is the aggregated areas within the boundaries of the reserves. The lands actually reserved are, however, only the vacant public lands therein, and these have been set aside and reserved for sale or settlement in order that they may be of the greatest use to the people.

Protection of the national forests, inaugurated by the Department of the Interior in 1897, has been continued during the past year and much has been accomplished in the way of preventing forest fires and the protection of the timber. There are now large tracts covered by forests which will eventually be reserved and set apart for forest uses. Until that can be done Congress should increase the appropriations for the work of protecting the forests.

The Department of Agriculture is constantly consulting the needs of producers in all the States and Territories. It is introducing seeds and plants of great value and promoting fuller diversification of crops. Grains, grasses, fruits, legumes, and vegetables are imported for all parts of the United States. Under this encouragement the sugar-beet factory multiplies in the North and far West, semitropical plants are sent to the South, and congenial climates are sought for the choice productions of the far East. The hybridizing of fruit trees and grains is conducted in the search for varieties adapted to exacting conditions. The introduction of tea gardens into the Southern States promises to provide employment for idle hands, as well as to supply the home market with tea. The subject of irrigation where it is of vital importance to the people is being carefully studied, steps are being taken to reclaim injured or abandoned lands, and information for the people along these lines is being printed and distributed.

Markets are being sought and opened up for surplus farm and factory products in Europe and in Asia. The outlook for the education of the young farmer through agricultural college and experiment station, with opportunity given to specialize in the Department of Agriculture, is very promising. The people of Hawaii, Puerto Rico, and the Philippine Islands should be helped, by the establishment of experiment stations, to a more scientific knowledge of the production of coffee, india rubber, and other tropical products, for which there is demand in the United States.

There is widespread interest in the improvement of our public highways at the present time, and the Department of Agriculture is co-operating with the people in each locality in making the best possible roads from local material and in experimenting with steel tracks. A more intelligent system of managing the forests of the country is being put in operation and a careful study of the whole forestry problem is being conducted throughout the United States. A very extensive and complete exhibit of the agricultural and horticultural products of the United States is being prepared for the Paris Exposition.

On the 10th of December, 1898, the treaty of peace between the United States and Spain was signed. It provided, among other things, that Spain should cede to the United States the archipelago known as the Philippine Islands, that the United States should pay to Spain the sum of twenty millions of dollars, and that the civil rights and political status of the native inhabitants of the territories thus ceded to the United States should be determined by the Congress. The treaty was ratified by the Senate on the 6th of February, 1899, and by the Government of Spain on the 19th of March following. The ratifications were exchanged on the 11th of April and the treaty publicly proclaimed. On the 2d of March the Congress voted the sum contemplated by the treaty, and the amount was paid over to the Spanish Government on the 1st of May.

In this manner the Philippines came to the United States. The islands were ceded by the Government of Spain, which had been in undisputed possession of them for centuries. They were accepted not merely by our authorized commissioners in Paris, under the direction of the Executive, but by the constitutional and well-considered action of the representatives of the people of the United States in both Houses of Congress. I had every reason to believe, and I still believe that this transfer of sovereignty was in accordance with the wishes and the aspirations of the great mass of the Filipino people.

From the earliest moment no opportunity was lost of assuring the people of the islands of our ardent desire for their welfare and of the intention of this Government to do everything possible to advance their interests. In my order of the 19th of May, 1898, the commander of the military expedition dispatched to the Philippines was instructed to declare that we came not to make war upon the people of that country, "nor upon any party or faction among them, but to protect them in their homes, in their employments, and in their personal and religious rights." That there should be no doubt as to the paramount authority there, on the 17th of August it was directed that "there must be no joint occupation with the insurgents"; that the United States must preserve the peace and protect persons and property within the territory occupied by their military and naval forces; that the insurgents and all others must recognize the military occupation and authority of the United States. As early as December 4, before the cession, and in anticipation of that event, the commander in Manila was urged to restore peace and tranquillity and to undertake the establishment of a beneficent government, which should afford the fullest security for life and property.

On the 21st of December, after the treaty was signed, the commander of the forces of occupation was instructed "to announce and proclaim in the most public manner that we come, not as invaders and conquerors, but as friends to protect the natives in their homes, in their employments, and in their personal and religious rights." On the same day, while ordering General Otis to see that the peace should be preserved in Iloilo, he was admonished that: "It is most important that there should be no conflict with the insurgents." On the 1st day of January, 1899, urgent orders were reiterated that the kindly intentions of this Government should be in every possible way communicated to the insurgents.

On the 21st of January I announced my intention of dispatching to Manila a commission composed of three gentlemen of the highest character and distinction, thoroughly acquainted with the Orient, who, in association with Admiral Dewey and Major-General Otis,

were instructed "to facilitate the most humane and effective exten
sion of authority throughout the islands, and to secure with the least
possible delay the benefits of a wise and generous protection of life
and property to the inhabitants." These gentlemen were Dr. Jacob
Gould Schurman, president of Cornell University; the Hon. Charles
Denby, for many years minister to China, and Prof. Dean C. Worcester, of the University of Michigan, who had made a most careful
study of life in the Philippines. While the treaty of peace was
under consideration in the Senate, these Commissioners set out on
their mission of good will and liberation. Their character was a
sufficient guaranty of the beneficent purpose with which they went,
even if they had not borne the positive instructions of this Government, which made their errand pre-eminently one of peace and
friendship.

But before their arrival at Manila the sinister ambition of a few
leaders of the Filipinos had created a situation full of embarrassment
for us and most grievous in its consequences to themselves. The
clear and impartial preliminary report of the Commissioners, which I
transmit herewith, gives so lucid and comprehensive a history of the
present insurrectionary movement that the story need not be here
repeated. It is enough to say that the claim of the rebel leader that
he was promised independence by an officer of the United States in
return for his assistance has no foundation in fact and is categorically
denied by the very witnesses who were called to prove it. The most
the insurgent leader hoped for when he came back to Manila was
the liberation of the islands from the Spanish control, which they
had been laboring for years without success to throw off.

The prompt accomplishment of this work by the American Army
and Navy gave him other ideas and ambitions, and insidious suggestions from various quarters perverted the purposes and intentions
with which he had taken up arms. No sooner had our army captured Manila than the Filipino forces began to assume an attitude of
suspicion and hostility which the utmost efforts of our officers and
troops were unable to disarm or modify. Their kindness and forbearance were taken as a proof of cowardice. The aggressions of
the Filipinos continually increased until finally, just before the time
set by the Senate of the United States for a vote upon the treaty, an
attack, evidently prepared in advance, was made all along the American lines, which resulted in a terribly destructive and sanguinary
repulse of the insurgents.

Ten days later an order of the insurgent government was issued
to its adherents who had remained in Manila, of which General Otis
justly observes that "for barbarous intent it is unequaled in modern
times." It directs that at 8 o'clock on the night of the 15th of February the "territorial militia" shall come together in the streets of

San Pedro armed with their *bolos*, with guns and ammunition where convenient; that Filipino families only shall be respected; but that all other individuals, of whatever race they may be, shall be exterminated without any compassion, after the extermination of the army of occupation, and adds: "Brothers, we must avenge ourselves on the Americans and exterminate them, that we may take our revenge for the infamies and treacheries which they have committed upon us. Have no compassion upon them; attack with vigor." A copy of this fell by good fortune into the hands of our officers and they were able to take measures to control the rising, which was actually attempted on the night of February 22, a week later than was originally contemplated. Considerable numbers of armed insurgents entered the city by waterways and swamps and in concert with confederates inside attempted to destroy Manila by fire. They were kept in check during the night and the next day driven out of the city with heavy loss.

This was the unhappy condition of affairs which confronted our Commissioners on their arrival in Manila. They had come with the hope and intention of co-operating with Admiral Dewey and Major-General Otis in establishing peace and order in the archipelago and the largest measure of self-government compatible with the true welfare of the people. What they actually found can best be set forth in their own words:

> Deplorable as war is, the one in which we are now engaged was unavoidable by us. We were attacked by a bold, adventurous, and enthusiastic army. No alternative was left to us except ignominious retreat.
>
> It is not to be conceived of that any American would have sanctioned the surrender of Manila to the insurgents. Our obligations to other nations and to the friendly Filipinos and to ourselves and our flag demanded that force should be met by force. Whatever the future of the Philippines may be, there is no course open to us now except the prosecution of the war until the insurgents are reduced to submission. The Commission is of the opinion that there has been no time since the destruction of the Spanish squadron by Admiral Dewey when it was possible to withdraw our forces from the island either with honor to ourselves or with safety to the inhabitants.

The course thus clearly indicated has been unflinchingly pursued. The rebellion must be put down. Civil government cannot be thoroughly established until order is restored. With a devotion and gallantry worthy of its most brilliant history, the Army, ably and loyally assisted by the Navy, has carried on this unwelcome but most righteous campaign with richly deserved success. The noble self-sacrifice with which our soldiers and sailors whose terms of service had expired refused to avail themselves of their right to return home as long as they were needed at the front forms one of the brightest pages in our annals. Although their operations have been somewhat interrupted and checked by a rainy season of unusual violence and duration, they have gained ground steadily in every direction, and now look forward confidently to a speedy completion of their task.

The unfavorable circumstances connected with an active campaign have not been permitted to interfere with the equally important work of reconstruction. Again I invite your attention to the report of the Commissioners for the interesting and encouraging details of the work already accomplished in the establishment of peace and order and the inauguration of self-governing municipal life in many portions of the archipelago. A notable beginning has been made in the establishment of a government in the island of Negros which is deserving of special consideration. This was the first island to accept American sovereignty. Its people unreservedly proclaimed allegiance to the United States and adopted a constitution looking to the establishment of a popular government. It was impossible to guarantee to the people of Negros that the constitution so adopted should be the ultimate form of government. Such a question, under the treaty with Spain and in accordance with our own Constitution and laws, came exclusively within the jurisdiction of the Congress. The government actually set up by the inhabitants of Negros eventually proved unsatisfactory to the natives themselves. A new system was put into force by order of the Major-General Commanding the Department, of which the following are the most important elements:

It was ordered that the government of the island of Negros should consist of a military governor appointed by the United States military governor of the Philippines, and a civil governor and an advisory council elected by the people. The military governor was authorized to appoint secretaries of the treasury, interior, agriculture, public instruction, an attorney-general, and an auditor. The seat of government was fixed at Bacolod. The military governor exercises the supreme executive power. He is to see that the laws are executed, appoint to office, and fill all vacancies in office not otherwise provided for, and may, with the approval of the military governor of the Philippines, remove any officer from office. The civil governor advises the military governor on all public civil questions and presides over the advisory council. He, in general, performs the duties which are performed by secretaries of state in our own system of government.

The advisory council consists of eight members elected by the people within territorial limits which are defined in the order of the commanding general.

The times and places of holding elections are to be fixed by the military governor of the island of Negros. The qualifications or voters are as follows:

(1) A voter must be a male citizen of the island of Negros. (2) Of the age of 21 years. (3) He shall be able to speak, read, and write the English, Spanish, or Visayan language, or he must own real property worth $500, or pay a rental on real property of the value of $1,000. (4) He must have resided in the island not less than one year preceding, and in the district in which he offers to register as a voter not less than three months immediately preceding the time he offers to register. (5) He must register at a time fixed by law before voting. (6) Prior to such registration he shall have paid all taxes due by him to the Government. Provided, that no insane person shall be allowed to register or vote.

The military governor has the right to veto all bills or resolutions adopted by the advisory council, and his veto is final if not disapproved by the military governor of the Philippines.

The advisory council discharges all the ordinary duties of a legislature. The usual duties pertaining to said offices are to be performed by the secretaries of the treasury, interior, agriculture, public instruction, the attorney-general, and the auditor.

The judicial power is vested in three judges, who are to be appointed by the military governor of the island. Inferior courts are to be established.

Free public schools are to be established throughout the populous districts of the island, in which the English language shall be taught, and this subject will receive the careful consideration of the advisory council.

The burden of government must be distributed equally and equitably among the people. The military authorities will collect and receive the customs revenue, and will control postal matters and Philippine inter-island trade and commerce.

The military governor, subject to the approval of the military governor of the Philippines, determines all questions not specifically provided for and which do not come under the jurisdiction of the advisory council.

The authorities of the Sulu Islands have accepted the succession of the United States to the rights of Spain, and our flag floats over that territory. On the 10th of August, 1899, Brig.-Gen. J. C. Bates, United States Volunteers, negotiated an agreement with the Sultan and his principal chiefs, which I transmit herewith. By Article I the sovereignty of the United States over the whole archipelago of Jolo and its dependencies is declared and acknowledged.

The United States flag will be used in the archipelago and its dependencies, on land and sea. Piracy is to be suppressed, and the Sultan agrees to co-operate heartily with the United States authorities to that end and to make every possible effort to arrest and bring

to justice all persons engaged in piracy.   All trade in domestic products of the archipelago of Jolo when carried on with any part of the
Philippine Islands and under the American flag shall be free, unlimited, and undutiable.   The United States will give full protection
to the Sultan in case any foreign nation should attempt to impose
upon him.   The United States will not sell the island of Jolo or any
other island of the Jolo archipelago to any foreign nation without
the consent of the Sultan.   Salaries for the Sultan and his associates
in the administration of the islands have been agreed upon to the
amount of $760 monthly.

Article X provides that any slave in the archipelago of Jolo shall
have the right to purchase freedom by paying to the master the usual
market value.   The agreement by General Bates was made subject
to confirmation by the President and to future modifications by the
consent of the parties in interest.   I have confirmed said agreement,
subject to the action of the Congress, and with the reservation,
which I have directed shall be communicated to the Sultan of Jolo,
that this agreement is not to be deemed in any way to authorize or
give the consent of the United States to the existence of slavery in
the Sulu archipelago.   I communicate these facts to the Congress for
its information and action.

Everything indicates that with the speedy suppression of the
Tagalo rebellion life in the archipelago will soon resume its ordinary
course under the protection of our sovereignty, and the people of
those favored islands will enjoy a prosperity and a freedom which
they have never before known.   Already hundreds of schools are
open and filled with children.   Religious freedom is sacredly assured
and enjoyed.   The courts are dispensing justice.   Business is beginning to circulate in its accustomed channels.   Manila, whose inhabitants were fleeing to the country a few months ago, is now a populous
and thriving mart of commerce.   The earnest and unremitting
endeavors of the Commission and the Admiral and Major-General
Commanding the Department of the Pacific to assure the people of
the beneficent intentions of this Government have had their legitimate effect in convincing the great mass of them that peace and
safety and prosperity and stable government can only be found in a
loyal acceptance of the authority of the United States.

The future government of the Philippines rests with the Congress
of the United States.   Few graver responsibilities have ever been
confided to us.   If we accept them in a spirit worthy of our race and
our traditions, a great opportunity comes with them.   The islands
lie under the shelter of our flag.   They are ours by every title of
law and equity.   They cannot be abandoned.   If we desert them we
leave them at once to anarchy and finally to barbarism.   We fling
them, a golden apple of discord, among the rival powers, no one of

which could permit another to seize them unquestioned. Their rich plains and valleys would be the scene of endless strife and bloodshed. The advent of Dewey's fleet in Manila Bay instead of being, as we hope, the dawn of a new day of freedom and progress, will have been the beginning of an era of misery and violence worse than any which has darkened their unhappy past. The suggestion has been made that we could renounce our authority over the islands and, giving them independence, could retain a protectorate over them. This proposition will not be found, I am sure, worthy of your serious attention. Such an arrangement would involve at the outset a cruel breach of faith. It would place the peaceable and loyal majority, who ask nothing better than to accept our authority, at the mercy of the minority of armed insurgents. It would make us responsible for the acts of the insurgent leaders and give us no power to control them. It would charge us with the task of protecting them against each other and defending them against any foreign power with which they chose to quarrel. In short, it would take from the Congress of the United States the power of declaring war and vest that tremendous prerogative in the Tagal leader of the hour.

It does not seem desirable that I should recommend at this time a specific and final form of government for these islands. When peace shall be restored it will be the duty of Congress to construct a plan of government which shall establish and maintain freedom and order and peace in the Philippines. The insurrection is still existing, and when it terminates further information will be required as to the actual condition of affairs before inaugurating a permanent scheme of civil government. The full report of the Commission, now in preparation, will contain information and suggestions which will be of value to Congress, and which I will transmit as soon as it is completed. As long as the insurrection continues the military arm must necessarily be supreme. But there is no reason why steps should not be taken from time to time to inaugurate governments essentially popular in their form as fast as territory is held and controlled by our troops. To this end I am considering the advisability of the return of the Commission, or such of the members thereof as can be secured, to aid the existing authorities and facilitate this work throughout the islands. I have believed that reconstruction should not begin by the establishment of one central civil government for all the islands, with its seat at Manila, but rather that the work should be commenced by building up from the bottom, first establishing municipal governments and then provincial governments, a central government at last to follow.

Until Congress shall have made known the formal expression of its will I shall use the authority vested in me by the Constitution and the statutes to uphold the sovereignty of the United States in those distant islands as in all other places where our flag rightfully floats. I shall put at the disposal of the Army and Navy all the means which the liberality of Congress and the people have provided to cause this unprovoked and wasteful insurrection to cease. If any orders of mine were required to insure the merciful conduct of military and naval operations, they would not be lacking; but every step of the progress of our troops has been marked by a humanity which has surprised even the misguided insurgents. The truest kindness to them will be a swift and effective defeat of their present leader. The hour of victory will be the hour of clemency and reconstruction.

No effort will be spared to build up the waste places desolated by war and by long years of misgovernment. We shall not wait for the end of strife to begin the beneficent work. We shall continue, as we have begun, to open the schools and the churches, to set the courts in operation, to foster industry and trade and agriculture, and in every way in our power to make these people whom Providence has brought within our jurisdiction feel that it is their liberty and not our power, their welfare and not our gain, we are seeking to enhance. Our flag has never waved over any community but in blessing. I believe the Filipinos will soon recognize the fact that it has not lost its gift of benediction in its world-wide journey to their shores.

Some embarrassment in administration has occurred by reason of the peculiar status which the Hawaiian Islands at present occupy under the joint resolution of annexation approved July 7, 1898. While by that resolution the Republic of Hawaii as an independent nation was extinguished, its separate sovereignty destroyed, and its property and possessions vested in the United States, yet a complete establishment for its government under our system was not effected. While the municipal laws of the islands not enacted for the fulfillment of treaties and not inconsistent with the joint resolution or contrary to the Constitution of the United States or any of its treaties remain in force, yet these laws relate only to the social and internal affairs of the islands, and do not touch many subjects of importance which are of a broader national character. For example, the Hawaiian Republic was divested of all title to the public lands in the islands, and is not only unable to dispose of lands to settlers desiring to take up homestead sites, but is without power to give complete title in cases where lands have been entered upon under lease or other conditions which carry with them the right to the purchaser, lessee, or settler to have a full title granted to him upon compliance with the conditions prescribed by law or by his particular agreement of entry.

Questions of doubt and difficulty have also arisen with reference to the collection of tonnage tax on vessels coming from Hawaiian ports; with reference to the status of Chinese in the islands, their entrance and exit therefrom; as to patents and copyrights; as to the register of vessels under the navigation laws; as to the necessity of holding elections in accordance with the provisions of the Hawaiian statutes for the choice of various officers, and as to several other matters of detail touching the interests both of the island and of the Federal Government.

By the resolution of annexation the President was directed to appoint five commissioners to recommend to Congress such legislation concerning the islands as they should deem necessary or proper. These commissioners were duly appointed and after a careful investigation and study of the system of laws and government prevailing in the islands, and of the conditions existing there, they prepared a bill to provide a government under the title of "The Territory of Hawaii." The report of the Commission, with the bill which they prepared, was transmitted by me to Congress on December 6, 1898, but the bill still awaits final action.

The people of these islands are entitled to the benefits and privileges of our Constitution, but in the absence of any act of Congress providing for Federal courts in the islands, and for a procedure by which appeals, writs of error, and other judicial proceedings necessary for the enforcement of civil rights may be prosecuted, they are powerless to secure their enforcement by the judgment of the courts of the United States. It is manifestly important, therefore, that an act shall be passed as speedily as possible erecting these islands into a judicial district, providing for the appointment of a judge and other proper officers and methods of procedure in appellate proceedings, and that the government of this newly acquired territory under the Federal Constitution shall be fully defined and provided for.

A necessity for immediate legislative relief exists in the Territory of Alaska. Substantially the only law providing a civil government for this Territory is the act of May 17, 1884. This is meager in its provisions, and is fitted only for the administration of affairs in a country sparsely inhabited by civilized people and unimportant in trade and production, as was Alaska at the time this act was passed. The increase in population by immigration during the past few years, consequent upon the discovery of gold, has produced such a condition as calls for more ample facilities for local self-government and more numerous conveniences of civil and judicial administration. Settlements have grown up in various places, constituting in point of population and business cities of thousands of inhabitants, yet there is no provision of law under which a municipality can be organized or maintained.

In some localities the inhabitants have met together and volun-

tarily formed a municipal organization for the purposes of local government, adopting the form of a municipal constitution and charter,
under which said officials have been appointed; and ordinances
creating and regulating a police force, a fire department, a department of health, and making provision for the care of the insane and
indigent poor and sick and for public schools, have been passed.
These proceedings and the ordinances passed by such municipalities
are without statutory authority and have no sanction, except as they
are maintained by the popular sentiment of the community. There
is an entire absence of authority to provide the ordinary instruments
of local police control and administration, the population consisting
of the usual percentage of lawless adventurers of the class that
always flock to new fields of enterprise or discovery, and under circumstances which require more than ordinary provision for the maintenance of peace, good order, and lawful conduct.

The whole vast area of Alaska comprises but one judicial district,
with one judge, one marshal, and one district attorney, yet the civil
and criminal business has more than doubled within the past year,
and is many times greater both in volume and importance than it was
in 1884. The duties of the judge require him to travel thousands of
miles to discharge his judicial duties at the various places designated
for that purpose. The Territory should be divided into at least two
districts, and an additional judge, district attorney, marshal, and
other appropriate officers be provided.

There is practically no organized form of government in the Territory. There is no authority, except in Congress, to pass any law,
no matter how local or trivial, and the difficulty of conveying to the
Congress an adequate conception and understanding of the various
needs of the people in the different communities is easily understood.
I see no reason why a more complete form of Territorial organization should not be provided. Following the precedent established in
the year 1805, when a temporary government was provided for the
recently acquired territory, then known under the name of Louisiana,
it seems to me that it would be advantageous to confer greater executive power upon the governor and to establish, as was done in the
case of the Territory of Louisiana, a legislative council having power
to adopt ordinances which shall extend to all the rightful subjects of
local legislation, such ordinances not to take effect until reported to
and approved by the Congress if in session, and if that body is not
in session then by the President. In this manner a system of laws
providing for the incorporation and government of towns and cities
having a certain population, giving them the power to establish and
maintain a system of education to be locally supported, and ordinances providing for police, sanitary, and other such purposes, could
be speedily provided. I believe a provision of this kind would be

satisfactory to the people of the Territory. It is probable that the area is too vast and the population too scattered and transitory to make it wise at the present time to provide for an elective legislative body, but the conditions calling for local self-government will undoubtedly very soon exist, and will be facilitated by the measures which I have recommended.

I recommend that legislation to the same end be had with reference to the government of Puerto Rico. The time is ripe for the adoption of a temporary form of government for this island; and many suggestions made with reference to Alaska are applicable also to Puerto Rico.

The system of civil jurisprudence now adopted by the people of this island is described by competent lawyers who are familiar with it, as thoroughly modern and scientific, so far as it relates to matters of internal business, trade, production, and social and private right in general. The cities of the island are governed under charters which probably require very little or no change. So that with relation to matters of local concern and private right, it is not probable that much, if any, legislation is desirable; but with reference to public administration and the relations of the island to the Federal Government, there are many matters which are of pressing urgency. The same necessity exists for legislation on the part of Congress to establish Federal courts and Federal jurisdiction in the island as has been previously pointed out by me with reference to Hawaii. Besides the administration of justice, there are the subjects of the public lands; the control and improvement of rivers and harbors; the control of the waters or streams not navigable, which, under the Spanish law, belonged to the Crown of Spain, and have by the treaty of cession passed to the United States; the immigration of people from foreign countries; the importation of contract labor; the imposition and collection of internal revenue; the application of the navigation laws; the regulation of the current money; the establishment of post-offices and post-roads; the regulation of tariff rates on merchandise imported from the island into the United States; the establishment of ports of entry and delivery; the regulation of patents and copyrights; these, with various other subjects which rest entirely within the power of the Congress, call for careful consideration and immediate action.

It must be borne in mind that since the cession Puerto Rico has been denied the principal markets she had long enjoyed and our tariffs have been continued against her products as when she was under Spanish sovereignty. The markets of Spain are closed to her products except upon terms to which the commerce of all nations is subjected. The island of Cuba, which used to buy her cattle and tobacco without customs duties, now imposes the same duties upon those products as from any other country entering her ports. She has therefore lost her free intercourse with Spain and Cuba without any compensating benefits in this market. Her coffee was little known and not in use by our people, and therefore there was no demand here for this, one of her chief products. The markets of the United States should be opened up to her products. Our plain duty is to abolish all customs tariffs between the United States and Puerto Rico and give her products free access to our markets.

As a result of the hurricane which swept over Puerto Rico on the 8th of August, 1899, over 100,000 people were reduced to absolute destitution, without homes, and deprived of the necessaries of life. To the appeal of the War Department the people of the United States made prompt and generous response. In addition to the private charity of our people, the War Department has expended for the relief of the distressed $392,342.63, which does not include the cost of transportation.

It is desirable that the government of the island under the law of belligerent right, now maintained through the Executive Department, should be superseded by an administration entirely civil in its nature. For present purposes I recommend that Congress pass a law for the organization of a temporary government, which shall provide for the appointment by the President, subject to confirmation by the Senate, of a governor and such other officers as the general administration of the island may require, and that for legislative purposes upon subjects of a local nature not partaking of a Federal character a legislative council, composed partly of Puerto Ricans and partly of citizens of the United States, shall be nominated and appointed by the President, subject to confirmation by the Senate, their acts to be subject to the approval of the Congress or the President prior to going into effect. In the municipalities and other local subdivisions I recommend that the principle of local self-government be applied at once, so as to enable the intelligent citizens of the island to participate in their own government and to learn by practical experience the duties and requirements of a self-contained and self-governing people. I have not thought it wise to commit the entire government of the island to officers selected by the people, because I doubt whether in habits, training, and experience they are such as to fit them to exercise at once so large a degree of self-government; but it is my judgment and expectation that they will soon arrive at an attainment of experience and wisdom and self-control that will justify conferring upon them a much larger participation in the choice of their insular officers.

The fundamental requirement for these people, as for all people, is education. The free schoolhouse is the best preceptor for citizenship. In the introduction of modern educational methods care, however, must be exercised that changes be not made too abruptly and that the history and racial peculiarities of the inhabitants shall be given due weight. Systems of education in these new possessions founded upon common-sense methods, adapted to existing conditions and looking to the future moral and industrial advancement of the people, will commend to them in a peculiarly effective manner the blessings of free government.

The love of law and the sense of obedience and submission to the lawfully constituted judicial tribunals are embedded in the hearts of our people, and any violation of these sentiments and disregard of their obligations justly arouses public condemnation. The guaranties of life, liberty, and of civil rights should be faithfully upheld; the right of trial by jury respected and defended. The rule of the courts should assure the public of the prompt trial of those charged with criminal offenses, and upon conviction the punishment should be commensurate with the enormity of the crime.

Those who, in disregard of law and the public peace, unwilling to await the judgment of court and jury, constitute themselves judges and executioners should not escape the severest penalties for their crimes.

What I said in my inaugural address of March 4, 1897, I now repeat:

> The constituted authorities must be cheerfully and vigorously upheld. Lynchings must not be tolerated in a great and civilized country like the United States. Courts, not mobs, must execute the penalties of the laws. The preservation of public order, the right of discussion, the integrity of courts, and the orderly administration of justice must continue forever the rock of safety upon which our Government securely rests.

In accordance with the act of Congress providing for an appropriate national celebration in the year 1900 of the establishment of the seat of Government in the District of Columbia, I have appointed a committee, consisting of the governors of all the States and Territories of the United States, who have been invited to assemble in the city of Washington on the 21st of December, 1899, which, with the committees of the Congress and the District of Columbia, are charged with the proper conduct of this celebration.

Congress at its last session appropriated five thousand dollars "to enable the Chief of Engineers of the Army to continue the examination of the subject and to make or secure designs, calculations, and estimates for a memorial bridge from the most convenient point of the Naval Observatory grounds, or adjacent thereto, across the Potomac River to the most convenient point of the Arlington estate property." In accordance with the provisions of this act, the Chief of Engineers has selected four eminent bridge engineers to submit competitive designs for a bridge combining the elements of strength and durability and such architectural embellishment and ornamentation as will fitly apply to the dedication, "A memorial to American patriotism." The designs are now being prepared, and as soon as completed will be submitted to the Congress by the Secretary of War. The proposed bridge would be a convenience to all the people from every part of the country who visit the national cemetery, an ornament to the Capital of the Nation, and forever stand as a monument to American patriotism. I do not doubt that Congress will give to the enterprise still further proof of its favor and approval.

The executive order of May 6, 1896, extending the limits of the classified service, brought within the operation of the civil-service law and rules nearly all of the executive civil service not previously classified.

Some of the inclusions were found wholly illogical and unsuited to the work of the several Departments. The application of the rules to many of the places so included was found to result in friction and embarrassment. After long and very careful consideration, it became evident to the heads of the Departments, responsible for their efficiency, that in order to remove these difficulties and promote an efficient and harmonious administration certain amendments were necessary. These amendments were promulgated by me in executive order dated May 29, 1899.

The principal purpose of the order was to except from competitive examination certain places involving fiduciary responsibilities or duties of a strictly confidential, scientific, or executive character which it was thought might better be filled either by noncompetitive examination, or in the discretion of the appointing officer, than by open competition. These places were comparatively few in number. The order provides for the filling of a much larger number of places, mainly in the outside service of the War Department, by what is known as the registration system, under regulations to be approved by the President, similar to those which have produced such admirable results in the navy-yard service.

All of the amendments had for their main object a more efficient and satisfactory administration of the system of appointments established by the civil-service law. The results attained show that under their operation the public service has improved and that the civil-service system is relieved of many objectionable features which heretofore subjected it to just criticism and the administrative officers to the charge of unbusinesslike methods in the conduct of public affairs. It is believed that the merit system has been greatly strengthened and its permanence assured. It will be my constant aim in the administration of government in our new possessions to make fitness, character, and merit essential to appointment to office, and to give to the capable and deserving inhabitants preference in appointments.

The 14th of December will be the One Hundredth Anniversary of the death of Washington. For a hundred years the Republic has had the priceless advantage of the lofty standard of character and conduct which he bequeathed to the American people. It is an in-heritance which time, instead of wasting, continually increases and enriches. We may justly hope that in the years to come the benig-nant influence of the Father of his Country may be even more potent for good than in the century which is drawing to a close. I have been glad to learn that in many parts of the country the people will fittingly observe this historic anniversary.

Presented to this Congress are great opportunities. With them come great responsibilities. The power confided to us increases the weight of our obligations to the people, and we must be profoundly sensible of them as we contemplate the new and grave problems which confront us. Aiming only at the public good, we cannot err. A right interpretation of the people's will and of duty cannot fail to insure wise measures for the welfare of the islands which have come under the authority of the United States, and inure to the common interest and lasting honor of our country. Never has this Nation had more abundant cause than during the past year for thankfulness to God for manifold blessings and mercies, for which we make rever-ent acknowledgment.

FOURTH ANNUAL MESSAGE.

EXECUTIVE MANSION, *December 3, 1900.*
To the Senate and House of Representatives:

At the outgoing of the old and the incoming of the new century you begin the last session of the Fifty-sixth Congress with evidences on every hand of individual and national prosperity and with proof of the growing strength and increasing power for good of Repub-lican institutions. Your countrymen will join with you in felicita-tion that American liberty is more firmly established than ever before, and that love for it and the determination to preserve it are more universal than at any former period of our history.

The Republic was never so strong, because never so strongly in-trenched in the hearts of the people as now. The Constitution, with few amendments, exists as it left the hands of its authors. The additions which have been made to it proclaim larger freedom and more extended citizenship. Popular government has demonstrated in its one hundred and twenty-four years of trial here its stability and security, and its efficiency as the best instrument of national de-velopment and the best safeguard to human rights.

When the Sixth Congress assembled in November, 1800, the population of the United States was 5,308,483. It is now 76,304,799.

Then we had sixteen States. Now we have forty-five. Then our territory consisted of 909,050 square miles. It is now 3,846,595 square miles. Education, religion, and morality have kept pace with our advancement in other directions, and while extending its power the Government has adhered to its foundation principles and abated none of them in dealing with our new peoples and possessions. A nation so preserved and blessed gives reverent thanks to God and invokes His guidance and the continuance of His care and favor.

In our foreign intercourse the dominant question has been the treatment of the Chinese problem. Apart from this our relations with the powers have been happy.

The recent troubles in China spring from the antiforeign agitation which for the past three years has gained strength in the northern provinces. Their origin lies deep in the character of the Chinese races and in the traditions of their Government. The Taiping rebellion and the opening of Chinese ports to foreign trade and settlement disturbed alike the homogeneity and the seclusion of China.

Meanwhile foreign activity made itself felt in all quarters, not alone on the coast, but along the great river arteries and in the remoter districts, carrying new ideas and introducing new associations among a primitive people which had pursued for centuries a national policy of isolation.

The telegraph and the railway spreading over their land, the steamers plying on their waterways, the merchant and the missionary penetrating year by year farther to the interior, became to the Chinese mind types of an alien invasion, changing the course of their national life and fraught with vague forebodings of disaster to their beliefs and their self-control.

For several years before the present troubles all the resources of foreign diplomacy, backed by moral demonstrations of the physical force of fleets and arms, have been needed to secure due respect for the treaty rights of foreigners and to obtain satisfaction from the responsible authorities for the sporadic outrages upon the persons and property of unoffending sojourners, which from time to time occurred at widely separated points in the northern provinces, as in the case of the outbreaks in Sze-chuen and Shan-tung.

Posting of antiforeign placards became a daily occurrence, which the repeated reprobation of the Imperial power failed to check or punish. These inflammatory appeals to the ignorance and superstition of the masses, mendacious and absurd in their accusations and deeply hostile in their spirit, could not but work cumulative harm. They aimed at no particular class of foreigners; they were impartial in attacking everything foreign.

An outbreak in Shan-tung, in which German missionaries were slain, was the too natural result of these malevolent teachings.

The posting of seditious placards, exhorting to the utter destruction of foreigners and of every foreign thing, continued unrebuked. Hostile demonstrations toward the stranger gained strength by organization.

The sect, commonly styled the Boxers, developed greatly in the provinces north of the Yang-Tse, and with the collusion of many notable officials, including some in the immediate councils of the Throne itself, became alarmingly aggressive. No foreigner's life, outside of the protected treaty ports, was safe. No foreign interest was secure from spoliation.

The diplomatic representatives of the powers in Peking strove in vain to check this movement. Protest was followed by demand and demand by renewed protest, to be met with perfunctory edicts from the Palace and evasive and futile assurances from the Tsung-li Yamen. The circle of the Boxer influence narrowed about Peking, and while nominally stigmatized as seditious, it was felt that its spirit pervaded the capital itself, that the Imperial forces were imbued with its doctrines, and that the immediate counselors of the Empress Dowager were in full sympathy with the antiforeign movement.

The increasing gravity of the conditions in China and the imminence of peril to our own diversified interests in the Empire, as well as to those of all the other treaty governments, were soon appreciated by this Government, causing it profound solicitude. The United States from the earliest days of foreign intercourse with China had followed a policy of peace, omitting no occasions to testify good will, to further the extension of lawful trade, to respect the sovereignty of its Government, and to insure by all legitimate and kindly but earnest means the fullest measure of protection for the lives and property of our law-abiding citizens and for the exercise of their beneficent callings among the Chinese people.

Mindful of this, it was felt to be appropriate that our purposes should be pronounced in favor of such course as would hasten united action of the powers at Peking to promote the administrative reforms so greatly needed for strengthening the Imperial Government and maintaining the integrity of China, in which we believed the whole western world to be alike concerned. To these ends I caused to be addressed to the several powers occupying territory and maintaining spheres of influence in China the circular proposals of 1899, inviting from them declarations of their intentions and views as to the desirability of the adoption of measures insuring the benefits of equality of treatment of all foreign trade throughout China.

With gratifying unanimity the responses coincided in this common policy, enabling me to see in the successful termination of these negotiations proof of the friendly spirit which animates the various powers interested in the untrammeled development of commerce and industry in the Chinese Empire as a source of vast benefit to the whole commercial world.

In this conclusion, which I had the gratification to announce as a completed engagement to the interested powers on March 20, 1900, I hopefully discerned a potential factor for the abatement of the distrust of foreign purposes which for a year past had appeared to inspire the policy of the Imperial Government, and for the effective exertion by it of power and authority to quell the critical antiforeign movement in the northern provinces most immediately influenced by the Manchu sentiment.

Seeking to testify confidence in the willingness and ability of the Imperial administration to redress the wrongs and prevent the evils we suffered and feared, the marine guard, which had been sent to Peking in the autumn of 1899 for the protection of the legation, was withdrawn at the earliest practicable moment, and all pending questions were remitted, as far as we were concerned, to the ordinary resorts of diplomatic intercourse.

The Chinese Government proved, however, unable to check the rising strength of the Boxers and appeared to be a prey to internal dissensions. In the unequal contest the antiforeign influences soon gained the ascendancy under the leadership of Prince Tuan. Organized armies of Boxers, with which the Imperial forces affiliated, held the country between Peking and the coast, penetrated into Manchuria up to the Russian borders, and through their emissaries threatened a like rising throughout northern China.

Attacks upon foreigners, destruction of their property, and slaughter of native converts were reported from all sides. The Tsung-li Yamen, already permeated with hostile sympathies, could make no effective response to the appeals of the legations. At this critical juncture, in the early spring of this year, a proposal was made by the other powers that a combined fleet should be assembled in Chinese waters as a moral demonstration, under cover of which to exact of the Chinese Government respect for foreign treaty rights and the suppression of the Boxers.

The United States, while not participating in the joint demonstration, promptly sent from the Philippines all ships that could be spared for service on the Chinese coast. A small force of marines was landed at Taku and sent to Peking for the protection of the American legation. Other powers took similar action, until some four hundred men were assembled in the capital as legation guards.

Still the peril increased. The legations reported the development of the seditious movement in Peking and the need of increased provision for defense against it. While preparations were in progress for a larger expedition, to strengthen the legation guards and keep the railway open, an attempt of the foreign ships to make a landing at Taku was met by a fire from the Chinese forts. The forts were thereupon shelled by the foreign vessels, the American admiral taking no part in the attack, on the ground that we were not at war with China and that a hostile demonstration might consolidate the antiforeign elements and strengthen the Boxers to oppose the relieving column.

Two days later the Taku forts were captured after a sanguinary conflict. Severance of communication with Peking followed, and a combined force of additional guards, which was advancing to Peking by the Pei-Ho, was checked at Langfang. The isolation of the legations was complete.

The siege and the relief of the legations has passed into undying history. In all the stirring chapter which records the heroism of the devoted band, clinging to hope in the face of despair, and the undaunted spirit that led their relievers through battle and suffering to the goal, it is a memory of which my countrymen may be justly proud that the honor of our flag was maintained alike in the siege and the rescue, and that stout American hearts have again set high, in fervent emulation with true men of other race and language, the indomitable courage that ever strives for the cause of right and justice.

By June 19 the legations were cut off. An identical note from the Yamen ordered each minister to leave Peking, under a promised escort, within twenty-four hours. To gain time they replied, asking prolongation of the time, which was afterwards granted, and requesting an interview with the Tsung-li Yamen on the following day. No reply being received, on the morning of the 20th the German minister, Baron von Ketteler, set out for the Yamen to obtain a response, and on the way was murdered.

An attempt by the legation guard to recover his body was foiled by the Chinese. Armed forces turned out against the legations. Their quarters were surrounded and attacked. The mission compounds were abandoned, their inmates taking refuge in the British legation, where all the other legations and guards gathered for more effective defense. Four hundred persons were crowded in its narrow compass. Two thousand native converts were assembled in a nearby palace under protection of the foreigners. Lines of defense were strengthened, trenches dug, barricades raised, and preparations made to stand a siege, which at once began.

From June 20 until July 17, writes Minister Conger, " there was scarcely an hour during which there was not firing upon some part of our lines and into some of the legations, varying from a single shot to a general and continuous attack along the whole line." Artillery was placed around the legations and on the over-looking palace walls, and thousands of 3-inch shot and shell were fired, destroying some buildings and damaging all. So thickly did the balls rain, that, when the ammunition of the besieged ran low, five quarts of Chinese bullets were gathered in an hour in one compound and recast.

Attempts were made to burn the legations by setting neighboring houses on fire, but the flames were successfully fought off, although the Austrian, Belgian, Italian, and Dutch legations were then and subsequently burned. With the aid of the native converts, directed by the missionaries, to whose helpful co-operation Mr. Conger awards unstinted praise, the British legation was made a veritable fortress. The British minister, Sir Claude MacDonald, was chosen general commander of the defense, with the secretary of the American legation, Mr. E. G. Squiers, as chief of staff.

To save life and ammunition the besieged sparingly returned the incessant fire of the Chinese soldiery, fighting only to repel attack or make an occasional successful sortie for strategic advantage, such as that of fifty-five American, British, and Russian marines led by Captain Myers, of the United States Marine Corps, which resulted in the capture of a formidable barricade on the wall that gravely menaced the American position. It was held to the last, and proved an invaluable acquisition, because commanding the water gate through which the relief column entered.

During the siege the defenders lost 65 killed, 135 wounded, and 7 by disease—the last all children.

On July 14 the besieged had their first communication with the Tsung-li Yamen, from whom a message came inviting to a conference, which was declined. Correspondence, however, ensued and a sort of armistice was agreed upon, which stopped the bombardment and lessened the rifle fire for a time. Even then no protection whatever was afforded, nor any aid given, save to send to the legations a small supply of fruit and three sacks of flour.

Indeed, the only communication had with the Chinese Government related to the occasional delivery or dispatch of a telegram or to the demands of the Tsung-li Yamen for the withdrawal of the legations to the coast under escort. Not only are the protestations of the Chinese Government that it protected and succored the legations positively contradicted, but irresistible proof accumulates that the attacks upon them were made by Imperial troops, regularly uniformed, armed, and officered, belonging to the command of Jung Lu, the Imperial commander in chief. Decrees encouraging the Boxers, organizing them under prominent Imperial officers, provisioning them, and even granting them large sums in the name of the Empress Dowager, are known to exist. Members of the Tsung-li Yamen who counseled protection of the foreigners were beheaded. Even in the distant provinces men suspected of foreign sympathy were put to death, prominent among these being Chang Yen-hoon, formerly Chinese minister in Washington.

With the negotiation of the partial armistice of July 14, a proceeding which was doubtless promoted by the representations of the Chinese envoy in Washington, the way was opened for the conveyance to Mr. Conger of a test message sent by the Secretary of State through the kind offices of Minister Wu Ting-fang. Mr. Conger's reply, dispatched from Peking on July 18 through the same channel, afforded to the outside world the first tidings that the inmates of the legations were still alive and hoping for succor.

This news stimulated the preparations for a joint relief expedition in numbers sufficient to overcome the resistance which for a month had been organizing between Taku and the capital. Reinforcements sent by all the co-operating Governments were constantly arriving. The United States contingent, hastily assembled from the Philippines or dispatched from this country, amounted to some 5,000 men, under the able command first of the lamented Colonel Liscum and afterwards of General Chaffee.

Toward the end of July the movement began. A severe conflict followed at Tientsin, in which Colonel Liscum was killed. The city was stormed and partly destroyed. Its capture afforded the base of operations from which to make the final advance, which began in the first days of August, the expedition being made up of Japanese, Russian, British, and American troops at the outset.

Another battle was fought and won at Yangtsun. Thereafter the disheartened Chinese troops offered little show of resistance. A few days later the important position of Ho-si-woo was taken. A rapid march brought the united forces to the populous city of Tung Chow, which capitulated without a contest.

On August 14 the capital was reached. After a brief conflict beneath the walls the relief column entered and the legations were saved. The United States soldiers, sailors, and marines, officers and men alike, in those distant climes and unusual surroundings, showed the same valor, discipline, and good conduct and gave proof of the same high degree of intelligence and efficiency which have distinguished them in every emergency.

The Imperial family and the Government had fled a few days before. The city was without visible control. The remaining Imperial soldiery had made on the night of the 13th a last attempt to exterminate the besieged, which was gallantly repelled. It fell to the occupying forces to restore order and organize a provisional administration.

Happily the acute disturbances were confined to the northern provinces. It is a relief to recall and a pleasure to record the loyal conduct of the viceroys and local authorities of the southern and eastern provinces. Their efforts were continuously directed to the pacific control of the vast populations under their rule and to the scrupulous observance of foreign treaty rights. At critical moments they did not hesitate to memorialize the Throne, urging the protection of the legations, the restoration of communication, and the assertion of the Imperial authority against the subversive elements. They maintained excellent relations with the official representatives of foreign powers. To their kindly disposition is largely due the success of the consuls in removing many of the missionaries from the interior to places of safety. In this relation the action of the consuls should be highly commended. In Shan-tung and eastern Chi-li the task was difficult, but, thanks to their energy and the co-operation of American and foreign naval commanders, hundreds of foreigners, including those of other nationalities than ours, were rescued from imminent peril.

The policy of the United States through all this trying period was clearly announced and scrupulously carried out. A circular note to the powers dated July 3 proclaimed our attitude. Treating the condition in the north as one of virtual anarchy, in which the great provinces of the south and southeast had no share, we regarded the local authorities in the latter quarters as representing the Chinese people with whom we sought to remain in peace and friendship. Our declared aims involved no war against the Chinese nation. We adhered to the legitimate office of rescuing the imperiled legation, obtaining redress for wrongs already suffered, securing wherever possible the safety of American life and property in China, and preventing a spread of the disorders or their recurrence.

As was then said, "The policy of the Government of the United States is to seek a solution which may bring about permanent safety and peace to China, preserve Chinese territorial and administrative entity, protect all rights guaranteed to friendly powers by treaty and international law, and safeguard for the world the principle of equal and impartial trade with all parts of the Chinese Empire."

Faithful to those professions which, as it proved, reflected the views and purposes of the other co-operating Governments, all our efforts have been directed toward ending the anomalous situation in China by negotiations for a settlement at the earliest possible moment. As soon as the sacred duty of relieving our legation and its dependents was accomplished we withdrew from active hostilities, leaving our legation under an adequate guard in Peking as a channel of negotiation and settlement — a course adopted by others of the interested powers. Overtures of the empowered representatives of the Chinese Emperor have been considerately entertained.

The Russian proposition looking to the restoration of the Imperial power in Peking has been accepted as in full consonance with our own desires, for we have held and hold that effective reparation for wrongs suffered and an enduring settlement that will make their re-currence impossible can best be brought about under an authority which the Chinese nation reverences and obeys. While so doing we forego no jot of our undoubted right to exact exemplary and deterrent punishment of the responsible authors and abettors of the criminal acts whereby we and other nations have suffered grievous injury.

For the real culprits, the evil counselors who have misled the Imperial judgment and diverted the sovereign authority to their own guilty ends, full expiation becomes imperative within the rational limits of retributive justice. Regarding this as the initial condition of an acceptable settlement between China and the powers, I said in my message of October 18 to the Chinese Emperor:

> I trust that negotiations may begin so soon as we and the other offended Governments shall be effectively satisfied of Your Majesty's ability and power to treat with just sternness the principal offenders, who are doubly culpable, not alone toward the foreigners, but toward Your Majesty, under whose rule the purpose of China to dwell in concord with the world had hitherto found expression in the welcome and protection assured to strangers.

Taking, as a point of departure, the Imperial edict appointing Earl Li Hung Chang and Prince Ching plenipotentiaries to arrange a settlement, and the edict of September 25, whereby certain high officials were designated for punishment, this Government has moved, in concert with the other powers, toward the opening of negotiations, which Mr. Conger, assisted by Mr. Rockhill, has been authorized to conduct on behalf of the United States.

General bases of negotiation formulated by the Government of the French Republic have been accepted with certain reservations as to details, made necessary by our own circumstances, but, like similar reservations by other powers, open to discussion in the progress of the negotiations. The disposition of the Emperor's Government to admit liability for wrongs done to foreign Governments and their nationals, and to act upon such additional designation of the guilty persons as the foreign ministers at Peking may be in a position to make, gives hope of a complete settlement of all questions involved, assuring foreign rights of residence and intercourse on terms of equality for all the world.

I regard as one of the essential factors of a durable adjustment the securement of adequate guarantees for liberty of faith, since insecurity of those natives who may embrace alien creeds is a scarcely less effectual assault upon the rights of foreign worship and teaching than would be the direct invasion thereof.

The matter of indemnity for our wronged citizens is a question of grave concern. Measured in money alone, a sufficient reparation may prove to be beyond the ability of China to meet. All the powers concur in emphatic disclaimers of any purpose of aggrandizement through the dismemberment of the Empire. I am disposed to think that due compensation may be made in part by increased guarantees of security for foreign rights and immunities, and, most important of all, by the opening of China to the equal commerce of all the world. These views have been and will be earnestly advocated by our representatives.

The Government of Russia has put forward a suggestion, that in the event of protracted divergence of views in regard to indemnities the matter may be relegated to the Court of Arbitration at The Hague. I favorably incline to this, believing that high tribunal could not fail to reach a solution no less conducive to the stability and enlarged prosperity of China itself than immediately beneficial to the powers.

Ratifications of a treaty of extradition with the Argentine Republic were exchanged on June 2 last.

While the Austro-Hungarian Government has in the many cases that have been reported of the arrest of our naturalized citizens for alleged evasion of military service faithfully observed the provisions of the treaty and released such persons from military obligations, it has in some instances expelled those whose presence in the community of their origin was asserted to have a pernicious influence. Representations have been made against this course whenever its adoption has appeared unduly onerous.

We have been urgently solicited by Belgium to ratify the International Convention of June, 1899, amendatory of the previous Convention of 1890 in respect to the regulation of the liquor trade in Africa. Compliance was necessarily withheld, in the absence of the advice and consent of the Senate thereto. The principle involved has the cordial sympathy of this Government, which in the revisionary negotiations advocated more drastic measures, and I would gladly see its extension, by international agreement, to the restriction of the liquor traffic with all uncivilized peoples, especially in the Western Pacific.

A conference will be held at Brussels December 11, 1900, under the Convention for the protection of industrial property, concluded at Paris March 20, 1883, to which delegates from this country have been appointed. Any lessening of the difficulties that our inventors encounter in obtaining patents abroad for their inventions and that our farmers, manufacturers, and merchants may have in the protection of their trade-marks is worthy of careful consideration, and your attention will be called to the results of the conference at the proper time.

In the interest of expanding trade between this country and South America, efforts have been made during the past year to conclude conventions with the southern republics for the enlargement of postal facilities. Two such agreements, signed with Bolivia on April 24, of which that establishing the money-order system is undergoing certain changes suggested by the Post-Office Department, have not yet been ratified by this Government. A treaty of extradition with that country, signed on the same day, is before the Senate.

A boundary dispute between Brazil and Bolivia over the territory of Acre is in a fair way of friendly adjustment, a protocol signed in December, 1899, having agreed on a definite frontier and provided for its demarcation by a joint commission.

Conditions in Brazil have weighed heavily on our export trade to that country in marked contrast to the favorable conditions upon which Brazilian products are admitted into our markets. Urgent representations have been made to that Government on the subject and some amelioration has been effected. We rely upon the reciprocal justice and good will of that Government to assure to us a further improvement in our commercial relations.

The Convention signed May 24, 1897, for the final settlement of claims left in abeyance upon the dissolution of the Commission of 1893, was at length ratified by the Chilean Congress and the supplemental Commission has been organized.

It remains for the Congress to appropriate for the necessary expenses of the Commission.

The insurrectionary movement which disturbed Colombia in the latter part of 1899 has been practically suppressed, although guerrillas still operate in some departments. The executive power of that Republic changed hands in August last by the act of Vice-President Marroquin in assuming the reins of government during the absence of President San Clemente from the capital. The change met with no serious opposition, and, following the precedents in such cases, the United States minister entered into relations with the new *de facto* Government on September 17.

It is gratifying to announce that the residual questions between Costa Rica and Nicaragua growing out of the Award of President Cleveland in 1888 have been adjusted through the choice of an American engineer, General E. P. Alexander, as umpire to run the disputed line. His task has been accomplished to the satifaction of both contestants.

A revolution in the Dominican Republic toward the close of last year resulted in the installation of President Jimenez, whose Government was formally recognized in January. Since then final payment has been made of the American claim in regard to the Ozama bridge.

The year of the exposition has been fruitful in occasions for displaying the good will that exists between this country and France. This great competition brought together from every nation the best in natural productions, industry, science, and the arts, submitted in generous rivalry to a judgment made all the more searching because of that rivalry. The extraordinary increase of exportations from this country during the past three years and the activity with which our inventions and wares had invaded new markets caused much interest to center upon the American exhibit, and every encouragement was offered in the way of space and facilities to permit of its being comprehensive as a whole and complete in every part.

It was, however, not an easy task to assemble exhibits that could fitly illustrate our diversified resources and manufactures. Singularly enough, our national prosperity lessened the incentive to exhibit. The dealer in raw materials knew that the user must come to him; the great factories were contented with the phenomenal demand for their output, not alone at home, but also abroad, where merit had already won a profitable trade.

Appeals had to be made to the patriotism of exhibitors to induce them to incur outlays promising no immediate return. This was especially the case where it became needful to complete an industrial sequence or illustrate a class of processes. One manufacturer after another had to be visited and importuned, and at times, after a promise to exhibit in a particular section had been obtained, it would be withdrawn, owing to pressure of trade orders, and a new quest would have to be made.

The installation of exhibits, too, encountered many obstacles and involved unexpected cost. The exposition was far from ready at the date fixed for its opening. The French transportation lines were congested with offered freight. Belated goods had to be hastily installed in unfinished quarters with whatever labor could be obtained in the prevailing confusion. Nor was the task of the Commission lightened by the fact that, owing to the scheme of classification adopted, it was impossible to have the entire exhibit of any one country in the same building or more than one group of exhibits in the same part of any building. Our installations were scattered on both sides of the Seine and in widely remote suburbs of Paris, so that additional assistants were needed for the work of supervision and arrangement.

Despite all these drawbacks the contribution of the United States was not only the largest foreign display, but was among the earliest in place and the most orderly in arrangement. Our exhibits were shown in one hundred and one out of one hundred and twenty-one classes, and more completely covered the entire classification than those of any other nation. In total number they ranked next after those of France, and the attractive form in which they were presented secured general attention.

A criterion of the extent and success of our participation and of the thoroughness with which our exhibits were organized is seen in the awards granted to American exhibitors by the international jury, namely, grand prizes, 240; gold medals, 597; silver medals, 776; bronze medals, 541, and honorable mentions, 322 — 2,476 in all, being the greatest total number given to the exhibit of any exhibiting nation, as well as the largest number in each grade. This significant recognition of merit in competition with the chosen exhibits of all other nations and at the hands of juries almost wholly made up of representatives of France and other competing countries is not only most gratifying, but is especially valuable, since it sets us to the front in international questions of supply and demand, while the large proportion of awards in the classes of art and artistic manufactures afforded unexpected proof of the stimulation of national culture by the prosperity that flows from natural productiveness joined to industrial excellence.

Apart from the exposition several occasions for showing international good will occurred. The inauguration in Paris of the Lafayette Monument, presented by the school children of the United States, and the designing of a commemorative coin by our Mint and the presentation of the first piece struck to the President of the Republic, were marked by appropriate ceremonies, and the Fourth of July was especially observed in the French capital.

Good will prevails in our relations with the German Empire. An amicable adjustment of the long-pending question of the admission of our life-insurance companies to do business in Prussia has been reached. One of the principal companies has already been readmitted and the way is opened for the others to share the privilege.

The settlement of the Samoan problem, to which I adverted in my last message, has accomplished good results. Peace and contentment prevail in the islands, especially in Tutuila, where a convenient administration that has won the confidence and esteem of the kindly disposed natives has been organized under the direction of the commander of the United States naval station at Pago-Pago.

An Imperial meat-inspection law has been enacted for Germany. While it may simplify the inspections, it prohibits certain products heretofore admitted. There is still great uncertainty as to whether our well-nigh extinguished German trade in meat products can revive under its new burdens. Much will depend upon regulations not yet promulgated, which we confidently hope will be free from the discriminations which attended the enforcement of the old statutes.

The remaining link in the new lines of direct telegraphic communication between the United States and the German Empire has recently been completed, affording a gratifying occasion for exchange of friendly congratulations with the German Emperor.

Our friendly relations with Great Britain continue. The war in

Southern Africa introduced important questions. A condition unusual in international wars was presented in that while one belligerent had control of the seas, the other had no ports, shipping, or direct trade, but was only accessible through the territory of a neutral. Vexatious questions arose through Great Britain's action in respect to neutral cargoes, not contraband in their own nature, shipped to Portuguese South Africa, on the score of probable or suspected ultimate destination to the Boer States.

Such consignments in British ships, by which alone direct trade is kept up between our ports and Southern Africa, were seized in application of a municipal law prohibiting British vessels from trading with the enemy without regard to any contraband character of the goods, while cargoes shipped to Delagoa Bay in neutral bottoms were arrested on the ground of alleged destination to enemy's country. Appropriate representations on our part resulted in the British Government agreeing to purchase outright all such goods shown to be the actual property of American citizens, thus closing the incident to the satisfaction of the immediately interested parties, although, unfortunately, without a broad settlement of the question of a neutral's right to send goods not contraband *per se* to a neutral port adjacent to a belligerent area.

The work of marking certain provisional boundary points, for convenience of administration, around the head of Lynn Canal, in accordance with the temporary arrangement of October, 1899, was completed by a joint survey in July last. The *modus vivendi* has so far worked without friction, and the Dominion Government has provided rules and regulations for securing to our citizens the benefit of the reciprocal stipulation that the citizens or subjects of either power found by that arrangement within the temporary jurisdiction of the other shall suffer no diminution of the rights and privileges they have hitherto enjoyed. But however necessary such an expedient may have been to tide over the grave emergencies of the situation, it is at best but an unsatisfactory makeshift, which should not be suffered to delay the speedy and complete establishment of the frontier line to which we are entitled under the Russo-American treaty for the cession of Alaska.

In this relation I may refer again to the need of definitely marking the Alaskan boundary where it follows the one hundred and forty-first meridian. A convention to that end has been before the Senate for some two years, but as no action has been taken I contemplate negotiating a new convention for a joint determination of the meridian by telegraphic observations. These, it is believed, will give more accurate and unquestionable results than the sidereal methods heretofore independently followed, which, as is known, proved discrepant at several points on the line, although not varying at any place more than 700 feet.

The pending claim of R. H. May against the Guatemalan Government has been settled by arbitration, Mr. George F. B. Jenner, British minister at Guatemala, who was chosen as sole arbitrator, having awarded $143,750.73 in gold to the claimant.

Various American claims against Haiti have been or are being advanced to the resort of arbitration.

As the result of negotiations with the Government of Honduras in regard to the indemnity demanded for the murder of Frank H. Pears in Honduras, that Government has paid $10,000 in settlement of the claim of the heirs.

The assassination of King Humbert called forth sincere expressions of sorrow from this Government and people, and occasion was fitly taken to testify to the Italian nation the high regard here felt for the memory of the lamented ruler.

In my last message I referred at considerable length to the lynching of five Italians at Tallulah. Notwithstanding the efforts of the Federal Government, the production of evidence tending to inculpate the authors of this grievous offense against our civilization, and the repeated inquests set on foot by the authorities of the State of Louisiana, no punishments have followed. Successive grand juries have failed to indict. The representations of the Italian Government in the face of this miscarriage have been most temperate and just.

Setting the principle at issue high above all consideration of merely pecuniary indemnification, such as this Government made in the three previous cases, Italy has solemnly invoked the pledges of existing treaty and asked that the justice to which she is entitled shall be meted in regard to her unfortunate countrymen in our territory with the same full measure she herself would give to any American were his reciprocal treaty rights contemned.

I renew the urgent recommendations I made last year that the Congress appropriately confer upon the Federal courts jurisdiction in this class of international cases where the ultimate responsibility of the Federal Government may be involved, and I invite action upon the bills to accomplish this which were introduced in the Senate and House. It is incumbent upon us to remedy the statutory omission which has led, and may again lead, to such untoward results. I have pointed out the necessity and the precedent for legislation of this character. Its enactment is a simple measure of previsory justice toward the nations with which we as a sovereign equal make treaties requiring reciprocal observance.

While the Italian Government naturally regards such action as the primary and, indeed, the most essential element in the disposal of the Tallulah incident, I advise that, in accordance with precedent, and in view of the improbability of that particular case being reached by the bill now pending, Congress make gracious provision for indemnity to the Italian sufferers in the same form and proportion as heretofore.

In my inaugural address I referred to the general subject of lynching in these words:

Lynching must not be tolerated in a great and civilized country like the United States; courts, not mobs, must execute the penalties of the law. The preservation of public order, the right of discussion, the integrity of courts, and the orderly administration of justice must continue forever the rock of safety upon which our Government securely rests.

This I most urgently reiterate and again invite the attention of my countrymen to this reproach upon our civilization.

The closing year has witnessed a decided strengthening of Japan's relations to other States. The development of her independent judicial and administrative functions under the treaties which took effect July 17, 1899, has proceeded without international friction, showing the competence of the Japanese to hold a foremost place among modern peoples.

In the treatment of the difficult Chinese problems Japan has acted in harmonious concert with the other powers, and her generous cooperation materially aided in the joint relief of the beleaguered legations in Peking and in bringing about an understanding preliminary to a settlement of the issues between the powers and China. Japan's declarations in favor of the integrity of the Chinese Empire and the conservation of open world trade therewith have been frank and positive. As a factor for promoting the general interests of peace, order, and fair commerce in the Far East the influence of Japan can hardly be overestimated.

The valuable aid and kindly courtesies extended by the Japanese Government and naval officers to the battle ship *Oregon* are gratefully appreciated.

Complaint was made last summer of the discriminatory enforcement of a bubonic quarantine against Japanese on the Pacific coast and of interference with their travel in California and Colorado under the health laws of those States. The latter restrictions have been adjudged by a Federal court to be unconstitutional. No recurrence of either cause of complaint is apprehended.

No noteworthy incident has occurred in our relations with our important southern neighbor. Commercial intercourse with Mexico continues to thrive, and the two Governments neglect no opportunity to foster their mutual interests in all practicable ways.

Pursuant to the declaration of the Supreme Court that the awards of the late Joint Commission in the La Abra and Weil claims were obtained through fraud, the sum awarded in the first case, $403,-030.08, has been returned to Mexico, and the amount of the Weil award will be returned in like manner.

A Convention indefinitely extending the time for the labors of the

United States and Mexican International (Water) Boundary Commission has been signed.

It is with satisfaction that I am able to announce the formal notification at The Hague, on September 4, of the deposit of ratifications of the Convention for the Pacific Settlement of International Disputes by sixteen powers, namely, the United States, Austria, Belgium, Denmark, England, France, Germany, Italy, Persia, Portugal, Roumania, Russia, Siam, Spain, Sweden and Norway, and the Netherlands. Japan also has since ratified the Convention.

The Administrative Council of the Permanent Court of Arbitration has been organized and has adopted rules of order and a constitution for the International Arbitration Bureau. In accordance with Article XXIII of the Convention providing for the appointment by each signatory power of persons of known competency in questions of international law as arbitrators, I have appointed as members of this Court, Hon. Benjamin Harrison, of Indiana, ex-President of the United States; Hon. Melville W. Fuller, of Illinois, Chief Justice of the United States; Hon. John W. Griggs, of New Jersey, Attorney-General of the United States; and Hon. George Gray, of Delaware, a judge of the circuit court of the United States.

As an incident of the brief revolution in the Mosquito district of Nicaragua early in 1899 the insurgents forcibly collected from American merchants duties upon imports. On the restoration of order the Nicaraguan authorities demanded a second payment of such duties on the ground that they were due to the titular Government and that their diversion had aided the revolt.

This position was not accepted by us. After prolonged discussion a compromise was effected under which the amount of the second payments was deposited with the British consul at San Juan del Norte in trust until the two Governments should determine whether the first payments had been made under compulsion to a *de facto* authority. Agreement as to this was not reached, and the point was waived by the act of the Nicaraguan Government in requesting the British consul to return the deposits to the merchants.

Menacing differences between several of the Central American States have been accommodated, our ministers rendering good offices toward an understanding.

The all-important matter of an interoceanic canal has assumed a new phase. Adhering to its refusal to reopen the question of the forfeiture of the contract of the Maritime Canal Company, which was terminated for alleged nonexecution in October, 1899, the Government of Nicaragua has since supplemented that action by declaring the so-styled Eyre-Cragin option void for nonpayment of the stipulated advance. Protests in relation to these acts have been filed in the State Department and are under consideration. Deeming itself relieved from existing engagements, the Nicaraguan Government shows a disposition to deal freely with the canal question either in the way of negotiations with the United States or by taking measures to promote the waterway.

Overtures for a convention to effect the building of a canal under the auspices of the United States are under consideration. In the meantime, the views of the Congress upon the general subject, in the light of the report of the Commission appointed to examine the comparative merits of the various trans-Isthmian ship-canal projects, may be awaited.

I commend to the early attention of the Senate the Convention with Great Britain to facilitate the construction of such a canal and to remove any objection which might arise out of the Convention commonly called the Clayton-Bulwer Treaty.

The long-standing contention with Portugal, growing out of the seizure of the Delagoa Bay Railway, has been at last determined by a favorable award of the tribunal of arbitration at Berne, to which it was submitted. The amount of the award, which was deposited in London awaiting arrangements by the Governments of the United States and Great Britain for its disposal, has recently been paid over to the two Governments.

A lately signed Convention of Extradition with Peru as amended by the Senate has been ratified by the Peruvian Congress.

Another illustration of the policy of this Government to refer international disputes to impartial arbitration is seen in the agreement reached with Russia to submit the claims on behalf of American sealing vessels seized in Bering Sea to determination by Mr. T. M. C. Asser, a distinguished statesman and jurist of the Netherlands.

Thanks are due to the Imperial Russian Government for the kindly aid rendered by its authorities in eastern Siberia to American missionaries fleeing from Manchuria.

Satisfactory progress has been made toward the conclusion of a general treaty of friendship and intercourse with Spain, in replacement of the old treaty, which passed into abeyance by reason of the late war. A new convention of extradition is approaching completion, and I should be much pleased were a commercial arrangement to follow. I feel that we should not suffer to pass any opportunity to reaffirm the cordial ties that existed between us and Spain from the time of our earliest independence, and to enhance the mutual benefits of that commercial intercourse which is natural between the two countries.

By the terms of the Treaty of Peace the line bounding the ceded Philippine group in the southwest failed to include several small islands lying westward of the Sulus, which have always been recognized as under Spanish control. The occupation of Sibutú and Cagayan Sulu by our naval forces elicited a claim on the part of Spain, the essential equity of which could not be gainsaid. In order to cure the defect of the treaty by removing all possible ground of future misunderstanding respecting the interpretation of its third article, I directed the negotiation of a supplementary treaty, which will be forthwith laid before the Senate, whereby Spain quits all title and claim of title to the islands named as well as to any and all islands belonging to the Philippine Archipelago lying outside the lines described in said third article, and agrees that all such islands shall be comprehended in the cession of the archipelago as fully as if they had been expressly included within those lines. In consideration of this cession the United States is to pay to Spain the sum of $100,000.

A bill is now pending to effect the recommendation made in my last annual message that appropriate legislation be had to carry into execution Article VII of the Treaty of Peace with Spain, by which the United States assumed the payment of certain claims for indemnity of its citizens against Spain. I ask that action be taken to fulfill this obligation.

The King of Sweden and Norway has accepted the joint invitation of the United States, Germany, and Great Britain to arbitrate claims growing out of losses sustained in the Samoan Islands in the course of military operations made necessary by the disturbances in 1899.

Our claims upon the Government of the Sultan for reparation for injuries suffered by American citizens in Armenia and elsewhere give promise of early and satisfactory settlement. His Majesty's good disposition in this regard has been evinced by the issuance of an irade for rebuilding the American college at Harpoot.

The failure of action by the Senate at its last session upon the commercial conventions then submitted for its consideration and approval, although caused by the great pressure of other legislative business, has caused much disappointment to the agricultural and industrial interests of the country, which hoped to profit by their provisions. The conventional periods for their ratification having expired, it became necessary to sign additional articles extending the time for that purpose. This was requested on our part, and the other Governments interested have concurred with the exception of one convention, in respect to which no formal reply has been received.

Since my last communication to the Congress on this subject special commercial agreements under the third section of the tariff act have been proclaimed with Portugal, with Italy, and with Germany. Commercial conventions under the general limitations of the fourth section of the same act have been concluded with Nicaragua, with Ecuador, with the Dominican Republic, with Great Britain on behalf of the island of Trinidad, and with Denmark on behalf of the island of St. Croix. These will be early communicated to the Senate. Negotiations with other Governments are in progress for the improvement and security of our commercial relations.

The policy of reciprocity so manifestly rests upon the principles of international equity and has been so repeatedly approved by the people of the United States that there ought to be no hesitation in either branch of the Congress in giving to it full effect.

This Government desires to preserve the most just and amicable commercial relations with all foreign countries, unmoved by the industrial rivalries necessarily developed in the expansion of international trade. It is believed that the foreign Governments generally entertain the same purpose, although in some instances there are clamorous demands upon them for legislation specifically hostile to American interests. Should these demands prevail I shall communicate with the Congress with the view of advising such legislation as may be necessary to meet the emergency.

The exposition of the resources and products of the Western Hemisphere to be held at Buffalo next year promises important results not only for the United States but for the other participating countries. It is gratifying that the Latin-American States have evinced the liveliest interest, and the fact that an International American Congress will be held in the City of Mexico while the exposition is in progress encourages the hope of a larger display at Buffalo than might otherwise be practicable. The work of preparing an exhibit of our national resources is making satisfactory progress under the direction of different officials of the Federal Government, and the various States of the Union have shown a disposition toward the most liberal participation in the enterprise.

The Bureau of the American Republics continues to discharge, with the happiest results, the important work of promoting cordial relations between the United States and the Latin-American countries, all of which are now active members of the International Union. The Bureau has been instrumental in bringing about the agreement for another International American Congress, which is to meet in the City of Mexico in October, 1901. The Bureau's future for another term of ten years is assured by the international compact, but the congress will doubtless have much to do with shaping new lines of work and a general policy. Its usefulness to the interests of Latin-American trade is widely appreciated and shows a gratifying development.

The practical utility of the consular service in obtaining a wide range of information as to the industries and commerce of other countries and the opportunities thereby afforded for introducing the sale of our goods have kept steadily in advance of the notable expansion of our foreign trade, and abundant evidence has been furnished, both at home and abroad, of the fact that the Consular Reports, including many from our diplomatic representatives, have to a considerable extent pointed out ways and means of disposing of a great variety of manufactured goods which otherwise might not have found sale abroad.

Testimony of foreign observers to the commercial efficiency of the consular corps seems to be conclusive, and our own manufacturers and exporters highly appreciate the value of the services rendered not only in the printed reports but also in the individual efforts of consular officers to promote American trade. An increasing part of the work of the Bureau of Foreign Commerce, whose primary duty it is to compile and print the reports, is to answer inquiries from trade organizations, business houses, etc., as to conditions in various parts of the world, and, notwithstanding the smallness of the force employed, the work has been so systematized that responses are made with such promptitude and accuracy as to elicit flattering encomiums. The experiment of printing the Consular Reports daily for immediate use by trade bodies, exporters, and the press, which was begun in January, 1898, continues to give general satisfaction.

It is gratifying to be able to state that the surplus revenues for the fiscal year ended June 30, 1900, were $79,527,060.18. For the six preceding years we had only deficits, the aggregate of which from 1894 to 1899, inclusive, amounted to $283,022,991.14. The receipts for the year from all sources, exclusive of postal revenues, aggregated $567,240,851.89, and expenditures for all purposes, except for the administration of the postal department, aggregated $487,-713,791.71. The receipts from customs were $233,164,871.16, an increase over the preceding year of $27,036,389.41. The receipts from internal revenue were $295,327,926.76, an increase of $21,890,-765.25 over 1899. The receipts from miscellaneous sources were $38,748,053.97, as against $36,394,976.92 for the previous year.

It is gratifying also to note that during the year a considerable reduction is shown in the expenditures of the Government. The War Department expenditures for the fiscal year 1900 were $134,774,-767.78, a reduction of $95,066,486.69 over those of 1899. In the Navy Department the expenditures were $55,953,077.72 for the year 1900, as against $63,942,104.25 for the preceding year, a decrease of $7,989,026.53. In the expenditures on account of Indians there was a decrease in 1900 over 1899 of $2,630,604.38; and in the civil and miscellaneous expenses for 1900 there was a reduction of $13,418,-065.74.

Because of the excess of revenues over expenditures the Secretary of the Treasury was enabled to apply bonds and other securities to

the sinking fund to the amount of $56,544,556.06. The details of
the sinking fund are set forth in the report of the Secretary of the
Treasury, to which I invite attention. The Secretary of the Treasury
estimates that the receipts for the current fiscal year will aggregate
$580,000,000 and the expenditures $500,000,000, leaving an excess of
revenues over expenditures of $80,000,000. The present condition
of the Treasury is one of undoubted strength. The available cash
balance November 30 was $139,303,794.50. Under the form of state-
ment prior to the financial law of March 14 last there would have
been included in the statement of available cash gold coin and bullion held for the redemption of United States notes.

If this form were pursued, the cash balance including the present
gold reserve of $150,000,000, would be $289,303,794.50. Such balance November 30, 1899, was $296,495,301.55. In the general fund,
which is wholly separate from the reserve and trust funds, there was
on November 30, $70,090,073.15 in gold coin and bullion, to which
should be added $22,957,300 in gold certificates subject to issue,
against which there is held in the Division of Redemption gold coin
and bullion, making a total holding of free gold amounting to $93,-
047,373.15.

It will be the duty as I am sure it will be the disposition of the
Congress to provide whatever further legislation is needed to insure
the continued parity under all conditions between our two forms of
metallic money, silver and gold.

Our surplus revenues have permitted the Secretary of the Treasury since the close of the fiscal year to call in the funded loan of
1891 continued at 2 per cent, in the sum of $25,364,500. To and
including November 30, $23,458,100 of these bonds have been paid.
This sum, together with the amount which may accrue from further
redemptions under the call, will be applied to the sinking fund.

The law of March 14, 1900, provided for refunding into 2 per cent
thirty-year bonds, payable, principal and interest, in gold coin of the
present standard value, that portion of the public debt represented
by the 3 per cent bonds of 1908, the 4 percents of 1907, and the 5
percents of 1904, of which there was outstanding at the date of said
law $839,149,930. The holders of the old bonds presented them for
exchange between March 14 and November 30 to the amount of
$364,943,750. The net saving to the Government on these transac-
tions aggregates $9,106,166.

Another effect of the operation, as stated by the Secretary, is to
reduce the charge upon the Treasury for the payment of interest
from the dates of refunding to February 1, 1904, by the sum of more
than seven million dollars annually. From February 1, 1904, to
July 1, 1907, the annual interest charge will be reduced by the sum of
more than five millions, and for the thirteen months ending August

1, 1908, by about one million. The full details of the refunding are given in the annual report of the Secretary of the Treasury.

The beneficial effect of the financial act of 1900, so far as it relates to a modification of the national banking act, is already apparent. The provision for the incorporation of national banks with a capital of not less than $25,000 in places not exceeding three thousand inhabitants has resulted in the extension of banking facilities to many small communities hitherto unable to provide themselves with banking institutions under the national system. There were organized from the enactment of the law up to and including November 30, 369 national banks, of which 266 were with capital less than $50,000, and 103 with capital of $50,000 or more.

It is worthy of mention that the greater number of banks being organized under the new law are in sections where the need of banking facilities has been most pronounced. Iowa stands first, with 30 banks of the smaller class, while Texas, Oklahoma, Indian Territory, and the middle and western sections of the country have also availed themselves largely of the privileges under the new law.

A large increase in national-bank-note circulation has resulted from the provision of the act which permits national banks to issue circulating notes to the par value of the United States bonds deposited as security instead of only 90 per cent thereof, as heretofore. The increase in circulating notes from March 14 to November 30 is $77,889,570.

The party in power is committed to such legislation as will better make the currency responsive to the varying needs of business at all seasons and in all sections.

Our foreign trade shows a remarkable record of commercial and industrial progress. The total of imports and exports for the first time in the history of the country exceeded two billions of dollars. The exports are greater than they have ever been before, the total for the fiscal year 1900 being $1,394,483,082, an increase over 1899 of $167,459,780, an increase over 1898 of $163,000,752, over 1897 of $343,489,526, and greater than 1896 by $511,876,144.

The growth of manufactures in the United States is evidenced by the fact that exports of manufactured products largely exceed those of any previous year, their value for 1900 being $433,851,756, against $339,592,146 in 1899, an increase of 28 per cent.

Agricultural products were also exported during 1900 in greater volume than in 1899, the total for the year being $835,858,123, against $784,776,142 in 1899.

The imports for the year amounted to $849,941,184, an increase over 1899 of $152,792,695. This increase is largely in materials for manufacture, and is in response to the rapid development of manufacturing in the United States. While there was imported for use

in manufactures in 1900 material to the value of $79,768,972 in excess
of 1899, it is reassuring to observe that there is a tendency toward
decrease in the importation of articles manufactured ready for consumption, which in 1900 formed 15.17 per cent of the total imports,
against 15.54 per cent in 1899 and 21.09 per cent in 1896.

I recommend that the Congress at its present session reduce the
internal-revenue taxes imposed to meet the expenses of the war with
Spain in the sum of thirty millions of dollars. This reduction should
be secured by the remission of those taxes which experience has
shown to be the most burdensome to the industries of the people.

I specially urge that there be included in whatever reduction is
made the legacy tax on bequests for public uses of a literary, educational, or charitable character.

American vessels during the past three years have carried about
9 per cent of our exports and imports. Foreign ships should carry
the least, not the greatest, part of American trade. The remarkable
growth of our steel industries, the progress of shipbuilding for the
domestic trade, and our steadily maintained expenditures for the
Navy have created an opportunity to place the United States in the
first rank of commercial maritime powers.

Besides realizing a proper national aspiration this will mean the
establishment and healthy growth along all our coasts of a distinctive
national industry, expanding the field for the profitable employment
of labor and capital. It will increase the transportation facilities
and reduce freight charges on the vast volume of products brought
from the interior to the seaboard for export, and will strengthen an
arm of the national defense upon which the founders of the Government and their successors have relied. In again urging immediate
action by the Congress on measures to promote American shipping
and foreign trade, I direct attention to the recommendations on the
subject in previous messages, and particularly to the opinion expressed in the message of 1899:

> I am satisfied the judgment of the country favors the policy of aid to our mer-
> chant marine, which will broaden our commerce and markets and upbuild our
> sea-carrying capacity for the products of agriculture and manufacture, which, with
> the increase of our Navy, mean more work and wages to our countrymen, as well
> as a safeguard to American interests in every part of the world.

The attention of the Congress is invited to the recommendation
of the Secretary of the Treasury in his annual report for legislation
in behalf of the Revenue-Cutter Service, and favorable action is
urged.

In my last annual message to the Congress I called attention to
the necessity for early action to remedy such evils as might be found
to exist in connection with combinations of capital organized into
trusts, and again invite attention to my discussion of the subject at

that time, which concluded with these words:

It is apparent that uniformity of legislation upon this subject in the several States is much to be desired. It is to be hoped that such uniformity, founded in a wise and just discrimination between what is injurious and what is useful and necessary in business operations, may be obtained, and that means may be found for the Congress, within the limitations of its constitutional power, so to supplement an effective code of State legislation as to make a complete system of laws throughout the United States adequate to compel a general observance of the salutary rules to which I have referred.

The whole question is so important and far-reaching that I am sure no part of it will be lightly considered, but every phase of it will have the studied deliberation of the Congress, resulting in wise and judicious action.

Restraint upon such combinations as are injurious, and which are within Federal jurisdiction, should be promptly applied by the Congress.

In my last annual message I dwelt at some length upon the condition of affairs in the Philippines. While seeking to impress upon you that the grave responsibility of the future government of those islands rests with the Congress of the United States, I abstained from recommending at that time a specific and final form of government for the territory actually held by the United States forces and in which as long as insurrection continues the military arm must necessarily be supreme. I stated my purpose, until the Congress shall have made the formal expression of its will, to use the authority vested in me by the Constitution and the statutes to uphold the sovereignty of the United States in those distant islands as in all other places where our flag rightfully floats, placing, to that end, at the disposal of the army and navy all the means which the liberality of the Congress and the people have provided. No contrary expression of the will of the Congress having been made, I have steadfastly pursued the purpose so declared, employing the civil arm as well toward the accomplishment of pacification and the institution of local governments within the lines of authority and law.

Progress in the hoped-for direction has been favorable. Our forces have successfully controlled the greater part of the islands, overcoming the organized forces of the insurgents and carrying order and administrative regularity to all quarters. What opposition remains is for the most part scattered, obeying no concerted plan of strategic action, operating only by the methods common to the traditions of guerrilla warfare, which, while ineffective to alter the general control now established, are still sufficient to beget insecurity among the populations that have felt the good results of our control and thus delay the conferment upon them of the fuller measures of local self-government, of education, and of industrial and agricultural development which we stand ready to give to them.

By the spring of this year the effective opposition of the dissatisfied Tagals to the authority of the United States was virtually ended, thus opening the door for the extension of a stable administration over much of the territory of the Archipelago. Desiring to bring this about, I appointed in March last a civil Commission composed of the Hon. William H. Taft, of Ohio; Prof. Dean C. Worcester, of Michigan; the Hon. Luke I. Wright, of Tennessee; the Hon. Henry C. Ide, of Vermont, and Prof. Bernard Moses, of California. The aims of their mission and the scope of their authority are clearly set forth in my instructions of April 7, 1900, addressed to the Secretary of War to be transmitted to them:

In the message transmitted to the Congress on the 5th of December, 1899, I said, speaking of the Philippine Islands: "As long as the insurrection continues the military arm must necessarily be supreme. But there is no reason why steps should not be taken from time to time to inaugurate governments essentially popular in their form as fast as territory is held and controlled by our troops. To this end I am considering the advisability of the return of the Commission, or such of the members thereof as can be secured, to aid the existing authorities and facilitate this work throughout the islands."

To give effect to the intention thus expressed, I have appointed Hon. William H. Taft, of Ohio; Prof. Dean C. Worcester, of Michigan; Hon. Luke I. Wright, of Tennessee; Hon. Henry C. Ide, of Vermont, and Prof. Bernard Moses, of California, Commissioners to the Philippine Islands to continue and perfect the work of organizing and establishing civil government already commenced by the military authorities, subject in all respects to any laws which Congress may hereafter enact.

The Commissioners named will meet and act as a board, and the Hon. William H. Taft is designated as president of the board. It is probable that the transfer of authority from military commanders to civil officers will be gradual and will occupy a considerable period. Its successful accomplishment and the maintenance of peace and order in the meantime will require the most perfect co-operation between the civil and military authorities in the islands, and both should be directed during the transition period by the same Executive Department. The Commission will therefore report to the Secretary of War, and all their action will be subject to your approval and control.

You will instruct the Commission to proceed to the city of Manila, where they will make their principal office, and to communicate with the Military Governor of the Philippine Islands, whom you will at the same time direct to render to them every assistance within his power in the performance of their duties. Without hampering them by too specific instructions, they should in general be enjoined, after making themselves familiar with the conditions and needs of the country, to devote their attention in the first instance to the establishment of municipal governments, in which the natives of the islands, both in the cities and in the rural communities, shall be afforded the opportunity to manage their own local affairs to the fullest extent of which they are capable and subject to the least degree of supervision and control which a careful study of their capacities and observation of the workings of native control show to be consistent with the maintenance of law, order, and loyalty.

The next subject in order of importance should be the organization of government in the larger administrative divisions corresponding to counties, departments, or provinces, in which the common interests of many or several municipalities falling within the same tribal lines, or the same natural geographical limits, may best be subserved by a common administration. Whenever the Commission is of the opinion that the condition of affairs in the islands is such that the central administration may safely be transferred from military to civil control they will report that conclusion to you, with their recommendations as to the form of central government to be established for the purpose of taking over the control.

Beginning with the 1st day of September, 1900, the authority to exercise, subject to my approval, through the Secretary of War, that part of the power of government in the Philippine Islands which is of a legislative nature is to be transferred from the Military Governor of the islands to this Commission, to be thereafter exercised by them in the place and stead of the Military Governor, under such rules and regulations as you shall prescribe, until the establishment of the civil central government for the islands contemplated in the last foregoing paragraph, or until Congress shall otherwise provide. Exercise of this legislative authority will include the making of rules and orders, having the effect of law, for the raising of revenue by taxes, customs duties, and imposts; the appropriation and expenditure of public funds of the islands; the establishment of an educational system throughout the islands; the establishment of a system to secure an efficient civil service; the organization and establishment of courts; the organization and establishment of municipal and departmental governments, and all other matters of a civil nature for which the Military Governor is now competent to provide by rules or orders of a legislative character.

The Commission will also have power during the same period to appoint to office such officers under the judicial, educational, and civil-service systems and in the municipal and departmental governments as shall be provided for. Until the complete transfer of control the Military Governor will remain the chief executive head of the government of the islands, and will exercise the executive authority now possessed by him and not herein expressly assigned to the Commission, subject, however, to the rules and orders enacted by the Commission in the exercise of the legislative powers conferred upon them. In the meantime the municipal and departmental governments will continue to report to the Military Governor and be subject to his administrative supervision and control, under your direction, but that supervision and control will be confined within the narrowest limits consistent with the requirement that the powers of government in the municipalities and departments shall be honestly and effectively exercised and that law and order and individual freedom shall be maintained.

All legislative rules and orders, establishments of government, and appointments to office by the Commission will take effect immediately, or at such times as they shall designate, subject to your approval and action upon the coming in of the Commission's reports, which are to be made from time to time as their action is taken. Wherever civil governments are constituted under the direction of the Commission such military posts, garrisons, and forces will be continued for the suppression of insurrection and brigandage and the maintenance of law and order as the Military Commander shall deem requisite, and the military forces shall be at all times subject, under his orders, to the call of the civil authorities for the maintenance of law and order and the enforcement of their authority.

In the establishment of municipal governments the Commission will take as the basis of their work the governments established by the Military Governor under his order of August 8, 1899, and under the report of the board constituted by the Military Governor by his order of January 29, 1900, to formulate and report a plan of municipal government, of which His Honor Cayetano Arellano, President of the Audiencia, was chairman, and they will give to the conclusions of that board the weight and consideration which the high character and distinguished abilities of its members justify.

In the constitution of departmental or provincial governments they will give especial attention to the existing government of the island of Negros, constituted, with the approval of the people of that island, under the order of the Military Governor of July 22, 1899, and after verifying, so far as may be practicable, the reports of the successful working of that government they will be guided by the experience thus acquired so far as it may be applicable to the condition existing in other portions of the Philippines. They will avail themselves, to the fullest degree practicable, of the conclusions reached by the previous Commission to the Philippines.

In the distribution of powers among the governments organized by the Commission, the presumption is always to be in favor of the smaller subdivision, so that all the powers which can properly be exercised by the municipal government shall be vested in that government, and all the powers of a more general character which can be exercised by the departmental government shall be vested in that government, and so that in the governmental system, which is the result of the process, the central government of the islands, following the example of the distribution of the powers between the States and the National Government of the United States, shall have no direct administration except of matters of purely general concern, and shall have only such supervision and control over local governments as may be necessary to secure and enforce faithful and efficient administration by local officers.

The many different degrees of civilization and varieties of custom and capacity among the people of the different islands preclude very definite instruction as to the part which the people shall take in the selection of their own officers; but these general rules are to be observed: That in all cases the municipal officers, who administer the local affairs of the people, are to be selected by the people, and that wherever officers of more extended jurisdiction are to be selected in any way, natives of the islands are to be preferred, and if they can be found competent and willing to perform the duties, they are to receive the offices in preference to any others.

It will be necessary to fill some offices for the present with Americans which after a time may well be filled by natives of the islands. As soon as practicable a system for ascertaining the merit and fitness of candidates for civil office should be put in force. An indispensable qualification for all offices and positions of trust and authority in the islands must be absolute and unconditional loyalty to the United States, and absolute and unhampered authority and power to remove and punish any officer deviating from that standard must at all times be retained in the hands of the central authority of the islands.

In all the forms of government and administrative provisions which they are authorized to prescribe the Commission should bear in mind that the government which they are establishing is designed not for our satisfaction, or for the expression of our theoretical views, but for the happiness, peace, and prosperity of the people of the Philippine Islands, and the measures adopted should be made to conform to their customs, their habits, and even their prejudices, to the fullest extent consistent with the accomplishment of the indispensable requisites of just and effective government.

At the same time the Commission should bear in mind, and the people of the islands should be made plainly to understand, that there are certain great principles of government which have been made the basis of our governmental system which we deem essential to the rule of law and the maintenance of individual freedom, and of which they have, unfortunately, been denied the experience possessed by us; that there are also certain practical rules of government which we have found to be essential to the preservation of these great principles of liberty and law, and that these principles and these rules of government must be established and maintained in their islands for the sake of their liberty and happiness, however much they may conflict with the customs or laws of procedure with which they are familiar.

It is evident that the most enlightened thought of the Philippine Islands fully appreciates the importance of these principles and rules, and they will inevitably within a short time command universal assent. Upon every division and branch of the government of the Philippines, therefore, must be imposed these inviolable rules:

That no person shall be deprived of life, liberty, or property without due process of law; that private property shall not be taken for public use without just compensation; that in all criminal prosecutions the accused shall enjoy the right to a speedy and public trial, to be informed of the nature and cause of the accusation, to be confronted with the witnesses against him, to have compulsory process for obtaining witnesses in his favor, and to have the assistance of counsel for his defense; that excessive bail shall not be required, nor excessive fines imposed, nor cruel and unusual punishment inflicted; that no person shall be put twice in jeopardy for the same offense, or be compelled in any criminal case to be a witness against himself; that the right to be secure against unreasonable searches and seizures shall not be violated; that neither slavery nor involuntary servitude shall exist except as a punishment for crime; that no bill of attainder or *ex-post-facto* law shall be passed; that no law shall be passed abridging the freedom of speech or of the press, or the rights of the people to peaceably assemble and petition the Government for a redress of grievances; that no law shall be made respecting an establishment of religion, or prohibiting the free exercise thereof, and that the free exercise and enjoyment of religious profession and worship without discrimination or preference shall forever be allowed.

It will be the duty of the Commission to make a thorough investigation into the titles to the large tracts of land held or claimed by individuals or by religious orders; into the justice of the claims and complaints made against such landholders by the people of the island or any part of the people, and to seek by wise and peaceable measures a just settlement of the controversies and redress of wrongs which have caused strife and bloodshed in the past. In the performance of this duty the Commission is enjoined to see that no injustice is done; to have regard for substantial rights and equity, disregarding technicalities so far as substantial right permits, and to observe the following rules:

That the provision of the Treaty of Paris pledging the United States to the protection of all rights of property in the islands, and as well the principle of our own Government which prohibits the taking of private property without due process of law, shall not be violated; that the welfare of the people of the islands, which should be a paramount consideration, shall be attained consistently with this rule of property right; that if it becomes necessary for the public interest of the people of the islands to dispose of claims to property which the Commission finds to be not lawfully acquired and held disposition shall be made thereof by due legal procedure, in which there shall be full opportunity for fair and impartial hearing and judgment; that if the same public interests require the extinguishment of property rights lawfully acquired and held due compensation shall be made out of the public treasury therefor; that no form of religion and no minister of religion shall be forced upon any community or upon any citizen of the islands; that, upon the other hand, no minister of religion shall be interfered with or molested in following his calling, and that the separation between State and Church shall be real, entire, and absolute.

It will be the duty of the Commission to promote and extend, and, as they find occasion, to improve the system of education already inaugurated by the military authorities. In doing this they should regard as of first importance the extension of a system of primary education which shall be free to all, and which shall tend to fit the people for the duties of citizenship and for the ordinary avocations of a civilized community. This instruction should be given in the first instance in every part of the islands in the language of the people. In view of the great number of languages spoken by the different tribes, it is especially important to the prosperity of the islands that a common medium of communication may be established, and it is obviously desirable that this medium should be the English language. Especial attention should be at once given to affording full opportunity to all the people of the islands to acquire the use of the English language.

It may be well that the main changes which should be made in the system of taxation and in the body of the laws under which the people are governed, except such changes as have already been made by the military government, should be relegated to the civil government which is to be established under the auspices of the Commission. It will, however, be the duty of the Commission to inquire diligently as to whether there are any further changes which ought not to be delayed, and if so, they are authorized to make such changes subject to your approval. In doing so they are to bear in mind that taxes which tend to penalize or repress industry and enterprise are to be avoided; that provisions for taxation should be simple, so that they may be understood by the people; that they should affect the fewest practicable subjects of taxation which will serve for the general distribution of the burden.

The main body of the laws which regulate the rights and obligations of the people should be maintained with as little interference as possible. Changes made should be mainly in procedure, and in the criminal laws to secure speedy and impartial trials, and at the same time effective administration and respect for individual rights.

In dealing with the uncivilized tribes of the islands the Commission should adopt the same course followed by Congress in permitting the tribes of our North American Indians to maintain their tribal organization and government, and under which many of those tribes are now living in peace and contentment, surrounded by a civilization to which they are unable or unwilling to conform. Such tribal governments should, however, be subjected to wise and firm regulation, and, without undue or petty interference, constant and active effort should be exercised to prevent barbarous practices and introduce civilized customs.

Upon all officers and employees of the United States, both civil and military, should be impressed a sense of the duty to observe not merely the material but the personal and social rights of the people of the islands, and to treat them with the same courtesy and respect for their personal dignity which the people of the United States are accustomed to require from each other.

The articles of capitulation of the city of Manila on the 13th of August, 1898, concluded with these words:

"This city, its inhabitants, its churches and religious worship, its educational establishments, and its private property of all descriptions, are placed under the special safeguard of the faith and honor of the American Army."

I believe that this pledge has been faithfully kept. As high and sacred an obligation rests upon the Government of the United States to give protection for property and life, civil and religious freedom, and wise, firm, and unselfish guidance in the paths of peace and prosperity to all the people of the Philippine Islands. I charge this Commission to labor for the full performance of this obligation, which concerns the honor and conscience of their country, in the firm hope that through their labors all the inhabitants of the Philippine Islands may come to look back with gratitude to the day when God gave victory to American arms at Manila and set their land under the sovereignty and the protection of the people of the United States.

Coincidently with the entrance of the Commission upon its labors I caused to be issued by General MacArthur, the Military Governor of the Philippines, on June 21, 1900, a proclamation of amnesty in generous terms, of which many of the insurgents took advantage, among them a number of important leaders.

This Commission, composed of eminent citizens representing the diverse geographical and political interests of the country, and bringing to their task the ripe fruits of long and intelligent service in educational, administrative, and judicial careers, made great progress from the outset. As early as August 21, 1900, it submitted a preliminary report, which will be laid before the Congress, and from which it appears that already the good effects of returning order are felt; that business, interrupted by hostilities, is improving as peace extends; that a larger area is under sugar cultivation than ever before; that the customs revenues are greater than at any time during the Spanish rule; that economy and efficiency in the military administration have created a surplus fund of $6,000,000, available for needed public improvements; that a stringent civil-service law is in preparation; that railroad communications are expanding, opening up rich districts, and that a comprehensive scheme of education is being organized.

Later reports from the Commission show yet more encouraging advance toward insuring the benefits of liberty and good government to the Filipinos, in the interest of humanity and with the aim of building up an enduring, self-supporting, and self-administering community in those far eastern seas. I would impress upon the Congress that whatever legislation may be enacted in respect to the Philippine Islands should be along these generous lines. The fortune of war has thrown upon this nation an unsought trust which should be unselfishly discharged, and devolved upon this Government a moral as well as material responsibility toward these millions whom we have freed from an oppressive yoke.

I have on another occasion called the Filipinos "the wards of the nation." Our obligation as guardian was not lightly assumed; it must not be otherwise than honestly fulfilled, aiming first of all to benefit those who have come under our fostering care. It is our duty so to treat them that our flag may be no less beloved in the mountains of Luzon and the fertile zones of Mindanao and Negros than it is at home, that there as here it shall be the revered symbol of liberty, enlightenment, and progress in every avenue of development.

The Filipinos are a race quick to learn and to profit by knowledge He would be rash who, with the teachings of contemporaneous history in view, would fix a limit to the degree of culture and advancement yet within the reach of these people if our duty toward them be faithfully performed.

The civil government of Puerto Rico provided for by the act of the Congress approved April 12, 1900, is in successful operation The courts have been established. The Governor and his associates, working intelligently and harmoniously, are meeting with commendable success.

On the 6th of November a general election was held in the island for members of the Legislature, and the body elected has been called to convene on the first Monday of December.

I recommend that legislation be enacted by the Congress conferring upon the Secretary of the Interior supervision over the public lands in Puerto Rico, and that he be directed to ascertain the location and quantity of lands the title to which remained in the Crown of Spain at the date of cession of Puerto Rico to the United States, and that appropriations necessary for surveys be made, and that the methods of the disposition of such lands be prescribed by law.

On the 25th of July, 1900, I directed that a call be issued for an election in Cuba for members of a constitutional convention to frame a constitution as a basis for a stable and independent government in the island. In pursuance thereof the Military Governor issued the following instructions:

Whereas the Congress of the United States, by its joint resolution of April 20, 1898, declared —

"That the people of the island of Cuba are, and of right ought to be, free and independent.

"That the United States hereby disclaims any disposition or intention to exercise sovereignty, jurisdiction, or control over said island except for the pacification thereof, and asserts its determination, when that is accomplished, to leave the government and control of the island to its people;"

And whereas, the people of Cuba have established municipal governments, deriving their authority from the suffrages of the people given under just and equal laws, and are now ready, in like manner, to proceed to the establishment of a general government which shall assume and exercise sovereignty, jurisdiction, and control over the island:

Therefore, it is ordered that a general election be held in the island of Cuba on the third Saturday of September, in the year nineteen hundred, to elect delegates to a convention to meet in the city of Havana at twelve o'clock noon on the first Monday of November, in the year nineteen hundred, to frame and adopt a constitution for the people of Cuba, and as a part thereof to provide for and agree with the Government of the United States upon the relations to exist between that Government and the Government of Cuba, and to provide for the election by the people of officers under such constitution and the transfer of government to the officers so elected.

The election will be held in the several voting precincts of the island under, and pursuant to, the provisions of the electoral law of April 18, 1900, and the amendments thereof.

The election was held on the 15th of September, and the convention assembled on the 5th of November, 1900, and is now in session.

In calling the convention to order, the Military Governor of Cuba made the following statement:

As Military Governor of the island, representing the President of the United States, I call this convention to order.

It will be your duty, first, to frame and adopt a constitution for Cuba, and when that has been done to formulate what in your opinion ought to be the relations between Cuba and the United States.

The constitution must be adequate to secure a stable, orderly, and free government.

When you have formulated the relations which in your opinion ought to exist between Cuba and the United States the Government of the United States will doubtless take such action on its part as shall lead to a final and authoritative agreement between the people of the two countries to the promotion of their common interests.

All friends of Cuba will follow your deliberations with the deepest interest, earnestly desiring that you shall reach just conclusions, and that by the dignity, individual self-restraint, and wise conservatism which shall characterize your proceedings the capacity of the Cuban people for representative government may be signally illustrated.

The fundamental distinction between true representative government and dictatorship is that in the former every representative of the people, in whatever office, confines himself strictly within the limits of his defined powers. Without such restraint there can be no free constitutional government.

Under the order pursuant to which you have been elected and convened you have no duty and no authority to take part in the present government of the island. Your powers are strictly limited by the terms of that order.

When the convention concludes its labors I will transmit to the Congress the constitution as framed by the convention for its consideration and for such action as it may deem advisable.

I renew the recommendation made in my special message of February 10, 1899, as to the necessity for cable communication between the United States and Hawaii, with extension to Manila. Since then circumstances have strikingly emphasized this need. Surveys have shown the entire feasibility of a chain of cables which at each stopping place shall touch on American territory, so that the system shall be under our own complete control. Manila once within telegraphic reach, connection with the systems of the Asiatic coast would open increased and profitable opportunities for a more direct cable route from our shores to the Orient than is now afforded by the trans-Atlantic, continental, and trans-Asian lines. I urge attention to this important matter.

The present strength of the Army is 100,000 men — 65,000 regulars and 35,000 volunteers. Under the act of March 2, 1899, on the 30th of June next the present volunteer force will be discharged and the Regular Army will be reduced to 2,447 officers and 29,025 enlisted men.

In 1888 a Board of Officers convened by President Cleveland adopted a comprehensive scheme of coast-defense fortifications which involved the outlay of something over one hundred million dollars. This plan received the approval of the Congress, and since then regular appropriations have been made and the work of fortification has steadily progressed.

More than sixty millions of dollars have been invested in a great number of forts and guns, with all the complicated and scientific machinery and electrical appliances necessary for their use. The proper care of this defensive machinery requires men trained in its use. The number of men necessary to perform this duty alone is ascertained by the War Department, at a minimum allowance, to be 18,420.

There are fifty-eight or more military posts in the United States other than the coast-defense fortifications.

The number of these posts is being constantly increased by the Congress. More than $22,000,000 have been expended in building and equipment, and they can only be cared for by the Regular Army. The posts now in existence and others to be built provide for accommodations for, and if fully garrisoned require, 26,000 troops. Many of these posts are along our frontier or at important strategic points, the occupation of which is necessary.

We have in Cuba between 5,000 and 6,000 troops. For the present our troops in that island cannot be withdrawn or materially diminished, and certainly not until the conclusion of the labors of the constitutional convention now in session and a government provided by the new constitution shall have been established and its stability assured.

In Puerto Rico we have reduced the garrisons to 1,636, which includes 879 native troops. There is no room for further reduction here.

We will be required to keep a considerable force in the Philippine Islands for some time to come. From the best information obtainable we will need there for the immediate future from 45,000 to 60,000 men. I am sure the number may be reduced as the insurgents shall come to acknowledge the authority of the United States, of which there are assuring indications.

It must be apparent that we will require an army of about 60,000, and that during present conditions in Cuba and the Philippines the President should have authority to increase the force to the present number of 100,000. Included in this number authority should be given to raise native troops in the Philippines up to 15,000, which the Taft Commission believe will be more effective in detecting and suppressing guerrillas, assassins, and ladrones than our own soldiers.

The full discussion of this subject by the Secretary of War in his annual report is called to your earnest attention.

I renew the recommendation made in my last annual message that the Congress provide a special medal of honor for the volunteers, regulars, sailors, and marines on duty in the Philippines who voluntarily remained in the service after their terms of enlistment had expired.

I favor the recommendation of the Secretary of War for the detail of officers from the line of the Army when vacancies occur in the Adjutant-General's Department, Inspector-General's Department, Quartermaster's Department, Subsistence Department, Pay Department, Ordnance Department, and Signal Corps.

The Army cannot be too highly commended for its faithful and effective service in active military operations in the field and the difficult work of civil administration.

The continued and rapid growth of the postal service is a sure index of the great and increasing business activity of the country. Its most striking new development is the extension of rural free delivery. This has come almost wholly within the last year. At the beginning of the fiscal year 1899–1900 the number of routes in operation was only 391, and most of these had been running less than twelve months. On the 15th of November, 1900, the number had increased to 2,614, reaching into forty-four States and Territories, and serving a population of 1,801,524. The number of applications now pending and awaiting action nearly equals all those granted up to the present time, and by the close of the current fiscal year about 4,000 routes will have been established, providing for the daily delivery of mails at the scattered homes of about three and a half millions of rural population.

This service ameliorates the isolation of farm life, conduces to good roads, and quickens and extends the dissemination of general information. Experience thus far has tended to allay the apprehension that it would be so expensive as to forbid its general adoption or make it a serious burden. Its actual application has shown that it increases postal receipts, and can be accompanied by reductions in other branches of the service, so that the augmented revenues and the accomplished savings together materially reduce the net cost. The evidences which point to these conclusions are presented in detail in the annual report of the Postmaster-General, which with its recommendations is commended to the consideration of the Congress. The full development of this special service, however, requires such a large outlay of money that it should be undertaken only after a careful study and thorough understanding of all that it involves.

Very efficient service has been rendered by the Navy in connection with the insurrection in the Philippines and the recent disturbance in China.

A very satisfactory settlement has been made of the long-pending question of the manufacture of armor plate. A reasonable price has been secured and the necessity for a Government armor plant avoided.

I approve of the recommendations of the Secretary for new ves-

sels and for additional officers and men which the required increase
of the Navy makes necessary.   I commend to the favorable action of
the Congress the measure now pending for the erection of a statue to
the memory of the late Admiral David D. Porter.   I commend also
the establishment of a national naval reserve and of the grade of
vice-admiral.   Provision should be made, as recommended by the
Secretary, for suitable rewards for special merit.   Many officers who
rendered the most distinguished service during the recent war with
Spain have received in return no recognition from the Congress.

The total area of public lands as given by the Secretary of the
Interior is approximately 1,071,881,662 acres, of which 917,135,880
acres are undisposed of and 154,745,782 acres have been reserved
for various purposes.   The public lands disposed of during the year
amount to 13,453,887.96 acres, including 62,423.09 acres of Indian
lands, an increase of 4,271,474.80 over the preceding year.   The
total receipts from the sale of public lands during the fiscal year
were $4,379,758.10, an increase of $1,309,620.76 over the preceding
year.

The results obtained from our forest policy have demonstrated its
wisdom and the necessity in the interest of the public for its continuance and increased appropriations by the Congress for the carrying on of the work.   On June 30, 1900, there were thirty-seven
forest reserves, created by Presidential proclamations under section
24 of the act of March 3, 1891, embracing an area of 46,425,529
acres.

During the past year the Olympic Reserve, in the State of Washington, was reduced 265,040 acres, leaving its present area at 1,923,-
840 acres.   The Prescott Reserve, in Arizona, was increased from
10,240 acres to 423,680 acres, and the Big Horn Reserve, in Wyoming, was increased from 1,127,680 acres to 1,180,800 acres.   A
new reserve, the Santa Ynez, in California, embracing an area of
145,000 acres, was created during this year.   On October 10, 1900,
the Crow Creek Forest Reserve, in Wyoming, was created, with an
area of 56,320 acres.

At the end of the fiscal year there were on the pension roll 993,529
names, a net increase of 2,010 over the fiscal year 1899.   The number added to the rolls during the year was 45,344.   The amount disbursed for Army pensions during the year was $134,700,597.24 and
for Navy pensions $3,761,533.41, a total of $138,462,130.65, leaving
an unexpended balance of $5,542,768.25 to be covered into the Treas-
ury, which shows an increase over the previous year's expenditure
of $107,077.70.   There were 684 names added to the rolls during
the year by special acts passed at the first session of the Fifty-sixth
Congress.

The act of May 9, 1900, among other things provides for an extension of income to widows pensioned under said act to $250 per annum. The Secretary of the Interior believes that by the operations of this act the number of persons pensioned under it will increase and the increased annual payment for pensions will be between $3,000,000 and $4,000,000.

The Government justly appreciates the services of its soldiers and sailors by making pension payments liberal beyond precedent to them, their widows and orphans.

There were 26,540 letters patent granted, including reissues and designs, during the fiscal year ended June 30, 1900; 1,660 trademarks, 682 labels, and 93 prints registered. The number of patents which expired was 19,988. The total receipts for patents were $1,358,228.35. The expenditures were $1,247,827.58, showing a surplus of $110,400.77.

The attention of the Congress is called to the report of the Secretary of the Interior touching the necessity for the further establishment of schools in the Territory of Alaska, and favorable action is invited thereon.

Much interesting information is given in the report of the Governor of Hawaii as to the progress and development of the islands during the period from July 7, 1898, the date of the approval of the joint resolution of the Congress providing for their annexation, up to April 30, 1900, the date of the approval of the act providing a government for the Territory, and thereafter.

The last Hawaiian census, taken in the year 1896, gives a total population of 109,020, of which 31,019 were native Hawaiians. The number of Americans reported was 8,485. The results of the Federal census, taken this year, show the islands to have a total population of 154,001, showing an increase over that reported in 1896 of 44,981, or 41.2 per cent.

There has been marked progress in the educational, agricultural, and railroad development of the islands.

In the Territorial act of April 30, 1900, section 7 of said act repeals Chapter 34 of the Civil Laws of Hawaii whereby the Government was to assist in encouraging and developing the agricultural resources of the Republic, especially irrigation. The Governor of Hawaii recommends legislation looking to the development of such water supply as may exist on the public lands, with a view of promoting land settlement. The earnest consideration of the Congress is invited to this important recommendation and others, as embodied in the report of the Secretary of the Interior.

The Director of the Census states that the work in connection with the Twelfth Census is progressing favorably. This national undertaking, ordered by the Congress each decade, has finally resulted in the collection of an aggregation of statistical facts to determine the industrial growth of the country, its manufacturing and mechanical resources, its richness in mines and forests, the number of its agriculturists, their farms and products, its educational and religious opportunities, as well as questions pertaining to sociological conditions.

The labors of the officials in charge of the Bureau indicate that the four important and most-desired subjects, namely, population, agricultural, manufacturing, and vital statistics, will be completed within the limit prescribed by the law of March 3, 1899.

The field work incident to the above inquiries is now practically finished, and as a result the population of the States and Territories, including the Hawaiian Islands and Alaska, has been announced. The growth of population during the last decade amounts to over 13,000,000, a greater numerical increase than in any previous census in the history of the country.

Bulletins will be issued as rapidly as possible giving the population by States and Territories, by minor civil divisions. Several announcements of this kind have already been made, and it is hoped that the list will be completed by January 1. Other bulletins giving the results of the manufacturing and agricultural inquiries will be given to the public as rapidly as circumstances will admit.

The Director, while confident of his ability to complete the different branches of the undertaking in the allotted time, finds himself embarrassed by the lack of a trained force properly equipped for statistical work, thus raising the question whether in the interest of economy and a thorough execution of the census work there should not be retained in the Government employ a certain number of experts not only to aid in the preliminary organization prior to the taking of the decennial census, but in addition to have the advantage in the field and office work of the Bureau of trained assistants to facilitate the early completion of this enormous undertaking.

I recommend that the Congress at its present session apportion representation among the several States as provided by the Constitution.

The Department of Agriculture has been extending its work during the past year, reaching farther for new varieties of seeds and plants; co-operating more fully with the States and Territories in research along useful lines; making progress in meteorological work relating to lines of wireless telegraphy and forecasts for ocean-going vessels; continuing inquiry as to animal disease; looking into the extent and character of food adulteration; outlining plans for the care, preservation, and intelligent harvesting of our woodlands; s'udying soils that producers may cultivate with better knowledge oι conditions, and helping to clothe desert places with grasses suitable to our arid regions. Our island possessions are being considered that their peoples may be helped to produce the tropical products now so extensively brought into the United States. Inquiry into methods of improving our roads has been active during the year; help has been given to many localities, and scientific investigation of material in the States and Territories has been inaugurated. Irri gation problems in our semiarid regions are receiving careful and increased consideration.

An extensive exhibit at Paris of the products of agriculture has made the peoples of many countries more familiar with the varied products of our fields and their comparative excellence.

The collection of statistics regarding our crops is being improved and sources of information are being enlarged, to the end that producers may have the earliest advices regarding crop conditions. There has never been a time when those for whom it was established have shown more appreciation of the services of the Department.

In my annual message of December 5, 1898, I called attention to the necessity for some amendment of the alien contract law. There still remain important features of the rightful application of the eight-hour law for the benefit of labor and of the principle of arbitration, and I again commend these subjects to the careful attention of the Congress.

That there may be secured the best service possible in the Philippine Islands, I have issued, under date of November 30, 1900, the following order:

The United States Civil Service Commission is directed to render such assistance as may be practicable to the Civil Service Board, created under the act of the United States Philippine Commission, for the establishment and maintenance of an honest and efficient civil service in the Philippine Islands, and for that purpose to conduct examinations for the civil service of the Philippine Islands, upon the request of the Civil Service Board of said islands, under such regulations as may be agreed upon by the said Board and the said United States Civil Service Commission.

The Civil Service Commission is greatly embarrassed in its work for want of an adequate permanent force for clerical and other assistance. Its needs are fully set forth in its report. I invite attention to the report, and especially urge upon the Congress that this important bureau of the public service, which passes upon the qualifications and character of so large a number of the officers and employees of the Government, should be supported by all needed appropriations to secure promptness and efficiency.

I am very much impressed with the statement made by the heads of all the Departments of the urgent necessity of a hall of public records. In every departmental building in Washington, so far as I am informed, the space for official records is not only exhausted, but the walls of rooms are lined with shelves, the middle floor space of many rooms is filled with file cases, and garrets and basements, which were never intended and are unfitted for their accommodation, are crowded with them. Aside from the inconvenience there is great danger, not only from fire, but from the weight of these records upon timbers not intended for their support. There should be a separate building especially designed for the purpose of receiving and preserving the annually accumulating archives of the several Executive Departments. Such a hall need not be a costly structure, but should be so arranged as to admit of enlargement from time to time. I urgently recommend that the Congress take early action in this matter.

I transmit to the Congress a resolution adopted at a recent meeting of the American Bar Association concerning the proposed celebration of John Marshall Day, February 4, 1901. Fitting exercises have been arranged, and it is earnestly desired by the committee that the Congress may participate in this movement to honor the memory of the great jurist.

The transfer of the Government to this city is a fact of great historical interest. Among the people there is a feeling of genuine pride in the Capital of the Republic.

It is a matter of interest in this connection that in 1800 the population of the District of Columbia was 14,093; to-day it is 278,718. The population of the city of Washington was then 3,210; to-day it is 218,196.

The Congress having provided for "an appropriate national celebration of the Centennial Anniversary of the Establishment of the Seat of the Government in the District of Columbia," the committees authorized by it have prepared a programme for the 12th of December, 1900, which date has been selected as the anniversary day. Deep interest has been shown in the arrangements for the celebration by the members of the committees of the Senate and House of Representatives, the committee of Governors appointed by the President, and the committees appointed by the citizens and inhabitants of the District of Columbia generally. The programme, in addition to a reception and other exercises at the Executive Mansion, provides commemorative exercises to be held jointly by the Senate and House of Representatives in the Hall of the House of Representatives, and a reception in the evening at the Corcoran Gallery of Art in honor of the Governors of the States and Territories.

In our great prosperity we must guard against the danger it invites of extravagance in Government expenditures and appropriations; and the chosen representatives of the people will, I doubt not, furnish an example in their legislation of that wise economy which in a season of plenty husbands for the future. In this era of great business activity and opportunity caution is not untimely. It will not abate, but strengthen, confidence. It will not retard, but promote, legitimate industrial and commercial expansion. Our growing power brings with it temptations and perils requiring constant vigilance to avoid. It must not be used to invite conflicts, nor for oppression, but for the more effective maintenance of those principles of equality and justice upon which our institutions and happiness depend. Let us keep always in mind that the foundation of our Government is liberty; its superstructure peace.

Theodore Roosevelt

September 14, 1901 to March 4, 1905

(First Term)

FIRST ANNUAL MESSAGE

WHITE HOUSE, *December 3, 1901.*

To the Senate and House of Representatives:

The Congress assembles this year under the shadow of a great calamity. On the sixth of September, President McKinley was shot by an anarchist while attending the Pan-American Exposition at Buffalo, and died in that city on the fourteenth of that month.

Of the last seven elected Presidents, he is the third who has been murdered, and the bare recital of this fact is sufficient to justify grave alarm among all loyal American citizens. Moreover, the circumstances of this, the third assassination of an American President, have a peculiarly sinister significance. Both President Lincoln and President Garfield were killed by assassins of types unfortunately not uncommon in history; President Lincoln falling a victim to the terrible passions aroused by four years of civil war, and President Garfield to the revengeful vanity of a disappointed office-seeker. President McKinley was killed by an utterly depraved criminal belonging to that body of criminals who object to all governments, good and bad alike, who are against any form of popular liberty if it is guaranteed by even the most just and liberal laws, and who are as hostile to the upright exponent of a free people's sober will as to the tyrannical and irresponsible despot.

It is not too much to say that at the time of President McKinley's death he was the most widely loved man in all the United States; while we have never had any public man of his position who has been so wholly free from the bitter animosities incident to public life. His political opponents were the first to bear the heartiest and most generous tribute to the broad kindliness of nature, the sweetness and gentleness of character which so endeared him to his close associates. To a standard of lofty integrity in public life he united the tender affections and home virtues which are all-important in the make-up of national character. A gallant soldier in the great war for the Union, he also shone as an example to all our people because of his conduct in the most sacred and intimate of home relations. There could be no personal hatred of him, for he never acted with aught but consideration for the welfare of others. No one could fail to respect him who knew him in public or private life. The defenders of those murderous criminals who seek to excuse their criminality by asserting that it is exercised for political ends, inveigh against wealth and irresponsible power. But for this assassination even this base apology cannot be urged.

President McKinley was a man of moderate means, a man whose stock sprang from the sturdy tillers of the soil, who had himself belonged among the wage-workers, who had entered the Army as a private soldier. Wealth was not struck at when the President was assassinated, but the honest toil which is content with moderate gains after a lifetime of unremitting labor, largely in the service of the public. Still less was power struck at in the sense that power is irresponsible or centered in the hands of any one individual. The blow was not aimed at tyranny or wealth. It was aimed at one of the strongest champions the wage-worker has ever had; at one of the most faithful representatives of the system of public rights and representative government who has ever risen to public office. President McKinley filled that political office for which the entire people vote, and no President — not even Lincoln himself — was ever more earnestly anxious to represent the well thought-out wishes of the people; his one anxiety in every crisis was to keep in closest touch with the people — to find out what they thought and to endeavor to give expression to their thought, after having endeavored to guide that thought aright. He had just been reelected to the Presidency because the majority of our citizens, the majority of our farmers and wage-workers, believed that he had faithfully upheld their interests for four years. They felt themselves in close and intimate touch with him. They felt that he represented so well and so honorably all their ideals and aspirations that they wished him to continue for another four years to represent them.

And this was the man at whom the assassin struck! That there might be nothing lacking to complete the Judas-like infamy of his act, he took advantage of an occasion when the President was meeting the people generally; and advancing as if to take the hand out-stretched to him in kindly and brotherly fellowship, he turned the noble and generous confidence of the victim into an opportunity to strike the fatal blow. There is no baser deed in all the annals of crime.

The shock, the grief of the country, are bitter in the minds of all who saw the dark days, while the President yet hovered between life and death. At last the light was stilled in the kindly eyes and the breath went from the lips that even in mortal agony uttered no words save of forgiveness to his murderer, of love for his friends, and of unfaltering trust in the will of the Most High. Such a death, crowning the glory of such a life, leaves us with infinite sorrow, but with such pride in what he had accomplished and in his own personal character, that we feel the blow not as struck at him, but as struck at the Nation

We mourn a good and great President who is dead; but while we mourn we are lifted up by the splendid achievements of his life and the grand heroism with which he met his death.

When we turn from the man to the Nation, the harm done is so great as to excite our gravest apprehensions and to demand our wisest and most resolute action. This criminal was a professed anarchist, inflamed by the teachings of professed anarchists, and probably also by the reckless utterances of those who, on the stump and in the public press, appeal to the dark and evil spirits of malice and greed, envy and sullen hatred. The wind is sowed by the men who preach such doctrines, and they cannot escape their share of responsibility for the whirlwind that is reaped. This applies alike to the deliberate demagogue, to the exploiter of sensationalism, and to the crude and foolish visionary who, for whatever reason, apologizes for crime or excites aimless discontent.

The blow was aimed not at this President, but at all Presidents; at every symbol of government. President McKinley was as emphatically the embodiment of the popular will of the Nation expressed through the forms of law as a New England town meeting is in similar fashion the embodiment of the law-abiding purpose and practice of the people of the town. On no conceivable theory could the murder of the President be accepted as due to protest against " inequalities in the social order," save as the murder of all the freemen engaged in a town meeting could be accepted as a protest against that social inequality which puts a malefactor in jail. Anarchy is no more an expression of " social discontent " than picking pockets or wife-beating.

The anarchist, and especially the anarchist in the United States, is merely one type of criminal, more dangerous than any other because he represents the same depravity in a greater degree. The man who advocates anarchy directly or indirectly, in any shape or fashion, or the man who apologizes for anarchists and their deeds, makes himself morally accessory to murder before the fact. The anarchist is a criminal whose perverted instincts lead him to prefer confusion and chaos to the most beneficent form of social order. His protest of concern for workingmen is outrageous in its impudent falsity; for if the political institutions of this country do not afford opportunity to every honest and intelligent son of toil, then the door of hope is forever closed against him. The anarchist is everywhere not merely the enemy of system and of progress, but the deadly foe of liberty. If ever anarchy is triumphant, its triumph will last for but one red moment, to be succeeded for ages by the gloomy night of despotism.

For the anarchist himself, whether he preaches or practices his doctrines, we need not have one particle more concern than for any ordinary murderer. He is not the victim of social or political injustice. There are no wrongs to remedy in his case. The cause of his criminality is to be found in his own evil passions and in the evil conduct of those who urge him on, not in any failure by others or by the State to do justice to him or his. He is a malefactor and nothing else. He is in no sense, in no shape or way, a " product of social conditions," save as a highwayman is " produced " by the fact than an unarmed man happens to have a purse. It is a travesty upon the great and holy names of liberty and freedom to permit them to be invoked in such a cause. No man or body of men preaching anarchistic doctrines should be allowed at large any more than if preaching the murder of some specified private individual. Anarchistic speeches, writings, and meetings are essentially seditious and treasonable.

I earnestly recommend to the Congress that in the exercise of its wise discretion it should take into consideration the coming to this country of anarchists or persons professing principles hostile to all government and justifying the murder of those placed in authority. Such individuals as those who not long ago gathered in open meeting to glorify the murder of King Humbert of Italy perpetrate a crime, and the law should ensure their rigorous punishment. They and those like them should be kept out of this country; and if found here they should be promptly deported to the country whence they came; and far-reaching provision should be made for the punishment of those who stay. No matter calls more urgently for the wisest thought of the Congress.

The Federal courts should be given jurisdiction over any man who kills or attempts to kill the President or any man who by the Constitution or by law is in line of succession for the Presidency, while the punishment for an unsuccessful attempt should be proportioned to the enormity of the offense against our institutions.

Anarchy is a crime against the whole human race; and all mankind should band against the anarchist. His crime should be made an offense against the law of nations, like piracy and that form of man-stealing known as the slave trade; for it is of far blacker infamy than either. It should be so declared by treaties among all civilized powers. Such treaties would give to the Federal Government the power of dealing with the crime.

A grim commentary upon the folly of the anarchist position was afforded by the attitude of the law toward this very criminal who had just taken the life of the President. The people would have torn him limb from limb if it had not been that the law he defied was at once invoked in his behalf. So far from his deed being committed on behalf of the people against the Government, the Government was obliged at once to exert its full police power to save him from instant death at the hands of the people. Moreover, his deed worked not the slightest dislocation in our governmental system, and the danger of a recurrence of such deeds, no matter how great it might grow, would work only in the direction of strengthening and giving harshness to the forces of order. No man will ever be restrained from becoming President by any fear as to his personal safety. If the risk to the President's life became great, it would mean that the office would more and more come to be filled by men of a spirit which would make them resolute and merciless in dealing with every friend of disorder. This great country will not fall into anarchy, and if anarchists should ever become a serious menace to its institutions, they would not merely be stamped out, but would involve in their own ruin every active or passive sympathizer with their doctrines. The American people are slow to wrath, but when their wrath is once kindled it burns like a consuming flame.

During the last five years business confidence has been restored, and the nation is to be congratulated because of its present abounding prosperity. Such prosperity can never be created by law alone, although it is easy enough to destroy it by mischievous laws. If the hand of the Lord is heavy upon any country, if flood or drought comes, human wisdom is powerless to avert the calamity. Moreover, no law can guard us against the consequences of our own folly. The men who are idle or credulous, the men who seek gains not by genuine work with head or hand but by gambling in any form, are always a source of menace not only to themselves but to others. If the business world loses its head, it loses what legislation cannot supply. Fundamentally the welfare of each citizen, and therefore the welfare of the aggregate of citizens which makes the nation, must rest upon individual thrift and energy, resolution, and intelligence. Nothing can take the place of this individual capacity; but wise legislation and honest and intelligent administration can give it the fullest scope, the largest opportunity to work to good effect.

The tremendous and highly complex industrial development which went on with ever accelerated rapidity during the latter half of the nineteenth century brings us face to face, at the beginning of the twentieth, with very serious social problems. The old laws, and the old customs which had almost the binding force of law, were once quite sufficient to regulate the accumulation and distribution of wealth. Since the industrial changes which have so enormously increased the productive power of mankind, they are no longer sufficient.

The growth of cities has gone on beyond comparison faster than the growth of the country, and the upbuilding of the great industrial centers has meant a startling increase, not merely in the aggregate of wealth, but in the number of very large individual, and especially of very large corporate, fortunes. The creation of these great corporate fortunes has not been due to the tariff nor to any other governmental action, but to natural causes in the business world, operating in other countries as they operate in our own.

The process has aroused much antagonism, a great part of which is wholly without warrant. It is not true that as the rich have grown richer the poor have grown poorer. On the contrary, never before has the average man, the wage-worker, the farmer, the small trader, been so well off as in this country and at the present time. There have been abuses connected with the accumulation of wealth; yet it remains true that a fortune accumulated in legitimate business can be accumulated by the person specially benefited only on condition of conferring immense incidental benefits upon others. Successful enterprise, of the type which benefits all mankind, can only exist if the conditions are such as to offer great prizes as the rewards of success.

The captains of industry who have driven the railway systems across this continent, who have built up our commerce, who have developed our manufactures, have on the whole done great good to our people. Without them the material development of which we are so justly proud could never have taken place. Moreover, we should recognize the immense importance of this material development of leaving as unhampered as is compatible with the public good the strong and forceful men upon whom the success of business operations inevitably rests. The slightest study of business conditions will satisfy anyone capable of forming a judgment that the personal equation is the most important factor in a business operation; that the business ability of the man at the head of any business concern, big or little, is usually the factor which fixes the gulf between striking success and hopeless failure.

An additional reason for caution in dealing with corporations is to be found in the international commercial conditions of to-day. The same business conditions which have produced the great aggregations of corporate and individual wealth have made them very potent factors in international commercial competition. Business concerns which have the largest means at their disposal and are managed by the ablest men are naturally those which take the lead in the strife for commercial supremacy among the nations of the world. America has only just begun to assume that commanding position in the international business world which we believe will more and more be hers. It is of the utmost importance that this position be not jeoparded, especially at a time when the overflowing abundance of our own natural resources and the skill, business energy, and mechanical aptitude of our people make foreign markets essential. Under such conditions it would be most unwise to cramp or to fetter the youthful strength of our Nation.

Moreover, it cannot too often be pointed out that to strike with ignorant violence at the interests of one set of men almost inevitably endangers the interests of all. The fundamental rule in our national life — the rule which underlies all others — is that, on the whole, and in the long run, we shall go up or down together. There are exceptions; and in times of prosperity some will prosper far more, and in times of adversity, some will suffer far more, than others; but speaking generally, a period of good times means that all share more or less in them, and in a period of hard times all feel the stress to a greater or less degree. It surely ought not to be necessary to enter into any proof of this statement; the memory of the lean years which began in 1893 is still vivid, and we can contrast them with the conditions in this very year which is now closing. Disaster to great business enterprises can never have its effects limited to the men at the top. It spreads throughout, and while it is bad for everybody, it is worst for those farthest down. The capitalist may be shorn of his luxuries; but the wageworker may be deprived of even bare necessities.

The mechanism of modern business is so delicate that extreme care

must be taken not to interfere with it in a spirit of rashness or ignorance.   Many of those who have made it their vocation to denounce the
great industrial combinations which are popularly, although with technical inaccuracy, known as "trusts," appeal especially to hatred and
fear.   These are precisely the two emotions, particularly when combined with ignorance, which unfit men for the exercise of cool and steady
judgment.   In facing new industrial conditions, the whole history of
the world shows that legislation will generally be both unwise and ineffective unless undertaken after calm inquiry and with sober self-
restraint.   Much of the legislation directed at the trusts would have
been exceedingly mischievous had it not also been entirely ineffective.
In accordance with a well-known sociological law, the ignorant or reckless agitator has been the really effective friend of the evils which he
has been nominally opposing.   In dealing with business interests, for
the Government to undertake by crude and ill-considered legislation to
do what may turn out to be bad, would be to incur the risk of such far-
reaching national disaster that it would be preferable to undertake
nothing at all.   The men who demand the impossible or the undesirable
serve as the allies of the forces with which they are nominally at war,
for they hamper those who would endeavor to find out in rational fashion what the wrongs really are and to what extent and in what manner
it is practicable to apply remedies.

All this is true; and yet it is also true that there are real and grave
evils, one of the chief being over-capitalization because of its many
baleful consequences; and a resolute and practical effort must be made
to correct these evils.

There is a widespread conviction in the minds of the American people
that the great corporations known as trusts are in certain of their
features and tendencies hurtful to the general welfare.   This springs
from no spirit of envy or uncharitableness, nor lack of pride in the
great industrial achievements that have placed this country at the head
of the nations struggling for commercial supremacy.   It does not rest
upon a lack of intelligent appreciation of the necessity of meeting
changing and changed conditions of trade with new methods, nor upon
ignorance of the fact that combination of capital in the effort to accomplish great things is necessary when the world's progress demands that
great things be done.   It is based upon sincere conviction that combination and concentration should be, not prohibited, but supervised and
within reasonable limits controlled; and in my judgment this conviction
is right.

It is no limitation upon property rights or freedom of contract to require that when men receive from Government the privilege of doing
business under corporate form, which frees them from individual
responsibility, and enables them to call into their enterprises the capital
of the public, they shall do so upon absolutely truthful representations

as to the value of the property in which the capital is to be invested. Corporations engaged in interstate commerce should be regulated if they are found to exercise a license working to the public injury. It should be as much the aim of those who seek for social betterment to rid the business world of crimes of cunning as to rid the entire body politic of crimes of violence. Great corporations exist only because they are created and safeguarded by our institutions; and it is therefore our right and our duty to see that they work in harmony with these institutions.

The first essential in determining how to deal with the great industrial combinations is knowledge of the facts — publicity. In the interest of the public, the Government should have the right to inspect and examine the workings of the great corporations engaged in interstate business. Publicity is the only sure remedy which we can now invoke. What further remedies are needed in the way of governmental regulation, or taxation, can only be determined after publicity has been obtained, by process of law, and in the course of administration. The first requisite is knowledge, full and complete — knowledge which may be made public to the world.

Artificial bodies, such as corporations and joint stock or other associations, depending upon any statutory law for their existence or privileges, should be subject to proper governmental supervision, and full and accurate information as to their operations should be made public regularly at reasonable intervals.

The large corporations, commonly called trusts, though organized in one State, always do business in many States, often doing very little business in the State where they are incorporated. There is utter lack of uniformity in the State laws about them; and as no State has any exclusive interest in or power over their acts, it has in practice proved impossible to get adequate regulation through State action. Therefore, in the interest of the whole people, the Nation should, without interfering with the power of the States in the matter itself, also assume power of supervision and regulation over all corporations doing an interstate business. This is especially true where the corporation derives a portion of its wealth from the existence of some monopolistic element or tendency in its business. There would be no hardship in such supervision; banks are subject to it, and in their case it is now accepted as a simple matter of course. Indeed, it is probable that supervision of corporations by the National Government need not go so far as is now the case with the supervision exercised over them by so conservative a State as Massachusetts, in order to produce excellent results.

When the Constitution was adopted, at the end of the eighteenth century, no human wisdom could foretell the sweeping changes, alike in industrial and political conditions, which were to take place by the beginning of the twentieth century. At that time it was accepted as a matter of course that the several States were the proper authorities to regulate, so far as was then necessary, the comparatively insignificant and strictly localized corporate bodies of the day. The conditions are now wholly different and wholly different action is called for. I believe that a law can be framed which will enable the National Government to exercise control along the lines above indicated; profiting by the experience gained through the passage and administration of the Interstate-Commerce Act. If, however, the judgment of the Congress is that it lacks the constitutional power to pass such an act, then a constitutional amendment should be submitted to confer the power.

There should be created a Cabinet officer, to be known as Secretary of Commerce and Industries, as provided in the bill introduced at the last session of the Congress. It should be his province to deal with commerce in its broadest sense; including among many other things whatever concerns labor and all matters affecting the great business corporations and our merchant marine.

The course proposed is one phase of what should be a comprehensive and far-reaching scheme of constructive statesmanship for the purpose of broadening our markets, securing our business interests on a safe basis, and making firm our new position in the international industrial world; while scrupulously safeguarding the rights of wage-worker and capitalist, of investor and private citizen, so as to secure equity as between man and man in this Republic.

With the sole exception of the farming interest, no one matter is of such vital moment to our whole people as the welfare of the wage-workers. If the farmer and the wage-worker are well off, it is absolutely certain that all others will be well off too. It is therefore a matter for hearty congratulation that on the whole wages are higher to-day in the United States than ever before in our history, and far higher than in any other country. The standard of living is also higher than ever before. Every effort of legislator and administrator should be bent to secure the permanency of this condition of things and its improvement wherever possible. Not only must our labor be protected by the tariff, but it should also be protected so far as it is possible from the presence in this country of any laborers brought over by contract, or of those who, coming freely, yet represent a standard of living so depressed that they can undersell our men in the labor market and drag them to a lower level. I regard it as necessary, with this end in view, to re-enact immediately the law excluding Chinese laborers and to strengthen it wherever necessary in order to make its enforcement entirely effective.

The National Government should demand the highest quality of service from its employees; and in return it should be a good employer. If possible legislation should be passed, in connection with the Interstate Commerce Law, which will render effective the efforts of different

States to do away with the competition of convict contract labor in the open labor market. So far as practicable under the conditions of Government work, provision should be made to render the enforcement of the eight-hour law easy and certain. In all industries carried on directly or indirectly for the United States Government women and children should be protected from excessive hours of labor, from night work, and from work under unsanitary conditions. The Government should provide in its contracts that all work should be done under "fair" conditions, and in addition to setting a high standard should uphold it by proper inspection, extending if necessary to the subcontractors. The Government should forbid all night work for women and children, as well as excessive overtime. For the District of Columbia a good factory law should be passed; and, as a powerful indirect aid to such laws, provision should be made to turn the inhabited alleys, the existence of which is a reproach to our Capital city, into minor streets, where the inhabitants can live under conditions favorable to health and morals.

American wage-workers work with their heads as well as their hands. Moreover, they take a keen pride in what they are doing; so that, independent of the reward, they wish to turn out a perfect job. This is the great secret of our success in competition with the labor of foreign countries.

The most vital problem with which this country, and for that matter the whole civilized world, has to deal, is the problem which has for one side the betterment of social conditions, moral and physical, in large cities, and for another side the effort to deal with that tangle of far-reaching questions which we group together when we speak of "labor." The chief factor in the success of each man — wage-worker, farmer, and capitalist alike — must ever be the sum total of his own individual qualities and abilities. Second only to this comes the power of acting in combination or association with others. Very great good has been and will be accomplished by associations or unions of wage-workers, when managed with forethought, and when they combine insistence upon their own rights with law-abiding respect for the rights of others. The display of these qualities in such bodies is a duty to the nation no less than to the associations themselves. Finally, there must also in many cases be action by the Government in order to safeguard the rights and interests of all. Under our Constitution there is much more scope for such action by the State and the municipality than by the nation. But on points such as those touched on above the National Government can act.

When all is said and done, the rule of brotherhood remains as the indispensable prerequisite to success in the kind of national life for which we strive. Each man must work for himself, and unless he so works no outside help can avail him; but each man must remember also that he is indeed his brother's keeper, and that while no man who refuses to walk can be carried with advantage to himself or anyone else, yet that each at times stumbles or halts, that each at times needs to have the helping hand outstretched to him.   To be permanently effective, aid must always take the form of helping a man to help himself; and we can all best help ourselves by joining together in the work that is of common interest to all.

Our present immigration laws are unsatisfactory. We need every honest and efficient immigrant fitted to become an American citizen, every immigrant who comes here to stay, who brings here a strong body, a stout heart, a good head, and a resolute purpose to do his duty well in every way and to bring up his children as law-abiding and God-fearing members of the community.   But there should be a comprehensive law enacted with the object of working a threefold improvement over our present system.   First, we should aim to exclude absolutely not only all persons who are known to be believers in anarchistic principles or members of anarchistic societies, but also all persons who are of a low moral tendency or of unsavory reputation.   This means that we should require a more thorough system of inspection abroad and a more rigid system of examination at our immigration ports, the former being especially necessary.

The second object of a proper immigration law ought to be to secure by a careful and not merely perfunctory educational test some intelligent capacity to appreciate American institutions and act sanely as American citizens.   This would not keep out all anarchists, for many of them belong to the intelligent criminal class.   But it would do what is also in point, that is, tend to decrease the sum of ignorance, so potent in producing the envy, suspicion, malignant passion, and hatred of order, out of which anarchistic sentiment inevitably springs.   Finally, all persons should be excluded who are below a certain standard of economic fitness to enter our industrial field as competitors with American labor.   There should be proper proof of personal capacity to earn an American living and enough money to insure a decent start under American conditions.   This would stop the influx of cheap labor, and the resulting competition which gives rise to so much of bitterness in American industrial life; and it would dry up the springs of the pestilential social conditions in our great cities, where anarchistic organizations have their greatest possibility of growth.

Both the educational and economic tests in a wise immigration law should be designed to protect and elevate the general body politic and social.   A very close supervision should be exercised over the steamship companies which mainly bring over the immigrants, and they should be held to a strict accountability for any infraction of the law.

There is general acquiescence in our present tariff system as a national policy. The first requisite to our prosperity is the continuity and stability of this economic policy. Nothing could be more unwise than to disturb the business interests of the country by any general tariff change at this time. Doubt, apprehension, uncertainty are exactly what we most wish to avoid in the interest of our commercial and material well-being. Our experience in the past has shown that sweeping revisions of the tariff are apt to produce conditions closely approaching panic in the business world. Yet it is not only possible, but eminently desirable, to combine with the stability of our economic system a supplementary system of reciprocal benefit and obligation with other nations. Such reciprocity is an incident and result of the firm establishment and preservation of our present economic policy. It was specially provided for in the present tariff law.

Reciprocity must be treated as the handmaiden of protection. Our first duty is to see that the protection granted by the tariff in every case where it is needed is maintained, and that reciprocity be sought for so far as it can safely be done without injury to our home industries. Just how far this is must be determined according to the individual case, remembering always that every application of our tariff policy to meet our shifting national needs must be conditioned upon the cardinal fact that the duties must never be reduced below the point that will cover the difference between the labor cost here and abroad. The well-being of the wage-worker is a prime consideration of our entire policy of economic legislation.

Subject to this proviso of the proper protection necessary to our industrial well-being at home, the principle of reciprocity must command our hearty support. The phenomenal growth of our export trade emphasizes the urgency of the need for wider markets and for a liberal policy in dealing with foreign nations. Whatever is merely petty and vexatious in the way of trade restrictions should be avoided. The customers to whom we dispose of our surplus products in the long run, directly or indirectly, purchase those surplus products by giving us something in return. Their ability to purchase our products should as far as possible be secured by so arranging our tariff as to enable us to take from them those products which we can use without harm to our own industries and labor, or the use of which will be of marked benefit to us.

It is most important that we should maintain the high level of our present prosperity. We have now reached the point in the development of our interests where we are not only able to supply our own markets but to produce a constantly growing surplus for which we must find markets abroad. To secure these markets we can utilize existing duties in any case where they are no longer needed for the purpose of protection, or in any case where the article is not produced here and the duty is no longer necessary for revenue, as giving us something to offer in exchange for what we ask. The cordial relations with other nations which are so desirable will naturally be promoted by the course thus required by our own interests.

The natural line of development for a policy of reciprocity will be in connection with those of our productions which no longer require all of the support once needed to establish them upon a sound basis, and with those others where either because of natural or of economic causes we are beyond the reach of successful competition.

I ask the attention of the Senate to the reciprocity treaties laid before it by my predecessor.

The condition of the American merchant marine is such as to call for immediate remedial action by the Congress. It is discreditable to us as a Nation that our merchant marine should be utterly insignificant in comparison to that of other nations which we overtop in other forms of business. We should not longer submit to conditions under which only a trifling portion of our great commerce is carried in our own ships. To remedy this state of things would not merely serve to build up our shipping interests, but it would also result in benefit to all who are interested in the permanent establishment of a wider market for American products, and would provide an auxiliary force for the Navy. Ships work for their own countries just as railroads work for their terminal points. Shipping lines, if established to the principal countries with which we have dealings, would be of political as well as commercial benefit. From every standpoint it is unwise for the United States to continue to rely upon the ships of competing nations for the distribution of our goods. It should be made advantageous to carry American goods in American-built ships.

At present American shipping is under certain great disadvantages when put in competition with the shipping of foreign countries. Many of the fast foreign steamships, at a speed of fourteen knots or above, are subsidized; and all our ships, sailing vessels and steamers alike, cargo carriers of slow speed and mail carriers of high speed, have to meet the fact that the original cost of building American ships is greater than is the case abroad; that the wages paid American officers and seamen are very much higher than those paid the officers and seamen of foreign competing countries; and that the standard of living on our ships is far superior to the standard of living on the ships of our commercial rivals.

Our Government should take such action as will remedy these inequalities. The American merchant marine should be restored to the ocean.

The Act of March 14, 1900, intended unequivocally to establish gold as the standard money and to maintain at a parity therewith all forms of money medium in use with us, has been shown to be timely and judicious. The price of our Government bonds in the world's market, when compared with the price of similar obligations issued by other nations, is a flattering tribute to our public credit. This condition it is evidently desirable to maintain.

In many respects the National Banking Law furnishes sufficient liberty for the proper exercise of the banking function; but there seems to be need of better safeguards against the deranging influence of commercial crises and financial panics. Moreover, the currency of the country should be made responsive to the demands of our domestic trade and commerce.

The collections from duties on imports and internal taxes continue to exceed the ordinary expenditures of the Government, thanks mainly to the reduced army expenditures. The utmost care should be taken not to reduce the revenues so that there will be any possibility of a deficit; but, after providing against any such contingency, means should be adopted which will bring the revenues more nearly within the limit of our actual needs. In his report to the Congress the Secretary of the Treasury considers all these questions at length, and I ask your attention to the report and recommendations.

I call special attention to the need of strict economy in expenditures. The fact that our national needs forbid us to be niggardly in providing whatever is actually necessary to our well-being, should make us doubly careful to husband our national resources, as each of us husbands his private resources, by scrupulous avoidance of anything like wasteful or reckless expenditure. Only by avoidance of spending money on what is needless or unjustifiable can we legitimately keep our income to the point required to meet our needs that are genuine.

In 1887 a measure was enacted for the regulation of interstate railways, commonly known as the Interstate Commerce Act. The cardinal provisions of that act were that railway rates should be just and reasonable and that all shippers, localities, and commodities should be accorded equal treatment. A commission was created and endowed with what were supposed to be the necessary powers to execute the provisions of this act.

That law was largely an experiment. Experience has shown the wisdom of its purposes, but has also shown, possibly that some of its requirements are wrong, certainly that the means devised for the enforcement of its provisions are defective. Those who complain of the management of the railways allege that established rates are not maintained; that rebates and similar devices are habitually resorted to; that these preferences are usually in favor of the large shipper; that they drive out of business the smaller competitor; that while many rates are too low, many others are excessive; and that gross preferences are made, affecting both localities and commodities.   Upon the other hand, the railways assert that the law by its very terms tends to produce many of these illegal practices by depriving carriers of that right of concerted action which they claim is necessary to establish and maintain non-discriminating rates.

The act should be amended.   The railway is a public servant.   Its rates should be just to and open to all shippers alike.   The Government should see to it that within its jurisdiction this is so and should provide a speedy, inexpensive, and effective remedy to that end.   At the same time it must not be forgotten that our railways are the arteries through which the commercial lifeblood of this Nation flows.   Nothing could be more foolish than the enactment of legislation which would unnecessarily interfere with the development and operation of these commercial agencies.   The subject is one of great importance and calls for the earnest attention of the Congress.

The Department of Agriculture during the past fifteen years has steadily broadened its work on economic lines, and has accomplished results of real value in upbuilding domestic and foreign trade.   It has gone into new fields until it is now in touch with all sections of our country and with two of the island groups that have lately come under our jurisdiction, whose people must look to agriculture as a livelihood. It is searching the world for grains, grasses, fruits, and vegetables specially fitted for introduction into localities in the several States and Territories where they may add materially to our resources.   By scientific attention to soil survey and possible new crops, to breeding of new varieties of plants, to experimental shipments, to animal industry and applied chemistry, very practical aid has been given our farming and stock-growing interests.   The products of the farm have taken an unprecedented place in our export trade during the year that has just closed.

Public opinion throughout the United States has moved steadily toward a just appreciation of the value of forests, whether planted or of natural growth.   The great part played by them in the creation and maintenance of the national wealth is now more fully realized than ever before.

Wise forest protection does not mean the withdrawal of forest re sources, whether of wood, water, or grass, from contributing their full share to the welfare of the people, but, on the contrary, gives the assurance of larger and more certain supplies.   The fundamental idea of forestry is the perpetuation of forests by use.   Forest protection is not an end of itself; it is a means to increase and sustain the resources of our country and the industries which depend upon them.   The preservation of our forests is an imperative business necessity. We have come to see clearly that whatever destroys the forest, except to make way for agriculture, threatens our well being.

The practical usefulness of the national forest reserves to the mining, grazing, irrigation, and other interests of the regions in which the reserves lie has led to a widespread demand by the people of the West for their protection and extension. The forest reserves will inevitably be of still greater use in the future than in the past. Additions should be made to them whenever practicable, and their usefulness should be increased by a thoroughly business-like management.

At present the protection of the forest reserves rests with the General Land Office, the mapping and description of their timber with the United States Geological Survey, and the preparation of plans for their conservative use with the Bureau of Forestry, which is also charged with the general advancement of practical forestry in the United States. These various functions should be united in the Bureau of Forestry, to which they properly belong. The present diffusion of responsibility is bad from every standpoint. It prevents that effective co-operation between the Government and the men who utilize the resources of the reserves, without which the interests of both must suffer. The scientific bureaus generally should be put under the Department of Agriculture. The President should have by law the power of transferring lands for use as forest reserves to the Department of Agriculture. He already has such power in the case of lands needed by the Departments of War and the Navy.

The wise administration of the forest reserves will be not less helpful to the interests which depend on water than to those which depend on wood and grass. The water supply itself depends upon the forest. In the arid region it is water, not land, which measures production. The western half of the United States would sustain a population greater than that of our whole country to-day if the waters that now run to waste were saved and used for irrigation. The forest and water problems are perhaps the most vital internal questions of the United States.

Certain of the forest reserves should also be made preserves for the wild forest creatures. All of the reserves should be better protected from fires. Many of them need special protection because of the great injury done by live stock, above all by sheep. The increase in deer, elk, and other animals in the Yellowstone Park shows what may be expected when other mountain forests are properly protected by law and properly guarded. Some of these areas have been so denuded of surface vegetation by overgrazing that the ground breeding birds, including grouse and quail, and many mammals, including deer, have been exterminated or driven away. At the same time the water-storing capacity of the surface has been decreased or destroyed, thus promoting floods in times of rain and diminishing the flow of streams between rains.

In cases where natural conditions have been restored for a few years, vegetation has again carpeted the ground, birds and deer are coming back, and hundreds of persons, especially from the immediate neighborhood, come each summer to enjoy the privilege of camping.   Some at least of the forest reserves should afford perpetual protection to the native fauna and flora, safe havens of refuge to our rapidly diminishing wild animals of the larger kinds, and free camping grounds for the ever-increasing numbers of men and women who have learned to find rest, health, and recreation in the splendid forests and flower-clad meadows of our mountains.   The forest reserves should be set apart forever for the use and benefit of our people as a whole and not sacrificed to the shortsighted greed of a few.

The forests are natural reservoirs.   By restraining the streams in flood and replenishing them in drought they make possible the use of waters otherwise wasted.   They prevent the soil from washing, and so protect the storage reservoirs from filling up with silt.   Forest conservation is therefore an essential condition of water conservation.

The forests alone cannot, however, fully regulate and conserve the waters of the arid region.   Great storage works are necessary to equalize the flow of streams and to save the flood waters.   Their construction has been conclusively shown to be an undertaking too vast for private effort. Nor can it be best accomplished by the individual States acting alone. Far-reaching interstate problems are involved; and the resources of single States would often be inadequate.   It is properly a national function, at least in some of its features.   It is as right for the National Government to make the streams and rivers of the arid region useful by engineering works for water storage as to make useful the rivers and harbors of the humid region by engineering works of another kind. The storing of the floods in reservoirs at the headwaters of our rivers is but an enlargement of our present policy of river control, under which levees are built on the lower reaches of the same streams.

The Government should construct and maintain these reservoirs as it does other public works.   Where their purpose is to regulate the flow of streams, the water should be turned freely into the channels in the dry season to take the same course under the same laws as the natural flow.

The reclamation of the unsettled arid public lands presents a different problem.   Here it is not enough to regulate the flow of streams. The object of the Government is to dispose of the land to settlers who will build homes upon it.   To accomplish this object water must be brought within their reach.

The pioneer settlers on the arid public domain chose their homes along streams from which they could themselves divert the water to reclaim their holdings.   Such opportunities are practically gone.   There remain, however, vast areas of public land which can be made available for homestead settlement, but only by reservoirs and main-line canals impracticable for private enterprise. These irrigation works should be built by the National Government. The lands reclaimed by them should be reserved by the Government for actual settlers, and the cost of construction should so far as possible be repaid by the land reclaimed. The distribution of the water, the division of the streams among irrigators, should be left to the settlers themselves in conformity with State laws and without interference with those laws or with vested rights. The policy of the National Government should be to aid irrigation in the several States and Territories in such manner as will enable the people in the local communities to help themselves, and as will stimulate needed reforms in the State laws and regulations governing irrigation.

The reclamation and settlement of the arid lands will enrich every portion of our country, just as the settlement of the Ohio and Mississippi valleys brought prosperity to the Atlantic States. The increased demand for manufactured articles will stimulate industrial production, while wider home markets and the trade of Asia will consume the larger food supplies and effectually prevent Western competition with Eastern agriculture. Indeed, the products of irrigation will be consumed chiefly in upbuilding local centers of mining and other industries, which would otherwise not come into existence at all. Our people as a whole will profit, for successful home-making is but another name for the upbuilding of the nation.

The necessary foundation has already been laid for the inauguration of the policy just described. It would be unwise to begin by doing too much, for a great deal will doubtless be learned, both as to what can and what cannot be safely attempted, by the early efforts, which must of necessity be partly experimental in character. At the very beginning the Government should make clear, beyond shadow of doubt, its intention to pursue this policy on lines of the broadest public interest. No reservoir or canal should ever be built to satisfy selfish personal or local interests; but only in accordance with the advice of trained experts, after long investigation has shown the locality where all the conditions combine to make the work most needed and fraught with the greatest usefulness to the community as a whole. There should be no extravagance, and the believers in the need of irrigation will most benefit their cause by seeing to it that it is free from the least taint of excessive or reckless expenditure of the public moneys.

Whatever the nation does for the extension of irrigation should harmonize with, and tend to improve, the condition of those now living on irrigated land. We are not at the starting point of this development. Over two hundred millions of private capital has already been expended in the construction of irrigation works, and many million acres of arid land reclaimed. A high degree of enterprise and ability has been shown in the work itself; but as much cannot be said in reference to the laws relating thereto. The security and value of the homes created depend largely on the stability of titles to water; but the majority of these rest on the uncertain foundation of court decisions rendered in ordinary suits at law. With a few creditable exceptions, the arid States have failed to provide for the certain and just division of streams in times of scarcity. Lax and uncertain laws have made it possible to establish rights to water in excess of actual uses or necessities, and many streams have already passed into private ownership, or a control equivalent to ownership.

Whoever controls a stream practically controls the land it renders productive, and the doctrine of private ownership of water apart from land cannot prevail without causing enduring wrong. The recognition of such ownership, which has been permitted to grow up in the arid regions, should give way to a more enlightened and larger recognition of the rights of the public in the control and disposal of the public water supplies. Laws founded upon conditions obtaining in humid regions, where water is too abundant to justify hoarding it, have no proper application in a dry country.

In the arid States the only right to water which should be recognized is that of use. In irrigation this right should attach to the land reclaimed and be inseparable therefrom. Granting perpetual water rights to others than users, without compensation to the public, is open to all the objections which apply to giving away perpetual franchises to the public utilities of cities. A few of the Western States have already recognized this, and have incorporated in their constitutions the doctrine of perpetual State ownership of water.

The benefits which have followed the unaided development of the past justify the nation's aid and co-operation in the more difficult and important work yet to be accomplished. Laws so vitally affecting homes as those which control the water supply will only be effective when they have the sanction of the irrigators; reforms can only be final and satisfactory when they come through the enlightenment of the people most concerned. The larger development which national aid insures should, however, awaken in every arid State the determination to make its irrigation system equal in justice and effectiveness that of any country in the civilized world. Nothing could be more unwise than for isolated communities to continue to learn everything experimentally, instead of profiting by what is already known elsewhere. We are dealing with a new and momentous question, in the pregnant years while institutions are forming, and what we do will affect not only the present but future generations.

Our aim should be not simply to reclaim the largest area of land and provide homes for the largest number of people, but to create for this new industry the best possible social and industrial conditions; and this requires that we not only understand the existing situation, but avail ourselves of the best experience of the time in the solution of its problems. A careful study should be made, both by the Nation and the States, of the irrigation laws and conditions here and abroad. Ultimately it will probably be necessary for the Nation to co-operate with the several arid States in proportion as these States by their legislation and administration show themselves fit to receive it.

In Hawaii our aim must be to develop the Territory on the traditional American lines. We do not wish a region of large estates tilled by cheap labor; we wish a healthy American community of men who themselves till the farms they own. All our legislation for the islands should be shaped with this end in view; the well-being of the average home-maker must afford the true test of the healthy development of the islands. The land policy should as nearly as possible be modeled on our homestead system.

It is a pleasure to say that it is hardly more necessary to report as to Puerto Rico than as to any State or Territory within our continental limits. The island is thriving as never before, and it is being administered efficiently and honestly. Its people are now enjoying liberty and order under the protection of the United States, and upon this fact we congratulate them and ourselves. Their material welfare must be as carefully and jealously considered as the welfare of any other portion of our country. We have given them the great gift of free access for their products to the markets of the United States. I ask the attention of the Congress to the need of legislation concerning the public lands of Puerto Rico.

In Cuba such progress has been made toward putting the independent government of the island upon a firm footing that before the present session of the Congress closes this will be an accomplished fact. Cuba will then start as her own mistress; and to the beautiful Queen of the Antilles, as she unfolds this new page of her destiny, we extend our heartiest greetings and good wishes. Elsewhere I have discussed the question of reciprocity. In the case of Cuba, however, there are weighty reasons of morality and of national interest why the policy should be held to have a peculiar application, and I most earnestly ask your attention to the wisdom, indeed to the vital need, of providing for a substantial reduction in the tariff duties on Cuban imports into the United States. Cuba has in her constitution affirmed what we desired, that she should stand, in international matters, in closer and more friendly relations with us than with any other power; and we are bound by every consideration of honor and expediency to pass commercial measures in the interest of her material well-being.

In the Philippines our problem is larger. They are very rich tropical islands, inhabited by many varying tribes, representing widely different stages of progress toward civilization. Our earnest effort is to help these people upward along the stony and difficult path that leads to self-government. We hope to make our administration of the islands honorable to our Nation by making it of the highest benefit to the Filipinos themselves; and as an earnest of what we intend to do, we point to what we have done. Already a greater measure of material prosperity and of governmental honesty and efficiency has been attained in the Philippines than ever before in their history.

It is no light task for a nation to achieve the temperamental qualities without which the institutions of free government are but an empty mockery. Our people are now successfully governing themselves, because for more than a thousand years they have been slowly fitting themselves, sometimes consciously, sometimes unconsciously, toward this end. What has taken us thirty generations to achieve, we cannot expect to see another race accomplish out of hand, especially when large portions of that race start very far behind the point which our ancestors had reached even thirty generations ago. In dealing with the Philippine people we must show both patience and strength, forbearance and steadfast resolution. Our aim is high. We do not desire to do for the islanders merely what has elsewhere been done for tropic peoples by even the best foreign governments. We hope to do for them what has never before been done for any people of the tropics — to make them fit for self-government after the fashion of the really free nations.

History may safely be challenged to show a single instance in which a masterful race such as ours, having been forced by the exigencies of war to take possession of an alien land, has behaved to its inhabitants with the disinterested zeal for their progress that our people have shown in the Philippines. To leave the islands at this time would mean that they would fall into a welter of murderous anarchy. Such desertion of duty on our part would be a crime against humanity. The character of Governor Taft and of his associates and subordinates is a proof, if such be needed, of the sincerity of our effort to give the islanders a constantly increasing measure of self-government, exactly as fast as they show themselves fit to exercise it. Since the civil government was established not an appointment has been made in the islands with any reference to considerations of political influence, or to aught else save the fitness of the man and the needs of the service.

In our anxiety for the welfare and progress of the Philippines, it may be that here and there we have gone too rapidly in giving them local self-government. It is on this side that our error, if any, has been committed. No competent observer, sincerely desirous of finding out the facts and influenced only by a desire for the welfare of the natives, can assert that we have not gone far enough. We have gone to the very verge of safety in hastening the process. To have taken a single step farther or faster in advance would have been folly and weakness, and might well have been crime. We are extremely anxious that the natives shall show the power of governing themselves. We are anxious, first for their sakes, and next, because it relieves us of a great burden. There need not be the slightest fear of our not continuing to give them all the liberty for which they are fit.

The only fear is lest in our overanxiety we give them a degree of independence for which they are unfit, thereby inviting reaction and disaster. As fast as there is any reasonable hope that in a given district the people can govern themselves, self-government has been given in that district. There is not a locality fitted for self-government which has not received it. But it may well be that in certain cases it will have to be withdrawn because the inhabitants show themselves unfit to exercise it; such instances have already occurred. In other words, there is not the slightest chance of our failing to show a sufficiently humanitarian spirit. The danger comes in the opposite direction.

There are still troubles ahead in the islands. The insurrection has become an affair of local banditti and marauders, who deserve no higher regard than the brigands of portions of the Old World. Encouragement, direct or indirect, to these insurrectors stands on the same footing as encouragement to hostile Indians in the days when we still had Indian wars. Exactly as our aim is to give to the Indian who remains peaceful the fullest and amplest consideration, but to have it understood that we will show no weakness if he goes on the warpath, so we must make it evident, unless we are false to our own traditions and to the demands of civilization and humanity, that while we will do everything in our power for the Filipino who is peaceful, we will take the sternest measures with the Filipino who follows the path of the insurrecto and the ladrone.

The heartiest praise is due to large numbers of the natives of the islands for their steadfast loyalty. The Macabebes have been conspicuous for their courage and devotion to the flag. I recommend that the Secretary of War be empowered to take some systematic action in the way of aiding those of these men who are crippled in the service and the families of those who are killed.

The time has come when there should be additional legislation for the Philippines. Nothing better can be done for the islands than to introduce industrial enterprises. Nothing would benefit them so much as throwing them open to industrial development. The connection between idleness and mischief is proverbial, and the opportunity to do remunerative work is one of the surest preventatives of war. Of course no business man will go into the Philippines unless it is to his interest to do so; and it is immensely to the interest of the islands that he should go in. It is therefore necessary that the Congress should pass laws by which the resources of the islands can be developed; so that franchises (for limited terms of years) can be granted to companies doing business in them, and every encouragement be given to the incoming of business men of every kind.

Not to permit this is to do a wrong to the Philippines. The franchises must be granted and the business permitted only under regulations which will guarantee the islands against any kind of improper exploitation. But the vast natural wealth of the islands must be developed, and the capital willing to develop it must be given the opportunity. The field must be thrown open to individual enterprise, which has been the real factor in the development of every region over which our flag has flown. It is urgently necessary to enact suitable laws dealing with general transportation, mining, banking, currency, homesteads, and the use and ownership of the lands and timber. These laws will give free play to industrial enterprise; and the commercial development which will surely follow will accord to the people of the islands the best proofs of the sincerity of our desire to aid them.

I call your attention most earnestly to the crying need of a cable to Hawaii and the Philippines, to be continued from the Philippines to points in Asia. We should not defer a day longer than necessary the construction of such a cable. It is demanded not merely for commercial but for political and military considerations.

Either the Congress should immediately provide for the construction of a Government cable, or else an arrangement should be made by which like advantages to those accruing from a Government cable may be secured to the Government by contract with a private cable company.

No single great material work which remains to be undertaken on this continent is of such consequence to the American people as the building of a canal across the Isthmus connecting North and South America. Its importance to the Nation is by no means limited merely to its material effects upon our business prosperity; and yet with view to these effects alone it would be to the last degree important for us immediately to begin it. While its beneficial effects would perhaps be most marked upon the Pacific Coast and the Gulf and South Atlantic States, it would also greatly benefit other sections. It is emphatically a work which it is for the interest of the entire country to begin and complete as soon as possible; it is one of those great works which only a great nation can undertake with prospects of success, and which when done are not only permanent assets in the nation's material interests, but standing monuments to its constructive ability.

I am glad to be able to announce to you that our negotiations on this subject with Great Britain, conducted on both sides in a spirit of friendliness and mutual good will and respect, have resulted in my being able to lay before the Senate a treaty which if ratified will enable us to begin preparations for an Isthmian canal at any time, and which guarantees to this Nation every right that it has ever asked in connection with the canal. In this treaty, the old Clayton-Bulwer treaty, so long recognized as inadequate to supply the base for the construction and maintenance of a necessarily American ship canal, is abrogated. It specifically provides that the United States alone shall do the work of building and assume the responsibility of safeguarding the canal and shall regulate its neutral use by all nations on terms of equality without the guaranty or interference of any outside nation from any quarter. The signed treaty will at once be laid before the Senate, and if approved the Congress can then proceed to give effect to the advantages it secures us by providing for the building of the canal.

The true end of every great and free people should be self-respecting peace; and this Nation most earnestly desires sincere and cordial friendship with all others. Over the entire world, of recent years, wars between the great civilized powers have become less and less frequent. Wars with barbarous or semi-barbarous peoples come in an entirely different category, being merely a most regrettable but necessary international police duty which must be performed for the sake of the welfare of mankind. Peace can only be kept with certainty where both sides wish to keep it; but more and more the civilized peoples are realizing the wicked folly of war and are attaining that condition of just and intelligent regard for the rights of others which will in the end, as we hope and believe, make world-wide peace possible. The peace conference at The Hague gave definite expression to this hope and belief and marked a stride toward their attainment.

This same peace conference acquiesced in our statement of the Monroe Doctrine as compatible with the purposes and aims of the conference.

The Monroe Doctrine should be the cardinal feature of the foreign policy of all the nations of the two Americas, as it is of the United States. Just seventy-eight years have passed since President Monroe in his Annual Message announced that "The American continents are henceforth not to be considered as subjects for future colonization by any European power." In other words, the Monroe Doctrine is a declaration that there must be no territorial aggrandizement by any non-American power at the expense of any American power on American soil. It is in no wise intended as hostile to any nation in the Old World. Still less is it intended to give cover to any aggression by one New World power at the expense of any other. It is simply a step, and a long step, toward assuring the universal peace of the world by securing the possibility of permanent peace on this hemisphere.

During the past century other influences have established the permanence and independence of the smaller states of Europe. Through the Monroe Doctrine we hope to be able to safeguard like independence and secure like permanence for the lesser among the New World nations.

This doctrine has nothing to do with the commercial relations of any American power, save that it in truth allows each of them to form such as it desires. In other words, it is really a guaranty of the commercial independence of the Americas. We do not ask under this doctrine for any exclusive commercial dealings with any other American state. We do not guarantee any state against punishment if it misconducts itself, provided that punishment does not take the form of the acquisition of territory by any non-American power.

Our attitude in Cuba is a sufficient guaranty of our own good faith. We have not the slightest desire to secure any territory at the expense of any of our neighbors. We wish to work with them hand in hand, so that all of us may be uplifted together, and we rejoice over the good fortune of any of them, we gladly hail their material prosperity and political stability, and are concerned and alarmed if any of them fall into industrial or political chaos. We do not wish to see any Old World military power grow up on this continent, or to be compelled to become a military power ourselves. The peoples of the Americas can prosper best if left to work out their own salvation in their own way.

The work of upbuilding the Navy must be steadily continued. No one point of our policy, foreign or domestic, is more important than this to the honor and material welfare, and above all to the peace, of our nation in the future. Whether we desire it or not, we must henceforth recognize that we have international duties no less than international rights. Even if our flag were hauled down in the Philippines and Puerto Rico, even if we decided not to build the Isthmian Canal, we should need a thoroughly trained Navy of adequate size, or else be prepared definitely and for all time to abandon the idea that our nation is among those whose sons go down to the sea in ships. Unless our commerce is always to be carried in foreign bottoms, we must have war craft to protect it.

Inasmuch, however, as the American people have no thought of abandoning the path upon which they have entered, and especially in view of the fact that the building of the Isthmian Canal is fast becoming one of the matters which the whole people are united in demanding, it is imperative that our Navy should be put and kept in the highest state of efficiency, and should be made to answer to our growing needs. So far from being in any way a provocation to war, an adequate and highly trained navy is the best guaranty against war, the cheapest and most effective peace insurance. The cost of building and maintaining such a navy represents the very lightest premium for insuring peace which this nation can possibly pay.

Probably no other great nation in the world is so anxious for peace as we are. There is not a single civilized power which has anything whatever to fear from aggressiveness on our part. All we want is peace; and toward this end we wish to be able to secure the same respect for our rights from others which we are eager and anxious to extend to their rights in return, to insure fair treatment to us commercially, and to guarantee the safety of the American people.

Our people intend to abide by the Monroe Doctrine and to insist upon it as the one sure means of securing the peace of the Western Hemisphere. The Navy offers us the only means of making our insistence upon the Monroe Doctrine anything but a subject of derision to whatever nation chooses to disregard it. We desire the peace which comes as of right to the just man armed; not the peace granted on terms of ignominy to the craven and the weakling.

It is not possible to improvise a navy after war breaks out. The ships must be built and the men trained long in advance. Some auxiliary vessels can be turned into makeshifts which will do in default of any better for the minor work, and a proportion of raw men can be mixed with the highly trained, their shortcomings being made good by the skill of their fellows; but the efficient fighting force of the Navy when pitted against an equal opponent will be found almost exclusively in the war ships that have been regularly built and in the officers and men who through years of faithful performance of sea duty have been trained to handle their formidable but complex and delicate weapons with the highest efficiency. In the late war with Spain the ships that dealt the decisive blows at Manila and Santiago had been launched from two to fourteen years, and they were able to do as they did because the men in the conning towers, the gun turrets, and the engine-rooms had through long years of practice at sea learned how to do their duty.

Our present Navy was begun in 1882. At that period our Navy consisted of a collection of antiquated wooden ships, already almost as out of place against modern war vessels as the galleys of Alcibiades and Hamilcar—certainly as the ships of Tromp and Blake. Nor at that time did we have men fit to handle a modern man-of-war. Under the wise legislation of the Congress and the successful administration of a succession of patriotic Secretaries of the Navy, belonging to both political parties, the work of upbuilding the Navy went on, and ships equal to any in the world of their kind were continually added; and **what was even more important, these ships were exercised at sea singly** and in squadrons until the men aboard them were able to get the best possible service out of them. The result was seen in the short war with Spain, which was decided with such rapidity because of the infinitely greater preparedness of our Navy than of the Spanish Navy.

While awarding the fullest honor to the men who actually commanded and manned the ships which destroyed the Spanish sea forces in the Philippines and in Cuba, we must not forget that an equal meed of praise belongs to those without whom neither blow could have been struck. The Congressmen who voted years in advance the money to lay down the ships, to build the guns, to buy the armor-plate; the Department officials and the business men and wage-workers who furnished what the Congress had authorized; the Secretaries of the Navy who asked for and expended the appropriations; and finally the officers who, in fair weather and foul, on actual sea service, trained and disciplined the crews of the ships when there was no war in sight — all are entitled to a full share in the glory of Manila and Santiago, and the respect accorded by every true American to those who wrought such signal triumph for our country. It was forethought and preparation which secured us the overwhelming triumph of 1898. If we fail to show forethought and preparation now, there may come a time when disaster will befall us instead of triumph; and should this time come, the fault will rest primarily, not upon those whom the accident of events puts in supreme command at the moment, but upon those who have failed to prepare in advance.

There should be no cessation in the work of completing our Navy. So far ingenuity has been wholly unable to devise a substitute for the great war craft whose hammering guns beat out the mastery of the high seas. It is unsafe and unwise not to provide this year for several additional battle ships and heavy armored cruisers, with auxiliary and lighter craft in proportion; for the exact numbers and character I refer you to the report of the Secretary of the Navy. But there is something we need even more than additional ships, and this is additional officers and men. To provide battle ships and cruisers and then lay them up, with the expectation of leaving them unmanned until they are needed in actual war, would be worse than folly; it would be a crime against the Nation.

To send any war ship against a competent enemy unless those aboard it have been trained by years of actual sea service, including incessant gunnery practice, would be to invite not merely disaster, but the bitterest shame and humiliation. Four thousand additional seamen and one thousand additional marines should be provided; and an increase in the officers should be provided by making a large addition to the classes at Annapolis. There is one small matter which should be mentioned in connection with Annapolis. The pretentious and unmeaning title of "naval cadet" should be abolished; the title of "midshipman," full of historic association, should be restored.

Even in time of peace a war ship should be used until it wears out, for only so can it be kept fit to respond to any emergency. The officers and men alike should be kept as much as possible on blue water, for it is there only they can learn their duties as they should be learned. The big vessels should be manœuvred in squadrons containing not merely battle ships, but the necessary proportion of cruisers and scouts. The torpedo boats should be handled by the younger officers in such manner as will best fit the latter to take responsibility and meet the emergencies of actual warfare.

Every detail ashore which can be performed by a civilian should be so performed, the officer being kept for his special duty in the sea service. Above all, gunnery practice should be unceasing. It is important to have our Navy of adequate size, but it is even more important that ship for ship it should equal in efficiency any navy in the world. This is possible only with highly drilled crews and officers, and this in turn imperatively demands continuous and progressive instruction in target practice, ship handling, squadron tactics, and general discipline. Our ships must be assembled in squadrons actively cruising away from harbors and never long at anchor. The resulting wear upon engines and hulls must be endured; a battle ship worn out in long training of officers and men is well paid for by the results, while, on the other hand, no matter in how excellent condition, it is useless if the crew be not expert.

We now have seventeen battle ships appropriated for, of which nine are completed and have been commissioned for actual service. The remaining eight will be ready in from two to four years, but it will take at least that time to recruit and train the men to fight them. It is of vast concern that we have trained crews ready for the vessels by the time they are commissioned. Good ships and good guns are simply good weapons, and the best weapons are useless save in the hands of men who know how to fight with them. The men must be trained and drilled under a thorough and well-planned system of progressive instruction, while the recruiting must be carried on with still greater vigor. Every effort must be made to exalt the main function of the officer — the command of men. The leading graduates of the Naval Academy should be assigned to the combatant branches, the line and marines.

Many of the essentials of success are already recognized by the General Board, which, as the central office of a growing staff, is moving steadily toward a proper war efficiency and a proper efficiency of the whole Navy, under the Secretary. This General Board, by fostering the creation of a general staff, is providing for the official and then the general recognition of our altered conditions as a Nation and of the true meaning of a great war fleet, which meaning is, first, the best men, and, second, the best ships.

The Naval Militia forces are State organizations, and are trained for coast service, and in event of war they will constitute the inner line of defense. They should receive hearty encouragement from the General Government.

But in addition we should at once provide for a National Naval Reserve, organized and trained under the direction of the Navy Department, and subject to the call of the Chief Executive whenever war becomes imminent. It should be a real auxiliary to the naval seagoing peace establishment, and offer material to be drawn on at once for manning our ships in time of war. It should be composed of graduates of the Naval Academy, graduates of the Naval Militia, officers and crews of coast-line steamers, longshore schooners, fishing vessels, and steam yachts, together with the coast population about such centers as life-saving stations and light-houses.

The American people must either build and maintain an adequate navy or else make up their minds definitely to accept a secondary position in international affairs, not merely in political, but in commercial, matters. It has been well said that there is no surer way of courting national disaster than to be "opulent, aggressive, and unarmed."

It is not necessary to increase our Army beyond its present size at this time. But it is necessary to keep it at the highest point of efficiency. The individual units who as officers and enlisted men compose this Army, are, we have good reason to believe, at least as efficient as those of any other army in the entire world. It is our duty to see that their training is of a kind to insure the highest possible expression of power to these units when acting in combination.

The conditions of modern war are such as to make an infinitely heavier demand than ever before upon the individual character and capacity of the officer and the enlisted man, and to make it far more difficult for men to act together with effect. At present the fighting must be done in extended order, which means that each man must act for himself and at the same time act in combination with others with whom he is no longer in the old-fashioned elbow-to-elbow touch. Under such conditions a few men of the highest excellence are worth more than many men without the special skill which is only found as the result of special training applied to men of exceptional physique and morale. But nowadays the most valuable fighting man and the most difficult to perfect is the rifleman who is also a skillful and daring rider.

The proportion of our cavalry regiments has wisely been increased. The American cavalryman, trained to manœuvre and fight with equal facility on foot and on horseback, is the best type of soldier for general purposes now to be found in the world. The ideal cavalryman of the present day is a man who can fight on foot as effectively as the best infantryman, and who is in addition unsurpassed in the care and management of his horse and in his ability to fight on horseback.

A general staff should be created. As for the present staff and supply departments, they should be filled by details from the line, the men so detailed returning after a while to their line duties. It is very undesirable to have the senior grades of the Army composed of men who have come to fill the positions by the mere fact of seniority. A system should be adopted by which there shall be an elimination grade by grade of those who seem unfit to render the best service in the next grade. Justice to the veterans of the Civil War who are still in the Army would seem to require that in the matter of retirements they be given by law the same privileges accorded to their comrades in the Navy.

The process of elimination of the least fit should be conducted in a manner that would render it practically impossible to apply political or social pressure on behalf of any candidate, so that each man may be judged purely on his own merits. Pressure for the promotion of civil officials for political reasons is bad enough, but it is tenfold worse where applied on behalf of officers of the Army or Navy. Every promotion and every detail under the War Department must be made solely with regard to the good of the service and to the capacity and merit of the man himself. No pressure, political, social, or personal, of any kind, will be permitted to exercise the least effect in any question of promotion or detail; and if there is reason to believe that such pressure is exercised at the instigation of the officer concerned, it will be held to militate against him. In our Army we cannot afford to have rewards or duties distributed save on the simple ground that those who by their own merits are entitled to the rewards get them, and that, those who are peculiarly fit to do the duties are chosen to perform them.

Every effort should be made to bring the Army to a constantly increasing state of efficiency. When on actual service no work save that directly in the line of such service should be required. The paper work in the Army, as in the Navy, should be greatly reduced. What is needed is proved power of command and capacity to work well in the field. Constant care is necessary to prevent dry rot in the transportation and commissary departments.

Our Army is so small and so much scattered that it is very difficult to give the higher officers (as well as the lower officers and the enlisted men) a chance to practice manœuvres in mass and on a comparatively large scale. In time of need no amount of individual excellence would avail against the paralysis which would follow inability to work as a coherent whole, under skillful and daring leadership. The Congress should provide means whereby it will be possible to have field exercises by at least a division of regulars, and if possible also a division of national guardsmen, once a year. These exercises might take the form of field manœuvres; or, if on the Gulf Coast or the Pacific or Atlantic Sea board, or in the region of the Great Lakes, the army corps when assembled could be marched from some inland point to some point on the water, there embarked, disembarked after a couple of days' journey at some other point, and again marched inland. Only by actual handling and providing for men in masses while they are marching, camping, embarking, and disembarking, will it be possible to train the higher officers to perform their duties well and smoothly.

A great debt is owing from the public to the men of the Army and Navy. They should be so treated as to enable them to reach the highest point of efficiency, so that they may be able to respond instantly to any demand made upon them to sustain the interests of the Nation and the honor of the flag. The individual American enlisted man is probably on the whole a more formidable fighting man than the regular of any other army. Every consideration should be shown him, and in return the highest standard of usefulness should be exacted from him. It is well worth while for the Congress to consider whether the pay of enlisted men upon second and subsequent enlistments should not be increased to correspond with the increased value of the veteran soldier.

Much good has already come from the act reorganizing the Army, passed early in the present year. The three prime reforms, all of them of literally inestimable value, are, first, the substitution of four-year details from the line for permanent appointments in the so-called staff divisions; second, the establishment of a corps of artillery with a chief at the head; third, the establishment of a maximum and minimum limit for the Army. It would be difficult to overestimate the improvement in the efficiency of our Army which these three reforms are making, and have in part already effected.

The reorganization provided for by the act has been substantially accomplished. The improved conditions in the Philippines have enabled the War Department materially to reduce the military charge upon our revenue and to arrange the number of soldiers so as to bring this number much nearer to the minimum than to the maximum limit established by law. There is, however, need of supplementary legislation. Thorough military education must be provided, and in addition to the regulars the advantages of this education should be given to the officers of the National Guard and others in civil life who desire intelligently to fit themselves for possible military duty. The officers should be given the chance to perfect themselves by study in the higher branches of this art. At West Point the education should be of the kind most apt to turn out men who are good in actual field service; too much stress should not be laid on mathematics, nor should proficiency therein be held to establish the right of entry to a *corps d'élite*. The typical American officer of the best kind need not be a good mathematician; but he must be able to master himself, to control others, and to show boldness and fertility of resource in every emergency.

Action should be taken in reference to the militia and to the raising of volunteer forces. Our militia law is obsolete and worthless. The organization and armament of the National Guard of the several States, which are treated as militia in the appropriations by the Congress, should be made identical with those provided for the regular forces. The obligations and duties of the Guard in time of war should be carefully defined, and a system established by law under which the method of procedure of raising volunteer forces should be prescribed in advance. It is utterly impossible in the excitement and haste of impending war to do this satisfactorily if the arrangements have not been made long beforehand. Provision should be made for utilizing in the first volunteer organizations called out the training of those citizens who have already had experience under arms, and especially for the selection in advance of the officers of any force which may be raised; for careful selection of the kind necessary is impossible after the outbreak of war.

That the Army is not at all a mere instrument of destruction has been shown during the last three years. In the Philippines, Cuba, and Puerto Rico it has proved itself a great constructive force, a most potent implement for the upbuilding of a peaceful civilization.

No other citizens deserve so well of the Republic as the veterans, the survivors of those who saved the Union. They did the one deed which if left undone would have meant that all else in our history went for nothing. But for their steadfast prowess in the greatest crisis of our history, all our annals would be meaningless, and our great experiment in popular freedom and self-government a gloomy failure. Moreover, they not only left us a united Nation, but they left us also as a heritage the memory of the mighty deeds by which the Nation was kept united. We are now indeed one Nation, one in fact as well as in name; we are united in our devotion to the flag which is the symbol of national greatness and unity; and the very completeness of our union enables us all, in every part of the country, to glory in the valor shown alike by the sons of the North and the sons of the South in the times that tried men's souls.

The men who in the last three years have done so well in the East and the West Indies and on the mainland of Asia have shown that this remembrance is not lost. In any serious crisis the United States must rely for the great mass of its fighting men upon the volunteer soldiery who do not make a permanent profession of the military career; and whenever such a crisis arises the deathless memories of the Civil War will give to Americans the lift of lofty purpose which comes to those whose fathers have stood valiantly in the forefront of the battle.

The merit system of making appointments is in its essence as democratic and American as the common school system itself. It simply means that in clerical and other positions where the duties are entirely non-political, all applicants should have a fair field and no favor, each standing on his merits as he is able to show them by practical test. Written competitive examinations offer the only available means in many cases for applying this system. In other cases, as where laborers are employed, a system of registration undoubtedly can be widely extended. There are, of course, places where the written competitive examination cannot be applied, and others where it offers by no means an ideal solution, but where under existing political conditions it is, though an imperfect means, yet the best present means of getting satisfactory results.

Wherever the conditions have permitted the application of the merit system in its fullest and widest sense, the gain to the Government has been immense. The navy-yards and postal service illustrate, probably better than any other branches of the Government, the great gain in economy, efficiency, and honesty due to the enforcement of this principle.

I recommend the passage of a law which will extend the classified service to the District of Columbia, or will at least enable the President thus to extend it. In my judgment all laws providing for the temporary employment of clerks should hereafter contain a provision that they be selected under the Civil Service Law.

It is important to have this system obtain at home, but it is even more important to have it applied rigidly in our insular possessions. Not an office should be filled in the Philippines or Puerto Rico with any regard to the man's partisan affiliations or services, with any regard to the political, social, or personal influence which he may have at his command; in short, heed should be paid to absolutely nothing save the man's own character and capacity and the needs of the service.

The administration of these islands should be as wholly free from the suspicion of partisan politics as the administration of the Army and Navy. All that we ask from the public servant in the Philippines or Puerto Rico is that he reflect honor on his country by the way in which he makes that country's rule a benefit to the peoples who have come under it. This is all that we should ask, and we cannot afford to be content with less.

The merit system is simply one method of securing honest and efficient administration of the Government; and in the long run the sole justification of any type of government lies in its proving itself both honest and efficient.

The consular service is now organized under the provisions of a law passed in 1856, which is entirely inadequate to existing conditions. The interest shown by so many commerical bodies throughout the country in the reorganization of the service is heartily commended to your attention. Several bills providing for a new consular service have in recent years been submitted to the Congress. They are based upon the just principle that appointments to the service should be made only after a practical test of the applicant's fitness, that promotions should be governed by trustworthiness, adaptability, and zeal in the performance of duty, and that the tenure of office should be unaffected by partisan considerations.

The guardianship and fostering of our rapidly expanding foreign commerce, the protection of American citizens resorting to foreign countries in lawful pursuit of their affairs, and the maintenance of the dignity of the nation abroad, combine to make it essential that our consuls should be men of character, knowledge and enterprise. It is true that the service is now, in the main, efficient, but a standard of excellence cannot be permanently maintained until the principles set forth in the bills heretofore submitted to the Congress on this subject are enacted into law.

In my judgment the time has arrived when we should definitely make up our minds to recognize the Indian as an individual and not as a member of a tribe. The General Allotment Act is a mighty pulverizing engine to break up the tribal mass. It acts directly upon the family and the individual. Under its provisions some sixty thousand Indians have already become citizens of the United States. We should now break up the tribal funds, doing for them what allotment does for the tribal lands; that is, they should be divided into individual holdings. There will be a transition period during which the funds will in many cases have to be held in trust. This is the case also with the lands. A stop should be put upon the indiscriminate permission to Indians to lease their allotments. The effort should be steadily to make the Indian work like any other man on his own ground. The marriage laws of the Indians should be made the same as those of the whites.

In the schools the education should be elementary and largely industrial. The need of higher education among the Indians is very, very limited. On the reservations care should be taken to try to suit the teaching to the needs of the particular Indian. There is no use in attempting to induce agriculture in a country suited only for cattle raising where the Indian should be made a stock grower. The ration system, which is merely the corral and the reservation system, is highly detrimental to the Indians. It promotes beggary, perpetuates pauperism, and stifles industry. It is an effectual barrier to progress. It must continue to a greater or less degree as long as tribes are herded on reservations and have everything in common. The Indian should be treated as an individual — like the white man. During the change of treatment inevitable hardships will occur; every effort should be made to minimize these hardships; but we should not because of them hesitate to make the change. There should be a continuous reduction in the number of agencies.

In dealing with the aboriginal races few things are more important than to preserve them from the terrible physical and moral degradation resulting from the liquor traffic. We are doing all we can to save our own Indian tribes from this evil. Wherever by international agreement this same end can be attained as regards races where we do not possess exclusive control, every effort should be made to bring it about.

I bespeak the most cordial support from the Congress and the people for the St. Louis Exposition to commemorate the One Hundredth Anniversary of the Louisiana Purchase. This purchase was the greatest instance of expansion in our history. It definitely decided that we were to become a great continental republic, by far the foremost power in the Western Hemisphere. It is one of three or four great landmarks in our history — the great turning points in our development. It is eminently fitting that all our people should join with heartiest good will in commemorating it, and the citizens of St. Louis, of Missouri, of all the adjacent region, are entitled to every aid in making the celebration a noteworthy event in our annals. We earnestly hope that foreign nations will appreciate the deep interest our country takes in this Exposition, and our view of its importance from every standpoint, and that they will participate in securing its success. The National Government should be represented by a full and complete set of exhibits.

The people of Charleston, with great energy and civic spirit, are carrying on an Exposition which will continue throughout most of the present session of the Congress. I heartily commend this Exposition to the good will of the people. It deserves all the encouragement that can be given it. The managers of the Charleston Exposition have requested the Cabinet officers to place thereat the Government exhibits which have been at Buffalo, promising to pay the necessary expenses. I have taken the responsibility of directing that this be done, for I feel that it is due to Charleston to help her in her praiseworthy effort. In my opinion the management should not be required to pay all these expenses. I earnestly recommend that the Congress appropriate at once the small sum necessary for this purpose.

The Pan-American Exposition at Buffalo has just closed. Both from the industrial and the artistic standpoint this Exposition has been in a high degree creditable and useful, not merely to Buffalo but to the United States. The terrible tragedy of the President's assassination interfered materially with its being a financial success. The Exposition was peculiarly in harmony with the trend of our public policy, because it represented an effort to bring into closer touch all the peoples of the Western Hemisphere, and give them an increasing sense of unity. Such an effort was a genuine service to the entire American public.

The advancement of the highest interests of national science and learning and the custody of objects of art and of the valuable results of scientific expeditions conducted by the United States have been committed to the Smithsonian Institution. In furtherance of its declared purpose — for the "increase and diffusion of knowledge among men" — the Congress has from time to time given it other important functions. Such trusts have been executed by the Institution with notable fidelity. There should be no halt in the work of the Institution, in accordance with the plans which its Secretary has presented, for the preservation of the vanishing races of great North American animals in the National Zoological Park. The urgent needs of the National Museum are recommended to the favorable consideration of the Congress.

Perhaps the most characteristic educational movement of the past fifty years is that which has created the modern public library and developed it into broad and active service. There are now over five thousand public libraries in the United States, the product of this period. In addition to accumulating material, they are also striving by organization, by improvement in method, and by co-operation, to give greater efficiency to the material they hold, to make it more widely useful, and by avoidance of unnecessary duplication in process to reduce the cost of its administration.

In these efforts they naturally look for assistance to the Federal library, which, though still the Library of Congress, and so entitled, is the one national library of the United States. Already the largest single collection of books on the Western Hemisphere, and certain to increase more rapidly than any other through purchase, exchange, and the operation of the copyright law, this library has a unique opportunity to render to the libraries of this country — to American scholarship — service of the highest importance. It is housed in a building which is the largest and most magnificent yet erected for library uses. Resources are now being provided which will develop the collection properly, equip it with the apparatus and service necessary to its effective use, render its bibliographic work widely available, and enable it to become, not merely a center of research, but the chief factor in great co-operative efforts for the diffusion of knowledge and the advancement of learning.

For the sake of good administration, sound economy, and the advancement of science, the Census Office as now constituted should be made a permanent Government bureau. This would insure better, cheaper, and more satisfactory work, in the interest not only of our business but of statistic, economic, and social science.

The remarkable growth of the postal service is shown in the fact that its revenues have doubled and its expenditures have nearly doubled within twelve years. Its progressive development compels constantly increasing outlay, but in this period of business energy and prosperity its receipts grow so much faster than its expenses that the annual deficit has been steadily reduced from $11,411,779 in 1897 to $3,923,727 in 1901. Among recent postal advances the success of rural free delivery wherever established has been so marked, and actual experience has made its benefits so plain, that the demand for its extension is general and urgent.

It is just that the great agricultural population should share in the improvement of the service. The number of rural routes now in operation is 6,009, practically all established within three years, and there are 6,000 applications awaiting action. It is expected that the number in operation at the close of the current fiscal year will reach 8,600. The mail will then be daily carried to the doors of 5,700,000 of our people who have heretofore been dependent upon distant offices, and one-third of all that portion of the country which is adapted to it will be covered by this kind of service.

The full measure of postal progress which might be realized has long been hampered and obstructed by the heavy burden imposed on the Government through the intrenched and well-understood abuses which have grown up in connection with second-class mail matter. The extent of this burden appears when it is stated that while the second-class matter makes nearly three-fifths of the weight of all the mail, it paid for the last fiscal year only $4,294,445 of the aggregate postal revenue of $111,631,193. If the pound rate of postage, which produces the large loss thus entailed, and which was fixed by the Congress with the purpose of encouraging the dissemination of public information, were limited to the legitimate newspapers and periodicals actually contemplated by the law, no just exception could be taken. That expense would be the recognized and accepted cost of a liberal public policy deliberately adopted for a justifiable end. But much of the matter which enjoys the privileged rate is wholly outside of the intent of the law, and has secured admission only through an evasion of its requirements or through lax construction. The proportion of such wrongly included matter is estimated by postal experts to be one-half of the whole volume of second-class mail. If it be only one-third or one-quarter, the magnitude of the burden is apparent. The Post-Office Department has now undertaken to remove the abuses so far as is possible by a stricter application of the law; and it should be sustained in its effort.

Owing to the rapid growth of our power and our interests on the Pacific, whatever happens in China must be of the keenest national concern to us.

The general terms of the settlement of the questions growing out of the antiforeign uprisings in China of 1900, having been formulated in a joint note addressed to China by the representatives of the injured powers in December last, were promptly accepted by the Chinese Government. After protracted conferences the plenipotentiaries of the several powers were able to sign a final protocol with the Chinese plenipotentiaries on the 7th of last September, setting forth the measures taken by China in compliance with the demands of the joint note, and expressing their satisfaction therewith. It will be laid before the Congress, with a report of the plenipotentiary on behalf of the United

States, Mr. William Woodville Rockhill, to whom high praise is due for the tact, good judgment, and energy he has displayed in performing an exceptionally difficult and delicate task.

The agreement reached disposes in a manner satisfactory to the powers of the various grounds of complaint, and will contribute materially to better future relations between China and the powers. Reparation has been made by China for the murder of foreigners during the uprising and punishment has been inflicted on the officials, however high in rank, recognized as responsible for or having participated in the outbreak. Official examinations have been forbidden for a period of five years in all cities in which foreigners have been murdered or cruelly treated, and edicts have been issued making all officials directly responsible for the future safety of foreigners and for the suppression of violence against them.

Provisions have been made for insuring the future safety of the foreign representatives in Peking by setting aside for their exclusive use a quarter of the city which the powers can make defensible and in which they can if necessary maintain permanent military guards; by dismantling the military works between the capital and the sea; and by allowing the temporary maintenance of foreign military posts along this line. An edict has been issued by the Emperor of China prohibiting for two years the importation of arms and ammunition into China. China has agreed to pay adequate indemnities to the states, societies, and individuals for the losses sustained by them and for the expenses of the military expeditions sent by the various powers to protect life and restore order.

Under the provisions of the joint note of December, 1900, China has agreed to revise the treaties of commerce and navigation and to take such other steps for the purpose of facilitating foreign trade as the foreign powers may decide to be needed.

The Chinese Government has agreed to participate financially in the work of bettering the water approaches to Shanghai and to Tientsin, the centers of foreign trade in central and northern China, and an international conservancy board, in which the Chinese Government is largely represented, has been provided for the improvement of the Shanghai River and the control of its navigation. In the same line of commercial advantages a revision of the present tariff on imports has been assented to for the purpose of substituting specific for *ad valorem* duties, and an expert has been sent abroad on the part of the United States to assist in this work. A list of articles to remain free of duty, including flour, cereals, and rice, gold and silver coin and bullion, has also been agreed upon in the settlement.

During these troubles our Government has unswervingly advocated moderation, and has materially aided in bringing about an adjustment which tends to enhance the welfare of China and to lead to a more beneficial intercourse between the Empire and the modern world; while in the critical period of revolt and massacre we did our full share in safe-guarding life and property, restoring order, and vindicating the national interest and honor. It behooves us to continue in these paths, doing what lies in our power to foster feelings of good will, and leaving no effort untried to work out the great policy of full and fair intercourse between China and the nations, on a footing of equal rights and advantages to all. We advocate the "open door" with all that it implies; not merely the procurement of enlarged commercial opportunities on the coasts, but access to the interior by the waterways with which China has been so extraordinarily favored. Only by bringing the people of China into peaceful and friendly community of trade with all the peoples of the earth can the work now auspiciously begun be carried to fruition. In the attainment of this purpose we necessarily claim parity of treatment, under the conventions, throughout the Empire for our trade and our citizens with those of all other powers.

We view with lively interest and keen hopes of beneficial results the proceedings of the Pan-American Congress, convoked at the invitation of Mexico, and now sitting at the Mexican capital. The delegates of he United States are under the most liberal instructions to co-operate with their colleagues in all matters promising advantage to the great family of American commonwealths, as well in their relations among themselves as in their domestic advancement and in their intercourse with the world at large.

My predecessor communicated to the Congress the fact that the Weil and La Abra awards against Mexico have been adjudged by the highest courts of our country to have been obtained through fraud and perjury on the part of the claimants, and that in accordance with the acts of the Congress the money remaining in the hands of the Secretary of State on these awards has been returned to Mexico. A considerable portion of the money received from Mexico on these awards had been paid by this Government to the claimants before the decision of the courts was rendered. My judgment is that the Congress should return to Mexico an amount equal to the sums thus already paid to the claimants.

The death of Queen Victoria caused the people of the United States deep and heartfelt sorrow, to which the Government gave full expres-sion. When President McKinley died, our Nation in turn received from every quarter of the British Empire expressions of grief and sym-pathy no less sincere. The death of the Empress Dowager Frederick of Germany also aroused the genuine sympathy of the American people; and this sympathy was cordially reciprocated by Germany when the President was assassinated. Indeed, from every quarter of the civilized world we received, at the time of the President's death, assurances of such grief and regard as to touch the hearts of our people. In the midst of our affliction we reverently thank the Almighty that we are at peace with the nations of mankind; and we firmly intend that our policy shall be such as to continue unbroken these international relations of mutual respect and good will.

SECOND ANNUAL MESSAGE.

WHITE HOUSE, *December 2, 1902.*

To the Senate and House of Representatives:

We still continue in a period of unbounded prosperity. This prosperity is not the creature of law, but undoubtedly the laws under which we work have been instrumental in creating the conditions which made it possible, and by unwise legislation it would be easy enough to destroy it. There will undoubtedly be periods of depression. The wave will recede; but the tide will advance. This Nation is seated on a continent flanked by two great oceans. It is composed of men the descendants of pioneers, or, in a sense, pioneers themselves; of men winnowed out from among the nations of the Old World by the energy, boldness, and love of adventure found in their own eager hearts. Such a Nation, so placed, will surely wrest success from fortune.

As a people we have played a large part in the world, and we are bent upon making our future even larger than the past. In particular, the events of the last four years have definitely decided that, for woe or for weal, our place must be great among the nations. We may either fail greatly or succeed greatly; but we can not avoid the endeavor from which either great failure or great success must come. Even if we would, we can not play a small part. If we should try, all that would follow would be that we should play a large part ignobly and shamefully.

But our people, the sons of the men of the Civil War, the sons of the men who had iron in their blood, rejoice in the present and face the future high of heart and resolute of will. Ours is not the creed of the weakling and the coward; ours is the gospel of hope and of triumphant endeavor. We do not shrink from the struggle before us. There are many problems for us to face at the outset of the twentieth century—grave problems abroad and still graver at home; but we know that we can solve them and solve them well, provided only that we bring to the solution the qualities of head and heart which were shown by the men who, in the days of Washington, founded this Government, and, in the days of Lincoln, preserved it.

No country has ever occupied a higher plane of material well-being than ours at the present moment. This well-being is due to no sudden or accidental causes, but to the play of the economic forces in this country for over a century; to our laws, our sustained and continuous policies; above all, to the high individual average of our citizenship. Great fortunes have been won by those who have taken the lead in this phenomenal industrial development, and most of these fortunes have been won not by doing evil, but as an incident to action which has benefited the community as a whole. Never before has material well-being been so widely diffused among our people. Great fortunes have been accumulated, and yet in the aggregate these fortunes are small indeed when compared to the wealth of the people as a whole. The plain people are better off than they have ever been before. The insurance companies, which are practically mutual benefit societies— especially helpful to men of moderate means—represent accumulations of capital which are among the largest in this country. There are more deposits in the savings banks, more owners of farms, more well-paid wage-workers in this country now than ever before in our history. Of course, when the conditions have favored the growth of so much that was good, they have also favored somewhat the growth of what was evil. It is eminently necessary that we should endeavor to cut out this evil, but let us keep a due sense of proportion; let us not in fixing our gaze upon the lesser evil forget the greater good. The evils are real and some of them are menacing, but they are the outgrowth, not of misery or decadence, but of prosperity—of the progress of our gigantic industrial development. This industrial development must not be checked, but side by side with it should go such progressive regulation as will diminish the evils. We should fail in our duty if we did not try to remedy the evils, but we shall succeed only if we proceed patiently, with practical common sense as well as resolution, separating the good from the bad and holding on to the former while endeavoring to get rid of the latter.

In my Message to the present Congress at its first session I discussed at length the question of the regulation of those big corporations commonly doing an interstate business, often with some tendency to monopoly, which are popularly known as trusts. The experience of the past year has emphasized, in my opinion, the desirability of the steps I then proposed. A fundamental requisite of social efficiency is a high standard of individual energy and excellence; but this is in no wise inconsistent with power to act in combination for aims which can not so well be achieved by the individual acting alone. A fundamental base of civilization is the inviolability of property; but this is in no wise inconsistent with the right of society to regulate the exercise of the artificial powers which it confers upon the owners of property, under the name of corporate franchises, in such a way as to prevent the misuse of these powers. Corporations, and especially combinations of corporations, should be managed under public regulation. Experience has shown that under our system of government the necessary supervision can not be obtained by State action. It must therefore be achieved by national action. Our aim is not to do away with corporations; on the contrary, these big aggregations are an inevitable development of modern industrialism, and the effort to destroy them would be futile unless accomplished in ways that would work the utmost mischief to the entire body politic. We can do nothing of good in the way of regulating and supervising these corporations until we fix clearly in our minds that we are not attacking the corporations, but endeavoring to do away with any evil in them. We are not hostile to them; we are merely determined that they shall be so handled as to subserve the public good. We draw the line against misconduct, not against wealth. The capitalist who, alone or in conjunction with his fellows, performs some great industrial feat by which he wins money is a welldoer, not a wrongdoer, provided only he works in proper and legitimate lines. We wish to favor such a man when he does well. We wish to supervise and control his actions only to prevent him from doing ill. Publicity can do no harm to the honest corporation; and we need not be over tender about sparing the dishonest corporation.

In curbing and regulating the combinations of capital which are, or may become, injurious to the public we must be careful not to stop the great enterprises which have legitimately reduced the cost of production, not to abandon the place which our country has won in the leadership of the international industrial world, not to strike down wealth with the result of closing factories and mines, of turning the wageworker idle in the streets and leaving the farmer without a market for what he grows. Insistence upon the impossible means delay in achieving the possible, exactly as, on the other hand, the stubborn defense alike of what is good and what is bad in the existing system, the resolute effort to obstruct any attempt at betterment, betrays blindness to the historic truth that wise evolution is the sure safeguard against revolution.

No more important subject can come before the Congress than this of the regulation of interstate business. This country can not afford to sit supine on the plea that under our peculiar system of government we are helpless in the presence of the new conditions, and unable to grapple with them or to cut out whatever of evil has arisen in connection with them. The power of the Congress to regulate interstate commerce is an absolute and unqualified grant, and without limitations other than those prescribed by the Constitution. The Congress has constitutional authority to make all laws necessary and proper for executing this power, and I am satisfied that this power has not been exhausted by any legislation now on the statute books. It is evident, therefore, that evils restrictive of commercial freedom and entailing restraint upon national commerce fall within the regulative power of the Congress, and that a wise and reasonable law would be a necessary and proper exercise of Congressional authority to the end that such evils should be eradicated.

I believe that monopolies, unjust discriminations, which prevent or cripple competition, fraudulent overcapitalization, and other evils in trust organizations and practices which injuriously affect interstate trade can be prevented under the power of the Congress to "regulate commerce with foreign nations and among the several States" through regulations and requirements operating directly upon such commerce. the instrumentalities thereof, and those engaged therein.

I earnestly recommend this subject to the consideration of the Congress with a view to the passage of a law reasonable in its provisions and effective in its operations, upon which the questions can be finally adjudicated that now raise doubts as to the necessity of constitutional amendment. If it prove impossible to accomplish the purposes above set forth by such a law, then, assuredly, we should not shrink from amending the Constitution so as to secure beyond peradventure the power sought.

The Congress has not heretofore made any appropriation for the better enforcement of the antitrust law as it now stands. Very much has been done by the Department of Justice in securing the enforcement of this law, but much more could be done if the Congress would make a special appropriation for this purpose, to be expended under the direction of the Attorney-General.

One proposition advocated has been the reduction of the tariff as a means of reaching the evils of the trusts which fall within the category I have described. Not merely would this be wholly ineffective, but the diversion of our efforts in such a direction would mean the abandonment of all intelligent attempt to do away with these evils. Many of the largest corporations, many of those which should certainly be included in any proper scheme of regulation, would not be affected in the slightest degree by a change in the tariff, save as such change interfered with the general prosperity of the country. The only relation of the tariff to big corporations as a whole is that the tariff makes manufactures profitable, and the tariff remedy proposed would be in effect simply to make manufactures unprofitable. To remove the tariff as a punitive measure directed against trusts would inevitably result in ruin to the weaker competitors who are struggling against them. Our aim should be not by unwise tariff changes to give foreign products the advantage over domestic products, but by proper regulation to give domestic competition a fair chance; and this end can not be reached by any tariff changes which would affect unfavorably all domestic competitors, good and bad alike. The question of regulation of the trusts stands apart from the question of tariff revision.

Stability of economic policy must always be the prime economic need of this country. This stability should not be fossilization. The country has acquiesced in the wisdom of the protective-tariff principle. It is exceedingly undesirable that this system should be destroyed or that there should be violent and radical changes therein. Our past experience shows that great prosperity in this country has always come under a protective tariff; and that the country can not prosper under fitful tariff changes at short intervals. Moreover, if the tariff laws as a whole work well, and if business has prospered under them and is prospering, it is better to endure for a time slight inconveniences and inequalities in some schedules than to upset business by too quick and too radical changes. It is most earnestly to be wished that we could treat the tariff from the standpoint solely of our business needs. It is, perhaps, too much to hope that partisanship may be entirely excluded from consideration of the subject, but at least it can be made secondary to the business interests of the country—that is, to the interests of our people as a whole. Unquestionably these business interests will best be served if together with fixity of principle as regards the tariff we combine a system which will permit us from time to time to make the necessary reapplication of the principle to the shifting national needs. We must take scrupulous care that the reapplication shall be made in such a way that it will not amount to a dislocation of our system, the mere threat of which (not to speak of the performance) would produce paralysis in the business energies of the community. The first consideration in making these changes would, of course, be to preserve the principle which underlies our whole tariff system— that is, the principle of putting American business interests at least on a full equality with interests abroad, and of always allowing a sufficient rate of duty to more than cover the difference between the labor cost here and abroad. The well-being of the wage-worker, like the well-being of the tiller of the soil, should be treated as an essential in shaping our whole economic policy. There must never be any change which will jeopardize the standard of comfort, the standard of wages of the American wage-worker.

One way in which the readjustment sought can be reached is by reciprocity treaties. It is greatly to be desired that such treaties may be adopted. They can be used to widen our markets and to give a greater field for the activities of our producers on the one hand, and on the other hand to secure in practical shape the lowering of duties when they are no longer needed for protection among our own people, or when the minimum of damage done may be disregarded for the sake of the maximum of good accomplished. If it prove impossible to ratify the pending treaties, and if there seem to be no warrant for the endeavor to execute others, or to amend the pending treaties so that they can be ratified, then the same end—to secure reciprocity—should be met by direct legislation.

Wherever the tariff conditions are such that a needed change can not with advantage be made by the application of the reciprocity idea, then it can be made outright by a lowering of duties on a given product. If possible, such change should be made only after the fullest consideration by practical experts, who should approach the subject from a business standpoint, having in view both the particular interests affected and the commercial well-being of the people as a whole. The machinery for providing such careful investigation can readily be supplied. The executive department has already at its disposal methods of collecting facts and figures; and if the Congress desires additional consideration to that which will be given the subject by its own committees, then a commission of business experts can be appointed whose duty it should be to recommend action by the Congress after a deliberate and scientific examination of the various schedules as they are affected by the changed and changing conditions. The unhurried and unbiased report of this commission would show what changes should be made in the various schedules, and how far these changes could go without also changing the great prosperity which this country is now enjoying, or upsetting its fixed economic policy.

The cases in which the tariff can produce a monopoly are so few as to constitute an inconsiderable factor in the question; but of course if in any case it be found that a given rate of duty does promote a monopoly which works ill, no protectionist would object to such reduction of the duty as would equalize competition.

In my judgment, the tariff on anthracite coal should be removed, and anthracite put actually, where it now is nominally, on the free list. This would have no effect at all save in crises; but in crises it might be of service to the people.

Interest rates are a potent factor in business activity, and in order that these rates may be equalized to meet the varying needs of the seasons and of widely separated communities, and to prevent the recurrence of financial stringencies which injuriously affect legitimate business, it is necessary that there should be an element of elasticity in our monetary system. Banks are the natural servants of commerce, and upon them should be placed, as far as practicable, the burden of furnishing and maintaining a circulation adequate to supply the needs of our diversified industries and of our domestic and foreign commerce; and the issue of this should be so regulated that a sufficient supply should be always available for the business interests of the country.

It would be both unwise and unnecessary at this time to attempt to reconstruct our financial system, which has been the growth of a century; but some additional legislation is, I think, desirable. The mere outline of any plan sufficiently comprehensive to meet these requirements would transgress the appropriate limits of this communication. It is suggested, however, that all future legislation on the subject should be with the view of encouraging the use of such instrumentalities as will automatically supply every legitimate demand of productive industries and of commerce, not only in the amount, but in the character of circulation; and of making all kinds of money interchangeable, and, at the will of the holder, convertible into the established gold standard.

I again call your attention to the need of passing a proper immigration law, covering the points outlined in my Message to you at the first session of the present Congress; substantially such a bill has already passed the House.

How to secure fair treatment alike for labor and for capital, how to hold in check the unscrupulous man, whether employer or employee, without weakening individual initiative, without hampering and cramping the industrial development of the country, is a problem fraught with great difficulties and one which it is of the highest importance to solve on lines of sanity and far-sighted common sense as well as of devotion to the right. This is an era of federation and combination. Exactly as business men find they must often work through corporations, and as it is a constant tendency of these corporations to grow larger, so it is often necessary for laboring men to work in federations, and these have become important factors of modern industrial life. Both kinds of federation, capitalistic and labor, can do much good, and as a necessary corollary they can both do evil. Opposition to each kind of organization should take the form of opposition to whatever is bad in the conduct of any given corporation or union—not of attacks upon corporations as such nor upon unions as such; for some of the most far-reaching beneficent work for our people has been accom-

plished through both corporations and unions. Each must refrain
from arbitrary or tyrannous interference with the rights of others. Organized capital and organized labor alike should remember that in the
long run the interest of each must be brought into harmony with the
interest of the general public; and the conduct of each must conform
to the fundamental rules of obedience to the law, of individual freedom,
and of justice and fair dealing toward all. Each should remember
that in addition to power it must strive after the realization of healthy,
lofty, and generous ideals. Every employer, every wage-worker, must
be guaranteed his liberty and his right to do as he likes with his property or his labor so long as he does not infringe upon the rights of
others. It is of the highest importance that employer and employee
alike should endeavor to appreciate each the viewpoint of the other
and the sure disaster that will come upon both in the long run if either
grows to take as habitual an attitude of sour hostility and distrust
toward the other. Few people deserve better of the country than those
representatives both of capital and labor—and there are many such—
who work continually to bring about a good understanding of this
kind, based upon wisdom and upon broad and kindly sympathy between
employers and employed. Above all, we need to remember that any
kind of class animosity in the political world is, if possible, even more
wicked, even more destructive to national welfare, than sectional, race,
or religious animosity. We can get good government only upon condition that we keep true to the principles upon which this Nation was
founded, and judge each man not as a part of a class, but upon his
individual merits. All that we have a right to ask of any man, rich
or poor, whatever his creed, his occupation, his birthplace, or his residence, is that he shall act well and honorably by his neighbor and by
his country. We are neither for the rich man as such nor for the poor
man as such; we are for the upright man, rich or poor. So far as the
constitutional powers of the National Government touch these matters
of general and vital moment to the Nation, they should be exercised
in conformity with the principles above set forth.

It is earnestly hoped that a secretary of commerce may be created,
with a seat in the Cabinet. The rapid multiplication of questions
affecting labor and capital, the growth and complexity of the organizations through which both labor and capital now find expression, the
steady tendency toward the employment of capital in huge corporations,
and the wonderful strides of this country toward leadership in the
international business world justify an urgent demand for the creation
of such a position. Substantially all the leading commercial bodies
in this country have united in requesting its creation. It is desirable
that some such measure as that which has already passed the Senate
be enacted into law. The creation of such a department would in itself

be an advance toward dealing with and exercising supervision over the whole subject of the great corporations doing an interstate business; and with this end in view, the Congress should endow the department with large powers, which could be increased as experience might show the need.

I hope soon to submit to the Senate a reciprocity treaty with Cuba. On May 20 last the United States kept its promise to the island by formally vacating Cuban soil and turning Cuba over to those whom her own people had chosen as the first officials of the new Republic.

Cuba lies at our doors, and whatever affects her for good or for ill affects us also. So much have our people felt this that in the Platt amendment we definitely took the ground that Cuba must hereafter have closer political relations with us than with any other power. Thus in a sense Cuba has become a part of our international political system. This makes it necessary that in return she should be given some of the benefits of becoming part of our economic system. It is, from our own standpoint, a short-sighted and mischievous policy to fail to recognize this need. Moreover, it is unworthy of a mighty and generous nation, itself the greatest and most successful republic in history, to refuse to stretch out a helping hand to a young and weak sister republic just entering upon its career of independence. We should always fearlessly insist upon our rights in the face of the strong, and we should with ungrudging hand do our generous duty by the weak. I urge the adoption of reciprocity with Cuba not only because it is eminently for our own interests to control the Cuban market and by every means to foster our supremacy in the tropical lands and waters south of us, but also because we, of of the giant republic of the north, should make all our sister nations of the American Continent feel that whenever they will permit it we desire to show ourselves disinterestedly and effectively their friend.

A convention with Great Britain has been concluded, which will be at once laid before the Senate for ratification, providing for reciprocal trade arrangements between the United States and Newfoundland on substantially the lines of the convention formerly negotiated by the Secretary of State, Mr. Blaine. I believe reciprocal trade relations will be greatly to the advantage of both countries.

As civilization grows warfare becomes less and less the normal condition of foreign relations. The last century has seen a marked diminution of wars between civilized powers; wars with uncivilized powers are largely mere matters of international police duty, essential for the welfare of the world. Wherever possible, arbitration or some similar method should be employed in lieu of war to settle difficulties between civilized nations, although as yet the world has not progressed sufficiently to render it possible, or necessarily desirable, to invoke arbitration in every case. The formation of the international tribunal which sits at The Hague is an event of good omen from which great consequences for the welfare of all mankind may flow. It is far better, where possible, to invoke such a permanent tribunal than to create special arbitrators for a given purpose.

It is a matter of sincere congratulation to our country that the United States and Mexico should have been the first to use the good offices of The Hague Court. This was done last summer with most satisfactory results in the case of a claim at issue between us and our sister Republic. It is earnestly to be hoped that this first case will serve as a precedent for others, in which not only the United States but foreign nations may take advantage of the machinery already in existence at The Hague.

I commend to the favorable consideration of the Congress the Hawaiian fire claims, which were the subject of careful investigation during the last session.

The Congress has wisely provided that we shall build at once an isthmian canal, if possible at Panama. The Attorney-General reports that we can undoubtedly acquire good title from the French Panama Canal Company. Negotiations are now pending with Colombia to secure her assent to our building the canal. This canal will be one of the greatest engineering feats of the twentieth century; a greater engineering feat than has yet been accomplished during the history of mankind. The work should be carried out as a continuing policy without regard to change of Administration; and it should be begun under circumstances which will make it a matter of pride for all Administrations to continue the policy.

The canal will be of great benefit to America, and of importance to all the world. It will be of advantage to us industrially and also as improving our military position. It will be of advantage to the countries of tropical America. It is earnestly to be hoped that all of these countries will do as some of them have already done with signal success, and will invite to their shores commerce and improve their material conditions by recognizing that stability and order are the prerequisites of successful development. No independent nation in America need have the slightest fear of aggression from the United States. It behoves each one to maintain order within its own borders and to discharge its just obligations to foreigners. When this is done, they can rest assured that, be they strong or weak, they have nothing to dread from outside interference. More and more the increasing interdependence and complexity of international political and economic relations render it incumbent on all civilized and orderly powers to insist on the proper policing of the world.

During the fall of 1901 a communication was addressed to the Secretary of State, asking whether permission would be granted by the President to a corporation to lay a cable from a point on the California coast to the Philippine Islands by way of Hawaii. A statement of conditions or terms upon which such corporation would undertake to lay and operate a cable was volunteered.

Inasmuch as the Congress was shortly to convene, and Pacific-cable legislation had been the subject of consideration by the Congress for several years, it seemed to me wise to defer action upon the application until the Congress had first an opportunity to act. The Congress adjourned without taking any action, leaving the matter in exactly the same condition in which it stood when the Congress convened.

Meanwhile it appears that the Commercial Pacific Cable Company had promptly proceeded with preparations for laying its cable. It also made application to the President for access to and use of soundings taken by the U. S. S. *Nero,* for the purpose of discovering a practicable route for a trans-Pacific cable, the company urging that with access to these soundings it could complete its cable much sooner than if it were required to take soundings upon its own account. Pending consideration of this subject, it appeared important and desirable to attach certain conditions to the permission to examine and use the soundings, if it should be granted.

In consequence of this solicitation of the cable company, certain conditions were formulated, upon which the President was willing to allow access to these soundings and to consent to the landing and laying of the cable, subject to any alterations or additions thereto imposed by the Congress. This was deemed proper, especially as it was clear that a cable connection of some kind with China, a foreign country, was a part of the company's plan. This course was, moreover, in accordance with a line of precedents, including President Grant's action in the case of the first French cable, explained to the Congress in his Annual Message of December, 1875, and the instance occurring in 1879 of the second French cable from Brest to St. Pierre, with a branch to Cape Cod.

These conditions prescribed, among other things, a maximum rate for commercial messages and that the company should construct a line from the Philippine Islands to China, there being at present, as is well known, a British line from Manila to Hongkong.

The representatives of the cable company kept these conditions long under consideration, continuing, in the meantime, to prepare for laying the cable. They have, however, at length acceded to them, and an all-American line between our Pacific coast and the Chinese Empire, by way of Honolulu and the Philippine Islands, is thus provided for, and is expected within a few months to be ready for business.

Among the conditions is one reserving the power of the Congress to modify or repeal any or all of them. A copy of the conditions is herewith transmitted.

Of Porto Rico it is only necessary to say that the prosperity of the island and the wisdom with which it has been governed have been such as to make it serve as an example of all that is best in insular administration.

On July 4 last, on the one hundred and twenty-sixth anniversary of the declaration of our independence, peace and amnesty were promulgated in the Philippine Islands. Some trouble has since from time to time threatened with the Mohammedan Moros, but with the late insurrectionary Filipinos the war has entirely ceased. Civil government has now been introduced. Not only does each Filipino enjoy such rights to life, liberty, and the pursuit of happiness as he has never before known during the recorded history of the islands, but the people taken as a whole now enjoy a measure of self-government greater than that granted to any other Orientals by any foreign power and greater than that enjoyed by any other Orientals under their own governments, save the Japanese alone. We have not gone too far in granting these rights of liberty and self-government; but we have certainly gone to the limit that in the interests of the Philippine people themselves it was wise or just to go. To hurry matters, to go faster than we are now going, would entail calamity on the people of the islands. No policy ever entered into by the American people has vindicated itself in more signal manner than the policy of holding the Philippines. The triumph of our arms, above all the triumph of our laws and principles, has come sooner than we had any right to expect. Too much praise can not be given to the Army for what it has done in the Philippines both in warfare and from an administrative standpoint in preparing the way for civil government; and similar credit belongs to the civil authorities for the way in which they have planted the seeds of self-government in the ground thus made ready for them. The courage, the unflinching endurance, the high soldierly efficiency, and the general kind-heartedness and humanity of our troops have been strikingly manifested. There now remain only some fifteen thousand troops in the islands. All told, over one hundred thousand have been sent there. Of course, there have been individual instances of wrongdoing among them. They warred under fearful difficulties of climate and surroundings; and under the strain of the terrible provocations which they continually received from their foes, occasional instances of cruel retaliation occurred. Every effort has been made to prevent such cruelties, and finally these efforts have been completely successful. Every effort has also been made to detect and punish the wrongdoers. After making all allowance for these misdeeds, it remains true that few indeed have been the instances in which war has been waged by a civilized power against semicivilized or barbarous forces where there has been so little wrongdoing by the victors as in the Philippine Islands. On the other hand, the amount of difficult, important, and beneficent work which has been done is well-nigh incalculable.

Taking the work of the Army and the civil authorities together, it may be questioned whether anywhere else in modern times the world has seen a better example of real constructive statesmanship than our people have given in the Philippine Islands. High praise should also be given those Filipinos, in the aggregate very numerous, who have accepted the new conditions and joined with our representatives to work with hearty good will for the welfare of the islands.

The Army has been reduced to the minimum allowed by law. It is very small for the size of the Nation, and most certainly should be kept at the highest point of efficiency. The senior officers are given scant chance under ordinary conditions to exercise commands commensurate with their rank, under circumstances which would fit them to do their duty in time of actual war. A system of maneuvering our Army in bodies of some little size has been begun and should be steadily continued. Without such maneuvers it is folly to expect that in the event of hostilities with any serious foe even a small army corps could be handled to advantage. Both our officers and enlisted men are such that we can take hearty pride in them. No better material can be found. But they must be thoroughly trained, both as individuals and in the mass. The marksmanship of the men must receive special attention. In the circumstances of modern warfare the man must act far more on his own individual responsibility than ever before, and the high individual efficiency of the unit is of the utmost importance. Formerly this unit was the regiment; it is now not the regiment, not even the troop or company; it is the individual soldier. Every effort must be made to develop every workmanlike and soldierly quality in both the officer and the enlisted man.

I urgently call your attention to the need of passing a bill providing for a general staff and for the reorganization of the supply departments on the lines of the bill proposed by the Secretary of War last year. When the young officers enter the Army from West Point they probably stand above their compeers in any other military service. Every effort should be made, by training, by reward of merit, by scrutiny into their careers and capacity, to keep them of the same high relative excellence throughout their careers.

The measure providing for the reorganization of the militia system

and for securing the highest efficiency in the National Guard, which
has already passed the House, should receive prompt attention and
action.   It is of great importance that the relation of the National
Guard to the militia and volunteer forces of the United States should
be defined, and that in place of our present obsolete laws a practical
and efficient system should be adopted.

Provision should be made to enable the Secretary of War to keep
cavalry and artillery horses, worn-out in long performance of duty.
Such horses fetch but a trifle when sold; and rather than turn them
out to the misery awaiting them when thus disposed of, it would be
better to employ them at light work around the posts, and when necessary to put them painlessly to death.

For the first time in our history naval maneuvers on a large scale
are being held under the immediate command of the Admiral of the
Navy.   Constantly increasing attention is being paid to the gunnery
of the Navy, but it is yet far from what it should be.   I earnestly
urge that the increase asked for by the Secretary of the Navy in the
appropriation for improving the markmanship be granted.   In battle
the only shots that count are the shots that hit.   It is necessary to
provide ample funds for practice with the great guns in time of peace.
These funds must provide not only for the purchase of projectiles,
but for allowances for prizes to encourage the gun crews, and especially
the gun pointers, and for perfecting an intelligent system under which
alone it is possible to get good practice.

There should be no halt in the work of building up the Navy,
providing every year additional fighting craft.   We are a very rich
country, vast in extent of territory and great in population; a country,
moreover, which has an Army diminutive indeed when compared
with that of any other first-class power.   We have deliberately made
our own certain foreign policies which demand the possession of a first-
class navy.   The isthmian canal will greatly increase the efficiency
of our Navy if the Navy is of sufficient size; but if we have an inadequate navy, then the building of the canal would be merely giving a hostage to any power of superior strength.   The Monroe Doctrine should be treated as the cardinal feature of American foreign
policy; but it would be worse than idle to assert it unless we intended
to back it up, and it can be backed up only by a thoroughly good
navy.   A good navy is not a provocative of war.   It is the surest
guaranty of peace.

Each individual unit of our Navy should be the most efficient of
its kind as regards both material and personnel that is to be found in
the world.   I call your special attention to the need of providing for
the manning of the ships.   Serious trouble threatens us if we can not
do better than we are now doing as regards securing the services of a

sufficient number of the highest type of sailormen, of sea mechanics. The veteran seamen of our war ships are of as high a type as can be found in any navy which rides the waters of the world; they are unsurpassed in daring, in resolution, in readiness, in thorough knowledge of their profession. They deserve every consideration that can be shown them. But there are not enough of them. It is no more possible to improvise a crew than it is possible to improvise a war ship. To build the finest ship, with the deadliest battery, and to send it afloat with a raw crew, no matter how brave they were individually, would be to insure disaster if a foe of average capacity were encountered. Neither ships nor men can be improvised when war has begun.

We need a thousand additional officers in order to properly man the ships now provided for and under construction. The classes at the Naval School at Annapolis should be greatly enlarged. At the same time that we thus add the officers where we need them, we should facilitate the retirement of those at the head of the list whose usefulness has become impaired. Promotion must be fostered if the service is to be kept efficient.

The lamentable scarcity of officers, and the large number of recruits and of unskilled men necessarily put aboard the new vessels as they have been commissioned, has thrown upon our officers, and especially on the lieutenants and junior grades, unusual labor and fatigue and has gravely strained their powers of endurance. Nor is there sign of any immediate let-up in this strain. It must continue for some time longer, until more officers are graduated from Annapolis, and until the recruits become trained and skillful in their duties. In these difficulties incident upon the development of our war fleet the conduct of all our officers has been creditable to the service, and the lieutenants and junior grades in particular have displayed an ability and a steadfast cheerfulness which entitles them to the ungrudging thanks of all who realize the disheartening trials and fatigues to which they are of necessity subjected.

There is not a cloud on the horizon at present. There seems not the slightest chance of trouble with a foreign power. We most earnestly hope that this state of things may continue; and the way to insure its continuance is to provide for a thoroughly efficient navy. The refusal to maintain such a navy would invite trouble, and if trouble came would insure disaster. Fatuous self-complacency or vanity, or short-sightedness in refusing to prepare for danger, is both foolish and wicked in such a nation as ours; and past experience has shown that such fatuity in refusing to recognize or prepare for any crisis in advance is usually succeeded by a mad panic of hysterical fear once the crisis has actually arrived.

The striking increase in the revenues of the Post-Office Department shows clearly the prosperity of our people and the increasing activity of the business of the country.

The receipts of the Post-Office Department for the fiscal year ending June 30 last amounted to $121,848,047.26, an increase of $10,-216,853.87 over the preceding year, the largest increase known in the history of the postal service. The magnitude of this increase will best appear from the fact that the entire postal receipts for the year 1860 amounted to but $8,518,067.

Rural free-delivery service is no longer in the experimental stage; it has become a fixed policy. The results following its introduction have fully justified the Congress in the large appropriations made for its establishment and extension. The average yearly increase in post-office receipts in the rural districts of the country is about two per cent. We are now able, by actual results, to show that where rural free-delivery service has been established to such an extent as to enable us to make comparisons the yearly increase has been upward of ten per cent.

On November 1, 1902, 11,650 rural free-delivery routes had been established and were in operation, covering about one-third of the territory of the United States available for rural free-delivery service. There are now awaiting the action of the Department petitions and applications for the establishment of 10,748 additional routes. This shows conclusively the want which the establishment of the service has met and the need of further extending it as rapidly as possible. It is justified both by the financial results and by the practical benefits to our rural population; it brings the men who live on the soil into close relations with the active business world; it keeps the farmer in daily touch with the markets; it is a potential educational force; it enhances the value of farm property, makes farm life far pleasanter and less isolated, and will do much to check the undesirable current from country to city.

It is to be hoped that the Congress will make liberal appropriations for the continuance of the service already established and for its further extension.

Few subjects of more importance have been taken up by the Congress in recent years than the inauguration of the system of nationally-aided irrigation for the arid regions of the far West. A good beginning therein has been made. Now that this policy of national irrigation has been adopted, the need of thorough and scientific forest protection will grow more rapidly than ever throughout the public-land States.

Legislation should be provided for the protection of the game, and the wild creatures generally, on the forest reserves. The senseless slaughter of game, which can by judicious protection be permanently preserved on our national reserves for the people as a whole, should be stopped at once. It is, for instance, a serious count against our national good sense to permit the present practice of butchering off such a stately and beautiful creature as the elk for its antlers or tusks.

So far as they are available for agriculture, and to whatever extent they may be reclaimed under the national irrigation law, the remaining public lands should be held rigidly for the home builder, the settler who lives on his land, and for no one else. In their actual use the desert-land law, the timber and stone law, and the commutation clause of the homestead law have been so perverted from the intention with which they were enacted as to permit the acquisition of large areas of the public domain for other than actual settlers and the consequent prevention of settlement. Moreover, the approaching exhaustion of the public ranges has of late led to much discussion as to the best manner of using these public lands in the West which are suitable chiefly or only for grazing. The sound and steady development of the West depends upon the building up of homes therein. Much of our prosperity as a nation has been due to the operation of the homestead law. On the other hand, we should recognize the fact that in the grazing region the man who corresponds to the homesteader may be unable to settle permanently if only allowed to use the same amount of pasture land that his brother, the homesteader, is allowed to use of arable land. One hundred and sixty acres of fairly rich and well-watered soil, or a much smaller amount of irrigated land, may keep a family in plenty, whereas no one could get a living from one hundred and sixty acres of dry pasture land capable of supporting at the outside only one head of cattle to every ten acres. In the past great tracts of the public domain have been fenced in by persons having no title thereto, in direct defiance of the law forbidding the maintenance or construction of any such unlawful inclosure of public land. For various reasons there has been little interference with such inclosures in the past, but ample notice has now been given the trespassers, and all the resources at the command of the Government will hereafter be used to put a stop to such trespassing.

In view of the capital importance of these matters, I commend them to the earnest consideration of the Congress, and if the Congress finds difficulty in dealing with them from lack of thorough knowledge of the subject, I recommend that provision be made for a commission of experts specially to investigate and report upon the complicated questions involved.

I especially urge upon the Congress the need of wise legislation for Alaska. It is not to our credit as a nation that Alaska, which has been ours for thirty-five years, should still have as poor a system of laws as is the case. No country has a more valuable possession—

in mineral wealth, in fisheries, furs, forests, and also in land avail
able for certain kinds of farming and stockgrowing. It is a territory
of great size and varied resources, well fitted to support a large permanent population. Alaska needs a good land law and such provisions
for homesteads and pre-emptions as will encourage permanent settlement. We should shape legislation with a view not to the exploiting
and abandoning of the territory, but to the building up of homes
therein. The land laws should be liberal in type, so as to hold out
inducements to the actual settler whom we most desire to see take
possession of the country. The forests of Alaska should be protected,
and, as a secondary but still important matter, the game also, and at
the same time it is imperative that the settlers should be allowed to
cut timber, under proper regulations, for their own use. Laws should
be enacted to protect the Alaskan salmon fisheries against the greed
which would destroy them. They should be preserved as a permanent
industry and food supply. Their management and control should be
turned over to the Commission of Fish and Fisheries. Alaska should
have a Delegate in the Congress. It would be well if a Congressional
committee could visit Alaska and investigate its needs on the ground.

In dealing with the Indians our aim should be their ultimate absorption into the body of our people. But in many cases this absorption
must and should be very slow. In portions of the Indian Territory
the mixture of blood has gone on at the same time with progress in
wealth and education, so that there are plenty of men with varying
degrees of purity of Indian blood who are absolutely indistinguishable
in point of social, political, and economic ability from their white
associates. There are other tribes which have as yet made no perceptible advance toward such equality. To try to force such tribes
too fast is to prevent their going forward at all. Moreover, the tribes
live under widely different conditions. Where a tribe has made considerable advance and lives on fertile farming soil it is possible to
allot the members lands in severalty much as is the case with white
settlers. There are other tribes where such a course is not desirable.
On the arid prairie lands the effort should be to induce the Indians to
lead pastoral rather than agricultural lives, and to permit them to
settle in villages rather than to force them into isolation.

The large Indian schools situated remote from any Indian reservation do a special and peculiar work of great importance. But, excellent
though these are, an immense amount of additional work must be done
on the reservations themselves among the old, and above all among the
young, Indians.

The first and most important step toward the absorption of the
Indian is to teach him to earn his living; yet it is not necessarily
to be assumed that in each community all Indians must become either

tillers of the soil or stock raisers. Their industries may properly be diversified, and those who show special desire or adaptability for industrial or even commercial pursuits should be encouraged so far as practicable to follow out each his own bent.

Every effort should be made to develop the Indian along the lines of natural aptitude, and to encourage the existing native industries peculiar to certain tribes, such as the various kinds of basket weaving, canoe building, smith work, and blanket work. Above all, the Indian boys and girls should be given confident command of colloquial English, and should ordinarily be prepared for a vigorous struggle with the conditions under which their people live, rather than for immediate absorption into some more highly developed community.

The officials who represent the Government in dealing with the Indians work under hard conditions, and also under conditions which render it easy to do wrong and very difficult to detect wrong. Consequently they should be amply paid on the one hand, and on the other hand a particularly high standard of conduct should be demanded from them, and where misconduct can be proved the punishment should be exemplary.

In no department of governmental work in recent years has there been greater success than in that of giving scientific aid to the farming population, thereby showing them how most efficiently to help themselves. There is no need of insisting upon its importance, for the welfare of the farmer is fundamentally necessary to the welfare of the Republic as a whole. In addition to such work as quarantine against animal and vegetable plagues, and warring against them when here introduced, much efficient help has been rendered to the farmer by the introduction of new plants specially fitted for cultivation under the peculiar conditions existing in different portions of the country. New cereals have been established in the semi-arid West. For instance, the practicability of producing the best types of macaroni wheats in regions of an annual rainfall of only ten inches or thereabouts has been conclusively demonstrated. Through the introduction of new rices in Louisiana and Texas the production of rice in this country has been made to about equal the home demand. In the Southwest the possibility of regrassing overstocked range lands has been demonstrated; in the North many new forage crops have been introduced, while in the East it has been shown that some of our choicest fruits can be stored and shipped in such a way as to find a profitable market abroad.

I again recommend to the favorable consideration of the Congress the plans of the Smithsonian Institution for making the Museum under its charge worthy of the Nation, and for preserving at the National Capital not only records of the vanishing races of men but of the animals of this continent which, like the buffalo, will soon become extinct unless specimens from which their representatives may be renewed are sought in their native regions and maintained there in safety.

The District of Columbia is the only part of our territory in which the National Government exercises local or municipal functions, and where in consequence the Government has a free hand in reference to certain types of social and economic legislation which must be essentially local or municipal in their character. The Government should see to it, for instance, that the hygienic and sanitary legislation affecting Washington is of a high character. The evils of slum dwellings, whether in the shape of crowded and congested tenement-house districts or of the back-alley type, should never be permitted to grow up in Washington. The city should be a model in every respect for all the cities of the country. The charitable and correctional systems of the District should receive consideration at the hands of the Congress to the end that they may embody the results of the most advanced thought in these fields. Moreover, while Washington is not a great industrial city, there is some industrialism here, and our labor legislation, while it would not be important in itself, might be made a model for the rest of the Nation. We should pass, for instance, a wise employer's-liability act for the District of Columbia, and we need such an act in our navy-yards. Railroad companies in the District ought to be required by law to block their frogs.

The safety-appliance law, for the better protection of the lives and limbs of railway employees, which was passed in 1893, went into full effect on August 1, 1901. It has resulted in averting thousands of casualties. Experience shows, however, the necessity of additional legislation to perfect this law. A bill to provide for this passed the Senate at the last session. It is to be hoped that some such measure may now be enacted into law.

There is a growing tendency to provide for the publication of masses of documents for which there is no public demand and for the printing of which there is no real necessity. Large numbers of volumes are turned out by the Government printing presses for which there is no justification. Nothing should be printed by any of the Departments unless it contains something of permanent value, and the Congress could with advantage cut down very materially on all the printing which it has now become customary to provide. The excessive cost of Government printing is a strong argument against the position of those who are inclined on abstract grounds to advocate the Government's doing any work which can with propriety be left in private hands.

Gratifying progress has been made during the year in the extension of the merit system of making appointments in the Government service. It should be extended by law to the District of Columbia. It is much to be desired that our consular system be established by law on a basis providing for appointment and promotion only in consequence of proved fitness.

Through a wise provision of the Congress at its last session the White House, which had become disfigured by incongruous additions and changes, has now been restored to what it was planned to be by Washington. In making the restorations the utmost care has been exercised to come as near as possible to the early plans and to supplement these plans by a careful study of such buildings as that of the University of Virginia, which was built by Jefferson. The White House is the property of the Nation, and so far as is compatible with living therein it should be kept as it originally was, for the same reasons that we keep Mount Vernon as it originally was. The stately simplicity of its architecture is an expression of the character of the period in which it was built, and is in accord with the purposes it was designed to serve. It is a good thing to preserve such buildings as historic monuments which keep alive our sense of continuity with the Nation's past.

The reports of the several Executive Departments are submitted to the Congress with this communication.

THIRD ANNUAL MESSAGE.

WHITE HOUSE, *December 7, 1903.*

To the Senate and House of Representatives:

The country is to be congratulated on the amount of substantial achievement which has marked the past year both as regards our foreign and as regards our domestic policy.

With a nation as with a man the most important things are those of the household, and therefore the country is especially to be congratulated on what has been accomplished in the direction of providing for the exercise of supervision over the great corporations and combinations of corporations engaged in interstate commerce. The Congress has created the Department of Commerce and Labor, including the Bureau of Corporations, with for the first time authority to secure proper publicity of such proceedings of these great corporations as the public has the right to know. It has provided for the expediting of suits for the enforcement of the Federal anti-trust law; and by another law it has secured equal treatment to all producers in the transportation of their goods, thus taking a long stride forward in making effective the work of the Interstate Commerce Commission.

The establishment of the Department of Commerce and Labor, with the Bureau of Corporations thereunder, marks a real advance in the direction of doing all that is possible for the solution of the questions vitally affecting capitalists and wage-workers. The act creating the Department was approved on February 14, 1903, and two days later the head of the Department was nominated and confirmed by the Senate. Since then the work of organization has been pushed as rapidly as the initial appropriations permitted, and with due regard to thoroughness and the broad purposes which the Department is designed to serve. After the transfer of the various bureaus and branches to the Department at the beginning of the current fiscal year, as provided for in the act, the personnel comprised 1,289 employees in Washington and 8,836 in the country at large. The scope of the Department's duty and authority embraces the commercial and industrial interests of the Nation. It is not designed to restrict or control the fullest liberty of legitimate business action, but to secure exact and authentic information which will aid the Executive in enforcing existing laws, and which will enable the Congress to enact additional legislation if any should be found necessary, in order to prevent the few from obtaining privileges at the expense of diminished opportunities for the many.

The preliminary work of the Bureau of Corporations in the Department has shown the wisdom of its creation. Publicity in corporate affairs will tend to do away with ignorance, and will afford facts upon which intelligent action may be taken. Systematic, intelligent investigation is already developing facts the knowledge of which is essential to a right understanding of the needs and duties of the business world. The corporation which is honestly and fairly organized, whose managers in the conduct of its business recognize their obligation to deal squarely with their stockholders, their competitors, and the public, has nothing to fear from such supervision. The purpose of this Bureau is not to embarrass or assail legitimate business, but to aid in bringing about a better industrial condition—a condition under which there shall be obedience to law and recognition of public obligation by all corporations, great or small. The Department of Commerce and Labor will be not only the clearing house for information regarding the business transactions of the Nation, but the executive arm of the Government to aid in strengthening our domestic and foreign markets, in perfecting our transportation facilities, in building up our merchant marine, in preventing the entrance of undesirable immigrants, in improving commercial and industrial conditions, and in bringing together on common ground those necessary partners in industrial progress— capital and labor. Commerce between the nations is steadily growing in volume, and the tendency of the times is toward closer trade relations. Constant watchfulness is needed to secure to Americans the chance to participate to the best advantage in foreign trade; and we may confidently expect that the new Department will justify the expectation of its creators by the exercise of this watchfulness, as well as by the businesslike administration of such laws relating to our internal affairs as are intrusted to its care.

In enacting the laws above enumerated the Congress proceeded on sane and conservative lines. Nothing revolutionary was attempted; but a common-sense and successful effort was made in the direction of seeing that corporations are so handled as to subserve the public good. The legislation was moderate. It was characterized throughout by the idea that we were not attacking corporations, but endeavoring to provide for doing away with any evil in them; that we drew the line against misconduct, not against wealth; gladly recognizing the great good done by the capitalist who alone, or in conjunction with his fellows, does his work along proper and legitimate lines. The purpose of the legislation, which purpose will undoubtedly be fulfilled, was to favor such a man when he does well, and to supervise his action only to prevent him from doing ill. Publicity can do no harm to the honest corporation. The only corporation that has cause to dread it is the corporation which shrinks from the light, and about the welfare of such corporations we need not be oversensitive. The work of the Department of Commerce and Labor has been conditioned upon this theory, of securing fair treatment alike for labor and for capital.

The consistent policy of the National Government, so far as it has the power, is to hold in check the unscrupulous man, whether employer or employee; but to refuse to weaken individual initiative or to hamper or cramp the industrial development of the country. We recognize that this is an era of federation and combination, in which great capitalistic corporations and labor unions have become factors of tremendous importance in all industrial centers. Hearty recognition is given the far-reaching, beneficent work which has been accomplished through both corporations and unions, and the line as between different corporations, as between different unions, is drawn as it is between different individuals; that is, it is drawn on conduct, the effort being to treat both organized capital and organized labor alike; asking nothing save that the interest of each shall be brought into harmony with the interest of the general public, and that the conduct of each shall conform to the fundamental rules of obedience to law, of individual freedom, and of justice and fair dealing towards all. Whenever either corporation, labor union, or individual disregards the law or acts in a spirit of arbitrary and tyrannous interference with the rights of others, whether corporations or individuals, then where the Federal

Government has jurisdiction, it will see to it that the misconduct is stopped, paying not the slightest heed to the position or power of the corporation, the union or the individual, but only to one vital fact— that is, the question whether or not the conduct of the individual or aggregate of individuals is in accordance with the law of the land. Every man must be guaranteed his liberty and his right to do as he likes with his property or his labor, so long as he does not infringe the rights of others. No man is above the law and no man is below it; nor do we ask any man's permission when we require him to obey it. Obedience to the law is demanded as a right; not asked as a favor.

We have cause as a nation to be thankful for the steps that have been so successfully taken to put these principles into effect. The progress has been by evolution, not by revolution. Nothing radical has been done; the action has been both moderate and resolute. There- fore the work will stand. There shall be no backward step. If in the working of the laws it proves desirable that they shall at any point be expanded or amplified, the amendment can be made as its desir- ability is shown. Meanwhile they are being administered with judg- ment, but with insistence upon obedience to them, and their need has been emphasized in signal fashion by the events of the past year.

From all sources, exclusive of the postal service, the receipts of the Government for the last fiscal year aggregated $560,396,674. The expenditures for the same period were $506,099,007, the surplus for the fiscal year being $54,297,667. The indications are that the surplus for the present fiscal year will be very small, if indeed there be any surplus. From July to November the receipts from customs were, approximately, nine million dollars less than the receipts from the same source for a corresponding portion of last year. Should this decrease continue at the same ratio throughout the fiscal year, the sur- plus would be reduced by, approximately, thirty million dollars. Should the revenue from customs suffer much further decrease during the fiscal year, the surplus would vanish. A large surplus is certainly undesirable. Two years ago the war taxes were taken off with the express intention of equalizing tl : governmental receipts and expendi- tures, and though the first year thereafter still showed a surplus, it now seems likely that a substantial equality of revenue and expenditure will be attained. Such being the case it is of great moment both to exer- cise care and economy in appropriations, and to scan sharply any change in our fiscal revenue system which may reduce our income. The need of strict economy in our expenditures is emphasized by the fact that we can not afford to be parsimonious in providing for what is essential to our national well-being. Careful economy wherever possible will alone prevent our income from falling below the point required in order to meet our genuine needs.

The integrity of our currency is beyond question, and under present conditions it would be unwise and unnecessary to attempt a reconstruction of our entire monetary system. The same liberty should be granted the Secretary of the Treasury to deposit customs receipts as is granted him in the deposit of receipts from other sources. In my Message of December 2, 1902, I called attention to certain needs of the financial situation, and I again ask the consideration of the Congress for these questions.

During the last session of the Congress at the suggestion of a joint note from the Republic of Mexico and the Imperial Government of China, and in harmony with an act of the Congress appropriating $25,000 to pay the expenses thereof, a commission was appointed to confer with the principal European countries in the hope that some plan might be devised whereby a fixed rate of exchange could be assured between the gold-standard countries and the silver-standard countries. This commission has filed its preliminary report, which has been made public. I deem it important that the commission be continued, and that a sum of money be appropriated sufficient to pay the expenses of its further labors.

A majority of our people desire that steps be taken in the interests of American shipping, so that we may once more resume our former position in the ocean carrying trade. But hitherto the differences of opinion as to the proper method of reaching this end have been so wide that it has proved impossible to secure the adoption of any particular scheme. Having in view these facts, I recommend that the Congress direct the Secretary of the Navy, the Postmaster-General, and the Secretary of Commerce and Labor, associated with such a representation from the Senate and House of Representatives as the Congress in its wisdom may designate, to serve as a commission for the purpose of investigating and reporting to the Congress at its next session what legislation is desirable or necessary for the development of the American merchant marine and American commerce, and incidentally of a national ocean mail service of adequate auxiliary naval crusiers and naval reserves. While such a measure is desirable in any event, it is especially desirable at this time, in view of the fact that our present governmental contract for ocean mail with the American Line will expire in 1905. Our ocean mail act was passed in 1891. In 1895 our 20-knot transatlantic mail line was equal to any foreign line. Since then the Germans have put on 23-knot steamers, and the British have contracted for 24-knot steamers. Our service should equal the best. If it does not, the commercial public will abandon it. If we are to stay in the business it ought to be with a full understanding of the advantages to the country on one hand, and on the other with exact knowledge of the cost and proper methods

of carrying it on.   Moreover, lines of cargo ships are of even more
importance than fast mail lines; save so far as the latter can be depended upon to furnish swift auxiliary cruisers in time of war.   The
establishment of new lines of cargo ships to South America, to Asia,
and elsewhere would be much in the interest of our commercial expansion.

We can not have too much immigration of the right kind, and we
should have none at all of the wrong kind.   The need is to devise
some system by which undesirable immigrants shall be kept out entirely, while desirable immigrants are properly distributed throughout
the country.   At present some districts which need immigrants have
none; and in others, where the population is already congested, immigrants come in such numbers as to depress the conditions of life
for those already there.   During the last two years the immigration
service at New York has been greatly improved, and the corruption
and inefficiency which formerly obtained there have been eradicated.
This service has just been investigated by a committee of New York
citizens of high standing, Messrs. Arthur V. Briesen, Lee K. Frankel.
Eugene A. Philbin, Thomas W. Hynes, and Ralph Trautman.   Their
report deals with the whole situation at length, and concludes with
certain recommendations for administrative and legislative action.
It is now receiving the attention of the Secretary of Commerce and
Labor.

The special investigation of the subject of naturalization under
the direction of the Attorney-General, and the consequent prosecutions
reveal a condition of affairs calling for the immediate attention of
the Congress.   Forgeries and perjuries of shameless and flagrant character have been perpetrated, not only in the dense centers of population, but throughout the country; and it is established beyond doubt
that very many so-called citizens of the United States have no title
whatever to that right, and are asserting and enjoying the benefits
of the same through the grossest frauds.   It is never to be forgotten
that citizenship is, to quote the words recently used by the Supreme
Court of the United States, an "inestimable heritage," whether it
proceeds from birth within the country or is obtained by naturalization; and we poison the sources of our national character and strength
at the fountain, if the privilege is claimed and exercised without
right, and by means of fraud and corruption.   The body politic can
not be sound and healthy if many of its constituent members claim
their standing through the prostitution of the high right and calling
of citizenship.   It should mean something to become a citizen of the
United States; and in the process no loophole whatever should be
left open to fraud.

The methods by which these frauds—now under full investigation with a view to meting out punishment and providing adequate remedies—are perpetrated, include many variations of procedure by which false certificates of citizenship are forged in their entirety; or genuine certificates fraudulently or collusively obtained in blank are filled in by the criminal conspirators; or certificates are obtained on fraudulent statements as to the time of arrival and residence in this country; or imposition and substitution of another party for the real petitioner occur in court; or certificates are made the subject of barter and sale and transferred from the rightful holder to those not entitled to them; or certificates are forged by erasure of the original names and the insertion of the names of other persons not entitled to the same.

It is not necessary for me to refer here at large to the causes leading to this state of affairs. The desire for naturalization is heartily to be commended where it springs from a sincere and permanent intention to become citizens, and a real appreciation of the privilege. But it is a source of untold evil and trouble where it is traceable to selfish and dishonest motives, such as the effort by artificial and improper means, in wholesale fashion to create voters who are ready-made tools of corrupt politicians, or the desire to evade certain labor laws creating discriminations against alien labor. All good citizens, whether naturalized or native born, are equally interested in protecting our citizenship against fraud in any form, and, on the other hand, in affording every facility for naturalization to those who in good faith desire to share alike our privileges and our responsibilities.

The Federal grand jury lately in session in New York City dealt with this subject and made a presentment which states the situation briefly and forcibly and contains important suggestions for the consideration of the Congress. This presentment is included as an appendix to the report of the Attorney-General.

In my last annual Message, in connection with the subject of the due regulation of combinations of capital which are or may become injurious to the public, I recommend a special appropriation for the better enforcement of the antitrust law as it now stands, to be extended under the direction of the Attorney-General. Accordingly (by the legislative, executive, and judicial appropriation act of February 25, 1903, 32 Stat., 854, 904), the Congress appropriated, for the purpose of enforcing the various Federal trust and interstate-commerce laws, the sum of five hundred thousand dollars, to be expended under the direction of the Attorney-General in the employment of special counsel and agents in the Department of Justice to conduct proceedings and prosecutions under said laws in the courts of the United States. I now recommend, as a matter of the utmost importance and urgency, the extension of the purposes of this appropriation, so that it may be available, under the direction of the Attorney-General, and until used, for the due enforcement of the laws of the United States in general and especially of the civil and criminal laws relating to public lands and the laws relating to postal crimes and offenses and the subject of naturalization. Recent investigations have shown a deplorable state of affairs in these three matters of vital concern. By various frauds and by forgeries and perjuries, thousands of acres of the public domain, embracing lands of different character and extending through various sections of the country, have been dishonestly acquired. It is hardly necessary to urge the importance of recovering these dishonest acquisitions, stolen from the people, and of promptly and duly punishing the offenders. I speak in another part of this Message of the widespread crimes by which the sacred right of citizenship is falsely asserted and that "inestimable heritage" perverted to base ends. By similar means—that is, through frauds, forgeries, and perjuries, and by shameless briberies—the law relating to the proper conduct of the public service in general and to the due administration of the Post-Office Department have been notoriously violated, and many indictments have been found, and the consequent prosecutions are in course of hearing or on the eve thereof. For the reasons thus indicated, and so that the Government may be prepared to enforce promptly and with the greatest effect the due penalties for such violations of law, and to this end may be furnished with sufficient instrumentalities and competent legal assistance for the investigations and trials which will be necessary at many different points of the country, I urge upon the Congress the necessity of making the said appropriation available for immediate use for all such purposes, to be expended under the direction of the Attorney-General.

Steps have been taken by the State Department looking to the making of bribery an extraditable offense with foreign powers. The need of more effective treaties covering this crime is manifest. The exposures and prosecutions of official corruption in St. Louis, Mo., and other cities and States have resulted in a number of givers and takers of bribes becoming fugitives in foreign lands. Bribery has not been included in extradition treaties heretofore, as the necessity for it has not arisen. While there may have been as much official corruption in former years, there has been more developed and brought to light in the immediate past than in the preceding century of our country's history. It should be the policy of the United States to leave no place on earth where a corrupt man fleeing from this country can rest in peace. There is no reason why bribery should not be included in all treaties as extraditable. The recent amended treaty with Mexico, whereby this crime was put in the list of extraditable offenses, has established a salutary precedent in this regard. Under this treaty the State Department has asked, and Mexico has granted, the extradition of one of the St. Louis bribe givers.

There can be no crime more serious than bribery. Other offenses violate one law while corruption strikes at the foundation of all law. Under our form of Government all authority is vested in the people and by them delegated to those who represent them in official capacity. There can be no offense heavier than that of him in whom such a sacred trust has been reposed, who sells it for his own gain and enrichment; and no less heavy is the offense of the bribe giver. He is worse than the thief, for the thief robs the individual, while the corrupt official plunders an entire city or State. He is as wicked as the murderer, for the murderer may only take one life against the law, while the corrupt official and the man who corrupts the official alike aim at the assassination of the commonwealth itself. Government of the people, by the people, for the people will perish from the face of the earth if bribery is tolerated. The givers and takers of bribes stand on an evil pre-eminence of infamy. The exposure and punishment of public corruption is an honor to a nation, not a disgrace. The shame lies in toleration, not in correction. No city or State, still less the Nation, can be injured by the enforcement of law. As long as public plunderers when detected can find a haven of refuge in any foreign land and avoid punishment, just so long encouragement is given them to continue their practices. If we fail to do all that in us lies to stamp out corruption we can not escape our share of responsibility for the guilt. The first requisite of successful self-government is unflinching enforcement of the law and the cutting out of corruption.

For several years past the rapid development of Alaska and the establishment of growing American interests in regions theretofore unsurveyed and imperfectly known brought into prominence the urgent necessity of a practical demarcation of the boundaries between the jurisdictions of the United States and Great Britain. Although the treaty of 1825 between Great Britain and Russia, the provisions of which were copied in the treaty of 1867, whereby Russia conveyed Alaska to the United States, was positive as to the control, first by Russia and later by the United States, of a strip of territory along the continental mainland from the western shore of Portland Canal to Mount St. Elias, following and surrounding the indentations of the coast and including the islands to the westward, its description of the landward margin of the strip was indefinite, resting on the supposed existence of a continuous ridge or range of mountains skirting the coast, as figured in the charts of the early navigators. It had at no time been possible for either party in interest to lay down, under the authority of the treaty, a line so obviously exact according to its provisions as to command the assent of the other. For nearly three-fourths of a century the absence of tangible local interests demanding the exercise of positive jurisdiction on either side of the border left the question dormant. In 1878 questions of revenue administration on the Stikine River led to the establishment of a provisional demarcation, crossing the channel between two high peaks on either side about twenty-four miles above the river mouth. In 1899 similar questions growing out of the extraordinary development of mining interests in the region about the head of Lynn Canal brought about a temporary *modus vivendi*, by which a convenient separation was made at the watershed divides of the White and Chilkoot passes and to the north of Klukwan, on the Klehini River. These partial and tentative adjustments could not, in the very nature of things, be satisfactory or lasting. A permanent disposition of the matter became imperative.

After unavailing attempts to reach an understanding through a Joint High Commission, followed by prolonged negotiations, conducted in an amicable spirit, a convention between the United States and Great Britain was signed, January 24, 1903, providing for an examination of the subject by a mixed tribunal of six members, three on a side. with a view to its final disposition Ratifications were exchanged on March 3 last, whereupon the two Governments appointed their respective members. Those on behalf of the United States were Elihu Root, Secretary of War, Henry Cabot Lodge, a Senator of the United States, and George Turner, an ex-Senator of the United States, while Great Britain named the Right Honourable Lord Alverstone, Lord Chief Justice of England, Sir Louis Amable Jetté, K. C. M. G., retired judge of the Supreme Court of Quebec, and A. B. Aylesworth, K. C., of Toronto. This Tribunal met in London on September 3, under the Presidency of Lord Alverstone. The proceedings were expeditious, and marked by a friendly and conscientious spirit. The respective cases, counter cases, and arguments presented the issues clearly and fully. On the 20th of October a majority of the Tribunal reached and signed an agreement on all the questions submitted by the terms of the Convention. By this award the right of the United States to the control of a continuous strip or border of the mainland shore, skirting all the tide-water inlets and sinuosities of the coast, is confirmed; the entrance to Portland Canal (concerning which legitimate doubt appeared) is defined as passing by Tongass Inlet and to the northwestward of Wales and Pearse islands; a line is drawn from the head of Portland Canal to the fifty-sixth degree of north latitude; and the interior border line of the strip is fixed by lines connecting certain mountain summits lying between Portland Canal and Mount St. Elias, and running along the crest of the divide separating the coast slope from the inland watershed at the only part of the frontier where the drainage ridge approaches the coast within the distance of ten marine leagues stipulated by the treaty as the extreme width of the strip around the heads of Lynn Canal and its branches.

While the line so traced follows the provisional demarcation of 1878 at the crossing of the Stikine River, and that of 1899 at the summits of the White and Chilkoot passes, it runs much farther inland from the Klehini than the temporary line of the later *modus vivendi*, and leaves the entire mining district of the Porcupine River and Glacier Creek within the jurisdiction of the United States.

The result is satisfactory in every way. It is of great material advantage to our people in the Far Northwest. It has removed from the field of discussion and possible danger a question liable to become more acutely accentuated with each passing year. Finally, it has furnished a signal proof of the fairness and good will with which two friendly nations can approach and determine issues involving national sovereignty and by their nature incapable of submission to a third power for adjudication.

The award is self-executing on the vital points. To make it effective as regards the others it only remains for the two Governments to appoint, each on its own behalf, one or more scientific experts, who shall, with all convenient speed, proceed together to lay down the boundary line in accordance with the decision of the majority of the Tribunal. I recommend that the Congress make adequate provision for the appointment, compensation, and expenses of the members to serve on this joint boundary commission on the part of the United States.

It will be remembered that during the second session of the last Congress Great Britain, Germany, and Italy formed an alliance for the purpose of blockading the ports of Venezuela and using such other means of pressure as would secure a settlement of claims due, as they alleged, to certain of their subjects. Their employment of force for the collection of these claims was terminated by an agreement brought about through the offices of the diplomatic representatives of the United States at Caracas and the Government at Washington, thereby ending a situation which was bound to cause increasing friction, and which jeoparded the peace of the continent. Under this agreement Venezuela agreed to set apart a certain percentage of the customs receipts of two of her ports to be applied to the payment of whatever obligations might be ascertained by mixed commissions appointed for that purpose to be due from her, not only to the three powers already mentioned, whose proceedings against her had resulted in a state of war, but also to the United States, France, Spain, Belgium, the Netherlands, Sweden and Norway, and Mexico, who had not employed force for the collection of the claims alleged to be due to certain of their citizens.

A demand was then made by the so-called blockading powers that the sums ascertained to be due to their citizens by such mixed commissions should be accorded payment in full before anything was paid upon the claims of any of the so-called peace powers. Venezuela, on the other hand, insisted that all her creditors should be paid upon a basis of exact equality. During the efforts to adjust this dispute it was suggested by the powers in interest that it should be referred to me for decision, but I was clearly of the opinion that a far wiser course would be to submit the question to the Permanent Court of Arbitration at The Hague. It seemed to me to offer an admirable opportunity to advance the practice of the peaceful settlement of disputes between nations and to secure for the Hague Tribunal a memorable increase of its practical importance. The nations interested in the controversy were so numerous and in many instances so powerful as to make it evident that beneficent results would follow from their appearance at the same time before the bar of that august tribunal of peace.

Our hopes in that regard have been realized. Russia and Austria are represented in the persons of the learned and distinguished jurists who compose the Tribunal, while Great Britain, Germany, France, Spain, Italy, Belgium, the Netherlands, Sweden and Norway, Mexico, the United States, and Venezuela are represented by their respective agents and counsel. Such an imposing concourse of nations presenting their arguments to and invoking the decision of that high court of international justice and international peace can hardly fail to secure a like submission of many future controversies. The nations now appearing there will find it far easier to appear there a second time, while no nation can imagine its just pride will be lessened by following the example now presented. This triumph of the principle of international arbitration is a subject of warm congratulation and offers a happy augury for the peace of the world.

There seems good ground for the belief that there has been a real growth among the civilized nations of a sentiment which will permit a gradual substitution of other methods than the method of war in the settlement of disputes. It is not pretended that as yet we are near a position in which it will be possible wholly to prevent war, or that a just regard for national interest and honor will in all cases permit of the settlement of international disputes by arbitration; but by a mixture of prudence and firmness with wisdom we think it is possible to do away with much of the provocation and excuse for war, and at least in many cases to substitute some other and more rational method for the settlement of disputes. The Hague Court offers so good an example of what can be done in the direction of such settlement that it should be encouraged in every way.

Further steps should be taken. In President McKinley's annual Message of December 5, 1898, he made the following recommendation:

"The experiences of the last year bring forcibly home to us a sense of the burdens and the waste of war. We desire in common with most civilized nations, to reduce to the lowest possible point the damage sustained in time of war by peaceable trade and commerce. It is true we may suffer in such cases less than other communities, but all nations are damaged more or less by the state of uneasiness and apprehension into which an outbreak of hostilities throws the entire commercial world. It should be our object, therefore, to minimize, so far as practicable, this inevitable loss and disturbance. This purpose can probably best be accomplished by an international agreement to regard all private property at sea as exempt from capture or destruction by the forces of belligerent powers. The United States Government has for many years advocated this humane and beneficent principle, and is now in a position to recommend it to other powers without the imputation of selfish motives. I therefore suggest for your consideration that the Executive be authorized to correspond with the governments of the principal maritime powers with a view of incorporating into the permanent law of civilized nations the principle of the exemption of all private property at sea, not contraband of war, from capture or destruction by belligerent powers."

I cordially renew this recommendation.

The Supreme Court, speaking on December 11. 1899, through Peckham, J., said:

"It is, we think, historically accurate to say that this Government has always been, in its views, among the most advanced of the governments of the world in favor of mitigating, as to all non-combatants, the hardships and horrors of war. To accomplish that object it has always advocated those rules which would in most cases do away with the right to capture the private property of an enemy on the high seas."

I advocate this as a matter of humanity and morals. It is anachronistic when private property is respected on land that it should not be respected at sea. Moreover, it should be borne in mind that shipping represents, internationally speaking, a much more generalized species of private property than is the case with ordinary property on land—that is, property found at sea is much less apt than is the case with property found on land really to belong to any one nation. Under the modern system of corporate ownership the flag of a vessel often differs from the flag which would mark the nationality of the real ownership and money control of the vessel; and the cargo may belong to individuals of yet a different nationality. Much American capital is now invested in foreign ships; and among foreign nations it often happens that the capital of one is largely invested in the shipping of another. Furthermore, as a practical matter, it may be mentioned that while commerce destroying may cause serious loss and great annoyance, it can never be more than a subsidiary factor in bringing to terms a resolute foe. This is now well recognized by all of our naval experts. The fighting ship, not the commerce destroyer, is the vessel whose feats add renown to a nation's history, and establish her place among the great powers of the world.

Last year the Interparliamentary Union for International Arbitration met at Vienna, six hundred members of the different legislatures of civilized countries attending. It was provided that the next meeting should be in 1904 at St. Louis, subject to our Congress extending an invitation. Like the Hague Tribunal, this Interparliamentary Union is one of the forces tending towards peace among the nations of the earth, and it is entitled to our support. I trust the invitation can be extended.

Early in July, having received intelligence, which happily turned out to be erroneous, of the assassination of our vice-consul at Beirut, I dispatched a small squadron to that port for such service as might be found necessary on arrival. Although the attempt on the life of our vice-consul had not been successful, yet the outrage was symptomatic of a state of excitement and disorder which demanded immediate attention. The arrival of the vessels had the happiest result. A feeling of security at once took the place of the former alarm and disquiet; our officers were cordially welcomed by the consular body and the leading merchants, and ordinary business resumed its acitivity. The Government of the Sultan gave a considerate hearing to the representations of our minister; the official who was regarded as responsible for the disturbed condition of affairs was removed. Our relations with the Turkish Government remain friendly; our claims founded on inequitable treatment of some of our schools and missions appear to be in process of amicable adjustment.

The signing of a new commercial treaty with China, which took place at Shanghai on the 8th of October, is a cause for satisfaction. This act, the result of long discussion and negotiation, places our commercial relations with the great Oriental Empire on a more satisfactory footing than they have ever heretofore enjoyed. It provides not only for the ordinary rights and privileges of diplomatic and consular officers, but also for an important extension of our commerce by increased facility of access to Chinese ports, and for the relief of trade by the removal of some of the obstacles which have embarrassed it in the past. The Chinese Government engages, on fair and equitable conditions, which will probably be accepted by the principal commercial nations, to abandon the levy of "liken" and other transit dues throughout the Empire, and to introduce other desirable administrative reforms. Larger facilities are to be given to our citizens who desire to carry on mining enterprises in China. We have secured for our missionaries a valuable privilege, the recognition of their right to rent and lease in perpetuity such property as their religious societies may need in all parts of the Empire. And, what was an indispensable condition for the advance and development of our commerce in Manchuria, China, by treaty with us, has opened to foreign commerce the cities of Mukden, the capital of the province of Manchuria, and An tung, an important port on the Yalu River, on the road to Korea The full measure of development which our commerce may rightfully expect can hardly be looked for until the settlement of the present abnormal state of things in the Empire; but the foundation for such development has at last been laid.

I call your attention to the reduced cost in maintaining the consular service for the fiscal year ending June 30, 1903, as shown in the annual report of the Auditor for the State and other Departments, as compared with the year previous. For the year under consideration the excess of expenditures over receipts on account of the consular service amounted to $26,125.12, as against $96,972.50 for the year ending June 30, 1902, and $147,040.16 for the year ending June 30, 1901. This is the best showing in this respect for the consular service for the past fourteen years, and the reduction in the cost of the service to the Government has been made in spite of the fact that the expenditures for the year in question were more than $20,000 greater than for the previous year.

The rural free-delivery service has been steadily extended. The attention of the Congress is asked to the question of the compensation of the letter carriers and clerks engaged in the postal service, especially on the new rural free-delivery routes. More routes have been installed since the first of July last than in any like period in the Department's history. While a due regard to economy must be kept in mind in the establishment of new routes, yet the extension of the rural free-delivery system must be continued, for reasons of sound public policy. No governmental movement of recent years has resulted in greater immediate benefit to the people of the country districts. Rural free delivery, taken in connection with the telephone, the bicycle, and the trolley, accomplishes much toward lessening the isolation of farm life and making it brighter and more attractive. In the immediate past the lack of just such facilities as these has driven many of the more active and restless young men and women from the farms to the cities; for they rebelled at loneliness and lack of mental companionship. It is unhealthy and undesirable for the cities to grow at the expense of the country; and rural free delivery is not only a good thing in itself, but is good because it is one of the causes which check this unwholesome tendency towards the urban concentration of our population at the expense of the country districts. It is for the same reason that we sympathize with and approve of the policy of building good roads. The movement for good roads is one fraught with the greatest benefit to the country districts.

I trust that the Congress will continue to favor in all proper ways the Louisiana Purchase Exposition. This Exposition commemorates the Louisiana purchase, which was the first great step in the expansion which made us a continental nation. The expedition of Lewis and Clark across the continent followed thereon, and marked the beginning of the process of exploration and colonization which thrust our national boundaries to the Pacific. The acquisition of the Oregon country, including the present States of Oregon and Washington, was a fact of immense importance in our history; first giving us our place on the Pacific seaboard, and making ready the way for our ascendency in the commerce of the greatest of the oceans. The centennial of our establishment upon the western coast by the expedition of Lewis and Clark is to be celebrated at Portland, Oregon, by an exposition in the summer of 1905, and this event should receive recognition and support from the National Government.

I call your special attention to the Territory of Alaska. The country is developing rapidly, and it has an assured future. The mineral wealth is great and has as yet hardly been tapped. The fisheries, if wisely handled and kept under national control, will be a business as permanent as any other, and of the utmost importance to the people. The forests if properly guarded will form another great source of wealth. Portions of Alaska are fitted for farming and stock raising, although the methods must be adapted to the peculiar conditions of the country. Alaska is situated in the far north; but so are Norway and Sweden and Finland; and Alaska can prosper and play its part in the New World just as those nations have prospered and played their parts in the Old World. Proper land laws should be enacted; and the survey of the public lands immediately begun. Coal-land laws should be provided whereby the coal-land entryman may make his location and secure patent under methods kindred to those now prescribed for homestead and mineral entrymen. Salmon hatcheries, exclusively under Government control, should be established. The cable should be extended from Sitka westward. Wagon roads and trails should be built, and the building of railroads promoted in all legitimate ways. Light-houses should be built along the coast. Attention should be paid to the needs of the Alaska Indians; provision should be made for an officer, with deputies, to study their needs, relieve their immediate wants, and help them adapt themselves to the new conditions.

The commission appointed to investigate, during the season of 1903, the condition and needs of the Alaskan salmon fisheries, has finished its work in the field, and is preparing a detailed report thereon. A preliminary report reciting the measures immediately required for the protection and preservation of the salmon industry has already been submitted to the Secretary of Commerce and Labor for his attention and for the needed action.

I recommend that an appropriation be made for building light-houses in Hawaii, and taking possession of those already built. The Territory should be reimbursed for whatever amounts it has already expended for light-houses. The governor should be empowered to suspend or remove any official appointed by him, without submitting the matter to the legislature.

Of our insular possessions the Philippines and Porto Rico it is gratifying to say that their steady progress has been such as to make it unnecessary to spend much time in discussing them. Yet the Congress should ever keep in mind that a peculiar obligation rests upon us to further in every way the welfare of these communities. The Philippines should be knit closer to us by tariff arrangements. It would, of course, be impossible suddenly to raise the people of the islands to the high pitch of industrial prosperity and of governmental efficiency to which they will in the end by degrees attain; and the caution and moderation shown in developing them have been among the main reasons why this development has hitherto gone on so smoothly. Scrupulous care has been taken in the choice of governmental agents, and the entire elimination of partisan politics from the public service. The condition of the islanders is in material things far better than ever before, while their governmental, intellectual, and moral advance has kept pace with their material advance. No one people ever benefited another people more than we have benefited the Filipinos by taking possession of the islands.

The cash receipts of the General Land Office for the last fiscal year were $11,024,743.65, an increase of $4,762,816.47 over the preceding year. Of this sum, approximately, $8,461,493 will go to the credit of the fund for the reclamation of arid land, making the total of this fund, up to the 30th of June, 1903, approximately, $16,191,836.

A gratifying disposition has been evinced by those having unlawful inclosures of public land to remove their fences. Nearly two million acres so inclosed have been thrown open on demand. In but comparatively few cases has it been necessary to go into court to accomplish this purpose. This work will be vigorously prosecuted until all unlawful inclosures have been removed.

Experience has shown that in the western States themselves, as well as in the rest of the country, there is widespread conviction that certain of the public-land laws and the resulting administrative practice no longer meet the present needs. The character and uses of the remaining public lands differ widely from those of the public lands which Congress had especially in view when these laws were passed. The rapidly increasing rate of disposal of the public lands is not followed by a corresponding increase in home building. There is a tendency to mass in large holdings public lands, especially timber and grazing lands, and thereby to retard settlement. I renew and emphasize my recommendation of last year that so far as they are available for agriculture in its broadest sense, and to whatever extent they may be reclaimed under the national irrigation law, the remaining public lands should be held rigidly for the home builder. The attention of the Congress is especially directed to the timber and stone law, the desert-land law, and the commutation clause of the homestead law, which in their operation have in many respects conflicted with wise public-land policy. The discussions in the Congress and elsewhere have made it evident that there is a wide divergence of opinions between those holding opposite views on these subjects; and that the opposing sides have strong and convinced representatives of weight both within and without the Congress; the differences being not only as to matters of opinion but as to matters of fact. In order that definite information may be available for the use of the Congress, I have appointed a commission composed of W. A. Richards, Commissioner of the General Land Office; Gifford Pinchot, Chief of the Bureau of Forestry of the Department of Agriculture, and F. H. Newell, Chief Hydrographer of the Geological Survey, to report at the earliest practicable moment upon the condition, operation, and effect of the present land laws and on the use, condition, disposal, and settlement of the public lands. The commission will report especially what changes in organization, laws, regulations, and practice affecting the public lands are needed to effect the largest practicable disposition of the public lands to actual settlers who will build permanent homes upon them, and to secure in permanence the fullest and most effective use of the resources of the public lands; and it will make such other reports and recommendations as its study of these questions may suggest. The commission is to report immediately upon those points concerning which its judgment is clear; on any point upon which it has doubt it will take the time necessary to make investigation and reach a final judgment.

The work of reclamation of the arid lands of the West is progressing steadily and satisfactorily under the terms of the law setting aside the proceeds from the disposal of public lands. The corps of engineers known as the Reclamation Service, which is conducting the surveys and examinations, has been thoroughly organized, especial pains being taken to secure under the civil-service rules a body of skilled, experienced, and efficient men. Surveys and examinations are progressing throughout the arid States and Territories, plans for reclaiming works being prepared and passed upon by boards of engineers before approval by the Secretary of the Interior. In Arizona and Nevada, in localities where such work is pre-eminently needed, construction has already been begun. In other parts of the arid West various projects are well advanced towards the drawing up of contracts, these being delayed in part by necessities of reaching agreements or understanding as regards rights of way or acquisition of real estate. Most of the works contemplated for construction are of national importance, involving interstate questions or the securing of stable, self-supporting communities in the midst of vast tracts of vacant land. The Nation as a whole is of course the gainer by the creation of these homes, adding as they do to the wealth and stability of the country, and furnishing a home market for the products of the East and South. The reclamation law, while perhaps not ideal, appears at present to answer the larger needs for which it is designed. Further legislation is not recommended until the necessities of change are more apparent.

The study of the opportunities of reclamation of the vast extent of arid land shows that whether this reclamation is done by individuals, corporations, or the State, the sources of water supply must be effectively protected and the reservoirs guarded by the preservation of the forests at the headwaters of the streams. The engineers making the preliminary examinations continually emphasize this need and urge that the remaining public lands at the headwaters of the important streams of the West be reserved to insure permanency of water supply for irrigation. Much progress in forestry has been made during the past year. The necessity for perpetuating our forest resources, whether in public or private hands, is recognized now as never before. The demand for forest reserves has become insistent in the West, because the West must use the water, wood, and summer range which only such reserves can supply. Progressive lumbermen are striving, through forestry, to give their business permanence. Other great business interests are awakening to the need of forest preservation as a business matter. The Government's forest work should receive from the Congress hearty support, and especially support adequate for the protection of the forest reserves against fire. The forest-reserve policy of the Government has passed beyond the experimental stage and has reached a condition where scientific methods are essential to its successful prosecution. The administrative features of forest reserves are at present unsatisfactory, being divided between three Bureaus of two Departments. It is therefore recommended that all matters pertaining to forest reserves, except those involving or pertaining to land titles, be consolidated in the Bureau of Forestry of the Department of Agriculture.

The cotton-growing States have recently been invaded by a weevil that has done much damage and threatens the entire cotton industry. I suggest to the Congress the prompt enactment of such remedial legislation as its judgment may approve.

In granting patents to foreigners the proper course for this country to follow is to give the same advantages to foreigners here that the countries in which these foreigners dwell extend in return to our citizens; that is, to extend the benefits of our patent laws on inventions and the like where in return the articles would be patentable in the foreign countries concerned—where an American could get a corresponding patent in such countries.

The Indian agents should not be dependent for their appointment or tenure of office upon considerations of partisan politics; the practice of appointing, when possible, ex-army officers or bonded superintendents to the vacancies that occur is working well. Attention is invited to the widespread illiteracy due to lack of public schools in the Indian Territory. Prompt heed should be paid to the need of education for the children in this Territory.

In my last annual Message the attention of the Congress was called to the necessity of enlarging the safety-appliance law, and it is gratifying to note that this law was amended in important respects. With the increasing railway mileage of the country, the greater number of men employed, and the use of larger and heavier equipment, the urgency for renewed effort to prevent the loss of life and limb upon the railroads of the country, particularly to employees, is apparent. For the inspection of water craft and the Life-Saving Service upon the water the Congress has built up an elaborate body of protective legislation and a thorough method of inspection and is annually spending large sums of money. It is encouraging to observe that the Congress is alive to the interests of those who are employed upon our wonderful arteries of commerce—the railroads—who so safely transport millions of passengers and billions of tons of freight. The Federal inspection of safety appliances, for which the Congress is now making appropriations, is a service analogous to that which the Government has upheld for generations in regard to vessels, and it is believed will prove of great practical benefit, both to railroad employees and the traveling public. As the greater part of commerce is interstate and exclusively under the control of the Congress the needed safety and uniformity must be secured by national legislation.

No other class of our citizens deserves so well of the Nation as those to whom the Nation owes its very being, the veterans of the civil war. Special attention is asked to the excellent work of the Pension Bureau in expediting and disposing of pension claims. During the fiscal year ending July 1, 1903, the Bureau settled 251,982 claims, an average of 825 claims for each working day of the year. The number of settlements since July 1, 1903, has been in excess of last year's average, approaching 1,000 claims for each working day, and it is believed that the work of the Bureau will be current at the close of the present fiscal year.

During the year ended June 30 last 25,566 persons were appointed through competitive examinations under the civil-service rules. This was 12,672 more than during the preceding year, and 40 per cent of those who passed the examinations. This abnormal growth was largely occasioned by the extension of classification to the rural free-delivery service and the appointment last year of over 9,000 rural carriers. A revision of the civil-service rules took effect on April 15 last, which has greatly improved their operation. The completion of the reform of the civil service is recognized by good citizens everywhere as a matter of the highest public importance, and the success of the merit system largely depends upon the effectiveness of the rules and the machinery provided for their enforcement. A very gratifying spirit of friendly co-operation exists in all the Departments of the Government in the enforcement and uniform observance of both the letter and spirit of the civil-service act. Executive orders of July 3, 1902; March 26, 1903, and July 8, 1903, require that appointments of all unclassified laborers, both in the Departments at Washington and in the field service, shall be made with the assistance of the United States Civil Service Commission, under a system of registration to test the relative fitness of applicants for appointment or employment. This system is competitive, and is open to all citizens of the United States qualified in respect to age, physical ability, moral character, industry, and adaptability for manual labor; except that in case of veterans of the Civil War the element of age is omitted. This system of appointment is distinct from the classified service and does not classify positions of mere laborer under the civil-service act and rules. Regulations in aid thereof have been put in operation in several of the Departments and are being gradually extended in other parts of the service. The results have been very satisfactory, as extravagance has been checked by decreasing the number of unnecessary positions and by increasing the efficiency of the employees remaining.

The Congress, as the result of a thorough investigation of the charities and reformatory institutions in the District of Columbia, by a joint select committee of the two Houses which made its report in March, 1898, created in the act approved June 6, 1900, a board of charities for the District of Columbia, to consist of five residents of the District, appointed by the President of the United States, by and with the advice and consent of the Senate, each for a term of three

years, to serve without compensation.   President McKinley appointed
five men who had been active and prominent in the public charities in
Washington, all of whom upon taking office July 1, 1900, resigned
from the different charities with which they had been connected.   The
members of the board have been reappointed in successive years.   The
board serves under the Commissioners of the District of Columbia.
The board gave its first year to a careful and impartial study of the
special problems before it, and has continued that study every year
in the light of the best practice in public charities elsewhere.   Its
recommendations in its annual reports to the Congress through the
Commissioners of the District of Columbia "for the economical and
efficient administration of the charities and reformatories of the District of Columbia," as required by the act creating it, have been based
upon the principles commended by the joint select committee of the
Congress in its report of March, 1898, and approved by the best ad-
ministrators of public charities, and make for the desired systematiza-
tion and improvement of the affairs under its supervision.   They are
worthy of favorable consideration by the Congress.

The effect of the laws providing a General Staff for the Army and
for the more effective use of the National Guard has been excellent.
Great improvement has been made in the efficiency of our Army in
recent years.   Such schools as those erected at Fort Leavenworth and
Fort Riley and the institution of fall maneuver work accomplish satisfactory results.   The good effect of these maneuvers upon the National
Guard is marked, and ample appropriation should be made to enable
the guardsmen of the several States to share in the benefit.   The
Government should as soon as possible secure suitable permanent
camp sites for military maneuvers in the various sections of the country.   The service thereby rendered not only to the Regular Army,
but to the National Guard of the several States, will be so great as to
repay many times over the relatively small expense.   We should not
rest satisfied with what has been done, however.   The only people
who are contented with a system of promotion by mere seniority are
those who are contented with the triumph of mediocrity over excellence.
On the other hand, a system which encouraged the exercise of social
or political favoritism in promotions would be even worse.   But it
would surely be easy to devise a method of promotion from grade to
grade in which the opinion of the higher officers of the service upon
the candidates should be decisive upon the standing and promotion
of the latter.   Just such a system now obtains at West Point.   The
quality of each year's work determines the standing of that year's class,
the man being dropped or graduated into the next class in the relative
position which his military superiors decide to be warranted by his
merit.   In other words, ability, energy, fidelity, and all other similar

qualities determine the rank of a man year after year in West Point, and his standing in the Army when he graduates from West Point; but from that time on, all effort to find which man is best or worst, and reward or punish him accordingly, is abandoned; no brilliancy, no amount of hard work, no eagerness in the performance of duty, can advance him, and no slackness or indifference that falls short of a court-martial offense can retard him. Until this system is changed we can not hope that our officers will be of as high grade as we have a right to expect, considering the material upon which we draw. Moreover, when a man renders such service as Captain Pershing rendered last spring in the Moro campaign, it ought to be possible to reward him without at once jumping him to the grade of brigadier-general.

Shortly after the enunciation of that famous principle of American foreign policy now known as the "Monroe Doctrine," President Monroe, in a special Message to Congress on January 30, 1824, spoke as follows: "The Navy is the arm from which our Government will always derive most aid in support of our * * * rights. Every power engaged in war will know the strength of our naval power, the number of our ships of each class, their condition, and the promptitude with which we may bring them into service, and will pay due consideration to that argument."

I heartily congratulate the Congress upon the steady progress in building up the American Navy. We can not afford a let-up in this great work. To stand still means to go back. There should be no cessation in adding to the effective units of the fighting strength of the fleet. Meanwhile the Navy Department and the officers of the Navy are doing well their part by providing constant service at sea under conditions akin to those of actual warfare. Our officers and enlisted men are learning to handle the battleships, cruisers, and torpedo boats with high efficiency in fleet and squadron formations, and the standard of marksmanship is being steadily raised. The best work ashore is indispensable, but the highest duty of a naval officer is to exercise command at sea.

The establishment of a naval base in the Philippines ought not to be longer postponed. Such a base is desirable in time of peace; in time of war it would be indispensable, and its lack would be ruinous. Without it our fleet would be helpless. Our naval experts are agreed that Subig Bay is the proper place for the purpose. The national interests require that the work of fortification and development of a naval station at Subig Bay be begun at an early date; for under the best conditions it is a work which will consume much time.

It is eminently desirable, however, that there should be provided a naval general staff on lines similar to those of the General Staff lately created for the Army. Within the Navy Department itself the needs of the service have brought about a system under which the duties of a general staff are partially performed; for the Bureau of Navigation has under its direction the War College, the Office of Naval Intelligence, and the Board of Inspection, and has been in close touch with the General Board of the Navy. But though under the excellent officers at their head, these boards and bureaus do good work, they have not the authority of a general staff, and have not sufficient scope to insure a proper readiness for emergencies. We need the establishment by law of a body of trained officers, who shall exercise a systematic control of the military affairs of the Navy, and be authorized advisers of the Secretary concerning it.

By the act of June 28, 1902, the Congress authorized the President to enter into treaty with Colombia for the building of the canal across the Isthmus of Panama; it being provided that in the event of failure to secure such treaty after the lapse of a reasonable time, recourse should be had to building a canal through Nicaragua. It has not been necessary to consider this alternative, as I am enabled to lay before the Senate a treaty providing for the building of the canal across the Isthmus of Panama. This was the route which commended itself to the deliberate judgment of the Congress, and we can now acquire by treaty the right to construct the canal over this route. The question now, therefore, is not by which route the isthmian canal shall be built, for that question has been definitely and irrevocably decided. The question is simply whether or not we shall have an isthmian canal.

When the Congress directed that we should take the Panama route under treaty with Colombia, the essence of the condition, of course, referred not to the Government which controlled that route, but to the route itself; to the territory across which the route lay, not to the name which for the moment the territory bore on the map. The purpose of the law was to authorize the President to make a treaty with the power in actual control of the Isthmus of Panama. This purpose has been fulfilled.

In the year 1846 this Government entered into a treaty with New Granada, the predecessor upon the Isthmus of the Republic of Colombia and of the present Republic of Panama, by which treaty it was provided that the Government and citizens of the United States should always have free and open right of way or transit across the Isthmus of Panama by any modes of communication that might be constructed, while in turn our Government guaranteed the perfect neutrality of the above-mentioned Isthmus with the view that the free transit from the one to the other sea might not be interrupted or embarrassed. The treaty vested in the United States a substantial property right carved out of the rights of sovereignty and property which New Granada then had and possessed over the said territory. The name of New Granada has passed away and its territory has been divided. Its successor, the Government of Colombia, has ceased to own any property in the Isthmus. A new Republic, that of Panama, which was at one time a sovereign state, and at another time a mere department of the successive confederations known as New Granada and Columbia, has now succeeded to the rights which first one and then the other formerly exercised over the Isthmus. But as long as the Isthmus endures, the mere geographical fact of its existence, and the peculiar interest therein which is required by our position, perpetuate the solemn contract which binds the holders of the territory to respect our right to freedom of transit across it, and binds us in return to safeguard for the Isthmus and the world the exercise of that inestimable privilege. The true interpretation of the obligations upon which the United States entered in this treaty of 1846 has been given repeatedly in the utterances of Presidents and Secretaries of State. Secretary Cass in 1858 officially stated the position of this Government as follows:

"The progress of events has rendered the interoceanic route across the narrow portion of Central America vastly important to the commercial world, and especially to the United States, whose possessions extend along the Atlantic and Pacific coasts, and demand the speediest and easiest modes of communication. While the rights of sovereignty of the states occupying this region should always be respected, we shall expect that these rights be exercised in a spirit befitting the occasion and the wants and circumstances that have arisen. Sovreignty has its duties as well as its rights, and none of these local governments, even if administered with more regard to the just demands of other nations than they have been, would be permitted, in a spirit of Eastern isolation, to close the gates of intercourse on the great highways of the world, and justify the act by the pretension that these avenues of trade and travel belong to them and that they choose to shut them, or, what is almost equivalent, to encumber them with such unjust relations as would prevent their general use."

Seven years later, in 1865, Mr. Seward in different commuications took the following position:

"The United States have taken and will take no interest in any question of internal revolution in the State of Panama, or any State of the United States of Colombia, but will maintain a perfect neutrality in connection with such domestic altercations. The United States will, nevertheless, hold themselves ready to protect the transit trade across the Isthmus against invasion of either domestic or foreign disturbers of the peace of the State of Panama. * * * Neither the text nor the spirit of the stipulation in that article by which the United States engages to preserve the neutrality of the Isthmus of Panama, imposes an obligation on this Government to comply with the requisition [of the President of the United States of Colombia for a force to protect the Isthmus of Panama from a body of insurgents of that country]. The purpose of the stipulation was to guarantee the Isthmus against seizure or invasion by a foreign power only."

Attorney-General Speed, under date of November 7, 1865, advised Secretary Seward as follows:

"From this treaty it can not be supposed that New Granada invited the United States to become a party to the intestine troubles of that Government, nor did the United States become bound to take sides in the domestic broils of New Granada. The United States did guarantee New Granada in the sovereignty and property over the territory. This was as against other and foreign governments."

For four hundred years, ever since shortly after the discovery of this hemisphere, the canal across the Isthmus has been planned. For two score years it has been worked at. When made it is to last for the ages. It is to alter the geography of a continent and the trade routes of the world. We have shown by every treaty we have negotiated or attempted to negotiate with the peoples in control of the Isthmus and with foreign nations in reference thereto our consistent good faith in observing our obligations; on the one hand to the peoples of the Isthmus, and on the other hand to the civilized world whose commercial rights we are safeguarding and guaranteeing by our action. We have done our duty to others in letter and in spirit, and we have shown the utmost forbearance in exacting our own rights.

Last spring, under the act above referred to, a treaty concluded between the representatives of the Republic of Colombia and of our Government was ratified by the Senate. This treaty was entered into at the urgent solicitation of the people of Colombia and after a body of experts appointed by our Government especially to go into the matter of the routes across the Isthmus had pronounced unanimously in favor of the Panama route. In drawing up this treaty every concession was made to the people and to the Government of Colombia. We were more than just in dealing with them. Our generosity was such as to make it a serious question whether we had not gone too far in their interest at the expense of our own; for in our scrupulous desire to pay all possible heed, not merely to the real but even to the fancied rights of our weaker neighbor, who already owed so much to our protection and forbearance, we yielded in all possible ways to her desires in drawing up the treaty. Nevertheless the Government of Colombia not merely repudiated the treaty, but repudiated it in such manner as to make it evident by the time the Colombian Congress adjourned that not the scantiest hope remained of ever getting a satisfactory treaty from them. The Government of Colombia made the treaty, and yet when the Colombian Congress was called to ratify it the vote against ratification was unanimous. It does not appear that the Government made any real effort to secure ratification.

Immediately after the adjournment of the Congress a revolution broke out in Panama. The people of Panama had long been discontented with the Republic of Colombia, and they had been kept quiet only by the prospect of the conclusion of the treaty, which was to them a matter of vital concern. When it became evident that the treaty was hopelessly lost, the people of Panama rose literally as one man. Not a shot was fired by a single man on the Isthmus in the interest of the Colombian Government. Not a life was lost in the accomplishment of the revolution. The Colombian troops stationed on the Isthmus, who had long been unpaid, made common cause with the people of Panama, and with astonishing unanimity the new Republic was started. The duty of the United States in the premises was clear. In strict accordance with the principles laid down by Secretaries Cass and Seward in the official documents above quoted, the United States gave notice that it would permit the landing of no expeditionary force, the arrival of which would mean chaos and destruction along the line of the railroad and of the proposed canal, and an interruption of transit as an inevitable consequence. The de facto Government of Panama was recognized in the following telegram to Mr. Ehrman:

"The people of Panama have, by apparently unanimous movement, dissolved their political connection with the Republic of Colombia and resumed their independence. When you are satisfied that a de facto government, republican in form and without substantial opposition from its own people, has been established in the State of Panama, you will enter into relations with it as the responsible government of the territory and look to it for all due action to protect the persons and property of citizens of the United States and to keep open the isthmian transit, in accordance with the obligations of existing treaties governing the relations of the United States to that Territory."

The Government of Colombia was notified of our action by the following telegram to Mr. Beaupre:

"The people of Panama having, by an apparently unanimous movement, dissolved their political connection with the Republic of Colombia and resumed their independence, and having adopted a Government of their own, republican in form, with which the Government of the United States of America has entered into relations, the President of the United States, in accordance with the ties of friendship which have so long and so happily existed between the respective nations, most earnestly commends to the Governments of Colombia and of

Panama the peaceful and equitable settlement of all questions at issue between them. He holds that he is bound not merely by treaty obligations, but by the interests of civilization, to see that the peaceful traffic of the world across the Isthmus of Panama shall not longer be disturbed by a constant succession of unnecessary and wasteful civil wars."

When these events happened, fifty-seven years had elapsed since the United States had entered into its treaty with New Granada. During that time the Governments of New Granada and of its successor, Colombia, have been in a constant state of flux. The following is a partial list of the disturbances on the Isthmus of Panama during the period in question as reported to us by our consuls. It is not possible to give a complete list, and some of the reports that speak of "revolutions" must mean unsuccessful revolutions.

May 22, 1850.—Outbreak; two Americans killed. War vessel demanded to quell outbreak.

October, 1850.—Revolutionary plot to bring about independence of the Isthmus.

July 22, 1851.—Revolution in four southern provinces.

November 14, 1851.—Outbreak at Chagres. Man-of-war requested for Chagres.

June 27, 1853.—Insurrection at Bogota, and consequent disturbance on Isthmus. War vessel demanded.

May 23, 1854.—Political disturbances; war vessel requested.

June 28, 1854.—Attempted revolution.

October 24, 1854.—Independence of Isthmus demanded by provincial legislature.

April, 1856.—Riot, and massacre of Americans.

May 4, 1856.—Riot.

May 18, 1856.—Riot.

June 3, 1856.—Riot.

October 2, 1856.—Conflict between two native parties. United States forces landed.

December 18, 1858.—Attempted secession of Panama.

April, 1859.—Riots.

September, 1860.—Outbreak.

October 4, 1860.—Landing of United States forces in consequence.

May 23, 1861.—Intervention of the United States forces required by intendente.

October 2, 1861.—Insurrection and civil war.

April 4, 1862.—Measures to prevent rebels crossing Isthmus.

June 13, 1862.—Mosquera's troops refused admittance to Panama.

March, 1865.—Revolution, and United States troops landed.

August, 1865.—Riots; unsuccessful attempt to invade Panama.

March, 1866.—Unsuccessful revolution.
April, 1867.—Attempt to overthrow Government.
August, 1867.—Attempt at revolution.
July 5, 1868.—Revolution; provisional government inaugurated.
August 29, 1868.—Revolution; provisional government overthrown.
April, 1871.—Revolution; followed apparently by counter revolution.
April, 1873.—Revolution and civil war which lasted to October, 1875.
August, 1876.—Civil war which lasted until April, 1877.
July, 1878.—Rebellion.
December, 1878.—Revolt.
April, 1879.—Revolution.
June, 1879.—Revolution.
March, 1883.—Riot.
May, 1883.—Riot.
June, 1884.—Revolutionary attempt.
December, 1884.—Revolutionary attempt.
January, 1885.—Revolutionary disturbances.
March, 1885.—Revolution.
April, 1887.—Disturbance on Panama Railroad.
November, 1887.—Disturbance on line of canal.
January, 1889.—Riot.
January, 1895.—Revolution which lasted until April.
March, 1895.—Incendiary attempt.
October, 1899.—Revolution.
February, 1900, to July, 1900.—Revolution.
January, 1901.—Revolution.
July, 1901.—Revolutionary disturbances.
September, 1901.—City of Colon taken by rebels.
March, 1902.—Revolutionary disturbances.
July, 1902.—Revolution.

The above is only a partial list of the revolutions, rebellions, insurrections, riots, and other outbreaks that have occurred during the period in question; yet they number 53 for the 57 years. It will be noted that one of them lasted for nearly three years before it was quelled; another for nearly a year. In short, the experience of over half a century has shown Colombia to be utterly incapable of keeping order on the Isthmus. Only the active interference of the United States has enabled her to preserve so much as a semblance of sovereignty. Had it not been for the exercise by the United States of the police power in her interest, her connection with the Isthmus would have been sundered long ago. In 1856, in 1860, in 1873, in 1885, in 1901, and again in 1902, sailors and marines from United States war ships were forced to land in order to patrol the Isthmus, to protect life and property, and to see that the transit across the Isthmus was kept open. In 1861, in 1862, in 1885, and in 1900, the Colombian Government asked that the United States Government would land troops to protect its interests and maintain order on the Isthmus. Perhaps the most extraordinary request is that which has just been received and which runs as follows:

"Knowing that revolution has already commenced in Panama [an eminent Colombian] says that if the Government of the United States will land troops to preserve Colombian sovereignty, and the transit, if requested by Colombian chargé d'affaires, this Government will declare martial law; and, by virtue of vested constitutional authority, when public order is disturbed, will approve by decree ratification of the canal treaty as signed; or, if the Government of the United States prefers, will call extra session of the Congress—with new and friendly members—next May to approve the treaty. [An eminent Colombian] has the perfect confidence of vice-president, he says, and if it became necessary will go to the Isthmus or send representatives there to adjust matters along above lines to the satisfaction of the people there."

This dispatch is noteworthy from two standpoints. Its offer of immediately guaranteeing the treaty to us is in sharp contrast with the positive and contemptuous refusal of the Congress which has just closed its sessions to consider favorably such a treaty; it shows that the Government which made the treaty really had absolute control over the situation, but did not choose to exercise this control. The dispatch further calls on us to restore order and secure Colombian supremacy in the Isthmus from which the Colombian Government has just by its action decided to bar us by preventing the construction of the canal.

The control, in the interest of the commerce and traffic of the whole civilized world, of the means of undisturbed transit across the Isthmus of Panama has become of transcendent importance to the United States. We have repeatedly exercised this control by intervening in the course of domestic dissension, and by protecting the territory from foreign invasion. In 1853 Mr. Everett assured the Peruvian minister that we should not hesitate to maintain the neutrality of the Isthmus in the case of war between Peru and Colombia. In 1864 Colombia, which has always been vigilant to avail itself of its privileges conferred by the treaty, expressed its expectation that in the event of war between Peru and Spain the United States would carry into effect the guaranty of neutrality. There have been few administrations of the State Department in which this treaty has not, either by the one side or the other, been used as a basis of more or less important demands. It was said by Mr. Fish in 1871 that the Department of State had reason to believe that an attack upon Colombian sovereignty on the Isthmus had, on several occasions, been averted by warning from this Government. In 1886, when Colombia was under the menace of hostilities from Italy in the Cerruti case, Mr. Bayard expressed the serious concern that the United States could not but feel, that a European power should resort to force against a sister republic of this hemisphere, as to the sovereign and uninterrupted use of a part of whose territory we are guarantors under the solemn faith of a treaty.

The above recital of facts establishes beyond question: First, that the United States has for over half a century patiently and in good faith carried out its obligations under the treaty of 1846; second, that when for the first time it became possible for Colombia to do anything in requital of the services thus repeatedly rendered to it for fifty-seven years by the United States, the Colombian Government peremptorily and offensively refused thus to do its part, even though to do so would have been to its advantage and immeasurably to the advantage of the State of Panama, at that time under its jurisdiction; third, that throughout this period revolutions, riots, and factional disturbances of every kind have occurred one after the other in almost uninterrupted succession, some of them lasting for months and even for years, while the central government was unable to put them down or to make peace with the rebels; fourth, that these disturbances instead of showing any sign of abating have tended to grow more numerous and more serious in the immediate past; fifth, that the control of Colombia over the Isthmus of Panama could not be maintained without the armed intervention and assistance of the United States. In other words, the Government of Colombia, though wholly unable to maintain order on the Isthmus, has nevertheless declined to ratify a treaty the conclusion of which opened the only chance to secure its own stability and to guarantee permanent peace on, and the construction of a canal across, the Isthmus.

Under such circumstances the Government of the United States would have been guilty of folly and weakness, amounting in their sum to a crime against the Nation, had it acted otherwise than it did when the revolution of November 3 last took place in Panama. This great enterprise of building the interoceanic canal can not be held up to gratify the whims, or out of respect to the governmental impotence, or to the even more sinister and evil political peculiarities, of people who, though they dwell afar off, yet, against the wish of the actual dwellers on the Isthmus, assert an unreal supremacy over the territory. The possession of a territory fraught with such peculiar capacities as the Isthmus in question carries with it obligations to mankind. The course of events has shown that this canal can not be built by private enterprise, or by any other nation than our own; therefore it must be built by the United States.

Every effort has been made by the Government of the United States to persuade Colombia to follow a course which was essentially not only to our interests and to the interests of the world, but to the interests of Colombia itself. These efforts have failed; and Colombia, by her persistence in repulsing the advances that have been made, has forced us, for the sake of our own honor, and of the interest and well-being, not merely of our own people, but of the people of the Isthmus of Panama and the people of the civilized countries of the world, to take decisive steps to bring to an end a condition of affairs which had become intolerable. The new Republic of Panama immediately offered to negotiate a treaty with us. This treaty I herewith submit. By it our interests are better safeguarded than in the treaty with Colombia which was ratified by the Senate at its last session. It is better in its terms than the treaties offered to us by the Republics of Nicaragua and Costa Rica. At last the right to begin this great undertaking is made available. Panama has done her part. All that remains is for the American Congress to do its part, and forthwith this Republic will enter upon the execution of a project colossal in its size and of well-nigh incalculable possibilities for the good of this country and the nations of mankind.

By the provisions of the treaty the United States guarantees and will maintain the independence of the Republic of Panama. There is granted to the United States in perpetuity the use, occupation, and control of a strip ten miles wide and extending three nautical miles into the sea at either terminal, with all lands lying outside of the zone necessary for the construction of the canal or for its auxiliary works, and with the islands in the Bay of Panama. The cities of Panama and Colon are not embraced in the canal zone, but the United States assumes their sanitation and, in case of need, the maintenance of order therein; the United States enjoys within the granted limits all the rights, power, and authority which it would possess were it the sovereign of the territory to the exclusion of the exercise of sovereign rights by the Republic. All railway and canal property rights belonging to Panama and needed for the canal pass to the United States, including any property of the respective companies in the cities of Panama and Colon; the works, property, and personnel of the canal and railways are exempted from taxation as well in the cities of Panama and Colon as in the canal zone and its dependencies. Free immigration of the personnel and importation of supplies for the construction and operation of the canal are granted. Provision is made for the use of military force and the building of fortifications by the United States for the protection of the transit. In other details, particularly as to the acquisition of the interests of the New Panama Canal Company and the Panama Railway by the United States and the condemnation of private property for the uses of the canal, the stipulations of the Hay-Herran treaty are closely followed, while the compensation to be given for these enlarged grants remains the same, being ten millions of dollars payable on exchange of ratifications; and, beginning nine years from that date, an annual payment of $250,000 during the life of the convention.

FOURTH ANNUAL MESSAGE.

WHITE HOUSE, *December 6, 1904.*

To the Senate and House of Representatives:

The Nation continues to enjoy noteworthy prosperity. Such prosperity is of course primarily due to the high individual average of our citizenship, taken together with our great natural resources; but an important factor therein is the working of our long-continued governmental policies. The people have emphatically expressed their approval of the principles underlying these policies, and their desire that these principles be kept substantially unchanged, although of course applied in a progressive spirit to meet changing conditions.

The enlargement of scope of the functions of the National Government required by our development as a nation involves, of course, increase of expense; and the period of prosperity through which the country is passing justifies expenditures for permanent improvements far greater than would be wise in hard times. Battle ships and forts, public buildings, and improved waterways are investments which should be made when we have the money; but abundant revenues and a large surplus always invite extravagance, and constant care should be taken to guard against unnecessary increase of the ordinary expenses of government. The cost of doing Government business shauld be regulated with the same rigid scrutiny as the cost of doing a private business.

In the vast and complicated mechanism of our modern civilized life the dominant note is the note of industralism; and the relations of capital and labor, and especially of organized capital and organized labor, to each other and to the public at large come second in importance only to the intimate questions of family life. Our peculiar form of government, with its sharp division of authority between the Nation and the several States, has been on the whole far more advantageous to our development than a more strongly centralized government. But it is undoubtedly responsible for much of the difficulty of meeting with adequate legislation the new problems presented by the total change in industrial conditions on this continent during the last half century. In actual practice it has proved exceedingly difficult, and in many cases impossible, to get unanimity of wise action among the various States on these subjects. From the very nature of the case this is especially true of the laws affecting the employment of capital in huge masses.

With regard to labor the problem is no less important, but it is simpler. As long as the States retain the primary control of the police power the circumstances must be altogether extreme which require interference by the Federal authorities, whether in the way of safeguarding the rights of labor or in the way of seeing that wrong is not done by unruly persons who shield themselves behind the name of labor. If there is resistance to the Federal courts, interference with the mails, or interstate commerce, or molestation of Federal property, or if the State authorities in some crisis which they are unable to face call for help, then the Federal Government may interfere; but though such interference may be caused by a condition of things arising out of trouble connected with some question of labor, the interference itself simply takes the form of restoring order without regard to the questions which have caused the breach of order—for to keep order is a primary duty and in a time of disorder and violence all other questions sink into abeyance until order has been restored. In the District of Columbia and in the Territories the Federal law covers the entire field of government; but the labor question is only acute in populous centers of commerce, manufactures, or mining. Nevertheless, both in the enactment and in the enforcement of law the Federal Government within its restricted sphere should set an example to the State governments, especially in a matter so vital as this affecting labor. I believe that under modern industrial conditions it is often necessary, and even where not necessary it is yet often wise, that there should be organization of labor in order better to secure the rights of the individual wage-worker. All encouragement should be given to any such organization, so long as it is conducted with a due and decent regard for the rights of others. There are in this country some labor unions which have habitually, and other labor unions which have often, been among the most effective agents in working for good citizenship and for uplifting the condition of those whose welfare should be closest to our hearts. But when any labor union seeks improper ends, or seeks to achieve proper ends by improper means, all good citizens and more especially all honorable public servants must oppose the wrongdoing as resolutely as they would oppose the wrongdoing of any great corporation. Of course any violence, brutality, or corruption, should not for one moment be tolerated. Wage-workers have an entire right to organize and by all peaceful and honorable means to endeavor to persuade their fellows to join with them in organizations. They have a legal right, which, according to circumstances, may or may not be a moral right, to refuse to work in company with men who decline to join their organizations. They have under no circumstances the right to commit violence upon those, whether capitalists or wage-workers, who refuse to support their organizations, or who side with those with whom they are at odds; for mob rule is intolerable in any form.

The wage-workers are peculiarly entitled to the protection and the encouragement of the law. From the very nature of their occupation railroad men, for instance, are liable to be maimed in doing the legitimate work of their profession, unless the railroad companies are required by law to make ample provision for their safety. The Administration has been zealous in enforcing the existing law for this purpose. That law should be amended and strengthened. Wherever the National Government has power there should be a stringent employer's liability law, which should apply to the Government itself where the Government is an employer of labor.

In my Message to the Fifty-seventh Congress, at its second session, I urged the passage of an employer's liability law for the District of Columbia. I now renew that recommendation, and further recommend that the Congress appoint a commission to make a comprehensive study of employer's liability with the view of extending the provisions of a great and constitutional law to all employments within the scope of Federal power.

The Government has recognized heroism upon the water, and bestows medals of honor upon those persons who by extreme and heroic daring have endangered their lives in saving, or endeavoring to save, lives from the perils of the sea in the waters over which the United States has jurisdiction, or upon an American vessel. This recognition should be extended to cover cases of conspicuous bravery and self-sacrifice in the saving of life in private employments under the jurisdiction of the United States, and particularly in the land commerce of the Nation.

The ever-increasing casualty list upon our railroads is a matter of grave public concern, and urgently calls for action by the Congress. In the matter of speed and comfort of railway travel our railroads give at least as good service as those of any other nation, and there is no reason why this service should not also be as safe as human ingenuity can make it. Many of our leading roads have been foremost in the adoption of the most approved safeguards for the protection of travelers and employees, yet the list of clearly avoidable accidents continues unduly large. The passage of a law requiring the adoption of a block-signal system has been proposed to the Congress. I earnestly concur in that recommendation, and would also point out to the Congress the urgent need of legislation in the interest of the public safety limiting the hours of labor for railroad employees in train service upon railroads engaged in interstate commerce, and providing that only trained and experienced persons be employed in positions of responsibility connected with the operation of trains. Of course nothing can ever prevent accidents caused by human weakness or misconduct; and there should be drastic punishment for any railroad employee, whether officer or man, who by issuance of wrong orders or by disobedience of orders causes disaster. The law of 1901, requiring interstate railroads to make monthly reports of all accidents to passengers and employees on duty, should also be amended so as to empower the Government to make a personal investigation, through proper officers, of all accidents involving loss of life which seem to require investigation, with a requirement that the results of such investigation be made public.

The safety-appliance law, as amended by the act of March 2, 1903, has proved beneficial to railway employees, and in order that its provisions may be properly carried out, the force of inspectors provided for by appropriation should be largely increased. This service is analogous to the Steamboat-Inspection Service, and deals with even more important interests. It has passed the experimental stage and demonstrated its utility, and should receive generous recognition by the Congress.

There is no objection to employees of the Government forming or belonging to unions; but the Government can neither discriminate for nor discriminate against nonunion men who are in its employment, or who seek to be employed under it. Moreover, it is a very grave impropriety for Government employees to band themselves together for the purpose of extorting improperly high salaries from the Government. Especially is this true of those within the classified service. The letter carriers, both municipal and rural, are as a whole an excellent body of public servants. They should be amply paid. But their payment must be obtained by arguing their claims fairly and honorably before the Congress, and not by banding together for the defeat of those Congressmen who refuse to give promises which they can not in conscience give. The Administration has already taken steps to prevent and punish abuses of this nature; but it will be wise for the Congress to supplement this action by legislation.

Much can be done by the Government in labor matters merely by giving publicity to certain conditions. The Bureau of Labor has done excellent work of this kind in many different directions. I shall shortly lay before you in a special message the full report of the investigation of the Bureau of Labor into the Colorado mining strike, as this was a strike in which certain very evil forces, which are more or less at work everywhere under the conditions of modern industrialism, became startlingly prominent. It is greatly to be wished that the Department of Commerce and Labor, through the Labor Bureau, should compile and arrange for the Congress a list of the labor laws of the various States, and should be given the means to investigate and report to the Congress upon the labor conditions in the manufacturing and mining regions throughout the country, both as to wages, as to hours of labor, as to the labor of women and children, and as to the effect in the various labor centers of immigration from abroad. In this investigation especial attention should be paid to the conditions of child labor and child-labor legislation in the several States. Such an investigation must necessarily take into account many of the problems with which this question of child labor is connected. These problems can be actually met, in most cases, only by the States themselves; but the lack of proper legislation in one State in such a matter as child labor often renders it excessively difficult to establish protective restriction upon the work in another State having the same industries, so that the worst tends to drag down the better. For this reason, it would be well for the Nation at least to endeavor to secure comprehensive information as to the conditions of labor of children in the different States. Such investigation and publication by the National Government would tend toward the securing of approximately uniform legislation of the proper character among the several States.

When we come to deal with great corporations the need for the Government to act directly is far greater than in the case of labor, because great corporations can become such only by engaging in interstate commerce, and interstate commerce is peculiarly the field of the General Government. It is an absurdity to expect to eliminate the abuses in great corporations by State action. It is difficult to be patient with an argument that such matters should be left to the States because more than one State pursues the policy of creating on easy terms corporations which are never operated within that

State at all, but in other States whose laws they ignore. The National Government alone can deal adequately with these great corporations. To try to deal with them in an intemperate, destructive, or demagogic spirit would, in all probability, mean that nothing whatever would be accomplished, and, with absolute certainty, that if anything were accomplished it would be of a harmful nature. The American people need to continue to show the very qualities that they have shown—that is, moderation, good sense, the earnest desire to avoid doing any damage, and yet the quiet determination to proceed, step by step, without halt and without hurry, in eliminating or at least in minimizing whatever of mischief or evil there is to interstate commerce in the conduct of great corporations. They are acting in no spirit of hostility to wealth, either individual or corporate. They are not against the rich man any more than against the poor man. On the contrary, they are friendly alike toward rich man and toward poor man, provided only that each acts in a spirit of justice and decency toward his fellows. Great corporations are necessary, and only men of great and singular mental power can manage such corporations successfully, and such men must have great rewards. But these corporations should be managed with due regard to the interest of the public as a whole. Where this can be done under the present laws it must be done. Where these laws come short others should be enacted to supplement them.

Yet we must never forget the determining factor in every kind of work, of head or hand, must be the man's own good sense, courage, and kindliness. More important than any legislation is the gradual growth of a feeling of responsibility and forbearance among capitalists and wage-workers alike; a feeling of respect on the part of each man for the rights of others; a feeling of broad community of interest, not merely of capitalists among themselves, and of wage-workers among themselves, but of capitalists and wage-workers in their relations to each other, and of both in their relations to their fellows who with them make up the body politic. There are many captains of industry, many labor leaders, who realize this. A recent speech by the president of one of our great railroad systems to the employees of that system contains sound common sense. It runs in part as follows:

" It is my belief we can better serve each other, better understand the man as well as his business, when meeting face to face, exchanging views, and realizing from personal contact we serve but one interest, that of our mutual prosperity.

" Serious misunderstandings can not occur where personal good will exists and opportunity for personal explanation is present.

" In my early business life I had experience with men of affairs of a character to make me desire to avoid creating a like feeling of resentment to myself and the interests in my charge, should fortune ever

place me in authority, and I am solicitous of a measure of confidence on the part of the public and our employees that I shall hope may be warranted by the fairness and good fellowship I intend shall prevail in our relationship.

" But do not feel I am disposed to grant unreasonable requests, spend the money of our company unnecessarily or without value received, nor expect the days of mistakes are disappearing, or that cause for complaint will not continually occur; simply to correct such abuses as may be discovered, to better conditions as fast as reasonably may be expected, constantly striving, with varying success, for that improvement we all desire, to convince you there is a force at work in the right direction, all the time making progress—is the disposition with which I have come among you, asking your good will and encouragement.

" The day has gone by when a corporation can be handled successfully in defiance of the public will, even though that will be unreasonable and wrong. A public may be led, but not driven, and I prefer to go with it and shape or modify, in a measure, its opinion, rather than be swept from my bearings, with loss to myself and the interests in my charge.

" Violent prejudice exists towards corporate activity and capital today, much of it founded in reason, more in apprehension, and a large measure is due to the personal traits of arbitrary, unreasonable, incompetent, and offensive men in positions of authority. The accomplishment of results by indirection, the endeavor to thwart the intention, if not the expressed letter of the law (the will of the people), a disregard of the rights of others, a disposition to withhold what is due, to force by main strength or inactivity a result not justified, depending upon the weakness of the claimant and his indisposition to become involved in litigation, has created a sentiment harmful in the extreme and a disposition to consider anything fair that gives gain to the individual at the expense of the company.

" If corporations are to continue to do the world's work, as they are best fitted to, these qualities in their representatives that have resulted in the present prejudice against them must be relegated to the background. The corporations must come out into the open and see and be seen. They must take the public into their confidence and ask for what they want, and no more, and be prepared to explain satisfactorily what advantage will accrue to the public if they are given their desires; for they are permitted to exist not that they may make money solely, but that they may effectively serve those from whom they derive their power.

" Publicity, and not secrecy, will win hereafter, and laws be construed by their intent and not by their letter, otherwise public utilities will be owned and operated by the public which created them, even though

the service be less efficient and the result less satisfactory from a financial standpoint."

The Bureau of Corporations has made careful preliminary investigation of many important corporations. It will make a special report on the beef industry.

The policy of the Bureau is to accomplish the purposes of its creation by co-operation, not antagonism; by making constructive legislation, not destructive prosecution, the immediate object of its inquiries; by conservative investigation of law and fact, and by refusal to issue incomplete and hence necessarily inaccurate reports. Its policy being thus one of open inquiry into, and not attack upon, business, the Bureau has been able to gain not only the confidence, but, better still, the co-operation of men engaged in legitimate business.

The Bureau offers to the Congress the means of getting at the cost of production of our various great staples of commerce.

Of necessity the careful investigation of special corporations will afford the Commissioner knowledge of certain business facts, the publication of which might be an improper infringement of private rights. The method of making public the results of these investigations affords, under the law, a means for the protection of private rights. The Congress will have all facts except such as would give to another corporation information which would injure the legitimate business of a competitor and destroy the incentive for individual superiority and thrift.

The Bureau has also made exhaustive examinations into the legal condition under which corporate business is carried on in the various States; into all judicial decisions on the subject; and into the various systems of corporate taxation in use. I call special attention to the report of the chief of the Bureau; and I earnestly ask that the Congress carefully consider the report and recommendations of the Commissioner on this subject.

The business of insurance vitally affects the great mass of the people of the United States and is national and not local in its application. It involves a multitude of transactions among the people of the different States and between American companies and foreign governments. I urge that the Congress carefully consider whether the power of the Bureau of Corporations can not constitutionally be extended to cover interstate transactions in insurance.

Above all else, we must strive to keep the highways of commerce open to all on equal terms; and to do this it is necessary to put a complete stop to all rebates. Whether the shipper or the railroad is to blame makes no difference; the rebate must be stopped, the abuses of the private car and private terminal-track and side-track systems must be stopped, and the legislation of the Fifty-eighth Congress which

declares it to be unlawful for any person or corporation to offer grant, give, solicit, accept, or receive any rebate, concession, or discrimination in respect of the transportation of any property in interstate or foreign commerce whereby such property shall by any device whatever be transported at a less rate than that named in the tariffs published by the carrier must be enforced. For some time after the enactment of the Act to Regulate Commerce it remained a mooted question whether that act conferred upon the Interstate Commerce Commission the power, after it had found a challenged rate to be unreasonable, to declare what thereafter should, prima facie, be the reasonable maximum rate for the transportation in dispute. The Supreme Court finally resolved that question in the negative, so that as the law now stands the Commission simply possess the bare power to denounce a particular rate as unreasonable. While I am of the opinion that at present it would be undesirable, if it were not impracticable, finally to clothe the Commission with general authority to fix railroad rates, I do believe that, as a fair security to shippers, the Commission should be vested with the power, where a given rate has been challenged and after full hearing found to be unreasonable, to decide, subject to judicial review, what shall be a reasonable rate to take its place; the ruling of the Commission to take effect immediately, and to obtain unless and until it is reversed by the court of review. The Government must in increasing degree supervise and regulate the workings of the railways engaged in interstate commerce; and such increased supervision is the only alternative to an increase of the present evils on the one hand or a still more radical policy on the other. In my judgment the most important legislative act now needed as regards the regulation of corporations is this act to confer on the Interstate Commerce Commission the power to revise rates and regulations, the revised rate to at once go into effect, and stay in effect unless and until the court of review reverses it.

Steamship companies engaged in interstate commerce and protected in our coastwise trade should be held to a strict observance of the interstate commerce act.

In pursuing the set plan to make the city of Washington an example to other American municipalities several points should be kept in mind by the legislators. In the first place, the people of this country should clearly understand that no amount of industrial prosperity, and above all no leadership in international industrial competition, can in any way atone for the sapping of the vitality of those who are usually spoken of as the working classes. The farmers, the mechanics, the skilled and unskilled laborers, the small shop keepers, make up the bulk of the population of any country; and upon their well-being, generation after generation, the well-being of the country and the race depends.

Rapid development in wealth and industrial leadership is a good thing, but only if it goes hand in hand with improvement, and not deterioration, physical and moral. The over-crowding of cities and the draining of country districts are unhealthy and even dangerous symptoms in our modern life. We should not permit overcrowding in cities. In certain European cities it is provided by law that the population of towns shall not be allowed to exceed a very limited density for a given area, so that the increase in density must be continually pushed back into a broad zone around the center of the town, this zone having great avenues or parks within it. The death-rate statistics show a terrible increase in mortality, and especially in infant mortality, in overcrowded tenements. The poorest families in tenement houses live in one room, and it appears that in these one-room tenements the average death rate for a number of given cities at home and abroad is about twice what it is in a two-room tenement, four times what it is in a three-room tenement, and eight times what it is in a tenement consisting of four rooms or over. These figures vary somewhat for different cities, but they approximate in each city those given above; and in all cases the increase of mortality, and especially of infant mortality, with the decrease in the number of rooms used by the family and with the consequent overcrowding is startling. The slum exacts a heavy total of death from those who dwell therein; and this is the case not merely in the great crowded slums of high buildings in New York and Chicago, but in the alley slums of Washington. In Washington people can not afford to ignore the harm that this causes. No Christian and civilized community can afford to show a happy-go-lucky lack of concern for the youth of to-day; for, if so, the community will have to pay a terrible penalty of financial burden and social degradation in the to-morrow. There should be severe child-labor and factory-inspection laws. It is very desirable that married women should not work in factories. The prime duty of the man is to work, to be the breadwinner; the prime duty of the woman is to be the mother, the housewife. All questions of tariff and finance sink into utter insignificance when compared with the tremendous, the vital importance of trying to shape conditions so that these two duties of the man and of the woman can be fulfilled under reasonably favorable circumstances. If a race does not have plenty of children, or if the children do not grow up, or if when they grow up they are unhealthy in body and stunted or vicious in mind, then that race is decadent, and no heaping up of wealth, no splendor of momentary material prosperity, can avail in any degree as offsets.

The Congress has the same power of legislation for the District of Columbia which the State legislatures have for the various States. The problems incident to our highly complex modern industrial civilization. with its manifold and perplexing tendencies both for good and for evil, are far less sharply eccentuated in the city of Washington than in most other cities. For this very reason it is easier to deal with the various phases of these problems in Washington, and the District of Columbia government should be a model for the other municipal governments of the Nation, in all such matters as supervision of the housing of the poor, the creation of small parks in the districts inhabited by the poor, in laws affecting labor, in laws providing for the taking care of the children, in truant laws, and in providing schools.

In the vital matter of taking care of children, much advantage could be gained by a careful study of what has been accomplished in such States as Illinois and Colorado by the juvenile courts. The work of the juvenile court is really a work of character building. It is now generally recognized that young boys and young girls who go wrong should not be treated as criminals, not even necessarily as needing reformation, but rather as needing to have their characters formed, and for this end to have them tested and developed by a system of probation. Much admirable work has been done in many of our Commonwealths by earnest men and women who have made a special study of the needs of those classes of children which furnish the greatest number of juvenile offenders, and therefore the greatest number of adult offenders ; and by their aid, and by profiting by the experiences of the different States and cities in these matters, it would be easy to provide a good code for the District of Columbia.

Several considerations suggest the need for a systematic investigation into and improvement of housing conditions in Washington. The hidden residential alleys are breeding grounds of vice and disease, and should be opened into minor streets. For a number of years influential citizens have joined with the District Commissioners in the vain endeavor to secure laws permitting the condemnation of insanitary dwellings. The local death rates, especially from preventable diseases, are so unduly high as to suggest that the exceptional wholesomeness of Washington's better sections is offset by bad conditions in her poorer neighborhoods. A special " Commission on Housing and Health Conditions in the National Capital" would not only bring about the reformation of existing evils, but would also formulate an appropriate building code to protect the city from mammoth brick tenements and other evils which threaten to develop here as they have in other cities. That the Nation's Capital should be made a model for other municipalities is an ideal which appeals to all patriotic citizens everywhere, and such a special Commission might map out and organize the city's future development in lines of civic social service, just as Major L'Enfant and the recent Park Commission planned the arrangement of her streets and parks.

It is mortifying to remember that Washington has no compulsory school attendance law and that careful inquiries indicate the habitual absence from school of some twenty per cent of all children between the ages of eight and fourteen. It must be evident to all who consider the problems of neglected child life or the benefits of compulsory education in other cities that one of the most urgent needs of the National Capital is a law requiring the school attendance of all children, this law to be enforced by attendance agents directed by the board of education.

Public play grounds are necessary means for the development of wholesome citizenship in modern cities. It is important that the work inaugurated here through voluntary efforts should be taken up and extended through Congressional appropriation of funds sufficient to equip and maintain numerous convenient small play grounds upon land which can be secured without purchase or rental. It is also desirable that small vacant places be purchased and reserved as small-park play grounds in densely settled sections of the city which now have no public open spaces and are destined soon to be built up solidly. All these needs should be met immediately. To meet them would entail expenses; but a corresponding saving could be made by stopping the building of streets and levelling of ground for purposes largely speculative in outlying parts of the city.

There are certain offenders, whose criminality takes the shape of brutality and cruelty towards the weak, who need a special type of punishment. The wife-beater, for example, is inadequately punished by imprisonment; for imprisonment may often mean nothing to him, while it may cause hunger and want to the wife and children who have been the victims of his brutality. Probably some form of corporal punishment would be the most adequate way of meeting this kind of crime.

The Department of Agriculture has grown into an educational institution with a faculty of two thousand specialists making research into all the sciences of production. The Congress appropriates, directly and indirectly, six millions of dollars annually to carry on this work. It reaches every State and Territory in the Union and the islands of the sea lately come under our flag. Co-operation is had with the State experiment stations, and with many other institutions and individuals. The world is carefully searched for new varieties of grains, fruits, grasses, vegetables, trees, and shrubs, suitable to various localities in our country; and marked benefit to our producers has resulted.

The activities of our age in lines of research have reached the tillers of the soil and inspired them with ambition to know more of the principles that govern the forces of nature with which they have to deal. Nearly half of the people of this country devote their energies to growing things from the soil. Until a recent date little has been done to prepare these millions for their life work. In most lines of human activity college-trained men are the leaders. The farmer had no opportunity for special training until the Congress made provision for it forty years ago. During these years progress has been made and teachers have been prepared. Over five thousand students are in attendance at our State agricultural colleges. The Federal Government expends ten millions of dollars annually toward this education and for research in Washington and in the several States and Territories. The Department of Agriculture has given facilities for post-graduate work to five hundred young men during the last seven years, preparing them for advance lines of work in the Department and in the State institutions.

The facts concerning meteorology and its relations to plant and animal life are being systematically inquired into. Temperature and moisture are controlling factors in all agricultural operations. The seasons of the cyclones of the Caribbean Sea and their paths are being forecasted with increasing accuracy. The cold winds that come from the north are anticipated and their times and intensity told to farmers, gardeners, and fruiterers in all southern localities.

We sell two hundred and fifty million dollars' worth of animals and animal products to foreign countries every year, in addition to supplying our own people more cheaply and abundantly than any other nation is able to provide for its people. Successful manufacturing depends primarily on cheap food, which accounts to a considerable extent for our growth in this direction. The Department of Agriculture, by careful inspection of meats, guards the health of our people and gives clean bills of health to deserving exports; it is prepared to deal promptly with imported diseases of animals, and maintain the excellence of our flocks and herds in this respect. There should be an annual census of the live stock of the Nation.

We sell abroad about six hundred million dollars' worth of plants and their products every year. Strenuous efforts are being made to import from foreign countries such grains as are suitable to our varying localities. Seven years ago we bought three-fourths of our rice; by helping the rice growers on the Gulf coast to secure seeds from the Orient suited to their conditions, and by giving them adequate protection, they now supply home demand and export to the islands of the Caribbean Sea and to other rice-growing countries. Wheat and other grains have been imported from light-rainfall countries to our lands in the West and Southwest that have not grown crops because of light precipitation, resulting in an extensive addition to our cropping area and our home-making territory that can not be irrigated. Ten million bushels of first-class macaroni wheat were grown from these experimental importations last year. Fruits suitable to our soils

and climates are being imported from all the countries of the Old
World—the fig from Turkey, the almond from Spain, the date from
Algeria, the mango from India. We are helping our fruit growers
to get their crops into European markets by studying methods of preservation through refrigeration, packing, and handling, which have
been quite successful. We are helping our hop growers by importing
varieties that ripen earlier and later than the kinds they have been
raising, thereby lengthening the harvesting season. The cotton crop
of the country is threatened with root rot, the bollworm, and the boll
weevil. Our pathologists will find immune varieties that will resist
the root disease, and the bollworm can be dealt with, but the boll
weevil is a serious menace to the cotton crop. It is a Central American
insect that has become acclimated in Texas and has done great damage. A scientist of the Department of Agriculture has found the
weevil at home in Guatemala being kept in check by an ant, which has
been brought to our cotton fields for observation. It is hoped that
it may serve a good purpose.

The soils of the country are getting attention from the farmer's
standpoint, and interesting results are following. We have duplicates
of the soils that grow the wrapper tobacco in Sumatra and the filler
tobacco in Cuba. It will be only a question of time when the large
amounts paid to these countries will be paid to our own people. The
reclamation of alkali lands is progressing, to give object lessons to
our people in methods by which worthless lands may be made productive.

The insect friends and enemies of the farmer are getting attention.
The enemy of the San Jose scale was found near the Great Wall of
China, and is now cleaning up all our orchards. The fig-fertilizing
insect imported from Turkey has helped to establish an industry in
California that amounts to from fifty to one hundred tons of dried
figs annually, and is extending over the Pacific coast. A parasitic
fly from South Africa is keeping in subjection the black scale, the
worst pest of the orange and lemon industry in California.

Careful preliminary work is being done towards producing our own
silk. The mulberry is being distributed in large numbers, eggs are
being imported and distributed, improved reels were imported from
Europe last year, and two expert reelers were brought to Washington
to reel the crop of cocoons and teach the art to our own people.

The crop-reporting system of the Department of Agriculture is being
brought closer to accuracy every year. It has two hundred and fifty
thousand reporters selected from people in eight vocations in life. It
has arrangements with most European countries for interchange of
estimates, so that our people may know as nearly as possible with what
they must compete.

During the two and a half years that have elapsed since the passage of the reclamation act rapid progress has been made in the surveys and examinations of the opportunities for reclamation in the thirteen States and three Territories of the arid West. Construction has already been begun on the largest and most important of the irrigation works, and plans are being completed for works which will utilize the funds now available. The operations are being carried on by the Reclamation Service, a corps of engineers selected through competitive civil-service examinations. This corps includes experienced consulting and constructing engineers as well as various experts in mechanical and legal matters, and is composed largely of men who have spent most of their lives in practical affairs connected with irrigation. The larger problems have been solved and it now remains to execute with care, economy, and thoroughness the work which has been laid out. All important details are being carefully considered by boards of consulting engineers, selected for their thorough knowledge and practical experience. Each project is taken up on the ground by competent men and viewed from the standpoint of the creation of prosperous homes, and of promptly refunding to the Treasury the cost of construction. The reclamation act has been found to be remarkably complete and effective, and so broad in its provisions that a wide range of undertakings has been possible under it. At the same time, economy is guaranteed by the fact that the funds must ultimately be returned to be used over again.

It is the cardinal principle of the forest-reserve policy of this Administration that the reserves are for use. Whatever interferes with the use of their resources is to be avoided by every possible means. But these resources must be used in such a way as to make them permanent.

The forest policy of the Government is just now a subject of vivid public interest throughout the West and to the people of the United States in general. The forest reserves themselves are of extreme value to the present as well as to the future welfare of all the western public-land States. They powerfully affect the use and disposal of the public lands. They are of special importance because they preserve the water supply and the supply of timber for domestic purposes, and so promote settlement under the reclamation act. Indeed, they are essential to the welfare of every one of the great interests of the West.

Forest reserves are created for two principal purposes. The first is to preserve the water supply. This is their most important use. The principal users of the water thus preserved are irrigation ranchers and settlers, cities and towns to whom their municipal water supplies are of the very first importance, users and furnishers of water power, and the users of water for domestic, manufacturing, mining, and other purposes. All these are directly dependent upon the forest reserves.

The second reason for which forest reserves are created is to preserve the timber supply for various classes of wood users. Among the more important of these are settlers under the reclamation act and other acts, for whom a cheap and accessible supply of timber for domestic uses is absolutely necessary; miners and prospectors, who are in serious danger of losing their timber supply by fire or through export by lumber companies when timber lands adjacent to their mines pass into private ownership; lumbermen, transportation companies, builders, and commercial interests in general.

Although the wisdom of creating forest reserves is nearly everywhere heartily recognized, yet in a few localities there has been misunderstanding and complaint. The following statement is therefore desirable:

The forest reserve policy can be successful only when it has the full support of the people of the West. It can not safely, and should not in any case, be imposed upon them against their will. But neither can we accept the views of those whose only interest in the forest is temporary; who are anxious to reap what they have not sown and then move away, leaving desolation behind them. On the contrary, it is everywhere and always the interest of the permanent settler and the permanent business man, the man with a stake in the country, which must be considered and which must decide.

The making of forest reserves within railroad and wagon-road land-grant limits will hereafter, as for the past three years, be so managed as to prevent the issue, under the act of June 4, 1897, of base for exchange or lieu selection (usually called scrip). In all cases where forest reserves within areas covered by land grants appear to be essential to the prosperity of settlers, miners, or others, the Government lands within such proposed forest reserves will, as in the recent past, be withdrawn from sale or entry pending the completion of such negotiations with the owners of the land grants as will prevent the creation of so-called scrip.

It was formerly the custom to make forest reserves without first getting definite and detailed information as to the character of land and timber within their boundaries. This method of action often resulted in badly chosen boundaries and consequent injustice to settlers and others. Therefore this Administration adopted the present method of first withdrawing the land from disposal, followed by careful examination on the ground and the preparation of detailed maps and descriptions, before any forest reserve is created.

I have repeatedly called attention to the confusion which exists in Government forest matters because the work is scattered among three independent organizations. The United States is the only one of the great nations in which the forest work of the Government is not concentrated under one department, in consonance with the plainest dictates of good administration and common sense. The present arrangement is bad from every point of view. Merely to mention it is to prove that it should be terminated at once. As I have repeatedly recommended, all the forest work of the Government should be concentrated in the Department of Agriculture, where the larger part of that work is already done, where practically all of the trained foresters of the Government are employed, where chiefly in Washington there is comprehensive first-class knowledge of the problems of the reserves acquired on the ground, where all problems relating to growth from the soil are already gathered, and where all the sciences auxiliary to forestry are at hand for prompt and effective co-operation. These reasons are decisive in themselves, but it should be added that the great organizations of citizens whose interests are affected by the forest-reserves, such as the National Live Stock Association, the National Wool Growers' Association, the American Mining Congress, the national Irrigation Congress, and the National Board of Trade, have uniformly, emphatically, and most of them repeatedly, expressed themselves in favor of placing all Government forest work in the Department of Agriculture because of the peculiar adaptation of that Department for it. It is true, also, that the forest services of nearly all the great nations of the world are under the respective departments of agriculture, while in but two of the smaller nations and in one colony are they under the department of the interior. This is the result of long and varied experience and it agrees fully with the requirements of good administration in our own case.

The creation of a forest service in the Department of Agriculture will have for its important results:

First. A better handling of all forest work; because it will be under a single head, and because the vast and indispensable experience of the Department in all matters pertaining to the forest reserves, to forestry in general, and to other forms of production from the soil, will be easily and rapidly accessible.

Second. The reserves themselves, being handled from the point of view of the man in the field, instead of the man in the office, will be more easily and more widely useful to the people of the West than has been the case hitherto.

Third. Within a comparatively short time the reserves will become self-supporting. This is important, because continually and rapidly increasing appropriations will be necessary for the proper care of this exceedingly important interest of the Nation, and they can and should be offset by returns from the National forests. Under similar circumstances the forest possessions of other great nations form an important source of revenue to their governments.

Every administrative officer concerned is convinced of the necessity for the proposed consolidation of forest work in the Department of Agriculture, and I myself have urged it more than once in former messages. Again I commend it to the early and favorable consideration of the Congress. The interests of the Nation at large and of the West in particular have suffered greatly because of the delay.

I call the attention of the Congress again to the report and recommendation of the Commission on the Public Lands forwarded by me to the second session of the present Congress. The Commission has prosecuted its investigations actively during the past season, and a second report is now in an advanced stage of preparation.

In connection with the work of the forest reserves I desire again to urge upon the Congress the importance of authorizing the President to set aside certain portions of these reserves or other public lands as game refuges for the preservation of the bison, the wapiti, and other large beasts once so abundant in our woods and mountains and on our great plains, and now tending toward extinction. Every support should be given to the authorities of the Yellowstone Park in their successful efforts at preserving the large creatures therein; and at very little expense portions of the public domain in other regions which are wholly unsuited to agricultural settlement could be similarly utilized. We owe it to future generations to keep alive the noble and beautiful creatures which by their presence add such distinctive character to the American wilderness. The limits of the Yellowstone Park should be extended southwards. The Canyon of the Colorado should be made a national park; and the national-park system should include the Yosemite and as many as possible of the groves of giant trees in California.

The veterans of the Civil War have a claim upon the Nation such as no other body of our citizens possess. The Pension Bureau has never in its history been managed in a more satisfactory manner than is now the case.

The progress of the Indians toward civilization, though not rapid, is perhaps all that could be hoped for in view of the circumstances. Within the past year many tribes have shown, in a degree greater than ever before, an appreciation of the necessity of work. This changed attitude is in part due to the policy recently pursued of reducing the amount of subsistence to the Indians, and thus forcing them, through sheer necessity, to work for a livelihood. The policy, though severe, is a useful one, but it is to be exercised only with judgment and with a full understanding of the conditions which exist in each community for which it is intended. On or near the Indian reservations there is usually very little demand for labor, and if the Indians are to earn their living and when work can not be furnished from outside (which is always preferable), then it must be furnished by the Government.

Practical instruction of this kind would in a few years result in the forming of habits of regular industry, which would render the Indian a producer and would effect a great reduction in the cost of his maintenance.

It is commonly declared that the slow advance of the Indians is due to the unsatisfactory character of the men appointed to take immediate charge of them, and to some extent this is true. While the standard of the employees in the Indian Service shows great improvement over that of bygone years, and while actual corruption or flagrant dishonesty is now the rare exception, it is nevertheless the fact that the salaries paid Indian agents are not large enough to attract the best men to that field of work. To achieve satisfactory results the official in charge of an Indian tribe should possess the high qualifications which are required in the manager of a large business, but only in exceptional cases is it possible to secure men of such a type for these positions. Much better service, however, might be obtained from those now holding the places were it practicable to get out of them the best that is in them, and this should be done by bringing them constantly into closer touch with their superior officers. An agent who has been content to draw his salary, giving in return the least possible equivalent in effort and service, may, by proper treatment, by suggestion and encouragement, or persistent urging, be stimulated to greater effort and induced to take a more active personal interest in his work.

Under existing conditions an Indian agent in the distant West may be wholly out of touch with the office of the Indian Bureau. He may very well feel that no one takes a personal interest in him or his efforts. Certain routine duties in the way of reports and accounts are required of him, but there is no one with whom he may intelligently consult on matters vital to his work, except after long delay. Such a man would be greatly encouraged and aided by personal contact with some one whose interest in Indian affairs and whose authority in the Indian Bureau were greater than his own, and such contact would be certain to arouse and constantly increase the interest he takes in his work.

The distance which separates the agents—the workers in the field—from the Indian Office in Washington is a chief obstacle to Indian progress. Whatever shall more closely unite these two branches of the Indian Service, and shall enable them to co-operate more heartily and more effectively, will be for the increased efficiency of the work and the betterment of the race for whose improvement the Indian Bureau was established. The appointment of a field assistant to the Commissioner of Indian Affairs would be certain to insure this good end. Such an official, if possessed of the requisite energy and deep interest in

the work, would be a most efficient factor in bringing into closer relationship and a more direct union of effort the Bureau in Washington
and its agents in the field; and with the co-operation of its branches
thus secured the Indian Bureau would, in measure fuller than ever before, lift up the savage toward that self-help and self-reliance which
constitute the man.

In 1907 there will be held at Hampton Roads the tricentennial celebration of the settlement at Jamestown, Virginia, with which the history of what has now become the United States really begins. I commend this to your favorable consideration. It is an event of prime
historic significance, in which all the people of the United States should
feel, and should show, great and general interest.

In the Post-Office Department the service has increased in efficiency,
and conditions as to revenue and expenditure continue satisfactory.
The increase of revenue during the year was $9,358,181.10, or 6.9 per
cent, the total receipts amounting to $143,382,624.34. The expendi-
tures were $152,362,116.70, an increase of about 9 per cent over the
previous year, being thus $8,979,492.36 in excess of the current rev-
enue. Included in these expenditures was a total appropriation of $12,-
956,637.35 for the continuation and extension of the rural free-delivery
service, which was an increase of $4,902,237.35 over the amount ex-
pended for this purpose in the preceding fiscal year. Large as this expenditure has been the beneficent results attained in extending the
free distribution of mails to the residents of rural districts have justified the wisdom of the outlay. Statistics brought down to the 1st of
October, 1904, show that on that date there were 27,138 rural routes
established, serving approximately 12,000,000 of people in rural districts remote from post-offices, and that there were pending at that time
3,859 petitions for the establishment of new rural routes. Unquestionably some part of the general increase in receipts is due to the increased postal facilities which the rural service has afforded. The revenues have also been aided greatly by amendments in the classification
of mail matter, and the curtailment of abuses of the second-class mail-
ing privilege. The average increase in the volume of mail matter for
the period beginning with 1902 and ending June, 1905 (that portion
for 1905 being estimated), is 40.47 per cent, as compared with 25.46
per cent for the period immediately preceding, and 15.92 for the four-
year period immediately preceding that.

Our consular system needs improvement. Salaries should be substituted for fees, and the proper classification, grading, and transfer
of consular officers should be provided. I am not prepared to say that
a competitive system of examinations for appointment would work
well; but by law it should be provided that consuls should be familiar,
according to places for which they apply, with the French German. or

Spanish languages, and should possess acquaintance with the resources of the United States.

The collection of objects of art contemplated in section 5586 of the Revised Statutes should be designated and established as a National Gallery of Art; and the Smithsonian Institution should be authorized to accept any additions to said collection that may be received by gift, bequest, or devise.

It is desirable to enact a proper National quarantine law. It is most undesirable that a State should on its own initiative enforce quarantine regulations which are in effect a restriction upon interstate and international commerce. The question should properly be assumed by the Government alone. The Surgeon-General of the National Public Health and Marine-Hospital Service has repeatedly and convincingly set forth the need for such legislation.

I call your attention to the great extravagance in printing and binding Government publications, and especially to the fact that altogether too many of these publications are printed. There is a constant tendency to increase their number and their volume. It is an understatement to say that no appreciable harm would be caused by, and substantial benefit would accrue from, decreasing the amount of printing now done by at least one-half. Probably the great majority of the Government reports and the like now printed are never read at all, and furthermore the printing of much of the material contained in many of the remaining ones serves no useful purpose whatever.

The attention of the Congress should be especially given to the currency question, and that the standing committees on the matter in the two Houses charged with the duty, take up the matter of our currency and see whether it is not possible to secure an agreement in the business world for bettering the system; the committees should consider the question of the retirement of the greenbacks and the problem of securing in our currency such elasticity as is consistent with safety. Every silver dollar should be made by law redeemable in gold at the option of the holder.

I especially commend to your immediate attention the encouragement of our merchant marine by appropriate legislation.

The growing importance of the Orient as a field for American exports drew from my predecessor, President McKinley, an urgent request for its special consideration by the Congress. In his message of 1898 he stated:

"In this relation, as showing the peculiar volume and value of our trade with China and the peculiarly favorable conditions which exist for their expansion in the normal course of trade, I refer to the communication addressed to the Speaker of the House of Representatives by the Secretary of the Treasury on the 14th of last June, with its ac-

companying letter of the Secretary of State, recommending an appropriation for a commission to study the industrial and commercial conditions in the Chinese Empire and to report as to the opportunities for
and the obstacles to the enlargement of markets in China for the raw
products and manufactures of the United States. Action was not taken
thereon during the last session. I cordially urge that the recommendation receive at your hands the consideration which its importance and
timeliness merit."

In his annual message of 1889 he again called attention to this recommendation, quoting it, and stated further:

"I now renew this recommendation, as the importance of the subject has steadily grown since it was first submitted to you, and no time
should be lost in studying for ourselves the resources of this great field
for American trade and enterprise."

The importance of securing proper information and data with a
view to the enlargement of our trade with Asia is undiminished. Our
consular representatives in China have strongly urged a place for permanent display of American products in some prominent trade center
of that Empire, under Government control and management, as an
effective means of advancing our export trade therein. I call the attention of the Congress to the desirability of carrying out these suggestions.

In dealing with the questions of immigration and naturalization it
is indispensable to keep certain facts ever before the minds of those
who share in enacting the laws. First and foremost, let us remember
that the question of being a good American has nothing whatever to
do with a man's birthplace any more than it has to do with his creed.
In every generation from the time this Government was founded men
of foreign birth have stood in the very foremost rank of good citizenship, and that not merely in one but in every field of American activity;
while to try to draw a distinction between the man whose parents
came to this country and the man whose ancestors came to it several
generations back is a mere absurdity. Good Americanism is a matter
of heart, of conscience, of lofty aspiration, of sound common sense, but
not of birthplace or of creed. The medal of honor, the highest prize
to be won by those who serve in the Army and the Navy of the United
States decorates men born here, and it also decorates men born in
Great Britain and Ireland, in Germany, in Scandinavia, in France, and
doubtless in other countries also. In the field of statesmanship, in the
field of business, in the field of philanthropic endeavor, it is equally
true that among the men of whom we are most proud as Americans
no distinction whatever can be drawn between those who themselves
or whose parents came over in sailing ship or steamer from across the
water and those whose ancestors stepped ashore into the wooded

wilderness at Plymouth or at the mouth of the Hudson, the **Delaware,** or the James nearly three centuries ago. No fellow-citizen of ours is entitled to any peculiar regard because of the way in which he worships his Maker, or because of the birthplace of himself or his parents, nor should he be in any way discriminated against therefor. Each must stand on his worth as a man and each is entitled to be judged solely thereby.

There is no danger of having too many immigrants of the right kind. It makes no difference from what country they come. If they are sound in body and in mind, and, above all, if they are of good character, so that we can rest assured that their children and grandchildren will be worthy fellow-citizens of our children and grandchildren, then we should welcome them with cordial hospitality.

But the citizenship of this country should not be debased. It is vital that we should keep high the standard of well-being among our wageworkers, and therefore we should not admit masses of men whose standards of living and whose personal customs and habits are such that they tend to lower the level of the American wage-worker; and above all we should not admit any man of an unworthy type, any man concerning whom we can say that he will himself be a bad citizen, or that his children and grandchildren will detract from instead of adding to the sum of the good citizenship of the country. Similarly we should take the greatest care about naturalization. Fraudulent naturalization, the naturalization of improper persons, is a curse to our Government; and it is the affair of every honest voter, wherever born, to see that no fraudulent voting is allowed, that no fraud in connection with naturalization is permitted.

In the past year the cases of false, fraudulent, and improper naturalization of aliens coming to the attention of the executive branches of the Government have increased to an alarming degree. Extensive sales of forged certificates of naturalization have been discovered, as well as many cases of naturalization secured by perjury and fraud; and in addition, instances have accumulated showing that many courts issue certificates of naturalization carelessly and upon insufficient evidence.

Under the Constitution it is in the power of the Congress "to establish a uniform rule of naturalization," and numerous laws have from time to time been enacted for that purpose, which have been supplemented in a few States by State laws having special application. The Federal statutes permit naturalization by any court of record in the United States having common-law jurisdiction and a seal and clerk, except the police court of the District of Columbia, and nearly all these courts exercise this important function. It results that where so many courts of such varying grades have jurisdiction, there is lack of uniformity in the rules applied in conferring naturalization. Some courts are strict and others lax. An alien who may secure n   _ation in one place might be denied it in another, and the intent   the constitutional provision is in fact defeated. Furthermore, the certificates of naturalization issued by the courts differ widely in wording and appearance, and when they are brought into use in foreign countries, are frequently subject to suspicion.

There should be a comprehensive revision of the naturalization laws. The courts having power to naturalize should be definitely named by national authority; the testimony upon which naturalization may be conferred should be definitely prescribed; publication of impending naturalization applications should be required in advance of their hearing in court; the form and wording of all certificates issued should be uniform throughout the country, and the courts should be required to make returns to the Secretary of State at stated periods of all naturalizations conferred.

Not only are the laws relating to naturalization now defective, but those relating to citizenship of the United States ought also to be made the subject of scientific inquiry with a view to probable further legislation. By what acts expatriation may be assumed to have been accomplished, how long an American citizen may reside abroad and receive the protection of our passport, whether any degree of protection should be extended to one who has made the declaration of intention to become a citizen of the United States but has not secured naturalization, are questions of serious import, involving personal rights and often producing friction between this Government and foreign governments. Yet upon these question our laws are silent. I recommend that an examination be made into the subjects of citizenship, expatriation, and protection of Americans abroad, with a view to appropriate legislation.

The power of the Government to protect the integrity of the elections of its own officials is inherent and has been recognized and affirmed by repeated declarations of the Supreme Court. There is no enemy of free government more dangerous and none so insidious as the corruption of the electorate. No one defends or excuses corruption, and it would seem to follow that none would oppose vigorous measures to eradicate it. I recommend the enactment of a law directed against bribery and corruption in Federal elections. The details of such a law may be safely left to the wise discretion of the Congress, but it should go as far as under the Constitution it is possible to go, and should include severe penalties against him who gives or receives a bribe intended to influence his act or opinion as an elector; and provisions for the publication not only of the expenditures for nominations and elections of all candidates but also of all contributions received and expenditures made by political committees.

No subject is better worthy the attention of the Congress than that portion of the report of the Attorney-General dealing with the long delays and the great obstruction to justice experienced in the cases of Beavers, Green and Gaynor, and Benson. Were these isolated and special cases, I should not call your attention to them; but the diffi-culties encountered as regards these men who have been indicted for criminal practices are not exceptional; they are precisely similar in kind to what occurs again and again in the case of criminals who have sufficient means to enable them to take advantage of a system of pro-cedure which has grown up in the Federal courts and which amounts in effect to making the law easy of enforcement against the man who has no money, and difficult of enforcement, even to the point of some-times securing immunity, as regards the man who has money. In criminal cases the writ of the United States should run throughout its borders. The wheels of justice should not be clogged, as they have been clogged in the cases above mentioned, where it has proved abso-lutely impossible to bring the accused to the place appointed by the Constitution for his trial. Of recent years there has been grave and increasing complaint of the difficulty of bringing to justice those crim-inals whose criminality, instead of being against one person in the Republic, is against all persons in the Republic, because it is against the Republic itself. Under any circumstance and from the very nature of the case it is often exceedingly difficult to secure proper punish-ment of those who have been guilty of wrongdoing against the Gov-ernment. By the time the offender can be brought into court the popular wrath against him has generally subsided; and there is in most instances very slight danger indeed of any prejudice existing in the minds of the jury against him. At present the interests of the innocent man are amply safeguarded; but the interests of the Govern ment, that is, the interests of honest administration, that is the interests of the people, are not recognized as they should be. No subject better warrants the attention of the Congress. Indeed, no subject better warrants the attention of the bench and the bar throughout the United States.

Alaska, like all our Territorial acquisitions, has proved resourceful beyond the expectations of those who made the purchase. It has be-come the home of many hardy, industrious, and thrifty American citi-zens. Towns of a permanent character have been built. The extent of its wealth in minerals, timber, fisheries, and agriculture, while great, is probably not comprehended yet in any just measure by our people. We do know, however, that from a very small beginning its products have grown until they are a steady and material contribution to the wealth of the nation. Owing to the immensity of Alaska and its ioca-tion in the far north, it is a difficult matter to provide many things essential to its growth and to the happiness and comfort of its people by private enterprise alone. It should, therefore, receive reasonable aid from the Government. The Government has already done excellent work for Alaska in laying cables and building telegraph lines. This work has been done in the most economical and efficient way by the Signal Corps of the Army.

In some respects it has outgrown its present laws, while in others those laws have been found to be inadequate. In order to obtain information upon which I could rely I caused an official of the Department of Justice, in whose judgment I have confidence, to visit Alaska during the past summer for the purpose of ascertaining how government is administered there and what legislation is actually needed at present. A statement of the conditions found to exist, together with some recommendations and the reasons therefor, in which I strongly concur, will be found in the annual report of the Attorney-General. In some instances I feel that the legislation suggested is so imperatively needed that I am moved briefly to emphasize the Attorney-General's proposals.

Under the Code of Alaska as it now stands many purely administrative powers and duties, including by far the most important, devolve upon the district judges or upon the clerks of the district court acting under the direction of the judges, while the governor, upon whom these powers and duties should logically fall, has nothing specific to do except to make annual reports, issue Thanksgiving Day proclamations, and appoint Indian policemen and notaries public. I believe it essential to good government in Alaska, and therefore recommend, that the Congress divest the district judges and the clerks of their courts of the administrative or executive functions that they now exercise and cast them upon the governor. This would not be an innovation; it would simply conform the government of Alaska to fundamental principles, making the governorship a real instead of a merely nominal office, and leaving the judges free to give their entire attention to their judicial duties and at the same time removing them from a great deal of the strife that now embarrasses the judicial office in Alaska.

I also recommend that the salaries of the district judges and district attorneys in Alaska be increased so as to make them equal to those received by corresponding officers in the United States after deducting the difference in the cost of living; that the district attorneys should be prohibited from engaging in private practice; that United States commissioners be appointed by the governor of the Territory instead of by the district judges, and that a fixed salary be provided for them to take the place of the discredited "fee system," which should be abolished in all offices; that a mounted constabulary be created to police the territory outside the limits of incorporated towns—a vast section now wholly without police protection; and that some provision be made to at least lessen the oppressive delays and costs that now attend the prosecution of appeals from the district court of Alaska. There should be a division of the existing judicial districts, and an increase in the number of judges.

Alaska should have a Delegate in the Congress. Where possible, the Congress should aid in the construction of needed wagon roads. Additional light-houses should be provided. In my judgment, it is especially important to aid in such manner as seems just and feasible in the construction of a trunk line of railway to connect the Gulf of Alaska with the Yukon River through American territory. This would be most beneficial to the development of the resources of the Territory, and to the comfort and welfare of its people.

Salmon hatcheries should be established in many different streams, so as to secure the preservation of this valuable food fish. Salmon fisheries and canneries should be prohibited on certain of the rivers where the mass of those Indians dwell who live almost exclusively on fish.

The Alaskan natives are kindly, intelligent, anxious to learn, and willing to work. Those who have come under the influence of civilization, even for a limited period, have proved their capability of becoming self-supporting, self-respecting citizens, and ask only for the just enforcement of law and intelligent instruction and supervision. Others, living in more remote regions, primitive, simple hunters and fisher folk, who know only the life of the woods and the waters, are daily being confronted with twentieth-century civilization with all of its complexities. Their country is being overrun by strangers, the game slaughtered and driven away, the streams depleted of fish, and hitherto unknown and fatal diseases brought to them, all of which combine to produce a state of abject poverty and want which must result in their extinction. Action in their interest is demanded by every consideration of justice and humanity.

The needs of these people are:

The abolition of the present fee system, whereby the native is degraded, imposed upon, and taught the injustice of law.

The establishment of hospitals at central points, so that contagious diseases that are brought to them continually by incoming whites may be localized and not allowed to become epidemic, to spread death and destitution over great areas.

The development of the educational system in the form of practical training in such industries as will assure the Indians self-support under the changed conditions in which they will have to live.

The duties of the office of the governor should be extended to include the supervision of Indian affairs, with necessary assistants in different districts. He should be provided with the means and the power to protect and advise the native people, to furnish medical treatment in time of epidemics, and to extend material relief in periods of famine and extreme destitution.

The Alaskan natives should be given the right to acquire, hold, and dispose of property upon the same conditions as given other inhabitants ; and the privilege of citizenship should be given to such as may be able to meet certain definite requirements. In Hawaii Congress should give the governor power to remove all the officials appointed under him. The harbor of Honolulu should be dredged. The Marine-Hospital Service should be empowered to study leprosy in the islands. I ask special consideration for the report and recommendation of the governor of Porto Rico.

In treating of our foreign policy and of the attitude that this great Nation should assume in the world at large, it is absolutely necessary to consider the Army and the Navy, and the Congress, through which the thought of the Nation finds its expression, should keep ever vividly in mind the fundamental fact that it is impossible to treat our foreign policy, whether this policy takes shape in the effort to secure justice for others or justice for ourselves, save as conditioned upon the attitude we are willing to take toward our Army, and especially toward our Navy. It is not merely unwise, it is contemptible, for a nation, as for an individual, to use high-sounding language to proclaim its purposes, or to take positions which are ridiculous if unsupported by potential force, and then to refuse to provide this force. If there is no intention of providing and of keeping the force necessary to back up a strong attitude, then it is far better not to assume such an attitude.

The steady aim of this Nation, as of all enlightened nations, should be to strive to bring ever nearer the day when there shall prevail throughout the world the peace of justice. There are kinds of peace which are highly undesirable, which are in the long run as destructive as any war. Tyrants and oppressors have many times made a wilderness and called it peace. Many times peoples who were slothful or timid or shortsighted, who had been enervated by ease or by luxury, or misled by false teachings, have shrunk in unmanly fashion from doing duty that was stern and that needed self-sacrifice, and have sought to hide from their own minds their shortcomings, their ignoble motives. by calling them love of peace. The peace of tyrannous terror, the peace of craven weakness, the peace of injustice, all these should be shunned as we shun unrighteous war. The goal to set before us as a nation, the goal which should be set before all mankind, is the attainment of the peace of justice, of the peace which comes when each nation is not merely safe-guarded in its own rights, but scrupulously recognizes and performs its duty toward others. Generally peace tells for righteousness; but if there is conflict between the two, then our fealty is due first to the cause of righteousness. Unrighteous wars are common, and unrighteous peace is rare; but both should be shunned. The right of freedom and the responsibility for the exercise of that right can not be divorced. One of our great poets has well and finely said that freedom is not a gift that tarries long in the hands of cowards. Neither does it tarry long in the hands of those too slothful, too dishonest, or too unintelligent to exercise it. The eternal vigilance which is the price of liberty must be exercised, sometimes to guard against outside foes; although of course far more often to guard against our own selfish or thoughtless shortcomings.

It these self-evident truths are kept before us, and only if they are so kept before us, we shall have a clear idea of what our foreign policy in its larger aspects should be. It is our duty to remember that a nation has no more right to do injustice to another nation, strong or weak, than an individual has to do injustice to another individual; that the same moral law applies in one case as in the other. But we must also remember that it is as much the duty of the Nation to guard its own rights and its own interests as it is the duty of the individual so to do. Within the Nation the individual has now delegated this right to the State, that is, to the representative of all the individuals, and it is a maxim of the law that for every wrong there is a remedy. But in international law we have not advanced by any means as far as we have advanced in municipal law. There is as yet no judicial way of enforcing a right in international law. When one nation wrongs another or wrongs many others, there is no tribunal before which the wrongdoer can be brought. Either it is necessary supinely to acquiesce in the wrong, and thus put a premium upon brutality and aggression, or else it is necessary for the aggrieved nation valiantly to stand up for its rights. Until some method is devised by which there shall be a degree of international control over offending nations, it would be a wicked thing for the most civilized powers, for those with most sense of international obligations and with keenest and most generous appreciation of the difference between right and wrong, to disarm. If the great civilized nations of the present day should completely disarm, the result would mean an immediate recrudescence of barbarism in one form or another. Under any circumstances a sufficient armament would have to be kept up to serve the purposes of international police; and until international cohesion and the sense of international duties and rights are far more advanced than at present, a nation desirous both of securing respect for itself and of doing good to others must have a force adequate for the work which it feels is allotted to it as its part of the general world duty. Therefore it follows that

a self-respecting, just, and far-seeing nation should on the one hand
endeavor by every means to aid in the development of the various
movements which tend to provide substitutes for war, which tend to
render nations in their actions toward one another, and indeed toward
their own peoples, more responsive to the general sentiment of humane
and civilized mankind; and on the other hand that it should keep prepared, while scrupulously avoiding wrongdoing itself, to repel any
wrong, and in exceptional cases to take action which in a more advanced stage of international relations would come under the head
of the exercise of the international police. A great free people owes
it to itself and to all mankind not to sink into helplessness before the
powers of evil.

We are in every way endeavoring to help on, with cordial good
will, every movement which will tend to bring us into more friendly
relations with the rest of mankind. In pursuance of this policy I
shall shortly lay before the Senate treaties of arbitration with all powers
which are willing to enter into these treaties with us. It is not possible at this period of the world's development to agree to arbitrate all
matters, but there are many matters of possible difference between us
and other nations which can be thus arbitrated. Furthermore, at the
request of the Interparliamentary Union, an eminent body composed
of practical statesmen from all countries, I have asked the Powers to
join with this Government in a second Hague conference, at which it
is hoped that the work already so happily begun at The Hague may
be carried some steps further toward completion. This carries out the
desire expressed by the first Hague conference itself.

It is not true that the United States feels any land hunger or enter-
tains any projects as regards the other nations of the Western Hemisphere save such as are for their welfare. All that this country desires is to see the neighboring countries stable, orderly, and prosperous. Any country whose people conduct themselves well can count
upon our hearty friendship. If a nation shows that it knows how to
act with reasonable efficiency and decency in social and political matters, if it keeps order and pays its obligations, it need fear no interference from the United States. Chronic wrongdoing, or an impotence which results in a general loosening of the ties of civilized
society, may in America, as elsewhere, ultimately require intervention
by some civilized nation, and in the Western Hemisphere the adherence
of the United States to the Monroe Doctrine may force the United
States, however reluctantly, in flagrant cases of such wrongdoing or
impotence, to the exercise of an international police power. If every
country washed by the Caribbean Sea would show the progress in stable
and just civilization which with the aid of the Platt amendment Cuba
has shown since our troops left the island, and which so many of

the republics in both Americas are constantly and brilliantly showing, all question of interference by this Nation with their affairs would be at an end. Our interests and those of our southern neighbors are in reality identical. They have great natural riches, and if within their borders the reign of law and justice obtains, prosperity is sure to come to them. While they thus obey the primary laws of civilized society they may rest assured that they will be treated by us in a spirit of cordial and helpful sympathy. We would interfere with them only in the last resort, and then only if it became evident that their inability or unwillingness to do justice at home and abroad had violated the rights of the United States or had invited foreign aggression to the detriment of the entire body of American nations. It is a mere truism to say that every nation, whether in America or anywhere else, which desires to maintain its freedom, its independence, must ultimately realize that the right of such independence can not be separated from the responsibility of making good use of it.

In asserting the Monroe Doctrine, in taking such steps as we have taken in regard to Cuba, Venezuela, and Panama, and in endeavoring to circumscribe the theater of war in the Far East, and to secure the open door in China, we have acted in our own interest as well as in the interest of humanity at large. There are, however, cases in which, while our own interests are not greatly involved, strong appeal is made to our sympathies. Ordinarily it is very much wiser and more useful for us to concern ourselves with striving for our own moral and material betterment here at home than to concern ourselves with trying to better the condition of things in other nations. We have plenty of sins of our own to war against, and under ordinary circumstances we can do more for the general uplifting of humanity by striving with heart and soul to put a stop to civic corruption, to brutal lawlessness and violent race prejudices here at home than by passing resolutions about wrongdoing elsewhere. Nevertheless there are occasional crimes committed on so vast a scale and of such peculiar horror as to make us doubt whether it is not our manifest duty to endeavor at least to show our disapproval of the deed and our sympathy with those who have suffered by it. The cases must be extreme in which such a course is justifiable. There must be no effort made to remove the mote from our brother's eye if we refuse to remove the beam from our own. But in extreme cases action may be justifiable and proper. What form the action shall take must depend upon the circumstances of the case; that is, upon the degree of the atrocity and upon our power to remedy it. The cases in which we could interfere by force of arms as we interfered to put a stop to intolerable conditions in Cuba are necessarily very few. Yet it is not to be expected that a people like ours, which in spite of certain very obvious shortcomings,

nevertheless as a whole shows by its consistent practice its belief in the
principles of civil and religious liberty and of orderly freedom, a
people among whom even the worst crime, like the crime of lynching, is
never more than sporadic, so that individuals and not classes are
molested in their fundamental rights—it is inevitable that such a
nation should desire eagerly to give expression to its horror on an
occasion like that of the massacre of the Jews in Kishenef, or when
it witnesses such systematic and long-extended cruelty and oppression
as the cruelty and oppression of which the Armenians have been the
victims, and which have won for them the indignant pity of the civilized world.

Even where it is not possible to secure in other nations the observance
of the principles which we accept as axiomatic, it is necessary for us
firmly to insist upon the rights of our own citizens without regard to
their creed or race; without regard to whether they were born here
or born abroad. It has proved very difficult to secure from Russia
the right for our Jewish fellow-citizens to receive passports and travel
through Russian territory. Such conduct is not only unjust and irritating toward us, but it is difficult to see its wisdom from Russia's
standpoint. No conceivable good is accomplished by it. If an American Jew or an American Christian misbehaves himself in Russia he
can at once be driven out; but the ordinary American Jew, like the
ordinary American Christian, would behave just about as he behaves
here, that is, behave as any good citizen ought to behave; and where
this is the case it is a wrong against which we are entitled to protest
to refuse him his passport without regard to his conduct and character, merely on racial and religious grounds. In Turkey our difficulties arise less from the way in which our citizens are sometimes
treated than from the indignation inevitably excited in seeing such
fearful misrule as has been witnessed both in Armenia and Macedonia.

The strong arm of the Government in enforcing respect for its just
rights in international matters is the Navy of the United States. I
most earnestly recommend that there be no halt in the work of upbuilding the American Navy. There is no more patriotic duty before
us a people than to keep the Navy adequate to the needs of this
country's position. We have undertaken to build the Isthmian Canal.
We have undertaken to secure for ourselves our just share in the trade
of the Orient. We have undertaken to protect our citizens from improper treatment in foreign lands. We continue steadily to insist on
the application of the Monroe Doctrine to the Western Hemisphere.
Unless our attitude in these and all similar matters is to be a mere
boastful sham we can not afford to abandon our naval programme.
Our voice is now potent for peace, and is so potent because we are
not afraid of war. But our protestations upon behalf of peace would

neither receive nor deserve the slightest attention if we were impotent to make them good.

The war which now unfortunately rages in the far East has emphasized in striking fashion the new possibilities of naval warfare. The lessons taught are both strategic and tactical, and are political as well as military. The experiences of the war have shown in conclusive fashion that while sea-going and sea-keeping torpedo destroyers are indispensable, and fast lightly armed and armored cruisers very useful, yet that the main reliance, the main standby, in any navy worthy the name must be the great battle ships, heavily armored and heavily gunned. Not a Russian or Japanese battle ship has been sunk by a torpedo boat, or by gunfire, while among the less protected ships, cruiser after cruiser has been destroyed whenever the hostile squadrons have gotten within range of one another's weapons. There will always be a large field of usefulness for cruisers, especially of the more formidable type. We need to increase the number of torpedo-boat destroyers, paying less heed to their having a knot or two extra speed than to their capacity to keep the seas for weeks, and, if necessary, for months at a time. It is wise to build submarine torpedo boats, as under certain circumstances they might be very useful. But most of all we need to continue building our fleet of battle ships, or ships so powerfully armed that they can inflict the maximum of damage upon our opponents, and so well protected that they can suffer a severe hammering in return without fatal impairment of their ability to fight and maneuver. Of course ample means must be provided for enabling the personnel of the Navy to be brought to the highest point of efficiency. Our great fighting ships and torpedo boats must be ceaselessly trained and maneuvered in squadrons. The officers and men can only learn their trade thoroughly by ceaseless practice on the high seas. In the event of war it would be far better to have no ships at all than to have ships of a poor and ineffective type, or ships which, however good, were yet manned by untrained and unskillful crews. The best officers and men in a poor ship could do nothing against fairly good opponents; and on the other hand a modern war ship is useless unless the officers and men aboard her have become adepts in their duties. The marksmanship in our Navy has improved in an extraordinary degree during the last three years, and on the whole the types of our battleships are improving; but much remains to be done. Sooner or later we shall have to provide for some method by which there will be promotions for merit as well as for seniority, or else retirement of all those who after a certain age have not advanced beyond a certain grade; while no effort must be spared to make the service attractive to the enlisted men in order that they may be kept as long as possible in it. Reservation public schools should be provided wherever there are navy-yards.

Within the last three years the United States has set an example in disarmament where disarmament was proper. By law our Army is fixed at a maximum of one hundred thousand and a minimum of sixty thousand men. When there was insurrection in the Philippines we kept the Army at the maximum. Peace came in the Philippines, and now our Army has been reduced to the minimum at which it is possible to keep it with due regard to its efficiency. The guns now mounted require twenty-eight thousand men, if the coast fortifications are to be adequately manned. Relatively to the Nation, it is not now so large as the police force of New York or Chicago relatively to the population of either city. We need more officers; there are not enough to perform the regular army work. It is very important that the officers of the Army should be accustomed to handle their men in masses, as it is also important that the National Guard of the several States should be accustomed to actual field maneuvering, especially in connection with the regulars. For this reason we are to be congratulated upon the success of the field maneuvers at Manassas last fall, maneuvers in which a larger number of Regulars and National Guard took part than was ever before assembled together in time of peace. No other civilized nation has, relatively to its population, such a diminutive Army as ours; and while the Army is so small we are not to be excused if we fail to keep it at a very high grade of proficiency. It must be incessantly practiced; the standard for the enlisted men should be kept very high, while at the same time the service should be made as attractive as possible; and the standard for the officers should be kept even higher—which, as regards the upper ranks, can best be done by introducing some system of selection and rejection into the promotions. We should be able, in the event of some sudden emergency, to put into the field one first-class army corps, which should be, as a whole, at least the equal of any body of troops of like number belonging to any other nation.

Great progress has been made in protecting our coasts by adequate fortifications with sufficient guns. We should, however, pay much more heed than at present to the development of an extensive system of floating mines for use in all our more important harbors. These mines have been proved to be a most formidable safeguard against hostile fleets.

I earnestly call the attention of the Congress to the need of amending the existing law relating to the award of Congressional medals of honor in the Navy so as to provide that they may be awarded to commissioned officers and warrant officers as well as to enlisted men. These justly prized medals are given in the Army alike to the officers and the enlisted men, and it is most unjust that the commissioned officers and warrant officers of the Navy should not in this respect have the same rights as their brethren in the Army and as the enlisted men of the Navy.

In the Philippine Islands there has been during the past year a continuation of the steady progress which has obtained ever since our troops definitely got the upper hand of the insurgents. The Philippine people, or, to speak more accurately, the many tribes, and even races, sundered from one another more or less sharply, who go to make up the people of the Philippine Islands, contain many elements of good, and some elements which we have a right to hope stand for progress. At present they are utterly incapable of existing in independence at all or of building up a civilization of their own. I firmly believe that we can help them to rise higher and higher in the scale of civilization and of capacity for self-government, and I most earnestly hope that in the end they will be able to stand, if not entirely alone, yet in some such relation to the United States as Cuba now stands. This end is not yet in sight, and it may be indefinitely postponed if our people are foolish enough to turn the attention of the Filipinos away from the problems of achieving moral and material prosperity, of working for a stable, orderly, and just government, and toward foolish and dangerous intrigues for a complete independence for which they are as yet totally unfit.

On the other hand our people must keep steadily before their minds the fact that the justification for our stay in the Philippines must ultimately rest chiefly upon the good we are able to do in the islands. I do not overlook the fact that in the development of our interests in the Pacific Ocean and along its coasts, the Philippines have played and will play an important part; and that our interests have been served in more than one way by the possession of the islands. But our chief reason for continuing to hold them must be that we ought in good faith to try to do our share of the world's work, and this particular piece of work has been imposed upon us by the results of the war with Spain. The problem presented to us in the Philippine Islands is akin to, but not exactly like, the problems presented to the other great civilized powers which have possessions in the Orient. There are points of resemblance in our work to the work which is being done by the British in India and Egypt, by the French in Algiers, by the Dutch in Java, by the Russians in Turkestan, by the Japanese in Formosa; but more distinctly than any of these powers we are endeavoring to develop the natives themselves so that they shall take an ever-increasing share in their own government, and as far as is prudent we are already admitting their representatives to a governmental equality with our own. There are commissioners, judges, and governors in the islands who are Filipinos and who have exactly the same share in the government of the islands as have their colleagues who are Americans, while in the lower ranks, of course, the great majority of the public servants are Filipinos. Within two years we shall be trying the experiment of an elective lower house in the Philippine legislature. It may be that the Filipinos will misuse this legislature, and they certainly will misuse it if they are misled by foolish persons here at home into starting an agitation for their own independence or into any factious or improper action. In such case they will do themselves no good and will stop for the time being all further effort to advance them and give them a greater share in their own government. But if they act with wisdom and self-restraint, if they show that they are capable of electing a legislature which in its turn is capable of taking a sane and efficient part in the actual work of government, they can rest assured that a full and increasing measure of recognition will be given them. Above all they should remember that their prime needs are moral and industrial, not political. It is a good thing to try the experiment of giving them a legislature; but it is a far better thing to give them schools, good roads, railroads which will enable them to get their products to market, honest courts, an honest and efficient constabulary, and all that tends to produce order, peace, fair dealing as between man and man, and habits of intelligent industry and thrift. If they are safeguarded against oppression, and if their real wants, material and spiritual, are studied intelligently and in a spirit of friendly sympathy, much more good will be done them than by any effort to give them political power, though this effort may in its own proper time and place be proper enough.

Meanwhile our own people should remember that there is need for the highest standard of conduct among the Americans sent to the Philippine Islands, not only among the public servants but among the private individuals who go to them. It is because I feel this so deeply that in the administration of these islands I have positively refused to permit any discrimination whatsoever for political reasons and have insisted that in choosing the public servants consideration should be paid solely to the worth of the men chosen and to the needs of the islands. There is no higher body of men in our public service than we have in the Philippine Islands under Governor Wright and his associates. So far as possible these men should be given a free hand, and their suggestions should receive the hearty backing both of the Executive and of the Congress. There is need of a vigilant and disinterested support of our public servants in the Philippines by good citizens here in the United States. Unfortunately hitherto those of our people here at home who have specially claimed to be the champions of the Filipinos have in reality been their worst enemies. This will continue to be the case as long as they strive to make the Filipinos independent, and stop all industrial development of the islands by crying out against the laws which would bring it on the ground that capitalists must not "exploit" the islands. Such proceedings are not only unwise, but are most harmful to the Filipinos, who do not need independence at all, but who do need good laws, good public servants, and the industrial development that can only come if the investment of American and foreign capital in the islands is favored in all legitimate ways.

Every measure taken concerning the islands should be taken primarily with a view to their advantage. We should certainly give them lower tariff rates on their exports to the United States; if this is not done it will be a wrong to extend our shipping laws to them. I earnestly hope for the immediate enactment into law of the legislation now pending to encourage American capital to seek investment in the islands in railroads, in factories, in plantations, and in lumbering and mining.